STALIN

The Fiery Colchidian (Plamennyi kolkhidets), a romanticized image of the young Stalin by the famous Georgian painter Irakli Toidze. Here the studious, determined Stalin is shown carrying a copy of Lenin's *What Is to Be Done?* and the journal *brdzola* (Struggle) for which he wrote articles. In fact, he was not Colchidian, that is from western Georgia, but Iberian or *kartveli*, from eastern Georgia. The author is grateful to the Toidze family—Irakli's grandson, Giorgi, and his mother, Rozaliia Borisovna Toidze—for permission to use this image. A search for the original painting has not been successful.

STALIN

PASSAGE TO REVOLUTION

RONALD GRIGOR SUNY

PRINCETON UNIVERSITY PRESS

PRINCETON & OXFORD

Library of Congress Cataloging-in-Publication Data

Names: Suny, Ronald Grigor, author.
Title: Stalin : passage to revolution / Ronald Grigor Suny.
Description: Princeton : Princeton University Press, 2020. | Includes bibliographical
    references and index.
Identifiers: LCCN 2019034217 (print) | LCCN 2019034218 (ebook) |
    ISBN 9780691182032 (hardback) | ISBN 9780691202716 (paperback) |
    ISBN 9780691185934 (ebook)
Subjects: LCSH: Stalin, Joseph, 1878–1953. | Soviet Union—History—Revolution,
    1917–1921—Biography.
Classification: LCC DK268.S8 S77 2020 (print) | LCC DK268.S8 (ebook) |
    DDC 947.084/2092 [B]–dc23
LC record available at https://lccn.loc.gov/2019034217
LC ebook record available at https://lccn.loc.gov/2019034218

British Library Cataloging-in-Publication Data is available

Editorial: Eric Crahan and Thalia Leaf
Production Editorial: Kathleen Cioffi
Text Design: Leslie Flis
Jacket Design: Faceout Studio
Production: Danielle Amatucci
Publicity: James Schneider and Kate Farquhar-Thomson
Copyeditor: Jennifer Harris

Jacket art: (Background) Map of Russian Empire, 1913 / Buyenlarge Archive / UIG /
Bridgeman Images. (Photograph) Josef Stalin, 1902. Sputnik / Alamy Stock Photo

This book has been composed in Arno Pro

Printed on acid-free paper. ∞

Printed in the United States of America

10 9 8 7 6 5 4 3 2 1

To Armena Pearl Marderosian
(January 1, 1949–November 3, 2012)
My life companion,
who never tired of asking questions

CONTENTS

ACKNOWLEDGMENTS

This book has had a long gestation. I signed the initial contract with my first editor, Nancy Lane, at Oxford University Press in 1987. She and subsequent editors patiently supported my decision to delay the writing as we watched the Soviet Union collapse and the archives open. Over the next decades I was able to work in both Moscow and Tbilisi, as well as at the Hoover Institution Archives at Stanford University, and discover materials that earlier biographers had been denied. I benefited enormously from the research of Aleksandr Orlovskii, Simon Sebag Montefiore, Olga Edelman, and Erik van Ree, fellow trollers in the documentary record of the young Stalin. Two young historians in Georgia— Giorgi Kldiashvili and Levan Avalishvili—provided a service, not only to me but also to all future historians and their homeland, by saving the archive of the Georgian Communist Party from the brink of destruction. They convinced Omar Tushurashvili of the Georgian Ministry of Internal Affairs of the importance to Georgia's history of the materials then disintegrating in the building of the then defunct Institute of Marxism-Leninism. The documents were rescued and moved to a secure location, in which I had the pleasure of being the first researcher to work.

Much of the work on this book (and other projects) was accomplished while I was a residential fellow at the Center for Advanced Study in the Behavioral Sciences in Stanford, California (2001–2002, 2005– 2006). CASBS is a place of active engagement with other scholars and the world beyond its beautiful hilltop. I am grateful to the two directors—Doug McAdams and Claude Steele—and the staff for the environment they created for all of us. It was on that pleasant hilltop where I met an extraordinary man of letters, Donald Lamm, whose reading and suggestions shaped the way I have told this story. Other inspirational environments have included Ann Arbor and the University of Michigan; Hyde Park and the University of Chicago, each with its own intense collectives of colleagues and students; Moscow, with long-time dear friends (Vahan Mkrtchian and family most importantly); Tbilisi and Erevan, where teachers of languages and besieged historians contributed to my completing this endeavor. Many friends and colleagues have read earlier drafts and offered invaluable comments. Susan Ferber, with whom I worked for many years on this and other books, is an editor who actually edits, and I appreciate enormously her improvements to the text. I also wish to thank my superb editor at Princeton University Press, Brigitta van Rheinberg, for her interest in this project and her diligence and intelligence in turning a manuscript too enamored of esoteric detail into a more readable and accessible book. She secured the services of two excellent readers—the gifted biographer and political scientist William Taubman, and the leading Western historian of Georgia, Stephen Jones—whose supportive and critical suggestions reshaped and further improved my work. When she moved upward at Princeton, she handed me on to Eric Crahan and the gifted professionals at the press, who guided the manuscript with great skill into print.

I am grateful particularly to my fellow Georgianists Oliver Reisner, Stephen Jones, and Beka Kobakhidze. Beka not only read and corrected a late draft of the manuscript but also contributed new sources from his deep knowledge of modern Georgian history. My comrade and critic Alex Szejman read various versions of the text, convinced me to put more of myself into it, but sadly did not live to see it in print. Colleagues in political science and history Geoff Eley, Charles King, Lars Lih, Norman Naimark, David Priestland, Alexander Semyonov, Lewis Siegelbaum, Milan Svolik, and Erik Van Ree carefully and critically read and commented on earlier drafts of this book. Their erudition and attention to detail and argument improved the text considerably.

Archives are often difficult places to work, and at times it seems to historians that archivists are there to prevent them from doing their work. My colleagues in the field are well aware of the frustrations that researchers face in working in Soviet and post-Soviet archives. At times materials that had been available are rendered inaccessible, while at other times unsuspected treasures appear. I will always remember the 1970s, when I worked in Tbilisi, living in hotels with my wife, Armena, reading forbidden newspapers in the Karl Marx Library, and calling over and over again to the archives only to be told that the desired materials were still in the process of *razsekretovanie* (unsecreting). I can testify that persistence was rewarded and the payoff was profound. My gratitude to the conscientious archivists who aided me is boundless. Over the years I have been fortunate to benefit from the advice and aid of Larissa Rogovaia, Andrei Doronin, Zinaida Peregudova, Olga Edelman, Albert Nenarokov, and others who have plowed the fertile Russian archives. Particularly valuable has been the diligent work of Olga Edelman, who collected and edited all the documents she was able to find on the young Stalin in archives, memoirs, and other sources. She and I shared our prospective books with each other, and we both benefited from our exchanges. The indispensable Oleg Khlevniuk, student assistants like Stephen Rapp, Tom Hooker, and Svetlana Dubinina, as well as sage advice from my close friend Valerie Kivelson and suggestions from previous Stalin biographers like Robert C. Tucker have all made this work better than it might have been. I am indebted to my extraordinary students at the University of Michigan, who read various versions of my manuscript and let me know what worked and what did not. I am especially grateful to Will Carter, who boarded with me for the last two years of this project, and whose company, intellectual curiosity, and discipline kept me healthy, happy, and grounded.

The last and most honorable place to express gratitude traditionally and deservedly belongs to those closest to the author—in this case, the three women who were forced for more than three decades to live with Stalin, they whose beautiful white cat was named "Soso" and gentle golden retriever was "Koba": Armena Pearl Marderosian, Sevan Siranoush Suni, and Anoush Tamar Suni. I dedicate this book to my most faithful companion for over forty years, our beloved and much missed Armena.

A NOTE ON DATING AND SPELLING

In this text dates in the Russian Empire are given according to the Julian calendar, which in the nineteenth century was twelve days behind, and in the twentieth century thirteen days behind, the Gregorian calendar used in the West. After February 1918 the Soviet government adopted the Western calendar. Dates for events in the West are given in the Gregorian calendar. Where confusion might arise, both dates are indicated.

Spelling of Russian, Georgian, and Armenian words and names are given in a modified Library of Congress style. Georgian words do not use capital letters, though I have used capitals for names of persons and places. For Stalin I have transliterated his original name from Georgian (Jughashvili) rather than from Russian (Dzhugashvili), and have done the same with Orjonikidze (not Ordzhonikidze). The soft sign in Russian (ь) is rendered by an apostrophe but will be left out in many proper names in the text. Some names widely known to English-language readers—for example, Trotsky, not Trotskii—will be rendered in their most familiar form. I have left out patronymics, which are commonly used in Russian but not in Armenian, Azeri, or Georgian.

For the city currently known as Tbilisi, in this book I have used the Russian name, Tiflis, which was most widely used at the time about which I am writing. Georgians knew the city then as *tpilisi*, and from 1936 on Soviet authorities officially designated the capital of Georgia Tbilisi.

A NOTE ON ARCHIVES

This book could not have been written without the opening of the formerly Soviet archives at the end of the 1980s and through the 1990s. Indeed, when I first proposed this work more than thirty years ago, I wrote an initial manuscript of about two hundred pages before realizing that the reforms then being carried out by Mikhail Gorbachev would make possible a completely different book. The end of the Soviet system and the subsequent disintegration of the USSR allowed a new scholarship based on the archives that were being "unsecreted." Over the last several decades I have been able to work in both Moscow and Tbilisi in the archives of the Communist Party and the Soviet state as one closed *fond* (collection) after another was opened to investigators.

In recording the sources in the notes, I have adopted a somewhat unorthodox method in the interest of clarity and accessibility for future scholars. The archival sources with which I have worked are recorded first in the notes, occasionally followed by references to publications where the documents can also be found. If I was not able to see the original and was compelled to rely on the work of other scholars, like Orlovskii and Edelman, whom I have found to be reliable, I refer first to the source from which I took the information and, if available, then indicate the archival source that the published work used. Given the citation style of various authors, some of these published archival references are not as complete as the ones I myself read. Still, my intention is to give as full a record of the sources as possible in order to facilitate the work of future scholars of Stalin and Soviet history.

ARCHIVAL REFERENCES

Archives in the former Soviet Union changed their names frequently after the collapse of the USSR in 1991. Here I use the most recent name of the archive with an appropriate abbreviation in the national language.

GARF   *Gosudarstvennyi arkhiv Rossiiskoi Federatsii* [State Archive of the Russian Federation]; formerly TsGAOR (*Tsentral'nyi gosudarstvennyi arkhiv Oktiabr'skoi Revoliutsii*) [Central State Archive of the October Revolution].

HIA   Hoover Institution Archives, Stanford, California.

RGASPI   *Rossiiskii gosudarstvennyi arkhiv sotsial'noi i politicheskoi istorii* [Russian State Archive of Social and Political History]; formerly RTsKHIDNI (*Rossiiskii tsentr khraneniia i izucheniia dokumentov noveishei istorii*) [Russian Center for the Preservation and Study of Documents of Recent History]; and during Soviet times: IMEL (*Institut Marksizma-Leninizma*) [Institute of Marxism-Leninism].

SEA   *sakartvelos erovnuli arkivi* [National Archive of Georgia]; formerly often referred to as GIAG (*Gosudarstvennyi istoricheskii arkhiv Gruzii*) [State Historical Archive of Georgia] is composed of two separate archives: the *sakartvelos tsentraluri saistorio arkivi* [Central Historic Archive of Georgia] (STsSA); and the *sakartvelos uakhlesi istoriis tsentraluri arkivi* [Central Contemporary History Archive of Georgia] (SUITsA).

SShSSA   *sakartvelos shinagan sakmeta saministros arkivi* [Archive of the Ministry of Internal Affairs of Georgia]; formerly *sakartvelos shinagan sakmeta saministros saarkivo sammartvelos II ganqopileba* [Second Department of the Archival Administration of the Ministry of Internal Affairs of Georgia] (SShSSSIIG); in Soviet times *sakartvelos komunisturi partiis tsentraluri komitetis arkivi* [Archive of the Central Committee of the Communist Party of Georgia], often referred to by his Russian initials GF IML (*Gruzinskii filial Instituta Marksizma-Leninizma*).

SSM   *i. v. stalinis sakhl-muzeumi* [Stalin House Museum, Gori].

I have indicated where the documents might be found by the conventional Russian terms: f. = *fond* (collection); op. = *opis* (list of holdings); d. = *delo* (file); ch. = *chast'* (part); l. = *list* (page), whether they are in Russian, Soviet, or Georgian archives.

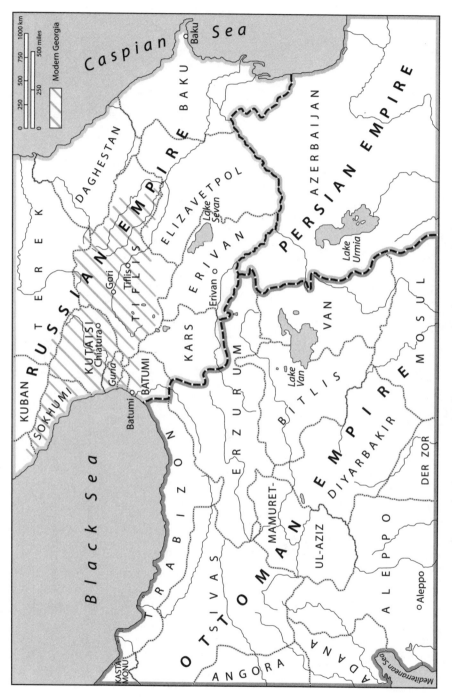

MAP 1. Caucasia (in the Russian Empire), the Ottoman East (Eastern Anatolia), and Persia, 1878–1914.

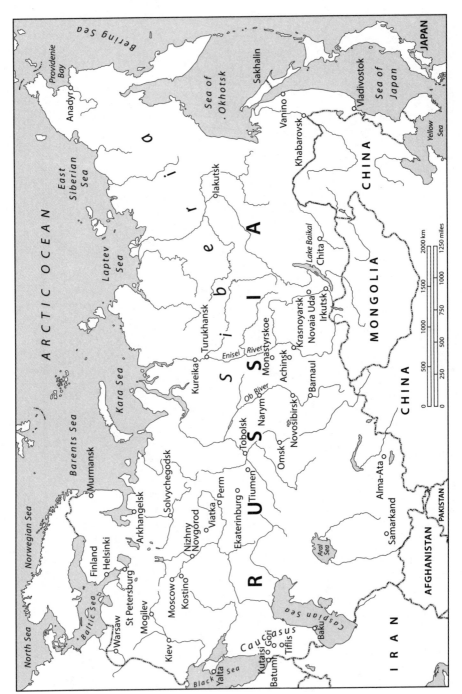

MAP 2. Russian Empire, 1878–1914.

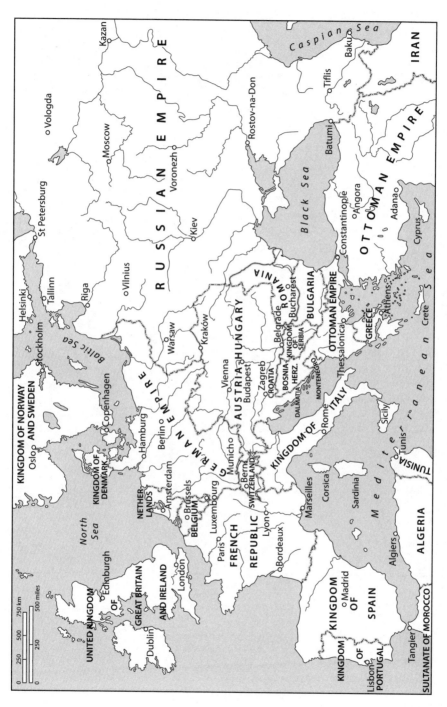

MAP 3. Europe, 1900.

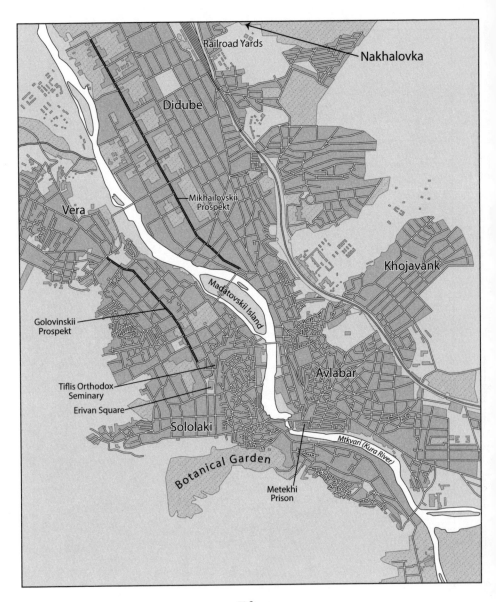

MAP 4. Tiflis, 1913.

STALIN

INTRODUCTION

FORTUNE'S KNAVE

No one can be regarded as a born criminal. One cannot look at Stalin in the same light in 1918, in 1924, or in 1937. It is the same person, and yet it is not. In the ten years after he succeeded Lenin, he changed markedly. Yet that is the difficulty of creating his political portrait: while apparently struggling for the ideals of socialism—however twistedly understood—he committed crime after crime.

—DMITRII VOLKOGONOV,
STALIN: TRIUMPH AND TRAGEDY (1991)

Do not expect more from the truth than it actually contains.

—RUSSIAN PROVERB

In the spring of 1924, Stalin's nemesis and rival, Lev Trotsky, told the "Old Bolshevik" Vladimir Smirnov, "Stalin will become the dictator of the USSR." "Stalin?" Smirnov reacted. "But he is a mediocrity, a colorless non-entity." "Mediocrity, yes," Trotsky mused, "non-entity, no. The dialectics of history have already hooked him and will raise him up. He is needed by all of them—by the tired radicals, by the bureaucrats, by the Nepmen, the kulaks, the upstarts, the sneaks, by all the worms that are crawling out of the upturned soil of the manured revolution."[1]

Stalin continues to fascinate—the central mystery within the riddle inside the enigma that was the Soviet Union. Ordinary in many ways, hardly a mediocrity, he rose to extraordinary heights. Toward the end of his life he was arguably the most powerful individual in the world. Yet at various earlier times he was seen as a "gray blur," "the man who missed the revolution," a "mediocrity" hooked by history. He was

Lenin's "marvelous Georgian," in wartime the "Generalissimo," and still later "history's villain."

Yet the telling of Stalin's life story has always been more than biography. There is wonder at the achievement—the son of a Georgian cobbler ascending the heights of world power, the architect of an industrial revolution and the destruction of millions of the people he ruled, the leader of the state that stopped the bloody expansion of fascism. Stalin's story is the story of the making of the Soviet Union and a particular vision of what he called socialism. His biographers have often placed historical imagination at the service of a specific politics of eroding (or lauding) the Stalinist inheritance. Such a life story cannot be separated from an evaluation of that life's work. In twenty-first century Russia visions of Stalin are deployed to justify yet another slide into authoritarianism, while in the West the entirety of the Soviet experience is often reduced to Stalin and Stalinism, the Great Purges, and the gulag. The drama of his life, the achievements and tragedies, are so morally and emotionally charged that they challenge the usual practices of historical objectivity and scholarly neutrality. As his heirs and victims have tried to make sense of Stalin, tales or rumors have been used to illuminate the dark corners of the Soviet past. Imaginative portraits, like those by great novelists like Alexander Solzhenitsyn or Vasilii Grossman, doubtless help us to sense the interior of the dictator's mind but contain fictions or at best half-fictions.[2] When it comes to Stalin, gossip is reported as fact, legend provides meaning, and scholarship gives way to sensationalist popular literature with tangential reference to the reliable sources.

Most elusive and obscure have been Stalin's early years—before he was Stalin. Here the lasting fascination with the demon dictator is matched by an irresistible temptation to make his childhood and youth "useful" by investing them with the first signs of the paranoid revolutionary-from-above of the 1930s, the arch criminal who presided over the death of millions. Those who "know" the autocratic Stalin of totalitarian Russia have read back the characteristics of the General Secretary into the young Stalin, emphasizing what fits—violence, paranoia, arrogance, and the need to dominate—and rejecting what does not— romanticism, literary sensibility, love for his homeland, and revolutionary idealism. As important as Stalin's early life was to the formation of his personality, the difficulties of reconstructing it from the few extant memoirs of his youth and scanty available documentation have led sometimes to flimsily built psychoanalytic speculation and at other times to fanciful arguments that Stalin must have been an agent for the tsar's *Okhrana* (political police).[3]

From the earliest attempts at understanding Stalin, biographers have drawn conclusions about the mature Stalin from the psychological, not to mention physical, blows suffered by the young Ioseb Jughashvili. His boyhood friend, Ioseb Iremashvili, later a political opponent, composed the first memoir of Stalin's childhood and made the primary psychological deduction later followed by other biographers: "Undeserved, terrible beatings made the boy as hard and heartless as his father himself. Since all men who had authority over others either through power or age reminded him of his father, there soon arose a feeling of revenge against all men who stood above him. From his youth the realization of his thoughts of revenge became the goal toward which everything was aimed." Stalin evidently evaluated his parents' disciplining differently from Iremashvili. When popular German biographer Emil Ludwig, known for his interviews with the political celebrities of the interwar years, met with Stalin in the Kremlin, he indelicately broached the issue of parental abuse: "What pushed you into opposition? Perhaps the bad treatment by your parents?" Stalin did not take the bait, however. "No," he answered. "My parents were uneducated people, but they treated me not badly at all."[4]

Reducing the complexity of the biographical subject to a single explanatory key, in this case parental abuse, impoverishes explanation, and most historians have been suspicious of a method that leaves so much out—culture and context, politics and ideas—and renders stated motivations suspect, reducing them to psychological functions (rationalization, compensation, sublimation). Stalin is without doubt one of the most tempting and, at the same time, least hospitable subjects for a biographer. Not particularly introspective, he left few intimate letters, no secret diary, and many dubious witnesses to his inner life. Moreover, Bolshevik political culture was hostile to open personal expression and

imposed on Stalin and other adherents an enforced modesty. Denial of
the importance of self was part of the Social Democratic tradition, and
even as a grotesque cult of Stalin's personality grew to gargantuan pro-
portions Stalin would continue, disingenuously, to claim that he dis-
liked all the fuss. At different times in his life Stalin created distinct
narratives about who he was. In the 1930s that narrative drew parallels
with Peter the Great and then with Ivan the Terrible. His earlier narratives were romances about Georgia, the revolutionary hero, the practical man of the underground, the hardened, steeled Bolshevik, who in
time became the Lenin loyalist, the man of the moderate middle, and
soon afterward the radical transformer of Russia's reality.

Yet for all his dissembling and deception, his playacting and postur-
ing, Stalin revealed himself through what he did and said in public
and—now that archives are open and more reliable testimonies have
come forth—in private as well. For the first time biographers are able
to place the man in his world, show his limits as well as talents, and work
toward a portrait that might explain the seemingly inexplicable. Stalin
was an exceptional individual because of what he became and what he
did, the positions he occupied in a tumultuous time, but like many
people in higher politics he was at the same time quite ordinary, a small
man placed in extraordinary circumstances.

In this study Stalin's psychological evolution is treated as the interplay
between the boy from Georgia's developing character and the social and
cultural environments through which Soso Jughashvili—later Koba, still
later Stalin—moved. Each of these environments—the ethnocultural
setting of Georgia, the revolutionary intelligentsia, the Marxist movement, the underground, prison and exile, on to the upper circles of Russian Social Democracy, the fire of civil war, the inner workings of the
Soviet political system, and the political cultures of socialism—imprinted
Stalin, changing him along the way. As life's experiences molded him,
what he was becoming modified what he had been. He was not born a
criminal and did not become a Caucasian bandit. Rather than a gangster
out to enrich himself, he was both the product of and participant in an
evolving culture of the underground revolutionary. Idealism and ideology, as well as resentment and ambition, impelled him to endure the risks

and recklessness of a political outlaw. He hardened himself, accepted the necessity of deception, ruthlessness, and violence—all these means justified by the end of social and political liberation. This is the story of how a political revolutionary was made, as well as the emergence of the revolutionary movement, its possibilities, ambitions, and trials.

Stalin lived almost exactly as long before the revolution as after, and the first third of his life was spent in Georgia. As a Georgian who rose to the top of the Russian Communist movement and as the architect of the Soviet multinational state, Stalin's story is part of a larger story of empires and nations, new forms of imperial construction and national ambitions. Born, raised, and educated in Georgia, this was the first cultural environment he experienced. Yet it is hard to claim that Jughashvili became Stalin because of something essentially Georgian, as there is no archetypical Georgian.[5] His boyhood country was a lively arena in which people defined and defended what they considered to be their culture and its values, often bitterly disagreeing with other members of the same ethnicity. Nationalists like to think of ethnic culture as harmonious and consistent, with those inside that culture sharing characteristics that differ radically from those outside. But Georgia was part of a larger Caucasian cultural sphere and embedded in the imperial Russian polity with its own cultural and social influences. Among Georgians values and behaviors were simultaneously shared and contested. Older traditions contended with novel divisions of power and shifts in status and gender hierarchies. Poets and politicians made claims about what was authentically "Georgian." In the half century before Stalin's birth there were those ready to "police" the boundaries of Georgian culture, tell others what was authentic and proper, and discipline deviants. Even as aspects of Stalin's ethnic culture were breaking down and being reformulated, while intellectuals turned their attention to what appeared about to be lost, young Soso Jughashvili, influenced by his doting mother, identified intensely with Georgia, its practices and preferences, the beautiful intricacies and cadences of its language, its music, and its hypermasculine gender regime.

A more mature Koba eventually broke through what he found to be the confining limits of nationality to identify with an explicitly anti-nationalist political party and its socialist future. In rapid succession Soso left the largely Georgian town of his birth and entered other cultural milieus: the seminary, the intelligentsia, the movement, and the party. By his twenty-first birthday he had become a professional revolutionary defined by a new culture, the political culture of Russian Social Democracy, with its specific forms of moral and personal behavior, its idealized self-representations of what constituted an *intelligent* (a radical political intellectual), and its elaborate codes of loyalty and sacrifice.

Elaborating the cultural worlds through which the young Stalin passed makes possible a fuller understanding of the sources of Stalin's particular psychology and the determinants of his personal and political trajectory. Understanding the man comes from setting him in his time and place, even though some parts of his inner workings undoubtedly remain elusive, buried in regions to which historians are not admitted. Poverty was the condition of the world into which he came. The constant and demanding attention and fierce adulation that his single present parent, his mother, focused on Soso fed his social resentment at his place in the scheme of things. Aware of being marginalized and at the same time talented, Soso found that hard work and discipline moved him to the front of the class. His inheritance from both parents was ambition.

The usual biographical narrative, with its organic continuity between boy, young adult, and mature man, is challenged by the reconstruction of the available fragments of Stalin's life that suggest a much more disjointed evolution in which Soso/Koba/Stalin shed one identity and took on another. The obedient child and priest-in-training became a rebel; the Georgian patriot became an assimilated Russian, though only in part and primarily in his public posture; the militant Bolshevik at times took on the coloring of a moderate. As he moved physically and psychologically away from Georgia, Stalin left behind a culture in which one's sense of personhood derived from family, friends, and nation and entered a world in which one defined one's own nature in line with a particular understanding of historical direction and the unforgiving imperatives of politics. By becoming a rebel against the existing order, revolutionaries like Stalin declared war on constituted authorities. For Marxists in the Russian Empire politics were less about compromise and persuasion and more about the violent, unforgiving confrontations found on the battlefield. A logic of war prevailed, one that required (sometimes with regret) the use of violence. Responding both to inner needs and external possibilities and challenges, deeply changed by the experiences of the seminary, underground, prison, revolution, civil war, and political power, the Stalin that emerged on the world stage was both a product of the successive cultures through which he passed and an actor making choices and defining himself in unprecedented and un-predictable historical circumstances.

During the Cold War, battalions of Soviet and Western scholars ex-plored the history of Russian Social Democracy, the Marxist movement that split irrevocably into Bolshevism and Menshevism by 1905 and whose radical wing led by Vladimir Lenin came to power in Octo-ber 1917. The stories they told were diametrically opposed to one an-other, each a product of the intellectual and political imperatives of their respective worlds. With the fall of the Soviet Union interest in the intri-cacies of the political struggles of the Marxist factions and their mean-ings and influences on the Soviet future evaporated. Yet at the same moment the less contentious environment of the post-Soviet period, along with the opening of Soviet archives, made possible a reevaluation of the history of Russian (and Georgian) Marxism and their respective and distinct labor movements. Since those movements and the Marxist underground were the major breeding grounds for Stalin and those around him, I have undertaken a fresh reading of the history of those movements out of which the Soviet experiment and Stalin himself emerged.

Understanding Stalin's psychological makeup, the cognitive under-standings and the emotions that drove him, in these spatial and tempo-ral contexts and influences has involved the careful construction of a mosaic of diverse pieces of information—from the variety of archival documents, official and unofficial memoirs, even photographs—until a legible portrait emerged. My aim was to evoke from that mosaic a credible and convincing interpretation of the evolution of the boy, Soso

Jughashvili, through the young Koba to the mature Stalin—an elucidation of his personal, psychological, and political formation that could shed light on his motivations and choices. In the end exploring where he was and when is fundamental to understanding who Stalin was, why he acted and thought as he did, and how he evolved into the confident, fearless rebel determined to lead.

Throughout this book I present a variety of alternative views of Stalin produced by his friends and enemies, biographers and hagiographers—many of them in the epigraphs opening each chapter—in order to illustrate how Stalin has stirred contradictory commentaries on his character, both by contemporaries and historians. In contrast to other biographies I have left narrative gaps where no available material exists and avoided speculating about what he "must have felt" or "might have thought." This book provides the evidence from which both a compelling story can be told as well as a caution that the line between history and fiction is too easily crossed. It also navigates between disciplines, to maintain the historian's sensitivity to time and place and the anomalies, particularities, and accidents that make up the deep texture of the past, while at the same time borrowing from political and social science concepts, techniques, and insights that can make forests out of empirical trees. In this way we might get closer to unraveling the deeper mysteries of Stalin and understand why a revolution committed to human emancipation ended up in dictatorship and terror.

GROWING UP GEORGIAN

1

THE GEORGIAN

Georgian was his native tongue; to the end he spoke Russian with an accent. Though he retained some native habits, his self-identification with Russians progressed very rapidly. One day his little daughter would be puzzled when her brother Vassily excitedly announced to her a new discovery: Father used to be a Georgian.

—ADAM ULAM, *STALIN, THE MAN AND HIS ERA* (1973)

I was 6 years old and did not know what it was to be a Georgian, and [my brother Vasilii] explained: "They went around in cherkesses and cut up everyone with kinjals."

—SVETLANA ALLILUEVA,
TWENTY LETTERS TO A FRIEND (1967)

For nineteenth-century travelers from Russia or Europe, Georgia was a land of drama and passion, savagery, and exotic Eastern culture. Poets and novelists depicted a country of majestic mountains and verdant valleys peopled by a Christian people who had fought for centuries to stave off the predations of neighboring Turks and Persians. Through the Great Caucasus, which separated Russia from Georgia, passage was difficult and dangerous. To those from the north and west, the men of the south were strong and silent, the women sultry, and the rivers always turbulent. Villagers and townspeople in both highlands and lowlands were noted for their hospitality. Strangers were always welcome and protected; a woman was able to stop a fight that might have proven deadly by dropping her handkerchief. At a near fatal moment at the beginning of the century, Georgian kings, threatened by Iran, petitioned the Russian tsar for protection. Russia answered by annexing the Georgian lands one by one and eventually abolishing the monarchy. The next one hundred years witnessed the most profound transformation of Georgian society since the coming of Christianity in the fourth century. United by the Russian Empire for the first time after three hundred years of fragmentation, Georgians began a gradual social metamorphosis that ended their rural isolation, eroded the power of the traditional landed nobility, and created an urban Georgian population for the first time in their history.

Georgia's relationship with Russia was ambiguous and could be read in very different ways. In the idiom of nationalism then spreading from Europe, Georgian intellectuals told the story of their country's fate as a fundamental clash of cultures, Russian and Georgian. In their telling, an ancient people with a deeply embedded ethnoreligious culture confronted an emasculating imperial power determined to annihilate their civilization and people through repression and assimilation. Opposed to that story, and ultimately far less influential among Georgians, was the defense of empire related by Russian officialdom and its supporters, a heroic tale of a great state tolerant of and caring for its constituent peoples, which then faced ungrateful and rebellious subjects thwarting the civilizing mission of a benevolent empire. Here repression, as with other imperial projects, was justified in the name of order and progress.

Each story left out the interplay with the other. Founded on sharp lines of difference between ethnic cultures, on the one hand, and between empire and nation, on the other, the conflicting narratives neglected the constitutive effects of imperial rule on the making of nations within the empire as well as the ways in which peoples shared, borrowed, and migrated between different cultures. Georgian and many non-Russian nationalist intellectuals spoke of the recovery of a constant, primordial nationhood that the empire was determined to suppress. Russians lauded the benefits of empire and promoted a patriotic identification of the tsar's subjects with the imperial enterprise. Generations of Georgian and other Russophilic intellectuals accepted that Russia was the path to Europe and a higher civilization. It was in this contested imperial setting, in a colonialized borderland experiencing the contradictions of subordination and progress, that Ioseb Jughashvili was born and within which he would grow.

Ioseb Jughashvili was born in Gori on December 9, 1879, to Bessarion (Beso) Jughashvili (ca. 1850–1909), a shoemaker, and his religious wife, Ketevan (Ekaterine, Keke) Geladze (1856/1860–1937).[1] Or so it is usually reported. Even this most basic of facts about the young Stalin is disputed. According to the *metricheski tsigni* (Record Book) of the Cathedral of the Assumption in Gori, the boy was born on December 6, 1878, and christened on the 17th, a year and three days earlier than Stalin himself usually claimed.[2] His childhood was not particularly distinct from that of other poor boys in Gori, and the mature Stalin rarely referred back to his early life. When the great Russian writer Mikhail Bulgakov wrote a play at the end of the 1930s about his youthful years, Stalin had the work suppressed, commenting, "All young people are alike, why write a play about the young Stalin?"[3] His biographers have had to rely on a few disjointed official records, the reminiscences of his boyhood friends, particularly those of Ioseb Iremashvili, and on the few details provided by his mother.[4] From these fragments a spare picture can be drawn. The boy was treasured by his mother, who bore the loss of two or three infants, all male, in five years, the last one two years after Ioseb's birth.[5] Usually referred to as Soso, the Georgian diminutive of Ioseb, he suffered a bout with smallpox that scarred his face permanently and an injury, probably incurred when he fell under a carriage, that shortened his left arm.[6] When he was ten or eleven he was again hit by a carriage, which rolled over his legs but left no permanent damage.[7] Yet many remember him as a boy who was physically active and quite strong, though among the shortest of the boys in his class, a good swimmer and wrestler, with a talent for singing and poetry, well-behaved and studious, but as rowdy and ready to misbehave as his friends. He was the best of the bunch with a slingshot. Clearly competitive, anxious to be the first or the best, Soso compensated for his height and disability with extra effort and his intellect.[8]

The future Stalin grew up in the periphery of a periphery, a frontier between European Russia and the Middle East.[9] Caucasia was the borderland where the Muslim world of the Ottomans and Persians met Christian Armenians and Georgians. He was born at a time when Georgia was undergoing particularly palpable social changes that affected even isolated Gori. Founded in the Middle Ages, Gori was originally built to house Armenian refugees who would eventually make up Georgia's trading and manufacturing middle class. Lying in an amphitheater with mountains around it, the town was up the Mtkvari River (the Kura) from Mtskheta, the ancient capital of Eastern Georgia (Kartli), and its successor, Tbilisi (known to the Russians and foreigners as Tiflis). In the 1870s Gori was little more than a big village, though it was the largest town in the district and the official center of the region. With about thirteen hundred buildings, ten of which were government offices, it was home to less than ten thousand people at the turn of the twentieth century. Gori boasted a medieval fortress, admired by the French novelist and traveler Alexandre Dumas when he changed horses in town in 1859, and had a modest cathedral, a theater, the religious school in which young Jughashvili would study, three hundred small shops, twenty-four inns or taverns, seventeen *duknebi* (pub-like wine and food cellars), four hotels, a state school, and one of the first pharmacies in the Caucasus. Most of the houses were small limestone dwellings, but almost all had an orchard or a vineyard attached. All but three of the roughly forty streets were twisted lanes, unpaved and dusty.[10] The Russian writer Maxim Gorky visited Gori in the early 1890s and described how "over the whole town lies the gray coloring of some kind of isolation and wild originality. The sultry sky above the town, the turbulent and troubled waves of the Kura nearby, the mountains at a distance with neatly placed holes—this is a city of caves; and still further, on the horizon, the eternal unmoving white clouds—there are the mountains of the Caucasian range, studded with silver, never melting snow."[11]

But change was coming to Gori. In 1872 the town was connected by rail west to the port of Poti on the Black Sea and east to Tiflis, and by 1883 one could take a train from Gori through Tiflis farther east to oil-rich Baku on the Caspian. With rail access to wider markets, villages ceased to be cut off. Towns received goods more easily from Russia and

Europe; and new enterprises, initiated primarily by the entrepreneurial Armenian middle class, undermined the protected production of local artisans. The railroad was a mixed blessing for Gori, which lost its prominence as a trading center, as many peasants preferred to make the journey to Tiflis for their purchases. Like many of his contemporaries, Soso Jughashvili was a first-generation town dweller. As Georgians came to the towns in the last decades of the nineteenth century, they found people of other religions and languages, Armenians and Russians primarily. Contact heightened awareness of the distinctions among peoples, even though the boundaries between ethnicities were repeatedly crossed, in school and through public activity. The very choice to speak Georgian on the streets or in the markets almost always excluded any Russians nearby. While difference did not necessarily imply hostility or conflict, people circulated in an environment marked by distinctions of ethnicity, social class, and religion, especially when ethnicity overlapped with class and differences in power. Very often Armenians occupied more privileged positions, as merchants or factory owners. Soso's father worked as a shoemaker for Armenian entrepreneurs. As a consequence, Georgian peasants like the Jughashvilis found themselves thrust into an unstable world in which their material condition was precarious, their sense of social status challenged, and their ethnic identity a refuge.[12]

Georgia had been part of the Russian Empire for less than a century when Soso was born, and for much of that time the Russian administration had not interfered with the customs or even the customary law of the Georgians. In a provincial capital like Gori the reach of Russian rule was limited. Yet the garrison stood as a reminder of tsarist power, and the execution of peasant rebels or "bandits" reinforced the impression that behind the tax collectors and local bureaucrats stood the army and the police. Georgian traditions, however, were intact, though changing, as were kinship and friendship networks. Through the year various religious holidays and popular festivals affirmed Georgians' preferred understanding of their history. The most important festival, the carnival of *qeenoba*, marked a long-ago conquest of Georgia by the Persian shah and a victorious uprising of the Georgians. Such invasions and rebellions were so numerous in Georgian history that the revelers referred to no specific battle. In Gori, as in Tiflis, two sides were formed, one symbolically representing the Persians, the other the Georgians. The shah's forces occupied the town until mid-day. Then the Georgian side came forth; fights broke out; and the shah was thrown into the river. In the evening a massive fistfight brought the festivities to a spirited end.[13]

Georgians were still largely a rural people, and ninety-five percent of Gori district's inhabitants were officially classified as peasants. In the state's eyes Soso Jughashvili was recorded as a peasant from his father's village, Didi-Lilo. The legal emancipation of landlord serfs had just been completed in the 1870s, and noble landlords only reluctantly and slowly granted permission for peasants to move freely from their villages. Peasants who lost their land or their jobs as household servants or had their plots reduced were compelled to find new work in the towns.[14] The first factories deserving of that name were opened in Tiflis and to the east in Baku. In 1860 an Englishman named Rooks opened the first "mechanized workshop," and five years later the Armenian Mirzoev established the first textile mill in Tiflis.[15]

From the beginning of the nineteenth century, when the Russian Empire annexed the Georgian kingdoms and principalities, European culture steadily filtered into the towns of South Caucasia, starting with the urban aristocracy and the commercial middle class. Already by the 1840s Georgian and Armenian townswomen in Tiflis, just a half day's journey from Gori, were either modifying their dress along European lines or adopting the latest fashions from Paris. The newer districts of the city were built not in the traditional Georgian styles, but according to the dictates of neo-classicism. "It is not to be forgotten," wrote the traveler A. L. Zisserman, "that [comparing] Tiflis in 1842 and 1878 is [like] Asia and Europe; now one has to search for oriental peculiarities, but then they simply hit you in the eye."[16] As Caucasian styles retreated, city life grew more distinct from village life, which remained bound to older local traditions. As a small city Gori shared in the changes affecting the rest of the South Caucasus, though not as dramatically as Tiflis or Baku. Gorians experienced a slower pace of life, without the dynamic diversity of a city or the attractions of a lively nightlife.

All through Soso's childhood there was a steady introduction of new products, styles, and possibilities for social mobility. Modernity was associated with Russia, and through Russia Europe, tradition with Georgia, and in Gori a certain suspicion of the novel and unfamiliar reigned. When one of their pals returned from a sojourn with his cultivated Armenian relatives in Tiflis, outfitted in a European-style sailor suit, complete with red pompom on his hat, Soso's Gori companions were both fascinated and appalled by his attire. Soso grabbed his hat roughly, and before the little sailor's grandmother could rescue him, he lay on the ground nearly naked.[17]

The Jughashvili family was not particularly distinguished from other peasants of the region, though at the end of the 1930s a report was published, probably in an effort to give Stalin a revolutionary pedigree, that Stalin's great-grandfather, Zaza, had led a peasant revolt.[18] Stalin's paternal grandfather, Vano, had two other children: a son Grigori, who it was later said had been killed by bandits, and a daughter, Pelageia, of whom nothing is known.[19] For reasons that remain obscure, Soso Jughashvili's family, on both sides, was socially ambitious, not content to remain in the traditional peasant milieu. Even before he had committed to Marxism the young Soso grew up in an environment in which the move from village to town and the metamorphosis from peasant to worker represented major improvements in social standing. But such moves were difficult, and life was as precarious, if not more, in the town as in the village. His father had moved up from peasant to craftsman. Soso would move even higher through the educational system available to a poor provincial Georgian. His mother would see to that. Yet both father and son experienced the tension between the ideal images of Georgian masculinity and the frustrations imposed by poverty that made it nearly impossible to realize the ideal.

His father's odyssey reproduced that of many of his generation. For all the tales of alcoholism and hooliganism that have attached themselves to his name, Beso Jughashvili appears to have been someone who sought a better life. He came from humble origins. His ancestors, the Gerelis (from the village of Geri), had raised livestock. From the word *jogi* (herd) the family was known as *mejogeebi* (herders or shepherds). As serfs, they worked for the noble Machabeli family. Because the

Osetins, a mountain people who competed with Georgians for land and power in the region south of the mountains, frequently attacked their village, the Machabelis resettled the family in Didi-Lilo.[20] After his father's death, Beso left the village to find work in Tiflis at the newly opened shoe factory of the Armenian manufacturer Adelkhanov. He soon rose to the rank of *master* (skilled worker). When another Armenian, Hovsep Baramov, opened a shoe workshop in Gori to supply the local garrison, Beso was invited to return to his native region. Although not formally educated, Beso had learned to speak the languages of the towns—Russian, Armenian, and "Turkish" (Azeri)—and even to read Georgian, a skill that few of his fellow workers could claim.[21] He was respected as someone who could recite from memory lines from the medieval Georgian epic, Shota Rustaveli's *vepkhistqaosani* (The Knight in the Panther's Skin). He soon was able to open his own workshop and bragged about how the son of a simple peasant had risen to become a master craftsman.[22] Almost all production in Gori was in the hands of self-employed artisans. Since larger workshops and factories in Tiflis and Russia were producing most of the new shoes, an independent craftsman like Beso more often than not did repair work. Business was good. He hired apprentices. And he prepared to seek a wife.

Ketevan Geladze, whom friends and relatives called Keke, was the daughter of Glakho and Melania, who lived in the village of Ghambareuli, not far from Gori. Her parents were serfs who had fled with their children from the village of Sveneti because they found their lords, the Amilakhvaris, unbearable. Swampy and chilly Ghambareuli, however, was a harsh refuge. Keke suffered from fevers and headaches, and her father soon died, leaving his wife with a daughter and two sons, Giorgi (Gio) and Sandala.[23] The family worked as gardeners for Armenian landlords, the Ghambarovs. With the serf emancipation of the 1860s her mother decided to move the family to Gori. Relatives gave them a piece of land on which the boys built a little house in the section of town called *rusisubani*, the "Russian district," because of a Russian army barracks. There Keke restored her health and developed into an attractive young woman.

Thanks to their mother, Keke and her brothers were taught to read and write in Georgian. For Georgian women literacy was rare.[24]

Beautiful by all accounts, "slender, chestnut-haired with big eyes" (by her own description), she was introduced to the handsome, musta-chioed Beso. Her brother, Gio, liked Beso and encouraged the marriage. At their introduction, unsure of him, Keke began to cry, but inside, she confesses, she was happy because all the local girls were attracted to Beso and envied her for catching the handsome young man. On May 17, 1874, at seventeen, she married him, in a ceremony that was traditionally Georgian, in the style befitting a *karachokheli*, "a fearless and irreproach-able knight."[25] Close friends of the family, Iakob Egnatashvili and Mikha Tsikhitatrishvili, themselves *karachokhelebi*, gave her away.

At first the marriage was a happy one. Settling in *rusisubani*, not far from the medieval fortress, *goristsikhe*, the Jughashvilis rented a one-room apartment in a small house. A fit, strong man, reputed to be the best shoemaker in Gori, Beso was moving up in the world.[26] The family lived better than the other workers in the shop, and one acquaintance noted, "they always had butter at home. Beso considered selling things shameful."[27] He went to church regularly with Keke's mother and pro-vided well for his family.[28] He was overjoyed by the birth of their first son, Mikheil. But when the boy died a few months later, his grief led him to drink. The death of his second son only compounded his despair. Keke remembered that Beso almost went mad. A fervent believer in the powers of Saint Giorgi the Victor of Geri, he made a pilgrimage to the Geri monastery and promised to make a sacrifice if his third child lived.[29] Faith for Beso, like that of many Georgians and Armenians, was tied up with ancient pagan traditions, like animal sacrifice and wishing trees, along with the more formal rituals of the church. At the time of Soso's birth, Beso embodied a model Georgian man: proud, strong, de-sirous of sons, pious, and a good provider. But that would soon change.

The birth of Soso was filled with anxiety. The family decided not to have Egnatashvili, who had already served twice, as the godfather. In-stead they invited their close family friend, Mikha Tsikhitatrishvili, hus-band of Maria.[30] When the baby became ill, the couple turned to prayer and made a pilgrimage to the holy shrine at Geristavi to save him. Soso was very weak and thin, constantly sick. Maria Tsikhitatrishvili breast-fed him when Keke was not home, and Keke reciprocated with Maria's

Sandro, five months younger than Soso.[31] Soso would not eat meat, only *lobio* (beans). His first word was *dunala*, which was used for everything shiny. At one point he stopped speaking altogether and started again only when his frightened parents made another trip to Geristavi. There they sacrificed a sheep and ordered a mass. When a nun in white appeared, the terrified boy threw himself into his mother's arms to avoid the "evil angel." In his mother's eyes Soso was a very sensitive child. When he saw his father drunk, he cuddled with his mother and urged her to visit the neighbors until his father fell asleep. He became more introverted and stopped playing as much with his friends. Gori boys played a game called *arsenaoba* that reenacted the exploits of the social bandit Arsena, a kind of Georgian Robin Hood. Instead Soso asked to be taught the poem celebrating Arsena's life.[32]

Over time Beso's alcoholism grew worse. He drank with his customers, toasting the shoes he had made for them. Egnatashvili tried but failed to stop him. His hands began to shake, and he could not work. He befriended a Russian, Poka, who matched his consumption of alcohol, downing vodka instead of wine. When Poka froze to death on a snowy road, it was Beso who buried him. Beso took on an apprentice, Dato Gasitashvili, who did the work that Beso was less and less able to do at the shop. But Dato soon opened his own business, and Beso's next choice was less successful. Vano Khutishvili simply fed Beso more drink. As the family's fortunes fell, they moved like nomads from house to apartment to living with other families. In ten years of marriage, from roughly Soso's fourth to fourteenth year, they moved nine times.[33]

Eventually Beso gave up his workshop completely. When Soso was five Beso moved back to Tiflis without his family, as was often the practice, to take up his old job at Adelkhanov's. Beso's "proletarianization" might be seen as a fall in status from independent artisan, but the move to Tiflis and factory work probably meant a higher and steadier income. Craftsmen could no longer effectively compete with mechanized shoe production. Beso thought enough of his new position as factory worker to force his son into the factory against the wishes of the boy's mother. Keke believed that her husband needed his son because he could no longer work well. Soso worked as an apprentice shoemaker briefly in

Tiflis, but at age six he contracted smallpox and nearly died. Keke retrieved her son and brought him back to Gori, terrified that her only surviving son would perish. Soso burned with high fever for three days. On the fourth day he was covered with red spots and blisters. Three days later they filled with pus, and in another ten days scabs formed. When the scabs fell off, they left deep, pitted pockmarks that Stalin would retain the rest of his life.[34]

Scarred but alive, Soso was adored by his parents, each in their own way. Beso wanted his son to be a worker but lost out to Keke, who was determined that her only son become a priest. Soso remained, according to Iremashvili and others, devoted to his mother, and she to him. In her memoir dictated later, Ketevan Jughashvili emphasized Soso's contemplative nature and his delight in reading and walking. She remembered his love for the music of the *duduki* (Caucasian flute), for birds, and daisies, which as an infant he called *zi zi*. Her mother carried the baby into the garden to hear the birds, and Keke taught Soso to walk by holding out a daisy, enticing him forward.[35] An independent child, he obeyed his parents when he felt like it. "When his mother called him and if he did not want to come, he stayed at his game."[36]

The boy was frail and prone to illness. "Like his mother," Davrishev recalled, "he had an emaciated face, somewhat pale, lightly marked by smallpox, a strong jaw, and a low, stern forehead. In general, he had the calm and reflective air of someone whose brain was busy with serious things, but without doubt he would give himself these airs to impress Kola and me, a bit younger than he, and show off. This calm apparently did not impede him at other times when he was angry to become brutal, to swear like a carter and to push things to the extreme."[37] But, thought Davrishev, all Georgians are like that.

No longer able to afford a place of their own, the Jughashvilis rented the second floor of the house of a friend, the priest Kristepore Charkviani. Soso was seven and adored by the Charkvianis' children. Against her husband's wishes and with tears in her eyes, Keke pleaded with the children to teach her son to read: "Children, I wish only that my child would not stay illiterate; bless you, please teach my child the alphabet, and he will make his way and not fail in life." When Beso left for work, the Charkviani children taught Soso in secret. But Beso figured out what was going on and exploded, "Do not spoil my child, or I will show you!" He forced the weeping Soso to go to his workshop, dragging him off by his ear. Keke was determined that Soso be educated, however. After a break, the lessons continued, interrupted when Soso grew tired and turned to play with the dolls of the young daughter of the family.[38] Years later, when he was in the third year of the Gori Seminary, Soso told his friend Giorgi Elisabedashvili of the deep love he felt for Father Charkviani's daughter and laughed at himself for being so smitten.[39]

To survive Keke depended on the kindness of friends. She wanted to work in a bakery or as a laundress to supplement their dwindling income, but proud, old-style Beso forbade his wife to work outside the home. The Charkvianis helped the family and treated them like relatives. Friends like Mariam, Egnate Egnatashvili's wife, sent baskets of fruit to the family.[40] To save herself and her son from her drunken husband, Keke moved in with her brothers. Twice Beso pleaded with Keke to be allowed to return to the family, but she rebuffed his attempts to reconcile with her. Keke was finished with him. Her brothers and Egnatashvili pressured her to compromise, and Giorgi blamed her for breaking up the family and preventing Soso from becoming a shoemaker. It was shameful, he said, for her to be without a husband. What would people say? Keke stood her ground and insisted that Soso would go to school. Her brother stopped speaking to her for a week, but she would not give in. The breakup of the family dragged on, a damaging, searing series of events that continued well into Soso's teenage years. His ties with his father, however, had been broken long before. For Beso, sending his son to school was a disgrace, and he eventually abandoned his family, probably in 1890 when Soso was eleven.[41]

Keke's dream that Soso enter the seminary and become a priest met yet another obstacle. Only sons of priests were accepted into the elementary church school. Again, friends came to the rescue. So that Soso could take the entrance examinations, Father Charkviani claimed that Beso was his deacon. The shoemaker's son passed with flying colors.[42]

In a society like Georgia, with strict ideas of honor and shame, Beso was seen as a failure.[43] He lost out to his wife. He stood between cultures, the agricultural past and the industrial future, less secure and determined than his strong-willed wife, who was ready to break with certain male-enforced conventions. Beso dressed in traditional Georgian clothes, the *chokha*, a long-sleeved coat that flared at the bottom, but appropriately, as a worker, wore a Russian cap. Keke, "even though poorer than others . . . wore the old traditional costume of Georgian women"—the flowing blue dress with long sleeves and the *chikhta*, the traditional headdress.[44] Those who knew her have claimed that Keke personified the ideal of Georgian womanhood—honest, gentle, and modest. This ideal was originally associated with noblewomen, but in the nineteenth century it was broadened into a national ideal. Graceful and sexually passive, a Georgian woman was supposed to be a virgin until marriage, keep a neat house, and be prepared at any time to receive guests with food and drink.[45] Her most important role was the raising of sons.[46] For Georgian patriots this was a woman's duty to the nation. In one of his best-known verses, "To a Georgian Mother," the Georgian nationalist poet Ilia Chavchavadze wrote: "Ah here, o mother, is thy task, Thy sacred duty to thy land: Endow thy sons with spirits strong, With strength of heart and honor bright, Inspire them with fraternal love, To strive for freedom and for right."[47] The poet both reflected and produced what he projected as the ideal for a Georgian woman.

Instead of being submissive and obedient, pushing against tradition and custom, Keke found the courage of the rebel and struck out on her own. With the help of friends she took in sewing to supplement the poor family income, and for a time she worked for the family of Damian Davrishev, the prefect of police. The head of the local church school, the Russian Belaev, sent laundry to Keke and paid her well. When Darejan and Liza Kulijanov opened a tailoring shop, she went to work as a seamstress and sewed dresses in their atelier for the next seventeen years. Keke was unusual for a Georgian woman of the time. Strong-willed, she was prepared to live without a man. She focused completely on her son. At the same time, she insisted on piety. Rituals were important and had to be faithfully observed. Once Soso refused to go to church to bless a watermelon and stood in one place refusing to move. For hours he stayed there, from morning to night, eventually catching a chill and fainting. Neither son nor mother would give in. She was not only determined but also ambitious for her son. Literate in Georgian, able to provide for her beloved offspring, Keke Jughashvili never gave up her dream that he would become a priest, even after he became the secular autocrat of the largest country in the world. When Soso's teacher, Simon Goglichidze, suggested that the boy transfer from the religious school to the local pedagogical institute, a school from which he could go on to the *gimnaziia* (classical high school) and university, Keke gratefully refused.[48]

Stalin's daughter, Svetlana Allilueva, had clear memories of her grandmother and of her father's affection and respect for her. "She was very devout and dreamt that her son would become a priest. She remained religious until her last days and when father visited her not long before her death she told him: 'It's a shame that you didn't become a priest.' . . . He repeated these words of hers with delight; he liked her scorn for all he had achieved, for the earthly glory, for all the fuss."[49]

Although poor, Keke made sure that her son was well-dressed. A friend remembered his good shoes, a heavy gray wool overcoat, and a winter hood, which Keke made for him.[50] Soso slept on a *kushetka* (couch), and when he outgrew it, Keke extended it with boards. Once his teachers, who periodically inspected the homes of their pupils, arrived in the rain to find Soso and his mother huddled in a corner away from the leaking roof.[51] Stalin considered his mother to have been intelligent, though uneducated. Resolute and willful, she bore the scorn of some in her society who considered such a brazen woman to be morally loose. When she died "around eighty years old," Svetlana Allilueva recalled, "My father grieved very much and often spoke about her later."[52]

While Soso's mother may not have been the perfect Georgian wife— she certainly did not defer to her husband—she erred on the side of power and principle. But Soso's father did not measure up to the strict masculine ideal of Georgian men. For Georgians to say "*katsia katsuri*" ("He is a man's man!"), one ideally would have to be fearless, determined, resolute, impetuous, assertive, and even possess a kind of repressed aggressiveness. Physically he should be tall, broad-shouldered, and strong; in personal relations he must be loyal to his family, friends, and nation. And he should be able to hold his alcohol and control his emotions.

Realizing the image of a *katsi* is extraordinarily difficult, but it is an ideal toward which one strives. Failure can mean not only loss of respect but also loss of honor. "It is better," the Georgians say, "to lose your head than your honor." It was terrible to be called *unamuso* (shameless, remorseless). Largely a man's business among the Caucasian peoples, honor brings with it prestige and status, even for the low born, but loss of honor is a sin, a kind of social death. However attenuated, even contorted, the meaning of honor and shame became later in Stalin's life, both his behavior and his image retained much of the masculine ideal of the *katsi*— toughness, disciplined emotions, and sobriety (at least in public).

If any social practice marks Georgia it is the *supra* (feast), the highly performative ritual of inviting, feeding, and elaborately toasting one's friends and visiting strangers. Abundance, display, even excess are obligatory for a successful *supra*. Essential for the master of a house is the periodic display of generosity at the feast, the fulfillment of one's reciprocal obligation to entertain, praise, and honor one's friends by lavishly wining and dining them. The table with its elaborate rituals—the *tamada* (toastmaster), strictly regulated toasts, enforced drinking, complexly harmonized group singing, all in an atmosphere of male camaraderie and female subordination—was the very center of traditional Georgian life.[53] In a culture that prides itself on occasional lavishness of food preparation and abundance, Beso could provide only modest fare—*lobio*, boiled potatoes, either eggplant or vegetables with ground meat, *lavashi* (flat bread) with onions. Most Gorians had their own orchards or vineyards outside the town, but there is no record that the Jughashvilis ever possessed one.[54] This ideal of the Georgian male, the proud Georgian host who spares nothing for his honored guests, was one of the few Georgian customs that Stalin maintained to the end of his life. But such a display of largesse was difficult, if not impossible, for his father, Beso Jughashvili, to achieve. A popular Georgian saying laments, "When your house is empty, where is your honor?"

Drunkenness and fighting were not unusual activities for Georgian men, or for that matter, Russians. Throughout the empire factory workers and artisans turned in their leisure time to heavy drinking and brawling. On weekends mass fistfights (*mushti-krivi* in Georgian, *kulach-nye boi* in Russian) were organized to let off steam or settle old scores. The governor of Gori outlawed *krivi* (boxing), but it went on anyway. Drinking bouts, carried on with wine in place of vodka, were deeply embedded in traditional male culture and were considered appropriate, even required, behavior for "true men." The proper way to drink was with friends, not alone, usually at a table laden with food, and ritualistically with toasts. One never took a drink on one's own but waited to be prompted. Being able to hold your liquor and drinking to the bottom of the glass were virtues. Drunkenness was common but restricted to specific occasions. Alcoholism and the loss of control, however, were unacceptable.

Whereas drinking and fighting were valued in Georgian male society, loss of control and uncontrollable drunkenness were signs of weakness. Beso fell far short of this Georgian ideal of *katsoba* (manliness). The unquestioned head of the household, a real *katsi* was made splendid by his wife's subordination to him. Beso's lack of authority within the family, challenged and defeated by his unbending wife, along with his inability to provide the means for display and magnanimity valued by Georgians, and his personal impotence (alcoholism) brought shame and dishonor on his family.

Beating a child, likewise, was unacceptable if done arbitrarily or in a stupor. Iremashvili claims that Soso was mercilessly beaten by his father and concludes that, "Through him Soso learned to hate people. The young boy matured far too early to independent thought and observation. Soso hated his father most of all, who drank most of his meager earnings, and through this forced his mother into exhausting night work at the sewing machine."[55] Soso's boyhood pal, Soso Davrishev, also remembered Beso brutally beating his son, thinking that it was very unusual for fathers to beat their sons so mercilessly. Usually a slap on the face was enough punishment to induce shame.[56] Kote Charkviani remembered that a drunk Beso even stormed into the school searching for Soso, but his classmates and teachers hid him and insisted that Soso was absent that day.[57] Strangely enough, however, Keke Jughashvili never mentions her husband beating her son. The greatest offenses hinted at in her memoirs are Beso's insults against herself that troubled Soso. In her first memoir Svetlana Allilueva remembers her father telling her not of beatings by his father but by his mother, and only in her second, *After One Year*, does she emphasize the cruelty of her father's father: "Sometimes [my father] told me about his childhood. Fights, crudeness were not a rare phenomenon in this poor, semi-literate family where the head of the family drank. The mother beat the little boy, the husband beat her. But the boy loved his mother and defended her; once he threw a knife at his father. [The father] then chased him, shouting, and neighbors hid [the boy]."[58]

Davrishev reports that Beso complained to his father, the popular prefect, about the "misconduct" of his wife, while Keke complained that her husband beat her and drank his wages away at Ignatashvili's tavern. He relates that Beso attempted to kill Davrishev's father, suspecting him of fathering Soso. The policeman did not prosecute his would-be assassin, but, known in town as *gizhi Beso* (crazy Beso), Beso had to leave Gori.[59] Estranged from family and friends, violent, erratic, and drunk, Beso Jughashvili represented a social and cultural failure in the eyes of his fellow Georgians.

In later years Stalin never revealed how he felt about these beatings nor recorded any specific memory of his father. The passing remark to Emil Ludwig in 1931 ("My parents were uneducated people, but they treated me not badly at all") contradicts his youthful companions' depiction of merciless abuse, but then unpleasant memories of childhood mistreatment are often repressed. As a young man he occasionally used Besoshvili (son of Beso) as his revolutionary nickname, indicating that there may have been some lingering affection or regret regarding this parent. Long after Soso had moved away from Georgian national values to Marxism he remembered his father in an oblique, disparaging reference. In his essay "Anarchism or Socialism?" written in 1906–1907, he recounted a story of a worker, evidently modeled on his father, who remained imbued with the consciousness of private property even after he had undergone proletarianization:

Let us take a shoemaker who owned a tiny workshop, but who, unable to withstand the competition of the big manufacturers, closed his workshop and took a job, say, at Adelkhanov's factory, not with the view to becoming a permanent wage worker, but with the object of saving up some money, of accumulating a little capital to enable him to reopen his workshop. As you see, the position of this shoemaker is *already* proletarian, but his consciousness is *still* non-proletarian; it is thoroughly petty bourgeois.[60]

As apparently revealing as this passage seems to be about the young Marxist's condescending view of his father, it also adds a meaningful role for the son. The shoemaker moves "up" to become a proletarian, but his consciousness lags behind. Social position in and of itself does not produce mentalities. For the Bolshevik propagandist the missing agent here is the political activist, the Social Democrat, who will assist the worker to become a politically conscious proletarian. This was the role that the young Stalin would seek for himself.

A childhood acquaintance, the Armenian Simon Ter-Petrosian, later to be a major Caucasian revolutionary (known later by his revolutionary pseudonym Kamo), remembered that Soso gained a reputation in Gori when he defended his father, who had unjustly been accused of not paying his debts.[61] A shopkeeper named Vasadze kept a book where he recorded what was owed him, and since Beso sometimes paid his debts while stupefied by drink, the crafty merchant claimed he had not paid. Beso realized what was happening and loudly protested, only to be dragged off to the police station. Then only eleven, and upset when he saw his mother in tears, Soso went to see Vasadze and somehow convinced him to drop the charges. The story made the rounds of the town, but no one could understand why the shopkeeper had admitted that it had been his mistake. Only many years later did Kamo ask Stalin what he had said to the merchant to change his mind. "Nothing special," Stalin answered. "I promised to set fire to his shop if Vasadze did not set right what he had done. Vasadze understood that I was not joking. That's all there was to it."[62]

Once Beso left Gori, Soso lost touch with his father. They met again in Tiflis sometime after the boy entered the seminary there in 1894.

When his cousin Ana Geladze visited him, they went to Beso's shoe shop, and Soso left with a pair of boots made by his father. From childhood through the rest of his life he loved wearing boots, recalled Geladze.[63] Soso's friend Kote Charkviani remembered that he saw Beso in Tiflis "dejected, . . . not the formerly self-satisfied, cleanly shaved man. He rented a small workshop on Mukhrani Street and repaired clothes." But he still loved his son and constantly talked about him. Soso and Kote visited him, and Beso reached into his pocket to give his last pennies to his son. There were no reproaches while Soso was present, but once when Beso ran into Kote, he was upset that Soso was "fighting against (Tsar) Nikolai, as if he were going to drag him from the throne."[64] It appears that Beso attempted to solicit help from his son when Soso was studying in the Tiflis Seminary, appealing to the rector: "My son is studying here. You see in what a poor condition I live. Please make him leave the seminary and help me, for I need someone to take care of me." A friend reports, "Soso was not moved by this story at all. He knew well that his father's words were empty and that he could not be removed from the seminary against his will. Therefore, he was not moved at all. Soso saw how helpless his father was, but what could he do; he had no means to help him."[65]

Stalin may not have known Beso's ultimate fate, and biographers have speculated about both the date and the manner of his death. Unsubstantiated accounts have it that he was killed in a drunken brawl, perhaps in 1890, perhaps later. Both boyhood friend Iremashvili and daughter Allilueva testified that Beso died violently, stabbed with a knife.[66] His wife, Ekaterine, told interviewer Jerome Davis in 1927 that when Soso was ten, "his father returned from work one night saying that he felt ill. He went to bed and died in his sleep."[67] Three years later she told an American interviewer in 1930 that her husband had been killed around 1890, and biographers Edward Ellis Smith, Robert McNeal, and Miklós Kun also affirmed that Beso probably lived until 1909.[68] His actual passing was much more mundane than a knife fight. With the opening of the Georgian archives, it can be confirmed that he died on August 12, 1909, in the Mikhailovskii Hospital in Tiflis of tuberculosis, colitis, and chronic pneumonia. He was buried in a pauper's grave.[69]

Soso lived in a family where his mother's breaking the near sacred convention of female submission undermined his father's traditional patriarchal authority. This reversal of roles profoundly affected the boy. As Allilueva reports, the beatings by his mother, the more impressive parent, were not resented. Her father told her "how [Keke] beat him when he was small and how she beat his father, who loved to drink. Her character, evidently, was strict and decisive, and this delighted father." Widowed early she "became even more severe. . . . Grandmother had her principles—the principles of a religious person who had lived a strict, hard, honest, and worthy life. Her firmness, obstinacy, her strictness toward herself, her puritan morality, her masculine character—all of this passed to my father. He was much more like her than like his father."[70]

2

THE PUPIL

In 1890, having entered the Gori Religious School, I first met the eleven year old Iosif Dzhugashvili. Our subjects were taught in Russian, and only twice a week did they teach us Georgian. Born in Mingrelia, I pronounced Georgian words with an accent. This caused the pupils to laugh at me. Iosif, on the other hand, came to my aid. Modest and sensitive, he approached me and said, "Hey, I will learn the Mingrelian language from you, and you will learn Georgian from me. This heartfelt move of a comrade deeply touched me.

—D. GOGOKHIA, "NA VSIU ZHIZN' ZAPOMNILIS' ETI DNI"
["WE REMEMBERED THESE DAYS OUR WHOLE LIFE"] (1937)

The streets of Gori were in a real sense Stalin's first school. "All the kids of Gori were raised together in the street," writes Soso Davrishev, "without distinction based on religion, nationality, or wealth, and they were looked after by the whole community."[1] But parents did not intervene in the quarrels of the boys and sometimes even punished tattletales. The boys roamed together in neighborhood gangs and learned the fundamentals of loyalty, honor, self-esteem, and how to deal with adversaries. They observed laws—not to be overly irreverent or to hurt the weaker among them.[2] Soso took the boys' codes seriously. According to a boyhood friend, Grigol Glurjidze, Soso surprised his friends once when he refused to kiss someone near him, as Georgian males customarily did with friends. When asked why, he said, laughing, "I don't want to be a Pharisee and kiss those whom I do not love."[3] Soso led the gang of the Maidan (square) district, but occasionally he joined a gang in a neighboring street led by David Machavariani. The boys of Machavariani's *pranguli ubani* (French Quarter), where the Georgian and Armenian

Catholics had their church, built their own fortress hidden in an abandoned sawmill. Elaborate initiations were required before a boy could be admitted to the gang, as well as a sworn oath never to lie, to fear none but God, never to betray a comrade, and to obey the gang leaders. Unwilling to obey Machavariani, Soso tried to take over the gang, and the two boys came to blows. Although he lost the fight to the older boy, Soso was acknowledged as second in command.[4] Machavariani was the one to think up the various pranks in which the gang engaged, and Soso "contented himself with the role of organizer, pushing the others to carry them out."[5]

Fighting was the way young boys interacted with each other. When challenged by a neighbor's son, Ioseb (Soso) Iremashvili, to a fight, Soso Jughashvili beat him handily though perhaps not fairly. Iremashvili recalled that Jughashvili and he fought to a draw, but as Iremashvili adjusted his clothes, Jughashvili jumped him from behind, wrestled him to the ground, and was declared the winner. The two boys kissed and became fast friends.[6] A third, younger Soso, Davrishev recalled his earliest memory of Soso Jughashvili as a fight over a *khachapuri* (Georgian cheese pastry). When the older Soso finished his half, he took Davrishev's piece and commenced eating it. A fight ensued, broken up only by the intervention of Davrishev's father, the local chief of police. Learning what had happened, Davrishev senior reprimanded his own son: Soso Jughashvili was a guest in their house, and by Georgian custom nothing could be refused him. To make peace Davrishev's grandmother gave Jughashvili a large piece of cake. When alone with his friend, Soso divided the cake carefully and, laughing, gave a piece to Davrishev. "You see, *viro* (you ass)," he said, "thanks to me, we have two pieces of cake. Take your piece, we are even."[7]

Soso was a skilled wrestler, and his favorite move was called *shuasarma*, catching his opponent under his leg. He loved fighting and cheered on his mates, particularly the *palavanebi* (champions) that he favored.[8] When victorious, he snapped his fingers, yelled, and spun on one foot.[9] His gang's principal enemy was the band around Stepko Romanov, who was known to humiliate his captives by tying their hands behind their backs and sending them out with their pants down around their ankles. The gangs from the various neighborhoods within the town fought not only among themselves but also against the gangs of the suburbs, made up of the sons of workers and artisans. Once, in such a battle, Soso was pitted against a suburban gang leader, Mishatka the *Molokan*, a boy older and stronger than he.[10] Although he defended himself fiercely, when it became clear he would lose, Soso picked up a large stone and smashed his opponent's head. Even though later Mishatka ambushed Soso and beat him mercilessly, Soso's friends admired his audacity.[11] Another time he provoked an older boy, Prtiani, to fight him, and though he was thrown ten times, he refused to give up. When his mother saw her bloodied son, she cried to the police chief, but he calmly reminded her that "when a clay pot clashes with an iron pot, it's the clay pot that is cracked and not the iron." Soso's friends later took their revenge on Prtiani.[12]

The son of an alcoholic, abusive father, Soso Jughashvili knew physical violence from an early age—either bearing it himself or witnessing beatings of his mother. Whether inside his home or out on the street, violence was woven into the fabric of Gorian life, in its play, its celebrations, and the visible presence of the Russian gendarmes. He grew up learning to defend himself, to play rough, and in the competitive world of the street to do what he thought necessary to win. At home he saw a weak, defeated man prone to physical violence, but outside he was determined to come out on top.

Reminiscences published a half century after his years in Gori all mention his role as leader of his mates. But those published in the Soviet Union, at the height of Stalinism, portray not only an active, athletic child, but also a prefiguration of the powerful leader of the party and state—Soso Jughashvili, boy *vozhd'* (leader). Besides playing the usual Georgian games, like *krivi* (boxing), *arsenaoba* (named after the legendary social bandit), or *chilikaoba* (stick kicking), picking flowers and making wreaths, composing *shairi* (traditional Georgian verse), the boy in these books dominates by his natural talents, all of which are turned toward helping his weaker, less intelligent companions. A voracious reader and star pupil, Soso is at the center of every group, and even adults listen to him with pleasure. This is standard hagiography, and uncritical acceptance of these accounts of Soso's character in his formative years leads precisely to the conclusions their creators intended.[13]

Without a father at home to reprimand him and his mother often absent, working away from home, Soso was more independent than most. Boys of this age took up smoking, to the dismay of their parents, picking up butts in the streets for their improvised pipes.[14] One of their favorite games was *lakhti*, in which one boy's belt is placed in the center of a ring of boys who whip him as he tries to retrieve it. Georgii Vardoian, who entered the seminary at eight, remembered Soso as a staunch fellow with great authority among the other children.[15]

A childhood friend, Maria Makharoblidze-Kubladze, remembered that Soso loved to ride in Zakaria Kuladze's phaeton and urged him to drive the open carriage faster and faster. He called the driver *nagizhari*, crazy one, and would pull Maria's pigtails, pretend to be the bandit Arsena Odzelashvili, and tell her that he had abducted her. Sometimes he pretended to be a priest and demanded that she allow him to put his hand on her head. It was *nagizhari*'s carriage under which Soso fell. *Nagizhari* almost went mad, because he loved Soso very much. When the boy needed money, *nagizhari* helped him out.[16] Already adept at role-playing, Soso skillfully cultivated friends who in time became devoted to him.

Soso loved nature, and together with his boyhood companions he climbed up to Gorisjvari, the ancient fortress atop the hill above the town, where they could see the panorama of the two rivers, the Liakhvi and the Mtkvari, which joined near Gori.[17] There they met the hermit monk Tomas, who fed them nuts and regaled them with legends from the Georgian past. In his halting Georgian, Tomas read to them from the Georgian medieval epic of Shota Rustaveli. Soso was enthralled by the tale, and if someone interrupted the monk, he snapped, "*gachumdi, viro* [quiet, you ass]!"[18]

One of the few entertainments for the young boys of the town was the occasional visit of the old *mestvire* (troubadour), Sandro, whom they followed through the streets, forgetting the enmities of the different neighborhoods, enraptured by his ballads of the bandits Arsena and Tato and the noble Giorgi Saakadze, the seventeenth-century collaborator with and later rebel against the Persians.[19] What news of Georgia or the outside world there was came either from the local barbers or the few copies of whatever Georgian-language publication circulated from hand to hand.[20] In the evenings older women would gather in groups outside their houses and talk until nightfall. Soso Jughashvili and his friends sat with the women, listening to their gossip as well as Bible stories. When he heard the story of Judas's betrayal of Jesus, Soso asked, "Why . . . didn't Jesus take up his sword? Why didn't his comrades defend Jesus?" His friend's grandmother reminded him that Jesus had sacrificed himself to save "all of us."[21]

Soso was mischievous and enjoyed breaking rules at times. He loved fried potatoes and walnut preserves, and when he saw his chance to snatch some preserves, he lifted his younger cousin, Ana Geladze, onto his shoulders so that she could reach up and take the jar. But Ana dropped the jar, and it broke. Soso ran off, and the adults found only Ana to spank.[22] Once when an old woman entrusted him with a sack of communion bread to be consecrated, Soso and his pals quickly consumed seven pieces. Then Soso convinced the boys to fill the sack with air and punch it until it burst with a loud noise. One of the choirboys told a teacher that he had seen Soso's friend Kote Charkviani with the sack, and the unfortunate Kote was nearly expelled from the school. Soso denounced the "spy" and aroused the others to despise him. When the opportunity arose, they beat him black and blue.[23] Tough and ready to hold his own in the rough world of Gori boys, young Soso convinced the school inspector that the seminarians be given gymnastics lessons like the boys in the secular school. He was passionate about boxing, which was forbidden for seminary students. Like his older schoolmates, Soso waited until dark, crept away secretly to box, and later complained about the pain in his hands.[24]

His boyhood friend Sandro Elisabedashvili noted that though Soso was the shortest of the boys in their grade, he was also the first in most things, very bold, and smart. "We all wanted him in our group."[25] Soso even taught Sandro how to swim—in his own way. He threw his friend into the water, and Sandro barely made it to shore. Sandro was upset; Soso had almost drowned him. Soso replied that in one month he would explain himself. A week later Sandro was able to swim, and Soso reminded him of the saying, "Necessity teaches everyone."[26]

Soso's confidence and firm sense of self-worth was nurtured by his mother, who adored and sacrificed for him. In an interview with an American journalist in 1927, Keke remembered that he was "a good boy" whom she rarely had to punish. "He studied hard, was always reading and talking, trying to find out everything." Not only was he the favorite of his teacher, he was the leader of the local gang of boys. "Once he demonstrated his superiority by going around a complete circle of trees by hanging from the branches by his hands without once touching the ground. A feat that none of the other boys succeeded in doing." The proud mother, who had always been ambitious for her only child, added, "He was very sensitive to the injustice all about us."[27] Soso, she told the interviewer, had never been strong, was often ill, and suffered at age seven from smallpox. Her tale about hanging from the tree suggests that what the boy Soso lacked in strength he made up for in willpower. More likely, in this story, he benefited from the imagination of his doting mother.

The firmness and obstinacy that the young boy acquired from his mother was evident in an incident that occurred while Soso was in the Gori religious school. The Georgian language teacher, I. Peradze, gave the students an assignment to visit Ateni Church and write about it. On the way to the church Soso and his mates were stopped by an angry group of peasants whose grapevines had been vandalized. They were convinced that Soso and the others were the culprits. The boys scattered, but Soso stood his ground. A peasant threatened to take Soso to the police if he did not give him the names of the other boys. At first Soso refused; then he gave completely false names. Once freed, he met up with his friends and reprimanded them for their cowardice. He then softened his reproach: "You actually did the right thing, fellows, to run away. If you hadn't or if someone other than I had stayed behind, then, I think, the peasant would have gotten out of him all the names, and it is possible that for nothing we would have been expelled from school.[28] Not only was Soso sure of himself, he was convinced that among the boys from Gori he was particularly able to extricate himself from a

dangerous situation. In his view strategic lying was on occasion necessary and justified.

Gori had four schools for the children of its eight thousand inhabitants:
a four-class secular school, a four-class church school, a teachers' school,
and a women's school. Keke chose the four-class religious school for her
son. Founded in 1817, it was the oldest school in Gori, and it had four
primary schools attached to it—one for Georgians, the others for Russians, Armenians, and Muslims. Children of clergy were admitted easily,
along with the scions of the gentry, but poor students needed sponsors.
In school it was difficult to avoid the privileges and disadvantages that
were tied to one's social class and nationality. Russia was an empire, and
as an empire it preserved, even produced, differences along the lines of
social and ethnic distinction—differences that were marked as superior
and inferior.[29]

The Gori religious school was the ground where empire met ethnicity. While there were many connections between the peoples of
Caucasia, the school one attended, along with language, religion, and
cultural traditions, separated Georgians from Russians, Armenians,
and Muslims. Their tongues were mutually unintelligible and difficult
for the other to learn. Although in the towns of Caucasia many spoke
both Russian and Georgian and often Armenian or Azeri as well,
people were aware of and sensitive about their ethnicity and religion. The
Orthodox religion bridged the differences between Russians and Georgians, as they were members of a single church. The tsar had subordinated the Georgian Church to the Russian, reducing its authority over
the Georgian faithful. Orthodoxy separated Georgians from the Armenians, who had their own autonomous "Apostolic" or "Gregorian"
church, as well as from the Muslims and Jews among them. For some
Georgians the need for Russian protection and the hope for a northern
route to European enlightenment inspired dedication, even affection,
for the tsarist empire. But increasingly for others Russia seemed a brutal master and its culture a debased version of Europe's. The imposition
of Russian law, including serfdom, tsarist bureaucratic absolutism, and
a cultural condescension toward local customs and practices, stirred

resentment and opposition among segments of the nobility and the peasants.[30]

The highpoint of Georgian Russophilia was reached a quarter century before Soso Jughashvili's birth, during the administrations of Viceroy Mikhail Vorontsov (1845–1854) and Prince Aleksandr Bariatinskii (1856–1862). Many Georgian nobles loyally served the tsar in government and the army, and the first generation of Georgian intellectuals (known as the *tergdaleulni*, drinkers of the waters of the Terek River) made their way to Petersburg and Moscow to acquire European learning. When they returned to their homeland, however, making their way down the Georgian Military Highway, through the Darial Pass along the Terek, these gentry intellectuals thought of themselves as *mamulishvilebi* (sons of the fatherland) with a new appreciation of what was most valuable in their own people.[31]

On September 1, 1888, three months before his ninth birthday, Soso entered school, thanks to the Russian headmaster, Belaev, who convinced resistant Beso to allow the boy to study.[32] A year or two older than most of the other students, Soso was also one of the shortest of the boys in his class. In the one extant photograph of his Gori class, dark-haired and round-faced Soso is standing in the back row, a half head shorter than the others, straining, it seems, to appear taller. A teacher remembered him as "thin, with a pale face, lively, and someone who looked you straight in the eyes, poorly dressed but clean."[33]

Schooling distinguished young boys like Soso from the peasants and simple workers among whom he had played. Education was a ladder to the priesthood or the intelligentsia. By the 1890s the nascent Georgian intelligentsia, largely made up of provincial noblemen, had displaced the religious elite as the principal definer of Georgian culture. In the absence of a Georgian state the intellectuals became the inventors and carriers of what they determined to be the recovered national traditions. As the architects of a new nationalist discourse, they disseminated ideas that held sway among the elite until challenged at the turn of the century by a particularly Georgian Marxism. At first, as national awareness spread from a narrow circle of writers to the broader readership of their newspapers and novels, the relationship between Georgian intellectuals and Russians remained symbiotic rather than conflictual. Stimulated by European and Russian ethnographic and philological studies, interest and pride in the Georgian language grew along with a new appreciation of folk music, Georgia's history, and ethnography.[34] By the 1870s, however, the vulnerability of Georgian culture before the twin threats of the Russian language and the attractions of a more Europeanized urban life convinced several Georgian journalists and teachers to promote the teaching of their own language. In 1879 a number of Georgian cultural nationalists in Tiflis formed the Society for the Spread of Literacy among Georgians and began to publish textbooks and grammars.[35]

Soso entered school when the rediscovery of Georgianness that Russian-educated Georgian intellectuals and political activists had promoted was being disseminated to a broader reading public. Poets like Rapiel Eristavi, Ilia Chavchavadze, and Akaki Tsereteli, the journalists Sergi Meskhi and Niko Nikoladze, and eventually political activists like the first generation of Georgian Populists and Marxists—as well as dozens of lesser-known school teachers, librarians, booksellers, grammarians, and chorus directors—inspired a new respect for the Georgian language and the promotion of its literary culture. Unlike many peoples of the Russian Empire, Georgians were privileged to have a history of statehood, a recoverable record of heroic battles preserved in the royal chronicles, and glorious periods of art and architecture physically present on the landscape.

Within the literary tradition that extended from medieval hymnographers through secular poets, three works stood as the principal pillars of Georgian literature: the translated Bible; Rustaveli's epic poem of the twelfth century, *vepkhistqaosani*; and the chronicles that collectively recorded the history of the Georgian monarchies, *kartlis tskhovreba* (The Life of Georgia). Committed to reviving the Georgian language and literature and preserving what they took to be the essence of their culture, poets, scholars, and journalists selected from the chaotic recording of events, traditions, and symbols to inspire a new sense of nationhood. Consonant with the developing national consciousness of other peoples, the first generations of Georgian nineteenth-century literati articulated a notion of nation based on the ethnic culture of the people, rather than primarily on religion, and emphasized harmony between nobles and peasants and development through education and economic growth.[36] Nobleman Ilia Chavchavadze (1837–1907), universally recognized as the most important nationalist writer and poet, urged Georgians to value their common culture. Rather than thinking of themselves as Kakhetians, Imeretians, Gurians, Svans, Mingrelians, or Kartlians, or dismissing the peasants as uncultured, they should think as a coherent nation: "If Georgian is not their common name, then what is common to all of them? . . . if the people of the countryside are not Georgians, then who are they?"[37] What is most notable in his question is the fact that Chavchavadze had to ask it at all.

For a boy with few prospects the door that education opened required reading knowledge not only of Georgian but of Russian as well. His mother had made sure that he knew the Georgian alphabet, but she did not speak Russian. Soso had resisted learning Russian in his preschool years. Keke sent him to a Miss Ter-Stepanova, who dismissed him after two months as someone "incapable of concentrating in order to learn Russian." She then sent him to the Davrishevs' scribe, Father Gogokhia, whose Russian was quite poor and who liberally used a large ruler to enforce discipline. Although Soso learned enough Russian to qualify for the Gori church school, his teacher was appalled that "instead of picking up Russian and grammar, [Jughashvili] spent his time reading Shota Rustaveli!"[38] Somehow, he managed to learn enough Russian to enroll in the second preparatory grade.[39] He continued to improve, and later when the school inspector, a teacher from the Tiflis Seminary, visited Gori and complained about the poor quality of Russian among the local religious students, he noted how impressed he was by Soso's use of Russian.[40]

Soso was ambitious and competitive. His teachers attest to his hunger for study. He worked hard and tried to please. In Gori, unlike his later years in Tiflis, he had no disciplinary problems in school.[41] One of his schoolmates, Petre Adamishvili, came to school with the advantage that his father insisted that only Russian be spoken at home. The anti-Georgian Russian instructor, Shiriaev, a poor teacher more interested in women than grammar, gave the students an assignment to write about what they had done on Sunday. Petre's essay was judged excellent, but Soso's merely good. Soso was determined to better his grade and befriended Petre to find out how to improve his language. Within a short time Soso received the highest grade. Another time he was upset that a fellow student had drawn a beautiful picture of Queen Tamar, the medieval ruler of Georgia. For a time, he did not bring any of his pictures to school. Then he appeared with a beautifully drawn portrait of Rustaveli, which he hung up on the wall for all to see. When some of his classmates doubted that he had actually drawn the picture, Soso sat down and drew it again.[42]

Soso was an inveterate reader and stole glances at books even at meals. He liked to play jokes, tell stories, and laughed easily. He loved singing even more than playing games, but never mastered the intricate Georgian dance (*lekuri*).[43] His schoolmates noticed that Soso did not play at recess. He just read or ate a piece of bread or an apple. He was not above correcting his teachers. When he embarrassed the unpopular mathematics teacher, Iluridze, by pointing out an error in his arithmetic, Soso became a hero celebrated by his classmates. "Soso never yielded first place to anyone. . . . He was first in his studies." He studied ancient Greek and corrected his teacher's grammar. He refused to cheat in school and would not give answers to Adamishvili. He even marked him down when he was class monitor for being late. "Improve yourself," he told him. "Don't be lazy; otherwise you will fail in life."[44]

Religion, more precisely Georgian Orthodoxy, was central to Soso's childhood. Not only was his mother devoted to her faith, not only were his principal mentors Orthodox priests, but Georgian culture was also rooted in a national Christianity. The alphabet, invented in the fifth century, had been devised for the purpose of reproducing the holy texts, and Georgia's written history from its inception was intimately tied to Christianity and the royal states. The national church, linked to the Eastern Orthodox Church in Byzantium, provided Georgians with a key element in their ethnic identification—Christians confronting the infidel worlds of paganism and Islam. For the premodern period ethnicity was more a matter of religious identification than of language or material culture, though the three together—language, religion, and way of

life—reinforced the understanding of who was Georgian (or Orthodox) and who was not. Like their neighbors, the Armenians, and the
Jews of the Old Testament, Georgians were an ethnoreligious group
that equated salvation with fidelity to the community and the church.

The Georgian Orthodox Church, which might have been a vehicle
for the preservation and promotion of Georgian religious culture, was
hobbled by its doctrinal and institutional subordination to the Holy
Synod of the Russian Orthodox Church. In 1811 the catholicos (head of
the church) was removed, sent into exile, and replaced by an exarch
appointed by the tsar. By the last decades of the century Georgian bish-
ops were sent elsewhere to serve, and Georgia's ecclesiastical hierarchy
was largely Russian.[45] Church authorities suppressed Georgian religious practices and the use of the vernacular in the service and in teaching. Yet in villages and provincial towns like Gori Orthodoxy retained
its grip on the faithful like Keke Geladze.

Memoirs by childhood friends testify to Soso's religious sensibilities.
Every evening before sleeping, he recited several times the *mamao ch-
veno* (Our Father), and in church he sat still, in a kind of meditation. If
he felt he had sinned or blasphemed, he stayed silent and prostrate for
hours. At such times, if anyone approached him or made a joke, he flew
into anger.[46] "In the seminary," his classmate A. Gogebashvili remembered, "the pupils of the upper classes had to read the psalms, the Book
of Hours, the Hymnus Acathistus [of the Orthodox Church], and other
prayers. As the best reader, Soso attracted much attention and trust in
the school, and he was assigned to teach us the reading of the psalms,
and only after being trained by him were we allowed to read in church.
Soso was considered the principal cleric, and at the celebratory church
services he was the main singer and reciter."[47]

A schoolmate, Grigol Razmadze, remembered that he, Soso, and four
friends climbed a tree by the Liakhvi River to watch the public hanging
of three "brigands."[48] Public executions were extremely rare by this
time, but the Russian authorities wanted to make an example of these
men. The condemned were social bandits, popular with the peasants
with whom they shared their booty. One was commuted on the gallows,
but the other two, Sandro Khubuluri and Tate Jinoshvili, were executed.

Soso's friends wondered if the condemned would suffer in hell. Confident at age thirteen that he understood divine justice, Soso did not hesitate to answer. "Soso Jughashvili resolved our doubts: 'They,' he said thoughtfully, 'have already borne punishment, and it would be unjust on the part of God to punish them again.'"[49] His friend Sandro Tsikhitatrishvili, then ten years old, a few years younger than Soso, could not sleep for days, and afterward could remember nothing of the event.[50] Soso, on the other hand, appeared unaffected by the horror of the execution, noting only the injustice meted out by the authorities to those whom simple Georgians revered. The execution had a profound effect on many people of Gori, who mixed the fate of the condemned with that of Jesus, and when local boys saw gendarmes in Gori, they would shout insults at them from afar and quickly disappear.[51]

The ideal future for boys in Gori was to emulate the national hero Giorgi Saakadze or the celebrated social bandit Arsena, but for Soso Jughashvili and a few others it was to become a *beri* (monk), "living alone on top of a mountain, close to God and praying for the salvation of his people."[52] While he lived in Gori with his pious mother, Soso appeared to be an observant Orthodox Christian. But several memoirs by his companions of the time, taken down almost half a century later when Stalin headed a state committed to atheism, construct a fanciful tale of an early onset loss of faith. Schoolmate Grigol Glurjidze remembered both the intensity of Soso's faith and, as he testifies, when he lost it. Soso was "a firm believer, punctually attending all the divine services, was the leader of the church choir," Glurjidze reports. "I remember he not only performed the religious rites but always reminded us of their meaning. But already in the third or fourth class, . . . he unexpectedly shocked me with clearly atheist declarations. We were lying in a meadow outside the city, talking about the rich and the poor; why was God so unjust as to force some people to be poor. 'You know, Grisha,' suddenly Soso said softly after a short pause, 'he is not unjust, he simply does not exist. They are deceiving us, Grisha.'" His friend could not believe what Soso had said. Soso then mentioned that he had a book for Grisha, which turned out to be by Darwin.[53] As farfetched as the memory of Darwin is, another Gori companion relates how Soso and a number of his closest companions—Petre Kaparadze and Glurjidze—sat at the feet of a local stationery seller and listened to him tell a story unlike that of the priests about the creation of the world.[54] As tantalizing as these later memoirs are, they cannot be taken on faith, for they served at the time of their production to underscore the precocious enlightenment of young Jughashvili. Whatever early doubts may have entered Soso's mind, the bulk of the evidence testifies that only after he moved on to the Tiflis Seminary did young Jughashvili lose his faith in God and replace it with a secular faith in social revolution.[55]

Georgia's religion, intertwined as it was with ethnic culture and patriotism, was seriously challenged by the tsarist authorities, who by the last quarter of the nineteenth century grew increasingly suspicious of nationalist expressions. At the moment when educated Georgians were thinking nationally, the imperial state hoped to create its own "imperial nation" of all the loyal subjects of the tsar. The tsarist government had grown fearful of non-Russian nationalisms, particularly after the Polish rebellion of 1863, and as it tried to repress expressions of the nation it only compounded the problem. Russian politicians and intellectuals struggled to articulate some sense of a "Russian nation," but they faced the great paradox of empire: that non-Russian peoples when confronted by the civilizing mission of the empire were often transformed by education, mobility, and exposure to the West into opponents of empire.[56] Many who had once been loyal servitors of the tsar earlier in the century turned into proponents of their nations, even as they attempted to conceive schemes for reconciling nation with empire short of full separation and sovereign statehood.

By the 1880s Emperor Alexander III (1881–1894) turned to a policy of cultural Russification directed toward expanding the use of Russian in educational and administrative institutions. Such a threat to an emerging national identity dramatically affected the Georgian intelligentsia. Imperial authorities haphazardly applied restrictions on local language and culture, which served only to inspire affection for what was most intimately connected to family and home. By the 1890s the affinities that Georgian intellectuals had felt for Russia had been tempered by the hostility and condescension that many Russian officials and clerics displayed toward non-Russians. When Soso Jughashvili entered the Gori religious school, some instruction was still given in Georgian. Within two years Russians replaced the Georgian teachers, and instruction in the Georgian language was reduced to twice a week.[57] Reacting to the harsh regime imposed by the Synod on the Georgian Church, many Georgian clerics and seminarians looked to what was specifically Georgian in their religion. Around the turn of the century a palpable nationalization of Orthodoxy was occurring in Georgia.

While schools and churches were required to use Russian, the language of daily communication in the house and on the street continued to be Georgian. In fact Georgian-language newspapers, journals, and books grew in number. Unwittingly the empire, with its face turned toward Europe, aided the very process of nation-making by fostering education and the means of communication (railroads, roads, and telegraphs) by which isolated, illiterate villagers grew to imagine they were part of a larger community, the nation.[58] Social mobility, the growth of cities, as well as the peace and security enforced by the imperial state, cultivated the ground from which nationalist intellectuals grew to become the most forceful voices of the nation.

One of Soso's first intellectual experiences was the struggle between Russian official culture and his own Georgian culture, an uneven contest in which Russian language and culture had the distinct advantage of the state's backing. Although most pupils could speak only Georgian, they were forbidden to use their own language in school. Prohibition only highlighted the value of Georgian. A seemingly innocent outlet for national sentiments was music, particularly choral singing. Among Georgian men, group singing, often accompanied with quantities of wine, was considered a quintessentially masculine activity. The choir director, Simon Goglichidze, discovered Soso's voice as soon as he entered school. Already in his first year at school Soso so excelled at singing that among the teachers he was known as *bulbuli* (the nightingale). The choir sang the work of Tchaikovsky and the composers of Russian sacred music. Apparently the intricate harmonies of Georgian polyphony were not considered appropriate for the school choir, though precisely at this time the first chorus for Georgian folk music was being formed in Tiflis. Soso, a proud and bold pupil, approached his teacher and asked why the choir could not sing folk songs as did the chorus of the secular school. When the school inspector made his next visit, this question was raised, and permission was granted for special hours in which Georgian music could be sung.[59] Soso himself, the story goes on, led his fellow students in renditions of folk favorites.[60] For Soso singing was an activity that brought him attention and praise, bound him to his fellow students, and impressed his teachers. Choir director Goglichidze reported that he had a pleasant, high voice, was knowledgeable about music, and occasionally substituted for the precentor, the one who prepared the worship service or sang first. "Little Soso had a great musical talent and a beautiful voice. When singing was being taught in the small room of the school, located at the edge of the street, people gathered at the doors and window to hear Soso sing." Discovering his talents, Soso was happy to perform. He wanted to stand out and in his own way be noticed. When the graduating students gathered to have the chorus photographed, Soso arrived with a bouquet of wildflowers and a watch, borrowed from a friend, around his neck, and on the watch chain, for reasons that remain obscure, the tooth of a rooster. [61]

In a school dominated by chauvinistic Russian administrators and instructors, most of Soso's teachers and priests looked down on the Georgians as an inferior people. They imposed on their pupils rote learning infused with ethnic discrimination. Students were not permitted out of their homes in the evening, and school supervisors spied on the families of students to enforce the curfew. Condescension and authoritarianism enforced by Russian and Russified pedagogues replaced the anarchic freedom in which Gori boys had reveled in their preschool years. School inspector Butyrskii was one of the worst of the administrators, a Russian nationalist who hated the Georgians and drove the Georgian students especially hard, referring to them as savages.[62] A Russian teacher, Vladimir Lavrov, called Georgian "a dog's language" and punished any student who spoke Georgian in his classroom. Soso organized seven of his fellow students in a plot against the teacher. Everyone was nervous except Soso. He asked Lavrov to come with him because he had some questions. Lured into an empty classroom on the top floor of the school, the teacher was confronted by several of the older, stronger boys, who threatened to beat him. He tried to speak, but Soso stopped him. "Don't you dare curse the Georgian language." He warned him that if he reported the students, he would be sorry. Lavrov soon changed completely. He became very accommodating to his students, smiled, and treated people courteously.[63] A schoolmate noted that Lavrov, known to the students as "the gendarme," respected Soso enough to make him his assistant and allow him to distribute the books to the class.[64]

Russian repression compelled Georgians to become more aware of their own language and traditions once they could no longer be taken for granted. The idea of Russian as higher culture presented the post-Emancipation generation of Georgian intellectuals with an unenviable dilemma—whether to reject the culture of the conqueror and remain isolated or to embrace it and lose what is unique in one's own culture. In the dominant discourse of modernity, already pervading Russia and Georgia, the modern and progressive were linked to Russia and Europe, the traditional and backward to Georgia and other imperial peripheries. Whatever the attractions in the abstract of Russian learning, the actual experience of Georgian students with their Russian teachers only served to alienate them from the ruling nationality. Like his mates, Soso was pulled in one direction by his love of his Georgian world, his mother, and his church, and in another toward the wider world of learning, an enlightenment that came with Russian.

In the harsh environment of the school students sought solace and support from fellow students and a few sympathetic Georgian teachers, like Soprom Mgaloblishvili and Zakaria Davitashvili.[65] Certain older students became models for younger pupils. In December 1893, when Soso was fifteen, eighty-seven students were expelled from the Tiflis Seminary for protesting the harsh regime there. Forbidden to remain in the city, many moved to Gori, and suddenly "the streets of Gori were full of seminarians," among them the lively young activist Lado Ketsk-hoveli, who was known to Soso. "To us younger people," one Gori student remembers, "they seemed to be some kind of martyrs; in general this event brought something new into our colorless lives; it shook us and sharply changed our formerly narrow thoughts."[66]

Soso suffered not only treatment as a cultural inferior in the Gori church school but also humiliation because he was poor. In June 1891 he successfully passed his examinations, but he was not permitted (for some time) to matriculate because his family had not paid the fees for further study.[67] In his final year, however, the church assembly decided to reward Soso's diligence, musical talent, and knowledge of school regulations by waiving tuition, giving him free textbooks and a stipend of three rubles a month.[68] While the church school did not give out medals as did the secular schools, it awarded Soso the *davitni*, the Georgian version of the Psalms, with an inscription praising a talented and successful pupil.[69]

In 1894, Soso's last year in the Gori church school, the Populist Arsena Kalandadze opened a bookstore in town where young people could meet and read.[70] A member of the Tiflis Society for the Spread of Literacy among Georgians, as well as a secret revolutionary group in Gori, Kalandadze set out to establish reading rooms open to all. Here Georgian literature and Russian classics like Pushkin and Turgenev were available, as well as anonymous radical works, all translated into Georgian. Like his schoolmates, Soso Jughashvili visited this reading room and there found an alternative to the prescribed education he received in the school. He is said to have read Daniel Chonkadze's novel *suramis tsikhe* (Surami Fortress), one of the few prose works in Georgian. A romantic melodrama of revenge by a betrayed lover, the novel had shocked genteel society when it appeared in 1859–1860 because of its condemnation of serfdom.[71] Reading such works gave young readers like Soso an alternative education, not only in Georgian instead of Russian, but more broadly humanist and populist, concerned with the welfare of the poorest members of society and the obligation of privileged intellectuals to serve the people. Literature was a second university. In both a national and a social sense Soso imbibed two separate kinds of education: one that attempted to subordinate strong-willed young Georgians to the Russian autocratic-bureaucratic order; the other that subverted the very bases of that order and held out a slim hope for something better.

3

KOBA

Soso's ideal and dream-figure was Koba. . . . Koba had become Soso's god, the sense of his life. He wanted to become another Koba, as famous a fighter and hero as he. The figure of Koba would live again in him. From now on he called himself Koba and would not have us call him by any other name. His face would shine with pride when we called him "Koba."

—IREMASCHWILI, *STALIN UND DIE TRAGÖDIE GEORGIENS*
[*STALIN AND THE TRAGEDY OF THE GEORGIANS*] (1931)

In the fearless and laconic Koba Soso Djugashvili found the first of his hero-identifications, a fit name and symbol for the heroic Soso that he envisaged himself as being. . . . [B]esides furnishing Soso with an idealized image of the hero as avenger, [Koba's story] conveyed to him the message that vindictive triumph is a cause to which a person can worthily devote his life.

—ROBERT C. TUCKER,
STALIN AS REVOLUTIONARY, 1879–1929 (1973)

When Soso Jughashvili arrived in Tbilisi, much of the world knew Georgia's most vibrant city by its Russian name, Tiflis. Set in the valley of the Kura (*mtkvari* in Georgian), with low mountains rising to the north and south, Tiflis was the cosmopolitan center of Russian imperial power in Caucasia. Visitors were impressed by a city where East met West. The ruins of the medieval fortress, called *nariqala*, stretched across the ridge of one of the hills on the right bank. An ancient Georgian church, *metekhi*, stood across the river on a promontory over the river, its stark beauty marred by the walls of a dreaded prison built by the Russians. In the old town, imprinted with Georgia's Persian past, narrow, curved streets wound between balconied houses set on the slopes of hills. Bazaars, caravanserais, and Turkish-style hot baths mingled with Armenian, Georgian, and Russian churches and mosques. Jews from Akhaltsikhe were about to start building their Grand Synagogue, not far from Soso's school. Just to the west of the expansive Erivan Square lay the broad imperial avenue, Golovinskii Prospect, where the palace of the viceroys, the finer hotels, theaters, and shops were located. Here was the European-style city built by the Russian state and the Armenian bourgeoisie that dominated much of the city's economy and politics. Up the slopes behind the square hung the wooden and stone houses of the townspeople (*mokalakeebi*) who dwelled in the desirable Sololaki district. Rising above the new city was the "holy mountain," *mtatsminda*, where half a century later, near a small church, Stalin's mother would be buried in a Georgian pantheon. Across the river was the "colony," settled by Protestant Germans, religious refugees who were renowned for their industriousness. Far from these central districts, to the north and west, near the railroad yards, were the workers' districts—Didube and Nadzaladevi—slums with muddy streets. Russians knew this latter district as Nakhalovka, since people spontaneously, without permission (*nakhal'no*), put up their own shacks. Two thousand men worked for the railroad shops, others in the soap mills, tanneries, tobacco plants, breweries, lumber and brickyards. Here was the nascent industrial Georgia, the home of an embryonic working class soon to become the hoped-for instrument of the youngest generation of Georgian intellectuals.

Tiflis was a very different place from Gori. In the small town people knew each other more intimately. The better-off felt a responsibility for the less fortunate. Neighbors took in orphans, and no one was left hungry or homeless. Funerals were attended by strangers as well as relatives and friends, and at the ensuing banquet a collection was taken up for the widow.[1] In Tiflis, newcomers had to fend for themselves, which meant finding one's place and creating a network of friends, linking up with other migrants from one's village. In the Caucasus friends, relations (even distant ones), and personal connections were essential to getting what one needed or wanted. Laws were incidental, rights nonexistent, and money merely a lubricant. More than in the closer quarters of Gori, in the big town money conveyed status, opened doors, and brushed aside customary practices and older ideas of honor and proper behavior.

Tiflis society was stratified along ethnic and class lines. At the top were the Russian officials, headed by the viceroy or governor-general. Equal in social status if not political power were the great Georgian nobles, the *tavadebi*, and the lesser nobles, the *aznaurebi*. Besides a few Russian princes and a Georgian cognac king, the prosperous brandy distiller David Sarajishvili, the wealthiest people of the city were Armenian factory owners—the Mantashevs, Tamashevs, and Adelkhanovs—who built the great houses and hospitals and patronized the schools. Armenian merchants in shops and stalls competed with the roving *kintos*, the peddler tricksters who sang songs about their wares.[2] At the bottom of city society were the artisans and factory workers, the peasants migrating in from the villages to seek a livelihood in the shops and factories that were appearing in the burgeoning urban economy. In the noisy squares and streets of Tiflis, Georgian competed with Russian, Armenian, and Azeri, and even young children used words of several languages.

English traveler James Bryce experienced the heat and bustle of the city some eighteen years before Soso arrived and was entranced by its exotic diversity. "[I]n Tiflis it is not the particular things to be seen in the city that impress themselves on one's memory: it is the city itself, the strange mixture of so many races, tongues, religions, customs." For Bryce, the city's character lay "in the fact that it has no one character, but ever so many different ones. Here all these peoples live side by side, buying and selling, and working for hire, yet never coming into any closer union, remaining indifferent to one another, with neither love, or hate, nor ambition, peaceably obeying a government of strangers who annexed them without resistance and retain them without effort, and held together by no bond but its existence."[3] In the "uneven cultural terrain" of a multicultural and multilingual city, Georgians, outnumbered by other ethnicities, "were, in a sense, visitors."[4]

When Soso and his mother journeyed to Tiflis in the summer of 1894, he was already familiar with the big city, having lived there briefly some years earlier. Fifteen years old, he was well-equipped for his new life, but, as his mother reports, he was anxious about coming to the town where his father lived. As the train approached the city, Soso began to cry, fearing that his father would kidnap him and force him to become a shoemaker. He told his mother that he would rather kill himself than follow his father's trade. Although Keke was also worried that Beso might show up, she calmed her son and assured him that as long as she was alive no one would be able to prevent him from receiving an education. They arrived in the morning around eleven. Beso was nowhere in sight, and Soso was enchanted by the city.[5] Keke had little money and could not afford an apartment, but she found a room in the old district of Anchiskhati with an Armenian woman who sent her family away temporarily to live in their home village. Keke befriended the woman, who thought that the visitor from Gori brought her good luck. When the landlady found a man to marry, she was so grateful that she refused to take rent money from Keke and instead gave her a *lechaki* (a traditional Caucasian head covering).[6]

Keke's next task was to find someone who could help her have Soso admitted into the Tiflis Seminary. With difficulty she found a distant relative, Kato Ananiashvili, whose neighbor, the priest Chagunava, worked as a steward in the seminary and was well-connected. The two women approached the priest's wife, Maka, and convinced her of Soso's talents. She then interceded with her husband, who also liked the boy and took him to the historian and ethnographer Tedo Zhordania. Together they helped him take the examinations. Keke reciprocated by quilting a blanket for Maka.[7] Thus, in typical Caucasian style Keke used relatives, friends, chance acquaintances, and gifts to improve her son's fortune.

Soso excelled in the entrance exams and won a state subsidy. The next problem was finding money to buy clothes for the new seminarian. Keke made a quick trip to Gori to earn some money, but she soon was told that Soso had done so well that this too had been taken care of. Though the stipend saved the Jughashvilis one hundred rubles—to them a fortune—Keke still had to come up with money for board. Again an acquaintance came to the rescue: Tedo Zhordania convinced the school to accept him into the dormitory with board paid by state stipend.[8] That left only the tuition money to be paid by Keke.

Separated from his mother for the first time in his life, Soso wrote to her twice a week, and the proud but lonely mother read his letters hundreds of times before going to sleep. She hung up an old-fashioned wall clock to break the silence, with no regard that it did not keep time. She missed her boy's physical presence, savoring as long as she could the sugar cubes that he sent as a gift at Christmas. The bond between the determined mother and her ambitious son was unusually strong, though Tiflis and the seminary would soon have a malignant effect on his studies and her dreams.[9]

At first, according to a fellow student, Soso held himself aloof. "Quiet, cautious, shy, bashful—that's how I remember Soso in his first days in the seminary, before I knew him."[10] Everyone looked at him with curiosity as he walked on the balcony or in the yard. They heard he wrote poetry, but hesitated to speak to him because of his shyness. Whatever psychological damage may have been done by a weak and alcoholic father, or by a strong, protective mother, was manifested in his new life by withdrawal. Soon he regained confidence as he made friends and repeated his success in schoolwork. Nine boys had come from Soso's school in Gori, among them Ioseb Iremashvili, and since the seminary had just reopened after being closed since the student protests the year before, Soso's class was joined by those who should have started earlier. Among these older boys was his friend Mikha Davitashvili, who was lame and something of a rebel.[11] Soso would spend the summer vacation with Mikha in his village, Tsromi. Banding together, the Gorians also associated with the boys from Telavi, fellow provincials.

For someone like Soso without a close, extended family and whose parents could supply little material or social support, friends were especially important. In both Georgian high culture and folk wisdom friendship, particularly male bonding, was treasured. Rustaveli's epic, the verses of which Soso (like his father before him) knew from memory, depicted men sacrificing and performing heroic deeds for their close friends.[12] Similarly, Georgian proverbs and sayings insist on the importance of loyal friends. "Show me your friends, and I will tell you who you are." The foundation of friendship is trust, an essential resource that Caucasians regarded as highly as honor. "A man who is not trusted has no honor; a man without honor cannot be trusted." Those who knew Soso as a young man frequently report that he drew a small circle of people around him and was able to extract loyalty from them. From the earliest records of Soso's youth, he could be seen forming such associations with himself at the center. The closeness of ties with friends, however, meant at the same time separation of the inner group from others.[13] Such groups of friends were needed in the highly competitive world of Georgian men where one's status depended on associations—family, friends, patrons, and clients. "Since Georgians are so competitive," one student of modern Georgia found, "the peer group becomes the natural arena for contest, as it is also the primary social reference group. This means that at the same time, young men are pushed to find their friends from among their potential rivals. This is why on the one hand we find the almost obsessive pre-occupation with trust, the sanctity with which friendship is treated; and on the other hand the ever present suspicion, uncertainty and insecurity."[14]

Along with loyalty and the comfortable sharing of confidences lurked an omnipresent possibility of betrayal. Friendship and family networks provide security and protection but cannot eliminate the fear of loss of trust or honor. By placing such high value on friendship, loyalty, and trust, the potential for disappointment and disillusion is heightened. Betrayal of a friend is the worst sin. The intensity of the emotions embedded in friendship is matched by the strength of the emotions when trust is broken.

Tiflis Seminary stood in the very heart of the city, just off Erivan Square.[15] A large stone block of a building, with a classical façade, the seminary is today the Georgian national art museum. It anchored the western edge of the square, near a caravanserai, and faced, at the far side of a grand expanse, the dramatic Moorish-style City Hall. The seminary was at the end of the old city and the start of the western town. While sons and daughters of the nobility more often enrolled in the local high school (*gimnaziia*) on Golovinskii Prospect, poorer male students had a choice of the technical school (*uchilishche*) or the seminaries—the Tiflis Orthodox Seminary or, across the river, the Nersesian Academy (*Jemaran*) for Armenians. For most of the boys subsidized seminary education was their only opportunity for a formal intellectual life and eventually university in Russia. For the teachers and administrators, the mission of the seminary was to prepare young boys for the priesthood. With a partial stipend from the Georgian Church Treasury (*Gruzinskoe Tserkovnoe Kaznacheistvo*), Soso began his studies on September 1, 1894.

At first Soso studied well and was in many ways a model student. At the end of his first year he was eighth in his class. The top spots were held by Russians—not surprising, since almost all the instruction was in Russian—with two Georgians in places just above Soso.[16] His highest mark, a perfect 5, was in Slavic singing. He was determined to be a priest, as his mother wished, but he was troubled by financial problems.[17] Just a month after entering the seminary he appealed humbly to the rector of the school, Archimandrite Seraphim, for funding for tuition. "Having completed my studies at the Gori Church School as the best student," he wrote, "with the permission of Your Reverence I presumed to take the entrance examination for the Tiflis Theological Seminary even though I do not have the money to continue my studies. I was fortunate to be successful in this examination and was admitted among the students of the Theological Seminary. However, since my parents are unable to provide for me in Tiflis, I am appealing with great humility to Your Reverence to admit me among those students who have half their tuition fees paid for them. I presume to mention here that throughout my studies at the Gori Church School I received assistance from the school funds."[18] At the end of September 1894, he pleaded to His Reverence to provide him with winter clothing to alleviate his mother from financial burdens and save him from sickness and the cold. Soso was even more abject in another petition in the summer after his first year:

> Your Reverence knows all about the pitiful circumstances of my mother, who takes care of me. My father has not provided for me for three years. This is his way of punishing me for continuing my studies

against his wishes. . . . At present my mother's eyes have weakened and as a consequence she is no longer able to work with her hands (the only source of income). . . . It is for this reason that I am applying to Your Reverence for the second time for full support, which would be the greatest mercy.

August 28, 1895

IOSIF DZHUGASHVILI, SUPPLICANT[19]

The rector rejected his request for a full stipend, but somehow with his mother working at menial jobs Soso managed to stay in school. A year later, at the time he was promoted to the third class, he had moved up to fifth place, with only one Georgian ahead of him.[20] His progress toward priesthood seemed assured.

In his first two years in the seminary Soso tried to please the clergy and reap the benefits offered by the teachers. In a note excusing an absence, he showed contrition (or a precocious ability to dissemble) for being late in returning from a funeral. Writing to the monk Ioanaki, who served as the "Father Supervisor," he related the following story:

I arrived in Gori on Sunday. The deceased had apparently stated in his will that he was to be buried next to his father near the village of Sveneti. The body was taken there on the Monday and the burial took place there on the Tuesday. I wanted to return on Tuesday night, but circumstances were such that even the strongest person's hands would have been tied. The mother of the deceased, who had suffered so cruelly at the hand of fate, begged me with tears in her eyes to be a son to her, even if just for a week. I simply could not reject the appeal of a weeping mother. I hope you will forgive me but I decided to stay. After all, the Father Supervisor usually allows leave to those who intend to travel home.[21]

Hardly a rebel, Soso was obedient in that first year in the Tiflis Seminary, submissive to authority, and diligent in his studies. One day one of the popular teachers, the nervous instructor of Russian language Albov, came into class with exceptional praise of a student's essay. Without pointing out to whom he was referring, the teacher told his pupils,

"Remember children this day. The author of this work is expected to play a great role in our public life." The students turned to their Russian classmates, certain that the talented student was among them. But, as a witness relates, "they looked at us with curiosity. Surprised, we noticed our Soso sitting with his head down and blushing. We gathered around him after the lesson. 'Leave me alone! Yes, it was I,' he said, nervously stroking his hair."[22]

As a teenager Jughashvili shared the nationalist sentiments then dominant among Georgian intellectuals and students. He sent his romantic and patriotic poetry to Ilya Chavchavadze's nationalist newspaper, *iveria*, and five poems were published in 1895, several under the pen name "Soselo," a diminutive of Soso.[23] The first, "*dila*" (Morning), was considered good enough to be reprinted in the widely used textbook, *deda ena* (Mother Tongue).[24] It begins lyrically with images of flowers awakening and birds singing, then shifts abruptly to a message for the nation:

> Flourish, adored world
> Rejoice, land of *iveria*
> And you, learned men of Georgia,
> Bring happiness to the Motherland [*samshoblo*][25]

Like the sense of obligation that Russian intellectuals felt toward the simple people, so in this youthful poem education was for a young Georgian a privilege that implied service to the homeland. Echoing a theme familiar to readers of *iveria*, the world was not to be left in misery but to be changed for the better by education and educated national actors.

The longest poem, "*mtvares*" (To the Moon) begins with a romantic call to the moon to keep moving, never bow its head, disperse the clouds (of ignorance), and smile tenderly on the world. "Sing a lullaby to *mqinvari*" (Mount Kazbeg), the peak that towers over Georgia.[26] The mood of the verse then changes and challenges:

> Know well, those who once
> Fell to the oppressors

Will rise again with hope
Above the holy mountain.

It ends with its young author ripping open his shirt, baring his breast to the moon, and with outstretched hands worshipping that which lights up the world.

Soso continued the themes of his first two poems in a third that also begins with a full moon drifting across the sky. Another nightingale accompanies the panpipe before the rhythm shifts and a dammed mountain spring gushes forth and the forest awakens:

When the man driven out by his enemy
Again becomes worthy of his oppressed country
And when the sick man, deprived of light
Again begins to see sun and moon;

Then I, too, oppressed, find the mist of sadness
Breaks and lifts and instantly recedes;
And hopes of the good life
Unfold in my unhappy heart.
And, carried away by this hope,
I find my soul rejoicing, my heart beats peacefully;
But is this hope genuine
That has been sent to me at these times?[27]

The themes of arousal and awakening were taken up again in his next poem, titled "*peletoni*" (Feuilleton), in which a prophet-like figure roams the country, "like a ghost," playing a *panduri*, the Georgian lute, and dispensing "truth itself and heavenly love."[28]

This voice made many a man's heart
Beat, that had been turned to stone;
It enlightened many a man's mind
Which had been cast into uttermost darkness.
But instead of glorification,
Wherever the harp was plucked,
The mob set before the outcast

A vessel filled with poison . . .
And they said to him: "Drink this, o accursed,
This is your appointed lot!
We do not want your truth
Nor these heavenly tunes of yours!"

Bitterly, the author speaks of the inability of "the mob" to understand the truth or the message of love. Instead, the ungrateful masses poison the minstrel who brings them music and light.[29]

Soselo's most widely reproduced poem was dedicated to the Georgian Romantic poet Rapiel Eristavi (1824–1901), who in his plays and poems championed the peasants.[30] In 1895 the patriotic poet Akaki Tsereteli organized a jubilee to mark the fiftieth anniversary of Eristavi's literary activity. Delegates gathered from all parts of Georgia in Tiflis for the occasion. The Social Democrat Irakli Tsereteli later declared that "this jubilee was witness to the national unity of the Georgian people. Under autocratic conditions only in this form could national feelings be shown. The jubilee of R. Eristavi turned from a purely literary celebration into the first national manifestation of the Georgian people."[31] All three of the major Georgian journals—*iveria*, *kvali* (Furrow), and *moambe* (Bulletin)—praised the event, which they interpreted as the fruit of seeds sown in the 1860s. In this jubilant atmosphere of national revival Soso Jughashvili enthusiastically shared the unifying enthusiasms of his country's leading intellectuals, as well as their sense of service to the poor. Reflecting the national celebration, the seventeen-year-old Jughashvili's poem praised the poet for his sensitivity to the peasants, his sacrifice to the people, and his songs to the motherland. He ended the poem with the plea "let my country grow sons like Eristavi."[32]

In 1896 Soso published a last poem, "*mokhutsi ninika*" (The Old Man, Ninika), in *kvali*, the progressive newspaper in which the first Georgian Marxists were appearing.[33] His peasant hero, the gray-haired Ninika, no longer can display the bare-chested, iron strength that had "piled up mountains of sheaves side by side." His knees cannot move the way they did, "scythed down by old age." But when he hears the singing of the young lads in the fields, he smiles, catching fire for a moment. Again, the poet points to the passing of the staff to a younger generation.

After this appearance the poet Soselo fell silent. He was about to turn in a new direction. The nationalist newspaper in which he had previously published, Chavchavadze's *iveria*, had been closed down for eight months for carrying on "harmful propaganda, aimed principally at students, against the Russian authority in the Caucasus, against the Russian language, and in general against Russian influence in any form and in any sphere."[34] In this atmosphere in which the government both repressed the Georgian language in schools and the church and then persecuted those who publicly stated that fact, the very act of a young seminarian writing poetry in his own language and sending it to nationalist or progressive newspapers was an affront to the Russifying regime and an affirmation of Soso's affinity to the values of Georgia's intellectual leaders.[35] His move to *kvali*, a more socially and politically radical newspaper, did not signal a move from nationalism to socialism at this point, since *kvali* was not yet identified with the Marxists. But both his poems and their publication in the leading intellectual outlets of Georgian writing testify to Soso's identification with the Georgian national intelligentsia and their hopes for liberal reform. The shoemaker's son had made a bold entry into the literary world, driven by his ambition, impatience, and belief in his own talents. He was determined to stand out and to succeed in this unfamiliar realm. Writing was a tool that could raise him up from his impoverished origins. The young poet's desire for enlightenment and a better life in Georgia, however, was tinged with a realism, even pessimism, about the possibility of change for the better. The older generation had to give way. The task of liberating Georgia falls on the young, particularly the educated. But this new generation must overcome the inertia and hostility of the philistine crowd.

In Georgia language was one of the battlefields on which Georgians tested their loyalties to their two "homelands," Georgia and Russia. The first generation of Georgian national intellectuals, like Ilia Chavchavadze, laid claim to leadership of the nation they were bringing into being. Their gentry nationalism asserted the value of Georgian language and culture and lauded the unity of all classes of the nation. Chavcha-vadze expressed hostility toward what he saw as destructive anti-national forces: the disruption of the traditional harmony and unity of Georgian society by Russian officials and the rapacious capitalist intrusions of Armenian merchants and industrialists. By the time he published an uncensored version of his *Letters of a Traveler* (1892), first written some thirty years earlier, his idea of a Georgia without capitalism or class strife had become an impossible utopia.[36] The old man grew increasingly conservative and closer to tsarist autocracy, while younger Georgian intellectuals were already moving toward a different vision. Rather than simple preservation of traditional culture and social harmony, the young radicals proposed aligning their country with what they understood as the direction things were actually going, with what appeared to be the movement of history—toward capitalism and industrialization, and beyond.

The city outside the seminary was a place of liberation for Soso. Inside the seminary was a world unto itself, a powerful shaper of its denizens, though not in the way that the clerical authorities intended. One of Soso's classmates, another Gorian, Domenti Gogokhia, remembered the seminary as a "stone sack." The life inside was colorless and monotonous. The boys rose at seven, were led to prayer, then had tea, and at the bell went off to class. A student read the prayer "To the Lord of the Heavens," and the lessons continued until two in the afternoon with few breaks. They lunched at three and were given two hours of free time until roll call at five. They were forbidden to leave the seminary in the evenings. After evening prayers, there was tea at eight, more lessons, and at ten they went to bed. It was a strict routine designed to inculcate obedience and deference.[37] Instead, for many it achieved just the opposite. Indeed, the Tiflis Seminary proved to be as much the crucible of revolutionaries as for priests. It was an unintended process of miseducation that pushed an intelligent but still quite ordinary adolescent into opposition. Thirty years later Stalin related to biographer Emil Ludwig the baleful influence of the priests. After dismissing the interviewer's implication that mistreatment by his parents led him to revolution, Stalin pointedly singled out his school. "The Orthodox seminary where I later studied is another matter. In protest against the humiliating regime and Jesuit methods that existed in the seminary, I was ready to become and actually became a revolutionary, an adherent of Marxism as a genuinely revolutionary teaching." Ludwig then asked him, "But do you not recognize any positive qualities in the Jesuits?" Stalin's answer impresses by its irony:

> Yes, they have a methodical quality, a perseverance in their work to achieve their bad ends. But the basis of their method is snooping, spying, prying into one's soul, humiliation—what can be positive in this? For example, the snooping in the dormitory. At the nine o'clock bell for tea, we go to the dining room, but when we return to our rooms, it turns out that in this time they have carried out a search and messed up drawers . . . what can be positive in this?[38]

The priests about whom Stalin complained were almost all Russians, openly contemptuous of Georgian culture and its language. When the rector of the seminary, Archimandrite Seraphim (Meshcheriakov), remarked that Georgian was a language of dogs, he provoked a student protest.[39] But his superior, the exarch of Georgia, Archbishop Vladimir (Bogoiavlenskii), defended the administrator against the students. The priests enforced the rules that prohibited the reading of newspapers or "outside" (*postoronnie*) books and forbade the speaking or reading of Georgian in the seminary. Contact with their native language was limited to the reading of religious texts in the archaic medieval Georgian language. Even there the obscure texts were explained with the help of Russian. Just a few years before Soso entered the seminary, Lado Ketskhoveli had convinced a teacher to allow a weekly reading of a secular work. The students debated whether to read the contemporary poets Akaki Tsereteli and Ilia Chavchavadze or the eighteenth-century David Guramishvili before deciding on Rustaveli's *vepkhistqaosani*. But when the teacher insisted that Russian be used to explicate the poem, the students voted unanimously to cancel the experiment.[40]

"The Georgian pupils," a Russian teacher at the seminary remembered, "seeing the consistently unjust and cruel treatment by the Russian rectors . . . not only did not acquire the Russian spirit . . . but on the contrary grew to hate the Russians, turn away from all things Russian and Russians, to feel that all Russians were worthless, judging by the wretched Russian monk-rectors, and for this reason to join together ever more strongly with one another."[41] Not only was the Russifying regime unable to stifle the growing interest in Georgian literature and traditions, but a subculture of the seminarians, built on a comradeship among young men and marked by a hostility toward the obscurantist priests, also rejected the worst aspects of Russian official culture—its dogmatism, condescension toward non-Russians, and sense of superiority as the ruling nationality. At the same time some students took learning much more seriously than their teachers, transgressing the limits set by the instructors and absorbing the countertradition of the Russian radical intelligentsia. Learning became the first act of rebellion, and the subversive force of self-education led many like Soso Jughashvili to shift from furtively reading forbidden books during church services to identifying openly with the political opposition.

As in lower schools the contrast between the humanistic ideals and values found in Georgian and Russian literature and the harsh routine of life in the seminary created an unbridgeable distance and a cold hostility between the Georgian students and the priests. The seminarians resisted the authorities, repeatedly protesting or staging strikes. In 1885 a seminarian, Silibistro Jibladze, had been exiled for slapping the rector, Pavel Chudetskii, and the next year nineteen-year-old Ioseb Laghiashvili stabbed and killed the despised administrator. About sixty students were expelled from the seminary, and the Russian exarch of the Georgian Church, Pavel, anathematized the whole of Georgia for the murder. In March 1890 the seminarians organized a weeklong strike, refusing to attend class until ten demands were met. The students wanted restoration of courses in Georgian language and history, polite treatment, and permission to subscribe to those legally published but critical newspapers of which the church authorities did not approve.[42] The strike ended in partial victory for the students, but three years later a second strike for similar ends had to be organized. Among the principal participants in that strike were the former seminarian Mikhail (Mikha) Tskhakaia, who a decade later would become Soso's patron in the revolutionary movement, and Soso's acquaintance from Gori, Lado Ketskhoveli. By the time young Jughashvili came to Tiflis, the seminary had already produced many of the intellectual rebels, including Jibladze, Tskhakaia, Noe Zhordania, and Pilipe (Filip) Makharadze, who would make up the first generation of Georgian Marxists.

Even as the harsh clerical regime enforced by Russians and Russified Georgian priests drove many students to resist the Russifying regime, it did not lead them to an anti-Russian nationalism. The dominant narrative of nationalists usually envisions a natural, visceral, emerging consciousness leading to demands for statehood as the inevitable result of a "rebirth" of national feelings. But in Georgia and Armenia, rather than developing a nationalist, separatist vision, the leading intellectuals considered a more benign integration into a reformed empire as the preferred and pragmatic political solution. In the complex imperial setting in which urban Georgians were entwined within a cosmopolitan society, an exclusivist ethnic nationalism proved less attractive than a commitment to enlightenment and progress within a more tolerant, liberalized empire. It was this mood that prevailed when Soso and his fellow seminarians established their study circles where they could read forbidden literature.

Late in 1896 the seminarian Seit Devdariani organized a study circle for which he had worked out an ambitious six-year reading program.[43] He and a number of other students, including Soso Jughashvili, were moved from the dormitory to a separate apartment because of their ill health. "Just after getting to know him," writes Devdariani, "I proposed that he join our circle. He was happy to and agreed. He didn't even ask about details about the circle, what its aims were. He was interested in its illegality. 'When? Where,' he asked me. . . . He stopped writing poems," and joined the circle that fall. Soso took an active part in the circle and soon "was the leader."[44]

The strict regime within the seminary, enforced by the despised inspector of the seminary, the Russified Georgian monk Dmitrii, forced the students to find a safe house for their circle meetings.[45] Devdariani rented a room at the foot of *mamadavita*, where they gathered from three to five.[46] As one of the poorest among his friends, Soso did not pay for the room, which cost five rubles a month, or the books from the library run by Zakaria Chichinadze, a rare book collector. Somehow they found copies of *The Communist Manifesto*, Marx's *The Erfurt Program*, and Engels's *The Development of Scientific Socialism*, which they borrowed for a few days and laboriously copied out by hand during the night. They were told that these were the only copies in all of Tiflis. The first volume of *Capital* cost twenty-five rubles, if it could be found, and poor seminarians could hardly afford to buy it. Soso's group read Marx's classical work from a handwritten manuscript painstakingly copied from the single available copy of the 1872 Russian translation in the Tiflis library.[47] When the inspector came by, they hid their readings under the blankets, and then continued reading and writing until morning.[48]

The ten student members of the secret circle were to begin with Georgian, Russian, and European literature, and go through natural science, sociology, and last the works of Marx and Engels. Different "sections" met separately to discuss economics, aesthetics, or literature. Anyone could attend any section, and the whole group met together to talk about organizational matters. Devdariani remembered that the students were already atheists, thanks largely to the clerical regime in the seminary, and were fascinated by questions like whether heat, light, or sound was material.[49] The two Sosos from Gori—Jughashvili and Iremashvili—were most impressed by the works of Georgian literature, in which the struggle for Georgian freedom was a constant theme, but no clear separation was made in their minds between national liberation and the social struggles of the poorer classes. Iremashvili remembered, "Soso and I often talked about the tragic fate of the Georgians. We were inspired by the poet Shota Rustaveli," who epitomized the chivalric ideals of the Georgian past.[50] Soso Jughashvili had found an alternative education, one steeped in humanistic literature, social and natural science. The church and religion fell rapidly away.

Soso's academic record worsened in his third year. By the time he was promoted to the fourth class Soso had fallen to fourteenth place in his class and, for the first time, into the second group (*razriad*) of students.[51] The next year, 1897–1898, his grades fell precipitously. Instead of earning the top grade of five, he wavered between threes and fours, with an occasional two. Bizarrely, only in deportment did he excel and achieve all fives.[52]

The student romantic had a personal hero with whom he identified—Koba, the protagonist of a novella by the Georgian writer Aleksandre Qazbegi (1848–1893). Iremashvili writes that Koba became a "God for Soso, gave meaning to his life."[53] Before he adopted the pseudonym Stalin, Jughashvili was known to friends and fellow revolutionaries as Koba, and until the end of his life close friends, particularly Georgians, referred to him by the name of his boyhood hero.[54] His friend and collaborator in the 1920s Nikolai Bukharin addressed pleading letters to Stalin "Dear Koba" before he was executed in 1938.

The writings of the popular author Qazbegi (Kazbegi) were being rediscovered and appreciated anew just as Jughashvili entered the Tiflis Seminary. His life's journey told a strange tale of descent from privilege to service to despair. Born in the mountain village of Stepantsminda, the first Georgian village in which a traveler from the north arrives, Qazbegi was descended from noblemen. His father and grandfather had been governors of Khevi, the highland region in which they lived, both under the last Georgian kings and under the Russians. Raised by a nurse, Qazbegi learned the folk tales and traditions of the *mokheveebi*, the Georgian mountaineers among whom he lived. As a nobleman he was sent to Tiflis *gimnaziia* for schooling and then on to the Moscow Agricultural Institute until illness forced him back to his homeland. Suddenly in the fall of 1870 Qazbegi broke with his family and his gentry roots, abandoned the family "palace," and freed the *mokheveebi* from all the taxes and obligations imposed by his father and grandfather. For seven years he lived the rugged life of a mountain shepherd, overcoming both the physical hardships and the suspicions of the poor herdsmen among whom he lived. "Those to whom I tried with all my soul to draw near alienated themselves from me," he wrote. "It was not easy for them to believe that a person who is allowed to steal from them could honestly want to work together with them, to become their brother."[55] Returning to Tiflis in 1879 Qazbegi began to write the series of memoirs and romantic tales that established his reputation as the chronicler of the unspoiled people of the mountains. Repeatedly harassed by the tsarist censors, his prolific output ceased abruptly in 1886, and he spent the last years of his life in a mental asylum.

Qazbegi's choice to give up a life of ease in order to bond with his people was consistent with the values expressed by the heroes he created in his stories. Their admiration for the threatened traditions of the mountain Georgians was matched by their anguish as the ideal customary life based on old customs and simple justice was destroyed with the coming of the Russians. The imposition of an alien administration and its attendant careerism and corruption was the backdrop to rebellion. Resistance to foreign rule was justified not on racial or ethnic grounds, but as an attempt to recover a dying way of life, as an act of cultural preservation. Qazbegi's stories and their author's tragic odyssey inspired those looking for a path to service.

The story *Patricide* (*mamis mkvleli*) concerns the ill-fated love of Iago, a poor serf, and Nunu, the daughter of "Poor Glakha," an outlaw who had killed a magistrate (*diambegi*) and his own innocent but dishonored wife.[56] Glakha's brother and sister-in-law give Nunu in marriage to the brother of a wealthy but dishonest official, Grigola. Falsely arrested and jailed, Iago is rescued by his friend, Koba, a man who embodies all the virtues of the mountain man. In a world of rampant official injustice, Koba uses his physical strength and daring to aid his friends and maintain the traditions of the mountains. To save the honor of Nunu and his own beloved Mariné, Koba kills a man and becomes an outlaw. The outlaws join together as adopted brothers, sealing their oath with exchanges of bullets, embraces, and kisses. They cross the Terek to the land of the Chechens and join Imam Shamil's rebellion against Russia.[57] Though Georgians and Chechens had had a long history of hostility, Koba and Iago believe that the mountain peoples should ally against the Russian invaders. Victory falls to the rebels, but just as it seems that

Nunu and Iago will be united, the treacherous Grigola conspires to have Iago killed and Nunu accused of the murder of her father. As she is being displayed in public before being exiled to Siberia, Nunu dies. Only Koba is left to mete out the justice that the corrupt Georgian officials deserve. As they move through the mountains, Koba fires the fatal shots. "'It is I, Koba! You are paying for the life of Iago!'—a voice was heard from the forest, and having cried out, it disappeared without a trace."

Vengeance is a theme central to the story *Patricide*, but this vengeance is not based on a personal disposition. Rather in Caucasian society vengeance is a socially sanctioned, even sacred, instrument required to restore a lost moral balance.[58] *Patricide* tells a story about the near impossibility to maintain two of the most fundamental values of the mountaineers, honor and friendship, with their associated obligations. In the society of the mountaineers insults and injustices cannot be tolerated by real men, and the ties of kinship and friendship demand that the pains suffered by those close to you be taken upon yourself (*sheni jiri me*). "These words are holy to a mountain man—better to die with honor than live in shame." In the new world created since the arrival of the Russians, what passes for justice is administered by the unjust, and men and women of honor fall victim to the unscrupulous and godless among their own people. In this new universe the victims cry, "Where is God, where is justice?" In the absence of alternatives vengeance is the only possible act of retribution, restoring a just and moral order in a society in which authorities are criminal. Against all odds and overwhelming opposition the vindictive Koba is the agent of the old justice seeking to resurrect the conservative utopia that had existed in times past.

Beginning with Chavchavadze, Georgian writers celebrated the purity and simplicity of the "Georgian" peoples of the mountains. However distinct their dialects and customs, in the nationalist imagination they were members of the greater Georgian nation. In this literary tradition mountain society is contrasted with the world of drunken Cossacks, corrupt and ambitious officials, and vain noblemen and compared favorably with the freer life of the North Caucasian mountain people who revolted against the Russians under Shamil to preserve the old way of life. The Chechens, Koba tells us, "have customs that are like our grandfathers', according to the tales." They elect their own judges and leaders, just as the Georgians did in the past. In both societies men and women are distinct and different. Men are required to be strong but to use their strength to defend honor, most importantly the honor of women and the homeland. Yet at the same time they can also be sensitive and appreciate beauty. Koba, for example, is able to play the *panduri*, the traditional Georgian plucked instrument, and to sing "songs of manliness." Women are chaste and modest and at crucial times play the role of peacemaker, able to stop a fight or feud by throwing down a kerchief between the antagonists. Marriages might be arranged, but they are to be based on love. The village is able to dissolve a loveless marriage. Last, in the inhospitable mountains where a single mistake can lead to death and where humans must help each other to survive, the greatest respect is shown to the stranger who becomes a guest. Even Russian prisoners of war are treated respectfully, as guests. As a binding element in mountain life, hospitality contrasts with the exploitative treatment by Cossacks and tsarist officials of people passing through the mountains. The tsarist official, Grigola, thwarts these traditional views by insisting on enforcing a contract based on monetary exchange.

In Qazbegi's stories the national struggle and the social are tightly intertwined. Inverting the imaginative Caucasus of Russian letters, in which Russia represented civilization and the Caucasus an exotic but barbaric threat, Qazbegi sets up the ideal society of the mountaineers as a standard of civilization against which the Russian intrusion becomes a form of barbarism.[59] In the hierarchy of higher and lower cultures, mountain Georgia's purer expression of honor and honesty is closer to God's natural order than lowland, urban, and Russian societies and represents an ideal in which people live in freedom, choosing their own authorities, and making their laws according to ancient practices. In Qazbegi's backward-gazing utopia, characters are not psychologically complex. Their one-dimensionality makes moral choices simple—the good is identified with conformity with the old customs;

evil is to give in to instincts and drives such as lust, greed, or personal ambition.

What attracted the young Jughashvili to Qazbegi and Koba? The tale, filled with passion, danger, rapid reversals, and violence, has all the dramatic elements of a well-told adventure story. But along with the romantic evocations of Georgia's natural beauty and the barely suppressed sexuality of several episodes, *Patricide* presented Soso with a vision of Russian oppression and Georgian resistance that perfectly matched his own experience both in Gori and in the Tiflis Seminary. It illuminated Soso's early life, reinforcing an experience of tension and conflict between indigenous Georgian concepts of respect, honor, and justice and the naked, arbitrary power of the Russians, which students like Soso came to perceive as illegitimate. The struggle against injustice justified, indeed required, taking up weapons. Violence was inscribed in what had to be done. Koba represented a noble ideal of a man of honor unwilling to submit to injustice. Turning away from the comforts of society and embracing the freedom of the outlaw as Koba did attracted Soso. Through his rebellion Koba (and Soso) became authentically Georgian.

Until his third year at the seminary Soso's boyhood had not been extraordinary. Poor, without an extended family or siblings, or even a father at home for much of his early life, the restless young Jughashvili possessed neither the material means nor the social status to rise very far within Georgia. But he was unwilling to accept the lot given him. Like many of his contemporaries, Soso experienced a double, even triple sense of inferiority and oppression. He was the son of a cobbler, officially registered as a member of the peasant estate; a provincial in a cosmopolitan city dominated by Russians and Armenians; and a Georgian faced by a newly aggressive nationalizing imperial regime prepared to deracinate the "inferior" culture of the non-Russians. Unable to reconcile who he was with what he hoped to be, or what the world was with what it ought to be, Soso faced a double "realization crisis": a broad social crisis for Georgians in general, buffeted by Russian cultural pressures and Armenian economic challenges, which made retention of old Georgian practices ever more difficult; and a personal crisis for a young ambitious man, who empathized with Georgia but could excel as a Georgian only by becoming a rebel.[60] Jughashvili initially sought restoration of a lost ideal, a typical goal of romantic nationalists, but the only way to achieve that was through radical opposition to the world around him. As Georgia's traditional, patriarchal ways were shaken by new social practices and ideas, Soso sought a way out, a way to realize himself by reinventing who he was to be.

BREAKING LEFT

4

APPRENTICE OF THE REVOLUTION

He entered the revolutionary movement of Transcaucasia with this "moral preparation," not as an idealist dreaming of a beautiful future, like my mother's parents, the Alliluevs; not as an enthusiastic writer, like Gorky, whose romantic hyperboles sang of the coming revolution and freedom; nor as a European-educated theoretician, like Plekhanov, Lenin, Trotsky, or Bukharin. High Ideals, with capital letters, did not impress this sober youth with his practical outlook on life. He chose the path of the revolutionary because burning within him was the cold flame of protest against a society in which he was at the bottom and was supposed to stay there forever. He wanted more, and there was no other path for him except revolution.

—SVETLANA ALLILUEVA,
TOL'KO ODIN GOD [ONLY ONE YEAR] (1969)

I remember the year 1898 when I was first assigned to a circle of workers from the railroad workshops. This was 28 years ago. I remember how in comrade Sturua's apartment in the presence of Jibladze (he too was then one of my teachers), Chodrishvili, Bochorishvili, Ninua, and other leading workers of Tiflis I received the first lessons in practical work. Compared to these comrades I was then a young man. Perhaps I was then a little more educated than many of these comrades. But as a practical worker I was then, undoubtedly, a beginner. Here, at that time, in the circle of these comrades I received my first fighting revolutionary baptism. Here, at that time, in the circle of these comrades, I became an apprentice of the revolution. As you see, my first teachers were Tiflis workers.

—JOSEPH STALIN, *ZARIA VOSTOKA [DAWN OF THE EAST]*
(JUNE 10, 1926)

In the passage from adolescence to adult revolutionary, the first vaguely political sensibility for Stalin was highly moralistic and emotional. Dominant was resentment, the emotion felt when others receive what is seen as not rightfully theirs, and one's own lot is not what one deserves. Only in his last teen years was an intellectual foundation slowly constructed, a story that explained his social and ethnic inferiority not as congenital or irredeemable, but as the product of exploitation, the abuse of power, and global forces of history. Soso Jughashvili's passage from studious seminarian and romantic Georgian nationalist onto the path to Marxist revolutionary took place after two years in the Tiflis Seminary. In what was the premier great reversal in his life, Soso first rejected the religion of his mother and his teachers and later the nationalism of many of his compatriots. He progressively shed his native culture, its values, codes, and habits, and shifted his personal and political allegiances, embracing those intellectuals who professed a cosmopolitan humanism and a dedication to serving the simple people. This was the first step that moved him away from Georgia toward Russia, from the periphery to the center. His gravitation toward the values of the radical Russian intelligentsia was in no way unique or extraordinary. Dozens of his contemporaries in the schools and seminaries of the Caucasus, Georgian and Armenian as well as Russian, were embarking on the same passage, exploring a world of forbidden books that gave meaning to their sense of social and ethnic oppression. While some of his mates accommodated themselves to the world around them and others remained nationalists and focused their intellectual and political energies on their own people, the more radical like Soso discovered socialism and immersed themselves in an empire-wide revolutionary movement.[1]

Just a decade earlier, another young man, far from the Caucasus, in a comfortable home near the Volga, underwent a similar conversion to politics. His sister, Anna, the most credible witness, reports that the boy, Vladimir Ulianov, had no explicitly political interests before the death of his beloved older brother, Aleksandr.[2] As a teenager, Vladimir resisted authority but found his intellectual pleasures in reading Turgenev.

Only after Aleksandr was executed in 1887 for his part in a plot against the tsar did Vladimir read and reread Nikolai Chernyshevskii's novel *What Is to Be Done?* in which the ideal revolutionary, Rakhmetov, was represented as a disciplined, resolute ascetic ready to sacrifice his personal well-being for the people. By the time Jughashvili began to read Marx, Vladimir Ulianov, using his revolutionary pseudonym, Lenin, was already recognized among northern radicals as a major force in the socialist movement. The lives of these two young men, the Russian eight years older than the Georgian, would eventually intersect and determine much of the fate of twentieth-century Russia.

Soso's progressive passage toward Lenin began with his forays into study circles, meeting the first Georgian Marxists, and his tentative introduction to workers. Like much of the rest of the Russian Empire, Georgia experienced a revival in political activity in 1894—the same year that Soso moved from Gori to Tiflis. The emperor Nicholas II ascended the throne, and liberal nobles pinned their hopes for broadening the range of expression in the country on the new young monarch. While the tsar's initial response dismissed their petitions as "senseless dreams," the long dormant oppositional elements in society—liberal gentry in local and provincial assemblies, educated professionals, and a growing number of revolutionary intellectuals—sought both legal and illegal means to expand their influence.

A small group of young intellectuals, which included the former seminarians Noe Zhordania, Pilipe Makharadze, and Mikha Tskhakaia, had been meeting since December 1892 to organize a political "party" around a revolutionary program. Zhordania and Makharadze had left the seminary with "wolves' tickets," certificates that prohibited them from entering a university.[3] Compelled to enroll in the Veterinarian Institute in Warsaw, they imbibed the dual intoxications of Marxism and the anti-tsarist nationalism of "Russian" Poland. Moving from one imperial periphery to another, their Polish experience solidified their opposition to Russian autocracy and an intense commitment to national liberation. The newly minted Marxists returned home confident that European Social Democracy laid out Georgia's path to the modern world. Not completely free of nationalist sentiments themselves, the young radicals nevertheless distanced themselves from the gentry nationalists around Chavchavadze and self-consciously adopted the internationalist language of Marxism. Inspired by both the traditions of Russian revolutionary Populism as well as Marx, they sought a way out of the double oppression they believed afflicted Georgia—the burden of Russian absolutism and the growing power of Armenian and foreign capital.

Zhordania and his associates began collaborating with the journal *kvali* (Furrow), whose editor, the liberal Giorgi Tsereteli, soon dubbed them *mesame dasi* (the third group) and thus the historic successors to the "enlighteners" of the 1860s (*pirveli dasi*, first group) and the liberal reformers of the 1870s (*meore dasi*, second group). Tsereteli reported in *kvali* the provocative speech of the firebrand "Silva" Jibladze at the funeral of the socialist writer Egnate Ingoroqva, who had chronicled the misery of the poor under the pseudonym "Ninoshvili." "Our contemporary life," Jibladze proclaimed, "presents two opposing camps or classes. On one side are the representatives of physical and mental labor; on the other are the bourgeois-capitalist parasites."[4] For young Georgian intellectuals, the funeral oration signaled that something dormant was awakening. For fledgling rebels like Soso Jughashvili the most energetic and exciting political message no longer centered on the nation but on the nascent working classes.

Although the group's ideological profile remained vague and eclectic, the polemic directed against Chavchavadze's newspaper, *iveria*, helped to clarify important distinctions. In the summer of 1894 a major programmatic article by Zhordania was, after much debate, approved by the group's members and published in the legal journal *moambe* (Bulletin). Here several themes that would be associated with the young Marxists were explicitly expressed: a commitment to social progress in a Westernizing direction (a challenge to Chavchavadze's nostalgia for agrarian, seigniorial Georgia); a willingness to work with other nationalities (as opposed to *iveria*'s passionate Armenophobia); and a reliance on the notion of class conflict both in their social analysis and in their political strategy (in contrast to Chavchavadze's ideal of social harmony under noble patriarchy).[5] Zhordania elaborated his class interpretation of Georgia's history and announced that "our country has already imperceptibly stood on the road of industry; the nation has already pushed its head into the capitalist vise."[6]

Zhordania's article, "Economic Development and Nationality," appeared within months of Soso Jughashvili's arrival in Tiflis and quickly became a major topic of conversation, particularly among students and young intellectuals. They sensed an infusion of energy in Georgian life and embraced the appearance of an *akhali taoba* (new generation). Its compelling analysis of Georgia's dual social and cultural humiliation converted many to the new thinking. Zhordania soon became the acknowledged leader of this emerging intellectual and political movement, and eventually the editor of *kvali*. While his path and Soso's would cross at crucial moments over their long careers, the two men could not have been more different. Zhordania, the son of impoverished nobles from a small town in Guria, Western Georgia, was a tall, slim man with a black beard, modest bearing, and aristocratic manners.[7] With his slight stutter, he reminded an acolyte of a village schoolteacher. His influence and power came from his writings. Applying historical materialism to the history of Georgia's national formation, Zhordania argued that while "language is the first sign of nationality," only real material transformation linked the disparate regions of Georgia and led to the consolidation of the nation. Just as economic development created a new Georgia, so in the future the national and the social struggles had to be combined in order to win freedom for the nation.

Zhordania's Marxism demystified the nation and rendered it a product of social forces. He provided Georgians with an ostensibly supranationalist analysis that offered a means of overcoming the dual oppression of Russian autocracy and Armenian capital but at the same time tied Georgia's future to a liberated Russia. His version of history placed Georgia on the same trajectory as the advanced capitalist countries of Western Europe and singled out the embryonic working class of the Russian Empire as the instrument that would bring down the whole apparatus of state and economic power. Instead of Russia as a whole, or Russians in general, depicted as the enemy of Georgia, Zhordania proposed that Georgia's emancipation required alliance with the progressive intellectuals and workers of Russia. He laid out the path by which backward, exoticized Georgia reached Europe and became part of the most advanced and progressive social movement of the time. For the younger generation like Soso and his friends, this analysis explained the changes in the social life of their country they were experiencing. Moreover, it ended their provincial isolation and linked their cause with that of the progressive, humanistic Russian writers that they had been reading. Georgian Marxists applauded the attacks of Georgii Plekhanov, the "father of Russian Marxism," on the peasant socialism of the Populists (*narodniki*), whose notion that Russia could avoid capitalism and remain a land of small peasant farming was contradicted by the country's rapid industrialization and urban growth in the last decades of the nineteenth century. The prognosis of the Marxists that Russia (and within it, Georgia) would repeat the experience of Europe and America—massive industry, urban concentration, the emergence of the proletariat—seemed daily to be confirmed.

The first Russian Marxists came out of the Populist movement but rejected its romanticization of the peasant and its attempt to avoid the path of West. Populists often relied on the actions of individuals, hopefully by word or deed, to stir up the peasant masses. When propaganda did not seem to work, a small number of militants turned to terrorism, spectacularly culminating in the assassination of the Emperor Alexander II in 1881.[8] Plekhanov and a few of his comrades abjured terrorism and turned instead to appropriating the ideas of Marx as a form of scientific historical and economic reasoning. He read *Capital* and found confirmation that the peasant commune could not survive the onslaught of capitalism and that Russia would necessarily reproduce the historic evolution of bourgeois Europe.[9] His view became the prevailing vision of the future for Russian Marxists. A stern and demanding patriarchal figure fully deserving of his title "Father of Russian Marxism," Plekhanov preached patience and moderation. Socialism demanded a high level of economic development and a mature political consciousness within the working class. Only passage through capitalism and industrialization could create a proletariat capable of carrying out the socialist revolution. The coming of socialism would require a long gestation, and no premature seizure of power by revolutionaries could hasten the process along. Plekhanov's enormous stature among Russian Marxists did not hinder Soso Jughashvili from becoming highly critical of his positions on a variety of issues, just as he had toward Plekhanov's Georgian counterpart, Zhordania.

As in Russia so in Georgia, intellectual (and eventually worker) interest in the ideas of Marx, as received through Plekhanov, swelled in the decade after 1891. Everywhere the Russian Marxists' prediction that Russia must follow Europe into industrialism seemed to be validated by the spurt in railroad building, the new industries promoted by the tsarist state, and even by the squalid ghettos in which newly forged workers lived. The disastrous famine of 1891 exposed the peasantry as passive and nearly helpless in the face of calamity and encouraged radicals to seek new allies among workers. The strikes among textile workers in the mid-1890s only ratified the decision to agitate in the cities. Moreover, Marxism had its own internal appeals—the inevitability of revolution, the model of Western development, and the promise of success. History seemed to be on the side of the Social Democrats.

At the same time *mesame dasi* confidently put forth its own claim to be the new leaders of the Georgian people. They easily overwhelmed their principal opponents, the pathetically poor and discouraged nobles. Georgians had neither a state of their own nor even an effective, politically potent dominant class. Unlike the Armenians in their midst, who could boast an entrepreneurial "bourgeoisie," Georgians were divided between a declining gentry and the mass of peasants suffering from the onslaughts of a market economy that drove many into the industrial suburbs of the towns. Marxists stepped into a political void, a vacuum of leadership, which gave the small Georgian intelligentsia, itself emerging from déclassé nobles and the sons of priests and teachers (and even cobblers), a weight in society far greater than its numbers would suggest. Here was the new generation of enlighteners that the poet Soselo had sought lyrically. Young *intelligenty* (politically committed intellectuals) became the definers of the national agenda in this moment of transition and cultural crisis.

Whatever emotional formation Soso had undergone within his family was reshaped by his attraction to the new intellectual culture of the Georgian radicals and the repulsion he and his fellow seminarians felt toward the clerics who controlled their lives and learning. In the seminary the harsh world of Russian dominance, represented by the priests, clashed with the student subculture—at once Georgian and hostile to the values of their largely Russian or Russified teachers. Just as in Gori, so in Tiflis, Soso steadily turned inward and grew more serious. His friend Vano Ketskhoveli noted that Soso changed from a child interested in games and fun into a "thoughtful, and it would seem taciturn person. He refused to play games and stayed with his books; finding some corner he read intensively."[10] Grades became unimportant to him. "Joseph stopped paying attention to the lessons," writes Gogokhia, another boyhood companion. "His grades fell to threes—he only sat for the examinations."[11] Following the example of upperclassmen, he abandoned religious studies. "In the end he even stopped singing in the seminary choir, something he had always done with pleasure."[12] Gradually those students attracted to socialism withdrew from the other seminarians.[13]

The new energy and political activism of the mid-1890s penetrated the walls of the seminary. The students of the seminaries and *gimnazii* (secular academies), at least those who were prepared to join the opposition, believed, like their elders, that if Georgia and its unique culture were to be preserved and nourished, the younger generation had to take itself seriously. Not just exceptional individuals but an entire generation of students appreciated the need for organization, discipline, and action. Soselo's poems had reiterated the special role of the young. Even though an industrial working class hardly existed in Georgia, and the Russian Empire was overwhelmingly a peasant country, for students like Soso the choice of Marxism was made with little effort. It had simply become the most vital and persuasive political synthesis for both Georgian and Russian radical intellectuals. Marxism attracted young converts with its analysis of the transformative trends experienced in everyday life and its prediction of a better world to come. It combined "scientific" explanation of their mundane experience with a romantic faith in future possibilities. For Soso, like other politically minded students, becoming a Marxist was to join the dominant current sweeping through the Georgian intelligentsia, to abandon their hermetic commitment to Georgia alone and open up to a more powerful international movement. Historian Yuri Slezkine has noted a similar evolution among radical young Russians: "A conversion to socialism was a conversion to the intelligentsia, to a fusion of millenarian faith and lifelong learning. It was an immediate step up socially and intellectually, as well as spiritually."[14]

From the memoirs of his fellow students Soso's rough passage through the seminary resembles a fractured mosaic. Two contrasting stories emerge. The memoirs and histories published in the Soviet Union in the 1930s and 1940s transformed the young Stalin into an iconic figure, a model of proper Bolshevik evolution. Removing all blemishes (even the pockmarks on his face) and elaborating his leadership qualities, his attentiveness to younger comrades, and his courage in standing up to the priests, the hagiographers eliminated the contradictions and complexities and nearly obliterated the boy Jughashvili. At the same time the hostile accounts of Stalin's rivals and enemies produced outside the Soviet Union painted an unrelentingly negative picture of a boy with a need to dominate weaker classmates and driven by a generalized hatred toward all authority. Yet both sympathetic and unsympathetic witnesses confirm that Soso was a dominant and popular figure among the seminarians and that he was among the most radical of his peers. Iremashvili and Razmadze tell of two "parties" being formed in the seminary, one for and one against Jughashvili.[15] Most students thought of the writers around *kvali* as cultural and political heroes, but Soso showed a studied irreverence toward them.[16] By 1898, Iremashvili reports, Soso was making fun of the *kvali* editors. While Devdariani, Iremashvili, and their friend Rutrushvili considered themselves close to the views of Noe Zhordania and Georgii Plekhanov, the "fathers" of Georgian and Russian Marxism, Iremashvili claims, improbably, that Soso was inspired by Bakunin, Blanc, and Lenin.[17] Here Iremashvili appears to be reading back into those earlier days distinctions between Marxists and other revolutionaries that emerged with clarity only much later. In a Soviet source another student, Petre Kapanadze, also remembered Soso being critical of Zhordania. He goes on to report that after reading an article by "Tulin," Soso supposedly said, "No matter what, I must see him."[18] "Tulin" was an early pseudonym of Lenin. Here, however, the mythmakers of the mature Stalin have stepped far beyond the plausible.

What is clear is that Soso and his friends in the study circle disagreed with Seit Devdariani's emphasis on a broad reading program and preferred focusing on natural science and economics. They argued for a whole year about the direction of their study. Drifting further from his romantic and humanistic interests in poetry and fiction, Soso wanted to read the Marxist literature immediately. In the spring of 1897 the dispute was taken outside the seminary to be adjudicated by the budding Marxists Jibladze and Makharadze, who lived together. They pronounced the reading program "too academic," apparently agreeing with Soso.[19] Even with the advice from their elders and despite their general agreement with Soso, most students, out of respect for Devdariani, continued to support him. Even Soso deferred to his friend. When a leader for the socioeconomic section of the circle was to be chosen, Devdariani proposed Khutsishvili. The other likely candidate was Soso, but he said that he did not want to insult his friend, Seit, or his opponent, and proposed that Khutsishvili be elected. Despite their intellectual and tactical differences, Soso and Seit remained close, discussing circle matters between meetings and even vacationing together. Nevertheless, after Devdariani left for university, the circle split, and Soso turned toward more "practical" material. Once or twice a week the circle, handpicked by Soso, gathered after dinner in secret, likely in the same rented room near *mamadaviti*. Soso, who visited bookshops and picked up bits and pieces from skimming, lectured his fellow students or read to them from borrowed books or pamphlets. Not too much should be made of this "split" in the circle, which reads too much like a prefiguration of future schisms, between "hards" and "softs" in the Georgian movement, and even more prematurely the division between Bolsheviks and Mensheviks. In fact, once Devdariani graduated in May 1898 and moved on to Iur'ev University in the Baltic region, Soso became the leader of his circle, the members of which now agreed with his program.[20]

The romantic humanism of the seminary poet was overwhelmed by reading Darwin and Marx, the most powerful available critics of the worldview of those in charge. These works revealed a harsh truth: that what they had been told before, by parents and teachers, was false. The world was without God. Religion was a deception. Appearances could mislead. Probing analysis, intensive learning, and science were the way to reveal the true nature of things. Rather than accepting what was being taught in the classroom or chapel, an effort had to be made to learn for oneself. If the original texts were unattainable, popularized pamphlets or hand-copied versions were read. Each issue of *kvali* was discussed as it appeared, and the seminarians often visited the newspaper's offices. Following a student tradition, Soso may also have edited a handwritten journal in Georgian, actually a notebook of about thirty pages, which was passed around from hand to hand twice a month.[21] Besides Darwin, Marx, Lev Tolstoy, and Victor Hugo, he read the work of the recently deceased writer Egnate Ingoroqva (Ninoshvili), whose story "Gogia Uishvili" was a particular favorite of his. In this tale, written in 1889, poverty and the arbitrary power of local officials drive the peasant Uishvili to suicide and his wife, Mariné, to madness. Humanity is eroded by material depravation and official humiliation. The peasants in the story share Gogia's misery, but their fear and self-interest prevent them from intervening to help. A single ray of hope remains that Gogia and Mariné's son, who returns to the ruined house of his parents, might escape their harsh fate.[22]

Soso's interests in the social and psychological world took over his life. He recommended that his friends read a book, *The Psychology of Feelings*, by a certain psychologist, Ribot.[23] Devdariani remembered that when his friend stayed with him in his home village, he sat in one place all day and read an illegal book, *The Struggle of the English Workers for Freedom*. Seit asked him why he did not take notes, and Soso replied that he relied on his memory. Devdariani noted that everyone was impressed by Soso's memory. Soso also invited the better-off Seit to Gori to stay at his mother's modest home. Keke was upset that she could offer only bread and cheese. "How guilty I feel, my son, that we are eating without wine," she moaned. "Perhaps, my son, the bedbugs have not allowed you to sleep." Embarrassed, Seit relied on his "Imeretian politeness" and answered that he had not been disturbed. Soso broke in, "Ah, as if he had not been disturbed. All night he was twitching his leg."[24]

A family friend, Giorgi Elisabedashvili, a few years younger than Soso, asked his father if it would be possible, now that he had finished the Gori religious school, to continue his studies with the help of Soso Jughashvili. His father agreed, and during the school holidays, in the first days of June 1898, Soso arrived by phaeton in the village of Akhaltsikhe, Kaspi district. Elisabedashvili loaded his baggage on his horse, and they walked to the family home. Loaded down with books, Soso began instructing his younger pupil right away, speaking of "the development of the struggle between workers and the parasites." Elisabedashvili felt chills, realizing how unprepared he was and how much more educated Soso was. His affection turned into deep admiration.[25] He was surprised that Soso had not brought any books by "our writers," but instead was weighed down with sociological and political economic volumes: Charles Letourneau's *Sociology*; Julius Lippert's *History of Culture*; Szymon Diksztajn's *The History of a Piece of Bread*; Friedrich Engels's *Origins of the Family, Private Property, and the State*; Mikhail Tugan-Baranovskii's *The Russian Factory*; Karl Kautsky's *Contemporary Nationalism*; Beltov's [Plekhanov] *The Monistic View of History*; *Psychology* by an unknown author; a textbook on geology; and Thomas Henry Huxley's lectures at an English university. Soso had created his own university; he had given up lyrical works for social science; and like the heroes of his poems he set out to "enlighten" first Elisabedashvili and then the local villagers.[26]

That summer Soso listened with pleasure to the peasants' songs—the *horoveli* (plowing song) and *namgalo* (sickle). Then he tried to explain to the villagers that the one who works should eat and that it was wrong that those who worked had to give up so much of what they had produced to those—the landlords, the church, and the state—who had not worked. The peasants listened with interest, but then turned away saying that this was their fate.[27] Soso explained to Elisabedashvili at length how he had earlier been enchanted by the peasants but had come to realize that the future lay with the workers. In what reads like a standard Social Democratic transition from Populist sympathies to Marxist consciousness, he related his intellectual odyssey:

From the time I started to read and write, I read through many books. I was interested in the works of Qazbegi, the poems of Rapael Eristavi, selected works of Ilia Chavchavadze, Lermontov, Pushkin, the heroic tales, etc. I saw neediness and poverty at home and around me. I was always interested in the affairs of those people and heroes who created something new and good to help the poor. I dreamt of growing up more quickly in order to have enough strength to take part in the struggle together with the poorest peasants. With this goal in mind at first I dreamt of becoming a village clerk and thought that this was the best way. . . . Then I dreamt of becoming a village headman [*mamasakhlisi*] in order to be connected to the greatest number of people and to help them. . . .

But time passed. . . . I became convinced that these were incorrect views and acquainted myself with the workers' question. I changed my views fundamentally, and all my sympathies gravitated to the side of the workers. . . . That is how I began to worry about the peasants and eventually concluded that liberating them was only possible with the help of and under the leadership of the working class. And I have never deviated from this path. This is the right path.[28]

As packaged as this tale appears, Soso's migration from a broad sympathy for "the people" to a reliance on the working class occurred sometime during his last years in the seminary. That transition to Marxist faith in the working class cannot with certainty be dated, but the influence of the *mesame dasi* socialists on Soso and his friends was palpable. Jughashvili acted as a rebel by his third year in the seminary, but his acts of insubordination involved little more than reading forbidden books, writing poems or singing in Georgian, and not properly greeting a teacher. He was reprimanded for laughing in church, for wearing a *furazhka* (military-style cap) in class, for carrying a book by Victor Hugo, for possessing something from the *Deshevaia biblioteka* (Cheap Library), talking in class, being late for morning prayers, and reading in church.[29] He deliberately failed to appear at church services, would not stand where he was supposed to, carried on conversations during the service, and for such offenses was sent to the punishment room (*kartser*).[30] At nine one evening Soso was reading to his friends in the dining room when they were accosted by one of the priests. Soso tried to hide the paper from which he was reading but was forced to give it up. The monk-inspector, Dmitrii Abashidze, reported: "It turned out that Jughashvili was reading from foreign books unsanctioned by the administration of the seminary, had made his own notes based on articles he had read, which he then passed on to the pupils Khadachidze, Nestroev, Davidov [Davitashvili], and Iremashvili. A search was made of these pupils but nothing forbidden was found."[31]

Simply remaining true to the language and culture of his childhood in the alien and oppressive world of the seminary led to clashes with the authorities. The directors of the seminary punished the students with low grades for behavior and a severe warning.[32] Students were particularly offended by the perennial searches of their lockers and their persons by the inspector Dmitrii, who discovered a notebook on Soso with articles for a student journal. Later the inspector broke open Soso's locker and found several illegal books. As he marched his victim upstairs, an upperclassman, Vaso Kelbakiani, bumped the monk violently, spilling the books on the floor. The two boys ran off with the evidence.[33] The assistant inspector, S. A. Murakhovskii, had better luck when he discovered Jughashvili reading Letourneau's *Literary Evolution of the Nations*.[34] This marked the thirteenth time Soso had been caught with books borrowed from the "Cheap Library."[35] Some time later Dmitrii forced Soso and his companion Grisha Makhtadze to burn a notebook in which humorous verses had been written. On January 18, 1899, Jughashvili was punished by loss of the privilege of going into the city for a month. The next day, Kelbakiani, then in his sixth year at the seminary, was expelled from the school.[36]

Soso found the spying and searches intolerable and protested to the inspectors, only enhancing his reputation as insubordinate. His conduct report for 1898–1899 reveals the disdain he held toward certain teachers. When several pupils of the fifth class were being searched, Soso "spoke up several times to the inspectors, expressing his discontent with the searches that are carried out from time to time among the pupils of the seminary and declared that such searches are not made in any other seminary." Father Dmitrii reported him to be "in general disrespectful and rude to the authorities, systematically refusing to bow to one of the teachers (A. A. Murakhovskii), as the latter has already repeatedly informed the inspectors." For insubordination Soso was reprimanded and confined to a cell for five hours.[37] These repeated acts of defiance were later embellished into the story of the "black spot," told by American reporter Jerome Davis. "Once when Father Dimitry, the seminary supervisor, entered Stalin's room after a search, the student went on reading without paying any attention to the intruder. Father Dimitry said, 'Don't you see who is standing before you?' Stalin rose, rubbing his eyes, and said, 'I don't see anything except a black spot before my eyes.'"[38] Davis claims that Dmitrii then recommended that Soso be expelled from the seminary.

At the end of the school year, on May 29, 1899, Soso Jughashvili was expelled from the seminary. The official explanation in the seminary records was that he had failed to take the final examinations for reasons unknown.[39] Years later his mother told a journalist that she had taken her son out of school because of his poor health. "When he went up to Tiflis from Gori and entered the seminary, he was fifteen years old and one of the strongest boys you ever saw. But then he studied too hard in the seminary, and by the time he was nineteen, he was so run down that the doctors said he might get tuberculosis. So I took him out of school. He did not want to go. I took him out."[40]

Seminary records confirm that, besides a toothache, Soso suffered twice from anemia and was sent to the out-patients' department (*ambulatoriia*) of the hospital.[41] In June 1898, at the end of his fourth year, he petitioned the rector of the seminary, Archimandrite Seraphim, for permission not to sit for an examination. "Due to my lung problems," he wrote, "I require prolonged periods of rest. I have been suffering from the disease, which became more serious during the examination period, for some time. I need extended relief from work and exertion and appropriate medical treatment. Therefore I humbly ask Your Holiness to grant me exemption from the repeat examination in Holy Scripture studies. This would make it possible for me to have some relief from this disease, which has been undermining my strength since the first grade."[42]

There is also a story that the authorities took away Soso's state subsidy. They may have finally discovered his secret reading circle.[43]

The most plausible explanation for Soso not completing the seminary remains his mother's: he was ill and she took him back to Gori. Three decades later Stalin would enhance the story of his leaving the seminary by claiming to have been expelled for Marxist propagandizing, but this does not jibe with the documentary record. Young Soso's grades actually improved in his last year at the seminary, as evidenced by the "copy of his final report card" issued to him four months after his expulsion. He received a "five" (excellent) in conduct, logic, and ecclesiastical singing and "fours" (very good) in thirteen other subjects, including history of the Bible, Greek, Georgian, Russian literature, and "secular history." The report noted that Jughashvili had been expelled because "for unknown reasons" he had failed to appear for his final examinations in his fifth year. As a result of his expulsion, he was "not entitled to the privileges enjoyed by those students who have completed their studies at the seminary." That essentially meant that he could neither become a priest nor go on to university.[44] The seminary authorities may have simply used the excuse of his absence at the examinations to rid themselves of a troublesome influence.

Why Soso's grades improved in his last year is difficult to explain. It appears that he was less concerned with acting up in the seminary than learning what he could in the time left in school. Intriguingly, it may have been a conversation with the editor of *kvali*, Noe Zhordania, that convinced the impatient Soso to stay in school that last year and take his studies more seriously. Sometime in late 1898, at the beginning of his last year at the seminary, Soso decided to visit Zhordania in his editorial offices. Soso was a foot soldier in a socialist platoon, far removed from the *mesame dasi* intellectuals around *kvali*. According to a noteworthy memory by Zhordania, the young seminarian told the veteran of Georgian Marxism that he was "a dedicated reader of your journal and your articles. They have had a great effect on me. I have decided to give up the seminary and carry these ideas into the workers' midst. Give me advice." Since good propagandists were scarce, Zhordania was pleased by Jughashvili's intention but decided to test the young man's intellectual breadth. After a few questions on history, sociology, and political economy, it became clear that Soso had a very superficial understanding based largely on articles from *kvali* and on Karl Kautsky's *The Erfurt Program*. Zhordania advised the seminarian to stay in school for another year and to take up self-education. "I will think about it," said Soso, and he left.[45] Zhordania feared that the workers would reject such an unsophisticated propagandist. Soso, on the other hand, was anxious to end his frustrating existence within the seminary and to immerse himself in the "movement." Reluctantly the new recruit to Marxism returned to the seminary, but the condescension that the older, more genteel *intelligent* displayed toward the youthful enthusiast did not long deter him. Younger activists were already moving in a different direction from the older *literati*. Around this time Soso decided to send an article critical of *kvali* to the newspaper. But the editors rejected it. "This is unheard of!" Soso angrily told Elisabedashvili. "They sit around so long and are unable to express a single sensible thought."[46]

Soso had by his last year moved beyond the intellectual limits of the school and probably had little interest in continuing. He was older than the other students, and the financial costs of attending were burdensome. He left the seminary without paying the 18 rubles, 15 kopecks that he owed for books or the last third of the tuition fees for 1898–1899.[47] He did not respond when the administration suggested that his debt of 680 rubles would be forgiven if he took up a position as a teacher in a church school or a temporary post in the church.[48] His education had prepared him for the priesthood, but he no longer had any interest in the church. He had no diploma, no possibility of continuing his education. He returned to Gori, but not to his mother's home. She was angry that he did not plan to return to school. Her plans for his future were shattered. Friends hid him for a few days in a garden in Ghambareuli and secretly visited and fed him.[49] There was an even greater fear that the police were after him. While he visited with Misha Davitashvili in Tsromi, the house of Misha's father, a priest, was searched. Nothing was found, but the atmosphere was growing tense. That summer and fall more than twenty students were removed from the seminary rolls, possibly because of the secret reading groups.[50]

With no definite plans he returned to Tiflis by the end of the year. There Jibladze, a founding member of *mesame dasi* who was very fond of Soso, found him a room in the apartment of the Kalandarashvili family across the Kura from the seminary.[51] He lived at 102 Mikhailovskii Prospect with his friend Davitashvili, and in December Vano Ketskhoveli, Lado's younger brother and a friend from both the Gori church school and the Tiflis Seminary, found both roommates jobs at the Tiflis Physical Observatory. There Soso began work on December 28, 1899, as a meteorologist—the only wage-paying job he would ever hold outside politics—and soon moved into one of the small rooms in the building. One of his co-workers, the former seminarian Beso Berdzenishvili, remembered that the hours were long (15 1/2 hours on the day shift and 11 1/2 on the night shift) and the pay low.[52] Soso was paid twenty rubles a month, and the atmosphere at the observatory was pleasant.[53] He exercised with the other employees in the garden where they improvised the branch of a tree for pullups.[54] How (or whether) Soso might have done pullups with his damaged left arm remains a mystery. Soso liked to ask the director of the observatory, "Rudof Fomich, what is higher than a human?" to which the director would answer, "The roof." Dissatisfied and still curious as to his boss's attitude toward religion, Soso at the first opportunity would repeat his question.[55]

Jughashvili lived with and depended on his former schoolmates, particularly those from Gori. Like a band of brothers, the circle of ex-students worked together, shared their meager resources, and acted as a surrogate family toward one another. In the Caucasus, as in Russia, the ties among schoolmates were a kind of kinship that required lifelong loyalty and mutual aid. Their work as meteorologists, however, was only a cover behind which the former seminarians began their propagandist work among the city's students and workers. Soso may have been briefly detained by the police at the beginning of 1900—his first arrest—but not for his political work. It turned out that his father, who was probably living somewhere in Tiflis, owed taxes to his native village, Didi-Lilo.

Unable to pay, Soso missed work for the first two weeks of the year, but his comrades came to his rescue and paid his father's arrears.[56] Around this time his friend from Gori Georgii Vardoian rented him a "conspiratorial" apartment, a secret hideaway unknown to the police. To Vardoian Soso Jughashvili was already a role model, someone with a "steady disposition." He copied Soso's mannerisms, his walk, his laugh, his way of speaking, and soon was known as "Soso's gramophone."[57]

Soso kept up his ties with friends in Gori and students who in various Tiflis schools were forming discussion groups. He coached seminarians, many of whom he knew either from Gori or as schoolmates. He often visited Gori and organized reading circles there, one made up of local artisans. He brought a small flag and made everyone swear to be true to each other and to be prepared to fight when it was time. He tutored students, among them Simon Ter-Petrosian (Kamo), and demanded that they learn Russian in order to read Marxist literature, train with weights, and learn the skills of "conspiracy," that is, not attracting the suspicion of the police. Soso had Ter-Petrosian hide a revolver in his aunt's house and used him to pass along books and leaflets to students. He supplied the glue to paste up the leaflets, which, it was reported, caused a sensation in the town.[58] On one of his trips home, Soso stopped a student, Porpire Epremidze, as he was about to enter the Gori religious school's church service. Out of the blue Soso asked him to relate the content and meaning of the Marxist pamphlet, *History of a Piece of Bread*. Epremidze stumbled through the story, mixing things up. Soso scolded him and told him to borrow the book from Siko Alimbarov and study it better.[59] Soso saw himself as pedagogue to his fellow students, and they accepted him as such.

As the new century began, the circles expanded, and students began paying dues to the local Social Democratic organization. Many of these students were then recruited as agitators and propagandists or even, later, as terrorists.[60] As in the seminary, so in the socialist movement, Soso gathered loyal sympathizers around him, acting as patron to willing clients and using them as needed. In one of the secular Russian-language schools, the brightest student, a bookish Lev Rozenfeld, and his friend Florenskii asked the administration to allow a student discussion group.

When permission was refused, Rozenfeld, Florenskii, and a student from another school, the future Bolshevik Suren Spandarian, organized a study circle outside the school. They moved from the home of one student to another, most often meeting in a room at the Pasteur Institute directed by the father of one of the students. The first report was by the young Irakli Tsereteli on "The Women in Turgenev's Works." From literature and science, the group moved to political economy. The circle attracted young people of both sexes, among them the future Bolsheviks Kogan, Viktor Kurnatovskii, and Prokopi Japaridze ("Alesha"). Sitting quietly in a corner, Soso, who had grown a beard and let his hair grow long, listened to a report by Rozenfeld on the political economy of the Russian liberal Petr Struve. Impressed by the speaker, he leaned over to his boyhood friend Davrishev and asked in Georgian, who is this *bichi* (boy)?[61] Jughashvili befriended Rozenfeld, and together with Spandarian, who was inseparable from Soso, they eventually left the discussion group for more serious Social Democratic circles. Later a leading Bolshevik and a close comrade of Lenin and Stalin's, Rozenfeld's fate was inextricably and fatally tied to the bearded youth he so casually met in Tiflis.[62] Known in history by his party name, taken from the Russian word for stone, he was the future Lev Kamenev.

5

BURNING BRIDGES

In the course of many years I met with him in various aspects of social life, mainly in revolutionary work, and until now I cannot find an explanation for all that happened with this person in his life career. They say and write that history does not know such an example. This is true, but it is not an explanation of the fact but only of its affirmation. It is as if nothing foretold such a rise for him! His biography, up until his dizzying elevation, is entirely uncomplicated. It is possible to say: until then he was a man without a biography.

—GRIGOL URATADZE, *VOSPOMINANIIA GRUZINSKOGO SOTSIAL-DEMOKRATA* [*MEMOIRS OF A GEORGIAN SOCIAL-DEMOCRAT*] (1968)

Karl Marx was himself not particularly enamored of Russia and was genuinely surprised in his last years when radicals in Russia took up his writings with great enthusiasm. After all, Marx was arguing that socialism would come about only after a fully developed capitalism had spawned an organized, politically conscious working class prepared to overthrow the owners of industry. Why would Russians living in a country with a pitiably small number of industrial workers take seriously a socialism dependent on an organized proletariat? Russia was the most peasant of the European great powers. It lagged behind the developing capitalist countries of the West where workers could be seen to be developing an awareness that they shared interests with other workers and believed that their interests were different from (and even fundamentally opposed to) the interests of the owning classes. But in Russia before 1890 such awareness was quite rare. What Marxists called "class consciousness" did not seem to arise either from their position as exploited factory workers or from some innate sense of class that existed within workers. Many activists in late nineteenth-century Russia, who had already given up hope that the tens of millions of peasants would become revolutionary, despaired when they contemplated how workers might gain class or socialist or revolutionary "consciousness." Yet as they entered the social world of workers, the socialists had a profound effect on the formation of workers' understandings, supplying new meanings that the men and women in the factories began to attach to their lives and futures. As Marxists made contact with workers in the last quarter of the nineteenth century, their particular discourse of class conflict and worker solidarity provided a language and vision that shaped the attitudes of significant numbers of workers.[1]

Few as they were, particularly in the peripheries of the Russian Empire, the socialists could be found wherever strikes occurred or trade unions, never very strong in prerevolutionary Russia, sprang up. The emerging movement, which styled itself "Social Democracy," had few active worker adherents, yet its growing influence was evident in workers' petitions and the demands of strikers. Workers' memoirs make abundantly clear that more and more workers (though far from all) accepted the socialists' representation of social reality—irreconcilable class antagonism between worker and capitalist, the inevitability of social revolution and the collapse of capitalism, and the central importance of workers in this historical drama. By 1905, when the empire's most socially and politically active workers in the major cities and large factories thought about politics, the dominant ideas came from the Marxists. Such influence was not unique in Europe—most German workers, for instance, supported the Marxist Social Democratic Party (SPD)—but it seemed to make less sense in peasant Russia that Marxism would take the field.

Soso Jughashvili came to socialism through reading and the fellowship of his classmates. He was anxious to convey what he believed was a liberating truth to those around him—students like himself, but even more importantly peasants and workers. Like other *propagandisti* of the time he soon discovered that disseminating knowledge to people whose lives were consumed by laboring to live was extraordinarily difficult, especially in the conditions of a police state. In the stratified society of the Russian Empire a social and psychological gulf separated workers from members of the radical intelligentsia who aspired to work with them. Often relations between socialist intellectuals and activist workers were far from harmonious. Not only did they speak differently and dress differently, but also their goals often diverged. At times workers simply wanted a larger piece of the economic pie, while the Marxists urged them to fight for more radical political goals. At other times certain workers were more militant than their self-styled intellectual leaders and prodded them to revolutionary action.

The socialists faced two separate social strands among the workers: the broad mass of workers, many of them recent recruits from the peasantry; and the activist workers, often referred to as "conscious" (*soznatel'nye*) or "leading" (*peredovye*) workers, who were usually skilled craftsmen or artisans. These more activist workers often contended with the socialists for leadership of the movement. Only in 1905 did the various strands come together in a more or less coherent labor movement indebted to organized Social Democracy.[2]

In the Caucasus, as in Russia proper, the first waged workers were really peasants who added to their income by doing occasional work in the towns. Recent migrants from the countryside, they often held some land in the villages, usually kept their families there, and continued to pay various obligations to the landlords.[3] Their workdays were long and protests in vain.[4] At the time that Soso was becoming interested in workers, very few workers in Georgia or the oil-producing center of Baku knew anything of the socialists, even though the Caucasus, as a place of exile for undesirables, housed some of the most distinguished radical intellectuals in the empire.[5] In the harsh political conditions of Russia in the 1890s, when possession of a radical pamphlet or a postcard with a photo of Marx on it could result in prison or exile, the only means of spreading the political word was in secret one-on-one or small group meetings. Conspiratorial circles attended by workers and intellectuals appeared and disappeared with regularity.

The workers that Soso met were the same few dozen Russians working in the railroad yards who filtered through these circles. Rather than unskilled factory "proletarians," they were skilled mechanics or crafts-men from the railroad repair shops, men with a degree of independence and control over their own work process that was unknown to the less skilled, usually less literate workers in the mills of Tiflis. They were much more responsive to the political outlook of the circles, which was revolutionary and socialist, at first Populist and by the turn of the century almost exclusively Marxist.[6] Most of them were Russian, since not many Armenians or Georgians could find work in the railroad repair shops until the mid-1890s.

The ephemeral circles of workers and occasional socialist visitors, first formed among Russians and later among Georgians and Arme-nians, reflected the ethnic and social divisions among workers. Russian workers who had come down from Tula, a metalworking center south of Moscow, had their own compatriot association (zemliachestvo), while Georgians, Russians, and Armenians had only infrequent contact with people from the other nationalities. Rank-and-file workers were usually migrants from Russia, sometimes retired soldiers who had served in the local garrisons, while the skilled craftsmen (mastera) were often for-eigners.[7] Russian socialists encouraged Georgian workers to set up their own study groups, and in 1894 the first circle made up of Georgian rail-road workers gathered for self-improvement and propaganda of their new ideas among their fellow workers.[8] Circles of Georgian workers began to proliferate only in the last years of the century, when fifteen to twenty such groups existed. Few Georgian workers knew Russian, and many felt closer to Armenian workers, the sons of another local people, than to their Russian fellow workers.[9] It was among these fledgling gath-erings of a few Georgian artisans or Russian railroad workers that Soso Jughashvili first tried his skills as a propagandist.

A politically active Russian worker, Sergei Alliluev, who two decades later would become Stalin's father-in-law, remembered that "until 1896 the work in the circles was sluggish. From 1896 the work livened up and expanded."[10] From their Georgian comrades the Russians in the circles heard about mesame dasi, the cluster of intellectuals around Zhordania, and that Marxist articles were appearing in kvali, but they knew nothing more about the group.[11] Even the Georgian workers had only infrequent contact with the Marxist intellectuals who were intent on preserving their legal bastion around *kvali*. Political activist Silibistro (Silva) Todria remembered later that he and his comrades met "with workers at semi-legal Sunday and evening courses, reading them lectures about everything, but not about the revolutionary movement. Attending these evening and Sunday courses, it is true, the workers gained a broader view of the world. . . . The intellectuals who read the workers lectures on astronomy or biology . . . did not go near them during strikes and would not allow them near for fear of persecution by the police and gendarmes. Only monetary aid was sometimes given in a roundabout way."[12]

Though they sometimes worked together, workers and the sympathetic intellectuals of *mesame dasi* were allied ideologically but not organizationally in the late 1890s. They maintained separate institutions—the workers' circles and the *kvali* board—despite the fact that many of those who qualified as *intelligenty* were by origin not much different from workers.[13] Younger activists from poor families, like Soso, who had received some secondary education but had not entered any of the free professions, occasionally crossed the social barrier between the intellectuals of *mesame dasi* and the workers. What identified students like Soso Jughashvili or Lado Ketskhoveli was education, which marked them as more privileged and advantaged than workers at the bench.

In the Russian Empire a self-conscious and distinct social and intellectual group, known as the *intelligentsiia*, found itself precariously perched between the privileged groups that ruled Russia—the regime itself, the nobility, and the state bureaucracy—and those they wished to serve—ordinary working people, peasants and urban workers. Although he was the son of an ordinary worker, Soso Jughashvili, by virtue of his education and his self-identification, considered himself an *intelligent*, and he would soon be recognized as such by the police. Russian and Georgian Marxists, who proudly adopted the name Social Democrats, made up the radical wing of the politically committed oppositional intelligentsia, along with the neo-Populist Socialist Revolutionaries and a few anarchists.[14] These radical *intelligenty* had their own particular identity and a fierce loyalty to particular values, conventions, and even ways of dressing. They made up a subculture of their own and modeled their behavior on a set of literary sources.

The mid-nineteenth-century novel *What Is to Be Done?*, by the journalist and philosopher Nikolai Chernyshevskii, provided a model of authenticity emulated by generations of young radicals. The hero of the novel, Rakhmetov, inspired idealistic young people to eschew love and luxury and adopt an ascetic style of life. Chernyshevskii wrote the novel in prison after his arrest in 1862, as he began an eighteen-year ordeal of imprisonment and exile. Like his heroes and heroines, Chernyshevskii empathized with the poor and oppressed in Russia and imagined the radical intelligentsia as the elite force that could move Russia toward the indispensable revolution. Absorbed by abstract philosophical concepts and systems of beliefs borrowed from the West, the *intelligenty* felt both alienated from the Russian world around them and a deep sense of "service" or "debt" to the people.[15] They believed confidently that they were the "conscious" element bringing enlightenment and liberation to the politically "unconscious" masses. At times, an elitist notion of teaching and leadership prevailed among some intellectuals; at others, the desire to learn from the people or fuse with them dominated. Reason and passion compelled them to act in the name of the people, while, at the same time, they sensed their separation from the very people in whose interest they thought they acted. Both intellectually and emotionally they felt themselves servants of the people and, in some sense, of their homeland with which they with difficulty allied themselves.

As an aspiring member of the radical intelligentsia, Soso Jughashvili adopted the views of its Marxist fringe as well as the peripatetic lifestyle of the rootless radical. From the time he left the seminary until some years after the revolution of 1917, he would have no permanent home. Abandoning school and the priesthood, he lived outside the law. His anchor was the new faith he had found, one that explained his personal position in the world, the social setting in which he found himself, and provided a path to a kind of salvation. By the first years of the new century the seminarian turned self-styled professional revolutionary presented himself as a particular hybrid intellectual, one with proletarian origins and the manners and style of a bohemian.

One worker activist, Giorgi Eradze, worked in the same organization as Jughashvili and remembered how despite his humble origins he fashioned himself as an *intelligent*. "The son of a cobbler, officially registered as a peasant, Koba had become an *intelligent* in the Tiflis Seminary, transforming from religious seminarian to secular activist." Eradze noted the profound ambivalence that Koba felt about intellectuals. "In the Russian intelligentsia tradition, which the Georgian intellectuals had absorbed, the *intelligent* was to serve the people, energize society, and oppose the overweening Russian state." Marxism presented the path to that service, a link to the workers. For Koba, however, his new identity as *intelligent* was combined with a deep suspicion of intellectuals who were not fully, actively engaged in the workers' movement or who wavered in their commitment. Even an unequivocal intellectual, Koba's future mentor Lenin, expressed such ambivalence about intellectuals. An intellectual both in the Western sense of a person seriously engaged in the life of the mind and in the Russian understanding of an *intelligent*, someone concerned with the fate of the people and searching for the means to "save" Russia, Lenin, like Koba, constantly expressed disdain for purely intellectual activity and for the hesitation and wavering of intellectuals. "[I]t is precisely its individualism and incapacity for discipline and organization that in general distinguishes the intelligentsia as a separate stratum of modern capitalist society. . . . This, incidentally, is a feature that unfavorably distinguishes this social stratum from the proletariat; it is one of the reasons for the flabbiness and instability of the intellectual, from which the proletariat is so often made to suffer."[16]

Soso Jughashvili the budding *intelligent* shared the view that intellectuals were too individualist, verbose, indecisive, and too concerned with the nuances of theory that cut them off from life. For Soso many of the older generation of Georgian Social Democrats, the esteemed leaders of *mesame dasi*, were excessively refined, unwilling to dirty their hands among the workers.[17] Workers, on the other hand, were the indispensable force to change the social order. Their necessary allies would be the Social Democratic *intelligenty*, who would explain how important the political struggle was. While he admired workers, being a worker was not enough for Soso—his father, after all, had been a worker. What was most admirable was the worker who sought knowledge and self-improvement, and who began to understand how freedom might be achieved. He himself had begun his life odyssey in poverty, without the social and family supports that protected and promoted many of his contemporaries. From his teenage poetry through his early political writings, as well as his adherence to the views of Marx and Lenin, a person emerged who combined the emancipatory ambitions of a Russian *intelligent* with a belief that he also possessed the most important qualities of a real proletarian. Soso idealized the workers and "went out of his way to show his appreciation of what he saw as the proletarian virtues of courage and steadfastness."[18]

A few so-called practical workers (*praktiki*) from the intelligentsia who wanted closer ties with their labor constituency attended meetings of workers. Sometimes a visiting *intelligent* (as often as not a student) would be questioned by workers about economics, but besides a rare inquiry about a mysterious word like "constitution" most workers showed little interest in the intellectuals' preoccupation with revolutionary politics.[19] Students taught Georgian workers arithmetic, geography, history, and political economy, as well as the Russian language, and the exposure to new ideas and a wider world changed minds. As they learned about the theories of Darwin, some workers abandoned their inherited religious beliefs. Proud of their new knowledge, men like the railroad depot worker Giorgi Chkheidze rejected the suggestion by the intellectual Jibladze that they had learned enough and needed only to know their interests and distinguish their enemies from friends.[20] Circle workers objected when the intellectuals sought to send some of the students expelled from schools abroad to learn about Marxism. The workers apparently were content to have their own more advanced workers, like Mikha Bochoridze or Zakaria Chodrishvili, read to them on Marxism and revolutionary history.[21]

Marxist concepts passed from visiting *intelligenty* to the "leading workers," who in turn influenced other workers' attitudes. The process was tedious and dangerous, but the effects of these discrete contacts with small propaganda circles permanently affected some workers' lives. Alliluev remembered his own conversion to revolution as a gradual process. Not yet politically minded when he met Fedor Maiorov, a fellow worker in the Tiflis railroad workshops, Alliluev was impressed by a man who followed the news of West European labor. Maiorov introduced Alliluev to Fedor Afanasev, a twenty-four-year-old firebrand and "the soul of the circles." "Here, in Afanasev's room," he remembered, "for the first time doubts crept into my head about the rightness of the order existing on the earth. . . . The change in my thinking, the break with old habits and conceptions occurred, understandably, not all at once. Gradually, day by day, under the influence of books and conversations with comrades, under the direct impression of the harsh school of my own life thoughts began to appear about the need for a struggle against the existing order. From a lone rebel, unable to subordinate his actions to a definite idea, I grew into a conscious participant in the general struggle of the working class."[22] Alliluev soon was attending Afanasev's circle and reading literature "of an agitational character," like Raffaello Giovagnoli's *Spartacus*, Ethel Voynich's *The Gadfly*, and Edward Bellamy's *Looking Backward*.[23] His experience of "awakening" to new views, of enlightenment and consciousness, was repeated by dozens, even hundreds, of other workers until tales of eyes opening and seeing clearly became an integral part of the writings of Russian and Georgian workers.[24]

A Georgian worker, Giorgi Chkheidze, remembered that he and his friends had initially been Georgian nationalists and believed that the nationalist poet and publicist Ilia Chavchavadze should be king of Georgia. "At that time I considered all Russians to be my enemies." One evening the carpenter Vaso Tsabadze spoke to their circle, astonishing them with the notion that workers of all nationalities had the same interests and must join together against their common enemy, the rich. What had originally been formed as a patriotic reading group almost immediately took on a Social Democratic character.[25] Among circle workers throughout Tiflis, Marxism rapidly became the standard explanation of the workers' situation and the future of Georgia's development.[26]

Soso and his friends had already made contact with politically active workers while seminarians. "One evening," Iremashvili recalled, "Koba and I went secretly from the seminary to *mtatsminda*, to a small house on a cliff that belonged to a railroad worker. Like-minded seminarians followed after us. There the Social Democratic organization of the railroad workers met with us," and together students and workers listened to a long report from a political exile who had escaped from Siberia on the inhuman treatment of political prisoners by the tsarist police.[27]

The socialist seminarians had embarked on activity that was exceedingly dangerous. The police were on the trail of the circles and knew of illegal publications by workers. An educational society, called the "New Reader," was publishing and propagating socialist material among Georgians. Workers were willing to pay three rubles annual dues and buy translations of key texts like Kudriatsev's "How People Lived Earlier" and Sviderskii's "Labor and Capital." A Batumi worker, G. Sogorashvili, had rendered the *Communist Manifesto* into Georgian in 1897, and excerpts were published in *kvali*.[28] The police soon began to investigate those who had books printed by "New Reader," arrested the leading Social Democrats—Fedor Afanasev, Ivan Luzin, and Georgii Francheski—and closed down the publishing operation. The police dragnet pulled in the young writer Aleksei Maksimovich Peshkov (Maxim Gorky), a friend of Afanasev, who had been active in Tiflis in 1891–1892, but the outcry from writers like Leo Tolstoy, Anton Chekhov, and Vladimir Korolenko soon led to his release.

The arrests in 1897–1898 and the police attention focused on the revolutionaries brought one phase of the local movement to a close and opened another. The crackdown had two immediate effects. The importance of the Russian workers' circles receded, and the Georgians, now assisted by a reactivated *mesame dasi*, began to dominate labor activity. Because of the danger of exposure, intellectuals ceded much influence to workers themselves. In sharp contrast to the movement in central Russia, workers almost exclusively ran the secret circles of the embryonic labor movement in Georgia.

Soviet sources, and Stalin himself, dated Jughashvili's work as a propagandist in workers' circles from January 1898—that is, when he was still more than a year from leaving the seminary. The railroad worker Dato Lortkipanidze remembered three decades later that Jibladze, one of the oldest and most respected Marxists, introduced a soft-spoken, thin young man to a conspiratorial meeting of their *aktiv* (a group of politically aware workers) that year and told them that this worthy young man, full of energy, would be working with them.[29] The worker Giorgi Ninua remembered that Jibladze brought Soso to Vano Sturua's apartment at no. 194 Elizaveta Street, where a group of railroad workers lived in two small rooms on the first floor.[30] Although he probably visited workers' circles at that time, and perhaps occasionally tested his skills as a propagandist, it is unlikely that Jughashvili worked in the circles on a regular basis until later that year, just before leaving the seminary. The future Menshevik Davit Sagirashvili remembered, half a century later, that as a boy of eleven he met the teenage Soso Jughashvili at the home of activist workers Zakaria and Mikha Chodrishvili in 1898. "He made a very vivid impression on me. . . . When I first met him, Soso was dressed very poorly according to the nihilistic style of clothes which was very much in fashion then, especially among the radical wing of the socialist revolutionaries. It was unpleasant to see the traces of pockmarks which were clearly visible on his thin and oblong face. At first sight, his eyes appeared to be without expression, but on closer look one could detect in them a barely visible flicker of animation. His eyes betrayed neither good nor evil." The boy noted that Soso "spoke in exceptionally pure Georgian. His diction was clear, and his conversation betrayed a lively sense of humor. Anyone debating with him could also perceive immediately that Soso possessed an abominably strong will power." Before leaving the meeting, he patted young Saghirashvili on the shoulder and said that he hoped that he "would choose the road of the common struggle for a brighter future. . . . [T]o my inexperienced eyes he was a very unusual and mysterious man."[31]

About this time, 1894–1898, when seminarian Soso Jughashvili was turning to Marxism, Georgian socialism gained a second wind. Caught between police repression and growing worker activism, the socialists intensely discussed the future direction of their beleaguered movement. Two issues emerged as paramount: the role of legal versus illegal work; and the vexing question of nationalities. The tsarist regime forbade the formation of unions or participation in strikes and permitted only the narrowest opening for educating workers. The practical workers who directly engaged workers in the circles criticized those socialists who spent their time on *kvali* and proposed that they engage in purely illegal work. In the fall of 1897 Zhordania returned to Georgia after more than four years traveling and studying in Europe. He met with the leading Georgian Marxists in Georgia in his home village, Lanchkhuti, immediately resuming his place as the recognized leader of *mesame dasi*. Zhordania reported on the European labor movement, and while there was general agreement with his views, dissension cropped up over the appropriate form of work, legal or underground. A larger meeting was called for November in Tiflis, where Zhordania found himself in the minority. The majority opposed legal work, which, they felt, could be left to the liberals. Only after much discussion was Jibladze, with his impeccable credentials as an activist, able to convince most of the others that legal means, especially publishing in *kvali*, would benefit the movement.[32] Makharadze, Tsabadze, Kaladze, and Tskhakaia remained opposed, but Zhordania was authorized to open negotiations with Giorgi Tsereteli about using *kvali* as an outlet for Social Democratic views.

The other vital issue that vexed the Georgian Marxists was what became known as the "national question" (*natsional'nyi vopros*): how to deal with ethnic and cultural tensions and how should a future Russian state be structured. Zhordania was more prepared to accommodate national concerns than most of his comrades. Opposing their acknowledged leader, the majority in Lanchkhuti held that the Social Democratic tactic should be to widen the gap between workers and the ruling classes. Concessions to national sentiments build bridges between the top and bottom of society and thereby weaken the workers' movement. The delegates from the Black Sea port of Batumi, Nikoloz Chkheidze, B. Melia, and Ivan Luzin, as well as all of the Russian participants in the meeting, strongly defended the view that the business of socialists involves social, not nationality, concerns.[33] Both of these divisive issues—legal versus illegal work and the degree of emphasis placed on nationality rather than class—would repeatedly involve Soso Jughashvili as he advanced in the movement. They would continue to be discussed for the next twenty years and never be completely resolved.

Zhordania stayed away from direct participation in the illegal labor movement but was kept informed of its activities by Jibladze, who was the effective head of the organization.[34] In January he became editor of *kvali*, which he soon transformed into the legal organ of the Social Democrats. The government censors, who feared ethnic separatism much more than the esoteric economic theories of Karl Marx, were far less vigilant about Zhordania's Marxist analysis than about the nationalist poetry in Chavchavadze's *iveria*. As *kvali* attacked the Georgian nationalists and the more vicious Russian chauvinists around the newspaper *Kavkaz*, its influence among students and workers grew rapidly. The Social Democrats turned their attention toward the workers' circles, initiating new circles in the industrial districts of Tiflis. Marxist literature arrived regularly from Saint Petersburg and from the Jewish Bund, and local activists were able to carry out more systematic propaganda instead of the informal and infrequent contacts between intellectuals and workers.[35]

As Soso finished his last year in the seminary, local workers turned more boldly to open political protest. In April 1898 several activist workers organized the first celebration of May Day in the Caucasus. Thirty-five workers, almost all of them Georgian, gathered outside the city, in Nadzaladevi, and listened to speeches on the significance of the holiday.[36] The socialists considered this dangerous and courageous display of solidarity with the European labor movement a sign of maturity on the part of the workers. Even more dramatic was the display of militancy by railroad workers at year's end. When the railroad authorities ordered wage cuts and the curtailment of free tickets for workers, several thousand railroad workers—repair shop workers, engineers, and conductors—went on strike with the active support of the local Social Democrats. In an attempt to divide the workers ethnically, representatives of management asked a workers' delegation if the Armenians had incited the strike. A Russian delegate answered that all workers, Russian, Georgian, and Armenian, were equally disturbed by conditions. Thereupon the entire delegation was arrested.[37] After three days the old wage levels and privileges were restored by order of the minister of communications, but not before thirty-six leaders were detained and exiled from Tiflis. This strike, the first major protest in which the Social Democrats worked closely with workers, provided a new confidence to workers. The number of secret circles increased, and several local Marxists began to reconsider their activity among workers. A small group of young militants remained dissatisfied by what they considered a moderate and "opportunistic" leadership.

Jughashvili almost certainly had no connection to the 1898 strike. But for an impatient activist like Soso being part of the workers' movement had become irresistible, and the strike may have been the catalyst for his request to be assigned to a workers' circle. A worker, Giorgi Ninua, who was a member of Soso's propaganda circle, did not mention Jughashvili's participation in the strike when he later wrote a short memoir, only that after the strike Soso discussed the results and organizational inadequacies with the workers.[38] Still a seminarian in 1898, Jughashvili probably began his propaganda activities as an instructor in a workers' "Sunday school," since Sunday was the one free day that the seminarians had. Here he taught six workers about capitalism, the labor movement, and the need for political struggle.[39] The first workers' circle to which he was assigned was a Russian rather than a Georgian one, and he led it from 1898 to 1901.

Soso was popular neither with the intellectuals in the movement nor with the workers, who preferred Lado Ketskhoveli. They adored Lado, since he smoked and drank with them in the *dukani* (café or bar) while Soso did not.[40] Soso's lectures were markedly different in theme from those of older adherents of *mesame dasi*, who spoke about astronomy, geography, or literature. Instead of the "propaganda" of the previous period, when education of the workers in a broad sense was the central purpose of the circles, Jughashvili and a few other activists stressed what was becoming known as "agitation"—a curriculum directed at immediate issues of workers' discontent. Here, as earlier in the seminary when he shifted the curriculum of Devdariani's circle in a more practical, less theoretical direction, Soso emphasized mundane, everyday needs. Ever the pragmatist, he displayed exceptional self-confidence to the point of taking on the revered leaders of *mesame dasi*. One of the workers from those days, Arakela Okuashvili, remembered an incident at a party just after he had been released from prison. As Okuashvili told his friends about prison life and how prisoners had communicated with one another through the prison alphabet, knocking out letters on the wall, Soso "whispered to me (he sat right next to me), why bother to tell them this, they will soon learn this themselves in prison." He then pulled a Georgian brochure out of his pocket and rudely started to read it. Okuashvili was annoyed. "We were drinking wine, having fun, and he at that moment began to read."[41]

A more positive (but suspicious) account of Soso's circle activity comes from Alliluev, who remembered meeting him for the first time early in 1899. Alliluev's account, published first in 1937, contradicts his earlier memoir where he more credibly claimed to have met Stalin for the first time in 1904.[42] In the 1937 memoir he conveys the preferred Stalinist image of the benevolent leader and the grateful led, but it also reinforces the view that Jughashvili was distancing himself from the leaders of *mesame dasi*. Soso was teaching in a railroad workers' circle that included Giorgi Telia, Prokopi Dolidze, and Giorgi Lelashvili. "All were very satisfied with their young propagandist who, carrying on conversations in a popular and understandable language about the importance of organizing workers' circles and the strike struggle, patiently explained all difficult questions." But at one point during the general discussion Soso "spoke very unflatteringly about Noe Zhordania, severely criticizing his political convictions." His young listeners were upset. "No one at that time had yet allowed himself to express aloud such sharply negative opinions about the leaders of the Social Democracy of Georgia." Lelashvili reported what Soso had said to the organizer of the circle, who in turn informed the person who had recommended the young propagandist. Still, in time the circle members got used to Soso's sharp remarks "against this or that leader of the local Georgian Social Democratic organization.[43]

Although it is doubtful that Alliluev met Soso as early as he claimed in 1937, the story of the young agitator's criticism of Zhordania is confirmed in a memoir less flattering of Soso—that of Zhordania, who recalled a visit by a very angry Jibladze sometime in 1899. As the organizer of workers' circles Jibladze had assigned a young intelligent to a workers' circle, only to discover that the propagandist had taken it upon himself to criticize the Tiflis organization and had convinced the workers to call for the dissolution of the leading committee. Though he could not recall the man's full name, Jibladze remembered that he was called "Soso." Zhordania recognized him as Jughashvili. Soon after, the committee took the circle away from Soso and transferred him to the railroad district.[44]

There is no easy explanation for what made Soso Jughashvili break with the leaders of *mesame dasi* and begin the leftward drift that eventually brought him to Bolshevism. Perhaps it was his deep distrust of all authority, as posited by Iremashvili, or an inability to accept the decisions of an older generation. It may have been Soso's disappointment with his reception by the editor of *kvali*, evident from Zhordania's brief memoir. He had little personal experience with displaying subordination or deference to a father figure, which was both unusual and upsetting to the leaders of *mesame dasi*. Yet within his generation he was not exceptional in his rebellion against paternalism, and his steady disaffection may have been less a matter of some deep-seated psychological need than a conscious political choice. Like a number of younger (and several older) revolutionaries, most immediately his mentor, Lado Ketskhoveli, Soso was anxious for more radical action.

The official Stalinist version, enshrined in Lavrentii Beria's semifictional history of Transcaucasian Social Democracy that became holy writ for Soviet readers in the 1930s and 1940s, claims that Jughashvili, Ketskhoveli, and Aleksandre Tsulukidze "joined" *mesame dasi* in 1898 and formed the "core of the revolutionary Marxist minority."[45] This deceptively simple description presents far too schematic a picture of the fluid Georgian political scene of the last years of the nineteenth century. It was not necessary to "join" *mesame dasi*, for it was more a generation of Marxist thinkers than an organized party. Rather than having an institutional structure or fixed program, *mesame dasi* was simply made up of those who shared the general analysis developed by Zhordania and those working with him on *kvali*. As in other Social Democratic groups at the turn of the century, allegiance to Marxism and some form of activity either in workers' circles or the press was sufficient to guarantee admittance to whatever meetings were held. In a stricter sense, however, the term *mesame dasi* was used to refer specifically to the initial group of Marxist intellectuals around Zhordania, and in this usage as well it could not be "joined." Newcomers like Ketskhoveli and Jughashvili, who were primarily circle propagandists or labor organizers rather than journalists, were a distinct subgroup within the broader Social Democratic movement. Their ties were with the workers' circles rather than the legal newspaper. Often more radical and plebian (with the notable exception of Prince Aleksandre Tsulukidze) than the west Georgian petty nobility that made up the inner core, the younger men were in the movement but not of it the same way that Jibladze, Severian Jugheli, or Zhordania were.[46] The distance that the younger men felt between themselves and their elders was all the greater because of the genuine disagreements with the strategy of the *mesame dasi* leadership that did not play to their strengths. The labor movement was growing restless and ever bolder, yet its intellectual leaders, so it seemed to the radicals, kept it restrained within a cautious politics of legalism or, at best, confined to the secret educational circles. The workers were proving more active and radical than their ostensible leaders.

The personal distance from the Zhordania core was complemented in Jughashvili's case by his closeness to the most important radical in the movement, Lado Ketskhoveli. The early career of Ketskhoveli closely paralleled that of Jughashvili, and Soso's unquestionable admiration and affection for Ketskhoveli were crucial in his ideological and political evolution.[47] The son of a village priest, Vladimir (Lado) Ketskhoveli was almost three years older than Soso Jughashvili. When he was eighteen he wrote a series of letters that were published in the newspaper *iveria* about life in his village, Tkviavi. Indignant at the lack of opportunity for the poor, he railed against the local nobles who thwarted the plans of a priest to open a religious school in the village.[48] His anger at the evident social injustices in rural Georgia was shaped first by his Populist older brother, Niko, and later by Soprom Mgaloblishvili, a teacher at the Gori church school. For three years Lado and Soso were students together in Gori. Lado preceded his younger friend to the Tiflis Seminary, where he led a literary circle and issued his own handwritten journal, *gantiadi* (Dawn). The seminarians were in touch with radical former students, like Mikha Tskhakaia, and with his help the students organized a protest against the strict regime in the seminary that ended in the expulsion of eighty-seven students, including Lado.

Tall and imposing with his full dark beard, Ketskhoveli entered the Kiev Seminary in 1894, only to be arrested two years later after a search of his room turned up a pamphlet by the Marxist writer Iulii Martov. Sent back to Georgia, he was living semi-legally in Tiflis by September 1897. Ketskhoveli was dismayed to find no "signs of 'movement'" among local workers, and in his disillusionment he contemplated moving to Russia proper. But the "'moles' of revolution," as a later Social Democratic pamphlet reported, had just begun to become active.[49] Working in a printing shop, learning the trade that he would later use for purposes of revolution, Ketskhoveli translated from Russian the influential pamphlet "Who Lives on What?" by the Polish Marxist Szymon Diksztajn. This little book, the first illegal Marxist booklet to be published in Georgian, explained in simple language and colloquial style the fundamentals of Marx's labor theory of value.[50]

Lado and Soso Jughashvili renewed their friendship during the years that Ketskhoveli worked at the print shop (1897–1899). In the summer of 1899 Lado "went underground" with plans to establish his own illegal printing press. He frequently met with his brother, Vano, Jughashvili, and others at the observatory, where discussions went on into the night. Here the younger activists forged the incipient opposition to the more moderate Social Democrats. Vano Ketskhoveli later wrote that during these early discussions Lado and Soso found they both admired Lenin. "One evening as they argued over Plekhanov's *Nashi raznoglasiia* [Our Differences], Lado and Soso compared Plekhanov unfavorably to Lenin. Agreeing with Lado that Lenin was to be praised both as a theorist and for his practical work, Soso added that 'Lenin stands closer to life than Plekhanov, and in the workers' movement Lenin plays a great role.'"[51] Here, again, memory must be challenged. This appears to be another effort to establish an early Leninist pedigree for a precocious Jughashvili. Differences and distinctions between Lenin and Plekhanov were not acute at that time, and Vladimir Ulianov did not use the pseudonym Lenin until 1901.

Lado tried to convince the editors of *kvali* of the need to move to more active tactics, strikes and protests, but at a special meeting called to discuss strategy, most of those present sided with the older men who had led the movement and argued that such open actions would lead to a crushing defeat. Their numbers were too small. Ketskhoveli walked out, slamming the door.[52] Undaunted, Lado found support for his point of view from Soso, Jibladze, Jugheli, and others.[53]

Soso impressed Lado, his brother remembered, but the two young radicals were soon separated. In the summer of 1899, during school vacation, Soso and his friend and future in-law Mikheil Monaselidze were visiting a schoolmate, V. T. Khakhanashvili, when Lado dropped in. "Soso and Lado began to speak about organizing an illegal printing press. The conversation was serious, and they went off into another room."[54] But at the end of 1899 Lado was involved in a strike of trolley workers and, betrayed to the police by one of the workers, he fled to Baku in mid-January.

According to historians of the Stalin era, the third principal member of the radical opposition to the *mesame dasi* leadership was Aleksandre (Sasha) Tsulukidze, later one of the original Georgian Bolsheviks. The scion of a west Georgian noble family, Tsulukidze's path to the revolutionary movement was far more intellectual than that of Jughashvili or Ketskhoveli. A sickly child, he read voraciously and wrote stories and poems. For a time he lived the idle life of a provincial gentry man, but in 1895 he joined a socialist circle in Kutaisi, Georgia's second largest city. Influenced by the Marxism of *mesame dasi*, Tsulukidze developed rapidly into a defender of Zhordania and a perceptive critic of the Populist and nationalist views of the opponents of *kvali*. His letters indicate that he was intoxicated by the power of Marx's analysis and the sheer intellectual joy of extending these perceptions into Georgian life. At the turn of the century, the very time when Stalinist historians would have him opposing the Zhordania leadership, Tsulukidze was writing a number of closely reasoned articles on literature and political economy in *kvali* that expressively developed the basic positions of Zhordania.[55]

Reading Tsulukidze's articles suggests that the incipient discontent of the militants in the Georgian Social Democratic movement should not be exaggerated. Before 1900 no divisions existed that approached the growing schism over political versus economic strategies among Social Democrats north of the Caucasus. The main thrust of the Georgian movement in the 1890s, both in the legal press and in the workers' circles, was directed toward the exposition of a Marxist analysis. While the Stalinist histories and memoirs written more than thirty years later argue for precocious militancy, there is no contemporary evidence that Jughashvili, Ketskhoveli, and Tsulukidze developed a systematic radical critique of the practice of the *mesame dasi* leaders, a kind of Bolshevism *avant la lettre*. Not until 1901 did embryonic tactical differences coalesce into a coherent alternative analysis and strategy.

Still, for younger Marxists like Jughashvili, the time had come for more action and less talk, more direct participation in the workers' movement and less journalism. Although the fundamental break in the Russian Social Democratic movement would not take place until 1903, the vexing questions that would animate Bolshevism and Menshevism— how to reach the workers, educate them to their central role in history, and facilitate through organization and inspiration the coming revolution—were already straining the ties that bound the diverse intellectuals and activists among Social Democrats. The full implications of these emergent tensions would be realized only as the labor movement in the first years of the new century grew beyond the bounds of its intellectual mentors. The new vitality of workers illuminated the inadequacies of the old strategies and forced revolutionary leaders to face the most divisive of reassessments. In that sense the ingredients that came together in Bolshevism already existed in an inchoate form within Social Democracy—even before Lenin outlined its fundamental principles in *Chto delat?* [*What Is to Be Done?*] (1902). Rather than Bolshevism being the creation of the particular personality with whom it would ever after be identified, in its initial form what evolved into Bolshevism was a response to severe problems that socialist intellectuals in a heavily policed state faced in their daily activity among workers.

At the very dawn of the new twentieth century Soso Jughashvili had become part of a daring group of revolutionaries. Joining the movement was more than just an intellectual or moral commitment or even an attachment to a vision of an alternative future. Linking his fate with the Social Democrats was also the rejection of his old life and the plans his mother had made for him, the replacement of religious Orthodoxy with "orthodox" Marxism and a new radical lifestyle. He even dressed like a socialist. "I often visited him in his shabby little room on Mikhailovskii Street," Iremashvili reports. "Koba wore all day a plain black Russian shirt with the red tie characteristic of all Social Democrats. In winter he wore an old brown coat over it. For headgear he had only a Russian cap. . . . He was always in his dirty shirt and unpolished shoes. All that reminded him of a 'bourgeois,' he hated deep in his soul. A white collar or a European suit was for him the uniform of the well-fed bourgeois."[56] Romantic idealism may still have excited the former seminarian, but resentment and hostility to those in power increasingly fueled his passion for the revolution.

6

THE OUTLAW

He had an amazing way of escaping from spies. I remember something he told me often: "I was walking by the [Viceroy's] palace, in front of the First Girls' Gymnasium at night and noticed a well-known spy in the shadows of the trees (a Georgian, he always dressed in a *chokha* and carried a walking stick). I did not avoid him but passed in front of him. He was frightened and thought that I was going to beat him and avoided me. I crossed the street, turned toward the Kalaubani Church, turned right, and came up behind him. I saw that he was looking for me. I continued along my way and did just what I had planned. That fool," Soso joked, "wasted my time, and I was late for my appointment." Soso was always proud and amused when he deceived the spies. "Damn, these spies seem to be our burden as well. Are we supposed to teach them how to behave?" Soso would say.

—GIORGI ELISABEDASHVILI, "MEMOIRS" (1948)

Although insensitive to the feelings of others, Koba is extremely easily hurt, exceedingly sensitive about his own feelings, and although it may seem startling, he is moody to the point of capriciousness. His reactions are primitive. Whenever he feels himself ignored or neglected, he is inclined to turn his back upon developments as well as upon people, creep into a corner, and moodily pull on his pipe and dream of revenge.

—LEV TROTSKY, *STALIN: AN APPRAISAL OF THE MAN AND HIS INFLUENCE* (1941)

Russian Marxism at the turn of the twentieth century was not a movement for the impatient. The coming revolution in Russia, according to Plekhanov, was to be a "bourgeois revolution," like that in France in

1789, to establish a liberal, capitalist society. Only much later, after significant economic and social progress, would the second, the "proletarian socialist" revolution, come about. Embedded in Plekhanov's vision were the very tensions that ultimately would divide Russian Social Democracy into two hostile parties and occupy much of Soso's intellectual energies: how would workers develop the revolutionary consciousness required to overthrow tsarism? What would the appropriate role of workers be in the bourgeois revolution? And what was the precise weight to be given leadership by intellectuals over self-direction by workers? Since a proper "bourgeoisie"—that is, the propertied middle class—hardly existed in Russia, and given its amorphous, still embryonic formation, the "bourgeois" or "liberal democratic" revolution would anomalously have to be made by workers. Plekhanov was confident that the objective laws of history would create a conscious and revolutionary working class and lead to the ultimate defeat, first, of autocracy and then, in a second, distant, socialist revolution, of the bourgeoisie.

In the intense debates with the Populists, Russia's Marxists rejected what they considered to be the "voluntarism" and subjectivism" of the Populists, played down the role of individual actors in history, and instead relied on the sweep of historical forces. They were confident that the development of new capitalist social relations would in time foster a radical, even revolutionary, awareness among industrial workers. Social Democrats were to act like "revolutionary bacilli" and further the growth of the workers' consciousness. Workers themselves, by virtue of their class position, would as rational beings come to understand that their interests lay in socialism and revolution. "Thus," one historian puts it, "having made consciousness the defining marker of working-class identity, Plekhanov created a perfect rational hero for his rational history."[1] Together the Social Democrats and their allies would shorten the phase of capitalism and facilitate the transition to socialism. Still, because of the unreliable native middle class, Russian workers were the lever with which tsarism would be overturned. In an often-quoted phrase Plekhanov told the founding congress of the Second International in 1889, "The revolution in Russia will triumph as a working class movement or not at all."[2] This was Plekhanov's paradox of the Russian revolution: it was the proletariat that would have to carry out the "bourgeois" revolution against the feudal order.

The Plekhanovian synthesis was accepted by most of Russia's Marxists of the 1890s as the authentic vision of Marx. At one extreme, in the hands of Petr Struve and the reformist "Legal Marxists," it was further reduced to a near-fatalistic economic analysis. The role of the revolutionaries was constrained to educating the workers in the true social science. As an "elite, recruited from the most advanced members of the intelligentsia and the working class, [their job] was apparently to sit back at least for the present and preside over the unfolding of the omniscient and omnipotent process of history."[3] For Plekhanov, however, the workers' own experience would bring them toward socialism, and the Marxists, who understood the flow of history, could accelerate their coming to consciousness and—quoting Marx—shorten and lessen the birth pangs of the turn to revolution.[4]

The Marxist strategy of circle propaganda appeared to many activists to be appropriate for the long period of revolutionary gestation. Propaganda, it was hoped, would do more than provide a small number of workers with a veneer of culture. Not only would the teachings of the Social Democrats enrich the lives of the workers, but also propaganda would bring them to understand fully their position under capitalism. Soso Jughashvili, however, found the slow motion of the propaganda strategy too constraining. While many *intelligenty* were content with fostering education and culture, others were frustrated by the lack of activity of workers satisfied with their new gentility. Two young Jewish activists in western Russia proposed a more effective strategy in an influential pamphlet, *Ob agitatsii* [On Agitation] (1894). Iulii Martov and Arkadii Kremer called on their comrades to "agitate" workers around mundane issues of wages, hours, and working conditions. By engaging in an active struggle for their own economic improvement, workers would gradually become more conscious of capitalist exploitation, perhaps even eventually joining the Social Democrats. By 1898 the agitational strategy had made powerful inroads among Social Democrats throughout the empire and appeared confirmed by the strike movement of the last years of the century. This more practical approach soon won over the leading Social Democratic circles in Russia's capital, Saint Petersburg, and a new organization was formed in the city—the Union of Struggle for the Emancipation of Labor (*Soiuz bor'by za osvobozhdenie truda*). Among its members was the young lawyer from the Volga region, Vladimir Ulianov.

As an activist in an illegal social movement, Soso was certainly aware of the rising star of Russian Social Democracy who had been signing his articles "Vl. Il'in" and now adopted the pseudonym "Lenin." Iremashvili remembered that Soso especially liked Lenin's writings.[5] Not yet thirty, the prematurely bald Lenin quickly gained the respect of his comrades in Russia, who called him "Old Man." Like many of his fellow Social Democrats, Lenin was impressed by the stunning emergence of a workers' movement and its success in 1897 of forcing the tsarist government to grant a modest law limiting working hours. The young Marxist from the Volga had made his reputation with a mammoth study, *The Development of Capitalism in Russia*, published in 1899, and a series of reviews and articles on the economic debates dividing Marxists and Populists.

As an enthusiastic reader of Marxist literature, Lenin was also taken by the example of the massive German Social Democratic movement and its Erfurt Program, which proclaimed that Social Democracy's task was to merge the active labor movement with the socialist ideas developed by Marx and Engels.[6] This merger could not be achieved, however, either by strictly political action or by strictly economic activity. In Russia an exclusively political tactic was associated with the Populist terrorists, while some in the labor movement had occasionally adopted an exclusively economic approach aimed at improving workers' material situation. Lenin was dismayed when enthusiastic supporters of the principle of agitation gravitated toward concentration on the economic struggle and subordinated politics to the fight for higher wages, shorter hours, and safer working conditions. Those Social Democrats who insisted on the importance of political struggle labeled their opponents who emphasized the workers' interest in economic improvement

ekonomisty (economists) and considered them insufficiently revolutionary. Lenin was one of the key polemicists against overemphasis on the
economic struggle.

Jughashvili had met and worked in Tiflis with Viktor Kurnatovskii
(1868–1912), who had known Lenin in exile and had signed his "Protest"
written against the "Credo" of the *ekonomisty* in August 1899. Issued as
a pamphlet, Lenin's answer set out in straightforward prose his understanding of what constituted the essence of Social Democratic strategy.
Their role was to lead the political struggle for democracy. "The experience of history," he wrote, "bears incontrovertible further witness to the
fact that the absence of political liberty or the restriction of the political
rights of the proletariat always make it necessary to put the political
struggle first."[7] As fighters for the liberation of the working class, for
democracy as well as socialism, Lenin, like most Social Democrats, believed that they had to use all means to achieve that liberation—
economic agitation, political education, and revolutionary organization.
The political struggle was aimed at overthrowing autocracy, establishing
democracy, and securing political freedoms, essential first steps to
spreading Social Democratic views. Lenin particularly emphasized that
it was imperative to build a party, not only to ensure leadership and
guidance for the workers, but also to realize the claim of Social Democracy to be the leading force in the oppositional movement.

Lenin's energy and active engagement with workers attracted Soso.
As a man with literary skills in Georgian, he turned his talents to the
daily struggle of the workers. Some sources credit Jughashvili with au-
thoring a leaflet of December 18, 1900, which demanded freedom of
expression and assembly, as well as the right to form unions and strike.[8]
A foot soldier in an inchoate and incoherent movement, Soso searched
for direction.

Precisely at the time when Social Democrats were discussing the
need for a unified national party, they found their ranks dividing between the *ekonomisty*, who favored the workers' own economic struggles
as a means toward politicization of labor, and the *politiki* (Politicals),
who called for a broader political struggle that would involve other
alienated social groups besides workers. Although few Social Democrats

ever lost sight of the ultimate need for a political struggle against the autocracy, those who concentrated on the economic struggle grew increasingly suspicious of socialist intellectuals who led workers into dangerous political confrontations with the state. The *politiki*, on the other hand, criticized the *ekonomisty* for limiting their strategy to the working class, effectively neglecting the other social classes—the peasantry and the liberal bourgeoisie—without which a revolution could not succeed. An intense political competition pitted the Marxists against the revived Populism of the Socialist Revolutionary Party (Socialist Revolutionaries), their major competitors on the Left, as well as the liberalism that a few years later coalesced into the Constitutional Democratic Party (Kadets). But Marxists ought not, wrote Lenin, to surrender their position at the head of the anti-tsarist struggle to either the liberals or the neo-Populists. This was not a time to wait but to organize.

Far from the Caucasus, where individual workers' circles operated relatively separately, the more politically oriented Social Democrats decided to create a unified political organization for the whole of Russia. Despite the pervasive presence of the police, representatives from Kiev, Moscow, Ekaterinoslav, and other cities with Marxist organizations met in a congress in early 1898 in the western Russian town of Minsk (now the capital of Belorus). Tiflis socialists elected Vaso Tsabadze as their delegate, but the local police held him back. After the Minsk congress declared the existence of the Russian Social Democratic Workers' Party (*Rossiiskaia sotsialdemokraticheskaia rabochaia partiia*, or RSDRP) and set up a central committee, almost all of the delegates who attended the congress were arrested. No central Marxist organization survived the police sweep, though several Social Democratic organizations throughout the country, including Tiflis, adopted the manifesto and resolutions of the congress, which expressed the views of the *politiki*.[9] The fledgling party launched so inauspiciously was the organization to which Soso Jughashvili would dedicate his life and the vehicle through which Stalin would rise to power.

As the lines between the economic and political strategies became clearer, local committees were set up, which were linked in name to the newly formed but largely nonexistent party. At the beginning of 1899 a few Social Democrats declared themselves the Tiflis Committee of the RSDRP.[10] No one elected this self-proclaimed leadership, made up primarily of workers, but it soon was widely acknowledged as the leading center of the Social Democratic movement in the city and took charge of all activities—propaganda, agitation, strikes, the printing of leaflets, and even terrorism.[11] The Tiflis Social Democrats organized the second secret celebration of the May Day labor holiday in 1899 with a defiant manifesto written by Zhordania in Georgian.[12] About seventy-five workers and intellectuals—Armenians, Georgians, and Russians— gathered in Avchala outside the city. Railroad workers unfurled red banners with "Down with the Autocracy" and "The Eight-Hour Workday" written on them. Lado Ketskhoveli and three workers spoke.[13] As in years past, activist workers were at the forefront of the movement. Intellectuals like Zhordania, who himself did no illegal work in order to keep his legal status, were respected but kept apart from the movement. At the same time those who considered themselves Social Democrats were required to read kvali, and once Zhordania took over the editorship they read it regularly. By the end of the 1890s socialist workers were "fanatical" supporters of kvali.[14]

The celebration of May Day was a courageous and deliberate identification of Caucasian workers with their proletarian contemporaries in more developed countries. The inaugural congress of the socialist Second International in 1889 had designated May 1 the annual international holiday of labor, and Social Democrats worked hard to bring the symbols and rituals of the international movement to the provinces of the Russian Empire. By the time May Day was marked in 1900, more than five hundred people, almost all of them workers, participated in two meetings outside the city despite a heavy rain. Gevork Gharajian (Karajaev) gave a long speech, and the worker Arakela Okuashvili also spoke. Orators attacked a Russian worker who tried to convince the crowd that peaceful means were adequate for improving conditions. In his first "public appearance" Soso Jughashvili made a passionate statement that pleased the young socialists present.[15] But the dominant mood in the crowd was one of caution and fear. When a lone horseman was sighted in the distance, the workers lowered their red banners, muddying them, until one speaker shamed them into raising them again. Later conflict arose over a suggestion to march through the city, and it was resolved that the following year's celebration would be held in town.[16] That evening worker participants met with leading intellectuals—Makharadze, Jibladze, and others (Zhordania may have been among them)—in Giorgi Tsereteli's apartment. The intellectuals had opposed holding a May Day demonstration because of the evident danger, but Jibladze conceded that next year the intellectuals would also take part.[17] By the following day the whole city had heard of the workers' marches.

Political life throughout the empire was rapidly reviving at the turn of the century. On May Day 1900, thousands of workers in the southern Ukrainian city of Kharkov demonstrated openly in the streets, revealing a new militancy that encouraged leading Marxists to think about building a Social Democratic party in Russia. Students became politically active for the first time in decades. Neo-Populists now had their own revolutionary party, the Socialist Revolutionaries. Although disunited and lacking a single authoritative political center, the Social Democrats of the Russian Empire were extraordinarily confident about their historic mission. The dispute over strategy between the young activists (*molodye*) and the older Social Democrats (*starye*) intensified. More meetings were held, but the discussions were overtaken by the growing radicalism of workers.[18] Within months of the organization of the Tiflis Social Democratic Committee, the workers' movement in Georgia took on new dimensions, becoming a serious actor in Georgian society and visible to the police. The number of strikes increased rapidly. Whereas from 1870 to 1900 there had been nineteen strikes at twelve industrial enterprises in Tiflis, in 1900 alone there were seventeen at fifteen enterprises.[19] The strike wave began with the horse-trolley line workers. Almost all drivers and conductors participated, some four thousand workers, and though the demands were strictly economic, the police attacked the strikers and arrested one hundred fifty workers. The Social Democrats Lado Ketskhoveli and Razhden Kaladze, who were identified as instigators of the work stoppage, fled to Baku. Yet, three months later, for reasons that remain unclear, all the demands of the workers (shorter workday, higher pay, elimination of certain brutal work rules) were satisfied.[20] Strikes followed throughout the city—among printers, to-bacco workers, leather workers, and in textiles—and almost all of them ended in victories for the workers. Printers throughout the city were able to end overtime work and gain pay raises, shorter hours, and ad-ditional holidays.[21]

No strike, however, matched that of the workers in the main railroad workshops in August 1900. For ten years worker Social Democrats had been active in the railroad yards, and one of them, a Georgian, Zakro Chodrishvili, carefully and diligently prepared the ground for the strike. The Social Democratic workers played the key organizing and sustain-ing role in the strike. Intellectuals, like Jibladze, Tsulukidze, Alesha Japaridze, and Soso Jughashvili, were also involved, but they had to defer to the activist workers.[22] Soso commissioned workers in his study circle to prevent strikebreakers from entering the railroad yards.[23] When a series of demands—for pay raises, abolition of evening over-time and fines, polite address, improvement in hygienic conditions—were rejected by the authorities, and five workers arrested, five thousand men went on strike.[24] This was a strike not against a private firm but a government enterprise, and this time the police came down hard on strikers and their supporters. Tiflis was declared to be in a "state of siege." Soldiers surrounded the workers' districts, and the police ar-rested more than fifteen hundred workers. Many were fined or exiled to Batumi, Baku, or their home villages. A number of Social Democrats were rounded up, and their period of relative freedom of maneuver came to an end. "Until the strike of 1900," Giorgi Chkheidze remem-bered, "we enjoyed full freedom; it is true that meetings were held se-cretly, but no one paid us much attention. During this strike the gen-darmes for the first time approached the doors of the railroad workshops."[25] After two weeks the strikers returned to work; not a single demand had been granted. The workers felt discouraged and con-fused, and those Social Democrats still at liberty could do little to com-bat their mood.[26]

Strikes continued into 1901—at the tobacco plants and the printing houses, and later in the year among tram drivers and the masseurs and employees of the popular hot baths. Soso and his comrades remained active, but as arrests cut down their number, there were not enough Social Democrats in the city for the work at hand.[27] Several prominent Russian Social Democrats, exiled to the Caucasus, joined their ranks, among them Mikhail Kalinin, the future president of the Soviet Union. N. Sokolovskii remembered attending a meeting organized by Jughash-vili in the Tiflis Observatory, along with veteran propagandists Nikolai Domostroev and Viktor Kurnatovskii. The discussion centered on con-tacts with workers, but no resolution was reached. At a second meeting in the apartment of another exile, Ippolit Francheski, it was decided that since older revolutionaries were already under police surveillance, the younger ones were to make contact with workers. Ultimately nothing came of this strategy, however, because the police were too closely watching suspected activists.[28] Soso's first major foray into the strike movement had ended in failure.

Politicized workers like Alliluev and the Social Democratic intellec-tuals shared a secret society enclosed within the larger social world of Tiflis. They were close friends, something like family, secretly sheltering and protecting one another from the police. Anna Allilueva, Sergei's daughter, remembered how as a child she observed the tall, gaunt Kurna-tovskii in his unbuttoned jacket, the gigantic Francheski, and Vladimir Radzevich meeting and drinking with her father in a garden above the Kura. Not overheard by the children were the conversations about Marx, the movement, and Lenin, with whom Kurnatovskii was person-ally acquainted. To Anna the young revolutionary Kalinin, a frequent visitor to her home, was simply "Uncle Misha."[29] In February and March 1901, the police picked up Kurnatovskii, Francheski, Makha-radze, Jibladze, and others. Zhordania left town for his father's house in the town of Lanchkhuti but managed to avoid arrest only until July. The police completed their sweep with a raid on the editorial offices of *kvali* and the liberal newspaper *Novoe obozrenie* (New Review).

On March 21, the police searched the observatory, but Soso was ab-sent at the time. They woke up his suite mate, Berdzenishvili, and noted the Marxist books in his room. When they went through Jughashvili's adjoining room, however, they found nothing, for Soso always returned books as soon as he read them. His caution paid off. Returning home that evening, Soso noticed an unusual group of men at the tram stop and decided not to get off. He rode to the train station and then circled back to his room after the police had left. When Berdzenishvili told him about the "uninvited guests," Soso prudently went into hiding.[30] He moved into one of the conspiratorial apartments set up by the Social Democrats—at first at 18 Narashenskaia Street. A few days later the police reported that Jughashvili had been a member of a "group of people from the intelligentsia, local natives as well as Russians, who according to information from police agents formed a Social Democratic circle that aims through systematic propaganda to incite among the local workers discontent with their condition, to inspire them with revolutionary ideas, and thus to help prepare a general revolutionary movement among the working class."[31]

The police crackdown obliterated the existing Social Democratic infrastructure in Tiflis. Nevertheless, the activist workers managed to organize an open demonstration to mark May Day 1901 in the city for the first time. The socialist intellectuals, including Soso Jughashvili, stayed away from the demonstration. On April 22, three thousand workers milled around the Soldiers' Bazaar and the Alexander Garden waiting for the firing of the noon cannon. At that signal Okuashvili unfurled a red silk flag. Workers marched back and forth "armed" with black palm branches and shouting "Down with Autocracy." The police attacked the demonstrators with their whips, beating Okuashvili and arresting him. His comrade Leonti Mamaladze drew a revolver and wounded a Cossack, whereupon the mounted soldiers trampled Mamaladze unconscious. Forty-one were arrested. Yet the event was considered a triumph by the workers and was commended in the labor press throughout the empire. The new Social Democratic newspaper *Iskra* (Spark) reprinted the story from the Armenian nationalist *Droshak* (Banner): "From this day the open revolutionary movement begins in the Caucasus."[32] Whether it might be taken as a sign of success or failure, the number of political prisoners in the Metekhi fortress rose from 16 in 1897 to 77 in 1898, 102 in 1899, and 224 in 1900.[33]

Although he did not speak at the demonstration, as one of its organizers Soso Jughashvili had worked with the illegal printing presses in the city that printed the leaflets for the demonstrations. Sought by the police, he left Tiflis for Gori, hiding somewhere in the town, though not at his mother's. There he visited his boyhood friend Iremashvili, who was completing his studies in order to become a teacher at the Gori church school. Returning to Tiflis, he moved from one hiding place to another, sleeping in basements, on cots lent by comrades. By the end of the year he was under constant police surveillance. The demonstration had made a deep impression on him. More than ever he was convinced of the need for a life-and-death struggle to strengthen the movement and bring down the regime.[34] The younger agitators were confident that their more radical tactics had been vindicated. Workers were emboldened by the open expression of solidarity on May Day. To raise money for the party Kamo, encouraged by Soso, shook down several Armenian capitalists, the tobacco kings Bozarjiants and Safarov, promising them protection from strikes if they paid up. Some of the factory owners asked how much it would cost to organize a strike at a rival's firm. He "liked the irony . . . that the bourgeoisie itself paid for the preparation of its overthrow."[35]

By this time Soso was already an adherent, as were most of his comrades, of the Social Democratic newspaper *Iskra*, with its determinedly political orientation. Conceived by Lenin and his close comrades at the time Martov and Aleksandr Potresov, the newspaper was intended to bring together the dispersed Social Democratic circles as the first step to a new party organization. After completing a term of Siberian exile, Lenin went abroad in August 1900 and negotiated with the founders of Russian Social Democracy, Plekhanov, Pavel Akselrod, and Vera Zasulich, and with great difficulty worked out collaboration on the project. Lenin and Plekhanov both had strong, dominating personalities and found working together very trying. Somehow, four months after Lenin settled in Munich, the first issue of *Iskra* appeared. In its lead editorial Lenin lamented that Russian labor was still divorced from socialism, and that "such a divorce condemns the Russian revolutionary movement to impotence." But with a Social Democratic party, he wrote, socialist ideas and political consciousness could be effectively instilled in the proletariat; with such an organization the working class could fulfill its great historic mission—"to emancipate itself and the whole Russian people from its political and economic slavery."[36] Lenin and his comrades understood that a party was essential to coordinate diverse interests and views into a coherent, effective movement. At the turn of the twentieth century, it took extraordinary confidence in Marxism to believe that Russia's diverse and disorganized workers could coalesce into a potent revolutionary force.

From its first issue at the end of 1900 *Iskra* represented the triumph of the idea of conscious political intervention by radical intellectuals into the burgeoning workers' movement. The workers were on the move, it declared; what they required for success were proper leaders. Lenin and his comrades revived the Populists' ideal of the full-time revolutionary. "We must train people who will devote not just their free evenings but their whole lives to the revolution." As in Western Europe, so in Russia, Marxist activists were to put forth the socialist message, inspire, and guide the workers toward revolution. If in Europe the revolution was to be directed against capitalism and the bourgeoisie, in Russia it was first to bring down the autocracy and open the way to a "bourgeois" order with greater political freedom.

Iskra's editorials and articles were marked by a militant, polemical tone and harsh criticism of opposing points of view, particularly within labor and socialist circles. The influence of the bold new newspaper was almost immediately felt among Social Democrats inside Russia, as well as those abroad, the returned exiles, *praktiki* (the "practicals," those working in the committees and with the workers) and *teoretiki* (the "theorists," those who wrote pamphlets and in the newspapers) alike. Many workers saw in *Iskra's* "political line" the authentic and militant voice of radical Social Democracy.[37] The networks of Marxists were fragile, and from their Munich base Lenin and his wife, Nadezhda Krupskaia, corresponded furiously with their agents, organizing transport of the newspaper and of brochures, and securing presses with which to print socialist material. But police crackdowns and older traditions of socialist activity continually frustrated Lenin's plan for a tight, centralized Social Democratic organization essentially run from abroad. When the street demonstrations and strikes that erupted throughout the country for over a year, beginning in March 1901, exposed the secret Social Democratic committees and the broader ranks of workers, the police and Cossacks reacted quickly, arresting radical leaders, closing down newspapers, and punishing worker participants. Yet the prestige of *Iskra* within the Social Democratic movement remained high, for the militant mood among workers, students, and radical intellectuals corresponded precisely with *Iskra*'s emphasis on political action.

Iskra's resonance reached the far south of the empire, where younger activists like Soso Jughashvili were enthralled by its passion. In the Caucasus the Social Democrats were quite unevenly organized. In Tiflis the workers' organization was solidifying, and the *mesame dasi* leadership had enormous prestige. But neither Baku, the center of oil production in the Russian Empire, nor Batumi, the developing port on the Black Sea, had well-established organizations. It was from these politically "less developed" towns that the challenges to the authority of *mesame dasi* would come. Baku possessed the largest population of industrial workers, but it housed a large Muslim and Armenian population.[38] Marxists, primarily young Georgian migrants from Tiflis, had only begun organizing workers' circles there in 1898. Abel Enukidze, one of the first and most active Social Democrats, remembered how activity intensified when Soso's friend, Lado Ketskhoveli, arrived at the end of 1899.[39] With his customary energy and tireless effort, Ketskhoveli joined Enukidze in setting up circles of oilfield and refinery workers and soon was acknowledged as the most capable organizer. As successful as he was in having Social Democratic leaflets and proclamations printed by legal printing houses in Tiflis, Ketskhoveli had concluded that the Baku organization needed an underground press. The Tiflis Social Democrats had closed down their illegal presses after the railroad workers' strike. Since the Baku workers' dues hardly sufficed to pay for the construction of a printing press, Lado sent Enukidze to Tiflis to convince the organization to help. In a bar near the railroad station he met with Jibladze, the leader of the organization "famous all over Georgia," and with Jughashvili, "then still a young member of the party."[40] They refused, however, to help unless the printing operation were placed under the control and direction of the Tiflis organization. Enukidze felt he was not empowered to agree, and after securing some type from printing-house workers who had formerly worked with Ketskhoveli, he returned to Baku. Ketskhoveli categorically rejected the conditions, and soon after the Georgian organization relented, gave 100 rubles to the Baku operation, and even sent typesetter Viktor Tsuladze to help.[41] The first leaflet appeared in Georgian and Russian, and a Social Democratic workers' movement in Baku took its first steps. Twelve people gathered in 1900 for the first May Day in the city. A year later, as the mounted police kept their distance, two hundred people celebrated May Day.[42]

The movement in Baku differed fundamentally from that in Tiflis. Initiated by socialist intellectuals rather than by workers as in Tiflis, that difference would have a profound effect not only on the relative fortunes of Bolsheviks and Mensheviks in the next decade but on Soso Jughashvili as well. Even more striking in the two cities, both of them with culturally diverse populations, was that ethnic tensions were far more intense in Baku. By prodding and propagandizing, Baku Social Democrats attracted workers, primarily Georgians, Russians, and, somewhat less successfully, Armenians, to their cause. Muslims, who made up the lowest paid and least skilled oil-field workers, remained indifferent to or ignorant of the socialist message. Living in their own parts of the city, Muslims had almost no contact with the police or state officials. Few knew Russian, and socialist propaganda was not available in their languages. Ketskhoveli took advantage of the relative isolation of the Muslims when he built a second, larger press, housing it in the home of an old Muslim who had no idea that his apartment was being used for illegal purposes. The press published in Georgian as well as Russian. Tied both to *Iskra* and the popular Russian-based Social Democratic paper, *Iuzhnyi rabochii* (Southern Worker), the Baku Social Democrats made their press available to both. This nonsectarian generosity infuriated Lenin, who advised them to break off all relations with newspapers other than *Iskra*. The Baku comrades soon obliged.[43] Their secret press, dubbed "Nina," became legendary in Marxist circles.

Though he remained in Tiflis, hiding in the apartments of friends and composing articles in Georgian, Soso was attracted to the more militant young Georgian Social Democrats in Baku. In the spring and summer of 1901 the Baku group, most immediately influenced by *Iskra*, decided that an illegal organ ought to be published in Georgian. Although they recognized the enormous influence of *kvali* in Georgia, Ketskhoveli and Enukidze argued that as a legal publication it was unable to put forth openly Social Democratic slogans. The time had passed, it was felt, when the movement could be limited to what the censors would permit to appear in sanctioned newspapers. Negotiations were held with Zhordania in Tiflis, but he opposed Baku's plan as a waste of money and possibly of labor. Ketskhoveli defended his position: "Legal Marxism corrupts the masses; it does not temper them for the struggle because it gives them a diluted Marxism." Worker comrades from Tiflis were sent to convince Ketskhoveli to publish pamphlets instead of a rival to *kvali*, but Lado persuaded them of the need for an underground paper. The Tiflis Committee reluctantly agreed but sought to maintain control over the Baku militants. Jugheli traveled to Baku and informed the Baku comrades that the editorial board would sit in Tiflis with only the technical operations remaining in Baku. Again Ketskhoveli and his comrades refused to submit and told Jugheli that the illegal newspaper would be answerable directly to *Iskra*.[44]

The first issue of the underground newspaper, *brdzola* (Struggle), appeared in September 1901 as the periodic publication "of a revolutionary Social Democratic group." Articles, letters, and notes came from Tiflis, as well as Baku, and Soviet sources claim that Soso Jughashvili wrote the lead editorial. This is highly unlikely, since Ketskhoveli, as the older, more influential figure in the movement, was the probable principal author of the editorial.[45] Whoever wrote it, the article gives a clear sense of the thinking of the group with which twenty-two-year-old Soso identified. Beginning with a critique of the reliance on circle propaganda and agitation, the editorial pointed out the limits of the legal press and the need for a "free newspaper." Setting out the tasks of the newspaper, the author emphasized that "the Georgian Social Democratic movement is not an isolated, exclusively Georgian workers' movement with its own program; it goes hand in hand with the whole Russian movement and, as it were, accepts the authority of the Russian Social Democratic Party. It is thus clear that a Georgian Social Democratic newspaper ought to present itself only as a local organ dealing mainly with local questions and reflecting the local movement." At the same time, given that Georgian workers do not read Russian, a Georgian revolutionary newspaper must provide news about national, even international, events and relate what other social elements besides workers are doing in the struggle for freedom.

The articles in *brdzola*, no. 1, demonstrate that by the fall of 1901 Soso and his comrades had established a distinct position within the Georgian movement. They had already absorbed the impulse from *Iskra* for greater unity and cohesion in the party and the need to move beyond agitation and propaganda. Autocracy, *brdzola* argued, can be defeated, but only by the working class. Yet labor's parochial discontents had to be linked with the larger structures of tsarism and capitalism. Social Democrats should take up the call for political freedom and civil rights. In another editorial attributed to Jughashvili, "The Russian Social Democratic Party and Its Immediate Tasks," the author argued that with the new century Social Democracy developed negative tendencies that saw the movement as everything and the goal as nothing. This was the position of those German Social Democrats, influenced by Eduard Bernstein, who favored evolutionary rather than revolutionary socialism.[46] Such moderates, reviled by the more radical as "Revisionists," emphasized economic improvement of workers' conditions with little attention to the revolutionary struggle. For Jughashvili, as for other *Iskra*ites, "Economism" and Revisionism were both nonrevolutionary forms of socialism. These strategies, which promoted the "spontaneous" economic movements among workers, ultimately came up against the police regime in Russia that turned every economic action into a political challenge to the regime.

Workers, according to the editorial, were not alone in their struggle. Whole nations were oppressed by tsarism:

> Oppressed peoples and religious groups are groaning in Russia; this includes Poles, who are driven from their homeland and whose sacred feelings are insulted, and Finns, whose rights and liberties granted historically are being brutally trampled by the autocracy.

Groaning also are the eternally persecuted and humiliated Jews, who are deprived even of those pathetic rights that other subjects of Russia enjoy—the right to live anywhere, the right to study in schools, the right to serve [in the army or state], et cetera. The Georgians, Armenians, and other nations are groaning, deprived of their right to have their own schools and work in state institutions, and required to submit to the shameful and oppressive policy of Russification that the autocracy carries out so zealously.

Students had shown the way into the political struggle, with massive street demonstrations, but "their weak hands are not able to hold up this heavy banner. For that are needed stronger hands, and in present conditions only the united power of the working people has sufficient strength." Brimming over with youthful passion and enthusiasm for the heat of battle, the editorial argued that "short-term" losses would only bring victory nearer:

> Each fighter falling in battle or torn from our ranks will give rise to hundreds of new fighters. For a while we will be beaten on the streets; the government will continue to emerge victorious from the street battles. But these will be "Pyrrhic victories." A few more victories like these, and the defeat of absolutism is unavoidable.

The editorial reaffirmed the Social Democratic principle that the workers in Russia must lead the whole democratic movement and not simply be helpmates for the bourgeois intelligentsia. Only with workers leading will a truly democratic constitution be established in Russia. Expressing the sentiments of many militant Social Democrats, *brdzola* concluded with a call for the formation of an independent workers' political party. This program, hardly original with Jughashvili and his friends, was part of the repertoire of ideas put forth by *Iskra*, which at that moment was being developed by Lenin, Martov, and others into a coherent strategic position.

The young militants around *brdzola* were more hostile to nationalism than the older generation around *kvali*, several of whom flirted with Georgian nationalism. An article in *brdzola*, nos. 2–3, on "Nationalism and Socialism," attributed later to Aleksandre Tsulukidze, made the standard Marxist claim that nations rose with the coming of capitalism. Socialists, however, must distinguish between the nationalism of ruling nations and the nationalism of oppressed nations.[47] Contemporary national states show centralizing tendencies, which in turn give rise to nationalist movements, even among nations that without repression would not have developed such movements. "Is there anything more natural," the author asked rhetorically, "than defending one's native language, inherited traditions with which one lived from childhood, against repression?" Socialists must support struggles against forced Russification or Germanization. "National freedom is part of personal and social freedom, and for this reason national freedom is an inseparable part of the broad democratic program of the proletariat." But Social Democrats must oppose the nationalism of ruling nations. "Nationalism is now the principal enemy of socialism, and the struggle with this enemy ought to be the main struggle. . . . We are convinced that the national idea in its development negates any kind of democracy, that even the nationalism of oppressed nations turns into the nationalism of oppressors when the interests of the bourgeoisie are put forth."

The *brdzola* group rejected isolation of or privileging the Georgian movement. Nationalism presented more danger than opportunity. An Armenian comrade remembered that Soso asked him to find Armenian type so that socialist literature could be printed for the local Armenian workers.[48] Whatever remained of Soso's commitment to the liberation of Georgia was now clearly seen as connected to the liberation of all the peoples of the empire and beyond. He had come a long way since his days as a patriotic poet.

FINDING LENIN

By May 1901 Lenin was working on a synthetic statement of *Iskra*'s position on the role of a revolutionary Social Democratic party and who might be admitted and who might not. What at the time it was written was an obscure polemic within a small illegal Russian party proved to be enormously influential once the Communists took power fifteen years after it appeared. This work, *What Is to Be Done?*, published in the spring of 1902, has been characterized as containing "all the essentials of what was later to be known as Leninism" and the doctrinal source of Soviet authoritarianism.[49] Because of whom Lenin would become, the pamphlet's original intentions and meanings have been stretched and distorted to explain everything from Lenin's personal proclivities for dictatorship to the tragic trajectory of Russia's revolution from its radically democratic aspirations to its degeneration into sanguinary autocracy. But at the moment the pamphlet appeared, its author was making an intervention in a very specific debate among Russia's Marxists. He set out to defend the positions of *Iskra* against the *ekonomisty*, who claimed that the *Iskra*ites were forcing workers into political confrontations. Workers, in the Economists' view, were primarily interested in the daily struggles for wages and working conditions, but out of that struggle they would gravitate spontaneously toward socialism. Lenin pleaded for an effective Social Democratic party uniting the disparate activities of the dozens of circles and organizations then functioning in an "amateurish" way inside Russia. Hostile to the terrorism of the Populists and the pusillanimous moderation of "bourgeois" liberals, Lenin called on Russia's workers to participate in the broad social opposition to tsarism and not isolate themselves within their own class ghettos.[50] The task of the party was to expand the outlook of workers from a narrow understanding of their own class interests to an inclusive vision of the interests of the whole society. Such an expansion could be achieved only by a struggle on the level of theory against any tendency of workers to be concerned solely with their own problems—in his words: a struggle against "spontaneity" and for political consciousness.[51]

Lenin broke with those activists who believed that Social Democrats should simply reflect the current level of consciousness of the average worker living and working under capitalism. "The history of all countries shows," he wrote in one of his most revealing phrases, "that the working class, exclusively by its own effort, is able to develop only trade-union consciousness."[52] This trade unionism involved a kind of "bourgeois" politics, expressing workers' interests within the framework of the existing capitalist economic and political order. The task of Social

Democrats was to instill in the workers awareness of the need for the political overthrow of autocracy, something that would not emerge automatically from the economic struggle but would come from "the sphere of relationships between all classes and the state and the government, the sphere of the interrelations between all classes."[53] Here the Social Democrats would play the key role. Lenin did not argue that the workers could not themselves gravitate toward socialism, as many of his critics would later claim. Rather, workers easily assimilated socialist ideas, for they were perfectly aware of their own misery. "The working class is spontaneously attracted by socialism, but the much more widely disseminated . . . bourgeois ideology no less spontaneously thrusts itself upon the workers even more."[54] In the uneven contest between socialist ideas and the hegemonic culture of the bourgeoisie, Lenin argued, workers would succumb to the dominant discourses of the ruling classes. The task of the Social Democrats, intellectuals and workers, was to struggle against the spontaneous accommodation to the status quo and prevailing culture and to lead the working-class movement away from simple trade unionism toward revolutionary consciousness.

"Modern socialism"—that is, Marx and Engel's understandings of the dynamics of capitalism and the development of the working class—was the product of intellectuals, and Social Democrats, both intellectuals and advanced workers, would bring that theoretical expression to the working class, which because of its experience could easily assimilate it. For Lenin, the party of revolutionary Social Democrats was to act neither as a "trade union secretary" advocating the immediate material interests of workers alone nor as disconnected leaders independent of the workers, but as tribunes of the whole people, expounding the need for political freedom. Social Democrats were tasked to prod the labor movement beyond its immediate trade unionist stage.

Under Russian conditions the party was to be made up "first and foremost of people who make revolutionary activity their profession." Lenin was "not proposing any monopoly of decision-making by the revolutionaries by trade."[55] He called for all distinctions between workers and intellectuals to be effaced. The organization was to be small, as secret as possible, made up of people who understood the art of working in the difficult conditions of a police state. They had to practice *konspiratsiia* (working secretly), "the fine art of not getting arrested."[56] Lenin concluded his essay with a call for the foundation of a central party newspaper that would become a collective organizer, linking up local struggles and engaging in political and economic exposures all over Russia. Around the newspaper an "army of tried fighters" would gather, "Social Democratic Zheliabovs," made up not only of intellectuals but also of "Russian Bebels from among our workers."[57] And the Russian proletariat, by destroying the most powerful support of European and Asian reaction—tsarism—will become "the vanguard of the international revolutionary proletariat."

Lenin's pamphlet was at one and the same time a relentless diatribe against the critics of *Iskra*, a plea for workers to reflect the aspirations of the whole of society, and an inspirational call for a new relationship between Social Democrats and workers. Unwilling to concede that the current stage of the average worker's consciousness required socialists to moderate their tactics, he insisted on an active intervention by politically conscious revolutionaries. Lenin refused to confuse the present with the future or to consider the labor movement either one-dimensionally determined by objective economic forces or fated to fall under the sway of the currently hegemonic ideology of the bourgeoisie. Conscious political activity by leaders, along with changing circumstances, offered positive perspectives for a revolutionary working class. Blame for the failure to develop such a movement was to be placed not on the workers but on intellectuals who were unable to raise Social Democratic consciousness among the rank and file. Lenin's insistence that full socialist consciousness under bourgeois hegemony required Social Democratic intervention was not unique to him, but his conviction that without Social Democrats the workers' movement would remain "bourgeois" would be interpreted by his opponents as a major revision of Plekhanov's orthodox synthesis that workers would simply gravitate naturally to socialism while intellectuals would accelerate that movement. The issues laid out in *What Is to Be Done?* had been widely discussed in Social Democratic circles for years, but no one before Lenin had exposed them so starkly.

Adherents of Lenin's views, like Soso Jughashvili, were enthralled to find such a frank defense—and elevation—of the necessary role of active Social Democrats—that is, people like themselves. Lenin's personal political style, expressively demonstrated in this book, would have a decisive influence on activists like Soso. Here sharp ideological distinctions, principled divisions, and purity of position were turned into virtues. Accommodation, compromise, and moderation were thrown aside in favor of an impatient commitment to action. Conciliation was in Lenin's view a negative quality for a militant revolutionary. Although Bolshevism or Leninism was not yet a fully formed political tendency, Lenin's language and proposed practice had an immediate appeal for certain Social Democratic activists and bred anxiety in others. For the *praktiki* inside Russia, those like Jughashvili working with workers or underground presses, Lenin's message was inspirational: "You brag about your practicality and you do not see (a fact known to any Russian *praktik*) what miracles for the revolutionary cause can be brought about not only by a circle but by a lone individual."[58] Not surprisingly, as the secret police reported, Lenin's pamphlet soon made "a great sensation" among revolutionary activists in Russia.[59] Enukidze remembers how he convinced a policeman to let him keep a confiscated copy of the book, which he then smuggled into Metekhi Prison in Tiflis after his arrest in September 1902.[60] Although it is not known when Jughashvili read *What Is to Be Done?*, his subsequent writings show the profound effect it had on his thinking. He was one of those "daring and determined" young men who found in this pamphlet a clear call to the exalted role they were to play. "[I]t applied to *all of us* in those years," writes N. Valentinov (Vol'skii). "'Daring and determination' were common to us all. For this reason *What Is to Be Done?* struck just the right chord with us, and we were only too eager to put its message into practice. In this sense, one may say, we were one hundred per cent Leninists at that time."[61] Years later Stalin marked Lenin's fiftieth birthday with a laudatory account of how the older man had influenced him. A book like *What Is to Be Done?*, he wrote, "completely reflected Russian reality and masterfully generalized the organizational experience of the best *praktiki*. . . . [T]he majority of Russian *praktiki* decisively followed Lenin."[62]

From Petersburg and Moscow in the north to Tiflis and Baku in the south, an unprecedented wave of labor unrest swelled year after year as the new century unfolded. In part due to the slowdown in industrial growth and the effects of an international economic crisis, the growing labor movement was also a response to a general discontent felt and expressed by more privileged members of Russian society. Workers were not the only social group in the empire excluded from political participation and public life. People of property also lived and worked without protection from the arbitrary and intrusive powers of the tsarist state. They too were plagued by censorship, lawlessness, and restrictions on ethnic and cultural expression.[63] Intellectuals and professionals, industrialists and merchants wanted to play a greater role in political affairs, and at the turn of the century liberal and radical elements in the middle strata of society formed discussion groups, held political banquets, and more openly expressed their dissatisfaction with the autocracy's isolation from educated and propertied society. In Caucasia the first years of the new century witnessed socialists and workers joining thousands of peasants in western Georgia in a massive opposition to the government. Even before the revolutionary year of 1905 a rising arc of worker and peasant militancy, growing violence and terrorism, and repeated and brutal repression by the state transformed Caucasia into a crucible of revolutionary activity. Though far from instigating these waves of action himself, as Soviet accounts would later portray, Soso was riding them. His decision to throw in his lot with the socialists and workers appeared to be the right one for this twenty-four-year-old with few other prospects.

By the fall of 1901 the labor movement in Tiflis had outgrown the bounds both of the tutelage of the "legal" intellectuals around *kvali* and the "illegal" Social Democrats attached to the Tiflis Committee. The increased police surveillance and repression of workers and socialists, however, prevented further open demonstrations. At night the police carried out house searches and arrests in various worker districts. By year's end a socialist source estimated that some five hundred police spies and "provocateurs" were operating in Tiflis. If accurate, that was an exceptionally high number.

No longer a seminarian protected by the walls of the seminary and patronized by the church, Soso Jughashvili had become a man hunted by the police. For the next fifteen years he would be under their surveillance, sometimes in their custody, at other times pursued by gendarmes and police spies. Hiding became a mode of survival. The repression of the priests gave way to the daily dangers of avoiding arrest. Violence was ever present, and not only from the arbitrary power of the police. Workers dealt with spies in their own way; they beat up or murdered policemen. A few Social Democrats encouraged the violence as a way to paralyze and disrupt the plans of the government. The Tiflis Committee was more cautious and opposed such "excesses." The government's own cruelty, however, fed the workers' anger and revenge, and the socialists were unable to stop them from taking matters into their own hands.[64]

Social Democrats throughout the tsarist empire were conflicted about the role that intellectuals would play in the burgeoning workers' movement. In Georgia the usual practice had been that workers themselves would be primarily responsible for their own organizations, while intellectuals would play an important auxiliary role. Zhordania vigorously supported this practice and dismissed the view that the people were a passive element on which the intelligentsia could act however they chose. Early on, in a series of articles in *kvali*, he wrote disdainfully about how the intelligentsia treats "the people . . . like babies unable to stand on their own feet, who need a master and a nurse. . . . In other words, for the juvenile people, a guardian is necessary. And who is this guardian? The intelligentsia, dedicated and full of paternalistic love, calls out—I am the patron and guardian." Zhordania had a different response: "No, Mr. 'intellectual.' . . . You look after yourself, the people lead themselves and can manage on their own; here your patronage has no place. Try and move a finger without the people![65] In Georgia, he proclaimed proudly, "the active role is played by the people themselves. It is harnessed in history's yoke; to harness the intelligentsia there instead of it is completely impossible. This is a groundless dream. The intelligentsia can only lubricate the wheel with grease and thus ease its rotation."[66]

Not all the local intellectuals, however, were ready to give in to worker dominance. Soso was one of the most reluctant. The very first Tiflis Committee had been made up largely of "advanced" workers and a few intellectuals. But through the first year of the new century worker discontent with the dominance of intellectuals and their chosen "workers" grew. One Social Democrat remembered the brewing crisis beginning when "the circle of Social Democratic intellectuals chose or, rather, appointed from their midst more compatible people to be members of the Committee. The composition of the Committee was exclusively of an 'intellectual' character. Everything that the Committee decided, everything that it proposed, was communicated to the workers; the Committee considered the mood and opinion of the more advanced workers; but in the majority of cases it did not draw workers to take their own, independent action and to discuss and decide important questions or bring them into the leading center." While intellectuals made the important decisions, "Workers carried out, in the main, practical work; they were given only the technical side of things. In this sense more or less conscious workers, standing close to the organization and to the committee, were only an 'appendage,' a 'tail' of the latter. Inexplicable was the stubborn tendency of some comrade intellectuals to deprive the workers of the chance to participate in the Committee."[67]

Soso was named in police reports—attending a meeting of workers and *intelligenty* on November 4, 1901, and again on the 11th. In the Milani *dukani* he spoke about the distribution of illegal literature and the need to unite all nationalities. He promised to work out an "instruction" for the next meeting.[68] On November 11, 1901, between twenty-five and forty workers elected from various factories and workshops gathered, along with a few intellectuals who had escaped arrest, to discuss the issues that divided them. Soso attended, and because so many Social Democrats had been picked up by the police, he had suddenly become an important intellectual in the local movement. His circle was prominent in the selection of the new city committee. Jugheli launched the discussion of the workers' demands: (1) to abolish the old way of organizing the committee and to establish an electoral system; and (2) to recognize and implement the principle of worker participation in the committee. The first demand was accepted without much debate, but the second split the meeting into three positions. Some proposed a purely intellectual committee, without workers; others preferred a joint committee with equal representation of workers and intellectuals; and still others favored a mixed committee with no fixed quotas. An Armenian intellectual, Gevork Gharajian, spoke in favor of workers electing whomever they wanted to all Social Democratic organizations. Then a young intellectual (not specifically identified in the source) spoke against having workers on the committee because of their lack of preparation and political awareness. Conspiracy would be impossible: "How can this be? The intellectuals will be in frock coats and starched shirts, while the workers are in shirtsleeves; isn't this inappropriate, not conspiratorial?" This comrade, described as "scrupulously 'energetic' in all affairs," addressed the workers directly: "Here they flatter the workers; I ask if among you there are even one or two who are appropriate for the committee of workers. Tell the truth, placing your hand on your heart."[69]

From all indications the "young comrade" was Jughashvili. The story is backed up by Sebastian Talaqvadze, who remembered that "Soso Jughashvili and Vaso Tsabadze were trying to convince those comrades in favor of elections that a committee chosen in such a manner would be in danger, that untrustworthy people—police agents—would be elected to the committee and the organization could collapse."[70] Gharajian recalled further that the "young comrade soon shifted his activity from Tiflis to Batumi, whence the Tiflis [party] workers received news of his incorrect attitude, hostile and disorganizing agitation against the Tiflis organization and its [party] workers. Such activities by some comrades, which were very harmful to the cause of the revolutionary proletariat, can be explained, of course, in most cases not by their principled attitudes to the general cause but only by individual characteristics, personal caprices, and aspirations for personal power."[71]

The workers rejected Jughashvili's view, voted in favor of a mixed committee, and by secret ballot elected three or four workers and the same number of intellectuals to serve on the new committee. Despite his position on the makeup of the committee, Soso was elected a member.[72] Sometime later a meeting was held in Avlabar, across the river from the center of Tiflis, where representatives of all the district committees in the city elected a new Tiflis Committee made up of five workers and five intellectuals. Soso may have been one of the intellectuals.[73] The joint committee, however, proved to be short-lived. Betrayed to the police by one of the intellectuals in February 1902, all but one member were arrested and imprisoned in the Metekhi fortress. At that point the intellectuals around *kvali* simply chose a new committee. In the increasingly policed state that tsarist Russia had become, democracy within the party proved fragile and fleeting.[74]

In the empire in which Soso lived, opposing the tsar and the propertied classes was a declaration of war. Here war was not simply the extension of politics; politics was a form of warfare. Nowhere in Russia was that war carried out with such ferocity as it was in the imperial peripheries, particularly in Caucasia. Strength, firmness, and fearlessness in the face of the enemy armed him for the expected battles ahead. The goals of the movement were deeply humanistic; the means needed to achieve them were anything but.

Soso was in but not of the Georgian Social Democratic movement. He stood at the edge, alienated from the acknowledged intellectual leaders. Marxist theorists, socialist activists, and their adherents together were constructing a "socialist movement," which was itself an imagined community of like-minded people dedicated to revolutionary transformation.[75] Like a nation, so the movement fought within itself over its self-definition and identity, working out the rules of admission and exclusion. The struggle among those within the movement was often as intense, if not as bloody, as the struggle with tsarism and capital. For long periods of his prerevolutionary career Soso Jughashvili devoted much of his energy and time to the intramural wars fought within the ranks of the Georgian and Russian Marxists.

By the end of 1901 Jughashvili had established a reputation among Social Democrats in the Georgian capital as an energetic, militant, but rather difficult comrade. He was estranged from many, though hardly all, in the Tiflis organization. Workers opposed his strong position on the intellectual dominance of the Tiflis Committee. He was convinced of the importance of the role of the intelligentsia, its mission of enlightening the benighted poor, and though he could affect the manners of a proletarian, he self-identified as an *intelligent*. A boyhood companion from Gori who later became a political enemy generously recalled, "It is necessary to say that at this time Stalin was not a great orator. On the other hand, as an organizer, he certainly had no equal among all our revolutionary youth in the Caucasus."[76] He had questioned on several occasions the authority of Zhordania and Jibladze and identified himself with the young radicals around Ketskhoveli. When he had spoken against Jibladze to the workers in his propaganda circle, the party organization took the circle away from him and transferred him to the railroad district. But there as well, as Zhordania later remembered, "he was unable to reconcile himself to the internal structure of the organization. In the new district and the new circle he continued to fight with the committee; he created his own group and began a personal campaign against Jibladze." Zhordania claims that the committee was forced to put him on trial before a party court; the court found him guilty and decreed: "Soso Jughashvili, as an incorrigible intriguer, is expelled from the organization."[77]

Zhordania's story cannot be corroborated by an independent record of such a party court.[78] Yet it is likely that Soso was reprimanded by some party group, probably by those around *kvali*, and may have had his circles taken away from him. For that reason he left for Batumi.

Certainly the atmosphere in Tiflis had become tense, hostile, and even dangerous. Not only did Soso need to hide from the police, but he was also alienated from the prevailing views of workers and his fellow Social Democrats. Ambitious, impatient, and self-confident, Soso had struck out at the older generation of Social Democrats and had been punished for his insubordination. Rather than give in, he moved on to an uncultivated terrain where he could spread his own ideas and bring in new recruits. Jughashvili could take advantage of the fact that the party was not yet centralized, that each city's Social Democratic organization was largely independent. Excluded from one he might find refuge in another. His behavior was interpreted by some as a personal striving for power, by others as a principled attempt to forge a more effective movement. Plausibly the two views are not in conflict: Soso's drive for power was connected to his confidence that his convictions were correct and necessary for the success of Social Democracy. What looks like cynicism and the instrumental use of others was for Jughashvili the choosing of appropriate tactics directed toward the desired political (rather than a merely personal) goal. Batumi, a city with almost no active Social Democratic involvement with workers, was a fresh field for the restless revolutionary. Failure in one city might be overcome by success in another.

7

TRIAL BY FIRE

I saw Koba (Stalin) for the first time in my life and had not even
suspected his existence. In appearance he was plain, his pockmarked
face made him look somewhat untidy. . . . In prison he wore a beard,
long hair combed back. His gait was ingratiating, with small steps. He
never smiled with a full, open mouth, only smiled. And the measure
of the smile depended on the dimension of the emotion aroused by
what had happened, but his smile never turned into an open laugh of
his whole mouth. He was completely imperturbable. We lived together
in the Kutaisi prison for more than half a year, and I never once saw
him outraged, lose control, become angry, shout, curse; in a word, he
conducted himself in no other way than in complete calm. And his
voice corresponded exactly to his "icy character" that those close to
him knew well.

—GRIGORII URATADZE, *VOSPOMINANIIA GRUZINSKOGO
SOTSIAL-DEMOKRATA [MEMOIRS OF A GEORGIAN
SOCIAL DEMOCRAT]* (1968)

Stalin began his political career with a weak education and an immea-
surable pretension. This young man felt the need to be a leader, but
since he did not merit it, he resolved to enhance himself by denigrating
other leaders. He was a mediocre orator, a monotone, managing to
attract listeners only by using big words; he was not a writer. Only
the purely organizational area was left for him to achieve the status
of leader. There he revealed a tenacity, a daring, and an exceptional
fidelity. . . . But personal ambition, which was his basic quality,
prevented him from carrying on this work well; it led to haste and
made him forget the procedures used in Tiflis. Hating all leading
comrades, he accused them of cowardice, mediocrity, betrayal of the
working class and called on the workers to engage in street

demonstrations. Within the organization he created his own group,
which obeyed him blindly and did not feel obligated to answer to the
local committee. The result of such secret work was the demonstration
of workers in front of the prison and their massacre by the authorities.

—NOE ZHORDANIA, "STALINI," BRDZOLIS KHMA ["STALIN,"
VOICE OF THE STRUGGLE], NO. 65 (OCTOBER 1936)

Of the three industrial centers in South Caucasia—Baku, Tiflis, and
Batumi—the last was the latest to develop. For three hundred years the
steamy port on the Black Sea had been under Ottoman rule. Batumi
entered the Russian Empire as a prize of the Russo-Turkish War of
1877–1878. Just five years later the town was linked by rail to the other
cities of Caucasia, and its excellent harbor provided a natural outlet for
oil products shipped or later piped from Baku. Batumi replaced Poti as
the principal port for South Caucasia, and almost all oil sent abroad
passed through the town. By 1898 eight plants were producing the tin
and wooden containers in which Baku oil was packed for export.[1] Considering that until 1902 Baku produced more oil than the entire United
States, this packing and shipping industry in Batumi was a major economic attraction for foreign capital and local labor. The "Bnito" plant,
owned by the Rothschilds, employed almost six thousand workers; the
Khachaturiants factory and the two plants owned by the Armenian oil
magnate Aleksandr Mantashev had another four thousand workers.[2]
Three thousand dockworkers made their living loading and unloading
the Black Sea ships.

Almost all recent immigrants to the town—Georgian peasants from
nearby rural Guria, Armenian refugees from Turkey, and local
Muslims—the workers were completely exposed to the whims of the
absentee industrialists. Before 1902 there was no factory inspection system in South Caucasia, except in Baku.[3] Holidays went unobserved, and
seven-year-old boys worked the same fifteen- to sixteen-hour shifts as
adults at the Mantashev plant. "In our factories," a Batumi worker wrote
to Iskra, "the justice of the fist rules as far as the workers are concerned.

Overseers, managers, engineers, and even the director beat the workers," who suffered from unsanitary and unsafe working conditions.[4] They lived in settlements on the outskirts of the town. The Georgian socialist writer Ingoroqva worked at Rothschild's plant at the end of the 1880s and described the living conditions of the town's workers:

> On one side of the city of Batumi, a little above the oil refineries, are strewn in one spot a bunch of wooden structures with large cracks, which more readily deserve to be called hovels than houses. Around them is ubiquitous mud and impassable swamp. The paths leading to them are such that in foul weather, if one is not careful, it is very easy to fall deep into the mud. The swamps with which this area abound are filled with various stinking pieces of filth, and the evil stench rising from them poisons and infects the surrounding atmosphere; such a smell hangs there constantly that a person used to clean air cannot pass through without covering his nostrils.[5]

The houses were unheated, with a single window to a room. Ten to twelve workers crowded together in the small, damp rooms. Dark and gloomy inside, the cracks and holes in the walls let in more wind than light.[6]

As in Tiflis and Baku, the workers were divided along ethnic lines. Many Georgian workers maintained close ties to their villages, often returning for harvest and planting. As mechanization reduced the number of hands required in some of the larger plants, such as Rothschild's, the peasant workers faced the unenviable choice of remaining in Batumi unemployed or returning to their already burdened families back home. The local Georgian Muslims, the Ajars, were particularly discriminated against. They would not be given factory work unless they paid a substantial bribe.[7] A letter to the Tiflis nationalist newspaper *iveria* noted that Georgians resented Armenian workers, who had recently arrived from Turkey "searching for a better fate and a piece of bread" and were willing to work for lower wages. "The competition between people with bellies swollen from hunger has taken on an ethnic character, as if the Georgian or Armenian by himself has some responsibility for this situation."[8]

Once the international economic slump of the early twentieth century hit Russian oil, Baku lost its competitive edge to American producers and was forced to curtail output. Rumors spread that Batumi's dependent industries would suffer as well, that Mantashev would close his plants and that Rothschild and smaller plants would follow.[9] Wages fell; unemployment grew. "Now we earn enough only for bread and water," a worker correspondent wrote, "in order not to starve to death. . . . It is hard to live like this, and unwillingly we ask the question: why do we suffer so? Our life has no joy; it is only a path to the grave. Wouldn't it be better for us to die, not at the bench, but fighting for freedom, for a better future?"[10]

Social Democracy had barely rooted in Batumi at the turn of the century. Ingoroqva and Mikha Tskhakaia had formed worker study circles in the early 1890s, and the future Menshevik leader Nikoloz Chkheidze, along with Georgii Francheski and Ivan Luzin, formed a rather academic Marxist study circle dedicated to reading and translating Marx in 1895–1896.[11] In their enthusiasm for their intellectual mentor they even reproduced and sold Marx's photograph. Their illegal literature and the photographs proved incriminating, and Francheskii, Luzin, and other adherents were arrested early in 1898. Chkheidze escaped arrest and for several years managed to live a dual life as a respected deputy to the city duma and, less obviously, as a Marxist propagandist. Known among workers for his passion for Marx's ideas, which he compared to the music of Beethoven, Chkheidze was nicknamed "Karlo." But as workers grew more militant, he retreated into his legal occupation, pessimistic about the possibility of an effective workers' organization in Batumi.[12]

Making contact with workers, under the watchful eyes of the ubiquitous police, was not easy. When on weekends or holidays workers from the workers' suburb of Bartskhana went for walks in the countryside, socialists engaged them in conversation. If they spotted the police, the discussions metamorphosed into dances or a soccer game.[13] Workers read the Social Democratic newspapers whenever they would find them. In 1901 the typesetter Lado Dumbadze brought the first issue of *brdzola* to Batumi and told his fellow workers: "Read this and become socialists; understand how your comrades in Tiflis are struggling and imitate their example."[14] When Giorgi Chkheidze, a worker member of the Tiflis Committee (no relative of Nikoloz), visited Batumi in late 1900, he met with "Karlo" and found him wary of underground work.[15] Thus, a fragile embryo of an underground Social Democratic movement existed in Batumi, but it was not directly linked to the prominent "legal" Marxists, Chkheidze and his close associate Isidore Ramishvili.[16]

Soso Jughashvili appeared in Batumi early in December 1901 to take up the unpromising task of stimulating underground activity. A decade younger than "Karlo," Soso's temperament and ambitions were radically different from the leaders of the local Marxist circles. He went to the Kaplan plant and had a worker ask Konstantine [Kotsia] Kandelaki to meet him at the factory gate. Kandelaki came out and saw a thin young man, who gave him a false name. Kandelaki said that the man he sought was busy and would come out soon. Tell him that Soso from Tiflis has come, replied Stalin. His suspicions allayed, Kandelaki then revealed that he was in fact the man he sought. "Ah, this is what is called *konspiratsiia*," said Soso, and he shook his hand. Kandelaki then took Soso to his room, and when he returned after work, they shared a meal. Soso lived with him and Kote Kalandarov, whom he knew from Tiflis.[17] The local intellectuals received him coldly, and the workers were somewhat suspicious. Evgeniia Sogorovaia saw him as a "typical intellectual," a kind person but a bit odd. He talked a lot about the movement but like other intellectuals was "not really fit for work." He asked to be employed as a propagandist. Instead she gave him a scarf to wear and plied him with tea.[18]

Slowly Soso began to win over a few activist workers. He learned that the police had gotten wind of his local residence. After verifying with a long-time worker that Silibistro Lomjaria, a foreman, was trustworthy, Soso moved into the apartment Lomjaria shared with his brother, Porpire, in the outlying workers' district, Gorodok.[19] Later he moved on to the rooms rented by the Darakhvelidze brothers in the marshy *chaobis dasakhleba* (swamp settlement), where the police were reluctant to search.[20] With little regard for the legalism and caution of the Batumi Marxists, he launched immediately into setting up one clandestine circle after another and tried to establish a secret printing press. Displaying his usual energy and self-assurance, he carefully screened potential members. He stood by a window while Domenti Vadachkoria walked by with his invitees, one by one. For reasons unknown, Soso rejected one of them.[21] On another occasion he had Kandelaki dismiss a meeting because he was suspicious of a certain drayman.[22] Soso was clearly in charge, even though "no one knew his name, this young man in a black shirt, a long summer overcoat, and a soft black hat."[23]

A young printer, Silva Todria, remembered that a man calling himself "Soso" arrived in Batumi and asked him to organize a circle of reliable printers and set up an illegal press to print proclamations. Todria responded immediately, and on Sunday about a dozen or more workers listened to the young agitator talk about the labor movement in the Caucasus, Russia, and abroad. Todria was impressed by how Soso's conversation differed from those of the Sunday school lecturers, who focused on history, Darwinism, and planetary movements. "Listen," he told Todria, "Don't be afraid, the sun will not leave its orbit. But you should learn how to carry on revolutionary work and help me to set up a little illegal printing press."[24] With an ironic smile Soso told those who would listen that he disagreed with Chkheidze and the propagandists who claimed that underground work was impossible in Batumi.[25] In the home of a worker named Jedelov Soso met with workers' representatives and found considerable division along ethnic lines among them. Jughashvili told those who had gathered to organize groups of ten workers for study. By year's end more than eleven such circles had been formed at factories. While Georgians and Russians attended the meeting, no contacts had yet been made with Armenian workers, and whole factories where Armenians worked (like the Sachaturov plant) were not represented. The local members of the Armenian revolutionary party, the *Dashnaktsutyun*, warned Armenians against joining the Social Democrats.[26] Activist Armenian intellectuals in Caucasia discouraged organization around economic concerns and encouraged their supporters to focus on the liberation of their fellow countrymen in the Ottoman Empire. Tsarist officials tried to exploit the tensions between Armenians and Georgians, and the Batumi police chief Chikovani some years later (1904) encouraged Georgian workers at the Mantashev plant to attack Armenians in retaliation for their having beaten a Georgian. An equal opportunity provocateur, he also tried to stir up Armenians against Georgians.[27]

Although worker activity remained quite modest, Jughashvili's organizational work appears to have been quite effective during his first months in Batumi. His advantage was that he positioned himself as a worker-*intelligent* and found a language with which to communicate with those workers anxious both to learn and to act. He stimulated a moribund movement and established close ties with a number of local workers, some of whom referred to him as "Christ!"[28] Using a familiar metaphor, he spoke of how Tiflis workers had woken from a dream and were ready to fight their enemies, while Batumi workers were still peacefully asleep.[29] Shortly after he arrived, he advised some workers that they should not work on Sundays, and later he told them that they should quit work at six in the evening. The workers agreed, and to their surprise the factory administration gave in to their pressure. This, writes Vadachkoria, was the first victory of what could not yet be called a labor movement.[30]

Workers of various nationalities, all of them men, joined Soso's circles. Their wives were not included but would stand guard in the courtyard or clean up traces of secret meetings. Within this secretive world of almost exclusively male workers, distant from the resident intellectuals, Soso impressed those with whom he made contact as a man of the people, simple, direct, and different from the local Marxists, who remained aloof from the underground movement. They were attracted by his boldness. A policeman noticed the newcomer in town. In order to ward off suspicion, Soso simply walked up to him, asked directions, and continued on.[31] "Comrade Soso differed sharply from other educated people," remembered Porpire Kuridze. "For this reason, we workers called him, such a young man, 'Pastor' [*modzghvari*]."[32] He went on to make a highly dubious claim: that Soso read only one book in Russian—by Hegel![33]

Several attempts were made to mediate between Soso and the old Batumi Social Democratic *intelligenty*. Workers asked Soso to meet with the local Marxists, but he refused. "I won't go to them," he insisted. Let them work with us or put money in our treasury. "They are people of the study who avoid street fights."[34] The Tiflis Committee sent Datiko Khartishvili, known as "Mokheve" (the man from Khevi), to try to reverse Soso's tactics, but Soso did not like Mokheve and was upset that he was being displaced by an envoy from Tiflis: "We have gathered good fellows in Batumi, but Mokheve is a completely different type. He gives nothing, and the sooner the leading organization frees itself of him the better for the workers."[35] When a number of Social Democratic workers— Mikha Bochorishvili, Archil Dolidze, and Zakaria Chodrishvili—were invited from Tiflis to settle the argument, they backed Soso, to the dismay of the older *intelligenty*.[36] Confidently staking out his own path, Soso was determined not to compromise either with the local *intelligenty* or with emissaries from Tiflis.

One of the first actions of the circle workers was a funeral demonstration in December for an Armenian known only as "the poor worker."[37] A few weeks later, on New Year's Eve, Jughashvili and twenty-five workers held a meeting, disguised as a celebration, at the home of the Lomjaria brothers, where they discussed the need for a revolutionary organization. Soso asked his comrades not to drink too much. Only at dawn did he raise his glass and pronounce a toast: "Should it be that each of us fall on the field of battle for justice, we ought not fear death. We know that the day of our death will come. Let's carry our lives to the cause of the workers' liberation." Mikha Gabunia exclaimed, "Just so God doesn't kill me in my bed!"[38] It was probably agreed here to choose representatives from each factory who would coordinate labor activity in the future.[39]

Just before the New Year, Soso's friend, Mkuriani, found him a job at the lumberyard of the Rothschild plant. There he would earn about thirty-five rubles a month.[40] But a few days later, a fire broke out in the yard, and the managers implored the workers to put out the fire, promising them a reward.[41] Soso joined the other workers in quenching the fire. The money he had earned so far had been spent, so like the others he was looking forward to the bonus.[42] Once the fire was out, however, only the most skilled workers and foremen were rewarded. Learning of this, Jughashvili called the workers together and proposed that a list of the firefighters be drawn up and that, together with workers of other plants, they demand not only their due compensation but also free Sundays as stipulated by the law of 1897. At just this time a new manager, Franz Gyon, took over the plant and granted both demands. One or two rubles from the reward given each worker were turned over to a workers' fund (*kassa*).[43] It was a small success, but one that raised Soso's credibility among the workers.

Although Social Democrats certainly laid the ground for a more militant attitude by workers in Batumi, the sudden explosion of labor activity in the new year was unexpected, and the actual outbreak of strikes was largely spontaneous and free of direct involvement of the Marxists. Soso was interested in mobilizing workers at the Mantashev plant, who were predominantly Armenian. He invited Georgii Godziev to come to Batumi to act as translator, but the effort flopped because the workers, who spoke the Western Armenian dialect from the Ottoman lands, had trouble understanding Godziev's Eastern Armenian spoken in the Caucasus.[44] When on January 31, 1902, the manager of the Mantashev plant, an Armenian named Ter Akopov, dismissed a worker for talking with friends during working hours, four hundred workers walked out. Upset about night work and impolite address by bosses, workers particularly despised Ter Akopov as a cruel manager always ready to use his fists. The strikers felt that such a flimsy excuse for dismissal placed them all in danger of arbitrary firing. The manager called the police, who set upon the workers with whips. One hundred and twelve men were arrested; many were exiled to their villages. Immediately they trickled back to Batumi. The other workers refused to return to work until their arrested comrades were released. Fearing further escalation, the factory owner himself petitioned for the workers' release, and on February 17, all but two were freed. By the next day the workers returned to the plant, and Ter Akopov and several hated "dog-masters" were fired.[45] Unified and determined, the workers had gained not just a significant victory but a new confidence.

The police were soon on the trail of the strike leaders, who had used the apartment where Soso and Kandelaki lived as their headquarters. Soso slipped off to the home of an Armenian, and Kandelaki moved to Lomjaria's.[46] In that same week (February 15) the police in Tiflis arrested most of the members of the local Social Democratic committee. The danger notwithstanding, the strikers had learned a number of lessons from their action. They could see how the state in the form of the police or the army acted to back up the industrialists. Any pretense of neutrality or fairness by the government was no longer convincing. To be effective, it appeared, negotiations with the bosses had to be backed up with the threat of strikes or even violence.

Less than two weeks later a much more serious strike broke out at the Rothschild plant. Considered the best-equipped factory in town, Rothschild had a relatively stable workforce, but when the management announced that about four hundred workers, mostly older men, many of them members of the socialist study circles, were to be laid off, this violated the workers' sense of entitlement to employment after years of service and sacrifice. On their own initiative five hundred workers left the plant and gathered in Bartskhana to listen to Kotsia Kandelaki. They turned away a representative from the managers and refused to negotiate until the dismissed workers were reinstated. As a report from a factory inspector indicated, workers' attitudes toward management were shifting:

> The majority of them has been working in the plants 5–10–15 years, and during this period [workers] have managed to live together with one another . . . like one big family, sharing the same interests and living exclusively by local factory work. For the last years through their common life and work an attitude has grown stronger that because of their work and strength the companies make great capital. What is more [the companies] . . . do not have any legal right willfully or capriciously to fire people, no matter what the cause, from work to which they have become accustomed, for which many have lost their health or been maimed, and, finally, without which they cannot exist since they know no other kind of trade and many of them, perhaps even a majority, have long ago cut any tie they had with the land.[47]

The moral logic articulated by the workers stemmed from their belief that employers had obligations toward loyal workers. The way they conceived the worker-employer relationship contradicted the owners' model of the employer possessing exclusive rights over whom to hire and fire.

Soso, who was known to the workers (and the police) as the "teacher of the workers," was at that time in Tiflis arranging for an underground printing press for Batumi, relying on his old ties in the Tiflis workers' circles to acquire the needed equipment. He had arrived toward the end of February dressed in Caucasian costume (*cherkeska*) and met with his Social Democratic comrades at the "conspiratorial apartment" of his fanatically loyal disciple, Kamo, whom he assigned to acquire the necessary materials for setting up a secret press.[48] Soso would carry back the type slugs in cigarette boxes to which Todria would add those he filched from the city printing press.[49] A worker was sent from Batumi to bring him back, and he returned immediately, having shaven off his beard and mustache. What happened? asked Kuridze. "I sold them in Tiflis," he joked.[50] He soon became the pivotal advisor to the strikers, working out their list of demands, among which were a call for an eight-hour day and polite treatment by supervisors.[51]

One by one various shops went out, until the strike encompassed the whole plant (about fifteen hundred people), except for the Turkish workers in the lumberyard. The workers demanded that they be paid for the days they were on strike. The military governor of Kutaisi Province, Major-General Aleksei Smagin, tried to have the workers meet with a representative of the factory inspectorate, but the workers refused. The governor himself came to Batumi, and about four hundred striking workers met with him on March 3. A delegation chosen by the workers read their demands to Smagin. One worker stepped forward and pronounced the words that Soso Jughashvili had instructed him to say: "Today the factory horses are not working, but nevertheless they are being fed. Shouldn't human beings be treated the same way as horses?" The governor replied, where is it the case that workers who are not working are paid. The worker was ready with an answer: "That's the way it was done when there was a fire in the Putilov Plant [in Saint Petersburg]. Until the factory was rebuilt, the workers received half of their salary."[52] The military governor smoothed his beard and replied, "As your father, I order you to start working tomorrow."[53] With that he turned and left. The strikers, a police informant noted, "people almost starving to death, obstinately refused to return to work."[54] That night the police cordoned off the plant and arrested the thirty-two delegates.

Soso met with his circle of Social Democratic workers to plan their next move.[55] The following evening he called a meeting of workers at the Souk-su cemetery outside Batumi. He opposed negotiations with the governor and proposed a demonstration to demand the release of the arrested workers. In an article some months earlier in brdzola, he (or one of his comrades) had written that street demonstrations were particularly effective in mobilizing the population around the socialist cause. The whips of the police were completely democratic; they did not discriminate whom they hit; and therefore they provided the movement a great service in revolutionizing the merely curious who came out to watch.[56] "Don't run or they will shoot," Soso cautioned the workers, suggesting that they sing revolutionary songs. The police, who found it hard to keep up with the growing labor movement, were probably aware of this meeting in the cemetery but did not know what the workers were about to do. A detective reported that he had been at a cemetery meeting but because of the dark could not make out the leaders, and "given that I had only weak Georgian, I was unable to tell exactly what the conversation was about."[57]

On March 8, just after mid-day, approximately six hundred workers marched down the central streets of town to the prison. From a garden Soso directed the demonstration. Since the demonstrators had not yet learned any revolutionary songs, they sang the popular song "Ali Pasha."[58] Joined by sympathizers from the town, they shouted that either their comrades should be freed or all the marchers arrested. From the Alexander Garden members of the intelligentsia threw stones at the police. The authorities agreed to release the thirty-two worker delegates and requested that the crowd return to their homes, not through the city, but by a more roundabout route. By this time Soso had joined the crowd, encouraging the workers, urging them to sing. From the prison the incarcerated workers shouted "Bravo," and from the crowd they shouted back in Georgian, "Tomorrow we will come and liberate you all."[59] As they made their way past the so-called deportation prison, the workers, now numbering about four hundred, were met by two companies of soldiers. They were quickly arrested and locked in barracks.

That evening Soso, who had avoided arrest, met with his worker comrades at the Darakhvelidzes' and urged a second demonstration that would categorically demand the release of those arrested. One worker, Beglar Melia, feared that a demonstration could result in deaths and suggested a more cautious approach. Another, Vadachkoria, agreed that such a march would lead to bloodshed and frighten the workers. Soso hit him on the shoulder and said, "You are no revolutionary." Offended, Vadachkoria said that he would not lead the Mantashev workers to the march. He and Soso stopped speaking to each other for some time.[60] The meeting, however, backed Jughashvili's proposal.[61]

The next day, March 9, at 9:30 in the morning, four hundred more workers, led by Teopil Gogiberidze and Mikhail Khrimiants, marched to the barracks from which workers were to be deported. Not only factory workers but also artisans joined the demonstration. Soso, Kandelaki, and Natalia Kirtadze-Sikharulidze were in the crowd.[62] In a festive, optimistic mood, they shouted, sang, and even danced the *lezginka.* They believed that they might be arrested but not that the soldiers would shoot. As the marchers passed the Mantashev plant, they yelled, "*Mantashevtsy,* traitors!" In the excitement Vadachkoria changed his mind and decided to join the crowd. When the soldiers tried to disperse the crowd, they were met with a hail of rocks. The soldiers raised their guns; someone in the crowd shouted: "They are using blanks, don't be afraid." The chief of the gendarmes warned the crowd three times to desist. He was struck in the head by a rock. Caught between the angry crowd and the prisoners behind them, the soldiers shot twice into the air, and when this had no effect they fired directly at the demonstrators. "The shots rang out," the police later reported, "and the first ranks of the attackers fell to the ground like mown grass."[63] The shooting took ten to fifteen seconds, but it seemed longer to those upon whom the volleys were aimed. "The rifles fired again and again," Kandelaki remembered. "The soldiers would not leave the fleeing workers alone. Somehow I made it to the barracks and saw a few dead workers lying in the mud. Here also were the wounded crying for help. Seeing this scene, I was shaken to the depths of my soul; my eyes filled with tears; I was strangled by anger."[64] The crowd scattered, leaving thirteen dead and dozens more wounded.[65] Women tended to the wounded and carried them off in stretchers.

Although no contemporary sources nor the trial record of the arrested workers place Soso at the scene, several memoirs published during Stalin's reign report that Soso participated in the demonstration of March 9, dressed in a worker's shirt and a short jacket, and indeed that he carried wounded Geronti Kalandadze from the scene.[66] One participant reports that a soldier tried to stab Soso with his bayonet, but David Charkviani pushed it away, only to be wounded himself. Soso tried to calm down the workers, told them to sing, and sang himself, but the situation soon got out of hand.[67] Kandelaki wrote twenty years after the events that Soso had been present. "Then I remembered Soso. We got separated. I was afraid, starting to search for his body among the dead."[68] After Kandelaki made it home, a phaeton arrived with Soso and the wounded Kalandadze.[69] "Soso was fierce in his anger; his eyes were blazing like lightning." He bandaged the wounded and sent them to a physician's assistant. He then called those present into another room and explained that it was essential to put out a leaflet and present their views on what had happened to the workers.[70]

Both friends and foes of Stalin agree that the twenty-four-year-old Jughashvili had urged the workers to demonstrate in front of the prison to liberate their comrades.[71] He had calculated that a peaceful demonstration would not be fired upon, but instead of just singing songs, protestors had thrown rocks and the soldiers fired.[72] Some workers condemned what Soso had done, but others excused him and blamed the authorities. The easy success of January, it had confidently been felt, could be repeated. Instead a terrible massacre had occurred. The young revolutionary obviously had miscalculated. Workers were stunned, angered, and confused by the shooting. They immediately shut down all factories in Batumi. Vadachkoria felt that his caution had been vindicated and told Soso so. "You are no revolutionary!" Soso repeated, and justifying what had happened, he explained his logic of a *politique de pire*, "the worse the better." "If the government had freed the workers, it would win their hearts, and workers would think that the government defends the interests not only of the rich but of the workers. That would have given birth to a false idea. And now especially the relatives of those workers who were killed or wounded will be indefatigable enemies of the autocracy."[73]

Rumors quickly spread throughout Russia and abroad of the "Batumi slaughterhouse." On March 12 more than five thousand, nearly half the total number of workers in the town, marched in the funeral of those killed. Nothing in the experience of Batumi workers had ever before aroused such mass opposition to the authorities as the bloodshed of the March days. Images of heroism and horror, of innocent worker victims and tsarist executioners, reinforced the expectations of both militants and moderates. Whereas those working in particular factories had organized earlier strikes and marches, the funeral demonstration encompassed the whole spectrum of working-class Batumi. Cossacks accompanied the marchers, who moved silently through the streets to avoid provoking the soldiers. A leaflet written by Soso may have been quietly distributed in the crowd, but the police who collected such leaflets did not find it. This time Soso is said to have urged calm and restraint. In her memoir about Comrade Soso that day, Vera Lomjaria recalled how he "taught us courage and hatred toward the enemy."[74] A leaflet from the "Batumi Social Democratic Movement" describing the mood that day reflected something quite different. "Bless you, Lord, for a just death!" it read. "You showed all the Caucasian workers how essential it is for them to have humane rule."[75] The victims were buried in a common grave; no speeches were given, no songs sung.

But not all the reactions were so calm. A leaflet distributed in Tiflis in the name of the Russian Social Democratic Workers' Party and signed "Printing Press of the Social Democrats" linked the government with the Rothschild firm to defend capital's interests and not the workers. Soldiers shot their unresisting brothers. "The government holds a banquet on the graves of our brothers and celebrates victory; what is to be done? Submit to this savage power? Shame and disgrace. Submit to whom? To the autocratic beast who drinks our blood? Submit to those who are ready to eat us? No, we will no longer say that. . . . Freedom will triumph."[76] And even more militant was an anonymous letter signed "Workers" sent to Police Captain Antadze: "Soon approaches the hour of your eternal rest, you who drank the blood of your brothers. . . . Death to you, faithful watchman of rotting and moldy autocracy. . . . Death to you, Judas, traitor."[77]

To the "legalists" like Nikoloz Chkheidze and Isidore Ramishvili, the "Batumi slaughterhouse" proved the recklessness of open demonstrations in the face of the police and soldiers. Their tactic of circle propaganda seemed vindicated, though at the same time it was clear that responsible Social Democrats would have to develop new forms of organization and tactics to encompass a labor movement that had outgrown the circles and Sunday schools. To activists like Jughashvili the large turnouts and the fighting spirit of the workers on March 8th and 9th and at the funeral on the 12th proved their readiness for a more determined challenge to the established economic and political order. The militancy of the editorials in *brdzola* seemed to echo the mood of the workers, and Soso repeated his pungent phrase in yet another leaflet, "To Society:" "They feed animals when they work and when they don't work; we are denied that right."[78]

The situation was extraordinarily dangerous. The police were closing in. Soso hid with the Darakhvelidzes, where a secret press had been set up just before the strike. A worker, Giorgi Modebadze, noticed that the home of Ivliane Shapatava was being watched when Soso was there working on the secret press along with Silva Todria and an Armenian whose name has been lost. A night superintendent, Chkhikvaidze, and two policemen tried to enter. Despina Shapatava stood with a stick in her hands and declared, "The children are asleep; your appearance and noise will wake them up and frighten them." Chkhikvaidze laughed and left. As the account written down in Soviet times concludes, "Thus

Despina Shapatava saved the printing press and Comrade Stalin."[79] The printers moved the press several times, ending up in the village of Makhmudia in the home of an Abkhaz peasant, Khashim Smyrba, who knew nothing of the revolutionary movement. The Social Democrats paid Khashim to build a special room for them and paid monthly rent. Khashim's neighbors watched as men disguised in the *chadra*, Muslim female dress, moved in and out of the house. Khashim and the other villagers thought that the printers were counterfeiters. When Soso explained to Khashim what they were doing, the old man was assured that Jughashvili was a good man. "Only, it is a shame that you are not a Muslim. . . . If you were, I would give you in marriage seven beauties such as you have never seen."[80] While Soso worked, Khashim carried the leaflets printed in his home to the market concealed in a basket covered with greens.[81]

The police were aware that activist workers were influenced by a "workers' teacher," but they had no information on who or where he might be. One of the workers who had been fired after participating in the strike offered to inform the police of the next gathering of the strike organizers if in return he was reinstated in the Rothschild factory.[82] On the evening of April 5, Soso and Kandelaki met with Turkish Armenian teamsters at Darispan Darakhvelidze's apartment. After the workers left, around ten, Soso and Kandelaki, who were living there, sat with Darakhvelidze and a high school student, Vano Ramishvili. At one in the morning, the police raided the Darakhvelidze house, too late to catch the workers but in time to arrest the four. They missed Soso's suitcase, which contained his manuscripts, books, and some leaflets; instead they picked up Godziev's valise, which contained nothing incriminating.[83] Darakhvelidze and the boy were released, but Soso and Kandelaki were held on suspicion of involvement in the recent strike and demonstration. Soso gave his real name and claimed that he had arrived in Batumi after March 9. Only at the moment of their arrest did Kandelaki learn that his comrade from Tiflis was named Ioseb Jughashvili.[84] The police chief was better informed and quickly concluded that Jughashvili was "a typical propagandist and, of course, does not want to tell us where his accomplices are."[85]

THE PRISONER

From the moment of his arrest in 1902 and for the next fifteen years, until the revolution of 1917, Soso's life would alternate between prison, escape, living underground in danger of arrest, rearrest, prison, and exile. This time he was held for a year in Batumi prison, a long single-storied warehouse of a building, before being transferred to the provincial prison in Kutaisi for another seven months. He was placed in Cell no. 1, along with another prisoner whom Soso suspected of being a police spy dressed as a worker.[86] The police, who now began a file on the suspected revolutionary, had little hard information on his role among the Batumi workers. One officer reported seeing Jughashvili in the crowd on March 9, but Soso tried to convince the police that he had not arrived in Batumi until the 15th. Soso searched desperately for a way to be released from prison. Three times he petitioned the highest state official (*glavnonachal'stvuiushchii*) in the Caucasus, Prince Grigorii Golitsyn, but to no avail. In one note he pleaded ill health and his duty as a son:

> My worsening cough and the merciless condition of my aged mother, abandoned by her husband twelve years ago and seeing in me the only support in her life, force me to apply for the second time to the Chancellery of the Governor-General with a humble request for freeing me from arrest, under police surveillance. I beg the Chancellery of the Governor-General not to leave me unheeded and to answer my petition.
>
> I. DZHUGASHVILI. NOVEMBER 23, 1902[87]

The police actually had no real evidence on Soso, but he soon made a careless mistake. A few days after his arrest, he threw two notes, addressed to Illarion (Darakhvelidze), from his cell window into the prison courtyard in the vain hope that someone sympathetic would pick them up. One asked that a message be taken to Iremashvili that "Soso Jughashvili has been arrested and asks that you inform his mother of this immediately." Iremashvili was instructed that Keke was to testify that her son had been in Gori all summer and winter and had not left before March 15. His aunt and uncle were also to back up his story. The second note asked Illarion to find out if someone had been sent from Tiflis and to tell him to bring Giorgi Elisabedashvili to Batumi to "direct matters."[88] As Trotsky was later to point out in his biography of Stalin, Soso's rash attempt to establish an alibi and to carry on the movement from his jail cell was a foolish breach of the elementary rules of conspiracy.[89] Two young companions of Jughashvili, workers from the Mantashev plant, made their way to Gori to find Keke and Iremashvili, who was teaching in a church school. Iremashvili was searched, Elisabedashvili arrested and sent to Batumi prison, and Keke Jughashvili was interrogated by the police.[90]

The notes convinced the police that Soso was directly involved in the recent strikes. Captain Jaqeli of the Kutaisi provincial gendarmes determined that Jughashvili and Kandelaki were "the principal leaders of the unrest produced by the Batumi workers." The police believed that Jughashvili had been a member of the Tiflis Social Democratic Committee and had been sent to Batumi as a propagandist where he was referred to as "the workers' teacher." Holding himself apart and unfamiliar to many workers, he made contact through Kandelaki, who was known to be his assistant.[91]

Inmates experienced prison differently. A veteran Caucasian Social Democrat described the tedium and agony that political prisoners experienced at the time of Soso's imprisonment. "As soon as the arrested person arrived in prison, accompanied by gendarmes or the city police, the senior supervisor thoroughly searches him, removing everything he had with him: paper, pencils, date book, wallet, money, tobacco and pouch, penknife, watch, etc." Then the prisoner was locked in a solitary cell, and "a real comedy is arranged for him: the prison doctor carries out anthropological or craniological research. He painstakingly measures the height and all organs of the completely undressed, nude prisoner, noting bodily peculiarities if he has them. . . . After these preliminary comedies, the incarcerated must sit alone in his cell and wait a long time. . . . Days, weeks, months pass without the gendarme or the procurator appearing to question him."

Prisoners lived in dark, narrow cells, often without being allowed to meet or talk with other inmates. Once a day, if they were lucky, they

were permitted to walk alone for ten to fifteen minutes "in a place especially designated for political prisoners." Unlike most prisons in central
Russia, those in Georgia had no closed toilets, only chamber pots. In
cells shared by several prisoners a common barrel (*parasha*) was used.
"Assuming that on one floor of the building there are thirty prisoners,
they have to wait their turn each morning a very long time. This was real
torture." Isolated, cut off from family who were not permitted to visit
for the first few months, the prisoners lived in darkness and damp, dirt
and dust, with mice and insects.[92]

Yet as physically difficult as prison was, the political prisoners by
most accounts bore up well, sustained by commitment to their cause.
The Social Democrat Baron Bibineishvili, who knew Jughashvili from
his days at the Tiflis Observatory in 1898, had oddly positive memories
of prison. "Prison gave us, the people of the underground, leisure time,"
he wrote. "Here we tried to understand what we had gone through,
made new plans, completed our studies, hardened ourselves, learned
about each other." Being incarcerated was simply "involuntary leisure."
The struggle narrowed to resistance to the prison administration and
the guards.[93] If the seminary was a school for revolutionaries, prison
was their university. Kote Tsintsadze was a teenager when he was arrested in Kutaisi. In the six months before his parents were allowed to
vouch for him, he was introduced to "advanced" workers and radical
intellectuals, as well as peasants from Guria, initiated into political economy, and entrusted with letters to carry to comrades outside. "Here for
the first time I saw and felt the power of the liberation movement." He
went on to the manganese mining region of Chiatura where in November 1904 he first met "Koba" Jughashvili and heard his lectures on the
divisions in the party. From then on he and his friend Vano considered
themselves to be Bolsheviks![94]

Memoirs written and published in Stalin's Soviet Union present Stalin as a man who while in prison maintained his revolutionary posture,
remaining close to the other political prisoners but extremely resistant
to the prison authorities. Inmates remembered that Soso kept a strict
regime, rising early, doing exercises, studying German and economics,
and spending much time writing letters. He liked to discuss his reading

with others and to criticize the authors.[95] Separated from the Batumi workers who continued the strike until the third week of June, Soso wrote a number of leaflets for them. "This is how," he wrote, "the factory administration and its protector, the government, greeted us when we appealed for truth and freely fought for our welfare."

> Revenge for blood, for the killing, against such a government that aggressively tramples on our citizenship. Blood for blood to such a lawgiver who tries to enslave and strangle us. Does the government really think it can calm us by force or meet us with bullets? No, its bayonets will not force us to be silent, and their severity will not extinguish our love for freedom. Take heart, brothers, justice is on our side; our strength is with us and our happiness depends on us.[96]

Two months after Soso's arrest the workers finally settled with the Rothschilds, but they received only a small relief payment rather than compensation for the dates lost during the four-month strike. Nevertheless, Soso considered the strike and the demonstrations a great victory for workers.[97] In prison he continued to act as a leader and participated in a number of protests—one against the exarch of Georgia who had come to inspect schools and prisons.[98] For this, he was sent to Kutaisi prison on April 19, 1903, which had a less lax regime than the Batumi jail. Here too he acted as leader and teacher to the politically charged prisoners. Sporting a hood of thin black material, he continued learning German.[99] Rather than addressing other prisoners with the more formal form *vy* (you), Soso insisted on using the familiar *ty* (thou). He mentioned to a fellow prisoner that when the agents of the tsar accompany a condemned man to the gallows, they use the formal form: "Please, come to the scaffold. Sit, and so forth."[100] He organized a demonstration by rebel peasants from Guria who had "sat," as the Russians say, for more than a year without coming to trial. He demanded bunks for the prisoners, who were forced to sleep on the cement floor, and baths twice a month. On July 28, 1903, at 9 a.m., the whole prison erupted. Political prisoners banged on the iron doors, and the noise resonated in the city, until the governor agreed to their demands. But the "politicals" were then separated from the other prisoners and placed in the worst cells in the prison.[101]

Natalia Kirtadze-Sikharulidze remembered that Jughashvili was solicitous of those he saw as comrades. He had once looked into the
women's cell and asked: "Are you bored, comrades?" He sent one of
the prisoners to her and asked that she stand near the window. She
took the prisoner for a police spy and snapped, "Go to the devil, whoever that Soso is, I don't know him." He stood up for her when an inspector hit her on the leg with his sword. That was no way to treat a
political prisoner, he said, especially a woman. On his demand the inspector was removed. Soso was determined to maintain the dignity of
the political prisoners. When he and other "politicals" were being removed to Kutaisi, he protested the shackles: "We are not thieves that
you have to bind our hands." When the prisoners arrived at the Kutaisi
railroad station, he directed that Natalia proceed ahead of the rest so the
people "see that women too are fighting against this lawlessness!" When
Soso heard that Natalia, alone in a separate cell, was crying, he sent her
a piece of bread with a note inside: "Mother Eagle, what do your tears
mean? Could it be that prison has broken you?"[102]

Grigol Uratadze, then a young Social Democrat, later a Menshevik,
remembered Soso's arrival in Kutaisi prison. Nearly every day new prisoners arrived, and those in jail were always anxious to learn what was
going on outside. When the group was brought from Batumi prison, the
inmates met in the prison yard. Jughashvili was the only intellectual
among the new arrivals. The Batumi workers were kept together in what
was known as "the workers' cell," and there he and another prisoner,
Dgebuadze, gave lessons in political economy, reading from Russian
and translating into Georgian the popular work of Aleksandr Bogdanov
on political economy.[103] The prisoners eagerly looked forward to the
evening lessons. Other cells studied the French Revolution, and right
under the eyes of the authorities the prison was turned into a workers'
university. The guards allowed books in the cells for fear of prisoners'
protests, and a mutual interest in keeping the peace maintained correct
relations between prisoners and their keepers. Occasionally, as when a
popular thief was carried off to be executed, protests broke out.

Uratadze remembered the prison not as a particularly unpleasant
experience but rather as a place of learning and solidarity with his fellow

prisoners. During the more than six months he spent close to Stalin in the Kutaisi prison, he saw the young Jughashvili as serious, unusually self-controlled, and misanthropic. "He was a very dry person, even dried out, if one can express it that way. When, for example, we went out for our walk and we all in separate groups headed for this or that corner of the prison yard, he, Stalin, walked alone with his small steps, back and forth, and if someone conversed with him, he opened his mouth in his cold smile and, maybe, said a few words. And by his lack of sociability he attracted the attention of all to himself."[104]

Uratadze never saw Soso lose his temper, but Elisabedashvili, who had been arrested because of Soso's imprudent note, remembered an incident when his pal was outraged. "As I passed Soso's cell, I heard swearing. Soso was infuriated, enraged, and was swearing at the person sitting in his cell, and he hit him several times. All this happened very fast. I saw it through the window. . . . The next day I learned that they had sent a spy to Soso's cell, and the fight was about that. They removed this disagreeable person immediately."[105] Many years later, in the fall of 1946, Stalin told a Georgian actor, a native of Guria, that he had spent idle hours in the Kutaisi prison learning folk songs from prisoners from the western Georgian regions of Guria, Mingrelia, and Imereti. He asked his guest to sing a Gurian song and sang along with him.[106]

While Soso sat in Georgian prisons, the police lost track of exactly where he was, and various officials wrote back and forth, convinced that he was at large but under police surveillance.[107] As his case went up and down the bureaucratic ladder, an official noted that Jughashvili was one of the four leaders of the Batumi Social Democratic Committee, along with Aleksandr Shatilov and an unknown Georgian from near Kazbek, probably Khartishvili (Mokheve). Jughashvili was known by the revolutionary pseudonym, *chopura* (Georgian for "pockmarked").[108] He was not tried together with the twenty-one workers arrested in connection with the March demonstrations. Nor was he mentioned in the indictment. Either there was only circumstantial evidence linking him to the demonstration or a decision had been made to separate the cases of the worker demonstrators and the Social Democrats arrested in Tiflis. The workers were tried in March 1903 and given short jail sentences.

Soso's case was decided "administratively," without a trial. He was sentenced to three years "under local observation" to be served in eastern Siberia. The local authorities asked for a more severe sentence, six years, but the ministry of justice and the emperor signed off on three. Jibladze, Jugeli, and others also received three years, but his senior comrades, Kurnatovskii and Francheski, both received four years. Soso's mother petitioned the authorities to release her son from prison but to no avail.[109] Soso appealed in vain to Prince Golitsyn, the highest civil authority in Caucasia, that he was suffering from consumption, claiming his health was worsening each day.[110] He remained in Kutaisi prison until early November when he was brought back to Batumi for a couple of days. He managed to send a note to Natalia Kirtadze-Sikharulidze, and she and Bebe Loshadze, a relative of Mikha Bochoridze, accompanied him to the ship. Sitting alone on the dock, his hair disheveled, Soso spied the old woman and asked, "Aren't you Mikho's aunt?" "I am," she answered. They talked briefly before the ship's whistle blew, and the exiles were boarded.[111] Some workers found out that Soso was being exiled and collected ten rubles to help him on the way.[112]

Jughashvili was sent into Siberian exile in late November 1903. The young man who left by ship for Siberia—a rather roundabout passage from the tropics to the tundra—was already perceived quite differently by his political allies and opponents. Respected by some and despised by others, he was seen by most as a militant activist. To those who had worked closely with him, he was a man of the people, simple, direct, and deeply committed to the workers. To the Marxist veterans of Georgian Social Democracy, he was a reckless intriguer, ambitious to a fault, and dangerous to the movement. These images would have an extraordinary longevity, reinforced and repeated throughout Stalin's life. Even as Jughashvili re-created his own persona and his official admirers transformed the miscalculation outside the Batumi barracks into a drama of heroism and sacrifice, others constructed their own version of an immature upstart whose ambition had led to unnecessary losses. As he approached his twenty-fifth birthday Jughashvili had achieved a notable reputation among Caucasian revolutionaries and Batumi workers. His second immersion into the revolutionary labor movement had ended dismally, but he was recognized, for better or for worse, as the instigator of one of the most significant revolutionary confrontations of the new century. A Socialist Revolutionary publication equated the Batumi slaughterhouse with other recent examples of tsarist repression: the clashes in Iakutsk, violence in Poltava, Kharkov, Saratov, Odessa, and the famous Obukhov Defense.[113]

Beginning his first journey out of Caucasia, Soso traveled by ship from Batumi to Novorossiisk, on to Rostov-na-Donu, then by train through Tsaritsyn and Samara on the Volga, on to Cheliabinsk in the Urals.[114] The Trans-Siberian railroad ran only as far as Irkutsk, from which the train was ferried across Lake Baikal. From there he moved by sledge another 230 kilometers to Novaia Uda, Balagansk district, Irkutsk Province, a tiny town inhabited by Russians and Buryats, deep in eastern Siberia. Called *etap* (transport under guard) in Russian, Soso's long journey was far easier than those made on foot by prisoners a generation earlier, the trek familiar to generations of readers acquainted with the exiled Decembrists of the 1820s or the unfortunates depicted by the American traveler George Kennan.[115] In the late 1920s Stalin told his family an extraordinary story about his long passage:

> During the *etap* it was my fate to come up against a psychotic safe-cracker, a giant of a man almost two meters tall. I made some harmless remark to him; perhaps I suggested that he shouldn't take so much tobacco from my tobacco pouch. The exchange ended in a fight. The idiot forced me to the ground, breaking several of my ribs. No one tried to help me. As I was coming round, it occurred to me that a politician must always make efforts to win allies. I spent the remainder of the journey whispering to the other non-political prisoners what this particular individual had been saying about them to the guards in one of the transit prisons. One night, towards the end of the journey, he finally got what was coming to him. The prisoners I had been stirring up threw a coat over his head and proceeded to beat the hell out of him. The safe-cracker from Kharkov had no idea about the identity of his attackers. He had even less idea about who had put them up to it.[116]

Soso reached his destination on November 27 in subzero weather, something he had never experienced before. He found lodging in the home of a poor peasant, Marta Litvintseva, where he stayed just over a month. Set in a hollow under Mount Kitkai, the village of Novaia Uda was divided into a poorer lower part called Zabolote (the Marsh) and an upper section where the better-off peasants and merchants lived. Soso stayed in one of the two rooms in a hut in Zabolote.[117] He had no money, and the state payment he was supposed to receive did not arrive. He almost immediately attempted to escape, but he was still dressed *po-kavkazski* (as a Caucasian), with his light coat, shoes with galoshes instead of the warm felt *valenki* (boots) that native Siberians or *chaldoni* (Russians living in Siberia) wore. He made it as far as the town of Balagansk, 70 *versts* (just over 46 miles) away, but in the dead of the Siberian winter his ears and nose were frostbitten. Abram Gusinskii, a fellow exile, heard a knock on the door. "Who is it?" he asked, and to his surprise he heard a familiar voice. "Open up, Abram, it's me, Soso." "A frozen, ice-covered Soso came in. For the Siberian winter he was very unwisely dressed: a felt cloak, a light Caucasian hat (*papakha*), and a foppish Caucasian hood (*bashlyk*)." He stayed a few days to warm up. Gusinskii's wife and daughter admired the *bashlyk*, and Soso in true Caucasian fashion made a present of it.[118] A few weeks later, on January 5, 1904, he dressed more warmly and fled again. This time he prepared a forged document signed by one of the Siberian superintendents affirming that he was supposedly an agent of the superintendent.[119] He convinced a local carter, who like others was angry at the police superintendent, that if he took him to the railroad station at Zimnaia he would lodge a complaint against the difficult official with an acquaintance of his. The carter agreed but demanded payment in vodka at every stop along the way. The trip took several days, with temperatures of 40 below. Soso was wrapped in a fur coat, but the driver brazenly unbuttoned his coat despite the frost and wind. Soso later told a friend, "His body clearly was full of spirit. A hearty people."[120] The trek on to the railhead at Irkutsk took several weeks, and then he sped by train back to European Russia in a week.[121] A suspicious person, possibly a police spy, spotted him on the train. Soso coolly stepped off the train at a station, approached a gendarme, showed him his fake identity card made out to a Siberian police superintendent, and demanded that the "spy" be arrested. "The gendarme detained the suspect, and at that moment the train pulled off, carrying away Comrade Soso."[122]

The police report on Soso carefully described his physical characteristics:

> Height: 2 arsh. 4½ versh. [roughly 5 feet 4 inches], average build that produces the impression of an ordinary person, hair on his head dark chestnut, mustache and beard chestnut, straight hair, without a part, eyes dark brown, average height, normal head size, straight forehead, not tall, long straight nose, long dark face covered with pockmarks from smallpox, the front molar on the right side of his lower jaw is missing, moderate height, sharp chin, quiet voice, average size ears, ordinary gait, a birthmark on his left ear, the second and third toes on his left foot are webbed.[123]

An ordinary man, not very different from others, Soso successfully eluded the police on the long way home. The ease with which he escaped gave rise to speculation that he had been connected to, even employed by, the tsarist secret services—that is, that he was an agent of the dreaded *Okhrana*. Such stories were widespread among Stalin's opponents—Georgian Mensheviks and anti-Communist Western journalists—but those archivists and historians who have worked in the tsarist police files have conclusively shown that these accounts were false, based on ideological wishful thinking rather than on any evidence. Soso's escape was more typical of political exiles than exceptional. Tsarist Russia was a vast continental country seriously undergoverned and underpoliced. In his memoir, *My Life*, Lev Trotskii (Leon Trotsky), who had escaped from Irkutsk Province the year before Soso, relates how common such escapes were at the time:

> The exiles were no longer willing to stay in their places of confinement, and there was an epidemic of escapes. . . . In almost every village there were individual peasants who as youths had come under the influence of the older generation of revolutionaries. They would

carry the "politicals" away secretly in boats, in carts, or on sledges, and pass them along from one to another. The police in Siberia were as helpless as we were. The vastness of the country was an ally, but an enemy as well. It was very hard to catch a runaway, but the chances were that he would be drowned in the river or frozen to death in the primeval forests.[124]

By the time he arrived in Batumi at the end of 1901, Soso Jughashvili had made his choice about his life's work: he was a professional revolutionary. He had consciously and confidently chosen a life of risk and possible imprisonment or death when other options were still open to him. His deepest motives remain obscure, but a picture emerges of an ambitious, impatient young man who had become embittered by his lot in life. His dominant emotion, evident both in memoirs of his youth and his own writings, appears to be resentment—the sense that he was deprived of what justly should have been his, while others had more than they deserved. His early romanticism and idealism ran up against the harsh impositions and insults at school and seminary. His curiosity and intelligence led him to the alternative education that the Russian intelligentsia and the first Georgian Marxists professed. Therein lay the promise of liberation from the social insignificance and ethnic inferiority imprinted on him by the imperial setting into which he had been born.

Soso's choice was neither the most self-interested nor the safest; it certainly held no guarantee of success or even long life. As a boy and an adolescent he took moral and political questions seriously, first as an Orthodox seminarian and then as a political rebel. Whether from psychic wounds that demanded revenge or ideological commitments bound tightly to utopian visions of a better human existence, Soso had concluded that his future lay with the generation that identified with an emancipated Russia, without tsars and capitalists. There was a way out: history and Marxist science provided both a path and an agent to turn the intolerable world upside down. Reason and emotion worked together to produce powerful impulses to take risks, endure hardships in order to punish the unjust and lift up the oppressed. Power would devolve to those must humiliated by the present order, people like him-self. In Soso's evolution personality, circumstances, and experience—emotional preferences as well as rational, self-interested choices—combined to shape the choices that he made. In contrast to what some psychohistorians have claimed, revolution is not pathology but a political alternative, a choice, among others.[125]

The young Ioseb Jughashvili had moved from religion to revolution, from the safety of the seminary to the dangers of the political underground. His youthful poetry and his identification with Koba combined both a sense of immediate injustice and the possibility for radical improvement with a cold realization that it was necessary to use violence against those who used violence to protect the status quo. He might have begun as a "Communist of the heart," but the vicissitudes of his early revolutionary career, particularly his baptism of fire in Batumi, forged a "Communist of the head." His rebellion was directed not only against the social and political order in which he lived but more particularly it took aim at the sanctified figures of authority that stood in his way—the priests in the seminary and later the high priests of the very movement in which he thrived: Plekhanov in Russia and Zhordania in Georgia. Marxism provided both a frame through which the present and the future could be viewed as well as a means to the end—a movement that linked intellectuals with workers in a struggle for power. His first models came from fiction—Rustaveli's knights and the mountaineer outlaw Koba—then from everyday experience. His comrade-in-arms Lado Ketskhoveli was the first in a series of heroic figures that Jughashvili would admire and emulate. Another was just emerging far from the Caucasus and Siberia, at the Second Congress of the newly formed Russian Social Democratic Workers' Party.

THE MAKING OF A BOLSHEVIK

8

ON THE MARGINS

I was repelled by the very qualities that would strengthen him . . .
namely, the narrowness of his interests, his pragmatism, his
psychological coarseness and the special cynicism of the provincial
who has been liberated from his prejudices by Marxism but who has
not replaced them with a philosophical outlook that has been
thoroughly thought out and mentally absorbed.

—LEV TROTSKY, *MOIA ZHIZN': OPYT BIOGRAFII* [*MY LIFE:
AN ATTEMPT AT AN AUTOBIOGRAPHY*] (1929)

He unquestionably loved to dominate, to lead, to rule over, to give out
authoritative orders. He surrounded himself exclusively with people
who bowed before him and submitted in everything to his authority:
he could not stand others who were different, and others could not
bear him very much, even among Bolsheviks.

—RAZHDEN ARSENIDZE, "IZ VOSPOMINANII O STALINE"
["FROM MEMOIRS ABOUT STALIN"] (1963)

While the young Soso Jughashvili languished in Batumi and Kutaisi
prisons and then traveled to Siberia, the political organizations of which
he was part underwent momentous changes. He was in a movement
that was about to become a party, yet he was cut off from that world. For
two years, isolated in prison and later thousands of miles from the Caucasus, the young revolutionary received only the most fragmentary reports about the efforts and ultimate failure to found a unified party at
the Second Congress of the Russian Social Democratic Workers' Party
(RSDRP).

At the turn of the century Marxism and Social Democracy were at one and the same time ideologies, movements, and political cultures. Participants subscribed, within limits, to ways of thinking and ways of behaving, or at least to a frame within which they might argue about ideas they shared. If they strayed too far from the boundaries of the ideology, or failed to convince others of the need to extend those boundaries, they found themselves outside the movement. This political culture stretched and shifted and at a certain point split into distinct, antagonistic cultures. Unable to live under the same roof, Russian Social Democracy ultimately set up separate households with different addresses: Bolshevism and Menshevism. In the nearly two years from his arrest in April 1902 until his return to the Caucasus in mid-January 1904, Jughashvili was unable to participate fully in Social Democratic activity. It is doubtful he yet knew of Lenin's provocative polemic *What Is to Be Done?*, which had been smuggled into Russia in March 1902.

Stalinist sources make much of Soso's ability to direct the revolution from behind bars, but in fact he was largely cut off from the inner workings of the party and the burgeoning labor movement, as they were both, separately and together, going through one of the most significant formative moments of their early existence. He may have learned of the growing number of political demonstrations in 1902 that gave way to a wave of strikes in southern Russia in 1903. In the summer of 1903, while the leading Social Democrats from Russia traveled westward, first to Brussels and then to London, for the second congress of their party, more than thirty thousand oil workers and railroaders went on strike in Baku. Most services in the city were brought to a standstill by July, and Social Democrats organized mass meetings that drew thousands of workers.[1] As the Baku strike wound down, the Tiflis Committee called a general strike in support of Baku, but this ill-organized action was criticized as "adventurous" by moderate Social Democrats from Batumi.[2] A strike in Batumi was more successful and was followed by walkouts in Poti and Chiatura. Soldiers fired on workers in the town of Khashuri, killing more than a dozen. Though the government managed to secure an uneasy calm in the towns by the end of July, the strikes of the summer opened new opportunities for the Social Democrats. By late 1903 the tiny party of Marxist intellectuals and worker activists had become the most influential force among urban workers throughout the empire. In South Caucasia they were particularly powerful among rail-road men and oil workers and, to the surprise of the more orthodox Marxists, among the peasantry of Western Georgia.

The rapid expansion of labor activity infused workers with a new confidence and increased resentment against manipulation by intel-lectuals. Once again, the wave of strikes in summer 1903 resulted from worker initiative rather than the work of Social Democrats.[3] Within the tiny Batumi organization that Soso had left behind, the tensions be-tween socialist intellectuals and workers strained relations. While Jughashvili was still in Batumi prison, local Social Democrats discussed the reorganization of underground work in the city. Isidore Ramishvili and Chkheidze, who had never appreciated Soso's interventions, invited Khartishvili (Mokheve) from Tiflis to come once again to help the lo-cals decide on the next step. While still in prison in Batumi, Soso prompted Kandelaki to invite Giorgi Elisabedashvili and D. Gham-bashidze to come to Batumi, to Mokheve's dismay. A roughness, a rude-ness, characterized the young men who were risking their lives in the labor movement. The discussions were divisive; the "leading organ-ization" split; and Soso's close friend Kandelaki came to blows with Mokheve in Kuridze's house.[4] About this time some Batumi workers sent a letter to the Petersburg Committee asking its mediation on sev-eral key issues.[5] The Batumi workers wanted to know if intellectuals should not limit themselves to "peaceful circle propaganda, while the inspiration and leadership of the movement was undertaken by the workers themselves." Were intellectuals, as the more conscious and revolutionary-minded part of the population, to march ahead of the workers "during street demonstrations, local and regional, factory and plant disturbances and other open protests against the exploitation by capitalists and the willfulness of the government?" In a situation where the main means of protest were political, how were demonstrators to act in the face of police repression? Should workers arm themselves with guns, knives, and *khanjalebi* (Caucasian daggers), or should they be content with sticks and stones? The Batumi workers recognized the need for an all-Russian party organization with a single, leading central committee, and they turned to Petersburg because they were unclear after the disastrous demonstration in March about tactics and unable to get satisfactory answers from their local intellectuals. The Petersburg Committee answered the Batumi workers by rejecting the idea that workers and intellectuals should be distinguished within the party. The party would be led by the most conscious, developed elements, whether they come from the intelligentsia or the working class. Petersburg declined, however, to make a recommendation about arming demonstrators, suggesting instead that the power of demonstrations came from their purposefulness and organization.

Soso's brief sojourn in Batumi left traces long after he had been exiled. The bloody days in March had turned some Batumi workers toward political, in contrast to purely economic, action.[6] Mirian Khomeriki, a worker at the Rothschild plant, tried to assassinate the factory director, Vensheidt. Some workers marked May Day for the first time in Batumi, not with a demonstration but by stopping work. The revival of the labor movement stimulated the more passive Social Democrats of Batumi to form an organizational committee to build up the underground. Three intellectuals sat with three worker members, and sometime at the end of 1902 or early in 1903 they formally constituted a Batumi Committee of the RSDRP.[7] On March 9, 1903, the committee made its presence felt for the first time in a demonstration to mark the first anniversary of the Batumi shootings. The ill-fated demonstration that Soso Jughashvili had instigated was taking on mythic dimensions. A crowd of three thousand workers, many of them armed, accompanied the lawyers defending those indicted for participating in the March days to the railroad station.[8] In June the town was placed under increased military protection, and in December five hundred additional soldiers were brought in. Dozens of workers were exiled to their villages, a move that proved to be a dangerous mistake for the tsarist authorities. The workers, themselves recent migrants from the countryside, infected their friends and relatives with revolutionary fervor. Within months a massive peasant movement spread through Guria and other parts of Western Georgia.

The proliferation of Social Democratic committees and other groups, like the Tiflis-based Union of Armenian Social Democrats, convinced the Caucasian Marxists that the time had come to form an all-Caucasian united committee to coordinate activity. In the latter half of March 1903, fifteen delegates, representing local committees and editorial boards, gathered in Tiflis for what was later referred to as the "first conference of Caucasian Social Democratic Organizations." The most controversial issue was the question of appointing or electing party organizations. Even though all those attending considered themselves supporters of *Iskra*, many were not convinced by Lenin's arguments for appointed committees. In a long and heated debate Pilipe Makharadze and Mikha Tskhakaia, both of whom would in the near future become staunch followers of Lenin, defended the practice of co-opting members onto committees, and in the end the Caucasian Social Democrats broke with the past practice of the Georgian movement that had usually tried to adhere to the principle of elections. Fourteen voted for the *Iskra* position, and only Zhordania voted against.[9]

The conference went on to select a Caucasian Union Committee (*Kavkazskii soiuznyi komitet*) as the leading party center in the region. Of its nine members only one, Mikha Bochoridze, was a worker. The others were intellectuals.[10] Staunchly *Iskra*ite, the Caucasian Union was deliberately conceived to expand the Social Democratic movement from its urban and Russo-Georgian bases to include all the nationalities of Caucasia. Although Georgians outnumbered the other adherents to the movement, two of the three intellectuals chosen as delegates to the forthcoming Second Congress of the RSDRP were Armenian: Arshak Zurabov from Batumi (though he had no connection with the movement there) and Bogdan Knuniants from Baku. The third, who would prove to be somewhat of a loose cannon, was Diomide Topuridze from Tiflis.[11] At its moment of organizational consolidation, Caucasian Social Democracy had placed the direction of the movement firmly in the hands of party intellectuals and effectively marginalized the leading workers. The place of the workers' in the movement, however, had hardly been resolved. It would arise again and tear Social Democracy in two.

THE SECOND CONGRESS

When the RSDRP congress delegates gathered in Brussels in late July, the majority of Russia's Social Democratic committees (excluding those affiliated with the Jewish Bund) supported *Iskra*'s position. They were convinced that the nascent working class, with their assistance and leadership, would play the principal revolutionary role in the overthrow of tsarist autocracy. But they could not agree on what the exact initiating role of Marxist intellectuals should be. Were they merely to support or more assertively lead? Should they encourage the workers' spontaneous activity or restrain their undisciplined eruptions? Within both Russian and Georgian society, Marxist intellectuals represented themselves not only as a European, Westernized cultural alternative to the more brutal aspects of life in the Russian Empire, but also as examples of dedication and sacrifice. Among the readers of *Iskra*, there was a general understanding for the need to combat localism and "amateurism" in the movement and to promote greater organization and discipline. Yet even as political activism throughout Russian society livened in 1903, Social Democratic leaders, particularly Lenin, sensed new dangers to their movement. The liberals around the newspaper *Osvobozhdenie* (Liberation) and the local and regional assemblies (*zemstva*) attracted many intellectuals and threatened to divert political energies into a more reformist course. The tsarist government was actively organizing official "police unions," the so-called *Zubatovshchina*, to contain workers in organizations congenial to the authorities. And the neo-Populists and their new Socialist Revolutionary Party, with its advocacy of peasant socialism and political terrorism as a legitimate weapon in the struggle, were proving seductive in many parts of Russia and Ukraine (though not in Georgia) to many potential recruits to Social Democracy.

Iskra had convinced its readers that the political struggle had to take precedence over the purely economic. Lenin set out to consolidate that victory and go beyond it to reconstitute the party as a kind of political army, with local committees carrying out the commands of the central leadership. The first major question to be debated was the right of nationality organizations, like the Jewish Bund, to represent exclusively a given nationality. One of the oldest and most successful socialist organizations in tsarist Russia, the Bund, founded in 1897, predated the RSDRP by a year and was one of the groups most heavily involved in the founding of the Russian party. Competing with the Zionists for the loyalty of the Jews in Russia and Poland, the Bundists were determined to maintain autonomous organizations, operating largely in Yiddish, to direct their activities among Jewish workers. Bund leaders wanted their organization to represent the "Jewish proletariat" within the Russian party, although other Social Democratic organizations could operate among Jewish workers. But the leading "Russian" Social Democrats, many of them of Jewish origins, like Iulii Martov, Pavel Akselrod, and the young Lev Trotsky, joined with Plekhanov and Lenin in opposing separate national organizations within the party. Where the Bund wanted a federal relationship with the party, most Social Democrats preferred a more centralized party without formally autonomous organizations within it. The delegates from the Caucasus came out forcefully against the Bund's position, which to them smacked too much of nationalism.[12] Exaggerating somewhat the degree of harmony among workers of different ethnicities, the delegate from Baku, Knuniants, held up the Caucasian party committees as examples of multinational cooperation, in which workers of different nationalities with diverse languages worked together. "I consider each member of the party to be a representative of the whole proletariat of all Russia," he proclaimed.[13] After four days of intense debate, the congress voted, 41 to 5, to reject the Bund's right to autonomous organization within the party.[14]

At the 1903 congress (which was forced to move from Brussels to London), delegates of various nationalities—the Armenian Zurabov, the Georgian Diomide Topuridze, the Jew Trotsky—casually labeled the Bundists "nationalists" for their insistence on a privileged role in organizing workers of a single nationality. But this most offensive of labels, which was often linked with terms of opprobrium like "bourgeois" or, worse, "petty bourgeois," was not applied to the supra-national position of the "Russians," who were marked as above or beyond nationality. Here nationalism was linked to specific non-Russians, while the approved stance of internationalism applied to those of any nationality who favored multinationality, joint work in common committees, and a centralized (which in practice could mean Russian-dominated) party.

The debate over the Bund was the first occasion on which the so-called national question engaged, and divided, Russia's Social Democrats. Often marginalized, the issue of how to deal with the non-Russian nationalities would not go away, and ultimately it would prove to be fundamental to the formation of the Soviet Union, the very shape that the socialist federation took, and its ultimate demise seventy-four years later. No other issue would define as powerfully Stalin's role in the party. A decade after this initial debate Lenin would assign him the task of elaborating the Bolshevik position on nationalism, its origins and consequences.

In their personal identification most Social Democrats effaced or suppressed their ethnicity. Marxist political culture insisted that nationality was less significant than social class, which was far more indicative of a person's affinities and attitudes. Yet in the Russian Empire nationality and class overlapped and reinforced one another.[15] Though far from these debates at the congress, Soso Jughashvili's primary identity was still as a Georgian Social Democrat, a Marxist *intelligent* of worker origin to be certain, but still embedded in a Georgian milieu. He had not yet resolved the tension between an ethnic sense of self and an "internationalist" Marxist. But the movement to which he adhered was in its practice and ideology determinately internationalist and assimilationist. Men and women like Soso from the margins of society and the peripheries of the empire found a conducive environment within Social Democracy that accepted them and declared them ethnically and socially equal to all others. Created in an imperial setting of legally imposed discrimination, the party offered a social space in which those discriminated against became empowered.[16] A Georgian like Soso did not, of course, become culturally Russian (*russkii*), but took on an all-Russian (*rossiiskii*) identity, an imperial sensibility that aimed to preserve the all-Russian state and its vast territories as much as possible while accepting the diversity of its peoples and their rights to self-expression.

In reviewing the party program the congress delegates turned from consideration of nationality within the party to the plank supporting "broad local and regional self-government." Martov spoke in favor of self-government for such border regions as Finland, Poland, Lithuania, and the Caucasus that "by their way of life and composition of the population differ from strictly [ethnic] Russian localities." Zhordania, who had arrived at the congress late, seconded the idea, as did the other delegates from the Caucasus.[17] Knuniants pointed out that even the tsarist state had recognized differences between central Russia and the borderlands: "Guaranteeing national culture does not contradict the interests of the proletariat of Russia; [in fact] it completely protects the workers from the influence of such [nationalist] elements."[18] Suspicious of any concessions to nationality, Lenin offered an amendment to remove "regional" from the plank, but his motion was defeated and Martov's version adopted. More controversial was Zhordania's motion on establishing equality of languages in all schools, institutions, and meetings, which won by only one vote. The top party leaders—Lenin, Martov, Plekhanov, and Trotsky—voted against it.[19] The delegates approved the general principle of "the right to self-determination for all nations entering into the body of the state," but rejected an amendment that added "and freedom for their cultural development."[20] Last, they approved an amendment by Trotsky that called for teaching in native languages on demand of the population.[21] With little enthusiasm for nationalism, or even much awareness of its elemental power, the Social Democrats made minimal concessions to national culture at this foundational moment. Their policy toward non-Russians was ambivalent, tepid, and lacking in precision. Even their support of the principle of national self-determination was ambiguous. While it recognized each people's right to national distinction, there was at this point no clear assertion of a right to political sovereignty. Only much later would the issue of forming independent national states arise, and Social Democrats would disagree bitterly over whether to support such demands.

Through the debate on the Bund and the party program, the *Iskra* bloc held firm, but when the congress turned to consider "organization regulations," deep divisions rumbled to the surface. Fundamentally, this was a discussion about what kind of political party the RSDRP would be. Lenin's view was embodied in his laconic definition of party membership: "Everyone is considered a member of the party who accepts the party program and who supports the party by personal participation in one of the party organizations."[22] Lenin's close associate and fellow member of the *Iskra* editorial board, Martov, favored a looser, more flexible definition of party membership. "Everyone is considered to belong to the RSDRP who accepts its program, supports the party by material means, and affords it regular personal assistance under the leadership of one of its organizations."[23] Behind these subtle distinctions was a fundamental difference between two ideas of a revolutionary political party. For Lenin the party would include both organizations of full-time revolutionaries and workers' circles (endorsed by the Social Democratic committees), but the party would primarily be an instrument to foster socialist consciousness in the working class, which in turn would eventually lead all of oppositional society. For Martov the party was to be broad, open to all supporters of the socialist cause, and distinct from the tight organization of revolutionaries that might be included within it. Martov's older ally, Akselrod, put it succinctly: "Given that we are a party of a class, we must think about not leaving outside the party people who consciously, even if not completely actively, are affiliated with this party."[24] A distinction had to be made between members of organizations, some of which had to be conspiratorial, and the much wider mass party of workers made up of more than Lenin's "leading ranks" of workers and intellectuals.

Lenin fought hard for his position. A broad party would invite all kinds of "opportunists" into its ranks, he claimed.[25] A narrow party would be able to lead effectively a whole range of various kinds of workers' organizations, from the most conspiratorial to the most "loose." He wanted real control of party members and organizations in the hands of the Central Committee. Zhordania opposed Lenin: who would be left in the party if we exclude all our "soldiers"; we would be an army of generals without an army.[26] But the grand old man of the party, Plekhanov, came down on Lenin's side. He mocked Akselrod's fear that some professor who considered himself a Social Democrat would be left out of the party by quoting Engels: "When you deal with a professor, you must first prepare yourself for the very worst." Better to keep out intellectuals contaminated with "bourgeois individualism" and representing "every kind of opportunism."[27] This anti-intellectual, anti-individualist theme that both Lenin and Stalin adhered to reverberated through the future debates of Russian Social Democracy, a movement led, ironically, by highly idiosyncratic intellectuals.

As esoteric and disconnected as the discussions at the Second Congress have seemed to distant observers, they actually touched upon the most vital concerns of a rapidly expanding social movement: how to coordinate and sustain collective action. Lenin wanted the party to be more closely identified with the organization of Social Democratic professionals, while Martov wanted the party identified with the labor movement more broadly. In a close vote (28 to 22, with one abstention) the delegates adopted Martov's formulation.[28] The *Iskra* bloc had broken, and Martov's followers, along with the Bundists and Economists, now outnumbered Lenin's supporters.[29] Their victory, however, proved to be fleeting. When the Bund delegates, followed by two *ekonomisty*, walked out of the congress a few days later, Lenin's minority was suddenly transformed into a bare majority. For the next year or so the loose factions were referred to simply as the "majority" and the "minority," but they proved to be remarkably durable. Soon the Leninists would be known as "Bolsheviks" (*bol'sheviki*, "majorityites") and the Martovites as "Mensheviks" (*men'sheviki*, "minorityites"). The loyalties of many to faction and faction leader grew over time more fervent than to the party as a whole.

Lenin met with his supporters, whom he regarded as the "hards" in contrast to Martov's "softs," and worked to solidify their dominance in the central party institutions: the editorial board of *Iskra* (referred to as the central organ, or CO), which had functioned for years as the principal ideological and organizational executive of the party; the Council of the Party; and the Central Committee (CC) to be elected at the congress.[30] With the congress divided against itself, Lenin's majority faction chose a three-man editorial board for *Iskra*—Martov, Lenin, and Plekhanov—eliminating Akselrod, Aleksandr Potresov, and Vera

Zasulich, all of whom had sided with Martov. But Martov refused to serve on the reduced board, and the two factions left the congress unreconciled and bitter. Lenin was bewildered by Martov's behavior on the editorial board. He had earlier discussed with Martov and Potresov the need for a new editorial board. Even Martov's sister, Lidia, and her husband, Fedor Dan, were perplexed and thought that Lenin's position more closely followed the original *Iskra* line.[31] Subsequent efforts by Lenin to end the factional struggle—a conciliatory letter to Potresov, his willingness to reconstitute the old editorial board—were rebuffed by the Martovites, who saw their defeat as a triumph of extreme centralism and a threat to the "self-activity" of the workers. Within a month Lenin turned to his followers with talk of "war against the minority" and the need to fill the party committees "with our own people." Martov boycotted *Iskra* and soon set out to replace Lenin's supporters with his own in the central party institutions.[32] In this bitter struggle for dominance in the party, both the self-proclaimed "minority" and "majority" blamed the other for the split. Each claimed that it held true to the old *Iskra* positions. Personal sensibilities, hurt feelings, and a sense of betrayal intensified real political differences. A year later Akselrod wrote to his friend Karl Kautsky, the most revered figure in the German Social Democratic Party, accusing Lenin of "Bonapartist methods together with a healthy dose of Nechaevan ruthlessness" and of being a man determined to create his own "administrative dictatorship" in the party no matter what.[33] What had begun as a dispute over defining party membership had escalated into a bitter battle of personalities over the very nature of the movement.

MAKING A MOVEMENT

While delegates debated in the summer heat in Belgium and England, and Soso Jughashvili languished in a Batumi prison, oil workers in Baku and railroad men and shop workers in Tiflis were in the streets in massive protests and strikes. Strikes spread to Batumi, Khashuri, and Chiatura in Georgia, and massive crowds shouted political slogans—"Down with Autocracy," "Long Live Freedom," and "Proletarians of all

Countries, Unite"—and waved red flags. Tiflis workers had already adopted and adapted the practices of Russian and European workers. If a single worker was fired in Tiflis, the whole workforce went out on strike. If someone was killed, an elaborate funeral-demonstration was held. When a comrade was sent into exile, people saw him off at the station. Such rituals, along with the use of powerful symbols like red flags, mobilized and sustained the passions of the participants. Anger at perceived injustice and hope that their actions would improve their lives brought workers out onto the streets and motivated them to risk their lives and fight against what at times looked like overwhelming force. Social Democrats and other revolutionary activists framed everyday grievances in particular ways, stressing the injustice of the existing order and its potential fragility.[34] Once blood was spilled, the bonds forged by emotion grew tighter. Rather than isolated, individual acts, strikes, protests, and demonstrations were conceived and explained as a "move-ment," something tied to events and people in Russia, Europe, and America.

In tsarist Russia the very forms of worker organization and protest that had become the currency of labor expression in Western Europe, namely strikes and trade unions, were illegal. Almost any action by workers, particularly collective actions, immediately took on political significance, a challenge to the law and the political order. Without le-gitimate avenues for dealing with grievances, even a demand for im-proved wages could escalate quickly into radical politics. The Social Democrats reinforced the idea that the economic and material discon-tents produced by capitalism were intimately connected to the auto-cratic political system. Bosses and officials, bureaucrats and the police were all part of the repressive apparatus that demanded deference and obedience from its subjects. The regime resisted thinking about workers as anything more than displaced peasants. Through their acts of resis-tance, workers were muscling their way into a kind of citizenship, de-manding recognition of their rights and some voice in their fate. The clash between an inflexible political structure and a newly emerging social class repeatedly exploded into violence, bloodshed, and eventu-ally revolution.

The first years of the twentieth century were years of increasing social violence in Caucasia. Strikes and demonstrations were met with gunfire by the police and army. The movement, however, was too widespread and disjointed for the Social Democrats to control. Shooting, killing, and dying were becoming routine in Caucasia, and a habit of imperial repression and violent resistance was accepted as a fact of life. Caucasian Social Democrats suffered many martyrs in the July 1903 strikes, but the most important victim of the police was Soso's friend and comrade Lado Ketskhoveli. The principal organizer of the Baku Social Democrats, active in the underground printing operation there for *Iskra*, Ketskhoveli was known to Lenin and his wife, Nadezhda Krupskaia, as "the father of Nina" (the Baku printing press). Hot tempered and militant, he shocked a meeting of Tiflis Social Democrats when someone suggested bringing onto the new Tiflis Committee an intellectual from a self-education circle. "This is no time to study philosophy!" he shouted. "Now the main thing is to know how to stick a dagger into the heart of an enemy!"[35] Arrested in September 1902, Ketskhoveli was transferred to the fortress-prison Metekhi, high on a Tiflis promontory overlooking the Kura. There he and his fellow Social Democrats read and discussed Lenin's *What Is to Be Done?*, and most of them—even future Mensheviks—agreed with the analysis.[36] The prisoners carried on a war of nerves with their jailors, flouting prison rules, talking to each other from the windows, cursing, and throwing things at them. They protested the filth, the bugs, the damp, and, when the guards closed their windows with shutters because of their insubordination, they complained about the lack of fresh air and light. To the annoyance of the wardens prisoners spoke in their "native dialects," which could not be understood by the authorities. Ketskhoveli spent his time drawing caricatures of his jailers, organizing fellow inmates, and signaling tobacco workers across the Kura.[37] His rebellious nature endeared him to his fellow prisoners, but he was feared and hated by the guards who considered him the leader of the rowdy prisoners.[38] On the morning of August 17, 1903, he was particularly bold, taunting the sentry: "You walk back and forth, corner to corner, you fool." He was warned three times to step back from his window and cease provoking the guard in the courtyard. He refused and taunted the guard, Dergilev, to shoot: "You would not dare to shoot; we are not dogs!" Even as the guard took aim, Ketskhoveli stood his ground. A single shot killed him almost instantly.[39]

"This was the first prison murder of a political inmate, and the news resounded like a clap of thunder throughout Georgia and the rest of the Caucasus."[40] Almost immediately the local organization published a brochure on Ketskhoveli extolling his virtues.[41] His personal commitment and ultimate sacrifice were seen as models of revolutionary integrity, and he was turned into a legendary figure. In the estimation of Soviet historians, Ketskhoveli was a Bolshevik before there were Bolsheviks, the kind of revolutionary militant who would have emerged as an important and influential party cadre. Streets would be named in his memory. Fatefully, he was the first of several Caucasian revolutionaries who were more prominent than the young Jughashvili but who fell in the struggle and opened the way for him to advance in the party.

Soso learned of Ketskhoveli's death while in Kutaisi prison, expressing what a great loss this was for the movement and gain for the "gendarmes." "That is why they killed him. But the death of one Ketskhoveli," he proclaimed, "will give birth to hundreds and thousands of new Ketskhovelis."[42] In early 1904 Soso reached Tiflis, a fugitive sought by the police. The future Menshevik David Sagirashvili remembered that when he met Soso at the home of Vladimir Akhmeteli sometime after his return: "Stalin was very angry and called for vengeance. His hatred of the Russians grew stronger, for he considered Ketskhoveli his teacher of revolutionary action."[43] Now a wanted man, Jughashvili had to move cautiously in Georgia. He dressed in a soldier's uniform.[44] Once it was noticed that the young revolutionary had fled from exile, the political police in Tiflis noted his name down in the list of "active participants in the Social Democratic organization that are reviving their activity."[45] Reaching his hometown, he hid in the house of Giorgi Geladze, his mother's brother. A neighbor who lived near the Jughashvilis, Maria Kitiashvili, visited the Geladze house a few evenings. Jughashvili asked her about her studies in school, advised her to read books on natural science rather than religious books, tousled her hair, and joked a lot.

Years later Kitiashvili reported that "Comrade Stalin's mother lived in constant worry about her son and cried about her dear Soso—where is he now, have the gendarmes taken him, what is he doing at the moment."[46] In an important sense Keke's Soso no longer existed. Even before her son returned to the Caucasus, he had become an outlaw who had chosen revolution as a profession. Around this time, at a moment when revolution was in the air, to friends and opponents alike he became known as Koba.[47]

9

BECOMING BOLSHEVIK

Comrade Koba did not impress one as a deeply educated Marxist, a
theorist in the true sense of that word, but what he knew had deep,
strong, and spreading roots. Besides that, he had the ability to use
what little he had skillfully and ably. The lack of an oratorical gift was
compensated a hundredfold by his exceptional polemical mastery with
which he fell upon his opponent and parried blows. . . . With the cool
composure and calm of a surgeon he logically, incontrovertibly showed
that [the Mensheviks] were not Marxists but Bernsteinians, petty-
bourgeois reformists, falsifiers and vulgarizers of Marxism.

—SERGO KAVTARADZE, "VOSPOMINANIIA" ["MEMOIRS"]
(PROBABLY WRITTEN IN THE 1930S BUT
KEPT IN THE ARCHIVES)

Class struggle, so central to the Marxists' understanding of historical
change, was only part of the toxic mix that threatened Russian rule at
the edges of empire in the first years of the twentieth century. In the
multiethnic mosaic of South Caucasia, Armenians, Georgians, and the
local Muslims had their own aspirations and complaints. Armenians
were angry at the tsar's order of June 12, 1903, to confiscate the estates
belonging to their national church. The Armenian Revolutionary Federation, known by its Armenian name *Dashnaktsutyun*, organized resistance. Any clergyman who gave in to the state's orders was assassinated.
On October 14, 1903, three Armenian militants, tied to the Armenian
Marxist *Hnchak* (Bell) Party, attacked the tsar's top official in the Caucasus, Prince Grigorii Golitsyn, stabbing him in the face, head, and
hand. His wife and nearby soldiers fought off the attackers, and the as-
sailants were killed. Eight months later Golitsyn left the Caucasus for

Russia proper. To replace him the emperor sent a trusted ally, Count Illarion Ivanovich Vorontsov-Dashkov, in the spring of 1905, elevating the position to the exalted rank of viceroy of the Caucasus.

In January 1904 the Japanese, without warning, attacked and devastated the Russian navy in the Yellow Sea. Defeats in the Pacific, the prolonged siege of the Russian base at Port Arthur in China, and unrest among non-Russian minorities in Caucasia, the Baltic region, Finland, and Poland tested Russia's ability to fight a foreign enemy while keeping order within its borders. In July Socialist Revolutionaries assassinated the head of the tsar's government, Minister of the Interior Viacheslav von Pleve. Recruits refused to serve in the unpopular war; and peasants in western Georgia, under the leadership of Social Democrats, demonstrated against the draft.[1] Caucasia and much of Russia were moving toward open and violent confrontation with tsarism. Yet one of the leading revolutionary parties, the Social Democrats, stood mired in the quicksand of debilitating political and personal quarrels.

Paramount among Koba's concerns was the internal struggle among the Social Democrats. In the Caucasus the faction that he would feel closest to, the "majority," was, for the moment, losing ground to the "minority." In the fall of 1903 the godfather of Russian Social Democracy, Georgii Plekhanov, wrote to his ally Lenin that he had been thinking a lot about Caucasian affairs and feared "the Caucasus is moving away from us." Far away in Europe, he proposed sending someone to represent the Central Committee, then dominated by the "majority," to the Caucasus.[2] Also concerned, Lenin and his wife, Krupskaia, who worked as the secretary of the Central Committee, agreed to send the trusted Gleb Krzyzanowski [Krzhizhanovskii] to Tiflis.[3] On October 20, 1903, Lenin wrote to the Caucasian Union Committee (CUC) congratulating them on "firmly holding that path on which they stood" and not heeding the slander spread against "the majority."[4] Jointly signing the letter with Plekhanov, he agreed with the CUC's condemnation of Topuridze, who had supported the "majority" during the London congress, but switched to the "minority" under the influence of Zhordania. The Caucasian Social Democrats had barred Topuridze from party work and briefly considered bringing him before a court of his comrades, but the regional committee decided not to proceed with a trial.[5] "Such a person does not deserve your political trust," warned Lenin.[6]

The leaders of the "majority" in Europe sensed the fragility of their victory at the Second Congress. At this point, only months after the delegates had dispersed from London, the leading Marxists in the Caucasus had not yet definitely divided into factions. Zhordania sent a letter to his Caucasian comrades critical of the Caucasian delegates to the congress who had sided with Lenin, but when the local Social Democrats discussed the letter they hesitated to rebuke their delegates. With little knowledge of what had transpired in London, and in the interest of party discipline, they agreed to obey all the resolutions that the delegates brought back. At this point in time the instinct of most party members was to adhere to the "majority," since it was presumed to reflect the will of the party congress. The "minority" represented an insurgent group unwilling to subordinate itself to that will. The principal worry was to avoid factionalism and divisiveness. Local Social Democrats gathered secretly in Tiflis in the second half of October 1903 for what they grandly declared was "the Congress of Transcaucasian Social Democratic Organizations." Topuridze, now firmly with the "minority," blamed Lenin for the party schism, but his fellow delegates to the London congress, Knuniants and Zurabov, refuted his accusations. The conference, suspicious of the wealthy Topuridze, chastised the "minority" for thwarting the "elementary principle of submission to the majority."[7] All participants except the young Irakli Tsereteli voted to approve the congress' resolutions.[8] Every Social Democratic organization in Caucasia came out for the congress majority, and even future Mensheviks like Noe Ramishvili, Archil Japaridze, and Noe Khomeriki were in a sense "Bolsheviks" until early 1905.[9] Thus, for well over a year after London the local Caucasian committees did not suffer from factional divisions.[10] True to their local traditions the Caucasian Social Democrats were not pleased with the London congress' decision to appoint, rather than elect, local party committees. The Caucasian Union Committee worked out a shrewd compromise: committees would be appointed but candidates selected only from those chosen by the members.[11]

More worrisome to some delegates to the Caucasian congress was the sense that a form of "Caucasian Bundism," a socialist nationalism or a nationalist socialism, was emerging. Since Georgians heavily dominated the Caucasian socialist movement everywhere but Baku, and most Armenian political activists were nationalist and focused on Armenians in the Ottoman Empire, Social Democracy in Georgia remained susceptible to nationalism, an anathema to more orthodox Marxists. Knuniants wrote passionately in *Iskra* that in the Caucasus Social Democracy had to be multinational and fight the good fight equally against the seizure of Armenian Church lands, the nationalism of the Georgian nobility, and the pogroms against the Jews.[12] Arshak Zurabov wrote to Plekhanov warning that "the Congress of the Caucasian Union revealed to a significant degree Caucasian Bundism, and it appeared that it had sunk deep roots, and it will be necessary in the future to expend much energy to deal with this if one particularly pays attention to the fact that this is a region of great activity and this bundism will be a more painful phenomenon than real bundism." He was particularly dismayed with the activities of Topuridze, who "as a real adventurist, exploited such sentiments and constantly tried to deepen and spread this frame of mind."[13] Nationalism rumbled just below the surface of Caucasian Marxism, and the consequences of ethnic conflicts would soon erupt in 1905.

While party organizations within Caucasia and Russia more broadly called for renewal of party unity, their émigré leaders continued their bitter fight for control of the central party institutions. In November, Plekhanov defected from Lenin and joined Martov. Appalled by Plekhanov's "trading with the Martovites," Lenin resigned from *Iskra* and the Council of the Party but stayed an "abroad" member of the Central Committee. "The situation is desperate," he wrote to a close comrade, "[our] enemies are triumphant and insolent, our [friends] are all furious."[14] Martov gloated in a private letter, "Lenin has been smashed. 'Robespierre has fallen,' said Plekhanov, and Plekhanov now abusively curses his former adjutants."[15] With Plekhanov's help, Martov's supporters took over *Iskra*, but Lenin refused to give up. Unwilling to reconcile himself with the new conciliatory mood among party leaders, he called for a new party congress and heated up the language of intraparty struggle by portraying it as combat between "the revolutionary wing" and "the opportunist wing." For Lenin "conciliationism" was now a sign of softness toward the internal enemy.

The schism between the "majority" and "minority" within the party fundamentally shaped the political culture of Russian Marxism as well as the political—even personal—formation of Soso Jughashvili. It would later have profound consequences for European, indeed world, socialist movements. The sources of the disputes were complex and involved principle as well as personality. Each side simplified irreconcilable differences into narratives justifying their position. The Mensheviks presented themselves as the more democratic and tolerant faction and viewed Lenin and his followers as the primary instigators of the division and chiefly responsible for the failure to reunite the party. The Menshevik narrative proved to be remarkably durable and was influential among Western historians. Here the Bolsheviks were intransigent authoritarians. Power-hungry Lenin was ruthlessly attempting to dominate the party. His war on democracy was a prefiguration of Soviet dictatorship.[16] From the other side, the Bolshevik narrative, which formed the basis of Soviet historiography, reversed the images of the Mensheviks. Here the Bolsheviks represented the rightful majority and the orthodox Marxists. Mensheviks were schismatics, unwilling to accept their defeat at the congress. Moreover, they were moving toward reformism and compromising the revolutionary energy of the increasingly militant workers. In fact, the initial break in the party was largely the fault of Martov and his supporters who were unwilling to accept the decisions of the congress majority.[17] Lenin's subsequent anger, frustration, and recalcitrance further deepened the split and made reconciliation unlikely. As rancorous as the mutual exchanges of accusations would be, there nevertheless would be occasions, in 1905–1906, and as late as 1917, when attempts would be made to bring the factions back together. Lenin on those relatively infrequent occasions appeared ready to compromise.

CHOOSING THE MAJORITY

Soon after he returned to the Caucasus at the beginning of 1904, Jughashvili moved through his old haunts in Batumi, Tiflis, and Kutaisi. As a known but somewhat marginalized party activist, he first tried to link up with the workers with whom he had associated in Batumi. Some of them remembered him fondly and sent him money for his flight back to the Caucasus.[18] Natalia Kirtadze-Sikharulidze, living in Batumi, heard a knock on the door after midnight: "'Who is it?' 'It's I, open up.' 'Who are you?' 'I am Soso.'" She did not believe it until he gave the password: "Hello a thousand times."[19] He stayed with her that night. Although no sources frankly admit that Soso and Natalia were more than comrades, his choice to first find refuge with her after his flight from Siberia, her support and their closeness, as well as his sharp reaction when she refused to go away with him, all support the impression that they were lovers.[20] The morning after their reunion she informed the local Social Democrats that Soso had arrived. Some were happy, but others were cold.[21]

Sergei Alliluev, who had come from Baku to Tiflis on a mission to bring back equipment and type for a secret printing press, remembered meeting Soso at the home of Mikha Bochoridze in Tiflis. Soso quizzed him about his work and advised him and his companion, Vasilii Shelgunov, not to travel on the train to Baku in the same car and to break up the equipment between them. The type would be sent along later with other comrades.[22] In his Stalinized memoirs written in the 1930s, the older, more experienced Alliluev is depicted taking advice from Soso, twenty-two years his junior, albeit an *intelligent*. Yet what rings true here is the younger man's confident, self-assured, even imperious manner in dealing with his fellow socialists, like Shelgunov, who was more than ten years older than Soso and had worked in Saint Petersburg with Lenin. Razhden Arsenidze, a prominent Menshevik, reinforces this impression. He remembers meeting Jughashvili shortly after his arrival in Batumi. Before him stood "a young man, dried up, bony, with a pale brown pockmarked face, with lively and sly eyes, alert, free spirited, presumptuous. With his first words he started to point out some, in his opinion, defects in our illegal literature: he did not like the insufficiently militant tone of the leaflets directed at the peasants of Mingrelia, who had not yet been attracted to the movement." When Arsenidze informed him "that the leaflets had been adapted so that the Mingrelian peasants would understand them and composed in a softer tone on the instructions of our Mingrelian worker comrades, who were taking up their distribution to raise the movement in their districts, he grew silent though a sly smile stayed on his face."[23]

Soso, who now increasingly was known as Koba, tried to reestablish his old contacts in Batumi. The usual practice for Social Democrats who moved from place to place, for whatever reason, was to notify the local party committee and work under its auspices.[24] But discontent lingered from his behavior during the 1902 "slaughterhouse," and the Batumi Social Democrats would not have him.[25] An old opponent, Isidore Ramishvili, led the committee and talked freely about the dark side of Koba's activities, even hinting that he was a police spy. The committee turned down Koba's request to work with the local organization, and Ramishvili called Natalia Kirtadze-Sikharulidze to the committee and shouted at her that she must drive Jughashvili from her home or be expelled from "our ranks." "This man escaped from Nicholas' hangman," she replied. "I will not drive him away, and as long as he needs to, he can live with me." But when she informed Koba of Ramishvili's demand, he left the apartment and moved in with Lavrenti Chichiradze. That night, however, he returned when he realized he was being watched. Soso was upset with the reception he had received. "I hurried back to do work, and they won't give me work."[26]

Roaming the town, he stayed the next month in eight or more apartments, spending "all his strength," committeeman Arsenidze remembered, "in establishing direct ties with workers, among whom he had a few acquaintances from his earlier work (in 1901–1902)."[27] For about two weeks he held meetings with them, secret conversations, exhorting them to take action, but to no avail. Too few Batumi workers were receptive to his arguments.[28] Ramishvili pursued him. When Koba moved in with S. Jibuti, his host later reported, "Ramishvili came to me three times and demanded that I not harbor Comrade Soso."[29] Arsenidze remembered, "He had come from exile to Batumi as if to his hometown where he had left a deep trace and hoped that he would be received with open arms. Not surprisingly, he was pained and disillusioned by the inadequate attention paid to him." He turned to Kirtadze-Sikharulidze once more, this time not only for shelter but for money to return to Tiflis. She asked Jibladze, but he refused to give anything, and finally, with help from Ermile Javakhidze, she found the money. "Where will you go, Soso," she asked, "if you get caught, who will help you?" He came up to her, parted her hair, and kissed her on the forehead. "Have no fear, comrade," he said, "for the workers' cause I am ready to give my life—and we will win!" Koba left for Tiflis "to try his luck."[30] He did not forget Natalia, however, and invited her to come and live with him in Tiflis. In a cryptic note, he wrote: "Sister Natasha, the medicine pre-scribed by the doctors there makes the doctors here laugh. If your illness worsens, come—there are good doctors here." Unable to leave her family, she rejected his proposal. Soso cared for her and was hurt by her refusal. Later when they met again in Batumi at the home of Iliko Shara-madze, he bitterly shouted at her, "Get away from me!" She was so in-sulted, she left the meeting and went home.[31] Hurt by Natalia's rebuff, Koba cut her off despite the help she had given him and how he had felt about her.

As in Batumi, so in Tiflis, Koba displayed an exaggerated sense of his own importance. He "did not appear in the committee but immediately announced himself at a meeting of advanced workers, where he pro-posed his own plan for revolutionary work. But the Tiflis comrades greeted him very coldly, even distrustfully and treated his plans with such irony that he waved his hand and quickly left, not sitting through to the end of the meeting." Some of his fellow Social Democrats saw Koba's actions as an attempt to recruit advanced workers to his side, to become their leader, and when necessary to direct them against the committee in order to take it over."[32] But in Tiflis Koba had a powerful patron in a senior Social Democrat, Mikha Tskhakaia, who after the wave of arrests in January 1904 had become the de facto head of the Caucasian Union Committee. To at least one comrade in the city, Tsetsiliia Bobrovskia (Zelikson), Soso appeared exceptionally energetic, while

Tskhakaia, whom everyone respected as a patriarch of the movement, a kind of icon, seemed old and garrulous.[33] For all the problems associated with the brash young activist, Tskhakaia thought he was worth recuperating. "In 1904," Tskhakaia remembered, "at the time of the Russo-Japanese War, one of my 'old' comrades (from the circle where I had worked), the unforgettable Comrade Rostom (Archil Dolidze), who worked legally in one of the Tiflis newspapers, wrote a conspiratorial note to me. . . . In the letter he told me that for a few months Comrade Soso, having fled from Siberia, had been searching for me, in Batumi and here in Tiflis, and wanted somehow to meet me. . . . I mentioned a place and time for the meeting." Koba told Tskhakaia about his flight and his problems in Batumi, and said that he would like to "start at the top with the Caucasian Union Committee . . . in order to do more productive conspiratorial work." Tskhakaia took the younger comrade under his wing, advised him to rest a while in Tiflis and become acquainted with the illegal literature about the Second Party Congress. He introduced him to Nina Alajalova and Datush Shaverdov, who would assist him.[34]

Poorly informed about party affairs after his time away, Koba was not immediately invited to join the CUC. Tskhakaia explained the schism at the Second Party Congress, and in February required him to write out a statement of his beliefs, a "credo." To check if he was sufficiently "internationalist," he was asked to write on socialist nationality policies. No copy of this document has surfaced, but years later the veteran Bolshevik Sergo Kavtaradze remembered the circumstances that led to it.[35] Jughashvili had apparently called for an autonomous Georgian Social Democratic party, and some of his comrades considered him to be a "Georgian Bundist"—that is, a nationalist socialist. In order to acquit himself, he had to defend the orthodoxy of his position. He took a few days and returned to Tskhakaia with a thick notebook, parts of which concerned the "national question."[36] The single hand-written copy of the "credo" was circulated to other party members.[37] Koba repudiated his notion of a separate Georgian party, and his patron Tskhakaia, who claimed to have been the "first Bolshevik" in the Caucasus, visited the local Marxists to defend him.[38] Koba survived this political gauntlet but found it difficult to participate in party organizations wary of him. Tskhakaia sent him to Kutaisi to work with the Imeretino-Mingrelian Committee of the party. A revolutionary on probation, he still had to prove himself. There he was involved in reforming the committee and setting up a printing press for the local Social Democrats. The press, hidden in Vaso Gogiladze's house, was a success and survived into early 1906.[39] Still he remained a marginal second-rank activist. Even the official Stalinist record does not place Koba at the Third Congress of the Caucasian Union in April or participating in the summer demonstration in Kutaisi.

Koba had returned to the Caucasus at a time, early 1904, when the local Social Democrats were not yet well informed about the schism that had taken place at the Second Party Congress.[40] But as he and others learned about the factional divisions, Koba sided with the "majority." This was an almost inevitable progression for the young socialist, given his elevated sense of the role of leadership in the generation of political consciousness. The watchwords of such a full-time Marxist revolutionary were discipline, organization, and struggle. A later police report, cited by Trotsky to discredit Stalin, states that Koba "has been active in the Social Democratic organization since 1902, at first as a Menshevik and later as a Bolshevik."[41] But such a statement is misleading. As vehement as the intraparty disputes were at the time, they were still between like-minded militants. With the majority and minority positions still poorly understood in the Caucasus, it should not be assumed that Koba was ever a Menshevik in any strict sense. His preferences in party organization— emphasizing the role of *intelligenty* and advocating appointed committees—made it extremely likely that he would adhere to the party majority. At the time joining the majority meant submission to the decisions of the Second Party Congress and its majority's positions, as well as acceptance of the orthodox Social Democratic vision of the party as the repository of socialist consciousness, which would be combined in time with the workers' movement through agitation, propaganda, and practical activity. In 1904 Koba, along with most Caucasian Social Democrats, simply, without much reflection, identified with the party majority. Far more remarkable is that once he made that choice he never looked back.

In a sense Bolshevik political culture was forged in 1904. A veritable war of pamphlets raged. The year opened with a major assault in *Iskra* by Pavel Akselrod on the ideas and practices that had emerged from Lenin's *What Is to Be Done?* Instead of a mass party in which workers would develop their own consciousness and activity, Akselrod claimed that Russian Social Democracy had created an organization in which "all party members had been transformed into screws and wheels of an apparatus that is run by an omniscient center according to personal discretion."[42] Even though he and others of the "minority" had earlier supported a tighter party, he denounced the "bureaucratic centralism" in the party and the dominance of the intelligentsia as no longer appropriate for a growing, mass workers' party. With Akselrod's intervention the "minority" had a clearly stated ideological content to its organizational struggle against the "majority."

In a densely detailed pamphlet, *One Step Forward, Two Steps Back: The Crisis in Our Party,* Lenin launched an extensive counterattack with his own account of the party schism and what it meant. He castigated the "minority" as defenders of the individualistic "bourgeois intelligentsia," a social stratum characterized by flabbiness and instability starkly contrasted with proletarian organization and discipline. Lenin endorsed the view that the Social Democratic Party "is the conscious spokesman of an unconscious process." It is a guide to the working class but not identical to the working class, which is varied and operates both consciously and without political direction. The party has divided into an orthodox, proletarian, revolutionary wing (the "majority") and an opportunistic, "radical" intelligentsia wing (the "minority"). Responding to Akselrod's accusation that the majority was Jacobin, Lenin proudly adorned that mantle: "A Jacobin who maintains an inseparable bond with the *organization* of the proletariat, a proletariat *conscious* of its class interests, is a *revolutionary Social Democrat.* A Girondist who yearns for professors and high school students, who is afraid of the dictatorship of the proletariat and who sighs about the absolute value of democratic demands is an *opportunist.*"[43]

Lenin wanted greater discipline in the party and opposed the minority's insistence on greater autonomy for local committees, which he believed would lead to disorganization and the infiltration of reformist rather than revolutionary tendencies. He quoted the eminent German Social Democrat Karl Kautsky approvingly: "Democracy does not mean absence of authority; democracy does not mean anarchy; it means the rule of the masses over their representatives, as distinct from other forms of rule where the supposed servants of the people are in reality their masters."[44] Desperately seeking the unity of their fledgling party, some Social Democrats believed that unity was best achieved by rallying around the old party leaders and *Iskra* (the self-styled "minority"). Others, however, held that unity had to be based on acceptance of the sovereign decisions of the Second Party Congress (those who identified as the "majority"). The touchstone of factional loyalty in 1904 was whether or not one agreed with Lenin's call for another party congress to reunite the party around the "majority." Three principal positions were taken by party members: Lenin and his closest supporters fought tooth and nail for the congress; others sided unequivocally with the "minority" and opposed a new congress that might result in legitimating the Leninists; while the so-called conciliationists tried to bring the two extremes closer together.

Most activists within Russia had had enough of the divisive strife among the top party leaders. In many ways the self-activization of workers and peasants was outgrowing the modest means of the squabbling socialists. Still, in the first half of 1904, the major Caucasian committees, even when they were made up of members supporting the "majority," generally adopted the "conciliationist" position rather than call unequivocally for the third party congress that Lenin thought essential. Devastated by police searches and arrests in January 1904, those Tiflis Social Democrats who remained free kept their heads down. Possession of pamphlets or socialist newspapers was enough proof to be held in jail. The police triumphantly, but prematurely, proclaimed that the Tiflis Social Democratic circle had been "liquidated!"[45]

In June 1904, Noe Zhordania, then still in Europe, wrote a circular letter "To the Caucasian Committees" in Georgian announcing his decisive adherence to the party "minority" and laying out his critique of Lenin's approach.[46] Zhordania read Lenin in the spirit of Akselrod. Both

Akselrod and Zhordania depicted Lenin as substituting a party of intellectuals for the workers' own movement. "Lenin completely distorts Marxism," Zhordania claimed, "in order to raise the political element above socialism, i.e., in order to give the party over to the intelligentsia."[47] He lashed out against the dominance of the party by intellectuals, rejecting Lenin's formulations in *What Is to Be Done?* "In Lenin's opinion," he contended, "not only socialist but political class consciousness of the workers is brought from outside, by other classes. . . . Thus, the proletariat must receive everything from another, from the non-proletarian." Zhordania considered this a degradation of the proletariat and an elevation of the intelligentsia. Lenin, he went on, "even denied such an indisputable fact that the economic struggle is the best means to lead the workers into the political arena. 'Political class consciousness can be brought to the workers *only from outside* (the emphasis is Lenin's), i.e., from outside the economic struggle.'" Accepting Lenin's vision of the party organization, Zhordania concluded, would lead to many proletarians being driven out of the party and "a complete dictatorship of the intelligentsia." Fortunately, he concluded, the party had rejected Lenin's formula. "If this plan had been adopted, then our party would have been social democratic only in name, and in fact would have turned into a closed little circle, a sect, the master of which would have been Lenin and Company. That would have been a Blanquist organization (that is, an organization for a *tight* circle of conspirators who each minute must listen to the orders of their chief) that would have forever eliminated from our party its proletarian spirit."[48]

Lenin answered his critics by throwing the minority's accusation back at his opponents and characterizing the "opposition" as largely made up of intellectuals. "In comparison with the proletariat," Lenin wrote, "the intelligentsia is always more individualistic as a result of the basic conditions of its life and work, which does not give it the direct broad uniting of forces, the direct experience of organized collective work. For this reason it is more difficult for intelligentsia elements to adapt to the discipline of party life, and a few who don't have the strength to deal with this task, naturally, raise the banner of rebellion against the necessary organizational restrictions, and they elevate their own spontaneous anarchism into a principle of struggle, wrongly designating this anarchism a striving for 'autonomy,' a demand for 'tolerance,' etc."[49] Lenin repeatedly rejected the Menshevik accusation that he favored the dominance of intellectuals over workers, an indictment that has clung to Bolshevism in both scholarship and the popular imagination. While Lenin emphasized the key role of Social Democrats (from the working class as well as the intelligentsia) in the development of political consciousness, he was neither particularly enamored of intellectuals playing the role of leaders nor of neglecting the vital contribution of "advanced workers." Ironically, some Bolsheviks understood Lenin's message precisely as mischaracterized by his opponents, and in turn they would be reprimanded by Lenin.

Menshevism was in the end a reaction to the formation of Bolshevism and, in its own self-representation, a return to an earlier, more European form of socialist practice and program. Zhordania's letter, along with Akselrod's articles, explained the nature of the factional split as Mensheviks saw it. It was not simply about the *Iskra* editorial board or sovereignty of the party congress; the schism was depicted as democracy versus dictatorship within the party. Soon after the Second Congress of the RSDRP in 1903, the minority became convinced that they understood the full implications of Lenin's proposals. Yet it was not until years later, when the defeats in 1905–1906 propelled many to reconsider the forms of organization and revolutionary extremism of Lenin, that a relatively stable vision congealed among his opponents.[50]

Even though he had great prestige among Georgian Social Democrats, Zhordania's letter did not immediately turn the Caucasian committees to the "minority." As he had explained in his letter, the committees were made up of intellectuals, and not surprisingly many *intelligenty*, like Koba, had affinities with an intellectual-led party. Efforts to end the disarray in the party failed, and the mood in the Caucasus shifted once again, briefly, in favor of the Leninists.[51] Confidence in the "conciliationist" Central Committee dissipated, and the Caucasian Union, Tiflis, Batumi, Imeretino-Mingrelian, and Gurian committees reversed their earlier decisions and, along with Baku, sided with Lenin's call for a third party congress.[52] In October, Rosaliia Zemliachka was able to report to

Lenin, "We have won a complete victory in the Caucasus."[53] All this shifting back and forth, discussions, meetings, and adopting of resolutions was a veritable school of factional politics, and Koba was an involved and avid student.

At the end of September or the beginning of October 1904, Koba wrote two revealing letters from Kutaisi to his friend Mikha Davitashvili, then studying in Leipzig. He began by requesting the most recent literature on the internal party disputes. "Here we need *Iskra* [at that moment in the "minority's" hands] (even though it is without sparks, but it is nevertheless needed. . . . You have to know the enemy well)." With a casual confidence, Koba went on to give his opinion on a variety of publications and personalities: On the brochure of Mikhail Olminskii (Galerka), "Down with Bonapartism!" he wrote, "Not bad. If he had beaten more forcefully with his hammer and deeper, it would have been better. His joking tone and request for mercy weakened his blows and ruined the reader's impression. This fault is even more evident when the author, clearly, knows our position well and beautifully clarifies and develops several questions. A person with our position ought to speak with a firm and unbending voice. On this score, Lenin is a real mountain eagle."[54]

This is the first fully documented reference to Lenin by Koba, and his affinity with the clarity and hardness of Lenin's position in the party disputes emerges with full force here. His metaphors reveal his preferences. A revolutionary Social Democrat should be hard, firm, unbending, and deliver, without mercy, blows to his enemies. Here he employs for the first time in a surviving document what would become one of his favorite metaphors: to beat (*bit'*).[55]

Koba then turned to Plekhanov's recent article in *Iskra*. The grand old man of Russian Marxism had come out in a series of essays against Lenin, one of which was titled "Centralism or Bonapartism," another "What Is Not to Be Done." Plekhanov had long been one of the most intransigent Russian Marxists, hard on the Economists and Revisionists, dismissive of deviance from his own orthodoxy. With the party united ideologically but divided over organizational questions, he instead called for compromise, greater flexibility, and tolerance. Plekhanov had concluded that Lenin had simply gone too far in extolling the indispensability of the intelligentsia for workers' coming to socialist consciousness. By failing to see that the degradations produced by capitalism would lead workers to socialism, Lenin had forgotten the central tenet of Marxism that "social being determines consciousness."[56] For Koba and those who agreed with Lenin that Social Democrats alone could lead workers from trade unionism to socialism, Plekhanov's views were heresy:

> This person has either gone completely mad or speaks from hatred and enmity. I think that both causes have a place here. I think Plekhanov has not kept up with the new questions; old opponents haunt him, and he repeats over and over again, in the old way: "social existence determines social consciousness," "ideas do not fall from the sky." As if Lenin says that the socialism of Marx would have been possible in the time of slavery or serfdom. Nowadays school children know that "ideas do not fall from the sky." But the point is that now we are speaking of something completely different. We long ago digested this general formulation; . . . now what interests us is how a system of ideas (the theory of socialism) is produced from separate ideas, how separate ideas and thoughts are connected into one well-structured system—and by whom the theory of socialism is worked out and brought together. Do the masses give their leaders the program and the base for the program or do the leaders [give it] to the masses?

Koba answered this question as he believed a "Leninist" would: The theory of socialism develops outside the "spontaneous movement" of the workers themselves "from the observation and study of the spontaneous movement of people by those armed with knowledge of our time." It followed that it was Social Democrats that "raise the proletariat up to the consciousness of its true class interests, to the consciousness of the socialist ideal, not to change this ideal or to adapt to the spontaneous movement. . . . Here is the significance of Leninist thought; I call this Leninist because no one has expressed this in the Russian literature with such clarity as has Lenin."

Koba and the Leninists staked out a clear position. Socialism required revolution, and revolution required the workers to understand that their real interests lay beyond capitalism. That understanding would not arise spontaneously from the workplace but had to be articulated and inculcated in the workers by the Social Democrats. Koba ended the letter announcing that the "majority" position triumphed in the Caucasus nearly everywhere and taking some credit for the victory. "Only the Kutaisi committee hesitated, but I managed to convince them, and after that they bowed before the majority." He dismissed the two-faced policy of the conciliationist Central Committee. "It (the CC) breaks its own neck, local and Russian comrades endeavor to do this. Everyone is sharpening their teeth."[57]

In his second letter to Davitashvili, written late in October or early November 1904, Koba began by apologizing for not writing earlier. He had been very busy. He thanked Mikha for sending various Social Democratic newspapers and other materials. Again he expressed strong opinions about various writers, praising Aleksandr Bogdanov's article against Rosa Luxemburg.[58] "(These people—Rosa, Kautsky, Plekhanov, Akselrod, Vera Zasulich, and the others, in my opinion, have worked out some kind of family traditions; like old acquaintances, they are not able to 'betray' one another; they defend one another as members of patriarchal tribes defended one another without looking at the guilt or innocence of a relative.) It is just this familial 'kinship' feeling that hinders Rosa from objectively looking at the party crisis (of course, there are other reasons as well, for example her poor knowledge of the facts, her spectacles that look from abroad, etc.) This, by the way, explains some of the unworthy actions of Plekhanov, Kautsky, and others."[59] Not forgetting his vendetta against Zhordania, Koba commented on the patriarch's letter to his Caucasian comrades. "This ass does not understand that it is not the *kvali* audience that he is facing. Where does he get off talking about organizational questions?" None of the grandees of European Social Democracy was too highly regarded not to come under the withering gaze of Koba Jughashvili as he approached his twenty-sixth birthday.

From his provincial perch Koba repudiated sentimentality, "family feelings," in politics. Instead of an emotional attachment to one's comrades, he proposed "objectively looking" at the situation and, if necessary, betraying "members of the patriarchal tribe." He went on to note Vladimir Bonch-Bruevich's "masterful expressions of the position of the majority!"[60] But he was angered by the inconsistencies of Plekhanov: "This is not the first time he contradicts himself. And he, perhaps, is even proud of this, considering himself the living embodiment of the 'dialectical process.' By itself inconsistency is a spot on the political physiognomy of a 'leader,' and it (the spot), undoubtedly, should be noted." Koba then turned to the burning question of leadership and consciousness, "the relationship of the led to the leaders."

> Galerka should have, in my view, shown that Plekhanov's theoretical war against Lenin is the purest Don Quixotism, a battle with windmills, since Lenin in his little book completely consistently supports the position of Karl Marx *on the origins* of consciousness. As for the question of tactics, Plekhanov's war is a complete muddle, characteristic of an "individual" moving into the camp of the opportunists. If Plekhanov had posed the question clearly, if only in such a form: "Who formulates the program, the leaders or those led?" Or further: "Who raises whom to understand the program, the leaders the led or the latter the former?" Or: "Maybe it is not desirable that the leaders raise the masses to understand the program, tactics, and principles of organization?" If Plekhanov had clearly presented these questions, in all their simplicity and tautologicality, . . . then perhaps, he would have been frightened by his intentions and would not have acted with such a fuss against Lenin. And in so far as Plekhanov has done this, that is, in so far as he has confused the question with phrases about "heroes and crowds," so he has deviated toward the side of tactical opportunism. To confuse questions is a characteristic of opportunists.[61]

In these private missives to a trusted friend, intellectual and political convictions combined with psychic needs and emotional affinities to cement his adherence to Lenin and the Bolsheviks and render impossible any affection for his opponents. Except for Lenin, whom he saw as a towering figure, a "mountain eagle," with whom he personally and intellectually identified and in many ways would emulate, Koba felt disdain, even contempt, for the elders of the party, in Georgia, in Russia, and in Europe. He had found his spiritual home, people enough like himself that he could expose some part of his inner life in a letter or an off-handed remark. Still, he held his cards close to his chest and waited for others to let their guard down first. Others might fly into a rage, but Koba's power came from his ability to restrain himself, to hold his emotions inside and wait for the right moment and the most effective way to react.

10

BACK IN THE GAME

The Soso Jughashvili that I knew, a good comrade, loyal in friendship, jovial, loving jokes, sociable and sensitive to human misery, does not accord with the Stalin of the Kremlin who, after the death of Lenin, eliminated without hesitation, by Machiavellian means, all his adversaries, friends or not, filled concentration camps without pity in order to have the workforce needed for great works of national interest, drowning in blood even his own land of birth, Georgia, that he loved so much.

—IOSEB DAVRISHEV, *AH! CE QU'ON RIGOLAIT BIEN AVEC MON COPAIN STALINE* [*AH! WHAT WE LAUGHED AT WITH MY FRIEND STALIN*] (1950)

Western Georgia was seething with revolution in late 1904, with Batumi the headquarters of the movement. But Koba could not regain his earlier position there. The local workers were armed, and even soldiers and officers, particularly the local artillery units, shared the anti-government mood. Propagandists and agitators worked openly, and from mid-1904 well into 1905 the authorities were powerless to prevent mass meetings or carry out arrests.[1] When the authorities attempted to recruit young men for the war with Japan, those drafted refused to serve and were beaten by those already in uniform.[2] In many ways the Social Democrats, particularly in Tiflis, lagged behind the militant workers and peasants in Western Georgia. Only at the end of November 1904 did the Conference of the Caucasian Union call for their activists to move beyond "narrow work" in circles to broader political agitation, street meetings, and open protests.[3] Once again promoting his protégé, Tskhakaia proposed that Koba be made a member of the Caucasian

Union Committee (CUC). He was, however, sent to Kutaisi province, a region where in contrast to Tiflis or Batumi the Social Democrats had little influence on workers. In the western Georgian mountain town of Chiatura, however, workers in the manganese mines were preparing to take action.

The largest city in western Georgia, Kutaisi, represented the backwater of the Caucasian labor movement. Two years earlier, the city had only one workers' circle, at Piralov's tobacco factory, though after a victorious strike of shop assistants in 1903, the number of circles increased. The city's Social Democratic committee was made up of intellectuals who avoided both the underground and mass revolutionary work. Two activists, Sergo Kavtaradze and Alesha Japaridze, tried to show that "Kutaisi is not a swamp." They plotted to rescue one of their arrested comrades, Noe Khomeriki ["Khunkhuz"], as he was being transported through the town.[4] The rescue went astray. Prokopi Lezhava started shooting despite the others having called off the operation and was killed. The prisoners managed to escape, but the local socialists considered their action to have been a mistake.[5]

Although he was one of the youngest socialists in town, Kavtaradze had studied *What Is to Be Done?* and claimed to "know it almost by heart."[6] He and his friends hoped for a new committee of full-time party activists, but lacking confidence to take on their elders, they sent Sebastian Talaqvadze to Tiflis to meet with the Caucasian Union Committee, inform them about the situation in Kutaisi, and request a comrade be sent to straighten things out. Tskhakaia told him that he would send "an experienced party worker, a good organizer," who "had sat in prison, been exiled, and escaped from exile. He is well grounded in Marxism." After a short pause, Tskhakaia went on: "I have to tell you that this comrade had been suspended from any party work by the [Caucasian] Union Committee because of his nationalist tendencies [uklon]. . . . He was a Georgian Bundist. He wanted to create an independent Georgian national Social Democratic party." The Union Committee "decisively condemned his platform as inconsistent with the interests of the struggle of the proletariat and the principles of internationalism and proposed that he seriously rethink the mistaken step he has taken, to understand and recognize the political fallaciousness of his separatist deviation and in that way return to the position of the RSDRP." This comrade "did not show himself for a while," but then gave the committee his "Credo." The committee recognized his "confession" as politically correct and acceptable. "In it he speaks of his errors and lays out his point of view on organizational, national, and other questions and asks to be considered completely in line with the positions of the party. The Union Committee decided to send him off on party work, and since there is the matter of strengthening your organization we give him as help to you."[7] Talaqvadze asked to see the Credo, but Tskhakaia told him there was only one copy, and he was not sure where it was.

Sent by the Caucasian Union Committee, Jughashvili arrived in Kutaisi at the end of July or the beginning of August 1904 and stayed in town until October. "Up to this time none of us knew him or had even heard of him," writes Kavtaradze. His debut was at a large meeting where he debated Grigol Lortkipanidze, a student well versed in Marxist theory, on the definition of a party member.[8] Koba spoke clearly, logically, and convincingly, Kavtaradze reported, and the meeting adopted a resolution later published in *Iskra*. Shortly after Koba's settling in Kutaisi the question was raised about reconstituting the Imeretino-Mingrelian Committee. He joined the other supporters of the "majority" in a plot to remove the "minority" members from the committee. "He spoke of conspiracy; the committee ought to consist of comrades that were unknown to the authorities; it ought to be organized deeply conspiratorially and not semi-legally as it has been up to now, visible to all; if not, the whole endeavor is doomed to inevitable collapse. He advised us to cut off any contact with the old committee members, who were probably known to the gendarmes and the police."[9]

One night in a dark alley off the Kutaisi boulevard, the conspirators worked out some organizational questions. At the end of the meeting, Jughashvili advised them to take on revolutionary pseudonyms. "Call me 'Koba,'" he said, "and you," turning to Kavtaradze, "will be Togo." Why, asked Kavtaradze, have you given me the name of the Japanese admiral who had destroyed the Russian fleet in the Battle of Tsushima.

Soso laughed and answered, "Not because of your appearance, just . . . simply that." "I never understood or could explain to myself," Kavtaradze later recalled, "the choice of such a strange nickname, a name that he continued to use with me right up to the last days of his life."[10]

The question arose what to do about the Menshevik Samson, the treasurer of the old committee. It was decided to invite him to a meeting and inform him that, for conspiratorial reasons, he was to be removed from the committee. "Comrade Koba said that a Menshevik in our underground organization is the same as opening the door to the street," Kavtaradze remembered. "We agreed that if the Union Committee interfered with our decision, we would unanimously stand behind our decision and argue that since we Bolsheviks were a separate faction with our own principled ideological platform, tactical organizational line, and leadership, we could not reconcile ourselves with a Menshevik informant in our midst; we considered this harmful to our cause. Comrade Koba declared that he would himself tell Samson about our decision and explain our reasoning. 'This way is better,' he added. . . . 'You are more timid. . . . You have closer personal relations with him. . . . This makes you uncomfortable. . . . For me, it is nothing.'"[11]

The meeting took place in a private room at the *sitsotskhlis tsqaro* [Source of Life] restaurant by the White Bridge over the Rioni River. When Koba informed Samson of the group's decision, Samson protested that he would complain to the Union Committee. Upset and insulted, he demonstratively left the table but, in true Georgian style, not before paying for everyone's food and drink. Koba joked, "We threw him off the committee, and yet he felt compelled to pay for us." The affair, however, was not over. Tskhakaia, a close friend of Samson's, arrived from Tiflis as representative of the CUC to insist that the treasurer be returned to the committee. The Kutaisi comrades were unimpressed by his argument, which did not touch on the need for conspiracy, and they did not understand "why we should tolerate a Menshevik, even a politically trustworthy one, though of no use to us, in our organization." Suddenly, unexpectedly, Koba took the floor and declared that he had changed his mind: he shared Tskhakaia's view and considered the committee's decision incorrect. "His sudden turn was like a stab in the back.

It was completely inexplicable and incomprehensible. 'What happened to him?'" Kavtaradze remembered thinking. Siding with his patron, Koba had neither prepared the others nor warned them of his change of mind during the break or the meeting. The next day the committee met in the home of Ivan K. on Balakhvan Street. "Our meeting quickly took on a tense and sharp character. We asked Koba to explain his action the day before." Koba argued that, first, it was necessary to act in that way because of party discipline, and it made no sense to argue with the Union Committee; second, the sole Menshevik could be rendered harmless, isolated, "the more so since he himself evidently does not claim an active role and is completely satisfied with being a nominal member of the committee."[12]

Koba's comrades were not satisfied. They had neither meant to dispute the Union Committee nor considered Tskhakaia's decision a final and binding one. Tskhakaia was obliged to take the objections of the Kutaisi comrades back to the CUC, and once it made its ruling, Kutaisi would accept that without hesitation. Kavtaradze spoke up: "The action of Comrade Koba has to be recognized as uncomradely, since he did not consider it necessary to consult with us about this nor even to warn us that he had changed his view that earlier he had so energetically justified and defended. . . . This was . . . unpleasant . . . uncomradely."

"I did not find it necessary to consult about what I considered correct," Koba answered with an ironic smile. Kavtaradze exploded. He leapt up and hurled a kerosene table lamp at him. Their comrades jumped on him, calming him down. "[I] thought about my wild temper. At that moment I heard his voice: 'It's a good thing that the lamp was not lit, or the whole house would have burnt down.' This was pronounced completely calmly, with a joking, good-natured tone. My malicious glare at him was met with a kind, friendly expression in his eyes. I felt myself disarmed. What kind of devil is this, I thought. . . . What kind of person is this? I do not understand."[13] The whole incident was covered up. The CUC members, Tsulukidze and Tskhakaia, were told about it, but they thought it best not to report it further.

The Imeretino-Mingrelian Committee ended up with five Bolsheviks and one Menshevik.[14] Koba stayed on and worked with the committee as it connected with the rebellious peasants of western Georgia and the manganese workers of Chiatura. Even Kavtaradze praised his efforts during that time.[15] Occasionally Koba traveled to Tiflis for meetings. In late August to early September, seven or eight Social Democrats favoring the "majority" met with Tsetsiliia Zelikson and her husband, Vladimir Bobrovskii, who had been sent by Lenin to work with the Caucasian Union Committee. Koba, Tskhakaia, and Tsulukidze attended the meeting.[16] It had taken almost nine months, but Koba had reestablished himself within the Social Democratic movement. Indeed, he was part of the core of the emerging Bolshevik faction.

The incident over the makeup of the committee did not end with the kerosene lamp. Koba was not above using dubious means against comrades with whom he disagreed, and a letter buried deep in the tsarist police files reveals that his opponents suspected him of a propensity for intrigue. Sometime late in September or early October 1904, the Social Democrat Noe Khomeriki ("Khunkhuz") wrote in Russian to someone called "Sa-ni," addressing him as "Comrade Old Man."[17] "As I learned, comrade Koba, if one may so call him, told you that supposedly we (I together with 'Khorosho') were against you and tried to get you to leave the local committee. I declare to you that nothing like that happened and what Koba passed on to you is a vile lie. Yes, a vile lie with the aim of discrediting me and another comrade ('Khorosho') in the eyes of the comrades." Khomeriki had indeed considered dropping Comrade Old Man from the committee but later changed his mind and was incensed by what Koba had told the comrade.

Khomeriki declared that he was "shocked that a person can be so impudent. I know in general that there are such people like this gentleman but I confess that I did not expect such 'boldness' from them. But it is said that they are capable of any means if only these means are justified by the end." That end is actually "the small-minded plans of this scum of our party, . . . to show the people that they are great men. But this is not compatible with honest work. God did not give them adequate talent for this, and so they have to resort to intrigue, lies, and other such charms to realize their plans. Any kind of fabrication serves their purpose."

Koba had lied, Khomeriki claimed, invented his own story, "nothing like that happened." Khomeriki had quarreled with Koba over the role of older comrades in the Kutaisi Committee. After he arrived in Kutaisi, he recommended to the Caucasian Union Committee that the older comrades be kept on the committee, and the CUC agreed. That "Don Quixote Koba" knew about this decision. "Before his (Koba's) leaving for Kutaisi I argued with him on this question. I told him that it was necessary for the old ones to stay in the organization, but he declared to me (Khorosho is my witness) that for him my words have no value since the U. C. [Caucasian Union Committee] had given him broad plenipotentiary powers . . . over whom to exclude from the organization. I said that the U. C. could not have given him such rights. . . . In a word, we parted with a very bad impression of him." Khomeriki and Khorosho reproached the Union Committee "for giving such a person their confidence," but the representative of the UC told them that no "plenipotentiary powers" had been given "and that they had nothing against the older comrades."

Khomeriki made it clear that in the end neither he nor Khorosho had been against the old comrades; it had been "Mr. Koba." "I am again surprised how he could so boldly say that we led him into error and were opposed to you. But something else here surprises me. How could you listen to him when he so clearly lied and when you probably knew what his goal and 'the meaning of his tales' were. I think that this was a sin on your part before the sacred cause of the people. I think that such 'filthy' personages ought to receive from us a rebuff when they want to bring into this great and holy cause dirt and filth. We ought to show them that this is a sacred matter, but if we hear them out without protest, we will without thinking push them once again into great filth and harm the cause of the people. But . . . maybe you doubted our honesty and in your soul you believed him?"

In this extraordinary document, a dedicated Social Democrat who believed he had suffered indignity and injustice at the hands of the young Koba warned his comrades that Koba was not to be trusted. Both Khomeriki's letter and Kavtaradze's memoir reveal the passions and divisions in the movement as well as Koba's willingness to bend the truth

in his own (or the movement's) interest and to do it with ease and conviction and without remorse.

Hardness had replaced sentimentality in the young man's personality.
What was important was the movement to which he had dedicated himself. What talents he had he turned to the defense of the Leninist model
of a revolutionary party: leadership by Social Democrats with coopta-
tion of workers and intellectuals onto committees. But this form of
organization flew in the face of the older practices of Georgian workers,
who had always favored electing committee members almost exclusively from among the workers. Around this time Koba was commissioned to debate those who opposed the Leninist version. He and Noe
Ramishvili met in Tiflis, an event recorded by another old Menshevik,
Davit Saghirashvili.[18] Koba arrived at the meeting "burdened with a big
stack of books. He also brought clandestine brochures and a copy of
Iskra." He and Ramishvili soon were embroiled in argument. "At first,
Koba remained calm and was in full self-control, avoiding sharp words.
However, when he sensed that the assembly began to side with his ad-
versary, . . . he began to get very angry and was soon out of order. He
called all of those present *petit bourgeois*. After having insulted everybody in the room, he left the meeting with two or three of his followers.
Vaso Tsabadze, who chaired the meeting proposed that we should close
our meeting earlier than scheduled and go home."[19]

Asatur Kakhoian remembered another party meeting in the Rothschild factory in 1904 where Koba and Ramishvili held one of their series
of debates. When the workers voted for Ramishvili's resolution, with
only Koba and Kakhoian voting for Koba's, Kakhoian was very upset.
"It's nothing, dear comrade," Koba told him. "In the final accounting,
you see, we will win. We have to work energetically and not lose heart."[20]
Rather than express discouragement or lose his temper, which rarely
occurred, Koba almost always displayed a cool self-control and concealed his discontent behind a wry smile.

Settled in his Kutaisi backwater, Koba engaged not only in partisan
polemics and snipes at his adversaries but took up more serious writing
as well. He clarified his ideas on key issues of nationality and leadership
in an article written for *proletariatis brdzola* (Struggle of the Proletariat),

the Georgian edition of the illegal Social Democratic newspaper published as well in Armenian and Russian.[21] In the unsigned article, which bears the marks of Jughashvili's somewhat pedantic and repetitive style, Koba defended the Social Democrats' policies toward non-Russian nationalities. He opposed the newly formed Georgian Revolutionary Party of Socialist Federalists, founded in April 1904 in Geneva, which sought to combine socialism with nationalism. They supported national territorial autonomy for Georgia, as well as nonterritorial cultural autonomy for all peoples.[22] Along with the Armenian Social Democratic Workers' Organization, the Socialist Federalists represented a specifically national version of socialism that, in Koba's view, isolated each nationality from others and ultimately worked to link proletarians with their class enemy, the bourgeoisie, simply because they shared certain cultural features. They shunted aside the central reality of class struggle.

Once a patriotic Georgian, Koba now denigrated any priority given to the nation. In answer to criticisms from the Socialist Federalists, Koba went on to explicate the principal points of the Social Democratic program on the national question. "Our party," he stated, "has shown us clearly that taken by themselves so-called 'national interests' and 'national demands' have no special value, that these 'interests' and 'demands' are worthy of attention only in so far as they move forward or might move forward the class self-consciousness of the proletariat, its class development."[23] Explicating the party program, he stated that Russian Social Democracy does not guarantee each nationality its own self-rule but supports "broad local self-government" for those places with different populations and conditions of life. He defended full civil rights and freedom to use one's native language as contributions to the development of the proletariat in its revolutionary struggle.

At the same time, however, the program clearly proclaims "the right to self-determination for all nations" (Article 9). Koba interpreted this to mean that while each nation would have the right to determine whether it would be independent or not and what form that independence would take, Social Democrats were obligated to strive to have the wishes of nations reflect the class interests of the proletariat. Here he tried with some difficulty to reconcile a principle that recognized the actuality of nations and their right to determine their own fate with the Marxist emphasis on the primacy of class in the struggle for socialism and socialism's preference for larger multinational states. The question of what self-determination would mean and by whom and how it was to be expressed would remain an unresolved dilemma for the Russian Social Democrats until the Russian Civil War of 1918–1921.

As 1904 progressed, political activity intensified throughout the empire. After the assassination of the repressive minister of internal affairs, von Pleve, in July 1904, the tsar appointed a more accommodating minister, Prince Petr Sviatopolk-Mirskii, who tentatively initiated a few reforms. Rather than placating the public, the concessions to society opened the sluices to a torrent of strikes and demonstrations. Two major ideologies stood opposed to the autocracy: liberalism and socialism. They had arisen together in Russia, gaining momentum in the 1890s and the first years of the new century. Rivals for public support, they nevertheless needed each other in the struggle against tsarism.[24] Over the last decade the Social Democrats had won over a loyal, if not always dependable, following among workers. The liberals found support in the *zemstva*, among some nobles, and the so-called third element, professionals— lawyers, teachers, and agronomists. Though the socialists labeled the liberals "bourgeois," Russian liberals had difficulty attracting the middle class of industrialists and capitalists, who in general depended on the good will and generosity of the tsarist state and therefore accommodated to the existing regime. The more moderate liberals around the *zemstva* remained wary of the more radical liberals in the Union of Liberation who called for the election of a constituent assembly, that is, a constitutional convention. Yet as economic conditions worsened in the early twentieth century and workers and peasants grew restive, more liberals became radical. As liberals moved to the left, moderate Social Democrats, those that identified with the "minority," grew more enthusiastic about the possibility of an alliance with the "bourgeoisie," represented in their view by the liberals.

Both within Russia and in Europe relations between party factions worsened through 1904. The "minority," now known as the Mensheviks, controlled all the central institutions of the party—the Central Committee, the Council of the Party, and the principal party newspaper, *Iskra*. Desperate to convene another party congress and reassert the "majority's" position in the organization, Lenin used his own newspaper, *Vpered* (Forward), to convince his fellow Social Democrats that compromise with the Mensheviks would weaken the revolutionary struggle. But even those close to Lenin often wavered, unconvinced that a congress should be called against the will of the highest party institutions.

The brief hegemony of the "majority" in the Caucasus reached its height at the conference of Caucasian Social Democrats held in Tiflis at the end of November 1904. Twelve delegates attended the meeting, chaired by Lev Kamenev, whom Koba had met a few years earlier as Rozenfeld.[25] Now a member of the "majority" faction, Kamenev had settled again in the Caucasus and had probably become reacquainted with Koba when he visited Kutaisi to make a report on party affairs. The conference, considered by some to be the first "Bolshevik" conference in Caucasia, resolutely took the position of the "majority" and echoed Lenin's call for a third party congress.[26] Responding to the increasingly radical mood in the country, the committee urged its adherents to move beyond the propaganda circles to broader political agitation, street meetings, and demonstrations against military recruitment.[27] Almost all the decisions were taken with a 10–1 vote. But outside the walls of the meeting room, the ground under the "majority" was shifting in the local organizations.

Influenced by Lenin's writings and his own experience in the Caucasus, Koba believed wholeheartedly in what might be called a "cadre party." Members of such a party are not mere adherents who agree with the party's program but "deployable personnel" who work actively for the party, accept its discipline, and carry out its tasks.[28] Members of the Leninist party become agents. The party becomes a political army. In an article for the first issue of *proletariatis brdzola*, Jughashvili wrote forcefully in his didactic manner of the need for a tight party made up of leaders, a "fortress" to which only worthy people were admitted, rather than a "patriarchal family" made up of anyone who agreed with the party's program. Without such a party the struggle could not be carried out successfully, he wrote; no army operates without its officers. He wholeheartedly embraced Lenin's formula for party membership against that of Martov.[29] A half a year later, he again took a classically Leninist position: "The carrier of this consciousness, Social Democracy, is obligated to infuse socialist consciousness into the workers' movement, to be ever at the head of the movement, not to look upon the spontaneous workers' movement from the side, not to trail along at the rear."[30] Koba employed Lenin's theory of hegemony from *What Is to Be Done?* Left to themselves, workers would succumb to the more powerful ideology of the bourgeoisie, and the spontaneous labor movement would move toward trade unionism rather than revolutionary socialism.[31] The cultural and ideological dominance of the bourgeoisie makes the Social Democratic party essential in the struggle for socialism. Not only material conditions push the working class toward socialism but the power of ideas as well, Koba wrote. His Marxism rejected any simple materialist determination of culture and thought. Ideas are products of the social world but once they come into existence they have "great influence on the movement of history."[32] Consciousness is not merely a response to environment and sensations but is in turn affected by ideas. According to the Leninist Koba, Social Democrats were essential as guides to the proletarians.

Social Democracy's remarkable ascendance among radical intellectuals and a growing number of workers both in Russia and the Caucasus suggests that Lenin and Koba's anxiety about the power of "bourgeois hegemony" may have been exaggerated. Early twentieth-century Russia was a realm in which neither liberalism nor nationalism enjoyed uncontested sway over significant groups of people. Rhetoric defending autocracy, the nobility, capitalism, and the church was daily undercut in the press and in whatever other channels of public expression existed. It was precisely the absence of a hegemonic bourgeois culture that permitted the rapid entry of Marxist and Socialist Revolutionary ideas through the cracks of censorship into the embryonic public sphere. By 1904–1905 economic and social discontent, along with the unpopular war with Japan, drove ordinary people into the streets, somewhat to the surprise of those who had been suspicious of the spontaneous revolutionary momentum of ordinary workers and peasants. Bolsheviks in particular would be forced to rethink the relationship of party to people. Witnessing the unleashed energy of the lower classes, Lenin expanded his view of the party from the vision of *What Is to Be Done?*, and Koba, like many other Bolsheviks, would have to adjust to the new direction in which the revolution propelled Social Democrats.

"[I]t is no exaggeration to suggest," one historian of the period states confidently, "that it was during the last four months of 1904, not in January 1905, that the revolution of 1905 began."[33] The year ended with a huge general strike in Baku, which achieved the first labor contract in Russia's history.[34] In Stalinist narratives Koba was the leader of the strike, but in fact moderate socialists, the Shendrikov brothers, led the strike, and Koba visited the city, probably in his capacity as a member of the Caucasian Union Committee, only briefly that December.[35]

All of society was on the move. While workers walked out and struck, the liberals organized a series of political banquets at which ideas for representative institutions were discussed. The Mensheviks were excited by the banquet campaign and urged the liberals to call for a constituent assembly while warning the workers to refrain from disturbances that might frighten the liberals. During the early years of *Iskra* Akselrod's formula, "hegemony of the proletariat in the bourgeois revolution," had held sway with all the editors of the paper, but once the liberal Union of Liberation and the Socialist Revolutionary Party appeared, some Social Democrats began to rethink that concept. When the liberals turned to political banquets to mobilize opposition to tsarism among the middle classes, the Menshevik editors of the "new" *Iskra* thought that the bourgeoisie could be radicalized and suggested having workers send delegations to the banquets with their more radical demands. Lenin, on the other hand, viewed the banquet liberals as "half-hearted" opponents who were in fact prepared to compromise with the autocracy. Instead of the banquet campaign, Lenin proposed that the workers prepare for an "all-national armed uprising."[36] In fact, when the workers approached the banquets, rather than convert the liberals, they frightened the participants with their uncouth behavior.[37]

At noon on December 20, a crowd of a thousand workers gathered near the railroad workshops in Tiflis and listened to a Social Democratic speaker, who shouted, "Down with the Autocracy!" The crowd marched off singing the Marseillaise and shouting slogans. On New Year's Eve the local liberals held a political banquet in the hall of the Tiflis Artists' Society. When the chairman, S. M. Chemizov, a member of the city duma, introduced the liberals' resolution calling for a Constituent Assembly, a Social Democrat proposed a more radical alternative demanding the destruction of the autocracy and the establishment of a democratic republic. Three hundred of the 450 present voted for the socialists' resolution.[38] One participant remembers that Koba was among those at the meeting who stood and sang the solemn, stirring revolutionary hymn, *Varshavianka*.[39] "On to the bloody battle, sacred and righteous, march, march forward, working people."[40] The Caucasus once again demonstrated that even its moderates were more radical than most in Russia. Of the thirty-eight banquets held in Russia, only eleven had come out for a constituent assembly.[41] Tiflis had gone even further, calling for a democratic republic. Russia and the Caucasus were rushing toward revolution.

REVOLUTIONARY UNDERGROUND

11

REVOLUTIONARY BAPTISM

Comrade Soso was a mobile leader. One could not notice any fatigue in him. He was upset only if something was hindering his work. I often saw Soso rushing with a cap on his head, with a blue sateen shirt on, a pistol at his waist, in a light coat. He moved so fast we called him *gezo* [the way]. He also swayed as he walked, and so we called him *kunkula* [person who staggers]. Only those of us close to him knew these illegal nicknames for him.

—GIORGI ELISABEDASHVILI,
VOSPOMINANIIA [MEMOIRS] (1948)

Yet the question, "What did Koba really do in 1905?" remains unanswered.

—LEON TROTSKY, *STALIN: AN APPRAISAL OF
THE MAN AND HIS INFLUENCE* (1939–1940)

Nine days after the New Year, thousands of workers, led by the radical priest Father Gapon, marched in solemn procession, holding icons and singing "God Save the Tsar," to the tsar's Winter Palace in Saint Petersburg. They were met with a volley of rifle shots that left at least 130 dead and 299 seriously wounded.[1] The January snow ran red in Russia's capital city, and the events reverberated throughout Russia and the world as "Bloody Sunday." "The indiscriminate shooting of unarmed people seeking to petition their sovereign for 'justice and protection,'" writes a historian of 1905, "had severed the psychological ties between the ruler and many of the ruled, ties that were intangible but indispensable for the maintenance of order. Masses of Russians no longer felt bound to obey the commands of a sovereign whose power had previously been accepted as hallowed by God and tradition."[2]

As the year unfolded, strikes and demonstrations, mutinies and armed clashes of workers and police, battles between peasants and soldiers on horseback, nearly brought the three-century-old monarchy down. Later the sporadic turbulence would be known as the "revolution of 1905," and those out on the streets, as well as those in the palaces, certainly felt that they were in the midst of a revolution. "1905 unsealed the lips of all," wrote Lev Trotsky. "The country that had been silent for a thousand years began to speak for the first time."[3] Yet applying the term "revolution" to this tumultuous year needs some explanation. No government fell; no new group or class came to power; and so the conventional meaning of revolution seems inappropriate. An older usage of "revolution," in the sense of a turning, fits much better. By the end of 1905, massive and sporadic risings of ordinary people, mutinies by soldiers, and sustained opposition by intellectuals, public figures, and industrialists convinced the government to make significant reforms that seriously compromised the autocratic powers of the emperor and gave Russia, for the first time in its history, a kind of semi-constitutional regime. The fundamental contradictions of Russian society and governance were not resolved, however. The new industrialized economy, with its growing number of factory workers, managers, and industrial entrepreneurs, fit awkwardly in a system in which no significant social group, except the highest nobility, was represented in the institutions of government. Society and state remained distant and alien to one another. For the next two years the revolutionary clashes would continue, particularly in the empire's peripheries, like Poland, the Baltic region, and the Caucasus.

In most of the biographies of Stalin this revolutionary interlude appears as a blank space. The young Stalin seems to have been absent at a time when the very workers and socialist intellectuals among whom he had been active clashed with the autocratic authority in Georgia. Trotsky spends thirty pages in his biography of his rival demonstrating how Stalin sat out the revolutionary year in Georgia, a dull editorial writer absent from any of the strikes, protests, or armed confrontations.

Yet in fact Jughashvili was deeply involved in the Caucasian revolution, and 1905 was a transformative experience that shaped the further evolution of the man who became Stalin. The Menshevik Razhden Arsenidze, no friend of Koba's, conceded that in "1905 Koba actually carried on energetic work, traveled through Guria, Imereti, Chiatura, Baku, Tiflis, threw himself from one end to the other." He then goes on to undercut Koba's hyperactivity. "But all his work was almost exclusively factional."[4] Popular biographer Simon Sebag Montefiore paints a quite different but equally monochromatic portrait by writing almost exclusively about Koba as terrorist and bandit. In fact, Koba in 1905 was engaged in three related areas of activity: besides his active engagement in the intraparty struggle with the Mensheviks, he wrote extensively for the Bolshevik press and led a clandestine armed band.

The revolution and its repression in Caucasia were marked by extraordinary violence.[5] For a brief time the rebel peasants and workers effectively eliminated the writ of the tsar in much of the Caucasus, and the tsarist regime responded as colonial masters with massive and bloody reprisals. In the weeks after Bloody Sunday, Tiflis railroad workers took the lead by walking out on January 18, beginning what soon became a general strike throughout the city. Printers and tobacco workers followed. Their demands were largely economic—the eight-hour day, higher wages, improvement in work conditions—but the socialists pushed them toward more political demands. Within days the workers held demonstrations and battled soldiers. Five thousand gathered on Batumi Square in the Tiflis suburb of Didube on the 19th.[6] When Kamo told Koba how many had been at the demonstration, Koba snapped back, "You're lying."[7] Barricades went up in the workers' districts of the city, and by the 23rd crowds filled the streets around the city center, Erivan Square, the nearby Soldiers' Bazaar, and Golovinskii Prospect that led into the "European" section of the city. They sang revolutionary songs, joked with one another, while the police, at first, held back. But when a crowd of two hundred emerged from Theater Lane carrying a red flag, singing the *Marseillaise* and shouting "Down with the Autocracy," the police attacked, along with mounted Cossacks and street cleaners armed by the authorities with clubs. The workers fought back with sticks and stones, retreating only after shots were fired. The Cossacks chased the fleeing demonstrators into the side streets and nearby courtyards and houses, flailing away with whips and cudgels.[8]

Revolutionaries formed secret groups to carry out assassinations of officials and plan robberies to finance the rebellion or secure arms. Even Social Democrats, who as Marxists traditionally condemned the tactic of individual terrorism, joined the anarchists, Populists, Armenian socialists, and Georgian Socialist Federalists, who advocated the use of bombs and targeted killing. The workers particularly hated the street cleaners, whom the police employed as informers. Once Kote Charkviani was having an argument with a street cleaner in Tiflis when he heard a familiar voice: "Beat him, Kote; don't be afraid; they are the tamed street dogs of the gendarmerie!" Chasing after him, Kote caught up with his boyhood friend, Jughashvili, then on the run from the police.[9]

The unrest in the city spread. Another demonstration—this time a funeral of a teacher, Nina Goliashvili, said to have been killed by the police—was held on the 30th. Two thousand people marched. The police charged into the crowd and were answered with a hail of stones. Other cities responded to the call from Tiflis. On January 25 the Batumi Social Democrats, wary of a strike, organized meetings of workers to explain the events in Petersburg, and the workers, despite the pleas of their cautious spokesmen, voted to strike. In Sukhumi, Kutaisi, Poti, and Chiatura, as well as along the railroad line, work stopped and shops closed. If shopkeepers tried to keep the stores open, the salespeople refused to serve customers, informing them that they were acting in solidarity with the strikers.[10] Peasants, incensed by the shooting of Baku workers the month before, joined the protests. Clergy urged the people not to pray for the imperial family, and portraits of the tsar were destroyed. Government institutions were boycotted, and revenge was taken on particular officials and government supporters. This time, unlike the demonstrations of 1901, thousands of people were involved, unafraid to do battle with the police and army. What had been isolated, uncoordinated protests four years earlier had turned into open rebellion.

The January strikes in the Caucasus were part of a wave of resistance, followed by repression, throughout the empire. In Warsaw soldiers put down a week-long general strike, killing nearly a hundred civilians. In Riga ten to fifteen thousand workers marched; soldiers gunned down seventy and wounded another two hundred. The explosion of militant activity should have shaken the Social Democrats out of their internecine squabbles over party structure. In some parts of Russia, as Trotsky put it, "the differences of opinion between the Mensheviks and the Bolsheviks passed from the domain of party regulations to the domain of revolutionary strategy."[11] But in Caucasia the January strike went on simultaneously with a decisive struggle between the majority and minority factions for control of the Social Democratic organizations.

By 1905 Koba was recognized in Georgia as both a leading Bolshevik activist and a theorist, someone familiar with Marxist literature, not only with the works of Lenin but also those by Marx, Engels, and Kautsky. He was appreciated not as an original thinker but someone able to explicate what was taken to be the orthodox Bolshevik position. While he was deeply involved in the controversies among Marxists, he firmly held the view that there was a correct Marxist view, something that could be called "scientific." He was convinced that the Mensheviks displayed an opportunistic, that is, unprincipled, approach to the struggle for socialism; they gave in to immediate concerns; they seized opportunities close at hand, repeatedly shifting their positions. They were typical intellectuals. The Bolsheviks, on the other hand, were characterized by firmness, dedication to principles, and unwillingness to compromise their views, which conformed to the tenets set out by the classical Marxist theorists. Describing the Bolsheviks, Koba described himself.

Bolsheviks had enjoyed dominance in most of the Caucasian committees, as well as the Caucasian Union Committee, for most of the time since the divisive Second Party Congress of 1903. Once *Iskra* became Menshevik, the CUC stopped distributing it and passed out the Bolsheviks' newspaper *Vpered* instead.[12] The Tiflis Bolsheviks managed to direct the local labor movement despite the earlier traditions of Georgian workers of having committees made up of workers, elected rather than appointed, with socialist intellectuals as advisors. While such practices never completely disappeared, Social Democratic intellectuals had gradually established themselves on the local and Caucasian committees along with the occasional worker representative. Most Social Democrats in South Caucasia had worked well with the Caucasian Union Committee through 1903 and 1904, and people from both factions sat together on local committees as well as the CUC. In Batumi, for example, the local committee had three intellectuals (two Mensheviks and one Bolshevik) and four workers (three Bolsheviks and one Menshevik). But when "documents" from the Second Party Congress began arriving by ship from Europe at the end of 1904, allegiances shifted.[13] These "documents" included: Lenin's *What Is to Be Done?* and *One Step Forward, Two Steps Back*, as well as Martov's *On Our Divergences.* A Georgian Menshevik later recalled that once workers in Batumi, already suspicious of intellectuals, read Lenin's plan for a party dominated by professional revolutionaries (who were most likely to be from the intelligentsia), they turned the local Social Democratic organization from Bolshevik to Menshevik.[14] In fact, this struggle for supremacy in the Georgian movement went on for months, and it would take a particular reading of Lenin by long respected socialist intellectuals to turn workers in Georgia toward Menshevism.

The vehemence and passion of the factional fights can be felt in a letter, full of sarcasm and latent violence, that Koba, then in Tiflis, wrote early in January 1905 to Lenin and Krupskaia, reporting on the efforts of V. A. Noskov (Glebov), who had been sent by the Menshevik-dominated Central Committee to swing committees away from militant Bolsheviks and reconcile the two factions.[15] For Koba the "conciliationist" Glebov was a "cunning fox who knows where to deliver blows! He sniffed out that the only stronghold (in truth, not very satisfactory, but at least a bulwark) of party-mindedness in Caucasia is the Union Committee, keeping, at least for a time, the wavering local committees in line. So look, he wants to remove the 'intermediating link' between the CC and the local committees in the interest of . . . 'centralism!' I am afraid that this young diplomat missed the mark." Koba noted that Glebov's "conservative position, seasoned with characteristic demagogy, pharisaism, and lies, inspired only disgust in most of our Caucasian comrades. . . . [T]he Union Committee took the most severe measures against him." Some comrades were confused by Glebov, as was the Tiflis Committee for a while, but in general "a most interesting struggle is going on. Glebov . . . is some kind of charlatan, whom one wants to punch in the face. So much the worse for him. We managed to let him leave with empty hands."[16]

A more formidable opponent followed Glebov. In January 1905 the patriarch of Caucasian Social Democracy, the revered Noe Zhordania, returned to the Caucasus and traveled from city to city on a campaign against the Bolsheviks. In his peripatetic wanderings Zhordania, with whom Koba had already clashed, had become acquainted with the leaders of European Marxism, Jules Guesde and Karl Kautsky, as well as the most prominent Russian Social Democrats, Plekhanov, Vera Zasulich, Lev Deich, and Lenin. As a delegate to the Second Party Congress, he had debated with the men of the "majority." His letters to his Caucasian comrades had spelled out the affinities of the Menshevik position with the traditional practices of Georgian workers and played on their suspicion of intelligentsia dominance. A Baku Bolshevik, Aleksandr Stopani, wrote to Lenin and Krupskaia about Zhordania's visit to the city.[17] "Here comes the well-known 'Caucasian ass' (that's what his own Mensheviks called him abroad), that is, Kostrov [Zhordania], and immediately he opens a campaign against Lenin (first having disorganized the work in Tiflis and Batumi where he behaved not even as a regular *rabochedelets* [Economist] but as a Zubatovist [someone who favors the unions backed by the police]), then against the majority; everything came down to Lenin on one side and Martov on the other." Zhordania was met with rapturous welcomes. "At meetings they shouted not 'Down with Autocracy' but 'Down with Lenin'; this is what an *Iskra* education means now. . . . [T]he well known ass distorted terribly and confused things." Zhordania reduced Lenin's views to a claim that "only members of committees can be members of the party. . . . He says that the majority is made up of the intelligentsia [which] wants its own exclusive dominion—that is, bourgeois democracy." He urges "'come to us, workers, with us you will be your own masters.'—this is all literally what is said and in the name of Martov, with citations from Martov and with curses for Lenin."[18]

Zhordania's sharp attacks on Bolshevism resonated among the Georgians. His admirer Noe Ramishvili headed the Tiflis Committee, and the Tiflis committeemen were upset with the CUC's insistence on centralization and subordination.[19] They had attempted to organize strikes and issue proclamations in January without the sanction of the Union Committee, which had opposed such actions. When Zhordania thrashed out the major issues dividing the party in a series of debates with Tskhakaia, he quickly won over his old comrades. On January 17 one of the strongholds of Lenin's followers fell to their rivals. The Tiflis Committee became Menshevik. After hearing the Menshevik arguments a worker approached the Bolshevik Lado Dumbadze and threatened, "Wait, you will see what we will do with you Bolsheviks, with the agents of Nicholas. We will show you what it means to be a 'Bolshevik.'"[20]

The contest for the party then turned to Batumi. The battle was intense, both physically and verbally. "A worker" wrote from Batumi (his letter intercepted by the police), "The Mensheviks from abroad spoke about [the Bolsheviks'] 'political intrigues' [*politikanstvo*], their 'Jacobinism,' 'Blanquism,' and above all about elections from below (almost from the absolutely lowest masses)." The workers were told not to give in to the intelligentsia, "which coming from a bourgeois milieu carries with it a 'bourgeois psychology.'" "The intelligentsia (by this word they mean the 'Bolsheviks') needs more than anything political freedom," said one orator from the 'minority' camp, "and for this reason they propose that we arm and one fine day make a revolution. No, comrades, our weapon is consciousness. For this reason we will develop until we all have consciousness." One of the comrades then asked the Menshevik spokesman, if they had to wait ten years for this consciousness, would the revolution wait for us? And the answer followed: "The bourgeoisie will make the revolution; let them spill their blood on the barricades."[21]

One of the most active Social Democrats in Batumi, Giorgi Eradze, worked at the Rothschild's plant. Years later, he remembered how the local organization shifted toward the Mensheviks.[22] The Batumi organization had been decimated by the arrest of about seventy people late in 1903 or early 1904, and when many of the arrested were released, they changed the method of operation in the organization to a top down one. Some preferred working in the old way, and conflicts developed. Eradze considered all the members of the local committee to have been either "Bolsheviks" or people who did not distinguish between factions.[23] He was aware of Koba's residual influence in Batumi, and as the conflict between factions came to a head, he tried to find an able propagandist to work among the workers, someone who could oppose Koba, whom he considered an "adventurist" because of his actions that had led workers into the bloody clash with the police two years earlier. He conceded that Koba was a strong propagandist but saw him as an intriguer who had tried to turn workers against Zhordania and Jibladze. Koba, he claimed, had once even concocted a scheme to counterfeit money. Tiflis could only spare Noe Ramishvili, and Eradze reluctantly accepted him as a balance weight to Koba. Both men arrived, sometime in March or April 1905, in time for a large meeting.[24]

The tall, gaunt Ramishvili was as tough an opponent as Koba was likely to face. Known in party circles as "Petr" or "Caucasian Petr," he was soon to be a major leader of the "Red Hundreds," a paramilitary group of fighters ready to kill those who threatened the Social Democrats. He would earn the title "General Menshevik," and his daring and ruthlessness led some to compare him in later years to Koba.[25] Late in the evening seventy to eighty people gathered in two ground floor rooms in the home of Ivane Mgeladze in the workers' district of Bartskhana. One of those present, Khariton Shavishvili, remembered that Ramishvili came in first, accompanied by his supporters. Few in the crowd knew him, though a couple embraced him. Three or four minutes later Koba entered, and those assembled cried out "Soso," and one after the other hugged him.[26] Ramishvili was the first to speak. As thin as Koba but slightly taller, he spent the next three and a half hours laying out the position of the Tiflis leaders. Koba frequently interrupted him. Then for an additional three hours, until 4:30 in the morning, Koba elaborated Lenin's arguments. He displayed his erudition by referring to the works of Marx, Engels, Lassalle, Kautsky, Plekhanov, Akselrod, Martov, and Aleksandr Martynov.[27] Over and over again he repeated,

"Lenin says."[28] The debate resumed the following evening and concluded on a third. According to both witnesses, Ramishvili dominated the debate, and the workers declared their allegiance to the Mensheviks. "And the morning ended with an unforgettable scene," writes Shavishvili. "The workers who had just made the decision to separate themselves from their 'Soso,' who had become 'Koba,' and would become 'Stalin,' went one by one to embrace him before leaving, tears in their eyes."[29]

After the debate, the Batumi organization was rebuilt in the old way; elections were held to a city conference of twenty people; then local committees were formed; and a city committee was created that sent a letter to the old Batumi Committee asking it to liquidate itself. Despite the new committee having the backing of most of the workers, the old committee refused to disband or give up its archives, claiming it had been legally appointed by the Caucasian Union Committee.[30] Koba was not about to "disarm."[31] Prepared to use any means necessary to turn the workers toward the Bolsheviks, "he lied and accused his opponents of lying, without a twinge of conscience," the Menshevik Arsenidze remembered. "Koba's face expressed neither embarrassment nor the slightest sign of shame. Only disappointment and bitterness that 'the means did not achieve its end,' that his intrigue had been exposed."[32] "I heard him several times at meetings of Georgian workers, but where Russian workers were also present. 'Lenin,' Koba said, 'is exasperated that God has sent him such comrades as the Mensheviks! Indeed, what kind of people are they! Martov, Dan, Akselrod—circumcised Yids [*zhidy*]. Yes, and that old grandma, Vera Zasulich. Go and try to work with them. You can't go into the struggle with them, neither can you celebrate at a banquet with them. Cowards and petty tradesmen!'" Koba was surprised that "his little escapade, which, in his opinion, should have made them laugh" upset the workers. "For a long time he blamed his failure on the machinations of Menshevik propagandists. 'Is it possible that Georgian workers don't know that Jews are a cowardly people and are no good in a fight?' he wondered."[33]

Koba excused his rough language and coarse expressions as the language of proletarians who were not educated in "delicate mannerisms and aristocratic eloquence." He spoke "simple, crude truths," he claimed. But his tone, Arsenidze notes, was often sarcastic and ironic, and "he used rude jokes like a hammer, often going beyond the bounds of propriety."[34] If one of the Mensheviks used such language or means, his comrades insulted the offender by calling him or her "the Menshevik Koba."[35]

With both Tiflis and Batumi siding with the Mensheviks, the Caucasian Union Committee, still primarily intellectual in composition, was left with little worker support. A few of Koba's friends—David Suliashvili, Mikha Davitashvili, and Gurgenidze—arrived in the city after the events of Bloody Sunday, giving up their academic studies, eager to participate in the burgeoning movement in the Caucasus. They met with Koba the first night and regaled him with stories about the disputes in the party emigration. Stalin was thrilled to see them, smiling the whole time, and reciprocated with details about the local situation: how the CUC was Bolshevik but the Tiflis Committee Menshevik. "You arrived at a good time," he told them. "We are waging a brutal war with the Mensheviks. We are hoping for your help. I will call a meeting of the Union Committee for the day after tomorrow; you also come and give a report on the events abroad." At the hastily convened meeting of the CUC in Sololaki, Davitashvili made his report, noting that Plekhanov had gone over to the Mensheviks.[36] The CUC had some advantages; it controlled the printing press and had just brought out the first issue of a legal weekly newspaper, *mogzauri* (Traveler), edited by Pilipe Makharadze, as a replacement to *kvali*, which had been closed down by the police. It also published the illegal *proletariatis brdzola*, to which Koba was a frequent contributor.

Refusing to give in to the upsurge in support for the Mensheviks, the Bolshevik CUC ordered the Menshevik Tiflis Committee to disband and appointed a rival committee. "We are convinced," it brazenly commented in a leaflet attacking the old committee, "that the organized workers do not even know about the abandonment of the Tiflis Committee. We are convinced, comrades, that it was not you but a group of people making up the Tiflis Committee that decided to take such a thoughtless step."[37] With the movement built up so painfully for almost a decade on the brink of dissolving, the city's Social Democrats called a meeting to try to resolve the conflict. In a small, smoke-filled room in Nakhalovka, with a single kerosene lamp flickering and most of the participants standing for lack of chairs, the opening of the meeting was delayed until Zhordania appeared. Highly respected, he was chosen to preside and read out a statement emphasizing the democratic principle of party organization. The Bolsheviks—Kamenev, Tskhakaia, Mikha Borchoridze, Davitashvili, and Jughashvili among them—faced newly minted Mensheviks like Noe Ramishvili and Noe Khomeriki. Koba defended the decision of the Second Congress. "You are usurpers," someone said to the Bolsheviks. "You don't consider the workers' [will]." Another shouted: "You want in [its first] twenty-four hours to dissolve an elected workers' committee." Koba stayed calm throughout and insisted that they vote on the resolution to dissolve the Tiflis Committee. Someone warned that there were suspicious people outside and the meeting had to end. A vote was quickly taken, and most of those present voted for the Mensheviks and refused to dissolve the Tiflis Committee.[38] The party was now officially divided; two city committees would compete for support, along with the Bolshevik Caucasian Union Committee. The bitterness between former comrades who together had built up an organization was palpable. Trust gave way to a deep sense of betrayal.

While important principles were at stake, not to mention which faction would hold paramount influence over the local workers' movement, the conflict quickly turned petty. The Union Committee refused to give up its printing press to the Menshevik committee until the workers themselves demanded it. Then the CUC handed over its handcranked press but kept the *amerikanka*, the more modern mechanized press. Workers called on the CUC to dissolve itself or merge with the "minority," but the CUC demanded that before it would consider merger, the Tiflis Committee had to drop three of its members. The workers were so angry that they came close to beating up the members of the Caucasian Committee. When the CUC printed its newspaper, *Listok bor'by proletariata* [Leaflet of the Proletariat's Struggle], the Mensheviks refused to have it distributed among the workers.[39] They had most of the workers and intellectuals on their side and were confident that they would soon prevail and end the party schism. Workers blocked Bolsheviks from working in the propaganda and agitation circles.[40] No comradeship was displayed as each side made slanderous attacks on members of the opposite faction. Noe Ramishvili accused Koba of being an agent of the government, a spy, a provocateur. Noe Khomeriki so antagonized the tubercular Tsulukidze at a meeting that he fell from the tribunal, coughing up blood, and died soon after. The Bolshevik Sebastian Talaqvadze witnessed a Menshevik agitator, Varden Jibuti, explain to a group of Gurian peasants that Mensheviks were poor proletarians while Bolsheviks were rich people who defend the interests of the capitalists.[41] Bolshevik agitator Nina Alajalova was heckled by Tiflis railroad workers, one of whom shouted: "Why do we listen to the Bolsheviks? They are against workers being in the party. The Bolsheviks want to command us like [tsar] Nicholas."[42] A Bolshevik woman wrote to a friend about the infighting in Tiflis, "The sooner we break the ties with this gang, the better for SD. And in my opinion those Bolsheviks who call themselves such but speak in favor of the Mensheviks, . . . thus giving the Mensheviks time to act the demagogue and thus corrupt the masses, . . . such opportunists are more dangerous than the Mensheviks themselves."[43] With the turn toward the "minority," the few supporters of Lenin, like Koba, were left like beached ships on the shoals of the Georgian movement, an embittered "general staff without an army."[44]

"By the end of 1904 and the beginning of 1905," writes the Menshevik Arsenidze, "a full break occurred between the Bolsheviks and the Mensheviks."[45] Lenin put it even more starkly: "In fact . . . it has turned out that there are two Russian Social Democratic Workers' Parties. One with the newspaper *Iskra*, called the 'official' central organ of the party, along with the Central Committee and [its committees]. . . . The other party with the newspaper *Vpered*, with the Bureau of Russian Committees of the Majority with [its] committees in Russia."[46] Fights broke out between the CUC and the local committees in the first months of 1905. In Kutaisi the Bolsheviks held out, thanks to Tskhakaia, Budu Mdivani, and Tsulukidze, but the Mensheviks won in Georgia's westernmost regions, Batumi, Imereti-Samegrelo, and Guria. While one Batumi committee and committees in Chiatura, Racha-Lechkhumi, and Baku adhered to the Bolsheviks, most other committees in Georgia went over to the Mensheviks.[47] "The workers everywhere demanded the elective principle," Arsenidze remembered, "and they would only recognize democratic organizations. They, the workers, said in general that the Bolsheviks were not a workers' party and that they, the workers, ought to be the bosses in their own party."[48] The Menshevik organizations resurrected the earlier practices of workers electing worker leaders and inviting intellectuals to work as propagandists. Occasionally intellectuals were coopted onto committees. Cells of ten members elected district committees, which then elected the city committee, which invited one or two intellectual propagandists to join it.[49]

A letter from the Caucasian Union Committee (March 19 [April 1]) to the editorial board of *Vpered* gave the Bolshevik headquarters in Geneva a stunning picture of the collapse of their faction in Caucasia. "What is going on here! Complete anarchy reigns. Trust and respect have been torn up by the root. Our Mensheviks have no scruples about what means they use to attract the masses to their side. The position of the majority is conveyed to the workers in the most distorted form." Party discipline is referred to as "the soldiers' discipline of the fist and the stick," and it is said that the Bolshevik "commanders" want the "workers to dance to the tune of their duduki [Caucasian flute]." "According to Lenin, they say, the worker himself is without political consciousness." The local workers "say they will hire intellectuals!" One Menshevik addressing a mass of workers told them that the Bolsheviks "think that you are an unconscious mass. No, they are mistaken! You already understand who are your enemies and who wish you well, and you should drive from your midst these bloodsuckers, these uninvited guests. Down with the majority, long live the minority!" In despair the Caucasian Union Committee reported, "Demoralization is complete." The workers have turned to terrorism: "they are often killing those they simply suspect." The Bolshevik Tiflis Committee decided to put out a proclamation against terrorism but when the workers learned about it, they "strictly forbad the committee to print this proclamation and even threatened that they would not recognize such a committee. . . . What comes next, we don't know."

Even though the party organizations were in disarray, the letter went on, "The revolutionary mood here is very high. Students, craftsmen, even petty traders are being organized. We don't have people to handle all this. In the villages there is also great excitement. The authority of the government has in fact been abolished. All officials, elders, bureaucrats have been driven out; all the offices and bureaus have been burnt down. They are sending troops from here to suppress [the peasants]." Evident from this plaintive letter was a picture of mobilized, radicalized workers anxious to take over their own representative institutions. In revolution the ordinary people wanted to lead, not be led.

The letter ended by apologizing for Koba's silence, using his current pseudonym: "Vano [Jughashvili] is sorry that he cannot write. He is constantly moving from place to place and is very busy."[50] The infighting among ostensible comrades, with its ferocity and bitterness, was yet another school through which Koba matriculated. Former friends became enemies. Trust, the assurance that one could rely on another, so essential among friends and political comrades, had been shattered. Old solidarities were torn asunder. Those on whom one had relied turned out to be devious opponents at a moment of heightened danger and political opportunity. Intraparty politics were less a matter of deliberation and persuasion and more a form of warfare in which opponents had to be defeated and rendered impotent. Both Bolsheviks and Mensheviks gave as good as they got. Koba threw himself into the partisan struggle with characteristic energy and determination. He was prepared to use guile, deception, or whatever was needed to win. Besides spending much of his time writing editorials and articles, he traveled frequently between Chiatura, Batumi, and Guria to hold back the Menshevik flood.[51]

Not only Bolsheviks, but all factions and parties used what means they possessed to beat their rivals. Once they took over the local party organizations in Tiflis and in Guria, the Mensheviks tried to prevent anyone from another faction or party from gaining ground with their constituents. When Koba's old friend, Davrishev, now a Socialist Federalist, tried to speak at a workers' meeting, the Menshevik Khomeriki called him a provocateur. Davrishev grabbed Khomeriki, put a revolver to his stomach, and demanded the right to speak. He spoke.[52] A printing worker later told Davrishev that because he was bourgeois and an intellectual, "a weathercock that generally turns with the wind," the workers could not trust him. Too many intellectuals have deceived the workers and used the workers' cause as a trampoline to advance their own personal ends." But, replied Davrishev, most of your leaders are intellectuals. "What about Marx, Engels, Plekhanov, Zhordania, what are they?" Yes, said the worker, "but they have been with us a long time. They have proven their fidelity to our cause; they have been in prison, Siberia. While you, you have just come; we don't know you. And then you sing us a new song . . . to divide us."[53]

With the conquest of the Tiflis Committee, the Social Democratic "minority" became fused with the Georgian workers' and peasants' movement. When the committee issued its monthly newspaper, *sotsialdemokrat*, edited by Zhordania, it appeared only in a Georgian edition, whereas the CUC's Bolshevik publications usually came out in two or three languages.[54] The Tiflis Committee planned to publish an Armenian edition but was unable to attract a single Armenian intellectual. When the Mensheviks approached an Armenian Menshevik in Switzerland, he agreed to come only if he could propagate the idea of party unity. The Tiflis Mensheviks refused.[55] Social Democracy in the hands of the Mensheviks in Georgia was rapidly becoming not only the most massive revolutionary movement in Caucasia but increasingly an ethnically Georgian movement.

In the midst of the spreading peasant uprising in western Georgia, strikes and demonstrations in the towns and cities, Bolsheviks in Georgia were reduced to an impotent sect. The only bright spot was in Baku, where the Bolsheviks sat together with Mensheviks and conciliationists on various committees.[56] But there too they desperately needed organizers and *literatory*. "Demoralization is absolutely complete," the Bolshevik Caucasian Union Committee wrote to the Bureau of the Central Committee in Saint Petersburg.[57] The Mensheviks were leading the peasant movement in Guria and driving Bolsheviks from their meetings. When Bolsheviks tried to organize discussions of factional differences, Mensheviks dismissed such matters as trivial. A Bolshevik complained to the editors of *Proletarii* that one Menshevik spoke of "raw consciousness," of the facts of life leading workers toward socialist consciousness, and flattered his audience with all kinds of compliments and promises of "mountains of gold." At a meeting in Guria a Menshevik told the peasants that they "had found a mine of socialism" in western Georgia. Three-quarters of Gurian peasants considered themselves members of the party.[58]

Once, by the late spring of 1905, Georgia became Menshevik, it remained under the sway of the heirs of *mesame dasi* until the Bolshevik Red Army drove Zhordania and his government out of Tiflis in February 1921. The Mensheviks' initial victory in the factional struggle flowed from influential personalities like Zhordania, Noe Ramishvili, and Khomeriki, who bested Koba, Tskhakaia, and other Bolsheviks in the lengthy debates over organization and strategy. The Menshevik message resonated with Georgian workers on at least two levels. Its anti-Leninist critique of dominance by intellectuals harkened back to the local tradition of worker control of committees. Furthermore, the Mensheviks were more closely connected to the *mesame dasi* and *kvali intelligenty*, who had great prestige among workers. And they "spoke Georgian" to their followers—not only in the literal sense (Koba and the Bolsheviks did that as well)—but in a national sense of fostering the Georgian aspects of the movement more intensely than Social Democracy's interethnic character. From 1905 through the early 1920s Menshevism was the actual national liberation movement of the Georgians, sweeping before it all its rivals—Bolsheviks, Socialist Federalists, and nationalists.

Zhordania's victory was not only a personal triumph that stemmed from his prestige in his homeland. He was a tough infighter, ready to caricature the Bolsheviks to the advantage of his faction. He played on the genuine fears of the Georgian workers that they were being marginalized in their own movement. Unwittingly the Bolsheviks aided him, for they appeared to act precisely in the ways that Zhordania described. In his letter to Lenin the Bolshevik Stopani admitted as much and called for a change in party practices. In "meetings with the Mensheviks," he wrote, "workers on the committees expressed dissatisfaction with the fact that nonworkers are in charge of all work. It is essential to put local, influential workers in the center of the organization (this has already been done but is still too little); it is essential that such organizational forms be worked out so that so-called advanced workers can influence and initiate matters; if this is not resolved, we will remain behind the movement and will lose much. The 'schism' does not interest all the conscious workers as much as the forms of organizational life, as much as their growth in Social Democratic work and the movement." Stopani then cautioned Lenin "to be very careful" with the calling of a new congress that would further divide the party. If the Bolsheviks appeared to be divisive, "our position among the masses will be extremely [difficult]."[59]

Anxious about the turn that events in Russia had taken, Lenin in Geneva reevaluated his tactics. In letters to his comrades, he was frank in his estimation of the problems that the Bolsheviks faced. "The Mensheviks have more money, more literature, more means of transporting it, more agents, bigger 'names,' more people working with them."[60] They were actively taking over committees, so the Bolsheviks feared, in order to convene a Menshevik-dominated congress of the party. Lenin called for expansion of the committees, the building of sub-committees, and the recruiting of younger people. He complained about the slowness of party members to act, underscored the need to learn from the workers, and scoffed at the faults of intellectuals.

Lenin repeatedly claimed that he wanted a broad workers' movement, which would possess its own organizations and be allied with a tight organization of revolutionary Social Democrats. The latter would include both intellectuals and workers, for Lenin opposed either excluding intellectuals from the "workers' party" as some *ouvrierists* may have preferred or keeping out workers as some radical committeemen advocated.[61] The Social Democrats, whatever their social origins, were charged with sending their forces among all classes of the population to prepare "the direct struggle for freedom."[62] Yet even as he favored placing workers on committees, Lenin opposed election of Social Democratic committees within Russia because of the danger of discovery by the police. In autocratic Russia Social Democrats had to be *konspira-tivnye* (secretive). Socialists could only preserve their organizations by adhering to the need for secrecy.

With the Japanese rout of the Russian military at Port Arthur and the killings on Bloody Sunday, it became clear to Lenin that revolution was on the horizon. He also sensed the limits of his own organizational strategy. He began to criticize precisely the tendencies within the party to which his own emphasis on the intellectual origins of socialist theory, centralized organization, and discipline had given rise. A month after Bloody Sunday, he wrote, "January 9, 1905 revealed all the gigantic reserves of revolutionary proletarian energy, and at the same time the utter inadequacy of the Social Democratic organization."[63] As editor of *Vpered* he published an article by one of the most humanist Bolsheviks, Anatolii Lunacharskii, critical of old practices. Lunacharskii asserted, "An organization of professional revolutionaries as a closed and autonomous group—this is pernicious Jacobinism; but a solid and centralized party, closely connected with the proletarian masses, aspiring to enlighten and organize it and guide it by revolutionary demonstrations to its true interests—this is a social democratic party."[64] Lenin, who long had a grudging admiration for the Jacobins, felt entitled to add a line to Lunacharskii's essay: "Only hopelessly stupid people could conclude that we are becoming bourgeois Jacobins."[65]

In autocratic Russia, with its embryonic civil society, internal party politics of the type on which Social Democrats had spent so much energy could function as a surrogate for the give and take of political competition in an open arena. A political party, even one like the RSDRP that was not contesting elections but working to overthrow the existing political order, worked at coordinating the aims, interests, and behavior of its members, making out of the many an instrument for winning and holding power. But for all the effort of the *Iskra*ites up to 1903, and the leaders of the two factions up to 1905, the RSDRP was a failure as a coordinator of its members around a shared strategy. Instead of creating a disciplined organization with a common, coherent program and marshaling its strength to mobilize working people, Social Democrats spun their wheels in the muddy byways of factional conflicts. Even so, despite dissipating time and energy in internal affairs, they managed at times to stimulate, at other times to channel, mass activity into a broad political struggle against autocracy, to redirect particular, local, and material grievances into a radical challenge to the regime.

In the half decade of serious Social Democratic organizing, from the turn of the century until 1905, the all-consuming groundwork of building a party infrastructure had created its own culture, that of the committeeman, which to some leading Bolsheviks appeared to have become an obstacle to developing a broad popular revolutionary movement. In her memoirs Krupskaia drew a devastating portrait of this type of party worker. "The 'committeeman' was usually a rather self-assured person. He saw what a tremendous influence the work of the committee had on the masses, and as a rule he recognized no inner-Party democracy. 'Inner-Party democracy only leads to trouble with the police. We are connected with the movement as it is,' the 'committeemen' would say." Particularly noxious for Krupskaia was the committeemen's attitudes toward the party leaders abroad. "Inwardly they rather despised the Party workers abroad, who, in their opinion, had nothing better to do than squabble among themselves—'they ought to be made to work under Russian conditions.' The 'committeemen' objected to the overruling influence of the Center abroad. At the same time they did not want innovations. They were neither desirous nor capable of adjusting themselves to quickly changing conditions."[66]

Working underground in small circles, contacting only a few loyal workers, and coming up occasionally to initiate a strike or speak to crowds, the committeemen had gotten use to caution and avoidance of unnecessary danger, to secretiveness, and to giving orders rather than listening to the voices of those they were meant to serve. Loyal to the organization, the committeemen had become conservative preservers of old practices rather than adaptive to changing revolutionary circumstances. For all their service up to 1905, the committeemen were now seen by Lenin as unable to adjust to the possibilities of more open struggle and eventually of legal politics.

While many Bolsheviks, as well as Mensheviks, fit the portrait of the committeeman, one of those who matched it most neatly was Koba Jughashvili. Suddenly in 1905 Social Democrats of both factions found themselves swamped by striking workers, mass demonstrations, and peasant uprisings. Both factions had to reevaluate their tactics. Even committeemen like Koba were compelled to engage in new forms of political activity, put aside their factional squabbles, and focus on the escalating struggle against the state.

12

THE COMMITTEEMAN

The general reasons why Bolshevik tactics appealed to Koba
are not far to seek. By temperament he belonged to the "hard"
brand of revolutionaries. Softness in any form was not one of his
characteristics. . . . Koba translated Lenin's arguments and instructions
into Georgian, and into action. He took part in building and guiding
the provincial military organization, which had at its disposal a very
efficient secret laboratory of explosives. . . . Koba's role in the new branch
of the party was not that of a combatant officer but of an organizer,
administrator, and inspirer.

—ISAAC DEUTSCHER, *STALIN,*
A POLITICAL BIOGRAPHY (1949)

Late in the summer of 1905, a young woman, Faro Knuniants, arrived in
Tiflis. She had been exiled to her hometown of Shusha (Shushi) in the
mountainous region of Karabakh after her arrest in Petersburg for involvement in an armed revolutionary band. Knuniants wanted to continue her work as a party propagandist.[1] When Shusha erupted in
Armenian-Muslim riots, her brother Bogdan, already a well-regarded
party member, and his wife, Liza, invited her to Tiflis where they had
prepared a false passport for her. Bogdan had to leave immediately for
the capital, so he gave Faro a note for Mikha Tskhakaia, then operating
as one of the leading Bolsheviks in the city. Mikha greeted her warmly
and sent her off to meet his protégé, Koba. When Liza learned that Faro
was to meet Koba, she smiled sarcastically, "Well, well, go on, then, to
that dried up seminarian [*sukhar'-seminarist*]." "Bogdan and I don't like
him. . . . He is a kind of Talmudist. And by the way, Bogdan has an amazing feel for people." Faro hesitated to go, but Liza assured her that

perhaps their first impressions were wrong. After all, Mikha had confidence in him, and "you're not going to him to have your children baptized."

The Tiflis Bolsheviks desperately needed propagandists. Their numbers and supporters had dwindled since the return of Zhordania. Beleaguered by hostile Mensheviks, they were struggling both to shore up their support and explain the profound differences with their rivals within the same party. When Knuniants arrived at Koba's, he looked her over from head to foot and asked why she had come. What did she need from him? "Small, thin, dark, he spoke so that he was hardly audible. . . . I gave him the note from Mikha. He read it and again examined me from foot to head." "You? A propagandist?" he asked suspiciously. "Yes," she answered, "and this is not my first year." "Do you realize how responsible this job is in the situation here in Tiflis?" he asked. "I suppose that it is no more responsible than in Petersburg or Baku," she shot back. Koba rudely interrogated her: "Where have you come from?" "How did you become acquainted with Mikha?" "Do you read newspapers?" "Which ones exactly?" Knuniants stood her ground. "What is this, an examination?" "Call it what you like," said Koba, "only you don't look at all like a propagandist." "If I were to look like one," retorted Knuniants, "they would immediately arrest me. . . . In your opinion what do I look like?" Koba "delayed his answer; then he smirked. 'Like a noblewoman.'" At that point Faro Knuniants wondered why she had to endure this second-degree, but "considering party discipline," she pulled herself together and allowed Koba, who was in charge of the local Bolshevik propagandists, to talk to her "as if she were a schoolgirl."[2]

Russian Marxism was replete with dilemmas. On the one hand, workers were thought to have a natural, spontaneous attraction for socialism, but left to themselves fell victim to the hegemony of bourgeois ideas and were easily seduced into nonrevolutionary accommodation with capitalism. Therefore, Social Democrats had to take the lead in the workers' movement. Yet Social Democrats were most often *intelligenty* who came from the middle classes, and "bourgeois intellectuals" were seen to waiver in the face of the revolutionary challenge. Intellectuals were warned to be wary of displacing workers altogether and losing touch with their designated constituents, yet for many socialists workers seemed unable to fulfill their historic role. They regarded Russian workers as degraded, humiliated, and prone to "spontaneous" acts of violence. At the same time they considered workers to be primed to become "advanced," "conscious," unwavering revolutionaries. The revolution under way was a bourgeois democratic revolution, but Russia's Marxists believed that in Russia only revolutionary workers could achieve that revolution. However, workers and their representatives, the Social Democrats, were not supposed to seize power and move on to the socialist revolution.[3] Both factions of the party wrestled with these dilemmas, expecting that events beyond their control would help resolve them.

At all levels of the party, activists were thinking through the meaning of the events in which they found themselves. What was the nature of this revolution? What was the proper strategy for revolutionary socialists? All Marxists in Russia believed that the unfolding revolution was a "bourgeois-democratic revolution"—that is, a revolution that would overthrow autocracy and its attendant "feudalism" and open the way to the further development of a capitalist economy and a liberal democratic political state. As they had over questions of party structure and the relationship of socialist intellectuals to workers, Mensheviks and Bolsheviks disagreed bitterly about how to achieve that revolutionary transformation. In December 1904 Lenin wrote explicitly about the necessity to plan for a workers' insurrection to overthrow the tsarist state. Martov, on the other hand, greeted Bloody Sunday with a less radical reaction: "Our task at the moment is not so much 'to organize' the people's revolution as to 'unleash it.'"[4] Much more willing than the Bolsheviks to focus on the revolutionary potential of the Russian middle class, the Mensheviks sought to ally with the liberals in the *zemstva*, the municipal dumas, and the newspaper *Osvobozhdenie* (Liberation). Martov wrote that in Russia the proletariat was the "lever of the political self-liberation of bourgeois society"; it was more radical than the bourgeoisie, certainly, but at this moment the goal was not socialism but the creation of a liberal society in which it could then compete for power against the bourgeoisie.[5]

Whereas the Mensheviks talked about "arming" the proletariat with revolutionary propaganda, Lenin spoke of the "technical" tasks of actually supplying them with arms. "The separation of the 'technical' side of the revolution from the political side of the revolution," he wrote, "is the greatest nonsense."[6] While Martov thought that the Russian revolution might be led by a general, a bureaucrat, or a priest like Father Gapon, Lenin pushed the Social Democratic committeemen to take up the leadership of the armed struggle. Lenin emphasized the revolutionary energy of the proletariat, but other Bolsheviks clung to the idea that workers were not yet politically "conscious" enough and needed to be guided by the Social Democrats. Koba's friend Kamenev told his fellow Bolsheviks that even in the revolutionary days of January the workers had not gone beyond the "bourgeois" idea that they could improve the situation of the working class under capitalism. Class contradictions had not developed enough in Russia to crystallize a proletarian consciousness; therefore, Social Democrats had to take the lead and guide the "spontaneous" excitement of the workers toward revolution.[7]

In the spring and summer of 1905, just as liberals and socialists were swept to the head of a burgeoning mass opposition, the two Social Democratic factions were as far apart as they would be in the coming few years. On March 12 the Menshevik-led Central Committee decided to give in and go along with the preference of most of the Social Democratic committees within Russia and agreed with the Leninists that a third party congress should be held as soon as possible. But suspicions remained high, and the Council of the Party, which was charged with reconciling differences between the Central Organ and the Central Committee, refused to sanction the congress. Recriminations about the proper election of delegates led the Mensheviks to withdraw from the congress on the eve of its opening in London and to hold their own meeting in Geneva. They were cautious about arming the workers or joining any provisional revolutionary government, unless the expected socialist revolution suddenly broke out in the advanced countries of Europe.[8]

THE (BOLSHEVIK) THIRD PARTY CONGRESS

The Third Congress, then, was primarily a Bolshevik gathering. Even so, for Lenin the results of the Congress were mixed. The debates exposed serious differences within his own faction. Thirty-nine people participated in the congress, five representing the Caucasus.[9] When Lenin pointed out that the Caucasus was entitled to only three mandates, Tskhakaia protested: "Whoever heard of anyone voting in the Caucasus! We settle all our business in a comradely way. Four of us have been sent, and the number of mandates doesn't matter."[10] There were no workers at the congress, and Lenin was concerned about the predominance of the committeemen. When discussion turned to the perennial and unavoidable question of the relationship of intellectuals to workers within party organizations, Aleksandr Bogdanov, a rising star among the Bolsheviks, presented a resolution that laid out the standard factional view: the party prefers the most democratic form of organization—that is, electing members to committees—but under the circumstances of present-day tsarist Russia such democracy was a luxury. However, restrictions on elections had been taken too far, and it was time to increase the role of internal party elections and bring more workers into the committees.[11]

Bogdanov's resolution, supported by Lenin, was mild. Yet there was a quick and hostile reaction. Kamenev protested that there was no problem between intellectuals and workers in party organizations. Lenin interjected from the floor: "Yes, there is." Later when a delegate from Saratov complained that many committees were cut off from the masses and were far too conspiratorial, arguing that it was essential to bring workers into the committees, Lenin again intervened: "Completely correct!" "The Saint Petersburg Committee has only one worker on it," delegate Rumiantsev reported, "despite the fact that it has been working for fifteen years." "An outrage," Lenin interjected. He could not keep still. "Bringing workers into the committees," he asserted, "is not only a pedagogical but a political task. Workers have a class instinct, and with a little political practice they fairly soon become staunch Social Democrats. I support the view that for every two intellectuals committees ought to have eight workers." When the delegate from Baku, "Alesha" Japaridze, said that he was astonished to hear people say that there were no workers able to be committeemen, Lenin shouted, "Listen! Listen!"[12] "I cannot sit quietly when they say that there are no workers worthy of being members of the committee."[13] No other issue inspired as much passion as this one, but in the end no resolution was adopted. While all Social Democrats welcomed an increase in politically conscious workers in party committees, they differed on how this might be accomplished. A majority of the delegates were unwilling to go along with Lenin and Bogdanov and reverse what had become Bolshevik orthodoxy for many activists on the leading role of the intellectuals—at least for the time being. In some ways Lenin's opponents at the congress—Kamenev, Aleksei Rykov, and others—fit the Menshevik image of a "Bolshevik" far better than did the leader of the faction.[14] Although he was not at the congress, Koba was closer to Kamenev on this point than to Lenin. They were more "Leninist" than Lenin himself.

Koba also shared Kamenev's hard line against the Mensheviks. But Koba's patron at home and one of the Caucasian delegates in London, Tskhakaia, pointed out that Mensheviks within Russia were not the same as those abroad who had fought so hard with the Bolsheviks. When he first read *Iskra* and *What Is to Be Done?*, Tskhakaia was impressed that the party had found such a clear expression of its positions. But many of the faults that delegates to the congress had attributed to the Mensheviks—lack of organization, "cooptation-mania"—were also true of the Bolsheviks. "We all, Menshevik comrades as well, were educated together, have worked together in friendship yesterday, and only today are we enemies." Unlike Koba, he opposed the notion that there was something unique in what was being called "Leninism." "I am not a Leninist, I am a party activist, a revolutionary Social Democrat, a Marxist."[15] Other Georgian Bolsheviks shared Tskhakaia's attitudes toward the Mensheviks, but not Koba. His intransigence estranged him not only from the Mensheviks with whom he had been debating but also from more conciliatory Bolsheviks like Tskhakaia.

When discussion at the Third Party Congress turned to the nature of the current revolution, Lenin staked out a definitively radical position.

He agreed that the revolution was bourgeois democratic, not proletarian socialist, but he opposed the Mensheviks' restraint of the workers. Optimistic about the possibility of success, he called for a "democratic dictatorship," which meant a tough, centralized government of the "democracy"—that is, the lower classes, the workers and the peasants, ready to use "terror" against the autocracy. "A democratic dictatorship," he pointed out, "is not an organization of 'order,' but an organization of war. Even if we seized Saint Petersburg and guillotined Nicholas, we would still have to deal with several Vendées. And Marx understood this perfectly when . . . he recalled the Jacobins. He said: 'The Terror of 1793 was nothing but the plebeian manner of settling accounts with absolutism and counterrevolution.' We also prefer to settle accounts with the Russian autocracy by 'plebian' methods and leave Girondin methods to *Iskra*."[16]

In its final resolutions the congress decided that the Social Democrats should work toward an armed uprising that would establish a provisional revolutionary government in which Social Democrats could participate. That government would guarantee elections to a Constituent Assembly that in turn would inaugurate a bourgeois democratic regime to develop the capitalist economy and expand the democratic possibilities for the working class to move eventually toward a socialist revolution. The Bolsheviks supported the peasant movements, though they treated the bourgeoisie and the liberal opposition with more caution. *Iskra* was to be replaced by a new central newspaper, *Proletarii*. Party membership was defined as *po-bol'shevistski*—that is, to include only those who supported the party by material means and personal participation in one of its organizations.[17] Even though they remained linked formally to the Mensheviks in a single Social Democratic party, the Bolsheviks at this point operated (at least at the top, if not in all local committees) as if they were an independent party, complete with their own Central Committee.

As a militant Bolshevik ventriloquizing Lenin, Koba laid out his own understanding of the factional differences in a long essay published first in Georgian in May 1905 and a month later in Russian and Armenian translations.[18] "A Few Words on Party Disagreements" was a reply to Zhordania's articles "Majority or Minority?" and "What Is the Party?" which appeared in *sotsial-demokrat* and *mogzauri*. Challenging Zhordania's claim that the Bolsheviks believed that workers on their own could not master the tenets of socialism, Koba succinctly explained the Bolshevik view in simple, stark sentences reinforced through repetition. When the workers' movement in Russia first appeared, he asserted, the *ekonomisty* were content to reflect the views of the workers themselves without promoting the Social Democratic vision. But the bearer of socialist consciousness, worker or intellectual, was, according to Social Democracy, "obligated to instill socialist consciousness into the workers' movement and not to observe the spontaneous labor movement from the side, not to trudge behind it."[19] Quoting Kautsky and Lenin, he affirmed, "Social Democracy is the union of the workers' movement with socialism." Each is meaningless without the other. Paraphrasing Lenin, he argued that workers have a natural attraction to socialism but cannot on their own develop the knowledge of "scientific socialism"—that is, the flow of history, the temporary nature of capitalism and its replacement by its negation, namely socialism. Such conceptions of overall social and historical development were first worked out by bourgeois intellectuals, some of whom linked up with the working class. The labor movement without socialism is a "ship without a compass, which will reach the other shore, but if it had a compass it would reach that shore faster and would meet fewer dangers."[20] Without the Social Democratic Party workers would wander aimlessly under the influence of bourgeois ideology, accepting trade unionism and capitalist labor laws for a time, but eventually, even without Social Democracy, they would find their way instinctively toward socialism. The task of Social Democrats is to shorten the trip by plotting out a more direct route.

Against Zhordania's charge that Leninism at its root contradicts Marxism, Koba methodically linked Lenin with Kautsky, with the old *Iskra*, and with orthodox Marxism. "It is clear," he asserted, "that the 'scornful attitude toward workers,' the 'exalting of the intelligentsia,' the 'unmarxist position of the majority,' and other such pearls that Menshevik 'critics' strew before us are nothing more than pretentious words, the fantasies of the Tiflis 'Mensheviks.'"[21] He referred to Zhordania as "stupid" and impertinently corrected his Georgian. He explained the abandonment of Lenin by his former comrades Martov, Plekhanov, Akselrod, Zasulich, and Aleksandr Potresov as personal pique and the unsteady wavering of intellectuals. Like Lenin, Koba condemned the Mensheviks as opportunists who shift their positions more often than one changes one's pocket handkerchiefs.[22]

The pamphlet, a Bolshevik reported to Geneva, "created a sensation" in Tiflis and attracted attention among the Bolshevik leaders abroad.[23] In October Lenin himself reviewed the piece and lauded the discussion on "bringing consciousness from without" as "an excellent presentation of the question."[24] In another response to *sotsial-demokrat*, Koba again accused the Mensheviks of deliberately distorting the Bolshevik position. "How is it that you cannot understand that in our opinion, in the opinion of Bolsheviks, it is Social Democracy that brings [*vnosit*] socialist consciousness to the workers' movement, and not only Social Democratic intellectuals? Why do you think that in the Social Democratic party there are only intellectuals? Can it be that you do not know that in the ranks of Social Democracy there are more advanced workers than intellectuals?"[25] Koba distinguished between the "attraction" [*vlechenie*] toward socialism that was born in the proletariat itself and socialist consciousness [*soznanie*] that comes from outside, from Social Democrats.

In a movement distinguished by the youth of its activists, Koba, just twenty-six years old, was by 1905 a known figure among the leading Bolsheviks both at home and abroad. One Menshevik, Kalistrate Dolidze, remembered years later: "Stalin especially stood out among all the comrades. He dressed plainly, did not like to play the dandy, and loved only to work."[26] His reports from the Caucasus were valued at Bolshevik headquarters in Geneva. His importance to the Bolsheviks was enhanced by the fact that he was one of the relatively few veterans of the faction still active in Georgia, the proverbial big fish in a small pond.

The Mensheviks' political sweep over most of Caucasia was a bewildering rout for Koba and the local Bolsheviks. On May 8 (21), 1905,

Koba wrote to Lenin, signing the letter "Vano." He began by excusing himself for being late with his letter: "I have to travel around the Caucasus all the time, speak in discussions, cheer up the comrades, etc. The Mensheviks carried on a campaign everywhere, and it was necessary to rebuff them. We had almost no one (and now very few, two or three times less than the Mensheviks), and we have to work for three."[27] Reporting on the state of the party in the Caucasus, he acknowledged that "Tiflis is almost completely in the hands of the Mensheviks. Half of Baku and Batumi as well are Menshevik. . . . Guria is in the hands of conciliators, who decided to go over to the Mensheviks. The trend of the Mensheviks is still rising. However, a sharp eye notices a reverse tendency, more and more evident in Tiflis and Batumi." The Union Committee was the one stronghold of the majority, but it did not have direct ties with workers; it operated through the local committees. He "strongly cursed" those in the CUC and the Tiflis Committee who a year earlier had "vacillated" and not done enough to prevent the Mensheviks from taking almost all the workers with them. Koba was convinced that the situation could easily be reversed if the Bolsheviks had a few more *literatory*, people who could write leaflets and pamphlets. Workers responded more to the written than to the spoken word. Moreover, he wrote, "the Mensheviks are not good organizers (they are not even organizers; in the best case they are narrow '*praktiki*' of the Bundist type, without broad thoughts, without strong will; these are vulgar sentimentalists of the preparty period, the period of worker-philia. . . . But they have 'wonderful' demagogues, party hooligans, trying to resolve everything well, everything pure. . . . Besides this, they have many people. And all this is significant at a moment of the rapidly heightening spontaneity of the masses (a revolutionary moment)—you see, they appeal to spontaneity."[28]

Once he had committed to Bolshevism and assimilated Lenin's ideas, Koba remained loyal to his faction. Georgian Social Democrats noted Koba's near sycophancy toward the Bolshevik leader. "He bowed before Lenin," wrote the Menshevik Razhden Arsenidze. "He lived by his arguments, his thoughts, copied him incomparably, so much so that we jokingly called him 'Lenin's left leg.'"[29] On June 20, in an apparent tribute to Lenin, Jughashvili published an article, the first that he signed "Koba," in the first number of the Georgian Bolshevik newspaper, *akhali tskhovreba* (New Life). It was titled "What Is to Be Done?" Here he called for an autocracy of the people, a term he borrowed from the Social Democrats' party program, to replace the tsarist autocracy. "The revolution and counterrevolution cannot be reconciled, the goat and wolf herded together."[30]

Yet Koba already in 1905 demonstrated a trait that would become evident periodically over the next two decades of his career. As fiercely polemical as he frequently was against the opponents of the Bolsheviks, and as opposed as he was to "conciliationism," he repeatedly vented his frustration at the lack of party unity. In a handwritten letter to the editorial board of *proletariatis brdzola*, he expressed his amazement at how the Caucasian Bolsheviks and Mensheviks pursued each other to the point of mutual destruction. Such behavior was perhaps tolerable in parties in bourgeois democracies but not for Russian Social Democracy.[31] Personally he was contemptuous of Georgian Mensheviks, but practically he was prepared both to polemicize against them and to work with them.

The local Mensheviks were not interested. Zhordania and his comrades exploited their stunning success among the activist workers and intellectuals by setting up their own Caucasian Bureau to oppose the CUC in April 1905.[32] That spring the Georgian Mensheviks reflected the caution and moderation of their Russian comrades. They took a strong stand against joining a provisional revolutionary government. Such a move, they argued, would lead to disillusionment of the workers with Social Democracy, for the party could not fulfill the vital needs of the working class in a bourgeois revolution.[33] Zhordania was convinced that the Russian proletariat was not yet conscious and organized enough to make its own revolution. Therefore, socialists must try to attract the bourgeoisie away from the government and bring them closer to the workers. "Otherwise, the defeat of the proletariat and the victory of the government is inevitable."[34] With terrorism by workers and peasants spreading throughout Caucasia, the Mensheviks came out strongly against such tactics, although at the same time they decided to form a "military technical commission" to find the means to arm workers and chose Noe Ramishvili as the representative of the Tiflis Committee on the commission.[35] In December he personally threw a bomb into the store of the Officers' Club, killing both soldiers and employees.[36]

As one of the most steady and consistent Leninists, Koba's stature rose in his dwindling faction. His principal refuge was far to the west of Tiflis, in the Chiatura region, where tens of thousands worked in manganese mines. A remote mountain valley along the banks of the Qvirila, Chiatura had for thirty years been a principal source of Russia's manganese. Social Democrats in the mining district were a close-knit group. Young and inexperienced, they wanted to work openly with the workers but were warned by the more tried propagandists to be more "conspiratorial." "All day long," Kote Tsintsadze remembered, "we sat in our rooms like hostages and would go out to the mines to chat with the workers only at night." They were appalled by the conditions in which the workers lived and worked. Workers were in the mines over fifteen hours, but the socialists would corral them after work at seven or eight in the evening and talk to them for another hour or so until the exhausted miners would doze or wander off. Yet they managed to form several dozen circles with ten to twenty workers in each, launch a demonstration adorned with red flag in January, and a major strike in February. They "taxed" the local businessmen to support the strike and planned the assassination of two informers. The murders, however, went badly, and the popular organizer Shakro Giunashvili was killed. To avenge their loss the Social Democrats launched an attack on the police station. Joined by peasants who had come to the market in town, they and armed workers found their targets. After releasing innocent officers and the wife and children of the chief, they shot the ones for whom they had come. They set the building on fire to force Shakro's killer out. Suddenly, he ran out of the stable, fell to his knees, and begged, "For the sake of Christ, have mercy!" "Ask Shakro for mercy, he will forgive you," they answered as three gunmen opened fire on him.[37] Enraged by the loss of a beloved comrade, Social Democrats had mobilized the rage of local workers and peasants to carry out summary justice, and in the process demonstrated the vulnerability of the state authority.

Bolsheviks and Mensheviks competed for the loyalty of the Chiatura workers, and several Bolshevik workers went to Kutaisi to request help from the local committee. First the sickly Tsulukidze was sent, followed by Koba.[38] Koba was already known in the district for having directed a propaganda circle there some months earlier. After his patron Tskhakaia reported to a mass meeting of Chiatura workers about the Third Congress, they responded enthusiastically to the call for an armed uprising and a provisional revolutionary government.[39] Hiding in the home of Jaqeli, a local worker, Koba set up a secret printing press in the basement and formed a "Red Hundreds" detachment of local fighters.[40]

The Menshevik Khariton Shavishvili met Koba in Chiatura and was impressed by his skills as a debater. Once when Koba was quoting Lenin's *What Is to Be Done?* a seminary student tried to embarrass him by yelling out, "Here, comrades, the roasted turkey lies!" Koba quickly retorted that the Mensheviks seemed to need a roasted turkey to make the revolution.[41] Koba made sure each time that he spoke last and used simple words and serene manner to win over the workers. In desperation the Mensheviks brought in Grigol Lortkipanidze, who had recently returned to Kutaisi from a two-year stint leading the student movement in Odessa. An experienced speaker, used to addressing large halls, he understood the mood of an audience. When Koba invited him to speak first, Lortkipanidze politely declined. Although both men clearly and carefully explained their faction's position, once again the victory went to the Menshevik.[42] A second debate with Lortkipanidze took place in the Darkveti district, one still held by the Bolsheviks. Here Koba spoke last. He brought up the burning issue of participation in a provisional revolutionary government, which the Bolsheviks favored and the Mensheviks opposed. He asserted that if the Social Democrats were not part of the government, the bourgeoisie in power would betray the revolution and drown it in blood. Arousing the audience to a fever pitch, he said that the Mensheviks wanted the proletariat to bleed for the bourgeoisie while the Bolsheviks preferred to spill the blood of the bourgeoisie for the benefit of the proletariat. The workers turned on

Lortkipanidze, punching him and nearly lynching him before his comrades were able to save him. This time the victory went to Koba.[43]

Where they could gather some supporters, Koba and his comrades set up a "committee," appropriating the name associated with sanctioned Social Democratic institutions. The proprieties and formalities of elections were foregone in the case of the Imereti and Chiatura committees.[44] The Bolsheviks held their own around Kutaisi as well and profited from the workers' impatience. There the Mensheviks spoke of the revolution coming in ten, maybe sixty years, "to which the workers answered with a smirk: 'In such a case, come here and teach our children and grandchildren, but right now, for us, you Mensheviks are superfluous; we want an armed organization; give us weapons, weapons.'"[45]

When the young Bolshevik Aleksandre (Sasha) Tsulukidze succumbed to tuberculosis, a grand funeral attracted some thirty to forty thousand marchers. Both Mensheviks and Bolsheviks were among the organizers. Koba, who had known Tsulukidze slightly, attended the funeral along with his comrades, marching for miles through a pouring rain.[46] At the gravesite in Khoni, some seventeen miles from Kutaisi, two choruses sang, and endless speeches were made in Georgian, Russian, and Armenian.[47] But Bolshevik support in western Georgia was thin, as a bizarre incident at the funeral revealed. While a large crowd remained in the city square listening to orations, the Bolsheviks organized a discussion in an adjacent building. The room was packed when Koba spoke, even though most of the listeners were not particularly sympathetic to the Bolsheviks. One worker asked, "Are we supposed to consider Bolsheviks real Social Democrats?" The Menshevik Arsenidze answered that as party members they ought to be so considered. When Koba rose to speak for the last time, several of his Bolshevik comrades in a grand gesture lifted him into the air and carried him out of the meeting into the square. No one outside paid much attention to the triumphal march; only the handful of Bolsheviks cheered. Embarrassed, Koba turned angrily on his comrades. "You carried me out, but where are the people?"[48]

Sergo Kavtaradze, who was close to Tsulukidze and maintained the link between the dying young man and the Social Democratic committee in Kutaisi, bristled at the thought that Jughashvili was a close friend of Tsulukidze's or that the latter had worked under the former. "I do not remember one instance when he [Tsulukidze] asked me about Comrade Koba, showed interest in him, or that Koba visited him. I saw Comrade Koba among other comrades on the balcony of his father's home for the first and only time the day of [Tsulukidze's] death."[49] As a fellow party member Koba ought to have been at the funeral, but exploiting the occasion, he used it to promote his factional position, only to be embarrassed by the limp response of those attending.

Through 1904 and well into 1905 the infighting went on, and out of this struggle, which would carry the Social Democrats from the moment of schism through the revolutionary cauldron of 1905, each faction gradually became clearer about its differences with the other, and not only formed a coherent reading of the political situation and the strategies to be derived from it, but became convinced of the reprehensible qualities of its opponents. The shared language and political culture of Social Democracy divided bitterly into two antagonistic movements. Members of both factions desperately wanted the party to achieve the unity that had never been obtained, but in the struggle for dominance of one understanding of the movement's needs over another, the personal and political differences that had shaken the party in 1903 hardened into what was gradually becoming two rival political parties.

By the summer of 1905, after a long period of confusion, the strategic and tactical differences between Bolsheviks and Mensheviks were evident to all who cared to know. Immediately after the Bolshevik Third Congress and the Menshevik conferences in Geneva and Tbsilisi, Lenin wrote a major pamphlet outlining his position on what divided Russian Social Democracy's strategy in the current revolution. *Two Tactics of Social Democracy in the Democratic Revolution* was published in Geneva in July 1905 and in its fundamentals remained the principal strategic line of the Leninists for the next twelve years.[50] All in all the Bolsheviks stayed closer to the original *Iskra* positions, while the Mensheviks, as a critical "minority," considered the tactics of yesteryear obsolete. Even though polemicists on both sides exaggerated the views of the other, five fundamental differences separated the factions. First, the Bolsheviks emphasized that socialist *theory* came from outside the working class, and even though workers might *instinctively* move toward socialism, the powerful ideological hegemony of bourgeois ideas required Social Democrats to accelerate and facilitate the infusion of socialist consciousness in the workers.[51] The Mensheviks argued that life itself pushes workers toward becoming socialist, that there is a natural gravitation toward socialism, and claimed that Lenin wanted "the complete dominance of the intelligentsia in the party and the subordination of the proletariat."[52]

Second, Bolsheviks desired a narrower, tighter, more centralized party with appointment of committees rather than local elections, which they considered dangerous in an autocratic police state. Lenin distinguished the workers' movement from the party, while Menshevik theorists, like Vera Zasulich, called for absorption of as much of the movement as possible into the party. Mensheviks advocated election of committees by members and wanted a broader party that included the maximum number of supporters and sympathizers of Social Democracy. For Mensheviks discipline and initiative came from the workers themselves; for Lenin discipline had to be imposed by the party. Both factions claimed they wanted more workers on committees and denigrated the opportunism of intellectuals, which each claimed was characteristic of the other.

Both Bolsheviks and Mensheviks agreed that the present revolution could only be a bourgeois democratic revolution. As Lenin put it, "Only the most ignorant people can ignore the bourgeois character of the present democratic revolution; only the most naïve optimists can forget how little as yet the mass of the workers know of the aims of socialism and of the methods of achieving it. . . . Whoever wants to move toward socialism by another path other than political democracy will inevitably arrive at absurd and reactionary conclusions in the economic and in the political sense." Not only was democracy on the agenda but capitalism as well. "In countries like Russia, the working class suffers not so much from capitalism as from the lack of capitalist development. The working class is therefore *undoubtedly interested* in the widest, freest, and speediest development of capitalism."[53]

But Lenin was much less enamored of political democracy than the Mensheviks would prove to be. "Bourgeois" political democracy was for him a means to an end, namely socialism, rather than an end in itself: "All political freedoms in general, on the soil of contemporary, that is, capitalist, productive relations are bourgeois freedoms. The demand for freedom expresses first of all the interests of the bourgeoisie. Its representatives first put forth this demand. Its supporters have everywhere, like masters, used this acquired freedom, shrinking it to measured and precise bourgeois doses, mixing it with the repression of the revolutionary proletariat by the most refined methods in peacetime and brutally cruel ones in stormy times."[54] Real democracy would be achieved only with socialism and the dispossession of bourgeois power.

The suspicion of liberal or "bourgeois democracy"—limited as it was to civil rights, parliamentary politics, and the influence in everyday life of privileges based in wealth and property—was inscribed in Marxism from the young Marx and Engels forward. Marxists held that material security and social equality for those without property were basic requirements for a truly democratic polity. There was no full democracy without socialism. All Social Democrats subscribed to the idea that progress ultimately required transcending capitalism and liberalism to the empowerment of ordinary people—that is, socialism. But Mensheviks and Bolsheviks disputed how to move toward democracy and through it to socialism. With whom would the working class ally in these revolutionary transitions?

The third and fourth differences between the factions had to do with which social classes in the empire Social Democrats might partner—the liberal bourgeoisie or the mass of peasants—and whether Social Democrats should join a bourgeois revolutionary government. Despite their hostility to the class of capitalists and industrialists that had long been closely tied to the autocracy, Mensheviks and Bolsheviks alike placed their hopes on this group to run a liberal regime once it had been established. The Mensheviks held that workers needed the bourgeoisie in order to have a successful revolution, and, therefore, they favored a closer relationship with the liberal bourgeoisie and worried about frightening the bourgeoisie and pushing it into the arms of the government. They opposed, however, joining a provisional revolutionary government with the bourgeoisie and preferred pressure "from without." The only concession that the Mensheviks made was that Social Democrats might seize power in certain rebellious cities and form "revolutionary communes." Should the proletariat of advanced countries begin the socialist revolution, then the Russian Social Democrats might strive for power. Only "if we should be finally swept into power," the Mensheviks reluctantly agreed, "against our will by the inner dialectics of the revolution at a time when the national conditions for the establishment of socialism are not yet mature, we would not back out."[55]

Bolsheviks were consistently more suspicious of the liberal bourgeoisie. Since the revolution was bourgeois-democratic, Lenin advocated alliance with the "revolutionary and republican" bourgeoisie, most importantly the peasantry, but not with the "liberal and monarchist bourgeoisie." Impressed by the radicalism of the villagers, Lenin proposed the formation of a provisional "revolutionary democratic dictatorship of the proletariat and the peasantry" that could then settle accounts with tsarism "in the Jacobin, or, if you like, the plebian way." But, he cautioned, "This does not mean, of course, that we necessarily propose to imitate the Jacobins of 1793, to adopt their views, program, slogans, and methods of action. Nothing of the kind. . . . If we live to the real victory of the revolution, we will have new methods of action appropriate for the character and goals of the party of the working class striving for a complete socialist revolution."[56] Once again invoking a positive image of the Jacobins who launched the Terror during the French Revolution, Lenin did not spell out what those "new methods" would be. The door was left open, if need be, for the use of violence, even state terror.

Rather than take fright, Lenin wanted the Social Democrats to look forward to a possible "complete victory" that would "enable us to rouse Europe." "The socialist proletariat of Europe will then throw off the yoke of the bourgeoisie and in its turn help us to carry out a socialist revolution."[57] Here Lenin stated starkly the wager that he would make in 1917:

seize power in a country not yet ready for a socialist revolution and gamble that Europe would come to Russia's rescue.

One the great ironies of the Russian revolutionary movement was that a major political party—the Social Democrats—that advocated the advancement of democracy generally saw the majority of Russia's population, the eighty-five percent that was peasant, not as a progressive force, but as a potential obstacle to the future progress and development of the country.[58] The Bolsheviks, however, were far more willing to support, work with, and even ally with the peasantry than were the Russian Mensheviks (in contrast to the Georgian Mensheviks). Russian Mensheviks were more orthodox in their suspicion of a petit bourgeois class that historically had repeatedly turned against the workers. Like other Marxists, Lenin saw the peasants as petit bourgeois producers, but he considered them capable of valiant revolutionary action. Rather than being instinctively socialist as were the workers, they were ultimately limited to the capitalist stage of history and the bourgeois revolution. Today's allies, they could easily become tomorrow's enemies—if they did not move beyond the bourgeois revolution. "In politics, as in all the life of society," he wrote in March 1906, "if you do not push forward, you will be hurled back. Either the bourgeoisie, strengthened after the democratic revolution . . . will rob both the workers and the peasant masses of all their gains, or the proletariat and the peasant masses will fight their way further forward. And this means—a republic and the full autocracy of the people."[59]

Last, the two factions differed on the armed uprising. As a Menshevik pamphlet put it: "According to the views of the 'majority,' it is possible to schedule a general uprising and carry it out by conspiratorial means: revolution is a technical problem. According to the view of the 'minority,' revolution is a fundamental change in social relations and, as such, presents itself as the result of social development; for this reason it usually takes a long time."[60] Given the Mensheviks' qualms about insurrection, doubts about the peasantry, and fear of frightening the bourgeoisie, it is not surprising that for many rank and file Social Democrats the Bolsheviks seemed the more militantly revolutionary wing of the party. As Lenin put it, "Real support in a general struggle is given to those who strive for the maximum . . . and not to those who opportunistically curtail the aims of the struggle before the fight."[61] He specifically criticized the suggestion of the Georgian Mensheviks that Social Democrats, rather than support an armed insurrection, which they believed would push the bourgeoisie to ally with the forces of order, should work toward an elected assembly that would declare a republic.[62] Lenin saw this as "betraying the revolution and converting the proletariat into miserable stooges of the bourgeois classes."[63] Yet in many ways the Georgian Mensheviks were the most "Bolshevik" of Mensheviks, as the revolutionary years would demonstrate. Together both factions in Caucasia employed terror, formed armed units, and fought the tsarist police and army. Georgian Mensheviks were wary about an armed insurrection but willing to use arms for self-defense.[64]

In 1905 Koba was the most orthodox of Bolsheviks. In a series of articles in *proletariatis brdzola*, many of which were not published in the original editions of his collected works, Koba castigated the Mensheviks for their disruption of party unity. Bolsheviks had made concessions, he wrote, like giving up *Iskra*, even though they had won the majority of votes at the Second Congress. "Surprising people," he wrote, "these Mensheviks, because they were not chosen, they boycotted the party institutions."[65] Writing in the eastern Georgian dialect, in contrast to the western in which *mesame dasi* leaders wrote, Koba defended the various positions taken by the Bolshevik Third Congress: the call for armed uprising and participation of Social Democrats in a provisional revolutionary government.[66] It was time for party committees to carry out the arming of the workers and form armed bands not only to fight for power, but to prevent the tsarist state from deploying "the dark forces of the country." Already in the last half year officialdom has mobilized "professional hooligans or politically uninformed and fanaticized elements from among the Tatars [Caucasian Muslims] for a struggle against the revolutionaries." Social Democrats must prepare using the strictest secrecy for the upcoming battles.[67]

From his return from exile early the year before, through 1905 and 1906, Koba's articles reverberated with the language of revenge for the fate of fallen workers. In one pamphlet, he called for "Blood for blood

and death for death—that is how we will answer! To arms, on to revenge, long live the insurrection."[68] A month later he wrote, "It will not
be the people begging them for mercy, rather it will be them crawling
at our feet. Then the autocracy will pay with its dark blood for the honest blood of the workers. And having trampled upon the corpse of the
autocracy with our feet, we will go forward to socialism victoriously."[69]
For Koba the time was ripe for action, and like Lenin he was prepared
to use violence to carry the revolution forward.

13

THE TERRORIST

[I]n the revolutionary bedlam, . . . Stalin flourished in a seething
atmosphere of relentless struggle. Illiterate ruffians and cutthroats like
Kamo [Stalin's boyhood friend and loyal soldier] always prosper in
lawless times, but Stalin was unusual—as adept at debating, writing
and organizing as he was at arranging hits and heists. The command,
harnessing and provocation of turmoil were his gifts.

—SIMON SEBAG MONTEFIORE, *YOUNG STALIN* (2007)

Violence is an intimate companion of revolution, and nowhere in the
Russian Empire was their embrace tighter than in Caucasia. As an ex-
tralegal challenge to the constituted order, by its very nature revolution
involves violence. Good will and noble intentions, revolutionaries understand, are insufficient to wrest power from those who possess it. For
Marxists the very possession of power and property rests on past and
present violence. In tsarist Russia there were no institutions through
which democratic forces were represented or could express themselves
peacefully. Public protests, strikes, and ultimately violent opposition to
the police and army were the available alternatives to elections and the
rule of law. Yet as essential as they thought violence might be in the
battle with tsarism and capital, Social Democrats in the Russian Empire
distinguished between acceptable and unacceptable uses of violence, as
well as necessary and excessive violence. They never celebrated the romance of violence or saw it as an embodiment of nobility or virtue. For
Marxists, as for soldiers, violence was a strategic instrument, a rational
choice that required suspension of normal humanity and morality.

In Russian the word *terror* may be used for both terrorism and terror,
but in the prerevolutionary period it usually referred to individual or

group violence by enemies of the state to further the revolution. Terrorism was a "weapon of the weak" against an intractable authority and was used to demonstrate the vulnerability and perversity of the present order. The *narodniki* (Populists) of the 1870s and 1880s in Russia argued that "propaganda of the deed" would stimulate the peasants to rebellion. Social Democrats usually condemned terrorism as an inappropriate tactic for a party aspiring to forge a mass movement and carefully elaborated the conditions under which it might be employed. They were prepared to kill enemies, and though they targeted those suspected of aiding the state authorities in some way, they would not condone the murder of civilians or the innocent.[1]

Initially the Marxists conceded that individual acts of terrorism could be employed defensively against those who threatened their organization (police spies, informers, policemen, and soldiers). Later, in the years of revolution, they allowed terrorism to be used offensively in anticipation of and preparation for an armed uprising.[2] Violence and terrorism was justifiable, however, only as self-defense, as an inspiration toward revolutionary heroism, or as retribution. Self-preservation, as well as a sense of justice, justified killing, but indiscriminate violence that might claim innocent victims was not acceptable.

Decades earlier Plekhanov's Marxist circle, the Liberation of Labor Group, had broken with the Populists primarily over the question of terrorism and emphasized instead the importance of mass propaganda. Yet even those early Marxists noted that terrorism might initially wound "the political monster" of autocracy that the workers would then bring down.[3] Social Democrats pointedly distinguished their tactics from the Socialist Revolutionaries, the Armenian Revolutionary Federation (*Dashnaktsutyun*), the Georgian Socialist Federalists, and the anarchists who employed individual terrorism against officials, police spies, and the vicious Black Hundred instigators of pogroms. Lenin, whose Populist older brother had been hanged as a terrorist, wrote that the Socialist Revolutionaries, the heirs of the Populists, damaged the anti-tsarist movement by incorporating terrorism into the arsenal of political struggle. Terrorism created "harmful illusions" detrimental to the revolutionary forces.[4] Even so, the Bolsheviks, and the Mensheviks with less enthusiasm, refused to reject terrorism in all circumstances. In one of his more sanguinary calls for revolutionary action, at the moment in October 1905 when it appeared a general uprising was at hand, Lenin justified the use of terrorism. "Of course, any extremism is bad; everything good and useful taken to an extreme can become, and even beyond known bounds absolutely becomes, evil and harmful," he cautioned. "Disorderly, unprepared petty terror, taken to an extreme, can only reduce and waste our forces. . . . But, on the other hand, it should not be forgotten in any case that now the slogan of the uprising is already proclaimed, the uprising has already begun. To begin attacks in favorable circumstances is not only right but the clear duty of every revolutionary. The murder of spies, policemen, gendarmes, the blowing up of police stations, the freeing of the arrested, the seizure of government money for the use of the uprising—such operations are already being carried out everywhere where the uprising has flared up, in Poland and in Caucasia, and every detachment of the revolutionary army ought to prepare immediately for such operations."[5]

In the revolutionary years of 1905–1907, the armed struggle between workers, peasants, and the state was most intense at the very edges of empire, in the western borderlands of Russia, Poland, the Baltic region, and in the Caucasus. Tsarist officials viewed the peoples of the peripheries from a greater distance, with less understanding and sympathy, and often with deep disdain and enmity. Particularly after the Polish insurrection of 1863, many in authority perceived non-Russians as untrustworthy, a potential threat to the unity and security of the empire. The peoples of the peripheries often returned their hostility and antagonism. In Caucasia the targeting of enemies by Social Democrats began earlier and became more pervasive than in much of the rest of Russia. Marxists and workers emulated the Socialist Revolutionaries and murdered police spies in 1901–1902. Some like G. Z. Lelashvili became specialists in such killings, and it was he who attacked the informer who turned in the Tiflis Committee in February 1902 with an axe.[6] Koba Jughashvili was actively involved in the uncivil war of society against the autocratic state and was ready to mete out rough justice to those who endangered or betrayed the cause. He pointed out a worker who had asked to attend an illegal meeting and confided, "That guy is a spook." When the same man was later seen in a policeman's uniform, the decision was made (and carried out) to kill him.[7]

Terrorism in the Caucasus was an integral part of the rebellion of society against the state. Thousands of attacks took place in the first decade of the twentieth century. Estimates run from about seven hundred to several thousand dead.[8] In an April 1908 letter, Prime Minister and Interior Minister Petr Stolypin admonished the Caucasian viceroy for the violence in his jurisdiction, claiming that in 1907 alone there were 3,060 terrorist acts (1,732 were robberies), in which 1,239 people had been killed and another 1,253 wounded.[9] Defending his administration a few months later, the viceroy questioned Stolypin's figures. There were, he asserted, only 689 murders and attempted murders "of a purely terroristic character" and only 183 were fatal. But he did admit that robberies ran to over four thousand in 1906 and only slightly less in the past year.[10] Even these figures, however, when combined with the Armenian-Muslim riots and the punitive expeditions of the tsarist armies, reveal Caucasia to have been one of the bloodiest regions of the empire in the revolutionary years. Political struggle had become armed resistance and retaliation. The party that dominated oppositional politics, the Georgian Mensheviks, did not shun violence the way its Russian counterparts did. Zhordania argued that terrorism could be employed as self-defense and in order to sow panic in police circles. Bombs in various parts of Tiflis disoriented the local administration and forced the authorities to think about their own safety.[11] The Menshevik Uratadze showed the same ambivalence in his memoirs: "In our view one good demonstration brought us closer to our goal than the assassination of a few ministers. But, as a weapon of self-defense, all our organizations resorted to it when necessary."[12]

Even before the news of Bloody Sunday reached the Caucasus, local workers and peasants were already in incipient revolt against the tsarist state. On the eve of the shootings in Saint Petersburg, the Tiflis Social Democrats had issued a proclamation, said to have been written by Koba, that urged the workers to avenge their fallen: "It is time to take revenge! It is time to avenge those glorious comrades brutally cut down by the tsarist bashibazouks in Yaroslavl, Dombrov, Riga, Petersburg. Moscow, Batumi, Tiflis, Zlatoust, Tikhoretskaia, Mikhailov, Kishinev, Gomel', Iakutsk, Guria, Baku, and other places! . . . It is time to destroy the tsarist government! And we will *destroy* it."[13]

For all the passion, even rage, in this cry for vengeance, the Marxists were not driven by irrational urges or emotional excesses. Rather they used violence selectively and instrumentally, the choice made coolly, rationally.[14] As revolutionaries, they manifested selective empathy rather than a generalized humanism. Outraged by the suffering of workers and peasants, they would at the same time plot in cold blood the murder of a police spy. The socialists usually opposed indiscriminate attacks on enterprises or employers, so-called economic terrorism, but they often gave in to pressure from the workers or the rebel peasants of Guria. When the Social Democrats hesitated and held back from using violence, workers took matters in their own hands and murdered foremen and factory directors, even workers who refused to participate in a strike. The workers considered that they were acting morally when they turned their weapons against those whom they saw as oppressors. Anger at what a boss or a policeman might have done to a fellow worker, as well as hatred of who they were as a class or a people, drove men and sometimes women into the streets. Emotion and reason reinforced one another. But rather than indiscriminate rage, workers and peasants targeted specific threats to their safety or violators of their sense of justice.

Bloody confrontations between workers, peasants, soldiers, and the tsarist police forced both Mensheviks and Bolsheviks to accept the notion of "the self-defense of the workers." They formed armed combat units of socialist workers and peasants to resist the attacks of anti-socialist and anti-Semitic "counter-revolutionaries." What began as self-defense soon metamorphosed into guerrilla bands and terrorist gangs prepared to assassinate enemy officials and rob banks to finance the cause. Both Koba and his friend Soso Davrishev, as well as other young militants from Gori and Tiflis, quickly organized such gangs.

The killings escalated steadily. Workers in Batumi carried out several terrorist acts in 1904–1905, including the assassination of Prince Levan

Gurieli, the head of the police in the Batumi region. Even more violent than the Social Democrats were the Socialist Federalists, the *Dashnaks*, and the Socialist Revolutionaries, the heirs of the Populists, most of whom fervently believed in the efficacy of terrorism and considered the cautious Social Democrats to be mere babblers. The Armenian revolutionary party, *Dashnaktsutyun*, killed the governor of Baku, Prince Mikhail Nakashidze, blaming him for the massacres of local Armenians, and the Social Democrats carried out the execution of Lieutenant General Fedor Griaznov, the chief of the Caucasian Military Headquarters, who a month earlier had ruthlessly suppressed rebellious workers in Tiflis. The newly emergent party of Georgian Socialist Federalists carried out an attack on the Tiflis police chief Kovalev on July 12, 1905. Davrishev participated with Prince Lenko Kherkheulidze in the attempt, but the bomb only wounded its target. The bomber, Lenko, was caught and stabbed to death in the police station.[15] Their party robbed 315,000 rubles from the Dusheti Treasury on April 12, 1906, and killed the Gori provincial police chief, Gugushvili, on March 15, 1907. As socialist nationalists influenced by the Socialist Revolutionaries, their terrorism targeted enemies of the nation, including Archbishop Nikon, the exarch of Georgia and a fierce defender of Russian interests in the Georgian Church.[16] In much of western Georgia all parties engaged in armed combat with tsarist authorities. Bolsheviks and Mensheviks, along with radicalized mine workers, launched frontal attacks on police stations and other state institutions in Chiatura and effectively controlled the region by the fall of 1905.[17] The most prominent target of the revolutionary assassins was Ilya Chavchavadze, the patriarch of Georgian letters and the most renowned gentry nationalist.

Targeted terrorism paled in the scope of violence before the mass killing of one nationality against another. Just after the January 1905 strikes, pogroms broke out in Baku. Somewhere in the center of the city, an Armenian killed a well-to-do Muslim. His compatriots then slaughtered several Armenians passing by.[18] For three days, February 6–9, local Muslims hunted down Armenians and beat or killed them. It was widely believed that local tsarist officials had incited the Muslims against the Armenians, who were considered by the authorities to be subversive revolutionaries.[19] Whatever the police's instigating role, witnesses reported that they took no action while the beatings and killings went on. Instead of dampening the radicalism of the workers, the interethnic riots stirred up greater anger at the regime. Koba was in Baku at the time and sent an armed band of five Social Democrats to try to stop the killing. On his orders another fifteen took the opportunity to steal type from a printing house.[20]

In Batumi seven or eight thousand people attended a demonstration near the Armenian church to protest the Baku events. When a red flag was unfurled, Cossacks charged into the crowd, killing at least seven people.[21] In Tiflis the city fathers feared that the riots would spread to their city, and Armenian and Muslim children were kept home from school.[22] Members of the city duma, which represented the propertied middle and upper classes, were appalled at the repression of the recent strikes and the police use of street cleaners as spies and vigilantes. "The broom, that peaceful instrument of cleanliness," Prince Argutinskii-Dolgorukov proclaimed in the duma chamber, "has been replaced by brutal sticks and clubs, which are exercised on the backs of innocent bystanders. All around us we are forced to witness at various hours of day and night how whole battalions of street cleaners, headed by representatives of the police, armed with sticks wander the streets of Tiflis ready to fight with the unarmed population."[23] A certain Babov echoed the general sentiments of the city's bourgeois elite, illustrating, perhaps unwittingly, how the "bourgeois revolution" was being carried out by workers. "The moment has come when everyone understands that it is impossible to tolerate further the absence of elementary rights of citizenship, the absence of guarantees of personal inviolability, freedom of speech, assembly, unions, and freedom of the press. If the workers had not shown civic courage and taken the initiative to demand these minimal rights, then all society, all of us, would have had to strike, for we are bound to raise our voice in defense of our rights."[24]

As the duma members called for liberal reforms, the "public" flooded into the city hall, forcing them to take a more radical position. On March 14, the city duma adopted the position of the Russian *zemstva* (provincial assemblies) and municipal councils calling for a permanent representative legislature in Russia.[25] With the danger of ethnic violence merging with the economic struggle of workers and the mass rising of West Georgian peasants, the tsarist government, both in Russia under Prime Minister Sviatapolk-Mirskii and in the Caucasus, under the newly appointed viceroy, Count Illarion Vorontsov-Dashkov, turned from outright repression to a more conciliatory policy—at least for a time.[26]

The tsarist state was shaken. The war with Japan had been lost, and Russia would be forced to sign a humiliating peace. With its armies stranded in the east, the government could not suppress the mutinies and uprisings breaking out in far-flung parts of the country. Sensing the weakness of the authorities, the Caucasian Bolsheviks responded to Lenin's admonition to organize the armed struggle. They quickly formed their own paramilitary forces, militias of militants, to carry out armed actions, primarily for the defense of party members and worker adherents.[27] But self-defense easily glided into terrorism—the killing of provocateurs and spies—and in the overheated atmosphere of revolution, terrorism soon turned from protecting ones' own to an operative means to overthrow the regime.

Not all the Bolsheviks were enthusiastic about forming armed gangs and the use of terror. Stepan Shahumian, a genteel Armenian intellectual and the exact contemporary of Koba (only two months older) who shared with him the leadership role among Tiflis Bolsheviks, opposed Koba's enthusiastic turn toward terror.[28] Shahumian would work with Koba in both Tiflis and Baku, but their natures could not have been more different. In contrast to Koba, whose entire life was taken up in party work, Shahumian held jobs outside to support his family. They rivaled each other in their commanding position among Caucasian Bolsheviks. Shahumian, one comrade wrote, was "soft, almost feminine by nature, compliant in personal relations with people," though "he suddenly opened before us a new feature of his character—hardness and extreme obstinacy in matters of social convictions. . . . He was fascinating not only as an unusual fighter but also in personal life, in personal relationships. And almost the principal element of his fascination was his deep truthfulness, which came out in all his actions, words, gestures, movements."[29] His premature death at the hands of anti-Bolsheviks in

1918, like that of Koba's mentor, Ketskhoveli, removed yet another Caucasian Bolshevik obstacle to Stalin's rise in the party.[30]

While Shahumian wrote articles for the Armenian Bolshevik newspaper *Kaits* (Spark) and spent much of his time working with adoring young party members, Koba went deep underground and remained invisible. His comrades took the public role, giving speeches and leading demonstrations. Koba dismissed any action short of organizing an armed uprising to be merely "liberal."[31] He gathered around him companions like Tsulukidze, Japaridze, Tsintsadze, Davitashvili, Buda Azanurashvili, and Budu Mdivani, and with those most willing carried out his own violent "agitation."[32] Particularly close to, and perhaps competitive with, Koba was the tall, handsome, gregarious Mdivani, who was said to have "princely manners," had a large family, loved company, often acted as *tamada* (toastmaster) at traditional Georgian feasts, and even acted on the stage. But unlike Koba, Budu could not stand the party's restrictions, its discipline, and he often broke the rules. A fine orator at large gatherings, he was indifferent to party meetings and debates about intraparty disputes. He seemed to have more friends among the Mensheviks than the Bolsheviks.[33]

Memoirists contrast Mdivani's character sharply with Koba's. The Menshevik Uratadze wrote that Mdivani had "a joyous character," but Koba "had none of that. This was a person of a dark character, ruthless, vengeful. At big gatherings he could not compare with Mdivani, but at party meetings he overshadowed Mdivani. You had to force Mdivani to work in the circles and, it seems, he attended these meetings only a few times, while Stalin went only there."[34] "Unlike the others, [Koba] had no desire to make appearances, to parade, to be admired by the crowd, to become drunk with the applause," his friend Davrishev wrote. "He preferred to set up printing presses, edit the mountains of brochures, put out journals like *proletariatis brdzola* and in this way to lead a hard life among the rival ideologies."[35] Koba was connected to a gang of activists known as *jgupi* (the group), led ostensibly by his protégé and friend Simon Ter-Petrosian, the famous "Kamo." But it was Koba who chose the members, bold and fearless sixteen- to twenty-year-olds, most of them like Kamo from Gori and its region.[36] As in his boyhood days in Gori and at the Tiflis Seminary, he surrounded himself with loyalists among whom he was the acknowledged leader.[37] He enforced the strict code of revolutionary conduct, marked by secrecy and discipline. When P. Dashtoian was given the task of preparing workers for the "fighting group," he met with D. Karapetian and three military cadets in an apartment on Freilinskaia Street, in the "bourgeois" part of Tiflis where Koba would also live. At some point Dashtoian told a worker that he had served as a soldier in Dusheti, in the foothills of the Caucasus Mountains, but had recently left the army. A few days later Shahumian warned him that Koba was very displeased by Dashtoian's careless breaking of the rules of conspiracy. Later Koba himself upbraided the former soldier: "Why are you telling your biography to everyone?"[38]

The *jgupi* found refuge in the Mtatsminda district of Tiflis, where Davrishev's militia also hid out. That district at the base of a mountain was considered safe since the local police chief, an Armenian, Davidov, had made an agreement with the revolutionaries that he would let them live there unharmed if they carried out no actions in his district. Koba's group, which holed up in the basement of a local café where they kept their arms, probably made the same agreement with Davidov, whom they knew from Gori where he had worked with Davrishev's father.[39] Each armed group needed money to buy arms, either from soldiers or Armenian revolutionaries, but Koba decided instead to raid weapons shops. Such breaches of revolutionary etiquette infuriated the Mensheviks.[40] Both Davrishev's group and the *jgupi* extorted money from shopkeepers, the publisher of the newspaper *Tiflisskii listok* (Tiflis Leaflet), and others. Koba's group probably operated for only two or three months, but they managed to carry out one of these "expropriations," while the rival militia also carried out one.[41]

In his readiness to use violence and his ability to suffer pain, no one matched Kamo, the audacious Armenian from Gori and Koba's loyal follower.[42] The son of a priest and educated in same Gori church school as Soso Jughashvili, Ter-Petrosian was closely attached to his hometown pal, and although he was from a family with higher status than Soso's, Ter-Petrosian deferred to his more intellectual friend. Soso supposedly tutored the younger boy, gave him fiction to read, and initiated him into a basic Marxism. One day Soso was lying down, reading a book, when in his faulty Russian Ter-Petrosian said *kamo* instead of *komu* (to whom). Soso jumped up, "Not *kamo, bicho* [boy], . . . remember that, *bicho*." He then dubbed him with the nickname, Kamo, which soon stuck as his revolutionary pseudonym.[43] At first Soso used him as a gofer, to notify comrades of meetings, distribute leaflets, and set up secret libraries.[44] Neither a propagandist nor an agitator, Kamo loved to fight and was always ready to take on the most dangerous tasks. He specialized in explosives, daring robberies that were christened "exes," as well as the elimination of enemies.[45] Quick to anger, he once beat a printer nearly to death because he kept singing while working.[46] For the party he gave into the intimate demands of the wife of a rich man in whose home he was hiding. "Since there was no other conspiratorial apartment, I had to endure this," he said. He was a simple soldier for the organization, but his exploits were so daring that his reputation as a fearless fighter took on legendary dimensions. A master of disguise, he once dressed as a *kinto*, a Tiflis street peddler, and carried a basket of peaches under which were hidden socialist leaflets. On another occasion he might be a student, a Georgian peasant, or even a prince. Once Davrishev came upon Kamo, who was about to shoot an Armenian for stealing money from an expropriation. Davrishev tried but failed to stop him. Kamo warned him to stay out of Bolshevik affairs. "Koba . . . will be furious, and you know that he is not always very pleasant."[47] The murder took place in the very district where they all hid out, and it led to the discovery of the arms cache and the hanging of Avaliani, a young member of *jgupi*. Later Davrishev was present when Koba reproached Kamo for the murder and compromising their secure area. But Koba then turned to Davrishev. "'Listen, Soso,' he said to me calmly pulling on his pipe, 'I beg you not to busy yourself with us. Kamo did what he had to do, and I advise you to act like us. I hope that you understand why. Now, I have a proposition to make to you: come with us, leave that Federalist party. We are old comrades from Gori, you remember our haunts. I think highly of you . . . and of your sincerity. Come with us while there is still time. . . . Or else . . .' 'Or else . . . what?' I said aggressively." Koba did not respond, "but his eyes suddenly became smaller, and his face hardened." As he left the room, he changed the mood and without explanation asked about their boyhood companion. "And Leva Rozenfeld [Kamenev]. Where is he? Still in Paris?"[48]

Rather than standing aside, as Trotsky imagined, or being absent in the revolutionary civil war that marked 1905 in Caucasia, Koba was the behind-the-scenes coordinator of armed bands that took vengeance on officials and collaborators, used violence to discipline their own members, and robbed the state treasury and shops for arms and the money needed to carry on their activities. Men like Kamo carried out the orders of men like Koba. The *jgupi* attacked the barracks of the Cossacks, startled them with gunshots, and when the Cossacks ran out of their barracks, they threw bombs at them.[49] They also, along with Davrishev's militia, protected the Jews when they were threatened by a pogrom. For their efforts they were rewarded with forty nickeled steel watches from Mendelsohn the jeweler.[50]

THE GURIAN REPUBLIC

All of Caucasian society was in turmoil, and while Koba worked with small groups of workers and activists, a massive peasant movement swept western Georgia and solidified the Mensheviks' authority among Georgians. In the towns a rough alliance formed between workers and liberal elements in the middle classes—the very cross-class coalition that Social Democrats had imagined was required to bring about revolution. Soldiers joined workers in mass meetings in the Tiflis suburb of Nakhalovka.[51] But it was the stunning mobilization of peasants that inflated a broad social movement that the government seemed unable to restrain.[52] The center of the peasant uprising was the southwestern province of Guria, once an independent Georgian principality and long a site of rebellion. Since the late nineteenth century the peasants and petty nobles of Guria had suffered from too little land for a growing population and falling prices for their corn. The coming of global trade and production for the agricultural market had a devastating effect on the smallholders of Guria, who were at one and the same time victims of American, Australian, and Indian competition and burdened by state taxes and obligations to their former lords.[53] Many Gurian peasants worked in Batumi, where they met local socialists. After the "slaughter-house" of 1902, the police drove many of them out of the city back into the countryside. There they brought their new knowledge to their fellow peasants, and in time rebellion gestated and was born.

Though they looked to the Mensheviks for leadership, Gurian peasants often took matters in their own hands. They boycotted landlords, refused to work for them, threatened them with death if they did not comply with their demands, and murdered the agents of the nobles who resisted them. For Georgian peasants retribution against those who endangered family and fortune was justified. Vengeance was the rough justice meted out in the absence of legitimate state authority. "We did not forgive such people," one Social Democrat remembered; "such people awaited an inevitable death."[54] This violence from below made it more difficult for the Social Democrats to hold their traditional line against the use of terrorism.

The western Georgian districts were placed under martial law as a respected government official, Sultan Krym-Girei, passed through villages to listen to peasant grievances. "Our demands," one villager told him, "can be expressed in three words: we want bread, justice, and freedom. . . . The police belong to the landlords. . . . When we asked for bread, they gave us stone; instead of help, the police offered us the whip. Recently we have lost all confidence in the government. We are convinced that working people can expect nothing good from it, and that is why we consider it necessary to form peasant committees, elected by all, in order to negotiate with the landlords and the state."[55] The monks and priests also exploit the people, he went on. "Their craft is hypocrisy, humility, and slavery; they advise turning to heaven, while they themselves are reaching into our pockets. Without some payoff, they will not say one word in prayer, and their steady chant is 'money, money, money.' We reject all payments to support the clergy and demand the separation of church and state, that is, let he who needs his prayers and blessings support the priest."[56] Another peasant told Krym-Girei that he had so little land that when he lay down, his head was on the land of one neighbor and his feet on that of another. Land ought to belong to the one who tills it.[57]

At first Georgian Social Democrats were wary of joining the peasant movement. Orthodox Marxists like "Karlo" Chkheidze were convinced that peasants could not be socialist. Many of the prominent Georgian Mensheviks were from western Georgia and knew the region well. Zhordania was from Lanchkhuti, not far from Uratadze's Gurian village. Noe Ramishvili, Evgeni Gegechkori, Noe Khomeriki, and Konstantine Kandelaki—all later ministers in the Georgian Menshevik government— had been students in the Kutaisi seminary, as had the Mensheviks Chkheidze and Gerasime Makharadze and the Bolshevik Mikha Tskhakaia.[58] The young activist, Grigol Uratadze, convinced Zhordania and Jibladze that the party must engage with the peasants.[59] Once committed, the Georgian Mensheviks found themselves directing the movement, despite the resistance of the "Russian" Menshevik leaders who remained suspicious of this "petit bourgeois" rebellion. Within months a basically lower class, nonproletarian, nonsocialist movement attracted tens of thousands of supporters into the Menshevik ranks, giving them not only the upper hand in the Caucasus but larger numbers of delegates to future party congresses.[60] Such a coalition of workers and peasants was referred to in Russian as *demokraticheskii* (democratic), that is, of the *demos*, the simple people. The inclusive term *demokratiia* (the democracy or working people) was distinguished from stricter class categories like proletarian or bourgeois. The Bolshevik notion of narrow party membership simply did not work for this mass movement, and the Caucasian Union Committee's attempt to establish separate "democratic" and Social Democratic committees fell by the wayside.[61]

The peasants of western Georgia responded quickly to the involvement of the intellectuals and workers from the towns. "Our movement is growing not by the day but by the hour," read a letter from the Imeretian-Mingrelian Committee in Kutaisi to the Bolshevik editors of *Vpered*.[62] Thousands gathered at mass meetings that a year earlier would have attracted only twenty or thirty people. The uprisings "began with great discontent, without any organization or conscious purpose (*soznatel'nost'*), and involved pillage, violence, and arson directed for the most part against noble landlords and princes. The discord and hostility between social estates steadily intensified until the time came for cruel, bloody reprisals. The committee was taken by complete surprise; we did not have enough propagandists to take the movement into our hands right away, and for this reason these savage displays of discontent of the peasant masses rising to their feet were said to have been initiated by the Social Democrats."[63] By the end of 1905, even the tsar's governor of the region advised people, "I have no power; go to the committee."[64]

The violence in the Caucasus worried the government enough that the new viceroy, Vorontsov-Dashkov, resolved that "in order to bring order to the territory peacefully, the help of all social forces is essential."[65] Arriving by train in Tiflis on May 5, 1905, "an oldish but well preserved man, with a dignified bearing and pleasant manner," he adopted a "soft" line toward the local peoples.[66] Determined to keep peace among the various nationalities of the Caucasus and pacify the rebels through concessions if possible, Vorontsov-Dashkov appointed an agronomist sympathetic to the Gurian peasants, Vladimir Staroselskii, governor of Kutaisi province. Soldiers were kept out of western Georgia, and martial law was lifted. Over a hundred peasants were released from prison in Mingrelia.[67]

Western Georgia was on fire, and Tiflis was a tinder box. The tsarist government had for years been particularly hostile to the Armenians, whom they saw as disloyal subversives. In 1903 Nicholas II had seized the properties of the Armenian Church, thus violating the agreement that the autocracy had made with the church in 1836. Almost immediately, the viceroy returned the properties and established links with local Armenian notables.[68] In September he ordered that teaching in the native languages of the Caucasus would be introduced into primary schools.[69] But the viceroy's reformist ambitions and conciliatory policies hardly had a chance. The tsar's chief advisor, Petr Stolypin, opposed them, and Vorontsov-Dashkov proved unable to end the terror and violence in the region.

Two days after the viceroy's arrival, a bomb thrown by Drastamat Kanaian (Dro) blew up the carriage of the governor-general of Baku,

Prince Nakashidze, killing him. Armenians and Muslims turned on each other in Erivan province. Muslims attacked Armenians in the town of Nakhichevan, looting shops and burning houses. Some twenty Armenian villages were attacked and razed, another ten partially destroyed. An Armenian force led by the Dashnak Nikol Tuman then counterattacked.[70] When Georgian clergy met to discuss the issue of greater independence (autocephaly) for the Georgian Orthodox Church, Cossacks broke into the seminary in the night, driving the priests who had been sleeping there into the streets and beating them with whips.[71] For eight days in June, the Social Democrats organized a general strike in Tiflis. All trams stopped; shops closed; and power was turned off in the city. When Russian workers refused to join the strike, strikers attacked and killed two of them. Combat squads of revolutionaries launched bomb attacks, killing Cossacks. Fifteen hundred Russian workers sympathetic to the tsarist regime and hostile to the rebellious Georgians, who they believed threatened the unity of the empire, marched through the streets singing patriotic songs and carrying icons.[72] They were prepared to back the government against the revolutionaries. To prevent the city exploding into interethnic violence, like Baku, the viceroy reinstated martial law and put a military governor in charge of the city.

The revolution was growing beyond the bounds of the exceedingly moderate reforms set out by the tsarist state. Throughout the country resistance by ordinary people was met by vicious repression by the state. When the citizens of the Black Sea port of Odessa went on strike following the mutiny of the battleship *Potemkin*, the government sent in troops, firing wildly into the fleeing crowds. At least a thousand people died and several thousand were wounded. In the Caucasus the viceroy held discussions with leading local figures on introducing *zemstva* in the Caucasus, but that concession was not enough. People were demanding more representative institutions. When in August the tsar agreed to allow elections for a consultative assembly (the so-called Bulygin Duma), discontented peasants in Guria marched—with portraits of Marx, Engels, and Lassalle, along with the tsar's portrait upside down—in support of a fully representative and empowered parliament.[73]

On August 22, the Tiflis City Duma met in the ornate Moorish style city hall on Erivan Square to discuss reforms. Crowds gathered outside. The atmosphere was tense, for public meetings were prohibited under the martial law in effect that summer. The people on the square demanded an open session and entry into the duma hall, but the acting mayor, the Armenian liberal Khristofor Vermishev, refused their demand. Speakers yelled at the deputies: "You are the representatives of the bourgeoisie. You have never been at the head of the movement. We always dragged you by the tail, and you, like cowards, hide behind the administration and the law. You care only for yourselves and not for the welfare of the people." Reluctantly, the duma members agreed to an open session. On August 25, two thousand people crowded into the semi-circular chamber of the duma. In the ensuing chaos, the Social Democrats took charge, condemning the "bourgeois" duma. On the 29th, the crowds found the duma locked. They broke in and occupied the building. Vermishev tried but failed to convince them to leave. Cossacks arrived and opened fire, killing at least twenty-three, perhaps as many as sixty-three; another two hundred were wounded.[74] Koba had just returned from a conference chaired by Tskhakaia in Kutaisi, and two days after the shootings he met with a number of Bolsheviks in Artem Torozov's apartment to draft a response.[75]

The August killings opened a chasm between the government and the people of the Caucasus. The moderate reformers in the duma became more radical, demanding a national assembly based on universal suffrage, but at the same time workers, peasants, and the radical intellectuals moved even further left. By the fall of 1905, as insurrection seemed the only means to their political ends, Mensheviks and Bolsheviks grew closer. Meeting in Kutaisi, Social Democrats resolved that not one kopeck, not one soldier would be provided to the government. Preparations were to be made for an armed uprising. When the conference moved to the village of Jimistaro, Koba appeared at night, reported on the "current moment," and left immediately for the city.[76] Moving stealthily through towns and villages, he plotted a robbery of the Kutaisi armory in the hope that they might capture two thousand rifles. His comrades attempted to dig under the walls but ultimately had to give up.[77]

By fall 1905 people from all social classes throughout Russia were pushing for constitutional reform. Railroad workers went out on strike in early October, and the strike spread across the country. Two-thirds of Tiflis workers walked out on the 15th, though Russian workers refused to strike. Koba attended the citywide meeting of Bolsheviks and Mensheviks called to work out a common strategy.[78] The Social Democrats, primarily Mensheviks but also Bolsheviks, led the strike committee and issued a proclamation "to all citizens," calling for a general strike, the end of martial law and summary executions, the removal of troops from revolutionary villages, and the freeing of all arrested and exiled persons. The city shut down for several days. In Guria peasants clashed with Cossacks.

To the shock and joy of nearly everyone, on October 17th, faced by a choice between concessions or setting up a military dictatorship, Nicholas II issued the historic manifesto granting his people civil rights and an elected national parliament, the State Duma. Essentially, the autocrat had ended the autocracy, consented to limit the absolute power of the emperor, and become a constitutional monarch—or so it seemed to many.

For the next few days, crowds poured onto Golovinskii Prospect, Tiflis's main boulevard, cheering the speakers from the revolutionary parties.[79] The demonstrators demanded that the orchestra of the state theater play the "Marseillaise." Thrilled by what had been achieved, and seeing it as a victory of the workers over the government, a crowd marched from the workers' district, Nakhalovka, to the viceroy's palace calling for the end of martial law and the freeing of political prisoners. The viceroy greeted a delegation from the crowd but refused to grant their demands.[80] Within days the news of the tsar's declaration spread to Batumi and Guria, where Cossacks and soldiers were at war with peasants. Only when the tsar's "October Manifesto" was read in public did the peasants decide to stop their military campaign against the state. The governor of Kutaisi province, Staroselskii, traveled to the villages to announce the October Manifesto without police protection, wearing a red shirt, and surrounded by revolutionaries carrying red banners.[81] Cossacks, however, went ahead and set fire to several villages.[82]

The "October Days" were the height of the so-called all-nation movement against autocracy. The manifesto was the great triumph of the allied forces of the middle and lower classes, the liberals and the socialists, but at the same time it also marked the downfall of the cross-class alliance.[83] Both in higher society and on the streets, people divided between those who considered the reforms a sign of the tsar's grace and generosity and those who deemed it a paltry gesture that did not go far enough. Already on October 21–22 Russian workers and chauvinist "Black Hundreds" (*Chernosotentsy*, ultranationalist, anti-Semitic supports of the autocracy) held patriotic demonstrations in Tiflis. Guarded by government soldiers, seven to eight thousand supporters of the government's gesture, led by railroad workers, marched solemnly through the streets holding aloft a portrait of the tsar and religious banners. People broke from the march to beat up bystanders; houses were set afire. On the second day, twenty to twenty-five thousand marched, singing "God Save the Tsar"; fights broke out with the oppositional forces; shots were fired at the demonstrators, and two bombs were thrown. Near the viceroy's palace, troops fired, killing several dozen people.[84] The tsar's concession had severed the once-united opposition to autocracy.

Revolutionaries emerged from the underground and employed the new possibilities for open meetings and legal newspapers. A liberal Tiflis duma deputy, Tamamshev, proposed to the Social Democrat Ashot Khumarian that he take over his paper, *Kavkazskii listok* (Caucasian Bulletin). Khumarian laughed off the proposal, until Koba and Shahumian changed his mind. The paper soon appeared as *Kavkazskii rabochii listok* (Caucasian Worker's Bulletin), the first legally published Bolshevik newspaper in Caucasia.[85] For Koba and other Bolsheviks the manifesto made it possible to organize "Red partisans" openly. Koba worked with Tskhakaia, Makharadze, Bochoridze, Mdivani, and the Menshevik Jibladze, while Kamo took care of technical details.[86]

At the same time the new freedom allowed the expression of pent up ethnic discontents and hostilities. Some Armenian nationalists in Tiflis considered raiding the Metekhi prison and freeing political prisoners before they were reined in by a respected Dashnak leader.[87] In Baku the "patriots" turned on the Armenians, always suspected of being subversive enemies of tsarism. The city turned into a battlefield, and sixty Armenians were killed and more than a hundred wounded.[88] In Kiev, Odessa, Minsk, Rostov-on-Don, Ekaterinoslav, and towns in central Russia, the supporters of the tsar attacked Jews, killing thousands.[89] The Left blamed the government for the pogroms. The government lauded the spontaneous manifestation of retribution by the crowds. The tsar wrote to his mother, "The impertinence of the socialists and revolutionaries had angered the people once more; and because nine-tenths of the troublemakers are Jews, the people's anger turns against them."[90] Defenders of the regime saw the Jews, Armenians, reformers, and socialists as traitors to be exterminated by "all true Russians." So read proclamations put out by the reactionaries, some of which were printed on a secret press in police headquarters in Saint Petersburg.[91]

The euphoric moment of triumph in October was a temporary pause in the upheavals of 1905. Neither side was prepared to retreat. The tsar wanted restoration. The revolutionaries wanted a fundamental transformation. There were battles yet to be fought, and victory was uncertain.

14

MEETING THE MOUNTAIN EAGLE

The careful scrutinizing of Lenin's behavior on that occasion doubtless reflected the desire of the younger man to model himself upon his hero. Lenin was for Djugashvili everything that a revolutionary leader ought to be, and that he too would like to be insofar as his capacities permitted. . . . Djugashvili's hero-worship of Lenin in no way conflicted with his own ambition and self-admiration. On the contrary, it fortified these feelings.

— ROBERT C. TUCKER, *STALIN AS REVOLUTIONARY* (1973)

The two months after the October Manifesto were a time of hope and anxious expectation that came to be known as the "days of freedom." The revolutionaries, buoyed by their earlier successes and excited by the possibility of greater victory, became even more radical in the last months of 1905. Mensheviks joined Bolsheviks in pushing for a popular revolution, and the two factions cooperated as never before. New political parties were formed; others that had been subject to police repression now operated in the open. The liberals organized into two new parties: the left-leaning Constitutional Democratic Party (Kadets), critical of the tsar's limited reforms, and the right-leaning Union of October 17 (Octobrists), generally supportive of the fledgling constitutional monarchy. Workers joined newly legalized trade unions and held round after round of meetings and marches. The feeling of freedom was euphoric, but it included fears for the future. Koba shared those feelings, though he spent the last months of the revolutionary year traveling across Russia to Finland, where he would meet Lenin for the first time. While he was on the move, Caucasia exploded in renewed waves of violence.

The stakes were high in late 1905. Revolution was a life and death struggle between the old state authorities and their supporters on one side, and the forces of reform and revolution, increasingly divided from one another, on the other. Workers did not trust the government and wanted to wrest concessions from their employers. In Petersburg they campaigned for the eight-hour day, which they sought to institute by revolutionary means—that is, by simply declaring it in effect and laying down their tools after eight hours. But the militancy of the Left alienated the middle classes and, as the more moderate Mensheviks had predicted, drove them closer to the government, tearing apart the very alliance that had made October possible. From mid-October moderates and liberals moved in one direction, while socialists and other radicals veered off in another. Parts of the middle and upper classes that had opposed the autocracy welcomed the October concessions, and the broad front of opposition to tsarism broke. The tsarist authorities were prepared to do whatever was necessary to pacify the population, from cautious constitutional reforms to brutal repression. In the months after October the authorities were in retreat, but time was on their side. As long as the war with Japan had raged, the tsar's army was tied up in the Far East. With the signing of the peace in August, troops could be moved to quell unrest in European Russia.

In Tiflis some deputies to the city duma were prepared to resume their duties, satisfied with the rights granted by the tsar.[1] On October 31 the duma reconvened for the first time since the August massacre. A worker shouted out, "We workers do not believe in these illusory hopes for freedom that some of the deputies believe in. The only freedom that will be ours is the one we seize by force." He was met by applause. The liberal deputy Argutinskii-Dolgoruki expressed his dismay at what had transpired: "For the first three days after the Manifesto, life seemed to be more beautiful. The fourth day showed us how little we can believe those who with one hand give us freedom but with the other shoot down innocent people. We can believe the Manifesto only when real guarantees come with the words." The duma decided to adopt the liberal program of the newly formed Kadet Party.

Instead of consolidating their partial victory over autocracy, workers and the major socialist parties—the Social Democrats, the Socialist Revolutionaries, and in the Caucasus, the Georgian Socialist Federalists, and the Armenian *Dashnaktsutyun*—wanted to continue the struggle for a fully democratic state, amnesty for prisoners, and a constituent assembly. The Bolshevik Central Committee waved the manifesto aside and called for the "transfer of state power to all the people." In various towns and cities of the empire—Saint Petersburg, Moscow, Odessa, and Baku (but not Tiflis) among them—workers elected their own deliberative councils (*soveti*), a novel institution that would eventually become the principal form of popular representation. Mensheviks in general were more receptive of the soviets than most Bolsheviks, particularly those who remained suspicious of spontaneous worker expression.

In late October the viceroy of the Caucasus, Vorontsov-Dashkov, decided to take a hard line against the peasant rebels in western Georgia, but he hesitated when a delegation of Georgian public figures pleaded that he consider a peaceful resolution to the Gurian question. But "Guria is in full revolt," he replied. The revolt had gone on for four years, and there was no peaceful solution, he concluded, because the Gurian peasants did not recognize the tsar's authority.[2] The viceroy placed his hopes for tranquility on the tsar's reforms. He wrote to the emperor, "The essential condition for tranquility [in Caucasia] is the strict observance of the principles proclaimed in the Manifesto of your Excellency of October 17. Any hint of breaking these principles excites minds, makes people lean toward new manifestations of violence, in the form of strikes, street disorders, and political murders. All our hopes are on the state duma and the representatives of the center."[3]

After some wavering and under pressure from the central government to bring order to Caucasia, he decided to send the Muslim Major-General Maksud Alikhanov-Avarskii, a man known for his ruthlessness, to western Georgia.[4] "Bloody Alikhanov," as he was known, lived up to his reputation. A fiercely loyal servant of autocracy, he proclaimed, "The Georgians will have cause to remember me for four generations."[5] He gave his troops full rein to attack villages, loot and pillage, burn the homes of the rebellious Gurians, beat and hang whomever they suspected to be rebels. An American journalist, Kellogg Durland, appalled by what he witnessed, asked the sanguine general whether it was true that women and children were being abused. "The general received these words quietly, but answered with some heat: 'The people of this province are bad, very bad, all bad. There is no other way to repress them other than the way my soldiers are now doing.'" Durland interjected that there were many different peoples in the region, "many different tribes and races—are none good?" "No!" replied Alikhanov. "They are all bad! The Georgians are the worst, but they are all against the government, and must be put down." Turning to French, he continued: "These people are terrorists, they are socialists, and revolutionists. When I hear that a man is a revolutionist or a socialist, I order my soldiers to burn down his house. It is the only way."[6]

By the last weeks of November, Caucasia was once again in the throes of civil war. As the tsar's troops marched into Guria, soldiers of the Tiflis garrison protested against their living conditions, poor food, and abuse by officers and called for freedom of assembly and an end to saluting. Four to five thousand marched through the streets, upset over the arrest of two of their comrades. Even the despised street cleaners turned from the government and expressed their support for the Social Democrats, who now emerged from the underground and operated openly.[7] Elsewhere in Georgia, in Batumi and Kutaisi, Cossacks went on a rampage, fired on workers, and the "Red governor" of Kutaisi, Staroselskii, effectively lost control of his province.[8]

As order broke down in the cities, Armenians and Muslims clashed again, this time in Elisavetpol (Gence, Ganja), and the government feared that it would soon spread to Tiflis. Armenians and Muslims anticipated that they would be attacked, and "Tatars" from the villages came armed to Tiflis to protect their urban compatriots. On November 22 shots were fired in the old city, and some twenty-five Muslims were killed. The local Muslims were outnumbered and outgunned by the Armenians. A Dashnak leader remembered, "Our military organization took full shape within twenty-four hours. We became the virtual rulers

of the city. The metropolitan police withdrew from the streets. Our pa-
trols even stopped Russian army officers to search them lest they might
transport arms to the Tartar [sic] quarters. The Tartar section was ringed
in by the chain of our armed forced, while most of the Armenians
moved to the more distant and safer parts of the city."[9]

The city held its breath. The army was no longer reliable, as some
units joined the revolutionaries and others sided with the counterrevolution. On the 23rd, with shots being fired in some districts, the Social
Democrats organized a protest strike that brought twenty thousand
people into the streets. They marched to the Viceroy's palace and informed him that the workers were prepared to convince both sides to
stop fighting. The next morning Vorontsov-Dashkov met with the Menshevik Isidore Ramishvili and the liberal mayor of the city, Aleksandr
Khatisian. "I was told," he reported, "that the Social Democrat workers
will take over the defense of the city. I have absolute confidence in both
of you. I want to know if Mr. Khatisian will assure me of the wisdom of
this plan, and if Mr. Ramishvili can equally assure me that the arms
which the government will supply to the workers will not be turned
against it."[10] To keep the peace the viceroy then made the extraordinary
gesture of issuing five or six hundred rifles to the Social Democrats, relying on their neutrality in the interethnic fight. Zhordania and Ramishvili were unable to convince the Dashnak leader Armen Garo (Garegin
Pastrmajian) to agree to the terms of the Muslims but agreed to stand
ready to repulse any move from the "Tatar" section of town.[11] On November 27 a crowd of armed Muslims attempted to cross over into the Armenian section of Tiflis. They were met by Social Democratic *druzhiny*
(bands or regiments), which blocked their way. The Muslims opened
fire, and the Social Democrats returned it. A worker from the railroad
depot, Razhden Sturua, fell dead, and two others were wounded
among the workers. After a full day of fighting, the Russian army intervened and separated the two sides. An unknown number of Muslims
were killed or wounded.[12] Even though the Social Democrats managed
to keep a precarious peace and prevent in Tiflis the kind of massacres
that had bloodied Baku, about fifteen hundred army officers, policemen, and Russian nationalists gathered on Artillery Square to protest

the Viceroy's lack of faith in his troops.[13] Vorontsov-Dashkov's temporary reliance on a revolutionary party revealed to all the profound momentary weakness of the tsarist state at the edge of its empire. Although they had promised to return the rifles after the immediate crisis subsided, the revolutionaries gave up few weapons.[14]

OUT FROM THE UNDERGROUND, INTO THE STREETS

The capitulation of the tsar in October convinced revolutionaries of all stripes that a final push might bring the regime to its knees. Lenin returned from exile in Switzerland to Saint Petersburg in November and succumbed immediately to the revolutionary excitement. He admonished his Bolshevik comrades not to concentrate so intently on the party and instead to open up to the broader workers' movement. When an overly orthodox Bolshevik, Bogdan Knuniants, wrote that Social Democrats had to choose between the soviet or the party, Lenin objected: Social Democrats should work in all kinds of organizations. The soviet, he wrote, should be seen as the "embryo of the *provisional revolutionary government*."[15] The soviet is not too broad an assembly but too narrow; it should invite deputies from the sailors, soldiers, peasants, and even the revolutionary bourgeois intelligentsia.[16] In his maiden article in *Novaia zhizn'* (New Life), the new legal newspaper of the Bolsheviks in Petersburg, Lenin called on the Social Democratic party to reorganize itself. The time had come to democratize the party committees, to introduce elections, and to open the party to more workers. Once again he emphasized the healthy impulses of the workers: "The working class is instinctively, spontaneously Social Democratic, and the more than ten years of work of Social Democracy has done a great deal to turn this spontaneity into consciousness." The time had come to form a legal party while preserving the underground apparatus. "Our party stagnated in the underground. It was choking for air in recent years. . . . The underground is collapsing."[17] In a pungent footnote Lenin wrote that he had proposed at the Third Congress that eight workers be brought into the party committees for every two intellectuals. "How obsolete this proposal has become!"[18] Now for every one intellectual there should be a few hundred worker Social Democrats. He ended by calling for a new party congress and the unification of the factions into a single revolutionary party. Rethinking his earlier views on the nature of the party and ready to work with the Mensheviks, he demonstratively shook hands, after two and a half years of bitter disputes, with his old comrade Martov when he visited the soviet's executive committee.[19]

Bolshevik militancy appeared to be vindicated in late 1905. Just as Lenin was calling, in Menshevik fashion, for a broadening of the party, the excitement of the moment pushed Martov and the Mensheviks closer to the Bolsheviks' vision of revolution. Both factions called for the reunification of the party. Martov's resistance to the centralized party with narrow membership evaporated once the party came out from the underground into the light of open political struggle. He was prepared to accept Lenin's formulation of party membership, for the party required "the greatest degree of uniformity, the greatest degree of centralization."[20]

Late in 1905 the Menshevik editors of the briefly published newspaper *Nachalo* (Beginning), Fedor Dan and Aleksandr Martynov, drew close to the young firebrand Trotsky, who wrote of "uninterrupted" or "permanent revolution." Given the proletariat's leadership of the bourgeois revolution, he proposed that the workers could not surrender power to an alien class and that the workers' party should establish a workers' government. Trotsky's scenario eliminated the separation in time of the bourgeois and proletarian revolutions, a conception integral to a more orthodox Marxism. To accusations that he was moving toward a "Populist" conception, he retorted that the workers' government would not immediately introduce socialism and that revolution in more advanced countries would have to come to the rescue of the Russian revolution.[21] Dan and Martynov also envisioned an uninterrupted revolution in Russia that would ignite a European socialist revolution that in turn would spark a global socialist revolution that would sweep Russia into it. Even Martov toyed with the idea of a socialist seizure of power but drew back, unsure if the proletariat was strong enough to hold power. Plekhanov, who had stayed behind in Switzerland, despaired that his comrades were becoming too radical. The proponent of the notion that the Russian liberation movement would triumph as a proletarian movement or not triumph at all now warned that he did not mean "that the historical tasks of the present time will be decided by the proletariat alone."[22]

Although he too was intoxicated by the swirl of revolution, Lenin remained more restrained than Trotsky and the most radical Bolsheviks and Mensheviks. He sometimes used the phrase "uninterrupted revolution" and warned that "we shall not stop halfway."[23] Tsarism, he believed, was no longer able to crush the revolution, but the revolution still was not powerful enough to crush tsarism. The workers' natural allies were the peasants, and together they could carry out the armed insurrection and establish a revolutionary dictatorship of the proletariat and the peasantry. This would not yet be the socialist revolution, for the peasants' ambitions did not extend beyond capitalism, but such an effort would carry the bourgeois revolution to its most democratic outcome—the establishment of full civil rights for all citizens and the election of a constituent assembly.[24] Both Lenin and Martov's position on the progress of the revolution made tactical sense: the revolution would remain bourgeois and limit itself to the overthrow of autocracy. But Trotsky's formula of uninterrupted revolution, which would drive the liberals from the revolutionary coalition, made more practical sense. Why would workers, having triumphed over autocracy, voluntarily leave the field of battle and turn power over to their class enemies, the bourgeoisie? Another revolution, twelve years later, would demonstrate the realism of Trotsky's stratagem.

The climax of the revolutionary year came in December. The government closed down the Petersburg Soviet and arrested its leaders (its chairman, Trotsky, among them). In response the workers of Moscow rose in revolt, and Tiflis, Rostov, and many other cities followed. Each of these insurrections was put down in turn, but nowhere as bloodily as in the old capital of Russia. When the workers built barricades in the Presnia district of Moscow and took over factories, the government ordered its troops to move in "decisively and mercilessly against anyone offering armed resistance." When the fighting ceased, over seven hundred rebels and civilians were dead, as many as two thousand wounded, with fewer than seventy police and soldiers killed.[25]

To support their Moscow comrades Tiflis's Social Democrats called a general strike and brought the city to a halt once again.[26] This was the last major manifestation of the revolutionary opposition.[27] The viceroy immediately declared martial law. General Fedor Griaznov, commander of the Caucasian Military Headquarters, ordered meetings banned and shops to be opened.[28] Workers of Didube and Nakhalovka resisted the soldiers as they entered the workers' districts, but radical and moderate Social Democrats disagreed about tactics. For ten days the tsarist forces battled the rebel population, killing over sixty and wounding over two hundred fifty. The divisions among workers and socialists took their toll. The radicals ordered a bombing of the Cossacks stationed at the Soldiers' Bazaar in the center of the city. Several were killed, and the enraged Cossacks retaliated by burning down the Social Democrats' printing plant, incinerating twenty-nine people living in the building. At that point people began to turn away from the socialists. With Moscow defeated, and the losses mounting, the strike bureau called off the strike on December 29.[29] The battle had been lost, even though fighting continued in Western Georgia. The city and soon the rest of Georgia stood exposed to the mercy of the army.

THE TAMMERFORS CONFERENCE

Koba was not in Tiflis at the time of the December uprising. As a seasoned *praktik* and known for his Bolshevik orthodoxy, he had been sent, along with Giorgi Telia, as a representative to a conference of the faction in Tammerfors (Tampere), Finland.[30] He traveled to Saint Petersburg, where he was to receive further instructions at the editorial office of *Novaia zhizn* (New Life), but by the time he arrived the tsarist forces had closed down the soviet and the office. He wandered the streets, unsure what to do next, when by chance he ran into an old acquaintance, Ivliane Kukulava. Even though his home was a storage place for weapons and therefore off limits to guests, Kukulava hid Koba in his apartment for two and a half days. Koba soon made the right contacts and went off to Finland.[31]

Forty-one delegates (fourteen of them workers) from twenty-six organizations gathered in the People's House under the protection of the local police chief, who happened to be a Finnish Social Democrat, and "Red Guard" units of metal workers.[32] The conference has gone down in history as the moment at which Lenin and the man who would become Stalin met. In later years when he embellished his acquaintance with Lenin, Stalin told of an earlier "meeting." Speaking to Kremlin cadets in 1924 at a memorial for Lenin, Stalin recalled his first contact with the late leader, a letter ostensibly received late in 1903 during his first exile in Siberia. "I first met Comrade Lenin in 1903," he said, not in person but through an exchange of letters. "Yet it left me with an indelible impression that remained with me throughout the entire tenure of my work in the Party."

> Familiarity with Comrade Lenin's revolutionary activity at the beginning of the nineties, and especially since 1901, after the appearance of *Iskra*, led me to the conviction that in Comrade Lenin we had an extraordinary man. I did not regard him then as only a leader of the Party, but as its actual creator, for he alone understood our Party's inner substance and its urgent needs. When I compared him with the other leaders of our Party, it always seemed to me that Comrade Lenin's companions-in-arms—Plekhanov, Martov, Axelrod, and others—ranked a whole head lower than Comrade Lenin, that by comparison with them, Lenin was not only one of the leaders, but a leader of the highest type, a mountain eagle who knew no fear in the fight and who boldly led the Party forward over the unexplored paths of the Russian revolutionary movement. That impression sank so deep into my soul that I felt the necessity to write about it to one of my close friends, who was at the time in emigration, requesting a reply from him.

As Stalin told the story, his friend answered with a letter along with

> a simple yet profoundly pregnant letter from Comrade Lenin, to whom it would seem my friend had shown my letter. Comrade Lenin's little letter was comparatively brief, but it subjected the practices of our Party to bold and fearless criticism and gave a remarkably clear and cogent exposition of the entire plan of the Party's work for the impending period. Only Lenin could write a letter about the

most complicated matters so simply and clearly, so cogently and boldly that each phrase did not so much speak as shout. That simple and audacious letter strengthened my conviction that in Lenin we had the mountain eagle of our Party. I cannot forgive myself that due to the habits of an old underground worker, I burned Comrade Lenin's letter along with many other letters. My acquaintance with Comrade Lenin began at that time.[33]

Most biographers of Stalin doubt the authenticity of this story.[34] Yet Stalin's tale both gives a clue to how Jughashvili, in 1903 a young militant of twenty-four, admired Lenin (that part of his story conforms to other sources from the time) and also reveals how the mature Bolshevik invented a past that linked him to the founder of the movement he aspired to lead. The qualities he ascribed to Lenin in 1924 were precisely those that he cultivated and claimed for himself—clarity, cogency, simplicity, fearlessness, and audacity.

The actual meeting took place two years later, in December 1905, and Stalin later reflected in a similar way about meeting his much-admired factional leader. "I was hoping the see the mountain eagle of our party, the great man, great not only politically, but, if you will, physically, because in my imagination I had pictured Lenin as a giant, stately and impressive. How great, then, was my disenchantment to see a most ordinary looking man, below average height, in no way, literally in no way, distinguishable from ordinary mortals."[35] Instead of playing the role of a "great man" and appearing at the conference late "so that the assembly may await his appearances with bated breath; and then, just before the 'great man' enters, the warning whisper goes up: 'Hush! . . . Silence! . . . He is coming,' " Lenin arrived early with no fanfare. Stalin considered the ritual of a late appearance important, "because it creates an impression, inspires respect." He was greatly disappointed "to learn that Lenin had arrived at the conference before the delegates, had settled himself somewhere in a corner, and was unassumingly carrying on a conversation, a most ordinary conversation with the most ordinary delegates at the conference. I won't deny that this seemed to me then some kind of violation of some kind of essential rule."[36]

What Stalin reported in 1924 as disappointment was a carefully scripted account that attested to Lenin's lack of pretension, his simple and democratic nature. By painting such an appreciative portrait of Lenin, Stalin indicated that he approved such behavior and that he too was a modest man, or at least aspired to appear unpretentious, simple, and democratic.[37] Of course, at the same time he notes that the "ritual" of the "great man" coming in late, creating an impression and inspiring respect, also had an important political and theatrical effect—a performance that in time he would exploit to the full.

The senior party leaders that he met in Tammerfors did not intimidate Koba. He participated as a delegate without hesitation. The conference echoed the Menshevik conference of a few weeks earlier and proposed an immediate merger of the factional centers and the convening of a unity congress.[38] Koba embraced this view.[39] But another issue—the Bolsheviks' attitude toward participating in the elections to the first national parliament, the State Duma—proved more controversial, and Koba was in the midst of the debate. Most Bolsheviks opposed running in the elections to the duma, and Koba had written several articles in the Georgian press advocating a boycott. Years later he remembered: "Close to Comrade Lenin were people—the 'Seven'—whom we provincial delegates labeled with all kinds of epithets; they had assured us that Il'ich [the affectionate patronymic used by those close to Lenin] was against the boycott and for elections to the duma."[40] Grigorii Aleksinskii, then a Bolshevik, remembered that "at this time—the end of 1905—Lenin did not behave as he had in emigration before his return to Russia; he considered the mood and opinion of the *nizy* [the lower echelons of the party and the workers] and showed a readiness for concessions." But "before everything else, he tried to form around himself a group of people loyal and unhesitatingly dedicated to him."[41]

On December 11 a new law formulated by Russian Prime Minister Sergei Witte had turned the duma from a deliberative into a legislative body and broadened the franchise to include workers and peasants. When Lenin read the law, he exclaimed to a fellow Bolshevik, B. I. Gorev, "We can use these elections to organize [our own] unauthorized soviets."[42] The lone Menshevik delegate to the congress, E. L. Smirnov

(Gurevich), made the same suggestion in a private conversation with some Bolsheviks, only to be met with scorn and angry accusations of betrayal. The next day at the conference Lenin as chair coyly announced that a group of delegates was proposing that Social Democrats ought to participate in the first two rounds of the elections for "agitational" purposes but then categorically refuse to vote for deputies. Like the other provincial delegates with whom he closely identified, Koba was fiercely opposed to participation. When the Menshevik Smirnov spoke against a boycott of the elections, Koba sharply answered him: "What's in your head is completely unimportant and not interesting to anyone. What in such circumstances is more useful is to do everything to secure the advance against reaction—that is very important."[43] When Gorev spoke in favor of participation in the elections, he was met with cries that he was an opportunist and conciliationist. Koba shouted out, "Why vote? Our tactic, the boycott, is the right one. Why change it?" Gorev turned to Lenin: "Vladimir Il'ich, please confirm that yesterday you yourself expressed this idea!" Lenin corroborated Gorev: "Comrades, I must confess that yesterday I was also of the same opinion as Comrade Igor' [Gorev's party nickname]." An explosion of laughter shook the conference. Lenin smiled and continued, "but today, having heard all your objections, I retreat in full battle order."[44] "You, activists from the localities, it is clear, of course, you know better the mood of the masses out there. You are the ones who should decide this question. . . . I have been so long in emigration that things are clearer to you."[45] Koba remembered that the delegates were stunned. "This was like an electric shock. We gave him an ovation."[46] Lenin had given in to the militant mood of his comrades in the trenches.[47]

Koba had made an impression on the top Bolshevik leaders. He was appointed to the commission, which included Lenin, to draw up the resolution on boycotting the duma elections. The resolution passed, and the meeting at Tammerfors was cut short so that delegates could return home to participate in the strikes and revolts. Davrishev reports that when Koba returned to Tiflis he indicated how impressed he had been by Lenin. "He explained to me one day that among all those 'phrasemongers' deprived of all sense of realism and living cloistered in a world of theoretical abstraction, Lenin seemed to him to be different, certainly a theoretician but one who keeps his feet on the ground." The feeling apparently was mutual. Lenin, so Koba claimed, saw the young man as one of the few attending Tammerfors who had practical revolutionary experience.[48]

By the time Koba reached Tiflis, however, the revolutionary wave was clearly receding. The government had found renewed will to crush its enemies. Even Sergei Witte, who had urged reforms and concessions, turned to repression. The tsar was surprised. He wrote to his mother: "Witte, since the happenings in Moscow, . . . has radically changed his views; now he wants to hang and shoot everybody. I have never seen such a chameleon of a man. That, naturally, is the reason why no one believes in him anymore. He is absolutely discredited with everybody, except perhaps the Jews abroad."[49] The next months were a time of bloody suppression of the revolutionary opposition, savage punitive expeditions against peasant villages, thousands of summary executions, the vengeful application of force "without any sentimentality" in Witte's words.[50] The tsar believed that "terror must be met with terror," and nowhere was this doctrine applied more fiercely than in the borderlands of the empire.[51]

15

GENDARME OF THE REVOLUTION

Koba was limitlessly proud, and his personal ambition overcame
all other feelings. He did not feel shame, had no understanding of
morality. Respect for himself or for others, awareness of what is called
human worth, was not apparent in him in the slightest degree. In general,
his relations with comrades were not based on friendship, love, or respect
but were based on subordination and their admiration of him. He used
them as a weapon, a machine, cared for them as one cares for livestock,
not more. Having used them up, he discarded them without regret or
sent them to the slaughterhouse!

—RAZHDEN ARSENIDZE, "IZ VOSPOMINANII O STALINE"
["FROM MEMOIRS ABOUT STALIN"] (1963)

Here [at the Fourth Party Congress] the future Stalin displayed
revolutionary common sense: if you want the peasant to help you with
the Revolution you must give him land. . . . And so the little-known
delegate from the Caucasus outlined tactics which, endorsed by Lenin
in 1917 with his "All land to the peasants," were one of the most
important reasons for the Bolsheviks prevailing in Russia and,
practiced by Mao Tse-tung in the 1930s and 1940s, carried the Chinese
Communists as well to victory. The future Stalin is already discernible:
with his brusqueness, his ability to cut the Gordian knot of Marxian
dialectics and propose a simple and effective slogan.

—ADAM B. ULAM, STALIN, THE MAN AND HIS ERA (1973)

Early in 1906 the British Embassy in Saint Petersburg reported to the
Foreign Office in London that the brutal pacification of the Caucasus
represented "a state of things hardly credible in a civilized country."

"Whole districts seem to have been given over to military executions by the Cossacks who appear to have behaved with inconceivable brutality. The surviving inhabitants have fled to the mountains where they endure great privations from hunger and cold. At one place 15 political prisoners were killed by letting steam into the cells where they were confined and this statement, though often repeated, has not been denied. The result of these operations has been to restore the tranquility which is not likely to be disturbed for some time to come."[1] The American ambassador, George L. Meyer, noted that much of Russia had "gradually become quieter" since the suppression of the Moscow insurrection, but the Caucasus was still in a "condition of complicated chaos."[2]

The government in Saint Petersburg was itself divided and indecisive in early 1906. The tsar continued to think of himself as an autocrat with unlimited powers who had graciously granted the October Manifesto to his people. He and his top officials were unsure whether they should return to the policy of concessions of the past October or the program of repression of December. The emperor's closest advisors, Minister of Internal Affairs Petr Durnovo and Commandant of the Court General Dmitrii Trepov, used their proximity to the emperor to undermine his confidence in Prime Minister Witte, whom they considered too "liberal." Durnovo and Trepov favored outright repression and opposed Witte's policy of pacification and reform. More powerful than the prime minister, Durnovo echoed Alikhanov-Avarskii when he told a journalist that he intended to inspire such terror in Russia and among its revolutionaries that the grandchildren of the current generation would never forget it.[3] Even Witte was not unequivocally committed to the new constitutional order, and once blurted out that the tsar could "on his free will" rescind the rights promised.[4] Weary and sick, the prime minister resigned his post in April, to be replaced by the aged and incompetent Ivan Goremykin.

Despite the terror launched by the government, the Caucasus remained at war with the state for some time to come. In western Georgia open fighting raged between Cossacks and peasants. While some of the revolutionary armed units had been dissolved, the rebels held on to their weapons, and Caucasia was pockmarked by small guerilla bands working independently. The Social Democrats were determined to continue the revolution. On January 8, the tsar advised his viceroy to use full military force. "I am certain that at the moment when you call out troops for the energetic suppression of disorders, they will rescue [us] from these most difficult circumstances," he wrote to Vorontsov-Dashkov. "Now it is already necessary *to bring this business* of suppression *to completion* by force of arms, not stopping before the most extreme measures."

As for Staroselskii, the lenient Kutaisi governor, the tsar labeled him "a real revolutionary, maintaining open relations with that party. Indeed, the place for him is [hanging from] a good willow tree! The example would be beneficial to many." The tsar saw the Caucasian revolution through his own understanding of the key ethnic actors and indicated his disapproval of Vorontsov-Dashkov's reputed favoring of the Armenians. "In my personal and long held opinion, it is impossible to have any trust in the Armenians; they are without question at the head of the whole conspiracy behind the insurrection in the Caucasus. Up to this point the Muslims have been the most loyal elements; God forbid they lose faith in Russian power. It is very regrettable if they see a preference [by the government] for the Armenians. Even the Turks make fun of our inability to deal with disorders, and this is an unpleasant realization."[5]

That same day Vorontsov-Dashkov reversed his earlier abrogation of martial law in western Georgia, dismissed Staroselskii, and named Alikhanov-Avarskii provisional governor-general of Kutaisi province. His order warned that insurrection would be met with merciless response.[6] Staroselskii had tried to quiet the rebellion in his province by negotiating with the revolutionary bands, which promised to return to their homes. But the military was already advancing. Alikhanov-Avarskii and his troops moved westward by train, breaking through the Surami railroad tunnel that rebels had blockaded. They took town after town, burning Qvirili and Natanebi, and executed rebels. Soldiers looted and set fire to Ozurgeti. An audacious soldier, impersonating a captain and leading a small band of men, arrested Staroselskii and delivered him to the newly appointed governor-general, who sent him under guard to Tiflis.[7]

The tide had turned in favor of the government. The back of the peasant revolution had been broken. Durnovo's "terror from above" aimed to destroy not only the revolutionary socialists but to damage the liberal opposition as well. The military or the government executed almost four hundred people in January 1906 alone, and arrested tens of thousands.[8] Yet resistance continued for another two years. In the Georgian provinces the government calculated that "terrorist acts" rose from 527 in 1905 to 950 in 1907.[9]

Violence, bloody repression, and terrorist resistance had become a daily occurrence in Caucasia—a school of revolution for Koba. He and other Social Democrats readily adopted the methods of the Socialist Revolutionaries and the Dashnaks. Koba and his men planned the assassination of the hated General Griaznov, the officer who had suppressed the rising of the Nakhalovka workers a few weeks earlier.[10] The task was assigned to a twenty-five-year-old railroad worker, Arsena Jorjiashvili, a member of the fighting group led by the Menshevik Jibladze. When Jorjiashvili did not act in the expected time, Koba called in Kote Tsintsadze and told him, "Prepare several good guys, and if Jorjiashvili fails to carry out this job in a week, then we entrust this task to you." Tsintsadze was happy to carry out the murder and readied two other comrades. But before they could act, on January 16, Jorjiashvili threw a bomb at the carriage of General Griaznov, killing the despised general.[11] Arrested at the scene, Jorjiashvili was soon executed, only to be resurrected as a martyr and the subject of popular ballads.[12]

As tsarist troops "pacified" Georgia, the Socialist Revolutionaries attempted to kill Martynov, the police chief of Tiflis, throwing a bomb at him from the window of the Noble *gimnazium*. The Cossacks broke into the school and killed Shio Chitadze, the director, a native son of Gori, attending a teachers' meeting.[13] The next day, members of Koba's *jgupi* threw a bomb at the Cossacks who had killed Chitadze. The four young assassins hid in a small house, surrounded by Cossacks. Rather than being taken, they killed themselves.[14] Assassinations continued for the next several years, culminating at the end of August 1907, with the ambush and killing of the nationalist bard of Georgia, Ilia Chavchavadze, near Mtskheta, the medieval capital of Georgia. Since Chavchavadze had moved over the years from his youthful liberalism to become a dedicated opponent of the revolutionary movement and socialism, he had many enemies. Everyone from the police to the Social Democrats has been blamed for the murders, which may have in fact been the result of robbery.[15] Koba was certainly not involved in the assassination of one of most venerated notables of Georgia, in whose newspaper he had published his teenage poems.[16] Although the Georgian Social Democrats had long been estranged from Chavchavadze, "Karlo" Chkheidze spoke at the funeral, noting that the socialists had built on his past opposition to serfdom and oppression.[17] Almost as an anti-climax, a year later the Orthodox exarch of Georgia, Nikon, was cut down. By that time terrorist attacks on individuals and "expropriations" of banks and the treasury had become rare events.

The bloody consequences of the battles with tsarism took its toll on Georgian revolutionaries. Some moved toward more moderate tactics, while others held firm to their faith in insurrection. The Social Democratic newspaper, *skhivi* (Ray), expressed its pessimism about the future of the revolution. "It is clear that for the whole of the Caucasus the revolution is a dream. There is no revolutionary movement in any of the Armenian-Tatar provinces; their peasantry nowhere takes part in the renewal of Russia. The provinces of Ganja, Erivan, Baku, and the Kars district do not exist for the revolution. The revolution's flag remained in the hands of the other peoples of the Caucasus—the Georgians, Russians, Osetins, and other small nationalities."[18]

Koba, however, remained militant. On the first anniversary of Bloody Sunday, he published a pamphlet comparing the unarmed clash of Petersburg workers with tsarist soldiers to the December uprising in Moscow. Both failed, in part because of the Social Democratic party had been divided and immersed in its internal squabbles but also because the proletariat had to learn that the only way to oppose weapons was with its own weapons. The only effective strategy was bold and fearless attack.[19]

Sometime at the beginning of 1906, Koba was seriously injured. Returning home one night, he noticed that he was being followed by a police spy. To escape he jumped onto a speeding horse-pulled tramcar, but he fell and smashed his face. People shouted that the tram had hit someone. Koba managed to slip away in the dark. Covered with blood, he barely made it to the home of a friend's aunt.[20] He was taken to Mikhailovskii Hospital and then, by Tskhakaia, to Mikha Bochoridze's apartment. Because that place was under surveillance, he moved to the apartment of Bebe Loshadze on Goncharnaia Street, where he was discovered by a military patrol. In bed with his head wrapped, his right eye completely bandaged, Koba convinced the officer that he could not move. While the soldier went off to find a cart, Koba made his escape. He found refuge, first, in the apartment of the teacher N. G. Akhmeteli on Tumanov Street, and then with his colleague Aleksandre Mikaberidze.[21] The police searched everywhere, stopping anyone suspicious, but thanks to friends and supporters, Koba was able to elude them.

He was undaunted by his predicaments and the setbacks of the revolutionaries. He dreamed that soon the Social Democrats would seize Tiflis. Several comrades remember him spreading out a map of the city and planning the armed takeover. When Mikaberidze's son ran to his father and told him that the "uncle" living with them was "playing soldiers," he looked in to check and saw Koba on the floor with tin soldiers on the city map spread before him. Asked what he was doing, Koba told him that the Tiflis party organization was preparing for an armed uprising, that a staff had been selected, and that he, Koba, had been named chief of staff. He was working out a plan where to build barricades.[22]

As he recovered from the accident, Koba met when he could with other party members, including Zhordania and the Mensheviks. The years 1906–1907 were a peaceful interlude in the intraparty conflicts. Both Bolsheviks and Mensheviks, Koba wrote, understood the current revolution to be a struggle not for socialism, but for democracy and political freedom. In an article signed "Besoshvili" (Beso's child), he railed against the formation of the new "Independence" party in Russia. Its founders, Father Gapon and Mikhail Ushakov, advocated that workers alone should be trusted, and not the Social Democratic intelligentsia, and that the political struggle should be rejected. Koba reiterated the connection between the economic and political struggles: "When there is no freedom of assembly, when strikes are forbidden, when unions are closed down, there the trade union struggle is crushed, and whoever wants the economic strengthening of the proletariat must struggle politically."[23] By "political" Social Democrats referred at this juncture not so much to a socialist seizure of power, which would have flown in the face of Friedrich Engels's caution about coming to power before conditions were appropriate, but to fighting for the fullest possible democracy, which would in turn make possible the propagation of the Social Democratic message to the broadest strata of society.[24]

A strong advocate of party unity, Koba was elected early in 1906 to the combined Tiflis Committee, one of the two Bolsheviks who sat with ten Mensheviks.[25] The Bolshevik-dominated Caucasian Union Committee was abolished, and a joint Executive Commission formed.[26] Georgian Bolsheviks now wrote for the same newspapers and worked together, uneasily, in a single organization, with the dominant Mensheviks led by Zhordania. Koba and Pilipe Makharadze joined the editorial board of the new legal Social Democratic newspaper, *gantiadi* (Dawn).[27] Mensheviks were in control of most Social Democratic organizations in Georgia, except in Chiatura and Kutaisi where the Bolsheviks still had the edge.[28] Yet neither faction was completely homogeneous. In Kutaisi the Bolshevik Baron Bibineishvili echoed the militants who insisted on armed resistance, while his factional comrade Sergo Kavtaradze argued that armed struggle was futile and that the *druzhiny* should be disbanded.[29]

The most divisive issue was whether the party should participate in the upcoming duma elections.[30] Zhordania and many of his closest associates adopted a classically Marxist position. Marx himself, in his 1850 "Address to the Communist League," had advised his comrades, "even where there is no prospect whatsoever of their being elected, the workers must put up their own candidates in order to preserve their independence, to count their forces and to bring before the public their revolutionary attitude and party standpoint."[31] Both Georgian and Russian Mensheviks would field candidates for the duma. Koba vehemently dissented. He warned that campaigning in elections to a "mongrel parliament" would raise false hopes in the workers and dampen their revolutionary spirit.[32] The very next day, March 9, the Tiflis organization, which earlier had come out for boycott, reversed itself by a vote of 42 to 8 and followed Zhordania's call to participate in the elections.[33] In Kutaisi party workers had supported the boycott until Tiflis Mensheviks sent intellectuals to convince them to change their minds. Koba later complained that the Tiflis Bolsheviks "learned of this and shamed the conspirators, saying that after this, unity is only a phrase." They decided not to oppose "the conspiratorial attempt of the Mensheviks" in order not to worsen relations.[34] Koba made a quick trip to Baku to speak on the controversy over duma elections and impressed a young Social Democrat, Raisa Okinshevich. "I clearly remember his figure. I remember how he was dressed: a long overcoat, not fully trimmed beard, a characteristically sharp face; he was smartly [dressed], a multicolored scarf with crossed stripes that looked like a Jewish Torah, and some sort of bowler hat on his head."[35] An interdistrict meeting representing Baku workers agreed to the boycott—by one vote.[36]

Unity was forced on the Social Democrats, both by the failures they had suffered and by workers tired of esoteric infighting. As winter turned to spring, local Mensheviks and Bolsheviks met to elect delegates to what would be known as the "unity congress," their first full all-Russian congress since the party schism in 1903. Differences were acute, and some activists agreed to work together only under pressure from workers. The Menshevik Giorgi Eradze told workers that they should elect intellectuals rather than workers as delegates to the forthcoming congress, for intellectuals would better understand the theoretical issues and could later explain them to workers.[37] Apparently the workers agreed. Koba was part of the delegation overwhelmingly made up of *intelligenty*. The journey was well-organized by the party but not without incident. Almost two dozen delegates traveled by train to Petersburg where they made contact with comrades who instructed them further how to proceed to Finland. From there they took a ship to Stockholm. The ship hit a rock, listed to one side, and delegates had to return to Finland and transfer to a second ship. One delegate, Osip Ermanskii, saw this as a bad omen for party unity.[38] After reaching Stockholm, Koba was pulled in by the Swedish police, interrogated by a Commissioner Mogren along with a constable and a translator named Aleksei. The police asked him if he had any funding from the Finns, whom the Swedes considered a security threat. Koba said he did not and identified himself as a political refugee, a national democrat named Ivan Ivanovich Vissarionovich. After agreeing to report regularly to the police while in the country, he was released along with other delegates.[39]

THE UNITY CONGRESS

At the Stockholm congress factionalism proved more powerful than common interests. Mensheviks and Bolsheviks met in separate caucuses; they even lived in different hotels. Koba stayed at the Hotel Bristol with Kliment Voroshilov, a fellow Bolshevik with whom he began a long friendship. Voroshilov remembered that they placed "another delegate by the name of Ivanovich in the same room with me. He was a thick-set, not-very-tall fellow, about my age, with a dark complexion and barely visible pockmarks on his face from childhood smallpox. He had surprisingly radiant eyes, and he was full of energy, cheerful, and buoyant."[40] Impressed by his citations of Marxist literature and Russian literature, his familiarity with poems and songs, Voroshilov quickly became friends with the young Georgian. Wandering about the city, sticking close to the historic center, marveling at the ease with which people of different social classes interacted with one another, Voroshilov noted that people passing by discretely watched a certain peacefully engaged fisherman, only to learn that he was the Swedish king. At least in Russia, he thought, the tsar does not deceive the people with such pseudo-democratic poses but simply, brutally crushes the working people.[41] What Koba thought and experienced on his first trip abroad must remain speculative. Voroshilov does not seem to have taken him along on his walks.

Thanks to the hospitality of the Swedish Social Democrats, the Fourth Congress of the Russian Social Democratic Workers' Party (RSDRP), which party historians would label the "unity congress," opened in the People's House on the city's waterfront. Of the almost one hundred forty people present, Mensheviks outnumbered

Bolsheviks. Twenty-three delegates (nineteen of them Mensheviks) represented Caucasia—the most prominent being Zhordania, Isidore Ramishvili, Grigol Uratadze, Stepan Shahumian, and Koba Jughashvili. Georgians were the third most numerous nationality at the congress, after Russians and Jews. As one of the largest, and therefore decisive delegations, the Caucasians, all but the four Bolsheviks, voted as a bloc following the lead of Zhordania. Much time was taken up with bitter battles over the proper mandates of the delegates. The credentials of both Shahumian as a Bolshevik representative of the tiny Erivan organization and Jughashvili as a Bolshevik delegate from Tiflis were questioned, and Zhordania had to defend the eleven mandates from Tiflis.[42]

The Bolshevik Grigorii Aleksinskii noticed the two Caucasian Bolsheviks, who appeared in their tall Caucasian sheepskin hats (*papakha*) and seemed to be very busy. He took Shahumian for a "blue-eyed Georgian" and noted that Stalin spoke Russian poorly. "His attempts to 'speak' at the Stockholm congress much amused his listeners."[43] At a factional meeting of the Bolsheviks, Koba polemicized with Anatolii Lunacharskii, a respected member of the Central Committee. Aleksinskii remembers how the young Caucasian mocked the older man: "Here now Comrade Voinov [Lunacharskii] has given a speech. Like a ballerina, he jimped, jumped, and nothing is left. When I came here they told me: you will see Comrade Voinov. This is a big fellow, a member of the CC. I came, looked at him. I see, what kind of member of the CC he is. Only an [ordinary party] member." "In his personal behavior," Aleksinskii went on, "Stalin gave an impression of a poorly educated, uncouth, wild, and crude person. Evidently he was able to preserve these traits until his death."[44]

Eighteen years later, once again reflecting on the appropriate posture of a leader, Stalin remembered that this "was the first time I saw Lenin in the role of the defeated. In no way did he look like those leaders who whimper and are despondent after a defeat. Just the opposite, the defeat turned Lenin into a ball of energy, inspiring his supporters to fight anew for the coming victory." With the Mensheviks posing as the victors, Lenin launched "merciless criticism." "I remember how we, the

Bolshevik delegates, clumped together, looked to Lenin, and asked for his advice." Several delegates were beaten down by fatigue and were despondent. "I remember how Lenin responded to their speeches, barely straining through his teeth, 'Don't whimper, comrades, we will win for sure because we are right.'"[45]

Four principal questions divided the congress: agrarian reform, elections to the duma, armed uprising, and relations with socialist parties of the non-Russian nationalities. Now that the revolutionary fervor of late 1905 had dissipated, no one was calling for the revolution "growing over" from bourgeois democratic to socialist. The extremism of the preceding year had evaporated. The Bolshevik resolution on armed insurrection failed to pass, and the congress rejected the Bolsheviks' call for a boycott of the elections to the state duma. On the all-important question of land, the congress adopted the Menshevik policy of "municipalization"—that is, the large landholdings of the nobles and other nonpeasants would be transferred to local governmental institutions, like the *zemstva*, and rented out to peasants, who would also keep their own land. In this way the most capitalist of enterprises would not be included in the land redistribution. Lenin's proposal that all land be nationalized and then turned over to the peasants was condemned as Populist rather than Marxist. He proposed an American-style distribution of land to potential productive farmers, rather than a Prussian-style large-scale farm economy with hired agricultural laborers. Nationalization and redistribution of land would hasten the collapse of "feudal" relations in the countryside, he believed, and would accelerate the development of agrarian capitalism. Lenin wanted the land reform to be carried out by the central government, while Mensheviks preferred "municipal" control of the land reform.

Jughashvili made his debut intervention at the congress during the heated debate over the agrarian question. He had published a series of articles a few months earlier that took a very radical position on the agrarian question—full seizure of agricultural land by the peasants without compensation to the landlords.[46] When earlier the Social Democrats had called only for the return of the so-called cutoffs (*otrezki*), land that had been taken from the peasants and given to the landlords in the Emancipation settlement of 1861, that tactic had aimed at encouraging a peasant movement. Now that the peasants had risen, Koba argued, their demands for all the land had to be recognized and supported. He emphasized that each approach had been appropriate for its time, but the moment had come to turn the land directly over to the peasants. Only confiscation of all the land and distribution directly to the peasants would eliminate the remnants of serfdom and open the way for the "free development of capitalism," the next stage in the evolution of the village. Having worked in western Georgia where all around him he had witnessed the most extraordinary peasant mobilization and seen ordinary villagers acting with political clarity and determination, Koba confidently proposed a solution more radical than Lenin's.

But he did not go as far as the Socialist Revolutionaries (SRs), who wanted full "socialization of the land," the parceling out of the land to the peasants in equal shares. Socialism, Koba insisted, does not come from the village but from the city. "Everyone knows [except apparently the Socialist Revolutionaries] that the city is more developed than the village, that the city is the leader of the village." Such a socialism as proposed by the SRs would be "a stillborn socialism."[47] Moreover, the SRs would establish socialism in the village while the towns were still capitalist. That would be "bourgeois socialism." The SRs wanted to battle against the development of capitalism, but socialism required the full development of capitalism. Although socialism lay in an indeterminate future, Koba outlined what he understood it to be: "The realization of socialism is the annihilation of commodity production, the abolition of a money economy, the destruction of capitalism to its foundations, and the socialization of all means of production."[48] The time for socialism in Russia, he affirmed, had not yet arrived.

In these articles Koba emphasized flexibility, rather than dogmatic consistency. "What becomes reactionary *tomorrow* might be revolutionary *today*."[49] "Each question ought to be posed dialectically, i.e., we should never forget that everything changes, that everything has its time and place, and, therefore, we should pose questions as well in accordance with concrete conditions."[50] He spoke with great assurance, critically evaluated alternative policies, and distinguished questions of principle from matters of practice. He quoted from the third volume of Marx's *Capital* as if it were the most natural thing for a provincial Social Democrat to have read it. He cited Kautsky to explain why the breakup of the landlords' estates, which were the principal producers for the market, and division of the land among smallholding peasants were not backward steps. Landlord estates, after all, were part of the serf-owning system. They were not capitalist producers, in his view, and, therefore, were destined to be replaced by a "petty bourgeois economy" of peasant proprietors.[51] Here too Koba was to the left of Lenin. This was the first foray of this young Georgian Marxist into the resolution of a vital policy question, the most fundamental economic problem in Russia. What he thought at the time mattered to few, but two decades later the ideas he was evolving on peasant agriculture and the nature of socialism would have life-and-death consequences for millions of people.

At the congress Koba explained that he favored full partition of the land (*razdel*) both because the peasants were demanding it and it was in line with the requirements of economic development. "Since we are making a provisional revolutionary alliance with the struggling peasants, we cannot fail to consider the demands of that peasantry. We ought to support those demands, if they generally and wholly do not contradict the tendencies of economic development and the process of the revolution."[52] Neither municipalization nor nationalization was acceptable. Full partition would be reactionary if the Russian village were already capitalist, but since it was precapitalist, *razdel* would be revolutionary. Only forests and water should not be redistributed but nationalized. Still, "the agrarian revolution has its goal, which above everything is primarily the liberation of the peasants. . . . If the liberation of the proletariat can be the task of the proletariat itself, then the liberation of the peasants can be the task of the peasants themselves."[53]

While Koba was prepared to accommodate peasant demands for full partition of the land, Lenin later criticized those supporting *razdel*: the duty of Marxists is not simply to interpret the world, he asserted, but to change it, not simply to give in to peasant demands but show peasants the way forward. "Municipalization is mistaken and harmful, *razdel* as a program is mistaken but not harmful. Therefore, I, of course, am closer to *razdel* and ready to vote" for it rather than for the Menshevik variant.[54] Koba defended Lenin from attacks by Plekhanov, who talked about the Bolshevik leader's "anarchist manner." Such accusations, he claimed, undermined the purpose of the congress, which was to unite the party. One could speak of Plekhanov's "Kadet manner," he slyly hinted, but that would not resolve the agrarian question.[55]

The difference between nationalization, which would redistribute free land and enhance production for the market, and *razdel*, which would turn all the land over to the peasants who would then divide it up into small plots, was significant. Nationalization was concerned with productivity; *razdel* with the strategy of alliance with the peasants during the revolution. Since peasants wanted the land as their own, and nationalization, as Zhordania pointed out in the debate, abolished private property in land, such a program would put Social Democracy in conflict with the peasants. *Razdel* (like municipalization) preserved the private property of the peasants.[56] In 1906 Lenin and his Bolshevik comrades lost on the agrarian question, and the Menshevik resolution favoring municipalization of the land won, 61 to 46 to 3.[57] Eleven years later, in the revolutionary year 1917, Lenin himself would abandon the idea of nationalization and give in to the peasant demand for *razdel*.[58]

For all the talk of unity, ending factionalism proved impossible. The Menshevik spokesman on the "current moment," Aleksandr Martynov, accused those like Lenin who insisted on the viability of an armed insurrection of reverting to the tactics of nineteenth-century utopian revolutionaries like the anarchist Mikhail Bakunin and the "Russian Jacobin" Petr Tkachev. Social Democrats, he insisted, should realize that the revolution had to gather its forces, defend itself, and refrain from launching fresh attacks on the autocracy. The means at hand were the elections to the state duma. Our Bolsheviks, Martynov concluded, are too emotional: "Among our comrades from the majority a new type of revolutionary has formed who has fire in his heart and his imagination, whose head is on fire and who is delirious with revolutionary phrases."[59]

Koba was one of those fiery Bolsheviks, and when he commented on the Menshevik evaluation of the "current moment" he laid out a stark choice for the party. "It is no secret for anyone that in the development of the socio-political life of Russia we notice two paths: the path of pseudo-reforms and the path of revolution. . . . We are on the eve of a new explosion, the revolution is on the rise, and we must carry it to the end." He opposed Martynov's notion that "the hegemony of the proletariat in the current bourgeois revolution is a harmful utopia." Mensheviks may prefer the "hegemony of the democratic bourgeoisie," but "if the class interests of the proletariat lead it to hegemony, if the proletariat ought to lead, not follow behind, the flow of the current revolution, then it is understandable that the proletariat ought not to refuse to take an active role in the organization of the armed uprising or the seizure of power." Koba cut through the complexities of the issue. The essence of the disagreements between Mensheviks and Bolsheviks was simple: "Either the hegemony of the proletariat or the hegemony of the democratic bourgeoisie—that is how the question stands in the party; that is what our disagreements are about."[60]

The stark choice had come down to insurrection or participation in the duma elections. Vehemently opposed to the Bolshevik position, Akselrod condemned their insurrectionary-conspiratorial tactic.[61] The best means to move toward full democracy, he argued, was through the duma, though the final battles would require a popular uprising. Lenin answered him, but without his usual force and enthusiasm, as if he were not fully committed to the boycott of the elections but merely going along with the young militants in his faction. He feared that the duma would aid the liberals more than the socialists and that workers might be tempted to think that there was a peaceful road to democracy.[62] Koba spoke briefly, mentioning that in Baku, the only heavily industrial center of the Caucasus, the workers had voted for a boycott of the duma. The Bolshevik tactic does not lull the workers to sleep as the Mensheviks do but wakes them up, he contended.[63] The Tiflis Menshevik, the worker Vlasa Mgeladze, rebuked Koba. In a passionate speech he pointed out that the vote in Baku was very close and did not represent the whole of the proletariat. Baku voted for the boycott because "our intellectuals . . . look on the proletariat as they look on the bourgeoisie; they think that the proletariat can be pulled by the ears and led wherever they want.

They frightened us and we were afraid. . . . I saw how they lied to the workers." He was interrupted by protests from the floor but went on: "They frightened us in Baku: they will arrest you. They told us that this duma is a Black Hundreds [that is, reactionary] one. . . . They frightened us, but who bears on its shoulders the mistakes of the intellectuals. We, the workers! And in order that this does not go on, I know only one way out: the political education of the workers themselves. But our leaders bother themselves very little about this."[64]

As expected, the congress voted in favor of participation in the duma, 62 to 43 to 3, almost the exact breakdown by faction as had occurred in the vote on the agrarian plank.[65] When the Caucasian Mensheviks proposed that Social Democrats participate in those elections to the duma that had not yet taken place (in Caucasia among other places), Lenin and Shahumian voted for that resolution. Koba abstained.[66] On the most radical issue of armed insurrection, the Bolsheviks insisted on the need of Social Democrats to arm workers and peasants, to carry out the technical work of organizing an uprising. The Mensheviks argued that the people were not yet sufficiently convinced that their interests and those of the government were incompatible. Therefore, more political work had to be carried out before the insurrection could succeed. Again, the Menshevik resolution prevailed.[67] Propaganda, not the direct arming of the people, was the order of the day. "Partisan" activities were also to end. The congress voted to cease all armed expropriations of money and terrorist activity, for they discredited and disorganized the party.[68] Bolsheviks in the Caucasus largely disregarded this particular resolution. That stance would have dire consequences for Koba.

Last, the congress discussed the issue of uniting with various national Social Democratic organizations—the Polish-Lithuanian, the Latvian, and the Jewish Bund. Unity with the first two was unproblematic, for they organized all workers in their territorial purview regardless of nationality. But the Bund was dedicated to working only with Jewish workers, and many Social Democrats considered that form of work contrary to the internationalist principles of their party. Zhordania stated bluntly that "if you unite with the Bund under these conditions, then you will gain the Bund and you will lose the Caucasus, where we are strong only because we build our organizations on other principles. . . . I declare that the Caucasian organizations will be destroyed at the moment that the Bund enters the party without rejecting first its organizational principle. If you want to disarm us in our struggle with Armenian and other nationalist organizations," then let the Bund in.[69] On this issue the Georgian Mensheviks lost, and Koba and Shahumian voted with Lenin to allow the Bund to enter the party, reversing the controversial decision of the Second Congress of the RSDRP. The concern for party unity overwhelmed the principle of internationalism, even though, exhausted, the delegates ended their congress on their feet singing the "Internationale."

The congress elected a united Central Committee, with seven Mensheviks and three Bolsheviks, to which five representatives of the national Social Democratic parties were later added. The editorial board of the "central organ" was entirely Menshevik. For the next year, until a fifth congress was held, the Mensheviks controlled the central party institutions. Lenin acknowledged this temporary defeat and called on all Social Democrats both to carry out the decisions of the congress and to engage in "free discussion of party questions, free comradely criticism" within united organizations. "We all agreed with the principle of democratic centralism, with the guarantee of the rights of any minority and any loyal opposition, to the autonomy of every party organization, with the recognition of electivity, accountability, and removability of all officials of the party. By really observing these principles of organization, in their honest and consistent realization, we see a guarantee from schisms, a guarantee that the battle of ideas in the party can and ought to be completely compatible with strict organizational unity, with submitting to all the decisions of the general congress."[70] Lenin made the point that he distinguished himself from the "minority" at the Second Congress, which had refused to submit to the Congress's decisions. At this moment unity and discipline were paramount—at least publicly. He referred to the Bolsheviks as "the former faction," relegating it to the party's past rather than future. His address expressed optimism about the direction in which the revolution and the working class were moving. There would be another day and another battle.

Despite the formal unity of the party, the factions continued to meet informally. The Bolsheviks gave up their separate Central Committee, but in the guise of a "financial group" they formed a "Bolshevik Center" made up of Lenin and two of his closest allies at the time, Aleksandr Bogdanov and Leonid Krasin.[71] Rather than eliminating factions, Grigorii Zinoviev later wrote, "The situation was such that two parties operated in the framework of one."[72]

In Caucasia the rhetoric of unity could not hide the growing fissure as each faction looked at the recent past and future possibilities differently. Koba and Shahumian did not sign Lenin's address from the "former faction of Bolsheviks," their identities tied firmly to the militant wing of the party. While Mensheviks increasingly concluded that Social Democrats and workers had gone too far in late 1905, that they had become too radical, those who continued to identify as Bolsheviks insisted that militant, even armed, opposition to tsarism was still essential at this time for a victorious revolution. For Mensheviks the December insurrection had been a clear defeat; to Bolsheviks it remained an inspiration, a moment when ordinary people had taken up arms against the government. Both factions should have been sobered by the events of December 1905. The Mensheviks saw their hopes for the liberal bourgeoisie misplaced and their fears confirmed. Frightened by the radicalism of the insurgents, the "bourgeoisie," as the Marxists conceived it, had stood by, not supported the workers, and basically capitulated to the new tsarist order. The Bolshevik anticipation that the peasants would back the workers had also not been realized—as least in Russia proper. "The brief 'days of liberty,' to be sure," wrote the Menshevik Fedor Dan, "showed that the Bolshevik assumption of a 'republican-democratic' peasantry as the ally of the working-class in the revolutionary struggle for a consistent 'political democracy' was no less illusory than the assumption of the Mensheviks of a revolutionary bourgeoisie under the influence of the proletariat."[73] In the next year the tactics of the factions diverged, with the Mensheviks committed to using the new legal possibilities of elections to the duma and the Bolsheviks holding steadfastly to the idea of organizing an armed uprising.[74]

POLITICS IN THE PUBLIC SPHERE

Koba did not rush back to Tiflis from the Stockholm congress. He wrote a friend, Mikheil Monaselidze, that he planned to visit his friend and Mikheil's brother-in-law, Aleksandre Svanidze, in Germany.[75] The seemingly innocent postcard had more behind it than was immediately apparent. Svanidze had earlier introduced Koba to his three sisters, the oldest of whom, Aleksandra, was married to Monaselidze. In 1905 Svanidze had asked Monaselidze if he could bring Koba to stay with them, and he agreed. He was not, however, to inform his sisters, who lived in the Monaselidze household, beforehand. Koba stayed in the Monaseldizes' apartment, and various of his comrades visited regularly. At some point one of the younger sisters, Ekaterine, caught his eye. The anodyne postcard had yet another message that could be read on the other side, which featured a painting by a radical Finnish artist, Eetu Isto, *The Attack*, painted in 1899 and the image widely distributed in 1905. An eagle, understood to represent Russia, was swooping down and ripping apart a large book labeled "Lex," defended by a blond maiden in the Finnish national colors, a white dress with a blue sash buckled with the coat of arms of Finland. Koba had chosen carefully an image that depicted the struggle between imperial power and a colonized periphery.

When Koba arrived back in Tiflis he looked quite different. "It was impossible to recognize him," wrote Aleksandra Monaselidze. "In Stockholm his comrades had forced him to buy a suit, a felt hat and a pipe; he looked like a real European. This was the first time we had seen Soso so well dressed."[76] He busied himself with newspaper work, raising money for the first legal Bolshevik newspaper in Georgian, *akhali tskhovreba* (New Life). Akhmeteli would be the official publisher, a front for the police, and Mikheil Monaselidze would run the press and function as editor. The paper lasted less than a month, but it was the first of a series of Bolshevik newspapers that operated with relative freedom for the next year.[77]

Koba missed the Caucasian elections, which had already been held. Not much had been expected from them since the tsar's electoral law was far from democratic.[78] Yet, so well organized and determined were the Caucasian Social Democrats that the results of the elections there stunned even the unsuspecting victors.[79] Social Democrats took nine out of ten precincts in Tiflis (the middle class Armenians of Sololaki voted for the Kadets) and crushed their opponents in Kutaisi and Batumi.[80] Even the nationalist Russian workers and the "Tatars" in Tiflis supported the Social Democrats, as did the peasants overwhelmingly. In the next rounds, in the electoral curiae, the Georgian Marxists came out ahead. Mensheviks took one seat from Tiflis city, one from Tiflis province, and all three seats from Kutaisi province.[81] The elections transformed the Georgian Mensheviks from a provincial into a national party. For the next decade they played a major role in the State Duma in Saint Petersburg, the center of Russian parliamentary life.

The existence of the duma changed the political landscape in Russia. Society had a voice in government for the first time in Russia. By the time the Caucasian deputies arrived in Saint Petersburg, the duma was already in full confrontation with the government. Led by the Kadets, the assembly had made a bold bid in its answer to the tsar's "Address from the Throne" to establish itself as a fully sovereign legislature. It called for radical land reform, amnesty for political prisoners, and a government responsible to the legislature. To the left of the Kadets was the large, amorphous group of deputies known as the *trudoviki* (laborers), who outpaced the Kadets in their call for abolition of capital punishment and censure of the government. Land reform was foremost in the minds of those representing the villages. Angered by Prime Minister Goremykin's rejection of their demands, the duma called for the resignation of the tsar's appointed cabinet. But the government, flush with a large loan from the French and confident that it had broken the back of the revolution, refused to cooperate with the duma, and Prime Minister Goremykin acted as if the legislature simply did not exist.

Outside the walls of the Tauride Palace, where the duma met, the public read about the duma's debates and learned of the government's recalcitrance. Those in power worried that the duma would pass its own legislation on the agrarian question and were concerned by the positive public impact of its proclamations and public debates. However ineffective the duma was as a legislature, its speeches resonated through-out the country. The Georgian Menshevik leaders were familiar figures throughout educated society. Zhordania was elected head of the eighteen-member Social Democratic caucus in the duma, though his pronounced stutter kept him from becoming a major orator.[82] His com-rades Dr. Ivane Gomarteli, Sergo Japaridze, and Isidore Ramishvili used the duma as a tribune to address the public outside the chamber's walls.[83] The tsarist government, Ramishvili proclaimed in his Gurian accent, should be tried for "criminal acts against the lives, property, and honor of Russia's citizens."[84] It did not matter that the speeches might be made to an empty hall since they were reported in the national press.

The question of whether to support the liberal Kadets in their quest for a government responsible to the duma or to simply use the parlia-ment as a platform from which to mobilize the masses divided the So-cial Democrats. The Menshevik-led Central Committee decided to work with the Kadets and demand a government answerable to parlia-ment, but the Bolsheviks were appalled at this compromise with the "bourgeoisie." The Caucasian leaders of the duma's Social Democratic caucus went along with the tactic of cooperation with the duma, even as their rhetoric in the chamber exposed their ultimate revolutionary intent.

While the most prominent Georgian Mensheviks were visible to the public eye, their Bolshevik and Menshevik comrades in Georgia worked in a penumbra. They operated both legally and illegally.[85] Koba lived for much of 1906–1907 in Tiflis on the second floor of a house at 3 Freil-inskii Street, a cul-de-sac. He and Shahumian, who was editing the Bolsheviks' Armenian paper *Kaits* (Spark), were the most important of the few Bolsheviks in town. Shahumian echoed Koba's sentiment that unity of the party was paramount. "We believe that our party has already matured so much with such a strong form it feels one and only one party obligation, that no sort of event can create a new split, a new 'schism' among us, even if that were wished by this or that influential body or groups, even if that were the Central Committee itself."[86] Dur-ing Koba's absence abroad the Tiflis police had discovered the underground printing press that the Social Democrats had set up at the end of 1903. Established in secret in Avlabar, a semi-rural suburb across the Kura from central Tiflis, the press had printed materials from both factions until March 1906, when the united Tiflis Committee turned the building above the press into the headquarters for preparing an armed insurrection. One room was dedicated to a bomb-making laboratory. But early on the morning of April 15 the police surrounded the building, searched it thoroughly, and discovered the press by descending into a dry well. The same day they arrested Social Democrats throughout the town.[87]

As the heavy hand of the police fell on the revolutionaries, it became impossible to organize mass demonstrations. But sporadic armed attacks kept the government at bay. The combat organization of the Georgian Socialist Federalists carried out a spectacular "expropriation." Dramatically, on April 13, six armed men dressed as soldiers, and led by an active officer, Captain Ioseb Gedevanishvili, made their way into the Dusheti treasury right under the gaze of the guards and made off with 315,000 rubles.[88] In the spring there was a spike in peasant unrest. "Red hundreds" took control of the eastern Georgian region of Telavi, and only in August were troops able to restore the government's authority.[89] Workers took advantage of the new freedoms and held thousands of meetings, organized unions, and went on strike. In Tiflis the city was brought to a halt once again by a transportation strike. Terrorist attacks took their toll on prominent officials. From April to July 1906 there were more than one hundred fifty mutinies in the armed forces throughout the empire.[90] The daily violence peaked on June 1, when almost ninety people were killed and seven hundred wounded in an anti-Jewish pogrom in the town of Bialystok, a more devastating repetition of the August 1905 pogrom in the same town.[91] Duma deputy Japaridze proposed that the duma call on the people "to take the defense of their lives and property into their own hands."[92] When the tsar ordered his viceroy to return one of his divisions to Kiev, Vorontsov-Dashkov wrote plaintively that such a transfer would strip the southern border of soldiers needed "for the preservation of the proper order in Kars and Erivan, the guarding of the border against raids by Kurds and Armenian bands, and the leaving in barracks of one or two battalions for drilling. . . . In central Russia rarely do the police have to act against the armed masses, but in Caucasia it is continually that way."[93]

As the wave of revolution heaved and fell, Koba avoided arrest, working primarily as a journalist, writing articles for the Georgian Bolshevik newspapers and polemicizing with opponents at meetings. Nikolai Eliava, who knew him at the time, noted that not only did Koba write articles for *elva* (Lightning), but "his basic work, as before, was done in the illegal organizations; this was his instinct. He was the soul of all the underground work."[94] Even Arsenidze, no friend of Koba's, grudgingly remembered how effective Koba was in the organization. "Of all the Bolsheviks, Koba was distinguished by his unquestionably enormous energy, his tireless ability to work, his insuperable passion to run things, and most of all his enormous and peculiar organizational talent."[95] Intense, unceasing meetings and discussions were Koba's stage. Even though they were formally members of the same party, Koba relentlessly attacked the Mensheviks. The railroad worker Dato Lortkipanidze remembered that the Menshevik leader Jibladze sent Koba to argue with the anarchists and that the young agitator had great success convincing workers not to join them.[96] Konstantine Dvali, a cousin of the Svanidzes, the family into which Koba would soon marry, remembered that Koba invited some people to go to a theater where the anarchist Komando Gogelia was lecturing. During the question period Koba put questions to the speaker and won over the audience, quoting from Bakunin and Kropotkin. The audience shouted, "Good job, you in the black shirt." His friends cheered "Koba," so that no one would know that the hero of the day was Soso Jughashvili.[97] During a discussion of the contentious issue of participation in a provisional revolutionary government once the autocracy was overthrown, Arsenidze, who considered Koba crude, dishonest, and untrustworthy, confronted him with a blunt question: "When you are in the government, you will be forced by circumstances sometimes to disperse the workers, to fight with them, in a word to become gendarmes; is this really acceptable to you?" Arsenidze was stunned by his answer, "as unexpected as a clap of thunder from a clear sky." Without hesitation Koba answered: "Yes, if it is necessary, we will be the gendarmes of the revolution."[98]

Sometime in 1906 Arsenidze chaired a meeting in the Tiflis district of Kharpukhi, where the Bolsheviks were in the minority as had become the case in most places in Georgia. "Koba glowered, acted very provocatively, was rude, and clearly tried to break up the meeting. I had to exchange some sharp words with him since the usual pleas had no effect on him. To my reprimand he reacted obscenely. He indecently answered that he had not taken off his trousers and that there was nothing improper in his behavior. I answered back that he was acting like a man without trousers and like 'someone walking around without underwear.' This popular expression had the meaning of 'streetwalker.' I thought that this retort would cause him to explode. Nothing of the kind happened: he only smiled maliciously with the left corner of his mouth and sat in his place. After a few minutes he stood and left the meeting." Shortly afterward, whistles were heard from the street, the signals that the police were coming. The meeting quickly broke up, but the participants soon realized that there were no police nearby. Arsenidze and his comrades were convinced that Koba had taken his revenge for the insult with this trick.[99]

At another secret meeting in Tiflis attended by a large group of party workers and craftsmen, Koba challenged the main speaker. He "began to cite Marx, but as always in his own peculiar way." The chairman, Vladimir Akhmeteli, who was a student of Marxism just back from Germany, "regarded Stalin's face for a long time in silence, smiled and, no longer able to endure, got up and cited from memory the words of Marx from the third volume of *Das Kapital* in a Georgian translation" to show that Koba "had a false and mistaken grasp on Marx." Not in the least perturbed, his face inscrutable and showing no emotion, Koba "calmly got up and said the following within the hearing of all those assembled: 'Whoever wrote that is the son of an ass; it ought to have been written as I said.' Everybody in the assembly laughed, and Stalin slowly got up and departed quickly." Remembering this incident, Davit Saghirashvili went on:

Having learned to simulate calm though a storm might rage within his breast, Koba-Stalin returned to the home of the Akhmeteli family, which had five sons. One of them, Mate, was a Bolshevik and considered himself Koba's friend. There, Koba renewed his dialectical debate with Vladimir Akhmeteli and reproached him by saying that surely he had falsified the text of Marx at that meeting. Vladimir lightly replied that he spoke about the current opinion on Marx's teachings, which differed so drastically from Koba's. He added, jokingly, that the divide between Koba and Marx is as great as the difference between Koba and the Chinese emperor. Then Vladimir proceeded to explain how Koba misunderstood Marx, giving his views on scientific socialism. This time, Koba showed his choleric temper by cursing his ideological teachers Marx and Engels. Later, in his Berlin exile, Akhmeteli would still recall Stalin's ferocity and brutality, which made many Georgians feel that Stalin might be capable of liquidating Marx and Engels if they were alive in his day.[100]

Ferocity of disagreement was embedded in Marxist political culture. The original texts were fair game for adherents of both evolutionary, reformist views as well as revolutionary approaches. The potential of division and schism and expulsion from the fold of agreement were always present. Koba fervidly defended his own views, an ardent partisan of Bolshevism, while at one and the same time an opponent of any formal schism of the Social Democratic party. For the three weeks in late June and early July 1906 that the Tiflis Bolsheviks were able to publish *akhali tskhovreba* legally, Koba wrote an article nearly every day and repeatedly touted the need for unity. As a key contributor, perhaps even the principal inspiration behind the paper, producing some twenty-seven articles, for the first time he began signing (seventeen of them) "Koba."[101] When the Socialist Federalists claimed that the split in the RSDRP was widening, Koba responded that "after the congress there is no schism between Bolsheviks and Mensheviks anywhere, not in any city, and, therefore, it cannot be gaining strength; and Bolsheviks and Mensheviks are working in common organizations; the majority of organizations are accepting the resolutions [of the congress]; and, therefore, between them there exists only differences of ideas, which cannot be called a schism."[102] He rejected the call by a worker writing in *simartle* (Truth]) that the party should either become a united party with a single tactic, a common road, or split.[103]

The battle of ideas, however, was intense. The moderate Menshevik Khomeriki, writing in *lampari* (Torch), castigated those in the party who favored an armed insurrection as "Blanquists." "Marxist tactics demand mass self-action. According to Blanquist tactics only conscious revolutionaries ought to act; the people, the masses, ought to be offered help. Marxism teaches us that a real struggle with the old regime is possible only when the revolutionary fire appears in the whole mass. . . . It has not been a long time since Blanquist tactics appeared in our party, but already it is evident that they are intolerable in the struggle for the liberation of the proletariat."[104] Koba countered that *lampari* echoed the liberals by labeling as Blanquists those who do not see the duma as some kind of revolutionary center. But the duma wants an autocracy of the big bourgeoisie, while the people want an "autocracy of the people."[105] "We do not say that the people are ready for an armed uprising. But we believe the situation is developing so that an uprising will break out, break out just as 'unexpectedly' as happened in January [1905] (in Petersburg) and in December—whether we want it or not, and that is why it is essential for us to prepare, energetically prepare for an uprising, etc."[106]

With overweening confidence, Koba predicted that a major revolutionary confrontation was fast approaching. The major sin of the Social Democrats was that they had not sufficiently worked to arm the people for the December 1905 insurrections and coordinate the events in various cities.[107] The Social Democratic congress had erred in rejecting the Bolshevik resolution calling for arming the workers and forming red detachments. For an insurrection to succeed it cannot merely defend; it must attack. As Marx put it, "Defense is the death of any armed uprising. . . . In a word, act according to the words of the greatest of the hitherto known masters of revolutionary tactics, Danton: boldness, boldness, and again boldness."[108] Koba had nothing positive to say about the duma or its Georgian Menshevik deputies—unlike Lenin who praised

Isidore Ramishvili's speeches.[109] Koba, Suren Spandarian, "Borchalin-skii," and "Mikho" signed a declaration that if the duma betrayed the revolution, then Social Democrats "must abolish the duma and move forward to an all-people constituent assembly."[110] When Koba tried to "correct" the local Mensheviks and affirm that Bolsheviks were not op-posed to adopting more moderate tactics like participating in political banquets, Tskhakaia felt compelled to defend him from Menshevik charges of "Jesuitism." "Why have you concluded that Koba is a Jesuit? Is argumentation from fact Jesuitism?"[111]

Koba's revolutionary rhetoric matched the mood of many young ac-tivists in Georgia. A letter from a Social Democrat named "Razhden" to his Menshevik comrade, Nestor Kaladze, reveals how Koba was re-garded by many of his comrades. Razhden feared that support of the duma would dissipate the revolutionary enthusiasm of ordinary people. "Our policy and tactics ought in every way to aid the development and strengthening in the people of a revolutionary spirit; of course, along with this it is necessary to develop the self-consciousness of the people as much as possible, although in time of revolution a revolutionary spirit is more valuable and more necessary than self-improvement." He proudly declared his allegiance to the Bolsheviks, singling out Lenin and Koba. "So, as you can see, by conviction I am a partisan of Lenin's, but from the heart and soul I also want the victory of Koba in our land. True, we do not have such leaders who have received higher education abroad, as you have, but I can say that now even Mensheviks approve the works of Koba. Let our leader be a real proletarian *intelligent*. It seems to me that this more closely fits the proletarian teachings than someone educated in the embraces of the nobles, a learned representa-tive of the free professions, a great intellectual."[112] Razhden valued Koba as that rare combination—a radical worker intellectual—that for him characterized Bolsheviks.

A few days after this letter, a number of Social Democrats left the Tiflis organization and formed what they called the Workers' Union of Social Democrats. Upset by the "personal self-regard, idol worship, and hierarchy in the party," they felt that nepotism reigned among the princes, nobles, officers, and ordinary people in the party. They cited

Comrade Koba, who had written that "democratism had not been fully implemented within the party."[113] Even though he was in the lesser wing of Georgian Social Democracy, for a number of Georgian Social Democrats, Koba had achieved recognition as a stalwart of the movement. He was a model revolutionary with few doubts about what he was doing, someone who possessed a coherent sense of his life's purpose. His confidence and self-assurance infected others around him. As someone who had risen from the people, the son of a worker, he could identify himself both as a man of the masses and an *intelligent*, someone close to the workers but not a worker himself. To young Social Democrats like Razhden and the militants of the Workers' Union, Koba was the kind of leader needed by the revolution.

16

THE PROFESSIONAL

He was able to influence certain kinds of people and achieved a great deal in this area. There were those who were prepared at his first call to do anything. But among propagandists and people of a higher intellectual level, he was less well-liked and appreciated, although literally everyone recognized him as one of the most energetic and essential party members in the Caucasus.

—TATIANA VULICH, "BOL'SHEVIKI V BAKU"
["BOLSHEVIKS IN BAKU"] (1949)

One could see, even in one so young at this time, that Stalin was already making an extraordinary ascent. The admiration and affection that enveloped him allowed him to impose an iron discipline on his followers and, if he thought it necessary, to sacrifice his best disciples for the success of his politics. . . . And, it was characteristic that this iron discipline was imposed not only on his young disciples and comrades of his own age, but also on his elders from whom he had learned and had nothing to teach! At this time already, Stalin knew how to attract them to him—and to become the uncontested boss of those in the group of old Marxists, much older and more cultured than he.

—KHARITON SHAVISHVILI, *PATRIE, PRISONS, EXIL* (1946)

Koba's personal life had long been subordinated to his political activity. He had friends, but many of them viewed him as distant and difficult to understand. He was a man who made it hard to know him. His smile, on which so many commented, was protective, a veil that separated him from those around him. Life as an outlaw had made close or romantic relationships extremely problematic. Sometime in 1906, however, Koba courted Ekaterine Svanidze, the sister of his seminary friend, Aleksandre Svanidze, who had become a Bolshevik.[1] Ekaterine, known as Kato, worked as a seamstress in the shop of a French dressmaker, Madame Hervieu, in Sololaki, the comfortable "bourgeois" district of Tiflis. Koba occasionally visited the shop or dropped in to chat with Ekaterine at the apartment she shared with her sister. Their premises were relatively safe. Even though there might be the occasional search by the police, no one was picked up unexpectedly. He sat all day and wrote in a corner reserved for him, a cigarette in his mouth.[2] At night Koba disappeared with his articles and returned only at two or three in the morning.[3] Sometimes he read socialist brochures to those around him or entertained them with jokes. "In his private life Comrade Stalin was a big jokester," Efim Sartania remembered. "In appearance Comrade Stalin was very severe, . . . but in fact he was a deeply feeling person."[4]

One evening, as Koba sat with Ekaterine in the rear boutique of the *couturier* Madame Hervieu, who was watching the street through a window, she rushed into the room in a panic: "The gendarmes!" she exclaimed, "save yourself!" Koba barely had time to rush to the roof and disappear into the night. The police commander of the raid was particularly upset that he had missed his prey, especially since it was the first time he had employed two dogs that the secret police had imported from Germany to chase fugitives.[5]

Despite the perils of married life, Koba decided to wed Ekaterine Svanidze. In order to please his mother, who approved of the quiet, pretty Kato, Koba agreed to a church wedding.[6] Kato's brother-in-law, Mikheil Monaselidze, searched for a priest to marry the couple, but no one was willing to overlook Koba's illegal status. Finally, he bumped into Khristisi (Kita) Tkhinvaleli, who had attended seminary with Koba and was now a priest at Saint David's Church. Kita agreed to perform the service but under two conditions: nothing would be said to the senior priest at the church, and the service would have to take place at one or two in the morning. Only a few could attend. In the early hours of July 16, 1906, Koba and Kato were wed, the ceremony witnessed by Davit Monaselidze and Giorgi Elisabedashvili on the groom's side, and

Mikhail Davidov and Mikha Tskhakaia on the bride's. Kostia Dvali sang in the choir. Ekaterine kept her maiden name, since her husband had no legal passport in which to register it, and the marriage was not recorded in her official documents.[7] At the reception afterward, Koba's friend and fellow Bolshevik Tskhakaia acted as the *tamada* (toastmaster), and among the dozen or so guests were Archil Dolidze; Kato's older sister, Aleksandra (Sashiko); her husband, Mikheil Monaselidze; and Kamo.[8] During the dinner Kote Tsintsadze offered Kato some candy wrapped in paper, but she refused to take it. "Good girl," Kote said. "She will make a worthy wife of a Bolshevik. No one will easily fool her, for this was empty paper." Everyone sang, Koba as well. Tskhakaia joked after the first course, as the second was brought in, "This, comrades, is a provocation. . . . You know, we socialists go hungry for two or three days; why did you not warn us in advance that there would be more dishes." Kamo remarked, "Where are the stupid police now? We are all here. Let them come and arrest us like sheep."[9]

From most accounts Koba loved his wife dearly, and his affection was reciprocated. But his revolutionary activities cruelly affected their life together. Those in Russia who chose to become professional revolutionaries, from the 1860s through the civil war of 1918–1921, often placed their party work above family. Four months after the wedding, while Koba traveled to Baku on party business, his wife was arrested. She lived with her sister and brother-in-law, the Monaselidzes, and Koba's close friend, Kamo, had asked them to care for a sick comrade unknown to them. The man stayed for two weeks and then left for Russia. Shortly afterward, he was arrested in Moscow, and the police discovered a note on him: "Freilinskii 3, seamstress Svanidze, ask for Soso." On November 13, the police interrogated Ekaterine about her husband. She denied that the person they sought lived with them, and Kato showed the gendarmes her passport to verify that she was not married. The police arrested Kato and seized two heavy sacks of books and the archive of *akhali tskhovreba*. Shortly afterward, the police also arrested her cousin, Spiridon Dvali, in whose house they found a store of weapons, and condemned him to death. It turned out that the man from Moscow, the Jewish "revolutionary" they had helped, was in fact a police spy.[10]

Sashiko Monaselidze turned frantically to the wife of the colonel of the gendarmes, Rechitskii, for whom she had sewn a dress, begging her to convince her husband to reduce Dvali's death sentence to exile and to release the pregnant Kato. Sashiko persisted with other influential people until Dvali was given four years hard labor and Kato was reassigned to a local jail. It turned out that the jailor's wife had worked as a seamstress along with Kato and Sashiko, and she insisted that Kato live with her and her husband. When Koba returned from Baku, "he was very depressed by what had happened." He wanted to see Kato, and Sashiko convinced the jailor's wife to allow Kato a visitor, a cousin from the countryside. There in the jailor's apartment, Koba and Kato met. Soon she was given her freedom for two hours a day to meet with her "cousin," and after a month and a half she was released.[11]

On July 8, 1906, after seventy-two days of tolerating the duma, the emperor dismissed the legislature, with the promise to call a new one in seven months. The Kadets and the more radical deputies, including Zhordania and Japaridze, quickly gathered in Vyborg in Finland where they issued a manifesto calling on the people to refuse to pay taxes or serve in the military. The Menshevik-dominated Central Committee of the RSDRP called for a general political strike, but other revolutionary parties at first refused to go along. Sailors at Kronstadt outside Petersburg and Sveaborg in the Helsinki harbor revolted, but the workers in Petersburg, particularly those in the large state factories who had responded in 1905 to such appeals, did not walk out.[12] Angry as peasants were at the government's inaction on the land question and other issues, few were prepared to turn out to support the duma. The tsar emerged from this crisis unscathed, and he promptly appointed a new government headed by the tough, competent Petr Stolypin. Known to both admirers and critics as "Russia's Bismarck," Stolypin worked for the next five years to suppress the revolutionary opposition, strengthen the state, carry out his own peasant reform from above, and preserve the sovereign power of the monarch. Caucasia was kept under martial law or emergency laws until the last flickers of revolutionary fire faded in 1911.

The expectations of the Bolsheviks that a new revolutionary wave was on the horizon proved to be erroneous, and they had to go underground. Lenin left Petersburg, where he had briefly been in the thick of events, even managing to speak to workers at public meetings. Hiding in semi-autonomous Finland, frustrated and melancholy, he received the news from the capital in a comfortable country house in Kuokkala. He wrote feverishly about current politics and played the card game *durak* [fool] with the Bogdanovs, who lived on the floor above. Meanwhile police spies penetrated their organization, and Social Democrats were hunted down and arrested. But Lenin and his followers were slow to change tactics.[13]

Koba received the news of the dispersal of the duma with a sense of vindication. In a piece on "International Counterrevolution," he claimed that "the false hopes of various liberals and other naïve people" that there is a constitution in Russia were replaced by an understanding that "here we have civil war, and that the struggle must be carried out as a war." "Russia's proletariat marches at the head of the *democratic* revolution and extends its fraternal hand to the European proletariat, which will begin the *socialist* revolution," which will not only eliminate the remnants of serfdom but of capitalism as well.[14] Later, in a pamphlet published in the summer of 1906, he presented a stark picture of a country on the brink of a revolutionary uprising. Deploying that most familiar Manichean cliché, "Who is not with us is against us," he proclaimed, "The coming battles are in the streets, not in the 'garrulous duma.' "[15] In order to establish the "autocracy of the people" (a democratic republic), the socialist proletariat, not the bourgeois liberals, must be the hegemon in Russia's democratic revolution. While Mensheviks saw the hegemony of the proletariat as a "dangerous utopia," Bolsheviks believed the workers and peasants ought to seize political power.[16] "The leader of the revolutionary street ought also to be the leader in the government of the revolution." He rejected supporting the "conciliationist" duma and again called for an armed uprising.

INTRIGUE IN THE TRANSCAUCASIAN SOCIAL DEMOCRATIC CONGRESS

With the closing of the duma, the Georgian deputies returned home in the summer, and most were arrested for signing the Vyborg Manifesto. Zhordania went into hiding and worked with the local Bolsheviks to organize an armed uprising. His Menshevik comrades were split between those like himself prepared to return to a revolutionary strategy and those who preferred the parliamentary route.[17] In early September the Social Democrats gathered in their fourth congress of Transcaucasian Social Democratic Organizations. It opened in Tiflis but was forced to move the very next day to Baku because of police spies. In the freer atmosphere of the Caspian town, they met in a hotel, fifty delegates, for a whole week. An armed unit under Vladimir Gogua guarded the congress.[18] Koba controlled the votes of the small delegation of six Bolsheviks.[19] The Mensheviks were divided into two equal groups of eighteen, one of which agreed with the Bolsheviks that the repressive policies of Stolypin were the precursor of an armed uprising of the popular masses about to break out, and another that concluded that preparatory political work was required before a new upsurge of the popular movement. Instead of favoring an armed uprising, this latter group proposed the slogan "Through the State Duma to the Constituent Assembly." Noe Ramishvili gave a fiery speech in which he defended the more radical line. Devdariani, now a Menshevik, argued that the political repression would grow stronger and that Social Democrats had to demonstrate greater flexibility in their tactics. They should use both legal and illegal means, exploit the duma and agitate for a constituent assembly, but only with the ripening of the revolutionary movement within the masses should they move to insurrection.[20]

Zhordania and Archil Japaridze sided with Ramishvili, and the Mensheviks presented two resolutions. "Here," recalled Arsenidze with malicious irony, "Stalin demonstrated his organizational wisdom." He decided to support the more moderate faction (to which Arsenidze and Devdariani belonged, and Zhordania in a change of heart had joined) against the radicals (Noe Ramishvili and Archil Japaridze). The moderates were primarily from the cities—Tiflis, Batumi, and Baku—while the radicals represented rural districts, like Guria. After four votes were taken, Koba threw the Bolshevik votes behind the moderate slogan in order to defeat the "fortress of Transcaucasian Menshevism."[21] But this merely led the Mensheviks to form a mediation committee that the next day came up with a compromise: revolutionary actions were permitted but the main task of the moment is participation in the election campaign and the parliamentary political struggle. This position was acceptable only to the Menshevik delegates. Koba, it turned out, had united most of the Mensheviks![22] For the rest of the congress Koba sat quietly behind his ironic smile.[23] Yet to his old friend Devdariani, he seemed to direct the Bolsheviks. Koba was not ready to go as far as Ramishvili and put all the eggs in the insurrectionary basket, a tactic he considered anarchistic, but neither was he in favor of using legal means alone.[24] The final resolution demanded that the next duma take power from the tsarist regime and convene a Constituent Assembly to create a new government.[25]

The congress also passed a resolution in favor of organizing a non-party workers' congress as an antidote to the harmful effects "of the intelligentsia-circle period of our party" that had convinced many workers that the RSDRP was not a workers' party and that they should not join it. The workers' congress was a favorite cause of the veteran Social Democrat Pavel Akselrod, and in the wake of the defeats of 1905 many Mensheviks, like Martov, came on board, anxious to "exploit all the opportunities generated by the legal concessions of the tsarist regime . . . to build a mass labor movement and mass labor party in Russia."[26] For the Caucasian Social Democrats, class solidarity was both enormously important and incredibly fragile, given the religious and ethnic divisions in the Caucasus. They were shaken by the repeated ethnoreligious clashes between Armenians and local Muslims, which their congress interpreted in impeccably Marxist terms: "The basic reason for the Armenian-Tatar clashes is the antagonism between the vestigial feudalism of the Caucasus represented by the Tatar khans, beks, and agalars, and the growing victorious capitalism represented by the Armenian bourgeoisie."[27] In its resolution on the "national question," the congress decided to follow the standard formula of the Russian Social Democrats and to demand only a regional administration for Transcaucasia, with full rights for all nationalities. They would allow "free use of native language in all local state, social, and judicial institutions and the right to study in one's native language," but would not encourage ethnic over class identification by establishing national territorial autonomy for the region or for any of the local peoples.[28]

Reflecting the new moderate mood of local Social Democrats, the congress also resolved to curtail the activities of the armed *druzhiny* in which activists like Koba played such a vital role but over which the party had lost control. "The experience of the last few years," the resolution read, "have clearly shown that the standing armed fighting *druzhiny* are turning into a self-contained power and are trying to achieve a dominant position in the party and to dictate to it their conditions." The party was not to arm the *druzhiny* in peacetime and urged local organizations "to take the most forceful measures to disarm those Red Hundreds that operate primarily in the villages, rob the local population in the name of the party, and by undermining the prestige of Social Democracy demoralize the party masses."[29] The resolution did not, however, demand the breakup of the *druzhiny*. In Caucasia both Mensheviks and Bolsheviks continued to set up *druzhiny* and carry out assassinations and robberies. Indeed, the most spectacular of all "expropriations," the famous "Tiflis ex," was to take place in the following year with Koba playing a small initiating role. The congress ended with the election of a regional committee [*Oblastnoi komitet*] of nine full members and five candidate members, all but one of them Menshevik.[30]

The divisive squabbles within the Caucasian movement were often more personal than ideological. Feelings ran high, and the personal was political, and the political was personal. Although the party remained formally united, the local Bolsheviks boycotted the committee and in early 1907 formed their own center, called the "Literary Bureau of Bolsheviks." Among its members were Koba, Shahumian, Tskhakaia, Pilipe Makharadze, Mikha Davitashvili, and Mikheil Okujava.[31] Here Koba's purported organizational skills seemed to fail hm. When Viktor Naneishvili arrived in Tiflis and joined the bureau he noted how poorly directed was the work of the local Bolsheviks. "Ties with the districts were weak, especially with the petty-bourgeois fourth and fifth districts (Avlabar and Vera). In the most influential first district (Nakhalovka, the railroad yards), and the second (the railroad depot, trolleys, factories), no ties existed at all." In the bureau itself there was great disorder, and the rules of conspiracy were not observed. Though only six or seven men were actual members of the bureau, some twenty to twenty-five attended meetings.[32] The Bolsheviks in Georgia had shrunk to a tiny faction in the burgeoning Social Democratic movement. Never again would they recover the influence they had had briefly in 1903–1904— that is, not until the Red Army invaded independent Georgia in February 1921.

KOBA AND THE ANARCHISTS

Newly married, keeping clear of the police, Koba spent much of late 1906 and early 1907 issuing a steady stream of articles, about unions, factory legislation, and most extensively against political anarchism. As in much of the Russian Empire, Caucasia had few anarchists. Social Democracy was overwhelmingly the most powerful revolutionary force in the region, and the anarchists posed no real threat to their dominance. Followers of the Russian prince Petr Kropotkin, the Georgian anarchists took advantage of the new possibilities opened by the revolution, and many of them—Varlaam Cherkezishvili [Cherkezov], Giorgi (Komando) Gogelia, his brother Shalva, and Mikheil Tsereteli—returned to Georgia.[33] They published their own newspapers—*nabati* (Tocsin), *khma* (Voice), and *musha* (Worker)—and took every opportunity to attack the Marxists on their philosophical flank. Anarchism might be called "the conscience of the revolution," for it mounted a telling moral critique of the Marxists, in this case primarily the actions of the Mensheviks. In a letter early in 1906, the anarchist Gogelia wrote to a friend that the dominant Social Democrats had effectively "abolished freedom of speech and thought for all non-Social Democrats." "All the horrors of a revolutionary government occurred here . . . with the help of a special gang called the group of Social Democratic terrorists. . . . Social

Democracy forbade meetings and even followed, with the help of their own secret agents, those who spoke at private meetings. Social Democracy stopped people on the streets, searched [them], and demanded documents to establish identity. . . . There were exemplary arrests. Social Democracy burned the literature of every other party."[34]

Koba, who had been reading Engels's philosophical works, *Anti-Duhring* and *Ludwig Feuerbach*, decided to take on the anarchists in the Georgian Bolshevik press. His series of articles, titled "Anarchism or Socialism?," appeared from late June 1906 through the first weeks of April 1907. Koba began his series respectfully. While acknowledging that anarchists did not have mass following, he argued that their ideas must nevertheless be taken seriously and confronted. "If the teachings of the anarchists express the truth, then it is self-evident that they will open the way and will gather the masses around them." If, however, their beliefs do not conform to reality, then they will evaporate into air. Here Koba demonstrated a simple pragmatism: correct ideas will find their followers and win out. But he immediately asserted that "we must consider anarchists to be real enemies of Marxism" against whom we must battle.[35] It was this battle of ideas in which he was now engaged.

Koba laid out what he took to be the Marxist position on philosophical materialism. Borrowing from Plekhanov's monist materialism, Koba's views on the material base of social reality and ideas were quite orthodox for the time: the world is real and external to our perceptions; and it is nature that gives rise to concepts in our head.[36] He opened with a favorite quotation from Marx's *The Poverty of Philosophy*—one that seemed confirmed by the transformations both in Russia and in his own life experiences: "In the world everything is in motion. . . . Life changes; forces of production develop; old relations are destroyed. . . . Eternal movement and eternal destruction and creation—that is the essence of life."[37] He reiterated Marx's epistemology: social being determines consciousness. "With the change of the economic foundation, the entire immense superstructure is *more or less rapidly transformed*."[38] He elaborated how people's ideas and behaviors changed with social transformation: "If our world outlook, if our habits and customs are determined by external conditions, if the unsuitability of legal and political forms rests on an economic content, then it is clear that we must help to bring about a radical change in the habits and customs of the people, and in the political system of the country."[39] Koba was taken by the permanence of struggle, of new forms contesting old forms, processes of growing and dying, evolutionary and revolutionary change. Historian Erik van Ree characterizes his philosophy as "a kind of biological Marxism, a Marxist 'Darwinism,' well adapted to an ideology of life-and-death class struggle."[40]

For Koba, Marxism was "not only a theory of socialism but a whole world view, a philosophical system from which logically flows proletarian socialism."[41] He doggedly defended the principal tenets of Marxism against the accusations of the anarchists that Social Democrats were more interested in dictatorial rule than socialism. Marxism, he made clear, favors preservation of state power after the revolution since compulsion would have to be used to wrest power from the bourgeoisie and pass it on to the proletariat. Certainly there would be a dictatorship, but it would represent the broad masses. Using the popular works of Arnould and Lissagaray on the history of the Paris Commune of 1871, Koba echoed Marx's lament that the Communards' reluctance to use force, indeed to initiate civil war, led to the defeat of the Parisian workers. He endorsed Engels' characterization of the Paris Commune as the actual example of the dictatorship of the proletariat, a form of rule radically democratic, directly representing through elections the great bulk of the population.[42]

Though to a present-day reader Koba's articles are a simple exposition of a true believer's faith, at the time they impressed young Georgians. Even the Socialist Federalist Davrishev, who was closer to the anarchists, was amazed when he read Koba's polemic. One day he met Cherkezov, the leader of the anarchists, at the lawyer Diazamidze's. "Who is this Koba?" Cherkezov asked. "I have read these brochures attentively. Between us, they astounded me; they read as if Lenin himself had produced them. He is very dangerous, this guy. He must be eliminated when there is a chance."[43]

ARMED INSURRECTION OR ELECTORAL POLITICS?

The revolution was clearly winding down by late 1906. Even Lenin, who kept up a steady drumbeat in favor of armed insurrection, came out for contesting the upcoming elections to the Second State Duma. At a second conference of Social Democrats held in Tammerfors (Tampere), Finland, early in November 1906, he and a group of fourteen delegates declared themselves in favor of participation, but he opposed a Menshevik idea that in some cases, in order to defeat reactionary candidates, the party could join in an electoral bloc with the liberal Kadets.[44] Lenin refused to give up his support for armed struggle, the so-called partisan war, even though the Menshevik-dominated Fourth Party Congress had condemned it. Armed action was necessary, he asserted, along with a variety of other forms of opposition, to overthrow tsarism.[45] Koba parroted Lenin's line in his introduction to a Georgian translation of Karl Kautsky's pamphlet on Russia's revolution, demonstrating justifiably that the German theorist also supported the Bolshevik strategy. Kautsky's pamphlet—"Triebkräfte und Aussichten der russischen Revolution" ("The Driving Forces and Perspectives of the Russian Revolution")—had just appeared and characterized the current Russian Revolution as neither bourgeois nor socialist but something in-between. His view corresponded quite closely to Lenin's notion of the "democratic" revolution. Instead of allying with the liberal bourgeoisie, Kautsky and Lenin agreed, the Social Democrats should turn toward the peasants.[46]

The elections to the Second State Duma stunned the liberals and radicals and demoralized the conservatives and the government. Despite Stolypin's efforts to influence the elections in a more conservative direction—subsidizing the Right and repressing the Left—urban voters and peasants cast their ballots for the liberal and even socialist opposition. Instead of the seventeen Social Democratic deputies elected to the First Duma, the party held sixty-five seats in the second. Together with Socialist Revolutionaries, *Trudoviki*, and other smaller groups, socialist delegates numbered 232, more than either the liberal center (192) or the Right (74). "The end result," one historian notes, "was a chamber in which the political extremes were strengthened at the expense of the Kadets."[47] Once again the Caucasus returned a heavily Social Democratic delegation. As the left-leaning newspaper *Kavkazskaia rech'* (Caucasian Speech) reported, there were no real conservative parties in Caucasia, no monarchists or Octobrists; the liberal Kadets took up the middle-class vote and were the most "right wing" party south of the mountains. "Caucasian nations, especially the Georgians and Armenians," it explained, "are completely opposed to religious and political conservatism." Here the struggle was between socialism and nationalism.[48] And sometimes socialists of different nationalities could not agree. The Armenian Social Democratic organization in Tiflis, for instance, refused to form an electoral bloc with the local, primarily Georgian, RSDRP organization.[49] It went without saying that the Marxist Social Democrats would not cooperate with the more populist and nationalist Armenian Revolutionary Federation (*Dashnaktsutyun*), which ended their boycott and also contested the elections to the Second Duma, nor with the similarly socialist nationalist Georgian Socialist Federalist Party.

In Georgia the Mensheviks swept the elections. Even in Kutaisi province, wrote the newspaper *Zakavkaz'e* (Transcaucasia), "The party of the proletariat has achieved a complete victory there where there is absolutely no proletariat."[50] The local administration reported that the attempt by the Georgian Socialist Federalists to "take in the whole Georgian people . . . captured almost nothing. They tried with all their strength to unite the proletariat, the agriculturalists, and the financial bourgeoisie of Georgia, but their forces brought in nothing: the proletariat in its mass follows the Social Democrats, and the bourgeoisie does not consider itself able to defend its own interests."[51]

In Tiflis city the Social Democrats chose two Georgians and one Armenian as their candidates. With the Mensheviks controlling the elections and largely excluding the Bolsheviks, Koba arranged the election of a Bolshevik committee that operated separately and tried to put forth its own candidates. But the Menshevik Tiflis Committee was no longer interested in working with their ostensible comrades from the opposing faction.[52] The Menshevik Arshak Zurabov replaced the Bolshevik

Shahumian. Choosing Zurabov did not please a Dashnak who shouted, "You have elected a swindler." Most notable among the Georgians elected from Kutaisi was Irakli Tsereteli, a nobleman, the son of the journalist Giorgi Tsereteli, and though a newcomer to Social Democracy, not yet twenty-five years old, fated to have a brilliant career ahead as orator and a key leader of the Mensheviks both in the Second Duma and, ten years later, in the February Revolution of 1917.[53]

Young Tsereteli was chosen chairman of the caucus and given the task of answering Prime Minister Stolypin's initial speech.[54] At the opening of the duma, the radical mood of the majority was clear. Left and liberal deputies refused to stand when the Right cheered for the absent emperor. Prime Minister Stolypin was suspicious of the opposition, and his police spies followed and harassed them. Yet he wanted to work with the duma and pass necessary legislation to institute a semi-constitutional order in order to forestall those close to the tsar, like Durnovo and Goremykin, who favored turning back toward autocracy. On March 6 the prime minister addressed the duma, emphasizing the importance of establishing a state based on law and on passing a land reform that would end the peasants' "forced attachment" to their communes.[55] Tsereteli then rose and with unexpected eloquence and power blasted the government for its repressive measures against workers and peasants, its defense of landlord privileges, and failure to carry out a meaningful land reform. The Right repeatedly interrupted the speech, shouting that it was a call for insurrection. Tsereteli answered that it was the government's policies that were calling the people to rebellion.[56] In the weeks that followed his comrades repeatedly provoked the conservatives and the government with speeches denouncing the impotence of the duma and the viciousness of the government's pacification policies. Japaridze spoke in favor of turning the duma into a weapon of the people to move the revolution forward.[57] When Zurabov criticized the army as ineffective in battle against the Japanese and only capable of suppressing its own people, even the Kadets moved to censure him. The liberals appeared to some to be moving toward the government. This famous "Zurabov incident" infuriated the tsar, who pressed his ministers to consider dissolving the duma.[58]

As the revolution switched to the parliamentary track, Koba managed through stealth and caution to live a relatively routine life—at least for a professional revolutionary. Eight months after the wedding, his son, Iakob, was born, on March 18, 1907. Koba took the event in stride, hardly changing his patterns. His brother-in-law remembered: "If the child began to cry while he worked, Soso grew nervous and complained that the child was disturbing his work; but when they fed the child and he calmed down, Soso kissed him, played with him, and flicked his nose. Caressing the baby, he called him '*patsan*' [laddie], and this name stuck with him for the rest of his life."[59] The new father's articles in *chveni tskhovreba* (Our Life) and *dro* (Time) focused on the duma, and the venom in these pieces was directed more at the moderate wing of Social Democracy than at the liberals or reactionaries.[60] Koba gave a simple sociological analysis of where and why the Mensheviks found support: in backward areas, small towns, wherever artisanal production dominated. This included the Caucasus. But in the centers of factory production and mechanized industry, like Saint Petersburg, Moscow, the Central Industrial Region, Poland, the Urals, and the Baltic provinces, where class consciousness was more highly developed, the Bolsheviks had the greater support.[61]

THE CONGRESS OF DISUNITY

By spring 1907, in the Caucasus as in Russia, Mensheviks and Bolsheviks only occasionally acted as comrades in the same party. The Mensheviks had control of the Tiflis and the Caucasian Regional Committees, and the Bolsheviks took refuge in their "literary bureau." The Mensheviks' radicalism of late 1905 and early 1906 had momentarily brought them closer to the Bolsheviks, but their flirtation with the Kadets opened a chasm between the two factions. When in March 1907 the Caucasian Social Democrats organized elections for delegates to the upcoming Fifth Party Congress, they chose one delegate for every three hundred party members. The Bolsheviks were unable to find that many people for their candidates, but the conference agreed to give them one delegate from Tiflis and one from Baku. The Bolsheviks, however, published a resolution in *dro* that declared: "We, as the fighting part of the proletariat, do not sympathize with nor share the tactics of the Mensheviks, who support the Kadets, their allies."[62] Tiflis then chose ten delegates, all Mensheviks. The Bolsheviks demanded greater representation. They went ahead and chose Tskhakaia as their representative from Baku and Asatur Kakhoian and Suren Spandarian (interestingly enough, two Armenians) as delegates from the southern Georgian district of Borchalo, a mixed Armenian-Muslim region that had few if any Social Democrats.[63] By April 8 the Bolsheviks had managed to collect only 572 votes, just enough they decided to select Koba as their delegate from Tiflis.[64] His right to be a delegate would be repeatedly challenged by the local Mensheviks.

Around April 16 Koba left Tiflis for the planned Social Democratic congress in Copenhagen. He traveled to Petersburg by way of Baku with Kakhoian. In Tiflis Koba gave Kakhoian some documents to hide inside his jacket. In Petersburg they joined up with other delegates and went immediately to the Finland Station for the train and ship to Stockholm. Koba asked for the documents, but Kakhoian felt insulted. "When it was dangerous, you demanded that they be with me, but now when all difficulties are behind us, you want to carry them yourself." Koba explained, "I am taking the documents from you at the most serious and dangerous moment. I gave the documents to you because there [in Georgia] the gendarmes and spies know me better than you, and here they are less experienced and astute. I am no less experienced than they; there is no question that I will be caught." In fact, the police at the Finland Station searched every passenger head to foot, but Koba made it through.[65] Voroshilov later remembered the circuitous route that the delegates took to the congress. From Stockholm they took a train to Malmö and a ferry that took the train cars to Copenhagen across the narrow straits. But arriving about April 23 they found that the Danish government refused to allow the congress, and the delegates were forced to return to Malmö. Neither the Swedes nor the newly independent Norwegians extended their hospitality to the Russian revolutionaries. Their train again crossed to Denmark by ship, on to Esberg, and from there they moved to London, where the *Morning Post* announced their arrival in its April 28 (May 11) edition.[66]

Koba may have detoured to Berlin to meet with Lenin. More likely, he saw Lenin in Copenhagen, where party members from the interior of Russia, like Koba a year and a half earlier, were dismayed to see the modest bald man whom they had assumed from his writings to be a giant.[67] They were also surprised by the dark, oddly dressed delegates from the Caucasus. By the time the congress opened on April 30 Stalin was settled—some sources claim—in the apartment of Arthur P. D. Bacon, rooming with Shahumian, who had replaced the arrested Spandarian as a Bolshevik delegate.[68] Bacon's son, also Arthur, later reminisced for London's *Daily Express* about "Mr. Ivanovich," who wore a loose moleskin jacket, heavy trousers, and soft boots and enjoyed his favorite treat, English toffee. "I bought him some every day," Arthur Bacon recalled. His memory after forty-three years was that the man who would become Stalin lived at the corner of Jubilee and Clark streets in Stepney, staying with a Russian cobbler and his wife. "I used to make a bit of pocket money by running errands or lighting someone's fire at a ha-penny a time. Stalin wrote a letter to someone a street or so away and wanted it taken round by hand. He couldn't write English, so the cobbler's wife addressed the envelope. When I'd lit the fire, she gave me the letter. And old Joe gave me two bob. That was money then, you know. What did I do with it? Spent it my boy."[69]

The congress was held in the Brotherhood Church on Southgate Road, Islington, a wooden building with bare walls "unadorned to the point of absurdity."[70] For nearly three weeks, the three hundred plus delegates, representing an estimated one hundred fifty thousand party members, sat in the Gothic hall and debated the fate of their withering revolution. Social Democratic parties representing various national organizations—the Jewish Bund, the Social Democratic Party of Poland and Lithuania, and the Latvian Social Democrats–attended as full members of the congress. Alongside the veteran intellectuals sat simple workers who had meticulously outfitted themselves in suits and stiff collars. Isidore Ramishvili remembered that he had to buy a starched shirt to be properly dressed at the congress or else, his comrades told him, "you will look like a naked man if you come casual to the congress.[71]

The two major factions were basically even in number (eighty-nine sided with the Bolsheviks to the Mensheviks eighty-eight), with the Georgians inflating the Menshevik numbers. But the Bolsheviks had the advantage of occasional support of the largest non-Russian groups, the Latvians and the Poles. Lenin came prepared for a fight. When he greeted the celebrated writer Maxim Gorky, who was staying with him and his wife, he "said jocularly: 'So glad you've come. I believe you're fond of a scrap? There's going to be a fine old scuffle here.'" Gorky was also unimpressed by Lenin's physical appearance on their first meeting: "I did not expect Lenin to be like that. Something was lacking in him. He rolled his 'r's' gutturally, and had a jaunty way of standing with his hands somehow poked up under his armpits. He was somehow too ordinary, did not give the impression of being a leader."[72]

Plekhanov, "in a frock coat, closely buttoned up like a Protestant pastor," greeted the delegates, but now the "Father of Russian Marxism" had been orphaned by most of his children, who would not go as far as he in supporting the "bourgeois" duma.[73] To one worker delegate Plekhanov appeared affected, pretentious, and "unlike a Russian." His "speeches were speeches for the mind, but we were filled with revolutionary feeling."[74] Lenin fidgeted all during Plekhanov's speech, laughing silently at remarks he thought absurd.

The first long debate focused on the Social Democratic deputies' work in the duma. Martov gave the report of the Central Committee. Trembling all over, swaying back and forth, "spasmodically unfastening the collar of his starched shirt and waving his hands about," he praised the tactic of working through the duma to forestall the reactionary forces and push the Kadets to the Left, an approach he believed essential as the working class was growing politically passive, on the one hand, and apt to turn to sporadic violence, on the other.[75] Bogdanov gave a long, blistering reply from the perspective of a Bolshevik. He reviewed how the Mensheviks in the duma had ignored the directives of the last party congress and turned the Central Committee into a

factional center. As an example he mentioned that the Russian Mensheviks had been prepared to vote for a Kadet appeal to the peasants that
proposed land reform but without specifying that nobles' land would
be confiscated without compensation. Lenin castigated the Menshevik
strategy as "liberal" and parliamentary in a time of revolution.[76] The
Caucasian Mensheviks joined him and rejected such a step.[77] But as the
leader of the duma Social Democrats, Tsereteli defended their work by
quoting the German Marxist August Bebel: "I would walk with the
devil and his grandmother if this were good for the proletariat."[78] His
comrade, Japaridze, emphasized that the Mensheviks thought of the
duma both as a tribune and as "a means to educate the proletariat
politically."[79]

Toward the end of his life the Menshevik delegate Isidore Ramishvili
remembered approaching Lenin after the debate on Menshevik relations with the liberal Kadets. He saw Lenin during a break in the pro-
ceedings resting on a gravestone in the churchyard and reproached him
for criticizing Martov and Martinov for sitting at the same table and
drinking tea with Kadet leader Pavel Miliukov.

> Lenin laughed wholeheartedly and replied: "You happen to be a
> naïve man. Did you not see with this accusation what a disorder
> I made for both of them? All means are good when they harm your
> opponent. You are a weak factionalist, but you are a good man. I hope
> you will not expose me if I tell you that I have even drunk tea with
> the Bishop of Samara. This is not a sin, but when you are fighting,
> even this harmless affair of your opponent you should sell it as a sin.
> If you persistently point to the forehead of your opponent, claiming
> that he has a black spot there, for others it will seem that there really
> is a black spot. This is what happened today, I have marked both of
> them with a black spot."[80]

Trotsky, who had arrived at the congress after a daring escape from
Siberian exile, gave a long, passionate speech lambasting both the Mensheviks' ties to the Kadets and a proposed Bolshevik resolution of no
confidence in the duma delegation.[81] Everyone had heard of Trotsky,
famous as the head of the Petersburg Soviet in 1905 and for his bold

defense at his trial in 1906. For his deeds he had been given a life sentence. When Gorky introduced himself to Trotsky in the church vestibule as an admirer, Trotsky returned the compliment: "I hope it is not necessary for me to say that I am your admirer."[82] One delegate later remembered, "If Lenin made no impression on us by his outward appearance, Trotsky impressed [us] very strongly."

> We were very happy that this [person who] was known for his activity in the Petersburg Soviet of W[orkers'] D[eputies], who had just escaped from exile, Comrade Trotsky looked like a "real" leader. . . . Standing outside of any faction, and often agreeing with neither the Bolsheviks nor the Mensheviks, Trotsky stunned us with the energy and brilliance of his speeches. Each of his sentences hit us like a whip. . . . Raging and ardent, he appeared the living incarnation of revolutionary energy and passion. Everything about him was expressive—both word and gesture. He spewed out simple and picturesque comparisons; saturated with feeling, exactly apt, they made an enormous impression.[83]

This congress was where Koba first saw and heard Trotsky, but the latter had no memory of the obscure Georgian and only learned of his presence at the congress decades later when he read Boris Souvarine's biography of Stalin.[84] The two men, both ambitious and self-important, were as different as salt and pepper in their public manner. Trotsky basked in his well-earned fame, while Koba remained low key and reserved, hardly visible at the congress.

Still unknown outside Bolshevik circles and the Caucasus, Koba and his comrades had to fight to stay at the congress. The Caucasian Mensheviks were determined to keep Bolsheviks out of their delegation, since they had very few followers in the Caucasus. They contested the suspicious mandates of Shahumian and Kakhoian from Borchalo, and Koba from Tiflis. There was no Social Democratic organization in Borchalo, they asserted, only a peasant group, and Shahumian had no right to be at this congress just as he had had no right to represent Erivan at the last.[85] But the Bolshevik majority at the congress decided to accept their mandates, granting them deliberative voices instead of votes.[86] Yet even with the right to speak Koba never addressed the congress. In sharp contrast to his confident performance at the last congresses, his only intervention this time in London was to join his comrades from the Caucasus—Shahumian, Tskhakaia, and Kakhoian—in two written corrections to the minutes of the congress. To the Kutaisi Menshevik Lortkipanidze's statement that the Caucasian Bolsheviks had not only opposed participation in the legislative activity of the duma but had even called for wiping the duma from the earth at the first opportunity, they replied that they had reacted to the Tiflis Menshevik newspaper *tsin* (Forward), which had declared support of the duma no matter what. The Bolsheviks wanted nothing to do with such liberal sentiments and held that if the duma betrayed the revolution, then Social Democracy should call for its abolition and move beyond the duma to a constituent assembly.[87] Their second declaration challenged the Menshevik claims to represent the proletariat of Caucasia and that the workers support the duma caucus's work. Of the eighteen thousand party members in the region, not more than six thousand were proletarians (one thousand in Baku, about four thousand in Tiflis province, and about one thousand in Kutaisi and Batumi provinces). The other twelve thousand were peasants and the lower middle class of the towns. Workers in Caucasia have no real knowledge of what the duma caucus has been doing.[88] Those two statements were the substance of Koba's contribution to the congress.

After interminable discussions, with the congress hopelessly divided, the Bolsheviks pushed for a resolution that seriously criticized the duma caucus, but the Latvian and Polish delegates refused to go along, and no resolution praising or criticizing the duma deputies was passed.[89] Social Democrats would continue to work through the Russian parliament, but the party's relationship to nonproletarian parties remained divisive. Lenin explained that the Bolsheviks believed that during the bourgeois revolution the Russian bourgeoisie would waver between revolution and reaction, using whatever weapons it could to keep back the proletariat. Martynov, speaking for the Mensheviks, reiterated their line that a militant position by Social Democracy would drive the liberals into the arms of the reactionaries. Trotsky argued that the

Mensheviks were pessimistic about the potential victory of the revolution. This time, thanks to the support of the Latvians and Poles, the Bolsheviks won (159 to 106 to 18), and the congress went on record against working with the "treacherous" liberals.[90] It then turned down Akselrod's pet proposal of convening a broad nonparty workers' congress and adopted a Bolshevik resolution that required the Social Democrats in the duma to use it, not for legislation, but as a tribune to expose the liberals and explain to the masses that the duma cannot realize their interests. This placed the duma deputies in an awkward position. Most of them were Mensheviks, but now they were constrained by the Bolshevik resolution of their party. The eminent Polish Jewish Marxist writer Rosa Luxemburg sided with Lenin and told the Mensheviks, "You don't stand on Marxism, you sit on it, rather lie down on it."[91]

The intense debates over resolutions demonstrated that this second congress convened to unify was far from unified. At a Menshevik caucus Noe Ramishvili lambasted the Russian Menshevik leaders, accusing them of "organizational opportunism" for their growing suspicion of the underground party. "The speech," Boris Nikolaevskii later reported, "had the impression of an exploding bomb. Tsereteli remembered that before it was finished, Martov came up to him and with a distorted face asked, 'What does this mean? Do the Georgians want to separate from the Mensheviks?'"[92] Archil Japaridze tried to mediate the conflict, but news of the "anti-Menshevik Georgian *bunt* [insurrection]" could not be contained.

Zhordania, a member of the commission on resolutions along with Lenin, remembered that at the time when the commission was wrangling over language, he encountered the Bolshevik leader outside the congress. "One time I was walking along the street after the fruitless work [of the commission] and heard a voice behind me: 'Kostrov, wait one second.' I looked and saw Lenin. I waited for him, and together we crossed to the other sidewalk." Lenin bluntly told him: "Georgians, don't mess in our affairs. You don't know our people, neither their psychology nor their lives nor way of life. And why do you hinder us working out our affairs in Russian ways? Get your autonomy, do in Georgia whatever you want; we won't interfere, and you shouldn't interfere in our affairs." Zhordania was shocked and suspected that Lenin was testing him. He told him that he could not give an answer without consulting with his comrades. "Very well," answered Lenin. "Pose that question; if you want, call me in, but remember my proposal: you Georgians don't interfere in our affairs, and we will not interfere in your party affairs. You see where the Russian working class is going; the majority of its delegation is Bolshevik; we know each other; the people are in a revolutionary mood. The Mensheviks are a kind of group of friends [sodruzhestvo], and for this reason they are not with us. You Georgian Social Democrats are the only thing that surprises me. You are also revolutionary like us. What do you have in common with the company of Martov and Dan?"[93] Zhordania agreed with Lenin that the Russian Mensheviks were "intellectuals without character" who avoided revolutionary action and hoped that everything would be decided by the state duma. Yet he decided not to mention his conversation to his Georgian comrades. Neither he nor Lenin ever spoke of the matter again. What was clear to both men as they parted, however, was that the Georgian Mensheviks were the most "Bolshevik" of all Mensheviks.[94]

One of the last, and shortest, debates at the congress was the one that most concerned Koba and his closest comrades—the party's attitude toward "partisan actions," that is, terrorism and expropriations. Overwhelmingly (170 to 35 to 52) the congress voted to disband the fighting units and refrain from robberies and individual killings.[95] Lenin, Kamenev, and Dubrovinskii among the Bolsheviks, along with the Latvian delegates, opposed the resolution. Most of the other Bolsheviks abstained.[96] In his militant mood Lenin was not interested in giving up the armed struggle, and Koba shared that view.

After the congress, Koba and Shahumian remained in London tending to their sick comrade, Tskhakaia, who was suffering from a toothache and high fever.[97] Koba moved on to Paris as he made his way home, while Tskhakaia, who was to follow, instead stayed abroad for the next ten years, until the revolution, when he returned with Lenin in the famous sealed train. Evgeniia Sogorova (Soghorashvili), who had known Koba from his Batumi days, arranged for him to stay for a week with Grigol Chochia in his apartment at Rue Michelet, 7.[98] Koba asked

Chochia for the passport of a recently deceased friend, and he soon left France under the name "Simon Dzvelaia."[99]

Silent at the congress, Koba shared his impressions of the gathering through a two-part article published in the first two issues of the Baku Bolsheviks' newspaper, *Bakinskii proletarii* (Baku Proletariat).[100] In this, his first major piece in Russian, he praised the congress both for reestablishing party unity and for the effective dominance of the Bolshevik faction. Mensheviks, who had chided their rivals for their reliance largely on intellectuals and professional revolutionaries—he claimed—in fact turned out to be less representative of industrial workers, more likely to be intellectuals, and more reflective of the countryside and artisans—in other words, "the half-bourgeois elements of the proletariat."[101] He continued his sociology of the congress by noting that the Menshevik faction was made up primarily of Jews and Georgians, while the Bolsheviks were overwhelmingly Russian, and then Jewish, Georgian, and so on. "For this reason one Bolshevik (probably Aleksinskii) joked that the Mensheviks were the Jewish faction, the Bolsheviks the true Russian, and therefore, it shouldn't disturb the Bolsheviks if we organized a pogrom in the party."[102]

The congress, he went on, reflected the polarization of the party. "There was no so-called center, or swamp, at the congress. Trotsky turned out to be 'a beautiful irrelevance.'"[103] The only Menshevik resolution to pass was on banning "partisan actions" (armed actions), but this was purely accidental since the Bolsheviks decided not to put up a fight on this one. He scorned the old Menshevik Akselrod's accusation that the party "has been since its origins and remains until this time the revolutionary organization not of the working class, but of the petty bourgeois intelligentsia for the revolutionary influence over this class."[104] Worker-Bolshevik delegates to the congress, he noted, had energetically proclaimed, "We are patriots of the party, . . . we love our party."[105]

By the first days of June, the peripatetic revolutionary relocated to Baku. Prospects for the Bolsheviks were dismal in Georgia, and on Lenin's suggestion Koba and Shahumian soon moved, with their families, to the oil capital of Russia.[106] Years later in a private conversation he expressed his disappointment with the Georgian workers who proved to be more "petty bourgeois" than proletarian and compelled him to leave his homeland. Stalin told the actor Vasadze that he had not only attacked the Mensheviks but the workers as well, since those that had land outside town did not appreciate the plight of those without land. "In a word, those with full bellies," he said, "do not understand those who are hungry."[107] Exiting Georgia was more than a physical move; it was another psychological break with the milieu that had shaped him in his first quarter century. But before he left Georgia for a future that would lead him far from his native land to heights that the son of a shoemaker and former seminarian could not have imagined, Koba embarked on one final, spectacular endeavor.

STAYING THE COURSE

17

THE TIFLIS "EX"

The Stalin of 1907 was a small, wiry, mysterious man of many aliases, usually dressed in a red satin shirt, grey coat, and his trademark black fedora. Sometimes he favoured a traditional Georgian *chokha*, and he liked to sport a white Caucasian hood, draped dashingly over his shoulder. Always on the move, often on the run, he used the many uniforms of Tsarist society as his disguises, and frequently escaped manhunts by dressing in drag.

—SIMON SEBAG MONTEFIORE, *YOUNG STALIN* (2007)

"In Europe," I said to him, "you are described either as the bloody Czar or as the bandit of Georgia. There are stories about bank robberies and the like which you are said to have organized in your youth for the benefit of the party. I would very much like to know how much of this we can believe.

Stalin began to laugh in that heavy way of his, blinked several times, and stood up for the first and only time in our three-hour interview. . . . The question of the bank robbery was the only one he would not answer—except to the extent that he answered it by passing it over.

—EMIL LUDWIG, *STALIN* (1942; BASED ON HIS INTERVIEW WITH STALIN, 1931)

"The year 1907," wrote the historian Isaac Deutscher, "was the year of the tsar's revenge."[1] Day by day the monarch grew angrier at the duma, one-third of which—the Social Democratic Left and its allies—wanted the abolition of the monarchy. The Right, both in the duma and the government, played to the tsar's fears of terrorism and pushed for dissolution of the duma and a return to the old autocratic system. Prime Minister Stolypin made an effort to work with the center, led by the Kadets, but they refused to go along with his moderate land reform and held out for expropriation of the gentry estates. He wrote wearily to the British historian Bernard Pares, "I am fighting on two fronts. I am fighting against revolution but for reform. You may say that such a position is beyond human strength and you might be right."[2]

Emotions ran high in the halls of the duma when the conservatives proposed a motion to condemn revolutionary terrorism. "Do none of you, gentlemen [of the Left]," queried the rightist deputy Vasilii Shulgin, "have bombs in your pockets?"[3] On May 15, 1907, the Kadets and the Leftist deputies defeated the anti-terrorist motion 215 to 146. For the liberals to have voted for it would have seemed a sanction for the summary military courts that the government was operating throughout the empire. Many of them, in fact, admired the sacrifices made by the revolutionaries and faulted the authorities and their allies as the initiators of violence.[4] Like Stolypin, the Russian parliament was caught between reform through state institutions and revolutionary action from outside the duma's walls, where both radicals on the left and reactionaries on the right were engaging in assassinations. Convinced that the duma would never support his program for land reform, Stolypin gave in to the pressure from the tsar and agreed to dissolve the duma. He announced in a closed session of the duma that Social Democratic deputies were to be arrested as participants in a conspiracy against the government. A few days later, on June 3, the government dissolved the duma, called for elections to a third duma but with a new, restricted franchise, and ordered the arrest of most of the Social Democratic deputies.[5]

The government had successfully carried out a *coup d'état* with the expectation that the coming elections would return a conservative majority that would back the government. Russia effectively had a new "constitution," what later observers would call the "Third-of-June System." The revised election law was even less representative of the people as a whole than was the former version. The votes of millions of peasants and workers did not count as much as those of "the provincial gentry—a small and shrinking social class, numbering approximately twenty thousand fully enfranchised voters in a nation of 130 million people." The landed nobles became "the dominant political force within the major elective institutions of the restricted old order."[6] In Caucasia representation of ethnic Russians was enhanced, while the votes of Armenian, Georgian, and Muslim peasants and workers were severely reduced. In Tiflis province, for example, of the fifty-five electors who would vote directly for deputies, landlords would have the right to choose twenty-nine and Russians would choose another twenty-one, while hundreds of thousands of peasants would choose only twelve, city dwellers fourteen, and workers two.[7]

Repression and some reform had divided the social forces that had nearly toppled the monarchy in 1905, and the scattered revolutionaries could no longer mount real resistance to the tsar. For the next five years the Russian empire experienced a period of "reaction," greater state repression, and, on the left, deep demoralization. With their immunity gone and accused of conspiracy, the Social Democratic deputies faced trial, imprisonment, and exile. They issued a dramatic protest:

> After June 3, the fig leaf of constitutionalism fell and [the government] stood in all its despotic nakedness before the land. Now they want to try us. . . . We understood perfectly that not only we are being tried—here old, autocratic Russia is trying new Russia straining for freedom. And with complete confidence in the inevitability of the approaching victory of freedom over arbitrariness we say: try us—it is itself tried by history.[8]

Stripped of some of their best-known leaders, who were in prison soon to be exiled, the Tiflis Social Democrats met secretly and decided that in the current environment they had better curtail open activities like mass meetings and demonstrations. But they would still participate in the elections to the Third State Duma and even contest the elections to the Tiflis municipal duma.[9] The local Bolsheviks, however, had one more desperate project under way—a sensational robbery to seize hundreds of thousands of rubles from the state treasury—the infamous Tiflis "ex" of June 13, 1907.

The great Tiflis robbery has become a matter of legend and myth. For popular biographers of Stalin, it resonates as the moment when the bandit nature of the future dictator was first revealed in full light.[10] But in fact Koba was peripheral to the robbery. Although he knew that it was being planned, and even supplied vital information to the perpetrators, he kept his distance from the actual event.[11] This was the usual practice of party members who were not members of the fighting (*boevye*) units. Indeed, the fighters usually gave up formally their membership in the party when they turned to such activity. For Menshevik opponents of the "partisan struggle" the robberies represented a serious breach of the resolutions adopted at the Fourth and Fifth Party Congresses. For Lenin and his Caucasian followers, the Tiflis "ex" was a means to an end, the end being financial support of the party, particularly the Bolshevik faction. The Bolsheviks were desperate for money, and expropriations of state funds seemed the best single stone to kill both the bird of need and the bird of counterrevolution. While Mensheviks worried about the effect the "exes" had on the morale and behavior of their supporters, the Bolsheviks considered terrorism an imperative part of the "partisan warfare" that disrupted the governmental machine.[12]

Kote Tsintsadze, who had worked with Koba in Chiatura and attended his wedding, was the pivotal figure in the Caucasian Bolsheviks' fighting group—until his arrest in late 1906.[13] The Menshevik Uratadze characterized Tsintsadze as "more a brigand than a political activist."[14] Trotsky remembered how Tsintsadze's "good-natured sarcasm and a sly sense of humor were combined in this tempered terrorist with a gentleness one might almost call feminine."[15] Tsintsadze reported in his memoirs that since Mensheviks and Bolsheviks were working together he asked one of the Mensheviks, Banurian, what Zhordania's views about the "exes" were. He was assured that Zhordania believed that despite the congress's rejection of expropriations, certain local organizations were permitted to engage in them when possible.

The two party factions sometimes carried out actions together, other times separately, and they always argued over the spoils. In May 1906 Tsintsadze, I. E. Lominadze, and Vano Kalandadze robbed a pawnshop but made off with very little cash. What they secured was mostly used to finance more serious exes.[16] Because Banurian proved to be an inadequate organizer, and many Mensheviks were not enthusiastic about exes, Tsintsadze decided to form his own Bolshevik group into which he recruited several men from his disbanded Chiatura band. Since most of those who carried out such actions were Bolsheviks, Tsintsadze felt that any money he secured with his group should go exclusively to the Bolshevik faction. Koba and other leaders agreed.

Shortly after Tsintsadze's arrest, Kamo returned from abroad and took over leadership of the group.[17] Already sporting a reputation as a particularly daring fighter, Kamo's deep-set, dark eyes, thick brows and mustache gave him the look of a stereotypic "Caucasian bandit." Once he had appeared at a gathering of Bolsheviks in Saint Petersburg with a round object wrapped in a napkin. "Everyone in the canteen stopped eating," remembered Krupskaia, "and began to stare at the striking visitor. 'He has brought a bomb,' most of them probably thought. But it was not a bomb, it was a watermelon. Kamo had brought the watermelon and some candied nuts as a treat for Ilyich [Lenin] and me."[18] This "naïve and affectionate comrade, . . . passionately devoted to Ilyich, Krasin, and Bodganov," was in close contact with Lenin and his wife. Her mother even helped him strap his revolvers on his back "with affectionate care."[19]

Kamo meticulously planned the Tiflis "ex," and though it was carried out with cool precision, it did not go as anticipated. Twelve of his band participated. The "expropriators" knew exactly the route and time the carriages with the postal money would come to Tiflis. Kamo had learned the needed intelligence from Grigol (Gigo) Kasradze, a postal worker from Gori, whom Koba had introduced to him.[20] Koba and Gigo knew each other from childhood in Gori, and Gigo remembered how much Soso liked to fight, how he and Iremashvili had sung so beautifully, and how Soso was disappointed in Zhordania's *kvali*. Koba visited Kasradze, whom had had not seen in a long time and told him to meet him at nine the next morning at Adam's Tea House, where he would introduce him to one of the best of their fighters. Koba introduced him to Kamo and left. Kamo instructed Kasradze to move to the financial office of the postal service and to learn when money was coming from Saint

Petersburg.[21] Koba also secured an important connection with another postal clerk, the Russian Voznesenskii, who had been a schoolmate of his at both the Gori and Tiflis seminaries and had been enthralled by the young Soselo's poem on the poet Eristavi. Meeting at a milk bar, Koba asked Voznesenskii to supply the needed information about the timing of the transport of postal funds. He agreed. At that point Voznesenskii ceased contact with Koba and dealt with Kamo and others.[22] Rumors could already be heard in the city that the revolutionaries would attempt a major theft, but the police chief did not believe what his own agents could not confirm.[23]

On the morning of June 13 two carriages entered Erivan Square, guarded by five Cossacks and two police constables. People on the streets had been warned away earlier by Kamo disguised as a cavalry officer complete with a Cherkess *kinjal* borrowed from Kato's father. They fled in various directions. As the first carriage passed by the Commercial Bank and the stores of Rotinov and Gavilov, a bomb was thrown from the left, exploding in front of the carriage. Smoke filled the square, and two more bombs exploded near the Rotinov shop. Those left in the square scattered. Three of Kamo's men dashed toward the police and, firing their Mausers, drove them away. The money was in the second carriage, which had not been damaged, and the explosions spooked the horses, which bolted and ran wildly across the square toward the Armenian Bazaar. Bachua Kuprashvili then threw his bomb at the horses, but at such close range that the blast propelled him into the air, and he landed unconscious. The horses lay dying, the carriage crumpled in the smoke and dust. Chiabrishvili grabbed the money sack and ran toward Veliaminov Street. There Kamo waited by his own carriage, shouting, cursing, firing his revolver to attract attention away from his comrades. Chiabrishvili gave him the sack, and Kamo drove off.[24] The robbers met at Mikha Bochoridze's apartment, but Bachua did not show up. Kamo was very upset, believing he had been killed. "Devil take the money; it would have been better to save our comrade. How could you leave him without help?" At that moment the wounded Bachua appeared, and Kamo exclaimed, "*Bicho* [boy], you see, even death cannot take us. Like cats from any height, we fall and we don't get hurt."

They had gotten away with 250,000 rubles. The money, however, would be extraordinarily difficult to use. The postal informant Voznesenskii found out that the serial numbers of the 500-ruble banknotes were known to the police, who sent them on to foreign banks. He rushed to the hideout of the robbers on Goncharnaia Street to warn them. Didebulov suggested they burn the money, but Kamo decided to take the risk and deliver it to higher party officials.[25] The "ex," carried out with such bravado and immediate success, soon became a virus that led to disaster for Kamo and others and a scandal among the Social Democrats.[26]

Kamo carried the money to Saint Petersburg in a simple woman's hatbox, and on to Lenin and Bogdanov in Kuokkala (today Repino) in Finland. Party members who tried to exchange the tainted bills were picked up in various parts of the continent. Kamo stayed in Europe, disguised as the insurance agent Dmitrii Mirskii, but on November 9, 1908, identified by a police spy who had infiltrated the Bolshevik court and was trusted by Lenin, he was arrested in Berlin. What followed is the fabled tale of his imprisonment and torture, his feigned madness, the return under guard to Russia, and his eventual escape in August 1911, aided by his old comrade Tsintsadze.

The Mensheviks were incensed at the Bolsheviks' brazen disregard for the decision of the Fifth Congress against expropriations. They began a series of investigations and trials, one in Tiflis that implicated Koba. Eventually Lenin was forced to give up the stolen money.[27] The Bolsheviks had long been desperate for funds, taking money from whatever source was available—the writer Maxim Gorky; his lover, the actress Maria Andreeva; the industrialist and patron of the arts (and revolutionaries) Savva Morozov; and after Morozov's suicide, his nephew, the young factory owner Nikolai Shmidt, who died in a tsarist prison cell either a suicide or a victim of the police. The intraparty squabbles over sharing the spoils of revolutionary robberies or inheritance from radicalized millionaires not only further divided Mensheviks from Bolsheviks but opened new cleavages among the Bolsheviks themselves.[28]

Koba's precise connection to the Tiflis "ex" remains disputed. He was probably not in Tiflis on June 13, though the exact date of his move to

Baku is unknown. He never personally took credit for the robbery, and early sources like Tsintsadze and Bibineishvili do not mention him. Indeed, during Stalin's life and even afterward, these episodes of Stalin's career as a revolutionary were not discussed nor was his role as terrorist mentioned in Soviet histories. Yet he never denied prior knowledge of the "ex," and it is indisputable that he knew about the plans to carry out the robbery. Indeed, the information that his contacts provided was crucial to the operation. The testimony of Voznesenskii and Kasradze, who worked at the post-telegraph, states that Koba brought them to Kamo to whom they gave information about the exact timing of the transport of money.[29] Koba's Gori schoolmate, Davrishev, believed that Stalin was behind this operation.[30] He noted that Koba worked through Kamo: "Stalin, sought also by the secret police, had one advantage over us. The police did not know him. . . . He had never spoken at a public meeting during the revolution. He rarely went out of his hiding place. He did not communicate with the outside world except through certain trusted comrades like Kamo Petrosian."[31] Boris Nikolaevskii, the Menshevik archivist who most carefully investigated the incident, concluded that Koba knew about the expropriation beforehand, certainly protected the participants and approved of the robbery, but probably was not directly involved in its planning or execution.[32]

The Tiflis-based regional committee of the party organized a commission, headed by Jibladze, to investigate Social Democrats involved in the Tiflis "ex." Jugheli told Kasradze to appear at the commission. There Kasradze told Zhordania and the others that he had participated in the Tiflis "ex" and that Kamo had received the money and sent it to the party center. When asked who introduced him to Kamo, Kasradze confessed that it had been Koba.[33] The commission concluded that the participants and organizers of the robbery, headed by Koba and Kamo, were to be excluded from the party. Kamo was furious at Kasradze when he heard about his testimony. Cursing him at length, he spit out, "I know why these lackeys questioned you. They are incompetent and get in our way."[34]

The sentence, together with the documents, was presented to the Fifth Congress of Transcaucasian SD organizations in February 1908, which agreed to expel all who had taken part in the activity of Kamo's group. Two representatives sent by the Central Committee, the Latvian K. Iu. Danishevskii and Zhordania, did not object to the resolution, which was then sent on to the Central Committee abroad. That committee, however, was at the time dominated by Bolsheviks, and nothing was done.[35] A few years after the Tiflis "ex," Martov, one of the fiercest opponents of terrorism and expropriations, wrote about this in his brochure, *Saviors or Destroyers?*[36]

> The Central Committee, then located within Russia, ordered a serious investigation of the Tiflis and Berlin affairs and the matter of money changing. The investigation abroad was assigned to the then-existing Foreign Bureau. In the Caucasus the Caucasian Regional Committee carried out the investigation. The Regional Committee identified a whole list of people who had taken part in the act of expropriation. Just before [the robbery] all these people had declared their resignation from the party's local organization. The Regional Committee ordered and publicized the exclusion of these people from the RSDRP, that is, taking into consideration that they had already left the local organization, they declared it impermissible to accept them into any other organization of the party.[37]

In 1911 Martov understandably did not name names, but in 1918 he fingered Stalin as one of those excluded from the party. Yet Martov's original article suggests that only those who had resigned from a party organization were later formally expelled. Stalin was not among those.

The Tiflis "ex" and the money it brought to the Bolsheviks proved to be poison pills. Socialists throughout Europe denounced the robbery, and disputes over which faction should receive the loot further exacerbated the existing tensions within the Russian party. Lenin, who had been enthusiastic about the "ex," realized that his faction was ensnared in a scandal that threatened its reputation abroad and the unity of the party inside Russia. A Georgian Social Democrat, Khariton Shavishvili, met Lenin in Geneva at the Café Landolt, a favorite watering hole for local socialists, and the disgruntled Bolshevik leader told him:

Dear comrade, in this period of terrible reaction in Russia, which finds its echo in Europe, the Mensheviks have raised some questions about the expropriation that our comrades carried out! At this moment when more than a dozen comrades have been arrested, ... when several hundred are in prison and being deported in Russia, all in danger of being hanged, it is a crime to bring such questions up for discussion in the Central Committee. The Mensheviks are turning into agents of the tsarist police.[38]

Shavishvili protested, but Lenin continued: "If they succeed in adopting such a resolution, our best comrades, including several Caucasians, will lose their lives." Shavishvili was sure that Lenin was speaking about Koba, then sitting in prison in Baku.[39] The issue came to a head in August 1908 when the Central Committee with its Bolshevik majority gathered in the Café Handwerk. Martov raised the painful issue of the "exes." Plekhanov declared that if the connection between the party and the robberies is confirmed, he would refuse to represent such a party in the Bureau of the Socialist International. Martov wrote to Noe Ramishvili in Leipzig to come to Geneva and testify about the "exes." When the Central Committee met again, Ramishvili reported on the findings of the Caucasian Regional Committee's investigation and mentioned the names Kote Tsintsadze, Stepko Intskirveli, Vano Kalandadze, and Kamo Ter-Petrosian, all of whom, he stated, worked under the direction of Comrade Koba. At that point Lenin interrupted and requested that Koba's last name not be given, to which Ramishvili replied, "I have no intention to do so, since he is well-known, without being named, as a Caucasian Lenin."[40] With that report the Mensheviks scored a victory: the party was clearly on record opposing such armed actions except in self-defense.

The saga of the Tiflis "ex" lasted into the early Soviet years. An extraordinary series of events brought Martov and Stalin face to face in court when the Soviet government was merely four months old. At the very end of March 1918 Martov wrote an article critical of the actions of the Menshevik government then operating in Georgia. Zhordania's administration had closed Bolshevik newspapers and fired upon a workers' demonstration in Tiflis's Alexander Garden in February. Martov advised his errant party comrades not to emulate the Moscow Bolsheviks' repressive political practices. In a pointed remark he then added, "That the Caucasian Bolsheviks from time immemorial have involved themselves in every kind of daring enterprise of the expropriatory variety is well known, at least to that same Comrade Stalin who in his own time was excluded from party organizations for his involvement in expropriations."[41] The very next day Stalin sent a memo to the Revolutionary Tribunal denying that he had ever been tried or expelled from a party organization. "Looking at the accusation thrown down by Martov as a dishonest trick by a person who has lost his balance, someone whose head has been smashed in open political battle and now in despair grasps at the 'last' means, vile slander—I request that the Revolutionary Tribunal call L. Martov (Tsederbaum) to account for slander in the press."[42]

Four days later, on April 5, the tribunal heard the case. Martov began by protesting that he was being charged by "Citizen" (not "Comrade") Stalin in the Revolutionary Tribunal and not a civil court. Stalin replied that such slander against a representative of a known political tendency was not personal but political. When asked to produce witnesses to prove his charge, Martov countered that none of the witnesses were in Moscow but in Petrograd, Baku, or Tiflis. He added that he had learned from former duma deputy Isidore Megrelishvili, who in 1908 was serving time in a Baku prison, that the Baku Committee, of which Stalin was then a member, was involved in an expropriation aboard the Caspian steamship *Nikolai I*.[43] Martov began to backtrack. He did not mean to claim that a party court or the organization as a whole had expelled Stalin from the party. "I know only that ten years ago we received information from Caucasian Menshevik comrades that the [Caucasian] regional [*oblastnoi*] committee had taken measures to cleanse the party of expropriators and that a number of activists, among them Citizen Stalin, were expelled from the party. That is all the information that I had when I wrote the article."[44]

The tribunal refused to call Martov's witnesses, primarily because they were far away and unreachable. Martov warned the court members to beware less they someday fall into such a court as he has. From the hall applause broke out, and the court was cleared. Martov insisted that without inviting witnesses "the past of Citizen Stalin will remain the past of an expropriator." "Martov," Stalin retorted sarcastically, "has earned the privilege of having the right to toss filthy accusations against any political person, without having in his hands a single fact nor even the shadow of facts."[45] The case was postponed, and the Menshevik historian and archivist Boris Nikolaevskii was sent to the Caucasus to gather affidavits for Martov. But the trial was never continued; the records of the first session were said to have disappeared; and the Tribunal issued a "social reprimand" to Martov for "insulting and damaging the reputation of member of the government."[46]

The documentary record that has been found of the Caucasian regional party commission reveals only Koba's role in providing vital information to the thieves and nothing about an expulsion from the party. Prominent Mensheviks, among them Martov, Zhordania, Arsenidze, and Lidia Dan remembered that a recommendation had been made by the local party organization to expel Koba from the party, but it was never carried out by higher party organs.[47]

A decade before this aborted trial Social Democrats, Mensheviks included, had been both fascinated by and critical of acts of terrorism. They had accepted the possibility of armed self-defense, assassinations of state officials and police spies, and expropriations of state treasure if it were tied to and contributed to the more important mass struggle. But in the peak years of revolution and terrorism, 1905 through 1907, the Bolsheviks more enthusiastically than their Menshevik counterparts promoted the armed struggle, the "partisan" movement as it was sometimes called, against the autocracy. Lenin's followers worried less about a descent into banditry, crime, or personal vendettas than Martov's did. By 1908–1909, with the full weight of Stolypin's "pacification" crushing the Left and the shocking disclosure that the leading Socialist Revolutionary terrorist, Evno Azef, had been a police provocateur for fifteen years, the glamour and glories of terrorism rapidly lost their earlier appeal.[48]

June 1907 is usually marked as the end of the 1905 revolution. One by one the various revolutionary parties gave up the armed struggle and turned to more peaceful forms of opposition. On October 2 the Third Party Conference of the Socialist Federalists decided to reject agrarian and factory terror but to continue political terror if it had political significance and was ordered by the party's Federative Committee.[49] Davrishev disbanded his armed group, for it seemed that an isolated revolution in Georgia had no chance of success without a revolution in central Russia. "The fate of our fatherland," he wrote, "is tied forever to that of Russia. For better or worse, that's the way it is." But that conclusion did not stop them from one last ex, a bold attack on the ship *Pushkin* on the Black Sea, which they relieved of money destined for a bank in Odessa.[50]

With their leaders out of the country, Koba and Kamo's group also dissolved after the Tiflis robbery.[51] There was not much a Bolshevik activist could do in Tiflis. The "ex" was a last hurrah of the "partisans." The strains between Bolsheviks and the dominant Mensheviks intensified once again. Koba soon moved his wife and son to Baku. With a still active working class and an influential Bolshevik committee, Baku appeared a land of opportunity. The move was momentous for Koba. Never again would he make Georgia his principal home. In his twenty-ninth year, Koba was stepping onto a broader stage, less provincial, less ethnonational—one might say, more cosmopolitan, more internationalist. In a real sense, he was becoming a man of the empire.

18

JOURNEYMAN FOR THE REVOLUTION

I remember . . . the years 1907–09 when I was sent by order of the party to work in Baku. Three years of revolutionary work among the workers of the oil industry tempered me as a practical fighter and as one of the local practical leaders. In contact with such advanced workers of Baku as Vatsek, Saratovets, Fioletov and others, on the one hand, and in the tempest of the deepest conflicts between workers and the oil industrialists on the other hand, I first discovered what it meant to lead large masses of workers. There, in Baku, I received, thus, my second baptism in revolutionary combat. There I became a journeyman for the revolution.

—IOSIF STALIN, TIFLIS (1926)

Although Koba lacked historical perspective, he was more than amply endowed with perseverance. During the years of reaction he was not one of the tens of thousands who deserted the party, but one of the very few hundreds who, despite everything, remained loyal to it.

—LEV TROTSKY, *STALIN* (1941)

Time and the antics of official historians have obscured Koba's activities in the so-called years of "reaction," 1907–1910, when he was in Baku. Trotsky, who writes more than most on his years in the oil capital, admitted finally that "very little is known about the Baku period of Stalin's life."[1] Yet one of his most eminent biographers, Isaac Deutscher, stressed the importance of this short span of activity in Stalin's political growth: "In going from Tiflis to the oil city on the Persian border, Stalin was really moving from his native backwater into the mainstream of national politics."[2]

Baku, the oil-producing center of the Russian Empire, had gained a deserved reputation of labor militancy to complement its fame as an exotic, untamed frontier town. A letter intercepted by the police observed, "Baku is a violent and wild city. There is not a day without two or three murders; the shooting does not stop day or night. They sometimes slaughter like beasts."[3] Armed bodyguards (*kochi*) accompanied men of wealth, and all, regardless of position, were asked to remove their guns before entering the post office.[4] In such an atmosphere it was strange indeed that some industrialists and labor leaders were interested in establishing legal, Western-style trade unions. The alternative to legality, however, was the constant escalation of even minor strikes into violent outbursts with revolutionary overtones. The memories of arson in the oil fields, political assassinations, and bloody clashes between Armenians and Muslims were still fresh in the minds of the managers. Neither capitalists nor the government wanted the flow of oil to central Russia to be cut off. Their accommodation of some worker demands was eased by rising oil prices. The well-known "liberalism" of the Baku bourgeoisie, thus, was just good business sense. As long as prices remained high, the industry was able to make concessions, particularly in wages, to the workers. This "liberal" attitude continued through 1907 and into 1908, but then prices fell, and concessions seemed too expensive.[5]

Essentially driven out of Georgia by the dominant Mensheviks, the Bolsheviks had decided to center their Caucasian operations in the more industrial setting of Baku.[6] "Destroyed by the Mensheviks in Georgia," Grigol ("Sergo") Orjonikidze later reported, "our faction decided to throw all its forces into Baku in order to push the Mensheviks out of the proletarian center of Transcaucasia."[7] Not only Koba, but his friends Davitashvili, Shahumian, Spandarian, Alesha Japaridze, and the young Sergo Orjonikidze, whom Koba had met in 1906, moved to Baku. From Russia several veterans of the Petersburg Soviet—Semen Vainshtein and Bogdan Knuniants—arrived, along with Kliment Voroshilov, R. Z. Zemliachka, Iurii Larin (Mikhail Lur'e), M. S. Olminskii, Elena Stasova, and Moisei Frumkin. Koba may have had a more personal reason for transferring to Baku. In the aftermath of the Tiflis "ex" the Mensheviks in Georgia were investigating the ties between party members and the robbery.[8] The police were also looking for Koba and were close to finding him. They reported on June 21, 1907, that "after the May arrests of Baku Bolsheviks, two unknown people, evidently Georgians, arrived in Baku; one with the party name Mikho, the other an unknown as yet delegate (Bolshevik) from the social-democratic congress in London, who will soon make a report about the above-mentioned congress."[9] Once again, just as in 1902 when he left Tiflis for Batumi, burning a bridge in one town meant a quick move to another.

His years in Baku determined much of Koba's future political life. He was now a mature party worker, entering his thirtieth year, and many of the people with whom he worked there—at least those who would survive into the 1920s—became the core around which the rising Stalin would form his close circle of loyalists. Koba met Andrei Vyshinskii in Baku.[10] The twenty-four-year-old Vyshinskii was a very influential Menshevik, a talented and well-prepared orator who spoke frequently at mass meetings and up and down the railroad line to Tiflis.[11] He renewed his acquaintance with Klim Voroshilov, who would rise to heights far above his limited abilities to become Stalin's People's Commissar of Defense of the Soviet Union. In his Baku days still a son of the working class and a newly minted Bolshevik, Voroshilov served as the secretary of the oil workers' union. Orjonikidze, Koba's fellow Georgian, would carry out tough assignments for Stalin both in Georgia in the early 1920s against deviant "National Bolsheviks" and later in Moscow as industrial tsar during the first Five Year Plans before taking his own life after a heated exchange with his patron.[12]

Others acquainted with Koba did not make it. Spandarian died in Siberian exile with Koba nearby. Knuniants, who never liked Koba and had left the Bolsheviks, had died a few years earlier in a Baku prison. Shahumian and Japaridze were cut down by anti-Bolsheviks in the desert of Turkmenistan after leading the short-lived Baku Commune of 1918. But those who endured the underground, prison and exile, and survived the revolution and civil war, 1917–1921, were among the few who stayed closest to Stalin longest. One can add to this list others who

worked in Baku or Tiflis at one time or another—Mikhail Kalinin
(1875–1946), who would become "president" of the Soviet Union; Sergei Kirov (1886–1934), head of the Azerbaijan Communist Party and
later party secretary of Leningrad whose assassination would eventually
lead into the Great Purges; Lavrenti Beria (1899–1953), whom Stalin put
in charge of Transcaucasia and later brought to Moscow to run his secret
police; and Anastas Mikoyan (1894–1978), the wily Armenian who rivaled Talleyrand for longevity in office under many different leaders.
These "Caucasians" rose in the party ranks along with Stalin until they
formed the core of his government in the 1930s.[13] They were Stalin's
team, the people who this most suspicious of men trusted more than
any others.

After the long journey from the London Congress of the Party, Koba
arrived in Baku in the first weeks of June 1907 at a most crucial moment.
Only a month earlier, the police had rounded up almost the entire Bolshevik underground. Party life had been moved inside prison walls.
Even though the Social Democrats maintained the façade of a single
party organization in Baku throughout the summer of 1907, this legacy
of the unifying tendencies of the revolutionary years did not prevent
Bolsheviks and Mensheviks from clinging to their factional identities
and separate trade unions. The dialogue between the Mensheviks and
the Bolsheviks on the issues of party unity and the relationship of the
party to the open labor movement continued without interruption.
When Koba set himself up in Baku, the city committee of the Russian
Social Democratic Workers' Party (RSDRP) was dominated by the
Mensheviks, who had reestablished the committee after a police raid in
early 1906. The Bolsheviks, after regrouping, retreated to the local party
committee in the suburb of Balakhany, which they used as the base for
their faction's activity.[14] A recent arrival in Baku, Nadezhda Kolesnikova
(1882–1964), who had participated in the December uprising in Moscow and escaped prison to work underground in Baku, remembered
that the Social Democrats all met at a milk bar called "Germaniia," but
Bolsheviks sat at a table in one corner and Mensheviks at another in the
opposite corner. Both factions, however, were served by waitresses who
were Mensheviks, since many woman workers, office personnel and

shop assistants, gravitated toward the more moderate wing of the party.[15] The organization had little money until Tsintsadze's armed band robbed a mail coach in the Kojori pass near Tiflis and brought 10,000 rubles to Shahumian.[16]

Koba moved from one comrade's apartment to another, living as did his comrades in the grimy oil drilling sections of the city.[17] He sometimes stayed with Alesha Japaridze, sometimes with Sergo Orjonikidze. In his memoirs Voroshilov recalled that Koba, with whom he had become acquainted earlier in London, came to visit him one evening because he had heard that a comrade was sick—"even though he was an extremely busy man and at the time we were not even such good friends as we were to become later during the Civil War. By the time he arrived I was no longer confined to bed. He was very pleased about this. He joked a great deal. He said that poetry and music elevate the spirit, which is good for health." Koba asked him if he liked poetry. "When I answered that I did, he asked me to recite a poem by Nekrasov. He called it an excellent poem that should be made known to as many workers as possible. Then we sang together the song 'I look up to the sky.' It turned out that he had a good voice and a fine ear for music."[18]

Koba returned briefly to Tiflis to gather his wife and infant son for the transfer to his new assignment.[19] A worker, Kirochkin, showed them the apartment of an oil worker on First Bailov Street, near a cave facing the Caspian Sea where the homeless found shelter.[20] The peripatetic life of a professional revolutionary sought by the police placed enormous burdens on family. Constant movement, one step ahead of informers and gendarmes, meant that wives and children could never be sure when the police might arrive or a husband or father would disappear. Children learned to keep silent, to dissemble, and at times act as couriers. Such a life required sacrifice of the expected comforts of home, stability, and predictability.[21] Koba's in-laws feared the worse for their beautiful Kato and her infant son in the noxious air, soot, and oil of industrial Baku. Their anxieties proved to be prophetic.[22]

Prime Minister Stolypin's dissolution of the Second State Duma and the government's crackdown on the Social Democrats had made open political activity by the Left much more difficult and dangerous. But the effects of the government's new course were not felt in Baku for nearly a year. In that time Baku workers enjoyed a degree of freedom and activity unknown in the rest of the empire. Russia's workers had gained some limited rights after 1905, though the labor laws were confused and contradictory. Economic strikes were permitted, but incitement to strike was prohibited; unions were allowed as mutual aid societies for workers but were forbidden to participate in strikes.

A writer for the newspaper of the Baku oil industrialists, *Neftianoe delo* (Oil Business), reflected the "liberalism" of at least some of the oil men. "That trade unions can play a great role in lessening the tensions between labor and capital, that the trade union movement is a powerful regulating factor in the struggle of labor with capital, and that it is one of the positive sides of the modern workers' movement, we do not doubt, and it is not necessary to prove this to anyone."[23] The writer's only regret was that Baku trade unions included only ten percent of the workers and therefore could not be considered the legitimate spokesmen of the working class as a whole. Two rival unions vied in Baku for the allegiance of the oil workers. The Union of Mechanical Workers, ostensibly "neutral" though in fact run by prominent Mensheviks, was a craft union made up largely of highly skilled Russian workers from the refineries and processing plants.[24] The competing Union of Oil Workers, set up in September 1906 by the Bolsheviks, was an industrial union, which aimed to represent all the workers in the oil industry regardless of craft or skill and appealed primarily to the Muslim workers.[25]

Each year Baku began shipping oil to central Russia in early April, when the Volga became navigable after the long Russian winter, and it continued until November. Stockpiles were built up along the Volga to satisfy the need for fuel in winter. Baku had always been able to supply a significant share of the oil that Russia needed, at least up to 1905. But during the revolutionary years, supply could not meet demand; prices shot up, and consequently many industries began to use coal and even wood instead of oil. Demand fell in 1906, and Baku industrialists feared additional losses in their markets. They grasped at any means to prevent the dislocations and shortages that resulted from strikes and arson.

Over forty-eight thousand men worked in the oil industry in Baku. The vast majority of these men (about ninety-two percent) was not native to the area but had come to find work in the fields and refineries. Young, most without their families, this Baku proletariat was made up of twenty-three different nationalities. One-quarter was Russian, another quarter Armenian, and nearly half Muslims, primarily Turkic speakers known to the Russians as "Tatars" and later as Azerbaijanis. Skilled workers tended to be Russian and Armenian, while the less skilled workers of the oil fields were largely Muslim.

Ethnicity overlapped with social advantages and disadvantages. While nearly two-thirds of Baku's workers were illiterate, Muslim workers were among the most poorly paid, the least educated, and the most politically passive. They had come from villages either in Russian Caucasia or Persia and tended to follow the lead of the Russian workers rather than develop their own movement. The higher paid and better educated tended to be Russian or Armenian. Led by the *Dashnaktsutyun*, Armenians of all social classes gravitated to their more national-oriented party.[26] The Russian workers, on the other hand, were the most active in the unions and in the party organizations, forming the backbone of the Union of Mechanical Workers (sixty-two percent of the membership) and of the local Social Democratic organization (about twenty-five hundred members). Russians made up the readership of the labor press. *Gudok* (Factory Whistle), the organ of the Bolshevik union, and *Promyslovyi vestnik* (Craft Bulletin), its Menshevik rival, had a joint circulation of about twenty-five hundred copies, almost exclusively among skilled Russian workers.[27] Baku, then, was one of the cities in Russia where Marxists had a mass following, but their influence was centered among the Russian workers, the more skilled, more literate, and materially better off.

If the word "proletariat" has any meaning, it certainly applied to the Baku workers. Almost every aspect of the workers' lives was affected by the industry. Those workers who lived outside the city proper in the oil-field districts came under the jurisdiction, not of municipal or state authorities, but of the Council of the Congress of Oil Industrialists. Everything from roads and water supply to medicine and schools had to be granted by the industrialists who ran the area as their private domain. Somehow, the "liberalism" of the industrialists, evident in their wage policy, did not extend to living and working conditions. The mass of the oil-field workers, those whom the message of the socialists reached last, lived in dismal, low shacks among the derricks. The industrialists did not keep their promises to build settlements in the hills away from the oil fields. The unusually poor conditions were somewhat offset by the relatively good wages and hours. Workers labored on average 9 hours a day, 55½ hours a week, slightly less than the average British or American worker at the time. Although prices rose along with wages, wages managed to rise at a more rapid rate. Real wages of even the poorest workers in Baku rose some fifteen percent from 1904 to 1907. The so-called mechanical workers of the factories did even better both in terms of real wages and shorter hours. All Baku workers enjoyed some improvement in their income in the years before 1907, unlike their comrades in Saint Petersburg who suffered a decline in their material condition.[28] But even for those workers who had steady jobs, the workweek left little time for leisure. Every day but Sunday belonged to the company. Still, it was just such better-off workers, not the poorest and most downtrodden, who aspired to improve their lives and believed that unions were the means to that end.

Koba joined his comrades in Baku just as the local socialists were turning ever more to the open labor movement. He had not yet really experienced this kind of work. In Tiflis he had been a circle propagandist. In Batumi he had been an underground agitator trying to mobilize workers. In 1905 and after he had worked as a journalist or been involved behind the scenes with militant fighters using terrorism and expropriations to advance the revolution. Now in Baku the old *komitetchiki* in the underground and the *praktiki* working in the labor movement were all required to readjust their conspiratorial and authoritarian habits to a movement in which newly awakened workers were participating. Koba, however, set out to find young fighters with whom to form a *druzhina* (fighting unit). Once again, despite the decision of the Fifth Congress disbanding such units, he brought together seven men, most of them Bolsheviks, as well as the Menshevik Vyshinskii, who were prepared to try to obtain weapons from the police and gendarmes.[29] He and David Zelindzon were among the most active in procuring arms.[30] Kavtaradze remembered that after the Tiflis expropriation they gathered in Baku, for they had learned that four million rubles were to be transported from the center of the city to Turkestan across the Caspian Sea. Koba connected a small group prepared for the robbery with sailors and instructed them to seize weapons from the naval arsenal. But the gendarmes got wind of their plans and on May 15, 1908, tried to arrest those living in the house where the band hid their weapons. One of them, Toma Chubinidze, was cut down by the Cossacks, and another, Stepko (Vano) Intskirveli, was shot. Kavtaradze immediately fled Baku, as did Koba briefly.[31]

Terrorism was a weapon that the Social Democrats employed when threatened. With workers less ready to turn toward revolution, they gave up the idea that terrorism might incite revolution and reverted back to the earlier view of terrorism as a weapon of self-defense. In contrast to the image painted by some historians of Koba as a sanguinary bandit, his attitude toward individual killing was based on a sober calculation of what was necessary—and what was excessive—for the success of the movement. When Tiflis Bolsheviks discovered that a certain Maksim Zharov was a police agent who had fled to Baku, they warned Shahumian who in turn informed the Mensheviks who had accepted him into their organization. But the Mensheviks did not believe Shahumian, and eventually the local Bolsheviks took matters into their own hands and killed him.[32]

Baku was not only a major city on the periphery of an empire but in the full sense it was a frontier town. Violence was an integral part of local life. The Baku Bolsheviks worried, however, about the spreading spontaneous violence in the city. They rejected *individual* terrorism in favor of revolutionary *mass* terror, which presumably meant a policy of the masses using violence against their enemies once a real revolutionary situation arose.[33] Even as he proposed setting up a self-defense squad in Bibi-Eibat, and the squad did its share of killing, Koba argued that it would not engage in individual terrorism but would serve as a "threat" to the forces of reaction, oil industrialists and Black Hundred gangs, to prevent the murder of Social Democratic workers.[34] At the same time workers took matters in their own hands and carried out what was euphemistically called "economic terror"—the murder of managers and other officials and the torching of plants and wells. The companies retaliated by hiring their own assassins and singled out particularly active workers. With the balance of violence clearly favoring their opponents, Koba tried to call off the "terror" soon after his arrival in the city, but younger party members resisted. The "chained dogs of capitalists" might have themselves to blame for their deaths, Koba emphasized, but the "anarchist actions" of workers must be combated.[35] He explained to those favoring terror that removing one boss would only lead to his replacement by another, even worse, and then by a third; "and there are as many bastards like that as they need."[36] When the Russian exarch of the Georgian Church was murdered, Koba excoriated such killings as damaging to the workers at a time when the proletariat had to gather its forces. But he was appalled by the call by the Georgian Menshevik daily, *napertskali* (Spark), to turn the killers over to the police "as the only means to cleanse this spot from us forever."[37]

Gradually the chary revolutionaries moved away from terrorism toward the legal labor movement. By the time the First Transcaucasian Congress of Social Democrats called for an end to all terrorism in February 1908, most of the fighters had either been arrested and exiled or killed. Koba plunged into both underground party work and the labor movement. Even with the restrictions on labor activity, Baku in 1907 presented a real possibility that an open, legal labor movement, protected by the new laws, might flourish in this semi-tropical periphery of the empire. Trade unions operated above ground; Social Democrats worked both in the open labor movement and secretly in the underground. "There," Lev Sosnovskii later remembered, "mass trade unions openly operated, workers' newspapers appeared. . . . The potential for propaganda and agitation was immeasurably greater than in other parts of Russia. The combination of the legal and underground revolutionary movement allowed us to expand our work here very broadly."[38] Workers were primarily interested at this point in improving their material security, and with a few exceptions—the May Day work stoppages and the

September 1907 strike in Bibi-Eibat to protest against the murder of the Muslim Social Democrat Khanlar—strikes were not politically motivated but aimed at increasing wages or securing bonuses. Strikes by individual factories tended to be more successful than broader strikes, for the competing firms hastened to settle with their own workers in order not to lose time while their rivals continued operating. Yet as "liberal" as Baku appeared to be, a potential model for bringing the empire's urban poor into a civil society, by 1907 victories for the workers in a labor dispute were daily becoming more difficult to secure.[39]

Already during the revolution of 1905 Baku workers began to demand recognition of their organizations by the industrialists. Factory committees had first appeared in Baku in the spring, and in October they were given a semi-legal status. The industrialists agreed that "the necessity for a leave of absence and also the length of the leave (not to exceed six weeks) will be determined by agreement between the administration and the factory committee of the enterprise."[40] Workers struck for "full recognition" of workers' organizations. Their demands compromised the power of capital and sought to establish the right of the committees to a say in hiring and firing. Industrialists were unwilling to give workers veto power on employment. That issue would remain a matter of contention up to and during the revolution of 1917.

The Bolsheviks who emerged from the revolutionary years in Baku were a chastened lot who had learned a stern lesson at the hands of rival labor leaders. Between 1904 and 1905 they had been outmaneuvered by a trade unionist movement led by the Shendrikov brothers, Gleb, Ilya, and Lev.[41] Only by emerging from their committee rooms and engaging in labor organizing in the oil-field districts were they able to build up a mass base for their faction. Social Democratic influence had grown apace in 1906 as the party began to articulate economic demands of the workers.[42] Even in those plants where Russian nationalists had enjoyed their greatest strength in 1905, the Social Democrats had been able to turn the workers toward strikes. The wave of strikes peaked in the summer of 1906 and fell until the beginning of 1907 when a new wave rose, this time among the unskilled oil-field workers. These men, largely uneducated and poorly paid, had seldom before initiated strikes. Now they demanded higher pay, increased bonuses, and an eight-hour day. Activity in the oil fields by the Bolshevik *praktiki* seemed to be paying off.

More and more of the old Social Democrats turned their attention away from work in the party organization toward the trade unions. This seemed to be where the action was. Yet even as old *komitetchiki* engaged in the open labor movement, the more committed underground activists from both factions found it difficult to emerge from conspiracy into the light of legality. Unlike the pre-1905 period when most Social Democratic committees in Russia had been appointed, purged, reappointed, and directed by agents of *Iskra* or the émigré leadership, during the revolutionary years the dominance by intellectuals had been severely challenged from below, resulting often in committees being elected, at least in part, by workers. In Baku such workers' democracy had been partially established within party organizations but usually only in the local committees. Rather than enter the principal party committees, workers gravitated to the trade unions, the factory committees, the committees of the unemployed, and other open labor groups.

Krupskaia's characterization of the *komitetchiki* as "rather self-assured" people who "were neither desirous nor capable of adjusting themselves to the quickly changing conditions" fit the picture in Baku. Working in the underground had isolated Koba and others from a wider, changing world. Living for years as an outlaw nurtured its own sense of reality in which danger was ever present; betrayal by enemies or false friends a constant concern; and sudden reversals of fortune to be expected. *Komitetchiki* like Koba were at home with interfactional politics, parsing the nuances of political positions, statements, even words.

As a *komitetchik* Koba was the last to adjust to the new possibilities for legal activities by the workers and had to face the fact that given the wave of strikes in 1907 and the ease with which the workers could organize in Baku, the trade unions enjoyed an influence greater than that of the party. By the summer of 1907 the division between the open labor movement and the underground party organization had developed to the point where the party was taking on a purely political character while the trade unions were concerned with economic matters. Members of the party tended to specialize in one aspect or the other. Japaridze became the effective leader of the Union of Oil Workers, while Koba disappeared "deep into the underground."[43] While participating somewhat in union affairs, Koba "gave most of his strength to party work, of which he was in charge."[44] Predictably, conflicts developed between the trade unionists and the committeemen. The party carried on its work "through influencing the trade union, the newspaper, the cooperatives, by infiltrating party members into the position of secretary or as members of the board of directors."[45] The trade unionists were caught between the workers who were playing a larger role in their own organizations and the party's ambition to dominate the unions. While all Bolsheviks agreed that the party's influence must be consolidated within the trade unions, Stopani, a Bolshevik who worked in the unions, remembered: "With reference to the degree and form of that consolidation there were also disagreements among ourselves: we had our own 'Left' (Koba-Stalin) and 'Right' (Alesha Japaridze and others, including myself); the disagreements were not on fundamentals but with reference to the tactics or the methods of establishing that contact."[46] Koba wanted to maximize party control over the trade unions while the more moderate Japaridze and Stopani argued for less control. Stopani recognized the trade union movement as "the most burning task for Baku in those days," but Koba feared the loss of primacy by the underground. His approach was that of pre-1905 Leninism: direction by the party activists (who were primarily *intelligenty*) rather than responding to worker initiative.

While the Mensheviks remained within the city proper, dealt primarily with skilled workers, and concentrated on small political meetings, the Bolsheviks were able to consolidate support among the unskilled Muslim proletariat of Baku's periphery. Among Menshevik leaders a narrative would later develop that more conscious and skilled workers tended to favor their approaches promoting an open and legal labor movement, while the less skilled and backward workers gravitated to the Bolsheviks and toward more elemental resistance.[47] But a simple deduction from social conditions or skill levels to factional allegiances does not take account of the influence of particular activists, where they were located, and what affiliations they had with specific workers.

Engaged in the economic struggle among the newly activated oil-field workers, the Bolsheviks set out to wrest the party committees from the Mensheviks and to call for a general strike. Starting in the oil-field districts where Bolshevism was strongest and fortified by newly arrived comrades and additional financial support, Bolsheviks took over one committee after another. At the end of June the district committee in Bibi-Eibat, where Koba was located, was reelected with Bolsheviks in control. The local committee then declared that the central Baku Committee was out of touch with the masses and should be reelected.[48] A short time later a delegates' meeting in Black City, the district to which Spandarian had been sent, replaced the Menshevik party organizer with a Bolshevik. The Mensheviks responded to this activity by calling a meeting of the Baku Committee; several Bolsheviks attended, only to walk out in protest. On July 8, Bolsheviks took over the newly elected Balakhany District Committee, which was henceforth led by Orjonikidze. The Balakhany Committee refused to recognize the authority of the Baku Committee and called for an organizational commission to convene a city conference. The Mensheviks objected to such a conference, but the local committees, most of which were already in Bolshevik hands, formed a nine-man organization commission in August (representing Balakhany, Bibi-Eibat, Black City, White City, the Maritime District, and the Muslim Social Democratic group, *Hummet*).

Koba was directly involved in the rough and tumble of intraparty politics, which were particularly intense in Baku. Even as he became somewhat engaged in the open labor movement, Koba preferred to stay hidden in the underground working primarily as a party organizer, a committeeman. He was considered the leading Bolshevik in the city, along with the blue-eyed Armenian Shahumian, who enjoyed a reputation as a Marxist theorist. Together Koba and Shahumian ran Marxist circles. One worker remembers that they discussed what books they might use to teach Marxism to the workers. Koba proposed several, but they were unavailable locally. Shahumian suggested Kautsky's *The Economic Teachings of Karl Marx*, but Koba claimed that there were "serious flaws" in that book. Nevertheless, he conceded, "we should be able to correct the errors in the process of teaching."[49]

Shahumian, his friend Spandarian, and Enukidze were willing to work with the Mensheviks, but Alesha Japaridze, usually a moderate, was on this matter adamantly opposed.[50] Koba looked for cooperation. As a member of the commission to bring the factions together, Koba helped organize the city conference, which met on October 25, in Khatisov's factory in Black City. No Mensheviks appeared, and in their absence a new, all-Bolshevik Baku Committee, which included Koba, was elected. Step by determined step the Bolsheviks had "conquered" the Baku organization in less than five months and secured greater support among workers. This kind of political maneuvering was Koba's forte. Working inside an organization, persistently recruiting adherents, he and his closest associates were relentless in consolidating their influence. Though they preferred one united Social Democratic organization with Bolsheviks on top, the Bolsheviks ended up alienated from their Menshevik comrades, with two parallel party organizations.[51]

This represented only a partial victory for the Bolsheviks and for Koba himself. The splitting of the Baku organization at a moment of revolutionary retreat did not escape the attention of the Central Committee, which favored unity. Noe Zhordania and Daneshevskii ("German"), a Latvian Bolshevik-conciliationist, were sent to arbitrate the dispute. They arrived in January 1908, and after gathering information pronounced in favor of the Mensheviks. The local Bolsheviks refused to accept the judgment and protested to the Central Committee. Despite the support from the delegates from the Central Committee, the Baku Mensheviks were unable to dislodge the Bolsheviks, who held on to the central city committee and the local committees in the surrounding oil fields.

Koba was sitting on a knife's edge. The Zhordania-Danishevskii commission saw him as pivotal both in the Tiflis "ex" and the Baku party schism. Yet when the investigators reported back to the Central Committee, no action was taken. Sometime later a Central Committee survey of Social Democratic activity in Russia reported regretfully that though "Baku is probably the only city in Russia where there still exists relatively free conditions for the activity of trade union and [party] organizations, and the unions manage to work together, the factional struggle within the party has taken on an embittered character" that has affected "the prestige of the party."[52]

CONFERENCE AND CONTRACT

In contrast to the repression in Georgia and throughout much of Russia, the authorities in Baku were ready to come to terms with the oil workers. On May 12, 1907, General N. F. Dzhunkovskii, the Baku agent of the viceroy of the Caucasus (and brother of V. F. Dzhunkovskii, renowned as Moscow vice governor), proposed that workers' representatives meet with the industrialists in a state conference to discuss the question of a general labor contract. Such conferences had been held in previous years but with no real results. The Social Democrats called a meeting of four district committees—Balakhany, Bibi-Eibat, Black City, and White City—which decided (52 to 2) against participation and in favor of a general strike. The Bolsheviks were pleased by the boycott of the conference, as were the Socialist Revolutionaries, the Armenian parties—the *Dashnaktsutyun* and the *Hnchaks*—and the Muslim SD group, *Hummet*. Only the Mensheviks and their union were for participation.[53] Distrust of yet another conference was widespread among the workers, and this played into the hands of the boycottists. General Dzhunkovskii renewed his offer in September, this time permitting workers to hold mass meetings at which they could elect representatives and eventually delegates to meet with the industrialists.[54]

Debate on participation in the state conference filled the pages of *Gudok* in the autumn of 1907. One of the first pieces, by Samartsev, the editor, argued in favor of participation as a means of unifying the stratified proletariat. The conference could work out a single labor contract for the whole oil industry and, like the contract of December 1904—the first labor contract in Russian history—it would tend to equalize wages and conditions of work. "The conference," he wrote, "can be a gate for us through which we can get off the narrow path of struggle within companies, of spontaneous actions, onto the broad highway of organized, unified action by all the masses."[55] Although a newcomer in the city, as a veteran of Social Democracy Koba replied to Samartsev in the following issue. He staked out a more radical position, opposing participation at this time because it would encourage conciliatory attitudes toward the industrialists. The unskilled workers, so recently awakened to strike activity, were still convinced that their best interests were served by extracting bonuses from the industrialists. Koba wanted to disabuse them of this "prejudice" and increase their hostility toward the bosses, in order to organize a general struggle of all workers against the oil industry: "The immediate task of advanced comrades is the desperate struggle for the unskilled workers, the struggle for the grouping of the unskilled workers around their skilled comrades by introducing into their consciousness unlimited distrust of the oil industrialists, by the removal from their heads of the harmful prejudices of petty traders and beggars."[56] Koba concluded by noting that a boycott would convince workers that only through a struggle, not through conferences, could workers improve their lives. His tone and outlook throughout the article remained uncompromising, wary of those who expected meaningful concessions from the industrialists in a conference.

Through the fall of 1907 meetings, discussions, and debates about the planned conference intensified among the workers. "The political life of the workers at this time was in full flower," wrote Iurii Larin.[57] He might have added that the bloom was a rare one in Russia, indeed one found only on the shores of the Caspian. After several weeks of meetings, workers voted by a two-thirds majority for boycotting the conference. They had accepted the same position as Koba. But hardly had the votes been counted when the leaders of the boycottist camp began to have doubts. During the weeks of open agitation subterranean differences among the Bolsheviks had surfaced. Japaridze and Shahumian, both of whom worked in Balakhany and were closely involved in the Union of Oil Workers, had never been enthusiastic about the boycott. Now they came out for participation. One night about two hundred workers met at an abandoned oil site in Balakhany and voted for participation. Other Bolsheviks gravitated toward participation. Koba remained opposed, hoping to convince the workers to engage instead in a general strike. Finally, a meeting was held in the laundry room of the Sabunchiny

Hospital. After a heated debate, the Bolsheviks voted to participate in the conference if certain preconditions were accepted by the state. This new position marked a defeat for the left wing of the Bolshevik organization and a victory for the more moderate trade unionists. Koba could not convince his comrades that a general strike was feasible given the low degree of organization and the lack of unity among the Baku workers. Most Bolsheviks were convinced that a general strike had little chance of success as winter was coming on, and the closing of navigation on the Volga would reduce the flow of oil from Baku.[58]

On November 7 the two major trade unions signed an agreement to support participation in the conference if preconditions were accepted by the state. A few days later the various Social Democratic factions—the Baku Committee of Bolsheviks, the Baku Organization of Mensheviks, the Armenian Social Democrats, and *Hummet*—all agreed to the new tactic. Only the Socialist Revolutionaries and the Dashnaks remained committed to unconditional boycott. With the workers on record as opposing the conference but the Social Democrats willing to urge participation if certain guarantees were met, the government was forced to negotiate with the trade unions on the preconditions to participation. The trade unions wanted to be able to have a say in the timing of the conference, to have its representatives meet periodically and guide the work of their delegation, to be free to hold meetings with workers, and to have special trade union delegates at the conference. The viceroy of the Caucasus announced that he did not object to the preconditions, but the Baku oil industrialists balked at the condition that union leaders play an influential role at the conference. Supported by protesting workers, the Social Democrats refused to consider participation without the unions. They believed that the future role of the trade unions was at stake. Though the municipal authorities and the oil industrialists preferred the elections to be held without trade union participation, this time they backed down and gave in to worker pressure.[59]

Trade unionism appeared triumphant in Baku, an oasis for workers in autocratic Russia. Unionist fever gripped both Bolsheviks and Mensheviks to the detriment of the party committees. "The political organization of Social Democracy almost ceased to operate at this time," wrote Larin. "All its party workers entered the campaign for the conference, and members signed up for the trade unions which in general began to attract greater attention of all the working masses as the legal center of the [campaign for participation in the] conference and boycottism."[60] The fears of Koba and the *komitetchiki* that the party underground would suffer with the turn toward the open economic struggle seemed to have been borne out. Yet instead of isolating themselves within the atrophying underground, the committeemen pragmatically joined the *praktiki* in the common struggle. Koba began to write articles in favor of participation in the conference, emphasizing that the conference was meaningful for the workers but only with the guarantees proposed by the Bolsheviks. Along with the rest of the Social Democrats, he advocated a fifth precondition to participation: that there be one labor contract for the whole industry instead of separate contracts for various groups of workers.[61]

In early 1908 thirty-five thousand workers cast their ballots for the four hundred representatives who would sit in the "workers' parliament" before and during the state conference. This was an extraordinary display of worker power and the peculiar openness of Baku politics. Nowhere else in the Russian Empire were the state and capital negotiating with workers and their socialist leaders. Two-thirds of those elected to the conference were either Social Democrats or sympathetic to them. Approximately nineteen thousand workers voted for the Bolshevik position (the conference with guarantees); eight thousand supported the original position of the Mensheviks, which some extreme Mensheviks still advocated (participation in the conference "no matter what"); and another eight thousand favored the Socialist Revolutionary–Dashnak boycott of the conference.[62] The election represented a great victory for the Social Democrats, especially the Bolshevik faction. Most workers recognized the Marxists as the spokesmen for the labor movement.

The urge to unity rose once again. The Social Democrats soon began to work out a plan for merging the two rival unions. But before the unions could unite, the police intervened. In January and February 1908, the new head of the city government (*gradonachal'nik*), General Folbaum, ordered the arrest of leading labor activists. Efforts at a merger of the unions collapsed, and divisions reappeared. The opening of the Council of Workers' Plenipotentiaries, which was to work out its position on the conference with industrialists, was delayed for two months while the bickering went on. In an article in *Gudok* Koba explained the differences between the two unions on the question of the authority of the council. The Bolshevik union held that the council should simply declare to the industrialists the expressed will of the proletariat—that is, a conference with guarantees—but the Menshevik union now argued that the council had no right to raise the question of a boycott without consulting the masses. Koba stated that the workers' representatives should present their demands as an ultimatum. The conference could be held only after the industrialists had accepted the five, non-negotiable preconditions of the workers.[63] Still confident that they could work out something with the authorities, the Baku Committee organized a citywide conference of the local organization in the People's House on March 15. About sixty to sixty-five people attended, including the leading Bolsheviks: Koba, Shahumian, Spandarian, Meshadi Azizbekov, Japaridze, and Mamed Mamediarov.[64] But the police had been tipped off that the meeting was to be held and surrounded the building. To avoid capture the delegates smashed a sealed door and found themselves in a hall where a play was being performed. Mixing with the crowd, they managed to escape in the commotion.[65] Ten days later, however, Koba was arrested.

By the time the Council of Workers' Plenipotentiaries held its first meeting at the end of March, the proposal by Dzhunkovskii was nearly a year old. In all that time the initiative had been in the hands of the workers who were to decide whether or not to negotiate with the industrialists. The decisive moves had been made by the workers, who followed the Bolsheviks first into boycotting the conference and then into agreeing to participate with preconditions. On April 26 the council finally voted 199 to 124 for participation with the five guarantees, but time was running out. The SRs and Dashnaks walked out of the meeting. Most of those leaving were Armenians, and the rest of the council taunted them: "Go elect a Catholicos; they are waiting for you in Ejmiadzin."[66]

"Reaction" finally creeped into Baku. The government had hardened its attitude toward the workers and Social Democrats. Stolypin wrote to Viceroy Vorontsov-Dashkov deploring the permissive policy of the Caucasian administration toward the revolutionaries and labor leadership. "In Baku daily tens of murders and expropriations occur openly and the guilty remain free." Stolypin rejected Vorontsov-Dashkov's analysis of the strikes as purely economic, for clearly visible was the activity of SRs and anarchists, "some of whom are Jews," destined to lead to an armed uprising. Stolypin made it clear to the Viceroy that he believed that the disorder in South Caucasia stemmed from the inertia of the local police, and he demanded a change in policy.[67] Just as the success of the Baku labor-industry conference seemed assured, the industrialists turned away from the cooperation on which the conference was founded. The oil industry was now in crisis. Oil prices had started a steady and rapid decline that made it unlikely that the industry would consider wage increases or amelioration of working conditions that would lead to substantial losses for investors.[68] On May 14 the local authorities settled the whole affair of the conference by arresting Japaridze, the head of the largest union in Baku. Almost a year after it had set in the rest of Russia, the "reaction" settled in Baku.

THE UNDERGROUND MAN SURFACES

When it had become futile to hold on to his opposition to the conference, Koba had made a pragmatic turn and came around to the open, semi-legalized labor movement. By December 1907 it was no longer possible to draw a distinction between Koba's new position and that of most Social Democrats. Having failed to win over the bulk of workers to Bolshevism in Georgia, Koba was not about to remain isolated from the workers in Baku. He adjusted his position and looked for ways to rebuild his faction's influence in Baku.

Yet his personal style, reputation for intrigue, and relentless competition with Shahumian for leadership created problems among the Bolsheviks. The two men were compelled to work together, but their temperaments and lifestyles made cooperation difficult. Shahumian was a dedicated family man, who eventually fathered four children. He wrote frequently to his beloved wife, Ekaterina, from prison and exile. Mikoyan remembered later that Shahumian respected Stalin but that there was no personal warmth between them. Ekaterina Shahumian had even stronger feelings about Koba and told Mikoyan that she considered him a *sklochnik* (divisive troublemaker), who schemed against Shahumian during their time together in Baku so that Koba and Spandarian could take over the leadership of the movement. Later Stalin himself confirmed that Ekaterina Shahumian could not abide him: "This woman, like a *samka* [female animal], thought only of her nestlings; she often looked hostilely at me when I pulled her Stepan into conspiratorial matters that could have meant prison [*pakhlo tiur'moi*]. It often happened that we with Spandarian would burst into their apartment and say, 'Stepan, get your things together, we are going to such and such illegal meeting.' Stepan immediately agreed and left. She could not hide her inimical attitude toward me."[69]

In time Shahumian grew frustrated with the viciousness of party infighting and accepted a position as director of the People's House that gave him legal status and a salary from the municipality. Tatiana Vulikh, who witnessed the tensions among the Bolsheviks when she worked in Baku for three months early in 1908, reported, "We knew that he left because he considered the tactic of the [party] committee mistaken but was unable to resist Stalin and preferred to leave. In general he was by character not very *boevoi* (militant). Stalin's adherents, of course, explained this in their own way: they said, he's an intellectual; the revolution exhausted him; he became demoralized and preferred a comfortable and well-paying position instead of the risk of revolutionary work." Vulikh dismissed what she considered an unfair characterization of Shahumian. "Stalin, Spandarian, and others were ready to characterize comrades who were of no use to them in this way." Shahumian, Budu Mdivani, and a few others, "were disturbed to different degrees by other tactical actions of Stalin and his supporters."[70]

According to Vulikh, Koba showed himself rarely, had almost no personal relations, and did not go out with others. His closest associates were Mdivani, who was quite popular, and Spandarian, "his closest friend and right arm, who unconditionally supported him in everything and defended him everywhere. Spandarian was very similar to Stalin in his entire moral makeup, though he had his own special 'qualities' not attributable to Stalin: namely, he was incredibly lazy, a sybarite, not careful in money matters, and a great womanizer." The Bolshevik Zemliachka told Vulikh later in Paris that all children under three in Baku looked suspiciously like Spandarian.[71]

A particularly unfriendly witness, Zhordania, attributed the rivalry between the two Bolshevik leaders less to moral character and more to power competition. He considered "all the Bolshevik intellectuals, generally speaking, marked by a thirst for power that they tried to achieve by any means. Given the circumstances of the period, this thirst to govern others could not go beyond the limits of the party. Shahumian and Koba opposed one another as pretenders to leadership." They were very different by nature. Shahumian "lacked cold bloodiness, became irritated in disputes, left meetings only to return immediately, was straight and sincere. Koba, in contrast, was taciturn, placid, serious, never raising his voice, and, what's more, it was impossible to figure out his true thoughts; he did not respond to insults on the field of battle but lay in wait patiently for an opportune moment to take his revenge." Not always the most trustworthy of informants, Zhordania tells an extraordinary story about how "this personal quarrel raged when Shahumian was arrested."

> Some years later, I met Shahumian and asked him at some point if the rumors [that Koba had denounced him to the police] were founded. His response was categorical: "I am persuaded that they express the truth. . . . I had a secret apartment where I spent nights; only Koba knew the address; yet that was the first thing that they [the police] mentioned to me when I was arrested."[72]

Whether in fact Koba had denounced Shahumian cannot otherwise be confirmed, but it is a very dubious story. In the years they worked together in Baku, 1907–1910, Shahumian was arrested only once, on April 30, 1909.[73] At that time Koba was in exile in Solvychegodsk. What is known, however, is that among Koba's Social Democratic comrades and opponents there were those who believed that to advance his own interests Koba was capable of betraying a comrade. And the rumors of his connections to the police never stopped.

At the same time Koba was admired by many of his fellow Social Democrats and workers. The Georgians in Baku "loved him very much, were proud of him, and considered him second after Lenin in the party."[74] Vulikh remembered him as a superb organizer who dedicated himself entirely to technical matters and did not have pretensions to become a theoretician.[75] One admirer was his future father-in-law, Sergei Alliluev, whose story of Koba as a generous and thoughtful friend fits the hagiographic mold of Stalinist memoirs. It also illustrates the kind of support and sharing that was an intimate part of the culture of the Social Democratic underground, a necessary practice in the network of those operating just outside the law. Living at the time illegally in Baku and unable to find work, Alliluev decided to try his luck in Saint Petersburg. At the end of July, on the advice of comrades, he approached Koba, who was living with his wife in a small one-floor house. Koba was reading. "He broke off from his book, stood up, and cordially said, 'Please come in.' I told Koba about my decision to move to Piter [Saint Petersburg]. My situation had forced me to take this step. 'Yes, you have to go,' Koba said. Suddenly he left the room, returning a few minutes later, offering Alliluev money. Seeing my confusion, he smiled. 'Take it, take it,' he said. 'You are going to a new city; you don't know many people there. You'll need it. . . . And you have a big family.' Then, squeezing my hand, Koba added, 'Good journey, Sergei.'"[76]

Creating loyalty in some and hostility, even hatred, in others, Koba's methods went beyond what most socialists thought acceptable and angered both Mensheviks and Bolsheviks. It was rumored that he hired thieves to obstruct Mensheviks on their way to meetings in Black City. In order to achieve a majority for his position at a gathering of workers and party members of both factions, Koba packed the room with Muslim workers who did not understand Russian. Their translator was a Koba supporter, and on cue they loyally voted as a bloc for his resolutions. The Bolsheviks Zemliachka and Aleksinskii complained to Lenin about Koba's shakedown of Baku industrialists. In order to raise money for the desperately poor party, he had invoices printed up on which the Baku Committee proposed a certain sum to be paid. Tall, strong, young men took the bills to various firms. No one refused to pay. Although Lenin was reported to have said that Koba is a "dumb Georgian" (*tupoi gruzin*) and promised to rein him in, nothing was done. Vulikh heard from several comrades that just before she arrived in Baku that Koba had fingered a worker as a police agent without having any definite proof. The worker was taken outside the city, "tried," condemned, and immediately shot. Such extreme actions troubled several of the comrades, particularly those from beyond the Caucasus.[77]

Preoccupied by politics, Koba neglected his young family. With no reliable income, they lived poorly in a small one-story house with the worker Alekseenko and his wife.[78] Kato was alone in the city for the roughly three months she lived there, without family, separated for the first time from Sashiko, the sister to whom she was so close. As the traditional Georgian woman she had been brought up to be, Kato bore her fate without complaining. Koba cared for her in his own way, but he subordinated family to work. As his pal Giorgi Elisabedashvili put it, "Soso loved her very much, but if you didn't know Soso's character well, you would not understand his love. Wife, child, friend were good for him only if they were not hindering him in his work and if they shared his views."[79] Koba's friends were pleased that their comrade had a good woman to take care of him and that she was loving and solicitous. She tried to find a job to help support the family, but it was impossible with a small child.[80] The heat in Baku was unbearable, and Kato soon became ill. She was weak, caring for a five-month-old infant. Sashiko and Koba both tried to convince her to join her sister in the countryside, but Kato would not leave her husband. "How can I leave Soso," she said, as if she felt that her life with him would be short.[81] After some delay Koba took her to her family in Tiflis in October. Kato's brother-in-law, Mikheil Monoselidze, indicted Koba for his treatment of his wife. "It was too hot in Baku. Soso would go early in the morning and return late at night while Kato sat at home with a tiny baby terrified that he would be arrested. Bad diet, little sleep, the heat, and stress weakened her, and she fell ill. Surrounded by strangers, she had no friends around her. Soso was so busy he forgot his family!"[82] When she seemed to improve, he brought her back to Baku. But her condition worsened, and after two or three weeks she died in his arms on November 22, 1907.[83]

Koba was devastated, and a photograph shows him standing sadly, head bowed, at her open coffin.[84] Monoselidze remembered, "Soso sank into deep grief. He barely spoke and nobody dared speak to him. All the time he blamed himself for not accepting our advice and for taking her to Baku in the heat."[85] Boyhood companion and later enemy Iremashvhili gives the canonical story of the effects of his loss on Koba. Before the coffin, Koba took his arm, pointed to the corpse, and said, "'Soso, this creature softened my heart of stone; she has died, and with her my last warm feelings for people.' He put his right hand on his chest: 'Here it is so desolate, so indescribably empty.'"[86] He left his child with Kato's mother, Sepora Svanidze, and for years made little effort to see him. Grief, arguably the most powerful human emotion, consumed him. He dropped out of sight for two months before plunging back into the turbulent politics in Baku.[87] As a sign of remembrance of his lost wife, he adopted, for a while, the pen name "K. Kato."

On the night of March 25 the police raided a number of "dens where criminal types hang out" and arrested a suspicious fellow with the passport in the name of Kogan Besov Nizharadze. It was in fact Koba, who soon revealed his real name but claimed he had lived more than a year in Leipzig after his escape from exile, returned to Russia only after the October Manifesto of 1905, and belonged to no illegal party or organization.[88] Despite all the rules of konspiratsiia, and Koba's acquired skills for staying out of the hands of the police, he was caught in a chance raid on a suspicious location. After his five months of underground activity Koba now had to operate from a cell in the Baku prison on the Bailov cape.

The regime was very lax in the prison. The political prisoners maintained active ties with their comrades on the outside. The prison was made for two hundred eighty prisoners, but in summer 1908 it held thirteen hundred, some for political offenses, others for purely criminal. The cells were kept open during the day, closed only at night, and prisoners wandered freely into the yard, where they played games, sang songs in choruses, traded cigarettes, and talked politics—a kind of "self-governing autonomous commune." The commune was largely divided into political factions, though some "'non-party' politicals" or "savages," remained outside the factions. Koba lived in the "Bolshevik" cell with Orjonikidze, Japaridze, Pavel (Sakvarelidze, Boris Legran, Slava Kasparov, Saratovets, S. Zhgenti, V. Sevriugin, N. Veprintsev (Peterburgets), M. Malkind, and others. "All on his own stood the well-known 'Christian socialist,' Sava Rostovskii, who went from cell to cell preaching the gospel of Tolstoy; Stalin could not abide him." While some played chess, Koba played *nardi* (backgammon), often through the night with Orjonikidze. The games were intense and could end with the tiles thrown off the board. Within the prison violence was common. Many convicts carried knives. Early on the "criminals" attacked the politicals, stole from them, beat them up; but a group of about twenty-five young Georgians, who admired the politicals, especially the Bolsheviks, gave an ultimatum to the criminals to desist. The threat worked, and a fragile peace was maintained within the grim walls.[89]

By that time the state had closed the door to negotiation, and the worker-industrialist conference was dead. As long as oil prices had been high, the tolerance of the industrialists and the state had not dissipated. Open labor organizations had flourished in Baku. But once the vice of the "reaction" began to close, the ephemeral nature of the mass organizations became apparent to all, and the real value of the party underground reasserted itself. Koba remained active and even while in prison continued to publish. He wrote a final article on the ill-fated conference, answering charges by the Mensheviks that Bolshevik militancy had destroyed the conference. He argued that the more mature proletariat of 1907 understood that such conferences were worthless unless their gains could be sustained and that could be accomplished only with full participation of the workers and their trade unions: a conference with guarantees or no conference at all! The blame for destroying the conference should fall not on the workers or their leaders but on the industrialists who feared such a conference.[90]

From cell no. 3 Koba participated in the lively debates held by the imprisoned revolutionaries. They sometimes went on for weeks. During one such debate, he laid out his position on the agrarian question. Upset by Koba's opponent, the SR Ilya Kartsivadze, Orjonikdize jumped to his friend's defense and slapped Kartsivadze. The offended debater challenged Orjonikidze to a duel, only to be reprimanded by his own faction and excluded from the SR caucus for violating revolutionary principles by resorting to such an archaic response.[91]

One of Koba's cellmates, the anarchist-communist Semen Vereshchak, later remembered Koba as so many others had as taciturn and unsociable. Unlike the other political prisoners Koba would associate with the ordinary criminals. When not engaged in factional debate he spent his time learning Esperanto, which he believed would be the language of the future. Several times, Vereshchak recalled, Koba started rumors about one or another prisoner being an *agent-provocateur*.[92] Yet a Bolshevik prisoner later remembered how Koba saved one of the prisoners threatened with execution. He conspired with the Bolshevik's wife, and on a visiting day the prisoner slipped away with the crowd of visitors, only after which the woman pretended not to have heard the signal to leave the prison. The guard slapped and cursed her, but it was already too late. The condemned man had disappeared.[93]

The experience of 1907–1908 had an important effect on Koba. He was not prepared to give up the open labor movement completely and pull back into the underground. He advocated "active involvement of the unions and our organization" to turn strikes into the "true means for the consolidation of the proletariat." "We must not forget that our organization will grow only to the degree of active involvement in all matters of the proletariat's struggle." He rejected a full retreat into the underground before the forces of reaction. Instead, the factory committees should be strengthened, imbued with the spirit of socialism, and united. This was the most urgent organizational task for the Social Democrats.[94] With these words Koba became silent, at least in print, for more than a year.

The revolution was behind them and, the Social Democrats hoped, before them as well. But in the years after 1905 party members in Russia agonized over what forms of struggle were possible. All Social Democrats inside Russia were faced with the reality of economic depression, a fall in labor activism, and the revived strength of the regime. Together they faced a strategic dilemma. The more actively they engaged in trade unionist and other legal activities, the more vulnerable they were to police persecution. Yet the deeper they retreated into the underground, the more tenuous their ties with the workers became. With shrinking support from the workers, the socialists either had to change their methods of operation or surrender to the mood of passivity.[95] Koba and the *komitetchiki* seemed vindicated in the next few years as the unions practically disappeared. The only center of Social Democratic activity that remained was hidden "deep in the underground." To emerge from the underground into the open labor movement would expose the few remaining cadres to the police.

As the Stolypin "reaction" closed down avenues for open organization, Social Democrats questioned whether European-style trade union activity was possible in Russia. Each faction attempted to deal with the potential of a legal labor movement and the actuality of continued police repression. One wing of Social Democracy believed that the time had come to concentrate on the legal labor movement, to broaden its appeal and deepen its roots among the working class and make it less political. Lenin would soon condemn the extreme manifestation of this movement as *likvidatorstvo* (liquidationism)—the effective elimination of the party underground. Another wing, tied to the traditions of the underground and the primacy of political work, opposed the new reliance on legal activity. The underground man Koba had fleetingly participated in the labor movement, and though he was cut off in prison from further activity, he observed the vicissitudes of Russian trade unionism struggling to survive in the years of "reaction."

Koba languished in Bailov prison as the organizations he had helped build disintegrated and hostility toward the party underground spread among Social Democrats and workers. The political prisoners elected Andrei Vyshinskii, I. P. Nadiradze, and Iustus their *starosty* (elders): Vyshinskii was linked to the kitchen, Iustus to transfers of prisoners, and Nadiradze to the administration. Koba and his comrades in cell no. 3 (among them Orjonikidze, Nadiradze, Pavel and Grigol Sakvarelidze), made several attempts to escape but failed each time. They had even managed to file through the bars, with Koba doing most of the work, and tie together a rope from sheets, but the needed signal from outside never came. On another occasion the worker I. Bokov agreed to exchange places with Koba during a group visit to the prison. Koba was to leave with the visitors disguised as Bokov, but the party organization declined to approve the plan.[96] His childhood friend and now cellmate Nadiradze through his wife arranged to have Keke Jughashvili come to Baku to see her son in the spring of 1908.[97]

Koba had arrived in Baku an underground man, a *komitetchik* of considerable experience, a militant and a fighter. In Baku he plunged first into party politics and helped to secure Bolshevik control over the organization. But as the open labor movement moved from success to success in its dealings with the industrialists, he was drawn into trade unionist activities. At no time did he either abandon the party underground or deny its primacy, but these first years in Baku were among the few in his life (along with his disastrous experience in Batumi six years earlier) in which he involved himself in the day-to-day economic struggle of the working class. The adaptation of Koba and other Baku *komitetchiki* to the open labor movement occurred earlier and more easily in Baku than elsewhere in Russia. Not until 1912 would Bolshevik committeemen in other parts of the country enter the trade unionist movement in significant numbers. At the end of this brief episode, however, he drifted back into the underground, where he remained, except for his years in prison and exile, until the revolution. In the dark years of the "reaction," Koba already prefigured ever more clearly the man who later became Stalin, both as a pragmatist and an organization man. After seven and a half months in prison in Baku, Koba was exiled on November 9, 1908, to Vologda Province in north-central Russia. By early summer of the next year he had escaped and was back in Baku.

19

THE REBEL DISARMED

I never really considered him a revolutionary, and I have told him this more than once to his face. Koba doesn't love the people; he despises them. His ambition may cost the party dear.

—ALEKSANDR SVANIDZE TO GALINA
SEREBRIAKOVA (1936)

Father loved Russia very strongly and deeply for his whole life. I do not know any other Georgian who forgot his own national characteristics as much and who so strongly loved everything Russian. Already in Siberia father loved Russia in a way that counts: the people, the language, and the nature. He always remembered the years of exile as if this were just fishing, hunting, and walks in the taiga. He preserved this love his whole life.

—SVETLANA ALLILUEVA, *DVADTSAT' PISEM K
DRUGU* [*TWENTY LETTERS TO A FRIEND*] (1967)

The tsarist exile system was porous and inefficient, relatively mild when compared to the gulag of Stalin's years in power when an archipelago of concentration camps dotted the USSR. In contrast to the Soviet system political prisoners were treated much more leniently than ordinary criminals, and though sickness and neglect led to the death of many committed revolutionaries, others managed to return to fight another day. Prison and exile were fundamental formative experiences for Koba. All in all he would be arrested six times, the first time in 1902, the last in 1913. He was exiled in 1903–1904, 1908–1909, 1910–1911, 1911–1912, a second time in 1912, and finally for his longest term, in 1913–1917. He escaped from exile five times: on January 5, 1904; on June 24, 1909; for a few days in early September 1911; then again on February 29, 1912; and on September 1, 1912. Koba's exile during his Baku years proved to be one of his shortest. But the trip to Vologda was his longest *etap*, the journey from beginning to end taking 110 days. He left the Bailov prison, his hands shackled. Koba was dressed in a loose, long belted shirt called a *tolstovka* or *kosovorotka*, pants over his boots, and a cap, a clear sartorial choice of identifying with Russians. Fellow prisoners bought him a warm coat and boots against his protests. Noticing his friends who had come out to send him off and made sure he wore the clothes they had bought for him, he smiled.[1] He was in a group with other prisoners from Baku, some of them Georgians, and together they were taken through Rostov-on-Don to Kursk, Tula, and Moscow, where they were held in the notorious Butyrskaia prison. There he met a worker from Tiflis, L. Z. Samchkuashvili, and a Social Democrat from Luhansk, Petr Chizhikov, with whom he would serve time in Vologda. After two months of police-escorted transport, he reached the provincial capital, Vologda, in north-central Russia sometime in January 1909.[2] He was locked up with about twenty political prisoners in a cold, damp cell. Every day a few prisoners died from typhus.[3] From there Koba was taken on to his designated place of exile, but weakened by the journey he came down with *typhus recurens* and was taken from the Viatka prison to the local *zemstvo* hospital. Once he recovered, he was sent on by train to Kotlas and then by sled for the last 27 kilometers on the frozen Vychegda River. Two weeks after his illness he arrived, on February 27, 1909, in the town of Solvychegodsk, where on the high banks above the Vychegda, as the town's name indicated (*sol'* in Russian means "salt"), Russians had mined salt since the Middle Ages.

Receiving his stipend of 7 rubles, 4 kopeks a month as a needy prisoner, Koba rented a room in a local house where he took his meals. As far from his past life as Solvychegodsk was, Koba found company in like-minded rebels. The long-time Bolshevik Iosif Dubrovinskii had arrived a week earlier but fled the town two days after Koba reached it.[4] Still, in June about fifteen people gathered around a bonfire by the river, among them Iakov Sverdlov, who would share yet another exile with

Koba and rise to become the head of the Soviet party bureaucracy, the Sekretariat, after the revolution. It was that position to which Stalin would succeed after Sverdlov's death and turn into his power base.[5] Koba also met a twenty-three-year-old noblewoman, the stately brunette Stefaniia Petrovskaia, who had been sentenced to two years exile in Vologda. She was living with another exile, her husband Pavel Tribulev, when Koba and she became more than friends. When her term of exile ended she went to Baku, where by that time, Koba had fled.[6] He also befriended a teacher, Tatiana Sukhova, another exile, who remembered years later how "Comrade Osip Koba" shivered in poverty in Solvychegodsk. He slept, indeed spent much of his time, on an improvised bed. "In the window was a wooden crate covered with planks and a bag of straw. On top of it were a flannel blanket and a pink pillowcase. Comrade Osip Koba would spend the night on that bed." Sometimes Sukhova found him lying there during the day as well. He suffered from the cold, lying wrapped in his overcoat, surrounded with books. "In his spare time Comrade Koba joined us in our walks more and more often. We even went rowing. He would joke a lot, and we would laugh at some of the others. Comrade Koba liked to laugh at our weaknesses."[7]

From his first days in Solvychegodsk Koba plotted his escape. He wrote to his friend Sergei Alliluev, who was then living in Saint Petersburg, to send him the address of his apartment and some money.[8] He contacted a certain "Vladik" in Tiflis (Vladimir Ter-Mirkurov), who sent a letter to Stepan Takuev, a Dashnak in Kiev, informing him that "Soso (Koba) has been writing from exile and requests that you send money for a return journey." But his Armenian contact was arrested, and Koba had to collect money from among the exiles. He confided in Sukhova. "Before his departure," she writes, "it turned out Comrade Osip Koba had no money. Sergei and Anton got hold of some money for him, and I gave him a few handkerchiefs for the trip. Comrade Osip Koba took them, and smiling remarked: 'One day I will give you a silk handkerchief in return.'"[9] On the evening before his escape, a fake card game was organized, and Koba "won" the pot of seventy rubles. His friends dressed him in a *sarafan*, a Russian peasant woman's tunic, and three friends—Sukhova, Sergei Shkarpetkin, and Anton Bondarev—rowed him down the river to Kotlas. They cut through a forest and crossed the Vychegda moving southwest on the Northern Dvina River, hiding in the bushes whenever another boat appeared. On June 24, 1909, his friends left him at a small railroad station just before the one train per day for Viatka was about to depart.[10]

Six months later Sukhova received a lighthearted postcard, dated November 1, from "Osip" sent from Baku: "Despite my promises, I remember, so often, up to now I have not sent you one postcard. This, of course, is swinishness. And I, if you like, beg forgiveness. From St[efaniia Petrovskaia] you will receive a letter. Until then, greetings. I live in general well, if you like, even very well. . . . Where are Anton and Sergei? Write. Osip."[11] On the front of the postcard was the painting by the Czech-German artist Anton Rober Leinweber, *David Dances before the Ark*. In 2 Samuel 6:14–22, David dances ecstatically before the ark to the disgust of Saul's daughter, Michal, who admonishes him for exposing himself half-naked before servant girls. David answers that he was dancing before the Lord, who chose him above Saul and his family to be king of Israel. And though he may look foolish in his own eyes, in the eyes of the servant girls he looked distinguished.

Koba cared about Sukhova, though how seriously is difficult to know. He often met women through his work or in exile with whom he had sometimes platonic, sometimes romantic relationships. But his attachments with women—except for his two wives—were casual, usually short-lived, punctuated with promises not carried out, and, if one can put it that way, utilitarian. Revolutionary culture—at least outside of the Caucasus where there were stricter, more traditional restrictions on male-female connections—was permissive about casual sex but almost without exclusion subordinated personal and romantic relationships to the ascetic demands of the movement. Given the circumstances of Sukhova's exile and Koba's escape and meanderings, she did not see him again until one day in 1912, as she tells it: "I was on my way to teach on Staronevskii Avenue [in Saint Petersburg]. Suddenly I felt a man's hand on my shoulder. It made me jump, but then a familiar voice addressed me. 'Don't be afraid, Comrade Tatiana, it's me.' And there was Comrade Osip Koba standing next to me, in the same clothes and boots but without the old, short winter coat. . . . We met that same evening at a workers' meeting. As we walked past the refreshment counter Comrade Koba took a red carnation and gave it to me."[12]

Saint Petersburg, the imperial capital, starkly reflected both the grandeur of empire and the squalor of most of its subjects, exposing the profound chasm between Russia's privileged upper classes and its peasants and workers. The center of the city stretched along the arrow-straight Nevskii Prospekt with its pastel palaces and ornate bridges. Across the Neva River and removed from the glitter of aristocratic life were the workers' quarters. Bridges, which were raised at night, further segregated the poor from the rich. Built on swampy ground by its namesake, Peter the Great, subject to the winds and cold rain from the Baltic, Petersburg was harsh and inhospitable to a visitor from the south. For half the year the days were short, cold, and damp, and the nights extended interminably. Police and their spies were ubiquitous, and for an illegal itinerant the city memorialized by Nikolai Gogol and Fedor Dostoevsky offered, not opportunity, but obscurity and danger.

Koba reached the capital around June 26, 1909, in the season when daylight in the far northern city extended far into the night. He searched for his friend Alliluev, who was not at his workplace when he arrived. Alliluev remembered that he was walking near Liteinyi Boulevard, not noticing where he was going, when suddenly someone blocked his path. Annoyed, he raised his head and saw Koba standing before him. They walked on together, and Koba told him that he had twice gone to the address that Alliluev had sent him but found no one at home. Koba was pale and weary.[13] Alliluev found him a place to stay, with a certain Melnikov, a relative of the concierge of his building. Years later Melnikov recalled "a young man who had black hair, a swarthy complexion, and a mustache" who dressed badly. "I gave him some underwear and a shirt to put on." Not a party member but willing to help out, Melnikov was told to watch out for police spies.[14] Alliluev also housed him with Kuzma Savchenko, who served with a cavalry regiment and was the brother of the apartment building's caretaker, Kanon, who arranged false papers for fugitives. There in the wing of a building where the right-wing duma deputy Vladimir Purishkevich lived, close to the barracks at the Tauride Palace, Koba hid out, right next to the comings and goings of the court officers' carriages.[15] Koba also visited his friend from Georgia, Silibistro Todria. His wife, Sofia Simakova, recalled that her husband came home during the workday and asked that lunch be prepared for his old friend Soso. Todria ran off to buy wine and fetch Soso. After potatoes, herring, and pickles, Soso asked to rest. "Stalin refused to lie down on our bed," Simakova writes. "He said that that was our place, and he would rather lie on the ground. I objected, but he insisted that I should make a bed for him on the floor. I swept the floor, of course, and then put down a blanket and gave Soso a pillow. He lay down, lit a cigarette, and began asking us about our life in Finland" where Todria worked on a secret printing press in Vyborg.[16] Koba spent only a few weeks in Saint Petersburg, but he used his time in the capital to have his comrades Vera Shveitser and Todria arrange a meeting with the Bolshevik duma deputy, Nikolai Poletaev, to discuss the publication of a newspaper.[17] By July 12 he was back in Baku. Now entering his thirties, Koba returned to party work, engaging in the debates and divisions that were paralyzing the Social Democrats. The police had him under surveillance almost as soon as he came to town, but they were confused as to who this "Koba" was. Somehow they were unable for months to identify him as Jughashvili, the fugitive from Solvychegodsk. He moved about with a false passport under the name Oganes [Hovhanes] Vartanovich Totomiants until he was again arrested eight months later on March 23, 1910.

ÉMIGRÉ SQUABBLES OVER PHILOSOPHY AND TACTICS

Koba returned to a shattered Baku party organization. The so-called years of reaction, 1907–1912, bled the RSDRP. Intellectuals abandoned the party, and workers deserted the unions. In Europe as well as Russia, Social Democrats argued over the corpse of 1905. The Menshevik and Bolshevik postmortems pulled in opposite directions. Lenin fought despair and wrote optimistically, "Wait, we will have another 1905. That is how the workers look at it. To the workers that year of struggle provided an example of *what is to be done*. To the intelligentsia and the renegade petty bourgeois it was a 'mad year,' an example of *what is not to be done.* To the proletariat, the study and critical assimilation of the experience of the revolution means learning to apply the methods of struggle *of that time more effectually,* learning to convert that October strike movement and December armed struggle into something broader, more concentrated and more class-conscious."[18] The Bolsheviks had banked on the revolutionary action of the workers, and, Lenin claimed, their faith in the workers had been vindicated in 1905 when they proved to be the major mass force in the revolutionary struggles. Mensheviks, he sneered, had placed their confidence in the liberal bourgeoisie and eventually reverted to their usual position of restraining the workers so as not to frighten the propertied classes who were slated to replace the autocracy.

The émigré leaders in Geneva, Paris, and other European cities turned on each other. Personality, politics, and philosophy not only further separated Mensheviks from Bolsheviks but tore apart both the Bolshevik and Menshevik factions as well. From the left the conflict stemmed from a philosophical challenge to Marxist materialism and an unwillingness to work within the possibilities of parliamentary politics. From the right disgust with the old practices of the party underground convinced some, like Aleksandr Potresov and the editors of the newspaper *Nasha zaria* (Our Dawn), that the future of the labor movement lay with trade unions and an emphasis on legal approaches.[19] Less convinced than the Leninists that the next revolutionary upsurge was on the horizon, many Mensheviks worked most energetically in the legal institutions, unions and the duma. Others, like Martov, Dan, and those around their newspaper *Golos sotsial-demokrata* (Voice of the Social Democrat), defended both the work of the trade unionists and the old underground party. Lenin's position also fell between those who favored legal work and the *komitetchiki* enamored of the underground.

Fearing arrest if he remained in Finland, which though somewhat autonomous was still part of the Russian Empire, Lenin had fled to Geneva in January 1908. After the heady exhilaration of the revolutionary years, this second European exile was more difficult than his first: it was "a flight from failure."[20] Doubting whether he would ever see Russia or revolution again, he confided, "I have a feeling as if I've come here to be buried."[21] Torn away from real politics for so long, distant from the everyday life of their constituents, the émigré socialists expressed their differences and petty personal annoyances in polemics that became the substitution for engagement in meaningful political conflict, compromises, and coalition building. Lenin confessed as much in a letter to Gorky: "Émigré life [*emigrantshchina*] is now a hundred times more oppressive than it was before the revolution. Émigré life and squabbling are inseparable." Then he reiterated his consistent confidence in the future: "But the squabbling will fall away. . . . And the development of the party, the development of the Social Democratic movement, will go on and on through all the devilish difficulties of the present situation."[22]

Their numbers dwindling from year to year, Bolsheviks maintained their own "Bolshevik Center" as a coordinating committee for their faction. But former activists were leaving party work, and several of Lenin's closest friends and comrades, most notably Aleksandr Bogdanov, Anatolii Lunacharskii, and Maxim Gorky, began to write vigorously about new philosophical thinking that to Lenin seemed to question the fundaments of Marxist materialism. Some saw Lenin as too moderate, too willing to work with legal institutions. Lenin's friend Gorky wrote to the dissident Bolshevik Bogdanov, "Lunacharskii is right when he says Lenin does not understand Bolshevism."[23] Most concerned about preserving the underground party organizations, even while not abandoning legal work with workers' organizations and in the duma, Lenin fought on two fronts: he pushed against Bolsheviks who wanted to boycott the Third State Duma elections and those Mensheviks who proposed a parliamentary alliance with the liberal Kadets. He was perturbed by what he considered new heresies that were appearing in the Bolshevik faction: *otzovizm* (the call for recalling the Bolshevik deputies from the duma); *ul'timatizm* (having the duma deputies read an ultimatum and then walk out); and *bogostroitel'stvo* ("God-Building," the view that Marxism was like an inspirational religion for workers, but built on science rather than the supernatural). Marooned in Geneva, sad, angry, but as pugnacious as ever, Lenin put aside some of his journalistic work and immersed himself in a deep study of philosophy. He believed that these philosophical questions were intimately tied to tactical political choices and became obsessively concerned with disputes about materialist ontology and epistemology.

The philosophical issues that animated Marxists for much of the first half of the twentieth century were never considered by them to be purely contemplative or speculative; they were tied to politics. Knowledge and political practice were inseparable. Turn of the century philosophers, however, exposed the limits of empiricism and positivism, that is, what could be observed and therefore was scientific. Idealism— the view that the world is the product of the mind—and philosophical materialism—the view that the world is objective, real, and made up entirely of matter—both go beyond the limits of observation and empirical verification and cannot be reconciled with the anti-metaphysical approach of positivism, which limits itself to the observable, testable world. Developments in late nineteenth- to early twentieth-century physics, like electromagnetic theory, relativity, and quantum theories, opened a new front in the philosophical wars between materialists and idealists. Traditional understandings of matter as permanent, hard, impenetrable, and inert were disrupted. Philosophers no longer saw matter as "material," or, in the words of the philosopher Bertrand Russell, "Matter has become a mere ghost."

As important Bolsheviks gravitated to Bogdanov, took up "God-building," or came out against the Social Democrats participating in the duma, Lenin decided to confront the dissidents within the faction. The "schism with Bogdanov," he wrote, was worse than that between the Mensheviks and the Bolsheviks. He threatened, "I will leave the faction as soon as the 'left' line and real 'boycottism' take over."[24]

For Lenin and many of his comrades, to think of the observable world as simply a product of mind or the senses, rather than objective and real, was intolerable. While accepting the new physics that seemed to confirm the fluidity of nature, Lenin resisted the shift among philosophers that seemed to posit a new idealism that saw the external world as a product of mind. Upset that such thinking attracted members of the Bolshevik faction like Bogdanov, Lenin wrote a book-length philosophical polemic, *Materialism and Empirocriticism* (1909), in which he famously argued that humans not only know the world through their senses but also that their perceptions correctly and accurately reflect the objective external world. Lenin would not accept that since humans can perceive and know only through sensations there is no independent nonsubjective way to verify the objective existence of the external world. Lenin was particularly disturbed by Bogdanov's embrace of the Austrian philosopher Ernst Mach, whom he considered (incorrectly) to be an idealist who claimed that physical objects were fictions and that only sense data were real. The Menshevik *Golos sotsial-demokrata*, as well, crowed that Machism was "a world view without a world."[25] Mach's views, however, were subtler than Lenin or the Mensheviks gave him credit. He held that science limits its investigations to phenomena perceivable by the senses, but scientific categories, rather than being an accurate picture of an underlying reality, were human constructions, conventions through which humans understand the world. This latter idea was anathema to Lenin.

As a great simplifier, the leader of the Bolsheviks liked dichotomies—idealists versus materialists, faith versus science, the bourgeoisie versus the proletariat, true revolutionaries versus opportunists. He condemned Bogdanov and his followers as idealist deviants. He took this controversy so seriously that he was willing to drive many of his most talented adherents from the Bolshevik faction. Lenin's singlemindedness and exaggerated sensitivity to deviation from what he considered actual Marxism profoundly influenced Bolshevik political culture, and Koba's own approach to philosophical and tactical matters.

Bolshevism continued to attract the most radicalized young intellectuals and embittered workers as it had in the revolutionary years 1905–1907 and would again when the labor movement revived in 1912. Leninists were generally perceived to be the more militant and aggressive of the two Social Democratic factions. There was a romantic, even millenarian impulse that propelled many into the perilous pursuit of revolutionary change, and when in the years after 1907 Lenin edged pragmatically toward combining underground revolutionary activity with exploitation of the new legal institutions, the "left" Bolsheviks resisted what looked like accommodation with the existing order. This pattern would repeat itself in the future—in 1918 in the crisis over Russia's surrender to imperial Germany at Brest-Litovsk, and again in 1921 in the transition from the radical program of "War Communism" to the moderation of the New Economic Policy. On several occasions Lenin would tear into what he called "left-wing infantilism," even as he zealously fought against those on his right, like the Menshevik "liquidators," whom he feared were abandoning the revolutionary struggle altogether. But in his "war on two fronts" Lenin was particularly strident and uncompromising in his reflexive readiness to use the most offensive language to caricature his opponents. This was a trait that his disciple Koba shared. Because of Lenin's great stature among his comrades, he encouraged a rhetoric and culture within the faction of bitter, exaggerated accusation and condemnation that in postrevolutionary years would have fatal effects on those who had employed it so loosely in less consequential circumstances.

In June 1909 Lenin called a conference "of the extended editorial board of *Proletarii*" in Paris to deal with Bogdanov and other rival Bolshevik approaches. The conference, which included Bolshevik members of the Central Committee, turned into a bitter debate over what constituted Bolshevism and what views would be tolerated in the faction. Lenin had effectively packed the meeting with his supporters, and Bogdanov was isolated, backed only by one or two others. Many of the Leninist core of the future Bolshevik Party emerged here: Lev Kamenev, Grigorii Zinoviev, Aleksei Rykov, Mikhail Tomskii, and Mikola Skrypnik. Kamenev, who had earlier favored boycott of the duma elections, recanted his leftism and came around to Lenin's position. Lenin pushed back against those who wanted to call for a "Bolshevik congress" to reconstitute the faction. Instead he spoke in the name of "partyness" (*partiinost'*) against any further schism in the RSDRP and urged joining with those "party Mensheviks" who repudiated the "liquidators." When the conference backed Lenin, condemning *otzovizm, ul'timatizm*, and *bogostroitel'stvo*, Bogdanov walked out. Veteran Bolsheviks refused to go along with Lenin's narrow definition of what constituted Bolshevism. Irritated and intransigent, he had weakened his own faction.

The "left" Bolsheviks—among them Lunacharskii (who wrote that "Scientific socialism is the most religious of all religions, and the true Social Democrat is the most religious of all human beings"), the historian Mikhail Pokrovskii, and the Baku veteran Martyn Liadov (M. N. Mandelshtam)—formed their own group and began publishing their own newspaper, *Vpered* (December 1909), appropriating the name of Lenin's earlier journal.[26] Bogdanov accused Lenin of abandoning "the entire political line of Bolshevism" and defended the heightened pedagogical role of Social Democrats in bringing revolutionary consciousness to workers that he took from the Lenin of *What Is to Be Done?* On tactics Bogdanov went along, unenthusiastically, with Lenin on the question of participating in the duma, but far more important to him was the pedagogical task of teaching workers. To this end he and his adherents organized a party school at Gorky's villa on Capri in 1909 and in Bologna in 1910–1911. Lenin, however, had been so impressed by the actions of workers in the revolution of 1905 that he now championed their ability to develop revolutionary views through revolutionary experience. To Bogdanov's educational approach, Lenin retorted, "Experience in the struggle enlightens more rapidly and profoundly than years of propaganda."[27] In one sense the conflict between Bogdanov and Lenin was a conflict between two Lenins—the Lenin of 1902 and the Lenin of 1905.[28] In another it was a struggle over the breadth or the narrowness of those who could be called Social Democrats. "Throughout 1909," writes Lenin biographer Robert Service, "he had behaved as if only his group inside Bolshevism and Plekhanov's inside Menshevism were legitimate constituent elements of the party."[29]

Bolsheviks inside Russia—even Koba in prison and exile—watched from the sidelines while the émigrés battered each other in polemical articles. Even though the examples and styles set by the party leaders flowed down into everyday behavior of rank-and-file members, the philosophical issues over the nature of reality seemed far less weighty to them than to Lenin and Bogdanov. The energy seeping out of the movement within Russia, they felt, was escaping even more rapidly because their theorists in Europe were preoccupied with questions of ontology and epistemology.

The elder statesman of Caucasian Bolshevism, Mikha Tskhakaia, was sympathetic to the Bogdanovites and *otzovizm*. He wrote from Paris to Baku, asking for Baku's mandate for the upcoming fifth conference of the RSDRP. Without Tskhakaia's express agreement, Shahumian circulated Tskhakaia's letter to comrades in Baku, including to those, like Koba, in prison. They answered with a letter signed by seven who agreed with the views of Koba. Shahumian then sent Koba's letter to Tskhakaia. In his own carefully crafted letter Shahumian replied that the Baku Bolsheviks were leaning toward giving the mandate to Lenin (which they later did). He hoped that Tskhakaia "will not interpret anything insulting for you, knowing full well that this is dictated by principled motives. Perhaps we have incorrectly evaluated your projected tendencies, but we are firmly convinced that Il'ich's position is correct and are, if not completely negative, then in any case greatly mistrustful of empirio-monism [Bogdanov's attempt to reconcile Marxism with Mach's views], etc." Baku Bolsheviks, he went on, "have become extremely interested in philosophy, we read and reread Dietzgen, Plekhanov, Bogdanov, and others."[30] Shahumian then reported that "Koba calls our intrafactional fight 'a tempest in a glass of water,'" and agreed that these philosophical disputes would not lead to a schism in the faction:

> No schism will come out of this. Curse each other a bit and this matter will end, but the positive result will be: improved acquaintance with the philosophical bases of Marxism and, it seems, a cleansing of new "isms" that wish to be added to Marxism. To us it seems the more incomprehensible occurrence in the party is the so-called "*otzovizm*." It seems absolutely unbelievable and extremely shameful that such views, such thinking can have a place in the ranks of a serious Social Democratic party.[31]

Koba's letter from prison to Tskhakaia was addressed to an "old friend" but one who had strayed. He confirmed that those in prison shared the view of those outside (*na vole*):

OK, let's get down to business. Where is the source of this "storm in a glass of water," which might turn into a real tempest? In "philosophical" disagreements? In tactical? In questions of organization, politics (relations to the "Left Menshies" and so forth)? In the self-regard of various egos? *Let's begin with philosophy.* . . . Should we separate all these tendencies one from the other and form around ourselves special factions? I think that if our party is not a sect—and it has not been a sect for a long time—it cannot break up into groups *according to philosophical* (gnoseological) tendencies. Of course, "philosophical" discussion is necessary and useful; we can only be happy about the well-known "philosophical" revitalization in our party "spheres." . . . But . . . discussion is one thing; abandoning the editorial board is something completely different.[32]

Koba considered Bogdanov's leaving *Proletarii* a desertion from his post. He was opposed to publishing the philosophical discussion in the newspaper, which would only result in fracturing the "party proletariat" into "various philosophical 'ists'." This was a bitter affair, he wrote, and would be even bitterer if "we, Russia's *praktiki,* were not able to call our nervous *literatory* to order."[33]

As for the substance of the (philosophical) differences, I personally think that your evaluation is completely correct. Of course, it is necessary to discard Plekhanov's "thing in itself," his peculiar understanding of materialism, his scornful attitude to Dietzgens, Mach, Avenarius, and others, as having nothing in common with the spirit of Marxism. But in just the same way it is necessary to discard Bogdanov's "panphysicism," his spiritualistic "universal substitution," and so forth. Empiro*criticism,* despite its good sides, is on the whole also unacceptable in view of its parallelism that only confuses things. We must stand on dialectical materialism (not Plekhanov's, but Marx-Engels'), developing and concretizing it in the spirit of J[oseph] Dietzgens, acquiring along the way the good sides of "Machism." Plekhanov's brushing aside of all "bourgeois philosophy" seems to me laughable and contradictory: were not Hegel and Holbach bourgeois philosophers, and is it not so that despite this Marx-Engels treated them and many others like people of science?[34]

Like Shahumian, Koba worked through the philosophical distinctions among Marxists and came to his own conclusions. But his paramount concern was that these disputes over materialism and perceptions not lead to further factional fractures. Bogdanov and Lenin had made it imperative that any party activist with serious pretensions to leadership would have to master the consequences of Machism and other philosophical interventions on Marxism. Koba made a serious effort to understand what was at stake in these debates, and while he was unwilling to take the nuances of the rival opinions as seriously as Lenin, he retained an interest in such questions. At key moments in his years at the head of the Soviet state Stalin would reengage in ongoing controversies within Marxist philosophy. But then he was not simply a minor participant but the ultimate arbiter of what was permitted to be true.

Not surprisingly, the comments by Koba on Marxist philosophy, his first excursion into the philosophical forest that seemed to question Lenin, were not published in the USSR in his lifetime—and then only after Nikita Khrushchev's exposure in 1956 of Stalin's crimes. When ammunition was needed in the 1960s to discredit Stalin's Leninist credentials, this letter was resurrected to demonstrate his "deviation." In fact, he was very close to Lenin and repeatedly emphasized that Lenin's position was the most sound. On political tactics he shared Lenin's views on the necessity to use the possibilities offered by trade unions, and other legal institutions, and he had come around to oppose boycott of the duma elections or recall of Social Democratic deputies. The boycott issue was a thing of the past now that Social Democrats had in fact been elected to the parliament. As for recall, "even Bogdanov himself (together with Il'ich) said that *otzovizm* is poorly understood Bolshevism!" Yet in this letter Koba's philosophical views were far more accommodating to Mach and Bogdanov than were Lenin's, less intransigent about compromise, and more open to working something out with Bogdanov.

Here Koba showed a supreme confidence about his understanding of the most sensitive issues facing party members. There was no hesitation to take on the giants of Social Democracy, even his revered Lenin. Discussing the party's attitude toward legal institutions, Koba pulled few punches:

> It is not worth speaking, for, if one takes into consideration the circumstances, that Il'ich *over*estimates the significance of such organizations, but that other comrades (for example, the Muscovites) *under*estimate it a little, the party has already decided the question. Of course, deviations from strict Bolshevism happen *accidentally* in one part of our faction headed by Il'ich (the question about the boycott of the Third Duma), but first of all, we are all guilty of this, for not once did we try (*seriously try*) in such cases to *establish the correctness of our position.*[35]

Koba ridiculed Kamenev's defense of the duma boycott as well as the *otzovisti*. But, he concluded, "Should we 'drive to the end' these chance deviations and make an elephant out of a fly?" He opposed turning these disputes into major, divisive issues, even as he held that Bogdanov should have observed party discipline and not walked out of the editorial board. "Is it really possible that there will never be an end to these anarchic exits from our faction?" Bogdanov's action was shameful. "I knew him as one of the few, serious, bright heads in the party and cannot stand such a frivolous walkout by him."

As for organizational policy, Koba favored unity of the Bolshevik faction as well as unity of the whole party:

> I think that Lenin's policy of rationally *putting* Bolshevism *into practice* (not simply *defending* but putting it into practice), demands sometimes some smoothing of the sharp corners of Bolshevism, [and] is the *only possible policy in the frame of a united party*. The unity of Social Democracy is no less essential than the unity of the faction—without such unity it is difficult to hold the banner high enough; Social Democracy will lose its influence among the proletariat. And I contend that if we want the unity of Social Democracy, then we must adopt the policy of Il'ich.[36]

Koba was willing to "let Bolshevism suffer a bit" by allowing various tendencies to continue. What was important was putting Bolshevik policy into practice. But, he continued, this has "nothing in common with conciliationism, for conciliationism is opportunism, that is, forgetting the basic interests of the faction." Instead he proposed "forgetting the transitory, non-essential interests of the faction for the good of its basic interests, and, this means, for the good of the unity of the party. That is why I think that the organizational policy of Il'ich (the relationship with the duma caucus, toward the left Mensheviks, etc.), as far as I am acquainted with it, seems at this moment to be the only sensible one."[37]

Still, as "Leninist" as he fashioned himself, a year later, after he had read Lenin's major work on materialism, Koba wrote critically about the older man's softness toward Plekhanov: "We precisely and correctly point to some more slips [promakhi] of Il'ich. It is right to point out that while Il'ich's materialism differs greatly from that of Plekhanov, contrary to the demands of logic (in the service of diplomacy), Il'ich tries to conceal [this]. In general I remain convinced that Il'ich's book is the only one of its kind that surveys the situation in Marxist philosophy."[38]

Apparently not amused by Koba's irreverent phrase, Lenin noted to Orjonikidze, "Nihilistic jokes about a storm in a glass of water show the immaturity of Koba as a Marxist." Soviet journalist Ilia Dubinskii-Mukhadze reconstructed Lenin's conversation with Orjonikidze from conversations he had with Old Bolsheviks. Walking arm in arm one evening in Paris, he writes, Lenin turned to his young comrade. "Sergo, are you familiar with the phrase 'a foreign storm in a glass of water.'" Orjonikidze understood that Lenin was referring to Koba. He had himself wanted to ask Lenin about Koba's views but had hesitated to bring up the subject, what with his Caucasian comrade "then languishing in exile." "Look here [Ish' ty], 'a foreign storm in a glass of water,'" repeated Lenin. "What nonsense! [Ekaia akhineia!]" "Vladimir Il'ich, don't!" Sergo pleaded. "Koba is our comrade! I am tied to him in many ways." "Of course, I know," Lenin willingly agreed. "I have the fondest memories of Stalin [sic]. I praised his 'Notes of a Delegate' on the London Congress of the party and especially 'Letters from the Caucasus.' But the revolution has not yet been victorious and has not given us the right to place personal sympathies and any pleasant memories above the interests of the cause. . . . You Caucasians value comradeship too highly." Lenin again frowned. "You say, 'Koba is our comrade,' you say, a Bolshevik, he will not betray [us] [deskat', bol'shevik, ne peremakhnet]. But are you shutting your eyes on what is inconsistent? Nihilistic jokes 'about a storm in a glass' show the immaturity of Koba as a Marxist. We won't delude ourselves. The disintegration and vacillation is extraordinarily great."[39]

Russian Social Democratic political culture involved a corrosive intensity of argument. Koba was able to give as well as take in the fierce disputes and debates that both invigorated and exhausted party members and workers. But at the same time he worried constantly that differences would lead to unnecessary divisions. Just weeks after Koba's return the Baku Committee of Bolsheviks adopted a resolution (August 2, 1909), condemning otzovizm and ultimatizm, along with bogostroitel'stvo. The resolution stated that while a "struggle of ideas" with these tendencies is imperative, and Bogdanov should be reprimanded for refusing to submit to the decisions of the majority of the editorial board, the Baku Committee disagreed with the Leninist majority on the editorial board of Proletarii about the necessity of "ejecting from our ranks" the supporters of the minority.[40] The local Bolsheviks demonstrated their ideological solidarity with Lenin but could not bring themselves to applaud the schism in the Bolshevik faction. Here the preferences of the more conciliatory Koba prevailed: unity of the Bolshevik faction but with fierce internal debate over divisive issues.

While visiting Tiflis Koba wrote a short, warm letter in Georgian to his former mentor Tskhakaia, then living in Geneva. "How are you doing, what are you doing, what makes you happy and what makes you sad? Write something, you son of a dog, why are you silent?" Turning more serious, he asked: "Could it be that these damn 'God tendencies' have driven us apart? From where you are they write that the split into factions is a fact, that both factions are already solidified into separate brigades, they have separate centers, etc. What a storm has burst upon us. What kind of wicked people you are. Did we really need this? In my opinion the 'Bogdanovtsy' are mistaken (look at the resolution of the Baku folks), and as for what seem to be useless quarrels, both sides are guilty [in Georgian, deserve death], the one and the other." He then turned to the situation in Caucasia. "There's nothing good to write about," he reported. "The situation in the organization is 'so-so.' Everyone 'collected their thoughts' and took off for business, personal business. (Except me, I have not yet managed to 'wise up.') In the last few days (here in Tiflis) we have had a conference with about 200 members represented. The Menshies kept separate (a split still exists), and I think they have about 400 (if not more) people."[41] Baku was better for the Bolsheviks (three hundred members) to the Mensheviks' "maybe up to a 100." Confidently he announced, "We are already uniting; the schism is over. They might be uniting in Tiflis—I have tried hard to unite them—and it is possible that my efforts will bear fruit. We want to call a Caucasian congress given that the regional committee no longer exists." In Baku leading Bolsheviks have either been arrested—among them Silia, Spandarian, and Japaridze, or like Shahumian "given up work (it has already been three months)." The police "are incessantly searching for your dedicated servant (that is, me). Let's see what will happen further." As if to indicate his opposition to further splintering of the Bolshevik faction, he ended the letter with "warmest [*plamennyi*] greetings to Maksimov [Bogdanov], Aleksinskii, Lunacharskii," and signed off, "Soso."[42]

Deeply disturbed by the fissiparous tendencies in the party, back in Baku, Koba followed a week later (November 12, 1909) with a letter to the editors of *Proletarii*, the Bolshevik newspaper abroad. At about that time Lenin found himself at odds with Zinoviev, Kamenev, and Dubrovinskii on internal party organizational matters.[43] Koba began by apologizing for not writing earlier in answer to the editors' letters because he and his comrades had been dealing with the problem of *provokatory* [police spies]. Speaking in the name of the Baku Bolsheviks, he expressed "our even greater conviction" that the editorial board had been wrong to expel Bogdanov. "Either working together was in principle harmful and impermissible, and then without waiting for him to break away it was necessary to throw them [the minority] out of the editorial board, or working together was possible, and then 'the whole question' comes down to a question of the behavior of Maximov

[Bogdanov] and his 'school.'" Koba believed that working together was "possible and imperative." "We understand the position of the editorial board being abroad, the foreign atmosphere, etc. But you ought to understand that we are not abroad, that you are writing for us, and what is expedient abroad is not always expedient for Russia." The Baku Bolsheviks, he concluded, supported the immediate convening of a Bolshevik conference "to rein in the Maximovists" and a parallel all-party conference. "The more the conference is delayed, the less light there will be, the better for them, the worse for the faction: delay gives them the possibility and time to organize, to cut off the path to the (straying) Russian comrades working together, which (note this!) is essential to remove from their heads all ultimatist dust."[44]

Shahumian reiterated Baku's opposition to Tskhakaia, the Bogdanovites, and the *otzovisti*. He was plugging away at reading the key works in the debate. "The three volumes of [Bogdanov's] *Empirimonism* are in any case with me on the table, and as much as possible I read them. I read his 'From the Psychology of Society.' Right now my attitude is very negative. His thesis on the identity of being [*bytie*] and consciousness destroys the whole system of Marx. But, I repeat, I consider my opinion not yet final until I am fully knowledgeable." He then asked Tskhakaia, "What are your relations now with Il'ich? In your first big letter you took up arms against him, and that letter in general had . . . a very bad impression on us. We are all completely on Il'ich's side. . . . The 'schism' that is beginning among the groups abroad . . . produced a terrible impression on us. How this reminds us of the time after the Second Congress! But this group is making a grave error if it thinks that it will influence the life of the party with these scandals. The old times have already passed."[45]

The "old times" had indeed passed in many different ways. The revolution was becoming a memory, and even the heady years when the duma was dominated by the liberals and socialists had ended with Prime Minister Stolypin's coup d'état of June 3, 1907. Russia's post-1905 political system was inherently contradictory, a kind of "constitutional autocracy." Autocracy means unlimited power by a single individual, while constitutionalism is defined by the limits that the laws place on arbitrary exercise of power. Although Nicholas II had granted his people rights and Fundamental Laws, he continued to proclaim himself an autocrat. But Stolypin thought of himself as a constitutionalist, supporting a monarchy that would self-limit itself to ruling within the law. Yet he opposed full parliamentary government in which the executive power would be responsible to the legislature. The vast majority of Russia's people had been effectively disenfranchised, and the non-Russians particularly suffered from the rising chauvinism, anti-Semitism, and condescension toward "minorities."

The Third Duma (1907–1912) was a pale shadow of the raucous assembly in which Tsereteli and Zurabov had taunted and antagonized the government. They and many of their fellow democrats had been arrested and exiled to Siberia, and the newly elected duma was dominated by the Right—extreme reactionaries, nationalists, and moderate conservatives like the Octobrists. By extra-constitutionally changing the franchise to over represent the landed nobility and propertied classes, Stolypin had acquired the parliament with which he believed he could work.[46] Still, the duma was arguably the only place in the empire where a degree of open political expression could reach a wide public.

The mix of gradual reform, particularly in the system governing peasant lands, with vicious repression of the radical opposition convinced many to give up revolutionary activity and find other paths to improving the plight of workers and peasants. In Baku the party organization and its influence continued to wither away throughout the years of "reaction." The Baku Committee was one of a mere half dozen Bolshevik committees operating inside Russia in mid-1909. By the end of that year Bolsheviks numbered only three hundred in Baku; two years later membership was down to two hundred, and by early 1913 to one hundred.[47] Yet despite the effective police infiltration into its ranks, the party continued to operate. As Trotsky's newspaper *Pravda* (Truth) reported: "Even in the period of the greatest decline, the party organizations existed: the Baku Committee and the Baku [Menshevik] Collective, but without the districts and without ties to the masses; not even because of the police but because of the general collapse. Some kind of work was carried on in the trade unions. An awakening in the masses began in

1909 in connection with the discussion of the law to introduce *zemstva* in the Caucasus and also in connection with the deliberations by the oil industrialists of the question of settlements and also the campaign for an anti-alcohol congress."[48] Still, with the loss of less-committed cadres, the two Social Democratic organizations shrank down to the original core of old party activists. As Shahumian put it, "Both 'collectives' consist almost exclusively of veterans [*stariki*] who do not think of giving way to despair and throwing away their Social Democratic organizations and liquidating them. It is evident that Baku is not favorable to our liquidators. The Baku Menshevik Collective has taken a sharply defined party position up to this time."[49]

Koba was one of those old party activists unwilling to give in to despair. After his escape from Solvychegodsk, he burrowed his way deep into the Baku underground. His presence in the city was unknown even to some of his comrades. But he and the Baku Bolsheviks revived the publication of *Bakinskii proletarii* and managed to put out two issues, with Koba's article on "The Party Crisis and Our Tasks." In this important article, one usually neglected by his biographers, Koba analyzed the lack of connectivity between party committees in various parts of Russia and the party's isolation from the broad masses.[50] The fracturing of the party was evident in the pages of its three principal newspapers: *Sotsial-Demokrat* (1908–1917), the official organ of the party, which included both Mensheviks and Bolsheviks on its editorial board until Martov and Dan left in June 1911; *Golos sotsial-demokrata* (1908–1911), which gravitated toward liquidationism and thus lost Plekhanov; and *Proletarii* (1908–1909), the Bolshevik newspaper edited by Lenin from which one of his closest collaborators, Bogdanov, walked out in 1909. To bring the various committees throughout Russia under some kind of common leadership, Koba proposed that the Central Committee create a new, all-Russian newspaper. To win back the masses he advocated bringing factory and plant party committees together in district and regional organizations. There "the most experienced and influential advanced workers" would take over the most important posts and carry out practical, organizational, and literary work. Involvement in union matters a year earlier had impressed Koba that even apparently limited economic issues had potential organizing benefits. "Don't forget," he wrote, "Bebels [that is, worker Social Democrats] do not drop from the skies; they are trained only in the course of work, by practice, and our movement now needs Russian Bebels, experienced and seasoned leaders from the ranks of the workers, more than ever before. . . . Workers with knowledge are few. But here is precisely where the help of experienced and active intellectuals comes in handy."[51] Workers must be bold, speak out, and have faith in their strength. "It is not so bad if you miss the mark on the first tries; twice you will stumble, but then you will learn to walk on your own, like 'Christ on water.'"[52]

Koba's apparent conversion from the *komitetchik* of years past to the advocate of increased workers' participation was neither abrupt nor complete, but he had moved to head off the genuine worker resentment of direction by intellectuals. While in Baku the party was holding back the workers, preventing them from confronting the oil capitalists, Koba praised the party workers of the Central District and the Urals, which "have been doing without intellectuals for a long time," as well as Sormovo, Lugansk (Donets Basin), and Nikolaev, where workers had published leaflets and even an illegal organ on their own.[53] He pointedly did not mention Tiflis, where he had witnessed worker influence in the Social Democratic committees, but where the Mensheviks had routed the Bolsheviks and positioned themselves successfully as spokespeople for workers' dominance in the committees as well as a mass peasant movement. Koba now outlined a subordinate role for intellectuals, akin to that practiced by his Georgian rivals. Intellectuals were to assist advanced workers and arrange discussion groups in which the theory and practice of Marxism would be studied. Koba also called for full use of legal possibilities—"from the floor of the duma and the trade unions to cooperative societies and burial funds"—and the creation of a central party newspaper to be published within Russia by the Central Committee, which would link local organizations to the center and end their isolation.[54]

In this article Koba summed up a long process of personal development while revealing some of his basic predilections. He combined various, even contradictory, aspects of what made a Social Democrat. He was still primarily a party man interested in building up that organization, but he recognized that legal and economic activity could serve the party and, in turn, the revolution. The choice between trade unionism and party work was perceived, as in the bygone days of *Iskra*'s struggle with the Economists, as a choice between reformism and revolution, and Koba mirrored Lenin's primary dedication to revolution. He was an activist, a *praktik*, rather than a theorist, but was about to launch himself into theory. However plebian his origin, he was himself an intellectual, though he shared Lenin's suspicion of intellectuals and extended it even further to those *teoretiki* abroad who tried to run the party from outside without firsthand knowledge of Russian conditions. To Koba and many socialists in Russia the émigrés appeared to be living in an unreal world of philosophical disputes and personalized intrigues.

20

LABOR AND LIQUIDATORS

Stalin, as a soldier in the army of Lenin, who between 1900 and 1919 [*sic*] transmitted his commands from abroad and prepared every campaign, acquired importance very slowly during those years; and right up to the Revolution he never once appeared in the foreground. When I asked him whether, in his opinion, a revolutionary could prepare himself better at home or abroad, Stalin did not give me a yes-or-no answer, but delivered himself as follows: "I consider Lenin an exception. Very few of those who were then living and working in Russia were as intimately acquainted with everything that happened as Lenin managed to be, from abroad."

—EMIL LUDWIG, *STALIN* (1942; BASED ON HIS
INTERVIEW WITH STALIN, 1931)

[I]ntellectually and politically Stalin was different from most of the historical figures in the Bolshevik movement. The other Bolshevik leaders were often political analysts, who knew the West well because they had lived there. More "European," easier to "read," they were interested in theoretical questions and intellectually superior to Stalin. He was less well-educated, with little experience of the outside world. He was secretive, intensely self-centered, cautious and scheming. His highly sensitive ego could be soothed, if by anything, only by a sense of his own greatness, which had to be unreservedly acknowledged by others.

—MOSHE LEWIN, *THE SOVIET CENTURY* (2005)

By the time Koba reengaged with the "movement" in Baku in 1909, there was no movement. For the Caucasian Bolsheviks the hope that Baku would continue to be a haven in the darkening storm was rapidly being extinguished. Russian oil entered hard times in 1908. The American financial crisis of the fall led to an extended depression in European heavy industry (1908–1909). Oil prices began to sink rapidly by 1909 and continued to fall until 1912.[1] Russia's exports suffered from the fierce competition of Standard Oil, the European Oil Union, and Shell, giant companies that in 1910–1911 deliberately lowered prices in an effort to drive Russia out of the market. The older, less efficient Russian companies could not keep up with the productivity of the more advanced Western firms or newer entrants into the field, like Rumania. Russian output fell each year (except 1910), and even in that peak year Russia produced only one-third what the United States produced.[2] By 1914 Baku's production was only a little more than half what it had been in 1901.[3]

The decline in oil prices and contraction of oil production had a devastating effect on Baku's workers and their trade unions. The gains that they had made in the preceding five years evaporated. Gone was the ephemeral liberalism of the industrialists, who now imposed new fines on workers for infraction of petty rules. Workers were forced to work overtime or at night under threat of being fired. The workday was lengthened in some plants by changing from three shifts (of eight hours) to two (of twelve hours). Fines and beatings were back, and some "kings of oil" even prohibited "their" workers to marry without permission.[4] The repression was greatest against the more skilled workers, particularly those who had been active in the labor movement.[5]

Unemployment rose. Threatened with joblessness, workers lost leverage vis-à-vis management. Wages were lowered in some factories, and the squeeze was put on workers to leave the unions. Strikes continued, but they were far fewer in number than in the preceding three years, and most of them ended in defeat for the workers. Management refused to recognize the factory committees, elected by workers since 1905, as bargaining agents, and they lost what authority they had built

up. Trade unions saw their membership dwindle from thousands of adherents to several hundred. Unemployed workers often left the city and
returned to their villages rather than starve in the grimy streets of Baku.

With little relief from the filth and noise of the oil wells and refineries,
one married worker described his living conditions: "The work at the
oil well is hard and dirty; besides that, you come home tired and there
is no place to dry out because there is no heater, and it is hard to dry out
with kerosene. The apartment itself is damp; it is getting damper and is
filled with some kind of stinking air. You come home late from work (it
is already getting dark), and you sit tired in a damp and gloomy apartment. If you have something to read, you read it, then have dinner and
go to sleep."[6] A skilled Russian worker, feeling lost in the multinational
environment of Caucasia, found other diversions: "We live badly, since
there are very few Russians. The majority are Moslems. There are no
forms of distraction except getting drunk, cursing, and fighting."[7]

The achievements of the Social Democrats withered quickly in 1908–
1909. Open work among workers became impossible. Armed guards at
factory gates refused admission to strangers. Yet retreat into the underground and return to the propaganda circles of the past appealed to no
one. Some *praktiki*, particularly Mensheviks, came out against the control of the labor movement by the underground party. Perceiving that
the workers were primarily interested in economic benefits and improvements in living conditions, these men and women could not reconcile themselves to the Bolshevik priorities of politics first, economics
second. A group of "syndicalists" stressing the priority of trade unionism
gathered around the newspaper *Gudok*, while those Mensheviks who
held more regard for the party and its politics considered putting out a
rival newspaper.[8] The stimulus to this antiparty feeling came in part
from the workers themselves. The editors of *Gudok* published a letter
from twenty members of the Bolshevik-run Union of Oil Workers severely criticizing the role of the party in the union:

> From the very beginning many comrades working in the union gave
> priority to ends peripheral to the union; they tried to use the union
> for tasks alien to it; instead of creative work, party elements brought

into the union party arguments and dissension, "the struggle for power," etc. As a consequence of this, all problems arising in daily life were not decided in our interest; they were not even discussed in open meetings. Usually they were decided by party organizations, and the union bodies, through their members, carried out these prepared, factional decisions.[9]

As far as these workers were concerned, union democracy had become a fiction, a victim of party interests. They called for the union to become independent of the party and to deal with the "daily struggle for bread." In Bibi-Eibat, the industrial district where Koba had operated, workers complained that the leadership tried to "paint the union in party colors."[10] The anti-political mood of the workers reflected the general attitude of other social classes. A Menshevik writer characterized the atmosphere in the city: "Recently the reactionary trend has penetrated and become strong in society. Not only is sympathy for revolution not to be seen, but just the opposite, dissatisfaction and hatred for it are growing."[11] The Bolsheviks, so closely identified with revolutionary and party politics, were victimized by this new mood. Shahumian wrote to his comrade, Tskhakaia, then living in Geneva, "The conditions of work, dear Mikha, have become terribly difficult: they literally crucify us, spit [on us] from all sides, humiliate [us]. Besides this, each day the reaction among the workers (the internal reaction) gains strength; the best comrades among the workers quit us at times. But we are not losing heart. Faith in the future and love for our cause provides us with inexhaustible energy."[12] Without support from workers the professional revolutionaries were "starving in the literal sense of the word." The local Bolsheviks could not even manage to raise enough money to buy an overcoat for Koba, when he was being exiled to Siberia.[13]

The nadir of the Baku labor movement was reached in 1910. In that year the number of workers shrank by fourteen percent (nearly seven thousand men).[14] Only eleven strikes occurred, of which five were successful.[15] Workers paid no attention to Social Democratic efforts to organize a May Day demonstration, and the holiday passed for the first time since 1901 without some kind of celebration. The Union of Oil

Workers, which in its heyday had had nine thousand members, was now down to twenty! The union building was closed. Five secretaries in a row had been arrested, several of them exiled. The Menshevik Union of Mechanical Workers was open, but—in Shahumian's words—"is also living out its days."[16] What was left of the legal labor movement was largely run by the Mensheviks, while the underground party was dominated by the Bolsheviks, who outnumbered their rivals there by two or three to one.[17] The legal labor organizations were in the hands of older workers, rather than intellectuals or younger workers. Among union workers there was complete indifference to party affairs.

Like Shahumian, Koba refused to give in to despair. He predicted that with unity of the party organizations and the merger of the competing unions, a "general economic strike" would meet success.[18] The strategy of using all legal means—unions, clubs, the anti-alcohol campaign, even the proposed creation of a *zemstvo*-like "self-government" for the oil-producing districts around Baku—as well as preserving the underground party organizations at least preserved the remnants of past achievements in anticipation of what might lie ahead.[19] He busied himself with the technical side of party work, particularly the secret press that published the Bolsheviks' newspaper and leaflets. When the owner of the building where the press was located demanded that it be moved by September 1909, Koba worked around the clock to put out one more issue of *Bakinskii proletarii*, visiting the printing shop every day. After Japaridze, who had been a central figure in Baku radical politics, had to flee for fear of arrest, Koba took over much of the direction of the faction.[20]

Then on August 28 one of Koba's closest collaborators, Suren Spandarian, was arrested. This shocked and frightened those still at liberty, especially since they had not yet found a new home for the secret press. The police were closely following the internal workings of the faction through their informers, and the Bolsheviks grew increasingly convinced that there were police agents among their activists. Suspicion fell on a Russian husband and wife, Aleksandr Prusakov and Evdokiia Kozlovskaia, who had been working with the press, and on the secretary of the Union of Oil Workers, Nikolai Leontev. First the husband disappeared, and after being questioned by party members, the wife also fled. The committee decided to "arrest" Leontev and hold him, try him, and kill him if found guilty of working with the police. Convinced of Leontev's guilt, Koba and Said Iakubov went to his apartment at 11 in the evening, and Koba declared, "Nikolai, you are a provocateur." Leontev began to tremble, and his wife threw herself on the bed crying. Iakubov held them at his place for several nights. Koba put out a leaflet denouncing these three and two other "provocateurs." Leontev was sent to Saint Petersburg with another party member, Nikolai Veprintsev, known as "Peterburgets," who subsequently reported back that indeed the union secretary worked for the secret police. When Leontev was returned to Baku, he demanded that he be given a party trial. If found guilty, he stated, he was ready to be killed. This bold gesture won the accused some sympathy, but ultimately Koba decided his fate. He convinced the others that since Leontev had given police information about them, they would be arrested after the killing. With so few Bolsheviks in Baku in 1909, carrying out killings would implicate leading party members. Eventually Leontev was sent out of Baku and dispatched by others.[21] Discussions involving all the revolutionary parties in the city about assassinating the *gradonachal'nik* (military mayor) of the city, Martinov, never went anywhere.[22]

The party organizations, both in the Caucasus and Russia proper, were riddled with police agents. It was difficult to know which comrades were dedicated to the revolution and which were about to turn their comrades in to the police. In November or December 1909, a high-ranking party member, Miron Chernomazov (1882–1917), was sent, ostensibly by Lenin, to Baku with a note to Shahumian requesting lists of the people in the Bolshevik *aktiv* (group of activists). He asked their names, their revolutionary pseudonyms, what kind of work they did and where. These questions aroused suspicions among local party members, and Koba denounced Chernomazov at one of the party meetings as a police spy. In fact, in this case, he was a little premature. Chernomazov probably started to work as a regular agent for the police only in 1913.[23] Known as "Miron" in party circles, Chernomazov was later secretary of the Bolsheviks' Petersburg newspaper, *Pravda*, in 1913–1914, but eventually he drew the suspicion of enough party members that Kamenev was ordered to remove him from the newspaper.[24]

The rumors that Koba was connected to the police persisted. One day a low-level employee of the *Okhrana* came up to Koba on the street and said to him, "I know that you are a revolutionary or a Social Democrat. . . . Here take this list; here are included the comrades who will be arrested in the near future." There were thirty-five people listed, and the fact that Koba had been given the list by a completely unknown person drew suspicion upon him. The Baku Committee met. The list was not read to them, but it was decided to choose a new committee of eleven who were not on the list. One by one the other Social Democrats were arrested.[25] In fact there was nothing unusual about people who were working for the police passing information to the political opposition. The exchange of information between police and party went in both directions. In 1909–1910 the police in Baku had at least four regular, paid informants among party members: "Mikhail" (Mikheil Koberidze); "Bystryi" (Speedy) (Aleksandr Donskoi); "Fikus" (Fig or Fig Tree) (Nikolai Erikov); and the Dashnak "Dorogoi" (Dear One) (Ivan Sarkisiants).[26] Particularly successful as a secret agent was Fikus, who had been a party member for over a decade, had become a member of the Balakhany Committee of the local party organization, and operated under the passport of David Bakradze, a revolutionary socialist killed by his own bomb while working in Persia. He turned over whatever information he had on the Social Democrats for payments that ranged from 35 rubles a month to as high as 70 to 80 for "special services."[27] But the party also had sympathizers within the ranks of the police.

Suspicion and uncertainty were imbedded in the culture of the underground. Anyone might be picked up at any moment. Koba was usually extremely careful. He avoided his earlier missteps. He took notes on a little pad at meetings; then he destroyed the pad. He never carried documents with him and never stayed overnight in the same part of the city where meetings were held.[28] When Alesha Japaridze quietly visited his wife in Baku, Koba and Orjonikidze dropped in to see their comrade on October 12, 1909. Suddenly the police arrived to arrest Japaridze. When the officer discovered the other men, he stationed guards at the front and rear doors and went off to telephone for authority to arrest all three. A 10-ruble note and a request to go and buy cigarettes was enough to convince one of the guards to leave his post, and Koba and Orjonikidze slipped away.[29]

As possibilities for socialist propaganda and even trade unionist work dried up in late 1908–1909, the Social Democrats resorted to "cultural" activity. The Menshevik newspaper declared: "In Baku there is no cultural life, almost no social organizations and institutions carrying on the fight with the terrifying backwardness of the broad masses of the population."[30] Mensheviks and Bolsheviks set up separate workers' clubs and reading rooms were set up. The lectures and libraries proved popular.[31] Koba performed in a play at the People's House in December 1907.[32] A few years later the Bolsheviks decided to present two plays to make money: Gorky's didactic *Children of the Sun*, in which the author had hoped to throw a bridge across the "deep abyss between the intelligentsia and the proletariat," played to half a house.[33] The thespian revolutionaries had more success with a later production of Aleksandr Ostrovskii's *The Guilty without Guilt*, a social melodrama with sudden turns of fate.[34] Social Democrats organized a campaign directed against alcoholism, the scourge of the working class.[35] "Drunkenness is a social ailment created by capitalism," read a Bolshevik resolution.[36] Even Koba spoke favorably of the fight against alcohol and saw the congress "as a means of agitating for the democratic and socialist demands of the proletariat."[37] The struggle for *kultura*—in the various meanings of "culture:" art, knowledge, and more refined behavior—along with the severely curtailed economic and political campaigns were the "fronts" on which the remaining Social Democrats determined to fight.

The strains of illegality, combined with the frustrations of ineffectuality, tore at the party regulars. Koba was involved in one dispute after another with erstwhile comrades. The Central Committee had sent 150 rubles to a party member, Sergei Seldiakov, who used the *klichka* "Kuzma," but insulted by several members of the Baku Committee he refused to turn over the money. Koba requested the funds several times, but the fiery-tempered Kuzma refused, "evidently not trusting Koba."[38] On March 16 the Baku Committee met to resolve the issue. Koba and

Kuzma each accused the other of *provokatorstvo* (being a police spy). This was an extraordinarily serious accusation since the organization had already decided that agent provocateurs were to be executed. Nothing came of the altercation, however, and the money was finally surrendered to Shahumian.[39] A year later Kuzma left the movement and immigrated to the United States.

The Mensheviks were in as much, if not more, disarray as the Bolsheviks, divided along the same lines of fracture as their émigré leaders. Within Russia their organizations and activists melted away. Fedor Dan reported to Akselrod at the end of 1907, "Menshevism as an organization simply does not now exist in Russia."[40] Even in Georgia where Mensheviks remained the dominant political movement, their faithful fell silent or went underground. The only voices that the broader public heard in the stillness were the Social Democratic deputies in the Third and Fourth State Dumas. From abroad Akselrod advocated a moderate course for the faction that was somewhat similar to Koba's: unity with open airing of ideological and tactical differences. But his close friend and collaborator, Martov, was embittered by the Bolsheviks' use of armed bands, in particular the Tiflis "ex." When he took the fight to them in the fierce denunciatory pamphlet *Saviors or Destroyers?* (1911), even the leading German Social Democrat, Karl Kautsky, who had been asked to arbitrate the split in the Russian party, denounced it as a "detestable brochure," a "senseless ... unearthing of mistakes of the past." Not Lenin, he wrote, but Martov should be censured for dividing the party.[41]

"Exes" were merely the most egregious illegal activity of the underground party. In the years of "reaction" Mensheviks became intolerant of the old practices of the illegal party organizations and emphasized the primacy of the legal institutions. At the contentious fifth conference of the Russian Social Democrats, held in Paris in January 1909, Lenin condemned this approach as "liquidationist." The Bolshevik resolution was adopted: to strengthen the RSDRP in the form it had built up during the revolutionary epoch; to maintain the traditions of its unfaltering struggle; to fight against deviations from revolutionary Marxism and against attempts, revealed among certain elements of the Party who had fallen under the influence of disintegration, to whittle down the party's slogans and to liquidate its illegal organizations. At the same time, it went on, party functions should steadily be transferred to Social Democratic workers themselves. The leading Menshevik representatives at the conference—Dan, Akselrod, and Noe Ramishvili—all with mandates from the Menshevik Transcaucasian Regional Committee protested that the conference did not adequately represent the party and aired their objections in a pamphlet issued in Geneva.[42] The conference accepted the Bolshevik resolution to call a party congress—one that would never be held in the form intended. *Sotsial-Demokrat* was declared the official organ of the whole party, and its editorial board included Lenin, Zinoviev, Kamenev, Martov, and the Polish Bolshevik Julian Marchlewski (1866–1925). Lenin's wife, Krupskaia, later wrote, "I remember Ilyich once remarking with satisfaction that it was good to work with Martov, as he was an exceedingly gifted journalist." But, she went on, "that was only until Dan arrived."[43]

Fedor Dan was a brilliant thinker, who along with Potresov expressed most forcefully the venerable Menshevik suspicion of the intellectual-dominated illegal party organizations. Married to Martov's sister, Lidia, Dan and his wife both in 1905 and again in 1917 lived in the big Tsederbaum apartment in Petersburg together with her siblings, but Dan and Martov, both strong personalities with firm views, often disagreed and fought fiercely with one another.[44] Early in 1910 Dan advocated using the traditional illegal activity to support the development of all legal institutions—the duma, courts, local governments, and the press. Lenin turned this tactic around and answered, "For Social Democrats the *legal* rallying [of the workers] is at the present moment one of the necessary weapons of the *illegal* party."[45] While he supported the legal labor movement, Lenin wanted it to be directed by the underground organizations. Only in this way could the revolutionary potential of the workers' movement be preserved against the ever-present danger of reformism. The target of Lenin's accusation, Potresov, rejected the label *likvidator* and stated that liquidationism was a "phantom of a morbid imagination" since the Russian Social Democratic party as "an integral and organized hierarchy of institutions" had already disintegrated."[46]

Old alliances were transformed by the liquidationist controversy. In February 1910 the old man of the party, Plekhanov, dramatically broke both with those he labeled "liquidators," as well as with those Mensheviks who refused to denounce them, like Martov and Akselrod, and allied uneasily with Lenin as a self-proclaimed "Menshevik-partyite" [Men'shevik-partiiets]. Most Menshevik leaders abroad never gave up on the underground organizations. But they saw them as aids and supports for the legal labor movement, not as the controlling agents. Akselrod and Martov were cautious in attacking the illegal party organizations though they both hoped to eliminate the elitist policies of the past by promoting legal work and "Europeanizing" the Russian party.[47] As Martov told the Georgian Menshevik Grigol Uratadze: "Yes, I am a liquidator! But not a liquidator of the Social Democratic party, not of the illegal organizations, but a liquidator of the Leninist bandit organizations and methods. And as long as we don't achieve this we will not have a real party or real organizations."[48]

Caucasian Bolsheviks remained close to Lenin on these tactical and organizational questions.[49] Through the fall of 1909, Koba moved between Baku and Tiflis, visiting close friends in Georgia, his conspiratorial apartment guarded by his faithful.[50] The local Bolsheviks organized a citywide conference of faction members to be held on the funicular on Mtatsminda, the mountain that rises in the center of the city. But when Koba and his comrade, Ilarion Mgeladze, approached, they saw the place surrounded by shpiki (police spies). Koba immediately went into hiding, and the conference was postponed a few days. When it reconvened in a worker's apartment, Koba was not present.[51]

Koba's desire for party unity was widely shared by his fellow Social Democrats. To bring the various factions back under a single leadership and organize another party conference to that end, a long plenary meeting of the party's Central Committee was held in Paris just after New Year, from January 2 (15) to 23 (February 5), 1910. For some attending, the plenum was an effort to rein in Lenin and reduce the influence of the bickering émigrés over the party inside Russia. Many of the party's "generals" attended: Lenin, Zinoviev, Kamenev, Bogdanov among the Bolsheviks; Martov, Zhordania, Noe Ramishvili from the Mensheviks;

and Trotskii, who considered himself outside of any faction. The question arose whether to include in the conference Social Democrats who worked in legal institutions but were not attached to a party group. A leaflet written by Koba before the plenum had supported Lenin's view that only *partiinye*, those connected to a party committee, should be invited.[52] On this issue Lenin and Zinoviev were defeated, and the more conciliatory Bolsheviks, like Dubrovinskii, prevailed. The plenum decided to throw out a broad net and invite those in the legal movement who were ready to establish firm organizational ties with local party centers.

Feelings still ran hot over the money taken in the Tiflis expropriation and from the so-called Schmidt inheritance, a considerable sum of money left to the Bolsheviks by Nikolai and Elizabeth Schmidt. The plenum decided to transfer the Schmidt funds to the Central Committee and German Social Democratic trustees, and to burn the Tiflis money. The plenum allowed the Russian-based members of the Central Committee to act on their own without sanction of the members abroad and ordered that factional centers, like the Bolshevik Center, were to be abolished. The factional newspapers—*Golos sotsial-demokrata* and *Proletarii*—were closed down, and as had been agreed a year earlier *Sotsial-Demokrat* was authorized as the single central party newspaper. Mensheviks wanted the editorial board to be "neutral" and insisted that a nonfactional person, either a Bundist or Trotsky, be appointed. But Lenin, who had a 4–1 majority on the board (three Bolsheviks and one Polish Social Democrat against Martov), proclaimed that if the old board were not kept, the Bolsheviks would leave and keep their factional newspaper. By one vote the plenum upheld Lenin.[53]

The efforts to bring the factions together were heroic but proved to be short-lived. With political activity outside the duma evaporating, and the labor movement becalmed, Lenin was particularly agitated and intemperate. By October 1910 he had launched a new Bolshevik newspaper, *Rabochaia gazeta* (Workers' Paper), and renewed the squabbles over the Schmidt money. He polemicized furiously through the next two years against Trotsky and his nonfactional attempts to bridge the chasm between Bolsheviks and Mensheviks. After a decade of infighting over the nature of the party, he was moving steadily toward the idea of creating a separate Bolshevik party. The problem, however, was that many of his close associates held far more conciliatory views toward dissident Bolsheviks, Mensheviks, and even *likvidatory*.

BAKU, BOGDAN KNUNIANTS, AND LIQUIDATIONISM

Disenchanted with the Social Democratic practices of the past, Baku workers were potentially fertile ground for the trade unionism and democratic inclinations of the *likvidatory*. Yet *likvidatorstvo* in Baku was a movement of generals without an army. Trade union *praktiki* with considerable reputation worked in the city—men like Larin, Sergei Ezhov (Martov's brother), and D. Koltsov—but with little palpable effect on the workers in the oil districts, where the Bolsheviks were entrenched. The liquidationist critique of party practice, however, touched a sensitive nerve, and the pain was felt by those who had spent the last decade in the underground. One of the most gifted of the *likvidatory* was a former underground man and one-time Bolshevik, the Armenian Bogdan Knuniants, a veteran of both the Caucasian movement and the revolutionary days in Saint Petersburg.[54] He had startled Lenin in 1905 by proposing that Social Democrats should work exclusively in party organizations rather than join the newly formed soviets. Just as Lenin was advocating greater support of the workers' own initiatives, Knuniants was ultra-Leninist, promoting party *intelligenty* over workers. Now he had moved to the opposite extreme, banking completely on the legal labor movement.

Before his early death Knuniants chronicled his odyssey from Bolshevism to *likvidatorstvo*. His posthumous account reveals the doubts shared by many Social Democrats in the wake of the aborted revolution and provides an alternative trajectory to that followed by Koba. He began plaintively to note, "By our world view we were a party of the working class, but by our composition almost exclusively an organization of the socialist intelligentsia. By our goals we were a class, socialist organization; in line with Russian life we became the ideological force of the bourgeois revolution in the absence of bourgeois political organizations. By our organizational plans we were a mass, democratic party given our tasks; in fact, by necessity we turned into an organization of conspiratorial circles, led by special cadres of professional revolutionaries recruited from the ranks of the radical intelligentsia. We strove for organized class warfare but were forced to carry on all work in the underground, outside the structured class organizations that we were not strong enough to build."[55]

Knuniants argued that before 1905 the Bolsheviks represented the party *stikhii* (elements), the actual people engaged in the revolutionary movement, while the Mensheviks were the upholders of Marxist thought. Ideologically Bolsheviks developed under Menshevik influence, but in practice Mensheviks acted *po-bol'shevistski* ("in a Bolshevik manner"). The year 1905 represented a break with the party's past, according to Knuniants. In that year the Bolsheviks developed their own ideology out of party practice: the theory of the democratic revolution replaced that of the bourgeois revolution. Bolsheviks, said Knuniants, moved away from Menshevik theory (and Marxism) but closer to Menshevik practice, for now they came out from underground and engaged in legal activities. Still Bolsheviks tended to be patriotic in their attitudes toward the old party organizations and resisted attempts to liquidate them. Knuniants concluded his first article with the claim that *likvidatorstvo* was an effort to bring Marxist theory (the notion of the coming bourgeois revolution) in line with Marxist practice (work toward creating a self-conscious working class).[56]

Knuniants' critique of Social Democratic practice was an indictment particularly of old-line Bolshevism. Like the other *likvidatory* he had concluded from practice that a party in which most of the work was done by intellectuals could not give the workers the self-confidence and self-sufficiency that they needed in order to develop a mass labor movement. As someone who had experienced working in the underground and had been in some ways more "Leninist" than Lenin, he provided insight into the mentality of someone like Koba:

The stupidest school for the education of a social activist is the conspiratorial organization. The weak development of a feeling of responsibility, the inability to deal with the public opinion of that milieu in which one must act, the exaggeration of the role of personality, not being used to constant control—all these are the products of the underground from which the great majority of us are not free. . . . The new workers' organizations, we repeat, are a good school for us intellectuals.[57]

Lenin's *What Is to Be Done?*, once the "gospel of all *praktiki*," had, according to Knuniants, turned the party not into a workers' party but into an organization of professional revolutionaries.[58] After the 1905 revolution the workers realized that their earlier exaggerated faith in the party had been misplaced and that they had to rely on their own powers. Therefore workers left the party: "By 1909 we already see our old organizations almost liquidated." Experience has demonstrated, concluded Knuniants, that in order to overcome the current crisis the Social Democrats must now build a party from below, not a new organization of professional revolutionaries centralized and directed from above, but an organization to aid the proletariat "in the difficult task of creating local organizations, a local press, with new activist cadres from the workers themselves."[59]

As can be seen from Knuniants's writings, *likvidatorstvo* was not so much an attack on the party and political activity in general (as it was often portrayed by its opponents) but rather a specific attack on the underground party led by professional revolutionaries. In Knuniants's words: "'Liquidators' (incidentally the title is completely absurd but is justified in relation to the old organization) do not liquidate the political organization of the proletariat altogether, do not deny the necessity for such an organization; they are critical only of the old roads traveled by the party and point out new ones."[60] The *likvidatory* were not denying the need for a political organization, but they held that a new party, legal and open, must be given priority over the illegal, conspiratorial party of the past. Their instincts reflected the grassroots democratic and participatory dynamics that had long inspired Menshevism.

Lenin, on the other hand, perceived an acute danger in too sharp a shift toward legality, and although he too wished to exploit all possibilities, legal and illegal, he firmly believed that in the tsarist police state the only revolutionary road toward the defeat of autocracy lay underground. Typically he exaggerated the dangerous implications of his opponents' tactics. To him the *likvidatory* seemed headed toward exclusively legal activity—that is, eventually to Economism, reformism, and the abandonment of the revolutionary struggle. Wary of where such views would lead the party, Lenin polemically linked the *likvidatory* to Mensheviks of various stripes and further to the "revisionists" and "opportunists" of West European socialist parties. Leading Mensheviks, however, were also aware of such danger. Martov wrote to Potresov on June 17, 1909: "Great care must be taken not to slip into a real 'liquidationism' of all elements of politics, and consequently of party-mindedness."[61]

As powerful as Knuniants' indictment of old party practices was, the liquidationist critique of party practice seemed extreme to many party members and even to those workers who had already spent nearly a decade working closely with the underground organization. Besides their lingering loyalty to Social Democracy, and despite their suspicion of intellectuals, workers could also see that their own local Bolsheviks were increasingly willing to engage in legal activity. Closer to the ground in industrial cities like Baku, workers were not nearly as divided as the party intellectuals were in Geneva or Capri. All kinds of socialists worked together, although the unorthodox insistence of the *likvidatory* on avoiding underground work led the Bolsheviks and their sympathizers to exclude them when the Baku organizations of Bolsheviks and Mensheviks merged in February 1911. Divided since 1907, the Bolshevik Committee and the Menshevik Leading Collective united on a platform that reasserted the traditional reliance on the illegal organization and the necessity of a struggle against the *likvidatory*. Each factional committee continued their separate existences, while a Central Committee of nine Bolsheviks and seven Mensheviks and an Executive Committee of five were to direct the party in Baku. The Bolsheviks, who made up a majority of the united organization, fell in general into the category of Leninists. There were no *Vperedisty* (followers of Bogdanov), and the few Bolshevik "conciliationists," who insisted that all factions unite, had to succumb to the will of the majority.[62]

For all their dedication to legal trade unions, the *likvidatory* in Baku were not able to dominate them or even win much of a following. With party unity partially achieved, it was not long before the two oil workers' unions, which had been negotiating for years, decided to merge. This was a defeat for the local *likvidatory*, who had consistently opposed joining with the Bolshevik union. With their merger and their renewed interest in legal activities, the "party" Social Democrats reasserted their traditional leadership over what was now a moribund labor movement.

The confirmation of the primacy of the party was clearly a victory for the staunchest party men, local Bolsheviks like Koba. Their attention turned now to the sticky problem of which socialist tendencies would be tolerated within the newly united organization. From its beginnings Russian Social Democracy had been a fissiparous movement. Repeated efforts to achieve greater unity and orthodoxy had consistently meant exclusion of those who would not conform. This time many Mensheviks, rejecting the reformist liquidationist tendency, were forced to adopt an essentially Bolshevik position putting the party above unions and to join the Bolshevik-dominated underground. The Bolsheviks by joining with some of the Mensheviks increased their influence in the fragile legal labor organizations, while the *likvidatory*, faced by a common front of Social Democrats, soon lost their tenuous hold on labor allegiances.

The experience of the Social Democrats of Baku demonstrated that in post-1907 Russia the maintenance of an underground party organization was an advantage, indeed an absolute necessity, for those working in the labor movement. Continuity and preservation of cadres were possible only with support from an illegal organization. For Mensheviks as well as Bolsheviks the last refuge in the face of the continuing governmental repression was the party underground. The *likvidatory*, on the other hand, tended to neglect the party and politics only to find that in a period of "reaction" the independence and initiative of workers necessary to form vital trade unions had been subdued by fear. Those socialists who tried to work in the legal labor movement were victims of the same harassment from the government as the revolutionaries concealed in the underground. But they were more exposed to the police because of their open activity. *Likvidatorstvo* remained an idea whose time had not come. A West European style of labor movement proved impossible in Baku, indeed in Russia more generally, not only because of the radical intelligentsia's traditions of the underground party but primarily because the workers themselves were economically too vulnerable and politically insecure. The tsarist government and most industrialists were not prepared to negotiate and compromise with an independent, organized workers' movement. If the *likvidatory* hoped all this would change with the industrial growth and labor activity already under way in 1912, they were to be bitterly disappointed.

When the labor movement revived in the years before World War I, it was the Leninists, not the *likvidatory*, who benefited. The underground had provided a place of retreat for the loyal remnants of Social Democratic practice. They would emerge in 1913 and 1914 to find in the prolonged economic struggles that mass base and eventually the political significance in the labor movement that earlier they had looked for in vain. Ultimately, however, the differences among party members proved greater than what the factions held in common. Within a few years Bolsheviks and Mensheviks would split decisively, and two opposing parties, still contending for the support of workers, ran parallel to one another into the coming years of war and revolution.

Koba's experience with the labor movement was not encouraging. Efforts to expand the legal labor movement during the "reaction" had proved impossible. No tactic seemed to work: neither acting as the self-defense units for besieged workers; nor emphasizing the legal labor movement and negotiation with the oil industry; nor retreat into cultural activities. Any success the open labor movement might have enjoyed was hostage to the willingness of capital and government to negotiate. The industrialists in their recalcitrance toward the unions made it difficult for the Social Democrats to demonstrate the effectiveness of collective bargaining as an alternative to more militant tactics. In general few workers were impressed by the benefits of legal and moderate action. Failures to make gains legally undermined the liquidators. Their thunder was stolen by party Social Democrats who, realizing their own losses due to neglect of legal activity and high-handed treatment of workers, rallied around a strategy based on both legal efforts and preservation of the illegal underground. Bolsheviks were frustrated, but they learned from experience. The workers had made it abundantly clear that they would no longer tolerate being subordinated to the political interests of the intelligentsia. Even a *komitetchik* like Koba got the message and came out for more worker participation within the party and the exploitation of legal possibilities.

WHAT KIND OF REVOLUTION? KOBA'S DEBATE WITH ZHORDANIA

Just before his arrest in March 1910 Koba sent off a "Letter from the Caucasus" that was published abroad in the central party journal. Koba took on his old rival, Zhordania, whom he accused of ideological and tactical liquidationism. Zhordania had made the standard Menshevik argument that neither the proletariat nor the liberal bourgeoisie by itself could achieve the democratic revolution in Russia. But he boldly rejected the venerated formula of Plekhanov that "the revolution would be victorious in Russia as a workers' movement or would not be victorious at all." Now workers had to wait for the middle bourgeoisie to become politically mature. Until then they had to be satisfied with a very moderate program, one that would be acceptable to the liberals, not one that would drive them into the arms of the reactionaries.[63] He defended the action of the workers in December 1905 as appropriate for that moment, but argued that the situation had changed with the turn toward reaction. Banking on the liberal bourgeoisie, Zhordania believed that the peasants remained unreliable and not one of the two principal forces of the revolution. Koba scorned this moderate strategy: "In a word, instead of the leading role of the proletariat leading the peasants, [we are given] the leading role of the Kadet bourgeoisie leading the proletariat by the nose." This he called "cheap liberal junk."[64]

Zhordania did not leave Koba's attack unanswered. He retorted that Koba had misunderstood his principal point, repeatedly distorted his words and their meaning, and mixed truth with lies. By personally taking on Koba, the revered patriarch of the Georgian Social Democrats acknowledged, perhaps unwittingly, the acquired stature of his younger opponent. Zhordania dismissed as utopian Koba's notion that the proletariat could lead the bourgeois revolution or realize its minimum program—for example, the eight-hour day—in the conditions of Russia's bourgeois revolution. The proletariat was unable to play the role of hegemon in the liberation struggle that it had played before. If it tried to "deviate from its historical path" the proletariat in a bourgeois revolution would eventually take "state power into its own hands." It would then try to use that power to advance its class interests, not the interests of its enemy, the bourgeoisie. This would mean social revolution, proletarian revolution, which Zhordania was convinced was not on the historic agenda.

Yet, he went on, "this does not mean that [the proletariat] in the future movement ought to become the tail of the bourgeoisie. . . . Without the proletariat the bourgeoisie cannot establish a new order. The struggle of the bourgeoisie or the proletariat alone cannot destroy the reaction." Opposed to Lenin's notion of a dictatorship of the proletariat and peasant (or leaning on the peasantry) in the bourgeois revolution, Zhordania wrote, "We continue to think that it is impossible to establish a bourgeois political order without or against the will of the bourgeoisie." Now was not the time for revolutionary manifestations but for class education and organization of the proletariat. "Of all the accusations of liquidation put forth in the 'Letter' against the author of the Georgian articles," he wrote, "only one is true—this is the liquidation of the idea of the hegemony of the proletariat in the liberation movement now and in the future." He ended with a brusque dismissal of his opponent. "Of course, from all that I have laid out above, it is clear that the 'Letter from the Caucasus' presents itself as a lampoon relying on people not knowing the Georgian language and the criticized article. This is one of those unscrupulous factional ways of fighting, which often were used earlier in localities and which now they want to bring onto the pages of the party press."[65]

Indeed, Koba's charge that Zhordania was guilty of liquidationism was pure demagogy and did not fit the dispute about which class would lead the bourgeois revolution. The accusations thrown back and forth were—in the words of a resolution of the Georgian Social Democrats— "to a significant degree exaggerated, being in general the fruit of the current period of social stagnation."[66] In fact, the Georgian Mensheviks were never advocates of liquidating the underground party. From his perch in Paris, Lenin often contrasted the Georgian with the Russian Mensheviks. Uratadze, who attended Lenin's lectures at the Longjumeau party school outside Paris in 1911, recalled that Lenin repeatedly commented that it was "surprising that the Georgian Mensheviks support Akselrod and Martov and not me! What is there in common between the Georgian Mensheviks and our ... Mensheviks? The Georgian Mensheviks, like us, firmly defend the illegal organizations, but our Mensheviks abolish them everywhere. Nevertheless, at the congresses [the Georgians] always support the liquidators.'"[67] Uratadze retorted, "in Georgia the local Bolsheviks say that one can tolerate Russian Mensheviks but that the Georgian Mensheviks are irredeemable opportunists, liquidators, and nationalists." "Is it true that they say that?" Lenin asked and loudly burst out laughing.[68]

The argument between Koba and Zhordania was embedded in the fundamental paradox of the Russian revolution: How could a bourgeois-democratic revolution be carried out in a country in which the bourgeoisie was so weak and so many of its elements tied to autocracy? And what would the workers and Social Democracy, a far more potent and massive political force, do in that revolution? Plekhanov himself entered the fray and, without knowing who Koba was, sided with the author of the "Letter from the Caucasus" and against Zhordania's revision of his cherished strategy. Instead of Social Democrats holding back the proletariat because it might frighten the liberal bourgeoisie, Plekhanov suggested that the Kadets would be less cowardly and indecisive if the revolutionary movement were as strong as possible, something that is only possible under the leadership of the proletariat.[69] At this moment Koba, an obscure provincial party activist, was being taken seriously by the older generation of party leaders. He was emerging from his Caucasian chrysalis.

The paradoxical role of workers in a bourgeois revolution would be resolved only in 1917 when Russian Mensheviks, to their detriment, held to the orthodoxy of the bourgeois revolution led by the bourgeoisie and the Bolsheviks ran ahead, secured the support of radicalized workers, and moved beyond the limits of the democratic revolution—only to find themselves stranded in a land hardly prepared for their vision of socialism. Ironically, the Georgian Mensheviks, whom Zhordania in 1910 warned against taking power in a "bourgeois revolution," reluctantly did precisely that in Tiflis in the revolution of 1917–1918.[70] They were able to establish in independent Georgia a relatively democratic government that resisted moving beyond capitalism to socialism and managed to last almost three years before the Red Army invaded Georgia and ended the Menshevik experiment. The principal masterminds behind that invasion were two Georgian Bolsheviks: Sergo Orjonikidze and Joseph Stalin.

On March 23, 1910, the very day that the Baku Committee issued the leaflet written by Koba celebrating August Bebel, the German worker who had risen to become a leading Social Democratic party leader and parliamentarian, the police arrested a man carrying a passport identifying him as Zakharii Grigorian-Melikiants.[71] Even though they found nothing incriminating on their prisoner, the police knew they had caught the elusive Jughashvili—the one that they referred to as "Molochnyi" (Milky).[72] That same day they also picked up Stefaniia Petrovskaia, with whom he had been living. Back in Bailov prison, both he and Petrovskaia were questioned three days later. Koba tried to weave an alibi:

I do not consider myself to belong to any political parties. I have lived in Baku about six months. I lived here without official registration. I slept where I could. My situation was quite unstable. I tried to find some kind of place but found nothing. . . . In Baku I bought from a person unknown to me a passport booklet without an expiration date that had been issued by the Baku police chief to Zakharii Krikorov Melikiants, but I did not live on that passport but lived without registration. The letter in Russian taken from me during the search addressed to Petrovskaia was given to me by a woman, and I did not have time to give it to Petrovskaia. I became acquainted with Stefaniia Leandrovna Petrovskaia while I was in exile in the town of Solvychegodsk in Vologda Province. . . . I did not live in the fortress in building no. 495, and I never had a passport with the name Oganes Vartanov Totomiants. I have never lived with Petrovskaia and was not cohabiting with her.[73]

Petrovskaia also denied having anything to do with the revolutionary movement or having any intimate connections to the other prisoner.[74]

Koba's comrades decided to try to have him moved from the common cell to a prison hospital, where he would receive better treatment. They took phlegm from a patient named Goriachev, who was ill with third-degree tuberculosis, and passed it off as Koba's. The doctor, Nesterov, was a drunkard and known as someone easily bribed. They paid for a diagnosis of third-stage tuberculosis, and Koba was moved to the hospital. Cavalry captain Fedor Gelimbatovskii, who had taken over as head of the Baku gendarmes, ordered that Petrovskaia be freed but that Jughashvili be given a more severe sentence: five years in the most distant part of Siberia. When he heard about the new sentence, Koba petitioned for leniency. Pleading that he was suffering from tuberculosis and was lying in the hospital, he ended by asking "your highness to allow me to enter into lawful matrimony with the inhabitant of Baku, Stefaniia Leandrovna Petrovskaia." In a second petition he spoke of Petrovskaia as "my wife." Koba's plea worked, and his sentence was reduced to the completion of his term of exile in Vologda and five years prohibition from living in the Caucasus. But the very day that the permission was granted for his marriage (September 23, 1910), Koba was taken from Baku prison and sent off to exile.[75]

Koba's marriage never took place. Petrovskaia eventually returned to Baku, and Koba pleaded with her to join him in Siberia. She refused, and he sent her postcards cursing her. Instead she married a Menshevik named Levine with whom she had a daughter named Rima. She worked with Shahumian on the legal Baku newspaper *Nasha zhizn'* (Our Life).

After the October Revolution Petrovskaia met with Stalin, evidently to renew their romance, but nothing came of it. She died shortly afterward in Moscow.[76] Koba had moved on. From fall 1910 when he left Baku, he never returned to full-time work in Caucasia. His prospects at that moment of defeat seemed dim, but as it turned out this exile led him ultimately to central Russia and to the vortex of Social Democratic activity. In the last years before world war and revolution, the cobbler's son from Gori had become a "master worker" for the revolution.

FROM OUTSIDE IN

21

THE ROVING AGENT

"Do you believe in Fate?" I asked.

He became very serious. He turned to me and looked me straight in the face. Then after a tense pause, he said: "No, I do not believe in Fate. That is simply a prejudice. It is a nonsensical idea." He laughed in his dark muffled way and said in German, "*Schicksal* [Fate], *Schicksal. . . .*"

"You have been through a hundred dangers," I said, "when you were banned and exiled, in revolutions and in wars. Is it merely an accident that you were not killed and that someone else is not in your place today?"

He was somewhat annoyed, but only for a moment. Then he said, in a clear, ringing voice:

"No accident. Probably there were inner and outer causes that prevented my death. But it could have happened by accident that someone else might be sitting here and not I. . . . Fate is contrary to law. It is something mystic. In this mystical thing I do not believe. Of course there were causes why I came through all these dangers. It could not have happened merely by accident."

—EMIL LUDWIG, *STALIN* (1942; BASED ON HIS
INTERVIEW WITH STALIN, 1931)

What for the radicals of the Left were years of "reaction," for more moderate elements in the country, and for the government of Stolypin, was a half-decade of reform. The prime minister maneuvered between the reactionary Right in the duma that hoped against hope for a return to the absolutism pre-1905, and the liberals and socialists who were calling for a government responsible to the duma or, even more militantly, for a democratic republic. Tsarist Russia remained, despite Stolypin's ambitions, a society where birth conveyed privilege and disadvantage, a world of social estates and institutionalized legal restrictions that rewarded the well-born and burdened those like Koba who were the offspring of peasants, workers, or non-Russians. In the first two decades of the twentieth century, increasing numbers of the tsar's subjects no longer were willing to accept the daily indignities of social discrimination, the inequities that birth and rank, property and propertyless-ness, determined. They no longer would acquiesce in being shut out of political decisions that affected their lives. With the regime compelled to resort to repression in order to hold the fragile polity together, the public mood darkened. A social glum comingled with personal disillusionment, even despair, gripped people at all levels of society. Pessimism, melancholy, and the untranslatable sorrow of the Russian word *toska* were repeatedly expressed in the press, art, poems, and novels. To many toward whom it was directed, the forced optimism about the future in Social Democratic exhortations sounded hollow.[1]

Stolypin in retrospect looms as a towering figure—the last chance for tsarism to find a path to survival in modern times. But his program was deeply contradictory. It sought to end the estate system and turn communal peasants into self-reliant farmers yet preserve the privileged position of the landholding nobility; to reduce restrictions on Jews and other religious groups but maintain the special role of the Orthodox Church that disdained, even vilified, those of other faiths; and to institute certain rights for Russia's "citizens" while driving labor organizations underground, closing down the critical press, and repressing radical expression. In the wake of the revolution, as the diverse non-Russian peoples of the empire's peripheries demanded recognition of their cultural and even political distinctiveness, Stolypin and his government, along with the majority in the duma, had not only moved to the Right but further toward Great Russian imperialism. Stolypin told the Third Duma, "The Russian Empire owes its origin and development to its Russian roots, and with its growth grew and also developed the autocratic power of the Tsars. To this Russian stem no foreign and alien flower may be grafted [cheers from the Center and Right]. Let our

Russian flower bloom on it."[2] To the Polish Kolo party, which advocated autonomy for Poland, he advised,

> Take our point of view, and acknowledge that the greatest blessing consists in being a citizen of Russia; hold up that emblem as high as it was held by the citizens of Rome and you will then style yourselves citizens of the superior kind, and will receive all manner of rights. . . . These are words which have caused the hearts of Russians to beat for centuries past: . . . undeviating loyalty to Russian historical traditions. These words form a counterpoise to Socialism, and magnify the country in opposition to those who desire its disruption, and finally they express loyalty to the death to [our] Tsar, who personifies Russia.[3]

After crushing rebels in Georgia, the Baltic region, Poland, and elsewhere, he and the emperor curtailed the long-standing political autonomy of the Grand Duchy of Finland in 1909–1910. The empire was to be a unitary state.

Empire and the nationalisms of non-Russians faced off against one another, and politicians of all stripes turned their attention to the "national question." The Right pushed for enhancing the position of "true Russians," while the Left debated possible solutions for maintaining a multinational state in an age of fissiparous nationalisms. The Menshevik duma deputy Evgeni Gegechkori spoke out in defense of the Georgian Orthodox Church, which, he said, had suffered for a century under Russian dominance and in favor of cultural and linguistic rights for Georgians. "In Georgia, in our homeland, they pass judgment in courts through translators; in schools they drive out the Georgian language and instruction takes place by the so-called natural method, once again through translators; and now holy rites and funerals will be carried out also with the help of translators."[4] But the government did not heed its non-Russian critics, or even the tsar's own Viceroy in the Caucasus, who repeatedly called for improving the treatment of the peoples he governed.[5]

Stolypin weakened his own position when he tried in early 1911 to pass the Western *Zemstvo* Act, which would have provided local

representational institutions in a region in which Polish landlords dominated socially and Russians were few in number. His usual allies broke
with him—first when he tried to substitute a national principle (defining electors by nationality to favor the Russians) for the estate principal
(defining electors by social estate to favor the nobility and therefore the
Poles), and later when he prorogued the duma for a few days in order
to implement the law. By this brazen flaunting of the constitution, the
prime minister lost the support of most of his political supporters. On
September 1 (14), 1911, in the presence of the tsar and his family, an
unstable Socialist Revolutionary who doubled as a police agent assassinated Prime Minister Stolypin in the Kiev Opera House. Imperial
Russia had lost its most effective politician and its last competent ministry. In the years left to it the monarchy remained authoritarian if not
absolutist, Russocentric if not Russifying, and defended the noble-
dominated system that it would take another revolution to displace. But
steadily, perceptibly both its social base and the public acceptance of its
legitimacy withered away.

Far from duma debates and court intrigues, after a month's journey beginning September 23, Koba reached Solvychegodsk, back to the place
of exile that he had escaped from just over a year earlier. From that day,
October 29, 1910, until six years and four months later when the February 1917 revolution freed him for good, he would spend all but seven
months in prison and exile. Yet it was in those half-dozen years that he
took on the revolutionary nom de guerre Stalin, was appointed to the
Bolshevik Central Committee, and wrote the book *Marxism and the
National Question*, which brought him to the attention of the broader
radical public. This was also the period when the Bolsheviks and Mensheviks, after years of futile attempts at unity, dissolved into two distinct
political parties even while maintaining a fictional connection to a single Russian Social Democratic Workers' Party.

   In Solvychegodsk Koba lived in the homes of peasant women, Grig-
orova and Maria Kuzakova. Many friends were gone by the time he
arrived. Viacheslav Skriabin, with whom he would work for much of his
life under his revolutionary pseudonym, Molotov, had just left, though

they learned of each other through Semen Surin, a Socialist Revolutionary, then an exile, later a police spy.[6] Surin described Koba as "a Caucasian Lenin"—at least that is how Molotov in his eighties remembered
the letter.[7] A woman with whom Koba would grow quite close, Serafima
Khoroshenina, described life in the town just before his arrival. "They
live poorly in our Solvychegodsk. Even the outdoor natural conditions
are appalling. Such impoverished, poor nature." She spoke disparagingly
of the locals as *meshchane* (petty bourgeois townspeople). "True, the
town is completely *meshchanskii*. Nothing touches the inhabitants;
the locals have learned nothing." Even more cheerless was the life of the
exiles. The "exiles are not alive, they are dead. Each person lives alone
with little interaction with others. When they meet, they have nothing
to talk about. There was once life, a lively life. There were factions and
colonies, there were many circles, but now there is nothing. We only
reminisce about our past life. . . . There are not even any get-togethers,
and the exiles drown their sorrows [*toska*] in wine. I too sometimes take
a drink."[8]

As lonely as he may have been, Koba did not give in to despair. He
immediately made contact with the Bolsheviks abroad, who inquired
about his position on the "damned questions" affecting the party. In a
long letter written on December 31, 1910, Koba laid out his ideas about
creating a center inside Russia for *praktiki*. This was an idea that was
particularly popular among the more conciliatory Bolsheviks like Viktor Nogin, Iosif Dubrovinskii, and Aleksei Rykov, disturbed by the
dominance of the émigrés in Paris.[9] He began with the "warmest greetings to Lenin, Kamenev, and others" and expressed his solidarity with
the alliance of Lenin and Plekhanov that brought all the *partiinye* Social
Democrats together.

> In my opinion the line of the bloc [Lenin-Plekhanov] is the only cor-
> rect one. 1) It, and only it, responds to the actual interests of our work
> in Russia, which demands the consolidation of all really party-
> minded elements; 2) it, and only it, hastens the process of freeing the
> legal organization from the weight of the liquidators, digging a hole
> between worker-Meks [Mensheviks] and the liquidators, scattering

and killing the latter. The struggle for influence in legal organizations is the topic of the day, an essential stage on the road to the resurrection of the party, but the bloc is the only means for the cleansing of such organizations of the trash of *likvidatorstvo*.[10]

He applauded "the hand of Lenin" evident in the planning of the new political bloc. "[H]e is a smart fellow [*muzhik*] and knows what's what [*gde raki zimuiut*, literally "where crabs winter"]. But this does not mean that any bloc is good. The Trotsky bloc (he would say, 'synthesis')—this is a rotten, unprincipled, Manilov-style amalgam of diverse principles, the unhelpful melancholy of an unprincipled person of 'good principles.'"[11] In contrast, the bloc of Lenin-Plekhanov "breathes life because it is deeply principled, based on the unity of views on the ways to resurrect the party."

> But this is a bloc, not a merger, precisely because the Beks [Bolsheviks] need their own faction. It is very possible that in the course of work the Beks will tame the Plekhanovites, but this is only a possibility. To sleep and hope for such an outcome, although it is very likely, is not something in any case we should do. The tighter the Beks work together, the better organized we act, the more chances we will have to tame them. We must, therefore, tirelessly hammer away on all anvils. I shall say nothing about the *Vperedisti*, because they are now of less interest than the Liquidators and the Plekhanovites. If they do wake up one of these days, all to the good, of course; but if not, well, never mind, let them stew in their own juice. That is what I think about things abroad.[12]

For Koba the success of Social Democracy required party unity based on clear, principled positions. Close allies could be brought around, but nothing should be left to chance. It was necessary to "hammer away on all anvils" and avoid linkages with unprincipled people like Trotsky.

He then turned to his own ideas on what should be done with the organizing of work within Russia. Here Koba's views did not conform completely to Lenin's. To head off the liquidators who had already penetrated the legal organizations and even had an underground center in

Russia, Koba proposed setting up a "central Russian group to coordinate the illegal, semi-legal, and legal work, first in the main centers (Saint Petersburg, Moscow, the Urals, the South)." "Call it what you like—the 'Russian section of the CC' or the auxiliary group of the CC—that makes no difference, but such a group is as necessary as air, as bread. At the present time lack of information, loneliness, and isolation reign among party workers in the localities and they are all becoming discouraged. This group could give fresh stimulus to the work and introduce clarity. And that would clear the road for the actual utilization of legal possibilities. And that, in my opinion, will start the revival of the party spirit." He was in favor of a conference of party workers who accepted the decisions of the January 1910 party plenum. "But we must act firmly and relentlessly and not fear reproaches from the Liquidators, Trotskyists, and *Vperedisti*. If the Plekhanovites and Leninists unite on the basis of work in Russia, they can afford to ignore all reproaches, no matter from what quarter they come. That is what I think about work in Russia." He concluded with words about himself. He noted that he had to serve another six months of his sentence, but was ready, "if the need for party workers is really acute" to "get away at once." He did not complain about his situation. "There is a decent crowd here in exile, and it would be a very good thing if they could be supplied with the illegal periodicals."[13]

Koba registered in the home of Kuzakova along with Serafima Khoroshenina, but their "civil marriage" lasted only a few days. On February 23 Khoroshenina was sent to the town of Nikolsk. Her transport occurred so suddenly that she was unable to say goodbye to Koba, and instead left him a postcard. When Koba was searched sometime later, the police found four letters from Khoroshenina in his pockets.[14] Such searches were routine, but intrusive and even frightening to the children of the house.[15]

A minor party activist, Mikhail Golubev, arrived in Solvychegodsk after his arrest in Saint Petersburg and soon befriended Grigorii Korostelev. They were told that a "Iosif Koba" was also exiled there and was very interested in what was going on in Russia. Golubev had already heard of Koba's activity in Baku from Vladimir Bobrovskii with whom he had served a prison term in Baku's Bailov prison in 1905, but "did not expect to meet such a simple and sociable person, as joyful, surprisingly easily and infectiously able to laugh as Comrade Stalin turned out to be. He lived in exile very modestly, even a little bit ascetically. In winter when it was 30 below he paraded around in a summer overcoat and beaver fur hat, sparing himself from the piercing winds only with the help of a hood."[16] They became friends, and Koba confided that he was torn between completing his term of exile or trying, once again, to escape and get back to his party work. He made it clear that rather than go abroad he wanted to work in Saint Petersburg. Korostelev and Golubev tried to convince him to serve out his term so that he could work both legally and illegally. He replied, "For professional revolutionaries there cannot be a legal situation until the revolution itself. In order to be legal, it is necessary to descend to a philistine."[17] This, he felt, was the problem with the so-called liquidators. By limiting themselves almost exclusively to activity permitted by the regime, they had to give up on what the authorities might construe to be revolutionary and threatening to the government.

As radical as Koba was, he, nevertheless, thought seriously that legal status might be an advantage. He fretted over this choice in a letter to Bobrovskii in Moscow. Introducing himself as Soso and reminding him that they had worked together in Tiflis and Baku back in 1904, he asked, "Do you remember Gurgen (the old man, Mikho) [Tskhakaia]. He is now in Geneva and . . . 'is recalling' the SD duma caucus. The old man has gone off his head, devil take him." "Il'ich and company are pressing me to come to one of the two centers without waiting for the end of my term of exile. I would like to serve out my term (being legal would give me more possibilities), but if the need is great (I am waiting for an answer from them), then, of course, I will take off." He admitted that he was "literally suffocating" without work and concluded with a few words about the internal party conflicts.

> You, of course, have heard about the "storm in a glass of water" abroad: the blocs—Lenin-Plekhanov, on one side, and Trotsky-Martov-Bogdanov, on the other. The attitude of workers to the first

bloc, as far as I know, is favorable. But in general workers have begun to look with scorn on those abroad. "Let them climb the walls as much as their souls like, but in our opinion whoever holds the interests of the movement dear should work, and the rest will work itself out." That in my view is for the best.[18]

He expressed the same strong feelings about the internal party bickering in a letter to his fellow exile, the Menshevik Aleksandr Shur. He had no intention, Koba said, to make the goal of his work "barking at *likvidatory* and *Vperedisti*." He would only "mock those people who bark."[19]

The factional center sent seventy rubles to facilitate Koba's escape, but to avoid police surveillance the money went to a student, Aram Ivaniants, then exiled and teaching in Vologda. Koba stayed with him a few days in Vologda, showed him the telegram indicating the money had been sent, but Ivaniants simply denied having received it. Whatever happened to the money can no longer be clarified, but the incident would ultimately come back to haunt Ivaniants. Years later, in the early 1920s, Ivaniants, then a ranking party official in Soviet Armenia, accidently ran into Stalin in Moscow, and the general secretary remembered their encounter. Ivaniants did not recall meeting Stalin in Vologda, though the Tatarinovs who lived there at the time did remember. Stalin wrote an accusation to party officials in the Caucasus, and Ivaniants was expelled from the party. Sometime in the 1930s Ivaniants wrote in desperation to Stalin pleading to be reinstated. Instead, in 1936 Ivaniants and his wife were arrested, and he was executed.[20]

Koba moved in with the exiled Doctor Dorrer for another two weeks. Then, even though he had no funds, he decided to make the journey to Saint Petersburg. The wife of an exiled Bolshevik, Sammer, who worked in the Vologda hospital, made up the paperwork that Koba needed to be admitted for treatment, and from there he was able to get away. At the end of February 1911 he made a brief trip to the capital, where he made contact with Alliluev, who set him up in the bleak room of an electrician named Zabelin. Alliluev had to supply a couple of chairs and a bed for "the comrade in hiding," Zabelin remembered. "One morning, at around ten o'clock, the person in question appeared at my apartment.

He moved in and slept there for two or three nights, then disappeared without a sign." Only much later did he learn whom he had housed.[21] After a week shopping in bookstores and visiting some of his Georgian friends, a somewhat pensive and depressed Koba returned to his place of exile.[22]

There was little to do in Solvychegodsk. Koba paid twenty-five kopecks to visit the local theater. Boredom and loneliness were relieved by a relationship with his landlady, Kuzakova. She later claimed that Koba was the father of her son, but the birth records show the boy was born in 1908, before Koba's arrival.[23] The Bolshevik Aleksandr Smirnov wrote to Koba in September that he had heard the Koba had again married.[24] Under the watchful eyes of the police, about ten exiled Social Democrats met together in one or another's rooms. There they made reports and discussed current politics—the tactics toward the state duma, whether there would be war between Russia and China. Golubev claims that Koba led the group, which included two Mensheviks, Lezhnev and Aleksandr Shur, a student from Kharkov University. Together they read Franz Mehring's three-volume *History of the German Social Democratic Party*.[25] When they tired of politics, they recited poetry or sang. Koba sang both Georgian and Russian songs. They made fun of Lezhnev, a rather handsome and cheerful youth who managed to seduce the Vologda prosecutor's wife. The cuckolded husband then had Lezhnev reclassified as a serious political offender and had him sent farther north, almost to the Arctic Circle. Generally the police tolerated these meetings, but for some reason they picked up Koba at one of them and incarcerated him for three days (June 23–26).[26]

Shur remembered Koba as a "thin, dark-skinned man" in a light black coat and soft black hat" who was kind enough to help him find a place to stay when he first came to town. Koba frequently visited him, sometimes several times a day. Most of Koba's reading was fiction, and he particularly liked reading in Georgian. When the Bolshevik Lunin organized an evening of readings in his rooms, a Dashnak named Khatisov recited his poems. Koba was very critical and "even expressed his opinion that a poet or writer cannot entirely lean on his artistic intuition but must improve himself incessantly. He has to learn a great deal."[27]

On June 27, 1911, Koba's term of exile was completed, and he was allowed on July 6 to move to the provincial capital, Vologda, a small town of twenty-one thousand inhabitants.[28] One of Russia's oldest towns, mentioned in the Novgorod Chronicles of 1147, Vologda was famous for Saint Sophia Cathedral, the Spaso-Prilutskii Monastery, its fine lace, as well as its tasty butter and cheese. The landscape was classic Russian heartland: flat with rivers, lakes, and forests. Under the watchful eye of the police, Koba asked for permission to stay there for two months, since he had no money with which to move. He had been banned from the Caucasus and from living in either of Russia's capitals. He settled first in the home of Bobrova on Malokozlenskaia Street, then with Novozhilova on Kalachnaia Street, and finally from late August in the Beliaeva home on Malo-Ekaterinskaia Street.[29] Koba had eyes for the landlady Maria Bogoslovskaia's daughter, who had recently divorced and brought her three children to live with her mother. Koba and Bogoslovskaia quarreled loudly, and as her servant Sofiia Kriukova testified, "They shouted and were almost at each other's throats. During their rows the names of women could be heard." Koba paid three rubles a month for a room, but the landlady's husband, a retired gendarme, was not happy that his wife rented to a political prisoner, an atheist. Whenever he went into Koba's room to pray before the house icon, he snooped around to see what the exile was reading. Kriukova, herself just a girl, remembered that Koba "liked my dress. Once, after a public holiday, when I returned from the village and went out into the kitchen to the sink, I noticed that Iosif Vissarionovich was watching me from behind the curtain. In those days I had long black hair, and I was wearing an attractive dress with a long skirt made of flowered Japanese cloth. Iosif Vissarionovich told me: 'That dress really suits you. In my home in Georgia girls your age wear dresses just like that.'"[30]

With time on his hands and needing company, he very quickly made contact with young people in town: Petr Chizhikov, a twenty-three-year-old worker known in Social Democratic circles as "Kuznets" [blacksmith]; his young fiancé, Pelegeia (Polia) Onufrieva; the former student and SR Meer Chernov, twenty-nine; the wife of the exiled student Nikolai Tatarinov; and Afroim Beirakh, who was associated with the SRs.[31] He was particularly close to Chizhikov, who worked as a clerk in the fruit store of Ishemiatov. Visiting Chizhikov daily, Koba carried on his party correspondence through him. Together they went every day to the post office to pick up mail. Koba would get it first, and the police noted that they were unable to find out to which address it was being sent or where it came from "because Dzhugashvili is evidently very familiar with the technical side of surveillance and behaves very carefully."[32] While Chizhikov was at work, Koba befriended Onufrieva. They would read quietly together. Polia was somewhat rebellious and had left her home village of Totma to live with Chizhikov. She despised the restrictive customs of the time. "He had a great many friends," Pelegeia Onufrieva, remembered, and he shopped in the stores of the Crimean Tatars and Georgians who sold fruit. "Iosif Vissarionovich, who loved fruit very much, often visited them. I remember that in the row of shops there was a fruit shop called 'Caucasia.' . . . He often called in there and usually left with a bag full of fruit. And then he would offer me some."[33] "In those days, for instance, one was not supposed to eat on the street. This made me uneasy, but . . . in the neighborhood there was a shady avenue bordered with trees. I went there on several occasions with Stalin, who often invited me to walk in that direction with him. Once we sat down on a bench and he offered me some fruit: 'Eat some. No one will see you here.'"[34]

They became quite close, though it was unconventional that an older man and a young girl should spend time together. "I behaved in all simplicity with him," Polia wrote. They talked about Koba's personal experiences, and he spoke about the death of his wife.

He told me how much he had loved her and how hard it was for him to lose her. "I was so overcome with grief," he told me, "that my comrades took my gun away from me. . . . I realized how many things in life we fail to appreciate. While my wife was still alive there were times when I didn't return home from work even at night. I told her when I left not to worry about me. But when I got home I would find her sitting there awake; she would wait up for me all night."[35]

He remembered her exquisite dressmaking. "Despite being a man," Polia said, "Stalin had good taste. . . . He talked a great deal about the southern landscapes, about how good life was there, how beautiful the gardens were and how attractive the buildings. He would often say to me: 'I know you would love it in the south. Come and see it for yourself. I'll give you a letter of recommendation, and you'll be treated as one of the family.'"[36]

As a kind of mentor, Koba lectured Polia on literature. She liked the erotic novel *Sanin* by Mikhail Artsybashev, but Koba told her, "It is not worth wasting your time on such things. . . . There is no merit in Artsybashev's work. He is vulgar."[37] Even as he stretched the rules of acceptable behavior with women, Koba fell back on the more puritanical gender culture of his homeland—long skirts for young girls and restraint on the sexual. When Koba was leaving Vologda, the seventeen-year-old Polia gave him a small cross as a gift and asked for a photograph. He declined to be photographed but reciprocated with a book, Marxist literary critic P. S. Kogan's *Essays on Western European Literature*. As a dedication he wrote: "To intelligent, nasty Polia from oddball [*chudak*] Iosif."[38] His relationship with Polia was probably quite innocent, with her husband part of their *troika*, but it had an erotic tinge to it. His last note to her exists only in Onufrieva's memory. From prison in Saint Petersburg, he wrote: "You know that I traveled to get married, but finally I ended up in prison. However, even now I am not bored. . . . I hope I will be free soon."[39]

Isolated and bored in the provinces, Koba read voraciously, making notes in the books. Other exiles from far away corresponded with him and discussed the restructuring of the party. His reputation was widespread in party circles far beyond the Caucasus. From Vologda Koba immediately contacted the editorial board of the Bolshevik newspaper, *Rabochaia gazeta* (Workers' Newspaper), which Lenin used as the tribune against "the half-anarchist tendency in the party that was called *otzovizm*" and "against the half-liberal tendency that was called *likvidatorstvo*." This newspaper was aimed at "the new generation of worker-Social Democrats" to help them "figure out the complex economic and social questions of the present day."[40] Koba had learned that the editors were attempting to get in touch with him, but he had not received the letter. He informed them that he wanted to work, but only in Moscow or Petersburg. He had outgrown the Caucasus and saw his future in the center of things. "In other places at the present time my work will be—and I am sure of this—very unproductive. It would be good to have a preliminary conversation with one of you about a plan of work, etc., perhaps with someone from the Russian section of the CC . . . if, of course, the Russian section of the CC is functioning. In a word, I am ready—the rest is your business."[41]

Party leaders abroad were trying to contact Koba for a new assignment. There had not been a major party conference for several years, and the central party institutions had atrophied. Bolsheviks and Mensheviks, working at cross-purposes, tried to lure party members to rival conferences. In order to gain support for a party conference that would adopt his narrow concept of party unity, Lenin had called a meeting of Bolshevik members of the Central Committee in Paris at the end of May 1911. Because the Foreign Bureau of the Central Committee, dominated by Mensheviks and *likvidatory*, opposed such a conference, this meeting set up the Organizational Commission Abroad (*Zagranichnaia Organizatsionnaia Komissiia*, ZOK). Koba, then in exile, and Shahumian, then in Baku, were among those nominated members of the commission, whose immediate tasks were to create a counterpart in Russia and lay the ground for a party conference. To this end Sergo Orjonikidze was sent to Russia, from city to city, to mobilize support.

As a roving agent he reported back that Baku was with the Leninists; the Urals were coming around but he could not be sure of Petersburg and Moscow. The Latvians were split, some with the Mensheviks and Trotsky, who planned their own conference, and others with the Bolsheviks. Proud Plekhanov, whose independence from either faction at this point was rendering him ever more irrelevant, refused to attend either conference. Optimistically Orjonikidze concluded, "Victory is already with those of us supporting the party."[42] Koba's old organization had hardened its position in the course of 1911, and Orjonikidze brought around both the local Bolsheviks and, after some hesitation, the Party Mensheviks.[43] Shahumian challenged those hesitant to join: you are "either with us, that is, with the Russian Social Democratic Workers' Party, or with the *likvidatory*, against the RSDRP. There is no other path."[44] The Baku Bolsheviks were uncompromising and refused to dissolve their old Baku Committee (as had been required as a condition of unification) until the new Baku Executive Committee took a positive decision in favor of Lenin's organizational commission to call a new party congress. Both in Baku and Tiflis the weakened party organizations were consolidating around a "party" position, discarding the few liquidators.[45]

Orjonikidze's mission had been thwarted by lack of money, and Shahumian had had to ask Sergo for fifty rubles to send urgently to Koba.[46] Shahumian was upset at the failure of the party leaders in Europe to maintain contact with Baku and send it the desperately needed publications and money. Just as Baku moved decisively toward Lenin, disaster struck. At a conference in Simon Enukidze's apartment in Baku at the very end of September, Shahumian gave in to the insistence of Orjonikidze, Shvarts, Zarnitsyn, and Spandarian to constitute themselves the *Russkaia kollegiia Organizatsionnoi Komissii* (ROK) and begin the planning of a party conference.[47] A second meeting was held at the Nauka Club, but the police were informed immediately.[48] The entire Baku Committee was arrested that night (September 30, 1911), along with a hundred others who were searched and taken in, among them Shahumian, Enukidze, Okhnianskii, and Chernomazov. Orjonikidze, who had stepped out for a moment to buy cigarettes, saw the police when he returned and escaped.[49] Even though no incriminating documents were found, these arrests destroyed the Bolshevik organization in Baku that Koba had spent so much time and energy carefully constructing.[50]

The police were aware that Koba was in direct contact with the party centers in Europe and had been told to come to the West to receive instructions as a mobile agent.[51] When he took off for Saint Petersburg on September 6, Chizhikov's passport in hand, the police were on his tail. According to the agent following him, Koba left the train station with an unknown traveling companion. Once again he made use of the network of trusted party members, many of them Georgian, that made it possible for an "illegal" like Koba to elude the police. He first tried his Tiflis and Baku buddy Sergei Alliluev but did not find him at home. Wandering in the rain along fashionable Nevskii Prospekt, hoping to meet up with someone he knew, by evening he finally ran into his friend Silva Todria, who was returning from work in a printing house. "This is very dangerous," said Todria. "Since the assassination of Stolypin, all the police are on alert. The gates and entry ways are locked at midnight.... You have to wake the attendant and show your passport. The owners of apartments are afraid of anyone suspicious." "Let's look for some furnished rooms ... somewhere not too far away," Koba proposed. They found a boarding house, the *Rossiia*, on Goncharnaia Street where the doorman looked long and carefully at him, turning Chizhikov's passport over in his hands.[52] He spent the night there and shaved off his beard. The police had lost him, but when he returned to the railroad station to retrieve his luggage, they sighted him. "Without a legitimate passport, altering his appearance, hiding from police detectives, [he] was forced to change his apartment daily."[53]

The next morning Todria picked Koba up, and they went to meet Alliluev on the Vyborg Side. His daughter, Anna, remembered the day she first met Koba. The doorbell rang, and she ran to open the door.

> I noisily cheered when I saw our adult friend Sila [Silva] Todria, but fell silent when I saw someone whom I did not know behind the short Sila. In a black overcoat, a soft hat, the unknown person was very thin. When he came into the entranceway, I noticed a pale face, attentive dark brown eyes under thick, sharply twisted eyebrows.
>
> "Is Papa home?" asked Sila. "We have come to him with a comrade."
>
> "He should return soon. Come in! Mama is in the dining room," I invited them in.
>
> They both came into the room, and, greeting my mother, Sila said, "Let me introduce our comrade; this is Soso."[54]

After dinner they noticed that police spies were hovering outside the apartment. Anna was sent to scout, and Koba was forced to wait before he could make his escape. That night he left with the electrician Zabelin and gave the police the slip by ducking into a dark alley. The Bolsheviks leaders abroad wanted Koba to help organize the forthcoming party conference, especially to bring around the non-Russian Social Democrats—the Latvians, the Poles, and the Jewish Bund. But when Stalin returned to the boarding house on the morning of the 9th, he was arrested and taken to the Petersburg Jail. On him the police found notes on his reading: "Questions of Political Economy"; "Notes on Sociology"; *Capital*, volume I; *Russian History*"; as well as a collection of conversational phrases in German, various German verbs, and Chizhikov's passport.[55]

His comrades were unable to find out what happened to him, and one of them wrote to Krupskaia, "Comrade Koba came here, but we do not know where he has disappeared to. We surmise that he has been arrested."[56] Lenin was anxious to make contact with Koba. Late in 1911 he was giving lectures at a Bolshevik party school in Longjumeau, outside of Paris, and tried to recruit the one Menshevik student, Grigol Uratadze, to find Koba and ask him to come to Paris. Uratadze agreed that this was not a difficult task but he wanted to inform Lenin that Koba had been expelled from the Baku Bolshevik group.[57] He expected that once the Bolshevik chief learned of Koba's expulsion he would take back his request. He was surprised by Lenin's reaction. "That is nothing," said Lenin. "It is just such people that I need."

These exclusions from groups are part of the practice of illegal work; they almost always occur through mistakes, by unverified declarations and facts, often based on misunderstandings. That's why it is not worth placing too much importance on this. Moreover, given that the exclusion was from one group or organization does not mean that he has been expelled from the party since only the party, and not a group, no matter how authoritative it might be, can expel someone from the party. The resolution of the Baku group, if it in fact occurred, requires investigation and confirmation. For this reason, despite your information, I all the same ask if you would pass on to him my assignment.[58]

Uratadze agreed to try to meet with Koba, thinking that he was in Caucasia. But at that moment Koba was being held in a Petersburg prison. He spent three months there until on December 14 the authorities ordered him sent him back to Vologda for an additional sentence of three years. Since his offense at this moment was only his illegal trip to the capital, he was released on his own recognizance and given a travel permit to move on his own to Vologda. He hid for about ten days in Petersburg. Spandarian and Vera Sveitser, who lived together as a couple, met with him in a chilly room in a small wooden house tucked into a courtyard on the Petersburg Side. Orjonikidze and the others met later in Sveitser's apartment to discuss the upcoming party conference in Prague. Then Koba left for Vologda.[59] He immediately went to see his closest friend, Chizhikov, and the same day he sent off a postcard to Chizhikov's wife, who was then in Totma: "Well, 'nasty' Polia, I am in Vologda and am kissing 'dear,' 'good' 'Petenka' [her husband]. We are sitting at the table and drinking to the health of 'intelligent' Polia. Drink as well for the health of the well-known to you 'oddball' Iosif."[60] Just before he fled from Vologda, Koba wrote one more affectionate note to Onufrieva. Here he joked: "I am here with your kiss, passed on to me by Petia [her husband]. I kiss you in return, yes, and not simply do I kiss you, but hotly (it doesn't pay to just kiss). Iosif."[61] And these last words were accompanied by a drawing of a couple kissing!

FOUNDING THE BOLSHEVIK PARTY: THE PRAGUE CONFERENCE, 1912

As peaceful and pleasant as Vologda might have been, Koba was anxious to keep active in the movement. He stayed for less than two months. By 1910 there were signs that the passivity and indifference of workers that had followed the June 2, 1907, coup d'état were dissipating. One could sense that the period of the counterrevolution was coming to an end. Following Stolypin's murder a series of ineffective prime ministers succeeded one another. After the death in November 1910 of the revered writer Lev Tolstoy, who had broken with the Orthodox Church and become an advocate of nonviolent resistance, students in Saint Petersburg and Moscow took to the streets to demonstrate their discontent, the first massive protests in several years. At the other end of society workers engaged in more work stoppages. And most dramatically, a few months after the Prague Conference, far from Petersburg in eastern Siberia, an event took place that had profound repercussions throughout Russia, especially for workers and Social Democrats. On April 4 (17), 1912, soldiers fired into a crowd of striking workers at the Lena goldfields.[62] Over a hundred protestors were killed. The brutal response to the killings by the minister of the interior, Aleksandr Makarov, in his comments in the duma—"Thus it has always been and thus it will be in times to come"—only exacerbated the bitter feelings in society. Within days strikes and demonstrations spread through Saint Petersburg. Month by month, year by year from 1912 to the outbreak of World War I in August 1914, strikes and protests grew in number and political radicalism. The "reaction" was giving way to what Soviet historians would later call "the new revolutionary upsurge."

From 1907 to 1911, during the "reaction," moderates, primarily Mensheviks but sometimes Socialist Revolutionaries and even Kadets, had been the acknowledged leaders of the trade unions in Russia's largest cities. Steadily, however, the fatal combination of workers being allowed to organize but being thwarted by the government from making any real gains led workers to more radical tactics and more militant leaders. With industrial production improving, workers had more potential leverage and began to feel their strength. Frustration plus opportunity fed their rage.[63] To the shock of the Mensheviks it was not the *praktiki* who had worked so long and hard in the labor movement who benefited from this new worker activism. One by one most of the important legal labor organizations, including those that the so-called *likvidatory* had spent much energy organizing, fell into the hands of Bolsheviks. The Union of Metal Workers, the largest union in Saint Petersburg, as well as the Union of Printers, a traditional base of the Mensheviks, both turned toward the Bolsheviks. Besides better wages, shorter hours, and improved working conditions, there was another issue of great personal importance to the workers. In their strikes they demanded that their dignity as human beings be recognized, that they be addressed politely with the plural form of the pronoun "you" (*Vy*)—the one used with deference between members of privileged society—and not with the singular (*ty*), the form used with children and social inferiors. What may have seemed a trivial matter in terms of their physical survival, the workers' insistence on proper treatment was in fact a challenge to the elaborate cultural hierarchy of subordination and elevation that underlay the system of imperial authority.[64]

Even as workers made it clear that they were no longer willing to live in social apartheid, separated by the rules, regulations, and restrictions— and in Saint Petersburg by the physical barrier of the Neva River—that kept them apart from the rest of society, they increasingly felt a bitter hostility toward the propertied classes, called in Russian *tsenzovoe obshchestvo* (census society), and a sense that the interests of the lower classes and those of the upper classes were fundamentally in conflict.[65] Decades of Social Democratic rhetoric and the experience of their own lives had profoundly shaped their view of themselves, their opponents, and their possible future. As Leopold H. Haimson summarized, "The insistence on equality *and* separateness should be viewed as a basic feature by the eve of the war, of the psychology and social and political behavior of Russia's working class."[66]

As they lost their influence among industrial workers, the Mensheviks despaired that younger workers and peasant immigrants were responsible for turning the Petersburg proletariat toward reckless adventurism. What Bolsheviks saw as conscious political maturity by the workers, Mensheviks thought of as immature, elemental, and emotional responses by callow, unschooled peasant-workers. In actuality, however, rather than "green youth," the Bolshevized workers of the capital were either young people who had been raised in the city but were too young to have experienced much of the difficult years of the "reaction" or they were young immigrants from the countryside who had broken with the village and quickly assimilated the radical rhetoric of the most militant agitators.[67] Once again as in 1905 the labor movement was outgrowing the party.

In the brief span while Koba remained in exile, his comrades gathered in Prague for the long-anticipated party conference. But rather than representing the diverse threads of Russian Social Democracy, the Prague Conference, which would go down in Soviet history as the Sixth, in fact was representative only of those Social Democrats who agreed with Lenin on the "narrow" composition of the party that eliminated the *Vperedisti*, the *likvidatory*, and the Mensheviks, except the Plekhanovites. Of the eighteen delegates who met in January 1912, all were Bolshevik except two Menshevik-partyites.[68] Despite elaborate precautions and evasive messages sent to suspected police agents, two of the Bolshevik delegates—Roman Malinovskii (Malinowski) and Alia Romanov (Aleksinskii)—were in fact employed by the Moscow branch of the tsarist secret police (*Okhrana*). As was standard practice of the secret police, neither agent knew of the other's connection to the *Okhrana*. On the very first day one of the Mensheviks, Iakov Zevin, questioned the representativeness of the conference. Lenin disingenuously claimed that everyone who wanted to help revive the party had been invited. The conference was essential, he said, to restore the central institutions of the party that were moribund. Indeed, the small meeting represented most of the existing Social Democratic organizations within Russia proper, and among the delegates were five workers. But even this small, select group had serious differences, and several of the delegates targeted Lenin for the sad state of the party. Sergo Orjonikidze, beloved for his forthrightness and enthusiasm (which led older delegates to call him "a child of nature"), complained about the direction of the party by those living abroad: "I am all the more convinced that there is ground for us [Bolsheviks and Mensheviks] to work together if only we did not have the 'damn abroad' and leaders who sit in Paris, San Remo, and so forth, and, understanding nothing, write directives and produce schisms. . . . [T]he guilt lies with the leaders issuing circulars."[69] Like Koba, he was not happy that Bogdanov and the *Vperedisti* had been driven from the Bolshevik faction since back in Russia many of them had fought the good fight against the *likvidatory* along with those defending the underground party.[70]

Lenin gave as good as he got. He laughed off the suggestion that his articles stirred up trouble. He asserted that one had to be forceful against the likes of Trotsky. "This man under the party flag, under cover of the legal party literature, on the quiet, smuggles liquidationism into the midst of the Russian workers. It was essential to expose that. It was necessary to show this to those who willingly or unwillingly play into Trotsky's hands." He stated frankly: "We have two parties—this is a fact. Their presence flows from the totality of Russian reality. In Russia the soil is being created in many places for the separation. That is where the schism is being created."[71] He made no apologies for the fractiousness in the party emigration. "As long as there is Stolypin's Russia, there will be an emigration, [and] it is [tied] to Russia by thousands of threads that no knives can cut apart."[72]

Lenin's ferocity toward *likvidatorstvo* can be explained by his unswerving commitment to a revolutionary overthrow of tsarism. For Lenin the turn of many Mensheviks toward the more moderate strategy was a shift away from revolution toward reformism, the same kind of heretical move of which a decade earlier the *Iskra* radicals had accused the *ekonomisty*. Largely ignored were the efforts of some Mensheviks like Martov's older brother, Ezhov, working in the legal labor movement, to create "initiative groups" (*initsiativnye gruppy*) directed at reviving the Menshevik underground. For Lenin compromise on vital strategic matters was anathema; conciliation with opponents was a betrayal of principle. Legal possibilities were to be exploited but not to the detriment of the true revolutionary instrument, the illegal, underground party committees. His views coincided with those Petersburg workers who felt that the *likvidatory* were simply too cautious, fearful that any aggressiveness on their part would lead the police to close their unions. These workers perceived the Mensheviks, who warned against linking the economic struggle with politics, to be holding them back, while the Bolsheviks urged them to escalate the strike movement from economic to political demands. In Lenin's view there was an affinity between the Menshevik emphasis on legal activity and their willingness to work with the liberals. When Martov, never a *likvidator*, argued that the alienation of the urban bourgeoisie from tsarism presented an opportunity for

Social Democrats in the upcoming elections to the Fourth Duma, Lenin snapped back that the bourgeoisie would sooner join the landed nobility than aid the struggle for democracy.[73] Through 1912–1913, he spelled out his strategy: to link the economic with the political struggle and turn the strike movement into a national general strike that would lead to the long-desired armed uprising.

While it is impossible to know for certain how the "bourgeoisie" might have acted if tsarism had allowed a more open arena for politics, both the Mensheviks and Bolsheviks made convincing arguments about how liberals and people of property might act in a revolutionary situation. The year 1917 illustrated the various possible scenarios. As long as the revolution did not move too far too fast, the liberals were willing to work with the moderate socialists—as long as their property and privileges were not threatened. But once the revolution moved rapidly from merely political (democratic) to a deeper social (socialist) revolution that implied the abolition of private property and hierarchies based on wealth and property, the "bourgeoisie"—at least many industrialists, entrepreneurs, and liberal intellectuals—shifted to the right and allied with whatever forces of order were available to prevent a slide into that unknown future called "socialism."

The dilemma facing all revolutionaries in Russia was that Stolypin's Russia was still a heavily policed state. The *likvidatory* insisted that possibilities for emerging from the underground existed, but *partiinye* Social Democrats insisted that open activity had severe limits. While legal organizations and institutions, like trade unions, workers' clubs, newspapers, and the duma operated, the tsarist regime regularly and arbitrarily would close down specific unions, even burn the clubs, and limit the possibility of lecturing workers. In Prague Lenin spoke of the need to have a party cell surrounded by a multitude of legal organizations and for Bolsheviks to win those groups over to Social Democracy. As Bolsheviks entered the labor movement, they encouraged the workers to engage in more confrontationist actions. Spandarian agreed that "the time of the old propaganda circles, with their students and female auditors who knew the biography of Marx, has gone." But it was still necessary "to create an illegal center in every city" to lead the economic and political struggle, for the trade unions are unable to carry on even the economic struggle.[74]

The underground that had barely managed to preserve itself during the "reaction" now had to reinvent itself and put its rhetoric of working with legal institutions into practice. At Prague the Leninist faction created its own Central Committee, with only two members from the emigration (Lenin and Zinoviev), one Menshevik-partyite (Shvartsman), and four Bolsheviks inside Russia (Orjonikidze, Spandarian, Goloshchekin, and Malinovskii). Incredibly, a police spy, Malinovskii, was a member of the top Bolshevik institution and soon to be elected a Bolshevik deputy to the Fourth State Duma, all the while being employed by the Moscow branch of the *Okhrana*.

Who was—what was—Roman Malinovskii (1876–1918)? In some ways he was the personification of one of Lenin and Koba's dreams—a real "Russian Bebel," a worker Social Democrat who had risen from the ranks of metalworkers to become a politically astute party activist. His rise had been spectacular. Born the son of Polish peasants, he wandered through a series of odd jobs and occupations—as a tinker, a tailor, and after three years in prison, a soldier—before taking a job as a lathe operator and union organizer at the Langenzipen Factory in Saint Petersburg in 1906. Displaying extraordinary energy and enthusiasm, and a gift for effective oratory, he became, in the words of one Menshevik, "the soul of the [metalworkers'] union."[75] After a second arrest in late 1909, he moved to Moscow. Six months later he was arrested once again, and this time he accepted the proposal that he become a secret agent of the Moscow *Okhrana* with a salary of one hundred rubles a month. The tall, sturdy, self-confident Malinovskii with his contacts in both factions of the Social Democratic Party now became police agent "Portnoi" (the tailor).

His debut in top party circles was at the Prague Conference in January 1912. He was a newly minted Bolshevik, and his patron, Lenin, admired this rough-hewn man of the people—someone not unlike Koba, whom he also promoted. "With such people" as Duma deputies Malinovskii, Aleksei Badaev, and Grigorii Petrovskii, he wrote to Gorky, "It is really possible to build a workers' party, though the difficulties will be incredibly great."[76] Lenin insisted that Malinovskii be elected to the Central Committee, against the objections of the delegates from inside Russia who did not really know him, and pushed for him to be one of the "party's" (actually, the Bolshevik faction's) candidates in the elections to the Fourth State Duma.[77] Elected by the workers' curia in Moscow, Malinovskii used his parliamentary immunity to become the leading public speaker for the Bolsheviks, vice chairman of the Social Democratic duma caucus, a prolific writer for the workers' press, and a key link between the party in Petersburg and Lenin and Krupskaia in Kraków, whom he frequently visited. He served with Stalin on the Russian Bureau of the Central Committee and in 1913 would be given the task to facilitate Stalin and Sverdlov's escape from Turukhansk. The irony becomes even more palpable when Lenin discussed with Malinovskii measures to stop the epidemic of Bolshevik arrests.[78] In fact, Malinovskii was responsible for the arrests of dozens of party members, some of whom would die in exile. Among those he fingered were those "conciliatory" Bolsheviks like Dubrovinskii and Nogin who were anxious to bring the party factions back together despite Lenin's preference. The maintenance of the schism was a principal goal of the police. Here Lenin's narrow conception of the party and the ambitions of the police coincided. Even Stalin was too conciliatory for Lenin. He berated the four Bolshevik deputies (not Malinovskii and Muranov) who had had their names listed on the masthead of the Menshevik *Luch* and pressured the deputies to break decisively with the Mensheviks in the duma caucus. Finally, in November 1913, with Stalin and Sverdlov out of the picture, Malinovskii led the Bolshevik "six" to split with the Menshevik "seven." The Menshevik deputy Akaki Chkhenkeli wrote to a friend, Malinovskii's "role in the schism was in all shapes and forms enormous. The schism in the faction would not have occurred without him, even with ten Lenins in Kraków."[79]

Shortly after the Prague conference two more Bolsheviks were coopted onto the Central Committee: Koba and I. S. Belostotskii, a former metalworker then working for the workers' insurance fund. Koba was also named a member of the Russian Bureau of the Central Committee, along with Spandarian, Orjonikidze, and Goloshchekin.

The Central Committee was disproportionately weighted with Caucasians: of the nine members three (Koba, Spandarian, and Orjonikidze) were from the Caucasus and had worked in Baku. Of the five candidate members (Shahumian, Elena Stasova, Mikhail Kalinin, Andrei Budnov, and Aleksandr Smirnov), the first three had worked at some point in the Caucasus. The oil center was a model of the kind of party unity Lenin favored.[80] Baku supplied Lenin with his "hardest" followers. They were accustomed to underground life and work, completely dedicated to the politicization of the labor movement, yet willing and able to use legal labor institutions. Throughout the years of "reaction" they had gone along with Lenin and refused to work with those socialists who saw the legal labor movement as the main arena for activity and the underground as a mere auxiliary.

Koba had ascended to the very pinnacle of the Bolshevik faction and was a full member of the small, tight Central Committee, which audaciously usurped the authority of the Social Democratic Party. He would remain a leading member of the Central Committee until his death in 1953. But in his new leadership role he cautiously staked out his own positions on the important concerns of the party, positions that did not always conform closely to the views of his mentor, Lenin.

22

THE MAN OF STEEL

This was in mid-April 1912, in the evening, at the apartment of Comrade Poletaev, where two duma deputies (Pokrovskii and Poletaev), two literary people (Olminskii and Baturin), and I, a member of the Central Committee (I, as an illegal, was staying with Poletaev, who had immunity [from arrest]) agreed on the platform of *Pravda* and put together the first issue of the paper. I do not remember if the closest co-workers on *Pravda*—Dem'ian Bednyi and Danilov—attended this meeting. . . . The technical and material base for the paper was already provided thanks to the agitation of *Zvezda*, with the support of broad masses of workers and mass voluntary collections of money for *Pravda* in plants and factories. . . . The difference between *Zvezda* and *Pravda* consisted only in the fact that the audience of *Pravda*, in contrast to *Zvezda*, consisted not only of advanced workers but of the broad masses of the working class.

—IOSIF STALIN, "K DESIATILETIIU 'PRAVDY'
(VOSPOMINANIIA)" ["TOWARD THE TENTH
ANNIVERSARY OF 'PRAVDA' (MEMOIRS)"] (1922)

The Bolshevik leaders deeply regretted that Koba had not been in Prague. Isolation can lead to deviation, and they feared that he was far more willing to work with Mensheviks of various tendencies than was Lenin. Krupskaia wrote to Orjonikidze on February 9: "I have received a letter from Ivanovich [Koba]; he is developing his own point of view on the situation, promises to give me his address in a month. It is clear that he is terribly isolated from everything, as if he had just fallen from the sky. If it were not for this, his letter would have produced the most depressing impression. It is regrettable, very regrettable, that he did not make it to the [Prague] conference."[1]

As Lenin planned to "Bolshevize" the Russian Social Democratic Workers' Party, or even to "build an all-Bolshevik party," Koba was precisely the kind of party activist that Lenin and Krupskaya valued most.[2] His origins were plebian, but he had imbibed the teachings of Marx. He was a faithful, intrepid Bolshevik. And he had the hardness of a seasoned underground agent. He may have exhibited the dubious traits of a *komitetchik* and not taken some of the nuances of Lenin's philosophical musings seriously enough, but he stayed in the fray, did not give up or give in. He was experienced both in the labor movement and the complexities of intraparty politics. He was weathered, tempered, a Bolshevik in the mold that Lenin admired. Like Malinowski, Koba was exactly the kind of Russian Bebel that Lenin had long sought.

To inform Koba about the Prague Conference, Orjonikidze traveled to Vologda in mid-February, and shortly afterward he wrote that he had been to see Koba and that "he remained satisfied with the outcome of the affair."[3] About two weeks later, during the night of February 28–29, Koba left Vologda and made his way to Moscow. He found his way to the newly raised Central Committee member Malinovskii's apartment, but he was not in town, and Koba saw only his wife and children. He moved on to Petersburg where he sought out his boyhood friend Sergo Kavtaradze, who was then studying at Petersburg University. Koba noticed that he was being followed and needed to hide out until dark. Kavtaradze remembered later:

> On one of the cold dark winter days in Petersburg, about eleven in the morning I was sitting studying for some course. There was a knock on the door, and into the room came Stalin (Koba). This was unexpected. I knew that he had been exiled. With his usual jolly and affable expression on his face, wearing a light overcoat in the fierce frost, after a few preliminary words of greetings, without taking off his coat, he said, "I will stay with you for a short time." "That goes without saying. . . . Take off your coat, warm yourself up, I will organize the tea." "No need. I will rest just a little. But here is the thing: I just came from Moscow, straight from the train to you. . . . In Moscow at the station I noticed I was being followed, and imagine, when I left the

coach here I saw the very same spy, who has followed me to your entrance-way. Right now he is hanging around on the street."[4]

Kavtaradze considered disguising Koba in women's clothing but then thought better of it. Koba waited until dark and then stealthily left the apartment. He stayed in the city for about a week, meeting with workers, moving from apartment to apartment. On March 2 Social Democratic workers in the city met and formed a central group to coordinate activity, the kind of model that Spandarian had mentioned in Prague.[5] Koba wrote to Krupskaia about both the successes and difficulties of the work in the capital. There was no money. "We don't have a kopeck. . . . Three of us are doing all the work; if you don't send money, we will have to search for work in order to exist. The mood is good. The workers are joining the organization. The work now is primarily to look for connections everywhere; we have to run around; we made reports in Nevskii, Vyborg, and Vasileostrov [districts]."[6] He managed, apparently, after one workers' meeting to find a kopeck or two to buy a red carnation for a female acquaintance.[7]

Koba had been given one of the most responsible and dangerous assignments of any party member, that of roving agent moving between cities, contacting local activists, persuading them to adopt the "correct" positions or to organize effective committees, all the while keeping the émigré leaders informed. By mid-March Koba was on his way to Tiflis, where he set up a workers' nucleus of the new Russian Bureau of the Central Committee of the Bolsheviks, which besides himself included Orjonikidze, Spandarian, and Stasova as secretary.[8] He traveled on to Baku and Moscow with police spies close behind. Moving and meeting were extremely difficult and dangerous. His friend Spandarian had preceded him to Baku and when he attempted to report on the Prague Conference in the hall of the Union of Oil Workers to give another report, he and nine others were arrested.[9]

Koba arrived in Baku after Spandarian's arrest. Accompanied by Muslim bodyguards, Koba moved through his secret abodes. He managed to write a leaflet "For the party!" and a May Day proclamation in the name of the Central Committee, but the latter was discovered by the police.[10] Realizing that police spies had penetrated the Baku organization, Shahumian and Kasparian wrote to their comrades advising them to desist from all party work given the danger of arrest.[11] Koba called a meeting of party workers to which he invited Mensheviks. But the Mensheviks, who claimed that they had been trying for four months to find Bolsheviks whom they might co-opt to their Leading Center, declined the invitation for fear of arrest, and asked Koba to remain in Baku a little longer until conditions became more favorable. Anxious to achieve party unity Koba regarded such behavior by the Mensheviks as schismatic and held his meeting on March 29. The "conference," which was probably merely a gathering of a few activists, decided to call on the Mensheviks to form a Leading Collective together with the Bolsheviks and to run a joint campaign for the upcoming elections to the Fourth State Duma. Indeed they agreed to cooperate with *likvidatory* during the elections, though this contradicted the resolutions of the Prague Conference.[12] In their desperate straits, with their leadership gone, and with the *likvidatory* no longer a threat, the local Bolsheviks were willing to make concessions in order to facilitate joint work by Social Democrats. It was a small transgression; in all other aspects the conference approved the Leninist resolutions adopted in Prague.

Koba no longer had the authority in Baku that he had enjoyed before his arrest and exile. He faced the same hesitance from the Baku Leading Center to meet with him that Spandarian had experienced. Local Social Democrats were concerned that there was a police agent inside the local Bolshevik circles.[13] But Lev Sosnovskii, a conciliatory Bolshevik who supported the Center, met the Menshevik Nikolaevskii, a member of the Leading Center, and told him that Koba had arrived in Baku and wanted to meet with the Center.[14] He convinced Nikolaevskii that if the Center continued to refuse to hear reports from representatives of Lenin's Central Committee, they would be guilty of narrow factionalism. Since Koba, like Spandarian, had no official standing with them, Nikolaevskii failed to persuade his comrades to meet with Koba. None of the other Center members, including the conciliatory Bolsheviks, wanted to hear Koba's report. They sent Nikolaevskii to talk to Koba alone.[15]

In the evening of March 29, 1912, Nikolaevskii met with Koba for the first time. He had heard about him the September before from Enukidze, who warned him that Koba had a vengeful nature and was capable of using any means to win in a factional fight. Such disregard of appropriate means was characteristic not only of Bolsheviks, said Enukidze, but of some Mensheviks as well, for example, "Petr Kavkazskii" (Noe Ramishvili), "who differed little from Koba."[16] Despite this warning, Nikolaevskii in fact found Koba to be relatively moderate in his statements about the political issues within the party. Whereas the Prague Conference had come out against preelectoral alliances with *likvidatory*, Koba told Nikolaevskii that he did not agree with this tactic. Koba was flexible on the question of organizational ties with *likvidatory* but would not openly oppose the resolution of the conference. He said that the Russian *likvidatory* were better than the covert *likvidatory* of the Menshevik Caucasian Regional Committee (*Obkom*) in Tiflis, and if we permitted agreements with the latter, we should permit them with the former. For Koba the *Obkom* was the principal enemy, made up of his long-time opponents among the Georgian Mensheviks. He also spoke against those abroad (*zagranichniki*) who did not know Russian reality well. "Ours are no better than yours," he said. He wanted the *praktiki* who carried on work in the underground to have their own center, which should direct party policy and to which those abroad should be subordinated. Demands for such a center came only from Tiflis and Baku—that is, from those resolutions on which Koba worked.[17]

"Stalin was very persistent," wrote Nikolaevskii, "in his attempts to find a common language with the Baku people that took a critical attitude toward the Transcaucasian *Obkom*, playing on the old (as I then already knew) irritation that the multi-national Baku organization felt toward the *Obkom*, which beginning in 1905 had become almost exclusively a *Georgian* center. . . . The *Obkom* after 1907–1908 did almost nothing in the area of Social Democratic propaganda among other nationalities."[18] Koba had no time for exclusively national movements. His identification with the multinational (or as Social Democrats would put it, "internationalist") party had long since been solidified. He had long ago left Georgia physically and spiritually—or, more precisely, Georgia, led by the Mensheviks, had left him.

Nikolaevskii told Koba that Baku's Leading Center had no organizational ties with the *Obkom*, but it also had decided not to establish organizational ties with Lenin's Bolshevized Central Committee. Locally, however, it would defend unification of the party and join with Bolshevik circles in Baku as long as the Bolsheviks did not demand a complete break with "*likvidatory* on the right and *otzovisti* on the left" and recognized the necessity of all Social Democrats to work together in the upcoming election campaign to the Fourth State Duma. Koba conceded that he would not speak of *likvidatory* and Menshevik-partyites but only of Mensheviks in general. They both agreed that the Bolsheviks and Mensheviks should work together in the election campaign and that leading Bolsheviks who had legal positions—like Stopani, Azizbekov, and Dr. Leo Okinshevich—should become candidates. When Koba proposed Mgeladze and members of the Balakhany cell as representatives, Nikolaevskii refused to accept them and told him that the Center suspected that the Balakhany Bolshevik cell had been penetrated by the police. Koba made fun of the Mensheviks being "afraid" of meeting Bolsheviks. When Nikolaevskii told him that even Shahumian suspected (incorrectly) that Mgeladze was a police agent, Koba spoke sharply about "meeting people in our midst" who are "much too suspicious" because "they do not like to be arrested" and in general have "intelligentsia manners."[19] Nikolaevskii had heard of the hostile personal relations between Koba and Shahumian, but he felt that since Shahumian was the "indisputable leader of the Baku organization of Bolsheviks, I did not have the right not to consider his opinion." Koba tried to convince Nikolaevskii to support the Prague Conference in some way, but Nikolaevskii was unwilling to go that far.[20]

Both deft and tough in negotiation, Koba nevertheless failed to attract the Baku Mensheviks to his point of view primarily because they feared exposure. Just before he left Caucasia, Koba reviewed his work in Baku in a letter sent to Stasova ("Zel'ma") in Tiflis, who was the key link to comrades abroad.[21] Koba explained how in the absence of an all-city Bolshevik center in Baku he tried to bring people from various district organizations together. Despite his best efforts he was unable to attract any Mensheviks, who had their own city center, but declined to come to his meeting because of their fears of arrest and police spies. "To my admonition that such behavior by the Mensheviks is the same as a schism, they answered, turning their eyes to the sky, that twice in four months the gendarmes were able to search out the Bolsheviks and imprison them but the Mensheviks were unable to find a single Bolshevik in Baku. Well . . . that is their factional logic." Baku's Social Democrats wanted to create a center independent of either faction that would work with the new Central Committee in Russia. They were prepared to recognize the resolutions of the Prague Conference, except the rejection of working with the *likvidatory* together in the upcoming duma elections. Koba's meeting proposed a new party conference and asked that the Central Committee begin negotiations with the Social Democratic organizations of various nationalities (for example, Jews, Latvians, and Poles). Stasova in Tiflis reported to their comrades, "Soso is alive and well and left for the north on the 30th of March." From her letter it is clear that Koba clung to a much broader conception of how the party should be restored than that favored by Lenin and the Prague Conference.[22]

Koba's movements exposed him to the police even more than before, at a time when the tsarist gendarmes were becoming more efficient in their work. As long as he could elude them, he was indispensable to Lenin. Krupskaia wrote that "it is essential that 'Ivanovich' be sent immediately to Piter [Saint Petersburg]."[23] She was well aware that Koba, while a much-needed agent, was somewhat independent minded and did not carry out the precise instructions of the Bolshevik leadership abroad. Although his primary allegiance was to the party leaders abroad and the Central Committee in Russia, he refused to subordinate his own views on tactics and organization to the dictates of either center.

As a roving agent, Koba was no longer intimately connected to a community of workers. Another agent, Martyn Liadov (Mandelshtam), opened his memoirs with the regret that "in the years of underground work, especially after some sort of meeting, I envied deep in my soul the local party activists. They grew up tied to local affairs; they closely knew one another; they had tight ties with the local masses. And I come to this or that town, hold two or three meetings, give two or three reports, and go off again to a new place. I felt somewhat lonely sometimes, especially after a few days spent in the good, close solidarity of a truly comradely atmosphere. But someone had to take on the responsibility of a roving agent, of a party *kommivoiazher* [*commis voyageur* (traveling salesman)]." On the road one had to be ever vigilant, make sure that no police spies were following you. "Here one can never be sentimental very long."[24]

Koba made his way north early in April, through Rostov-on-Don where he saw Shveitser (as he had on his way south). They met at seven in the evening, first at a school, then in the first-class restaurant of the railroad station. "This is how we managed to hide from the street informers and tell each other about the state of party affairs. Stalin told me details of [her lover] Suren's [Spandarian's] arrest."[25] He moved on to Moscow where he conferred with Orjonikidze on April 7, a week before the police picked up the younger Georgian. Koba eluded the police by not emerging from the train on which they expected him.[26] By the next week he was back in Petersburg in the apartment of Bolshevik duma deputy, Poletaev, who involved him in writing for the newspapers *Zvezda* (Star) and the brand new legal daily of the Bolsheviks, *Pravda* (Truth). Unlike his last visits, this time Koba was not trailed by secret agents.

PRAVDA

Activists within Russia like Koba, as well as duma deputies and writers around the Bolsheviks' more intellectual newspaper, *Zvezda*, were enthusiastic about a daily like *Pravda*, written more simply and directly for the workers. There was a sense that émigrés and intellectuals were too invested in the divisive interfactional fights that workers found tedious. Lenin, however, was skeptical about a legal daily, fearing that it would encourage workers to overvalue the legal, gradualist road to reform.[27] Because he was a fugitive, Koba could not work openly with the newspapers, but he furtively made contact with the young Viacheslav

Molotov, then working on *Pravda*. They met at a dentist's office on Porokhovaia Street, along with Sverdlov. Late in his life Molotov recalled that Stalin edited the first issue of *Pravda*.[28]

Koba relished his new authority and quickly took to the role of directing and dictating. As a Central Committee member, he helped initiate the campaign for elections to the Fourth State Duma, though he complained that there was not enough money for an effective operation.[29] Stasova wrote in April 1912, "Sergo and Ivanovich keep giving orders but say nothing about what is happening around us."[30] Koba "almost single-handedly edited [the first] three issues of the paper."[31] He composed a proclamation for the upcoming May Day.[32] Turning out short journalistic pieces rather than more thoughtful theoretical excursions for *Zvezda* and *Pravda,* he featured the shootings at the Lena Goldfields in a number of his articles. He wrote of three stages in the wave of strikes: first defensive strikes two years earlier; then offensive strikes with economic demands a year and a half ago; and now the political demands of the present.[33] The massacre in Siberia, he declared, was the proof that moderate legal methods—the circulation of a petition in support of workers' rights (which did not resonate widely with workers), the legalistic methods of the *likvidatory,* and the compromises with autocracy of the Kadets—were doomed to failure. The patience of the country had come to an end. "The shootings at Lena broke the ice of silence."[34] "It was not long ago—just a year ago—that the zealots of the 'legal party,' the Messers Liquidators, with noise and clamor opened the so-called petition campaign," but that campaign led nowhere but to the Lena shootings. "The lessons of life, evidently, are not wasted even on the liquidators. The intoxication with petitions, it seems, has begun to pass."[35]

Although he was always willing to denounce the *likvidatory* publicly, Koba's more moderate proclivities toward party unity were evident in his unsigned lead editorial in *Pravda,* "Our Goals."

We think that a powerful movement full of life is unthinkable without differences—only in a cemetery does a "full identity of views" exist! But this does not mean that the points of difference are greater than the points of similarity. Far from it! As much as advanced party work-ers might disagree, they cannot forget that they, regardless of faction, are exploited the same; that they, regardless of faction, are equally without rights. For this reason *Pravda* will, above all else, call for the unity of the class struggle of the proletariat, for unity no matter what. As much as we must be uncompromising with our enemies, so we must demand from ourselves pliability [*ustupchivost'*] in our relations with one another. War to the enemies of the working class, peace and friendly working together within the movement—that is what will guide *Pravda* in its daily work.[36]

Here, as one of the principal writers and editors of the newspaper, Koba was setting a conciliatory tone that angered Lenin.

Pravda was remarkably successful. Taking up the cause of the Lena workers touched a nerve that excited all of society. Even leading Men-sheviks could not but envy the paper's influence. Martov, who was then back in Russia, wrote to Akselrod that the new "Bolshevik daily *Pravda* has taken a very moderate tone and even blabs 'unity' phrases. They have brought that conciliator Olminskii (Galerka) onto the editorial board."[37] And in a note to Petr Garvi, one of the Mensheviks who might justifiably be called a "liquidator," Martov wrote, "The tone taken by *Pravda* undoubtedly testifies to the fact Lenin has almost no one to serve as his 'conscience' in Russia."[38] *Pravda*'s tone was precisely what annoyed Lenin. The moderate editors either suppressed or altered his articles, cleansing them of abusive or abrasive words and phrases, par-ticularly those aimed at the Kadets or the *likvidatory*. He complained to the editors: "*Pravda* does not know how to fight. It does not attack, does not pursue either the Kadets or the liquidators. . . . Does this really look like Marxism?"[39] When *Pravda*'s circulation fell in the summer of 1912, Lenin struck back at the editors' treatment of his articles: "By avoiding 'painful questions,' *Pravda* and *Zvezda make themselves* dull, monoto-nous, uninteresting, noncombative organs. A socialist organ *must* con-duct polemics."[40]

By June 1912 Lenin had moved from Paris to the Polish city of Kraków, the capital of Austro-Hungarian Galicia, to be closer to the action in

Russia. Kraków was more convenient as a bridge to the *praktiki*. Yet even though they were closer physically to Russia, the émigré leaders fretted over their contact with their members in Russia and fought to increase their influence over both the press and the duma deputies. Lenin wrote to members of the Central Committee that he was "*terribly*" upset and worried about the "*complete* disorganization of our (and your) connections and ties." Referring to Koba, he used one of his aliases: "From Ivanovich there is nothing. What's going on with him? Where is he? How is he? It is devilishly necessary to have a legal person in Piter or near Piter, as our affairs are in bad shape there. The war is raging and is difficult. We have no information, no leadership, no supervision of the newspaper."[41]

Koba was essentially put in charge of the newspaper. He signed the articles with various pseudonyms—K. S., S., K. S—n, K. Salin, K. Solin, K. St.—until in January 1913, at the end of a major piece in *Sotsial-Demokrat*, he unveiled his new identity, K. Stalin. Sveitser remembered that her friend had been upset when he opened up *Zvezda* to find his article signed "K. Solin. He smiled and said, 'I do not like meaningless, borrowed names.'"[42] After that the editorial board coined no new names for him. He was Stalin—the man of steel [*stal'*].

As busy as he was, Stalin was anxious to move abroad, and he wrote to a comrade in Paris inquiring about a passport. He claimed he needed to leave Russia by April 25.[43] He didn't make it. The very day that the first issue of *Pravda* appeared, April 22, he was arrested as he left Poletaev's apartment to meet Molotov. The police had been watching the apartment. This time he was sentenced more severely: three years in Narym Territory, Tomsk province in western Siberia. Shortly after he was picked up, the Petersburg Committee was arrested, and the Russian Bureau effectively collapsed: Filipp Goloshchekin had already been caught; Stasova would be arrested in June; and soon after D. M. Shvartsman was also picked up.[44] Only I. S. Belostotskii and Malinovskii remained free. In his role as secret police agent Malinovskii was probably responsible for the demise of the Bureau. He left Belostotskii untouched, one can assume, to divert suspicion from himself.

On July 2, 1912, Koba was taken on the *etap* to Siberia. He traveled first to Tomsk by train and from there aboard the steamship *Kolpashevets* to the town of Narym on the Ob River. The very name of the place, which means "marsh" in the Selkup (Ostiak-Samoed) language, describes its desolate landscape. A fortified outpost founded in the sixteenth century, it was the place where Russians collected tribute from the indigenous peoples of the region. Almost from its founding Narym was used as a place of exile for the tsar's undesirables. On his way to Narym, in the village of Kolpashevo, Koba met other exiles—Vereshchak, with whom he had shared a cell in Baku; the Socialist Revolutionary Semen Surin; and the Bolsheviks Sverdlov, Mikhail Lashevich, and Ivan Smirnov. Surrounded by forests and swamps, Narym was less hospitable than Kolpashevo. It held about one hundred fifty houses and about one thousand inhabitants. There were three hundred exiles living there at the time. The town appropriately had been designated a site for exile as its harsh winters cut it off from the rest of Russia for three months a year. There Koba lived for thirty-eight days in the little wooden house of a peasant, Iakov Alekseev, at the edge of a lake. Alekseev and his family, nine people in all, lived in the front part of the house; the other room usually housed three or four political exiles. His hostess, Evfrosinia Alekseeva, remembered her guest some thirty years later. He stayed "for two months in my house. It all began when he arrived at my home and it was no use me saying that we were short of space. He went into the exiles' room, looked around, talked with his comrades, then moved in with the two other exiles. . . . He wore a Russian embroidered, open-necked white shirt, which left his chest exposed."[45] Once again Koba humbly petitioned the authorities for amelioration of his condition. On July 18 he wrote to the Tomsk police superintendent: "In view of absence of any real means for survival I request Your Excellency to grant me a food and living allowance and some money for clothing for the time of my stay under police supervision in Narym Territory."[46]

Koba had barely arrived before, once again, he began planning his escape. He seemed uninterested when a twenty-five-year-old local housewife, Lukeria Tikhomirova, spotted him at a dance. He sat quietly to the side, drinking very little, smoking his pipe. He did not react when she said, "So young, and already smoking a pipe!" Instead he played with her two-year-old niece, who sat on his lap and ate the apples he offered her.[47] Koba asked his host and his brother to aid him escape. Alekseeva remembered, "When he set off he said, 'I am leaving my books for the comrades.' My sons Yakov and Agafon took him by boat to the river port. Before his departure he offered us apples and sugar from the parcel he had received. It also contained two bottles of good vodka."[48] When at twilight on September 1 they boarded a small boat, Koba asked, "Will we make it on this?" The peasants assured him, "We'll make it." They rowed through a dark, moonless night and delivered their charge by the road to Kolpashevo. They asked when they would see him again. "Expect me when you see me," he answered, and left his books with them. Their mother was upset that her men took the books, which Koba might need when he returned. They were convinced, however, that he would not be back.[49] When the police checked in the next day, they found only his roommate, Mikhail Nadezhdin, who informed them that Koba had gone to Kolpashevo. For more than a year the police searched Narym province for the escaped prisoner, but he had long since headed back to the capital.[50]

By steamship he made his way to Tomsk and then by train on to Saint Petersburg. Around September 12 Kavtaradze met him on Nevskii.

His appearance was not right for Nevskii Prospekt. He had an overgrown beard, a crumpled cap on his head; he was dressed in a threadbare jacket on top of a black shirt; his pants were also wrinkled, his shoes worn down. He looked like a skilled proletarian and stood out sharply against the background of respectable Nevskii Prospekt. "I have come from Narym," Stalin said, "I made it to Piter fairly successfully. . . . But here is the problem. I had a secret rendezvous, went there, but no one was there. . . . It's good at least that I met you.[51]

Kavtaradze sent Koba first to no. 44 Kolomenskaia Street, and in the evening took him to no. 10 Sablinskaia Street, the home of the widow of a rear admiral. Georgian students lived at both these addresses. Even though he was now in the center of Russian Social Democratic activity, when it was necessary Koba still moved in the dependable circles of his countrymen. The day after Koba arrived in the city, the gendarmes carried out massive arrests of Social Democrats, and once again the entire Petersburg Committee was rounded up. This time, however, Koba eluded his captors, even though the Baku police informed Saint Petersburg that he might try to meet Alliluev.[52] In fact he did visit the Alliluevs, often resting in the middle of the day on a metal bed in their tiny room off the kitchen. He took the children—Anna, Fedia, and Nadia, his future wife, then a girl of eleven—for a ride in a sleigh. "Every word caused us to laugh. Soso laughed with us: and at how our driver lavished praise on the poor frozen horse, and at how we squealed when we were thrown in the air by each snowdrift, and when we were thrown out of the sleigh." The apartment became a meeting place during the election campaign for the Fourth State Duma. On occasion Koba asked Alliluev's wife, Olga, to accompany him somewhere in order to avoid police suspicion.[53]

Competing with the Mensheviks for the loyalty of the workers, the Petersburg Bolsheviks were burdened by the absence of their major intellectuals and leading activists. The Mensheviks operated openly, and Dan and Potresov were available to advise their duma deputies. The Bolshevik leaders were either in prison, exile, abroad, or, like Koba, operating in the penumbra of politics, furtively moving in the dark to avoid the police. Koba busied himself with editorial work and the elections, as Nikolai Krestinskii remembered.[54] "His short stay in Petersburg and his work on *Pravda* in 1912 (September–December) coincided with the most difficult moment in the life of *Pravda* and our 'Piter' organization. This was the period of the preelection struggle with the Mensheviks. Conciliatory tendencies were strong even among workers, and great endurance and firmness were needed in order not to allow an agreement with the Mensheviks in the elections to the workers' curiae." Stalin carried out that work as well as directing the work of the Bolsheviks in the Fourth State Duma. "It was essential to set up the Bolshevik nucleus within what was at first a united Social Democratic faction and with the help of *Pravda* to create this nucleus of support for the capital's workers. Comrade Stalin began this work."[55]

ELECTIONS AND DUMA POLITICS

Social Democrats in the capital were swept up in the revived labor movement and the elections. When Bolshevik activists Inessa Armand and Georgii Safarov arrived in Saint Petersburg in the summer of 1912 to reestablish the faction's organization, which had been destroyed after massive strikes in May, they sensed the exceptional influence that *Pravda* enjoyed among the workers.[56] But Safarov also noted that there was much ambivalence about the Prague Conference among their old comrades, local Bolshevik intellectuals. Rather than Leninist orthodoxy on the question of inclusion in the party, Petersburg activists wanted to throw out a wide net. The *likvidatory* benefited from this mood, and Safarov and his co-organizer, the Franco-Russian party worker Armand, had to plead the Leninist case that in the upcoming elections Bolsheviks should run their own independent Bolshevik candidates. The *Pravda* board was hesitant about this position, and a heated discussion ensued before the majority came around.[57] Still, the Leninists' influence was growing, and when *likvidatory* held elections under the slogan of "unity" for the conference sponsored by Trotsky in Vienna (August 1912), it was evident that the workers were moving leftward toward the Bolsheviks. In the charged atmosphere of the capital, deeply saturated with the fallout of the Lena massacres, voters went to the polls to elect the Fourth—and last—State Duma.

Arriving in the city just as the voting was taking place, Koba engaged for the first time in an election campaign. Taking on his new pseudonym, the one that would become more widely known than his real name, Stalin was now not only a key Bolshevik operative in the city but at the vortex of the burgeoning oppositional movement. First as a response to the Lena killings, then continually fueled by the voices in the liberal and radical press as well as by debates in the duma that castigated the regime's callousness, student demonstrators and striking workers grew ever more radical in their demands, turning away from the liberals and *likvidatory*. Unlike 1905–1907, the expression of social discontent did not spread in the prewar years to the countryside but remained within the cities, nowhere more powerfully than in Saint Petersburg.

And, though the liberal and even conservative press was critical of the government's handling of Lena, in contrast with the earlier revolutionary years, middle- and upper-class people, except for students, did not join the workers in their protests. The Menshevik vision of a bourgeois revolution with workers and people of property struggling together failed either to correspond to the social dynamics of the period or to attract workers. Rather it was the more extreme picture sketched by the Bolsheviks—of the whole of propertied society, liberals, conservatives, and reactionaries alike, as the enemy of the working class—that brought people out of the factories into the streets. Here "Bolshevism offered Russia's workers . . . a strategy, or more precisely an image of a strategy, to achieve [a] brighter future."[58] The Social Democrats provided the historical narrative with its larger meaning, the road map for workers out of their squalor and deprivation that inspired and further radicalized many of them.

The elections to the duma demonstrated the radicalization and social polarization of the Russian people. The Left (Social Democrats and Kadets) and the Right (Nationalists and Rightists) increased their delegations in the duma, while the Octobrists, who now constituted the center and were the party on which the government had depended for support, lost representatives. In the all-important second curiae of the cities, where Kadets had usually done well with middle class constituents, voters favored those who stood to the left of the liberals. Government manipulation of the elections and mobilization of the Orthodox clergy to vote for the Rightists cost the Octobrists votes but failed to prevent the general leftward shift of most of the voters. Octobrists lost to the more liberal Kadets, and Kadets to Social Democrats. Many Octobrists were no longer prepared to cooperate with the tsarist regime, appalled at the government's interference in the elections. As the country approached the world war, the opposition to tsarism was spreading from the bottom to the top of society, and at the same time, the lower and upper classes were pulling away from each other, both more suspicious about the aims and intentions of the other.[59] The growing social polarization reaped the whirlwind for the radical tactics of the Bolsheviks, both on the eve of World War I and again in the revolutionary year, 1917.

This was Stalin's first direct engagement with electoral politics. *Pravda's* editors operated as a Bolshevik general staff during the elections. Meetings were held with workers, far from the center, in the proletarian district, Narvskaia zastava, or secretly in forests outside of town to avoid the police and their spies. The Mensheviks and Bolsheviks argued ferociously for their platforms. With the Socialist Revolutionaries boycotting the elections, the Social Democrats were the workers' preferred choice. In Stalin's view the elections demonstrated the poverty of the legalism of *likvidatorstvo*. Three camps faced each other: revolutionary Social Democracy; the counterrevolutionary Right; and the conciliators.[60] All Social Democrats, except a few *otzovisti*, had been for participating and electing deputies from their faction.

The election process was deliberately structured in a series of rounds to restrict the votes of the lower classes. First, voters (*izbirateli*) in each class curia (workers, peasants, people with the *tsenz* [adequate property qualification]) voted for plenipotentiaries (*upolnomochennye*), who then voted for electors (*vyborshchiki*), who actually voted, along with electors from other social curiae for the duma deputies. In round one of the elections from the workers' curia not all workers were permitted to vote. The government had temporarily disenfranchised twenty-one of the largest Petersburg factories. Nevertheless, in September the voters in the workers' curia chose eighty-two plenipotentiaries: twenty-six anti-liquidators, fifteen liquidators, and forty-one Social Democrats and nonparty representatives who did not identify with either camp. The police prevented those elected to caucus before their official assembly, but many secretly gathered outside the city where Bolsheviks and Mensheviks argued for over five hours. The plenipotentiaries met in their assembly on October 5 and chose six electors, four of them from *Pravda's* list. Workers meanwhile protested the government's exclusion of the large plants, and when the government gave in, additional elections were held for plenipotentiaries. All over the city factory workers overwhelmingly adopted a *Nakaz* (instruction) drawn up by the Petersburg Committee to be given to the Social Democratic duma deputies. Stalin is said to have been the author, and as the ranking Central Committee member in the city, he must have drafted or played an editorial role in its composition. Lenin urged *Pravda* to publish it "in a prominent place in large print."[61] But the editors of *Pravda* apparently thought it too radical, and it was instead published abroad in *Sotsial-Demokrat*.[62] The *Nakaz* called for a struggle on two fronts—against the feudal bureaucratic order and against the liberal bourgeoisie—and ordered Social Democratic deputies not to engage in simple legislative activity but to use the duma floor as a tribunal to proclaim the working class's ambitions.

With the additional plenipotentiaries from the formerly excluded factories, a second assembly chose three Bolsheviks and three Mensheviks as electors. The Bolshevik *Nakaz* was unanimously adopted. Finally, the electors from the workers' curia met on October 20 with electors from the other curiae to choose the actual duma deputies. Most of the electors from the workers' curia wanted the Menshevik P. I. Sudakov as their deputy, though Lenin was disturbed by Sudakov's defection from the Bolsheviks to the Mensheviks.[63] But the ambitious and venal Bolshevik Aleksei Badaev had broken party rules and placed himself in contention. Sudakov lost the election, probably because he was Jewish, and more conservative electors voted for the Russian candidate, Badaev.[64]

With the elections over, Social Democrats could count thirteen deputies: seven Mensheviks and six Bolsheviks. Once again Caucasia, particularly Georgia, gave the Mensheviks their support. Besides the Georgians, Akaki Chkhenkeli and Nikoloz Chkheidze, the deputy from Baku, Matvei Skobelev (1885–1938), was also a Menshevik. Eugeniusz Jagiełło, a member of the Polish Socialist Party, was elected from Warsaw thanks to the votes of the local Jewish parties. The Social Democrats in the duma were divided whether he should be accepted into the caucus. The Mensheviks were prepared to accept him, but the Bolsheviks were opposed because he had been supported by the bourgeoisie.[65] Ultimately, the seven Mensheviks voted to invite him to become a member with a voice but no vote. Lenin was pleased by that decision, and Stalin accepted Jagiełło as not a "fully legitimate member of the Social Democratic faction."[66]

The Mensheviks in the duma were primarily intellectuals, many of them practiced in writing and speaking in public. They had been chosen by the provincial electoral assemblies representing various classes. Three were workers, but the most influential members of their delegation were professionals, the three from the Caucasus: Chkheidze was a journalist, Skobelev an engineer, and Chkhenkeli a lawyer. Though the Mensheviks dominated the duma caucus, they were far from united. The Georgians worried that their Russian Menshevik comrades were losing the workers because of their lukewarm attitude toward the strikes. Eventually the Mensheviks in the duma followed the Georgians and condemned *likvidatorstvo*. But they distinguished themselves from the Bolsheviks by holding firm to the notion that there was no possibility for revolutionary success without allying with the Kadets, the leading "bourgeois" liberal party. Their vain hope that the liberals might become even more radical left the Mensheviks waiting for something that did not come. Their passivity was all the more evident as the Bolsheviks went from victory to victory on the wave of worker militancy.

The Bolshevik deputies were mainly from the working class, and with the exception of Malinovskii were somewhat uneasy about performing in the duma.[67] Molotov, then working at *Pravda*, remembered later that Badaev "was a lightweight," an "honest man, though poorly educated and not very active. But he had a capacity for work. After he'd been elected he came to see us at *Pravda* and said, 'I'm not very educated. It will be difficult for me to work in the Duma. Can't you give me a book where I can read what I am supposed to do, and what Bolshevism is? I'll read this book, remember it, and follow it.' But no matter, he then improved."[68] Despite the fact that Badaev, like many of the Mensheviks, had been chosen by a provincial assembly, the Bolsheviks claimed that their six deputies were the truer representatives of Russia's working class since they had been elected by the workers' curiae in the six principal industrial provinces (Saint Petersburg, Moscow, Ekaterinoslav, Kharkov, Vladimir, and Kostroma). Four metal workers and two textile workers made up their delegation. Stalin acted as a liaison between the newly elected Bolshevik deputies and the factions' leaders in Kraków. Meeting with the deputies secretly, sometimes in Badaev's apartment, Stalin was as determined as the leaders abroad to guide their duma members and keep them from drawing too close to the Mensheviks or liberals. He wanted the deputies to meet with the Central Committee in Austrian Poland before the duma opened, but the conference could not be arranged in time.[69]

Oddly, the old political disputes from his Georgian days followed Stalin to Petersburg. At one point he was living with his friend Todria and his wife, Sofiia. The landlady of the apartment building did not like the "dark one" and forbad Sofiia to allow him to come into the apartment. He stayed away for a few days but eventually returned. There he crossed paths with two old nemeses, Zhordania and Jibladze. He remarked to his hostess, "They are old people. There's nothing to talk to them about!"[70] At a moment when it was essential that the Social Democrats needed to work together, they found it impossible. The Bolsheviks asked that the caucus be run not by simple majority rule, but as a federation with each faction being equally represented. As the leader of the duma Mensheviks, Chkheidze, Stalin's old enemy from Batumi, refused. The Social Democrats split into two caucuses, cooperating on occasion but competing intensely for the support of their public. Malinovskii, who had been elected from the Moscow workers' curia, was chosen leader of the Bolshevik deputies. From that favored position he reported regularly to his police handlers on the activity of the faction.

Some radicalized workers printed leaflets calling for a one-day political strike for November 15 (28), the day set for the opening of the Fourth Duma. The Menshevik newspaper *Luch* (Ray of Light) opposed the strike, and ultimately the Social Democratic duma caucus, Bolsheviks included, did as well. Thousands of workers marched to the Tauride Palace, where the duma met, to register their presence as a social force, even though the Social Democrats had cautioned against the manifestation. Lenin was appalled that workers' deputies had not backed the "remarkable proletarian instinct" of the protesting workers.[71] He wrote to Stalin suggesting that the "mistake of November 15 must be 'corrected'" by more determined action for the upcoming eighth anniversary of Bloody Sunday in January.[72] Stalin obliged by writing a radical proclamation for the anniversary.[73]

Lenin remained quite discontented with the direction of *Pravda*, and the émigrés hoped that Stalin might effect the necessary changes. On October 21 (November 3), 1912, Krupskaia requested Stalin's presence in Kraków, and a week later he left for the Polish city. Crossing the border was always a dangerous operation, and Stalin had no reliable contacts on the route to Austria. On the train to the border he grew angry at two passengers in his cabin who were reading a right-wing newspaper out loud. His patience exhausted, he burst out, "Why are you reading this rubbish? You ought to read other newspapers." The couple abruptly left the cabin.[74] When early in the morning the train approached his stop, Dąbrowa Górnicza, he jumped out of the last carriage to avoid the police of at the station. In the semi-darkness of the dawn he walked south toward Austria, but he no longer had the address of his local contacts, having destroyed it. In one version of the story he walked through the nearby market several times, when an unfamiliar man stopped him and asked if he was looking for someone or needed a place to stay. The kind stranger, who turned out to be a Polish shoemaker, took him home. In another, which he told to the Polish ambassador to the Soviet Union, Stanisław Kot, during the Second World War, he saw a light in a peasant's hut, where a cobbler was mending shoes. He knocked, and when asked who was there, he answered, "A revolutionary."[75] Stalin told the stranger that his father had been a shoemaker, and the two bonded. The Pole offered to guide him to the border, led him through the woods, all the while Stalin wary that he might be turned over to the police. About an hour from the border, the shoemaker pointed him in the right direction. When Stalin offered him money, the Pole refused. "No, that's not necessary. I did not do this for money. We are both sons of oppressed nations; we ought to help each other." They shook hands firmly and separated, never to see the other again.[76]

The man soon to become one of the Bolsheviks' leading experts on the nationality question learned another lesson about ethnic hostilities across the border at the Trzebinia station where he sat down at a large restaurant to eat. He ordered his food, but no one served him. As he told the story to Kot,

I went up to the buffet and said sharply: "This is scandalous; everybody else has been served except me." The waiter filled a plate with soup and handed it to me. Then there was another bell, a train for Cracow arrived and everyone rushed to get in. In my fury I threw the plate on the floor, flung a rouble at the waiter and flew out.

When he arrived in Kraków, he went straight to Lenin's apartment.

We hardly greeted each other when I burst out:

"Lenin, give me something to eat at once, for I'm half dead; I've had nothing since yesterday evening." Lenin replied: "Why didn't you eat at Trzebinia; there's a very good restaurant there." "The Poles wouldn't give me anything to eat." And I told him the whole story. "But what language did you order the food in?" he asked. "Why, in Russian of course. I don't know any other."

"What a fool you are, Stalin! . . . Don't you know that the Poles think of Russian as the language of their persecutors?" "But how could I order anything when I don't know Polish?" "How? Why, just point to what you wanted and you'd have got it." I remembered that advice, and whenever I went to a shop for cigarettes I pointed and put down my money and always got what I wanted."[77]

Stalin traveled three times to Kraków for consultations at the end of 1912 and in the first months of 1913. Several other members of the Central Committee and the duma deputies Malinovskii and Matvei Muranov also met with Lenin and Zinoviev.[78] By this time, however, Lenin was depending on Stalin as his key liaison to deal with the duma caucus, *Pravda*, and other matters.[79] Krupskaia wrote to him that "everything sent to [*Pravda*] should be seen by you and without your approval nothing should be done."[80] The editorial board was changed, but the newspaper's tone did not shift very much. From Kraków they wrote to Stalin, "For God's sake, take the most energetic steps to get [*Pravda*] away from [Poletaev] and put it formally in Muranov's name; in particular, take over the funds and the subscription money. Without these we are lost."[81] Stalin was in regular contact with the Bolshevik duma deputies, most of whom were unwilling to go along with Lenin and break completely with Chkheidze and the Mensheviks. They wanted to hold together in a single parliamentary caucus—all except Malinovskii, who touted the police position that breaking up the caucus was to the regime's advantage. Most of the Social Democratic deputies wanted *Pravda* to merge with the Menshevik *Luch*, which Lenin condemned as "liquidationist." In December 1912, eleven of the thirteen Social Democratic deputies voted to merge the two newspapers, and three days later, Mensheviks were listed as contributors to *Pravda*.[82] Lenin was furious.

In his letters to Stalin, written in a kind of code to "Vasilev," Lenin gave him specific instructions on what to do with the *Pravda* board and how to handle the Mensheviks' support of the Polish duma deputy and their attacks on the Bolshevik, Badaev. Cryptically he wrote, "As soon as possible, chase Vasilev out of there, otherwise you won't be saved, for he is needed and has already done the most important things."[83] This meant that, once again, he wanted Stalin in Kraków. The letters from Krupskaia grew more insistent, somewhat annoyed at Stalin's lack of deference toward the Bolshevik leaders.

> Dear friend, finally we received today a more or less detailed letter from you. By the way, it is not completely clear, it seems, if you intend, even given the situation, to come yourself . . . together with four friends. If this is so, then we categorically insist on your coming. Many questions are coming to a head . . . so that even independently of the conditions of your health your presence is absolutely required. And we categorically demand it. You have no right to proceed differently.[84]

The next day she asked for the most detailed report, budget numbers, income, and expenses.[85] Just before he left Petersburg, Stalin attended a meeting to reestablish the Petersburg Committee, and a few days later a committee made up of workers, with himself as Central Committee representative, was established.[86] Then, finally, around December 18, 1912, he left for Kraków.

His route this time was rather elaborate. A Finnish worker, A. V. Shotman, made the arrangements. On the eve of his departure Stalin met with Kalinin, Muranov, Petrovskii, Smoilov, and Shotman at Eino Rakhia's apartment on Finland Prospect to confer about the duma's work and his journey. Then he went on a shunting train to a small suburban station to avoid the spies at the Finland Station in the city. Just over the Finnish border he was met and taken on to Marienham in the Åland Islands, the westernmost point of the Russian Empire, whence he took a steamship to Germany and made his way to Austria.[87] Stalin intended to stay one and a half weeks, as he wrote to Kamenev in Paris. In a postscript to Stalin's letter, Zinoviev added his own "warm greetings" to the associate with whom he and Kamenev would be most closely associated right up to their executions in 1936. "The public is great here. Business will be a bit cleaner than in Prague. Too bad you are not here. Grigorii."[88]

In desperation Lenin had called a meeting of the Central Committee, Bolshevik duma deputies, and other party activists. The police, thanks to Malinovskii, knew exactly where Stalin was and the names of those present. Besides Stalin and Zinoviev, Lenin and Krupskaia, the duma deputies Badaev and Petrovskii attended, along with the worker Medvedev, and one of the editors of the Bolshevik theory journal, *Prosveshchenie* [Enlightenment], Aleksandr Troianovskii, and his wife, Elena Razmirovich. The meeting revamped the Central Committee, whose members now included Lenin, Zinoviev, Stalin, Petrovskii, Malinovskii, Sverdlov, Filipp, Spitsa, and Belostotskii. Stalin was named a member of the Central Committee's Russian Bureau along with Malinovskii, Petrovskii, and Sverdlov.[89] Essentially, Stalin was now one of the five or six most empowered Bolsheviks.

The Troianovskiis' young governess, Olga Veiland, was present at the Bolshevik gathering in Kraków and from an adjoining room listened to the discussions. "Koba did not speak very loudly. He talked in a deliberate, measured manner. He set out his thoughts with indisputable logic. Sometimes he went through the other room so he could pace up and down while listening to the speeches of the other comrades." Once when the discussions dragged on particularly long into the night, he slept in Lenin's kitchen on a blanket on the floor. Apparently, he was not sleeping well since Zinoviev had to reprimand him once for yawning during the conference.[90]

The resolutions of that January 1913 gathering affirmed the hard position of the Leninists. *Pravda* was chastised for its softness toward the more moderate Mensheviks.[91] Lenin chided Sverdlov for thinking that Stalin was exaggerating the need for reform at *Pravda*, then sent him to Petersburg to become co-editor with Stalin and to reorganize the editorial board. "In fact [*Pravda*] and its proper set up is the *nail* of the situation." Not reforming the newspaper will lead to "material and political bankruptcy."[92] Sverdlov managed to complete that task to Lenin's satisfaction just before he was arrested. He was picked up in deputy Petrovskii's apartment. The police were supposedly prohibited from violating the immunity of elected officials, but in this case they simply disregarded the rule.

Stalin remained free for another month. The situation was extraordinarily precarious as the police used the information from their secret agents to decimate the socialists' infrastructure. Stalin recommended to the Central Committee that the next editor of *Pravda* should be someone with legal status, and either he or Sverdlov suggested Koba's comrade from Baku Stepan Shahumian. Intrigued by the offer, the Armenian Bolshevik, who was living in exile with his family in Astrakhan, traveled to Petersburg and spent much of March and April working on the newspaper. He lived with the Alliluevs. The night editor was Miron Chernomazov, who unknown to his comrades, had been recruited by the police after an arrest. Shahumian knew him from Baku and asked that he be removed. The Bolshevik duma deputies objected. Shahumian, frustrated by the disagreements with the editorial board and fearful that he was drawing attention from the police, returned discouraged to the south.[93] Only after greater suspicion fell on Chernomazov was the secret agent removed and replaced by Lev Kamenev, who turned out not only to be a fine editor but able to turn the paper onto the path demanded by Lenin.

More than just a member of the Central Committee, Stalin had joined the inner circle of the Bolshevik faction. He was now one of Lenin's chief lieutenants, along with Kamenev and Zinoviev. A roving agent like Orjonikidze, he was in touch both with the émigré center and party members in various cities from Caucasia to Petersburg. He was an editor of the popular *Pravda* and closely involved in the politics of the Social Democratic caucus in the duma. The short time that he spent abroad, from late December 1912 to mid-February 1913, proved to be extraordinarily busy and productive. From Kraków he wrote to a comrade in Petersburg that "the problem is that the atmosphere here is impossible; everyone is ridiculously busy, occupied the devil only knows how." He remembered to send greetings to his friends in Narym, to "Andrei" [Sverdlov], and concluded, "With me things here are in general not bad."[94] He wrote an especially warm letter to his old friend Kamenev but also complained about his situation in Kraków.

Dear friend!

I kiss you on the nose, Eskimo-style. Devil take me. I miss you terribly. Really, I miss you, I swear on my dog! There is no one for me here, no one to talk to heart-to-heart, devil take you. Can you really not come over to Kraków?

Like Lenin he was upset by the failure of some of the Bolshevik deputies to support the November 15 protest and by their defection to the Menshevik *Luch*. But he did not agree with him that a "tough policy" had to be taken toward the caucus or that the *nizy*, the party rank-and-file and workers, had to be mobilized against the deviant Bolsheviks. "The six [Bolshevik duma deputies]," he cautioned, were not fully Bolshevik; they "have not yet matured to the point of accepting a tough policy. They are not yet prepared. We must first consolidate the six and then beat the majority of the caucus with them, as Ilia [Muromets] beat the Tatars with a Tatar."[95] In a couple of months, he advised, we might attract one or two deputies to our side and gain a majority in the caucus. "Then we can beat the *caucus of liquidators*; this is a much better approach. We have to work and hold off a little with the tough policy." He regretted that he had missed one meeting of the caucus, "and that was enough time for the six to slip up stupidly with *Luch*. In a word, we must wait a bit."[96] He soon was on his way to Vienna where, on Lenin's instructions, he was to write on the problem of nationalities. This simple assignment had repercussions, unimaginable at the time both for Stalin personally and for his country.

23

THE EXPERT

Those few weeks that Comrade Stalin spent with us were devoted entirely to the national question. [He] involved everyone around him in the study. Some analyzed Otto Bauer, others Karl Kautsky. This was our sole topic of conversation at the time. Little Galochka, . . . who loved being in adult company, often complained about it: "You're always talking about the nations!"

—OLGA VEILAND, "IZ AVSTRIISKOI EMIGRATSII"
["FROM THE AUSTRIAN EMIGRATION"]

I read in the Bolshevik magazine *Prosveshchenie* an article on the national question with the signature, strange to me then, of J. Stalin. The article attracted attention mainly because, through the banal monotonous text, there flashed occasionally original ideas and brilliant formulas. Years afterwards I learned that the article had been inspired by Lenin and in the manuscript of the apprentice there could be seen the hand of the master.

—LEON TROTSKY, *PORTRAITS,
POLITICAL & PERSONAL* (1977)

Nationalism was the specter haunting Communism in Europe at the turn of the century. In Russia whatever emotional attachments most peasants and workers felt toward their language, culture, or ethnic compatriots were simply taken for granted as part of the mélange of loyalties, affinities, and identities with which they lived in their daily lives. But for small groups of intellectuals and politicians the nation had become a touchstone for politics. The wars and revolutions of nineteenth-century

Europe were often inspired by the rhetoric of the nation, tales of resisting imperial oppression, gathering one's cultural brethren under a single flag, or recovering the lost patrimony of nationhood. A narrative of rising from darkness into light, emerging from blindness into consciousness, of renaissance and rebirth excited the educated men and women who engaged in the construction of national mythologies and histories. New states based on the national principle rather than dynasticism—Greece, Serbia, Italy, Rumania, and Bulgaria—inspired peoples who had yet to achieve statehood, among them the Poles, Irish, Ukrainians, Armenians, Georgians, and others in the Austrian, Ottoman, and Russian empires. For several of the nationalities living under the Romanovs the revolution of 1905 was a moment of mass mobilization around the symbols of national resistance to imperial rule. The Georgian peasant movement, even though led by Marxists, was tinged with national sentiments as well as social resentments, the two too intricately interwoven to dissect from one another. The Menshevik Akaki Chkhenkeli, later a deputy to the Fourth State Duma, noted that 1905 was "the greatest moment for the development of Georgian people's consciousness of their nationhood. It did not exist as a whole nation [before]; now it exists as a whole nation. A new period of development has begun—a time when toiling masses become the carriers of national solidarity."[1] From the podium of the Duma Chkhenkeli, along with his fellow Georgians Evgeni Gegechkori and Nikoloz Chkheidze, as well as Polish and other non-Russian deputies, publicly raised issues of religious, linguistic, and cultural rights.[2] In the neighboring Hapsburg Empire, as the Austrian Marxists reported, the fallout from 1905 had a radicalizing effect, particularly on the Slavic nationalities. The question of one's primary loyalty to the empire versus one's own ethnic "nation" no longer could be brushed aside.

MARXISTS PONDER THE QUESTION OF THE NATION

When it came to thinking about the emergence of the nation-form and the unexpected power of nationalism, Marxists were on their own. Their mentors and guides, Marx and Engels, had left them "neither a systematic theory of the national question, a precise definition of the concept of a 'nation,' nor a general political strategy for the proletariat in this domain."[3] Optimistic that the development of the bourgeoisie, free trade, and the world market worked to lessen national differences and antagonisms, Marx had boldly proclaimed that the workers had no fatherland and were by nature internationalist rather than nationalist. Workers might after the revolution constitute themselves as the nation only to hasten the process of eliminating national boundaries and conflicts between peoples.[4] Nationalism was a harmful phenomenon generated by the bourgeoisie, which sought to control national markets and exploit ethnic suspicions as a means to dominate the proletariat. Marx and Engels considered nations to be historical communities that were capable of unity into a state. Rather than determined by language or ethnic culture, a nation was formed by the historical development of a distinct economic system, which resulted in a national solidarity among the people and a shared psychology. The formation of states and nations within them was progressive and contributed to the development of capitalism, but over time the capitalists' own economic activity paradoxically—Marx might say "dialectically"—created the conditions for the ultimate end of nations and nationalism. As an early theorist of what today we label "globalization," Marx predicted that the expansion of the capitalist mode of production, its sweeping away of national peculiarities, and the creation of a world market would undermine the foundations of the nation. "All that's solid melts into air, all that's holy is profaned."[5] Once the working class takes power, national differences and hostilities will "vanish still faster" until, presumably, when communism and a classless society has been created, nations would disappear altogether. For Marx and Engels nationalism was reducible to economic causes, and they usually set aside cultural or psychological factors as explanations for the formation and durability of national loyalties.

Since nations were connected to states and implicated in economic development, Marx and Engels did not propose an abstract right of all nations to self-determination and statehood. Rather they argued that some peoples would not achieve the sufficient size, territory, and capacity to form a viable state. In general Marx and Engels preferred larger states—for example, a united Germany—because they could advance the development of capitalism more rapidly. These "historyless peoples" (*geschichtslose Völker*), like the Czechs and other Slavs in the Austrian Empire, did not have a right to self-determination as did larger peoples, like the Germans or Hungarians.[6] Engels carried this notion further than his mentor and spoke of Austrian Slavs as "national refuse" who would be annihilated or at least absorbed by the Germans or Hungarians.

Both Marx and Engels supported national liberation movements in Poland and Ireland, struggles that they saw as directed against two great imperial powers: Russia, the gendarme of Europe; and Britain, whose global reach defied the setting sun. Liberation of oppressed nations weakened the reach of reactionary and liberal states as well as the hegemony of national bourgeoisies over their own workers. "Any nation that oppresses another," wrote Marx, "forges its own chains." To his successors Marx bequeathed both his positive evaluation of national consolidation for larger peoples and his support for anti-imperial movements to rise up against oppressive empires—two attitudes that were difficult to reconcile. To confuse matters further, Marx and Engels both condemned the brutality of British and French colonialism and simultaneously noted the progressive, civilizing effects of empire. Their backing of particular nationalist movements was primarily strategic. The relevant question was: would a particular national struggle aid the development of society in the proper historical direction, first from feudalism to capitalism, and later from capitalism to socialism? As important as national solidarities were for economic and historical progress, for Marx and Engels it was the horizontal solidarities of class that ultimately were decisive, not the vertical solidarities so dear to nationalists that linked the top of the nation with the bottom.

As early as 1887, just four years after Marx's death, the young Karl Kautsky laid out his understanding of a Marxist theory of the nation. The child of capitalist commodity production, the nation arose as a "community of language" and a "community of territory." In 1896 the Second International resolved that all nations had a "right to self-determination," a vague formulation that could mean anything from cultural rights or autonomy all the way to sovereign statehood. At the same time Marxists, particularly those in the multinational empires of the Romanovs and Hapsburgs, desperately desired to keep their large, economically advantageous states intact. Opposed to nationalism but in favor of self-determination, anti-imperialist and supporting national liberation yet discouraging nationalism and separatism, the Marxists' dilemma was somehow to justify the country's survival after the revolution without driving minority nationalities into the arms of the nationalists.

Russian Social Democrats shared Marx, Engels, and Kautsky's economic analyses of nations and nationalism, believing that nations were a product of a certain stage of historic evolution. Lenin preferred Kautsky's "historical-economic theory" of the nation as territorialized *Sprachgemeinschaft* (language community) to the Austro-Marxist "idealist" theory of nation as *Kulturgemeinschaft* (cultural community).[7] Even though nationalism was a kind of delusion that led people away from their authentic class interests, in the age of bourgeois hegemony nations were real entities with which victorious revolutionaries would have to deal.

In their discussions of the "national question," the Social Democrats divided the problem into three parts. First there was a cluster of theoretical questions: What are nations? Where did they come from, and what would become of them in the future? Were nations becoming more like one another, with acculturation and assimilation their ultimate fate, or were they becoming more divergent and belligerent? A second cluster confirmed the confidence of the Social Democrats that history was on their side and that they would eventually be taking over the reins of state power. How should the future multinational state be organized, on a centralized or federalist model? Should the various peoples of the socialist republic be granted nonnational regional autonomy that did not take ethnicity into consideration or national cultural autonomy that would privilege cultural and linguistic differences? Were national rights best guaranteed by territorial autonomy or by the intricate formula of the Austrian Marxists, extraterritorial national cultural autonomy, in which individuals carried their nationality and attendant rights wherever they might live?

The third set of questions, and the ones the Russian Social Democrats would take up first, were on party organization. Should the party be centralized or federalist? And should various national groups have their own distinct Social Democratic party? Most of the major leaders of Russian Social Democracy were committed to a centralized party and rejected the petitions of the Jewish Bund at their Second Party Congress in 1903 for special privileges in organizing the Jewish workers and for a federal tie to the RSDRP. As young Koba wrote in *brdzola*, "The Georgian Social Democratic movement does not represent in isolation only the Georgian workers' movement with its own program; it goes hand in hand with the All-Russian movement, and, consequently, is subordinated to the Russian Social Democratic Party."[8] Three years later, however, Lenin and the Bolsheviks were willing to compromise on this issue and admit the Bund, the Latvian, Polish, and Lithuanian Social Democrats, to the RSDRP, though not on a federal basis. Zhordania and the Georgian delegates were vociferous in their opposition to the Bund and continued to denounce the idea of organizing workers on the basis of nationality.[9] Local party committees were supposed to be made up of members of any and all nationalities. At their Kraków conference in February 1913, the Bolsheviks reaffirmed their commitment to multinational committees, criticized the Bund, and praised the Caucasians for their model organizations.[10] Lenin wrote that the "sad experience of half-federation" (1907–1911) was something that the party had to learn from; it had to campaign for "unity at the bottom." The Bund had not followed the resolution of the 1906 congress and united with other nationalities locally.[11] Less obviously the Georgian Mensheviks, even as they maintained rhetorically the principle of multinationality, steadily moved toward becoming a nearly exclusively Georgian organization. The ideal party organization for Lenin and the Bolsheviks, given the diverse ethnic makeup of its workers, was Baku, the crucible in which Koba had shed his Georgian apparel and been forged into an internationalist Social Democrat.

The Social Democrats of Caucasia could not leave the national question alone. It was too vital for their movement and their political prospects. Before Stalin emerged as a principal spokesman for the Bolsheviks on this issue, his fellow Caucasian, Shahumian, was engaged in a dialogue with Lenin about nationalism, federalism, and the place of nationality in the future socialist state. Shahumian penned his first major piece on the issue in 1906 and struggled to conceptualize the nation as both a "natural" and a "social" phenomenon—natural in the actual existence of millions of people of "more or less the same religion, morals, and traditions" living on one territory; and social in its historical existence as a political organism.[12] Naturalizing the nation was problematic for a Marxist, but at this time, Shahumian had a somewhat Darwinian sense of a struggle between united peoples, as well as with nature, for existence.[13] Several years later he took a more historical approach, highlighting the agency of the bourgeoisie in uniting tribes into national states to secure larger markets and gain advantages in economic competition with foreigners.[14] Having abandoned his earlier enthusiasm for national cultural autonomy and federalism under Lenin's unsparing criticism, Shahumian wrote in favor of a centralized state, which, in his view, was most appropriate for the proletariat.

> For the proletariat of a small nation, for example, the Armenians, the Russian proletariat is closer in interests and demands than the Armenian bourgeoisie, and it knows that uniting with the proletariat of the Russians, the Georgians, and of other nations in a common state parliament, it will be better able to protect its own economic needs than if it were forced to deal with the Armenian bourgeoisie in a "national" parliament.[15]

Regional self-government, which he distinguished from regional autonomy (there would be no reserved powers for the regions), was a means to reconcile "political centralization and administrative decentralization."[16]

Nearly a decade later, in 1913–1914, Lenin and Shahumian continued their intense correspondence on the fraught issue of nationalism. With

Stalin in prison and then exile, Lenin continued his search for someone, preferably a Caucasian Bolshevik, to collect material and write on this question. When Shahumian revealed to Lenin that he favored Russian as a state language for the future democratic state, Lenin sternly replied that he "completely disagreed."

> The Russian language had a progressive significance for those small and backward nations—no doubt of that. But is it possible that you do not see that it would have had a progressive significance in still greater measure if there had not been compulsion? . . . No, I absolutely disagree with you, and I find you guilty of royal Prussian socialism!![17]

Psychology, Lenin went on, was paramount in solving the national question, and "the slightest compulsion pollutes, dirties, reduces to nothing the indisputable progressive significance of centralization, large states, one language." Economics, he went on, is even more important than psychology, and with Russia already a capitalist society, economic forces will require homogenization of language. He also took Shahumian to task for not fully supporting regional autonomy. "We are for democratic centralism unconditionally. We are against federalism. We are for the Jacobins against the Girondists. But to be afraid of autonomy—in Russia . . . have mercy, this is funny! This is reactionary." The limits of autonomy would be determined by the central parliament, so there was no need to worry if some rights were reserved for localities.[18]

Shahumian had also argued that the right of self-determination would necessarily mean the right to autonomy and a federal tie to the center, but Lenin rejected that reading. He strongly opposed federalism because it weakened the economic tie and was incompatible with the type of unitary state he envisioned. "Do you want to separate? Go to the devil if you can cut the economic tie, or, rather, if the yoke and friction of 'coexistence' are such that they spoil and ruin the economic relationship. You don't want to separate? Then, please, don't decide for me; don't think that you have the 'right' to federation."[19] Lenin won this argument at the time, but on this fraught matter Shahumian would ultimately prove more prescient than Lenin. The future Soviet Union would formally enshrine national self-determination in its constitution, and Lenin himself would eventually agree that this would require national cultural territorial autonomy and a federal connection between the various national entities and the center.

As early as 1903 the RSDRP adopted a program in which only local and regional, not national cultural, autonomy was proposed. A nationality could determine that it wished to secede, but the Social Democrats might or might not support that effort. If the nationality decided not to secede, it could join the unitary socialist state where it would enjoy its cultural rights, but neither national territorial autonomy nor a federal tie to the state would be granted.

The questions of what is a nation and what should be the future shape of the postrevolutionary state again became matters of deep and immediate concern to Lenin at the end of 1912 and through the prewar years. Even as a long-time opponent of national cultural autonomy and federalism, both of which he thought would impede economic development and encourage nationalism, he remained a strong backer of the self-determination of nations. But while recognizing this right, he consistently maintained that support for national independence had to be subordinated to the interests of the proletarian struggle. Here was a loophole through which all kinds of mischief would be allowed, pragmatic choices made that would contradict the right of national self-determination. Even more ominously, the Bolsheviks in power, with Stalin a major proponent of a strong unified state, would compromise Lenin's early warnings against "the slightest compulsion" of a centralizing state.

MARXISM DIVIDED OVER THE NATION

The contentious debates and disagreements among the Social Democrats on the national question belie a conclusion that there is a single, fixed Marxist theory of nation formation and nationalism. Instead the moral and political attitudes of Marxists toward nationalism through the last century and a half have tended to be pragmatic, tactical, flexible, and contingent on historical specifics. A critic might call them "opportunistic," but the wide range of Marxists, who so often argue more vociferously with one another than with their opponents, might at least agree that their pragmatic and strategic statements were related to their assessment of which approach would lead to the advancement of socialism, the elusive beacon on which they all set their course.

Nations were real things to Second International Marxists. The classical (what some would call "orthodox") Marxist view of the nation, as articulated by most Social Democrats of the early twentieth century, began with the supposition that nations were products of history, not of nature, and that they were generated by material processes such as the need for national markets, state policies protecting those markets, and long-distance trade. Therefore, nations were objective, real, material, not merely the product of consciousness or a national spirit (*Geist*). They would continue to exist after the revolution and the building of socialism, even as the nationless proletariat dissolved antagonistic nationalisms. Not all nationalities would be preserved, however; small "historyless" peoples would merge into larger, more vital nations. "National ruins," like the Czechs, would disappear in what Engels posited as a Darwinian competition for economic and political survival. Nationalism, then, was progressive only at the moment of the struggle against the *ancien regime* and feudalism and as anti-imperialism, but not in its atavistic aspirations to preserve national culture as a value in itself. National liberation was to be applauded only when it aided and was subordinated to the movement for social emancipation. Horizontal class loyalties—workers of one nation joining with workers of other nations—were to be promoted, not vertical national loyalties—workers with the bourgeoisie of their own nation.

Nationalism, on the other hand, was a form of consciousness that arose as the nation was being formed, a subjective expression of the nation. This chronology—nation before nationalism—would be reversed in late twentieth-century nationalism theory in the work both of non-Marxists, like Elie Kedourie and Ernest Gellner, and Marxists, like Benedict Anderson and Eric J. Hobsbawm.[20] They would propose that nations were a product of human action, of invention and imagination, as much if not more than of historical processes and greater social communication. In other words, nationalism—thinking and talking about "the nation" and acting as if it existed or ought to be brought into existence—forged nations (in both senses of that verb) and made them a reality, rather than the other way around.[21]

Based as it was largely on the emergence of nations in Western Europe, Marxist theory labeled nationalism "bourgeois," as it emerged with the ascent of the propertied middle class and, in their reading, worked fundamentally in the interests of the possessing classes rather than the workers. But in most of Eastern Europe and the Russian Empire, where capitalist middle classes were weak or largely absent, nationalism was more the expression of patriotic intellectuals, scholarly clerics, journalists, village teachers, lawyers, and artists.[22] Imperial authorities saw these diverse public figures as threats to the great empires of the east. Although the Social Democrats and nationalists alike sought to overthrow autocracy, the former hoped to preserve the existing states' contours and, in many cases, its central authority, while the latter wanted either to break up the empire or win autonomy for its constituent nationalities.

At the furthest left pole of European Social Democracy, theorists like the Polish-German-Jewish radical Rosa Luxemburg (1871–1919); the Dutchman Anton Pannekoek (1873–1960), author of *Klassenkampf und Nation* (Class Struggle and Nation) (1912); and Josef Strasser (1870–1935), author of *Der Arbeiter und die Nation* (The Worker and the Nation) (1912), argued that no account should be taken of nationalism.[23] No concessions should be made to that bourgeois phenomenon. Luxemburg believed that Social Democrats should not defend the right of nations to self-determination since nations were kinds of fictions that in the real world were divided into classes. She and her comrades opposed those socialist nationalists at the opposite pole, like Józef Piłsudski (1867–1935), leader of the Polish Socialist Party (*Polska Partia Socjalistyczna* or PPS), the Jewish Bund, the Georgian Socialist Federalists, or the Armenian Revolutionary Federation (*Dashnaktsutyun*), who held that primary weight should be given to the national struggle. These parties claimed that socialism was subordinate to the needs of the nation and that there was no fundamental antagonism between the two in the long run. Between the two extremes were the German Social Democrats

(SPD), the Russian Social Democrats, and the Austro-Marxists, who recognized the power of nationalism and feared that it potentially could weaken the proletariat's unity and class resolve against the bourgeoisie. The solution proposed by the Austro-Marxists was founded on the contention that the nation was a "cultural community" (Karl Renner) rather than a merely material, economic entity. Faced by the national "awakenings" of Czechs, Slovaks, Croats, Hungarians, and others, the socialists in the Hapsburg Empire decided in 1897 to reorganize their party into a federal union of national parties. Two years later, their Brünn Congress unanimously accepted the principle of national cultural autonomy as a base for the federal multinational socialist state of the future. Austro-Marxists were optimistic that if socialists got the architecture right, the ethnically diverse state could be maintained intact.

In 1907 Otto Bauer published his powerful and provocative work, *Die Nationalitatinfrage und de Sozialdemokratie* (The National Question and Social Democracy).[24] Indebted to the discussions of a group of critical Marxist thinkers around the journal *Der Kampf* (The Struggle), Bauer's treatise was a sophisticated and subtle exploration of the nature of the nation-form. Here he presented a communication theory of national formation. First, the ruling classes came together, bound by a common culture and promoting a national language and education in that language that marked their nation off from others. With the coming of capitalism, the isolation of peasants in their villages ended as they were drawn into the national educational system and cultural life of the nation. Workers too were affected, but the process of integration would only be completed under socialism. For Bauer shared history was the effective cause of nation formation. Combining Marx with Darwin, Bauer proposed that rather than something constant and unchanging, the nation is "a process of becoming, determined in its essence by the conditions under which the people struggle for their livelihood and for the preservation of their kind."[25]

Language and culture were the means through which the nation was produced. Rejecting racial concepts of the nation, Bauer wrote, "Common descent alone establishes only a race, never a nation." "The nation is the totality of men bound together through a common destiny into a community of character [*Charaktergemeinschaft*]," which arose from a community of fate [*Schicksalsgemeinschaft*]. But he rejected the notion that national character was fixed. Rather, it was a kind of filter—psychological structures, styles, and tastes—through which more general social processes were experienced and interpreted by different peoples. Different nations have different "codes of representation."[26] For Bauer culture mattered, as did feelings. "Few of us would be able even to say the word 'German' without its resonating with a peculiar emotional overtone."[27]

Renner and Bauer went further than the recognition of national cultural autonomy adopted at the Brünn Congress. Instead of *territorial* autonomy, they proposed *extraterritorial* national cultural autonomy. Individuals no matter where they lived would have a say in the linguistic and cultural matters affecting their nation and could vote for their national council. As Bauer put it, "the nation does not represent for us a certain number of individuals who are somehow superficially held together. Rather, the nation exists in every individual as an element of his specificity, as his nationality." Produced by society, nevertheless, the nation manifests itself as a "character trait of individuals," "the product of inherited characteristics and transmitted cultural elements that the ancestors of every member of the nation have produced in continued interaction with the other members of their society."[28] The propositions of Renner and Bauer were particularly attractive to nationalities whose members lived scattered throughout the empire—Germans in Austro-Hungary, Armenians in Russia and the Ottoman Empire, Jews in both Russia and Austro-Hungary—and consequently parties of those peoples favored this approach. Some Caucasian Mensheviks also gravitated toward the ideas of the Austro-Marxists. But to Lenin and Stalin they were blasphemous.

STALIN ON THE NATIONAL QUESTION

For some years the Georgian Mensheviks had been moving away from strict adherence to the party program on nationalities. Chkhenkeli, one of the most nationalist of the Caucasian Mensheviks, was influenced by Karl Renner's *Staat und Nation* (State and Nation) and argued that loyalty to a multinational state could coexist with love for one's nationality. He considered himself a Social Democrat but felt that Georgian Social Democracy "was and is a national party; . . . it is the expression of the Georgian people's aspirations."[29] Unlike most Social Democrats, Chkhenkeli held that under capitalism national cultures would not wither but continue to flourish. He soon became the principal spokesman among Mensheviks for national cultural autonomy, advocating local communes that would govern in Georgia within a broader autonomous Caucasia with its own parliament (Seim).

Zhordania, writing under the pseudonym "An" and known in party circles as "Kostrov," was Stalin's fiercest and most constant opponent on the question of the nation. He polemicized with Stalin in the pages of *Sotsial-Demokrat*. His Marxist narrative posited that Georgia had not constituted a nation when the Russians annexed the kingdoms at the beginning of the nineteenth century. The imperial Russian regime stimulated economic and social development, and the Russians brought to Georgia a higher form of political administration to replace an inferior one. Georgia was led by princes and feudal lords who wanted to preserve the old order and resisted tsarist power, becoming in a sense the first nationalists in Georgia. The bourgeoisie in Georgia, in contrast, was not nationalistic and quite willing to work with the Russians. Because Georgians did not have capital, they had to live with foreign (Armenian and Russian) political and economic forces that helped built up its civil society. As a result, he concluded, though the intelligentsia was nationalist, the people of Georgia were anti-nationalist.

In 1912 Zhordania married his earlier historical analysis to theories then being propagated by Marxists in Austria. He argued that two national principles, territorial and cultural, had existed, but capitalism had wiped out the territorial. Therefore, the Georgian Socialist Federalists and other nationalists who favored national autonomy or statehood were retrograde. Workers were fusing socialism and national culture into a single liberation movement. He opposed territorial national cultural autonomy, which would lead to oppression of minority nationalities, and favored instead extraterritorial national cultural autonomy with

members of each nationality voting for their own national cultural institutions no matter where they lived.[30] The idea of national cultural
autonomy in one form or another—territorial or extraterritorial—won
over most Mensheviks. The Social Democrats attending the August 1912
Vienna conference initiated by Trotsky came out in favor of the principle of territorial cultural autonomy for Russia's non-Russian people, but
other socialists—the *Dashnaktsutyun* and the Jewish Bund—adopted
the Austro-Marxist notion of extraterritorial national cultural
autonomy.

These defections from the party program infuriated Lenin, who opposed both forms of national cultural autonomy, and prompted Stalin
to write his "Letter from the Caucasus" denouncing the move.[31] A few
months later, however, on December 7 (20), a majority of the Social
Democratic duma caucus supported the concept of national cultural
autonomy. As soon as the news reached Kraków, Krupskaia sent a note
to Stalin and Malinovskii in Petersburg that an article on the national
question was needed.[32] Lenin angrily wrote to the Russian Bureau of
the Central Committee (basically to Stalin as the principal member still
at large):

> Dear friends! The news about the inclusion by the liquidators of
> "cultural-national autonomy" [in the caucus's declaration to the
> duma] has finally incited us to anger! No, there is a limit to every-
> thing! The people who are destroying the party want now to destroy
> completely its program. . . . By doing this they have *started* a war. It is
> essential to think about war and to wage it energetically.[33]

In a second letter he called the caucus's action "a mockery" of the six
who voted against including this plank.[34]

Stalin entered this swirling debate on nations and nationalism at the
very end of 1912. Arriving in Kraków he was generally in a good mood,
though he missed his old friends, as Lenin noted in his own letter to
Kamenev. "Everyone sends you the biggest greetings, especially Malinovskii and Koba, who are all frightfully sorry that you are not here."[35]
Sometime during Stalin's stay in the Polish city, Lenin commissioned
him to write an article on the issue of nationalism and suggested he

move to Vienna to work on the piece. The Austrian capital was the site of the most intense discussions on nationalism, the home of the Austro-Marxists advocating national cultural autonomy. It was also the home of Aleksandr Troianovskii, one of the editors of the Bolsheviks' theoretical journal, *Prosveshchenie*, who in the mid-1930s would serve as Stalin's ambassador to the United States.[36]

Stalin was already drafting an article, for as early as January 6, Troianovskii had written to his fellow editors that he had received a version of the article the day before. One of the other editors, M. A. Sevelev, had sent him Stalin's draft, and Troianovskii returned it to Petersburg. Stalin was too busy in Kraków to do much writing, and around the 25th of the month he moved to Vienna on an assignment to prepare Lenin's report on the Kraków conference for publication in Paris. He lived with Troianovskii and his wife, Elena, and her daughter by an earlier marriage, Galina, in their three-room apartment at 30 Shenbrunner-Shossishstrasse, where he was given his own room. The Troianovskiis lived well. Troianovskii was a wealthy, handsome young man with dark thick eyebrows and a full, drooping mustache. His closely cropped hair was a legacy of his years as an artillery officer. Aleksandr tutored the children of rich Russians, and they both, especially Elena, received money from relatives back home. "Their guest seemed to them somewhat gloomy and not very gregarious, but they explained that by the fact that perhaps this was the first time he had to live with an intellectual [*intelligentsiia*] family."[37]

Stalin quickly began revising his piece on nationalities. Since he had very little German, he read materials in Russian translation and had others translate the relevant passages from articles by Kautsky, Bauer, or from *Die Neue Zeit* (New Time), the German Social Democrats' theoretical journal.[38] A Russian student was hired to find books in the library and translate. The young Olga Veiland, who lived with the Troianovskiis, also helped. "Once he called me to his temporary study and asked me to translate a piece from *Neue Zeit*," she wrote in her unpublished memoirs. "We sat down together. I was nervous about whether I could translate the text properly, but I soon stopped worrying because Comrade Stalin quietly and patiently helped me to find the most suitable expressions. I was surprised that he knew in advance what was coming up in the text."[39] In her old age, after many years working as a Soviet official and with the Communist International (Comintern), Veiland remembered that Stalin had been fond of her but that she was more attracted to the young Nikolai Bukharin. In her meeting with Stalin biographer Miklós Kun many years later, Veiland embellished her story: "Koba had problems with cleanliness. I washed many of his shirts in Vienna. They were filthy. He never washed his hands before lunch, and when he got up from the table he would belch with satisfaction."[40]

It was in Vienna that Stalin met Bukharin, a future friend, ally, and victim, who was a frequent visitor to the Troianovskii apartment. He also first ran into his postrevolutionary nemesis, Trotsky, who remembered his "yellow eyes" with a "glint of animosity."[41] Stalin made no effort to befriend Trotsky, whom he had seen before from a distance and knew from his writings as an opponent of Bolshevism. Stalin was staying briefly with the former Menshevik duma deputy from Baku, Matvei Skobelev, the scion of a wealthy merchant, who worked with Trotsky and financed his newspaper, *Pravda*. Trotsky recalled the odd entrance of the stranger.

> In 1913 I sat in the Vienna apartment of a fellow exile, before the samovar. We drank fragrant Russian tea and we meditated, naturally, on the overthrow of tsarism. Suddenly, without a preceding knock, the door opened and in it appeared a person unknown to me—of average height and rather thin, with a sallow face on which could be seen pockmarks.
>
> The new arrival held in his hand an empty glass. Uttering a guttural sound which could, had one wished, have been taken for a greeting, he approached the samovar. He silently filled his glass with tea and, as silently, left. I looked questioningly at my friend, who said: "That was the Caucasian, Dzhugashvili, my fellow countryman. He recently entered the Central Committee of the Bolsheviks and is evidently beginning to play an important role."
>
> The unexpected entrance and disappearance, the a priori enmity of manner, the inarticulate greeting, and, most importantly, the

morose concentration of the stranger made a confused but unusual impression on me.[42]

Stalin's time in Austria was short, and he was not satisfied with the results of his research and writing. He wrote to Malinovskii, whom he addressed affectionately as *druzhischche* (old chap or good buddy), that he was "writing all kinds of nonsense. We shall see." He told him that Lenin was worried about the Bolshevik *Pravda* and the duma caucus, and that he would be seeing Lenin soon. He asked him to tell Sevelev not to publish his article on the national question but to send it back to him as soon as he can, "if possible even today."[43] A few days later Troianovskii repeated Stalin's request with some annoyance: "We are waiting for Stalin's article on the national question. Why don't you send it? Did you receive the telegram? Do not print it, but send it immediately to us."[44] Troianovskii had doubts about Stalin's argument and wanted clarifications. That same day, January 22 (February 4, 1913), he pushed harder: "Vasilii insistently demands . . . that the article on the national question be returned to us here [in Vienna]."[45] It arrived the next day.

Both Stalin and Troianovskii traveled to Kraków in early February to attend a Central Committee meeting that would deal with the national question and the journal *Prosveshchenie*. There Lenin and Stalin thoroughly discussed the issue of nationalities. Stalin wrote, and Lenin edited the piece. Although he would later write his own article on the subject (and some historians argue that he was not content with Stalin's piece), in fact Lenin was pleased with Stalin's approach. He wrote to Gorky, "As for nationalism I am in complete agreement with you that it is necessary to get busy on this. We have a marvelous [*chudesnyi*] Georgian here who has settled in and is writing a big article for *Prosveshchenie*, having collected *all* the Austrian and other materials. We are applying ourselves to this." He went on to refute Gorky's criticism of the Bolshevik resolution on this matter as "merely a formal reply, bureaucratic."

No. This is not merely a formal reply. Our SDs in the Caucasus—Georgian + Armenian + Tatar + Russian—have worked together in a single SD organization more than ten years. This is not a phrase but the proletarian solution to the national question. The only solution. The same is true in Riga: Russians + Latvians + Lithuanians; only the separatist Bund has drifted off. The same in Vilna.[46]

In a later letter to Kamenev, Lenin expressed annoyance that Troianovskii was not happy with Koba's article and had raised a fuss. Because his wife favors national cultural autonomy, Lenin argued, Troitanovskii wanted the essay to be a discussion piece. "Of course, we are absolutely against this. The article is *very good*. This is a fighting issue, and we will not give one iota of our principled position against the Bund bastards. It's possible this will 'blow over,' but . . . tenez vous pour averti! [Be on your guard!]"[47] And again, a month later, after Stalin's arrest in Petersburg, he reiterated to Kamenev, "Koba managed to write a big (for three issues of *Prosveshchenie*) article on the national question. It is good! One has to wage war for the truth against the separatists and opportunists from the Bund and from the liquidators."[48]

Stalin's essay, his most significant foray into Marxist theory before the revolution, appeared in three issues of *Prosveshchenie* in the first months after Stalin's final arrest and exile.[49] The author set out to accomplish three tasks: defend the principle of national self-determination; demolish the policy of national cultural autonomy of the Austro-Marxists, Mensheviks, and Bundists; and demonstrate the superiority, from a Marxist point of view, of noncultural regional autonomy. Stalin began with a stark, firm definition of the nation, one that would have enormous consequences for the peoples of the Soviet Union. In his famous formulation a nation "is a historically evolved stable community of people, arising on the base of a community of language, territory, economic life, and psychological makeup [*sklad*], manifesting itself in a community of culture."[50] And further, on its origins: "A nation is not merely a historical category but a historical category belonging to a definite epoch, the epoch of rising capitalism. The process of the elimination of feudalism and the development of capitalism was at the same time a process of amalgamation of people into nations."[51] Stalin's definition of nation was counterposed to Bauer's, which he considered divorced "from the soil" and "something mystical, intangible, and supernatural."[52]

For Stalin national autonomy in any form contradicted the flow of history and the progress of class struggle. Territorial national cultural autonomy was unworkable because nationalities were not compactly settled in one contiguous area and would, as capitalism moves into a higher stage, become more mobile and dispersed. Likewise, extraterritorial national cultural autonomy was inconceivable since dispersed members of a nationality take on different characteristics in different places and grow more like the majority population. "Is it conceivable that, for instance, the Germans of the Baltic Provinces and the Germans of Transcaucasia can be 'welded' into a single nation?"[53] Once industry and class struggle develop, "one cannot seriously speak of the 'cultural community' of a nation when the masters and the workers of a nation have ceased to understand one another. What 'community of fate' can there be when the bourgeoisie thirsts for war and the proletariat declares 'war on war'?"[54]

Stalin supported the right of nations to determine freely their own fate. But though they had the right to autonomy or independence, this did not mean that such moves would always be good for a given nation, especially for its majority, its "laboring strata."[55] He distinguished between national cultural autonomy, which preserved the integrity of the state, and only went as far as to recognize cultural rights and national self-determination, which conveyed the possibility of secession and sovereignty. In specific cases Social Democrats would support the solution that benefited best working people. In the opinion of the Bolsheviks this was regional autonomy. It was not the task of Social Democrats, he argued, "to occupy themselves with 'organizing' nations, 'constituting' nations, 'creating' nations" (although this is precisely what the Bolshevik heirs of the Social Democratic Party would do once they took power).[56] What Bauer was proposing was a "subtle form of nationalism."[57] Once full democracy was established, even bourgeois democracy as in Switzerland, national cultural rights would be guaranteed without autonomy or special institutions.[58] "The only solution," he claimed, "is regional autonomy for such defined units as Poland, Lithuania, the Ukraine, the Caucasus, etc."

> The advantage of regional autonomy consists, first of all, in the fact that it does not deal with a fiction without a definite territory. Then it does not divide up people according to nations; it does not strengthen national barriers;—on the contrary, it breaks down these barriers and unites the population in order to open the road to division of another kind, division according to class. Finally, it makes possible in the best way the use of national resources of the region and the development of the productive forces, without waiting for the decisions of a common center—functions that are not characteristic of national-cultural autonomy.[59]

As a person born and educated in the empire's borderlands, who for long periods of time had lived in the depths of Russia among the most isolated Russians, Stalin was keenly sensitive to the ethnic diversity of the huge country in which he lived and of the hierarchies of cultures, peoples, and power. In Stalin's view there were higher and lower cultures, and national homogenization as in Western Europe was far from what was evident in Caucasia or other imperial peripheries. Georgia itself displayed diversity and ethnic tensions rather than homogeneous consolidation of a nation. Latching on to another opportunity to continue his long running feud with Zhordania, Stalin tore into the Menshevik leader, who had turned toward national cultural autonomy. Such a resolution, Stalin wrote, would aid the larger nationalities, like the Georgians and Armenians, but efface the rights of Mingrelians, Abkhazians, Ajars, Svans, Osetins, Lezgins, and other peoples with "primitive culture."[60] Regional autonomy was far more appropriate for Caucasia, for the "national problem in the Caucasus can be solved only *by drawing the backward nations and peoples into the common stream of a high culture.*"[61] While he appeared to appreciate the distinct cultures of smaller peoples, his evolutionary approach acknowledged the amalgamating history of nations under capitalism and his personal approval for the assimilation of less developed peoples into more highly developed cultures. What might look like internationalism or from another point of view a kind of Russian nationalism is better described as an imperial vision—acknowledgement of diversity combined with a statist conviction that ultimately greater consolidation would occur. Central to the imperial vision were the ideas that some peoples were superior to others and that the inferior peoples would ultimately benefit from the *mission civilisatrice*, the developmentalist, civilizing program, of the imperial center.[62]

Like Lenin, Stalin did not have any romantic or affective attachment to the nation. His youthful attachment to Georgia had eroded over time. There was no need in his mind to preserve national distinctions as if they were rare species that one might regret would soon be extinct. Instead there was a cool acceptance of the social processes that at one time in history brought nations into being and at another doomed them to oblivion. Stalin agreed with Bauer that because the Jews have no definitive territory of settlement they would eventually disappear as a nation. Indeed in his reading the Jews were not a nation precisely because they were not attached to the soil. And they had no "large and stable stratum associated with the soil, which would naturally rivet the nation, serving not only as its framework but also as a 'national' market."[63] Inevitably, he posited, Jews will assimilate into other nations. Here his analysis ironically coincided with that of the Zionists, who also argued that Jews could not survive as a nation in diaspora; in their view a national future required being wedded to the soil, eventually in Palestine. The Bund, on the other hand, envisioned a future for the Jews in Europe but only if the processes of assimilation were thwarted and the specific culture and language (Yiddish) were preserved. For Stalin this was a case of "bourgeois nationalism": "The maintenance of everything Jewish, the preservation of all the national peculiarities of the Jews, even those that are patently noxious to the proletariat, the isolation of the Jews from everything non-Jewish, even the establishment of special hospitals—that is the level to which the Bund has sunk."[64]

From his book and subsequent letters while in exile, the essential elements of Stalin's views on nations become clear. His tight, empirical definition of nation was inclusive and cumulative—that is, it was based on the historic accumulation of factors that when taken together constitute the nation. Language, economic life, territory, and psychological makeup are the necessary conditions for a stable community of culture. That community had a durability that socialists had to take seriously but ought not to promote. Therefore, he favored a centralized multinational state, one that would maintain the existing contours of Russia, was wary of the separation of nationalities from Russia, and followed Lenin in opposing federal ties and cultural autonomy in any form. All cultural and civil rights of the peoples of the new socialist state would be protected, however.

As a disciplined party member, he recognized the principle of national self-determination but not with the fervor that Lenin exhibited. Their emphases were quite different. Lenin was prepared to push hard against the reluctance of many of his comrades to accept national self-determination to the point of separation because he was convinced that imperial coercion by states and dominant nationalities was at the base of the nationalism of ethnic minorities in multinational states. Stalin was more satisfied that the guarantee of national cultural and linguistic rights in the future democratic and socialist states would be sufficient. Having lost his earlier enthusiasm for the nation, Stalin's imperial "internationalism" unhesitatingly subordinated national claims to the overriding interests of the proletariat. That proletariat would subtly be identified over time with Russia. In the evolutionary hierarchy of civilizations and cultures proletarian was superior to peasant, and Russian to the cultures of the other peoples of the empire.

Now that he had reached the top of the Bolshevik faction, in his view the more Russian of the two Social Democratic factions in the empire, Stalin's transition from youthful Georgian nationalist through Marxism to staunch "internationalist" was, at least in his writings and rhetoric, complete. His discussion of his own people revealed his antagonism to the contention of Georgian nationalists that Georgia was an ancient nation with primordial origins in the distant past. He took what we would call today a modernist, rather than a primordialist, approach to explain the making of the Georgian nation:

The Georgians before the [abolition of serfdom in the 1860s–1870s] inhabited a common territory and spoke one language. Nevertheless, they did not strictly speaking, constitute one nation, for, being split up into a number of disconnected principalities, they could not share a common economic life; for centuries they waged war and pillaged each other by inciting the Persians and Turks against each other. . . . Georgia came onto the scene as a nation only in the latter half of the nineteenth century, when the fall of serfdom and the growth of the economic life of the country, the development of means of communication, and the rise of capitalism instituted a division of labor among the various districts of Georgia, completely shattered the economic self-sufficiency of the principalities, and bound them together into a single whole.[65]

He did not reproduce the nationalist narrative of ancient origins that forged a nation continuous through time nor did he resort to the racist explanation of national character as natural character. Rather his somewhat stolid materialism depicted the nation as a modern form of community indebted to the revolutionary transformation of capitalism, while implying that Georgian nationhood also was greatly assisted by the annexation by the Russian Empire, the forceful abolition of the Georgian kingdoms and principalities, and the administrative-bureaucratic amalgamation that took place in the century of Russian rule. His historical narrative coincided with Zhordania's original Georgian Marxist account, though their preferred resolutions of the problem of nationality diverged. Although in his definition of nation Stalin mentioned psychological makeup, in his social historical narrative he elides any mention of the role of intellectuals or ideas. For Stalin the nation was a product of economic and social forces and had, like any historical phenomenon, its own history, its beginning and end.

As Trotsky later grudgingly conceded, "*Marxism and the National Question* is undoubtedly Stalin's most important—rather, his one and only—theoretical work. On the basis of that single article, which was forty printed pages long, its author is entitled to recognition as an outstanding theoretician." But he went on to discredit the authenticity of Stalin's originality and achievement. "What is rather mystifying is why he did not write anything else of even remotely comparable quality either before or after. The key to the mystery is hidden away in this, that Stalin's work was wholly inspired by Lenin, written under his unremitting supervision, and edited by him line by line."[66] Trotsky's assessment is ungenerous, understandably as it was written by a defeated opponent of the dictator, but captures the closeness of what Stalin composed and his intellectual, if not editorial, indebtedness to Lenin.

Stalin continued to think about and compose articles on the national question while in his final exile (1913–1917) in Turukhansk in eastern Siberia. One piece he had written earlier appeared in *Prosveshchenie* shortly after his arrest.[67] He wrote several times to Malinovskii and Zinoviev about other articles he hoped to see published. At the end of November 1913, he asked Malinovskii if he knew anything about Zinoviev's promise that several his pieces would appear in a separate brochure. "The point is that if this is true, then it is worth adding one more chapter to the articles (this I would be able to do in a few days, if only you let me know), and then I hope (I have the right to hope) that there will be an honorarium (in this God-forsaken territory where there is nothing except fish, money is as necessary as air). I hope that you will stand behind me and try to obtain the honorarium."[68] Zinoviev mentioned the article to Troianovskii in a note of March 12 (25), 1914: "A big article against the new book of Kostrov (Niradze) on cultural national autonomy arrived from Stalin. It deals only with this theme. You will be satisfied."[69] For reasons that remain obscure, however, the article was held up. Indeed, it was never published. Because Troianovskii favored the idea of national cultural autonomy, he may have had a hand in preventing the article's publication. David Riazanov, a renowned expert on Marx, asked in a letter of September 1913 to Troianovskii whether he wanted to launch a debate in *Prosveshchenie* on the article by "a certain Stalin."[70]

In a letter on February 5, 1916, to his "dear friend" Kamenev, then exiled in Ialansk, Eniseisk Province, Stalin reviewed his plans for a series of articles that would make up the second part of his study of Marxism and the national question.[71] After complaining that he had not received any letters from him, he wrote:

> In answer to Grigorii's [Zinoviev] question about "the plans for my work on the national question," I can say the following. Right now I am writing two big articles: 1) the national movement in its development, and 2) war and the national movement. If one were to combine in a single collection 1) my brochure "Marxism and the National Question," 2) the big article that has not appeared yet but has been approved for publication, "On Cultural-National Autonomy" (the same one about which you asked Avilov), 3) the post-script to the last article (I have an outline), 4) the national movement in its development, and 5) war and the national movement—as I say, bring together all this in one collection, then, maybe, you would have something suitable for what you mentioned in your letter to Suren [Spandarian], the publication of a book "on the theory of the national movement" (or the question).[72]

He then went on to detail his current thinking on the vexed question of nationalism.

> The content of the brochure "National Question and Marxism" is well known; it is necessary only to add a little to it (the brochure). The content of the article "Cultural-National Autonomy" also is well known, at least to Il'ich [Lenin] and Grigorii [Zinoviev]. A "Post-script" criticizes the articles of An. [Zhordania] in the Trotskyist [newspaper] Bor'ba [Struggle]. The plan of "the national movement in its development" (this article will soon be ready) is as follows: 1) forms of national oppression, 2) birth of the national movement [in the epoch of primitive accumulation], 3) the blossoming of the movement [in the first stage of industrial capitalism], 4) the decline of the national movement [in the highest stage of industrial capitalism], 5) imperialism and the national movement, 6) conclusion.[73]

In discussing his plans for the essay on war and the national movement, he indicated that he planned to write about "the continuous growth of the accumulation of capital; the basic requirements of industrial capital-ism; the export of primarily industrial capital (the export of financial and especially commodity capital is not characteristic in this case); and the unavoidable condition for accumulation [which] is demand," as well as about "imperialism as political expression." On the "national state," he intended to explain "the insufficiency of the old frame of the 'national state,'" how that state would be broken up and multinational states would be formed.

> From here comes the tendency to seizures and war (Russia and other agrarian countries exporting capital, primarily financial and indus-trial, aiming toward seizures [of new territory] for other goals and for other reasons that are not characteristic of contemporary war). From here come the various appeals of the warring states to the na-tional instincts of the nationalities, intended to be included within one or another state. From here comes the faith in national liberation, which without doubt excites the national movement, whether the masters of the game want this or not.[74]

He noted "the popularity of the principal of national self-determination as a counterweight to the principle of annexation" and referred to "the clear weakness (economic and otherwise) of small states and the popu-larity of the idea of a narrow union of states, not only military but also economic." He meant to demonstrate "the insufficiency of a completely independent existence of small and medium-sized states and the fiasco of the idea of national separation" as well as reveal the strength of "na-tional instincts" and "the popularity of the idea of autonomy of regions where one or another nationality dominates." His solution to the na-tional problem would be "a broadened and deepened union of states on the one hand and autonomy of national regions within states on the other, projecting the broadening of the old political framework that no longer corresponds to the new stage of capitalism."

> I am speaking about something that is happening by itself without the will of the proletariat. As for the latter [the will of the proletariat] it ought to express itself in the declaration of the autonomy of

national territories within multinational states [*gosudarstva natsional'nostei*] in the struggle for the united states of Europe, i.e., for the most democratic forms of the projected broadening of [political] frameworks.[75]

He asked Kamenev to send his letter on to Lenin, as it seemed that he had a more dependable way to communicate with the center.

So, if the collection works in such a form, then it is possible to say that it is almost ready. If this doesn't work, let Il'ich and Grigorii write in detail, that is, let them give me a detailed order, and I will try to do whatever I can.[76]

Far from Europe in Siberian exile, Stalin was certain that the Great War, the product of the imperial appetites of the European Great Powers, was stimulating nationalism from the Atlantic to the Urals. Most revealing in his sketch of his thinking in 1916 are his preferences for large multinational states, an outcome that he believed corresponded to the present stage of capitalist development *and* his ambiguous dismissal of "national separation." Without clarifying what he meant, Stalin seemed to be attacking the right to "national separation" that Lenin fiercely defended, though one could also read this sentence to mean that like Lenin he recognized the right but did not advocate actual separation. More forthrightly, instead of the party's position on regional autonomy, here Stalin proposed autonomy for national territories within multinational states that would be included in a large United States of Europe. Both this move from regional to national autonomy and his support for a United States of Europe were points that differed from positions staked out by Lenin and in his own 1913 articles.

Stalin's support for national autonomy demonstrates a shift toward a greater recognition of nationality and its durability than either Lenin or Luxemburg acknowledged. Lenin was prepared at a certain historical stage to allow nationalism to flourish and play itself out. In early 1916, emphasizing the importance of respecting the national aspirations of peoples, Lenin confidently wrote, "Just as mankind can achieve the abolition of classes only by passing through the transition period of the dictatorship of the oppressed class, so mankind can achieve the inevitable merging of nations only by passing through the transition period of the complete liberation of all the oppressed nations, i.e., their freedom to secede."[77] Stalin, like Lenin, appreciated the immediate power of nations and nationalism but was much more reluctant to make concessions to them. He wanted to move beyond the nation-state to multinational states and momentarily bought into the idea of an eventual United States of Europe.[78] Emphasis ought to be placed on utilizing the emerging class solidarities to confront nationalism.

Frustrated by the delay in publishing his article, Stalin wrote a few weeks later to the Bolshevik Center in Switzerland, through Inessa Armand, asking "what has been the fate of the article of K. Stalin 'On Cultural-National Autonomy.' Has it appeared in print, or maybe it was lost somewhere? It has been more than a year, and I cannot find out anything. Send me a postcard with news of the article."[79] The article never appeared, and its fate is unknown.

Stalin's work on the national question was appreciated by his fellow Bolsheviks but was hardly the final word on the subject. Lenin followed Stalin's major published article with his own "Critical Notes on the National Question," which he did not publish, and a long piece for *Prosveshchenie*—"The Right of Nations to Self-Determination"—which he did. But he acknowledged the importance of Stalin's articles in a piece he published in *Sotsial'demokrat*. "In the theoretical Marxist literature this situation and the basis of the national program of Social Democracy has already been illuminated recently (first of all, the articles of Stalin brought this forward)."[80] Both Lenin and Stalin publicly emphasized their faithfulness to the party program, criticized both those Mensheviks and Bundists who adopted the position of "national cultural autonomy" and those on Lenin's left, like Rosa Luxemburg, who would not support the right to national self-determination. Lenin repeatedly made it clear that while he was for the right of oppressed nations to secede from states oppressing them, Marxists need not promote secession, for they were, as far as possible, for preserving large multinational states. Russia was on the eve of a bourgeois-democratic revolution, and "the formation of independent national states is the tendency of all bourgeois-democratic revolutions."[81] Therefore, the Russian proletariat and the workers' party were faced with paradoxical tasks: they must "fight against all nationalism and, above all against Great Russian nationalism," while simultaneously recognizing "the right of nations to self-determination, to secession."[82] While Stalin's published work on the national question conformed closely to Lenin's views, in his Siberian musings, which never came to fruition, he appeared to be looking for a less drastic alternative to secession—that is, national autonomy within multinational states. That strategic paradox of how to grant national self-determination but prevent secession was left unresolved by Lenin and Stalin and would emerge as a major source of conflict among Bolsheviks after they took power. The national question, which more than anything else brought Lenin and Stalin together, would at the end of the older man's life strain their collaboration to the breaking point.

24

THE EXILE

The criminal Balanovskii, nicknamed "Seagull," robbed a peasant woman. Upset by this event, the political exiles organized a comradely court at which Stalin appeared. Completely unexpectedly for all, Stalin made a long speech defending the thief and declared that theft was the basic profession of Balanovskii and that he was a product of the capitalist system. For this reason, not only should he not be tried, but it is essential to win him over to our side since people like him were needed by all those fighting for the destruction of the capitalist order.

—G. I. KARGANOV, "IZ PROSHLAGO STALINA"
["FROM STALIN'S PAST"] (1929)

Once or twice, accidently happening upon a meeting of the Bolshevik Central Committee, [in Turukhansk, Siberia, the anarchist Aleksandr (Alesha) Ulanovskii] saw Stalin. In contrast to Sverdlov, who cared for people and whom everyone loved, Stalin was closed up and morose. For example, when he came to the meeting, he did not greet anyone. . . . Toward Bolsheviks, as with Social Democrats in general, Alesha had contempt: they argued about trifles! He was bored by their affairs— who is a Menshevik, who is an *otzovist*—you think there is a difference. . . . And about Stalin he said: "I was with him once in Turukhansk territory. I was known to all the exiles, but he—who was that one?" Stalin in exile was not especially popular.

—NADEZHDA AND MAIA ULANOVSKIE, *ISTORIIA ODNOI SEM'I [THE HISTORY OF A FAMILY]* (1982)

In mid-February 1913 Stalin returned to Saint Petersburg from Austria and took up where he had left off, working with and reorganizing the editorial board of *Pravda*. He settled in the apartment of the duma deputies Aleksei Badaev and Fedor Samoilov on Shpalernaia Street and wrote immediately to his friend Troianovskii in Vienna that he had arrived but had little to report. "A bacchanalia of arrests, searches, roundups—it is impossible to go out in public." He did meet with the six Bolshevik duma deputies, and they worked out a "proclamation" to mark the holiday honoring women workers on February 17. He sent greetings to "Galochka," Troianovskii's wife's daughter, and promised to send chocolates.[1] The *Okhrana* already knew that he had returned to Saint Petersburg.

Shortly after Stalin returned from abroad, the four Bolshevik deputies who had lent their name to the Menshevik newspaper *Luch* in a gesture of unity a few months before now publicly withdrew their collaboration. Whether Stalin had any influence on their decision is not known, but he may have conveyed Lenin's disapproval of their conciliatory attitude toward the *likvidatory*. The duma caucus was pulling apart, and Stalin wrote in *Pravda* of the need to preserve the unity of the Social Democratic deputies.[2] This was not his position alone. Social Democrats of both factions were concerned about a schism, but neither faction would give in to the demands of the other. Meeting in September 1913, in the village of Poronin near the Carpathian Mountain resort of Zakopane in Austrian Poland, the Bolsheviks, with Lenin leading the charge, expressed their support for unity but complained that the Menshevik "seven" was restricting the Bolshevik "six" from speaking in the duma. The Bolsheviks reaffirmed their radical difference from the Mensheviks by calling for developing the current rise in strikes into a general political strike that would lead to an armed uprising against tsarism. Their strategy appeared to the Mensheviks to be directed against not only the autocracy but the bourgeoisie, which the Mensheviks hoped to keep on the side of reform rather than reaction. After a year of failing to work together, in October 1913 the Social Democrats split into two caucuses. Relying on their majority, the Mensheviks had refused to accede to the Bolshevik demand that each faction have the same voting power in the caucus' decisions. The split ended the last institutional collaboration of Bolsheviks and Mensheviks.

The intensity of the factional hostility at the moment of rising worker activity is evident in a letter that Trotsky in Vienna wrote to Chkheidze in Petersburg on March 24, 1913—a letter that would come back to haunt Trotsky in the 1920s when it came to light during his power struggle with Stalin and his allies. Trotsky began by complimenting Chkheidze on his speeches in the duma and expressed his joy at the letters that workers were writing to *Luch*. But then he vented against "Master Lenin, this professional exploiter of every kind of backwardness in the Russian workers' movement. Not a single intelligent, untransformed European socialist believes that a schism is possible from such marginal disagreements as Lenin fabricates in Kraków." He wrote of Lenin's "circle intrigues and unprincipled schismatic behavior." However, he went on, "the spontaneous pull of the workers toward unity is so irresistible that Lenin has to play systematically at hide-and-seek with his readers, speaking of unity from below while creating a schism from above. . . . In a word, the whole edifice of Leninism is built at the present time on lies and falsification and will bring down on itself the poisonous beginning of its own disintegration."[3]

About this time rumors were heard that the duma deputy Malinowski, member of the Bolshevik Central Committee, was in fact working for the police. A note signed "Ts" appeared in the Menshevik newspaper *Luch* to that effect. The Bolsheviks suspected that the author was one of the Tsederbaums, the prominent Menshevik family of Martov and his sister, Lidia Dan. In fact, it was a lesser Menshevik, Tsioglinskii. Stalin found Lydia Dan and asked for a short meeting. Eventually they had a brief, disjointed conversation. Lidia Dan remembered him as "Vasilii," though the Mensheviks called him "Ioska the Pockmarked." Stalin demanded that the Mensheviks stop their "slander" against Malinowski and threatened that something would happen (Dan later could not remember what) if it did not cease.[4] Ironically, Stalin was under police watch because of Malinowski's reports and close to being picked up, but neither he nor Lenin gave the slightest credence to the rumors.

Stalin remained free in the capital only a week. In a long business-like letter sent abroad—and intercepted by the police—he noted that the situation among the Social Democratic duma deputies had improved but complained that he desperately needed help, more people, "legals" who could work with the duma and the press. Trying to control things "from outside" was impossible, he wrote. He was negotiating with Poletaev about the newspaper, but the former editor had laid down conditions. As before he is "acting like a bek [a Muslim potentate]" and wants to hire whomever he wants. The editorial board would include him, the Menshevik duma deputy Gegechkori, and the Bolshevik Pokrovskii. Gegechkori insisted that Zhordania be brought on as well. Poletaev said that he would not publish any articles by Zhordania but count him formally as one of the co-workers. "In a word, we have a little adventure."[5] Stalin delayed and said that he would give his answer in two weeks.

But Stalin did not have two more weeks. Saturday evening, February 23, on Malinowski's suggestion, he attended a charity masquerade ball meant to raise money for *Pravda*.[6] Malinowski was warned by his police handler to stay as far away from Stalin as possible, for his arrest was imminent. There, in the buffet of the Kalashnikov Grain Exchange, as he sat with several duma deputies waiting for the concert to begin, he was pointed out by a secret agent. Although nothing incriminating was found on him, he refused to give his name and was arrested. For such an experienced conspirator attending the ball had been a reckless exposure, a risk that he foolishly allowed himself to take. In a letter to Lenin, the poet Demian Bednyi ranted about the naïve error that "the Georgian" had made.

The day before yesterday our kind "diusha-gruzinchik" [little Georgian person] "has been tossed into prison." The devil took him or some fool led him to this "evening." This was simply brazenness—to go there. I did not know that he was in Piter and was flabbergasted seeing him in such a populated place. "Aren't you leaving," I said. But he didn't leave. . . . The seizure of the Georgian crushed me. I had the feeling that I had landed on the path of disaster along with everyone else who will be aided by the renewal of reaction. "Some people" get in the way and "some people" "sit firmly." [Here "sit" meant "to be in jail."][7]

For two weeks Stalin was held in the jail of the Petersburg *Okhrana* division. On March 7, he was moved to the Petersburg Provincial Gendarme Administration Prison and interrogated. Krupskaia wrote to the Bolshevik Nikolai Podvoiskii in Petersburg, worried about Stalin's health. "You must take care of Vaska. It is clear that he does not have endurance [*neprochen*], is sick too often." She evidently did not realize that he had been arrested, for she wanted him to help organize the daily work of *Pravda*.[8] Lenin and Stalin were still not in agreement about how to deal with the deputies and the Mensheviks, and Krupskaia complained in a follow-up letter about the weak and indecisive approach of *Luch* to the struggle against liquidationism and specifically about Stalin's article which "gave over too much" in relations with the liquidators.[9] The situation for the Bolsheviks was unstable everywhere. Leading activists had been arrested. In early May in Tiflis a major trial ended with Suren Spandarian, Vera Shveitser, Elena Stasova, and several others sentenced to prison and exile, effectively wiping out the leadership of the Bolshevik organization in Georgia.[10] A month later, the minister of interior, N. A. Maklakov, signed the order to exile Iosif Dzhugashvili to Turukhansk for four years. This left the police spy Malinowski in charge of the Bolsheviks in Petersburg.

Turukhansk was more than three thousand miles from Saint Petersburg. The exiles went by train through Vologda, Viatka, across the Urals into Siberia. They left the train at Krasnoiarsk, the provincial capital on the Enisei River. From there they traveled by boat nearly a thousand miles north, through the town of Eniseisk, to Monastyrskoe. Part of the way was on foot, but most of it in large rowboats. North of Eniseisk clouds of biting midges tortured them, even when they covered their faces with nets. Locals helped them with food when the guards would allow it.[11] Turukhansk was an enormous territory that stretched along the Enisei River from Eniseisk to the Arctic Ocean. More than a million and a half square kilometers, larger than England, France, and Germany taken together, it held only twelve to fifteen thousand inhabitants when Stalin arrived. Taiga and swamps passed into permanently frozen tundra further north. The treeless, flat wastes of much of the region echo the Sami origin of the word from which tundra evolved: *tunturi*, barren land.[12] The landscape itself was the prison. Fallen trees, swampy ground in summer, and great frozen expanses for three quarters of the year were better than walls or guards to prevent escape.

The long polar winter, during which temperatures might fall as far as 65 degrees below freezing, extends for nine months of bitter cold and dark nights, and when it breaks in mid-May, the rivers thaw and the ice roads turn to mud. Russians have a special word—*rasputitsa*—for that time in the spring after May and in the fall until November when the roads become impassable. The only reliable road in Stalin's time was the river. In the warmer months small boats and even a steamship plied the waters; in winter the Enisei became an ice road trod by horses, reindeer, and dog sleds. But there were times when the ice was breaking up on the river, the roads were too muddy for travel, and the northern villages were completely cut off from the rest of Russia. The river flowed north, and hearty women rowers were employed to move the boats down river. To travel south, upstream toward the last outposts of civilization, the boats were pulled by dogs that ran along the banks.

The town of Monastyrskoe (today Turukhansk), the region's administrative center, lay at the confluence of the Enisei and the Lower Tunguska rivers. Monastyrskoe had a post and telegraph office (it was the end of the line), a branch of the state bank, a school, hospital, two grocery shops, the police headquarters, and a jail. With only forty to fifty houses, there were no cultural amenities at all—no theater, no library— though there was a small white church. Klavdia Sverdlova, the wife of the exiled Bolshevik Iakov Sverdlov, remembered, "In the long northern winter Monastyrskoe drowned in enormous snowdrifts. The streets were deserted and dead; only the howling of a blizzard broke the heavy silence of the gloomy polar night. Rarely, very rarely, could one hear the crunch of steps of a lone passerby hurrying to get out of the severe cold."[13] A decade and a half earlier the tubercular Martov had spent time in Turukhansk, while his then friend and comrade, Lenin, sat out the last years of the nineteenth century in Shushenskoe, 280 miles south of Krasnoiarsk. Stalin's ordeal would be far worse.

After the long journey of twenty-six days, in shackles most of the time, Stalin arrived in Monastyrskoe on August 10, 1913. He was sick and exhausted. While the weary Georgian was still on his way to his final place of exile, Lenin and his comrades plotted the escape of their invaluable agents, Stalin and Sverdlov. Lenin sent Stalin 120 rubles. The Central Committee later set aside another 100 rubles for the escape. Malinowski was privy to these plans, and enjoying Lenin's confidence despite the festering rumors that he was a police spy, he immediately warned his handlers about the escape plans. The Enisei police were informed just after Stalin arrived in Monastyrskoe. The chief officer there was an Osetin who had worked in Baku, Ivan Kibirov. He had been transferred from the Caucasus to the far north evidently because of some error or misdeed he had committed. Stalin wrote a petition to the local authorities, as he had often done before, pleading that because he had no means of sustenance, he ought to be granted a state subsidy.[14] But Kibirov had other plans for him. At first he was placed in the village of Miroedikha, 27 kilometers south of Monastyrskoe. Miroedikha had been where the long-time Bolshevik "Innokentii" Dubrovinskii, a particular favorite of Lenin and Krupskaia, had perished over a year earlier when he fell (or threw himself) into the frigid Enisei. Some memoirists remember that when Stalin arrived in the village he took over the library of the deceased Dubrovinskii, to the dismay of the other exiles.[15] Such rare and valuable comforts were supposed to be shared among all the exiles.

He soon was moved to Kostino, still further south, another 120 kilometers, where he lived in the bathhouse of the Shadrin family. The woman of the house, Tatiana, cooked his meals and remembered him as happy, as he read, wrote, hunted, and fished.[16] He dashed off a short letter to Zinoviev in Kraków. "As you can see I am in Turukhansk. Did you receive the letter from the road. I am sick and must get better. Send money. If my help is needed, write; I will come immediately. Send books, Strasser, Pannekoek, and Kautsky."[17] His situation became increasingly desperate. He explained to Malinowski at the end of November,

Hello friend. It is embarrassing somewhat to write this, but one must. It seems I have never experienced such terrible conditions. My money has all gone; some kind of suspicious cough caused by the ever stronger frosts (37 degrees below) has begun; my general condition is sickly; there are no reserves of bread, sugar, meat, or kerosene (All the money has gone for the normal expenses, clothes, and shoes). And without reserves everything is expensive here. . . .

There is no money, friend. I do not know how I will get through the winter in such a situation. . . . I have no rich relatives or acquaintances; there is positively no one to whom I can turn, and I turn to you, yes, and not only to you, but to Petrovskii and to Badaev. My request consists of this: if the SD caucus has any funds for repressed people left, let it, the caucus, or better the bureau of the caucus, issue me some help, even if only sixty rubles. Pass my request along to Chkheidze and say that I also ask him to take my request close to his heart; I ask him not only as a countryman [zemliak] but principally as the chairman of the [duma] caucus. . . . This matter has to be dealt with today and the money sent by telegraph, because to wait further means starvation and I am quite emaciated and sick. . . . Can it really be that I am condemned to be chilled here for four years? . . . Yours, Iosif.[18]

Sverdlov and his fellow Bolshevik Goloshchekin had also been exiled in Turukhansk, to the riparian village of Selivanikha. Exiles moved somewhat freely between the towns along the river, at least the ones close to Monastyrskoe, and Stalin visited his comrades there in mid-September. Sverdlov mentioned the visit in a letter to Malinowski, "I just bid farewell to Vaska; he was my guest for a week. Did you receive our letters sent about a week ago? Tomorrow morning he is already leaving Monastyrskoe to go home." They were in desperate need of money, and Sverdlov hoped that the extension of the telegraph line would result in their receiving the promised funds. "If you have money for me or Vaska, . . . send it," along with a card that it has been sent.[19] The money, if delivered, was to be used for an escape. Stalin attached his own note, mentioning that he desperately needed the honorarium for his article on nationalism. In a postcard to Zinoviev he complained that he had not yet received the books of Kautsky and the others. "That's foul. Now I have in hand a new brochure of Kostrov (in Georgian), and I would like to deal with everything at once.[20] Once more I ask you to send [those books]." Stalin was eager to take on once again his long-time nemesis, Zhordania, and maintain his own authority on the issue that had propelled him into the maelstrom of party political discussions, the national question. He mentioned his terrible cough, that he had received some money, and that he had seen Sverdlov. "He has settled in well; the main thing he is healthy. He, like K. St., falls apart here without work." He kept up his interest in party affairs and claimed he was pleased that the duma caucus had finally split decisively into a Bolshevik and Menshevik group, even though he had not been very keen about a split while he was in Petersburg. "I am very glad (and how!) that your affairs in the homeland are going so satisfactorily. It couldn't be otherwise: who and what can stand up against the logic of things? I am happy that the split in our caucus took place now and not half a year ago: now no thinking workers can think of the split as unexpected and artificial."[21]

Although he was thinking about escape, Stalin also prepared for a long stay. He and a group of political exiles appealed to the editor of *Sovremennyi Mir* (Modern World) to give them a free subscription since the rising cost of living had made it impossible for them to pay for the newspaper.[22] He wrote to a certain G. Belinskii in France asking him, as a member of the Society for Intellectual Aid to Russian Exiles, to send him some books: a French-Russian pocket dictionary and some English newspapers.[23] Whether the books reached him is doubtful, for Stalin was about to be moved.

The harshness of this exile was felt on the body. The almost complete lack of fresh vegetables and fruit gave rise to scurvy and a kind of sleeping sickness. The cold, dark, and dampness broke down many of the exiles. Stalin complained repeatedly about money and his sickness and hunger. In December 1913 he wrote three letters to Tatiana Slovatins-kaia.[24] In the first one, he wrote, "Tatiana Alesandrovna! I have no choice but to mention this: necessity compels it. I have no money and have even run out of food."[25] He requested that she try to recover the clothes he had left in the holding prison in Petersburg.[26] Later he thanked her for her parcel but said that she "really did not need to buy new undergarments" for him. "I only asked for my old ones to be sent. Yet you bought me a new set, spending money you yourself can ill afford. I don't know how I can repay you, my darling sweetheart!"[27] Finally, he made another plea. "My darling, my need is increasing hour by hour. I am in dire straits. To make things worse, I have even fallen ill. I have a permanent cough. I need milk, but . . . that would take money, and I have none. My darling, if you can get hold of a little money, please forward it to me at once. I have no strength to wait any longer."[28]

His tone was quite different with the higher party officials from whom he expected much more. "You said in your letter of November 9 that you would send me my 'debt' in little pieces," he wrote to Zinoviev. "I would like that you send it as soon as possible in however little pieces (if it is money, send it straight to me in Kostino). I say this because I need money desperately. All this would be nothing if I were not sick, but this damned illness requiring a way out (that is, money) makes one lose balance and patience. I am waiting. As soon as I receive the German books, I will add to the article and send it off in a revised version. . . . Your Iosif."[29]

And again just after the New Year: "Why, friend, are you silent?" he asked Zinoviev. "In your place some time ago a certain N. wrote, but I swear by my dog, I do not know him. From you there has not been a letter already for three months." Speaking of himself in the third person, he went on: "Stalin sent to *Prosveshchenie* a big, very big article 'On Cultural-National Autonomy.' The article, it seems, is good. He thinks that he will receive a nice honorarium for it and will thus be freed from the need to turn to this or that other place for money. I suggest that he has the right to think in this way. In fact: the article criticizes the brochure of Kostrov (in the Georgian language) in connection with the shared propositions of the cultural autonomists. Well, I squeeze your hand. My greetings to acquaintances."[30]

The money finally arrived, and Malinowskii, using an obscure code, noted on a postcard: "Brother, until we sell the horse, I have requested 100 rubles." That money, earmarked for the escape, was sent to

Monastyrskoe addressed to Sverdlov.[31] The police, however, were on top of the plot. Kibirov took away Stalin's state subsidy for February through the first twenty days of June.[32] On February 24 the police chief wrote that the prisoners "Jughashvili and Sverdlov intended to escape from their place of exile. If they don't manage to go south, then they will take the first steamboat to the mouth of the Enisei." He ordered that they both be exiled "to a place further north of Monastyrskoe where there are no other exiles, and that two overseers be sent along especially to observe them."[33] Sverdlov wrote quickly to his sister, Sarra. "I write on the fly just a pair of lines. Iosif Dzhugashvili and I are being transferred 180 versts further north, 80 versts north of the Arctic Circle. We will be cut off from the post. Once a month there is delivery, which is often late, practically not more than eight to nine deliveries a year." He asked that money be sent addressed to someone else.[34]

Monastyrskoe or the nearby towns of Selivanikha, Kostino, and Miroedikha would have been harsh enough for political exiles, but Stalin and Sverdlov were sent far downriver to the truly forsaken settlement of Kureika. "It is not an exaggeration to say," wrote Vera Shveitser, "that it was located at the edge of the earth."[35] Positioned some twenty kilometers north of the Arctic Circle, at the time it was the northernmost settlement in Turukhansk territory, more a collection of log cabins than a functioning village. It lay at the confluence of the Kureika River and the Enisei. From that point north the only road was the Enisei, which broadened out as it flowed to the Arctic Sea. Even at Kureika one bank could not be seen from the other. Surrounded by forest and tundra, with wild animals roaming outside the circle of huts, Kureika had but eight houses in which thirty-eight men and twenty-nine women lived, roughly eight to nine in a house. The riverboat came by rarely and primarily to carry off the graphite that was mined in the region.[36]

Stalin and Sverdlov arrived on horseback and were put together in the home of Aleksandr Taraseev. A quarter century later, to mark Stalin's sixtieth birthday, Anfisa Taraseeva, the mother of the large family huddled in the small house, remembered their arrival, suitcase and bedroll in hand. Two gendarmes accompanied them, which was odd since usually a single policeman traveled with as many as five or six prisoners.

"We thought," she later wrote, "these are very dangerous criminals."[37] She recalls that Stalin, whom they called "Osip," enjoyed playing with her children, loved singing and dancing, and even provided folk medicine to the local peasants. He read and wrote late into the night. Taraseeva reports that once Stalin brought home some fresh meat from the hunt and prepared to cook it, but when he went out to fetch wood for the fire, his dog, Tishka, had finished off his supper. "Iosif Vissarionovich hit him in the stomach, and Tishka howled. Iosif Vissarionovich was left hungry until the next day's fishing. He banned Tishka from the house for two days, taught him good: 'It is forbidden to take. Fetch.' He split his sides laughing, guffawing. Tishka lived with him until his departure."[38]

Despite his illness, Stalin would not give up on the idea of escape. In a letter to duma deputy Grigorii Petrovskii, which was meant for Malinowskii, he mentioned that a Georgian in Petersburg had proposed that he settle there, but he needed money for the journey. "I wrote to him over four months ago but have not had an answer until now. Wouldn't just two words explain this misunderstanding to me?" he added cryptically.[39] He mentioned that he had had a note saying that "the horse would be sold," and he would receive one hundred rubles. Comrade Andrei (Sverdlov) received the money, but "I think that it belongs to him and only him." Nothing has come from Sister Nadia (Krupskaia) either. "In short, a whole pile of misunderstandings."

> I explain all this thus: there were, evidently, discussions about my transfer to serve in Piter. But discussions remained discussions, and Kosta [Malinowskii] decided on someone else, on Andrei, and for this reason sent 100. . . . Am I speaking truthfully, brother? I beg you, friend, to give me a straight and clear answer. I urge you not to answer me with silence as you have done up until now. . . . A clear answer is needed not only because much depends on it, but because I love clarity, as you do. I hope in all things you love clarity.[40]

He followed up with another letter to Malinowski on April 10, congratulating him and Badaev for their speeches in the Duma and article on freedom of the press. "From my soul I am happy that your speeches will be discussed in workers' meetings. In my opinion, this is the only correct method of work, so well adopted by the collective of Petersburg workers. That's the way we should look at each question affecting the workers. In general, my soul is joyful seeing how skillfully, how masterly the faction and the Piter collective uses each and every legal possibility." So far removed from the center of politics, Stalin spoke as if he were in the thick of it. Pretending not to be Stalin, he mentioned that he would tell Stalin that he should write more often, and asked for materials that he would pass on to Stalin, who would then write articles on the fundamentals of Marxism and the organizational side of the national question, as well as a popular article "accessible for workers" on the national question. Then he complained, "Someone, it seems, is spreading rumors that I will not remain in exile until the end of my sentence. Nonsense! I declare to you and swear on my dog that I will stay in exile until the end of my sentence (until 1917). I once thought of leaving, but I have now abandoned that idea, completely dropped it. There are reasons for this, and, if you want, I will someday write to you in detail about this."[41]

The letter to Malinowski was written too late. Events in the capital had turned the world of the Bolsheviks upside down. Malinowski, long suspected of ties to the police, had unexpectedly resigned from the duma and fled abroad.

Doubts about Malinowski had continued to spread within Bolshevik ranks, even as the spy's status in the party and in Russian politics rose, along with his government paycheck. On December 13, 1913, the young Bukharin wrote from Vienna to Lenin detailing his suspicions about the duma deputy.[42] Troianovskii and his wife, Elena Razumovich, were convinced they had irrefutable evidence that Malinowski worked for the police.[43] Lenin dismissed these accusations as he had others earlier. He was more concerned about Malinowski being too far to the left, too passionate, and too enamored of his new position and power.[44] By late 1913–early 1914, the pressure of the schizophrenic life of a police agent who was simultaneously a high party loyalist began to affect Malinowski. He was drinking heavily, acting more erratically, and becoming rude and temperamental with his colleagues. At the same time the new deputy minister of the interior, V. F. Dzhunkovskii, had serious qualms about the potential public scandal if it were discovered that the police had a spy in the duma.[45] On April 22, 1914, Dzhunkovskii surreptitiously informed Mikhail Rodzianko, the chairman of the duma, that Malinowski was his agent and, in exchange for the chairman's silence, promised he would soon have him resign as a deputy and leave the country. On May 8 Malinowski tendered his resignation. When his fellow deputies tried to talk to him at his apartment that evening, they were met by a distraught, drunk, hysterical Malinowski brandishing a revolver and his passport. He soon disappeared into Europe.

Lenin was "in disbelief." "This, of course, gives food for the worst thoughts. . . . Malinowski is accused of being a provocateur. You can imagine what it means! Very improbable but . . . you can imagine how much I'am [sic] worried."[46] A Bolshevik tribunal was set up in Poronin, and Malinowski testified in his own defense. Not only did Lenin and his comrades acquit Malinowski, but the chief spy catcher in the Russian socialist movement, Vladimir Burtsev (1862–1942), suppressed his suspicions and publicly affirmed Malinowski's innocence. Nevertheless, Malinowski had breached his responsibilities and party discipline by abandoning his duma post, and consequently he was stripped of all party posts.

The denouement of the Malinowski affair is as bizarre as the affair itself. The former spy fought and was wounded during the world war. When it was falsely reported that he had been killed, Lenin wrote a laudatory obituary for him. In a German prisoner of war camp Malinowski once again took up the socialist cause and propagandized fellow prisoners. Lenin refused to believe the ever-louder accusations of his guilt, and he even wrote to Malinowski several times during the war, concerned about his situation. Unaware that several of his lieutenants exiled to Siberia were there because of Malinowski's denunciations, Lenin informed him, "I got some news recently from friends who ended up in Siberia; it was not bad."[47] Only in 1917, on his way back to revolutionary Russia, did Lenin admit his error. In May he testified before an investigatory commission that was in possession of the archives of the *Okhrana* and other incriminating testimony. His own evaluation was that the Bolsheviks had gained more than did the police from the legal press and their deputies in the duma. From the German camp, Malinowski petitioned to be returned to Russia to stand trial. In October 1918 he arrived in Petrograd, wandered about "unable to get himself arrested" until he went to party headquarters at the Smolny Institute and announced who he was. He claimed that "he could not live outside the revolution" and wanted to "wash away the sins of his life with blood."[48] He was tried in Moscow on November 5, spoke for six hours in an attempt to explain his actions, and was shot early the next morning in the gardens of the Kremlin.

Malinowski's defection stunned the Bolsheviks. With Malinowski's flight from Saint Petersburg, Stalin lost one of his most important links to the party center. Whether he suspected the rumors that Malinowski was a police spy is not known, but he would one day realize that someone he had trusted and on whom he had depended had betrayed him and those close to him. Chronically suspicious and prone to doubt others, Stalin learned a bitter lesson: traitors can be concealed within the ranks of the party itself.

In Kureika Sverdlov and Stalin were almost completely isolated from their comrades. In the three-month summer the land was impassable, and the only access to the outside world was the single steamship that plied the Enisei. In winter the snow was several meters deep. Sverdlov suffered from nerves and headaches. He mentioned in a letter how much the irregular mail delivery agitated him. "You live, you wait, it comes and you receive one or two letters. One is furious, disappointed. Now the waiting will be worst, and stronger will be the reaction in case of disenchantment." A neat, hard-working intellectual with refined manners, Sverdlov found life with Stalin difficult. He needed quiet for his work, and there was often no kerosene for the lamp. His weak eyes needed more light than the available candles afforded him. He tried to keep up with his French while Stalin studied English. They took walks when the weather was good. The sun shone twenty-four hours a day, but it was hard to find the time and peace needed for serious writing. On March 22, 1914, he wrote:

I do not live alone in the room. We are two. With me is the Georgian Jughashvili, an old acquaintance whom I met in another exile. A good fellow [*khoroshii paren'*], but too much an individualist in everyday life. I am an advocate of minimal order. On this matter I sometimes become very nervous. But this is not so important. Far worse is the fact that there is no isolation from the owners of the house. Our room is next to the owners and there is no separate entrance. The owners have children. Naturally, they hang around for hours with us. They sometimes get in the way. The adults in the village drop in all the time. The come, sit, don't say a word for a half hour, and then suddenly get up, "Well, have to go, goodbye." They leave, but soon someone else comes in and the same thing is repeated. And they come right at the best part of the day for getting work done—in the evening.

The two Bolsheviks read well into the night, but there was little pleasure in reading; there was no good fiction or poetry. Sverdlov finished by noting, "The thirst for life is too strong to be satisfied all the time with dead material."[49]

Years later Stalin joked about how he tricked Sverdlov into doing most of the chores around the house. Going off for the post was like a "long-awaited holiday." The one who made the trip was freed from housework. "I loved to sneak away an extra time for the post," Stalin laughed, and Sverdlov then had to heat the stove and clean up. Anna Allilueva, Stalin's sister-in-law, tells of a meeting in 1919 when Sverdlov and Stalin remembered those days. "How many times I tried to fool you, to evade housework," Stalin said. "I woke up, it happened, when I was on duty and lay there as if I was snoozing." "And you think that I didn't notice this?" Sverdlov asked good-naturedly and laughed. "I absolutely noticed."[50] Nikita Khrushchev remembered Stalin telling how Sverdlov carefully washed his plates and spoons while Stalin let his dog, Iasha, lick his clean. To annoy Sverdlov, who was known locally as Iasha, Stalin gave the same name to his pet.[51] In May 1914 Sverdlov wrote: "There is a comrade with me. But we know each other too well. Besides this, saddest of all, in the conditions of exile, prison, a person is laid bare before expose the real nature of the imperialist war and pressure the Provisional Government to begin immediately negotiations to bring the war to an end.[31] While Lenin would have nothing to do with the government, Stalin would try to move it toward negotiations. Half a century later, toward the end of his life, Molotov bluntly referred to Stalin's position as a "mistake." He was even surprised that this article appeared in Stalin's collected works: "Why did Stalin include it in his collected works. After all, Stalin mastered the exceptional language of the propagandist—classical language, precise, terse, and clear. Yet he got this notion in his head. But he made a mistake."[32]

THE REVOLUTION DEEPENS

Whatever the desires and conceptions of professional revolutionaries, the revolution had a life of its own. People who in an earlier life had been the subjects of others now were actors in their own right. Workers marched for the eight-hour day and respectful address, and industrialists reluctantly gave in to their demands. Soldiers longed for an end to the war and to return home where they expected to obtain land. Exhausted by battle, they were prepared to fight for Russia, to defend the country, but were reluctant to launch an attack. As patriots, however, they hoped for victory. They resented the workers who wanted to limit their working day while soldiers were on duty all the time. They marched behind a banner suggested by the "bourgeois" press: "Soldiers to the Trenches, Workers to the Benches." The Soviet leaders feared that the army might turn away from the soviets in favor of the government, and toward the end of March they began a campaign to win back the soldiers. Their March 14th resolution proved popular: defense of the revolution until the war could be brought to an end.

The Mensheviks at the head of the Soviet adjusted their initial internationalist sympathies to the patriotic mood of many of the soldiers. But it was not until the arrival from Siberia on March 20 of the Georgian Menshevik Irakli Tsereteli that the moderates found a genuine leader. Exiled for ten years, since his arrest after the prorogation of the Second Duma, Tsereteli returned with the acquired authority of one who had suffered under tsarism. He was a renowned speaker and was able to present the Soviet with a vision of unifying all "the vital forces of the nation," which included both the democracy and bourgeois elements. When he rose to speak, the hall fell silent. Stalin arrived late and listened. In the unifying atmosphere of the moment, Isidore Ramishvili, who had long been hostile to Stalin, embraced him. When Tsereteli finished, Ramishvili asked Soso, as he called him, "Are you going to speak or not? I know you do not agree with him." Stalin agreed but declined to speak. "You [Bolsheviks] probably are waiting for your conductor [*dirizhor*]," Ramishvili joked. "Without him you do not have your own opinion." "That is also true," Stalin replied, laughing.[33]

Tsereteli's views on the war were diametrically opposed to those of Lenin and the radical Bolsheviks, who emphasized class polarization and inevitable struggle. He outlined a policy of "revolutionary defensism": support of the army's military efforts along with a campaign for peace "without reparations or annexations." The Executive Committee of the Soviet accepted his formulation on March 22, and it became the official position of the Soviet. Tsereteli soon became the most influential leader of the Petrograd Soviet. But his strategy of revolutionary defensism was completely unacceptable to most of the Bolsheviks. Trotsky would remark later that Tsereteli was brilliant and a man of integrity, but "as is often the case in history, it took a revolution to prove that Tsereteli was not a revolutionary."[34]

Had Russian society not been so polarized, the top (*verkhy*) and the bottom (*nizy*) so hostile to each other, Tsereteli's notion of uniting "all the vital forces of the nation" might have succeeded, but with the people of property and privilege ever more fearful of the *demos*, and the *demokratiia* becoming more radical, Lenin's gamble to secure a government of the lower classes would increasingly become more popular. The very usage of the word *demokratiia* exposed the chasm between the propertied classes and those who had only their labor to sell. The democracy stood opposed to the *burzhui* (the bourgeois). The people (*narod*) saw themselves as the democracy, and democracy took on the meaning of people power (*narodovlastie*).[35] Language gave meaning to experience; it created its own truths; and as historian Boris Kolonitskii has commented, "The language of democracy in 1917 was strongly influenced by the language of class, by the language of the socialists, which dominated during the revolution."[36]

By April soldiers, like workers, began to view the Provisional Government as bourgeois representatives of propertied society and implicated in the imperialist war. By standing behind the Soviet, men in arms effectively secured the first revolution of 1917.[37] But they had taken sides in the struggle between the Soviet and the Provisional Government. The government may have had the support of the Allied Powers, but ordinary Russian soldiers provided the muscle for the Petrograd Soviet. A day after the Soviet came out for a "democratic peace" without reparations or territorial annexations, Foreign Minister Miliukov indicated his opposition to the Soviet policy and reiterated that the war aims of his government were the same as those of the deposed tsarist government. The old regime had had grandiose plans for taking control of Istanbul and dividing up parts of Ottoman Armenia. Since the Soviet was clearly the more powerful partner in the fragile arrangement of dual power, Soviet negotiators easily forced the government to back down and agree that there would be no annexations and that the self-determination of all peoples would be recognized. It appeared that a crisis had been averted. When the First All-Russian Conference of Soviets opened on March 29, it expressed its "most energetic support" of "democratic principles in the realm of foreign policy," that is, renunciation of "programs of conquest," annexations, and indemnities imposed by victors on the vanquished.[38]

Stranded in Switzerland, Lenin intervened in the debates among Bolsheviks with his "Letters from Afar." He was both surprised by the February Revolution and ecstatic that the unexpected had happened. It was a "miracle" in a sense, but one that had to be explained by an analysis of historical forces that also pointed to the future. "How could such a 'miracle' have happened," he asked rhetorically, "that in only eight days . . . a monarchy collapsed that had maintained itself for centuries, and that in spite of everything had managed to maintain itself throughout the three years of the tremendous, nationwide class battles of

1905–1907?" His answer was clear: The "all-powerful 'stage manager,' this mighty accelerator was the imperialist world war. . . . The war shackled the belligerent powers, the belligerent groups of capitalists, the 'bosses' of the capitalist system, the slave-owners of the capitalist slave system, to each other with *chains of iron. One bloody clot*—such is the social and political life of the present moment in history." For Lenin the Provisional Government was tied hand and foot "to imperialist capital, the imperialist war, the plunder policy." Even though this was a bourgeois revolution, that did not mean that workers should support the bourgeoisie. Rather the workers ought to open the eyes of the people to the deceptions of bourgeois politicians. This "first revolution engendered by the imperialist world war" would not be the last, and "the first stage of this first revolution, namely, of the *Russian* revolution of March 1, 1917 . . . will certainly not be the last." First there will be the formation of a democratic republic, and then the people will move on to socialism, which alone can give them "*peace, bread,* and *freedom.*"[39]

Late in March deputies from local soviets all over Russia gathered in Petrograd to elect an authoritative and permanent soviet executive committee. It was to replace the Executive Committee of the Petrograd Soviet, which had ascended to power in March without any sanction outside the city. "The conference performed this task in a rather rough-and-ready way," wrote Sukhanov. "It simply elected sixteen people to supplement our Executive Committee and decided to consider this institution the fully authorized All-Russian Soviet organ."[40] That enlargement marked the end of the internationalists' dominance of the Soviet.

Bolshevik delegates to the Soviet gathering took the opportunity to meet in their own initial postrevolutionary conference (*soveshchanie*). The Kamenev-Stalin leadership in Petrograd maintained its moderate approach. Stalin, who continued to play a minor role in the new Soviet Executive Committee, gave the first major speech at the conference, on March 29, on the vexed issue of the attitude toward the Provisional Government. Not nearly as fiercely hostile to the Provisional Government as Lenin, he nevertheless conceded that eventually the government "must (it must objectively) be transformed into the bulwark of counter-revolution, not a tsarist counterrevolution—we face no danger from that side—but an imperialist counterrevolution."[41] The party must play for time, not force events, which will only drive away bourgeois forces toward counterrevolution.[42] He proposed, "We ought to wait until the Provisional Government has exhausted itself, when, in the process of fulfilling the revolutionary program, it discredits itself. The only organ able to take power is the soviet of workers' and soldiers' deputies on an all-Russian scale."[43] Stalin did not agree with the Russian Bureau's resolution that the soviets "should exercise the most decisive control over all the actions of the Provisional Government and its agents" and instead sided with the resolution of the Krasnoiarsk Soviet "to support the Provisional Government in its activities only in so far as it follows a course of satisfying the demands of the working class and the revolutionary peasantry."[44] This was precisely the formula proposed by the Mensheviks and Socialist Revolutionaries. Other speakers agreed with Stalin's characterization of the government as counterrevolutionary, but they differed as to what the radical opposition ought to do. Wladimir Woitinsky, who soon would leave the Bolsheviks and join the Mensheviks, spoke of the Provisional Government as "a clerk of the Soviet" and predicted a peaceful transfer of power.[45] The Ukrainian Bolshevik Mykola Skrypnyk equated "support" for the government with a vote of confidence, something that could not be contemplated. Another saw the government as "the captive of the revolution," which must be supported. Apparently affected by the debate, Stalin shifted his position. The conference refused to go as far as "support" of the government, and Stalin tactfully withdrew that phrase. "It is not logical to speak of supporting the Provisional Government; on the contrary, it is more appropriate to say that the government must not hinder us carrying out our program."[46] Bolsheviks would put pressure on the government but not struggle against it. The government was already organizing the counterrevolution, he announced, and in the resolution he sponsored with Kamenev there was no mention of support, only pressure on the government to radicalize the revolution.[47] Reacting to the mood of his fellow Bolsheviks, Stalin showed a pragmatic willingness to bend to the prevailing opinion.

Formally Bolsheviks and Mensheviks remained factions within a single Social Democratic Party. With the advent of the revolution party members throughout the country came together in an orgy of unity. A delegation of Mensheviks came to the Bolshevik conference to discuss the resolution on the war and consider the possibility of unification. The issue of the war, however, proved to be fatally divisive. Neither faction was completely committed to a single position; there were internationalists and defensists in both camps, though Bolsheviks were overwhelmingly against the war. After a lively debate the conference decided not to back the war resolution of the Soviet's Executive Committee but to come up with an independent alternative.[48] The conference then discussed a proposal by Tsereteli to unify the two factions. Consistent with his long-time propensity toward unity of the party, Stalin supported Tsereteli's suggestion, but proposed unification *only* with those who accepted the decisions of the Zimmerwald and Kienthal conferences. Molotov protested: Tsereteli calls himself a Zimmerwaldist but he wants a broader unity. This would be incorrect politically and organizationally. Skrypnyk agreed that unification was possible only with those who rejected revolutionary defensism and shared the Bolshevik position on the Provisional Government. Molotov's close friend, Zalutskii, was more brutal: "A philistine might proceed simply from a wish for unity, but not a Social Democrat."[49] Stalin argued that disagreements were inherent to party life, but finally conceded, "it is impossible to unite what cannot be united." He agreed that there could be no compromise with those who favored revolutionary defensism.[50] Related resolutions from Stalin and Molotov were approved, and Stalin was selected, along with Kamenev, Ivan Teodorovich, and Nogin, to represent the Bolsheviks in negotiations with the Mensheviks and was personally charged with giving the major report.[51] As a major party leader, who had demonstrated both moderation and, when confronted with insurmountable opposition, a supple ability to change his mind, he was elected to work with soviet representatives on the planning of the first all-Russian congress of soviets.[52]

The Bolshevik conference moved into another key with the arrival of Lenin. On April 3 Lenin and Zinoviev reached the Finland Station in Petrograd in a closed train that the German government had allowed to pass from Switzerland through Germany and Scandinavia. They were greeted with a tumultuous welcome. But Lenin immediately stunned both his closest comrades and his socialist rivals with the radicalism of his speeches as he traveled across the city in an armored car, stopping at various corners to address the crowds, and finally from the balcony of the Kshesinskaia Mansion, then serving as Bolshevik headquarters.[53] He was particularly caustic to Kamenev. "What is this you have been writing in *Pravda*? We have seen several issues and really swore at you."[54] "The party was as unprepared for Lenin," Trotsky later wrote, "as it had been for the February Revolution."[55] Stalin was not among those who met Lenin at the station. He was attending a meeting to work out plans for unifying the Bolsheviks, Mensheviks, and independent Social Democrats.[56]

Lenin would that very next day make such unity impossible by his own appearance at the Bolshevik conference.[57] The members of the Petersburg Committee enthusiastically agreed with Lenin's views.[58] But at a meeting of Bolsheviks and Mensheviks on April 4, called by the Mensheviks, others were shocked by Lenin's radical ideas on the betrayal of the moderate socialists, on the government, and the war. One venerable Bolshevik, now a Menshevik, Iosif Goldenberg (1873–1922), claimed, "Lenin has now made himself a candidate for the one European throne that has remained vacant for thirty years—the throne of Bakunin! Lenin's new words echo something old—the superannuated truths of primitive anarchism."[59] At that meeting only the radical feminist Aleksandra Kollontai supported him.[60] "Everyone was dumbfounded," Molotov remembered. "I was ready to lay down my life for certain goals, but the goals had suddenly changed; one needed to think things over again and that was not so simple. Lenin had opened our eyes."[61]

Pushing against the confusion and division in the ranks of the Social Democrats, Lenin presented his "April Theses" in speeches to ordinary people and in written form to both the Bolsheviks and Mensheviks, reiterating his conviction that the imperialist war had transformed the political landscape and made an international socialist revolution a real possibility. "Revolutionary defensism is treason to socialism," he proclaimed.[62] Instead Russian soldiers should be encouraged to fraternize with the enemy. "No support for the Provisional Government; the utter falsity of all its promises should be made clear, particularly of those relating to the renunciation of annexations. Exposure in place of the impermissible, illusion-breeding 'demand' that *this* government, a government of capitalists, should *cease* to be an imperialist government." As Lenin conceived it, the revolution had passed from a first phase, which had placed power in the hands of the bourgeoisie, to a second stage, which must place the power in the hands of the proletariat and the poorest peasantry. Rather than a parliamentary republic, which would be a step backward, the Bolsheviks should advocate a republic of soviets, the abolition of the police, the army, and the bureaucracy.

As for the calling of the Constituent Assembly, the constitutional convention to decide on the future form of the Russian state, Lenin "attacked the Provisional Government for *not* having appointed an early date or any date at all, for the convocation of the Constituent Assembly." He "argued that *without* the Soviets of Workers' and Soldiers' Deputies the convocation of the Constituent Assembly is not guaranteed and its success is impossible." Yet, he cautioned, the revolution was still "bourgeois" rather than socialist. "It is not our *immediate* task to 'introduce' socialism, but only to bring social production and distribution of products under the *control* [that is, supervision] of the soviets of workers' deputies." Still, the bourgeoisie could not be trusted to carry out a genuinely democratic revolution. That task now fell to the workers and soldiers.[63] Turning toward the peasant question, Lenin advocated the most radical solution—alliance with the poorest peasants, the landless *batraki*, who should be encouraged to form their own soviets and set up collectivized agricultural enterprises; and seizure of landlord estates by the people who worked the land. "What is the peasantry? We do not know. There are no statistics, but we do know it is a force. If they take the land, be assured that they will not give it up to you, nor will they ask your permission."[64]

With confidence in his own analysis, Lenin refused to give in to the temperate mood of the moment. He wanted to drop the party's name "Social Democrat," discredited by the "social chauvinists" who supported the world war, in favor of "Communist." He was even opposed to having Bolsheviks make demands to the Provisional Government, since making demands implied a degree of support for the government and some expectation of possible satisfaction. This was too conciliatory a position for Lenin. Once again he insisted on stark presentations of essentials as the only way to clarify the murky confusion of the debates on power and the war. Principled stands were needed. "Even if it is necessary to remain in a minority—so be it. It is a good thing to give up for a time the position of leadership; we must not be afraid to remain in the minority." "We must speak to the people without using Latin words. We must speak simply, intelligibly. . . . Our line will prove right. . . . All the oppressed will come to us, because the war will bring them to us. They have no other way out."[65] His eyes focused on a goal that was not yet attainable. As he had put it in 1905, "One cannot engage in a struggle without expecting to capture the position for which one is fighting."[66]

But many Bolsheviks were not yet convinced by Lenin's characterization of the revolution or his tactics. Living together at the time, Stalin and Molotov "discussed at length what Lenin meant by the socialist revolution." The younger Molotov more quickly identified with Lenin, Stalin more gradually.[67] He left Kamenev alone to defend the position adopted by *Pravda*, which rejected Lenin's notion that the bourgeois-democratic revolution was growing over into a socialist revolution. Kamenev feared that moving toward that radical interpretation would turn the Bolsheviks into "a group of Communist propagandists" and not a party relevant to the "revolutionary mass of the proletariat."[68] The workers themselves were not ready for socialism, Kamenev went on. When factory owners deserted the armament factories, the workers refused to take them over, instead limiting themselves to creating a "constitutional factory"—that is, a completely democratic work regime within the plant. This was still within the limits of the bourgeois revolution, although it was a significant step in the direction of socialism.[69]

While Lenin was prepared to move the country toward a government modeled on the Paris Commune of 1871, Kamenev, like most other Social Democrats obsessed with French precedents, pointed out that Russia had not yet gone through 1789 or 1848.[70]

The showdown came with the All-Petrograd Conference of Bolsheviks (April 14–22), which coincided with the first major break in the alliance of the Soviet and the government. Lenin opened the conference, once again emphasizing how the imperial war had presented socialists with a completely new, unexpected opportunity. Bolsheviks had to adjust to a novel situation and not simply try to learn from past revolutions. "Old Bolsheviks," he claimed, believed that because there was no dictatorship of the proletariat and peasantry, the bourgeois revolution is not complete. "But," Lenin proclaimed, "the Soviet of Workers' and Soldiers' Deputies is that dictatorship"—even though it has surrendered power to the bourgeoisie. At the moment there was no imperative to seize power. Bolsheviks were in the minority, and they would not act as Blanquists and take power as a minority. Patience and caution, not civil war, was the order of the day. The only way out was to win a majority in the soviets and to transfer all power to them. Only then could the world war be brought to an end.[71]

Kamenev faulted Lenin for providing no practical solutions for the short run. The Soviet was not prepared to take power nor were the Bolsheviks ready to call for the immediate overthrow of the Provisional Government. Indeed what Lenin advocated was "prolonged work" to explain to people the class nature of the current government and to increase Bolshevik representation in the Soviets (a very conventional parliamentary approach). A commission to which Lenin, Stalin, and Kamenev were elected came up with a resolution that basically reflected Lenin's approach and passed overwhelmingly. Lenin was gradually but steadily bringing his party to his position and providing the Bolsheviks with a lucid political profile: uncompromising opposition to the current government and to the war, and pushing the revolution toward more radical reforms that would move it closer to socialism.[72] The implication of the Bolshevik position was that the more democratic the revolution in Russia, the more likely that the soviets would take power, and the greater the prospective for the socialist revolution in Europe that would move the Russian Revolution toward socialism.[73]

Seven years after these tumultuous disagreements within the party, at a time when the Communist Party debated Trotsky's book *Lessons of October*, Stalin conceded publicly that he had erred in the first months of the revolution. He retold the story of March and April 1917 with an uncharacteristic display of political humility. He mused that at the time "there existed together, side by side and simultaneously, both the dictatorship of the bourgeoisie and the dictatorship of the proletariat and peasantry. . . . There was as yet no serious conflicts between the two dictatorships." Tactically, he said, "a new orientation of the Party was needed in the new conditions of struggle," and the majority of the party in Petrograd "groped its way toward this new orientation. It adopted the policy of pressure on the Provisional Government through the Soviets on the question of peace" but "did not venture to step forward at once from the old slogan of the dictatorship of the proletariat and peasantry to the new slogan of power to the Soviets."

> The aim of this halfway policy was to enable the Soviets to discern the actual imperialist nature of the Provisional Government on the basis of the concrete questions of peace, and in this way to wrest the Soviets from the Provisional Government. But this was a profoundly mistaken position, for it gave rise to pacifist illusions, brought grist to the mill of defensism and hindered the revolutionary education of the masses. At that time, I shared this mistaken position with other Party comrades and fully abandoned it only in the middle of April, when I associated myself with Lenin's theses.

Since in 1924 Stalin was allied with Zinoviev against Trotsky, he made it clear that "Comrade Zinoviev . . . utterly and completely [*tselikom i polnost'iu*] shared the point of view of Lenin." That view represented a "new orientation," which Lenin gave to the party "in his celebrated April Theses."[74]

In his 1924 reconstruction of 1917, Stalin played down the conflicts in the party at the time and accused Trotsky of gloating "maliciously over the past disagreements among the Bolsheviks" and depicting "them as a struggle waged as if there were almost two parties within Bolshevism. But, firstly, Trotsky disgracefully exaggerates and inflates the matter, for the Bolshevik Party lived through these disagreements without the slightest tremor." Stalin then finished with a telling defense of freewheeling intraparty discussions. "Secondly, our Party would be a caste and not a revolutionary party if it did not permit different shades of opinion in its ranks. Moreover, it is well known that there were disagreements among us even before that, for example, in the period of the Third Duma, but they did not shake the unity of our Party."[75] In retrospect, had Stalin heeded his own words and permitted "different shades of opinion" within the party a different Communist Party would have emerged than the one forged under Stalin.

Lenin's arrival meant the de facto dethroning of Stalin and Kamenev. As an editor of *Pravda* Stalin turned to writing routine articles, on the war and the national question, without engaging in the raging controversy within the party. Day by day he gravitated closer to the positions of Lenin. To those who said that opposing the Provisional Government was tantamount to undermining the unity of the revolution, he countered, "Revolution cannot satisfy each and everyone." Only the Soviet should be supported.[76] Nothing good could be expected from bourgeois ministers, he wrote in *Pravda*.[77] As for the peasants plowing land abandoned by landlords, "It would be a reactionary utopia to hold back this beneficial process of purging the revolution from unneeded elements."[78] "He who tries to stand still during a revolution," he wrote, "will inevitably fall behind, and he who falls behind will find no mercy: the revolution will push him into the camp of counterrevolution."[79]

THE FATAL COALITION

As the Bolshevik conference wound down, Foreign Minister Miliukov, the most prominent liberal politician in the country and leader of the Kadet Party, once again challenged the Soviet's position on the war. Miliukov sent a note to the Allies that called for a "victorious conclusion" to the war and assured the Western powers that Russia would honor its obligations.[80] The note starkly exposed the differences between the Soviet and the government, and the Soviet leaders were furious and demanded an explanation. Workers and soldiers took to the streets, surrounding the Mariinskii Palace, where the government met. The Bolsheviks supported the demonstrations, and some militants from the Bolshevik Military Organization called for the immediate overthrow of the government. Lenin later saw this as too sharp a turn to the left, an "adventurist," "inept" move.[81] Yet once again ordinary people demonstrated that real power lay with the Soviet, and the government was forced to back down. The "April Crisis" also revealed the deep divide in the country between the upper classes, military officers, and liberal politicians on one side, and the soviets, the "democracy," and radical parties on the other. The question of power, of what kind of government Russia would have, was raised once again, but not yet resolved.

Although the moderate socialists dominated both in the Petrograd Soviet and the upcoming Congress of Soviets, the Mensheviks and Socialist Revolutionaries felt the ground slipping under their feet in Petrograd as workers and soldiers became increasingly hostile to the Provisional Government. Already in the April Crisis the Petrograd garrison, which numbered over two hundred thousand soldiers and provided the muscle for or against the revolution, had responded only to the orders of the Soviet Executive Committee rather than to those from its ostensible commander, General Lavr Kornilov. The Bolsheviks, who had always been keenly aware of the necessity of armed strength, created their own Military Organization, led by Vladimir Nevskii, who pointedly told his comrades, "No matter how well-armed the working class is, the triumph of the revolution without the participation of the huge military mass is impossible."[82] As part of their effort to win over the garrison, the Bolsheviks published *Soldatskaia Pravda* (Soldiers' Truth), for which Stalin occasionally wrote. Some fifty thousand copies circulated in the city, and Bolshevik influence grew steadily at the expense of the SRs. Their support was greatest among the sailors of the Kronstadt Naval Base and in radicalized units like the First Machine

Gun Regiment. Soldiers were wary of the government and particularly the flamboyant Minister of War Kerenskii, who spoke of restoring "iron discipline" in the army and threatened to transfer recalcitrant troops to the front.

Dvoevlastie appeared doomed. On the right stood those, like the right liberal Miliukov and top army officers, who wanted to strengthen the government and eradicate Soviet influence over it. On the left were the Bolsheviks who called for "All Power to the Soviets." In the center were those left liberals and moderate socialists, Mensheviks and Socialist Revolutionaries, who were being forced to realize that a coalition government made up of liberals and socialists was now necessary. Prime Minister Prince Georgii Lvov asked Chkheidze to raise with the Executive Committee of the Soviets the question of Soviet members entering the government. For most Mensheviks and the left wing of the SRs participation with bourgeois politicians in a coalition government contradicted long-standing socialist traditions, and initially they voted against it.[83] But a few days later the minister of war, Aleksandr Guchkov, resigned his post, and the Executive Committee feared that the minister was conspiring with the conservative general Lavr Kornilov, and possibly the Kadet Party, to launch a military attack on the government. The Lvov government threatened to resign. Backed into a corner the moderate socialists agreed to join the government.

On May 1 the Soviet Executive Committee voted to support a coalition government. Bolsheviks, Menshevik-Internationalists (the group led by Martov), and radical "Left" SRs voted against the measure. Two days later Miliukov resigned from the government, which he considered dominated by the Soviet. The Socialist Revolutionary leader, Viktor Chernov, became minister of agriculture, and the Menshevik Matvei Skobelev, minister of labor. Tsereteli took the largely symbolic post of minister of post and telegraphs. Pulled by events into joining the government, the moderate socialists had crossed into unknown and dangerous territory, and it would prove impossible for them to retreat. Although they were a minority in an essentially "bourgeois" government, from this point on the moderate socialists were implicated in whatever the government accomplished or, as it turned out, failed to accomplish. On a whole series of issues the government had no choice but to accept the program of the Soviet: "peace without annexations and indemnities"; democratization of the army; increased state *kontrol'* ("control" in the sense of supervision) of industry; and regulation of agriculture in the interests of the peasantry. Liberal ministers found it more and more difficult to accept the direction that the government was taking. Within months the government, representing antagonistic elements in a polarizing society, became progressively paralyzed.

The Mensheviks, who had always been more tolerant of the middle classes than the Bolsheviks, and the Socialist Revolutionaries, who helplessly watched their support among soldiers seep away, were caught in a dissolving middle. In the eyes of the *demokratiia* they were bound tightly as members of the government to the bourgeoisie and to continuing the war. The great fear of the Mensheviks had long been that worker militancy would alienate even the "progressive bourgeoisie" (like the left Kadets) and lead to counterrevolution. Most Mensheviks could not bring themselves to believe in a government of the soviets. On the other hand, when the Kadet minister of trade and industry, Vasilii Stepanov, suggested that the government renounce socialism in order to attract greater support among the propertied classes, the socialist ministers refused.[84]

The coalition government was founded on what turned out to be the false hope that "the vital forces of the nation" would cooperate and create a democratic polity. But long-standing and increasing social polarization was pulling the country into antagonistic camps. The government could move neither decisively to the left and grant workers their demands for higher wages and greater *kontrol'* of production or peasants the land nor to the right and suppress the soldiers' committees and soviets and create an army-backed dictatorship. War that led to defeat, inflation that wiped out workers' wages, and hunger for land frustrated by the unwillingness of the government to grant it to them radicalized soldiers, workers, and peasants. Those who owned the industries grew more resistant to concessions to labor. Officers yearned for victory while their men wanted nothing more than to go home. The major liberal party became increasingly suspicious of *demokratiia* in both senses of the word—the lower classes and representation of the people—and grew ever more conservative. Right Kadet Vasilii Maklakov lamented, "Russia had received in the revolution more freedom than she could manage." And Miliukov asked rhetorically, "What reason is there for continuing the revolution?" [85] To put it simply, the top of society was moving to the right, while the bottom was moving to the left.

27

REAPING THE WHIRLWIND

Stalin, moreover, was a great actor. He acted a host of parts with
consummate skill. . . . But more than anything, Stalin tried to play the
part of the dedicated pupil and comrade-in-arms of the great Lenin.

—DMITRII VOLKOGONOV,
STALIN, TRIUMPH AND TRAGEDY (1988)

Standing outside government and refusing to collaborate with middle-
and upper-class parties and society, the Bolsheviks were able to reap
the whirlwind as the populace become ever more discontented and politically radical. All failures of the coalition government redounded to
their benefit. Bolsheviks gathered in the last week of April in what they
labeled the Seventh Conference of the RSDRP (Bolsheviks). As usual
Lenin opened the conference with a reminder that the Russian Revolution was an outgrowth of the imperialist war, and though the Russian
proletariat had the "great honor to start" the revolution, it was only part
of "a global proletarian movement that, for example, in Germany, is
growing day by day stronger and stronger."[1] At the moment, however,
Russia was between a bourgeois revolution, which had been completed,
and the proletarian, which had not yet begun. It was not yet clear how
far the peasants would advance beyond the bourgeois stage. The task of
the Bolsheviks was to increase the number of soviets and to win them
over to the radical party. Lenin essentially proposed an educational mission for the Bolsheviks: "We are at the moment in a minority; the
masses do not yet believe us. We can wait: They will come over to our
side when the government reveals itself."[2] He even moderated his call
to turn the imperialist war into a civil war and promoted instead "long,
peaceful, and patient class propaganda. . . . We are for civil war but only

when it is led by a [politically] conscious class. . . . Until then we reject this slogan, but only until then."[3] Still, the soviets should take power, not to move immediately to socialism but to take the first steps in that direction.

Kamenev again rose as the principal opponent of Lenin's analysis that the revolution was moving beyond the bourgeois-democratic stage. Consistent with what Lenin contemptuously referred to as "Old Bolshevism," Kamenev found it difficult to alter the time-honored sense of the historical stages. He repeated that Lenin's strategy placed the party in the odd position of supporting neither the current Soviet nor the government, neither the idea of Soviet control nor of the agreements that the Soviet had made with the government.[4] Rykov agreed: "The more the party stands for the point of view of a socialist revolution, the more it will turn into a propaganda circle." Socialism will come from the developed countries of the West, he predicted, for Russia was "the most petit bourgeois country in Europe."

Stalin indicated the distance he had moved from Kamenev. Whereas his recent ally advocated Soviet *kontrol'* over the government, Stalin now ridiculed the notion that the Soviet would "control" the government when in fact it was retreating before the bourgeois ministers. With victory in his grasp Lenin turned toward conciliation and noted that there was not very much distance between his views and Kamenev's, except on the question of control, which Lenin did not support. To Rykov he countered that it was not necessarily true that socialism would come from more industrially developed countries. "It is not possible to say who will begin and who will end. This is not Marxism but a parody of Marxism."[5] As might have been expected, given his position as *primus inter pares*, Lenin prevailed, and his resolution passed overwhelmingly. The differences between the "Old Bolsheviks," not ready to concede that the "bourgeois revolution" was over, and Lenin, who wanted the soviets to take steps toward socialism, were papered over as the party staked out a relatively firm position on the left of the political spectrum. The goal was "Soviet Power," which all Bolsheviks agreed was necessary both to extend democracy as far as possible and to bring the war to an end.

On the last day of the conference Stalin made his report on what was often treated as a secondary issue, the "national question." As one of the most prominent Bolsheviks from the ethnic borderlands of the empire, and the author of a major tract on the subject, he was recognized as the party's principal spokesman on matters dealing with non-Russians.[6] His report to the conference was short and perfunctory, but it aroused a heated discussion. The question of policies toward the dozens of nationalities had already become acute with the weakening of central authority in the country. Finns, Ukrainians, and Poles vigorously presented demands for autonomy, even independence. Into this maelstrom Stalin offered simple, overly schematic solutions that he had worked out during his brief sojourn in Austria, and his long exile in Turukhansk. They paralleled the essentials of Lenin's own views, but he rather crudely correlated national oppression (*natsional'nyi gnet*) with specific social classes. In Russia, where the landed aristocracy held sway, national oppression was unusually brutal, resulting in pogroms and massacres, whereas in more democratic states, like Britain and Switzerland, where aristocratic power had given way, minorities were treated more tolerantly.[7] The optimal solution to the problem of national oppression, then, was to create a full democracy purged of that "social chorus" that benefits from ethnic discrimination.

In practice this meant first that each nation should decide if it wished to stay within the Russian state or become independent. In the current conflict between Finns and the Provisional Government the Bolsheviks must stand with the Finns "since it is inconceivable to recognize the forced holding of any people within the bounds of a united state." "If we, Social Democrats, refuse the Finnish people the right to express their will to separate and the right to realize that will, then we would be continuing the policies of tsarism."[8] But, he qualified, recognizing the *right* to independence did not obligate the Social Democrats to support separation in every case. Personally, he pointed out, he was against the separation of Transcaucasia from Russia, though if the people demanded it the party should not oppose it. As Lenin had frequently argued, so Stalin agreed, the lack of trust felt by non-Russians toward Russia was a product of tsarism that would dissipate with the end of imperial oppression. Once agreeing to join Russia, non-Russian peoples would enjoy regional autonomy with guarantees of full equality in education, religion, and other matters concerning national minorities.[9] But the party opposed federalism, a "transitory" stage toward greater unity. Russia had already achieved that unity.

Stalin's principal opponent in the ensuing debate was Piatakov, a militant activist who had already made a name for himself during the war with his polemic against Lenin's views on nationality. Piatakov and the "section on the national question" proposed a far more radical resolution than Stalin's. The party's slogan should be: "Borders Be Gone!" (*Proch' granitsy!*). Not only did the resolution dismiss extraterritorial national cultural autonomy, as did Stalin and Lenin, but it opposed breaking up large multinational states into small nation-states, which in the era of imperialism and the approaching socialist revolution represented "a harmful and reactionary utopia." "The international party of the proletariat, at a time when the majority on a European scale is on its side, cannot consider the will of the majority of a nation if that will diverges from the will of its proletarian minority." For this reason the leftists rejected the slogan "the right of nations to self-determination" as "an empty phrase without any definite content."[10]

In his remarks Piatakov made it clear that only the will of the proletariat should be considered by Social Democrats. He believed that "Stalin posed the question purely metaphysically when he spoke of the will of the nation and not the will of a class." Outflanking Stalin on Marxist grounds, Piatakov insisted on the primary of class over nation. But he went further to claim that the era of the nation-state was over. Whereas defending the national state against feudalism had been progressive, "now it was a reactionary factor directed against socialism." Piatakov personalized his statement by focusing on Stalin, who, "for example, said that he was personally against the separation of Transcaucasia. But a political party cannot suppose that each individual comrade will express his personal opinion."[11]

Although this was an old debate that went back at least to 1903 and the Second Party Congress, Bolsheviks were caught on the horns of several dilemmas. They wanted both large economically advantaged states as well as national self-determination, which was likely to lead to fragmentation into smaller nation states. They wanted to move beyond nationalism to class solidarity, yet they sought allies among those still intoxicated with the nation. Lenin attempted to square the circle by emphasizing morality and strategy rather than Marxist theory. One of the few Bolsheviks to appreciate the benefits of a nuanced policy toward non-Russians, he queried the leftists, "Why should we, the Great Russians, who oppress more nations than any other people, refuse to recognize the right of Poland, Ukraine, Finland to be independent?" "A people that oppresses other peoples cannot themselves be free."[12] Nations ought to have the right to join or separate from other states. To deny Finland independence, as the Provisional Government does, is pure chauvinism. Granting Finns full freedom to decide will raise its trust in Russia, and then they will not want to separate. The method of the socialist revolution is to tell states to withdraw their armies from other states: "Germany, take your troops out of Poland; Russia, take your troops out of Armenia—anything else is a fraud."[13]

Two delegates from national regions—Feliks Dzierżyński from Poland and Pilipe Makharadze from Georgia—supported Piatakov, while Zinoviev backed self-determination.[14] As one of the oldest Marxists in Georgia, Makharadze evoked his authority as a man from the national borderlands and stated that the abstract slogan of national self-determination was harmful for regions like Transcaucasia. He pointed out that Stalin's resolution contained a contradiction between the blanket proclamation of a principle that permitted independence and the proviso that each case would be considered in light of what might be advantageous for the proletariat.[15] Stalin ignored Makharadze's sharp rebuke and ended the debate by posing the choice of resolutions as equivalent to supporting the Provisional Government over the Finns or British imperialism over a free Ireland. Do Social Democrats favor the oppressing classes or the people fighting against imperialism? "We must support any movement directed against imperialism."[16] Lenin and Stalin's more moderate and strategically motivated resolution, with its reservations about absolute agreement to independence, passed 56 for, 16 against, 18 abstaining, while Piatakov's failed, 11 to 48 to 19.[17]

When the elections to the Central Committee took place, Stalin's star appeared to be ascendant. He came in third in the number of votes cast (97), after Lenin (104) and Zinoviev (101) and just before Kamenev (95).[18] His patron was none other than Lenin. As Molotov remembered many years later, "Before the election of members to the Central Committee, Lenin spoke for Stalin's candidacy. He said Stalin had to be in the Central Committee without fail. He spoke up for Stalin in particular, saying he was such a fine party member, such a commanding figure, and you could assign him any task. He was the most trustworthy in adhering to the party line. That's the sort of speech it was. Of course, we voted in concord. So that's how it went."[19] Stalin, the dedicated party worker, the consummate insider, patronized by none other than Lenin, had secured a place at the top of a political party that was contending for state power. His patron valued him as someone who carried out the tasks assigned and, for all his occasional divergences, adhered to the party line. Diligence, perseverance, and loyalty had paid off.

The turmoil of the revolutionary year fractured and remade the political parties competing for influence and power. In early May a number of revolutionary luminaries returned to Russia, among them Trotsky, Lunacharskii, Martov, and Akselrod. Mensheviks met in their own conference, but instead of unifying, the party divided between internationalists led by Martov and revolutionary defensists led by Tsereteli. Martov and the Menshevik-Internationalists, as they characterized themselves, rejected the coalition with the bourgeoisie, which had become the touchstone of the majority of their party comrades. Suddenly the acknowledged leader of the Mensheviks, the man who had done as much as Lenin to cause the party to break into two factions, was a man without a significant party. Trotsky and Lunacharskii were also somewhat isolated. They joined the so-called *Mezhraionka* (Interdistrict Group) that included local and returning Social Democrats who favored unifying the various factions. Choosing sides was imperative in the rapidly radicalizing revolution, with social polarization accelerating. While Martov and the Menshevik-Internationalists remained distinct from the Bolsheviks, the *Mezhraiontsy*, who also were internationalist on the war and opposed to the coalition government, joined the Bolshevik party two months later. Trotsky's decision to join the Bolsheviks propelled him to power within half a year; Martov's choice to remain outside the two factions left him rudderless in turbulent waters.

In 1917 the Bolsheviks operated not as a tightly centralized party in which orders that came down from above were faithfully carried out without question but as a loose and disputatious collection of strong-willed activists who had to be persuaded of the right course to take. Through the revolutionary year, they had no coercive force with which to discipline their members. Persuasion and prestige were the instruments to win over dissidents. Lenin was able to use his stature as long-time leader to convince others to follow him, but he never had the kind of complete domination of the party that Stalin would achieve. He had to employ all his skills as logician and strategist to bring resolute party loyalists around. On May 30 he made several long pleas to the Petersburg Committee not to publish its own newspaper. He argued that Petersburg was not simply another locality but "the geographic, political, revolutionary center of all Russia. All Russia follows the life of Petersburg."[20] He informed the committee of the ongoing negotiations with Trotsky, "a powerful literary force," to have him edit a popular Bolshevik newspaper. Trotsky, however, was a thorn in the side of many Bolsheviks, even when he was championed by Lenin. Mikhail Tomskii expressed the lingering suspicions of many Bolsheviks and declared that Trotsky was "a whale that swayed this way and that."[21] On issue after issue Lenin insisted that deference to the Central Committee was extremely important. The Kronstadt Soviet had recently declared that it had taken power in the fortress-city, but this "doubtlessly caused harm to the party. That is why control [by the Central Committee] is essential." He pulled out all the stops with an apocalyptic prediction of what might lie ahead: "Such are the objective external conditions. Firing upon our party is always possible. We must expect this," and referring to the events of June 1848, "We stand on the eve of the 'June Massacres.'"[22] But in this case Lenin's arguments did not work.[23] The Petersburg Committee voted against him.[24]

THE JUNE CRISIS

By late spring 1917 Petrograd workers signaled their disaffection from the coalition government and the moderate leaders of the Soviet at the First Conference of Petrograd Factory Committees, which opened at the end of May. Frequently elected and reelected by workers, these committees more closely reflected the shifting mood of the workers and were consistently more militant than the soviets. When fuel, raw materials, and money failed to reach the factories, angry workers perceived the disruption in production as deliberate sabotage by the factory owners. In addition they were appalled by the government's plans to "unload" Petrograd by sending up to one hundred thousand workers to other parts of the country. The government, concerned about disorder and potential hunger in the city, may have been well-intentioned, but their actions were interpreted as counterrevolutionary. Some committees established *kontrol'* in their factories in an attempt to maintain production.[25] As *kontrol'* slipped from supervision to actual takeover of the factory, the Mensheviks, SRs, and liberals resisted such expansion of worker authority, which would only antagonize further the owners of industry. The Bolsheviks applauded it. At the Conference of Factory Committees, Lenin's resolution demanding "actual workers' *kontrol'*" of production passed overwhelmingly. Workers and the radical Left considered government supervision and regulation (*gosudarstvennyi kontrol'*) of the capitalists to be a dismal failure. At roughly the same time the workers' section of the Soviet, day by day more and more Bolshevik, accepted a Bolshevik-inspired resolution against "unloading" workers from the capital.[26] The Bolshevik slogan "All Power to the Soviets" appealed to workers in the city. What was clear was that Petrograd, not the country as a whole, would determine the fate of the revolution.

The moderate socialists fared better in the municipal elections to the twelve district dumas in the city than in the elections to the factory committees or local soviets. Mensheviks and SRs won fifty-six percent of the nearly eight hundred thousand votes cast, while the Kadets and nonsocialists won only twenty-two percent, and the Bolsheviks just over twenty percent. But the Bolsheviks could crow about their majority in the workers' district of Vyborg and their plurality on Vasilevskii Island. Mensheviks faced the stark reality that their victory came largely thanks to the votes for the SRs in districts with little industry. The only bastion of worker support on which the Mensheviks could reliably count was their traditional ally, the literate, highly skilled printers.[27] Those Mensheviks in government, progressively losing touch with the workers, interpreted the results of the municipal elections as a victory, and in a familiar Menshevik response assumed that the Bolshevized workers, unlike their printers, were "ignorant" and "backward."[28]

Stalin, along with Sverdlov, threw himself into the party's campaigns in the local elections. With humor heavily laced with irony and sarcasm, he reviewed in *Pravda* the "real and imaginary political parties contesting the elections, including one called the 'Party Slightly to the Left of the Kadets.'" These elections, he wrote, were not about the tinning of sinks and the proper layout of good toilets but were closely connected to national political issues. He deployed a new favorite word, one that Mensheviks had been using, *obuzdanie* (bridle, restraint), to condemn the Kadets, who were hobbling the revolution. The Bolsheviks were in his view the polar opposite of the Kadets and the only real alternative to the false socialists of the Revolutionary Defensist bloc.[29] When the results of the elections began to come in, Stalin interpreted them as demonstrating the deep social divide in the city and country. Even though the moderate socialists won the majority of the votes, he emphasized that the elections exposed the complete defeat of the Kadets and the growth of support for the Bolsheviks. With only about twenty-three to twenty-five thousand party members in the city and a circulation for *Pravda* of only ninety to one hundred thousand, the party won over seven times the number of supporters than it had members. Not only did it win in the Vyborg district, but it gained votes from unexpected quarters—women, shopkeepers, petty bureaucrats, tradesmen, and artisans. "In short, the mass voter *already* has left the Kadets, but it has not *yet* come over to our party; it has stopped halfway . . . where it found its worthy leader—the bloc of Mensheviks and SRs."[30]

In a review of the revolutionary crisis he characterized the coalition government as continuing the Miliukov-Guchkov policies on the war, only in softer, more appealing language about freedom. The coalition government even deported, without trial or judicial investigation, the Swiss socialist and organizer of the Zimmerwald Conference Robert Grimm, because of rumors that he was working toward a separate peace between Russia and Germany. "It is clear that the Provisional Government is steadily sliding into the embrace of the counterrevolution."[31] Miliukov was already writing that after exiling Grimm, one might ask why Lenin, Trotsky, and their comrades were still walking around freely. "We wish that sometime Lenin and his comrades will be deported as well."[32] The choice, Stalin wrote, is to go forward against the bourgeoisie and transfer power to the working people or to go backward and continue the war and the "openly counterrevolutionary policies."[33]

Growing Bolshevik influence among workers and soldiers in and near Petrograd was not matched in much of the rest of Russia. The Revolutionary Defensists were far more popular outside the capital than within. When the First All-Russian Congress of Soviets opened on June 3 they could count on an enormous majority. Of the more than 800 delegates they had almost two-thirds; the Bolsheviks only 105; Martov's Internationalists but 35; and the *Mezhraionka* just slightly more.[34] Tsereteli confidently opened the congress by declaring, "At the present moment, there is not a political party in Russia that would say: Hand the power over to us, resign, and we will take your place. Such a party does not exist in Russia." From the floor an even-more confident Lenin interjected a single word, "*est'*." ["It does exist!"] Tsereteli dismissed him: "Gentlemen, this is not the time for that kind of game. . . . In order to solve the problems of the country, we must unite and have a strong government." When he was given the floor, Lenin was characteristically bold and sarcastic:

> The proceeding orator, Citizen Minister of Post and Telegraphs . . . said that there is no political party in Russia that would express willingness to take all state power into its hands. I say: Such a party exists! No party has a right to refuse power, and our party does not refuse it. Our party is ready at any moment to take all power into its hands.[35]

He was greeted by both applause and laughter but continued to explain the connection, as he saw it, between a government of capitalists and the continuation of the war.

> Our first step, were we in power, would be to arrest the biggest capitalists, to sever all the threads of their intrigues. Unless this is done, all talk about peace without annexations is only empty words. Our second step would be to address ourselves to all peoples, over the heads of their governments, and to tell them that we consider all capitalists to be bandits.[36]

Kerenskii, well known for his rhetorical skills and very popular with the delegates, defended the government's policies as necessary for preserving democracy. Rather than the Russian Revolution of 1917 ending up like the French Revolution of 1789 or the Russian Revolution of 1905 in a "triumph of reaction," the Russian socialist parties must "hold on to the revolutionary conquests already made; to see to it that comrades who have been released from prison do not return there; that Comrade Lenin, who has been abroad, may have the opportunity to speak here again and not be obliged to flee back to Switzerland." After five days of debate the Congress approved by a huge majority the Menshevik-SR resolution to support the coalition government.

To the radicals the Congress was a great disappointment, and militant soldiers and sailors were anxious to hold a demonstration to impress the delegates with their discontent. Pushed by the mood of their constituents, the Bolshevik Military Organization brought the question of what action to take to the Central Committee. Lenin, Sverdlov, Stalin, and G. F. Fedorov strongly backed having a demonstration. Vladimir Nevskii, who had made the original proposal, insisted that the demonstrators be armed.[37] But Nogin, Zinoviev, Kamenev, and Krupskaia were against what they considered an ill-timed action that could end in disaster for the Bolsheviks. Divided and unable to secure firm support, the Central Committee decided to postpone a decision until a future meeting. That same day, June 6, the Petersburg Committee took up the same issue, and Stalin attended in order to speak in favor of the demonstration. He feared that if the Provisional Government were not challenged, it would soon turn on the Bolshevik party and try to crush it. The party "must call the masses to battle not only when the situation has reached the boiling point. Since we are an organization possessing influence, we have the duty to awaken the spirit of the masses." "Our duty is to repulse [the offensive of the government]. Our duty is to organize this demonstration—a review of our strength. Seeing armed soldiers, the bourgeoisie will hide."[38]

The situation heated up quickly. Anxious about unrest in the city, the Provisional Government responded to a provocative seizure of the printing press of a right-wing newspaper by anarchists by ordering them to give up their headquarters in the earlier requisitioned Durnovo Villa. The anarchists appealed to the Vyborg workers, and the Congress of Soviets decided to avert a confrontation by remanding the order of the government. That same day, June 8, the Central Committee decided that Bolsheviks would support the soldiers' demonstration, even though doubts were raised as to whether workers would join in defiance of the will of the Soviet. The principal slogan was to demand the transfer of power to the Soviet, even though it was run by moderates who did not intend to take power. Other slogans would include "Down with the Ten Capitalist Ministers!" and "Time to End the War!" The demonstration was scheduled for June 10, and the anarchists and the *Mezhraiontsy* also agreed to march. Soldiers would be armed in order to protect civilians.

Stalin was tasked with writing the proclamation that would appear in the Bolshevik newspapers. He rolled out all the complaints of workers and soldiers—rising prices, the lack of supplies, the transfer of soldiers to the front, and the threat of hunger—and finished by listing the Bolshevik slogans under which its supporters should march.[39] A clash was brewing between the Soviet and the street. The Georgian Menshevik and former duma deputy Gegechkori read out Stalin's proclamation to the congress. In the ensuing uproar, at just after midnight on the 10th, the Congress voted unanimously to prohibit street demonstrations in Petrograd for three days. Even the Bolshevik delegation to the Congress, which included Kamenev and Nogin, apparently unaware of the Central Committee's final decision, voted against the demonstration. At the last minute, at 2 a.m., as the possibility of a bloody outcome came closer, those Bolsheviks fearful of exposing the workers prevailed on the Central Committee to call off the march.[40]

The clash had been averted—or at least postponed. But Tsereteli believed that the Bolsheviks had conspired to seize power and had to be disarmed. At a meeting of Congress delegations, he declared, "We must take weapons away from those revolutionaries who do not know how to handle them with dignity." Excitedly, Kamenev exclaimed, "Mr. Minister, if you are not throwing words into the winds, you have no right to limit yourself to a speech; arrest me and try me for conspiracy against the revolution." He and the Bolshevik delegates then stormed out of the meeting.[41] Most of the delegates were not prepared to go as far as Tsereteli. As Martov put it, disarming the Bolsheviks would mean disarming the proletariat and even the soldiers, and the Congress did not have that kind of power. One would have to set up a military dictatorship of the bourgeoisie.[42] Ultimately, the Congress rejected Tsereteli's motion and merely chastised the Bolsheviks and prohibited future armed demonstrations without Soviet permission. The next day the Congress censured the Bolsheviks but took no stronger measures against them. It also announced it would sponsor its own demonstration on the 18th.

Stalin was upset by the Central Committee's decision to cancel the demonstration. From March to June he had moved from the right of the party to the left. Along with the Latvian Ivars Smilga, he submitted his resignation to the Central Committee, but their requests were denied.[43] On June 11 the Petersburg Committee met in a postmortem discussion on the demonstration that had not taken place.[44] Lenin and Zinoviev were uncomfortable with the retreat that they had called but calmly defended their decisions. Lenin justified the cancellation as unavoidable and presented the June 10 "event" as a revolutionary turning point. In his view Tsereteli had decisively shown himself to be a true counterrevolutionary. In the current context maximum calm and patience were called for. "We should not give cause for attack."[45]

Stalin soon reconciled himself to the temporary retreat called by the party leadership. When the anarchists decided to hold their own demonstration on the 14th, he criticized such "uncoordinated" actions and praised the more disciplined approach of the Bolsheviks, who had given up the idea of the demonstration once the Congress of Soviets had opposed it. Many Bolshevik supporters were also sympathizers of the anarchists, and the Bolsheviks did not want to be outflanked on the left. Yet they feared that odd, uncoordinated actions could provoke bloodshed and aid those opposed to the Soviet. The anarchists eventually backed down and decided to join the march sanctioned by the Soviet, though they chose to be armed, unlike most others. As attention turned to the Soviet-sponsored demonstration called for June 18, the Bolsheviks mobilized as many demonstrators as possible to march under Bolshevik slogans.[46]

The moderate leaders of the Soviet were confident that the demonstration would reveal their popularity among the masses and expose the weakness of the Bolsheviks. At the Executive Committee meeting on the eve of the demonstration, "Tsereteli triumphantly addressed the Bolsheviks, especially Kamenev, in an indignantly didactic speech: 'Here we have before us now an open and honest review of the forces of the revolution. Tomorrow there will be demonstrating not separate groups but all the working class of the capital, not against the will of the Soviet, but at its invitation. Now we shall all see which the majority follows, you or us. This isn't a matter of underhand plots but a duel in the open arena. Tomorrow we shall see.' Kamenev was discreetly silent."[47]

June 18 turned out to be an open but peaceful battle of banners and slogans. The Bolsheviks managed to have their own demonstration within the demonstration. At nine in the morning the band started up playing the *Marseillaise*. At the head of the parade were Chkheidze and the other Soviet leaders, who then stood by the Field of Mars to review the marchers. To their embarrassment most of the 400,000 demonstrators carried Bolshevik slogans. Sukhanov, the Menshevik chronicler of the revolution and a member of the Soviet Executive Committee, was stunned by what he saw:

But what was the political character of the demonstration? "Bolsheviks again," I remarked, looking at the slogans, "and there behind them is another Bolshevik column." "Apparently the next one too,"

I went on calculating, watching the banners advancing towards me and the endless rows going away towards Michael Castle a long way down the Sadovoy. "All Power to the Soviets!" "Down with the Ten Capitalist Ministers!" "Peace for the hovels, war for the palaces!" In this sturdy and weighty way worker-peasant Petersburg, the vanguard of the Russian and the world revolution, expressed its will. The situation was absolutely unambiguous. Here and there the chain of Bolshevik flags and columns was interrupted by specifically SR and official Soviet slogans. But they were submerged in the mass; they seemed to be exceptions, intentionally confirming the rule. Again and again, like the unchanging summons of the very depths of the revolutionary capital, like fate itself, like the fatal Birnam wood—there advanced towards us: "All Power to the Soviets!" "Down with the Ten Capitalist Ministers!"[48]

What had been planned as a display of support for the Soviet and the coalition government turned out to be a Bolshevik triumph. In a review of the demonstration Stalin noted the "endless forest of banners," the overwhelming presence of workers and soldiers in contrast to earlier marches, and the absence of the bourgeoisie. The Kadets had boycotted the demonstration. "And, really," Stalin wrote, "the bourgeoisie not only did not participate, they literally went into hiding."[49]

THE WAR ON WAR

Despite the dismay that the moderate Soviet leaders felt during the demonstration, the coalition government, backed by the Congress of Soviets, had reason to believe that the *demokratiia* in most of Russia, outside Petrograd, was on its side. The same day as its awkward showing on the streets of the capital, the government, egged on by the minister of war, launched the "Kerenskii Offensive" against the Germans. The Congress supported the attack, casting a fatal die that would resolve the balance of power between the coalition government on one side and the radical opposition led by the Bolsheviks on the other. Each side operated from its own logic. The Soviet-government coalition was pursuing the war, and consequently its attitude toward the soldiers hardened. It condemned fraternization with the enemy, called for greater discipline, and sent reinforcements to the front. Much of the middle and upper classes in Petrograd were pleased that the government had launched an offensive. Perhaps engaging the army in battle, it was thought, would end its disintegration.

The Bolsheviks operated from a different logic. Their future lay with the failure of the government's war policy. Within days the offensive faltered, for many soldiers simply did not want to fight. Whatever patriotism they had felt a few months earlier had dissipated as they longed for their homes and villages. "What good is the land and freedom to me if I am dead?" they complained.[50] Entire regiments and divisions mutinied and refused to attack. Kerenskii's impassioned speeches inspired some soldiers, but others "voted with their feet" and deserted in droves. Turning their fists on their officers, the soldiers organized mass meetings and passed resolutions against the offensive. Bolshevik propaganda was only part of the cause of soldier disaffection, but Bolshevism was the heir of their discontent. As the historian of the Russian army Allan K. Wildman concluded, "The formation of the Coalition cabinet with Kerenskii as War Minister and the Soviet's acquiescence in the fateful decision to launch a new offensive created a new political situation: revolutionary institutions, of which the front committees were a part, were now coresponsible for government policies, including the offensive, leaving the soldier masses with no outlets for their strivings other than illicit actions inspired by Bolshevik slogans."[51] Opposition to war, and particularly the offensive, mutated into what was called "trench Bolshevism," soldiers shifting their loyalty to the one major party that offered an alternative to carrying on the war.

THE JULY DAYS

The Bolshevik leadership was caught between its most furious and active followers, who demanded an immediate end to the coalition government and a seizure of power in the name of the Soviet, and the moderate socialists, who dominated the Soviet and refused to take power.

Lenin remained cautious about acting prematurely. The transfer of power, he told Podvoiskii, a leader of the Military Organization, would not be peaceful but would require guns. Yet if the masses were provoked into action too early, this would bring down counterrevolutionary repression. "It is necessary to give the proletariat instructions to the effect that all organization of its strength, in the final analysis, is for an armed uprising if not in days, if not in the coming weeks, then in any event in the near future."[52] Many military units, as well as Bolshevik military organizations, were ready to act. Once the offensive began, holding back certain regiments seemed impossible. A *vystuplenie* (public manifestation) could in a flash turn into a *vosstanie* (uprising). Lenin tried to calm the waters in an address to the All-Russian Conference of Bolshevik Military Organizations on June 20, and it seemed to work, at least for a few weeks.

> We must be especially attentive and careful, so as not to be drawn into a provocation. . . . One wrong move on our part can wreck everything. . . . If we were now able to seize power, it is naïve to think that having taken it we would be able to hold it.

The only possible form of revolutionary government was the Soviet, yet Bolsheviks were insignificant minorities in the soviets of both capitals, Moscow and Petrograd, which "shows that the majority of the masses are wavering but still believe the SRs and Mensheviks. . . . How can we push the petty bourgeoisie to power, if this petty bourgeoisie is already able but does not want to take it." And he concluded, "Events should not be anticipated. Time is on our side."[53]

The failure of the offensive fueled the anger of the most militant soldiers, particularly the First Machine Gun Regiment, who feared transfer to the front and imagined the dissolution of their unit.[54] The machine gunners discussed organizing another demonstration in early July with the Bolshevik military organizations, members of which encouraged action despite the Central Committee's appeal for patience. Such a move by armed soldiers would be tantamount to a military coup.

At the same time that the crisis at the bottom of society was heating up, a simultaneous crisis blew up at the top. Emissaries from the

Provisional Government had negotiated an agreement in Kiev with the nationalist Ukrainian Rada granting limited autonomy to Ukraine. But when they returned to Petrograd on July 2 and attempted to convince the rest of the government to accept their settlement, four of the five Kadet ministers resigned their posts. The government now had six socialist and only five "capitalist" ministers.

The next day the machine gunners rallied other military units and took to the streets demanding the end of the Provisional Government. They occupied the Finland Station and took positions on the major bridges over the Neva. Ten thousand sailors from Kronstadt and thirty thousand workers from the Putilov Factory came out in favor of the insurrection. Although not initiated by the Bolsheviks, many party members joined, even encouraged, the uprising, while others tried to restrain the rebels. But holding back the demonstrators was like standing in the way of an avalanche. The movement was beyond the control of any party. Bolsheviks were unsure whether they should act as firemen or incendiaries. The Central Committee voted twice not to participate in the demonstration, which in any case was banned by the Soviet. Stalin, who had become a member of the All-Russian Central Executive Committee (TsIK) of the Soviets on June 24, was sent by the Central Committee to read the party's statement opposing the demonstration into the record of the Executive Committee's session.[55] The party's ambivalence could be heard in the voice of Tomskii, who told a conference of Bolsheviks at the time, "We must obey the decision of the Central Committee, but we need not rush to the factories to put out the fire since we did not light it and we cannot put fires out for everybody."[56]

Like other members of the Bolshevik leadership, Stalin was both confused and swept along by events. The poet Demian Bednyi later related a story, perhaps apocryphal, of Stalin receiving a telephone call from a Kronstadt sailor, who asked advice about whether the sailors should come armed or unarmed to the demonstration. Stalin puffed on his pipe, stroked his mustache, and answered, "We scribblers always carry our weapons—our pens—with us wherever we go. As to your weapons, comrade, you can be the best judges of that."[57] Stalin moved about the city on that fateful July 3. He and Sverdlov met with members of the Bolshevik military organizations upstairs in a master bedroom at the Kshesinskaia Mansion, while in the ornate art nouveau hallways and outside the house factory workers and men in uniform milled about awaiting orders that did not come. No longer able to prevent the demonstration, the Bolsheviks had to decide whether to join a movement aiming at the government's overthrow or stand aside as observers. Sverdlov, Podvoiskii, Nevskii, and others—though not Stalin—spoke from a balcony to the crowd, urging them to return to the Vyborg district. But that appeal had no effect, and eventually the party's central Military Organization announced it was ready to support a march to the Tauride Palace, where the Soviet met, to present the demands of the demonstrators. Other Petersburg Bolshevik institutions also agreed to back the demonstrators and their call for Soviet Power. At the Tauride Palace the workers' section of the Soviet, after a walkout of the Mensheviks and SRs, passed a resolution agreeing with the demonstrators. This marked the first Bolshevik majority in the section.

As demonstrators moved up Nevskii Prospekt, the grand avenue that cut through the most fashionable district of the city, shots were fired. At the shopping arcade, *Gostinyi dvor*, a grenade was thrown; people were wounded, some killed; and the crowd retreated into the courtyard of the Armenian Church built by Catherine the Great. But the march continued until crowds numbering more than sixty thousand surrounded the Tauride Palace, locking the Soviet members inside. Chkheidze and Woytinski tried to calm people down and convince them to leave. They failed. Trotskii and Zinoviev stirred them with visions of Soviet Power. There were no forces around to defend the palace, but the crowd did not attempt to rush in. As dawn was about to break, the tired and disgusted protestors drifted off, determined to renew their struggle the next day.

In the early morning of July 4 the Bolshevik Central Committee met and decided it would lead a "peaceful but armed" demonstration later that day. Stalin drafted a leaflet by four in the morning that proclaimed the collapse of the coalition government and the need for Soviet Power. They sent for Lenin, who had been resting in Finland the last five days. Late in the morning twenty thousand Kronstadt sailors arrived in a motley flotilla. They marched to the Kshesinskaia Mansion, and there a reluctant Lenin spoke to them about self-restraint and vigilance. Soviet Power, he said, would win in the end. But the anger and anxiety of the crowds, soon to turn into rage, could not be contained. At the Tauride Palace they shouted down the SR leader Viktor Chernov. "Take power, you son-of-a-bitch, when it is given to you."[58] Even Trotsky could not calm the crowd, though he managed to rescue the pitiable Chernov, who had been manhandled and thrown into a car by the Kronstadters.

With the government about to fall, and unable to appease the people in the street, Tsereteli and other Soviet leaders decided they had to order troops loyal to the government to come from the Northern Front and put down the rebellion. To discredit the Bolsheviks and win over the garrison, Minister of Justice Pavel Pereverzev, an SR, released documents that claimed to show that Lenin was in the pay of the Germans. The former Bolshevik duma deputy Grigorii Aleksinskii was authorized to publish the material the next day and reveal, falsely, that Lenin was a German agent. The accusations seemed plausible to many. After all Lenin had returned to Russia on the famous "sealed train" with the aid of the Germans and, it was claimed, had been given money—the infamous and imaginary "German gold"—that the party used to advance its agenda. His aims—to bring the war to an end and overthrow the Provisional Government—coincided to some degree with those of the Germans, but as he saw it, Lenin was acting to advance the revolution, globally if possible (that is, in Germany as well), which was not consistent with the interests of the German Empire.[59]

The effect of these accusations was electric, and within hours many who had marched with the Bolsheviks turned against them or melted back into their barracks and workshops. As the mood shifted the Soviet leaders became emboldened. Workers met with them to present their demands: "We trust the Soviet, but not those whom the Soviet trusts."[60] But the Soviet leaders no longer trusted these workers either. For Tsereteli the coalition government represented the great majority of Russia, while the radical Petrograd workers, soldiers, and sailors were a misled minority of the whole population.

The tide turned extremely quickly. By early morning of the 5th, troops arrived to defend the Soviet. Mikhail Liber from the Soviet

Executive Committee demanded that the Bolsheviks remove their armored cars from the Kshesinskaia Mansion and persuade the sailors who had taken over the Peter-Paul Fortress to leave. The fortress was in the hands of the Military Organization. The Bolsheviks tried to secure a guarantee of the sailors' safety. But the next day, July 6, the military commander of the Petrograd District, A. Kuzmin, telephoned an ultimatum that the Bolsheviks must surrender their positions in three-quarters of an hour or face an armed attack. The Central Committee dispatched Stalin to mediate between the Soviet and the soldiers. As a representative of the Soviet Executive Committee, he went to the Soviet first. "What do you want?" asked Stalin. "Do you want to shoot us? We are not rising against the Soviets."[61] The Menshevik Boris Bogdanov said that they wanted to prevent bloodshed. Stalin and Bogdanov then went to Kuzmin's headquarters, where they were received coldly. The order had already been given, they were told. Disgusted that civilians were as usual holding him back, Kuzmin grudgingly gave in to the Soviet representatives. Stalin later told his comrades that it had been clear to him that the military wanted to teach the workers, soldiers, and sailors a bloody lesson.[62]

Stalin and Bogdanov went unarmed to the fortress, where they faced thousands of enraged sailors. Bogdanov told them, "There are two of us; we are unarmed. You are armed, and there are more than two thousand of you. You will always have time to kill us, but first you must give up." Stalin did not argue with the furious men. He simply stated, "There is no other way out except capitulation. You have to submit, give up your weapons, and return to Kronstadt."[63] The commandant of the Military Organization, Aleksandr Ilin-Zhenevskii, asked Stalin whether they should give up. He answered bitterly, "There is nothing else left."[64] Gradually the sailors calmed down and slipped back to their island fortress. Having put their lives on the line Stalin later sent Bogdanov a bizarre message: "Well done [*Molodets*], Bogdanov! With one stomach you disarmed the sailors [*Odnym briukhom razoruzhil matrosov*]!"[65]

Once the insurrection had been put down soldiers quickly switched sides. Even Bolshevized regiments expressed regret for their mistakes. The crowds had been for Soviet Power, but the Soviet refused to take power. As its members, backed by soldiers, sang the *Marseillaise*, Martov snapped, "A classic scene from the start of a counterrevolution!"[66]

Some four hundred people had been killed in the two-day uprising, a civil war in microcosm. The July Days were a bloody clash between two visions of revolution: one "bourgeois" and inclusive of all classes; the other, socialist, with the lower classes in power to the exclusion of others. The Bolsheviks, caught between their desire for Soviet Power and their belief that insurrection at this time could not succeed, hesitated, wavered, only eventually to go along with the demonstrators. Lenin had not been enthusiastic about the ill-timed insurrection, but he did not try to stop it. Kalinin reported that when asked if this was the beginning of a seizure of power, Lenin replied, "We shall see—right now it is impossible to say!"[67] The radical workers, sailors, and soldiers had gambled and lost, and the Bolsheviks had to pay for their adventure. *Pravda*'s publishing house was destroyed, the workers there arrested. The Kshesinskaia Mansion was occupied, and the Bolsheviks driven out. Some Bolsheviks, like Martyn Latsis, hoped to rejuvenate the movement by declaring a general strike, but Lenin immediately acknowledged defeat and called for a tactical retreat. Lenin and Zinoviev went into hiding. Kamenev, Trotsky, Lunacharskii, and others went to jail.

The room that the Alliluevs had reserved for Stalin now came into play. Its intended occupant was in no immediate danger, but Lenin needed a hideout. He had first taken refuge in the apartment of former duma deputy Poletaev, but that apartment was well known to the authorities. Olga Allilueva met Lenin at Poletaev's and suggested he move into their spare room. Since they had only recently acquired this apartment, though convenient to the center of the city, the address and their connection to the Bolsheviks were known to very few. Lenin and Zinoviev moved in on July 7 and stayed for two days before taking off for greater safety near the customs border with Finland. Anna Allilueva remembered coming home and worrying when the door was not immediately opened. Her father greeted her strangely, carefully locked the door, and then told her that they had guests. Entering the dining room, she was introduced to Lenin. (Her memoir, written at the height of Stalinism, does not mention Zinoviev, who had been shot in the Great Purges.) She indicated how surprised she was to see him since in town there were rumors that he had fled to Kronstadt. Stalin arrived a few hours later and took tea with Lenin in his room. Before he left, he asked Olga whether she was able to find groceries, given the shortages in Petrograd. "You look, Olga, feed him as you would your own." She understood Stalin's concern, but it went without saying that a guest would be treated as well as possible. When Stalin left, she simply laughed. Lenin also inquired about Stalin's eating. "Take care of him, Olga Evgenevna, he is somewhat gaunt." Somehow the family made out. Stalin occasionally brought what he could find to the apartment, and Olga Allilueva proved to be very inventive with pea soups.[68]

Stalin came to see Lenin almost every day, sometimes with Orjonikidze, Nogin, or Stasova. They discussed whether Lenin should give himself up. Stalin and Orjonikidze were against exposing Lenin to the Provisional Government. "Cadets will kill Lenin," Stalin said, "before they deliver him to prison."[69] It was decided to send him to the resort of Sestroretsk, a short train ride from the city on the Finnish Gulf. Olga bandaged Lenin in an effort to disguise him, but Lenin felt that the bandages drew attention to him. He suggested that they shave off his beard and mustache, and Stalin took on the task of his barber. Wearing Sergei Alliluev's worker's cap and baggy overcoat, Lenin was completely unrecognizable as the European intellectual with the bowler hat who had disembarked from the sealed train three months earlier. He left with Stalin and Alliluev, looking in their eyes like a Finnish peasant. Lenin walked on ahead, alone, with his two comrades keeping watch some distance behind.[70]

While Lenin was at the Alliluevs, Stalin stayed with Molotov and Petr Zalutskii, both of them bachelors, and Ivars Smilga and his wife. The apartment was large and located on the other side of the river from downtown, in the so-called Petersburg Side. Molotov in old age recalled that while they were together Stalin admitted he had been wrong earlier in the revolution. "You were the nearest of all to Lenin in the initial stage, in April." Their new relationship, however, did not prevent

Stalin from stealing Molotov's girlfriend, Marusia.[71] Stalin was hesitant to compromise the Alliluevs and told them, "I very much want to move in with you. But I think that now is not the time. They will begin surveillance on the apartment. Because of me there could be unpleasantness for you." "Don't worry, Iosif, about us," Olga said. "We are used to being followed. I would only be happy to have your presence in the apartment, but if this is dangerous for you, of course it is better to wait." A week later Olga informed him that there was no one observing the apartment and he should move in. "You can rest, have a good sleep, live a more normal life."[72]

That evening, late, he moved in. He seemed a bit preoccupied, Anna remembered. He drank tea with the family and retired to his room. But instead of sleeping he paced back and forth for many hours. In the morning he emerged to find the Alliluevs already at the breakfast table. "Ah," he said, "I slept well as I have not been able for a long time."[73] Before leaving he told Olga that she should not worry if he did not return for a day or two. There was much to do, and he had to be careful about his movements. Indeed his pattern was irregular. Dropping in at any hour, he changed clothes, drank some tea, perhaps napped for half an hour, and left abruptly. His belongings—manuscripts, books, some clothes—were packed in the wicker basket that he had brought from Siberia. He went around in his old threadbare jacket that Olga futilely attempted to repair. She finally demanded that he buy a new suit. "I know, I know," Stalin acknowledged. "But I have no time for this. If you would help." Given the assignment Olga and Aunt Mania made the rounds of the stores until they found a suit to fit Stalin. He was pleased and asked Olga to sew pads into the jacket. Because of his chronically sore throat, he did not wear stiff collars and ties. The women obliged him, sewing two high black velvet collars onto the jacket.[74]

Living in the Alliluev apartment was the closest Stalin had been to a semblance of family life since he left Gori almost a quarter century earlier. Young Fedia was in and out, and as the school term neared, Nadia returned from Moscow. Exceptionally tidy, she took to straightening up the apartment. The noise of furniture being moved woke Stalin. "What's going on here? What is the commotion?" Seeing Nadia in her apron, a brush in her hand, he exclaimed, "Oh, it's you! Well, it is immediately clear that a true housewife has taken things in hand!" "So what! Is that a bad thing?" Nadia said, standing her ground. "Absolutely not! It's very good!" said Stalin. "Bring order, bring it . . . show them all." This was the girl, almost sixteen, that he had known as a child, soon to become his aide and then his second wife, twenty-four years younger than he.[75]

Nadia and her mother sat up at night waiting for Sergei and Stalin to return. With Lenin and Zinoviev in hiding across the Finnish border in Razliv, Kamenev and Trotsky in prison, Stalin was now the highest-ranking member of the most important opposition to the government and the Soviet. Through the summer of 1917, at the moment when Bolsheviks were isolated and persecuted, Stalin was his party's pivotal person. Bolshevik prospects were at their nadir. The Mensheviks and SRs formed a new coalition government with Kerenskii at its head. It quickly adopted measures to establish discipline in the army and greater order in the city. The death penalty was restored at the front, and Kornilov, a general known for his anti-revolutionary views, was named Supreme Commander of the Russian Army. To the Left their predictions of ensuing counterrevolution appeared to be fulfilled. With the party weakened but hardly discouraged, Stalin and those still active mustered what limited resources they had. Yet ominous news from the front—the Germans had broken through Russian defenses and were advancing—and the deteriorating economic conditions closer to home were producing a tide that would soon carry the Bolsheviks to power.

28

THE DARK BEFORE

Nineteen-seventeen was a large milestone on the path of Stalin's rise. Being at the center of revolutionary events, taking part in the deliberations of the Bolshevik Central Committee, acting as one of the party's leading organizers, he greatly matured as a man of politics. It was then, as Trotsky much later observed, that he achieved the status of a recognized member of the Bolshevik general staff and "definitely became Stalin." . . . Moreover, although he won little glory during the year of revolution, he gained much influence in party affairs.

—ROBERT C. TUCKER, *STALIN AS REVOLUTIONARY* (1973)

I didn't consider him a genius, but I think he was a great person. . . . He was close to a genius in tactics; in theory and strategy he was weaker. In our party I consider Lenin alone to be a genius. . . . Stalin had an astounding capacity for work. . . . He had a thorough knowledge of what he needed and stuck to the point. And he considered a question in all its aspects. This was politically important. . . . Of course, Lenin was superior to Stalin. I always thought so. He was superior in the theoretical sense, in his personal qualities. But no one could surpass Stalin as a practical worker [party organizer].

—VIACHESLAV MOLOTOV, *MOLOTOV REMEMBERS* (1993)

Dragged into the July insurrection, vilified by the press, their supporters scattered and confused, the Bolsheviks needed to regroup. Before the top leaders fled or were arrested, Sverdlov set up a modest, secret head-quarters for the Central Committee in an apartment not far from the city center. Around a samovar on the dining table the members drank tea and planned their next moves. On July 6 Zinoviev, Kamenev, and Stalin, along with Podvoiskii of the Military Organization, listened while Lenin laid out his recalibration of what was to be done. He presented a sober analysis of the party's defeat followed by a characteristically radical guide to the way ahead. The workers, he assured his comrades, would soon abandon all illusions about the moderate socialists. Whereas up to July Lenin had been prepared to cede power to soviets led by other socialist parties, he now concluded that the Mensheviks and Socialist Revolutionaries and the Soviet had turned themselves into "the fig leaf of the counterrevolution."[1] This left the Bolsheviks as the only party committed to carrying the revolution forward. In his view the peaceful phase of the revolution had ended with the "July Days." Both legal and illegal means would have to be employed, just as in the years 1912–1914, and for the time being no precipitous or uncoordinated action should be taken. Power would eventually pass to soviets, but at the moment it could not be transferred to these discredited soviets. When the time was ripe, however, an armed uprising by the proletariat would be necessary. "The goal of the armed uprising can only be the transfer of power into the hands of the proletariat supported by the poorest peasantry in order to realize the program of our party."[2]

This abrupt withholding of support for the soviets, the institutions which above all others had signaled to Lenin that Russia had moved beyond the bourgeois revolution, was as much a shock to his comrades as had been the "April Theses" three months earlier. In the next few days Lenin elaborated his view that the "revolutionary proletariat, after the experience of July 1917, independently [*samostoiatel'no*] must take state power into its hands—without this there *cannot be* a victory of the revolution. The only way out is for the proletariat to be in power supported by the poorest peasants or semi-proletariat."[3] Few Bolsheviks rushed to embrace his new strategy. Giving up on the soviets was too great a step to take. The small group that gathered that day went on to agree that the Bolsheviks should continue their legal activities despite the danger. In any case, though Lenin entertained the thought, his comrades were adamant that Lenin and Zinoviev would not give themselves up for arrest.[4]

That same night the Provisional Government ordered the arrests of those who had organized armed resistance to the constituted authorities. These "traitors to the nation and the revolution" included Lenin, Zinoviev, Kamenev, Trotsky, and Lunacharskii. Dozens of arrests of party members and their active supporters followed; certain rebellious military units were disbanded, among them the First Machine Gun Regiment; and for a time public assemblies were banned. The right-wing newspaper *Petrogradskaia gazeta* [Petrograd Newspaper] ran a cartoon of a fat man hanging from the gallows with the caption "Lenin wants to occupy a high post? . . . Well? A position is ready for him!!!"[5] The venerable founder of Russian Marxism, Plekhanov, now a fervent patriot, declared categorically, "It has been definitely established that German agents took part in organizing the July disturbances," which were "an integral part of a plan formulated by the foreign enemy to destroy Russia." Without hesitation he proposed, "The revolution must crush everything in its way immediately, decisively, and mercilessly."[6]

The defeat of the Bolsheviks encouraged the political Right, those who had had influence and power in the old regime and saw a chance to regain some degree of what they had lost. In a majestic ceremony the church buried the seven Cossacks killed during the insurrection. Prime Minister Kerensky spoke of heroes, homeland, the Russian state, and its enemies, anarchy and disorder.[7] The rhetoric of nation and state contrasted with the Bolsheviks' language of class and counterrevolution. Even the music played by one side, the *Marseillaise,* cancelled out the strains of the *Internationale* sung by the other. Rightists linked the Bolsheviks not only to the Germans but to their perpetual enemy, the Jews. "Save Russia, save the motherland!" right-wing deputy Vladimir Purishkevich shouted, as he called for hanging the initiators of the insurrection.[8] Pro-government soldiers grabbed suspected Bolsheviks or anarchists off the street and threatened to kill them (and did in the case of one young Bolshevik). Kamenev, who had turned himself in against Lenin's advice, complained that no accusations had been presented to him a week after his imprisonment.

The repression of the party was haphazard and slipshod, and in time it let up. Kamenev was the only Central Committee member in jail. No matter how confident their opponents had been in the days following the insurrection, the moderate socialists were aware that the Bolsheviks still enjoyed great support among the Petrograd workers and in many military units. Even when the victory of the government appeared to be complete, there were clear signs that it was far more hollow than it seemed. The war remained extraordinarily unpopular. Still, Kerensky's government, pressured by its European allies, was determined to pursue it. Inflation had wiped away any wage gains by workers achieved in the first months of the revolution. People refused to obey the government's order to turn in their weapons, and the vindictive repression of the Bolsheviks offended many soldiers and workers and gave credence to the radicals' branding of the moderates as counter-revolutionaries. The government itself was seriously divided, and it was several weeks before Kerensky finally formed the second coalition government with eight socialist ministers and seven liberals—the first government in Russia with a socialist majority. But to hold together this fragile coalition the ministers were no longer to act as representatives of their parties or (in the case of the socialists) to be answerable to the Soviet.

The abortive insurrection in July baldly exposed the political choices left to the revolution. The Revolutionary Defensists, their influence eroding rapidly, held out for a coalition government with both moderate socialists and Kadets represented—that is, a parliamentary "bourgeois democracy." This solution, however, became less and less tenable every day. Martov's Menshevik-Internationalists favored a government of all the socialist parties, a solution referred to as either homogeneous socialist government (*odnorodnoe sotsialisticheskoe pravitel'stvo*) or homogeneous democratic government (*odnorodnoe demokraticheskoe pravitel'stvo*). This inclusive form of government was not only a possible alternative to a Bolshevik government but was in the minds of many what "Soviet Power" actually meant—a democratic multiparty socialist government. The most likely outcomes, however, were either a dictatorship of the Right, backed by the army and the propertied classes, or a dictatorship of the Left, a Bolshevik government or left coalition disguised as soviet democracy.

Stalin was not enthusiastic about Lenin's new strategy of distancing the party from the Soviet, yet he did not come out openly against it. In Lenin's absence the Central Committee met in a special conference (*soveshchanie*) on July 13–14 with members of the Military Organization, representatives from Moscow, and possibly some delegates from the *Mezhraionka*. Stalin and Sverdlov were the principal leaders at this meeting, which was deeply divided. V. Volodarskii, a leading member of the Petersburg Committee, Viktor Nogin of the Military Organization, and Aleksei Rykov, emerging as a prominent leader, strongly opposed Lenin's new theses, while Sverdlov, Molotov, and Maksimilian Savelev spoke in favor.[9] How Stalin voted is not known, but his subsequent behavior indicates that he neither fully adopted Lenin's new position nor completely shared the point of view of most of his comrades. The final vote was 10 to 5 against Lenin, and the Central Committee's resolution reflected a much milder position on the current situation than Lenin's. The government was characterized as having a dual character, in part petty bourgeois with some misguided worker support and in part tied to the big bourgeoisie, the landowning nobility, and foreign capital. The Mensheviks and SRs were characterized simply as traitors to the revolutionary proletariat and contributing to the counterrevolution. "Only a state authority which will be supported by the proletarian masses and the poorest strata of the peasantry and which will resolutely and firmly implement the program of the workers . . . will be viable." That authority required "the concentration of all power in the hands of the revolutionary proletarian and peasant Soviets."[10] Unspecified was whether these soviets were the current ones or reconstituted ones, but the majority of those at the meeting made it clear that they were not ready to break as decisively with Soviet Power as Lenin proposed. The resolution left open the possibility of future cooperation with the Mensheviks and SRs and did not speak of the end of the peaceful period of the revolution or of preparation for an armed uprising. The only concession to Lenin was that the old slogan, "All Power to the Soviets," was not explicitly proposed in the resolution.[11]

Upset by the moderation of his comrades, Lenin penned a long article, "On Slogans," that opened with a rebuke: "All too often in the past when history has made a sharp turn, even progressive parties have been unable to adapt quickly to new situations and have repeated slogans that were valid before but had now lost all meaning." The slogan for transfer of power to the soviets, he claimed, sounded now like "Don Quixotism or like a sneer."[12]

Unconvinced, the Petrograd Bolsheviks gathered in an emergency conference (actually the continuation of one that had been broken off during the "July Days"). The Central Committee assigned Stalin to present the various reports to conferences and the congress in July and August, as Molotov remembered later, "obviously under Lenin's orders."[13] In the absence of Lenin, Zinoviev, Kamenev, and Trotsky, all in hiding or prison, Stalin played the key role, though not very well. He had swung in a few months from moderate to militant among Bolsheviks, and as a "grey blur" in the eyes of those outside the party, he was not targeted for arrest. Now as representative of the scattered Central Committee, he began his report with a defense of the Bolsheviks' initial hesitation to support the workers' and soldiers' demonstration in early July. With the offensive against the Germans under way, the party had not wanted to be blamed for the expected failure at the front. But once the insurrection began, the Bolsheviks had no "right to wash their hands and stand aside."[14] As a proletarian party their responsibility was to give the movement "a peaceful and organized character, not setting a goal of a revolutionary seizure of power." He likened the party's dilemma to its decisions on Bloody Sunday, 1905, when it had to support the march of the workers to the Winter Palace even though no one "knew where the devil they were going." Even though the Bolsheviks had acted responsibly, the Mensheviks and SRs in the evening of July 4 called them traitors to the revolution. By that act, Stalin asserted, the Soviet leaders "had betrayed the revolution, torn asunder the united revolutionary front, and formed an alliance with the counterrevolution." When the Bolsheviks peacefully gave up their positions at the Kshesinskaia Mansion and the Peter-Paul Fortress, the Central Executive Committee of the Soviet broke its promises and turned on them. Power, said Stalin, was no longer in the hands of the Soviet "but in the hands of a military-Kadet clique that is setting the tone of counterrevolution." "Our task," he said, "is to gather our forces, to strengthen the existing organizations and hold back the masses from premature actions. It would be to the advantage of the counterrevolution to excite us to fight right now, but we must not give in to provocation, we must show the maximum revolutionary restraint. This is the general tactical line of the Central Committee of our party."[15]

Lenin had promoted Stalin's rise and had repeatedly relied on him to come around to his positions. The performances of his protégé here and at the forthcoming party congress were tests of Stalin's leadership qualities.[16] The challenge was great, and he met it with considerable difficulty. Besides the report on the July Days, Stalin also presented the principal report "on the current moment," usually the prerogative of Lenin or a similarly eminent leader. Not as definitive as Lenin on the counterrevolutionary nature of the Soviet leaders—they were helpmates rather than active counterrevolutionaries—Stalin nevertheless repeated his mentor's characterization that the period of the peaceful development of the revolution was over. The workers were moving toward taking power, but the bourgeoisie would not let this happen without a fight, while the petty bourgeoisie, the vast majority in Russia, was wavering, sometimes allying with the Bolsheviks, sometimes with the Kadets.[17] The Soviet had given in to the bourgeoisie, isolated the Bolsheviks, and by doing so had opened the way to counterrevolution. The moderate socialists blamed the Bolsheviks for the soldiers' reluctance to fight, but in fact the blame belonged to the revolution that gave every citizen the right to ask, why this war. A period of sharp conflicts and confrontations had begun, but Bolsheviks must remain steady, well organized, and use legal means. There could be no unity with the Mensheviks and SRs, except with the Left SRs (those around Boris Kamkov) and the Menshevik-Internationalists (around Martov).

Stalin was challenged from the floor. He claimed that the Bolsheviks could have seized power in the July Days, but without the support of the provinces they could not have held it.[18] Right now Bolsheviks would not turn power over to the existing soviets, and if the party proved victorious it would have to create a better kind of soviet. When asked whether the Soviet Executive Committee was to be obeyed, Stalin

equivocated. As members of the Executive Committee, the Bolshevik faction obeyed its decisions, but as members of the party they would act independently.[19] As for the soviets, Bolsheviks were unconditionally for those soviets with a Bolshevik majority but not for those allied to the counterrevolution.[20] Delegates asked Stalin to show them the theses of Lenin, but Stalin had to admit that he did not have them with him.[21] As he remembered, they made the point that the counterrevolution had triumphed and that "All Power to the Soviets" was a quixotic slogan. Power had to be transferred to a class not to a specific institution. Volodarskii insisted that the counterrevolution had not yet won, that one should not judge the masses by the actions of their leaders. While these "caliphs for an hour" like Kerenskii, Tsereteli, [Nikolai] Avksentev, and others have moved to the right, the masses were moving to the left.[22] He chided Stalin for not conveying the sense of the July 13–14 special conference, which had resolved that Bolshevik presence in the soviets hindered the soviets from further collaboration with the bourgeoisie.[23] Therefore there was no need to drop the old slogan. Veinberg and others supported him. To abandon the slogan of "All Power to the Soviets" would be harmful and would leave much of the democratic forces behind, to the advantage of the Mensheviks and SRs.

Strong support for Lenin and Stalin's position came from Molotov, who was consistently on the left of the party. Power, he said, had slipped from the soviets into the hands of the bourgeoisie, and therefore Bolsheviks could not fight to give power to those soviets that had betrayed the proletariat. Abram Slutskii agreed that the new situation required a new slogan, one that called for a dictatorship of the proletariat supported by the poorest strata of the peasantry but not necessarily in the institutional form of the soviets. But, warned Prokhorov, in the present situation a dictatorship of the proletariat could be sustained only by bayonets, not with the backing of the majority of the population.[24]

When given the chance to answer his critics Stalin accused them of imprecision in their understanding of his position. In rapid fire he parried their questions but without shedding much light on the principal differences. His view was that the soviets were not simply reactionary but counterrevolutionary; they had applauded when Tsereteli declared that Lenin was to be arrested. Those comrades who said that the dictatorship of the proletariat was impossible because the proletariat constituted only a minority of the population understood majorities mechanically. "The soviets represent only 20 million elements organized by them but thanks to their organization they are the leaders of the population." "As Marxists we ought to say: the matter is not in institutions but in which class's policy the institution carries out. We are unconditionally for those soviets in which we have a majority. And we will try to create such soviets." He then presented the resolution adopted by the Central Committee in its July 13–14 special conference with representatives of the Moscow and Petersburg organizations.[25] It was discussed in detail the next day, though Stalin did not attend that session. The reigning confusion continued.[26]

On the final day of the conference, July 20, the discussion turned to the election of delegates to the party congress, which was set to convene in five days. Volodarskii and Stalin proposed that the conference choose delegates, even though local committees had not been warned and there was no quorum. Stalin understood that this was a less than democratic method of choosing delegates, but he argued that the party was working in exceptional circumstances and there was too little time and too much work to delay any further. Bolsheviks should operate as they had in 1905. The conference went along with their proposal, though almost half of those present voted against it. Stalin suggested that a commission be set up to write appeals to the workers and soldiers, and he was elected to it. When it was written, the appeal was fiercely worded, starkly contrasting the Bolsheviks who had stood with the workers in July with the Mensheviks and SRs who had gone over to the counterrevolutionary bourgeoisie.[27] Any lingering spirit of unity with former comrades had long before evaporated.

Bolshevism appeared to many in the summer of 1917 to be in disarray and not much of a threat to the Menshevik-SR Soviet. Hardly the monolithic party of the Cold War stereotype, the Bolsheviks, nevertheless, were united around a set of fundamental convictions: there would be no collaboration with the nonsocialist parties; the soviets, wrong-headed as many were at the moment, provided the best chance for democratic government; the proletariat should ally with the peasants rather than the liberal bourgeoisie; and the war was imperialist and had to be brought to an immediate end. These core attitudes were carried over from the years in prerevolutionary opposition into the revolution. For all the rhetoric about a democratic revolution that had animated Social Democrats, including Bolsheviks, in the decades leading up to the fall of tsarism, the Bolshevik leaders, tempered by revolutionary struggles, were by the summer of 1917 prepared to disenfranchise all but the lower classes, push aside the moderates in the soviets, and work to "Bolshevize" whatever institutions they were able.

The pesky divisions in the debates in which Stalin was a key player were largely about short-term tactics rather than basic strategic choices or the party's desired goals. Disputatious but hardly in disarray, the Bolsheviks took advantage of what limited opportunities they had. Legal methods were the means of choice for the time being, but agitation was difficult without newspapers. Both *Pravda* and *Soldatskaia Pravda* had been closed, their presses destroyed. The Bolshevik Military Organization found a press and began publishing a newspaper, *Rabochii i Soldat* (Worker and Soldier), which for the next month was the only Bolshevik journal.

Stalin submitted short articles almost daily, articulating the arguments that Lenin and other Bolsheviks had expressed: the counterrevolution was ephemeral and would soon pass, and the future lay with a new revolution that would realize the people's power.[28] He harped on the servility of the Mensheviks and SRs before the Kadets.[29] The message resonated among soldiers, at least in the more radical units, and the Military Organization, although vilified by some and criticized for its radicalism, steadily, assiduously regained its footing within the garrison. As they retreated, many Bolsheviks blamed the Military Organization for the catastrophe that had befallen the party. But Lenin was not as hard on it as some. "It is necessary to help them," he told Sverdlov, "but there should be no pressure and no reprimands. To the contrary, they should be supported: those who don't take risks never win; without defeats there are no victories."[30]

The top Bolshevik leaders pushed to tighten their hold on the fissiparous party. They were wary of any Bolshevik organization other than the Central Committee having an independent newspaper. Stalin worked closely with several people in the Military Organization's leadership, and when the Central Committee grew suspicious once again of the organization's independence, he was sent to deal with the problem. The Central Committee decided it would take over *Rabochii i Soldat*, since it had no newspaper of its own, and in rather high-handed manner on August 4 it resolved that neither the Military Organization nor the Petersburg Committee was to be permitted to publish its own journals. The Central Committee appointed Stalin, Grigorii Sokolnikov, and Vladimir Miliutin to the editorial board, to be joined later by Podvoiskii from the Military Organization and Volodarskii from the Petersburg Committee.[31] But the arrangement did not work. Neither the Military Organization nor the Central Committee found working on a single newspaper easy. With different constituencies and different functions, the two groups had their own distinct interests. After the Provisional Government closed down *Rabochii i Soldat*, two separate newspapers appeared on August 13—*Proletarii* from the Central Committee and *Soldat* from the Military Organization. Stalin informed Podvoiskii that the Central Committee would control *Soldat* as well as its own newspaper. The Military Organization protested Stalin and Smilga's brusque intervention, bridling at the "unprincipled way, violating the most elementary principles of party democracy," in which Stalin and Smilga had acted. Stalin had promised that the Central Committee would support *Soldat*, but at the August 13 meeting of the Military Organization and the Central Committee he sharply told the representatives of the Military Organization that "once a decision of the Central Committee is made, it must be carried out without any discussion." The Military Organization protested:

> Unfortunately the Military Organization must state that such *impermissible* measures and steps are not accidental, but *from the moment* of the change in the former makeup of the Central Committee have become the real system of persecution and repression of an

extraordinarily strange character in relation to the whole larger organization. The Central Bureau of the Military Organizations demands from the Central Committee the *immediate normalization of the question of the forms* of mutual relations of these two organizations.[32]

Although the Central Committee had slapped down the Military Organization, informing its leaders that they could not act as an independent political center, it permitted *Soldat* to continue. However, a Central Committee member would sit on its editorial board with the right of veto. Sverdlov and Dzierżyński, but not Stalin, were chosen as liaisons with the Military Organization.[33] The incident revealed a style of leadership that Stalin, when unconstrained by more powerful figures, would deploy in the future. Operational habits from the days of the underground carried over into the open politics of the revolutionary year. Within the party central control from above overrode independence and initiative from below; expediency trumped consultation.

THE (BOLSHEVIKS') SIXTH CONGRESS

What would be known as the Sixth Congress of the RSDRP (Bolsheviks) opened on July 26 (August 8). Even the cardinal number indicating how many congresses had been held reflected the sharp break with their former, now estranged, Menshevik comrades. By enumerating the congress as "Sixth," the Bolsheviks included the "Third," which they had held without the Mensheviks in 1905. Stalin presented the first major report, on the activity of the Central Committee in the last two and a half months, and defended the leadership's choices supporting the "spontaneous" actions of workers and soldiers on July 3rd to give the movement a degree of organization. The Bolsheviks, he stated, had not tried to seize power or to overthrow the soviets; they simply wanted the soviets, in which they were a minority, to take power, which they refused to do.

What kind of mass party would we be if we pass by the mass movement! Our party always moved with the masses. By blaming us for involving ourselves in the movement, Tsereteli and the others have signed their own death sentence. They speak of spilling blood, but the spilling of blood would have been worse if [our] party had not become involved in the event. We played the role of a regulator. . . . Our party was the only party who stayed with the masses in their struggle with counterrevolution, and we did this in order to emerge with honor from the situation being created.[34]

In hindsight the Bolsheviks presented themselves as firemen instead of incendiaries.

The Sixth Congress was a nationwide gathering of a young party emerging into the open arena of politics. Of its 264 delegates just over a third were Russian, a tenth Jewish. Most were quite young, in their twenties or thirties, with a median age of twenty-nine. Most had entered the party before 1914, the largest number in the revolutionary years of 1905–1907. Few had worked abroad; many had served time in prison or exile. In the debate that followed Stalin's report, several delegates criticized the Central Committee for acting as the local committee of the Petrograd Bolsheviks rather than the national center for the whole party. Not enough had been done to explain to the provinces why the June 10 demonstration had been called off and the July 3–4 demonstration had been supported. Stalin acknowledged the criticism but explained that Petrograd was the battering ram of the revolution. The provinces reacted to what happened in Petrograd. The congress then turned to the question of whether Lenin and Zinoviev should surrender to the authorities. Volodarskii thought that a trial would demonstrate their innocence and indict instead the Soviet leaders. Another delegate proposed turning the trial of Lenin into the Russian version of the infamous Dreyfus Affair, in which an innocent Jewish captain in the French army had been wrongly accused of spying for Germany. But the delegates followed Bukharin and unanimously rejected the idea of giving up their leaders. The congress listened with enthusiasm to the speeches of Konstantin Iurenev from the *Mezhraionka* and Iurii Larin from the Menshevik-Internationalists. To stormy applause Larin defended the slogan "All Power to the Soviets," which Lenin was determined to drop.

Rather than destroy the soviets and create new institutions, Larin insisted that the internationalists must win over the existing soviets. Once again Lenin's abrupt course adjustment met resistance.

A rising star among Bolsheviks, the young Nikolai Bukharin had already gained a reputation as a theorist on imperialism. He delivered the first of two reports on the current moment, explaining in classic Marxist terms why the war, now a world war, was continuing. Not only were the ruling classes of the capitalist countries set on expanding their carnage across the globe but they also were using this mass slaughter to put down the revolutionary movement in their own countries.[35] After a lively debate and a ten-minute break, the floor was given to Stalin to analyze the forces at play in the revolution. Such "current moment" reports were normally assigned to the most revered leaders of the party. In the absence of Lenin, Trotsky, Kamenev, Zinoviev, and others, Stalin stepped into an unusual spotlight. In his simplified sociology he outlined the principal actors in the overthrow of tsarism—the proletariat, the peasantry, the liberal bourgeoisie, and Allied capital—but noted that from the beginning these temporarily united forces had different aims and ambitions. The landlords and capitalists, the liberal bourgeoisie and Allied capital, simply wanted a small revolution to wage a big war. Three factors contributed to the rise of the counterrevolution: the revolution went too far for the bourgeoisie; the failures at the front discredited the revolution in the eyes of the broad petty bourgeois masses (the peasantry); and Allied capital supported the coalition government. The Mensheviks and SRs were responsible for the counterrevolution since they had refused to have the Soviet take power when it had been given to them. "Our misfortune is that Russia is a petty-bourgeois country, which follows the SRs and Mensheviks, who move in tandem with the Kadets; and until that moment when the peasantry is disenchanted with the idea of the collaboration of the top [of society] with the bottom, we will suffer and the revolution will come to nothing."[36] But, he optimistically concluded, the war and the consequent economic ruin would continue to undermine the government, which could not survive without the backing of the Soviet. He reiterated his accusation that by not taking power the Soviet leaders had allowed the counterrevolution to organize and ended the possibility of a peaceful transfer of power. His position on the nature of the revolution had shifted definitively toward Lenin's. He took on those "comrades who said that capitalism is poorly developed in our country and it is utopian to pose the question of a socialist revolution. They might have been right if it had not been for the war, if there had been no economic devastation."[37] In his proposed resolution he implied that a catastrophic situation might arise in which the proletariat, led by the Petrograd workers, might have to seize power, even without the mass of the population, having concluded that such a second revolution was necessary.[38]

The first to rise after Stalin's report was a delegate from Moscow, long-time party member Nikolai Angarskii. He sharply disagreed with Stalin's formulations, labeling them un-Marxist. The only moving forces of the revolution of 1917, as in 1905, were the proletariat and the peasantry. He accused Stalin of being too cautious, of delaying the push to power, and promoting a "tactic of despair." More pessimistically, Evgenii Preobrazhenskii expressed dissatisfaction with Stalin's proposed resolution, fearing that there would not be another revolutionary upturn. There could be an alliance of the counterrevolutionary bourgeoisie, capitalists, landlords, and peasants. He did not think that the slogan "All Power to the Soviets" should be abandoned. Iurenev agreed. "There is no way out except the transfer of power to the soviets."[39]

Central Committee member Miliutin defended Lenin and Stalin's call for a new slogan. It made no sense at present, he said, to pass power to the soviets. A government can be formed that is based on the proletariat and the poorest stratum of the peasantry.[40] And so the debate went, swirling around the question of which way the "petty bourgeoisie" would shift. Would peasants support the liberals and moderate socialists or swing to the left and back the Bolsheviks? Volodarskii pleaded that the congress not throw the baby out with the bathwater. They should not condemn the soviets as a form because they do not like the current content. For a revolution that is something greater than a bourgeois revolution but not yet a socialist revolution, he suggested a modified slogan (though hardly one that tripped off the tongue or rang in the ears): "All Power to the Proletariat, Supported by the Poorest Peasantry and the Revolutionary Democracy Organized in the Soviets of Workers', Soldiers', and Peasants' Deputies."[41]

When the debate resumed the next day, July 31, several comrades suggested that Stalin be given the floor to clarify certain formulations in his resolution. What would replace the soviets? What would be the Bolsheviks' relationship in practice with the existing soviets, and in particular with those in which the party held a majority? What was meant by "the poorest peasantry" and how were they to be organized?[42] Stalin replied that he did not speak against soviets as forms of worker organization but opposed giving power to soviets that were dominated by anti-revolutionary parties. Soviets were only one type of revolutionary organization, he said, "a purely Russian one," but workers may find others. No one was for overthrowing the soviets. As for defining the poorest peasants, he claimed that the villages were already dividing into upper and lower elements. Those who needed land in order to live, those with little land and one or no horses were the ones that had to be organized and brought over to the side of the proletariat. And he repeated his formula from the earlier Petrograd conference. "In general, the soviets are the most appropriate form of organization of the masses, but we ought to speak not of *institutions* but point out the *class content*; we ought to strive to have the masses also differentiate *form* from *content*."[43] His explanations were met with applause. Stalin had held his own before his critics, though he had hardly silenced them.

The Bolsheviks were seriously divided in their estimation of where the revolution was headed. Alesha Japaridze from Baku chastised Stalin for conflating provincial soviets with the moderate Central Executive Committee in Petrograd. Local soviets were being radicalized, he said. In Baku, for example, Bolsheviks were a tiny minority of the deputies in the soviet, yet their resolutions regularly were adopted.[44] Sokolnikov disagreed with Stalin that Bolsheviks had been ready to form a united revolutionary front stretching from the SRs to the Bolsheviks, but then agreed with Stalin that the soviets were no longer "organs of an uprising," and a cautious period of winning over the peasants had begun. When he ended with a call for peasants to support the proletarian avantgarde, he was met with loud applause. The speakers swung back and forth: Viktor Nogin for Soviet Power; Petr Zalutskii against the old slogan; Ivar Smiga calling for boldness rather than caution; Andrei Bubnov sneering at the soviets as rotten.[45] Eight speakers wanted to retain the familiar slogan; six opposed it. Finally, a committee was set up to work out a final resolution based on Stalin's draft. Stalin joined the committee and presented its resolution to the Congress.[46] As the delegates reviewed each point of the resolution, Stalin confidently defended it. When Preobrazhenskii suggested a modification that emphasized Russia's dependence on the predicted European revolution, Stalin objected, anticipating one of his most important theoretical shifts half a decade later. The Russian Revolution, he confidently asserted, could lead Europe and the world to socialism:

> The possibility is not excluded that Russia will be the country that blazes the trail to socialism. So far no country has enjoyed such freedom as exists in Russia; none has tried to realize workers' control over production. Besides, the base of our revolution is broader than in Western Europe, where the proletariat is completely alone in its confrontation with the bourgeoisie. Here the workers have the support of the poorest strata of the peasantry. Finally, in Germany the machinery of state power is functioning incomparably better than the imperfect machinery of our bourgeoisie, which is itself a payer of tribute to European capital. It is necessary to give up the outworn idea that Europe alone can show us the way. There is a dogmatic Marxism and a creative Marxism. I stand on the ground of the latter.[47]

In this remarkable statement Stalin foreshadowed his future dispute with Preobrazhenskii, Trotsky, and the Communist Left over whether the European revolution was necessary for the victory of socialism in Russia or whether Russia was able to build "socialism in one country." The founders of Marxism, Marx and Engels, had explicitly excluded the possibility of socialism in a single country, but their successor, Karl Kautsky, had allowed that several socialist states might coexist in a capitalist world, their relatively autarkic economy surviving in a national setting. Lenin had held that a socialist victory was unlikely in all countries at once, and, therefore, it might be possible in some or even one country. Then the proletariat of that country would stand opposed to the whole of the capitalist world. However, in Lenin's view the possibility of a final victory of socialism in a backward, peasant country like Russia was precluded. There socialism would collapse unless it were aided by socialist victories in more developed states. In line with Lenin, Stalin proposed that the socialists could take power in Russia more easily than in Europe and begin the transition to socialism.[48] His passionate words promoting a novel historical role for Russia convinced the Congress, and ultimately his resolution was approved unanimously, with four abstentions.[49]

Divided though they were, the Bolsheviks managed to agree on a new slogan: "Complete Liquidation of the Dictatorship of the Imperialist Bourgeoisie." The resolution looked as if it had been cobbled together from conflicting points of view. From the Muscovites the resolution called for protecting mass organizations, especially the soviets, from counterrevolutionary assaults.[50] Blame for the country's turn to the right was laid on the village and city petty bourgeoisie and the "conciliationist" SR and Menshevik parties that they followed and that had eased the victory of the counterrevolution. The imperative importance of the revolution abroad was acknowledged. "To take power is easy. It is necessary to hold it, to realize socialist reforms. For this the support of the revolutionary workers in the West is essential. . . . Without such ties and support the united imperialists of Russia and the West will easily smother the Russian Revolution."[51]

The Congress ended with the election of the Central Committee. Although he was reelected, Stalin was this time not among the highest vote-getters. Lenin received 133 out of 134 votes, Zinoviev 132, Kamenev and the newly inducted party member, still in jail, Trotsky, 131 each.[52] Both Kamenev, who was particularly critical of Lenin in 1917, and Trotsky, who had a long record of disagreements with the Bolshevik leader, received high numbers of votes, almost matching one Leninist loyalist, Zinoviev, and besting another, Stalin.

Bolsheviks, like other Social Democrats, were an argumentative lot. They were Protestants without an infallible pope. Many were well-read in the classics of Marxism and kept abreast of the controversies at party congresses and conferences and in the party press. For all their protestations against intellectuals they were dedicated to an intellectual endeavor—using a body of political theory and historical interpretation to analyze the politics of the moment and predict possible outcomes. Marxism was their sociology. Strategy followed from their reading of the class configuration in Russia and in Europe. The Bolsheviks were a party that would prove to be ready to rule and would display remarkable skills in running a fragmented country. But, for all of their vaunted organizational capacities, their party was very hard to govern. Unruly and fractured, Bolsheviks were often difficult to congeal into a coherent political instrument. A constant cry for discipline accompanied them along the road to power and the subsequent years in power.

In the summer of 1917 Stalin was the de facto leader of the Bolsheviks in Petrograd, a placeholder while Lenin, Zinoviev, Kamenev, and Trotsky were either in hiding or jail. At the August 4 meeting of the newly elected Central Committee, he received the most votes for membership on the editorial board of the party newspaper. Trotsky was rejected by a single vote.[53] The next day Stalin was elected to the *uzkii sostav* (small inner group) of eleven, which would operate between sessions of the Central Committee. The smaller group met on the 6th and chose Stalin as one of three members to serve on a commission dealing with the elections to the Constituent Assembly. He was also assigned the task of negotiating with the rightist SR Abram Gots on the Central Executive Committee of Soviets about the case of Kamenev, who was suspected of having been a police spy under the tsars. The charge was absurd, but it was not until the end of August that he was cleared. Again and again Stalin was given not only technical tasks to accomplish but important political assignments. Having won a reputation for competence in practical matters, he was also charged with important propaganda and agitational work. Along with Sokolnikov and Moisei Uritskii, he drew up the guidelines for Bolshevik speakers (*agitatory*) to use in the public campaign against the Stockholm peace conference.[54] He was placed on the editorial boards of *Vpered* (Forward), formally the newspaper of the *Mezhraiontsy* and briefly of the Bolshevik Central

Committee, and *Prosveshchenie* (Enlightenment), the party's theoretical journal. He reworked the party's resolution on the Moscow State Conference, condemning the Soviet leaders' participation.[55]

For Stalin, like other Bolsheviks, the major brake on the further radicalization of the revolution was the mood and motion of the peasants. Since capitalism was not highly developed in the Russian countryside, he noted that the class differentiation between richer and poorer peasants had not become acute. Middle and rich peasants dominated the rural soviets, and this meant that the villages contributed to the "conciliationist" policy of the soviets and the coalition government.[56] The Bolsheviks needed to free the poorest peasants form the richer ones and bring them over to the "fraternal family" of urban workers. This was not an easy task, as Bolsheviks would repeatedly discover once they were in power.

In rural Russia the Marxist sociology that aided the Bolsheviks so well in Moscow, Petrograd, and Baku failed them. Notions of class polarization could not be exported so simply into the countryside. Russian villagers had their own internal interests and their own parochial conflicts. Their squabbles were about family, relationships between men and women, elders and the young. Attempts to sow class conflict within the villages proved a nearly impossible task. The villages were usually remarkably united against outsiders, especially tax collectors, recruiters, and other officials. Peasant anger primarily targeted the landlords, not other peasants. Yet it was precisely the peasants, at least the poorest strata, whom the Bolsheviks, in stark contrast to the Mensheviks, conceived of as the essential ally of the workers. While the villages remained a foreign land for the Bolsheviks, they attracted significant support among peasants with guns—that is, the soldiers, who were weary of war and wanted to go home. Stalin was prepared to ally with those peasants, soldiers and sailors, whose roots went back to the village, but not with "professors and students."[57] For Lenin and Stalin politics was war, and revolutions, like war, were ultimately decided by men with guns in the right place at the right time.

29

ON THE EVE

[A]lthough Stalin lied whenever it was useful to do so, . . . the fundamental political and ideological concepts with which he operated nevertheless expressed his understanding of reality.

As far as can be ascertained, Stalin was a true believer. . . .

Generally speaking, the greatest crimes in history have been committed by the sincere—those who believe in their hearts that they are justified in committing their acts.

—ERIK VAN REE, *THE POLITICAL THOUGHT OF JOSEPH STALIN* (2002)

In Petrograd and a few other large cities, the most active forces of the revolution were moving inexorably toward a more radical vision—a social, if not yet socialist, revolution that would depose people of property, turn factories over to the control of the workers and land over to the peasants. All parties agitated among ordinary people to turn them toward their perspective, but, as the Menshevik Sukhanov noted, Bolsheviks were especially committed to what American political campaigners a century later would call their "ground game."

> Yes, the Bolsheviks were working stubbornly and without let-up. They were among the masses, at the factory-benches, every day without a pause. Tens of speakers, big and little, were speaking in Petersburg, at the factories and in the barracks, every blessed day. For the masses they had become their own people, because they were always there, taking the lead in details as well as in the most important affairs of the factory or barracks. They had become the sole hope, if only because since they were one with the masses they were lavish with

promises and sweet but simple fairy tales. The mass lived and breathed together with the Bolsheviks. It was in the hands of the party of Lenin and Trotsky.[1]

Consistent with their own claims about themselves, Bolsheviks were accepted by increasing numbers of workers and soldiers to be the most revolutionary of the major Russian political parties. The Menshevik vision, which the SRs basically adopted, was limited to a democratic revolution inclusive of all classes and determined to develop the country in alliance with the bourgeoisie. It corresponded well with the actual economic potential and social evolution of Russia, still a predominantly peasant country, but in the revolutionary capital such a restrained politics had lost its appeal.

Late in July Stalin reviewed and contrasted the Bolsheviks' Petrograd conference with the Mensheviks' and predicted the revival of his party's fortunes. "They say that Bolshevism has been liquidated and buried. Too early did the gravediggers bury us. We are alive, and the bourgeoisie more than once will become agitated and will tremble from the sound of our voice."[2] The strained optimism of the Bolsheviks was vindicated within weeks of their sixth congress. Even with their newspapers shut down and leaders in hiding or prison, they managed to gain support, in part because of the worsening conditions of daily life and in part from the popular revulsion against the government's (and Soviet's) repression of the Bolsheviks. On August 7 the workers section of the Soviet, meeting for the first time since the July Days, voted overwhelmingly for a Bolshevik resolution condemning the persecution of the radical left as "a blow to the revolutionary cause."[3] Left SRs voted with the Bolsheviks, their estrangement from their more moderate comrades growing day by day. When two weeks later elections were held for the Petrograd City Duma—elections, it should be remembered, that represented all classes in the city unlike elections to the soviets—the Bolsheviks surprised themselves by polling the second highest number of votes (183,624), behind the leader, the SRs (205,659), and well ahead of the Kadets (114,483). The Menshevik vote had evaporated to 23,552. The elections exposed the chasm between the socialists, who took seventy-eight percent of the vote, and the liberals with just below twenty-one percent. One-third of the voters cast ballots for the Bolsheviks, who could claim the largest vote gains of any party since the May elections.[4] The elections confirmed one of the most robust findings of political science: when the economy is bad, voters turn away from those in power. With the Left advancing through democratic elections, the Right, along with many liberals, looked for a more authoritarian answer to what they understood to be a grave danger to the nation.

Fearful about the future, liberals moved closer to the military and more conservative forces. In late July at their ninth congress the Kadets applauded their leader Miliukov's pledge to fight the Left to save the motherland. The liberals were ready to join with army officers, army chief-of-staff General Kornilov, gentry landowners, industrialists, the Orthodox Church, the Don Cossacks, and Russian nationalists to restore order and struggle against socialism.[5] In early August at a trade and industrial conference in Moscow, the financier Pavel Riabushinskii calumniated the socialists in the government as "a pack of charlatans" and threw back at the Marxists their own conceptualization of the present revolution. "We ought to say . . . that the present revolution is a bourgeois revolution, that the bourgeois order which exists at the present time is inevitable, and since it is inevitable, one must draw the completely logical conclusion and insist that those who rule the state think in a bourgeois manner and act in a bourgeois manner."[6]

The leader of the Union of Landlords, N. N. Lvov, joined the chorus and announced that he was "organizing groups of industrialists, bankers, Kadets, and others" in order to "boldly defend our interests, because by defending property, we defend statehood."[7] The former minister of war and leader of the conservative Octobrist Party, Aleksandr Guchkov, collected money to be given to General Kornilov "for the purpose of organizing an armed struggle against the soviets."[8] The counterrevolution was not a figment of the Bolshevik imagination but real people consolidating forces and funds to carry out their program. This shift to the right of the principal liberal parties and the propertied classes left the Mensheviks and SRs, along with some left liberals, as the isolated defenders of the government. When Riabushinskii accused the Soviet leaders of fostering disorder, Stalin turned his words against him in an article, "What Do the Capitalists Want?" Defending the soviets from the worst charge of treason, he claimed that it was not the Soviet leaders but the capitalists who were responsible for the war, the arrests of radicals, and the introduction of capital punishment.[9]

Much of the revolution took place in meetings of one sort or another—committees, soviets, conferences, and congresses—punctuated by demonstrations and the occasional armed clashes. The government and the Central Executive Committee of the Soviets desperately sought a broader base of support to legitimize their power and institutionalize their authority. On August 12 a State Conference was convened in Moscow, bringing Kadets together with Mensheviks, SRs, and an array of political and public figures. The moderate socialists wanted to demonstrate their willingness to work with the propertied classes, and Chkheidze, in the name of the Central Executive Committee of the Soviets, promised that his associates would consider "the interest of the whole country, of the revolution, above the interests of classes or specific groups of the population."[10] But the Right and liberals like Miliukov rebuffed the socialists' overtures. They now saw Russia's salvation in a strong government ready to resist popular demands. The conference was opened and closed by the prime minister, but Kerenskii's speeches dragged on interminably and undermined rather than reinforced his authority.

While outside the hall Moscow workers, who in general were less radical than workers in Saint Petersburg, held a nearly unanimous general strike, inside the hall the emerging hero of the Right was General Kornilov, who had already presented a program of greater discipline, the curtailing of the power of committees, and the extension of the death penalty from the front to the rest of the country. As historian William G. Rosenberg writes, "After months and even years of stressing the need for Russian national unity, of great fear of mass unrest and a deep concern for civil law and order, Miliukov and his supporters among the Petrograd Kadets were girding for civil war."[11] When Stalin editorialized about the State Conference, he characterized it as the place where the counterrevolution was being hatched. He noted that Miliukov was wildly applauded when he said that it was necessary to annihilate Bolshevism, only to be answered timidly by Tsereteli that the "revolution (read: counterrevolution!) is not yet experienced in the struggle against the danger from the left."[12]

KORNILOVSHCHINA

Each month of 1917 had its own crisis. The revolution that brought down tsarism in February–March was followed by the "April Crisis" over the issue of the war; the fall of the first Provisional Government and the formation of the Coalition Government in May; the aborted and sanctioned June demonstrations; and the "July Days" when the Soviet refused to yield to the demands of radical workers, soldiers, and sailors to take power. August began peacefully enough. The shifting balance of power between the government, backed by the Soviet, and the radicals was tectonic, one side moving away from the other until a new crisis erupted—all against the background of the ongoing war. The Germans were advancing and forced the evacuation of Riga, just three hundred miles from the capital. The mood among hungry and frustrated workers and soldiers grew uglier. When the Kadet Andrei Shingarev tried to address a mass meeting and mentioned the fatherland, an angry worker shouted, "A worker has no fatherland—he has a fist!" Such words, said Shingarev, would lead to people chopping each other's heads off, as in the French Revolution. A sailor yelled out, "And your head should be chopped off too."[13] Just five months later, while lying in hospital, Shingarev was murdered by enraged Baltic sailors.

What Bolsheviks cheered as the "deepening of the revolution"—more strikes, protests, and peasant seizures of land—liberals and moderate socialists decried as anarchy and chaos. The principal generator of radicalism, most analysts concluded, was the war—a war that Russia was losing and was daily becoming more unpopular. The war effort could not be sustained, and the burden of fighting was undermining the economy. Inflation and the lack of supplies in the cities turned the anger of ordinary people against those in power. Futilely searching for a peaceful end to the war, the moderate socialists centered their hopes on a peace conference in Stockholm. The Bolshevik party decided against joining the "defensists" and "social patriots" in the Swedish capital. Once again taking an independent position, Kamenev came out on August 6 for participation in the Stockholm Conference. It was his personal opinion, Kamenev declared, that the Bolsheviks should reconsider their position. Lenin was incensed and wrote that he considered Kamenev's behavior "the height of stupidity, if not baseness."[14] Kamenev had no right, Lenin wrote, to speak against a decision of the party. "To go to a conference with social-imperialists, with ministers, with accomplices of butchery in Russia is shameful and treacherous."[15]

Commissioned by the Central Committee to lay out the party's position on the Stockholm Conference and the war, Stalin derided the efforts of European and Russian moderate socialists to try to negotiate a peace in Stockholm.[16] The Bolshevik position was that only Soviet Power could bring an end to the war. Now more journalist than organizer or activist, Stalin gave vent in a series of articles to his concern that the Bolsheviks were being blamed for the catastrophic defeats at the front. But, he noted, even conservative newspapers admitted that the army had been inadequately prepared for the Kerenskii Offensive. If investigations into the cause of the defeats are held, he wrote, then representatives of the soldiers should participate. Soldiers should also be given supervision over their commanders, and those officers under suspicion should be suspended.[17] He went on to accuse the moderate socialists of fraternizing with the very generals who in their hatred of the revolution blame the defeats on their soldiers though they themselves are responsible for the military catastrophe.[18] The surrender of Tarnopol (Ternopil), Chernivitsi, and Riga, he suggested, was part of a plan to crush the revolution.[19] The conspiracy, he believed, was bigger than the Russian army and the bourgeoisie. It included "the sharks of West European imperialism," who were prepared to use the defeats to bring about "the triumph of an imperialist dictatorship."[20] Stalin, who assiduously read and reported on the newspapers of the anti-Bolsheviks, seized on a provocative statement by Riabushinskii. The outspoken leader of the industrialists had coldly predicted, "It is necessary that the long bony hand of hunger and national impoverishment seize by the throat those false friends of the people, the members of the various committees and soviets, in order that they come to their senses." The counterrevolution, Stalin pointed out, regards the growing crisis as an opportunity not to be missed.[21]

Stalin's suspicions about conspiracies, as exaggerated and imaginative as they were in part, were hardly unfounded. The supreme commander of the army, General Kornilov, who feared that a Bolshevik uprising was imminent, told a subordinate that it was "high time to hang the German agents and spies headed by Lenin" and to "disperse the Soviet of Workers and Soldiers in such a way that it would not reassemble anywhere."[22] High government officers negotiated with General Kornilov on how to implement his program of greater discipline and order. Kerenskii himself wavered on the question of a dictatorship and gave confusing signals that were conveyed by self-appointed intermediaries to Kornilov, who finally ordered troops to move toward Petrograd. Kerenskii panicked, believing that Kornilov intended to establish his own military dictatorship. He convinced the cabinet to grant him emergency powers, and he immediately fired Kornilov. The ambitious general, who was said by a fellow officer to have the heart of a lion and the brain of a sheep, claimed that he had had Kerenskii's agreement to march on the capital and refused to resign his post. By this act the army commander was in mutiny, and Kerenskii declared him a traitor. The stock market rose rapidly in anticipation of Kornilov's victory.

The mild Sunday of August 27, the day Kornilov announced his intention "to come to the aid of the dying motherland," also marked the six-month anniversary of the February Revolution.[23] That evening the Central Executive Committee of Soviets, still dominated by the Mensheviks and SRs, met to support Kerenskii. The Bolsheviks remained highly suspicious of the prime minister, and when he suggested forming a six-man Directory to act as the government, Lunacharskii in the name of the Bolsheviks called for the transfer of all power to the soviets.[24] The sense that they faced an immediate threat to the revolution convinced the deputies to give their support to Kerenskii and to form a Committee for Struggle against Counterrevolution. Despite Lenin's refusal to collaborate with the Mensheviks and SRs, Bolsheviks in the Soviet agreed to fight alongside them against Kornilov's forces.

Since the Bolsheviks were the party most closely linked to organized workers and radical soldiers, their participation in the resistance to Kornilov was essential. As Sukhanov remembered, "The Military Revolutionary Committee, in organizing the defence, had to set in motion the masses of workers and soldiers, and these masses, in so far as they were organized, were organized by the Bolsheviks and followed them. At that time theirs was the only organization that was large, welded together by elementary discipline, and united with the democratic rank-and-file of the capital." The Military Revolutionary Committee was impotent without them. "It could only have passed the time with makeshift proclamations and flabby speeches by orators who had long since lost all authority."[25]

The Bolsheviks went into action, along with activists from other parties, and took up posts around the city. The workers were armed and formed into detachments. Railroad workers blocked the path to Petrograd and convinced the soldiers to lay down their arms. Kornilov was arrested, and the threat to the government—and the revolution—quickly dissipated. But this crisis—the *Kornilovshchina*—a confused attempt to stop the shift to the left, only accelerated the final collapse of the Coalition Government.

Stalin's editorial in *Rabochii* the day after Kornilov's defeat repeated his argument about the long-standing plot of the counterrevolutionaries to smother the revolution. The Kadets, he contended, were deeply implicated in the conspiracy. They had left the government just before Kornilov acted. "It could not be an accident that in July, as in August, the Kadets happened to be in the same camp with the traitors at the front and the most evil counterrevolutionaries in the rear against the Russian people." "The conspiracy is continuing," he wrote. Plans were afoot to convene yet another conference, this one organized by the so-called revolutionary democracy, to bring together "all the vital forces of the country." But the workers, Stalin asserted confidently, prefer to fight their enemies rather than to meet with them.[26]

In late September–early October Stalin published a major multipart article, "The Conspiracy against the Revolution," which appeared serially in *Rabochii put'* (Workers' Way).[27] Using the documents from the commission investigating the *Kornilovshchina*, he indicted Kerenskii, the Kadets, and others as co-conspirators. He agreed, with appropriate irony and a nice rhyme, that the conspiracy (*zagovor*) was in actuality carried out in agreement (*dogovor*) with Kerenskii. "The government of Kerenskii not only knew about this whole hellish plan but itself took part in working it out, and together with Kornilov intended to realize it."[28] This was not a mutiny against the Provisional Government, not simply an "adventure" of an arrogant general, but a well-formed conspiracy against the revolution. The Bolsheviks, he wrote over and over again, had been right all along about the connections. Stalin's disposition to see intrigues, plots and malevolent schemes as the underlying cause of events meshed neatly with the messy events, misguided intentions, and clumsy, even farcical, missteps of actors with competing ambitions.

In the aftermath of the *Kornilovshchina* large numbers of workers and soldiers, even those who had doubted the Bolsheviks after the July Days, became convinced that they could no longer trust the government or the propertied classes. Soldiers wanted an immediate end to the war and threatened to desert if peace were not achieved. Essentially the soldiers themselves, by fraternizing with the enemy, refusing to obey the orders of their commanders, and deserting were declaring an end to the war on the Eastern Front. Convinced that Kerenskii and the Provisional Government had colluded with Kornilov, they turned away in greater numbers from their former SR spokesmen toward the Bolsheviks. Early in the morning of September 1, the Petrograd Soviet adopted a resolution presented by Kamenev to form a revolutionary government that would establish a democratic republic. This was the first time the full Soviet had accepted a Bolshevik resolution—and significantly one that called for a government that excluded all representatives of the middle and upper classes and would be made up exclusively of "representatives of the revolutionary proletariat and peasantry."[29] The next day, however, Kerenskii announced the formation of a five-man Directory, and the Executive Committee of the Soviets, elected at the First Congress of Soviets and far more moderate than the Petrograd Soviet, agreed to convene a Democratic State Conference, rather than wait for the next Congress of Soviets, to decide what kind of government would govern Russia. One last futile effort was to be made to preserve the "bourgeois revolution."

MOMENTARY COMPROMISE

From afar Lenin feared that some Bolsheviks, anxious about the danger from the Right, might go too far in supporting the Central Executive Committee of Soviets and the Kerenskii government. In a letter to the Central Committee, written on August 30, he evaluated the situation with his characteristic sharpness.[30] "The uprising of Kornilov was extremely unexpected (at such a time and in such a form unexpected) and is without doubt a huge turning point. Like any huge turning point it demands a new look and a change in tactics. And, as with any reevaluation, it is necessary to be extra careful in order not to be unprincipled." He worried that some comrades were prepared to form a bloc with the SRs to support the war against the Germans. "We will become defensists *only after* the transfer of power to the proletariat, *after* the proposal of peace, *after* the destruction of the secret treaties and the ties to the banks, *only after*. Not the taking of Riga *nor the taking* of Piter makes us defensists." He finished the letter with praise for the editorials in *Rabochii*, many of which had been written by Stalin.

As a member of the editorial boards of the various Bolshevik newspapers that succeeded one another, Stalin wrote almost daily about the threat from both the government and the "conciliationist" Mensheviks and SRs. He condemned the Directory as a "screen hiding the alliance with the Kadets; the dictatorship of Kerenskii as a mask shielding itself from the indignation of the people."[31] He rejected the idea that the government was a non-Kadet government, even though no members sat as official party representatives in the cabinet. The policies of Kerenskii and the moderate socialists, though ostensibly socialist in nature, did not represent a truly radical program of land to the peasants, workers' control, and an end to the war.[32]

In Lenin's words the surge throughout the country in support for the Bolsheviks among politically active ordinary people was truly "dizzying." The party itself had given up its attempt to be a (supposedly) centralized (but in actuality fractured) organization and gave in to being a much looser mass party with hundreds of thousands of adherents. The distress of war and the despair about the future radicalized people only tangentially connected to or affiliated with the Bolsheviks. In Helsinki the soviet leaders proclaimed the local executive committee to be the government of Finland. In Tashkent the soviet, led by Left SRs, took power in the city. Late in September Bolsheviks won a majority in the elections to the Moscow City Duma.

Still in hiding in Finland, Lenin was so impressed both by the radicalism of the popular forces there and by the Petrograd Soviet leaders' resistance to Kornilov that he moderated his strategic stance and called once again for "All Power to the Soviets." He published an unusual article "On Compromises," in which he returned (it turned out briefly) to the idea of peaceful competition with the other socialist parties.[33] "Like any other political party," he wrote, "our party strives for political dominion for *itself*."[34] But if the Mensheviks and SRs were willing to take power, the Bolsheviks would refrain "from revolutionary methods of struggle."[35] But even before he sent off the article, he learned of the Soviet's acceptance of Kerenskii's Directory, and he backed away. "After reading Saturday's and today's, Sunday's, papers," he added in a postscript, "I say to myself: perhaps it is already too late to offer a compromise. . . . Yes, to all appearances, the day when by chance the path to peaceful development became possible has *already* passed."[36] In a follow-up essay, "The Russian Revolution and Civil War," he warned that only a soviet government could avoid civil war. An alliance of the socialist parties would render a bourgeois counterrevolution impossible.[37] Lenin was willing to work with the other socialists if they came out for a transfer of government power to the soviets and broke completely with the liberals. He feared, however, that the Mensheviks and

Right Socialist Revolutionaries were unlikely to make such a move. He was right.

Three days later Stalin moderated his position, once again following Lenin's lead. He noted the significance of the move to the left of the SRs and Mensheviks. Their break with the Kadets was still only formal, but "such a break as a beginning is a huge step forward."[38] He remained suspicious, however, of the upcoming Democratic State Conference, which he doubted would be able to come up with a solution to the all-important question of Russia's government.[39] Along with Trotsky, Kamenev, Miliutin, and Rykov, Stalin was elected to a commission to write up a declaration to be read at the conference.[40] Their statement called for Soviet Power in the center and the provinces. Anyone insisting on continuation of the Coalition Government, they wrote, was leading the country into civil war. A second Congress of Soviets must urgently be convened.

The Bolsheviks carried the tactic of compromise with other socialist parties into the grand gathering of almost fifteen hundred socialist party members and democratic civic activists that convened on September 14 at Petrograd's Aleksandrinskii Theater. The key question for the delegates was: Would the next government be a continuation of the Coalition Government, already shown to be paralyzed as it stretched between the extremes of a polarized society, or a government of the lower classes alone, a homogeneous democratic or socialist government? Both Kamenev and Trotsky spoke in favor an "all-democratic" government, with Kamenev advocating a broader coalition of lower class forces beyond the socialist parties, and Trotsky proposing an eventual transfer of power to the soviets.[41] After four days of deliberation the conference delegates voted on the question of the government. Given the preponderance of moderates in the hall, they first accepted in principle the possibility of coalition with the bourgeoisie. Next, still reeling from the Kornilov mutiny, they rejected any collaboration with the Kadets or any group that had supported Kornilov. Finally, they voted down their own amended resolution. In the end the conference achieved nothing except to expose the divisions among the "democratic" forces. The moderate socialists would not give up the idea of alliance with some part of the bourgeoisie, especially now that a soviet government would most probably mean Bolshevik dominance. The Bolsheviks, Left SRs, and more radical elements would not accept another coalition with the liberals. The whole issue was then passed on to another gathering, the so-called Preparliament, to be made up of delegates from the Democratic Conference. Meanwhile, with no resolution achieved, Kerenskii went ahead and formed a new coalition cabinet, the third in three months, which included Kadets as well as a majority of moderate socialists and was formally committed to a socialist program.[42] In his view the government, not the Preparliament, was the higher authority in Russia.

Even moderate Bolsheviks were appalled at the actions of the moderate socialists. The Central Committee voted not to use the word "comrade" when addressing such people.[43] In his comments on the Democratic Conference Stalin opened boldly: "The fundamental question of a revolution is the question of power." Trying to reconcile the break with the Kadets with some kind of coalition with capitalists, as SR leader Chernov desired, was impossible. This only opened the door for Kerenskii to form whatever government he wished.[44] Stalin enthusiastically took up the revived slogan, "All Power to the Soviets." Lenin's experiment with less vivid formulas was over now that the soviets of both capitals were turning to the Bolsheviks.[45] Stalin repeatedly mentioned in his articles the fate of the Tashkent Soviet, which after declaring Soviet Power, had been overthrown by a punitive military force sent by the Provisional Government.[46] This was a kind of warning that the struggle between government and soviets had come down to who could bring men with guns to carry out their orders. Stalin targeted the SR party, then in the process of disintegration. At the Preparliament the Left SRs had introduced a motion to turn the land over to the peasantry immediately. Right SRs voted against the motion, and centrists like Chernov abstained. Unity with such a party, he argued, was senseless.[47] But, in fact, the gravitation of the Left SRs toward the Bolsheviks gave Lenin's urban-based party at least a claim to a broad base of support in the villages. The alliance of these two radical parties was an essential factor in the ability of the Bolsheviks to take and hold power in the coming months.

PLANNING INSURRECTION

On September 25 a Bolshevik-Left SR majority took over the Petrograd Soviet and elected Trotsky its chairman. The Soviet immediately refused to support Kerenskii's coalition government. Both Trotsky and Kamenev now awaited the late October convening of the Second All-Russian Congress of Soviets, at which they expected power to be formally transferred to the Left. But by this time Lenin had long lost patience with his early September strategy of compromise with the moderate socialists. Already in mid-September he frantically wrote a series of letters to his comrades in Petrograd explaining that the "Bolsheviks, having obtained a majority in the soviets of workers' and soldiers' deputies in both capitals, can and *must* take state power in their own hands."[48] He called on them to learn the art of insurrection now that they had, in contrast to July, the unquestioned support of the workers. "All the objective conditions exist for a successful insurrection."[49] Once again Lenin was among the most militant members of his party. "The Mensheviks and Socialist Revolutionaries," he reminded his comrades, "even after the Kornilov revolt, refused to accept our compromise of peacefully transferring power to the soviets. . . . They have again sunk into the morass of mean and filthy bargaining with the Kadets. Down with the Mensheviks and Socialist Revolutionaries! . . . Ruthlessly expel them from all revolutionary organizations. No negotiations, no communications with these friends of the . . . Kornilovite landowners and capitalists."

Once again Lenin in exile had gone too far for his comrades in Petrograd. Instead of publishing Lenin's militant articles and letters, the Petrograd Bolsheviks either printed his conciliatory articles from earlier in September or severely cut his later pieces. Kamenev tried (and failed) to have the Central Committee reject formally Lenin's suggestions and oppose all open "street actions."[50] Lenin feared that Kerenskii was conspiring to use the army against the Bolsheviks while his party passed resolutions and acted in a "purely 'constitutional' spirit."[51] Frustrated by the party leaders' unwillingness to take power immediately and their preference to wait for the Congress of Soviets, he resigned from the

Central Committee so that he could freely campaign for insurrection among the party rank and file. No one in the Bolshevik leadership took this moment of pique seriously, and Lenin continued to barrage Petrograd with demands to "save the revolution."[52] Many Bolsheviks, however, were not convinced that a seizure of power before the Congress was necessary.

At the opening of the Preparliament, on October 7, Trotsky attacked the government as a tool of the counterrevolutionary bourgeoisie, and the Bolsheviks demonstratively walked out.[53] Stalin pointed out in an editorial that for many moderate socialists the Preparliament was seen as an alternative to the soviets, just as the Constituent Assembly would be.[54] Instead, he claimed, Soviet Power would be the realization of the dictatorship of the proletariat and peasantry and would require the elimination of bureaucrats and officers of the old regime. State officials and army commanders would be elected. There would be no violence against the masses, though there would be restrictions on their enemies.[55]

Three days later, October 10, Lenin slipped into Petrograd and met secretly with the Central Committee at the apartment of the Menshevik-Internationalist Sukhanov, invited there by his wife, a Bolshevik, who had made sure that her husband would be out for the night. Twelve sat around the dining room table.[56] "The majority is with us now," Lenin stated unequivocally, and "the political situation is fully ripe for the transfer of power." "To wait for the Constituent Assembly, which clearly will not be with us, is senseless." The masses were tired of words and resolutions.[57] Strongly opposed to a seizure of power, Kamenev and Zinoviev feared that the wavering peasantry was at that moment closer to the bourgeoisie than to the Bolsheviks. They would vote for the SRs, and the soldiers would desert rather than fight a revolutionary war. They did not wish to gamble the fate of the revolution "on one card." Bolshevik influence was growing and would be significant in the Constituent Assembly, which would in turn have to lean on the soviets. "Constituent Assembly plus soviets—this is the combined type of state institution toward which we are going. On that political base our party has the greatest chance for a real victory." Moreover, there was no guarantee of support from abroad.[58] Their arguments failed to convince those gathered, and in a historic vote Lenin's call for an armed insurrection as the new "order of the day" was approved by a vote of 10 to 2. Those present then chose a Political Bureau of seven "for political leadership in the short term." The seven selected were: Lenin, Zinoviev, Kamenev, Trotsky, Stalin, Sokolnikov, and Andrei Bubnov.[59]

The decision taken on October 10 and reaffirmed by the Central Committee six days later was fateful. Seizing power before the Congress of Soviets was to meet, and well before the Constituent Assembly had even been elected, meant that Lenin and the Bolshevik leaders (except Kamenev and Zinoviev) were prepared to gamble that the Bolsheviks with the backing of the Left SRs and the soviets could hold power on their own and did not need the democratic sanction of the mass of peasants. It was a step toward civil war, even though Stalin and other writers claimed just the opposite. Lenin mentioned that it may once have been possible to compromise with the Mensheviks and SRs, but they refused to end their collaboration with the liberals. The masses were now with the Bolsheviks, but they were changeable and could move away from the party if it did not act.[60] Reviewing the mood among workers and soldiers, the various reporters from the districts indicated that it was not very clear how many people were for an uprising. Metal workers, for example, Aleksandr Shliapnikov reported, were for the Bolsheviks, but a Bolshevik uprising was not popular, and rumors about an insurrection stirred up panic. Workers' meetings expressed an unwillingness to take the initiative against the government. They had been chastened by the failure in July and were now much more cautious. Yet they repeatedly stressed that if the government made the first move, they would respond.[61]

Kamenev, Zinoviev, and others were doubtful that the wager on an armed uprising would pay off. The moment was not right, and the risks and uncertainties were too great. Stalin, however, spoke strongly in favor of an insurrection:

One can say, we must wait for an attack on us, but what is an attack; the raising of prices of bread, sending Cossacks to the Don region, etc.—all these are already attacks. How long should we wait if there is not a military attack? What Kamenev and Zinoviev suggest objectively leads to the possibility that the counterrevolution will organize; we will retreat endlessly and lose the whole revolution. Why can't we give ourselves the possibility of choosing the day and the conditions so that we don't give the counterrevolution the possibility of organizing.

Stalin emphasized the readiness of Europe to join Russia in revolution. Therefore, the victory of the socialists was far more likely in October than in had been in July or August.

Let's move to the analysis of international relations, [which] shows that there should be greater faith [in victory]. Here there are two lines: one line holds the course on the victory of the revolution and leans on Europe, the second does not believe in the revolution and calculates that we will be merely an opposition. The Petrograd Soviet has already stood on the path of an uprising by refusing to sanction the transfer of troops [to the front]. The fleet has already risen up as it has moved against Kerenskii.[62]

Lenin too answered the doubters. "If one says that the uprising has matured, then speaking about conspiracies is uncalled for. If a political uprising is necessary, then it is necessary to treat insurrection as an art. And it has already matured."[63] The vote was 19 to 2, with 4 abstentions.

Distraught at what he considered a precipitous and dangerous action, Kamenev resigned from the Central Committee, and he and Zinoviev published their objections to the Bolsheviks' initiating an uprising in Gorky's newspaper *Novaia zhizn'* (New Life). Lenin was furious at what he considered an act of treachery and demanded that Kamenev and Zinoviev be expelled from the party. "I say straight out, that I do not consider these two to be comrades any longer, and with all my strength before the Central Committee and before the congress, I will fight for the exclusion of both from the party."[64] The question was taken up at the next Central Committee meeting on October 20. Sverdlov read out

Lenin's letter calling Zinoviev and Kamenev "strikebreakers" who could not be tolerated within the party ranks. "This is not easy to write about formerly close comrades, but I consider wavering here a crime, for otherwise a party of revolutionaries that did not punish such strike-breakers would perish."[65] Stalin opposed expelling the two from the party, falling back on his constant preference for party unity. "It is neces-sary," he said, "to preserve the unity of the party; it is proposed to obli-gate these two comrades to obey the will of the Central Committee but to let them remain in the Central Committee."[66] Kamenev's resignation was accepted by a vote of 5 to 3 (though it never went into effect).

Rumors spread about the planned insurrection. Trotsky stated in the Soviet that no date had been set for an uprising. Zinoviev wrote to the editors of *Rabochii put'* the next day that he and Kamenev agreed with Trotsky's statement in the Soviet that no date had been set for an upris-ing unless there was "a first attempt of the counterrevolution to smash the congress [of soviets]." Then "we will answer with a counterattack, which will be merciless and which we will carry through to the end."[67] He also took the opportunity to mention that he disagreed with Lenin "on a controversial question" but that it was necessary now to close ranks. Stalin wrote a declaration in the name of the editorial board ex-pressing the hope that Zinoviev and Kamenev's statements would end this matter. "The sharpness of the tone of Comrade Lenin's article does not change the fact that basically we remain in agreement with his views."[68] The rash of resignations was becoming infectious. At the Cen-tral Committee meeting Stalin announced that he wanted to resign from the editorial board of *Rabochii put'*, but it was resolved that in view of the fact that Stalin's declaration had been written in the name of the edi-torial board, it was a matter for the editorial board to decide. The Cen-tral Committee would neither discuss his declaration nor accept his resignation.[69]

In the run up to the October insurrection the key organizer and orator in the Bolshevik camp was the newly minted party member, Trotsky. He was everywhere at once, "tearing himself away from work on the revolutionary staff, [he] personally rushed from the Obukhovsky plant to the Trubochny, from the Putilov to the Baltic works, from the riding-school to the barracks; he seemed to be speaking at all points simultaneously. His influence, both among the masses and on the staff, was overwhelming." In Sukhanov's opinion, "He was the central figure of those days and the principal hero of this remarkable page of history."[70]

The divisions in the Bolshevik leadership—between Lenin who wanted an immediate insurrection; Kamenev and Zinoviev who opposed it; and others including Trotsky and Stalin willing to wait until the Second Congress of Soviets to take power—evaporated when Prime Minister Kerenskii decided to act first. Desperate to rid the city of the radical military units, he used the pretext of the German advance to order the Petrograd garrison to the front. But the soldiers refused to move and angrily called for Soviet Power. The Soviet hastily passed a resolution, written by Trotsky, which accused Kerenskii of preparing to surrender the capital to the Germans, and set up a committee to defend the revolution.[71] Soon to be known as the Military-Revolutionary Committee, this body, often chaired by Trotsky, was to take on the major role in organizing the insurrection. Some days later at its October 16 session, the Bolshevik Central Committee designated Stalin, Sverdlov, Uritskii, Dzierżyński, and Bubnov to be the "Military-Revolutionary Center" (a party body, not to be confused with the Military-Revolutionary Committee of the Soviet). Far less important, indeed hardly active, this "Center" would be credited by later Soviet historians with much of the critical activity that in fact was carried out by the Soviet Military-Revolutionary Committee.[72]

Lenin plotted the uprising like a military campaign. He convinced the Bolshevik Military Organization to overcome their doubts about the potential success of the uprising and rejected their plea for delay. "Time is on the side of the government," he claimed. Delay would "only give the government more time to destroy the Bolsheviks with loyal troops brought in from the front." He emphasized that he wanted to present the Congress of Soviets with a fait accompli.[73] Lenin suggested the Military-Revolutionary Committee of the Petrograd Soviet direct the actual event. For Stalin the moderate socialists had become "strikebreakers of the revolution." Having lost faith in the soviets they sided with the Preparliament and Kerenskii's government.[74] He and other Central Committee members prepared for the upcoming Congress of Soviets. Stalin would speak on his special field—the national question.[75]

In many ways what would be known as the "October Revolution" was a contest between the Soviet, now Bolshevized, and the Kerenskii government for supremacy over the Petrograd garrison. On October 21–22 the Soviet's Military-Revolutionary Committee announced that soldiers would obey no orders except those from the Soviet. This was in fact the first act in the overthrow of the Provisional Government. Once the garrison recognized the Soviet as its commander, power was in the hands of Petrograd's Bolsheviks. "No one took it for a coup d'état," Sukhanov wrote later. "And no wonder. The decision, after all, did not really change the situation: even earlier the Government had had no real power or authority. . . . Now the garrison had declared officially, urbi et orbi, that it did not recognize the Government and was subject to the Soviet. . . . Nevertheless, this is a fact: by October 21st the Provisional Government had already been overthrown, and was nonexistent in the territory of the capital."[76]

The next day the Military-Revolutionary Committee, after protracted speeches by Trotsky, won over the formerly reluctant soldiers of the Peter-Paul Fortress and took control of the Kronverk Arsenal across a small strait from the Fortress. Kerenskii responded by shutting down the Bolshevik newspapers. Some of the members of the Central Committee and of the Military-Revolutionary Committee gathered at party headquarters in the Smolny Institute to discuss launching the insurrection. Trotsky and others urged restraint. In the afternoon of October 24 Stalin met with Bolshevik delegates to the Second Congress of Soviets, which was scheduled to open the next day. He informed them, "within the Military-Revolutionary Committee there are two points of view. The first is that we organize an uprising at once, and the second is that we first consolidate our forces. The Central Committee has sided with the second view."[77] Sharing the same position, Trotsky also spoke:

The government is powerless; we are not afraid of it because we have enough strength. . . . Our task is to defend ourselves and gradually to expand our sphere of authority so as to build a solid foundation for tomorrow's Congress of Soviets. The views of the entire country will be revealed tomorrow; and Petrograd will not be alone in responding to its summons.[78]

The Military-Revolutionary Committee sent troops to reopen the Bolshevik printing houses. Stalin's editorial, reflecting his sense that the insurrection should follow the Congress, appeared in *Rabochii put'*:

The present impostor government, which was not elected by the people and which is not accountable to the people, must be replaced by a government recognized by the people, elected by the representatives of the workers, soldiers and peasants, and accountable to these representatives. . . .

If you want this, muster all your forces, rise as one man, organize meetings and elect your delegations and, through them, lay your demands before the Congress of Soviets which opens tomorrow at Smolny.[79]

Kerenskii desperately tried to rally the Preparliament to support him, but even after a long, excited speech, he failed. They voted no confidence. His power was slipping away. Isolated, with only some young military cadets, the Women's Battalion, and a few other units prepared to defend his ministers sitting in the Winter Palace, he left the city to find loyal troops.

Lenin sent a note through Krupskaia to his comrades urging them not to delay any longer. "With all my might I urge comrades to realize that everything now hangs by a thread; that we are confronted by problems which are not to be solved by conferences or congresses (even congresses of soviets), but exclusively . . . by the struggle of the armed people." The government had to be arrested that very night or everything would be lost. The insurrection that he had desired and fought for so long was at hand. Desperately, frantically, he wrote, "History will not forgive revolutionaries for procrastinating when they could be victorious today (and they certainly will be victorious today), while they risk losing much tomorrow; in fact, they risk losing everything. If we seize power today, we seize it not in opposition to the soviets but on their behalf. . . . The seizure of power is what an uprising is about; its political goal will be explained after the seizure." Unsure of what the delegates to the Congress might decide, though minute by minute it was becoming evident that they would not back the Coalition Government, Lenin preferred the street, not the Congress, to decide the fate of the revolution.

> It would be ruinous or a formality to wait for the wavering vote of the 25th of October; the people have the right and obligation to decide such questions not through voting but by force; the people have the right and obligation in critical moments of a revolution to give directions to their representatives, even their best representatives, not to wait for them.[80]

He then put on a wig, wrapped a bandage around his face, and made his way through the streets stealthily to the Bolsheviks' command center at Smolny.[81]

From the time of Lenin's arrival at headquarters, the Bolsheviks went on the offensive. By the next morning, October 25 (November 7), the city was in the hands of the Military-Revolutionary Committee. The Bolshevik Central Committee met in Room 36, on the second floor of Smolny. Lenin, Trotsky, Stalin, Zinoviev, Kamenev, and the others awaited news that the Winter Palace had been taken—a largely symbolic conclusion to their "revolution." But even before the Red forces entered the palace, or the Congress of Soviets had opened, Lenin drafted a manifesto declaring the overthrow of the Provisional Government and the passing of power to the Military-Revolutionary Committee of the Petrograd Soviet.

Huddled in Smolny, the Bolshevik leaders drew up a list of the new government. Trotsky suggested calling its members "people's commissars" instead of ministers. "Yes, that's very good," said Lenin. "It smells of revolution. And we can call the government itself 'the Council [Soviet] of People's Commissars.'" In mid-afternoon the Petrograd Soviet

met, and after listening to Trotsky and Lenin the deputies enthusiastically approved the seizure of power. A deputy shouted out that they
were anticipating the will of the Congress of Soviets. Having overcome
his earlier hesitation of seizing power before the Congress met, Trotsky
dismissed him. "The will of the Second Congress of Soviets has already
been predetermined by the fact of the workers' and soldiers' uprising.
Now we have only to develop this triumph."[82]

The congress opened late that evening. Of its 670 delegates, almost
half, 300, were Bolsheviks; 193 SRs (most of them Left SRs); 68 Mensheviks; 14 Menshevik-Internationalists; and the rest from smaller parties and groups.[83] The sound of fighting for the Winter Palace could be
heard in the hall, and Martov rose to request negotiations for a peaceful
end to the conflict. He proposed that a united, democratic government
be formed, one acceptable to all the democratic forces. His proposal was
unanimously accepted. But suddenly the Menshevik and Right SR
deputies announced that in view of the Bolsheviks' criminal action in
overthrowing the government, they were withdrawing from the congress. By this impulsive and rash move, the moderates left the field open
to the radicals. As historian Alexander Rabinowitch notes, "by pulling
out of the congress, the moderate socialists undercut efforts at compromise by the Menshevik-Internationalists, the Left SRs, and the Bolshevik moderates. In so doing, they played directly into Lenin's hands,
abruptly paving the way for the creation of a government which had
never been publicly broached before—that is, an exclusively Bolshevik
regime."[84]

Martov attempted to save the situation by introducing another resolution, condemning the Bolshevik "coup d'état" and reiterating the need
for negotiations to create an "all-democratic government."[85] Trotsky
rejected Martov's characterization. "A rising of the masses requires no
justification. What has happened is an insurrection, not a conspiracy. . . .
No, here no compromise is possible. To those who have left and to those
who tell us to do this we must say: You are miserable bankrupts, your
role is played out; go where you ought to go: into the dustbin of history!"[86] Martov bolted from the congress with his small band of

Internationalists. His proposal for negotiations with more moderate elements went with him. Only Bolsheviks and Left SRs were left in the congress, which now was the most influential political institution in the whole of Russia.

"So the thing was done," wrote Sukhanov about the exit of the Menshevik-Internationalists. "We had left, not knowing where or why, after breaking with the Soviet, getting ourselves mixed up with counter-revolutionary elements, discrediting and debasing ourselves in the eyes of the masses, and ruining the entire future of our organization and our principles. And that was the least of it: in leaving we completely untied the Bolsheviks' hands, making them masters of the entire situation and yielding to them the whole arena of the revolution." Perhaps, he thought, history could have moved in a different direction. "A struggle at the Congress for a united democratic front might have had some success. . . . By quitting the Congress and leaving the Bolsheviks with only the Left SR youngsters and the feeble little *Novaya Zhizn* group, we gave the Bolsheviks with our own hands a monopoly of the Soviet, of the masses, and of the revolution. By our own irrational decision we ensured the victory of Lenin's whole line."[87]

Early the next morning the last defenders of the Winter Palace surrendered. Much of the city had slept through the insurrection and was unaware that one world had come to an end and another begun. At 5 a.m., the congress accepted Lenin's manifesto declaring that state power was now in the hands of the soviets. In the next two days it approved Lenin's decrees on peace and land, and on October 27, it sanctioned the formation of a new, revolutionary government. Lenin would be chairman, and Trotsky agreed to become people's commissar of foreign affairs. Stalin was named people's commissar of nationalities. His mandate, as yet not clearly spelled out, would be to deal with the more than half of the country's population who were not ethnically Russian.

The October Revolution has been seen by both its opponents and many historians not so much as a popular uprising or insurrection but as a Machiavellian conspiracy by power hungry men, a coup d'état carried out behind the backs of the masses. The evidence can be read in a variety of ways, but it is clear that workers and soldiers in the city of Petrograd overwhelmingly supported both the Soviet and its Bolshevik leaders by October. The taking of power in the October days was determined by which side—the Kerenskii government and its moderate socialist supporters or the Soviet and the Bolsheviks—was able to call armed men out into the streets. Provoked by the Petrograd Soviet's takeover of the garrison, Kerenskii attacked first, and the Military-Revolutionary Committee of the Soviet responded. Like Nicholas II just eight months earlier, Kerenskii was unable to find sufficient loyal troops to resist the armed forces that had turned on him.

The revolution began, radicalized, and was decided, at least in 1917, in and by Petrograd. Most of the city's activated population had become convinced by fall that Soviet Power was the answer to its desire for an end to the war, recovery of the economy, and their own political empowerment. Fearing counterrevolution from the Right, the liberals, and the army, they opted for a government of all the socialist parties, rejecting the Menshevik view that "all the vital forces of the nation" ought to be represented. Lenin's analysis of the balance of forces in the city proved correct, and his initiative and timing was a gamble that he won. The Congress of Soviets then ratified what had already been decided in the streets.

October was a radical turning point in politics, a new imagination of the nation that excluded the upper and middle classes, the clergy, the high command of the army, and propertied society from political participation. This was a new understanding of democracy; only the *demokratiia*, the lower and working classes, would rule. Yet those excluded opposed the narrowing of the *pays legal* to the rule of those over whom they had ruled, and a civil war raged over the vast landscape of Russia for the next four years. In that ferocious fighting what had been the most radically democratic political arena since the Paris Commune descended into a dictatorship of one party, the Bolsheviks, from 1918 self-described as Communists. In that restricted political arena Stalin, the son of a Georgian cobbler, the seminarian regenerated as Marxist journalist, propagandist, and theorist, the relatively obscure committee-man of the Bolshevik underground found the milieu he required to rise swiftly to prominence and, eventually, absolute power. In eight months in 1917, the obscure underground conspirator and party loyalist had risen from being the tsar's prisoner in Siberia to one of the most powerful men in Russia. Never again would others control his life. Now he would command, and others would obey.

CONCLUSION

THE ROAD TRAVELED

Given . . . that we are dealing with a figure known for meticulously staging his appearances, a case can be made for the idea that all the various Stalins glimpsed by observers were authentic. . . . This tortuous, bloody, intensely dramatic and deeply personal path was also one component of a historical "motherboard"—in other words, it was also an impersonal product. . . . He was less well-educated, with little experience of the outside world. Capable of leading discussions and conducting arguments, he was no orator. He was secretive, intensely self-centered, cautious and scheming. His highly sensitive ego could be soothed, if by anything, only by a sense of his own greatness, which had to be unreservedly acknowledged by others.

—MOSHE LEWIN, *THE SOVIET CENTURY* (2005)

Like most successful politicians Stalin was a practiced performer. He learned to play numerous roles as he moved from provincial poverty to state power. The journey he traveled was a painful educational odyssey. Skills were acquired as the hard experiences of an outlaw life toughened him. Stalin grew up with models of a weak, irresponsible father and a strong, principled mother. Beso Jughashvili was a failure as husband and father; he could not reliably provide for his wife and son. Alcoholic and abusive, he was not a "true man" to his family or society. A *katsi* gained respect as much by restraint, in using violence or in drinking, as he did in earning a living, entertaining friends, and being loved and obeyed by his wife and children. Beso failed in all aspects, while Keke took over the role of the man of the family, became the head of the household, protected and promoted her son, and provided an example of hardness, strength, stubborn insistence on and faith in her chosen ideals. Already in the Gori church school Soso Jughashvili showed devotion, even fanatical dedication, to his system of belief, at the time the Orthodoxy of his mother's church. Once committed to a faith he did not easily display doubt. When he shifted beliefs he did so abruptly, radically, decisively, as when he gave up Christianity for Marxism. From his school and seminary he picked up the elements of his own pedagogy: explanations could be, should be, conveyed in plain language. He sought clarity, simplicity, not theoretical complication. With Marxism, particularly in its Leninist version, he believed he had discovered how the world works. More than that, he had acquired the means to change it.

Stalin's political education took place largely in the bowels of the party underground, in the intense partisan infighting between Mensheviks and Bolsheviks. Here he sharpened his polemical tools, deploying what minor oratorical skills he had, but largely relying instead on simple exposition of fundamentals. His own lack of conceptual facility actually aided him in presenting a reduced message plainly to plain folk, and he gained a following that appreciated this quality. Stalin was able to tell a comprehensible story, a clear narrative, repeating themes or words over and over again that made them intelligible to his audience. He instinctively grasped what political psychologists have noted: that a simple idea repeated, no matter how absurd or untruthful, has a greater impact than a more sophisticated but complicated conception.

The young Soso did not have the full, extended support of a close and loving family, as did Lenin, but he acquired successive circles of friends, comrades, and subordinates on whom he depended for help as he made his way through two precarious decades of outlaw life. He was able to evince devotion from others, like the fanatical Kamo. Yet his relationship with friends was instrumental, based on a calculation as to their usefulness. He could feel deeply about those whom he needed, like the Alliluevs, and had a soft, erotic side that he showed to the many women who passed through his life. But he could turn hostile quickly, hold grudges, and callously dismiss those whom he considered enemies.

Revolution was his profession, and through his work in the party underground and with workers in Baku and Saint Petersburg, hardened by the violence of 1905–1907 and his suffering in prison and exile, he

arrived in 1917 a man who had preserved his own ideals and was prepared as a pragmatic Marxist to use the means necessary to further the
Bolshevik cause. Sentimentality had largely been suppressed. Empathy
had eroded.[1] In their place was a Machiavellian calculus—discipline,
toughness, violence, even cruelty were requirements in this bitter
political battle.

In the Georgia in which he grew up violence was an everyday
occurrence—in the family, from the state, against the state. There was
arbitrary, unjustified violence, like that suffered from his father, and violence sanctioned by tradition, by the great epics of Georgian literature
and the stories of modern writers like Qazbegi. Revenge could be a
necessary, even ennobling, pursuit, the effecting of a rough justice, the
righting of an unbearable wrong. For a revolutionary violence was simply a basic tool of the trade. Without it came defeat; with it, victory.

From his earliest years in Gori he was ambitious, anxious to change
his place in the world and willing to take risks to do it. He wanted to
stand out, to succeed, but his was a controlled ambition, concealed
under a diffident demeanor. He did not announce himself but lurked,
hid behind a sly smile, waited for others to expose themselves first.
Many people remarked on his sense of humor, his love of jokes, but
many more noted how he stood apart or sat silently to the side, watching, observing, and sizing up the situation. His smile was ironic, sar-
donic, not engaging. He governed his emotions carefully. What passion
he had was reserved for his work and the cause to which he had given
his life.

In the years leading up the revolution he was willing to work with
those he admired and respected, like Lenin, but he was contemptuous
of those elders like Zhordania or Plekhanov or movement veterans like
Trotsky with whom he disagreed. Stalin was endowed with self-
confidence that passed beyond the boundary into arrogance. His disdain for those with whom he disagreed extended even to Friedrich Engels, whom in postrevolutionary years he would refer to privately as
incorrect or "foolish."[2] While Lenin was flexible and changed his mind
about people, able to ally with Trotsky or contemplate working with
Martov, whom he valued even though they had fought against one

another for over a decade, Stalin found that kind of compromise difficult. Whether it was resentment, jealousy, or disgust, he was unable to
subordinate his affective disposition toward such people to what might
better serve the movement. He did not appreciate refinement or gentility but preferred a rougher manner, affecting what he took to be a proletarian toughness. He operated best with acolytes like Suren Spandarian or Kamo, but was less able to get along with more independent
people like the genteel Stepan Shahumian or the punctilious Iakov
Sverdlov. His relationship with long-time comrades like Kamenev or
Orjonikidze was even more complicated, as the power and position of
each of these men shifted within the Bolshevik hierarchy. Like Lenin he
could be contemptuous of intellectuals, even though in the scheme of
things he was an *intelligent*. His intellectual interests, however, were directed toward confirmation rather than questioning. He was not introspective like Sverdlov. He appreciated the plainness of ordinary people.
His nature was narrow, not as open and generous as Lenin's.

Through the years of revolution in Caucasia and the long odyssey
through the underground and in exile his earlier idealism fell away before what worked in practice. A realist's calculation of means and ends
eliminated his youthful romanticism. But he was more than a simple
pragmatist. By the time he was Koba, he had a reputation within Georgian Social Democracy both as a talented organizer and an untrustworthy intriguer. He acted on his impulses, personal and political, and
was ready without much reflection to deceive or lie or turn on his comrades without consideration of what he may have promised or committed to earlier. His self-assuredness led him to dogmatism. In contrast to
Marx or Lenin, doubt was foreign to him.[3] At age twenty-five he had
strong opinions that were resistant to change. Yet when faced by strong
opposition to his convictions, he was able for practical reasons to shift
quickly and decisively, as the incident over his "credo" demonstrated.
To rejoin the movement and win over Tskhakaia, his patron, Koba abandoned his "Georgian Bundism" and accepted with little hesitation the
party's position against autonomous national political units.

Russia became more important to him than Georgia. His conviction
that Russian culture and society were more modern, more proletarian,

and therefore superior to the cultures of the peoples of the periphery, particularly those of the southern and eastern borderlands, grew stronger in the postrevolutionary years of civil war. Nation was subordinated to what was thought to be internationalism but would in time evolve into empire, the inequitable rule of some over others. In a variation of the theme proposed long before by Marx and Engels, that some small nations were *geschichtslose*, Stalin accepted the imperial notion that selected nations were on the right side of history and others were fated to be pulled by force into the light of modernity.[4]

His pragmatism led him to moderation rather than any extreme. The early impulsiveness that had resulted in the massacre of workers in Batumi and Soso's first arrest and exile may have tempered him. Although there were moments of exuberant militancy, as in the revolutionary years 1905–1907 and 1917, a degree of caution overlain with suspicion preserved him while on the run. The underground required a cool deliberation as well as wariness in choosing one's companions. Prudence and watchfulness were necessary qualities for survival. In his years in power Stalin would raise the practice of "vigilance" (*bditel'nost'*) to a supreme virtue for Soviet citizens. By that time, the novelist Alexander Solzhenitsyn mused, suspicion had become his ideology. Rather than being the most radical of revolutionaries, until his fiftieth birthday Stalin was (with a few notable exceptions) a man of the middle, ready to compromise, to accommodate others in order to achieve the goal at hand. Uncomfortably, he distinguished himself from Lenin in the squabbles over the Bolshevik Left—Bogdanov and the *otzovisti*—and was not convinced that the philosophical arguments that Lenin considered so vital were important enough to divide their faction. In 1917 he was at first close to his moderate friend Kamenev, and only after Lenin's return to Russia in April did he shift his position and recognize that young Molotov had been more correct than he in the principal strategic questions. Unlike Lenin he usually emphasized the need for party unity, for bringing various factions and subfactions together. Lenin, in contrast, was ready at times to split the party when he saw differences of principle, even to stand all alone against those whom he considered misguided. Yet it would be Lenin's tactics that Stalin would employ after the revolution. At one and the same time he would speak about unity only to divide, isolate his adversaries, and solidify a core around himself. When he considered it necessary or advantageous, he adopted the most extreme and radical measures against opponents, resistant peasants and officials, in 1928–1932 and again in 1936–1938. In the name of unity he would carry out the massive, murderous elimination of those labeled "Enemies of the People."

More than any other episode, the crucible that forged him as a revolutionary was the first revolution, the one that ultimately failed, 1905–1907. Talk of violence gave way to the actual exercise of terrorism. The imperial government was determined to crush the rebellion and preserve the empire, and a sanguinary civil war tore the Caucasus apart. The revolutionaries took up arms, first in self-defense and then more aggressively to punish their enemies and make a desperate effort to take power. Tsarism responded to the rebellion of workers and peasants with sanguinary repression, demonstrating that the state and those who benefited from the existing order would never surrender their privileges, property, and power without bloodshed. Like other Bolsheviks Stalin read the defeat not as a need to be more cautious in the future, but as a bitter lesson that carrying the fight to the finish, however ferocious that might be, was the only road to victory.

Revolution was not normal politics. It quickly became something beyond compromise and negotiation. Revolution was war, in fact the most devastating of wars, civil war, war within society and against the state, in many ways war without mercy. Such a war carried its own imperatives: the clear defining of enemies; the willingness to kill so as not to be killed; the subordination of feeling to what was needed to achieve victory. This logic of war—we versus them, destroying the enemy while preserving your own—became fundamental to his thinking. Once politics or any conflict is reconceived as war, the most extreme means, including killing ones' enemies and those who might support them even in the future, is legitimized and normalized.

Before coming to power Russian revolutionaries had very different motives from those after the October victory. Before 1917 Stalin was animated by a complex of ideas and emotions, from resentment and hatred to utopian hopes for justice and empowerment of the disenfranchised. Social Democracy universally was about democracy, the empowerment of ordinary working people and the end of unearned privilege of the well-born. The revolution at hand was a bourgeois-democratic one until the imperialist war of 1914 opened the way to a more rapid transition to a proletarian-socialist revolution. That project of democracy, revolution, and socialism empowered a poor young man from the borderlands of the empire, and combined with the anti-nationalist, anti-imperialist program embedded in Marxism erased the disadvantages of an ethnic Georgian or Jew or Tatar. Soso Jughashvili imbibed the democratic and socialist humanism that he discovered in both the Russian intelligentsia and the heroes and values of Georgian and Russian literature, while Koba came to appreciate how cruel the struggle to change the world would be.

Over time the humane sensibilities of the romantic poet gave way to hard strategic choices. Feelings for others were displaced or suspended and were trumped by personal and political interests. What originated as empathy for the plight of one's people (the Georgians), a social class (the proletariat), or humanity more broadly was converted to a rational choice of instruments to reach a preferred end. Empathy was replaced by an instrumental cruelty. Once in power those earlier emotions and ideals were subordinated to the desire to hold on to the power so arduously and painfully acquired. Power became a key motivator as the imperatives of the new conditions in which Bolsheviks found themselves forced them to make unanticipated choices. "Possession of power," wrote Immanuel Kant, "debases the free judgment of reason."[5] But power was seldom simply about personal aggrandizement or advancement. Based on convictions derived from experience, history, and Marxism, power also served the commitment to a certain vision of the future.[6]

The boy from Gori became a "great man"—that is, a powerful arbitrator of the fate of millions. His decisions as head of state and party decided who would live and who would die. He explained to his aged mother, regretful that he had not become a priest, that he had become something like a tsar. That "greatness" was not prefigured in Gori or

Tiflis or Baku. But the passage through those places, as well as Petersburg and Siberia, fashioned the man who in a world he could not have anticipated was determined to stamp his will on the Soviet people. He was the product not only of the circumstances in which he had been born and grew up, the excesses of imperial rule in the Caucasus, but also of his own ambition, his desire to move somehow beyond the limits that poverty and empire had imposed on him. From his earliest days he understood that education was the road to emancipation. With Marxism and the Social Democratic Party he found the way to change his world. Whether it was fate or luck, he had survived the trials of the revolutionary outlaw and emerged a tempered leader. The trials ahead—civil war, an unexpected political rise to unchallenged autocrat, a revolution initiated by the state against the bulk of the population, and another world war—damaged and destroyed others, but Stalin survived. History had hooked him and lifted him high. A revolutionary made by revolutions, for the remainder of his life he became the maker and breaker of revolutions.

1. A drawing of Stalin's childhood home in Gori. National Parliament Library
of Georgia. For his help in securing photographs from Georgian archives and
collections, the author is most grateful to historian Irakli Khvadagiani.

2. The reconstructed house-museum of Stalin's childhood home in
Gori. Photograph by Bernhard Kabelka, taken October 6, 2014.

3. The town of Gori as seen from the fortress, goristsikhe. Georgian National Archive, Central Archive of Cinema-Photo-Phono documents [SEA].

4. Stalin's mother, Ketevan (Ekaterine, Keke) Geladze (1856/1860–1937). Georgian MIA Academy Archive, II Division (former IMEL Archive) [SShSSA].

5. Stalin's father, Bessarion (Beso) Jughashvili (c.1850–1909). Georgian MIA Academy Archive, II Division (former IMEL Archive) [SShSSA].

6. The boy Stalin, Soso Jughashvili, center top row, in the Gori Religious School. Georgian MIA Academy Archive, II Division (former IMEL Archive) [SShSSA].

7. The student Soso Jughashvili, in his Gori Religious School days. Georgian MIA Academy Archive, II Division (former IMEL Archive) [SShSSA].

8. Soso Jughashvili and his Gori schoolmates, 1893. Georgian MIA Academy
Archive, II Division (former IMEL Archive) [SShSSA].

9. Soso in the Gori Religious School. Georgian National Archive,
Central Archive of Cinema-Photo-Phono documents [SEA].

10. Tiflis (Tbilisi), the Old City. Georgian National Archive, Central
Archive of Cinema-Photo-Phono documents [SEA].

11. Tiflis (Tbilisi), the view from the Botanical Garden. Georgian National
Archive, Central Archive of Cinema-Photo-Phono documents [SEA].

12. Soso (Koba) Jughashvili, second from left top row, in the Tiflis Seminary. Georgian
MIA Academy Archive, II Division (former IMEL Archive) [SShSSA].

13. Soso (Koba) Jughashvili, a young seminarian (1894–1899). Georgian MIA
Academy Archive, II Division (former IMEL Archive) [SShSSA].

14. Pushkin Street and Square, Tiflis. On the left, the caravanserai; in the distance, the Tiflis Seminary where Stalin studied, now the Georgian Museum of Fine Arts. Tiflisi Hamqari Photo Archive.

15. The young Vladimir Lenin (1870–1924), seated center, and fellow members of the Saint Petersburg League of Struggle for the Emancipation of the Working Class in 1897. His friend and later Menshevik opponent, Iulii Martov (1873–1923), is seated to Lenin's left, and the later Bolshevik, Gleb Krzyzanowski (1872–1959), is seated to Lenin's right. ITAR-TASS News Agency/Alamy Stock Photo.

16. Batumi, the port on the Black Sea where Stalin led a famous strike in 1902. National Archive of Georgia, Central Archive of Cinema-Photo-Phono documents [SEA].

17. Stalin (top row center) and fellow prisoners in the Kutaisi Prison, 1903. Georgian MIA Academy Archive, II Division (former IMEL Archive) [SShSSA].

18. Stalin, known then as Koba, with a reputation as a budding revolutionary.
Georgian MIA Academy Archive, II Division (former IMEL Archive) [SShSSA].

19. Koba, the romance of revolution. Georgian MIA Academy
Archive, II Division (former IMEL Archive) [SShSSA].

20. Georgii Valentinovich Plekhanov (1856–1918), known as the "Father
of Russian Marxism." Hoover Institution Archive [HIA].

21. Noe Zhordania (1868–1953), the leader of the Georgian Mensheviks. Tbilisi State University Center of Research of Georgian Democratic Republic.

22. Nikolai ("Karlo") Chkheidze (1864–1926), a leading Georgian Menshevik. Georgian National Archive, Central Archive of Cinema-Photo-Phono documents [SEA].

23. Simon Ter Petrosian ("Kamo") (1882–1922), Stalin's dedicated disciple, terrorist, master of disguise. Hoover Institution Archive [HIA].

24. Baku, the oil-rich city on the Caspian, a view of the cathedral. Georgian National Archive, Central Archive of Cinema-Photo-Phono documents [SEA].

25. Baku, the oil fields of Bibi-Eibat. Georgian National Archive, Central Archive of Cinema-Photo-Phono documents [SEA].

26. Stalin's first wife, Ekaterine ("Kato") Svanidze (1885–1907).

27. Grief-stricken Koba at the funeral of his wife, Kato, 1907. Georgian MIA Academy Archive, II Division (former IMEL Archive) [SShSSA].

28. Stepan Shahumian (1878–1918), considered the
"Caucasian Lenin." Sputnik/Alamy Stock Photo.

29. A rather dandyish young Stalin. National
Parliament Library of Georgia.

30. Grigol ("Sergo") Orjonikidze (1886–1937), a loyal comrade of Stalin's until they broke in 1937, and he committed suicide. Georgian National Archive, Central Archive of Cinema-Photo-Phono documents [SEA].

31. Stalin, the mature revolutionary. Georgian National Archive, Central Archive of Cinema-Photo-Phono documents [SEA].

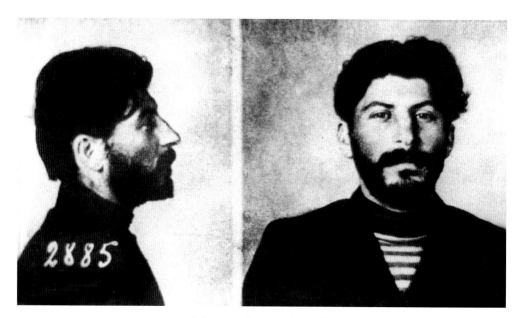
32. Stalin in a police mug shot, Baku, 1908.

33. Stalin in a police record, Baku 1910. Georgian MIA Academy
Archive, II Division (former IMEL Archive) [SShSSA].

34. Roman Malinovskii (1876–1918), Bolshevik duma deputy
and police spy. Photography studio of Bulla, 1913.

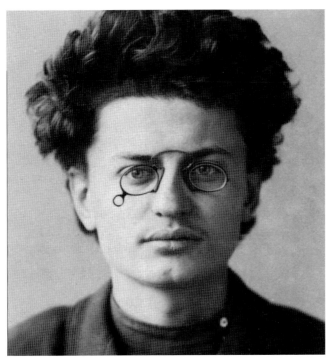

35. Lev Trotsky (1879–1940), shown here in 1905, was Stalin's principal enemy after the revolution of 1917. Hoover Institution Archive [HIA].

36. Stalin, standing third from the left, with his fellow exiles in Turukhansk, Siberia, summer 1915. His close associate Suren Spandarian (1882–1916) stands to his right and Lev Kamenev (1883–1936), a close comrade of Lenin's and a victim of Stalinist repression, stands to his left, then duma deputy Grigorii Petrovskii, Linde, Iakov Sverdlov (1885–1919), in white, Filip Goloshchekin (1876-1941), and an unknown figure; seated left to right are duma deputy Fedor Samoilov; Vera Sveitser (1887–1950), Spandarian's wife with whom Stalin briefly lived after Spandariari's death; and deputies Aleksei Badaev and Nikolai Shagov. Mul'timedia art muzei, Moscow/Moskovskii dom fotografii.

37. In this post-revolutionary doctored photograph, Stalin, standing second from left, is with his fellow exiles in Turukhansk, Siberia, where he spent the years 1913–1917. Kamenev, Goloshchekin, and others have been excised from the photograph. Georgian National Archive, Central Archive of Cinema-Photo-Phono documents [SEA].

38. Lenin in disguise, July 29, 1917, without his beard and uncharacteristically wearing a worker's cap. Sputnik/Alamy Stock Photo.

39. Stalin as commissar after the Bolshevik seizure of power in October 1917. Georgian National Archive, Central Archive of Cinema-Photo-Phono documents [SEA].

HISTORIANS LOOK AT STALIN

A HISTORIOGRAPHICAL DISCUSSION

The historiography on the young Stalin has undergone its own historical evolution but not in a single direction.[1] A narrowing of perspective, what might be called the Bolshevization of the historical past, marked Soviet historical writing in the 1920s. Yet during that decade Soviet historiography, enriched by memoirs of participants—for example, Abel Enukidze and Pilipe Makharadze—and a raucous search for an acceptable Marxist approach by Bolshevik historians, was considerably more informative and inclusive than the published works of history that were permitted during the long, dark years of Stalinism, roughly from 1930 to the early 1950s.

Stalinist history was whitewashed; blemishes left out; and the cult of the hero, the party, and the Soviet state became the idols at which historians were forced to worship. After Stalin's infamous letter to the journal *Proletarskaia Revoliutsiia* in October 1931, even the slightest criticism of Lenin or Stalin became a punishable offense. The threat of what was euphemistically called in Russia "administrative measures" was usually enough to encourage self-censorship by the historical profession. Stalin personally forbade any thorough biography of the leader, and only a short biography was published in 1939. The principal text on Stalin before the revolution of 1917 was the printed version of Lavrenti Beria's 1935 speech "On the Question of the History of Bolshevik Organizations in Transcaucasia," which made Koba the central figure in the resistance to tsarism south of the Caucasus. At the end of the 1930s and during the war years documents on the young Stalin and his time in exile in Siberia were collected, compiled, and occasionally published, but whatever was written about Stalin was too intimately connected with the interests of the Soviet state to be left to the independent authority of professional historians.

During the Khrushchev years (1953–1964), the figure of Stalin almost disappeared from Soviet historical writing, only to reemerge intermittently in the Brezhnev period (1964–1982). With the coming to power of Gorbachev (1985–1991), formerly restricted archives were opened to scholars, and a more honest evaluation of the sources became possible. From the first exchange programs between Soviet and Western scholars in the early 1960s, some sharing of information and ideas contributed to a more critical historiography, particularly of the revolutions of 1917 and Stalinism, though outside the USSR the young Stalin remained trapped in the shadows of a primitive psychohistory.

In the West biographies proliferated with the rise of academic Sovietology during the Cold War, and the general outlines of a master narrative fell securely into place with the accounts by Roy Medvedev, Robert C. Tucker, Adam B. Ulam, Ronald Hingley, Robert Slusser, and Robert McNeal.[2] More popular and sensationalist versions were produced by Robert Payne, Edward Ellis Smith, H. Montgomery Hyde, and Alex de Jonge.[3] The story of the abused boy from Gori who rose to become one of the three principal power brokers on the world stage was unified around a single motivation, an all-consuming and uncompromising drive to power, that integrated the fragments of his life into a unified narrative. The answers to the central mystery, why did he do what he did the way he did it, were sought by some with the aid of psychoanalysis, but ultimately they returned to the irreducible drive for power. The very thing that needed explanation became the source of the explanation and was itself beyond further examination. As is often the case in biographies, the disjunctures and anomalies of human experiences, the effects of radically different contexts, were smoothed away in service to a literary imperative to give meaning and recognizable shape to the life as a whole.

The major Stalin biographers of the 1930s, Boris Souvarine and Lev Trotsky, specifically rejected the crude psychoanalysis that reduced Stalin's initial political formation to relationships within his family. Trotsky's portrait of Stalin was colored by his political struggle with Stalin and Stalinism, and he admitted being "repelled by the very qualities that would strengthen him."[4] As Peter Beilharz pointed out, Trotsky refused to allow Stalin "any kind of power of initiative" and failed to recognize that his intellectual limitations were more than compensated by his political acumen.[5] A decade later Trotsky's political disciple, Isaac Deutscher, "an unrepentant Marxist," quite deliberately set out to "study the politics rather than the private affairs of Stalin" and produced a monumental history of the formation of the Soviet Union, which soon became one of the interpretations most influential on the post-Stalin generation of Soviet specialists.[6] This work challenged the liberal and conservative orthodoxies of the Cold War years and sought to rescue socialism from its popular conflation with Stalinism.

In the late 1940s the temptation to make sense of the seemingly senseless brutality of the Stalin era led Gustav Bychowski, a clinical professor of psychiatry in New York City, to make the first explicitly psychoanalytic reconstruction of Stalin's early life. Basing his analysis on Ioseb Iremashvili, Bychowski argued that Stalin's reach for power was the "struggle of the son against the father," a repetition of the kind of succession struggles that go on in "primitive tribal societies."[7] His Stalin was a man driven by a deep pathology, an identification with his native land's enemy, a thirst for flattery, whose inner impulses were shaped by the violence of the revolution.

About the time that Bychowski was writing, a young American diplomat stationed in Moscow was himself engaged in psychological investigation. While still in the USSR, Robert C. Tucker repeatedly read Karen Horney's *Neurosis and Human Growth* and was impressed by her concept of the "neurotic character structure." Tucker's Stalin wanted political power in order to become the "acknowledged leader of the Bolshevik movement, a second Lenin." His rise to power and his autocracy were to be understood as the outcome of four major influences— Stalin's personality, the nature of Bolshevism, the Soviet regime's historical situation in the 1920s, and the historical political culture of Russia ("a tradition of autocracy and popular acceptance of it"). The rough treatment by his father and the great love of his mother created a psychological tension in the young Stalin, simultaneously "the feeling of a conqueror, that confidence of success that often induces real success" and "anxieties and threats to self-esteem." It was only a small step to the militant Marxism of Lenin and to a psychological identification with his new hero. "Lenin was for Djugashvili everything that a revolutionary leader ought to be, and that he too would like to be insofar as his capacities permitted."[8] Rather than a psychoanalysis of Stalin, Tucker's work used psychoanalytic insights to discover Stalin's deepest motivations. On the whole the work is redeemed by the care and tentativeness of the psychological speculation and the more traditional reliance on other factors. But at times one has the feeling that Tucker, like other practitioners of psychohistory, "comes to the past with an understanding and explanation already in hand; the understanding and explanation do not emerge from the past itself but are the products of a theoretical model. In short, it is often less accurate to say that the model is applied to the past than that the past is applied to the model."[9]

While psychology cannot be avoided in a biography, most Stalin biographers leave Freud, his disciples, and psychoanalysis out of their analysis. In his sprawling biography of Stalin, political scientist Adam Ulam rejected a specific model of psychoanalysis and instead of psychopathology emphasized rational choices.[10] Shaped by "years of conspiracy, with its suspicions and betrayals," as well as "the notion of historical forces so deeply ingrained in Marxism-Leninism," Stalin became "a man who operated as a conspirator throughout much of his life, even when dictator."[11] Ulam elevated politics and ideology as explanatory factors, resisting "the temptation to read into the personality of the young Georgian socialist and agitator all and already full developed characteristics of the dictator."[12] How does one explain all the "little Stalins," like Orjonikidze, Molotov, and Mikoyan, who did not have the brutalized childhood of their leader? The real villain in Ulam's story is not Stalin's father, or even Stalin himself, but the particular view of history as a constant struggle between the forces of light and darkness that endowed the Bolsheviks with the sense of historic mission and enabled them to stifle their scruples and protect their power.

Two major studies of Stalin appeared in the second decade after the Soviet collapse by the journalist and novelist Simon Sebag Montefiore. Long obsessed by Stalin and Caucasia, Montefiore's initial foray into Staliniana was a comic novel, *My Affair with Stalin*, in which a malevolent eleven-year-old adopts Stalin's tactics to dominate his schoolmates.

Reborn as a popular historian, he is the author of a well-regarded biography of Prince Grigorii Potemkin, Catherine the Great's advisor and lover (those two positions often went together). A prodigious researcher, he mined Russian and Georgian archives, assisted by historians in Russia and Georgia with the required language skills, traveled to Stalin's birthplace, Georgia, to his various homes and hideaways as far away as war-torn Abkhazia, dug up unpublished memoirs, and carried on numerous interviews with anyone who knew Stalin and would talk to him (including most of his living descendants, with the notable exception of the reclusive Svetlana Allilueva, Stalin's daughter).

His study of *Young Stalin* begins in the "Wild East," an exoticized Georgia where for many foreigners the locals were savage and noble, the terrain majestic and wild. Even what is familiar in Montefiore's story is told in a vivid narrative rich with new details and sensational revelations. Leading us through the less well-explored years of Stalin's revolutionary evolution, Montefiore focuses almost exclusively on his personal rather than political side. He is more interested in Stalin's women than in Social Democracy and the labor movement. Young Stalin is already a "gangster godfather, audacious bank robber, killer, pirate and arsonist," a Marxist fanatic with a need to command and dominate.[13] The savage Caucasus was the essential environment in which this "murderous egomaniac" was nurtured.[14] The violence of the Russian Empire's southern periphery, both that of rebellious workers and peasants, anarchists and Marxists, as well as the state's brutal reprisals shaped Stalin's conviction that bloodshed and terror were necessary means to his desired ends. "Only in Georgia," writes Montefiore, "could Stalin the poet enable Stalin the gangster."[15] Even his human side, such as it was, was perverse. He neglected his devout and devoted mother, subordinated his first wife to his revolutionary work, which likely led to her death, and took up with whatever woman, regardless of age, who could satisfy his appetites. Stalin as womanizer is a new angle on the man of steel, but the evidence for his sexual exploits, while tantalizing, is extremely thin.

Montefiore's portrait is often overwrought, and though this does not fall into the category of psychohistory, as an explanation of Koba's path to power, it fails like many in that genre to deal adequately with his politics and thought. There is almost nothing on his intense involvement in the Bolshevik versus Menshevik factional squabbles or his role as a theorist of nationalism. Geography is insufficient as context for a historian. Growing up in autocratic Russia where suppression of open political dissent convinced thousands of people that the only way out of backwardness and oppression was by taking up arms, Stalin was in one sense not very unusual. But in another he was unique. His particular talents and lack of scruples enabled him to climb rapidly up the ladder of party politics, impressing Lenin and his own loyalists.

Reading through dozens of biographers, not all of which are reviewed here, it appears that there is a kind of justice when a great despot like Joseph Stalin, who made millions suffer during his lifetime, suffers at the hands of his biographers. Approaches differ, as we have seen, and yet without exception the biographers we have surveyed, from Trotsky to Montefiore, have drawn dark and sanguinary pictures of a worthy successor to Ivan the Terrible. In the first volume of a planned trilogy, Princeton University historian Stephen Kotkin aims to give a less tendentious and more balanced interpretation of the dictator and his times, without excusing or avoiding the viciousness of his rise to power and rule. Here too, however, one that misses some essentials of Stalin's personal and political formation. Kotkin focuses on the context in which Stalin took advantage of the chances he was given and avoided the pitfalls of years as an underground revolutionary, repeated Siberian exiles, and the violent clashes of the Russian Revolution and Civil War. Stalin's considerable talents as politician, organizer, and infighter are highlighted here in contrast to earlier portrayals of Stalin as a "mediocrity" or a "grey blur." Yet the wide-angle lens of the author sometimes loses sight of his protagonist, a secretive political operator who left no diary and few personal letters to flesh out his personal and more intimate moments.

The prerevolutionary Stalin is only lightly sketched in Kotkin's breezy run through his first thirty years. Abjuring Freudian analysis and explicitly avoiding relating the mature Stalin to his upbringing, the author leaves the reader with a richness of context but a thinness of explanation of how Jughashvili grew into Stalin. He deprives the reader of any sense of how Stalin's early experience as a writer and an outlaw influenced what the former seminarian became. The authoritarian preferences of Stalin's mentor and superior, Vladimir Lenin, paved the way for a dictatorship by a person whom few suspected would be the likely successor. Lenin recognized the strengths of Stalin's character—his toughness, even ruthlessness—and his talents—organization, the ability to knock heads and get things done—and had him appointed to the key position in the party apparatus. In contrast to Trotsky but like most successful politicians, Stalin was skilled in attracting supporters, loyalists whose ascendency was accelerated by their closeness and fidelity to their potent patron. With the mammoth amount of new archival material now available, Kotkin details better than any previous account how in the first decades of the Soviet Union the viciousness of the personal conflicts that brought down, one after another, the opponents of Stalin in a real sense buried the original aims of the revolution.

"The fundamental fact about him," writes Kotkin, "was that he viewed the world through Marxism."[16] He was "marinated in Communist ideology."[17] Yet here again, as in many of the earlier biographies, there is little discussion of Soso Jughashvili's gravitation from romantic Georgian nationalist to "Russian" Marxist, passionately, doggedly concerned with intricacies of party organization and the nuances of Marx's historical analysis of social change. Marxism is a collection of diverse and often contradictory understandings of history and the present, a sociology of capitalism with little prescription for what would follow. Marxist movements are fraught with disputes and conflicts that have at times led to the physical elimination of opponents. Here, however, the intensity of the differences and debates within the party are reduced to personality, and the author treats Stalin's philosophical universe with hostility tempered by condescension. As in other biographies Stalin is seen as an ambitious and talented intriguer, a man who combined pathological suspiciousness with overweening self-confidence (perhaps stemming from underlying insecurity). More intelligent than usually given credit he posed as a proletarian and expressed pride in his rudeness. Above all he was a survivor.

It is no accident that biographies are among the best-selling books dealing with history. Personalities, especially of celebrated figures, offer readers apparently easy access to dense and difficult questions about politics. But the emphasis on personality, so essential in a biography, can lead to an overemphasis on the determining effect of the personal characteristics and a neglect of context and social forces. Some Stalin biographers, like Trotsky, Deutscher, Tucker, and Ulam, have come closest to locating the life of this exceptional individual in its historically constructed context and the particular social and intellectual conjunctures that shaped the experiences through which he was made and transformed. Others, like the psychohistorians in particular, discount context too radically; and still others, like Kotkin, do not take the emotional and intellectual evolution of their subject as seriously as they might. Even after reading the work of dozens of biographers, puzzles and underexplored aspects of the Stalin story remain: the ethnographic culture of Georgia, the complex history of Russian Social Democracy, and the brutal effects of imperial rule on colonized peoples. Great historical conjunctures, like revolutions and wars, the contingencies of particular events, and the interactions of major historical actors require complexly conceived questions and explanations that avoid the neat and deceptive harmonies of organic narratives. Besides balance and whatever neutrality is achievable, open-endedness, admission of ignorance, irony, and paradox must be admitted into the study of Stalin and Stalinism.

The problem of Stalin will be with us as long as anyone is concerned with the history of Russia and revolutions. Russia has often been seen as a country fatally doomed to violence and authoritarianism. Explanations have been deployed from environment, national character, and ideology that in unmediated ways predetermine outcomes. Biography should lead us in a different direction, toward the examination of motivation and choice. The contingencies and contradictions of human experience allow us to come away with a sense that while people cannot choose the circumstances in which they live, the choices they make matter enormously. Rather than Russia's repeated fatal fall into despotism—a powerful trope that the Stalin story may convince us is true—other paths might have been taken. After all, ordinary people rose up repeatedly throughout Russian (and Soviet) history in the hope that they might alter the everyday repression of the regimes in which they lived.

The story of the Russian revolutionary movement and the Soviet experience has never just been about one country at one time but about the hopes, rightly or wrongly placed, for alternatives in human history. Biographers who decide to explore the evolution of Stalin might do well to do what they do best and introduce complexity, skepticism, and uncertainty into their stories. Historians are great advocates of context—temporal and spatial, cultural and social—along with the other four "cons" of historical writing: contingency, conjuncture, contradiction, and, yes, confusion. Accidents and chance play influential roles in the processes that in the past have determined the failure of empires and the victories of seemingly marginal parties and people. But those successes and defeats occur in time and space and are complexly determined by prior events and human choices, the consequences of which cannot be predicted. Neither context nor structures, institutions nor environments, fix human choices one-dimensionally. Consider the improbability of Ioseb Jughashvili, a small, wiry child whose affections circled around singing, wrestling, poetry, Georgian Orthodoxy, and nationalism, who could have died from typhus or Siberian frost or a well-aimed bullet, but who was lifted through adversities and reversals to the pinnacle of political power in a faltering revolutionary state. Once Stalin had captured the state, he was in a position to make decisions that had global consequences—limited as they had to be by the world in which he found himself, and his own understandings and preferences. How he came to be that person in that place is the subject of this book.

NOTES

INTRODUCTION: FORTUNE'S NAVE

1. Leon Trotsky, *Stalin: An Appraisal of the Man and His Influence*, ed. and trans. Charles Malamuth (New York: Harper & Brothers, 1941; paperback edition: New York: Grosset & Dunlap, no date), pp. 392–393.

2. Aleksandr Solzhenitsyn, *V kruge pervom* (New York: Harper & Row, 1968); *The First Circle*, trans. Thomas P. Whitney (New York: Harper & Row, 1968); Vasilii Grossman, *Zhizn' i sud'ba* (Moscow: Knizhnaia palata, 1988); *Life and Fate*, trans. Robert Chandler (New York: Harper & Row, 1985). See also Anatolii Rybakov, *Deti Arbata* (Moscow: Sovetskii pisatel', 1987); *Children of the Arbat*, trans. Howard Shukman (Boston: Little, Brown, and Co., 1988).

3. One of the first psychoanalytic discussions of Stalin was by Gustav Bychowski, "Joseph V. Stalin: Paranoia and the Dictatorship of the Proletariat," in Benjamin B. Wolman (ed.), *The Psychoanalytic Interpretation of History* (New York and London: Basic Books, 1971), pp. 115–149. For the theory that Stalin was a police agent before the revolution, see Isaac Don Levine, *Stalin's Great Secret* (New York: Coward-McCann, 1956); Edward Ellis Smith, *The Young Stalin: The Early Years of an Elusive Revolutionary* (New York: Farrar, Straus, and Giroux, 1967); and H. Montgomery Hyde, *Stalin: The History of a Dictator* (New York: Farrar, Straus, and Giroux, 1972). For a fuller discussion of psychohistorical and other approaches to Stalin, see Ronald Grigor Suny, "Making Sense of Stalin: Some Recent and Not-So-Recent Biographies," *Russian History*, XVI, 2–4 (1989), pp. 435–448; expanded as "Making Sense of Stalin: His Biographers," in *Red Flag Wounded: Stalinism and the Fate of the Soviet Experiment* (London and New York: Verso Books, 2020); and the historiographical appendix to this volume, "Historians Look at Stalin: A Historiographical Discussion."

4. I. V. Stalin, *Sochineniia* (Moscow: Gosudarstvennoe izdatel'stvo politicishekoi literatury, 1946–1952), XIII, p. 113.

5. For an account that emphasizes the centrality of an essentialized Georgian identity, particularly its purported romanticism and chronic violence, to Stalin's formation, see Simon Sebag Montefiore, *Young Stalin* (London: Weidenfeld & Nicolson, 2007; New York: Alfred A. Knopf, 2007), p. 11.

CHAPTER 1. THE GEORGIAN

1. The Hungarian historian Miklós Kun gives the birth date for Keke Geladze as February 5, 1860, based on the archival record of her death on June 4, 1937, in the former archives of the Communist Party of the Soviet Union. [Miklós Kun, *Stalin: An Unknown Portrait* (Budapest, New York: Central European University Press, 2003), p. 35; RGASPI, f. 558, op. 11, d. 1549]; Aleksandr Ostrovskii gives the date 1856 for her birth, which he took from the obituary in *Zaria vostoka*, June 8, 1937 [A. Ostrovskii, *Kto stoial za spinoi Stalina* (Saint Petersburg: Neva; Moscow: OLMA-PRESSA, 2002), p. 88]. This valuable work is a close review of archival materials

on Stalin's early life, primarily organized to show that he was not a police agent. Much of the material in Ostrovskii comes from his research in the Georgian party archives in Tbilisi [SShSSA] and the Stalin Museum in Gori [SSM], where he read through Russian-language memoirs of people who knew the young Stalin and his family. Soviet archivists collected dozens of memoirs of young Stalin in the 1930s and 1940s, only a few of which have been published. While such sources must always be approached with caution and a few are suspect in their schematic and hagiographic character, many others contribute details and stories that are corroborated in other sources and appear to this researcher to be reliable.

2. SShSA, f. 440, op. 2, d. 38, l. 12; I. Kitaev, L. Moshkov, and A. Chernev, "Kogda rodilsia I. V. Stalin," *Izvestiia TsK KPSS*, no. 11 (310) (November 1990), pp. 132–134; Edvard Radzinskii, *Stalin* (Moscow: Vagrius, 1997), pp. 17–18 [translation: Edvard Radzinsky, *Stalin*, trans. H. T. Willets (New York: Doubleday, 1996); references will be from the English translation unless otherwise noted]. In her collection of documents on the young Stalin, archivist Olga Edelman demonstrates that Stalin was aware of the true date of his birth. [Olga Edelman, *Stalin: Biografiia v dokumentakh* (unpublished manuscript), p. 2; page numbers in my citations refer to the manuscript that Ms. Edelman allowed me to read and cite before the actual publication, which occurred too late for inclusion here.]

3. From a conversation between Edvard Radzinskii and Elena Sergeevna Bulgakova, the playwright's widow, cited in Radzinsky, *Stalin*, p. 11.

4. Joseph Iremaschwili, *Stalin und die Tragödie Georgiens: Erinnerungen* (Berlin: Verfasser, 1932); V. Kaminskii and I. Vereshchagin, "Detstvo i iunost' vozhdia: dokumenty, zapiski, rasskazy," *Molodaia gvardiia*, 1939, no. 12, pp. 22–101; H. R. Knickerbocker, "Stalin, Mystery Man Even to His Mother," *New York Evening Post*, December 1, 1930. Stalin's mother dictated her memoirs of her marriage and her son's early life to L. Kasradze on August 23, 25, and 27, 1935, shortly before her death. [Ekaterine Giorgis asuli Jughashvili, "chemi mogonebani," SShSSA, f. 8, op. 2, ch. 1, d. 15.] An incomplete version of the memoir is available in Georgian and English in *saarkivo moambe/The Archival Bulletin*, no. 1 (April 2008), pp. 45–49; no. 2 (July), pp. 80–83. The memoir was published in full in Georgian: *stalinis dedis mogonebebi: shinagan sakmeta saministros arkividan* (Tbilisi: SShSSA, 2012), with an introduction by R. G. Suny. The English translation, without the introduction, was published as *My Dear Son: The Memoirs of Stalin's Mother, Keke Jughashvili* (Kindle edition: Amazon, 2012) [https://www.amazon.com/My-Dear -Son-Memoirs-Stalins-ebook/dp/B0084GH2BW/ref=sr_1_2?s=books&ie=UTF8&qid =1533601360&sr=1-2&dpID=512YKNxAWoL&preST=_SY445_QL70_&dpSrc=srch]. All references are to the archival version.

5. The marriage of Vissarion Jughashvili and Ketevan [Ekaterine] Geladze was registered on May 17, 1874, before the archdeacon Khakhanov and subdeacon Kvinkidze. Nine months later, their first son, Mikhail (Misho), was born, on February 14, 1875, and died exactly a week later, a day after his baptism, according to the records of births and deaths in Gori; Georgi (Glakho) was born on December 24, 1876, and died just before his six-month birthday on June 19, 1877. There is an archival reference to a second Georgi, born on October 5, 1880, but there is no written record of his death, perhaps because he was stillborn or died so soon after his birth, before being baptized. [Card file of Stalin's life, RGASPI, f. 71, op. 10, d. 404; d. 275; Miklós Kun, *Stalin: An Unknown Portrait*, pp. 8, 10.] In her memoir Keke Jughashvili mentions the death of only two sons.

6. Radzinskii gives this medical report, dictated by Stalin, and found in his personal archive: "Atrophy of the shoulder and elbow joints of the left arm. Result of a contusion at the age of six, followed by a prolonged septic condition in the region of the elbow joint." [Radzinsky, *Stalin*, p. 30.]

7. Ostrovskii, *Kto stoial za spinoi Stalina*, p. 99.

8. Edelman, *Stalin: Biografiia v dokumentakh*, p. 10.

9. Alfred J. Rieber argues that Stalin's political character was fundamentally shaped by his origins in a borderland of the Russian Empire and the need to negotiate his Georgian and Russian identities through the mediation of a proletarian identity. ["Stalin, Man of the Borderlands," *American Historical Review*, CVI, 5 (December 2001), pp. 1651–1691; and "Stalin as Georgian: The Formative Years," in Sarah Davies and James Harris (eds.), *Stalin: A New History* (Cambridge: Cambridge University Press, 2005), pp. 2–44.]

10. G. Bukhnikashvili, *Gori: Istoricheskii ocherk* (Tbilisi: Zaria vostoka, 1947), pp. 74–75.

11. First published in *Nizhegorodskii listok* (1896); Bukhnikashvili, *Gori*, p. 86.

12. Ronald Grigor Suny, *The Making of the Georgian Nation* (Bloomington, IN, and Stanford, CA: Indiana University Press in association with the Hoover Institution Press: 1988; London: I. B. Taurus & Co., 1989; second edition: Bloomington: Indiana University Press, 1994), pp. 139–144. All references are to the second edition.

13. Kaminskii and Vereshchagin, "Detstvo i iunost' vozhdia," pp. 49–50; Iosif Grishashvili, *Literaturnaia bogema starogo Tiflisa* (Tbilisi: Merani, 1977), pp. 18–20. [This latter work is a translation from the original Georgian *dzveli tpilisis literaturuli bogema* (Tiflis, 1927), an idiosyncratic collection of poems and ethnographic detail on the traditions and customs of Tiflis.]

14. For a more complete discussion of these social changes, see Suny, *The Making of the Georgian Nation*, pp. 96–112, 144–156.

15. Bukhnikashvili, *Gori*, p. 73.

16. A. L. Zisserman, *Dvadtsat' piat let na Kavkaze. 1842–1867*, I (Saint Petersburg, 1879), p. 10; for a discussion of Europeanization in Georgia, see N. G. Volkova and G. N. Dzhavakhishvili, *Bytovaia kul'tura Gruzii XIX–XX vekov: Traditsii i innovatsii* (Moscow: Nauka, 1982), pp. 185–195.

17. Joseph Davrichewy, *Ah! Ce qu'on rigolait bien avec mon copain Staline* (Paris: Éditions Jean-Claude Simoën, 1979), pp. 62–63. A Georgian, whose last name (Davrishashvili) had been Russified as was often the case in the mid-nineteenth century, Davrishev grew up with Stalin in Gori. He was the son of the prefect of police of Gori and his Armenian wife. He later joined the Georgian Socialist Federalist Party, a rival to the Social Democratic Party to which Stalin adhered, and was very active in the 1905 revolution in Georgia before immigrating to France. He first wrote his memoirs in the 1930s, but publication was hindered by the Soviet embassy in France, a representative of which convinced Davrishev to send his manuscript to the Soviet Union. It was never returned, and after meeting another boyhood friend from Gori, David Machavariani, in 1950, he wrote his memoirs again, using material from his friend. That manuscript was turned over to a publisher in 1965, but the author died two years later, and the publication was delayed until 1979. Despite its checkered publication history, Davrishev's memoir appears to me to be reliable for the most part. Even though he promotes his friend Koba to a more prominent position in Georgian Social Democracy than warranted, he nevertheless

provides a picture that conforms closely to other sources. My thanks to Claire Mouradian for alerting me to this memoir.

18. Kaminskii and Vereshchagin, "Detstvo i iunost' vozhdia," p. 24.

19. Ibid. The daughter is not mentioned in this source but by Kun, *Stalin: An Unknown Portrait*, p. 10.

20. Osetins speak an Indo-European language related to Iranian and live on both sides of the Caucasus Mountains. Iremashvili is the source for the many rumors that Beso Jughashvili was an Osetin, rather than a pure Georgian, and believes that his origin accounts for his crudeness and lack of culture (Iremaschwili, *Stalin und die Tragödie Georgiens*, p. 12). It is impossible to verify the question of Beso's ethnic origins, but the account by a Georgian patriot who might wish to exonerate the Georgian people of the crimes of their most infamous son makes this particular claim highly suspect. Beso's ancestors came from a village in the north of Georgia that was at times beset by Osetins, and the available sources indicate that he identified as a Georgian. In her memoir Keke Jughashvili never mentioned that her husband Beso was Osetin.

21. Ostrovskii, *Kto stoial za spinoi Stalina*, p. 86.

22. Kaminskii and Vereshchagin, "Detstvo i iunost' vozhdia," pp. 24–25; Simon Ter-Petrosian (Kamo), *Stalin: Moi tovarishch i nastavnik* (Moscow: Iauza-Press, 2017), p. 12. This last work is a purported memoir of Kamo written just before his death in 1922 on the suggestion of Maxim Gorky. It appeared only after the disintegration of the Soviet Union, having been preserved by a friend, Irakli Kapanadze, and his relatives. Like many memoirs about Stalin, suspicions exist about its veracity. Olga Edelman believes it is a fraud, and parts of it read like the standard hagiography of the Stalinist era. But other parts, interspersed throughout, appear authentic and may be the original bits of Kamo's own hand before Kapanadze or someone else edited and supplemented his text. I have used material from Kamo's memoirs that appear plausible and in most cases are confirmed by other sources.

23. *saarkivo moambe/The Archival Bulletin*, no. 1 (April 2008), p. 45.

24. In Tiflis province only nine percent of women could read (twenty-seven percent of town women and only two percent of country women). [*Pervaia vseobshchaia perepis' naseleniia rossiiskoi imperii, 1897 g. Pod redaktsiei N. A. Troinitskogo. Obshchii svod po imperii rezultatov razrabotki dannykh pervoi vseobshchei perepisi naseleniia, proizvedennoi 28 ianvaria 1897 goda*, 2 volumes (Saint Petersburg: TsSKMVD, 1905), p. xii.]

25. *Karachokhelebi* were known for their knightly qualities, but they were not an order of knights by definition. The word *karachokheli* means a man in a black *chokha* (a combination of the Persian word *kara*, which means "black," and *chokha*, traditional Georgian apparel). Another pronunciation of this word is *karachekheli*, but Keke uses *karachegeli*. [Ostrovskii, *Kto stoial za spinoi Stalina*, p. 88; Kaminskii and Vereshchagin, "Detstvo i iunost' vozhdia," p. 26; Grishashvili, *Literaturnaia bogema starogo Tiflisa*, p. 13.

26. Mariia (Masho) Kirillovna Abramidze-Tsikhitatrishvili, "Vospominaniia o sem'e Vissariona Dzhugashvili," SShSSA, f. 8, op. 2, ch. 1, d. 1, l. 143. Born in 1860 in Gori, Mariia Abramidze-Tsikhitatrishvili knew Glakho Geladze's family from her childhood.

27. Ostrovskii, *Kto stoial za spinoi Stalina*, p. 93; memoir of David Gasitashvili, SShSSA, f. 8, op. 2, ch. 1, d. 8, ll. 196, 200.

28. Ekaterine Giorgis asuli Jughashvili, "chemi mogonebani," SShSSA, f. 8, op. 2, ch. 1, d. 15, l. 7.

29. Ibid., l. 8.

30. Mariia (Masho) Kirillovna Abramidze-Tsikhitatrishvili, "Vospominaniia o seme Vissariona Dzhugashvili," SShSSA, f. 8, op. 2, ch. 1, d. 1, l. 144; Aleksandr Mikhailovich Tsikhitatrishvili, "Vospominaniia o tovarishche Staline," RGASPI, f. 558, op. 4, d. 665, l. 107.

31. Mariia (Masho) Kirillovna Abramidze-Tsikhitatrishvili, "Vospominaniia o seme Vissariona Dzhugashvili," SShSSA, f. 8, op. 2, ch. 1, d. 1, l. 144.

32. Ekaterine Giorgis asuli Jughashvili, "chemi mogonebani," SShSSA, f. 8, op. 2, ch. 1, d. 15, ll. 10–13. Today there is a monument in the city of Mtskheta to Arsena.

33. Ostrovskii, *Kto stoial za spinoi Stalina*, p. 94.

34. Mariia (Masho) Kirillovna Abramidze-Tsikhitatrishvili, "Vospominaniia o seme Vissariona Dzhugashvili," SShSSA, f. 8, op. 2, ch. 1, d. 1, l. 144.

35. Ekaterine Giorgis asuli Jughashvili, "chemi mogonebani," SShSSA, f. 8, op. 2, ch. 1, d. 15, ll. 10–11.

36. Mariia (Masho) Kirillovna Abramidze-Tsikhitatrishvili, "Vospominaniia o seme Vissariona Dzhugashvili," SShSSA, f. 8, op. 2, ch. 1, d. 1, l. 143b.

37. Davrichewy, *Ah! Ce qu'on rigolait bien avec mon copain Staline*, pp. 60–61.

38. Kote Charkviani, "Vospominaniia," SShSSA, f. 8, op. 2, ch. 1, d. 54, ll. 202–205.

39. G. Elisabedashvili, "Vospominaniia," SSM, f. 3, ch. 1, d. 1955–146, ll. 6–7.

40. Ekaterine Giorgis asuli Jughashvili, "chemi mogonebani," SShSSA, f. 8, op. 2, ch. 1, d. 15, l. 19.

41. Ibid., ll. 24, 26–28; Ostrovskii, *Kto stoial za spinoi Stalina*, pp. 103–105.

42. Ekaterine Giorgis asuli Jughashvili, "chemi mogonebani," SShSSA, f. 8, op. 2, ch. 1, d. 15, ll. 12–17.

43. On the concepts of honor and shame, see J. G. Peristiany (ed.), *Honour and Shame: The Values of Mediterranean Society* (Chicago: University of Chicago Press, 1966). Some ethnographers a generation ago characterized cultures in the Mediterranean and Middle East, Georgia among them, as honor and shame societies. "Honour," writes one anthropologist, "is the value of a person in his own eyes, but also in the eyes of his society. It is his estimation of his own worth, his *claim* to pride, but it is also the acknowledgement of that claim, his excellence recognized by society, his *right* to pride." [Julian P. H. Pitt-Rivers, "Honour and Social Status," in Peristiany (ed.), *Honour and Shame*, p. 21.] But the idea of honor differs from society to society, and even between social groups within a society. In some it is tied to wealth; in others the poor possess their own kind of honor. Yet in general honor supposes a moral or material hierarchy: honor distinguishes some people from others and places them in a higher (or lower) relationship to others. [Pierre Bourdieu, "The Sentiment of Honour in Kabyle Society," in Peristiany (ed.), *Honour and Shame*, p. 228.] While it is difficult to characterize a whole society as centered around honor and shame, language and behavior in many societies, Georgian and Caucasian more broadly, often employ such notions.

44. Iremaschwili, *Stalin und die Tragödie Georgiens*, p. 10.

45. Yochanan Altman, "A Reconstruction, Using Anthropological Methods, of the Second Economy of Soviet Georgia," PhD dissertation, Centre of Occupational and Community Research, Middlesex Polytechnic, 1983, chapter 4, p. 9.

46. Iremaschwili, *Stalin und die Tragödie Georgiens*, pp. 8–11.

47. English translation by Venera Urushadze, *Anthology of Georgian Poetry* (Tbilisi: Sabchota Sakartvelo, 1958), p. 57. Ilia Chavchavadze (1837–1907) was one of the leading figures in the Georgian national movement of the nineteenth century. Educated in Russia, he founded the newspaper *iveria* and the Georgian National Bank. Toward the end of his life he became more conservative, served in the Russian State Council, and stoked the anti-Armenian sentiments of nationalistic Georgians. Yet during Soviet times he was revered as a Georgian patriot; his statue stood on the main street in Tbilisi, and in 1987 he was canonized by the Georgian Orthodox Church as Saint Ilia the Righteous (*tsminda ilia martali*).

48. "Vospominanie o Staline tov. S. Goglichidze (1932 g.), byvshyi pedagog," SEA, f. 2417, op. 1, d. 211, ll. 1–16. [The original is in handwritten Georgian; the author has a Russian translation.]

49. Svetlana Allilueva, *Dvadtsat' pisem k drugu* (New York: Harper & Row, 1967), p. 145. [English translation: Svetlana Allilueva, *Twenty Letters to a Friend* (New York: Harper & Row, 1967).]

50. "Neopublikovannye materialy iz biografii tovarishcha Stalina," *Antireligioznik*, no. 12 (1939), p. 19.

51. "Vospominanie o Staline tov. S. Goglichidze."

52. Allilueva, *Dvadtsat' pisem*, p. 145.

53. In the post-Soviet period Georgian scholars began to examine the *supra* as an element of civil society, and a few questioned its antiquity, seeing it as an "invented tradition" of the late nineteenth century. See Gia Nodia, *kartuli supra da samokalako sazogadoeba* (Tbilisi: mshvido-bis, demokratiisa da ganvitarebis kavkasiuri instituti, 2000); Paul Manning, "Socialist *supras* and Drinking Democratically: Changing Images of the Georgian Feast and Georgian Society from Socialism to Post-Socialism" (http://www.dangerserviceagency.org/cv.html#4); and his *Semiotics of Drink and Drinking* (London and New York: Continuum, 2012), pp. 148–176.

54. Much useful information on the history and customs of Gori can be found in Bukhni-kashvili, *Gori: Istoricheskii ocherk*.

55. Ibid., p. 11.

56. Davrichewy, *Ah! Ce qu'on rigolait bien avec mon copain Staline*, p. 74.

57. Kote Charkviani, "Vospominaniia," SShSSA, f. 8, op. 2, ch. 1, d. 54, ll. 206–207.

58. Allilueva, *Dvadtsat' pisem'*, p. 313; *Twenty Letters*, p. 360.

59. Davrichewy, *Ah! Ce qu'on rigolait bien avec mon copain Staline*, pp. 27, 30.

60. I. V. Stalin, *Sochineniia* (Moscow, 1946–1952), I, pp. 314–315.

61. Simon Ter-Petrosian (1888–1922) (Kamo) was born in Gori, remained close to Stalin most of his life, and was a simple soldier of the revolutionary movement. His audacity, frequent escapes, and simulated madness while in captivity enhanced his legend. He was a master of disguise and is treated in the literature as a romantic figure. But his role should not be exaggerated. He was one of the rank-and-file fighters among the revolutionaries, not the acknowledged leader in all instances. Kamo was killed while riding his bicycle in Tiflis.

62. Ter-Petrosian, *Stalin*, pp. 15–16.

63. Anna Andreevna Geladze-Nikitina, "Moi vospominaniia o Staline," SShSSA, f. 8, op. 2, ch. 1, d. 9, l. 21.

64. Kote Charkviani, "Vospominaniia," SShSSA, f. 8, op. 2, ch. 1, d. 54, ll. 212–213.

65. G. Elisabedashvili, "Vospominaniia," SSM, f. 3, ch. 1, d. 1955–146, ll. 22–23.

66. Iremaschwili, *Stalin und die Tragödie Georgiens*, p. 12; Allilueva, *Dvadtsat' pisem*, p. 145n.

67. Jerome Davis, *Behind Soviet Power: Stalin and the Russians* (New York: Readers' Press, 1946), p. 15.

68. Ekaterine Giorgis asuli Jughashvili, "chemi mogonebani," SShSSA, f. 8, op. 14, d. 160, ll. 1–8; Robert H. McNeal, *Stalin: Man and Ruler* (New York: New York University Press, 1988), p. 336, n. 15; Kun, *Stalin: An Unknown Portrait*, p. 18.

69. RGASPI, f. 71, op. 1, d. 275; Montefiore, *Young Stalin*, p. 184.

70. Allilueva, *Dvadtsat' pisem*, pp. 145, 189. The last line appears only in the English translation. [Allilueva, *Twenty Letters*, p. 204.]

CHAPTER 2. THE PUPIL

1. Davrichewy, *Ah! Ce qu'on rigolait bien avec mon copain Staline*, p. 49.

2. Ibid., p. 49.

3. "Neopublikovannye materialy iz biografii tovarishcha Stalina," p. 19.

4. Ibid., pp. 72–73.

5. Ibid., p. 76.

6. Iremaschwili, *Stalin und die Tragödie Georgiens*, p. 5.

7. Davrichewy, *Ah! Ce qu'on rigolait bien avec mon copain Staline*, pp. 38–39.

8. Radzinskii relates a memory by a boyhood friend of Soso's, Mikhail Peradze, about fights between the boys of the upper town (the poorer section) and the lower town (where merchants and better-off people lived). Though smaller than the others, Soso managed to come up behind stronger opponents. The source for this story, like others in the book, is not footnoted but appears to be from the Stalin *fond* in the Presidential Archive of the Russian Federation in which Radzinskii was permitted to work. [Radzinsky, *Stalin*, p. 28.]

9. Petr Kapanadze, "Soso Dzhugashvili-Stalin v goriskom dukhovnom uchilishche i v tbilisskoi dukhovnoi seminarii (Vospominaniia)," RGASPI, f. 558, op. 4, d. 665, ll. 89–90.

10. *Molokane* (milk-drinkers) are members of a Russian religious sect.

11. Davrichewy, *Ah! Ce qu'on rigolait bien avec mon copain Staline*, pp. 46–47.

12. Ibid., pp. 82–83.

13. For example, reminiscences published on the eve of World War II of the boy Stalin repeatedly mention that he sang in both Georgian and Russian and studied Russian very hard and with great success. This diligence in learning Russian served as an example to Soviet students at the very moment when Russian was being promoted by the state as the lingua franca of the USSR and a new law requiring non-Russians to study the language in school had been passed. ["Neopublikovannye materialy iz biografii tovarishcha Stalina," pp. 17–21.]

14. Davrichewy, *Ah! Ce qu'on rigolait bien avec mon copain Staline*, p. 70.

15. Georgii Fedorovich Vardoian, "Vospominaniia," SShSSA, f. 8, op. 2, ch. 1, d. 7, l. 64.

16. Maria Makharoblidze-Kubladze, "Vospominaniia," SShSSA, f. 8, op. 2, ch. 1, d. 9, ll. 257–258.

17. Iremaschwili, *Stalin und die Tragödie Georgiens*, p. 6.

18. Davrichewy, *Ah! Ce qu'on rigolait bien avec mon copain Staline*, p. 86.

19. Ibid., p. 53. Arsena was a social bandit (*qachaghi* in Georgian), a kind of Robin Hood. Half a century later, when Stalin ruled the Soviet Union, films were made in Georgia celebrating Arsena and Giorgi Saakadze (ca. 1570–1629). In 1940 Stalin commented that Saakadze was a progressive figure who fought for unification of Georgia and the absolutist power of the monarch against the princes. [Erik van Ree, *The Political Thought of Joseph Stalin: A Study in Twentieth-Century Revolutionary Patriotism* (London and New York: RoutledgeCurzon, 2002), p. 304, n. 35.] Tato Tsulikidze was a simple thief, not a social bandit who robbed from the rich and gave to the poor and was not celebrated in song. [See A. S. Frenkeliia, *K istorii razboia na Kavkaze: Tato Tsulukidze* (Tiflis, 1892); I thank Beka Kobakhidze for this last reference.]

20. Davrichewy, *Ah! Ce qu'on rigolait bien avec mon copain Staline*, pp. 65, 69. Davrishev mentions *tsnobis purtseli* (Newssheet), published from 1896 to 1906, as one of the newspapers that was read in Gori, but it began its run after Soso Jughashvili left for the Tiflis Seminary.

21. Ibid., pp. 39–40.

22. Anna Andreevna Geladze-Nikitina, "Moi vospominaniia o Staline," SShSSA, f. 8, p. 2, ch. 1, d. 9, ll. 19–20.

23. Kote Charkviani, "Vospominaniia," SShSSA, f. 8, op. 2, ch. 1, d. 54, l. 208.

24. "Vospominanie o Staline tov. S. Goglichidze (1932 g.), byvshyi pedagog," SEA, f. 2417, op. 1, d. 211, ll. 1–16. [The original is in handwritten Georgian; the author has a Russian translation.]

25. Sandro Solomonovich Elisabedashvili, "Vospominanie ob Iosife Vissarionoviche Staline," SShSSA, f. 8, op. 2, d. 16, l. 143.

26. Ibid., l. 144.

27. Davis, *Behind Soviet Power*, p. 15.

28. Sandro Solomonovich Elisabedashvili, "Vospominanie ob Iosife Vissarionoviche Staline," SShSSA, f. 8, op. 2, d. 16, ll. 145–146.

29. For a discussion of the concepts and practices of empires and nations, see Valerie A. Kivelson and Ronald Grigor Suny, *Russia's Empires* (New York: Oxford University Press, 2017), pp. 75–88.

30. See the chapter "Emancipation and the End of Seigneurial Georgia," in Suny, *The Making of the Georgian Nation*, pp. 96–112.

31. For an illuminating discussion of the Georgian intelligentsia's relationship with European modernity and Russian imperialism, see Paul Manning, *Strangers in a Strange Land: Occidentalist Publics and Orientalist Geographies in Nineteenth-Century Georgian Imaginaries* (Boston: Academic Studies Press, 2012).

32. Ekaterine Giorgis asuli Jughashvili, "chemi mogonebani," SShSSA, f. 8, op. 2, ch. 1, d. 15, l. 18.

33. "Vospominanie o Staline tov. S. Goglichidze."

34. See, for example, the programmatic article by Petre Umikashvili, "sakhalkho simgherebisa da zghaprebis shekreba [The Collection of Folk Songs and Tales]," *droeba*, no. 22 (1871); H. Paul Manning, "Describing Dialect and Defining Civilization in an Early Georgian Nationalist Manifesto: Ilia Ch'avch'avadze's 'Letters of a Traveler,'" *Russian Review*, LXIII, 1 (January 2004), p. 33.

35. Oliver Reisner, "The Tergdaleulebi: Founders of Georgian National Identity," in *Forms of Identity: Definitions and Changes*, ed. Ladislaus Löb, István Petrovics, and György E. Szonyi

(Szeged, Hungary: Attila Jozsef University, 1994), pp. 125–137; Reisner, "Die georgische Alpha-betisierungsgesellschaft: Schule nationaler Eliten und Vergemeinschaftung," *Jahrbücher für Geschichte Osteruropas* 48, no. 1 (2000), pp. 66–89; and Reisner, *Die Schule der Georgischen Nation: Eine sozialhistorische Untersuchung der nationalen Bewegung in Georgien am Beispiel der "Gesellschaft zur Verbreitung der Lese- und Schreibkunde unter den Georgiern" (1850–1917)* (Wiesbaden: Reichert Verlag, 2004).

36. For an extended treatment of the Georgian national movement, see James William Robert Parsons, "The Emergence and Development of the National Question in Georgia, 1801–1921," PhD dissertation in History, University of Glasgow, 1987; and Suny, *The Making of the Georgian Nation*, pp. 113–143.

37. Il. Chavchavadze, "zogierti ram," *droeba*, no. 24, March 7, 1876; cited in Austin Jersild and Neli Melkadze, "The Dilemmas of Enlightenment in the Eastern Borderlands: The Theater and Library in Tiflis," *Kritika* 3, no. 1 (2002), p. 38.

38. Davrichewy, *Ah! Ce qu'on rigolait bien avec mon copain Staline*, pp. 60–61.

39. Ostrovskii, *Kto stoial za spinoi Stalina*, p. 97.

40. "Vospominanie o Staline tov. S. Goglichidze."

41. Ibid.

42. Petr Adamishvili, "Tovarishch Stalin v Goriiskom dukhovnom uchilishche," SShSSA, f. 8, op. 2. ch. 1, d. 1, ll. 226–235, 238–239.

43. Davrichewy, *Ah! Ce qu'on rigolait bien avec mon copain Staline*, p. 71.

44. Adamishvili, "Tovarishch Stalin v Goriiskom dukhovnom uchilishche," SShSSA, f. 8, op. 2. ch. 1, d. 1, ll. 226–235, 238–239.

45. Mikhail Agursky, "Stalin's Ecclesiastical Background," *Survey* XXVIII, no. 4 (Winter 1984), p. 2.

46. Reported by David Machavariani to Davrishev. [Davrichewy, *Ah! Ce qu'on rigolait bien avec mon copain Staline*, p. 47.]

47. Ostrovskii, *Kto stoial za spinoi Stalina*, p. 102; A. Gogebashvili, "Vospominaniia" SShSSA, f. 8, op. 2, ch. 1, d. 89, l. 2.

48. The Russian writer Maxim Gorky witnessed the same public execution in Gori on February 13, 1892; [*Nizhegorodskii listok* (1896); Bukhnikashvili, *Gori*, p. 85; Boris Piradov, "K istorii rannikh revoliutsionnykh sviazei A. M. Gor'kogo (Gruziia, 1891–1892), in *Stat'i o Gor'kom: Sbornik* (Moscow: Gosudarstvennoe izdatel'stvo khudozhestvennoi literatury, 1957), pp. 70–75.]

49. "Neopublikovannye materialy iz biografii tovarishcha Stalina," p. 20; McNeal, *Stalin*, p. 5. For a different version of this episode, see *Stalin: K shestidesiatiletiiu* (Moscow: Khudoshchest-vennaia literatura, 1940), p. 20.

50. Mariia (Masho) Kirillovna Abramidze-Tsikhitatrishvili, "Vospominaniia o seme Vissari-ona Dzhugashvili," SShSSA, f. 8, op. 2, ch. 1, d. 1, l. 146.

51. Davrichewy, *Ah! Ce qu'on rigolait bien avec mon copain Staline*, p. 59. Davrishev has an account of the execution, though his father prevented him from witnessing it.

52. Reported to Davrishev by Machavariani, a boyhood friend who later grew hostile to Stalin and immigrated to Turkey. [Davrichewy, *Ah! Ce qu'on rigolait bien avec mon copain Staline*, pp. 47–48.]

53. "Neopublikovannye materialy iz biografii tovarishcha Stalina," p. 19; Grisha Glurjidze, "Vospominaniia," SShSSA, f. 8, op. 2, ch. 1, d. 9, ll. 159–160; McNeal, *Stalin*, p. 4.

54. Davrichewy, *Ah! Ce qu'on rigolait bien avec mon copain Staline*, p. 93.

55. One other memoir, by Giorgi Elisabedashvili, also claims that Soso "was not a believer." [G. Elisabedashvili, "Vospominaniia," SSM, f. 3, ch. 1, d. 1955–146, l. 6; "Moi vospominaniia o tovarishche Staline," RGASPI, f. 558, op. 4, d. 665.] The bulk of the evidence, however, suggests that Soso did not abandon his faith until he had entered the Tiflis Seminary.

56. Olga Maiorova, *From the Shadow of Empire: Defining the Russian Nation through Cultural Mythology, 1855–1870* (Madison: University of Wisconsin Press, 2010); Kivelson and Suny, *Russia's Empires*, pp. 140–226.

57. For an account of education at the Gori church school in the 1860s, see Sofrom Mgalob-lishvili, *Vospominaniia o moei zhizni* (Tbilisi: Merani, 1974).

58. Theorists of nationalism have long emphasized the importance of social communication in the development of a sense of nation. Among the most important works in this genre are: Karl Deutsch, *Nationalism and Social Communication: An Inquiry into the Foundations of Nationality* (Cambridge, MA: MIT Press, 1953); Ernest Gellner, *Nations and Nationalism* (Oxford: Basil Blackwell, 1983); and Benedict Anderson, *Imagined Communities: Reflections on the Origin and Spread of Nationalism* (London and New York: Verso Books, 1991). See also the review of scholarly treatment about nationalism by Geoff Eley and Ronald Grigor Suny, "Introduction: From the Moment of Social History to the Work of Cultural Representation," in Eley and Suny (eds.), *Becoming National, A Reader* (New York: Oxford University Press, 1996), pp. 3–37.

59. Kote Charkviani, "Vospominaniia," SShSSA, f. 8, op. 2, ch. 1, d. 54, ll. 207–208.

60. Kaminskii and Vereshchagin, "Detstvo i iunost' vozhdia," pp. 41–42. Iremaschwili, *Stalin und die Tragödie Georgiens*, p. 7–8.

61. "Vospominanie o Staline tov. S. Goglichidze."

62. Kaminskii and Vereshchagin, "Detstvo i iunost' vozdia," p. 39.

63. Sandro Solomonovich Elisabedashvili, "Vospominanie ob Iosife Vissarionoviche Staline," SShSSA, f. 8, op. 2, d. 16, ll. 147–149.

64. Ostrovskii, *Kto stoial za spinoi Stalina*, p. 102; A. Gogebashvili, "Vospominaniia," SShSSA, f. 8, op. 2, ch. 1, d. 89, l. 3.

65. Ostrovskii, *Kto stoial za spinoi Stalina*, p. 98.

66. I. Z. Ketskoveli, "Nekotorye epizody iz zhizni i deiatel'nosti Lado," in Zinaida Gegeshidze, N. V. Sturua, and Sh. I. Chivadze (eds.), *Lado Ketskhoveli: Sbornik dokumentov i materialov* (Tbilisi: Sabchota Sakartvelo, 1969), pp. 107–108.

67. RGASPI, f. 71, op. 10, d. 404.

68. Ibid.; Marekh Khutsishvili, "A Love of Justice," *gamarjveba* (Gori), December 21, 1979, p. 2; article translated in *Joint Publications Research Service Reports* [JPRS], no. 75784 (May 29, 1980), "USSR Report: Political and Sociological Affairs," no. 1037, pp. 45–46.

69. "Vospominanie o Staline tov. S. Goglichidze."

70. Populism (*narodnichestvo*) was a radical political movement that attracted young people in the Russian Empire in the last third of the nineteenth century with its faith in the possibility of peasant revolution and the creation of a village-based socialism that avoided capitalism.

71. Donald Rayfield, *The Literature of Georgia: A History*, 2nd, revised edition (Surrey, UK: Curzon Press, 2000), pp. 153–154.

CHAPTER 3. KOBA

1. Davrichewy, *Ah! Ce qu'on rigolait bien avec mon copain Staline*, pp. 65–66.

2. My father, George (Gurken) Suny, repeatedly told me about the songs of the *kintos*.

3. James Bryce, *Transcaucasia and Ararat: Notes of a Vacation Tour in 1876* [3rd edition] (London: Macmillian and Co., 1878), pp. 155–156. Bryce (1838–1922) was a historian and diplomat, the author of *The American Commonwealth* (1888) and later Britain's ambassador to the United States (1907–1913). As Viscount Bryce, he was the responsible editor of *The Treatment of Armenians in the Ottoman Empire, 1915–16: Documents Presented to Viscount Grey of Fallodon, Secretary of State for Foreign Affairs* (London: Hodder & Stoughton, 1916), the major British indictment of the Ottoman deportations and massacres of Armenians during World War I.

4. Manning, *Strangers in a Strange Land*, p. 18.

5. Ekaterine Giorgis asuli Jughashvili, "chemi mogonebani," SShSSA, f. 8, op. 2, ch. 1, d. 15, l. 30.

6. Ibid., l. 31.

7. Ibid., ll. 32–33.

8. "Vospominanie o Staline tov. S. Goglichidze."

9. Ekaterine Giorgis asuli Jughashvili, "chemi mogonebani," SShSSA, f. 8, op. 2, ch. 1, d. 15, ll. 33–34.

10. Seid Devdariani, "Soso Stalin v Tbilisskoi seminarii," SShSSA, f. 8, op. 2, ch. 1, d. 12, l. 176; Ostrovskii, *Kto stoial za spinoi Stalina*, p. 112. Devdariani's memoirs were written in 1935.

11. Mikheil Davitashvili was a close associate of Jughashvili's until his death in 1916 in World War I.

12. "Rustaveli's chivalrous ideal puts male friendship and courtly love on the same plane." [Donald Rayfield, *The Literature of Georgia: A History* (Oxford: Clarendon Press, 1994), p. 77.]

13. On the psychological effects of intergroup relations, see Henri Tajfel and John C. Turner, "The Social Identity Theory of Intergroup Behavior," in W. G. Austin and S. Worchel (eds.), *The Social Psychology of Intergroup Relations* (Monterey, CA: Brooks Cole, 1981), pp. 10–11.

14. Altman, "A Reconstruction, Using Anthropological Methods," ch. 4, p. 16. Much of the discussion here of patterns of Georgian friendship is indebted to the fieldwork and analysis of Altman, who worked among Georgian Jews who had immigrated to Israel. Altman's findings confirm and corroborate my own observations and experiences during visits and research stays in Georgia (1966, 1972, 1975–1976, 1988, 2008, 2012, 2017, and 2018), as well as conclusions reached from reading Georgian historical and literary texts.

15. For histories of the Tiflis Seminary, see Karlo Chelidze, *tbilisis sasuliero seminarias revolutsiuri tsarsulidan* (Tbilisi: tbilisis universitetis gamomtsemloba, 1988); and Z. Chikviladze, "tp. sasuliero seminaria gasuli saukunis me-80 tslebshi," *revoliutsiis matiane*, 1924, no. 4, pp. 143–150.

16. SSSA, f. 440 [Tiflisskaia dukhovnaia seminariia], op. 2, d. 1, l. 26.

17. Davrichewy, *Ah! Ce qu'on rigolait bien avec mon copain Staline*, p. 116.

18. RGASPI, f. 558, op. 1, d. 4325, ll. 1–2; Edelman, *Stalin: Biografiia v dokumentakh*, p. 41; Kun, *Stalin: An Unknown Portrait*, pp. 22–23. Seraphim was rector of the seminary in 1894–1895 and 1897–1899; Father Dmitrii acted as rector in between. Father Germogen (Georgii Dolganov) succeeded Seraphim and later served as metropolitan of Tsaritsyn, and in Saratov.

19. RGASPI, f. 558, op. 1, d. 4324, ll. 1–2; d. 4326, ll. 1–2; Edelman, *Stalin: Biografiia v doku-mentakh*, pp. 42–43, 46; Kun, *Stalin: An Unknown Portrait*, p. 13; Ostrovskii, *Kto stoial za spinoi Stalina*, p. 125.

20. RGASPI, f. 440, op. 2, d. 1, l. 16; f. 440, op. 3, d. 3, l. 255; f. 440, op. 3, d. 4, l. 36a.

21. Kun, *Stalin: An Unknown Portrait*, pp. 23–24; Kun writes that the original of this document is in the archive of Bishop Germogen in the Saratov State Archive and was published in "a collection of sources" on Stalin, 1951, pp. 30–31, but the bibliographical reference is incomplete.

22. Kote Charkviani memoirs, SShSSA, f. 8, op. 2, ch. 1, d. 54, ll. 209–211.

23. *Iveria* (Iberia, Hiberia) is what the ancient Greeks called eastern Georgia, and it is used frequently to refer to Georgia. In Georgian, Georgia is *sakartvelo*.

24. The poem was first published in *iveria*, no. 123, June 14, 1895. *deda ena* was first compiled by the grammarian Iakob Gogebashvili, who died in 1912; Stalin's poem was selected by his successor and published in the 1916 edition. [Donald Rayfield, "Stalin the Poet," *Poetry Nation Review*, no. 41 (1984), pp. 44–47.]

25. Translation by the author. For the original Georgian and a translation, see Robert Payne, *The Rise and Fall of Stalin* (New York: Simon and Schuster, 1965), p. 47; or Rayfield, "Stalin the Poet," p. 44. Stalin's poems have been published in Georgian, with inadequate English translations, in *ioseb stalinis—soselos leksebi* (Tbilisi, 1999).

26. First published in *iveria*, no. 218, October 11, 1895, and signed "*soselo.*"

27. First published in *iveria*, no. 203, November 28, 1895; translation by Rayfield, "Stalin as Poet," p. 45.

28. Published in *iveria*, no. 280, December 25, 1895; translation by Rayfield, "Stalin as Poet," p. 45.

29. Stalin's poetry is discussed by Rayfield, *The Literature of Georgia*, pp. 182–184.

30. First published in *iveria*, no. 234, October 29, 1895. See also M. Kelendzheridze, "Stikhi iunogo Stalina," *Rasskazy o velikom Staline*, II (Tbilisi: Zaria vostoka, 1941), pp. 67–70. Jughashvili's poem honoring Eristavi was reprinted in a jubilee collection in 1899 that also included poems by Chavchavadze and Akaki Tsereteli. Two poems of Jughashvili were reprinted in Kelenjeridze's *teoria sitqvierebisa kartuli saliteraturo samagalito nimushebis garchevit* [The Theory of Literature with a Selection of Exemplary Models of Georgian Literature] (Kutaisi, 1899). In 1907 Kelenjeridze included the verses to Eristavi in his *kartuli krestomatia* [Georgian Collection of Readings].

31. I. G. Tsereteli, "Zametka o stikhotvorenii Stalina, 1895 g.," HIA, Nikolaevsky Collection, no. 15, box 10, item 79.

32. Russian translations of Stalin's poems are available in I. V. Stalin, *Sochineniia. Tom 17, 1895–1932* (Tver': Severnaia korona, 2004), pp. 1–6.

33. This poem was signed "*sozeli,*" *kvali*, no. 32, July 28, 1896, p. 574. An English translation can be found by Rayfield, "Stalin as Poet," p. 46.

34. V. S. Bakhtadze, *Ocherki po istorii gruzinskoi obshchestvenno-ekonomicheskoi mysli (60–90 gody XIX stoletiia)* (Tbilisi: Izdatel'stvo Tbiliskogo gosudarstvennogo universiteta, 1960), p. 166.

35. While almost all biographers of Stalin believe him to be the author of the six poems attributed to him, one writer seriously doubts his authorship. "If Stalin wrote the poems attributed to him, they show not only that he possessed an impressive style never later manifested, but that

his character changed radically." [Edward Ellis Smith, *The Young Stalin: The Early Years of an Elusive Revolutionary* (New York: Farrar, Straus, and Giroux, 1967), p. 42.] There is, however, little doubt that Stalin wrote these poems and later, when his interests changed, abandoned poetry altogether.

36. For an excellent discussion of this important work, see H. Paul Manning, "Describing Dialect and Defining Civilization," pp. 26–47.

37. Ostrovskii, *Kto stoial za spinoi Stalina*, p. 111; *Molodaia gvardiia*, 1939, no. 12, p. 65.

38. I. V. Stalin, *Sochineniia*, XIII, pp. 113–114.

39. Agursky, "Stalin's Ecclesiastical Background," p. 2–3. Agursky carefully documents the high degree of right-wing sentiment and Russian chauvinism among Russian priests in Georgia. Archbishop Vladimir, later as metropolitan of Moscow, as well as other priests who served in Georgia—the exarch Archbishop Flavian (Gorodetskii) (1898–1901), the rector of the seminary Archimandrite Germogen (Dolganev) (1898–1900) and his successor Archimandrite Stefan (Arkhangelskii), and Archpriest Ioann Vostorgov, at one point in charge of Georgian ecclesiastical schools—all became members of the reactionary and chauvinistic "Black Hundreds" movements, even to the point of joining the Union of the Russian People and/or the Union of the Archangel Michael.

40. Z. G. Porakishvili, "Lado v tiflisskoi dukhovnoi seminarii," in *Lado Ketskhoveli*, pp. 121–122.

41. *Iz vospominanii russkago uchitelia Pravoslavnoi Gruzinskoi Dukhovnoi Seminarii* (Moscow, 1907), p. 6.

42. P. Makharadze, "rogor gavkhdi marksisti. (chemi mogonebata erti gverdi)," *revoliutsiis matiane*, 1923, no. 1 (March), p. 80.

43. Iremaschwili, *Stalin und die Tragödie Georgiens*, p. 17. Devdariani (1879–1937) later became a Menshevik.

44. Devdariani, "Soso Stalin," SShSSA, f. 8, op. 2, ch. 1, d. 12, l. 176.

45. David, Prince Abashidze, took the name Dmitrii when he became a monk. Though himself a Georgian noble, he was known as fanatically Orthodox and pro-Russian. In 1900 he became rector of the Aleksandrovsk Missionary Seminary, and three years later moved to Poti on the Black Sea. In 1905 he was recalled from Georgia and later served in Ukraine, Tashkent, and from 1913 as bishop of Simferopol. In 1917 he was the only Georgian clergyman who refused to recognize the autocephaly of the Georgian Church. Although he supported the Whites in the Civil War, he continued as a monk in Kiev through the 1920s and survived the Great Purges when the Kievan clergy was decimated. [Agursky, "Stalin's Ecclesiastical Background," pp. 9–11.] He died in December 1943 and was canonized as Saint Antonii by the Russian Orthodox Church in 2012. [I thank Beka Kobakhidze for this information.]

46. "Vospominaniia Seida Devdariani" [an interview with Melikhov, June 7, 1936], SShSSA, f. 8, op. 2, ch. 1, d. 12, l. 210; D. Gogokhiia, "Na vsiu zhizn' zapomnilis' eti dni," *Rasskazy starykh rabochikh Zakavkaz'iia o velikom Staline* (Moscow: Molodaia gvardiia, 1937), p. 13.

47. G. Parkadze, "Iz vospominanii o nelegalnykh stalinskikh kruzhkakh," *Zaria vostoka*, no. 46, February 26, 1939; Kaminskii and Vereshchagin, "Detstvo i iunost' vozhdia," p. 71. See also Devdariani's memoirs in RGASPI, f. 558, op. 1, d. 665. Zakaria Chichinadze, a pioneer in the Georgian workers' movement, published the works of progressive Georgian authors and lent

out books. "Chichinadze's ability to survive as a publisher of new popular literature was an indication of growing levels of literacy among Georgian urban youth. Censorship of Georgian materials was lax. His bookshop and publishing house—which produced most of the *tergdaleulni*'s works—along with the editorial offices of *kvali* and *iveria*, became the gathering place for seminarians. [Stephen F. Jones, *Socialism in Georgian Colors: The European Road to Social Democracy, 1883–1917* (Cambridge, MA, and London: Harvard University Press, 2005), p. 53.]

48. Devdariani, "Soso Stalin," SShSSA, f. 8, op. 2, ch. 1, d. 12, l. 177.

49. Ibid., l. 178.

50. Iremaschwili, *Stalin und die Tragödie Georgiens*, p. 18.

51. Ibid., f. 440, op. 2, d. 5, l. 122.

52. Ibid., f. 440, op. 2, d. 3544, l. 2 ob.

53. Ibid.

54. Iremashvili jumbles the story of Koba somewhat, and several biographers, including Trotsky, have followed his account. But their emphasis, perfectly correctly, was on Koba's struggle against tsarist oppression and his love for his homeland. Robert C. Tucker, one of the few biographers of Stalin who made the effort to read the original story (in translation), was struck less by the "nationalistic romanticism" and more by "the theme of vengeance [that] runs through the novel like a red thread. . . . To a boy of Soso's background who longed to be a new Koba, [the story] could suggest—or at any rate prepare the mind for—a vision of the hero as revolutionary." [Robert C. Tucker, *Stalin as Revolutionary, 1879–1929* (New York: W. W. Norton, 1988), pp. 80–82.]

55. From his "Shepherd Memoirs," translated and reprinted in Aleksandr Kazbegi, *Izbrannoe* (Tbilisi: merani, 1974), p. 14.

56. The Georgian original of the story can be found in *kartuli proza, XI: aleksandre qazbegi, motkhrobebi* (Tbilisi: sabchota sakartvelo, 1986), pp. 180–425.

57. Imam Shamil (1797–1871), an Avar, was the leader of an anti-tsarist rebellion in the North Caucasus from 1834 to 1859. A revered figure among the Chechen and Daghestani peoples, Shamil was also admired as a courageous warrior by the Russians.

58. Armenians, who have historically endured multiple massacres and deportations, as well as genocide in the early twentieth century, have used the word *vrezh* (revenge) as a name for male children.

59. For a discussion of Russian literary treatment of the Caucasus, see Susan Layton, *Russian Literature and Empire: Conquest of the Caucasus from Pushkin to Tolstoy* (Cambridge: Cambridge University Press, 1994); and Harsha Ram, *The Imperial Sublime: A Russian Poetics of Empire* (Madison: University of Wisconsin Press, 2006). Also, see Susan Layton, "The Creation of an Imaginative Caucasian Geography," *Slavic Review* XLV, no. 3 (Fall 1986), pp. 470–485; and Agil' Gadzhiev, *Kavkaz v russkoi literature pervoi poloviny XIX veka* (Baku: Novaia tipografiia, 1982).

60. The idea of a "realization crisis"—the decline in capacity to realize the form of life dictated by the dominant values of one's society—has been taken from Judith Stacey, *Patriarchy and Socialist Revolution in China* (Berkeley: University of California Press, 1983).

CHAPTER 4. APPRENTICE OF THE REVOLUTION

1. On the transformation of young people in the Russian Empire to revolutionary engagement, see Susan K. Morrissey, *Heralds of Revolution: Russian Students and the Mythologies of Radicalism* (New York: Oxford University Press, 1998); Marina Mogilner, *Mifologiia podpol'nogo cheloveka': Radikal'nyi mikrokosm v Rossii nachala XX veka kak predmet semioticheskogo analiza* (Moscow: NLO, 1999); and Yuri Slezkine, *The House of Government: A Family Saga of the Russian Revolution* (Princeton, NJ: Princeton University Press, 2017).

2. On Lenin's early life, see A. I. Ul'ianova-Elizarova, *O Lenine i sem'e Ul'ianovykh. Vospominaniia, ocherki, pis'ma, stat'i* (Moscow: Politicheskaia literatura, 1988); and Robert Service, *Lenin: A Biography* (Cambridge, MA: Harvard University Press, 2000), pp. 13–90.

3. Zhordania became the acknowledged leader of the Georgian Mensheviks, a member of the Russian State Duma, and the prime minister of independent Georgia (1918–1921); Makharadze was a prominent figure among Georgian Bolsheviks and one of the leaders of the republic after the Sovietization of the country in 1921.

4. *kvali*, no. 22, May 22, 1894.

5. *moambe*, 1894, nos. 5–6. For more complete discussions of the conflicts in Georgian intellectual life at the end of the nineteenth century, see Parsons, "The Emergence and Development of the National Question in Georgia," pp. 298–321; and Suny, *The Making of the Georgian Nation*, chapter 6, "The Emergence of Political Society," pp. 113–143.

6. *moambe*, 1894, nos. 5–6.

7. Grigorii Uratadze, *Vospominaniia gruzinskogo sotsial-demokrata* (Stanford, CA: Hoover Institution, 1968), p. 11.

8. The Populist movement (*narodnichestvo*) in Russia was a radical pro-peasant association of revolutionaries who favored preserving the peasant commune and relied on peasants primarily as a revolutionary force to overthrow tsarism. It should not be confused with other usages of the word "populism" in other countries. Even the Populists of the 1870s, who favored peasant revolution and refused any privileged role for industrial workers, acquired their image of Western capitalism from Marx and helped to propagate his ideas. [A. Walicki, *The Controversy over Capitalism: Studies in the Social Philosophy of the Russian Populists* (Oxford: Oxford University Press, 1969), p. 132.] They concluded that the vicious social system described by Marx ought to be prevented from seeding itself in Russia and that "bourgeois" political forms, like parliamentary institutions so enamored by Russia's liberals, were a sham. Intervention in the processes of history by extraordinary individuals conscious of their moral and political goals could prevent the coming of capitalism and create the possibility in Russia of a peasant socialism based on the village commune. Walicki concludes that "Russian Populism was not only an ideological reaction to the development of capitalism *inside* Russia—it was also a reaction to the capitalist economy and socialist thought of the West," including the socialism of Marx. [Ibid., p. 26.]

9. Marx himself, writing from England, was less fatalistic than his followers in Russia and conceded to the Populists that Russia would be able, if it acted soon enough, to avoid "the same process of dissolution that constitutes the historical evolution of the West." But Plekhanov and his circle advanced their own highly determinist view that a bourgeois revolution and capitalism were inevitable in Russia. See the contrasting prefaces to the 1882 Russian edition of *The Communist Manifesto* by Marx and Plekhanov; for more on these variant interpretations of Marx's

analysis, see Teodor Shanin (ed.), *Late Marx and the Russian Road: Marx and the "Peripheries of Capitalism": A Case Presented by Teodor Shanin* (New York: Monthly Review Press, 1983).

10. Kaminskii and Vereshchagin, "Detstvo i iunost' vozhdia," p. 67.

11. Gogokhiia, "Na vsiu zhizn' zapomnilis' eti dni," p. 12.

12. Remembered by Grigori Razmadze, "Neopublikovannye materialy iz biografii tovarishcha Stalina," *Antireligioznik*, no. 12 (1939), p. 21.

13. Iremaschwili, *Stalin und die Tragödie Georgiens*, p. 20.

14. Slezkine, *The House of Government*, pp. 36–37.

15. Razmadze, "Neopublikovannye materialy iz biografii tovarishcha Stalina," p. 21.

16. Iremaschwili, *Stalin und die Tragödie Georgiens*, p. 16.

17. Ibid., p. 22.

18. P. Kapanadze, "Ia dolzhen uvidet' Lenina," *Rasskazy starykh rabochikh Zakavkaz'ia*, p. 26.

19. Devdariani, "Soso Stalin," SShSSA, f. 8, op. 2, ch. 1, d. 12, l. 180.

20. Ibid., l. 181. In his famous speech about Stalin's early revolutionary career, Beria spoke of two circles in the seminar, a senior and a junior one, but there are no sources corroborating such a pair. Moreover, he lists members of the junior circle who did not study at the seminary. [Ostrovskii, *Kto stoial za spinoi Stalina*, p. 128.] Iur'ev University, formerly Dorpat University, is now the University of Tartu, Estonia.

21. Ibid., p. 14. A late Soviet study of these "uncensored" periodicals in Georgia makes no mention of a journal edited by Jughashvili. The journals were usually literary outlets for poetry and stories composed by students in Georgian. A drawer (or box) was used as the "drop" for the unsigned articles, which the editor then gathered and copied in a notebook. [Sh. E. Gagoshidze, *Russkaia revoliutsionnaia mysl' i gruzinskaia beztsenzurnaia pressa* (Tbilisi: sabchota sakartvelo, 1986), pp. 45–49.]

21. RGASPI, f. 71, op. 10, d. 404.

22. For a Russian translation, see Egnate Ninoshvili, *Izbrannoe* (Tbilisi: Zaria vostoka, 1957), pp. 166–184.

23. Grigorii Parkadze, "I. V. Stalin v seminarii," RGASPI, f. 558, op. 4, d. 665, l. 139. Théodule-Armand Ribot (1839–1916) was a French psychologist, the author of *La psychologie des sentiments* (Paris, 1896), who emphasized the material and physical elements that influenced mental life.

24. Devdariani, "Soso Stalin," SShSSA, f. 8, op. 2, ch. 1, d. 12, l. 178. Imereti is the western part of Georgia.

25. G. Elisabedashvili, "Moi vospominaniia o tovarishche Staline," SShSSA, f. 8, op. 2, d. 16, ll. 133–134.

26. Ibid., ll. 139–140.

27. Ibid., ll. 135–137.

28. Ibid., ll.138–139.

29. RGASPI, f. 71, op. 10, d. 404. The *Deshevaia biblioteka* was a series of inexpensive, small-format books published by Aleksei Suvorin from 1879 to 1912 that made otherwise inaccessible literature available to ordinary people.

30. Edelman, *Stalin: Biografiia v dokumentakh*, pp. 52–53.

31. Ostrovskii, *Kto stoial za spinoi Stalina*, p. 148; RGASPI, f. 558, op. 4, d. 53, l. 1.

32. Gogokhiia, "Na vsiu zhizn'," pp. 14, 16.

33. Kaminskii and Vereshchagin, "Detsvo i iunost' vozhdia," pp. 84–85; Ostrovskii, *Kto stoial za spinoi Stalina*, pp., 149, 150; RGASPI, f. 558, op. 4, d. 60, ll. 1–4.

34. Charles Letourneau (1831–1902) was the prolific author of a series of popular books on evolution in various realms of human activity. Among his works were: *L'évolution du mariage et de la famille* (1888); *L'évolution politique dans les diverses races humaines* (1890); *L'évolution juridique dans les diverses races humaines* (1891); *L'évolution de la propriété* (1892); *L'évolution littéraire dans les diverses races humaines* (1894) [the book that Jughashvili was caught reading]; and *La condition de la femme dans les diverses races et civilizations* (1903).

35. Kaminskii and Vereshchagin, "Detsvo i iunost' vozhdiia," p. 71.

36. Ibid. p. 85.

37. Ibid., p. 84.

38. Davis, *Behind Soviet Power*, p. 16.

39. Kaminskii and Vereshchagin, "Detsvo i iunost' vozhdiia," p. 86.

40. H. R. Knickerbocker, "Stalin Mystery Man Even to His Mother, Post Interviewer Finds," *New York Evening Post*, December 1, 1930, p. 2.

41. SSSA, f. 440, op. 2, d. 10, ll. 19a, 22a, 24a.

42. Signed, I[osif] Jughashvili, petitioner. June 3, 1898; RGASPI, f. 558, op. 1, d. 4327; Kun, *Stalin: An Unknown Portrait*, p. 27.

43. Devdariani, "Soso Stalin," SShSSA, f. 8, op. 2, ch. 1, d. 12, l. 181; Ostrovskii, *Kto stoial za spinoi Stalina*, pp. 150, 151.

44. Kun, *Stalin: An Unknown Portrait*, pp. 31–32; RGASPI, f. 558, op. 4, d. 65; f. 71, op. 10, d. 275.

45. N. Zhordania, "stalini," *brdzolis khma*, no. 65 (October 1936); N. Vakar, "Stalin po vospominaniiam N. N. Zhordaniia," *Posledniia novosti* (Paris), December 16, 1936, p. 2.

46. G. Elisabedashvili, "Moi vospominaniia o tovarishche Stalina," SShSSA, f. 8, op. 2, d. 16, l. 142.

47. RGASPI, f. 558, op. 4, d. 65; Kun, *Stalin: An Unknown Portrait*, p. 32.

48. RGASPI, f. 558, op. 4, d. 65, l. 4; Kun, *Stalin: An Unknown Portrait*, pp. 32–33; Ostrovskii, *Kto stoial za spinoi Stalina*, p. 155; SEA, f. 440, op. 2, d. 82, l. 59.

49. Ostrovskii, *Kto stoial za spinoi Stalina*, p. 152; Maria Makharoblidze, SShSSA, f. 8, op. 2, ch. 1, d. 32, ll. 258–259.

50. Ostrovskii, *Kto stoial za spinoi Stalina*, p. 154; SEA, f. 440, op. 1, d. 1612; op. 2, d. 81, 82.

51. Dmitrii Kalandarashvili, "Iz moego proshlogo," SShSSA, f. 8, op. 2, ch. 1, d. 20, l. 76.

52. Kaminskii and Vereshchagin, "Detstvo i iunost' vozhdia," p. 89; Ostrovskii, *Kto stoial za spinoi Stalina*, pp. 157–158; B. Berdzenishvili, *Zaria vostoka*, February 25, 1938; N. L. Dombrovskii, "Vospominaniia," RGASPI, f. 558, op. 4, d. 651, ll. 50–51.

53. Dombrovskii, "Vospominaniia," (1934), in SShSSA, f. 8, op. 2, ch. 1, d. 15, l. 242.

54. Edelman, *Stalin: Biografiia v dokumentakh*, p. 86; "Iz vospominanii K. L. Dombrovskogo, 1934," RGASPI, f. 558, op. 4, d. 651, ll. 50–53.

55. Ibid., l. 257.

56. Ostrovskii, *Kto stoial za spinoi Stalina*, pp. 158–160; SEA, f. 440, op. 1, d. 1612; op. 2, d. 81, 82. Olga Edelman found no record of this incident in the police archives and concluded that it never took place, even though it is mentioned in Elisabedashvili's memoirs. Stalin himself was

suspicious of those who wrote memoirs of his childhood and referred to them as "fairy tale hunters, liars (perhaps 'conscientious' liars), and sycophants." [Jan Plamper, *The Stalin Cult: A Study in the Alchemy of Power* (New Haven, CT: Yale University Press, 2012), p. 123; RGASPI, f. 558, op. 11, d. 1121, l. 24.]

57. Georgii Fedorovich Vardoian, "Vospominaniia," SShSSA, f. 8, op. 2, ch. 1, d. 7, l. 66. Vardoian later became a Menshevik, formally leaving the party in 1923 at the Tiflis Congress of Former Mensheviks. His memoirs were written in 1945.

58. Porfirii Merabovich Efremidze, "Epizody iz zhizni tovarishcha Stalina," SShSSA, f. 8, op. 2, d. 16, ll. 283, 285; Ter-Petrosian, *Stalin*, pp. 26–30.

59. Efremidze, "Epizody," l. 282.

60. G. Elisabedashvili, "Vospominaniia," SSM, f. 3, ch. 1, d. 1955–146, ll. 24–31.

61. Davrichewy, *Ah! Ce qu'on rigolait bien avec mon copain Staline*, pp. 118–119. Davrishev was Rozenfeld's schoolmate and good friend.

62. Ibid., pp. 111–112.

CHAPTER 5. BURNING BRIDGES

1. See the essays by Reginald E. Zelnik, Mark D. Steinberg, Heather Hogan, S. A. Smith, and Hiroaki Kuromiya in Lewis H. Siegelbaum and Ronald Grigor Suny (eds.), *Making Workers Soviet: Power, Class, and Identity* (Ithaca, NY: Cornell University Press, 1994).

2. The literature on the early formation of the Russian working class and Social Democracy is impressive. Among the most important works, one should mention Leopold H. Haimson, *The Russian Marxists and the Origins of Bolshevism* (Cambridge, MA: Harvard University Press, 1955); Allan K. Wildman, *The Making of a Workers' Revolution: Russian Social Democracy, 1891–1903* (Chicago: University of Chicago Press, 1967); Jerry Surh, *1905 in St. Petersburg* (Stanford, CA: Stanford University Press, 1989); Heather Hogan, *Forging Revolution: Metalworkers, Managers, and the State in St. Petersburg, 1890–1914* (Bloomington: Indiana University Press, 1993); Victoria Bonnell, *Roots of Rebellion: Workers' Politics and Organizations in St. Petersburg and Moscow, 1900–1914* (Berkeley: University of California Press, 1983); Tim McDaniel, *Autocracy, Capitalism, and Revolution in Russia* (Berkeley: University of California Press, 1988); Mark Steinberg, *Moral Communities: The Culture of Class Relations in the Russian Printing Industry, 1867–1907* (Berkeley: University of California Press, 1992); Reginald Zelnik (ed.), *Workers and Intelligentsia in Late Imperial Russia: Realities, Representations, Reflections* (Berkeley: University of California Press, 1999); Michael Melancon and Alice K. Pate (eds.), *New Labor History: Worker Identity and Experience in Russia, 1840–1918* (Bloomington, IN: Slavica, 2002); and Barbara Engel, *Between Fields and the City: Women, Work, and Family in Russia, 1861–1914* (Cambridge: Cambridge University Press, 1995).

3. F. Makharadze, *Ocherki revoliutsionnogo dvizheniia v Zakavkaz'i* (Tiflis: Gosizdat Gruzii, 1927), pp. 45–48.

4. M. Chodrishvili, *chemi avtobiograpi* (Tiflis, 1927), pp. 77–78. The first strike (in the Tiflis arsenal in 1862) resulted in the dismissal of all strikers. The strikes of Tiflis textile workers at the Mirzoev mill in 1872 and at the Zeitser Factory six years later were defensive attempts by workers to resist cutbacks in wages and extension of the workday beyond the customary fourteen hours. They too failed, and workers hesitated to risk all on such fruitless activity.

5. Among them was Vasilii Vasil'evich Bervi-Flerovskii (1829–1918), author of the Populist tract *Polozhenie rabochego klassa v Rossii* (The Situation of the Working Class in Russia) (Saint Petersburg, 1869).

6. The earliest Georgian workers' circle of which I have a record was formed in 1880 by Zakaria Chichinadze. Artisans and students from the trade schools gathered in Tiflis to read Georgian stories, like "Tale of a Poor Man" or "The Bandit Kako" by Ilia Chavchavadze. In 1889 the workers decided to publish their own handwritten journal, *musha* (Worker). [Gagoshidze, *Russkaia revoliutsionnaia mysl'*, pp. 135–136.] A *Rabochii soiuz* (Workers' Union) operated in Tiflis for nearly two years (1887–1889) and distributed Populist material to interested Russian workers until the police, tipped off by an informer, rounded up the leaders. The authorities considered this a dangerous group, for as one of the circle's members later testified, its purpose "was to prepare the workers for an open protest against the government . . . and to demand the changing of the existing state order." [V. P. Mailian, *Deiatel'nost russkikh marksistov v Zakavkaz'e (s 1880-kh godov po 1903 god)* (Erevan: Haiastan, 1984), pp. 13–19.]

7. S. A. Alliluev, *Proidennyi put'* (Moscow: Gosudarstvennoe izdatal'stvo politicheskoi literatury, 1956), p. 21.

8. Filipp Makharadze, *K tridtsatiletiiu sushchestvovaniia tiflisskoi organizatsii: Podgotovitel'nyi period, 1870–1890 (Materialy)* (Tiflis: Sovetskii Kavkaz, 1925), pp. 48–49.

9. G. Chkheidze, "chemi mogonebani," *revoliutsiis matiane*, 1923, no. 5, pp. 87–88. Armenians usually worked in factories owned by Armenians, like the tobacco mills of Bozarjiants and Efianjiants. They kept to themselves, and if at all politicized responded to their national parties, the Dashnaktsutyun (Armenian Revolutionary Federation) or the Hnchak (Bell) Party, which were more committed to the revolutionary struggle against the Ottoman Empire than against Russian autocracy. The first Armenian workers' circle to be influenced by Marxism was formed in Tiflis in 1898 and is sometimes referred to as the Union of Workers of Tiflis. Caught between their nationalist countrymen and the relative indifference of socialists of other nationalities toward the Armenians, the few Armenian Social Democrats complained that little effort was being made to organize their workers. Georgian Social Democrats, on the other hand, argued that most Armenian workers in Georgia understood Georgian as well as they did their own native language and considered themselves to be more Georgian than Armenian. It seemed to them a waste of limited resources to translate everything into Armenian. [S. T. Arkomed (Gevork Gharajian), *Rabochee dvizhenie i sotsial-demokratiia na Kavkaze: S 80-kh godov do 1903 g.* (Geneva, 1910; 2nd edition (Moscow-Petrograd: Gosizdat, 1923), pp. 53–54, 179–180. References are to the second edition.]

10. Sergei Alliluev, "Moi vospominaniia," *Krasnaia letopis'*, 1923, no. 5, p. 170. Alliluev (1866–1945) was the father of Stalin's second wife, Nadezhda Allilueva, and the author of several memoirs.

11. Alliluev, *Proidennyi put'*, p. 29.

12. S. Todriia, "Na zare rabochego dvizheniia (1893–1903 g.g.)," in M. Orakhelashvili et al. (eds.), *Chetvert' veka bor'by za sotsializm* (Tiflis, 1923), pp. 195–196.

13. Edelman, *Stalin: Biografiia v dokumentakh*, p. 89; "Iz zakliucheniia tovarishcha prokurora sudebnoi palaty Khlodoskogo po delu Kurnatovskogo i dr.," November 30, 1902, GARF, f. 124, op. 10, d. 124, 1901, l. 72; ll. 124 ob.–125 ob., ll.128–130.

14. For their movement Russians borrowed the term "Social Democracy," a clear reference back to the German Social Democrats. As one of Plekhanov's most moderate comrades, Lev

Deutsch, pointed out, "In the whole civilized world the name 'Social Democracy' was associated then with the concrete, peaceful and parliamentary party whose activity was characterized by almost complete avoidance of all kind of determined, revolutionary methods of struggle." [Walicki, *The Controversy over Capitalism*, pp. 154–155.] Russia's Marxists principally identified with the revolutionary rhetoric of people like Karl Kautsky rather than the parliamentary practice of the majority of German Social Democrats, which was precluded by Russia's autocratic political system until 1906.

15. "The more strenuously he [*sic*; the *intelligent*] sought to mold his image of himself in the light of some rarefied Western model," writes historian Leopold H. Haimson, "the more he felt compelled to suppress or deny the emotions and the memories that still bound him to his Russian environment. But, however suppressed or denied, these feelings and memories continued to govern much of his life." [Leopold H. Haimson, *The Making of Three Russian Revolutionaries: Voices from the Menshevik Past* (Cambridge and New York: Cambridge University Press; and Paris: Éditions de la Maison des sciences de l'homme, 1987), p. 7.]

16. V. I. Lenin, *Shag vpered, dva shaga nazad (Krizis v nashei partii)* (Geneva, 1904), reprinted in V. I. Lenin, *Polnoe sobranie sochinenii* [henceforth, *PSS*] (5th edition: Moscow: Izdatel'stvo politicheskoi literatury, 1958–1965), VIII, p. 254.

17. Georgi Eradze, "Interviews with Leopold H. Haimson," [unpublished manuscript, Menshevik Project, Columbia University], interview no. 5, pp. 10–11.

18. Erik van Ree, "The Stalinist Self: The Case of Ioseb Jughashvili (1898–1907)," *Kritika*, XI, 2 (Spring 2010), pp. 259–260.

19. G. Chkheidze, "dzvirpasi da mudam dauvitsqari zakro chodrishvili," *revoliutsiis matiane*, 1923, no. 1 (March), pp. 94–95; Sevastii Talakvadze [Sebastian Talaqvadze], *K istorii kommunisticheskoi partii Gruzii. Chast' I. (Dva perioda)* (Tiflis: Izdatel'stvo Glavpolitprosveta SSRG, 1925), pp. 22, 41n.

20. G. Chkheidze, "chemi mogonebani," no. 5, p. 87.

21. Talakvadze, *K istorii kommunisticheskoi partii Gruzii*, I, p. 43.

22. Alliluev, *Proidennyi put'*, pp. 24, 26. On Maiorov and Afanasev, see Mailian, *Deiatel'nost' russkikh marksistov*, pp. 22–75.

23. Alliluev, "Moi vospominaniia," p. 170. Spartacus was the Roman slave who led a massive revolt in 72 AD and centuries later became part of both the nationalist and socialist pantheons of rebel heroes. The 1874 Italian novel *Spartaco, racconto storico del secolo VII dell 'era romana,* by Raffaello Giovagnoli (1838–1915), was popular among leftists in Russia and was the source for the Soviet ballet (1956) by Aram Khachaturian (1903–1978). *The Gadfly* (London: Heinemann, 1897) is a romantic adventure novel by Ethel Lillian Voynich (1864–1960), an Irish feminist who married a Russian revolutionary nobleman. Extraordinarily popular in Russia, the novel remained part of the Soviet canon, and a Russian film version (*Ovod*, 1955) featured a score by Dmitrii Shostakovich. In his futuristic novel *Looking Backward* (1888), Edward Bellamy (1850–1898) depicted a utopian state socialist society in the year 2000.

24. The autobiographical and personal writings of Russian workers in their transition from being politically "unconscious" to becoming self-aware and politically active have been sensitively explored in the work of Reginald Zelnik and Mark D. Steinberg. See, for example, Zelnik,

A Radical Worker in Tsarist Russia: The Autobiography of Semen Kanatchikov (Stanford, CA: Stanford University Press, 1986); and Steinberg, *Proletarian Imagination: Self, Modernity, and the Sacred in Russia, 1910–1925* (Ithaca, NY: Cornell University Press, 2002).

25. G. Chkheidze, "chemi mogonebani," *revoliutsiis matiane*, 1923, no. 4, pp. 172–173.

26. Talakvadze, *K istorii kommunisticheskoi partii Gruzii*, I, pp. 21–22. In 1896 two of the Georgian circles formed a joint "leading center" that included Georgian workers, the trusted Russian worker Alliluev, and technicians then working at the railroad depot. All had passed through Social Democratic circles. Circles throughout Tiflis were united around the center, and at the end of 1896 several of them assisted workers in the strikes at local tobacco factories. [F. Makharadze, *K istorii kommunisticheskoi partii Zakavkaz'ia* (Tiflis, 1923), p. 203; *revoliutsiis matiane*, 1925, no. 2 (12), p. 63.] This group is sometimes referred to as the first Tiflis Social Democratic Committee, but that honor should be reserved for the committee set up in 1899, after the first congress of the Russian Social Democratic Workers' Party (RSDRP) in 1898.

27. Iremaschwili, *Stalin und die Tragödie Georgiens*, p. 19.

28. Mailian, *Deiatel'nost' russkikh marksistov v Zakavkaz'e*, p. 43; P. V. Gugushvili, *Karl Marks v gruzinskoi publitsistike i obshchestvennosti do 1898 goda* (Tbilisi: Akademiia nauk Gruzinskoi SSR, 1963), pp. 269, 271.

29. "Vospominanie rabochego zheleznoi dorogi D. Lordkipanidze (1934 g.): V kakikh usloviiakh i gde poznakomilsia s Stalinom," SEA, f. 2417, op. 1, d. 227, ll. 1–11 [originals in Georgian; Russian translation in author's possession].

30. *Zaria vostoka*, July 17, 1939; Arakel Okuashvili, *Zaria vostoka*, September 18, 1935; Ostrovskii, *Kto stoial za spinoi Stalina*, pp. 130–131.

31. Roy Stanley De Lon, "Stalin and Social Democracy, 1905–1922: The Political Diaries of David A. Sagirashvili [Davit Saghirashvili]," PhD dissertation, Georgetown University, 1974, pp. 168–169.

32. Most of those who supported Zhordania later became Mensheviks. [Menshevik Project, Columbia University, no. 8, pp. 1–2.]

33. Uratadze, *Vospominaniia gruzinskogo sotsial-demokrata*, p. 16; N. N. Zhordaniia, *Moia zhizn'* (Stanford, CA: Hoover Institution Press, 1968), pp. 26–27. See also the memoir by Isidore Ramishvili, written in 1935–1936 before his execution and hidden by his family: *mogonebebi* (Tiflis: gamomtsemloba artanuji, 2012). Ramishvili notes how sympathetic Zhordania was to Georgian nationalism in the late 1890s, refusing to separate himself from the views of Ilia Chavchavadze (pp. 262–263). [I am grateful to Beka Kobakhidze for this reference.]

34. Zhordania, *Moia zhizn'*, p. 29.

35. Arkomed, *Rabochee dvizhenie i sotsial-demokraty na Kavkaze*, p. 49.

36. Talakvadze, *K istorii kommunisticheskoi partii Gruzii*, I, p. 28; Filipp Makharadze, *Ocherki revoliutsionnogo dvizheniia v Zakavkaz'i*, p. 72. Zhordania himself later claimed to have written the proclamation, but he may have had in mind the proclamation for May Day, 1899 [Zhordaniia, *Moia zhizn'*, p. 290].

37. *Rabochee delo*, 1899, nos. 2–3; Arkomed, *Rabochee dvizhenie*, pp. 47–48.

38. Kaminskii and Vereshchagin, "Detstvo i iunost' vozhdia," p. 78.

39. Kote Kalandarov, "Stalinskaia shkola bor'by," *Rasskazy starykh rabochikh Zakavkaz'ia o velikom Staline*, pp. 42–43.

40. "Vospominaniia Arakela Okuashvili o revoliutsionnoi deiatel'nosti," (1935), SShSSA, f. 8, op. 2, ch. 2, d. 165, ll. 23–25.

41. Ibid., l. 24.

42. For the discussion of Alliluev's memoirs, see Ol'ga Edel'man, *Stalin, Koba i Soso: Molodoi Stalin v istoricheskikh istochnikakh* (Moscow: Izdatel'skii dom Vysshei Shkoly Ekonomiki, 2016), pp. 99–102.

43. S. A. Alliluev, "Vstrechi s t. Stalinym," *Proletarskaia revoliutsiia*, 1937, no. 8, p. 154; Kaminskii and Vereshchagin, "Detstvo i iunost' vozhdia," p. 75. In this account Alliluev claims he met Stalin in 1898, but in his later, more complete memoir he reveals that he did not return to Tiflis until spring of 1899. [Alliluev, *Proidennyi put'*, pp. 30–31.] One must conclude that Alliluev's first meeting with Stalin was in 1904.

44. N. Zhordania, "stalini"; N. Vakar, "Stalin po vospominaniiam."

45. Lavrenti Beria, *On the History of the Bolshevik Organizations in Transcaucasia: A Lecture Delivered at a Meeting of Active Workers of the Tiflis Party Organization, July 21–22, 1935* (London: Lawrence and Wishart, 1939).

46. Those among *mesame dasi* who became leading Georgian Mensheviks—Zhordania, Evgeni Gegechkori, Nikoloz (Karlo, Nikolai) Chkheidze, and Irakli Tsereteli—were all of noble origin; the latter three were never seminarians but went through *gimnazii* and university education. Social origin, and the attendant sense of cultural endowment and entitlement, distinguished these men from the priest's sons (Tskhakaia and Makharadze) and the cobbler's son (Stalin), who joined the Bolsheviks. Uratadze makes the point that Stalin and his closest comrades were never members of *mesame dasi* and that the very term ceased to apply to Social Democrats after the Russian Social Democratic Workers Party (RSDRP) was formed in 1898. [Uratadze, *Vospominaniia gruzinskogo sotsial-demokrata*, p. 15.]

47. A number of Stalin biographers have emphasized the importance of this relationship. Tucker sees it as "something akin to hero-worship." And he quotes Abel Enukidze's remarks that "Comrade Stalin has many times emphasized with astonishment the outstanding capabilities of our deceased comrade, Ketskhoveli, who already at that time was able to raise questions in the spirit of revolutionary Marxism." [Tucker, *Stalin as Revolutionary*, p. 89; A. Enukidze, *Nashi podpol'nye tipografii na Kavkaze* (Moscow: Novaia Moskva, 1925), p. 24.]

48. *iveria*, no. 172, August 12, 1894; *Lado Ketskhoveli: Sbornik dokumentov i materialov* (Tbilisi: sabchota sakartvelo, 1969), p. 16.

49. From a 1903 brochure, reprinted in *Lado Ketskhoveli: Sbornik dokumentov i materialov*, p. 75.

50. Szymon Diksztajn (1858–1884), who had translated *Capital* into Polish, was the author of the well-known pamphlet, "Kto chem zhivet? (Who Lives on What?)," published first in Polish in 1881 (*Kto z czego żyje?*) and in Russian in 1885 by Plekhanov's group "Osvobozhdennie truda" (Liberation of Labor). For the early history of Marxism in Russian Poland, see Norman M. Naimark, *The History of the "Proletariat": The Emergence of Marxism in the Kingdom of Poland, 1870–1887* (Boulder, CO: East European Quarterly, 1979).

51. I. Z. Ketskhoveli, "Nekotorye epizody iz zhizni i deiatel'nosti Lado," *Lado Ketskhoveli: Sbornik dokumentov i materialov*, p. 109.

52. Ostrovskii, *Kto stoial za spinoi Stalina*, p. 156; Alliluev memoirs, RGASPI, f. 668, op. 1, d. 2, ll. 114–115.

53. Ostrovskii, *Kto stoial za spinoi Stalina*, p. 156; A. Okuashvili memoirs, SShSSA, f. 8, op. 2, ch. 2, d. 165, l. 10.

54. V. T. Khakhanashvili, "Zashchitnik ugnetennykh," *Lado Ketskhoveli: Sbornik dokumentov i materialov*, p. 125.

55. See his articles in *kvali*, 1898, nos. 44, 45, 48; 1899, nos. 16, 19, 22, 23, 42, 43, 46, 47, 48, 49; 1900, nos. 15, 33, which are translated into Russian and reprinted in Aleksandr Tsulukidze, *Sochineniia*, trans. and ed. P. Sharia (Tbilisi: Zaria Vostoka, 1945), pp. 1–68.

56. Iremaschwili, *Stalin und die Tragödie Georgiens*, p. 24.

CHAPTER 6. THE OUTLAW

1. Anna Krylova, "Beyond the Spontaneity-Consciousness Paradigm: 'Class Instinct' as a Promising Category of Historical Analysis," *Slavic Review*, LXII, 1 (Spring 2003), p. 11.

2. Samuel H. Baron, *Plekhanov: The Father of Russian Marxism* (Stanford, CA: Stanford University Press, 1963), p. 163; for a slightly different version of this phrase, see G. V. Plekhanov, *Sochineniia*, ed. David Riazanov (Moscow-Petrograd, 1923–1927), vol. IV, p. 54.

3. Leopold H. Haimson, *The Russian Marxists and the Origins of Bolshevism* (Cambridge, MA: Harvard University Press, 1955), p. 57.

4. Robert Mayer, "Plekhanov, Lenin, and Working-Class Consciousness," *Studies in East European Thought*, XLIX (1997), pp. 165–175.

5. Iremaschwili, *Stalin und die Tragödie Georgiens*, p. 25.

6. Lenin's allegiance to the Erfurt Program and the basic strategies developed by Karl Kautsky is a central theme of Lars Lih's *Lenin Rediscovered: What Is to Be Done? in Context* (Leiden and Boston: Brill, 2006), particularly pp. 111–158.

7. V. I. Lenin, *PSS*, IV, p. 171.

8. Ostrovskii, *Kto stoial za spinoi Stalina*, p. 164; RGASPI, f. 71, op. 10, d. 169, ll. 23–25.

9. The *ekonomisty* were victorious only in Saint Petersburg, the Union of Russian Social Democrats Abroad, and a few other organizations, though not for long.

10. This first Tiflis Committee included the workers Al. Shatilov, Vaso Tsabadze, Zakaria Chodrishvili, Arakela Okuashvili, and Mikha Bochoridze and several intellectuals active in the labor movement, Silibistro Jibladze, Severian Jugheli, and Dimitri Kalandarishvili.

11. Menshevik Project, no. 11, p. 9; G. Chkheidze, "chemi mogonebani," *revoliutsiis matiane*, 1923, no. 5, p. 90.

12. Menshevik Project, no. 11, p. 8.

13. Makharadze, *Ocherki revoliutsionnogo dvizheniia*, p. 72; Talakvadze, *K istorii kommunisticheskoi partii Gruzii*, I, p. 29; Menshevik Collection, no. 1; see also K. Macharadze's memoirs in *Novyi put'*, 1927, no. 15.

14. "Vospominaniia Arakela Okuashvili o revoliutsionnoi deiatel'nosti," SShSSA, f. 8, op. 2, ch. 2, d. 165, ll. 7, 11, 22.

15. Iremaschwili, *Stalin und die Tragödie Georgiens*, p. 26.

16. Arkomed, *Rabochee dvizhenie i sotsial-demokratiia na Kavkaze*, pp. 56–58, 181.

17. "Vospominaniia Arakela Okuashvili o revoliutsionnoi deiatel'nosti," SShSSA, f. 8, op. 2, ch. 2, d. 165, ll. 33–34.

18. Ostrovskii, *Kto stoial za spinoi Stalina*, p. 161; Alliluev, "Vospominaniia," RGASPI, f. 668, op. 1, d. 2, l. 144.

19. E. V. Khoshtaria, *Ocherki sotsial'no-ekonomicheskoi istorii Gruzii. Promyshlennost', goroda, rabochii klass (XIX v.–nachalo XX v.)* (Tbilisi: metsnieroba, 1974), p. 213.

20. *brdzola*, no. 2–3; Arkomed, *Rabochee dvizhenie i sotsial-demokratiia na Kavkaze*, p. 64; Makharadze, *Ocherki revoliutsionnogo dvizheniia*, pp. 78–79; Talakvadze, *K istorii kommunisticheskoi partii Gruzii*, I, pp. 32–33.

21. Arkomed, *Rabochee dvizhenie i sotsial-demokratiia na Kavkaze*, pp. 65–66.

22. Talakvadze, *K istorii kommunisticheskoi partii Gruzii*, I, pp. 33–35.

23. Edelman, *Stalin: Biografiia v dokumentakh*, pp. 91–92; P. D. Khurtsilava, "Nashim kruzhkom rukovodil tovarishch Stalin," *Rasskazy starykh rabochikh Zakavkaz'ia o velikom Staline*, pp. 34–35.

24. S. Alliluev, "tp. rkinis gzis sakhelosnoebis mushata gapitsva 1900 tsels," *revoliutsiis matiane*, 1926, 2 (15), pp. 67–71.

25. G. Chkheidze, "dzvirpasi da mudam dauvitsqari zakro chodrishvili," *revoliutsiis matiane*, 1923, 1 (March), p. 97.

26. The fullest account of the strike can be found in Arkomed, *Rabochee dvizhenie i sotsial-demokratiia na Kavkaze*, pp. 59–64.

27. Ibid., p. 68.

28. N. Sokolovskii, "Stranichka k istorii partii v Gruzii (Iz lichnykh vospominanii)," *Zaria vostoka*, no. 51, August 17, 1922. Sokolovskii recalls that the meeting was held in early 1899, but this is clearly too early. Jughashvili did not live at the observatory until late in 1899, and Kurnatovskii did not arrive in Tiflis until the fall of 1900. The meeting was held sometime between Kurnatovskii's arrival and his arrest in March 1901.

29. A. S. Allilueva, *Vospominaniia* (Moscow: Sovetskii pisatel', 1946), pp. 19–21. This memoir, somewhat hagiographic both in reference to Lenin and Stalin, displeased Stalin, and Anna Allilueva was arrested. For a translation of much of this memoir as well as the memoir of Sergei Alliluev, see David Tutaev (trans. and ed.), *The Alliluyev Memoirs: Recollections of Svetlana Stalina's Maternal Aunt Anna Alliluyeva and Her Grandfather Sergei Alliluyev* (New York: G. P. Putnam's Sons, 1968).

30. B. Berdzenishvili, "Iz vospominanii," *Zaria vostoka*, no. 46, February 25, 1938; Kaminskii and Vereshchagin, "Detstvo i iunost' vozhdia," p. 95.

31. Kaminskii and Vereshchagin, "Detstvo i iunost' vozhdia," p. 96.

32. *Iskra*, no. 6, July 1901. A fuller description of the demonstration is in Arkomed, *Rabochee dvizhenie i sotsial-demokratiia na Kavkaze*, pp. 75–79.

33. "Vospominaniia Arakela Okuashvili o revoliutsionnoi deiatel'nosti," SShSSA, f. 8, op. 2, ch. 2, d. 165, l. 34; Ostrovskii, *Kto stoial za spinoi Stalina*, p. 162; SShSSA, f. 8, op. 5, d. 1, l. 72.

34. Iremaschwili, *Stalin und die Tragödie Georgiens*, p. 27.

35. Ter-Petrosian (Kamo), *Stalin*, pp. 65–73.

36. *Iskra*, no. 1, December 1, 1900.

37. Allan K. Wildman, *The Making of a Workers' Revolution: Russian Social Democracy, 1891–1903* (Chicago: University of Chicago Press, 1967), p. 213.

38. The Armenian Revolutionary Federation (Dashnaktsutyun, the Dashnaks), founded in 1890, had begun organizing Armenian workers in Balakhany, an oil-drilling district outside Baku

city, in the early 1890s. By the time the party's founder, Kristafor Mikaielian, visited Baku in 1894 the workers' group numbered several hundred. The Dashnaks, however, were less interested in specific issues of labor than they were with preparing Armenians and their neighbors, both in the Russian and the Ottoman empires, for the coming revolution. [Ishkhan Mirzabekian, "Kristafor Mikaielian," *Arev* (Baku), no. 48, March 6 (19), 1918.]

39. A. S. Enukidze, "Istoriia organizatsii i raboty nelegal'nykh tipografii R. S.-D.R.P. na Kavkaze za vremia ot 1900 po 1906 god," *Proletarskaia revoliutsiia*, no. 2 (14) (1923), p. 109. Abel Enukidze (1877–1937) was one of the most active Social Democrats in the Caucasus, primarily in Baku. He was an early adherent of Bolshevism, knew Stalin from 1899, and worked in the party organizations of Baku, Tiflis, Rostov-on-Don, and Saint Petersburg. After the October Revolution he was the secretary of the Central Executive Committee of the Soviets from 1918 until his arrest in 1935. He was executed in 1937.

40. Enukidze, "Istoriia organizatsii i raboty nelegal'nykh tipografii," pp. 110–112.

41. In the original 1923 source Tsuladze is referred to as "Vaso," but an editor corrected the name in *Lado Ketskhoveli*, p. 135n.

42. A. Enukidze, "K dvadtsatipiatiletiiu bakinskoi organizatsii," in *Dvadtsat' piat' let bakinskoi organizatsii bol'shevikov* (Baku, 1924), pp. 11–13; Leonid Borisovich Krasin ("Nikitin"). *Gody podpol'ia. Sbornik vospominanii, statei i dokumentov* (Moscow-Leningrad, 1928), pp. 41–42.

43. Enukidze, "Istoriia organizatsii i raboty nelegal'nykh tipografii," pp. 116–117.

44. Ibid., pp. 118–120.

45. *brdzola* has been reprinted in a bilingual edition (Georgian and Russian): *brdzola/ Bor'ba*, nos. 1–4 1901/IX–1902/XII (Tbilisi: Sabchota Sakartvelo, 1988). The lead editorial attributed to Stalin is reprinted in *brdzola/Bor'ba*, pp. 6–9 (in Georgian), 104–106 (in Russian), and in Russian in I. V. Stalin, *Sochineniia*, 13 vols. (Moscow: Politicheskaia literatura, 1948–1952), I, pp. 3–10. The article was unsigned, and although authorship can never be completely certain, Soviet publications have consistently attributed it to Jughashvili, even as late as 1988. The Menshevik Razhden Arsenidze, who lived for a time with Severian Jugeli, a friend of Ketskhoveli's and a contributor to *brdzola*, makes a strong case against Soso's authorship. He claims that the early articles were by Ketskhoveli and Jugheli. [R. Arsenidze, "Iz vospominanii o Staline," *Novyi zhurnal*, no. 72 (June 1963), pp. 226–227.] Most probably the editorial was either written by Lado Ketskhoveli, who "wrote and printed almost all of the first number of the newspaper *brdzola*," or the product of various drafts to which several members of the group of Social Democrats around *brdzola* contributed. [*Lado Ketskhoveli: Sbornik dokumentov i materialov*, p. 77.]

46. *brdzola/Bor'ba*, pp. 28–36, 124–130; I. V. Stalin, *Sochineniia*, I, pp. 11–31. The article was unsigned.

47. "natsionalizmi da sotsializmi" (Nationalism and Socialism), *brdzola*, no. 2–3, November–December 1901, in *brdzola/Bor'ba*, pp. 53–58, 145–149; reprinted in Aleksandre Tsulukidze, *tkhzulebani* (Tbilisi: sabchota sakartvelo, 1967), pp. 84–94.

48. Edelman, *Stalin: Biografiia v dokumentakh*, p. 100; "Iz vospominanii Ashota Khumariana," translated from Georgian, RGASPI, f. 558, op. 4, d. 651, ll. 214–215.

49. Robert Conquest, *V. I. Lenin* (New York: Viking Books, 1972), p. 32. Lenin's *Shto delat'?* can be found in V. I. Lenin, *PSS*, VI, pp. 1–192; for the most reliable English translation, see Lih, *Lenin Rediscovered*.

50. This point is at the center of Robert C. Tucker's analysis in "Lenin's Bolshevism as a Culture in the Making," in his *Political Culture and Leadership in Soviet Russia: From Lenin to Gorbachev* (New York: W. W. Norton, 1987), pp. 33–40.

51. Scholars disagree whether Lenin was fundamentally pessimistic about the workers' capability to achieve socialist consciousness on their own or optimistic about their potential but emphasizing a role for the Social Democrats in facilitating and accelerating the development of consciousness. For the pessimistic view, see Reginald E. Zelnik, "Worry about Workers: Concerns of the Russian Intelligentsia from the 1870s to *What Is to Be Done?*" in Marsha Siefert (ed.), *Extending the Borders of Russian History: Essays in Honor of Alfred J. Rieber* (Budapest, New York: Central European University Press, 2003), pp. 205–226. For the challenge to the "textbook" version of the centrality and meaning of *What Is to Be Done?*, see Lih, *Lenin Rediscovered*. Robert Mayer argues that Lenin's pessimism in *What Is to Be Done?* was a momentary departure from his usual optimism about workers spontaneously generating a socialist consciousness, a position he held before and shortly after the years 1899–1903. ["The Status of a Classic Text: Lenin's *What Is to Be Done?* after 1902," *History of European Ideas*, XXII, 4 (1996), pp. 307–320.]

52. V. I. Lenin, *PSS*, V, p. 30.

53. Ibid., p. 79.

54. Ibid., p. 41, n.

55. Lih, *Lenin Rediscovered*, p. 464.

56. Ibid., p. 447. Lih shows conclusively that the Russian term *konspiratsiia* should not be confused with the English word *conspiracy*, which is equivalent to the Russian *zagovor*.

57. Lenin, *PSS*, V, p. 171; Andrei Ivanovich Zheliabov (1851–1881) was a leading Populist revolutionary, an adherent of the terrorist People's Will, executed for participation in the assassination of Alexander II. August Bebel (1840–1913), a founder of the German Social Democratic Party, rose from humble beginnings as a worker to become a deputy in the German parliament. He was the author of a principal socialist defense of the rights of women, *Woman and Socialism* (1879), and can be credited with the first public political speech, on the floor of the Reichstag, supporting rights for homosexuals (1898). The reference to "Russian Bebels" was to turning workers into Social Democratic activists equivalent to those from the intelligentsia.

58. V. I. Lenin, *Shto delat'?*, *PSS*, VI, p. 107. Lars T. Lih argues convincingly that *What Is to Be Done?* was "a pep talk to the *praktiki*," a challenge to them to carry the socialist word to the masses, which in 1902 were receptive to Social Democracy and already moving toward revolution. [Lars T. Lih, "How a Founding Document Was Found, or One Hundred Years of Lenin's *What Is to Be Done?*" *Kritika*, 4 (1), pp. 5–49; 47.]

59. Quoted in Mayer, "The Status of a Classic Text," p. 311. For thoughts about why workers were receptive to Lenin's ideas, see Reginald E. Zelnik, "Russian Bebels: An Introduction to the Memoirs of the Russian Workers Semen Kanatchikov and Matvei Fisher," Part I, *Russian Review*, XXXV, 3 (July 1976), pp. 249–289; Part II, ibid., 4 (October 1976), pp. 417–447; and Henry Reichman, "On Kanatchikov's Bolshevism: Workers and Intelligenty in Lenin's *What Is to Be Done?*" *Russian History/Histoire Russe*, XXIII, 1–4 (1996), pp. 27–45.

60. Enukidze, "Istoriia organizatsii i raboty nelegal'nykh tipografii," pp. 133–134.

61. Nikolay Valentinov, *Encounters with Lenin* (Oxford: Oxford University Press, 1968), p. 27.

62. I. Stalin, "Lenin kak organizator i vozhd' RKP," in I. V. Stalin, *Sochineniia*, IV, p. 309.

63. The connections between labor unrest and the "general mobilization of society" are explored in Laura Engelstein, *Moscow 1905: Working-Class Organization and Political Conflict* (Stanford, CA: Stanford University Press, 1982).

64. Arkomed, *Rabochee dvizhenie i sotsial-demokratiia na Kavkaze*, p. 81.

65. *kvali*, March 15, 1898, pp. 201–203; Jones, *Socialism in Georgian Colors*, p. 69; also pp. 63–64.

66. Menshevik Project, no. 18, p. 11.

67. Ibid., p. 82.

68. RGASPI, f. 71, op. 10, d. 404.

69. Arkomed, *Rabochee dvizhenie i sotsial-demokratiia na Kavkaze*, p. 84. Jughashvili had been elected sometime in 1901 to the Avlabar district committee, along with the worker Giorgi Chkheidze. [G. Chkheidze, "dzvirpasi da mudam," p. 97.] The police also noted that on November 11, Jughashvili attended a gathering of about twenty-five people at no. 9 Kuba Street, which was to elect a new Tiflis Committee. [RGASPI, f. 71, op. 10, d. 404.]

70. Jones, *Socialism in Georgian Colors*, p. 106; S. T. Talaqvadze, "sakartvelos revolutsionuri modzraobis tsarsuli (1870 tslidan 1905 tslamde meore natsili)," *revoliutsiis matiane*, 1923, no. 4, p. 30.

71. Arkomed, *Rabochee dvizhenie i sotsial-demokratiia na Kavkaze*, p. 84.

72. Edelman, *Stalin: Biografiia v dokumentakh*, pp. 104–105; "Iz doneseniia nachal'nika Tiflisskogo GZHU general-maiora Debilia v Department politsii," July 5, 1902, no. 3324, GARF, f. 102, d. 7, 1902 g., d. 175, ll. 92 ob.–93a ob.; RGASPI, f. 558, op. 4, d. 82 (photocopy).

73. This first elected committee included the workers Zakaria Chodrishvili, Arakela Okuashvili, Giorgi Chkheidze, Vaso Tsabadze, and Kalistrate Gogua and the intellectuals Gevork Gharajian (Arkomed), Severiane Jugheli, Kishishiants (Keshishev), Jughashvili, and Sergei N. Starosenko, who turned out to be a police agent. [G. Chkheidze, "chemi mogonebani," *revoliutsiis matiane*, 1923, no. 5, p. 91.] Although some accounts—by Arakela Okuashvili, E. E. Smith, and others—state that "there is no evidence that Soso was even elected a committee member" [Smith, *The Young Stalin*, p. 89], Ostrovskii and Erik van Ree, using police documents and memoirs, correctly place Jughashvili on the committee, though only for a brief time. He did not appear at the second meeting of the committee on November 25, 1901. By that time he had been sent by the committee to Batumi as a propagandist. [Ostrovskii, *Kto stoial za spinoi Stalina*, pp. 173–175; Erik van Ree, "The Stalinist Self."]

74. The Social Democratic worker Giorgi Eradze opposed Jughashvili's position on the composition of Social Democratic circles. He recalled that after he criticized the intellectuals' insistence on political struggle in a speech at the funeral of a railroad worker late in 1901, rumors spread that Eradze was anti-intellectual. Jughashvili, many of the seminarians, and a few comrades close to him, like Noe Ramishvili and Penia Chigishvili, attacked Eradze's argument that workers did not distinguish between economic and political struggles and would carry on both at once. [Georgii Eradze, "Interviews with Leopold H. Haimson," unpublished manuscript, Menshevik Project, Columbia University, interview no. 5, pp. 10–11.]

75. The phrase "imagined communities" applied to nations originates with the influential book by Benedict Anderson, *Imagined Communities: Reflections on the Origin and Spread of Nationalism* (London: Verso, 1983). Thinking of the revolutionary movement as a transnational

"imagined community" was suggested by William H. Sewell Jr. at a conference on Anderson's work at the University of Chicago, October 10–11, 2008.

76. Davrichewy, *Ah! Ce qu'on rigolait bien avec mon copain Staline*, p. 160.

77. N. Zhordania, "stalini," *brdzolis khma* (Voice of the Struggle) (Georgian Social Democratic monthly, published in Paris), no. 65, October 1936; excerpts translated into Russian by N. Vakar, "Stalin po vospominaniiam N. N. Zhordaniia," *Posledniie novosti* (Paris), December 16, 1936, p. 2. On the Tiflis "court of honor," see also *brdzolis khma*, 1930, no. 3, to which Bertram D. Wolfe [*Three Who Made a Revolution: A Biographical History* (New York: The Dial Press, 1948; Briarcliff Manor, NY: Stein & Day, 1984), p. 420] and E. E. Smith make reference. Smith quotes: "From his earliest days of activity among the workers, he attracted attention by his intrigues against the real leader of the social-democratic organization, S. Dzhibladze [Jibladze]. He was warned, but took no notice and continued to spread slanders intending to discredit the authorized and recognized representatives of the social-democratic movement, thus attempting to manage the local organization. He was brought before a party court of honor and found guilty of unjustly slandering Dzhibladze and was, by a unanimous vote, excluded from the Tiflis social-democratic organization." [*The Young Stalin*, p. 89.] Another Social Democrat, later Menshevik, Grigol [Grigorii] Uratadze, also refers to the party court, but he is reporting events about which he heard but did not witness: "This was the first party court that the Social Democratic organization of Georgia created in order to judge a party comrade. The court consisted of district representatives. After the interrogations the court unanimously decided to exclude him from the Tiflis organization as a slanderer and an incorrigible intriguer. After this sentence his circles in which he had been active were taken away from him. Then he left Tiflis for Batumi." [Uratadze, *Vospominaniia*, p. 67.]

78. This incident should not be confused with another accusation that Stalin faced a party court after the famous Tiflis "Ex," a sensational robbery carried out by local Social Democrats in 1907. Stalin would later dispute that he had ever been tried and expelled by a party court, even taking the case to trial when Iulii Martov made such an accusation in 1918. For an account of the trial, see Wolfe, *Three Who Made a Revolution*, pp. 469–472; Wolfe mentions that the records of the trial were lost, but they can now be found in RGASPI, f. 558, op. 2, d. 3.

CHAPTER 7. TRIAL BY FIRE

1. I. S. Chulok, *Ocherki istorii batumskoi kommunisticheskoi organizatsii (1890–1921 gody)* (Batumi: Sabchota Adzhara, 1970), pp. 12–13.

2. *Stalin i Khashim (1901–1902 gody). Nekotorye epizody iz batumskogo podpol'ia. S predisloviem N. A. Lakoba* (Sukhum: Abkhazskoe partiinoe izdatel'stvo, 1934), p. 11. This volume contains both factual and fictionalized material and was compiled under the auspices of Stalin's close associate Nestor Lakoba, the most powerful political figure in Abkhazia until his death in 1936. For an evaluation of the book as a dubious source, see Kun, *Stalin: An Unknown Portrait*, pp. 47–51.

3. Factory inspection was introduced in Tiflis province in 1902 after the series of strikes in 1901 and covered seventy-one enterprises with 4,556 workers. In Kutaisi province it covered eighteen enterprises with a total of 3,846 workers. [Khoshtaria, *Ocherki sotsial'no-ekonomicheskoi istorii Gruzii*, p. 128. Slightly different figures are given on pages 200–201.]

4. *Iskra*, no. 16, February 1, 1902.

5. Quoted from G. Tsereteli, *Ignatii Ingorokva* (Tiflis, 1905), pp. 11–12.

6. Ibid. An earlier description of Batumi and the railroad to Tiflis by Lord Curzon can be found in George N. Curzon, *Persia and the Persian Question*, vol. I (first edition: 1892; reprinted: London: Frank Cass, 1966), pp. 59–66.

7. Osman Gurgenidze, "Agitator i propagandist bol'shevizma," *Batumskaia demonstratsiia 1902 goda* (Moscow: Partizdat TsK VKP(b), 1937), p. 113.

8. From an unpublished correspondence to the newspaper *iveria* in 1900. [Gugushvili, *Karl Marks v gruzinskoi publitsistike i obshchestvennosti do 1898 goda*, pp. 65–66.]

9. *Vtoroi s"ezd RSDRP, iiul'–avgust 1903 goda: Protokoly* (Moscow: Gosudarstvennoe izdatel'stvo politicheskoi literatury, 1959), p. 681.

10. *Iskra*, no. 16, February 1, 1902.

11. Nikoloz Chkheidze (Karlo, Nikolai) (1864–1926) was born into a petty noble Georgian family, educated at Odessa University and the Kharkov Veterinary Institute, where he first read Marx's *Capital*, volume I. He moved to Batumi in 1898 and became the intellectual mentor of many local workers and socialist intellectuals. Elected to the Third and Fourth State Dumas (1907–1917), Chkheidze gained a reputation as a fearless orator and headed the Social Democratic caucus. In 1917 he chaired the Petrograd Soviet and in close alliance with Irakli Tsereteli was a principal leader of the Menshevik "Revolutionary Defensists." With the Bolshevik takeover in October he returned to Georgia, served as chairman of the Transcaucasian Seim and later the Georgian Constituent Assembly, and headed the Georgian delegation to the Paris Peace Conference. In exile he and Tsereteli broke with Zhordania and the more nationalist Georgian Social Democrats, and in June 1926 Chkheidze committed suicide. [Ziva Galili y Garcia and Ronald Grigor Suny, "Chkheidze, Nikolai Semenovich," in George Jackson and Robert Devlin (eds.), *Dictionary of the Russian Revolution* (Westport, CT: Greenwood Press, 1989), pp. 120–123. On Chkheidze's ten years as chair of the Social Demcratic caucus in the Russian State Duma, see Gela Saitidze, *ati tseli sakhelmtsipo satatbiros praktsiis sataveshi* (Tbilisi: tbilisis sakhelmtsipo universitetis gamomtsemloba, 2001).]

G. Ia. Francheski was born in Odessa in 1870 and became an active Social Democrat in Georgia in the late 1890s, working with Chkheidze in Batumi until his arrest on February 27, 1898.

12. Chulok, *Ocherki istorii batumskoi kommunisticheskoi organizatsii*, pp. 21–27. In 1900 Chkheidze and his comrade, Isidore Ramishvili, organized a Sunday school for workers. Two hundred workers and twenty teachers participated in the teaching of cultural history, natural science, arithmetic, and Georgian language. Only in 1901 did "one propagandist, a Social Democrat, who used advanced workers who had arrived from Tiflis, found an advanced circle that then served as the ferment for spreading Social Democratic ideas among workers." [*Vtoroi s"ezd RSDRP*, p. 681; Chulok, *Ocherki istorii batumskoi kommunisticheskoi organizatsii*, p. 37.]

13. *Stalin i Khashim*, pp. 13–14.

14. Lado Dumbadze, "chemi mogonebani," *revoliutsiis matiane*, 1926, no. 1 (14), p. 89.

15. G. Chkheidze, "dzvirpasi da mudam," p. 97.

16. Isidore Ramishvili (1859–1937) was a leading Menshevik. He was elected to the First State Duma in 1906, but after his arrest two years later he was in exile in Astrakhan until the revolution of 1917. He was a member of the Executive Committee of the Petrograd Soviet, and after the

October Revolution he returned to Georgia, where he was elected to the Constituent Assembly of the independent republic of Georgia. After the Bolsheviks invaded Georgia, he gave up politics, was repressed in the 1930s, and was executed in 1937.

17. Konstantin Kandelaki, "Kak ia poznakomilsia i rabotal s tovarishchem Stalinym" (1935), SShSSA, f. 8, op. 2, ch. 1, d. 20, ll. 239–240. Kandelaki later became a Menshevik, an elected deputy to the Second State Duma, and minister of finance in the independent Georgian republic (1918–1921). In *Stalin i Khashim* Stalin's residence is given as the home of the Mantashev worker Chkhaidze on Tiflis Street (p. 14).

18. Kandelaki, "Kak ia poznakomilsia i rabotal s tovarishchem Stalinym," SShSSA, f. 8, op. 2, ch. 1, d. 20. l. 247.

19. Kishvardi Tsertsvadze, "Organizator bor'by rabochikh i krest'ian," *Batumskaia demonstratsiia 1902 goda*, pp. 79–80; *Stalin i Khashim*, p. 16.

20. *Stalin i Khashim*, pp. 17–18.

21. Ostrovskii, *Kto stoial za spinoi Stalina*, p. 179; D. A. Vadachkoriia, "Vospominaniia," RGASPI, f. 558, op. 4, d. 537, l. 1.

22. Domentii Vadachkoriia, "Organizator revoliutsionnykh boev batumskikh rabochikh," *Batumskaia demonstratsiia 1902 goda*, p. 108.

23. Ostrovskii, *Kto stoial za spinoi Stalina*, p. 179; Vadachkoriia, "Vospominaniia," RGASPI, f. 558, op. 4, d. 537, l. 1.

24. S. Todria, "Nezabyvaemye dni," *Rasskazy starykh rabochikh Zakavkaz'ia o velikom Staline*, p. 30; Edelman, *Stalin: Biografiia v dokumentakh*, p. 134.

25. S. Todria, "Budni batumskogo podpol'ia," dated Tiflis, March 13, 1935, RGASPI, f. 558, op. 11, d. 1494, ll. 91–96.

26. Vadachkoria reports that the Dashnaks killed one Armenian worker with thirty-five knife wounds and beat up another worker propagandist ["Organizator revoliutsionnykh boev," p. 108].

27. Domentii Vadachkoriia, "Velikii organizator revoliutsionnykh boev," SShSSA, f. 8, op. 2, ch.1, d. 7, ll. 21–22.

28. Grigorii Kasradze, "Vospominaniia o velikom Staline," SShSSA, f. 8, op. 2, ch. 1, d. 22, l. 18.

29. *Stalin i Khashim*, p. 15.

30. Vadachkoriia, "Velikii organizator revoliutsionnykh boev," SShSSA, f. 8, op. 2, ch.1, d. 7, ll. 16–17.

31. Todria, "Budni batumskogo podpol'ia," RGASPI, f. 558, op. 11, d. 1494, l. 91.

32. Porfirii Kuridze, "Tovarishch Stalin—Organizator bor'by batumskikh rabochikh," *Batumskaia demonstratsiia 1902 goda*, p. 68.

33. Porfirii Kuridze, "Vospominaniia," RGASPI, f. 558, op. 11, d. 1494, l. 98. Montefiore mistakenly identifies this book as Gogol; in Russian *Gegel* is Hegel, not Gogol. [*Young Stalin*, p. 79.]

34. RGASPI, f. 558, op. 11, d. 1494, l. 98.

35. Kandelaki, "Kak ia poznakomilsia i rabotal s tovarishchem Stalinym," SShSSA, f. 8, op. 2, ch. 1, d. 20, l. 267.

36. RGASPI, f. 558, op. 11, d. 1494, l. 96. "Mokheve" was suspicious of intellectuals and, according to one memoir, wanted the *intelligenty* to be subordinated to the workers within the

organization. [G. Elisabedashvili, "Moi vospominaniia o tovarishche Staline," RGASPI, f. 558, op.4, d. 665, l. 50.]

37. Chulok, *Ocherki istorii*, p. 39.

38. RGASPI, f. 558, op. 11, d. 1494, ll. 98–99.

39. Stalinist and the majority of post-Stalinist Soviet accounts claim that the first Batumi Committee of the RSDRP was elected that evening, but earlier memoirs by participants make no mention of an election. [See, for example, Tengiz Zhgenti, "batumi 1901–1905 tslebshi," *revoliutsiis matiane*, 1928, no. 3 (20), p. 96.] The monograph by Ilia Chulok presents evidence that the committee was formed sometime at the end of 1902 (after Jughashvili's arrest) and the beginning of 1903. [*Ocherki istorii*, pp. 40–45.] At some point the Batumi Social Democrats reconstituted themselves as an "Organizational Committee" to begin laying the ground for a party organization and a city committee. [*Vtoroi s"ezd RSDRP*, p. 682.] Thus, Stalin had nothing to do with the formation of the Batumi Committee and was never a member of it.

40. Ostrovskii, *Kto stoial za spinoi Stalina*, p. 180.

41. Montefiore hints broadly that Jughashvili set the fire, based on his reading of Konstantine Kandelaki's memoirs, but there is no direct evidence of his involvement. [*Young Stalin*, pp. 77, 343; SShSSA, f. 8, op. 2, ch.1, d. 20, l. 248; see also the memoirs of D. A. Vadachkoria in RGASPI, f. 558, op. 4, d. 537.]

42. Kandelaki, "Kak ia poznakomilsia i rabotal s tovarishchem Stalinym," l. 248.

43. Zhgenti, "batumi 1901–1905 tslebshi," pp. 95–96; Porfirii [Porpire] Lomdzhariia, "Stalin organizoval nas na bor'bu s tsarizmom i burzhuaziei," *Batumskaia demonstratsiia 1902 goda*, p. 44; Ostrovskii, *Kto stoial za spinoi Stalina*, p. 180; Alliluev memoirs, RGASPI, f. 558, op. 4, d. 668, l. 107; Osman Gurgenidze memoirs, RGASPI, f. 558, op. 11, d. 1519, ll. 48–49; Noi Boguchava, "Vospominaniia," SShSSA, f. 8, op. 2, ch. 1, d. 6, l. 221.

44. Ostrovskii, *Kto stoial za spinoi Stalina*, p. 181; G. Godziev memoirs, SShSSA, f. 8, op. 2, ch. 1, d. 10, ll. 292–293.

45. *Iskra*, no. 20, May 1, 1902; Arkomed, *Rabochee dvizhenie i sotsial-demokratiia na Kavkaze*, pp. 112–113.

46. Kandelaki, "Kak ia poznakomilsia i rabotal s tovarishchem Stalinym," SShSSA, f. 8, op. 2, d. 20, l. 252; Ostrovskii, *Kto stoial za spinoi Stalina*, p. 183.

47. Khoshtaria, *Ocherki sotsial'no-ekonomicheskoi istorii Gruzii*, p. 198.

48. G. Elisabedashvili, "K 35-letiiu batumskoi organizatsii leninsko-iskrovskogo napravleniia," *Batumskaia demonstratsiia 1902 goda*, p. 118.

49. Edelman, *Stalin: Biografiia v dokumentakh*, pp. 142–143; K. Kandelaki, "Stalinskie proklamatsii," *Rasskazy starykh rabochikh Zakavkaz'ia o velikom Staline*, pp. 81–83.

50. RGASPI, f. 558, op. 11, d. 1498, l. 100.

51. Arkomed, *Rabochee dvizhenie i sotsial-demokratiia na Kavkaze*, pp. 113–116; Zhgenti, "batumi 1901–1905 tslebshi," p. 97.

52. Olga Edelman, "Soso v Batume, 1902," *Neprikosnovennyi zapas*, no. 90 (4/2013) [http://www.nlobooks.ru/node/3857]; T. Gogoberidze, "Tovarishch Stalin nas uchil pobezhdat'," *Batumskaia demonstratsiia 1902 goda*, pp. 100–101. The story of the Putilov fire was false; there is no record of a fire in that factory and workers being paid for the time lost.

53. Edelman, *Stalin: Biografiia v dokumentakh*, p. 144; T. Gogoberidze, "Tovarishch Stalin uchil nas pobezhdat'," *Batumskaia demonstratsiia 1902 goda*, pp. 100–101.

54. Edelman, *Stalin: Biografiia v dokumentakh*, p. 146; "Donesenie ad'iutanta Kutaiskkogo GZHU poruchika Ol'shevskogo v Departament politsii," March 10, 1902, No. 398, GARF, f. 102, OO. 1902, d. 4, ch. 38, l. A, ll. 20–21.

55. His circle included Vadachkoria, Beglar Melia, Ilarion Darakhvelidze, and Pilipe Kikava. [Vadachkoriia, "Velikii organizator revoliutsionnykh boev," SShSSA, f. 8, op. 2, ch.1, d. 7, l. 17.]

56. *brdzola*, 1901, nos. 2 and 3; I. V. Stalin, *Sochineniia*, I, pp. 26–27.

57. Olga Edelman, *Stalin, Koba i Soso*, p. 60; "Iz doneseniia nachal'nika Kutaisskogo GZHU polkovnika Stopchanskogo v Department politsii," March 22, 1902, GARF, f. 102, OO. 1898, d. 5, ch. 59, l. "A," l. 4.

58. Kuridze, "Tovarishch Stalin—Organizator bor'by batumskikh rabochikh," p. 69. Vadachkoria says that Jughashvili marched with the workers on March 8. [Vadachkoriia, "Velikii organizator revoliutsionnykh boev," p. 19.] For a rendition of the song "Ali Pasha," go to https://www.youtube.com/watch?v=Ir5WffFfXRQ.

59. Edelman, *Stalin: Biografiia v dokumentakh*, p. 149; "Iz doneseniia nachal'nika Kutaisskogo GZHU general-maiora Stopchanskogo v DP," March 12, 1902, No. 400, GARF, f. 102, OO. 1902, d. 4, ch. 38, l. A, ll. 22–25.

60. Vadachkoriia, "Velikii organizator revoliutsionnykh boev," SShSSA, f. 8, op. 2, ch.1, d. 7, ll. 19–20.

61. Pavel Dolubadze, "My borolis' pod rukovodstvom velikogo Stalina," *Batumskaia demonstratsiia 1902 goda*, p. 84.

62. Kandelaki, "Kak ia poznakomilsia i rabotal s tovarishchem Stalinym," SShSSA, f. 8, op. 2, d. 20, ll. 258–259.

63. Edelman, *Stalin: Biografiia v dokumentakh*, p. 149; "Iz doneseniia nachal'nika Kutaisskogo GZHU general-maiora Stopchanskogo v DP," March 12, 1902.

64. Kandelaki, "Kak ia poznakomilsia i rabotal s tovarishchem Stalinym," SShSSA, f. 8, op. 2, d. 20, l. 258.

65. *Iskra*, no. 20, May 1, 1902; no. 26, October 15, 1902; Kasradze, "Vospominaniia o velikom Staline," SShSSA, f. 8, op. 2, ch. 1, d. 22, l. 178; Porfirii Lomdzhariia, "Stalin organizoval nas na bor'bu s tsarizmom i burzhuaziei," *Batumskaia demonstratsiia 1902 goda*, p. 47; Ostrovskii, *Kto stoial za spinoi Stalina*, p. 185; P. Lomdzhariia, "Vospominaniia," RGASPI, f. 558, op. 4, d. 665, l. 251. Eventually fourteen people died and as many as fifty were wounded, according to the estimates of Chulok. [*Ocherki istorii batumskoi kommunisticheskoi organizatsii*, p. 82n.]

66. Illarion Darakhvelidze, "O revoliutsionnoi rabote tovarishcha Stalina v Batumi," *Batumskaia demonstratsiia 1902 goda*, p. 60.

67. Kasradze, "Vospominaniia o velikom Staline," SShSSA, f. 8, op. 2, ch. 1, d. 22, l. 178.

68. Montefiore, *Young Stalin*, p. 80; SShSSA, f. 8, op. 2.1, d. 20, ll. 155–222.

69. Kandelaki, "Kak ia poznakomilsia i rabotal s tovarishchem Stalinym," SShSSA, f. 8, op. 2, d. 20, l. 259.

70. Ibid.

71. In *Stalin i Khashim*, a work prepared a few months before Laverenti Beria's famous speech on Stalin's role in Caucasian Social Democracy, Jughashvili is shown urging on the workers and saying: "The soldiers will not shoot at us, and do not fear their commanders. Beat them right on the head, and we will achieve the liberation of our comrades!" [p. 31; *Stalin i Khashim*

(Sukhum edition), p. 22]. Beria's subsequent account skirts this point and does not mention Jughashvili urging on the workers. [L. Beria, *On the History of the Bolshevik Organizations in Transcaucasia* (Moscow: Foreign Languages Publishing House, 1948), p. 32.]

72. Kasradze, "Vospominaniia o velikom Staline," SShSSA, f. 8, op. 2, ch. 1, d. 22, l. 178.

73. Vadachkoriia, "Velikii organizator revoliutsionnykh boev," p. 20.

74. Vera Lomdzhariia, "Stalin vospital v nas muzhestvo i nenavist' k vragu," *Batumskaia demonstratsiia 1902 goda*, p. 92.

75. Edelman, *Stalin: Biografiia v dokumentakh*, p. 154; GARF, f. 102, op. 1898, d. 5, ch. 59, l. A, ll. 2–20b (translated from Georgian in the Kutaisi Province Gendarme Administration [GZHU]).

76. Edelman, *Stalin: Biografiia v dokumentakh*, pp. 152–153; GARF, f. 102, DO. 1898, d. 5, ch. 52, l. A, ll. 17–180b, 28–320b.

77. Edelman, *Stalin: Biografiia v dokumentakh*, p. 151; GARF, f. 102, OO. 1898, d. 5, ch. 59, l. A, ll. 26–260b. (translated from Georgian by the Kutaisi GZHU).

78. Edelman, *Stalin: Biografiia v dokumentakh*, pp. 126, 155–157; GARF, f. 102, OO. 1898, d. 5, ch. 59, l. "A," ll. 28–320b.

79. Ostrovskii, *Kto stoial za spinoi Stalina*, p. 185; E. Avaliani-Sharoeva memoirs, SShSSA, f. 8, op. 2, ch. 1, d. 1, l. 168.

80. *Stalin i Khashim*, pp. 34–35.

81. On Khashim, see Edelman, *Stalin: Biografiia v dokumentakh*, pp. 126–127.

82. Edelman, *Stalin: Biografiia v dokumentakh*, p. 128; "Donesenie nachal'nika Kutaisskogo GZhU polkovnika Stopchanskogo v Departament politsii, 22 aprelia 1902 goda," GARF, f. 102, op. 1898, d. 7, 1902 g.; d. 175, ll. 51–53.

83. *Batumskaia demonstratsiia 1902 goda*, pp. 177–178; Ostrovskii, *Kto stoial za spinoi Stalina*, p. 187; I. M. Darakhvelidze, "Vospominaniia," SShSSA, f. 8, op. 2, ch. 1, d. 12, l. 87; RGASPI, f. 558, op. 4, d. 80, l. 1. Ivan (Vano) Ramishvili was a cousin of Isidore Ramishvili and was wearing his relative's overcoat at the time of his arrest.

84. Kandelaki, "Kak ia poznakomilsia i rabotal s tovarishchem Stalinym," SShSSA, f. 8, op. 2, ch. 1, d. 20, ll. 263–265.

85. Edelman, *Stalin: Biografiia v dokumentakh*, pp. 159–160; "Donesenie nachal'nika Kutaisskogo GZHU polkovnika Stopchanskogo v Department politsii," April 22, 1902, no. 664, GARF, f. 102, op. 1898, d. 7, 1902 g; d. 175, ll. 51–53.

86. G. Elisabedashvili, "K 35-letiiu batumskoi organizatsii leninsko-iskrovskogo napravleniia," *Batumskaia demonstratsiia 1902 goda*, p. 120.

87. Ostrovskii, *Kto stoial za spinoi Stalina*, p. 187, p. 197; RGASPI, f. 558, op. 4, d. 619, l. 173.

88. From police records published in *Batumskaia demonstratsiia 1902 goda*, p. 178.

89. "One cannot help pausing with amazement at the carelessness with which Koba subjected two of his comrades to danger." [Trotsky, *Stalin*, p. 34.]

90. Police documents in *Batumskaia demonstratsiia 1902 goda*, pp. 182, 186; Iremaschwili, *Stalin und die Tragödie Georgiens*, p. 28; G. Elisabedashvili memoirs, SSM, f. 3, ch. 1, d. 1955–146, ll. 32–40.

91. *Batumskaia demonstratsiia 1902 goda*, p. 181; Edelman, *Stalin: Biografiia v dokumentakh*, p. 128.

92. Arkomed, *Rabochee dvizhenie i sotsial-demokratiia na Kavkaze*, pp. 159–169.

93. Baron Bibineishvili memoirs, written in Tiflis, December 19, 1929 [RGASPI, f. 558, op. 11, d. 1493, l. 14].

94. K. Tsintadze, "chemi mogonebani (1903–1920 tslamde)," *revoliiutsiis matiane*, 1923, no. 2–3 (7–8), pp. 115–117; *rogor vibrdzodit proletariatis diktaturistvis* (Tiflis, 1927), pp. 9–11.

95. Natalia Kirtadze-Sikharulidze, SShSSA, f. 8, op. 2, ch. 1, d. 43, ll. 213–214; *Batumskaia demonstratsiia 1902 goda*, pp. 86, 88, 97–98, 120, 136; Natalia Kirtadze-Sikharulidze, "Iz vospominanii o vozhde," ibid., pp. 85–89.

96. Edelman, *Stalin: Biografiia v dokumentakh*, pp. 131–132; "Donesenie nachal'nika Kutaiss-kogo GZhU general-maiora Stopchanskogo v Departament politsii," June 25, 1902, GARF, f. 102, OO. 1902, d. 4, ch. 38, l. A, ll. 39–400b; June 27, 1902, GARF, f. 102, DO. 1898, d. 5, ch. 52, l. A, ll. 36–38.

97. Edelman, *Stalin: Biografiia v dokumentakh*, pp. 168–169; Soso's leaflet of June 29, 1902, translated from Georgian into Russian in *Batumskaia demonstratsiia 1902 goda*, pp. 30–33.

98. Varlam Kalandadze, "Tovarishch Stalin v batumskoi tiur'me," *Batumskaia demonstratsiia 1902 goda*, pp. 134–136.

99. Edelman, *Stalin: Biografiia v dokumentakh*, pp. 210–211; "Vospominaniia Sakva-relidze P. D.," *Kommunist*, May 18, 1935; RGASPI, f. 558, op. 4, d. 658, ll. 303–307.

100. Edelman, *Stalin: Biografiia v dokumentakh*, p. 211; D. Lolua, "Stalin v kutaisskoi tiur'me," *Batumskaia demontratsiia1902*, pp. 137.

101. Ostrovskii, *Kto stoial za spinoi Stalina*, pp. 201–202; T. Zhgenti, *Zaria vostoka*, October 5, 1935.

102. Natal'ia Kirtadze-Sikharulidze, SShSSA, f. 8, op. 2, ch. 1, d. 43, ll. 213–214; *Batumskaia demonstratsiia 1902 goda*, pp. 86, 88, 97–98, 120, 136; Natal'ia Kirtadze-Sikharulidze, "Iz vospominanii o vozhde," ibid., pp. 85–89.

103. Aleksandr Bogdanov, *Kratkii kurs politicheskoi ekonomiki* (Moscow: Izdatel'stvo knizh-nogo sklada A. M. Murinovoi, 1897).

104. Uratadze, *Vospominaniia gruzinskogo sotsial-demokrata*, pp. 69–72.

105. G. Elisabedashvili, "Vospominaniia," SSM, f. 3, ch. 1, d. 1955–146, ll. 34–35.

106. Edelman, *Stalin: Biografiia v dokumentakh*, p. 200; A. A. Vasadze, "Pravda o Staline glazami aktera," in V. Gogiia (ed.), *Chelovek iz stali Iosif Dzhugashvili* (Moscow: Knizhnyi mir, 2015), pp. 228–229.

107. Ostrovskii, *Kto stoial za spinoi Stalina*, pp. 196–198.

108. *Batumskaia demonstratsiia 1902 goda*, p. 190.

109. RGASPI, f. 71, op. 10, d. 405.

110. Edelman, *Stalin: Biografiia v dokumentakh*, p. 206; RGASPI, f. 558, op. 4, d. 619, l. 172.

111. Edelman, *Stalin: Biografiia v dokumentakh*, p. 224; "Iz vospominanii Babe Lashadze-Bochoridze," translated from Georgian, 1934, RGASPI, f. 558, op. 4, d. 658, l. 217.

112. Natalia Kirtadze-Sikharulidze, "Vospominaniia," SShSSA, f. 8, op. 2, ch. 1, d. 43, l. 215; Ostrovskii, *Kto stoial za spinoi Stalina*, pp. 202–203; B. Loshadze-Bochoradze, *Gudok*, December 20, 1939.

113. *Batumskaia boinia: Obvinitel'nyi akt po delu batumskikh rabochikh, s predisloviiem* (n. p., 1902), p. 7. Strikes and protests throughout the empire were marked by violent clashes with police and soldiers. The most noted event occurred on May 7, 1901, when workers at the

Obukhov Steel Mill in Saint Petersburg fought police and army units; seven workers were killed, scores wounded. [Heather Hogan, *Forging Revolution: Metalworkers, Managers, and the State in St. Petersburg, 1890–1914* (Bloomington: Indiana University Press, 1993), p. 52.]

114. Kun, *Stalin: An Unknown Portrait*, p. 61; RGASPI, f. 71, op. 10, d. 404.

115. George Kennan, *Siberia and the Exile System*, 2 vols. (New York: The Century Company, 1891).

116. Recounted, with slight changes, from Kun, *Stalin: An Unknown Portrait*, p. 61, no source given except that the story was overheard by Levon Shahumian, the son of the martyred Bolshevik Stepan Shahumian.

117. K. Chernenko, *Stalin v sibirskoi ssylke* (Krasnoiarsk: Kraevoe izdatel'stvo, 1942), p. 24. The "responsible editor" of this book was Konstantin Chernenko (1911–1985), then secretary of the Krasnoiarsk party committee for propaganda, who later rose to serve briefly as general secretary of the Communist Party of the Soviet Union (1984–1985) between Iurii Andropov and Mikhail Gorbachev.

118. Ostrovksii, *Kto stoial za spinoi Stalina*, p. 206; A. A. Gusinskii memoirs, RGASPI, f. 558, op. 11, d. 1494, ll. 119–120.

119. In the archival original of Domenti Vadachkoria's memoirs, he wrote, "Comrade Soso told us how he fled from his place of exile" and relates this story. [Ostrovksii, *Kto stoial za spinoi Stalina*, p. 215; SShSSA, f. 8, op. 2, ch.1, d. 7, l. 21.]

120. Chernenko, *Stalin v sibirskoi ssylke*, pp. 32–33.

121. For other stories about Stalin's first exile, see Kun, *Stalin: An Unknown Portrait*, pp. 61–63; Montefiore's chapter, "The Frozen Georgian: Siberian Exile," in *Young Stalin*, pp. 94–102; and the collection of materials edited by K. Chernenko, *Stalin v sibirskoi ssylke*.

122. Domentii Vadachorkiia, "Organizator revoliutsionnykh boev batumskikh rabochikh," *Batumskaia demonstratsiia 1902 goda*, p. 112.

123. Edelman, *Stalin: Biografiia v dokumentakh*, p. 235; "Tsirkuliar Departamenta politsii o litsakh, podlezhashchikh rosysku po delam politicheskim," Mat. 1, 1904, No. 5500, GARF, f. 102, OO. 1904, d. 6, ch. 313, l. 150b; GARF, f. 102, op. 260, d. 11, ll. 110, 1190b.

124. Leon Trotsky, *My Life: An Attempt at Autobiography* (New York: Pathfinder Press, 1970), pp. 131–132.

125. Some psychohistorians have argued that personality defects lead to political pathologies like revolution. See, for examples, Arthur P. Mendel, *Michael Bakunin, Roots of Apocalypse* (New York: Praeger, 1981); Philip Pomper, *Lenin, Trotsky, and Stalin: The Intelligentsia and Power* (New York: Columbia University Press, 1991); Tucker, *Stalin as Revolutionary*; and Anna Geifman, *Thou Shalt Not Kill: Revolutionary Terrorism in Russia, 1894–1917* (Princeton, NJ: Princeton University Press, 1993).

CHAPTER 8. ON THE MARGINS

1. For an interesting account of the strikes in Transcaucasia in 1903, see S. A. Ratova (K. I. Zakharova-Tsederbaum), "Vseobshchaia stachka v 1903 godu na Kavkaze i Chernomorskom poberezh'e (K istoriiu rabochego dvizheniia v Rossii)," *Byloe*, II, 6 (18) (June 1907), pp. 97–117.

2. Razhden Arsenidze (Misha), "Interviews with Leopold H. Haimson," Inter-University Project on the History of the Menshevik Movement, Columbia University, Interview I, p. 4.

These interviews and other Georgian materials can be found in the Boris I. Nikolaevsky Collection, Hoover Institution Archives.

3. "The full measure of the Marxist intelligentsia's alienation from the class it purported to lead came to light as a result of the summer strikes of 1903. . . . Paradoxically, the strikes occurred, not because of Social Democratic leadership but in spite of it." [Wildman, *The Making of a Workers' Revolution*, p. 251; see also, J.L.H. Keep, *The Rise of Social Democracy in Russia* (Oxford: Oxford University Press, 1963)].

4. Kandelaki, "Kak ia poznakomilsia i rabotal s tovarishchem Stalinym," SShSSSIIG, f. 8, op. 2, ch. 1, d. 20, l. 267.

5. *Iskra*, no. 23, August 1, 1902.

6. *Vtoroi s"ezd RSDRP*, p. 683.

7. Ibid., p. 682; Chulok, *Ocherki istorii batumskoi kommunisticheskoi organizatsii*, p. 48.

8. Tengiz Zhgenti, a participant in the demonstration, claimed in 1923 that a proclamation written by Jughashvili at about this time was read throughout Guria and caused peasants to weep. It strains credulity to think that Jughashvili was able to write such a proclamation and have it reach Batumi from Siberia, yet Zhgenti's testimony comes early in the Soviet period, long before the Stalinization of historiography was established. [T. Zhgenti, "Iz istorii kompartii v Gruzii. (Vospominaniia)," in M. Orakhelashvili et al. (eds.), *Chetvert' veka bor'by za sotsializm. Khrestomatiia po istorii R.K.P.* (Tiflis, 1923), pp. 213–215.]

9. "Doklad III S"ezdu RSDRP o deiatel'nosti Kavkazskogo Soiuza za 1903–1905 gg.," by M. Tskhakaia, *Tretii S"ezd RSDRP, aprel'–mai 1905 goda: Protokoly* (Moscow: Gosizpolit, 1959), pp. 606–610. Later memoirs contradict Tskhakaia's report and claim that the elective principle triumphed. See, for example, Arsenidze, unpublished interviews, in HIA, Nikolaevsky Collection, box 667, series 279, folder 4–5, nos. 1–3, 104.

10. Sebastian Talakvadze claims that no workers were elected to the CUC, but a careful reading of his short history leads one to doubt its reliability on some points. For example, he writes that Jughashvili was elected a member of the CUC though at the time he was in exile. [Talakvadze, *K istorii kommunisticheskoi partii Gruzii*, I, pp. 79–80.] The intellectuals on the committee were Silibistro Jibladze, Bogdan Knuniants, Pilipe Makharadze, Diomide Topuridze, Mikha Tskhakaia, Aleksandre Tsulukidze, Noe Zhordania, and Arshak Zurabov.

11. Arshak Zurabov (Zurabian) (pseudonyms: Bekov, Rashid-bek) (1873–1920) had a long career in the Social Democratic movement from the mid-1890s until the end of his life. He became a Bolshevik in 1903 but moved to the Mensheviks in 1906. Elected the following year a deputy to the Second State Duma, he was arrested and sent to Siberia when the tsar dismissed the new legislature. He escaped abroad, and in later years was a Menshevik-Internationalist. On his return to the Caucasus after the revolution, he stood on the left of his party, sympathetic to the idea of Soviet power.

Bogdan Knuniants (alias Ruben, Rusov) (1878–1911) became a Bolshevik after the Second Congress of the RSDRP. He participated in the Petrograd Soviet of 1905 but turned critical of Leninist Bolshevism in the years 1908–1910. Arrested in 1910, he died in prison the following year.

Diomide (Dmitrii) Topuridze (alias Isai, Isari, Karskii) (1871–1942) became a Menshevik, active in the Georgian party, and held various governmental positions during the independent Georgian republic (1918–1921).

12. In the debate Topuridze said, "The Bund wants to be the representative not only of a territorially bounded proletariat but of the whole Jewish proletariat, and to be its only representative. I can call such a principle nothing other than nationalistic, since here the Bund is guided not by the general bases of Social Democracy but only by the proletariat belonging to a given nation. The point of departure is not language, not material conditions, not the level of consciousness, but membership in the Jewish nationality, the Jewish religion. This principle can be called nationalistic." [*Vtoroi s"ezd RSDRP, iiul'-avgust 1903 goda: Protokoly* (Moscow: Gosudarstvennoe izdatel'stvo politicheskoi literatury, 1959), p. 78.]

13. Ibid., p. 62.

14. Ibid., p. 107.

15. For a discussion of the construction of ethnic and class identities in tsarist Russia and the USSR, see Ronald Grigor Suny, *The Revenge of the Past: Nationalism, Revolution, and the Collapse of the Soviet Union* (Stanford, CA: Stanford University Press, 1993).

16. This is the argument of Liliana Riga, *The Bolsheviks and the Russian Empire* (Cambridge: Cambridge University Press, 2012), who sees Bolshevism in particular as "a movement of assimilating—but socially marginalized—outsiders seeking belonging, identity, and position in a less autocratic and exclusionary, universalist political imaginary." (p. 20). Rather than an exclusively class alienation, the engine of radicalization was the imperial setting in which ethnic stratification, discrimination, blocked mobility, and the disproportionate burdens of empire mobilized peripheral people to risk their lives and misfortunes. Riga argues that there were elective affinities between certain marginalized social actors who were "both culturally assimilating and suffering illiberal socioethnic exclusions or repressions" and the Bolsheviks' class narrative that promised a more egalitarian political order in the future (p. 21).

17. *Vtoroi s"ezd RSDRP*, p. 183. Zhordania was a nonvoting delegate, but his views were very influential.

18. Ibid.

19. Ibid., p. 187.

20. Ibid., pp. 190–192.

21. Ibid., p. 198.

22. Ibid., p. 425.

23. Ibid., p. 262n.

24. Ibid., p. 262.

25. "'Opportunism' was the catch-all term in international Social Democracy for deviations from orthodoxy in the direction of reformism. The main versions of opportunism that upset the *Iskra*-ites were Bernstein revisionists abroad and economists at home." [Lih, *Lenin Rediscovered*, pp. 283–284.] Eduard Bernstein (1850–1932) was a prominent German Social Democrat, who developed the idea of "evolutionary socialism" that would be reviled as "Revisionism" by those Marxists, like Karl Kautsky and Lenin, who favored a revolutionary rather than reformist road to socialism. Eventually, after World War I, the very term "Social Democracy" would come to be identified with a reformist, democratic, nonrevolutionary strategy in contrast to Communism, which maintained a commitment to the revolutionary overthrow of capitalism.

26. *Vtoroi s"ezd RSDRP*, pp. 275–278.

27. Ibid., pp. 271–272.

28. At the Fourth Party Congress (1906), which had a Menshevik majority, the delegates adopted Lenin's formulation of membership. By that time most Social Democrats saw Martov's definition as overly broad and no longer thought of Lenin's as including *only* full-time revolutionaries and members of Social Democratic committees. [Lih, *Lenin Rediscovered*, pp. 520–521.]

29. *Vtoroi s"ezd RSDRP*, p. 279.

30. The Party Council (*Sovet partii*) was in a sense the highest party organ, a five-person body that was to reconcile disputes between the two bodies elected independently at the congress: the Central Committee, operating clandestinely inside Russia and guiding the various local party committees, and the Central Organ (*Iskra*), operating in Europe and directing the ideological and intellectual life of the party. The council was to have five representatives, two each from the CC and the CO and an impartial chairman (which turned out to be Plekhanov).

31. Leopold Haimson, "Men'shevizm i bol'shevizm (1903–1917): Formirovanie mentalitetov i politicheskoi kul'tury," in Ziva Galili, Albert Nenarokov, and Leopold Haimson (eds.), *Men'sheviki v 1917 godu: Ot ianvaria do iiul'skikh sobitii* (Moscow: Progress-Akademiia, 1994), p. 23.

32. *Pis'ma P. B. Aksel'roda i Iu. O. Martova* (Berlin: Russkii Revoliutsionnyi Arkhiv, 1924), pp. 91–92; Keep, *The Rise of Social Democracy in Russia*, p. 134.

33. Letter of Aksel'rod to Kautsky, May 22, 1904, Kautsky Archive, International Institute of Social History, Amsterdam; quoted in Abraham Ascher, *Pavel Axelrod and the Development of Menshevism* (Cambridge, MA: Harvard University Press, 1972), p. 208. For Marxists, Bonapartism referred to deceptive dictatorial tendencies akin to the practices of Louis Bonaparte (Napoleon III, 1851–1870); Sergei Nechaev (1847–1882) was a revolutionary Populist, whose slogan "the end justifies the means" was manifested in the murder of an associate who disagreed with Nechaev's methods.

34. For the role of emotions in social movements, see Ron Aminzade and Doug McAdam, "Emotions and Contentious Politics," in Ronald R. Aminzade, Jack A. Goldstone, Doug McAdam, Elizabeth J. Perry, William H. Sewell Jr., Sidney Tarrow, and Charles Tilly, *Silence and Voice in the Study of Contentious Politics* (Cambridge: Cambridge University Press, 2001), pp. 14–50.

35. Baron [Varfolomei Efimovich] Bibineishvili, *Za chetvert' veka (Revoliutsionnoe bor'ba v Gruzii)* (Tiflis, 1925; Moscow-Leningrad: Molodaia gvardiia, 1931), p. 34.

36. Enukidze, "Istoriia organizatsii i raboty nelegal'nykh tipografii," pp. 134–135.

37. Ibid., pp. 135–137.

38. Alliluev was in Metekhi prison at the time. [S. Alliluev, "Moi vospominaniia," *Krasnaia letopis'*, no. 5 (1923), pp. 173–175.]

39. GARF, f. 102, 1902, d. 7; d. 175; *Krasnyi arkhiv*, no. 6 (91), pp. 271–275; Edelman, *Stalin: Biografiia v dokumentakh*, pp. 188–189.

40. From the memoir of Stalin by the Menshevik Davit Saghirashvili, in De Lon, "Stalin and Social Democracy, 1905–1922," p. 173.

41. *lado ketskhoveli. misi tskhovreba da revoliutsionuri mogvatseoba* (Tiflis: kavkasiis kavshiri rusetis sotsialdemokratiuli mushata partiisa, 1903).

42. Dzuku Lolua, "Stalin v kutaisskoi tiur'me," *Batumskaia demonstratsiia 1902 goda*, p. 138.

43. From the memoir of Stalin by the Menshevik David Sagirashvili, in De Lon, "Stalin and Social Democracy, 1905–1922," p. 173. Sagirashvili seems to claim that Stalin was in Tiflis at the time of Ketskhoveli's death, but in fact he was still in Kutaisi prison about to be exiled to Siberia.

44. Vera Lomdzhariia, "Stalin vospital v nas muzhestvo i nenavist' k vragu," *Batumskaia demonstratsiia 1902 goda*, p. 94.

45. RGASPI, f. 71, op. 10, d. 405.

46. "Neopublikovannye materialy iz biografii tovarishcha Stalina," p. 18.

47. Vera Lomdzhariia, *Batumskaia demonstratsiia 1902 goda*, p. 94.

CHAPTER 9. BECOMING BOLSHEVIK

1. M. M. Shakhnazarian, *Krest'ianskoe dvizhenie v Gruzii i sotsial-demokratiia* (Moscow: Kolokol, 1906), pp. 83–84.

2. N. I. Bukharin, V. I. Molotov, and I. I. Skvortsov-Stepanov (eds.), *Leninskii sbornik* (Moscow-Leningrad: Gosudarstvennoe izdatel'stvo, 1928), VII, p. 113; *Perepiska V. I. Lenina i rukovodimykh im uchrezhdenii RSDRP s partiinymi organizatsiiami, 1903–1905 gg.*, I (Moscow: Mysl', 1974), pp. 201–202.

3. *Leninskii sbornik*, VII, p. 116.

4. Ibid.; *Perepiska V. I. Lenina*, pp. 206–207.

5. Arsenidze, unpublished interviews, I, ii, pp. 8–9; R. Arsenidze, "Vospominaniia ob I. G. Tsereteli, (iz perepiski R. Arsenidze s B. I. Nikolaevskim)," Nikolaevsky Collection, Hoover Institution Archives, no. 15, box 10, item 78; *Pis'ma P. B. Aksel'roda i Iu. O. Martova*, pp. 97–99.

6. One prominent Bolshevik, Osip Piatnitskii, remembered Zhordania's choice of the minority over the majority as capricious: Zhordania "followed the majority (Lenin and Plekhanov) all along, but when the Congress decided to close all local press organs and leave only the *Iskra* as the central organ of the Party, he was offended because they closed the Georgian organ, of which he was the editor, and switched over to the minority of the Congress." [Osip Piatnitskii, *Memoirs of a Bolshevik* (London, 1933; reprint: Westport, CT, 1973), p. 60.]

7. *Leninskii sbornik*, vol. VII, pp. 116–117.

8. Irakli Tsereteli (1881–1959) was a leading Georgian Menshevik, one-time editor of *kvali*, and a deputy to the Second State Duma who was exiled to Siberia and liberated only with the February Revolution of 1917. He soon emerged as the most important figure in the Petrograd Soviet, leader of the "Revolutionary Defensist" wing of Russian Menshevism, and minister of posts and telegraphs in the Provisional Government. With the victory of the Bolsheviks, he moved to Georgia, where he was a deputy in the Transcaucasian Seim and leader of the Social Democratic caucus in the Georgian parliament. He later immigrated to the West, eventually settling in the United States.

9. F. Makharadze, "Iz istorii," *Chetvert' veka bor'by za sotsializm*, p. 204. "In the interests of truth," wrote Makharadze, one of the earliest Caucasian Marxists and a dedicated Bolshevik, "I ought to note here that the factional struggle in Transcaucasia became strained only afterward, after the crushing of the revolution of 1905; during the revolutionary clashes of 1905 both

factions acted together in friendship." [Ibid.] At the very end of 1903, the Caucasian Union passed a resolution and sent it to the "Foreign Section" of the party in Europe, calling for an end to the "petty disagreements" that were dividing the party and to come together under the leadership of the central party institutions—all of which at this point were held by the majority. [*Perepiska V. I. Lenina*, p. 424.] The Batumi Committee as well was disturbed by the discord (*smuta*) in the party and expressed its "complete confidence" in the Central Committee. [*Kak rozhdalas' partiia bol'shevikov* (Leningrad, 1925), pp. 299–300.]

10. Arsenidze, unpublished interviews, I, ii, pp. 8–10. Yet they were not free from conflict. When Topuridze was elected to the Caucasian Union Committee, which included members from the various local SD committees in the Caucasus, other comrades refused to work with him. The controversial candidate graciously withdrew, thereby winning even greater respect among those who supported him. [Letter from A. G. Zurabov from Tiflis to G. V. Plekhanov, in *Perepiska V. I. Lenina*, pp. 214–216.]

11. *Pis'ma P. B. Aksel'roda i Iu. O. Martova*, pp. 98–99.

12. Kavkazets, "Nekotorye voprosy nashei taktiki i organizatsii (Posviashchaetsia Bundu)," *Iskra*, no. 51, October 22 (November 4), 1903; reprinted in B. M. Knuniants, *Izbrannye proizvedeniia, 1903–1911* (Erevan: Aipetrat, 1958), pp. 51–56.

13. *Leninskii sbornik*, VII, p. 117; *Perepiska V. I. Lenina*, pp. 214–216. Zurabov ended his letter expressing pessimism about the Caucasian organization. Of those elected to the CUC who adhered to the "majority," two lived in other towns and the third was close to the Socialist Revolutionaries and favored the use of terrorism.

14. *Perepiska V. I. Lenina*, p. 252.

15. Letter from Martov to Aksel'rod, November 4, 1903, in *Pis'ma P. B. Aksel'roda i Iu. O. Martova*, p. 97.

16. Historian John Keep, for example, interprets Lenin's actions as arising from "fanatical determination to exercise personal control over the Party's fortunes. A lesser man might have been reconciled to his defeat. But for Lenin the odds he faced were of no account: even if he stood alone he was convinced that his ideas were correct and his leadership essential for the Party's well-being. Not only did he refuse to accept the November settlement: he set out to undermine it, employing every subterfuge that came to his mind." [Keep, *The Rise of Social Democracy in Russia*, p. 138.] What Keep calls "this private vendetta" was interpreted by the supporters of the "majority" as Lenin's effort to respect the decisions taken at the Second Party Congress and restore the authority of the Central Committee, which had been usurped by Plekhanov and the new *Iskra* board.

17. In a letter written at the end of 1903 explaining the party schism to his comrades in Baku, the congress delegate Bogdan Knuniants wrote that Lenin (and Plekhanov at the time) wanted a Central Committee made up of people "in solidarity with the editorial board [of *Iskra*] and firmly standing on the principles of revolutionary Social Democracy," while Martov's "minority" "wanted to bring into the CC people of various shades of Iskraism, . . . to create a 'coalition government,' as they then liked to express it." [Knuniants, *Izbrannye proizvedeniia*, p. 60.] Lars Lih sees these events as "a palace coup at *Iskra*. An editor [Lenin] selected by the Congress was out, the editors rejected by the Congress were in." [*Lenin Rediscovered*, p. 497.] Lenin, in his view, was defending the sovereignty of the party congress. [Ibid., p. 491.]

18. Ostrovskii, *Kto stoial za spinoi Stalina*, p. 212; Fedor Gogoberidze memoirs, RGASPI, f. 558, op. 4, d. 665, l. 70b.

19. Natal'ia Kirtadze-Sikharulidze, "Iz vospominanii o vozhde," *Batumskaia demonstratsiia 1902 goda*, p. 89.

20. Montefiore is convinced that Stalin "enjoyed a love affair with the young woman, the first but not the last with his many landladies and conspiratorial comrades." Kirtadze, after all, was "aged twenty-two, a peasant beauty and SD sympathizer whose husband had disappeared." He bases this claim on "Batumi folklore," and conjectures drawn from Kirtadze's own memoirs and Stalin's later proposals. [*The Young Stalin*, p. 78.]

21. Natali'ia Kirtadze-Sikharulidze, "Vospominaniia," SShSSA, f. 8, op. 2, ch. 1, d. 43, l. 215.

22. S. Alliluev, "Vstrechi s tovarishchem Stalinym," *Proletarskaia revoliutsiia*, no. 8 (1937), pp. 154–155; S. Ia. Alliluev, *Proidennyi put'* (Moscow: Gosudarstvennoe izdatel'stvo politicheskoi literatury, 1956).

23. Arsenidze, "Iz vospominanii o Staline," p. 218.

24. Uratadze, *Vospominaniia gruzinskogo sotsial-demokrata*, p. 57.

25. Ibid., p. 67.

26. Kirtadze-Sikharulidze, "Vospominaniia," SShSSA, f. 8, op. 2, ch. 1, d. 43, ll. 215–216.

27. Ostrovskii, *Kto stoial za spinoi Stalina*, p. 213; Arsenidze, "Vospominaniia ob I. G. Tsereteli (iz perepiski R. Arsenidze s B. I. Nikolaevskim)," HIA, Nikolaevsky Collection, no. 15, box 10, item 78.

28. Arsenidze, "Vospominaniia ob I. G. Tsereteli."

29. Ostrovskii, *Kto stoial za spinoi Stalina*, p. 213; S. Jibuti, *Zaria vostoka*, January 10, 1937. Jibuti's article accusing Ramishvili was published two months before the latter's execution.

30. Kirtadze-Sikharulidze, "Vospominaniia," SShSSA, f. 8, op. 2, ch. 1, d. 43, l. 216; Arsenidze, "Iz vospominanii o Staline," pp. 218–219.

31. Kirtadze-Sikharulidze, "Vospominaniia," SShSSA, f. 8, op. 2, ch. 1, d. 43, ll. 216–217.

32. This event was reported to Arsenidze by Tiflis Committee member D. Kakheladze; Arsenidze, "Iz vospominanii o Staline," p. 219.

33. "Beseda s tov. Bobrovskoi, Ts. S.," SShSSA, f. 8, op. 2, ch. 1, d. 6, l. 178; Ts. Zelikson-Bobrovskia, *Zapiski riadovogo podpol'shchika (1894–1914)*, Part I (Moscow: Giz, 1922), pp. 67–68.

34. Ostrovskii, *Kto stoial za spinoi Stalina*, p. 217; Mikha Tskhakaia, "Vospominaniia," RGASPI, f. 157, op. 1, d. 54, ll. 17–18.

35. Service, *Stalin: A Biography*, pp. 54–55, tells the story of the "credo." It is taken from S. Kavtaradze, *tsarsulis purtslebi* [Papers from the Past], vol. I, pp. 17–20, a memoir, written in Georgian, which was translated for Service by Zakro Megreleshvili [Zakaria Megrelishvili]. Kavtaradze's account of the "credo" is available in Russian; SShSSA, f. 8, op. d. 279, ll. 30–32.

36. Ostrovskii, *Kto stoial za spinoi Stalina*, p. 218; Mikha Tskhakaia memoirs, RGASPI, f. 157, op. 1, d. 54, l. 18.

37. Eventually Koba published his views on this question, presumably based on his "credo," in *proletariatis brdzola* (Struggle of the Proletariat), no. 7, September 1, 1904; the Russian translation can be found as "Kak ponimaet sotsial-demokratiia natsional'nyi vopros?" in I. V. Stalin,

Sochineniia, I, pp. 32–55. Stalin evidently was concerned about his early writings and his "credo," as is clear from a letter he wrote to Sebastian Talaqvadze at the Georgian Branch of the Institute of Party History in Tiflis on January 2, 1925: "I received the materials (my articles) and thank you. I request: 1) do not publish them and other materials without my sanction, 2) send me, if possible, the whole run of *dro* and *akhali droeba*, for there are a whole series of my articles without signature in [those newspapers], 3) find somehow in the archive of the Union Committee my article 'Credo' written at the beginning of 1904, 4) send me the run of the illegal newspapers *Bor'ba* [*brdzola*] and *Bor'ba proletariata* [*proletariatis brdzola*]. With comradely greetings. I. Jugashvili (Stalin)." [RGASPI, f. 558, op. 1, d. 2667, ll. 1–2; Ostrovskii, *Kto stoial za spinoi Stalina*, pp. 48–49.]

38. See V. D. Mochalov's notes in R. Kosolapov (ed.), *Slovo tovarishchu Stalinu*, 2nd edition (Moscow: Paleia, 2002), p. 463.

39. Ostrovskii, *Kto stoial za spinoi Stalina*, pp. 218–219; Mikha Tskhakaia, "Vospominaniia," RGASPI, f. 157, op. 1, d. 54, l. 18; S. I. Kavtaradze memoirs, SShSSA, f. 8, op. 2, ch. 1, d. 19, ll. 22–23; I. V. Stalin, *Sochineniia*, I, p. 421.

40. Arsenidze, "Iz vospominanii o Staline," pp. 218–219.

41. Report from 1911 by Karpov, chief of the Tiflis Okhrana; published in *Zaria Vostoka*, December 23, 1925; cited in Trotsky, *Stalin*, p. 50.

42. Pavl Aksel'rod, "Ob"edinenie rossiiskoi sotsialdemokratii i eia zadachi," *Iskra*, no. 55, December 15, 1903; no. 57, January 15, 1904; reprinted in part in *Men'sheviki: Dokumenty i Materialy, 1903–1917* (Moscow: Rosspen, 1996), pp. 54–67; Ascher, *Pavel Axelrod*, p. 197.

43. V. I. Lenin, *PSS*, VIII, p. 370. See Lars Lih's comments on this passage in Lih, *Lenin Rediscovered*, pp. 524–525.

44. V. I. Lenin, *PSS*, VIII, p. 388.

45. GARF, f. 124, op. 13, d. 137, ll. 1–40b.

46. RGASPI, f. 17, op. 1, d. 168, translation from Georgian; GARF, f. DP, OO., 1905 g., m. d., 118, ch. 3, l. 21a, b; perlustration. My translation is from the handwritten Russian version in RGASPI.

47. RGASPI, f. 17, op. 1, d. 168, ll. 10–100b.

48. RGASPI, f. 17, op. 1, d. 168, ll. 17–170b. In socialist rhetoric Blanquism refers to the views of the French revolutionary Louis Blanqui (1805–1881), who famously favored revolution by a small group of insurgents, rather than relying on a mass workers' movement. Blanquism, then, was employed by socialists as a term to criticize those who favored seizure of power by a small group of conspirators. Engels saw him as a socialist by sentiment, not of ideas, and Rosa Luxemburg accused Lenin of Blanquism because of his emphasis on a centralized and conspiratorial party.

49. *Perepiska V. I. Lenina i rukovodimykh im uchrezhdenii RSDRP*, II, p. 417. The entire letter can also be found in V. I. Lenin, *Polnoe sobranie sochinenii*, IX, pp. 13–21.

50. "Indeed, it is fair to state that Menshevism did not really begin to take shape as a distinct political movement, and especially as a political culture, until after the collapse of the great revolutionary expectations of 1905, and the searing criticism and self-criticism that . . . revolutionary maximalism generated within the Menshevik camp." [Haimson, *The Making of Three Russian Revolutionaries: Voices from the Menshevik Past*, p. 8. For knowledge and deep

sensitivity to the voices of Russian Social Democracy, particularly its Menshevik wing, the writings of Leopold Haimson are unrivaled. Long engaged in interviewing the last survivors of the movement and in publishing their memoirs, Haimson has through his work (and that of several of his students, like Allan K. Wildman and Ziva Galili, as well as the Soviet historian, Albert Nenarokov) illuminated the contours of the rival political cultures of Russian Social Democracy.

51. *Perepiska V. I. Lenina i rukovodimykh im uchrezhdenii RSDRP*, II, pp. 387–390; A. V. Maskuliia, *Mikhail Gregor'evich Tskhakaia* (Moscow, 1968), p. 75; Levan Ebanoidze, *sakartvelos bolshevikuri organizatsiebi 1905–1908 tslebis revolutsiis periodshi* (Tbilisi, 1959), p. 159; Z. A. Akubzhanova, "KSK RSDRP v period podgotovki III s"ezda . . . ," pp. 143–144; *Kak rozhdalas' partiia bol'shevikov: Literaturnaia polemika 1903–04 gg. Sbornik* (Leningrad, 1925), p. 350.

52. *Perepiska V. I. Lenina i rukovodimykh im uchrezhdenii RSDRP*, III, pp. 45, 47.

53. Ibid., p. 88.

54. The letter can be found in a translation from Georgian done by Stalin in RGASPI, f. 558, op. 1, d. 3, l. 1–4. The published text has some minor changes. [I. V. Stalin, *Sochineniia*, I, pp. 56–58.]

Several Bolsheviks took pen names that reflected their connection to the party masses—for example, Olminskii adopted the name "Galerka" (cheap seats) and Bogdanov was "Riadavoi" (rank and file). Mikhail Olminskii (1863–1933) was an early adherent to Bolshevism, who from 1920 to 1928 headed *Istpart*, the Commission for the Study and Collection of Materials on the History of the October Revolution and the Party.

55. Daniel Rancour-Lafferiere in *The Mind of Stalin: A Psychoanalytic Study* (Ann Arbor, MI: Ardis, 1988) makes much of Stalin's use of metaphors of hitting and kicking and argues that this son of a cobbler had a special fondness for feet, boots, and kicking.

56. For a discussion of Plekhanov's views in 1903–1904, see Samuel H. Baron, *Plekhanov: The Father of Russian Marxism* (Stanford, CA: Stanford University Press, 1963), pp. 231–253.

57. I. V. Stalin, *Sochineniia*, I, pp. 56–58; Sergo Kavtaradze remembered that there were two committees in Kutaisi, that the Bolshevik one met with Zemliachka and strongly backed Lenin while the Menshevik one did not. Koba, he suggests suspiciously, might have convinced a group of wavering Social Democrats who approached him for advice. [SShSSA, f. 8, op. 15, d. 279, l. 70.]

58. Jughashvili had read the pamphlet by Galerka [Olminskii] and Riadovoi [A. A. Bogdanov], *Nashi nedorazumeniia* (Geneva: Kooperativnaia Tipografiia, 1904), in which various essays by these two authors appear. Aleksandr Bogdanov (1873–1928) was a physician, philosopher, and radical Bolshevik. His disputes with Lenin over elections to the State Duma as well as philosophical questions led to his expulsion from the leading ranks of the faction and defined what Bolshevism became and failed to become. Later he was a founder of the Proletcult (Proletarian Culture) movement in the early Soviet period and an initial contributor to systems theory.

59. *Perepiska V. I. Lenina i rukovodimykh im uchrezhdenii RSDRP*, III, pp. 223–226; reprinted with some changes in I. V. Stalin, *Sochineniia*, I, pp. 59–61. Whereas in the original letter Koba speaks of "the majority" (*bol'shinstvo*), in the latter publication it is changed to Bolsheviks (*bol'sheviki*). The latter term was just coming into usage in 1904 but had not yet replaced "the majority."

60. Vladimir Dmitrievich Bonch-Bruevich (1873–1955) was a Social Democrat from 1895 and adhered to the Bolshevik faction. Close to Lenin, he wrote a popular memoir of the Bolshevik leader. He was interested in religious questions, wrote a scholarly treatise on the Dukhobors, and in Soviet times was director of the Museum of the History of Religion and Atheism in Leningrad. His older brother, Mikhail (1870–1956), was an officer in both the tsarist and Soviet armies.

61. I. V. Stalin, *Sochineniia*, I, pp. 60–61.

CHAPTER 10. BACK IN THE GAME

1. V. Taratuta, "Kanun revoliutsii 1905 goda na Kavkaze, *Proletarskaia revoliutsiia*, no. 1 (48) (January 1926), pp. 210–216.

2. Shakhnazarian, *Krest'ianskoe dvizhenie v Gruzii*, pp. 83–84.

3. Z. A. Akubzhanova, "Kavkazskii Soiuznyi komitet RSDRP v period podgotovki III s"ezda RSDRP (do nachala pervoi russkoi revoliutsii)," *Trudy (Institut istorii partii pri TsK KP Azerbaidzhana—Filial In-ta M. L. pri TsK KPSS*, no. 26 (1962), p. 145.

4. The pseudonym "Khunkhuz" is the Russian version of the Chinese *hunghutsu*, the frontier bandits of the Far East. [My thanks to Aleksander Semyonov for pointing out the origin of the name.]

5. S. Kavtaradze, "Vospominaniia, I," SShSSA, f. 8, op. 15, d. 279, ll. 2–6.

6. Ibid., p. 25.

7. Ibid., l. 31.

8. Grigol Lortkipanidze (1881–1937) served as minister of education and minister of defense in the independent Republic of Georgia. After the fall of the Menshevik government, he chose to stay in the Soviet Union. He was tortured and died in 1937. His memoirs written in the early 1920s were published as *pikrebi sakartveloze* [Thoughts on Georgia] (Tbilisi: tbilisis sakhelmtsipo universitetis gamomtsemloba, 1995).

9. S. Kavtaradze, "Vospominaniia, I," SShSSA, f. 8, op. 15, d. 279, ll. 45–46.

10. Ibid., l. 46.

11. Ibid., l. 47.

12. Ibid., ll. 48–50.

13. Ibid., ll. 50–51.

14. Ibid., l. 51. The new committee formed in July 1904 consisted of Jughashvili, Sergo Kavtaradze, N. Kartsivadze, Aleksandre Tsulukidze (as the representative of the CUC), and Mikheil Okujava, along with Baron [Bartiome, Varfolomei] Bibineishvili, apparently the only member of the former committee. [Bibineishvili, *Za chetvert' veka*, p. 80.]

15. "Vospominaniia Sergo Kavtaradze, I," SShSSA, f. 8, op. 15, d. 279, l. 52.

16. Ostrovskii, *Kto stoial za spinoi Stalina*, p. 220; Ts. S. Zelikson-Bobrovskaia memoirs, RGASPI, f. 558, op. 4, d. 658, l. 7.

17. The Menshevik Noe Khomeriki (1883–1924), minister of agriculture under the independent Georgian republic (1918–1921), was captured and executed by the Soviet authorities after the unsuccessful August Uprising organized by the Mensheviks in 1924. The letter was found by the police when they searched the home of Varvara Khojashvili. [GARF, f. 102, OO., 1904, d. 5, ch. 11, "A," ll. 174–175ob.] The letter, first shown to me in the late 1980s by a Soviet archivist,

Zinaida Peregudova, was published only after the fall of the Soviet Union by B. F. Dodonova, "'A tsel'... ta, chtoby pokazat'sia narodu velikim chelovekom,' Politsiia i soratniki ob I. V. Staline," *Otechesvennye arkhivy*, no. 4 (1995), pp. 77–80.

18. Noe Ramishvili (1881–1930) was second in importance only to Noe Zhordania for much of the history of Georgian Menshevism. He was the first prime minister of independent Georgia, 1918, and after the Sovietization of Georgia he led the anti-Soviet Prometheus movement from emigration until he was assassinated in Paris by a Soviet agent. [HIA, Okhrana Collection, index xvii n, box 201, folder 5a.]

19. De Lon, "Stalin and Social Democracy, 1905–1922," pp. 177–178. Saghirashvili speculates that Tsabadze, who knew Stalin well from Gori, may have feared that Stalin would expose the meeting to the police.

20. Asatur Kakhoian, "Vmeste so Stalinym na s"ezde," SShSSA, f. 8, op. 2, ch. 1, d. 22, l. 221.

21. Unsigned, "rogor esmis sotsial-demokratias natsionaluri sakitkhi?" appeared in *proletariatis brdzola*, no. 7, September 1, 1904; Russian translation, "Kak ponimaet sotsial-demokratiia natsional'nyi vopros?" in I. V. Stalin, *Sochineniia*, I, pp. 32–55.

22. *Programma gruzinskoi revoliutsionnoi partii sotsialistov-federalistov, utverzhdennaia s"ezdom v 1904 g.* (n.p., n.d.), pp. 4–7; Talakvadze, *K istorii kommunisticheskoi partii Gruzii*, I, pp. 95–98; Zhordania, *Moia zhizn'*, p. 40.

23. I. V. Stalin, *Sochineniia*, I, p. 42.

24. Abraham Ascher, *The Revolution of 1905: Russia in Disarray* (Stanford, CA: Stanford University Press, 1988), pp. 29–31.

25. Well connected to the party leadership, Rozenfeld (Kamenev) corresponded regularly with Lenin and Krupskaia, who received his letters warmly. He had been arrested in Moscow on February 15, 1904, returned to the Caucasus in the summer, and when he failed to be accepted at Iur'ev University, he returned to Tiflis in the fall. On the congress, see Taratuta, "Kanun revoliutsii 1905 goda na Kavkaze," pp. 214–215; and Ebanoidze, *sakartvelos bolshevikuri organizatsiebi*, pp. 162–164. It is not certain that Koba Jughashvili was among the twelve delegates representing Tiflis, Baku, Batumi, and the Imeretino-Mingrelian committees, though Ostrovskii claims he was. [Ostrovskii, *Kto stoial za spinoi Stalina*, p. 222.]

26. Jones, *Socialism in Georgian Colors*, p. 121. The resolutions of the conference are available in V. V. Adoratskii, V. M. Molotov, and M. A. Savel'ev (eds.), *Leniniskii sbornik* (Moscow: Gosudarstvennoe isdatel'stvo, 1930), XV, pp. 249–253, and in *Perepiska V. I. Lenina i rukovodimykh im uchrezhdenii RSDRP*, III, pp. 215–223.

27. Kamenev, Tskhakaia, Prokopi Japaridze, Vladimir Nevskii, and someone named Rybkin (Letuchii) were chosen as delegates for the Third Party Congress. [*Tretii s"ezd RSDRP: Protokoly*, p. 469.]

28. The view of the Bolshevik party as a "cadre party" was dominant in the Sovietological literature of the Cold War years and was in large part the result of reading *What Is to Be Done?* and deducing from that text the actual practices and singular beliefs of the Bolsheviks. See, for example, Philip Selznick, *The Organizational Weapon: A Study of Bolshevik Strategy and Tactics* (Glencoe, IL: Free Press, 1960) [First edition published by the Rand Corporation in 1952], pp. 18–20. [My thanks to Martin Krieger for bringing this book to my attention.]

29. I. V. Stalin, "Klass proletariev i partiia prolitariev," *Sochineniia*, I, pp. 62–73.

30. Ibid., p. 93. The pamphlet was translated into Russian and published by the Caucasian Union Committee: *Vskol'z o partiinykh raznoglasiiakh* (Tiflis: Tipografiia soiuza, 1905) [SShSSA, f. 153, op. 1, d. 356, ll. 1–17; copy in author's possession]; the translation in *Sochineniia*, I, pp. 89–130, is slightly different and was made later directly from the Georgian version.

31. Ibid., pp. 98–99.

32. Ibid., p. 119.

33. Ascher, *The Revolution of 1905: Russia in Disarray*, p. 58.

34. E. L. Keenan, "Remarques sur l'histoire du mouvement révolutionnaire à Bakou (1904–1905)," *Cahiers du monde russe et soviétique*, III, 2 (April/June 1962), pp. 225–260; Ronald Grigor Suny, *The Baku Commune, 1917–1918: Class and Nationality in the Russian Revolution* (Princeton, NJ: Princeton University Press, 1972), pp. 35–36.

35. Ostrovskii and Edelman compare the published and unpublished versions of Zelikson-Bobroskaia's memoirs and show conclusively that Stalin briefly visited Baku only in December 1904 and, contrary to the Stalinist versions of the story promoted by Emelian Iaroslavkii, he was not the organizer and leader of the December strike. [Ostrovskii, *Kto stoial za spinoi Stalina*, p. 224; *Pravda*, December 26, 1939; Ts. S. Zelikson-Bobrovskaia memoirs, RGASPI, f. 558, op. 4, d. 658, ll. 9–11; Edelman, *Stalin: Biografiia v dokumentakh*, pp. 289–295; "Iz besedy s Ts. S. Bobrovskoi-Zelikson," May 6, 1948, RGASPI, f. 558, op. 4, d. 658, ll. 7–12.]

36. V. I. Lenin, *PSS*, VII, pp. 5–20.

37. Haimson, "Men'shevizm i bol'shevizm (1903–1917): Formirovanie mentalitetov i politicheskoi kul'tury," p. 24.

38. *Iskra*, no. 86, February 3, 1905; *Listovki kavkazskogo soiuza RSDRP* (Moscow, 1905), pp. 231–234; Megrian, pp. 51–53.

39. Ostrovskii, *Kto stoial za spinoi Stalina*, p. 224; A. Zakomodlin memoirs, RGASPI, f. 558, op. 4, d. 651, ll. 59–61.

40. For a rendition of *Varshavianka*, see https://www.youtube.com/watch?v=8-C-tjQKoTY. The lyrics were written by the Bolshevik Gleb Krzyzanowski.

41. Ascher, *The Revolution of 1905*, p. 67; Terence Emmons, "Russia's Banquet Campaign," *California Slavic Studies*, X (1977), pp. 45–86.

CHAPTER 11. REVOLUTIONARY BAPTISM

1. Abraham Ascher, *The Revolution of 1905: Russia in Disarray* (Stanford, CA: Stanford University Press, 1988), pp. 91–92.

2. Ibid., pp. 206–207.

3. Trotsky, *Stalin*, pp. 65–66.

4. R. Arsenidze, "Iz vospominanii o Staline," pp. 228–229. Razhden Arsenidze (1880–1965) joined the Menshevik wing of Georgian Social Democracy right after the party factions formed in 1903–1904. Exiled to Siberia by the tsarist regime, he returned to Georgia in 1917, was elected to the parliament of the independent Georgian republic, and served as minister of justice. After the invasion of the Red Army, he fled to France, where he wrote memoirs and gave valuable interviews on the Menshevik movement.

5. The best short account of the 1905 revolution in Caucasia, and one that emphasizes the extraordinary violence of that year in that place, is Anahide Ter Minassian, "Particularités de la

révolution de 1905 en Transcaucasie," in François-Xavier Coquin and Céline Gervais-Francelle (eds.), *1905, La premiére révolution russe* (Paris: Publications de la Sorbonne, 1986), pp. 315–337.

6. Letter from the Tiflis Committee of the RSDRP to the Editorial Board of *Vpered*, January 20 (February 2), 1905, in *Perepiska V. I. Lenina i rukovodimykh im uchrezhdenii RSDRP s partiinymi organizatsiiami, 1905–1907: Sbornik dokumentov v piati tomakh, tom I, kniga 1* (Moscow: Mysl, 1979), pp. 121–122.

7. Edelman, *Stalin: Biografiia v dokumentakh*, p. 302; B. Bibineishvili, *Kamo* (Moscow: Staryi bol'shevik, 1934), pp. 80–81.

8. V. Nevskii, "Ianvarskie dni 1905 goda na Kavkaze," *Proletarskaia revoliutsiia*, no. 4 (27) (1924), pp. 40–64; *Revoliutsiia 1905 goda v Zakavkaz'i: Khronika sobytii, dokumenty i materialy, po materialam Muzeia revoliutsii Gruzii* (Tiflis: Istpartotdel TsK KP(b) Gruzii, 1926), pp. 3–7, 11; N. Badriashvili (compiler), *1905 god v Tiflise. Fakticheskie materially po dannym muzeia i arkhiva Tifliskogo Soveta R.K i K. D. i gazetnykh khronik* (Tiflis: Izdatel'stvo Tiflisskogo soveta R. K. i K. D., 1926), pp. 5, 8–9.

9. Kote Charkviani memoirs, SShSSA, f. 8, op. 2, ch. 1, d. 54, ll. 214–215.

10. Most of the strikers were Georgians; the Armenian workers in Armenian-owned factories were among the poorest paid and the least involved in the labor movement. Women workers were generally not included, and in Batumi they protested that they had not been recruited for revolutionary activity. As suddenly as it had started, the strike ended. Just after they called off the Tiflis strike, on January 31, the Social Democrats brought the Batumi strike to a close as well. [Arsenidze, unpublished interviews, II, pp. 8–9; Eradze, Interview 5, August 6, 1962, pp. 34–37; Interview 6, pp. 1–2, 5, 8–9; T. I. Vulich, in HIA, B. I. Nikolaevsky Collection, box 207, folder 8; V. A. Starosel'skii, "Krest'ianskoe dvizhenie v Kutaisskoi gubernii," *Byloe*, I, 9 (September 1906), p. 236.]

11. Trotsky, *Stalin*, p. 53.

12. Police report from Tiflis, GARF, f. 102, op. 1904, d. 5, ch. 11, l. b, ll. 98–99.

13. Arsenidze, unpublished interviews, I, p. 7.

14. Ibid., pp. 8–9.

15. V. A. Noskov (1878–1913), one of whose pseudonyms was "Glebov," had become a Social Democrat as a young man in the 1890s. He was elected a member of the Central Committee at the Second Party Congress from the "majority," but became a "conciliationist" interested in mending relations between factions. After the 1905 revolution, he left political activity and at age thirty-five killed himself.

16. *Perepiska V. I. Lenina i rukovodimykh im uchrezhdenii RSDRP s partiinymi organizatsiiami 1903–1905 gg.*, III (Moscow: Mysl', 1977), pp. 460–461.

17. Aleksandr Stopani (1871–1932) was a professional revolutionary from 1892. He adhered to the Bolsheviks at the Second Congress of the RSDRP and was active in the Caucasus. In Soviet times he was active in the Society of Old Bolsheviks and a member of the Soviet Supreme Court. He is buried near the Kremlin wall.

18. *Proletarskaia revoliutsiia*, no. 5 (40) (May 1925), pp. 22–27; *Perepiska V. I. Lenina i rukovodimykh im uchrezhdenii RSDRP s partiinymi organizatsiiami, 1905–1907*, I, kn. 2 (Moscow: Mysl', 1979), pp. 147–149.

19. The alliance of Zhordania and Noe Ramishvili was a powerful combination that would continue through the years of the independent Georgian republic (1918–1921), when Zhordania

served as prime minister and Ramishvili as the tough minister of the interior. In his memoirs the National Democrat Geronti Kikodze remembered Zhordania's gentle directness and approachability in contrast with the hardness of Noe Ramishvili: "No one had ever seen this pale, emaciated man smile. His energetic gestures, laconic, commanding style, and sullen facial expression indicated a dictatorial bent." [Kikodze's memoirs were published in January 1989 in *mnatobi* (Light), and reviewed by Elizabeth Fuller, "Filling in the 'Blank Spots' in Georgian History: Noe Zhordania and Joseph Stalin," *Report on the USSR*, March 31, 1989, pp. 19–22; Talakvadze, *K istorii kommunisticheskoi partii Gruzii*, I, pp. 112–113.]

20. S. Khanoian, "V podpol'e," in A. Rokhlin (ed.), *Dvadtsat' piat' let bakinskoi organizatsii bol'shevikov (Osnovnye momenty razvitiia bakinskoi organizatsii)* (Baku: Bakinskii rabochii, 1924), p. 235. Vladimir Osipovich Levitskii-Tsederbaum (ed.), *Za chetvert' veka: Revoliutsionnye vospominaniia, 1892–1917 g.g.* (Moscow-Leningrad: Gosudarstvennoe izdatel'stvo, 1927), p. 235. Other sources on the factional struggle in early 1905 include: *mogzauri*, February 20, 1905; *Sotsialdemokrat*, nos. 2, 3, and 4; and the memoirs of Sh. Eliava in *revolutsiis matiane*, no. 11.

21. Letter signed "Rabochii" from Batumi, sent through Tiflis to Leipzig to be printed in *Vpered*. [GARF, f. 102, op. 1905, d. 5, ch. 11, 1.B, ll. 16–170b.]

22. Georgii Eradze, Menshevik Project, Columbia University, Interview with Leopold H. Haimson, 5, August 6, 1962, p. 20.

23. Ibid., p. 22.

24. Eradze dates this meeting sometime in 1904, and it is possible that there were two debates between Koba and Ramishvili, as Koba traveled in the summer of 1904 debating Mensheviks. But it is more likely that it was in March–April 1905 that the decisive debate took place, after which a new Batumi Committee led by Mensheviks was chosen. In my account here I have consolidated Eradze's unpublished memoir with that of Khariton Shavishvili's published account. [Khariton Chavichvily (Shavishvili), *Patrie, prisons, exil* (Paris: Défense de la France, 1946).] Khariton Shavishvili (1886–1975) was the representative of the independent Democratic Republic of Georgia to the League of Nations.

25. Police report, 1907, August 9, GARF, f. 102, op. 1907, d. 197, ll. 6–100b.

26. Chavichvily, *Patrie, prisons, exil*, pp. 70–71.

27. Aleksandr Martynov (1865–1935) was a Menshevik theorist, who earlier had been an *ekonomist* and after the 1917 revolution joined the Communist Party.

28. Chavichvily, *Patrie, prisons, exil*, p. 75.

29. Ibid., p. 79.

30. Georgii Eradze, Menshevik Project, Columbia University, Interview with Leopold H. Haimson, 5, August 6, 1962, pp. 24–31.

31. Chavichvily, *Patrie, prisons, exil*, p. 80.

32. Arsenidze, "Iz vospominanii o Staline," pp. 220–221.

33. Ibid., p. 221. Arsenidze goes on to say that he does not mean to accuse Koba of anti-Semitism but merely to show that whatever his view on the Jews he was prepared to use such language for his political purposes. Koba displayed here the ubiquitous practice of characterizing different nationalities by attributing to them essential features. Such assertions of national character fed into stereotyping of different cultural groups, xenophobia, and anti-Semitism.

34. Ibid., pp. 220–221.

35. Ibid., p. 222.

36. Edelman, *Stalin: Biografiia v dokumentakh*, pp. 365–367; "Iz vospominanii Davida Suliashvili," 1934, translated from Georgian, RGASPI, f. 558, op. 4, d. 651, ll. 170–175.

37. Menshevik Project, no. 4, pp. 8–11; Edelman, *Stalin: Biografiia v dokumentakh*, pp. 365–367; "Iz vospominanii Davida Suliashvili."

38. D. S., "meore qrilobis shemdeg (mogoneba)," *revoliutiis matiane*, 1928, no. 3 (20), pp. 139–140.

39. Police report from Tiflis, GARF, f. 102, op. 1904, d. 5, ch. 11, l. b, ll. 98–99.

40. M. G. Toroshelidze in a letter from Tiflis to Lenin in Geneva, in *Perepiska V. I. Lenina i rukovodimykh im uchrezhdenii RSDRP s partiinymi organizatsiiami, 1905–1907*, I, kn. 2, p. 180.

41. Talakvadze, *K istorii kommunisticheskoi partii Gruzii*, I, p. 118, n. 1.

42. N. N. Aladzhalova, *Iz bol'shevitskogo podpol'ia: Vospominaniia* (Tbilisi: sabchota sakartvelo, 1963), p. 20. The best account of Zhordania's victory over the Bolsheviks is given by Stephen F. Jones in *Socialism in Georgian Colors*, pp. 120–127.

43. Letter from "tvoia" from Berlin to Anna Avakova Shakhaniants in Moscow, March 3, 1905, in HIA, Okhrana, index xxa, folder 1a.

44. *Perepiska V. I. Lenina i rukovodimykh im uchrezhdenii RSDRP s partiinymi organizatsiiami, 1905–1907*, I, kn. 2, p. 180.

45. Arsenidze, unpublished interviews, I, pp. 180–181.

46. *Perepiska V. I. Lenina i rukovodimykh im uchrezhdenii RSDRP s partiinymi organizatsiiami, 1905–1907*, I, kn. 1, p. 127; M. Leman, "Iz proshlogo kavkazskikh bol'shevistskikh organizatsii," *Proletaraksaia revoliutsiia*, no. 5 (40) (May 1926), pp. 11–18.

47. Talakvadze, *K istorii kommunisticheskoi partii Gruzii*, I, p. 119.

48. Arsenidze, unpublished interviews, I, p. 97.

49. Ibid., pp. 7–8.

50. *Perepiska V. I. Lenina i rukovodimykh im uchrezhdenii RSDRP s partiinymi organizatsiiami, 1905–1907 gg.*, II, kn. 1 (Moscow: Mysl', 1982), pp. 20–21.

51. Talakvadze, *K istorii kommunisticheskoi partii Gruzii*, I, pp. 121–122.

52. Davrichewy, *Ah! Ce qu'on rigolait bien avec mon copain Staline*, pp. 158–159.

53. Ibid., p. 159.

54. See Mikha Tskhakaia's letter to *Vpered*, in *Perepiska V. I. Lenina i rukovodimykh im uchezhdenii RSDRP s partiinymi organizatsiiami, 1905–1907*, II, kn. 1, p. 143.

55. Shahumian's letter to Lenin, ibid., pp. 218–219.

56. *Perepiska V. I. Lenina i rukovodimykh im uchrezhdenii RSDRP s partiinymi organizatsiiami, 1905–1907*, II, kn. 2, pp. 99–101, 189, 192.

57. Ibid., II, kn. 1, p. 301.

58. Ibid., II, kn. 2, p. 90.

59. *Proletarskaia revoliutsiia*, no. 5 (40) (May 1925), pp. 22–27; *Perepiska V. I. Lenina i rukovodimykh im uchrezhdenii RSDRP s partiinymi organizatsiiami, 1905–1907*, I, kn. 2, pp. 147–149.

60. *Perepiska V. I. Lenina i rukovodimykh im uchrezhdenii RSDRP s partiinymi organizatsiiami, 1905–1907*, I, kn. 1, p. 221.

61. *Ouvrierist*, from the French word for "worker" (*ouvrier*), was a term used among Marxists in Europe to describe those who held that the movement and its party should be made up purely

of workers. Few in Russia took such a position, though the accusation of *rabocheliubstvo* (worker loving) was made against opponents who denigrated the role of intellectuals.

62. V. I. Lenin, "Samoderzhavie i proletariat," *Vpered*, no. 1 (December 22, 1904 [January 4, 1905], in *PSS*, IX, pp. 126–136.

63. V. I. Lenin, "Dolzhny li my organizovat' revoliutsiiu?" in *PSS*, IX, pp. 264–265.

64. A. V. Lunacharskii, "Tverdyi kurs," *Vpered*, no. 5, February 7, 1905; Robert C. Williams, *The Other Bolsheviks: Lenin and His Critics, 1904–1914* (Bloomington and Indianapolis: Indiana University Press, 1986), p. 65.

65. Ibid.

66. N. K. Krupskaya, *Reminiscences of Lenin* (New York: International Publishers, 1970), pp. 124–125.

CHAPTER 12. THE COMMITTEEMAN

1. Called Shushi by Armenians and Shusha by Azerbaijanis, this town was the cultural and political center of the contested region of Karabakh [Gharabagh in Armenian]. In August 1905 Armenians and Muslims fought each other in the town, and hundreds were killed.

2. Aleksandr Rusov, "Pis'mo," *Znamia*, no. 9 (September 1987), pp. 135–136. Rusov was a great nephew of Bogdan Knuniants, and he published letters from Faro Knuniants, who became a high party official after the revolution and married Aleksandr Pavlovich Serebrovskii (1884–1937/1938), whom Lenin appointed head of the Baku oil industry in 1920.

3. As Reginald E. Zelnik put it, "Marxist agitators . . . were still committed to a contradictory notion: that whereas the movement's goal at this stage should be the overthrow of autocracy and its replacement with the kind of liberal-democratic political order that Marxists associated with a capitalist economy, workers should also be waging a class war against the entire capitalist system, thereby challenging the very heart of that system, private ownership." ["Worry about Workers: Concerns of the Russian Intelligentsia from the 1870s to WHAT IS TO BE DONE?" in Marsha Siefert (ed.), *Extending the Borders of Russian History: Essays in Honor of Alfred J. Rieber* (Budapest and New York: CEU Press, 2003), p. 213.]

4. [Unsigned, but written by Iiuli Martov], "Deviatoe ianvaria," *Iskra*, no. 85, January 27 (February 9), 1905.

5. I. Martov, "Revoliutsionnye perspektivy," *Iskra*, no. 90 (March 3, 1905); excerpts reprinted in *Men'sheviki: Dokumenty i materialy, 1903–1917 gg.* (Moscow: Rosspen, 1996), pp. 103–107.

6. V. I. Lenin, "Dolzhny li my organizovat' revoliutsiiu?" *Vpered*, no. 7 (February 1, 1905); reprinted in *PSS*, 9, p. 272.

7. *Tretii s"ezd RSDRP (aprel'–mai 1905 goda): Protokoly* (Moscow: Gosudarstvennoe izdatel'stvo politicheskoi literatury, 1959), p. 147.

8. *Men'sheviki. Dokumenty i materialy. 1903–fevral' 1917 gg.*, pp. 107–129.

9. The Caucasian Union Committee delegates were: Tskhakaia, Kamenev, Nevskii, "Alesha" Japaridze, and Riabkin. [*Tretii s"ezd RSDRP, Aprel'-Mai 1905 goda. Protokoly* (Moscow: Gosudarstvennoe izdatel'stvo politicheskoi literatury, 1959), p. 469.] The congress took place April 12–27 (April 25–May 10), 1905.

10. Krupskaya, *Reminiscences of Lenin*, p. 123. The Menshevik Tiflis Committee sent a letter to the congress protesting its legality and pointing out that a congress could be called only by

the Council of the Party, which in this case had not authorized this congress. [*Tretii s"ezd RSDRP*, pp. 307–309.]

11. *Tretii s"ezd RSDRP*, p. 254.

12. Ibid., pp. 255, 259, 267, 262, 332. Japaridze's claim was challenged by R. S. Zemliachka [Zalkind]: "Not long ago I traveled around the Caucasian committees. I was together with Comrade Golubin [Japaridze] at the committee meeting in Baku, and I was surprised that there were so few workers in the committees. In the Baku Committee at that time there was one worker. (Golubin: Two). In Batumi one, in Kutaisi—not one. And only in the Tiflis Committee were there a few workers. Is it possible that the Caucasian comrades prefer intellectual committeemen to worker committeemen?" [Ibid., p. 334.]

13. Ibid., p. 333. For a different view of these discussions at the Third Party Congress, see Lih, *Lenin Rediscovered*, pp. 540–543.

14. On this conflict, see Krupskaya, *Reminiscences of Lenin*, pp. 126–127; and Trotsky, *Stalin*, pp. 61–63. Aleksei Rykov (1881–1938) was a moderate Bolshevik. He succeeded Lenin as head of the Soviet government in 1924 and held that post until replaced by Viacheslav Molotov in 1931. He was identified with the Bukharin wing of the party and opposed Stalin's policies toward the peasantry. He was tried along with Bukharin in 1938 and executed.

15. *Tretii s"ezd RSDRP*, pp. 339–341.

16. *Tretii s"ezd RSDRP*, p. 194. For socialists the experience of the French Revolution of 1789, the Jacobin "reign of terror" of 1793, and the Paris Commune of 1870–1871 framed their understanding of the process of revolution. Girondins were the more moderate faction among French revolutionaries, while the Jacobins were the strongest advocates of terror as an instrument of rule. The Vendée was the region in the west of France where a massive resistance to the revolutionary government in Paris was viciously repressed.

17. B. Gorev, "Za kulisami pervoi revoliutsii: Otryvki iz vospominanii o deiatel'nosti peterburgskikh bol'shevikov vo vtoroi polovine 1905 goda," *Istoriko-revoliutsionnnyi biulleten'*, no. 1 (January 1922), p. 12.

18. Edelman, *Stalin: Biografiia v dokumentakh*, pp. 340–341; *Proletarii*, no. 12, August 16 (3), 1905; ibid., no. 15, September 5 (August 23), 1905.

19. I. V. Stalin, "Korotko o partiinykh raznoglasiiakh," *Sochineniia*, I, p. 93; the original Georgia article can be found in i. v. stalini, "gakvrit partiul utankhmoebaze," *tkhzulebani* (Tbilisi: sakhelgami politikuri literaturis sektori, 1947), pp. 86–124.

20. I. V. Stalin, *Sochineniia*, I, pp. 102–103.

21. Ibid., pp. 115–116.

22. Ibid., p. 127.

23. *Perepiska V. I. Lenina i rukovodimykh im uchrezhdenii RSDRP s partiinymi organizatsiiami, 1905–1907*, III, kn. 1, p. 103.

24. V. I. Lenin, "'Bor'ba proletariata,'" *PSS*, 11, pp. 386–387.

25. "Otvet Sotsial-Demokratu," I. V. Stalin, *Sochineniia*, pp. 164–165.

26. Kalistrat Dolidze, "I. V. Stalin na stokgol'mskom s"ezde," SShSSA, f. 8, op. 2, ch. 1, d. 15, l. 212.

27. Handwritten letter from Vano in Tiflis to Lenin in Geneva, RGASPI, f. 558, op. 1, d. 938, ll. 1–4; reprinted in *Perepiska V. I. Lenina i rukovodimykh im uchrezhdenii RSDRP s partiinymi organizatsiiami, 1905–1907*, II, kn. 1, pp. 294–297. An account written in the late 1930s mentions

that Koba attended and spoke at a number of meetings in the homes of Ivane Mgeladze (the debate with Ramishvili, which he dates May 1905), and others. Later, in the summer of 1905, Illarion Darakhvelidze traveled with Koba, who stayed in Gomi, and went on to Chokhatauri, Chiatura, and Batumi. [Illarion Darakhvelidze, "O revoliutsionnoi rabote t. Stalina v Batume," *Batumskaia demonstratsiia 1902 goda* (Moscow, 1937), p. 62.] On July 29, Koba arrived in the village of Partskhma in Guria and lived with the peasant Sepe Tsintsadze. [T. Zhgenti, *1905 tseli guriashi* (Tbilisi, 1936), p. 113.]

28. *Perepiska V. I. Lenina i rukovodimykh im uchrezhdenii RSDRP s partiinymi organizatsiiami, 1905–1907,* II, 1, pp. 294–297.

29. Arsenidze, "Iz vospominanii o Staline," p. 223.

30. I am grateful to Professor Robert Himmer for a copy of the original of this article, unpublished in I. V. Stalin, *Sochineniia,* and to Stephen Rapp for his translation of key passages.

31. Letter of May 10, 1905, RGASPI, f. 558, op. 1, d. 17, ll. 1–2.

32. *Men'sheviki: Dokumenty i materialy. 1903–fevral' 1917 gg.* (Moscow: Rosspen, 1996), pp. 130–133.

33. This allergy to participation in government would be fatally reversed in 1917 to the detriment of the Mensheviks in Russia. The Bolsheviks, who in 1905 were prepared to join such a provisional government, would twelve years later take precisely the opposing position and benefit from worker radicalism.

34. Arsenidze, unpublished interviews, I, pp. 10–11; Ebanoidze, *sakartvelos bolshevikuri organizatsiebi,* pp. 174–175; *Sotsial-Demokrat,* no. 1. The resolutions of this conference are published in *Men'sheviki: Dokumenty i materialy, 1903–fevral' 1917 gg.,* pp. 130–133.

35. *Men'sheviki: Dokumenty i materialy. 1903–fevral' 1917 gg.,* pp. 130–133. The prevalent fear among the Social Democrats was that the ethnic and religious differences in Caucasia could lead to violence, as had happened in Baku. Taking a strong stand against nationalism, the conference opposed any notion of territorial autonomy for the peoples of the Caucasus or a federation for the future Russian republic. Rather they called for local government elected equally by all peoples of the region and guaranteeing the use of one's native language. The conference also rejected cooperation with the newly formed Georgian Socialist Federalist Party, *sakartvelo,* as well as with the Armenian *Dashnaktsutyun* and the *Hnchak* Party, all of which they considered too nationalistic. [*Konferentsiia kavkazskikh sotsial-demokraticheskikh rabochikh organizatsii* (Geneva: Partiia, 1905), pp. 4–5.]

36. Edelman, *Stalin: Biografiia v dokumentakh,* p. 351; S. T. Arkomed, "Krasnyi terror na Kavkaze i okhrannoe otdelenie," *Katorga i ssylka,* no. 6 (13) (1924), pp. 71–83.

37. K. Tsintsadze, "chemi mogonebani," *revoliutsiis matiane,* no. 2 (1923), pp. 117–122; no. 3 (1923), pp. 68–70; Kote Tsintsadze, *rogor vibrdzodit proletariatis diktaturistvis (chemi mogonebani 1903–1920 tslamde)* (Tbilisi, 1927), pp. 12–18.

38. Ostrovskii, *Kto stoial za spinoi Stalina,* pp. 232–233; M. E. Bibineishvili memoirs, SSM, d. 43/1, l. 2.

39. K. Tsintsadze, "chemi mogonebani," p. 121. Tskhakaia reported that people discussed Lenin's *What Is to Be Done?* and *One Step Forward, Two Steps Backward,* and he suggested that the former be reprinted, as there were only five or six copies in all of Caucasia. The first book, which Lenin already considered historic and less relevant to the current revolutionary moment, was reprinted only in 1907 in a collection of Lenin's works, *Za 12 let.*

40. Ostrovskii, *Kto stoial za spinoi Stalina*, pp. 232–233; G. Nutsubidze memoirs, SSM, d. 509, l. 1.

41. Chavichvily, *Patrie, prisons, exil*, p. 94.

42. Ibid., pp. 100–101.

43. Ibid., pp. 111–112.

44. Arsenidze, "Iz vospominanii o Staline," p. 229.

45. Letter of Tskhakaia to Lenin, June 28, 1905, in *Perepiska V. I. Lenina i rukovodimykh im uchrezhdenii RSDRP s partiinymi organizatsiiami, 1905–1907*, III, 1, p. 120.

46. Memoirs of Domenti Dolidze, SShSSA, f. 8, op. 2, ch. 1, d. 15, l. 201.

47. *Perepiska V. I. Lenina i rukovodimykh im uchrezhdenii RSDRP s partiinymi organizatsiiami, 1905–1907*, III, 1, p. 122.

48. Arsenidze, "Iz vospominanii o Staline," pp. 230–231; memoirs of I. Bakhtadze, SShSSA, f. 2417, op. 1, d. 568, ll. 1–4. After the funeral Koba participated in three days of discussions between Bolsheviks and Mensheviks in various homes in Khoni on the conferences that had been held in London and Geneva. [Ostrovskii, *Kto stoial za spinoi Stalina*, p. 233; *kommunisti* (Tiflis), no. 233, October 6, 1935.]

49. "Vospominaniia Sergo Kavtaradze." Sergo (Sergei) Kavtaradze (1885–1971) became a Trotskyist in the 1920s and was imprisoned several times, eventually sentenced to death. But Stalin intervened, and he was brought into the Soviet foreign service. He served as vice minister of foreign affairs under Molotov and Soviet ambassador to Rumania.

50. V. I. Lenin, *PSS*, XI, pp. 3–131.

51. Both Lenin and Koba spoke of workers' instincts in 1905 and their natural tendency to move toward socialism. In a very suggestive article, Anna Krylova argues that this new attention to instinctual drives, feelings, and sense in Bolshevik writing at the moment of the first revolution was a solution to the dichotomous opposition of spontaneity characteristic of workers and consciousness embedded in Social Democrats that he struggled with in *What Is to Be Done?* ["Beyond the Spontaneity-Consciousness Paradigm"]. "In the Bolshevik vision, the conscious and the instinctual constitute the two extremes of the desirable worker-self" (p. 22).

52. *"Bol'shinstvo" ili "Men'shinstvo"?* (Geneva: Tipografiia Partii, 1905), p. 11. This pamphlet was authored by N. Khomeriki and N. Ramishvili, with a foreward by Fedor Dan and an appendix by Irakli Tsereteli.

53. V. I. Lenin, *PSS*, XI, pp. 16, 37.

54. Ibid., p. 101.

55. *Iskra*, no. 110, May 15, 1905; Esther Kingston-Mann, "Lenin and the Challenge of Peasant Militance: From Bloody Sunday, 1905 to the Dissolution of the First Duma," *Russian Review*, XXXVIII, 4 (October 1979), p. 439.

56. Lenin, *PSS*, XI, p. 48.

57. Ibid., p. 71.

58. Esther Kingston-Mann, "Deconstructing the Romance of the Bourgeoisie: A Russian Marxist Path Not Taken," *Review of International Political Economy*, X, 1 (February 2003), pp. 93–117.

59. V. I. Lenin, *PSS*, XII, p. 265; Kingston-Mann, "Lenin and the Challenge of Peasant Militance," p. 446.

60. *"Bol'shinstvo" ili "Men'shinstvo"?*, p. 26. This pamphlet was translated from Georgian articles in *sotsial-demokrat*, nos. 1–3.

61. V. I. Lenin, *PSS*, XIII, p. 221; Kingston-Mann, "Lenin and the Challenge of Peasant Militance," p. 455.

62. V. I. Lenin, *PSS*, XIII, pp. 50–54.

63. Ibid., p. 84.

64. The Bolshevik Pilipe Makharadze made this point in his book, *1905 tseli amierkavkasiashi* (Tiflis: sakhelgami, 1926) [*The Year 1905 in Transcaucasia*], which is cited in V. Tsuladze, "Bol'shevizm v Gruzii," Menshevik Collection, Columbia University, pp. 4–5.

65. From an unsigned article, "From the Party, published in *proletariatis brdzola*," August 15, 1905, and attributed by the Institute of Marxism-Leninism to Stalin [RGASPI, f. 71, op. 10, d. 179, ll. 221–223]. This particular article had been set in type but ultimately was not published in Stalin's collected works. It was published in the post-Soviet collection of Stalin's works: *Stalin. Trudy, II (1905–Mai 1906)*, ed. R. I. Kosolapov (Moscow: Prometei info, 2013), pp. 242–244.

66. *proletariatis brdzola*, no. 10, July 15, 1905; I. V. Stalin, *Sochineniia*, I, pp. 131–137.

67. The first part of the article was published in *proletariatis brdzola*, no. 11, August 15, 1905; reprinted in Russian translation, along with the previously unpublished second part, in I. V. Stalin, *Sochineniia*, I, pp. 138–159. See also an article on the Provisional Government and the Bolsheviks' tactics attributed by the Institute of Marxism-Leninism to Stalin, published in *proletariatis brdzola*, July 1 (14), 1905. Here the author repeated the Leninist position: "Bolsheviks are for a revolutionary government of the proletariat and poor peasants. There cannot be an all-Social Democratic government because the proletariat is only a small part of the population. The government would be the in the form of the democratic dictatorship of the proletariat and peasantry."

68. From a pamphlet of August 1905, attributed to Stalin by the Institute of Marxism-Leninism, RGASPI, f. 71, op. 10, d. 169, ll. 189–190; Erik van Ree, "Stalin's Bolshevism: The First Decade," *International Review of Social History*, XXXIX (1994), p. 369.

69. From another pamphlet attributed to Stalin by the Institute of Marxism-Leninism, RGASPI, f. 71, op. 10, d. 169, l. 296; van Ree, "Stalin's Bolshevism," p. 369.

CHAPTER 13. THE TERRORIST

1. On Russian terrorism and its relationship to the original Russian Social Democrats, see Norman Naimark, *Terrorists and Social Democrats: The Russian Revolutionary Movement under Alexander III* (Cambridge, MA: Harvard University Press, 1983). A more condemnatory account of terror originating in personal pathology can be found in Anna Geifman, *Thou Shalt Kill: Revolutionary Terrorism in Russia, 1894–1917* (Princeton, NJ: Princeton University Press, 1993).

2. An excellent discussion of the use of violence in Caucasia is available in Erik van Ree, "Reluctant Terrorists? Transcaucasian Social-Democracy, 1901–1909," *Europe-Asia Studies*, LX, 1 (January 2008), pp. 127–154. Van Ree demonstrates that the Social Democrats at first used terrorism defensively, then offensively during the revolutionary years 1905–1907, only to revert to the defensive use in the postrevolutionary period. He also argues against the psychohistorical idea that revolutionary violence was the result of personal pathology of the perpetrators and contends that terrorism in the Russian Empire "arose as a product of the deep-seated party culture of *Konspiratsiya*, characterised by a particular war mentality" (p. 130).

3. Geifman, *Thou Shalt Kill*, p. 85.

4. V. I. Lenin, "Pochemu S.-D. dolzhna ob"iavit' voinu S.-R.?" *PSS*, VI, p. 375. This article, written in 1902, was not published until 1923. For a full study of Lenin's views on violence, see James Ryan, *Lenin's Terror: The Ideological Origins of Early Soviet State Violence* (New York: Routledge, 2012).

5. V. I. Lenin, "Zadachi otriadov revoliutsionnoi armii," *PSS*, XI, pp. 341–342. This article was not published until 1926.

6. RGASPI, f. 124, op. 1, d. 1102, l. 5.

7. Van Ree, "Reluctant Terrorists?" p. 131; D. A. Vadachkoria memoirs, RGASPI, f. 558, op. 4, d. 537; quoted in Montefiore, *Young Stalin*, pp. 75–76.

8. Geifman, *Thou Shalt Kill*, p. 23.

9. "Bor'ba s revoliutsionnym dvizheniem na Kavkaze v epokhu stolypinschiny. (Iz perepiski P. A. Stolypina s gr. I. I. Vorontsovym-Dashkovym.)," *Krasnyi arkhiv*, 3 (34) (1929), p. 187.

10. Ibid., p. 204.

11. Zhordaniia, *Moia zhizn'*, p. 44.

12. Uratadze, *Vospominaniia gruzinskogo sotsial-demokrata*, p. 130.

13. "Rabochie Kavkaza, pora otomstit'," in I. V. Stalin, *Sochineniia*, I, pp. 74–80. Bashibazouks were irregular mercenaries in the Ottoman army who were known for their lack of discipline, plundering, and brutality toward their enemies.

14. As Erik van Ree puts it, "This selective approach to terrorism confirms once again that the social democrats were rational strategists. . . . If one would insist on classifying them in psychological terms, it can be suggested that they represented an extreme case of the political instrumentalisation of morality and suffered from an excess rather than from a lack of rationality." [van Ree, "Reluctant Terrorists?" p. 152.]

15. *Revoliutsiia 1905 goda v Zakavkaz'i*, pp. 162–163.

16. For the investigation of the murder of Exarch Nikon, see Dzhemal Gamakhariia and Tatiana Erokhina (eds.), *Materialy ob ubiistve Ekzarkha Nikona (Sofiiskii) i nekotorye voprosy tserkovnoi istorii (1908–1913)* (Tbilisi-Riazan: Saari, 2016).

17. The best source for the revolution in Chiatura is K. Tsintsadze, *rogor vibrzodit proletariatis diktaturistvis*, pp. 19–38.

18. Ostrovskii, *Kto stoial za spinoi Stalina*, p. 229; *Novoe obozrenie* (Tiflis), February 8, 1905; O. V. Edelman, "Mezhnatsional'nye stolknoveniia v Baku 7–10 fevralia 1905 goda v doumentakh Departamenta politsii," *Russkii sbornik: Issledovaniia po istorii Rossii*, XXII (2017), pp. 343–412.

19. Luigi Villari, *Fire and Sword in the Caucasus* (London: T. Fischer Unwin; New York: James Pott, 1906), pp. 169–170. Villari was a gifted observer who traveled throughout the South Caucasus in 1905 and visited "every important centre of political unrest" (p. 7). See also Ronald Grigor Suny, "Images of the Armenians in the Russian Empire," in Richard G. Hovannisian (ed.), *The Armenian Image in History and Literature* (Malibu, CA: Undena, 1981), pp. 105–137. On the pogroms, see Cecilia Bobrovskaya, *Twenty Years in Underground Russia: Memoirs of a Rank-and-File Bolshevik* (Chicago: Proletarian Publishers, 1976), pp. 110–112.

20. Ostrovskii, *Kto stoial za spinoi Stalina*, p. 230; RGASPI, f. 558, op. 4, d. 583, ll. 13–14, 17, 45.

21. Zhgenti, "batumi," *revolutsiis matiane*, 1928, no. 3 (20), pp. 120–121.

22. Badriashvili, *1905 g. v Tiflise*, pp. 17, 19.

23. Ibid., p. 11.

24. Ibid., p. 15.

25. Ibid., pp. 22, 28.

26. For an assessment of Vorontsov-Dashkov, see D. I. Ismail-Zade, *I. I. Vorontsov-Dashkov—administrator, reformator* (Saint Petersburg: Nestor-istoriia, 2008).

27. These "combat squads," Erik van Ree has shown, "were no terrorist units. Their job was to protect the party and workers' organizations. They were moreover expected in due course to evolve into a revolutionary army, the instrument of the armed uprising." [van Ree, "Reluctant Terrorists?" p. 134.]

28. Ia. Davtian, "Tiflisskaia voennaia organizatsiia v 1906–1907 g.g.," *Proletarskaia revoliutsiia*, no. 4 (16) (1923), p. 144. The information about the opposing currents among the Caucasian Bolsheviks comes from N. N. Zhordania, "Staline," a French translation of his article "stalini" in *brdzolis khma*, no. 65 (October 1936). [HIA, Nicolaevsky Collection, series 90, box 144 (reel 123).]

29. Manucharian in *Bakinskii rabochii*, no. 211 (1922); cited in G. B. Garibzhanian, "S. G. Shaumian v emigratsii," *Patma-banasirakan Handes*, I (24) (1964), pp. 136–137.

30. Stepan Shahumian (1878–1918) was a competitor of Koba Jughashvili for the role of "Caucasian Lenin." He was the leader of the so-called Baku Commune, a Bolshevik-led government in 1918. The differences between Shahumian and Jughashvili were acute. Shahumian was usually opposed to terrorism; there is no mention in any sources of his being involved in the activities of the armed *druzhiny*; and during his administration in Baku in 1917–1918 the Bolsheviks did not use state terror to hold on to power. When his government lost a crucial vote in the local soviet, Shahumian and his comrades stepped down. He died as one of the famous "Twenty-Six Baku Commissars" executed by anti-Communists in the deserts of Turkmenistan during the Russian Civil War.

31. Arsenidze, "Iz vospominanii o Staline," pp. 228–229.

32. Davrichewy, *Ah! Ce qu'on rigolait bien avec mon copain Staline*, p. 173. Davrishev also mentions Shahumian in this company, though it is unlikely that he engaged in terrorism.

33. This characterization of Mdivani is from Uratadze, *Vospominaniia gruzinskogo sotsial-demokrata*, pp. 208–210. Polikarpe (Budo) Mdivani (1877–1937) was a leading Georgian Bolshevik, who was a key member of the leadership that Sovietized Georgia in 1921. He was a member of the "national Communists" who defied Stalin and Orjonikidze's efforts to subordinate Soviet Georgia within a Transcaucasian Soviet Federated Socialist Republic. Later he sided with the Trotskyist Left Opposition, and in 1937 he was found guilty of treason, and shot, as were his wife, daughter, and sons.

34. Ibid., p. 209.

35. Davrichewy, *Ah! Ce qu'on rigolait bien avec mon copain Staline*, pp. 173–174.

36. Ibid., p. 174.

37. Arsenidze, "Iz vospominanii o Staline," pp. 219, 223.

38. P. Dashtoian, "Vospominaniia o tov. Staline," SShSSA, f. 8, op. 2, ch. 1, d. 12, ll. 112–113.

39. Davrichewy, *Ah! Ce qu'on rigolait bien avec mon copain Staline*, p. 175.

40. Ibid., pp. 176–177.

41. Ibid., pp. 180–182; P. Dashtoian, "Vospominaniia o tov. Staline," SShSSA, f. 8, op. 2, ch. 1, d. 12, ll. 112–113.

42. Bachua Kuprashvili, a member of the Tiflis Bolshevik *druzhina*, took issue with the elevation of Kamo above the rest. "Our military organization was called the Kamo group for some

reason, but it is not correct. We brought Kamo into our group a year after the group had been organized by the center. He participated only in one action but was given credit for everything." [Bachua Kuprashvili memoirs, SShSSA, f. 8, op. 2, ch. 1, d. 624, ll. 26.]

43. Bibineishvili, *Kamo*, p. 34. A version of the story can be found in Vardoian, "Vospominaniia," SShSSA, f. 8, op. 2, ch. 1, d. 7, l. 70.

44. Bibineishvili, *Kamo*, p. 46.

45. Montefiore sees Kamo as one of Stalin's "henchmen," a "gangster," a "psychotic" bank robber. [*Young Stalin*, pp. 4–5, 310.] Geifman has an even darker view of Kamo as a pathological killer, "an individual whose derangement became a catalyst for violent behavior that in the prevailing circumstances of the era happened to take revolutionary form." [*Thou Shalt Kill*, p. 167; on his mental condition, see pp. 322–323, nn. 99–101.]

46. Bibineishvili, *Kamo*, pp. 49, 54, 68.

47. Davrichewy, *Ah! Ce qu'on rigolait bien avec mon copain Staline*, pp. 188–189.

48. Ibid., p. 189. While this account rings true, one remains suspicious about Davrishev's recall of the exact conversation half a century earlier.

49. Ibid., p. 200. The members of the Tiflis Bolshevik *druzhina* that would carry out the "expropriations" included Eliso Lominadze, Vano Kalandadze, Bachua Kuprashvili, Datiko Chiabrishvili, Iliko Chachiashvili, Akaki Dalakishvili, Arkadi Elbakidze, Teopile Kakrishvili, Kamo, and others. [Bibineishvili, *Kamo*, p. 98.]

50. Ibid., p. 191.

51. Varl. Kalandadze and Vl. Mkheidze, *Ocherki revoliutsionnogo dvizheniia v Gurii* (Saint Petersburg: Epokha, 1906), pp. 35–36; *Revoliutsiia 1905 g. v Zakavkaz'i*, pp. 16, 33.

52. For the origins of the Gurian peasant revolt, see the excellent chapter in Jones, *Socialism in Georgian Colors*, pp. 129–158; and for historical background to the revolt, Kenneth Church, "From Dynastic Principality to Imperial District: The Incorporation of Guria into the Russian Empire to 1856," PhD dissertation in history, University of Michigan, 2001.

53. Suny, *The Making of the Georgian Nation*, pp. 144–154; Church, "From Dynastic Principality to Imperial District."

54. R. Arsenidze, unpublished interviews, HIA, Nicolaevsky Collection, box 667, folders 4–5, pp. 103–104; van Ree, "Reluctant Terrorists?" p. 137.

55. Kalandadze and Mkheidze, *Ocherki revoliutsionnogo dvizheniia v Gurii*, pp. 40–41.

56. Ibid., p. 44. This quotation, ostensibly by a peasant, is taken from a Social Democratic pamphlet and is probably the paraphrase of the authors. But the sentiments, as corroborated by other sources, were those of the Gurian peasants.

57. *Revoliutsiia 1905 goda v Zakavkaz'i*, p. 18.

58. Jones, *Socialism in Georgian Colors*, p. 140.

59. Uratadze, *Vospominaniia gruzinskogo sotial-demokrata*, pp. 44–46.

60. Jones, *Socialism in Georgian Colors*, p. 132. "Georgian delegates made up a quarter of the Menshevik wing at the RSDLP Stockholm congress in 1906 and almost a third (28.9 percent) at the Fifth RSDLP (London) Congress of 1907. At the Fifth Congress, around 30 percent of all Georgian delegates were from Guria," which Bolshevik Grigorii Aleksinskii called the "citadel of Menshevism."

61. Uratadze, *Vospominaniia gruzinskogo sotsial-demokrata*, pp. 170–172; Jones, *Socialism in Georgian Colors*, pp. 143–144.

62. *Perepiska V. I. Lenina i rukovodimykh im uchrezhdenii RSDRP s partiinymi organizatsiiami, 1905–1907*, II, kn. 1, p. 203.

63. Ibid., p. 204.

64. Arsenidze, unpublished interviews, II, p. 4.

65. *Revoliutsiia 1905 goda v Zakavkaz'i*, pp. 35–36.

66. Villari, *Fire and Sword in the Caucasus*, p. 130.

67. Ibid., p. 45.

68. Suny, "Images of the Armenians in the Russian Empire," pp. 31–51.

69. Badriashvili, *1905 g. v Tiflise*, p. 79.

70. *Revoliutsiia 1905 goda v Zakavkaz'i*, p. 42; Simon Vratzian, "The Armenian Revolution and the Armenian Revolutionary Federation (Part II)," *Armenian Review*, III, 4, p. 65.

71. *Iz vospominanii russkogo uchitelia Pravoslavnoi Gruzinskoi Dukhovnoi Seminarii* (Moscow: Russkaia pechatia, 1907), pp. 73–84. An investigation into the incident found that the police action had been permitted by the ethnic Russian exarch of the Georgian Church, Aleksei, and the rector of the seminary, Nikandr (Fenomenov).

72. *Revoliutsiia 1905 goda v Zakavkaz'i*, p. 42; Jones, *Socialism in Georgian Colors*, pp. 169–170.

73. Uratadze, *Vospominaniia gruzinskogo sotsial-demokrata*, p. 110. Ferdinand Lassalle (1825–1864) was a prominent German socialist, the founder of the All-German Workers' Association, which evolved into the German Social Democratic Party. His advocacy of universal manhood suffrage influenced Chancellor Otto von Bismarck. Marx criticized Lassalle's conception of the socialist state in his famous essay, *Critique of the Gotha Program*. Lassalle was killed in a duel over the woman he loved.

74. Kh. A. Vermishev, *Iz nedavnego proshlogo. 29 avgusta 1905 g. v Tiflisskoi gorodskoi dume* (Baku, 1917); Badriashvili, *1905 g. v Tiflise*, p. 70, 73; Eradze, Interview, no. 7, pp. 46–48; *Iskra*, no. 111, September 24, 1905, p. 7; *Revoliutsiia 1905 g. v Zakavkaz'i*, pp. 65–66.

75. Ostrovskii, *Kto stoial za spinoi Stalina*, p. 235.

76. Bibineishvili, *Za chetvert' veka*, p. 82.

77. Ostrovskii, *Kto stoial za spinoi Stalina*, p. 235.

78. Ibid., p. 237.

79. *Revoliutsiia 1905 g. v Zakavkaz'i*, pp. 78–80.

80. Ibid., pp. 159–160.

81. S. V. Maglakelidze, *Vladimir Aleksandrovich Starosel'skii (Dokumenty i materialy)* (Tiflis, 1969), p. 136.

82. Sh. Gortsev [Shalva Natadze], *Kak gruzinskie krest'iane boriutsia za svobodu* (Moscow: Tipografiia A. P. Paplovskago, 1906), pp. 20–22.

83. "From this moment on, . . . the power and cohesion of the revolutionary forces slowly but surely began to decline, to the rising chorus of the mutual recriminations of the various opposition and revolutionary parties." [Leopold H. Haimson, "The Parties and the State: The Evolution of Political Attitudes," in Cyril E. Black (ed.), *The Transformation of Russian Society* (Cambridge, MA: Harvard University Press, 1960), p. 131.]

84. Estimates of those killed range from thirty-six to forty-one; *Revoliutsiia 1905 g. v Zakavkaz'i*, pp. 83–84, 159–160; Badriashvili, *1905 god v Tiflise*, pp. 94, 99.

85. Ostrovskii, *Kto stoial za spinoi Stalina*, p. 238; A. Khumarian, *Zaria vostoka*, April 21, 1936; SShSSA, f. 8, op. 2, ch. 1, d. 50, ll. 163–167. Koba did not write for this newspaper, but Shahumian was a frequent contributor.

86. Ostrovskii, *Kto stoial za spinoi Stalina*, p. 238; Talakvadze, *K istorii Kommunisticheskoi partii Gruzii*, I, p. 143.

87. *Bank Ottoman: Memoirs of Armen Garo*, ed. Simon Vratzian, trans. Haig T. Partizian (Detroit: Armen Topouzian Publisher, 1990), pp. 159–160.

88. Ascher, *The Revolution of 1905: Russia in Disarray*, p. 254.

89. Charters Wynn, *Workers, Strikes, and Pogroms: The Donbass-Dnepr Bend in Late Imperial Russia, 1870–1905* (Princeton, NJ: Princeton University Press, 1992); Robert Weinberg, *The Revolution of 1905 in Odessa: Blood on the Steps* (Bloomington, IN: Indiana University Press, 1993); Gerald Surh, "Ekaterinoslav City in 1905: Workers, Jews, and Violence," *International Labor and Working-Class History*, no. 64 (Fall 2003), pp. 139–166.

90. Ascher, *The Revolution of 1905: Russia in Disarray*, p. 259.

91. Ibid.

CHAPTER 14. MEETING THE MOUNTAIN EAGLE

1. Badriashvili, *1905 god v Tiflise*, pp. 89–94.

2. *Revoliutsiia 1905 goda v Zakavkaz'i*, pp. 87–89.

3. *Krasnyi arkhiv*, 1 (26) (1928), p. 101.

4. Telegram from Vorontsov-Dashkov to the Minister of War, December 31, 1905, in *Revoliutsiia 1905 goda v Zakavkaz'i*, p. 142.

5. Report from the British Embassy in Saint Petersburg to London, February 28 and March 26, 1906, FO 181/869, BDFA; cited in Ascher, *The Russian Revolution of 1905: Russia in Disarray*, p. 334.

6. Hiroaki Kuromiya and Georges Mamoulia, *The Eurasian Triangle: Russia, the Caucasus and Japan, 1904–1945* (Berlin: Walter de Gruyter, 2016), p. 55; Kellogg Durland, *The Red Reign: The True History of an Adventurous Year in Russia* (New York: Century Co., 1908), pp. 111–112. On July 16, 1907, in Aleksandropol Dashnaks assassinated Alikhanov-Avarskii, throwing a bomb into his carriage.

7. *Kavkazskii rabochii, listok*, no. 2, November 23, 1905; no. 4, November 27, 1905.

8. V. A. Starosel'skii, "'Dni svobody' v kutaisskoi gubernii," *Byloe*, II, 7 (19) (July 1907), pp. 278–303; Maglakelidze, *Vladimir Aleksandrovich Starosel'skii*, pp. 107–110.

9. *Bank Ottoman: Memoirs of Armen Garo, the Armenian Ambassador to America from the Independent Republic of Armenia*, ed. and intro. Simon Vratzian; trans. Haig T. Partizian (Boston: Hairenik Press, 1948), p. 162.

10. Alexander Khatissian, "The Memoirs of a Mayor," *Armenian Review*, II, 3 (7) (Autumn: September 1949), p. 45.

11. *Bank Ottoman: Memoirs of Armen Garo*, pp. 166–170.

12. *Kavkazskii rabochii, listok*, no. 5, November 29, 1905. Armen Garo reports five hundred Muslims killed, and eight Armenians, sixty wounded. [*Bank Ottoman: Memoirs of Armen Garo*, p. 171.]

13. *Kavkazskii rabochii listok*, no. 6, November 30, 1905.

14. On the Armenian-Muslim clashes in Tiflis, 1905, see Isidore Ramishvili, *mogonebebi* (Tbilisi: artanuji, 2012), pp. 356–369.

15. V. I. Lenin, "Nashi zadachi i sovet rabochikh deputatov," *PSS*, XII, p. 63. This article, written in Stockholm as Lenin traveled to Russia, was not published at the time and was discovered only in 1940. The emphasis is in Lenin's text.

16. Ibid., p. 66.

17. "O reorganizatsii partii," ibid., p. 86.

18. Ibid., p. 90.

19. Gorev, "Za kulisami pervoi revoliutsii," p. 15. Agents of the Bolshevik Central Committee were sent to the provinces to invite participation in a party congress. Kamenev was sent to the Caucasus. This congress, it turned out, became the Bolshevik Tammerfors conference because many organizations could not attend, and the Moscow insurrection prevented representation from that city.

20. Ascher, *The Revolution of 1905: Russia in Disarray*, p. 285; from Martov's "Zadachi obedineniia," *Nachalo* [note incomplete in Ascher].

21. Leon Trotsky, *Permanent Revolution and Results and Prospects* (New York: Pioneer Publishers, 1965), pp. 194–195, 207, 237. The full working out of his theory was written while in prison and the relevant essay originally published as "Itogi i perspektivy," in *Nasha revoliutsiia* (Saint Petersburg: N. Glagolev, 1906).

22. Ascher, *The Revolution of 1905: Russia in Disarray*, p. 286; "Beseda s G. V. Plekhanovym," *Rus*, October 23, 1905, p. 3.

23. V. I. Lenin, *PSS*, XI, p. 222; Robert Service, *Lenin: A Political Life, I: The Strengths of Contradiction* (Bloomington: Indiana University Press, 1985), p. 130.

24. These ideas were expressed by Lenin in a series of articles in *Novaia zhizn'*, nos. 9, 11–14, 19, 21–22, 27, November 10–December 2, 1905; V. I. Lenin, *PSS*, XII, pp. 83–93, 99–105, 123–128, 129–141.

25. Engelstein, *Moscow, 1905*, pp. 214–221.

26. The initial Tiflis strike bureau of ten, largely Menshevik, was expanded to include members of other factions and parties. Jones places Jughashvili on the committee, but at about this time he was on his way to Tammerfors (Tampere) in Finland for a Bolshevik conference. [*Socialism in Georgian Colors*, p. 193.]

27. The Social Democrats hoped for support from the armed Armenians. Many Dashnaks were prepared to join the protest, but their military commander, Armen Garo, refused to participate. [*Bank Ottoman: Memoirs of Armen Garo*, pp. 171–172.]

28. The strike committee, made up of Mensheviks and Bolsheviks, was divided between those who argued that the strike should be turned into an insurrection and those who opposed such a radical move. Its executive committee was quite radical, and Zhordania and Isidore Ramishvili, along with a Bolshevik "Kora," proposed continuing the strike even after Moscow had been crushed. They called for terrorist attacks on Cossacks. The Bolshevik Tskhakaia and the Menshevik Arsenidze supported the more moderate position of the committee majority [Arsenidze, "Iz vospominanii o Staline," *Novyi zhurnal*, no. 72 (1963), pp. 231–232.]

29. *Revoliutsiia 1905 goda v Zakavkaz'i*, pp. 125–134; *Chetvert' veka bor'by za sotsializm*, p. 212; Arsenidze, unpublished interviews, II, pp. 21–24, 35–38.

30. Giorgi Telia (1880–1907) was born in a village and worked as a domestic servant, before becoming first a Menshevik and then a Bolshevik. Stalin admired the self-taught activist and journalist and wrote his obituary. [I. V. Stalin, "Pamiati tov. G. Teliia," *Sochineniia*, II, pp. 27–31.]

31. Ostrovskii, *Kto stoial za spinoi Stalina*, p. 239; SSM, d. 222, ll. 2–4. The Caucasian Union Committee meeting at which Koba and Telia were selected as delegates was held on November 26. Petr Montin was also chosen to attend, but he was murdered in December. His funeral in Baku occasioned a massive protest-demonstration.

32. Grigorii Aleksandrovich Aleksinskii, "Vospominaniia," unpublished, copy in HIA, B. I. Nicolaevsky Collection, series no. 230, box 302, p. 52; Gorev, "Za kulisami pervoi revoliutsii," p. 16.

33. This translation is from Trotsky, *Stalin*, p. 48; the original speech can be found in I. V. Stalin, *Sochineniia*, VI, pp. 54–55.

34. See, for example, Tucker, *Stalin as Revolutionary*, p. 122, where he writes, "This story is a blend of fact and fantasy." Also, Philip Pomper, *Lenin, Trotsky, and Stalin: The Intelligentsia in Power* (New York: Columbia University Press, 1990), p. 170. No trace of that letter has ever been found, even though Lenin and Krupskaia kept copies of their correspondence. One has to conclude that Stalin simply invented this episode to achieve the desired political effect of linking him from his earliest years to Lenin.

35. I. V. Stalin, *Sochineniia*, VI, p. 54.

36. Ibid.

37. Robert Himmer argues in an intriguing article that Stalin was truly disappointed when he met and observed Lenin, that he likely had expected Lenin to be of the same humble background as he, and that he experienced a "sense of distance between himself and Lenin." ["First Impressions Matter," p. 79.] Robert C. Tucker, on the other hand, interprets the event through the Freudian lens of identification with one's hero. [Tucker, *Stalin as Revolutionary*, pp. 134–135.]

38. On the Menshevik conference in Saint Petersburg, November 22–24, 1905, see the resolutions published in *Men'sheviki: Dokumenty i materialy*, pp. 147–148.

39. Aleksinskii, "Vospominaniia," p. 52. Grigorii Aleksinskii (1879–1967) joined the Bolsheviks in 1905. He was elected to the Second State Duma in 1906 and emigrated abroad when the duma was prorogued. He broke with Lenin in 1909 and joined the ultra-left wing of Bolshevism led by Aleksandr Bogdanov. He moved to the right and supported the Russian war effort in 1914. In 1917 he published documents claiming that Lenin was a German agent. He left Russia in 1918.

40. I. V. Stalin, "Rech' na sobranii v moskovskom komitete RKP (b) po povodu 50-letiia so dnia rozhdeniia V. I. Lenina, 23 aprelia 1920 g.," *Sochineniia*, IV, p. 316.

41. Aleksinskii, "Vospominaniia," p. 54.

42. Gorev, "Za kulisami pervoi revoliutsii," p. 16.

43. G. Kramol'nikov, "Konferentsiia bol'shevikov v Tammerforse v 1905 g. (11–17 dekabria st. st.)," *Trudy pervoi vsesoiuznoi konferentsii istorikov-marksistov, 28/xii—1923–4/I—1929*, I (Moscow: Kommunisticheskaia akademiia, 1930), p. 225; see also B. I. Gorev, *Iz partiinogo proshlogo. Vospominaniia 1895–1905 gg.* (Leningrad: Gosudarstvennoe izdatel'stvo, 1924).

44. Gorev, "Za kulisami pervoi revoliutsii," pp. 16–17.

45. P. F. Kudelli, "Na Tammerforsskoi konferentsii," in *Ob Il'iche: Vospominaniia pitertsev* (Leningrad: Lenizdat, 1970), pp. 134–135.

46. I. V. Stalin, *Sochineniia*, IV, p. 317.

47. Fifteen years later in his famous pamphlet *"Left-wing" Communism: An Infantile Disorder*, Lenin noted that the boycott of the duma in 1905 had been the correct tactic in the midst of the revolution, but the Bolshevik boycott of the First State Duma in 1906 was an error, though "a small and easily remediable" one. The idea of boycotting the Duma elections in 1907–1912 was, for Lenin, a "serious mistake and difficult to remedy," and led to deep divisions among the Bolsheviks. [V. I. Lenin, *PSS*, XLI, pp. 17–18.]

48. Davrichewy, *Ah! Ce qu'on rigolait bien avec mon copain Staline*, p. 213.

49. Edward J. Bing (ed.), *The Secret Letters of the Last Tsar* (New York, 1938), p. 211; Ascher, *The Russian Revolution of 1905: Russia in Disarray*, p. 328.

50. Ascher, *The Russian Revolution of 1905: Russia in Disarray*, p. 330.

51. Bing, *Secret Letters*, pp. 205–206; Ascher, *The Russian Revolution of 1905: Russia in Disarray*, p. 333.

CHAPTER 15. GENDARME OF THE REVOLUTION

1. Ascher, *The Russian Revolution of 1905: Russia in Disarray*, p. 334; Report from the British Embassy in Saint Petersburg to London, February 28 and March 26, 1906, FO 181/869, BDFA.

2. Abraham Ascher, *The Revolution of 1905: Authority Restored* (Stanford, CA: Stanford University Press, 1992), p. 9.

3. Ascher, *The Revolution of 1905: Authority Restored*, p. 14.

4. Ibid., pp. 11–13. The best account of the emperor's role in the revolution is Andrew Verner, *The Crisis of Russian Autocracy: Nicholas II and the 1905 Revolution* (Princeton, NJ: Princeton University Press, 1990).

5. A fragment of the letter is published in *Revoliutsionnoe dvizhenie v Armenii, 1905–1907 g.g.: Sbornik dokumentov i materialov* (Erevan: Aipetrat, 1955), p. 166; and in Maglakelidze, *Vladimir Aleksandrovich Starosel'skii*, pp. 114–115.

6. *Revoliutsiia 1905–1907 g.g. v Gruzii. Sbornik dokumentov*, ed. Sh. V. Tsarageishvili, comp. S. Maglakelidze and A. Iovidze (Tbilisi: sakhelgami, 1956), pp. 536–537. Bold type used for emphasis in original.

7. Starosel'skii, "'Dni svobod' v kutaisskoi gubernii," *Byloe*, II, 7 (19) (July 1907), pp. 301–306; Varlam Kalandadze and Vladimir Mkheidze, *Ocherki revoliutsionnogo dvizheniia v Gurii*, pp. 84–90; see also V. A. Starosel'skii, *Dni svobod*, ed. V. P. Ratiani (Tbilisi: metsniereba, 1985).

8. Ascher, *The Revolution of 1905: Authority Restored*, pp. 21–22. Ascher estimates that the British Embassy's estimates of arrests by March 1906 of 17–70,000 are too low (p. 22).

9. S. Fuks, "Bor'ba s revoliutsionnym dvizheniem na Kavkaze v epokhu stolypinshchiny. (Iz perepiski P. A. Stolypina s gr. I. I. Vorontsovym-Dashkovym)," *Krasnyi arkhiv*, no. 3 (34) (1929), pp. 204–205; Jones, *Socialism in Georgian Colors*, p. 198.

10. In his biography of Stalin, Trotsky repeats what he learned from Kote, who claimed that Koba brought him into the plot to kill the general, asking him to form his own armed band, but Menshevik assassins carried out the deed before the Bolshevik group acted. [Trotskii, *Stalin*, I, ed. Iu. G. Fel'shtinskii (Benson, VT: Chalidze Publications, 1985; Moscow, 1990), pp. 147–148.]

Arsenidze mentions those comrades who worked with Jughashvili in his fighting group and died as a result: Vano Kalandadze, S. Koridze, Eli[so] Lominadze, and Intskrivali. ["Iz vospominanii o Staline," p. 223.]

11. Tsintsadze, *rogor vibrdzodit proletariatis diktaturistvis*, p. 40.

12. *Krasnyi arkhiv*, 1 (26) (1928), p. 124; Menshevik Project, no. 2, p. 3. Davrishev claims that Jorjiashvili was a member of Jughashvili's *jgupi* and probably was accompanied by Kamo that day. [Davrichewy, *Ah! Ce qu'on rigolait bien avec mon copain Staline*, pp. 216–217.] That would mean that Stalin ordered and organized the killing. But Stephen F. Jones and an earlier source show that Jorjiashvili was a member of Silva Jibladze's group. [Jones, *Socialism in Georgian Colors*, p. 197; Arshak Megrabiantsi, "rogor mokles generali griaznovi 1906 tsels," *revoliutsiis matiane*, 1923, no. 4, pp. 203–205; Talakvadze, *K istorii kommunisticheskoi partii Gruzii*, I, p. 149n.

13. Mgaloblishvili, *Vospominaniia*, pp. 130–133, 173.

14. Davrichewy, *Ah! Ce qu'on rigolait bien avec mon copain Staline*, p. 219.

15. Who killed him and his wife remains a mystery to this day. Geifman uses a very dubious source to convict the Bolsheviks of this murder. [*Thou Shalt Kill*, pp. 95–96.]

16. Montefiore is ambivalent about Koba's involvement with Chavchavadze's assassination and believes that his associate Sergo Orjonikidze was behind it. [*Young Stalin*, p. 179.]

17. *chveni gza* (Our Road), September 11, 1907. Zhordania wrote a more critical piece on Chavchavadze, *bneli dalebi* (Dark Forces) in *chveni gza*, October 9, 1907.

18. "rusetis revoliutsia da kavkasia," *skhivi*, no. 13, January 5 (18), 1906, p. 1.

19. "Dve skhvatki," I. V. Stalin, *Sochineniia*, I, pp. 196–205.

20. A. S. Svanidze-Monaselidze, "Vospominaniia o tovarishche Staline," SShSSA, f. 8, op. 2, ch. 1, d. 43, l. 150.

21. Ostrovskii, *Kto stoial za spinoi Stalina*, pp. 242–243; B. Loshadze-Bochoridze memoirs, RGASPI, f. 558, op. 4, d. 658, ll. 222–223; SEA, f. 153, op. 1, d. 764, ll. 181–182; N. Akhmeteli memoirs, SShSSA, f. 8, op. 2, ch. 1, d. 3, ll. 293–295.

22. Ostrovskii, *Kto stoial za spinoi Stalina*, pp. 243–244; N. Akhmeteli memoirs, SShSSA, f. 8, op. 2, ch. 1, d. 3, ll. 298; A. N. Mikaberidze memoirs, SSM, d. 278, l. 6; Ruben Dashtoian memoirs, SSM, d. 118, l. 1.

23. I. Besoshvili, "damoukidebelta partia da sotsialdemokratia," *gantiadi*, no. 5, March 10 (233), 1906. This article, "The Independence Party and Social Democracy," was not reprinted in I. V. Stalin, *Sochineniia*.

24. Lih, *Rediscovering Lenin*, p. 101. From Lenin's writings it is clear that the struggle for democracy was paramount as a necessary environment in which the proletariat could imbibe the message of Social Democracy and go on to fight for socialism. What is ambiguous in Lenin is whether the political freedoms associated with bourgeois democracy had value beyond their instrumental contribution to the socialist revolution.

25. Arsenidze, unpublished interviews, II, pp. 12–13.

26. Ebanoidze, *sakartvelos bolshevikuri organizatsiebi*, p. 374.

27. Uratadze, *Vospominaniia gruzinskogo sotsial-demokrata*, pp. 203–204.

28. Jughashvili had been elected to the Social Democratic committee in Kutaisi in the fall of 1905, along with Budu Mdivani, Rostom (Archil) Dolidze, Al. Japaridze, Sergo Kavtaradze, and Mikha Okujava. [Talakvadze, *K istorii kommunisticheskoi partii Gruzii*, I, pp. 147–148.]

29. Bibineishvili, *Za chetvert' veka*, pp. 130–131.

30. On this period, see Isidore Ramishvili, *mogonebebi*, pp. 378–411.

31. Cited in Lih, *Lenin Rediscovered*, p. 52.

32. "sakhemtsipo satatbiro da sotsial-demokratiis taktika" ["The State Duma and the Tactics of Social Democracy"], *gantiadi* [Dawn], no. 3, March 8 (21), 1906; "Gosudarstvennaia duma i taktika sotsial-demokratii," *Sochineniia*, I, pp. 206–213. Jughashvili's article was a reply to "sakhemtsipo satatbiros archevnebi da chveni taktika" ["The Elections to the State Duma and Our Tactics"] by a Menshevik writer, who argued that the elections would increase the influence of Social Democracy. [*gantiadi*, no. 2, March 7 (20), 1906.] About this time Jughashvili published three articles in the Social Democratic newspaper *elva* (Lightning) that were not reprinted in his *Sochineniia*: "politikuri kameleonebi" ["Political Chameleons"], *elva*, no. 3, March 15, 1906; "kidev ertkhel politikur kameleonebze" ["Once More on Chameleons"], *elva*, no. 5, March 17, 1906; *elva*, no. 7, March 19 (31), 1906.

33. Jones, *Socialism in Georgian Colors*, p. 199. At the time the Tiflis organization numbered about 3,300 members, of which about 300 were Bolsheviks. [*Chetvertyi (Ob''edinitel'nyi) s''ezd RSDRP, aprel' (aprel'–mai) 1906 goda: Protokoly* (Moscow: Godudarstvennoe izdatel'stvo politicheskoi literatury, 1959), pp. 338–339.]

34. Ibid., p. 333.

35. Ostrovskii, *Kto stoial za spinoi Stalina*, pp. 245; Raisa Okinshevich, "Vospominaniia," SShSSA, f. 8, op. 2, ch. 1, d. 37, l. 200.

36. *Chetvertyi (Ob''edinitel'nyi) s''ezd RSDRP*, p. 314.

37. Eradze, interview 7, pp. 73, 78.

38. Eradze, interview 9, pp. 7–8; O. A. Ermanskii, *Iz perezhitogo (1887–1921 gg.)* (Moscow, Leningrad: Gosudarstvennoe izdatel'stvo, 1927), pp. 90–91.

39. M. Stugart, *Dagens Nyheter*, March 22, 2004; Service, *Stalin: A Biography*, p. 604. [My thanks to Björn Rahmström for assistance with the Swedish article.]

40. Kliment Voroshilov, *Razkazy o zhizni: Vospominaniia*, I (Moscow: Izdatel'stvo politicheskoi literatury, 1968), p. 246. This memoir was published after Nikita Khrushchev's denunciation of Stalin at the Twentieth Party Congress is 1956, and Voroshilov makes the obligatory reference to the "enormous mistakes" that Stalin made in his long career (p. 248).

41. Ibid., pp. 248–249.

42. *Chetvertyi (Ob''edinitel'nyi) s''ezd RSDRP*, pp. 338–339; Edelman, *Stalin: Biografiia v dokumentakh*, pp. 394–399; A. Lunacharskii, "Stokgol'mskii s''ezd," *Proletarskaia revoliutsiia*, 1926, no. 5 (52), p. 97.

43. Aleksinskii, "Vospominaniia," p. 184.

44. Ibid.

45. I. V. Stalin, "O Lenine: Rech' na vechere kremlevskikh kursantov," January 28, 2924, in I. V. Stalin, *Sochineniia*, VI, p. 56.

46. "The Agrarian Question" was published in *elva*, nos. 5 (March 17, 1906), 9 (March 22), and 10 (March 23), and "On the Agrarian Question" in the same newspaper, no. 14 (March 29). They were all signed "I. Besoshvili." [I. V. Stalin, *Sochineniia*, I, pp. 214–229, 230–235.]

47. I. V. Stalin, *Sochineniia*, I, p. 219.

48. Ibid.

49. Ibid., p. 232.

50. Ibid., p. 233.

51. Ibid., pp. 224–225.

52. *Chetvertyi (Ob"edinitel'nyi) s"ezd RSDRP*, p. 79.

53. Ibid.

54. Ibid., p. xxxvii.

55. Ibid., p. 78.

56. Ibid., p. 109. Stephen F. Jones points out that "privately, the Georgians were skeptical of the Menshevik alternative of municipalization. Most saw it as second best to the private distribution of land and were unsure of its potential support in Guria. Jughashvili expressed what most of the Georgian representatives were thinking—nationalization and municipalization would make 'union between the revolutionary peasantry and proletariat impossible.' Land privatization was the most realistic solution." [Jones, *Socialism in Georgian Colors*, p. 214.]

57. *Chetvertyi (Ob"edinitel'nyi) s"ezd RSDRP*, p. 163.

58. Forty years after the agrarian debate, when the collection of Stalin's works were published in the USSR, Stalin criticized his younger self as a "young Marxist who had not yet become a full Marxist-Leninist" and did not understand the full significance of Lenin's position. [I. V. Stalin, *Sochineniia*, I, pp. xi–xiv.]

59. *Chetvertyi (Ob"edinitel'nyi) s"ezd RSDRP*, pp. 192–199; the quotation is from p. 199.

60. Ibid., pp. 224–225.

61. Ibid., pp. 246–277.

62. Ibid., pp. 282–285.

63. Ibid., p. 311.

64. Ibid., p. 314.

65. Ibid., p. 326.

66. Ibid., pp. 357–358.

67. Ibid., pp. 392–394.

68. Ibid., pp. 401–402, 527–528.

69. Ibid., p. 435.

70. Ibid., p. 520.

71. Leonid Krasin (1870–1926) was close to Bogdanov and admired by Lenin. A successful electrical engineer, he was involved in bomb making and robberies for the Bolsheviks. He served as people's commissar of foreign trade from 1920 to 1924 and negotiated the Anglo-Soviet trade agreement of 1921 that ended the economic blockade of Soviet Russia.

72. G. Zinov'ev, *Istoriia Rossiiskoi Kommunisticheskoi Partii (bol'shevikov): Populiarnyi ocherk* (Moscow and Petrograd: Gosudarstvennoe izdatel'stvo, 1923), p. 124. On the history of the "Bolshevik Center," see HIA, Nicolaevsky Collection, box 3, folder 11, "Materialy po istorii marksistskogo dvizheniia v Rossii," Section 4, Part 1; see also "K istorii 'Bol'shevistskogo tsentra," in B. I. Nikolaevskii, *Tainye stanitsy istorii* (Moscow: Izdatel'stvo gumanitarnoi literatury, 1995), pp. 9–92; see also B. I. Nikolaevskii, "V preddverii polnogo raskola," *Voprosy istorii*, 210, no. 7, pp. 3–37.

Grigorii Zinoviev (1883–1936) was one of Lenin's most important Bolshevik allies, particularly from 1905. He was the long-time head of the Petrograd party organization and together with Lev Kamenev and Stalin made up the triumvirate that briefly dominated the Communist Party of the Soviet Union at the end of Lenin's life and shortly after his death. He headed the

Comintern (Communist International, 1919–1926) and was a key figure in the campaign against Lev Trotsky. Defeated by Stalin in the power struggle of the mid-1920s, Zinoviev and Kamenev were tried in the first of the Great Purge trials and condemned to death.

73. Theodore Dan, *The Origins of Bolshevism*, ed. and trans. Joel Carmichael (New York: Harper & Row, 1964; Schocken Books, 1970), pp. 380–381.

74. F. Makharadze, "Iz istorii," *Chetvert' veka bor'by za sotsializm*, p. 204; see Lenin's articles criticizing the Mensheviks' support of the Kadets and the First State Duma through the first half of 1906. [V. I. Lenin, *PSS*, XII, XIII.]

75. Ostrovskii, *Kto stoial za spinoi Stalina*, p. 248; postcard to M. Monaselidze, RGASPI, f. 558, op. 1, d. 5095, l. 1; Edelman, *Stalin: Biografiia v dokumentakh*, pp. 432–433.

Aleksandre Svanidze (1886–1941), a Bolshevik who became Stalin's brother-in-law, served as a government official in Soviet Georgia and as a diplomat in Germany before being accused of being a German spy, arrested in 1937, and shot, along with his sister, Mariko, in 1941.

76. A. S. Svanidze-Monaselidze, "Vospominaniia o tovarishche Staline," SShSSA, f. 8, op. 2 ch. 1, d. 43, l. 154.

77. Ostrovskii, *Kto stoial za spinoi Stalina*, p. 248; M. M. Monaselidze, "Vospominaniia," SSM, d. 287, op. 1, l. 10. When after five issues *gantiadi* was closed down by the police, it was immediately replaced by *elva*, which ran for twenty-eight issues. After that the Bolsheviks published a series of legal newspapers—*akhali tskhovreba* (New Life), *akhali droeba* (New Times), *mnatobi* (Luminary), *chveni tskhovreba* (Our Life), and *dro* (Time)—until 1907, after which they were able to print, once again, only illegal publications.

78. Women and millions of the poorest in the population—agricultural laborers, construction workers, servants, and day laborers—were not permitted to vote. The elections were in stages, with various parts of the population—landowners, townspeople, peasants, workers—voting for electors, who then met in curiae (class and property-determined groups) to choose the actual deputies. People with property were vastly over-represented. It took 90,000 workers to elect an elector, 30,000 peasants, but only 2,000 landowners. In Russia proper, with the Social Democrats and Socialist Revolutionaries boycotting most of the elections, the liberal Kadet party emerged with the largest delegation of deputies in the First State Duma.

79. The contest was between the liberal Kadets, the Social Democrats (in alliance with the Armenian Marxists of the Hnchak Party), and an electoral coalition of the Socialist Federalists, the Georgian Democratic Party, and the Radical Party, primarily an intelligentsia party led by Aleksandr Argutinskii-Dolgorukii, a very popular Tiflis notable, a former *narodovolets* (radical Populist) who broke with the local Kadets because they included compromised figures like former mayor Khristopor Vermishev. [N. N. Zhordaniia, "Izbiratel'naia kampaniia v Tiflise," *Otkliki sovremennosti*, no. 4 (1906), pp. 138–139.] The principal Armenian revolutionary party, the *Dashnaktsutyun*, had decided to boycott the elections, but some Bolsheviks, notably Shahumian, participated in the campaign. [Arsenidze, unpublished interviews, I, pp. 18–19.] Shahumian was an elector (*vyborshchik*), spoke at the curia that elected the actual deputies, and voted for Zhordania.

80. N. N. Zhordaniia, "Izbiratel'naia kampaniia v Tiflise," pp. 138–147.

81. Kadets took one seat from Tiflis province and another ten from Muslim and Armenian provinces; a right-wing independent landowner took a seat from Batumi-Sukhumi; and in line with an electoral agreement with the Social Democrats, a Socialist Federalist won a seat in Tiflis

province. The deputies elected from Georgia to the First State Duma were: the Mensheviks Zhordania (Tiflis), Isidore Ramishvili (Kutaisi), Svimon Tsereteli (Kutaisi), Ivane Gomarteli (Kutaisi), Sergo Japaridze (Tiflis); the Socialist Federalist Ioseb Baratashvili (Tiflis); independent Prince Prokopi Shervashidze (Batumi); and the Kadet Artemii Aivazov (Tiflis).

82. The word "caucus" [*fraktsiia* in Russian] will be used to indicate the group of deputies in the Duma adhering to a particular party affiliation—for example, the Social Democratic caucus; the word "faction" [also *fraktsiia* in Russian] will be used to indicate a group of party members adhering to a particular line—for example, the Bolsheviks, Mensheviks, *otzovisty* or *likvidatory*.

83. *Men'sheviki: dokumenty i materialy*, pp. 190–203.

84. Ibid., pp. 190–191; Jones, *Socialism in Georgian Colors*, p. 202.

85. Only about ten percent of Tiflis party members, some five hundred people, favored the Bolsheviks. [Davtian, "Tiflisskaia voennaia organizatsiia v 1906–1907 g.g.," p. 143.]

86. *Kaits*, no. 34, July 5, 1906.

87. *Avlabarskaia nelegal'naia tipografiia kavkazskogo soiuznogo komiteta RSDRP (1903–1906 gg.): Sbornik materialov i dokumentov* (Tbilisi: Gosizdat Gruzinskoi SSR, 1954), pp. 12–13, 41–42. Among those arrested were David Rostomashvili, Mikha Bochoridze, Pilipe Makharadze, Mikha Tskhakaia, and Nina Alajalova.

88. Kuromiya and Mamoulia, *The Eurasian Triangle*, p. 53; V. I. Lenin, *PSS*, XIV, p. 418, n. 4.

89. Ascher, *Revolution of 1905: Authority Restored*, pp. 126–127.

90. Ibid., p. 157; John Bushnell, *Mutiny amid Repression: Russian Soldiers in the Revolution of 1905–1906* (Bloomington: Indiana University Press, 1985).

91. Ibid., pp. 146–150; see also Shlomo Lambroza, "The Pogroms of 1903–06," in John D. Klier and Shlomo Lambroza (eds.), *Pogroms: Anti-Jewish Violence in Modern Russian History* (Cambridge: Cambridge University Press, 1992), pp. 195–247.

92. Ascher, *Revolution of 1905: Authority Restored*, p. 153.

93. Letter from Vorontsov-Dashkov to Tsar Nicholas II, August 16, 1906. [*Krasnyi arkhiv*, 1 (26) (1928), pp. 103–105.]

94. Edelman, *Stalin: Biografiia v doumentakh*, p. 411; "Iz vospominanii N. Eliava," translated from Georgian, 1948, RGASPI, f. 558, op. 4, d. 658, ll. 425–426.

95. Arsenidze, "Iz vospominanii o Staline," p. 235.

96. "Vospominanie rabochego zheleznoi dorogi D. Lordkipanidze (1934 g.): V kakikh usloviiakh i gde poznakomilsia s Stalinom," SEA, f. 2417, op. 1, d. 227, ll. 1–11 (original in Georgian; Russian translation in author's possession).

97. Konstantin Tadeorovich Dvali, "Vospominaniia o tovarishche Stalina," SShSSA, f. 8, op. 2, ch. 1, d. 12, ll. 120–121.

98. Arsenidze, "Iz vospominanii o Staline," pp. 222–223.

99. Ibid., p. 221–222.

100. From the diaries of Davit Saghirashvili, cited in De Lon, "Stalin and Social Democracy," pp. 178–180. Akhmeteli (1875–1942) was the ambassador from independent Georgia to Germany in 1919–1921.

101. RGASPI, f. 71, op. 10, d. 183, ll. 18–183.

102. *akhali tskhovreba*, no. 3, June 22, 1906; RGASPI, f. 71, op. 10, d. 183, ll. 173–176. This article, "Survey of the Press," is unsigned, attributed to Stalin by the Institute of Marxism-Leninism, but was not published in his collected works.

103. *akhali tskhovreba*, no. 16, July 9, 1906; RGASPI, f. 71, op. 10, d. 183, ll. 199–201.

104. "ori taktika," *lampari*, no. 45, June 18 (July 2), 1906.

105. *akhali tskhovreba*, no. 8, June 29, 1906; no. 10, July 2, 1906; RGASPI, f. 71, op. 10, d. 183, ll. 189–195. Koba wrote several replies to Khomeriki's accusation, defending himself with quotations from Marx and Engels. For the one that was later reprinted in his collected works [*akhali tskhovreba*, no. 19, July 13, 1906], see I. V. Stalin, *Sochineniia*, I, pp. 241–246.

106. *akhali tskhovreba*, no. 15, July 8, 1906; RGASPI, f. 71, op. 10, d. 183, ll. 196–198.

107. Ibid., pp. 269–270.

108. Ibid., pp. 270–271.

109. "Duma i narod," *Vpered*, no. 15, June 11, 1906; V. I. Lenin, *PSS*, XIII, pp. 215–217. For Ramishvili's speech, see *Men'sheviki: Dokumenty i materialy*, pp. 190–191.

110. RGASPI, f. 558, op. 1, d. 4549.

111. M. Tskhakaia, "Obzor pechati," *akhali tskhovreba*, no. 18, July 12, 1906.

112. Letter from "Razhden" to Nestor Fomich Kaladze, GARF, f. 102, d. 5, 1910, ch. 79, ll. 87–89.

113. *akhali tskhovreba*, no. 18, July 12, 1906; RGASPI, f. 71, op. 10, d. 183, ll. 137–141.

CHAPTER 16. THE PROFESSIONAL

1. For the family genealogy of Ekaterine Svanidze, see A. V. Ostrovskii, "Rodstvennye sviazi pervoi zheny I. V. Stalina (beseda s R. M. Monaselidze)," *Iz glubiny vremen*, no. 7 (1996), pp. 189–196.

2. G. Elisabedashvili, "Vospominaniia o tovarishche Staline," RGASPI, f. 558, op. 4, d. 665, l. 72.

3. A. Svanidze-Monaselidze, "Vospominaniia o tovarishche Staline," SShSSA, f. 8, op. 2, ch. 1, d. 43, l. 149.

4. Recorded conversation with Efim Sartania (1935), SShSSA, f. 8, op. 2, ch. 1, d. 43, l. 61.

5. Davrichewy, *Ah! Ce qu'on rigolait bien avec mon copain Staline*, pp. 227–228.

6. Stalin's daughter, Svetlana Allilueva, wrote what she had been told about her father's first marriage: "This quiet, pretty girl had pleased his mother, and at her insistence the wedding was in a church. But the marriage was not arranged only by his mother; the bride was the sister of the Georgian Bolshevik Aleksandre Svanidze, and marriages and family celebrations were used for meetings of the underground. Father soon left, and then was exiled, and the young woman suddenly died, leaving her little boy, Iasha [Jacob], to whom she had passed on her quiet disposition." [*Tol'ko odin god*, p. 318; *Only One Year*, p. 367.]

7. Dvali, "Vospominaniia o tovarishche Stalina," SShSSA, f. 8, op. 2, ch. 1, d. 12, l. 121; Ostrovskii, *Kto stoial za spinoi Stalina*, pp. 249–250; Svanidze-Monaselidze, "Vospominaniia o tovarishche Staline," SShSSA, f. 8, op. 2, ch. 1, d. 43, l. 155; M. M. Monaselidze, SSM, d. 287/1, l. 14; SEA, f. 440, op. 2, d. 39, ll. 36–37; SShSSA, f. 8, op. 5, d. 213, ll. 43–44; RGASPI, f. 71, op. 1, d. 275, l. 31.

8. Vladimir Alliluev, *Khronika odnoi sem'i: Alliluevy-Stalin* (Moscow: Molodaia gvardiia, 2002), p. 108.

9. Svanidze-Monaselidze, "Vospominaniia o tovarishche Staline," SShSSA, f. 8, op. 2, ch. 1, d. 43, l. 154.

10. Ibid., l. 156.

11. Ibid., ll. 155–156; Ostrovskii, *Kto stoial za spinoi Stalina*, pp. 250–252; M. M. Monaselidze, SSM, d. 287, op. 1, ll. 14–16; SEA, f. 153, op. 1, d. 3440, ll. 323–329.

12. Sailors on the ship "Memory of Azov" lying near Revel (Tallinn) took over the ship and sailed to the port, but when they tried to rally other ships there was no response. [*Piatyi (Londonskii) s"ezd RSDRP, aprel'–mai 1907 goda: Protokoly* (Moscow: Gosudarstvennoe izdatel'stvo politicheskoi litertury, 1963), p. 773, no. 63.] The Menshevik-led Central Committee of the RSDRP gave a thorough analysis of the failed resistance in July. See "Pis'mo TsK RSDRP k mestnym organizatsiiam ob itogakh iiul'skoi politicheskoi stachki," *Men'sheviki: Dokumenty i materialy*, pp. 217–221; and Ascher, *Revolution of 1905: Authority Restored*, pp. 228–238.

13. Krupskaya, *Reminiscences of Lenin*, pp. 153–156.

14. *akhali tskhovreba*, no. 20, July 14, 1906; reprinted in I. V. Stalin, *Sochineniia*, I, pp. 247–249.

15. I. V. Stalin, *Sochineniia*, I, pp. 251–252.

16. Ibid., p. 257.

17. Arsenidze, unpublished interviews, II, pp. 39–40.

18. Devdariani, "Soso Stalin," SShSSA, f. 8, op. 2, ch. 1, d. 12, l. 181.

19. The other delegates were Mensheviks, most from the larger centers—Tiflis (22), Baku (6), and Guria (2). [Arsenidze, "Iz vospominanii o Staline," p. 233.] Of the forty-three delegates with voting rights, twenty-four were intellectuals and nineteen workers. [*Men'sheviki: Dokumenty i materially*, p. 485.] There were also fifteen delegates with voice but no vote. Each delegate was said to represent three hundred party members, and the Tiflis organization, remarkably large, numbered some six thousand members. [*Sotsial'demokrat* (Saint Petersburg), no. 3, October 13, 1906.]

20. "Vospominaniia Seida Devdariani," SShSSA, f. 8, op. 2, ch. 1, d. 12, ll. 205–206.

21. Devdariani, "Soso Stalin," SShSSA, f. 8, op. 2, ch. 1, d. 12, l. 182.

22. Arsenidze, "Iz vospominanii o Staline," pp. 233–234; Arsenidze, unpublished interviews, I, pp. 14–16.

23. Devdariani, "Soso Stalin," SShSSA, f. 8, op. 2, ch. 1, d. 12, l. 183.

24. "Vospominaniia Seida Devdariani," SShSSA, f. 8, op. 2, ch. 1, d. 12, l. 209.

25. *Men'sheviki: Dokumenty i materially*, pp. 221–225; *Sotsial'demokrat* (Saint Petersburg), no. 3, October 13, 1906; no. 7, November 18, 1906.

26. Leopold H. Haimson, *Russia's Revolutionary Experience, 1905–1917: Two Essays* (New York: Columbia University Press, 2005), p. 6.

27. *Sotsial'demokrat* (Saint Petersburg), no. 7, November 18, 1906.

28. Menshevik Project, Georgian Collection, no. 14, p. 24.

29. *Men'sheviki: Dokumenty i materialy*, pp. 224–225.

30. Devdariani and Isidore Ramishvili represented Baku; other members included Zhordania, Archil Japaridze, Jibladze, Noe Ramishvili, and Shahumian. Koba Jughashvili was probably not a member, though one source is not sure. ["Vospominaniia Seida Devdariani," SShSSA, f. 8, op. 2, ch. 1, d. 12, ll. 209–210.]

31. Ebanoidze, *sakartvelos bolshevikuri organizatsiebi*, p. 398.

32. Viktor Naneishvili, "tpilisis organizatsia reaktsiis khanashi (1907–10 ts.ts.)," *revoliutsiis matiane*, 1928, no. 1 (18), p. 165.

33. Varlaam Cherkezishvili (1846–1925), better known as V. Cherkezov, was a major anarchist writer and critic of Marxism. Influenced by Petr Kropotkin, he was the author of important brochures and helped write the program of the Georgian Socialist Federalist Party. He died in poverty in London.

34. Letter from Giorgi Gogelia in Sukhumi to Lidia in Geneva, HIA, Okhrana Collection, index no. xvii n, box 200, folder 2a.

35. Stalin, *Sochineniia*, I, p. 373.

36. For an excellent discussion of Stalin's philosophical views, see Erik van Ree, "Stalin as Marxist Philosopher," *Studies in East European Thought*, LII (2000), pp. 259–308.

37. Karl Marx, *The Poverty of Philosophy*.

38. Karl Marx, *A Contribution to the Critique of Political Economy*.

39. Stalin, *Sochineniia*, I, p. 386; *Works*, I, p. 386.

40. van Ree, "Stalin as Marxist Philosopher," p. 271.

41. Stalin, *Sochineniia*, I, p. 374.

42. Stalin, *Sochineniia*, I, pp. 367–372; *Works*, I, pp. 368–372. Arthur Arnould (1833–1895) was an anarchist, a member of the First International, and an elected member of the Paris Commune. He wrote the *Histoire populaire et parlementaire de la Commune de Paris*, 3 vols. (Brussels: Kistemaeckers, 1878). Prosper-Olivier Lissagaray (1838–1901) was a journalist, an active participant in the Commune, and the author of the sympathetic *Histoire de la Commune de 1871*, 2 vols. (Paris, 1876). For Marxists the Paris Commune was a virtual historical primer from which strategic and tactical lessons could be learned. For a discussion, see the appendix, "The Marxist Image of the Commune," in Suny, *The Baku Commune, 1917–1918*, pp. 353–362.

43. Davrichewy, *Ah! Ce qu'on rigolait bien avec mon copain Staline*, p. 212.

44. V. I. Lenin, *PSS*, XIV, pp. 97–105, 447–448, n. 69.

45. V. I. Lenin, "Partizanskaia voina," *Proletarii*, no. 5, September 30, 1906; V. I. Lenin, *PSS*, XIV, pp. 1–12.

46. "Predislovie k gruzinskomu izdaniiu broshiury K. Kautskogo 'Dvizhushchie sily i perspektivy russkoi revoliutsii,'" I. V. Stalin, *Sochineniia*, II, pp. 1–13; Moira Donald, *Marxism and Revolution: Karl Kautsky and the Russian Marxists, 1900–1924* (New Haven, CT, and London: Yale University Press, 1993), pp. 80–107.

47. Roberta Thompson Manning, *The Crisis of the Old Order in Russia: Gentry and Government* (Princeton, NJ: Princeton University Press, 1982), p. 294.

48. *Kavkazskaia rech'*, no. 18, November 10, 1906.

49. Ibid., no. 28, November 23, 1906. In Baku, however, the RSDRP and the local committee of the Armenian Social Democratic Workers' Organization agreed to work together in the elections along with the Muslim Social Democratic group, *Hummet*.

50. *Zakavkaz'e*, no. 22, January 27, 1907.

51. "Kopiia doneseniia Pomoshchika Nachal'nika Kutaisskago Gubernskago Zhandarmskago Upravleniia v Sukhumskom okruge," 1907, February 17, GARF, f. 102 [Departament politsii, Osobyi otdel], op. 1907, d. 180, ch. 5, ll. 9–10.

52. Arsenidze, unpublished interviews, I, p. 18.

53. The Georgian deputies were: from Tiflis city—Archil Japaridze, a nobleman who had embraced Marxism as a student, at the time the de facto leader of the Tiflis Committee, and a good friend of Tsereteli; from Tiflis province—Severian Jugheli, the son of a clergyman, and

Nikoloz Katsiashvili, a peasant; from Kutaisi—Gerasime Makharadze (1881–1937), twenty-six years old, a student of eastern languages, and V. B. (Chola) Lomtatidze (1879–1915), twenty-eight, a peasant from Guria. [*Zakavkaz'e*, no. 22, January 27, 1907; no. 24, January 30, 1907; no. 28, February 4, 1907; no. 30, February 7, 1907; no. 31, February 8, 1907; no. 32, February 9, 1907.]

54. I. G. Tsereteli, "Vo vtoroi gosudarstvennoi dume (Iz vospominanii)," HIA, Boris Niko-laevsky Collection, no. 15, box 10, item 75, pp. 5–10, 14–16.

55. Ascher, *The Revolution of 1905*, II, pp. 304–305.

56. *Men'sheviki: Dokumenty i materialy*, pp. 230–236.

57. Ascher, *The Revolution of 1905*, II, p. 311.

58. Manning, *The Crisis of the Old Order in Russia*, pp. 311–312; Ascher, *The Revolution of 1905*, II, pp. 314–317; F. A. Golovin, "Zurabovskii intsident, izlozhenyi v vospominaniiakh o Stolypine," *Krasnyi arkhiv*, XIX, 6 (1926), pp. 129–146; see also F. A. Golovin, "Vospominaniia F. A. Golovina o II gosudarstvennoi dume," *Istoricheskii arkhiv*, no. 4 (1959), pp. 136–165; no. 5, pp. 128–154; no. 6, pp. 56–81.

59. Ostrovskii, *Kto stoial za spinoi Stalina*, p. 253; M. M. Monaselidze, "Vospominaniia," SSM, d. 287/1, l. 14. Iakob Jughashvili (1907–1943) was raised by aunts and his grandmother after his mother's death. Estranged from his father, he attempted suicide after an enraged Stalin objected to him marrying. "He can't even shoot straight," Stalin reportedly remarked. As a Red Army artillery officer, Iakob was captured by the Germans near Smolensk early in World War II. His father refused to exchange him for Marshall Friedrich von Paulus—"I will not trade a marshal for a lieutenant"—and he was killed in Sachsenhausen concentration camp. He was survived by two children, Evgenii (1936–2016), whose claim to his paternity has been questioned, and Galina (1938–2007).

60. I. V. Stalin, *Sochineniia*, II, pp. 14–26. Many of the articles of early 1907, signed and un-signed and accredited by the Moscow party archivists to Stalin, have not been published in his collected works—for example, "Tiflisskaia sotsial-demokraticheskaia konferentsiia," *dro*, nos. 11, 12, 14 (signed Ko . . .); "Gazeta 'Isari' i agrarnyi vopros," *dro*, no. 19, April 1 (14), 1907.

61. "Peredovoi proletariat i piatyi s"ezd partii," I. V. Stalin, *Sochineniia*, II, pp. 32–34.

62. Uratadze, *Vospominaniia gruzinskogo sotsial-demokrata*, p. 181.

63. Ibid., p. 182.

64. Ostrovskii, *Kto stoial za spinoi Stalina*, p. 253; B. Liudvigov, "K istorii vyborov bol'shevistskogo delegata ot Tiflisskoi organizatsii RSDRP na V s"ezd," *Zaria vostoka*, March 11, 1939.

65. Asatur Kakhoian, "Vmeste so Stalinym na s"ezde," SShSSA, f. 8, op. 2, ch. 1, d. 22, ll. 222–223.

66. Voroshilov, *Rasskazy o zhizni (vospominaniia)*, I, pp. 336–337.

67. K. Gandurin, *Epizody podpol'ia: (Vospominaniia starogo bol'shevika)* (Moscow: Molodaia gvardiia, 1934), p. 19.

68. Ibid.; Ostrovskii, *Kto stoial za spinoi Stalina*, pp. 253–255; Trotsky, *Stalin*, I, pp. 156–157; SShSSA, f. 8, op. 2, ch. 1, d. 22, l. 139.

69. "I lit Stalin's fire in London—in 1907. He wore same style coat, liked toffee—and tipped 2s. Mr. Bacon Remembers," *Daily Express*, January 5, 1950.

70. Maxim Gorky, *Days with Lenin* (1924) (London: M. Laurence, 1933), p. 5.

71. Isidore Ramishvili, *mogonebebi*, p. 437; Ramishvili discusses the congress, pp. 436–442.

72. Gorky, *Days with Lenin*, pp. 4, 5.

73. Ibid., p. 9.

74. Gandurin, *Epizody podpol'ia*, p. 36.

75. Gorky, *Days with Lenin*, p. 10; *Piatyi (Londonskii) s"ezd RSDRP*, pp. 73–88.

76. Ibid., pp. 129–132.

77. *Piatyi (Londonskii) s"ezd RSDRP*, p. 109.

78. Ibid., p. 194.

79. Ibid. p. 239.

80. Isidore Ramishvili, *mogonebebi*, p. 440.

81. *Piatyi (Londonskii) s"ezd RSDRP*, pp. 257–266.

82. Leon Trotsky, *My Life: An Attempt at Autobiography* [1929] (New York: Pathfinder Press, 1970), pp. 202–203.

83. Edelman, *Stalin: Biografiia v dokumentakh*, pp. 471–472; K. Gandurin, "O Londonskom s"ezde RSDRP (1907 g.)," in *V s"ezd partii (Londonskii)* (Moscow, 1923), pp. 126–127, 132.

84. Leon Trotsky, *Stalin: An Appraisal of the Man and His Influence* (New York: Harper & Brothers, 1941), p. 90; Boris Souvarine, *Stalin: A Critical Survey of Bolshevism* (New York: Longmans, Green & Co., 1939), pp. 106–109.

85. *Piatyi (Londonskii) s"ezd RSDRP*, pp. 540–542.

86. Ibid., p. 232.

87. Ibid., pp. 326, 349.

88. Ibid., p. 350.

89. Ibid., pp. 347–348, 357–358.

90. Ibid., pp. 493, 610–613.

91. Gorky, *Days with Lenin*, p. 16.

92. B. I. Nikolaevskii, "Pamiati I. G. Tsereteli. Stranitsy biografii," *Sotsialisticheskii vestnik*, no. 12 (1959), p. 245; Jones, *Socialism in Georgian Colors*, pp. 216–217.

93. N. Zhordania, *Moia zhizn'* (Stanford, CA: Hoover Institution, 1968, p. 53; HIA, Nicolaevsky Collection, box 144 [reel 123], pp. 64–65. The account in the archival record is slightly different from the printed version and has been used here.

94. Isidore Ramishvili remembered Akselrod telling him, "It's not a disaster that we have Bolsheviks, but the disaster is that in Russia and primarily in the Caucasus the Mensheviks are Bolsheviks." [*mogonebebi*, p. 439.]

95. *Piatyi (Londonskii) s"ezd RSDRP*, pp. 582.

96. A Menshevik present at the congress, and later a historian of the movement, Boris Nikolaevskii, saw Lenin as isolated within his own faction. Few voted with him on this last resolution. [HIA, Nicolaevsky Collection, box 3, folder 11, pp. 37–39.] The Central Committee elected in London included five Bolsheviks, four Mensheviks, one Latvian, and two Poles.

97. Ostrovskii, *Kto stoial za spinoi Stalina*, p. 255; M. Tskhakaia, RGASPI, f. 157, op. 1, d. 18, l. 6.

98. Ostrovskii, *Kto stoial za spinoi Stalina*, p. 255; G. I. Chochia, SShSSA, f. 8, op. 2, ch. 1, d. 56, ll. 19, 22.

99. Ostrovskii, *Kto stoial za spinoi Stalina*, p. 255; G. I. Chochia, SShSSA, f. 8, op. 2, ch. 1, d. 56, ll. 24–25.

100. I. V. Stalin, "Londonskii s"ezd Rossiiskoi Sotsial-Demokraticheskoi Rabochei Partii (Zapiski delegata)," *Sochineniia*, II, pp. 46–77.

101. Ibid., p. 50.

102. Ibid., pp. 50–51.

103. Ibid., p. 51.

104. Ascher, *Pavel Axelrod*, p. 264.

105. Ibid., p. 75.

106. Naneishvili, "tpilisis organizatsia reaktsiis khanashi (1907–10 ts.ts.)," p. 167.

107. Edelman, *Stalin: Biografiia v dokumentakh*, pp. 496–497; Vasadze, *Pravda o Staline glazami aktera*, pp. 257–259.

CHAPTER 17. THE TIFLIS "EX"

1. Isaac Deutscher, *The Prophet Armed. Trotsky: 1879–1921* (London: Oxford University Press, 1954), p. 175.

2. Manning, *The Crisis of the Old Order in Russia*, p. 323.

3. Ascher, *The Revolution of 1905: Authority Restored*, p. 324.

4. Geifman, *Thou Shalt Kill*, pp. 214–220.

5. "Stolypin and his government knowingly violated the constitution . . . by radically transforming the electoral system." [Ascher, *The Revolution of 1905: Authority Restored*, p. 357.]

6. Ibid., p. 325.

7. *Izbiratel'nyi zakon v gosudarstvennuyu dumu po Kavkazu* (Baku, 1912), p. 15.

8. Originally published in *Ternii bez roz (Sbornik v pol'zu osuzhdennykh SD deputatov vtoroi Gosudarstvennoi Dumy)* (Geneva, 1908); based on the translation in Alfred Levin, *The Second Duma: A Study of the Social Democratic Party and the Russian Constitutional Experiment* (New Haven, CT: Yale University Press, 1940), p. 349.

9. Arsenidze, unpublished interviews, III, pp. 55–56; N. N. Zhordaniia, "Gorodskie vybory v Tiflise," *Otzvuki* [Saint Petersburg], August 1907, pp. 70–78.

10. Simon Sebag Montefiore begins his account of the young Stalin with a dramatic recreation of the events of June 13, 1907, and refers to those who carried out the "expropriation" as "gangsters" and their inspiring leader as a "murderous egomaniac." [*Young Stalin*, pp. 1–11.]

11. See Kun's long discussion of Koba's involvement in the Tiflis "ex" and his discovery of an important source connecting him to expropriations in Caucasia [Kun, *Stalin*, pp. 68–84]; as well as Edelman's thorough investigation of the controversies over Koba and Kamo's roles in the "ex" and later accusations that he had been excluded from the party for his role in those events. [Edelman, *Stalin: Biografiia v dokumentakh*, pp. 486–496; and the documents, pp. 503–506.]

12. Ibid., p. 166. Uratadze quotes from the memoirs of Kote Tsintsadze, first published in *revoliutsiis matiane*, and then as a separate book, *rogor vibrdzodit proletarariatis diktaturistvis*, pp. 41–45, 49, 71–72.

13. Kote Tsintsadze (1887–1930) was a Bolshevik from the time of the party schism. He worked closely with Koba Jughashvili and Kamo as part of the "fighting organization" that carried out terrorist acts and "expropriations." He was the first chairman of the Soviet Georgian political police, the Cheka, but broke with Stalin and Sergo Orjonikidze and sided with those party members who wanted greater autonomy for Soviet Georgia. Labeled a "national deviationist" Tsintsadze was exiled from Georgia, joined the Left Opposition, and drew close to

Trotsky from 1923. He was expelled from the Communist Party in 1927, arrested in 1928, and died in prison of tuberculosis.

14. Ibid., p. 163.

15. Leon Trotsky, *Portraits: Personal and Political* (New York: Pathfinder Press, 1976), p. 95.

16. K. Tsintsadze, *rogor vibrdzodit proletariatis diktaturistvis*, pp. 40–44.

17. Ibid., p. 164.

18. Krupskaya, *Reminiscences of Lenin*, p. 154.

19. Ibid., p. 155.

20. Bibineishvili, *Kamo*, p. 119.

21. Kasradze, "Vospominaniia o velikom Staline," SShSSA, f. 8, op. 2, ch. 1, d. 22, ll. 20–25, 54.

22. This information comes from Voznesenskii's testimony to a three-man Social Democratic investigatory commission in Tiflis, the materials of which were sent to a party disciplinary commission investigating Maxim Litvinov's role in expropriations. [Kun, *Stalin,* pp. 77–79; RGASPI, f. 332, op. 1, d. 53.]

23. Bibineishvili, *Kamo*, p. 119.

24. Ibid., pp. 121–122; ; see also, Edelman, *Stalin: Biografiia v dokumentakh,* pp. 500–501; and the account by Kamo's wife, S. F. Medvedeva-Ter-Petrosian, *Geroi revolutsii ("Tovarishch Kamo")* (Moscow-Leningrad, 1925), pp. 32–36; see also, S. F. Medvedeva-Ter-Petrosian, "Tovarishch Kamo," *Proletarskaia revoliutsiia,* 1924, no. 8–9 (31–32), pp. 117–148.

25. Kun, *Stalin,* p. 78; RGASPI, f. 332, op. 1, d. 53.

26. Kun, *Stalin,* pp. 122–123.

27. That story has been told well by Wolfe, *Three Who Made a Revolution,* pp. 376–381; and by Robert Williams, *The Other Bolsheviks,* pp. 114–116. See also, Nikolaevskii, *Tainye stranitsi istorii,* pp. 47–50, 88 n. 78.

28. Williams, *The Other Bolsheviks,* pp. 58–61, 78–79, 117–119, 122–124, 164–166.

29. Ostrovskii, *Kto stoial za spinoi Stalina,* p. 257; Kasradze, "Vospominaniia," SShSSA, f. 8, op. 2, ch. 1, d. 22, ll. 54–55, 61–62.

30. Davrichewy, *Ah! Ce qu'on rigolait bien avec mon copaine Stalin,* p. 237.

31. Ibid., pp. 227–228. Davrishev speaks of Koba being arrested at this time: "Nevertheless, one day, despite all his prudence, he was arrested." But Koba left Tiflis in June 1907 and was not arrested until March 1908 in Baku.

32. Nikolaevskii, *Tainye stranitsii istori,* p. 88 n. 78.

33. Grigorii Kasradze, "Vospominaniia o velikom Staline," SShSSA, f. 8, op. 2, ch. 1, d. 22, ll. 61–62.

34. Ibid., l. 62.

35. Arsenidze, "Iz vospominanii o Staline," p. 232; B. I. Nikolaevsky, *Materialy. Vokrug prazhskoi konferentsii,* HIA, Nicolaevsky Collection.

36. L. Martov, *Spasiteli ili uprazdniteli? (Kto i kak razrushal RSDRP)* (Paris: Izdanie Golosa sotsial-demokrata, 1911).

37. Martov, *Spasiteli ili uprazdniteli?,* p. 23; Ostrovskii, *Kto stoial za spinoi Stalina,* pp. 257–258.

38. Khariton Chavichvily, *Révolutionnaires russes à Genève en 1908* (Geneva: Poésie Vivante, 1974), p. 65.

39. Ibid.

40. Ibid., pp. 68, 77, 82–83, 86.

41. Iiulii Martov, "Eshche ob artilleriiskoi podgotovke," *Vpered*, no. 51 (297), March 31 (18), 1918, p. 1.

42. RGASPI, f. 558, op. 2, d. 3, l. 4.

43. Ibid., l. 9.

44. Ibid., l. 11.

45. Ibid., ll. 13–18, 24.

46. Wolfe, *Three Who Made a Revolution*, pp. 470–471. Historian Bertram D. Wolfe, who had been a Communist and later a severe critic of the Soviet Union, interviewed Rafael Abramovich, Boris Nikolaevskii, and Samuel Levitas, all witnesses to the trial, to put together his account.

47. Dan claims that a plenary session of the Central Committee held in Paris in 1908 excluded participants of the Tiflis organization, among them Koba, in a secret, unpublished resolution. Martov reported that another plenum held in 1909 reinstated them. [Boris Sapir (ed.), *From the Archives of L. O. Dan* (Amsterdam: Stichting Internationaal Instituut Voor Sociale Geschiedenis, 1987), p. 101; Martov, *Spasiteli ili uprazdniteli?*, p. 23.]

48. On the Social Democrats and terrorism, see Geifman, *Thou Shalt Kill*, pp. 84–122; on Azev, see Boris Nikolajewsky, *Azeff the Spy: Russian Terrorist and Police Stool* (Garden City, NY: Doubleday, 1934).

49. HIA, Okhrana, XXa, folder 2, "Revoliutsionnaia partiia sotsialistov-federalistov Gruzii."

50. Davrichewy, *Ah! Ce qu'on rigolait bien avec mon copaine Stalin*, pp. 233, 236–237.

51. Ibid., pp. 237–239. By 1908 Davrishev had left Georgia, settled briefly in Lausanne, where he began his studies. But the Russian secret police managed to have him arrested and tried for a provocation against a Russian subject; he was acquitted but expelled from Switzerland. He settled in Paris, where he broke with all Georgians, went to university, and eventually became an aviator, one of the first "Russian" pilots. Both the Russian and French police continued to follow him. Later he fought for the French air force in World War I. Sometime after the war, in the 1930s, he received an offer from Stalin to return to the Soviet Union and to take up a job as chief of security in the Belovezhskaia Pushcha with the rank of colonel. He refused the offer (pp. 252–253). Stalin sent General Giorgii Iurevich Gordon to see Davrishev in Paris. Apparently, Stalin had seen Davrishev's book, *Dans l'air et dans la boue*, with its dedication in Georgian "To I. V. Stalin in memory of Gori and the revolution of 1905." On seeing the dedication, Stalin smiled and said, "Wait, he is still alive, this hunter. I thought he had died a long time ago, that old bandit." (p. 252).

CHAPTER 18. JOURNEYMAN FOR THE REVOLUTION

1. Trotsky, *Stalin*, p. 116.

2. Isaac Deutscher, *Stalin: A Political Biography*, 2nd edition (Oxford: Oxford University Press, 1967), p. 101. References are to the paperback edition.

3. Letter dated December 5, 1907, GARF, 102, op. 1907, d. 5, ch. 3, l. 107.

4. K. Zakharova-Tsederbaum, "V gody reaktsii," *Katorga i ssylka*, 1929, no. 11 (60), p. 76.

5. Iurii Larin, *Rabochie neftianogo dela (Iz byta i dvizheniia 1903–1908 gg.)* (Moscow, 1909), p. 65.

6. Naneishvili, "tpilisis organizatsia reaktsiis khanashi (1907–10 ts.ts.)," p. 167. Of the three principal leaders of the Tiflis Bolsheviks in 1907, Koba and Shahumian moved to Baku, and Tskhakaia stayed abroad until 1917.

7. Sergo Ordzhonikidze, "Bor'ba s men'shevikami," *Dvadtsat' piat' let bakinskoi organizatsii bol'shevikov* (Baku, 1924), p. 42. The career of Grigol (Grigorii, Sergo) Orjonikidze (1886–1937) rose and fell with Stalin. He rose to the top of the Soviet hierarchy with the support of his powerful patron, engineered the Soviet invasion of independent Georgia in 1921, defeated the more nation-oriented Georgian Communists in the early 1920s, and played a major role in Soviet industrialization in the 1930s before taking his own life after a quarrel with Stalin.

8. The Menshevik chronicler Boris Nikolaevskii, who was then working in Baku, believes this to have been the case. [B. I. Nikolaevsky, *Materialy. Vokrug prazhskoi konferentsii* (HIA, Nicolaevsky Collection).] Nikolaevskii (1887–1966) was a Menshevik activist, who later became a prominent historian and archivist of the movement. His collection of documents and memoirs is located in the Hoover Institution Archive at Stanford University.

9. GARF, f. 102, op. 1907, d. 5, ch. 3, l. 49.

10. Andrei Vyshinskii (1883–1954) was a Menshevik when he met Koba in Baku. He joined the Bolsheviks only in 1920 but rose rapidly to become Stalin's prosecutor in the show trials of the 1930s and later minister of foreign affairs in the late 1940s and Soviet ambassador to the United Nations.

11. Seid Devdariani, "V Baku. Do ob"edineniia," SShSSA, f. 8, op. 2, ch. 1, d. 12, l. 190.

12. For a biography of Orjonikidze, see Oleg Khlevniuk, *In Stalin's Shadow: The Career of "Sergo" Ordzhonikidze* (New York: M. E. Sharpe, 1995).

13. For the story of Stalin's associates at the height of their power, see Simon Sebag Montefiore, *Stalin: The Court of the Red Tsar* (London: Weidenfeld & Nicholson, 2003); Oleg V. Khlevniuk, *Master of the House: Stalin's Inner Circle* (New Haven, CT, and Stanford, CA: Yale University Press and Hoover Institution Press, 2009); and Sheila Fitzpatrick, *On Stalin's Team: The Years of Living Dangerously in Soviet Politics* (Princeton, NJ: Princeton University Press, 2015).

14. Ina Jordania (Zhordaniia) and L. Zhgenti, "Rabochee dvizhenie v Baku i bol'sheviki" (unpublished manuscript in the Russian Archive, Columbia University in the City of New York), p. 23. This central city committee in no way reflected the actual following of the Menshevik faction among the workers. The committee had been elected neither by workers nor by other party members, but had been largely self-appointed. Arrests frequently forced changes in the committee's composition. Thus, at any given time the makeup of the committee was quite arbitrary and unrelated to the popularity of either faction. In any case, the Mensheviks had gained control of the committee in 1906, the first time since 1904, and they retained a dominant influence until the Bolsheviks unseated them in the autumn of 1907. [V. Nogin, "1906 god v Baku," *Dvadtsat' piat' let*, pp. 16–18.]

15. N. N. Kolesnikova, *Po dorogam podpol'ia (Iz vospominanii)* (Baku, 1966), p. 54.

16. K. Tsintsadze, "chemi mogonebani," *revoliutsiis matiane*, 1923, no. 2, pp. 114–115.

17. Koba settled in Bibi-Eibat; Shahumian settled with his wife and three children in Balakhany, the oldest of the oil-field districts, and later moved into the city proper to edit the party newspapers, *Bakinskii proletarii* (Baku Proletariat) and later *Bakinskii rabochii* (Baku Worker). [N. Kolesnikova, "Kak bol'sheviki zavoevali Baku," *Dvadtsat' piat' let*, pp. 221–222.]

18. Kun, *Stalin*, p. 88; RGASPI, f. 74, op. 1, d. 240; op. 2, d. 130.

19. G. Elisabedashvili, "Vospominaniia," SSM, d. 1955/146, ll. 51–56.

20. Ibid.; Ostrovskii, *Kto stoial za spinoi Stalina*, p. 258; RGASPI, f. 558, op. 4, d. 2035, ll. 4–5.

21. The toll on the revolutionary's family is an ongoing theme of A. S. Allilueva, *Vospominaniia*.

22. For an appreciation of what women and their families tied to the revolutionary movement experienced, see Barbara Evans Clements, *Bolshevik Women* (Cambridge: Cambridge University Press, 1997).

23. *Neftianoe delo*, X, January 15, 1908, p. 8. By "liberalism" among Baku oil industrialists I am referring to their willingness to negotiate with workers and even Social Democrats. As for party affiliation, Baku entrepreneurs leaned toward the Octobrist Party rather than the more liberal and reformist Kadets, who in turn found some supporters among Armenian intellectuals and indusrialists. [My thanks to Alexander Semyonov for pointing this out.]

24. Larin, *Rabochie neftianogo dela*, p. 22; Ina Jordania (Zhordaniia) and L. Zhgenti, "Rabochee dvizhenie v Baku i bol'sheviki."

25. Deutscher, *Stalin*, p. 99.

26. Larin, *Rabochie neftianogo dela*, pp. 15. The population of Baku as a whole was 206,751, according to a local census of October 22, 1903. [Ibid., p. 7.]

27. Ibid., p. 127. Sixty-four percent of all Baku workers were illiterate (according to the 1903 census), but of the Russian workers only 40 percent could not read, while 53.6 percent of Armenians and 89.1 percent of Muslims were illiterate. [Ibid., p. 32.]

28. Ibid., pp. 30, 55, 58n. The average Baku worker received thirty percent more for a nine-hour workday than the average worker in the imperial capital.

29. An internal party letter of February 1908, intended only for Bolsheviks in Baku, opposed the Menshevik argument that all *druzhiny* be dissolved. The letter argued that the London Congress called for the dissolution of "special military *druzhiny*" but not of self-defense units [*druzhiny samooborony*]. In Baku, the letter claimed, special military units had ceased to exist long ago, and only self-defense units and their staffs were operating. ["Pis'mo k tovarishcham. Nuzhna li nam somooborona?" GARF, f. 102, op. 1908, d. 5, ch. 3, ll. 13–130b.] After the London Congress the existing *druzhina* was disbanded, but later self-defense units were re-created. [Edelman, *Stalin: Biografiia v dokumentakh*, p. 515; A. Rogov, "Na revoliutsionnoi rabote v Baku," *Katorga i ssylka*, 1927, no. 6 (35), pp. 103–104.]

30. Ostrovskii, *Kto stoial za spinoi Stalina*, p. 261; Ivan Bokov, "Vospominaniia," SSM, d. 49, l. 16; I. Bokov, RGASPI, f. 558, op. 4, d. 5 n. 83, ll. 24–25; David L'vovich Zelindzon, "Avtobiografiia," RGASPI, f. 1241, op. 1, d. 719, ll. 5–7.

31. Ostrovskii, *Kto stoial za spinoi Stalina*, p. 264; S. I. Kavtaradze, "Vospominaniia" SShSSA, f. 8, op. 2, ch. 1, d. 19, l. 33; I. Bokov memoirs, RGASPI, f. 558, op. 4, d. 583, ll. 24–25.

32. Naneishvili, "tpilisis organizatsia reaktsiis khanashi (1907–10 ts.ts.)," pp. 173–174.

33. *Bakinskii proletarii*, no. 4, May 15, 1908, pp. 2–3.

34. Erik van Ree, "Reluctant Terrorists?" pp. 141–142; Ivan Bokov memoirs, RGASPI, f. 558, op. 4, d. 658, ll. 39–41; d. 583, ll. 24–25; Edelman, *Stalin: Biografiia v dokumentakh*, pp. 542–543; "Iz vospominanii Bokova Ivana Vasil'evicha," March 1937, RGASPI, f. 558, op. 4, d. 658, ll. 39–41.

35. I. V. Stalin, "Ekonomicheskii terror i rabochee dvizhenie," *Sochineniia*, II, pp. 110–113; "Neftepromyshlenniki ob ekonimicheskom terrore," ibid., pp. 114–127; Erik van Ree, "Reluctant

Terrorists?" pp.146–147; Sibrat Gaurov memoirs, RGASPI, f. 558, op. 4, d. 658, ll. 129–130, 134; Efend'ev memoirs, RGASPI, f. 558, op. 4, d. 658, l. 431; d. 577, l. 4. Nikolaevskii writes that in 1908 Koba favored economic terror, while Shahumian was opposed, but Koba's own articles argue against economic terror. [B. I. Nikolaevsky, *Materialy. Vokrug prazhskoi konferentsii*, HIA, Nicolaevsky Collection, box 548 [reel 434], p. 119.

36. Edelman, *Stalin: Biografiia v dokumentakh*, p. 513; "Iz vospominanii Sibrata Gafurova," 1935, RGASPI, f. 558, op. 4, d. 658, ll. 129–130.

37. I. V. Stalin, "Lakeistvuiushchie 'sotsialisty,'" *Sochineniia*, II, pp. 128–130.

38. "Sosnovskii, Lev Semenovich (avtobiografiia)," *Deiateli SSSR i revoliutsionnogo dvizheniia Rossii: Entsiklopedicheskii slovar' Granat* (Moscow: Sovetskaia Entsiklopediia, 1989), p. 693.

39. Larin, *Rabochie neftianogo dela*, p. 41. In 1906, 85 percent of strikes in Baku were won by the workers; in January/February 1907, only 47 percent of strikes were successful and by May/June a mere 9.5 percent. In 1907 no pay was given for strike days. The strikes were largely spontaneous, unorganized affairs, in which the trade union occasionally participated. In general the oil-field workers tended to win their strikes more often than the factory and refinery workers. [Ibid., p. 72.]

40. Ibid., p. 43.

41. Keenan, "Remarques sur l'histoire révolutionnaire à Bakou, 1904–1905," pp. 225–260.

42. Prokofii Aprasionovich Dzhaparidze ("Alesha"), *Izbrannye stat'i, rechi i pis'ma, 1905–1918 gg.* (Moscow, 1958), p. 30.

43. The expression was originally Nogin's, who visited Baku in this period and wrote later: "In the deep underground was Stalin (Koba), well known in the Caucasus in those days and forced to hide in the Balakhana oil fields." [Trotsky, *Stalin*, p. 123.]

44. A. Stopani, "Iz proshlogo nashei partii, 1904–1908 gg.," *Iz proshlogo: Stat'i i vospominaniia iz istorii bakinskoi organizatsii i rabochego dvizheniia v Baku* (Baku, 1923), p. 18. This article, published while Lenin was still alive, establishes the central role that the twenty-three-year-old Koba played in the Baku underground.

45. I. Shitikov-Samartsev, "Partiia v rabochikh raionakh, 1905 i 1906 gg," *Dvadtsat' piat' let*, pp. 210–211.

46. Stopani, "Iz proshlogo nashei partii," p. 18.

47. The sociological conclusion that recently arrived and less experienced peasant workers favored the Bolsheviks would become a Menshevik orthodoxy in the years just before World War I. For Martov's views, shared by the historian Leopold H. Haimson, see Haimson, "The Problem of Social Stability in Urban Russia, 1905–1917 (Part I)," *Slavic Review*, XXIII, 4 (December 1964), pp. 632–642.

48. Z. G. Ordzhonikidze, *Put' bol'shevika. Stranitsy iz zhizni G. K. Ordzhonikidze* (Moscow: Gosudarstvennoe izdatel'stvo politicheskoi literatury, 1956), p. 61.

49. Published in 1887 and revised in 1903, Kautsky's work was a popular explanation of Marx's economic theories, translated into Russian in 1888 as *Ekonomicheskie ucheniia Karla Marksa v populiarnom izlozhenii K. Kautskogo*; Edelman, *Stalin: Biografiia v dokumentakh*, p. 545; "Iz vospominanii Sibrata Gafurova," 1935, RGASPI, f. 558, op. 4, d. 658, ll. 130–131.

50. Seid Devdariani, "V Baku. Do ob"edineniia," SShSSA, f. 8, op. 2, ch. 1, d. 12, l. 194.

51. The Mensheviks later changed the name of their committee to "Leading Collective," but refused to subordinate themselves to the Bolshevik Committee. The Bolsheviks expressed

opposition to a schism in the local party organization. Spandarian wrote that the Mensheviks had been the real schismatics since they had not called for new elections to the Baku Committee. The Bolshevik organizational commission had unanimously called for unification with the Mensheviks, who replied by calling a separate conference and refusing to negotiate with the Bolsheviks. [Suren Spandarian ("Timofei"), *Stat'i, pis'ma i dokumenty* (Moscow: Gosudarstvennoe izdatel'stvo politicheskoi literatury, 1958), p. 115.]

52. "Obzor deiatel'nosti organizatsii Rossiiskoi Sotsial-Demokraticheskoi Rabochei Partii, sostavlennyi na osnovanii pisem i soobshchenii s mest," May 8, 1908, GARF, f. 102, op. 1908, d. 5, ch. 61, ll. 44–51.

53. Larin, *Rabochie neftianogo dela*, p. 75.

54. Ibid., p. 84.

55. Kochegar (I. Shitikov-Samartsev), "Nuzhno idti na soveshchanie s neftepromyshlennikami?," *Gudok*, no. 3 (September 10, 1907). The labor contract of 1904, called the "crude oil constitution," established a nine-hour day and a minimum wage, but the industry did not observe these conditions. The Social Democrats argued that a new labor contract would be enforceable now that trade unions had been established in Baku.

56. Ko . . . , "Nado boikotirovat' soveshchanie," *Gudok*, no. 4 (September 29, 1907); I. V. Stalin, *Sochineniia*, II, p. 84.

57. L. A. Rin [Iurii Larin], *O soveshchanii s neftepromyshlennikami* (Baku, 1907), p. 104.

58. Ibid.; Ordzhonikidze, *Put' bol'shevika*, p. 44.

59. Larin, *Rabochie neftianogo dela*, pp. 106–108.

60. Ibid., pp. 105–106.

61. "Pered vyborami," *Gudok*, no. 14 (January 13, 1908); I. V. Stalin, *Sochineniia*, II, pp. 87–91; see also Stepan Shaumian, "K 'soveshchaniiu' s piat'iu rabochimi garantiiami," in S. G. *Izbrannye proizvedeniia, 1902–1916 gg.*, 2 vols. (Moscow: Gosudarstvennoe izdatel'stvo politicheskoi literatury, 1957–1958), I, pp. 241–248.

62. I. V. Stalin, *Sochineniia*, II, pp. 141–142. Larin gives slightly different figures: out of 35,000 votes cast (75 percent of the oil workers), about 24,000 or 69 percent were cast for the conference with preconditions. [Larin, *Rabochie neftianogo dela*, p. 119.]

63. K. Kato, "Mezhdu prochim," *Gudok*, no. 23 (March 16, 1908); this article, although signed with Stalin's pseudonym, was not reprinted in *Sochineniia*. In this same issue of *Gudok* there is another article by Stalin that does not appear in his *Sochineniia*: K. Kato, "Bezgramotnost' ili provokatsiia?" In this article Stalin replies to an attack by the liberal newspaper *Baku* on the Union of Oil Workers, in which the writer claimed that the union was run undemocratically. Stalin pointed out that the union was now too large for full meetings (he claimed 8,000 members) but that the delegates' meetings represented various points of view.

64. Meshadi Azizbekov (1876–1918) was one of the first Caucasian Muslim Marxists, served as people's commissar of internal affairs in the short-lived Bolshevik government in Baku in 1918, and perished as one of the Twenty-Six Baku Commissars.

Mamed Mamediarov (1875–1933) was an early Azerbaijani Social Democrat, a founder of the Muslim socialist group Hummet. He served in the Soviet period as Azerbaijan's people's commissar of social security (1922–1927).

65. Ostrovskii, *Kto stoial za spinoi Stalina*, p. 265; *Baku*, March 18, 1908; *Bakinskii rabochii*, December 20, 1939.

66. Larin, *Rabochie neftianogo dela*, pp. 136–137. A short time before the Armenians had elected the head of their national church, the Catholicos, in the holy city Ejmiadzin, not far from Erivan.

67. Letter of April 11, 1908, from P. A. Stolypin and I. I. Vorontsov-Dashkov, "Bor'ba s revoliutsionnym dvizheniem na Kavkaze v epokhu stolypinshchiny. (Iz perepiski P.A. Stolypina s gr. I. I. Vorontsovym-Dashkovym)," *Krasnyi arkhiv*, 1929, no. 3 (34), pp. 187–202, 195, 196.

68. Ibid., pp. 88, 138.

69. Anastas Mikoyan, *Tak Bylo: Razmyshleniia o minuvshem* (Moscow: Vagrius, 1999), p. 347.

70. T. I. Vulikh, "Bol'sheviki v Baku," HIA, Nicolaevsky Collection, series 133, box 207, folder 9 [reel 179], p. 2.

71. Ibid., pp. 2–3.

72. N. Zhordania, "Staline," pp. 9–10. This text is taken from a French translation of Zhordania's article, "stalini," in *brdzolis khma* [Voice of the Struggle], no. 65, October 1936. Copy in the collection of the author.

73. Kh. A. Barsegian, *Stepan Shaumian: Dokumental'naia letopis' zhizni i deiatel'nosti* (Erevan: Aisatan, 1973), p. 105.

74. Vulikh, "Bol'sheviki v Baku," p. 2–3.

75. Ibid.

76. Alliluev, *Proidennyi put'*, p. 134; A. S. Allilueva, *Vospominaniia*, p. 112.

77. Ibid., p. 6. Nikolaevskii, who worked in Baku in 1911, also heard this story. [HIA, Nicolaevsky Collection, series 133, box 207, folder 15.]

78. Edelman, *Stalin: Biografiia v dokumentakh*, p. 548; "Iz zapiski besedy s Alekseenko," RGASPI, f. 558, op. 4, d. 658, ll. 3–6.

79. G. Elisabedashvili, "Vospominaniia," SSM, d. 1955/146, ll. 54–56.

80. Ibid.

81. A. S. Svanidze-Monaselidze, "Vospominaniia o tovarishche Staline," SShSSA, f. 8, op. 2, ch. 1, d. 43, l. 157.

82. This translation is from Montefiore, who has the best account of Koba's treatment of his first wife and his grief at her death. [*Young Stalin*, pp. 163–166.] It is based on the memoirs of Giorgi Elisabedashvili and Aleksandra Svanidze-Monoselidze in the SSM, 1955/146, ll. 51–56; and 87.1955–368, ll. 1–16, respectively; and those of Mikheil Monoselidze in SShSSA, f. 8, op. 2, ch. 1, d. 34, ll. 317–54.

83. Edelman, *Stalin: Biografiia v dokumentakh*, p. 549; "Iz vospominanii M. Monaselidze," RGASPI, f. 558, op. 4, d. 651, l. 267.

84. Available in Montefiore, *Young Stalin*; Ostrovskii, *Kto stoial za spinoi Stalinia*; and other publications.

85. Montefiore, *Young Stalin*, p. 166.

86. Iremashvili, *Stalin und die Tragödie Georgiens*, p. 40.

87. Conversation with Efim Sartania, SShSSA, f. 8, op. 2, ch. 1, d. 43, l. 61.

88. Edelman, *Stalin: Biografiia v dokumentakh*, pp. 559–565.

89. Ibid., p. 566, 575–577; "Iz vospominanii Sakvarelidze P. D.," published in the Georgian newspaper *kommunisti*, May 18, 1935, translated from Georgian, RGASPI, f. 558, op. 4, d. 658, ll. 315–320; A. Rogov, "Iz zhizni bakinskoi tiur'my," *Katorga i ssylka*, 1927, no. 8 (37), pp. 126–130.

90. Koba, "Soveshchanie i rabochie," *Bakinskii proletarii*, no. 5 (July 20, 1908); I. V. Stalin, *Sochineniia*, II, pp. 134–145.

91. Olga Edel'man, "Bityi/nebityi vozhd': Stalin, knizhka Marksa i bakinskaia tiurma v stalin-iane," *Neprikosnovennyi zapas*, 2017, no. 2 [http://magazines.russ.ru/nz/2017/2/bityjnebityj -vozhd-pr.html]. This episode was reported originally in P. D. Sakvareldize's memoirs published in *kommunisti* and found in RGASPI, f. 558, op. 4, d. 658, ll. 318–322; Edelman, *Stalin: Biografiia v dokumentakh*, pp. 577–580.

92. Semen Vereshchak, "Stalin v tiur'me (vospominaniia politicheskogo zakliuchennogo)," *Dni* (Paris), January 22, 1928; January 24, 1928. Vereshchak, who has often been referred to as a member of the Socialist Revolutionary Party, later worked in the independent Georgian Re-public with the Mensheviks and fled with them to Paris when the Red Army invaded in Febru-ary 1921. Edelman is doubtful about Vereshchak's veracity; see her "Bityi/nebityi vozhd'" and *Stalin: Biografiia v dokumentakh*, pp. 686–688.

93. Edelman, *Stalin: Biografiia v dokumentakh*, p. 579; "Iz vospominanii Vatseka Ivana Prokop'evicha," RGASPI, f. 558, op. 4, d. 658, l. 114.

94. I. V. Stalin, *Sochineniia*, II, pp. 144–145.

95. *Golos sotsial-demokrata*, nos. 10–11, November–December 1908.

96. Ostrovskii, *Kto stoial za spinoi Stalina*, p. 303; memoirs of Bagdasar Ovchinian, SShSSA, f. 8, op. 2, ch. 1, d. 37, l. 122; B. Bibineishvili, *Zaria vostoka*, October 4, 1935.

97. Ostrovskii, *Kto stoial za spinoi Stalina*, pp. 303–304; memoirs of I. P. Nadiradze, SShSSA, f. 8, op. 2, ch. 1, d. 35, ll. 41, 47–48.

CHAPTER 19. THE REBEL DISARMED

1. Edelman, *Stalin: Biografiia v dokumentakh*, p. 584; I. V. Vatsek, "V gody polpol'ia," *Rasskazy starykh rabochikh Zakavkaz'ia o velikom Staline*, pp. 104–105.

2. Ostrovskii, *Kto stoial za spinoi Stalina*, pp. 300–302; memoirs of Tat'iana Sukhovaia, RGASPI, f. 558, op. 4, d. 647, l. 267; memoirs of Akima Semenov, RGASPI, f. 558, op. 4, d. 658, ll. 339–340.

3. Ostrovskii, *Kto stoial za spinoi Stalina*, pp. 300–302; memoirs of F. V. Blinov, RGASPI, f. 558, op. 4, d. 647, ll. 33–39; Edelman, *Stalin: Biografiia v dokumentakh*, pp. 585–588.

4. Iosif Dubrovinskii ("Innokentii") (1877–1913) was a Bolshevik whom at various times Lenin considered to be too conciliatory toward the Mensheviks. A member of the Central Committee, he was exiled to Turukhansk just before Stalin and, suffering from tuberculosis, he drowned himself in the Enisei River.

5. Ostrovskii, *Kto stoial za spinoi Stalina*, p. 308. Iakov Sverdlov (1885–1919) was a leading Bolshevik, who shared the Turukhansk exile with Stalin. More a party operative than a theorist, Sverdlov served as chairman of the All-Russian Executive Committee of the Soviets (VTsIK), the de facto head of the Russian Soviet Republic, until his untimely death in an influenza epidemic.

6. Ibid., pp. 308–309.

7. Edelman, *Stalin: Biografiia v dokumentakh*, p. 600; "Iz vospominanii T. Sukhovoi," RGASPI, f. 558, op. 4, d. 647, ll. 270–271.

8. S. Ia. Alliluev, "Vstrechi s tovarishchem Stalinym: Otryvki iz vospominanii," *Pravda*, December 22, 1939.

9. Kun, *Stalin: An Unknown Portrait*, p. 98.

10. Ibid.; Ostrovskii, *Kto stoial za spinoi Stalina*, pp. 309–310; Edelman believes the story about the card game is pure fiction, but Sukhova's account is accurate. [*Stalin: Biografiia v dokumentakh*, pp. 592, 601.]

11. Edelman, *Stalin: Biografiia v dokumentakh*, p. 601; RGASPI, f. 558, op. 1, d. 4372, l. 1.

12. Kun, *Stalin: An Unknown Portrait*, pp. 101–102; RGASPI, f. 558, op. 4, d. 647. Kun believes that Koba had a romance with Sukhova. Montefiore agrees and goes on to write, "In his short time in Solvychegodsk, he was to find two mistresses among the small group of politicals. He was never a womanizer, but even in these years of penniless obscurity he was never without at least one girlfriend, and often more. Indeed in exile be became almost libertine." [*Young Stalin*, p. 177.]

13. A. S. Allilueva, *Vospominaniia*, pp. 110–111.

14. Kun, *Stalin: An Unknown Portrait*, p. 98; RGASPI, f. 558, op. 4, d. 647.

15. A. S. Allilueva, *Vospominaniia*, pp.111–112.

16. Kun, *Stalin: An Unknown Portrait*, p. 98; RGASPI, f. 558, op. 4, d. 647.

17. Edelman doubts the accuracy of Shveitser's account of Koba's meeting with Poletaev. [Edelman, *Stalin: Biografiia v dokumentakh*, pp. 604, 637–638.]

18. V. I. Lenin, "K otsenke russkoi revoliutsii," *Proletarii*, May 10 [23] 1908); *PSS*, XVI, pp. 40–41.

19. Aleksandr Potresov (1869–1934) was one of the original editors of *Iskra* and after the Second Party Congress sided with the Mensheviks. He edited *Nasha zaria* and was an advocate of what Lenin condemned as "liquidationism," concentrating exclusively on the legal labor movement. In 1914 along with Plekhanov he defended Russia's war effort. He left Russia in 1925 and died in Paris.

20. Wolfe, *Three Who Made a Revolution*, p. 475.

21. N. K. Krupskaia, *Reminiscences of Lenin* (Moscow: Foreign Languages Publishing House, 1959), p. 162. This is the English translation of Krupskaia's memoirs, *Vospominaniia o Lenine* (Moscow: Gosudarstvennoe izdatel'stro, 1931).

22. Letter to Gorky, April 11, 1910, in V. I. Lenin, *PSS*, XLVII, p. 251.

23. Georges Haupt and Jutta Scherrer, "Gor'kij, Bogdanov, Lenin. Neue Quellen zur ideologischen Krise in der bolschewistischen Fraktion (1908–1910)," *Cahiers du monde russe et soviétique*, XIX, 3 (July–September 1978), p. 323.

24. Letter to V. V. Vorovskii, July 1, 1908, V. I. Lenin *PSS*, XLVII, p. 160.

25. *Golos sotsial-demokrata*, nos. 4–5 (April 1908); cited in Williams, *The Other Bolsheviks*, p. 132.

26. Nina Tumarkin, "Religion, Bolshevism, and the Origins of the Lenin Cult," *Russian Review*, 1 (January 1981), pp. 35–46.

27. V. I. Lenin, "Politicheskaia stachka i ulichnaia bor'ba v Moskve," *Proletarii*, no. 21, October 17 (4), 1905; *PSS*, XI, p. 350.

28. This is the argument of John Eric Marot, "Alexander Bogdanov, *Vpered*, and the Role of the Intellectual in the Workers' Movement," *Russian Review*, XLIX, 3 (July 1990), pp. 241–264, who sees Bogdanov as a continuation of the Lenin of *What Is to Be Done?* but distinct from his

views after 1905. Critical comments on Marot's article can be found in the Walicki and Sochor articles in the same special issue of *Russian Review*.

29. Service, *Lenin, I*, p. 189.

30. Shaumian's letter to Mikha Tskhakaia, July 27, 1909, in Shaumian, *Izbrannye proizvedeniia*, I, pp. 267–269; *Pis'ma*, pp. 151–153; Edelman, *Stalin: Biografiia v dokumentakh*, pp. 580–581. The writings of Joseph Dietzgen (1828–1888), a friend of Marx, became influential in Russia at the turn of the century. The author of *The Nature of Human Brain Work* (1869), he believed that socialism was the future religion of science. He argued that socialists needed to recognize that humans are motivated by emotion and a need for faith. Marx praised his work.

31. Ibid.

32. Letter of Koba to Mikha Tskhakaia, 1908, RGASPI, f. 558, op. 1, d. 5262, ll. 1–6; Edelman, *Stalin: Biografiia v dokumentakh*, pp. 581–583.

33. Ibid. Koba used the word *praktik* here as activists in the field with positive connotation, even though it was used in contrast to *komitetchik* and *teoretik*. *Praktik* was also employed for those who worked directly with workers, particularly trade unionists.

34. Ibid.

35. Ibid.

36. Ibid.

37. Ibid.

38. Letter signed K. Stefin from Baku to Stefik [M. Torchelidze] in Geneva, December 26, 1909, GARF, f. 102, op. 1910, d. 5, ch. 6l.B, ll. 5–70b; Edelman, *Stalin: Biografiia v dokumentakh*, pp. 662–663.

39. Il'ia Moiseevich Dubinskii-Mukhadze, *Ordzhonikidze* (Moscow: Molodaia gvardiia, 1963), pp. 92–94. In the 1967 edition, the harshest criticisms of Stalin (for example, "immaturity of Koba as a Marxist") were removed (pp. 75–76). While the first edition was published during Khrushchev's time, the second was issued during Brezhnev's when criticism of Stalin had been restricted. The first edition, while eminently readable, is a popular account without footnotes and was written at a time when Soviet historians were directed to be critical of Stalin. On the other hand, Dubinskii-Mukhadze based his work on archival and published sources as well as conversations with those involved in the events and had spent time with Orjonikidze.

40. This resolution was published in Stalin, *Sochineniia*, II, pp. 166–168.

41. The Bolshevik Tiflis Committee put out a news release on this conference. [*Izveshchenie o tiflisskoi gorodskoi konferentsii*, GARF, f. 102, op. 1909, d. 5, ch. 61, ll. 116–1180b.]

42. "Pis'mo Stalina M. Tskhakaia," November 5, 1909, translated from Georgian by Sh. Chivadze, May 15, 1950, RGSAPI, f. 558, op. 1, d. 4516, ll. 1–2; Edelman, *Stalin: Biografiia v dokumentakh*, pp. 658–659.

43. "Draft Resolution of the Executive Commission (November 1909), in Richard Pipes (ed.), *The Unknown Lenin: From the Secret Archives* (New Haven, CT, and London: Yale University Press, 1996), pp. 22–23.

44. Letter of Stalin to *Proletarii*, November 12, 1909, RGASPI, f. 558, op. 1, d. 26, ll. 1–10b; Edelman, *Stalin: Biografiia v dokumentakh*, pp. 659–660.

45. Shaumian, *Pis'ma*, pp. 155–156; Shaumian, *Izbrannye proizvedeniia*, I, pp. 285–288.

46. Of the 441 deputies in the Third Duma only 18 were Social Democrats and 14 *trudoviki* (peasant socialists). South Caucasia, with its six million people, had its duma representation reduced to six: the young Evgenii Gegechkori from Kutaisi province, the old Marxist Nikoloz Chkheidze from Tiflis, both Mensheviks; a Georgian "Progressive"; an Armenian socialist; a Muslim; and a right-wing Russian. Once again the Mensheviks dominated the tiny Social Democratic faction, but their erstwhile liberal allies, the Kadets, had by this time lost their radical edge.

47. Arutiunov, *Rabochee dvizhenie v Zakavkaz'e v period novogo revoliutsionnogo pod"ema*, pp. 74–75.

48. *Pravda* (Vienna), no. 11, March 18, 1910.

49. *Rabochaia gazeta*, no. 3, February 8 (21), 1910.

50. "Partiinyi krizis i nashi zadachi," *Bakinskii proletarii*, no. 6, August 1, 1909; no. 7, August 27, 1909; Stalin, *Sochineniia*, II, pp. 146–158.

51. Ibid., p. 152.

52. Ibid., p. 153.

53. Ibid., p. 153.

54. Ibid., pp. 157–158.

CHAPTER 20. LABOR AND LIQUIDATORS

1. P. A. Daniel-Bek, *Russkii neftianoi eksport i mirovoi rynok v period s 1904 po 1911 g.: Ekonimicheskii etiud*, ed. P. B. Struve (Petrograd, 1916), p. 89.

2. M. I. Ushakov, *Neftianaia promyshlennost' v Rossii* (Saint Petersburg, 1912), p. 198.

3. G. A. Arutiunov, *Rabochee dvizhenie v Zakavkaz'e v period novogo revoliutsionnogo pod"ema (1910–1914 gg.)* (Moscow and Baku, 1963), p. 47.

4. *Bakinskii proletarii*, no. 7, August 27, 1909; I. V. Stalin, *Sochineniia*, II, p. 160.

5. The conditions of the Baku workers during the "reaction" were exhaustively documented by a group of statisticians under the direction of the Bolshevik Aleksandr Stopani. The wage payment system had a paternalistic quality about it. The oil industrialists took away from the worker discretionary power over a significant portion of his income and tied workers to management through a system of favors and bonuses. [A. M. Stopani, *Neftepromyshlennyi rabochii i ego biudzhet* (Baku, 1916). For a useful summary of Stopani's work, see A. D. Bok, "Usloviia byta rabochikh-neftianikov g. Baku," in N. Druzhinin, ed., *Usloviia byta rabochikh v dorevoliutsionnoi Rossii (po dannym biudzhetnykh obsledovanii)* (Moscow, 1958), pp. 59–95.]

6. Stopani, *Neftepromyshlennyi rabochii*, p. 145.

7. Ibid., p. 147.

8. *Golos sotsial-demokrata*, nos. 8–9, July–September 1908, p. 38.

9. *Gudok*, no. 38, October 23, 1908.

10. *Golos sotsial-demokrata*, nos. 8–9, July–September 1908, p. 38.

11. Ibid.

12. Shaumian, *Izbrannye proizvedeniia*, I, p. 285.

13. Ibid., p. 287.

14. A. N. Guniev and I. V. Strigunov (eds.), *Rabochee dvizhenie v Azerbaidzhane v godakh novogo revoliutsionnogo pod"ema (1910–1914 gg.): Dokumenty i materialy*, 2 vols. (Baku: Izdatel'stvo Akademii Nauk Azerbaidzhanskoi SSR, 1967), I, p. 34.

15. Arutiunov, *Rabochee dvizhenie v Zakavkaz'e v period novogo revoliutsionnogo pod"ema*, p. 159.

16. Shaumian, *Izbrannye proizvedeniia*, I, pp. 295–296. By early 1911, the Mensheviks' "neutral" union numbered only 129 members. [*Baku*, no. 1, January 1, 1911; Arutiunov, *Rabochee dvizhenie v Zakavkaz'e v period novogo revoliutsionnogo pod"ema*, p. 164.]

17. *Sotsial-Demokrat*, no. 12, March 23, 1910; Stalin, *Sochineniia*, II, p. 187. See also, *Golos sotsial-demokrata*, no. 23, November 1910; this article was probably written by Muravsky (identified by Boris Nikolaevsky).

18. K. Ko . . . , "K predstoiashchei obshchei zabastovke," *Bakinskii proletarii*, no. 7, August 27, 1909; I. V. Stalin, *Sochineniia*, II, pp. 159–168; see also the proclamation of the Baku Committee, "O dekabr'skoi zabastovke i dekabr'skom dogovore (Po povodu piatoi godovshchiny)," December 13, 1909, in *Sochineniia*, II, pp. 169–173.

19. K. Stefin, "Pis'ma s Kavkaza," *Sotsial-Demokrat*, no. 11, December 13 (26), 1910; I. V. Stalin, *Sochineniia*, II, pp. 174–187.

20. Ostrovskii, *Kto stoial za spinoi Stalina*, p. 314.

21. Ibid., pp. 315–318, 322–323. Ostrovskii, who worked in the local archives, concluded that the Baku police had only one informer, code name "Estonets," and that none of those accused in Koba's leaflet were guilty. [Ibid., p. 318.] In fact there were several police informers. The reconstruction of the tale of the police agent Nikolai Leontev comes from Edelman, *Stalin: Biografiia v dokumentakh*, pp. 654–656; and from a number of revised memoirs of Said Iakubov, RGASPI, f. 558, op. 4, d. 658, ll. 462–463, 446–448; and Sibgat Gafurov, RGASPI, f. 558, op. 5, d. 558, ll. 133–134.

22. Edelman, *Stalin: Biografiia v dokumentakh*, pp. 620–621.

23. *Delo provokatora Malinovskogo* (Moscow: Respublika, 1992), p. 271, n. 105.

24. V. I. Lenin, "Prodelki respublikanskikh shovinistov" [first published in *Volksrecht*, No. 81, April 5, 1917], *PSS*, XXXI, pp. 79–82; Kolesnikova, *Po dorogam podpol'ia*, pp. 105–108; V. Dzhanibekian, *Provokatory. Vospominaniia, mysli i vyvody* (Moscow, 2000), pp. 260–273.

25. Garsevan Varshamian, "Vospominaniia," SShSSA, f. 8, op. 2, ch. 1, d. 7, ll. 100–101; Ostrovskii, *Kto stoial za spinoi Stalina*, p. 323. Varshamian's memoirs were written in 1935.

26. Ostrovskii, *Kto stoial za spinoi Stalina*, pp. 472–473.

27. Edelman, *Stalin: Biografiia v dokumentakh*, p. 606.

28. Varshamian, "Vospominaniia," SShSSA, f. 8, op. 2, ch. 1, d. 7, ll. 101.

29. V. Khodzhishvili [Varvara Japaridze], *Zhizn'—podvig. Vospominaniia o P. A. Dzhaparidze* (Baku, 1979), p. 61; Ostrovskii, *Kto stoial za spinoi Stalina*, p. 318.

30. *Bakinskii professional'nyi vestnik*, no. 1, February 21, 1909.

31. Zakharova-Tsederbaum, "V gody reaktsii," pp. 90–96.

32. Ostrovskii, *Kto stoial za spinoi Stalina*, p. 263. After the play A. P. Gevorkiants, Spandarian, and V. I. Kolesnikov went into the city; Kolesnikov invited them all home, but Koba refused, and the group went to greet the New Year in a restaurant. [A. P. Gevorkian memoirs, SShSSA, f. 8, op. 2, ch. 1, d. 8, l. 265.]

33. M. B. Koz'min and L. I. Ponomarev, *A. M. Gor'kii v portretakh, illiustratsiiakh, dokumentakh, 1868–1936* (Baku, 1966), p. 158.

34. N. N. Kolesnikova, *Po dorogam podpol'ia*, pp. 93–95.

35. *Sotsial-Demokrat*, no. 11, February 13 (26), 1911; Stalin, *Sochineniia*, II, p. 191, 407.

36. Kolesnikova, *Po dorogam podpol'ia*, p. 98.

37. Stalin, *Sochineniia*, II, p.192.

38. Police report, April 12, 1910 [GARF, f. 102, op. 1910, d. 5, ch. 6l.B, ll. 31–32].

39. Police report, June 1910, GARF, f. 102, op. 1910, d. 5, ch. 6l.B, ll. 38–40; Edelman, *Stalin: Biografiia v dokumentakh*, pp. 616–617.

40. Letter of Dan to Aksel'rod, December 6, 1907, Axelrod Archive, International Institute of Social History (Amsterdam); cited in Ascher, *Pavel Axelrod*, p. 273.

41. Letter of Kautsky to Lunacharskii, August 9, 1911, Nicolaevsky Collection, HIA; cited in Ascher, *Pavel Axelrod*, p. 276.

42. P. Aksel'rod, F. Dan, and N. Semenov, *Otchet kavkazskoi delegatsii ob obshchepartiinoi konferentsii* (Paris: Tsental'noe biuro zagranichnykh grupp RSDRP, 1909).

43. Krupskaya, *Reminiscences of Lenin*, p. 193.

44. Leopold H. Haimson (ed.), in collaboration with Ziva Galili y Garcia and Richard Wortman, *The Making of Three Russian Revolutionaries: Voices from the Menshevik Past* (Cambridge: Cambridge University Press; Paris: Editions de la maison des sciences d l'homme, 1987), pp. 4–5.

45. F. Dan, "Bor'ba za legal'nost," *Golos sotsial-demokrata*, III, nos. 19–20 (January–February 1910); V. I. Lenin, "'Golos' likvidatorov protiv partii (otvet 'Golosu sotsial-demokrata')," *PSS*, XIX, pp. 205–206; Ascher, *Pavel Axelrod*, p. 279.

46. A. Potresov, in *Nasha zaria*, no. 2 (1910), pp. 61–62; Ascher, *Pavel Axelrod*, p. 280. A small group of intellectuals in Saint Petersburg, led by Potresov, published the theoretical journal *Nasha zaria* (Our Dawn) (1910–1914).

47. P. Aksel'rod, "Istochniki raznoglasii mezhdu tak-naz. partiitsami i tak-naz. likvidatorami," *Golos sotsial-demokrata*, III, no. 23 (November 1910); Ascher, *Pavel Axelrod*, p. 281.

48. Uratadze, *Vospominaniia gruzinskogo sotsial-demokrata*, p. 242.

49. The Baku Committee, for example, adopted a resolution backing the position Lenin took in the January 1910 Central Committee meeting in Paris. While the CC was ready to have Social Democrats who were working in legal organizations participate in the forthcoming all-party conference, Lenin and the Baku Committee wanted only representatives from party organizations. Stalin wrote the Baku resolution. [I. V. Stalin, *Sochineniia*, II, pp. 197–200.]

50. Memoirs of Vaso Qiasashvili, *komunisti* (Tbilisi), December 12, 1935, p. 233.

51. I. Mgeladze (Vadini), P. Sabashvili, Germane Napetvaridze, and E. Karseladze, "bolshevikebis mushaoba tpilisshi 1909–10 tslebshi. mogonebani," *revoliutsiis matiane*, 1925, no. 1 (11), p. 159.

52. I. V. Stalin, *Sochineniia*, II, pp. 199–200.

53. B. I. Nikolaevskii, "Materialy," HIA, Nicolaevsky Collection, box 5, folder 2.

54. A Bolshevik veteran who gravitated toward the Mensheviks in the years of the "Reaction," Knuniants and his wife were not particularly fond of Koba, whom they considered too dogmatic. After the collapse of the Petersburg Soviet of 1905, Knuniants was arrested and exiled to Siberia. He escaped abroad, and early in 1908 returned illegally to Baku, where he made contact with his comrades. But soon afterward he left the Bolshevik organization and began working in the legal labor movement, writing for the Menshevik *Gudok* and *Bakinskii professional'nyi vestnik* (Baku Trade Union Bulletin) and lecturing in the Nauka Club. Steadily he moved toward *likvidatorstvo*. On September 29, 1910, he was arrested. While in prison he

contracted typhus and died on May 14, 1911. Bolsheviks and Mensheviks alike attended his funeral, and Shahumian, a long-time friend, wrote the obituary. [*Rabochaia gazeta*, no. 6, September 22 (October 5), 1911; Shaumian, *Izbrannye proizvedeniia*, I, pp. 343–345.] In a letter to Tskhakaia, Shahumian wrote, "As one slain, I have not been able to take up my pen all week. . . . The best comrade has died—one of my best friends—Knuniants. . . . Painful! I cannot continue." [Shaumian, *Pis'ma*, p. 162.]

In the several Soviet accounts and collections of documents concerning Knuniants, there is no mention of his conversion to Menshevism or his writings on *likvidatorstvo*. See, for example, O. G. Indzhikian, *Bogdan Knuniants* (Erevan, 1961), p. 238. Indzhikian merely says that Knuniants made certain mistakes and "wavered on questions of party tactics" after his return to Baku. This is explained by "his very long absence from direct party work, his sick condition, and the influence of Reaction."

55. B. Radin-Knuniants, "Odin iz itogov," *Nasha zaria*, no. 5 (May 1911), p. 52.

56. Ibid., pp. 53–54, 57–59.

57. B. Radin-Knuniants, "Staroe i novoe (okonchanie)," *Nasha zaria*, nos. 7–8 (1911), p. 39.

58. *Nasha zaria*, no. 6 (1911), p. 22.

59. Ibid., pp. 34–35, 42.

60. Ibid., no. 6 (1911), p. 18.

61. Israel Getzler, *Martov: A Political Biography of a Russian Social Democrat* (Cambridge: Cambridge University Press, 1967), p. 125. For one of the best discussions of Lenin and *likvidatorstvo*, see Neil Harding, *Lenin's Political Thought, Vol. I: Theory and Practice in the Democratic Revolution* (New York: St. Martin's Press, 1977), pp. 260–273.

62. *Sotsial-Demokrat*, no. 28–29, November 5 (18), 1912; Arutiunov, *Rabochee dvizhenie v Zakavkaz'e v period novogo revoliutsionnogo pod"ema*, p. 100; A. M. Raevskii, *Alesha Dzhaparidze: Politicheskii siluet* (Baku, 1931), pp. 25–26.

63. *dasatsqisi* (Beginning), no. 4, March 1908; cited in I. V. Stalin, *Sochineniia*, II, pp. 191–195.

64. I. V. Stalin, *Sochineniia*, II, pp. 195–196. A Russian translation of Zhordania's article, "Burning Questions," can be found in the Menshevik Project at Columbia University.

65. An. [Zhordania], "Po povodu Pis'ma s Kavkaza," *"Diskussionnyi listok" (Prilozhenie k gazete "Sotsial-Demokrat")*, no. 2, May 25 (June 7), 1910.

66. Resolution of a conference of Georgian Social Democratic Organizations held in Guria, fall 1910, in *Golos sotsial-demokrata*, no. 25 (May 1911).

67. Uratadze, *Vospominaniia gruzinskogo sotsial-demokrata*, p. 224.

68. Ibid.

69. G. V. Plekhanov, "Predislovie," to S. T. Arkomed, *Rabochee dvizhenie i sotsial-demokratiia na Kavkaze* (Geneva: Chaulmontet, 1910; 2nd edition: Moscow-Petrograd, 1923), pp. 21–22.

70. Suny, *The Making of the Georgian Nation*, pp. 185–208.

71. I. V. Stalin, *Sochineniia*, II, pp. 201–208.

72. "Donesenie nachal'nika Bakinskogo okhrannogo otdeleniia rotmistra P. P. Martynova v Departament politsii," March 24,1910, GARF, f. 102, op. 1910, d. 5, ch. 61.B, ll. 18–19; Edelman, *Stalin: Biografiia v dokumentakh*, pp. 666–667.

73. Ostrovskii, *Kto stoial za spinoi Stalina*, pp. 326–327; RGASPI, f. 558, op. 4, d. 635, ll. 410b–42.

74. Ibid., l. 44.

75. Elizaveta Adamovna Esaian, "Iz vospominanii o tov. Staline," SShSSA, f. 8, op. 2, ch. 1, d. 16, ll. 292–293; Ostrovskii, *Kto stoial za spinoi Stalina*, pp. 328–334; RGASPI, f. 558, op. 4, d. 635, ll. 19, 24–740b, 91, 94; d. 628, l. 17; Edelman, *Stalin: Biografiia v dokumentakh*, pp. 672–675.

76. Edelman, *Stalin: Biografiia v dokumentakh*, p. 634; from the memoirs of E. G. Bekker, written in 1975. ["V rabochem Baku," published by S. F. Korneeva, *Golosa istorii: Tsentral'nyi muzei revoliutsii, Sbornik nauchikh trudov*, Issue 22, book 1 (Moscow, 1990), p. 19.]

CHAPTER 21. THE ROVING AGENT

1. In his study of worker writers, Mark D. Steinberg notes, "These proletarian intellectuals took no pleasure in indeterminacy, paradox, or irony. They wanted to see the world with greater clarity, certainty, and faith. To their visible sorrow, they could not." [*Proletarian Imagination: Self, Modernity, and the Sacred in Russia, 1910–1925* (Ithaca, NY, and London: Cornell University Press, 2002), p. 9.]

2. Cited in Abraham Ascher, *P. A. Stolypin: The Search for Stability in Late Imperial Russia* (Stanford, CA: Stanford University Press, 2001), p. 217.

3. Ibid., p. 218.

4. His speech was reprinted in *Zvezda*, no. 15 (51), March 8 (21), 1912.

5. I. I. Vorontsov-Dashkov, *Vsepoddanneishii otchet za vosem' let upravleniia Kavkazom* (Saint Petersburg 1913), pp. 6–16.

6. *Sto sorok besed s Molotovym: Iz dnevnika F. Chueva* (Moscow: Terra, 1991), p. 240.

7. *Molotov Remembers: Inside Kremlin Politics. Conversations with Felix Chuev*, ed. Albert Resis (Chicago: Ivan R. Dee, 1993), p. 164. This is the English translation of *Sto sorok besed s Molotovym*.

8. Ostrovskii, *Kto stoial za spinoi Stalina*, p. 336.

9. Viktor Nogin (1878–1924) was a prominent Moscow Bolshevik, a "conciliationist" after 1905, who tried to reunite the Social Democratic Party. He favored a socialist coalition government of all the left parties in October 1917. He was an important trade official for the Soviet government.

   Iosif Dubrovinskii ("Innokentii") (1877–1913) joined the Bolsheviks after the party schism in 1903 and was active in the Moscow uprising in 1905. Exiled to Turukhansk where he met Stalin, he drowned in the Enesei River in 1913.

10. RGASPI, f. 558, op. 1, d. 28, ll. 1–4; B. I. Nikolaevskii, *Materialy. Vokrug prazhskoi konferentsii*, Nicolaevsky Collection, HIA, pp. 154–155; I. V. Stalin, *Sochineniia*, II, pp. 209–212. The archival text is slightly different from published text—for example, Kamenev is not mentioned in *Sochineniia*.

11. The landowner Manilov is a lifeless, empty, easily fooled landowner in Nikolai Gogol's *Dead Souls*.

12. RGASPI, f. 558, op. 1, d. 28, ll. 1–4; B. I. Nikolaevskii, *Materialy. Vokrug prazhskoi konferentsii*, Nicolaevsky Collection, HIA, pp. 154–155; I. V. Stalin, *Sochineniia*, II, pp. 209–212.

13. Ibid.

14. Ostrovskii, *Kto stoial za spinoi Stalina*, p. 341.

15. Kun, *Stalin: An Unknown Portrait*, p. 104.

16. Memoirs of Iv. Mikh. Golubev, RGASPI, f. 71, op. 10, d. 276, p. 205; from the mock-up for a book, *I. V. Stalin v tsarskoi ssylke na severe*, that apparently was never published.

17. Ibid., pp. 209, 206.

18. Letter from Solvychegodsk, signed Iosif, to Moscow, to the teacher Bobrovskaia, for Vl. S. Bobrovskii, January 24, 1911, RGASPI, f. 558, op. 1, d. 29, l. 1; Dubinskii-Mukhadze, *Ordzhonikidze* (1963), pp. 92–93, fn. 1; Ostrovskii, *Kto stoial za spinoi Stalina*, p. 337–338; *Zaria vostoka*, December 23, 1925; Edelman, *Stalin: Biografiia v dokumentakh*, p. 722.

19. From a letter from Moisei Lashevich in Iarensk to Riakovskii in Paris, quoting Koba's letter to Shur, GARF, f. 102, op. 1911, d. 5, ch. 14, l. 2; Ostrovskii, *Kto stoial za spinoi Stalina*, p. 345; Edelman, *Stalin: Biografiia v dokumentakh*, pp. 748–749.

20. A. Antonov-Ovseenko, *Portret tirana* (Moscow: Gregoi Peidzh, 1995), pp. 328–334; RGASPI, f. 558, op. 1, d. 5097, ll. 1–10b; Edelman, *Stalin: Biografiia v dokumentakh*, pp. 751–752.

21. Kun, *Stalin: An Unknown Portrait*, p. 109; RGASPI, f. 558, op. 4, d. 447.

22. Ostrovskii, *Kto stoial za spinoi Stalina*, pp. 338–339; memoirs of V. L. Sheitser, RGASPI, f. 161, op. 1, d. 20, l. 37.

23. Kun, *Stalin: An Unknown Portrait*, p. 119, n. 41; Ostrovskii, *Kto stoial za spinoi Stalina*, p. 342.

24. "Delo departamenta politsii deloproizvodstvo ob Iosife Vissarionoviche Dzhugashvili, klichka 'Koba', August 17, 1911," RGASPI, f. 558, op. 1, d. 5377, ll. 17–170b.

25. Korostelev and Golubev were members, along with Mikheil Kalandadze, Grigorii Zhavoronkov, Lunev, Fedor Siatrovskii, and Ivan Petrov. [Memoirs of Iv. Mikh. Golubev, RGASPI, f. 71, op. 10, d. 276, p. 207.]

26. Ostrovskii, *Kto stoial za spinoi Stalina*, pp. 341–342; Kun, *Stalin: An Unknown Portrait*, p. 112; RGASPI, f. 558, op. 4, d. 540.

27. Kun, *Stalin: An Unknown Portrait*, p. 112; RGASPI, f. 558, op. 4, d. 540.

28. RGASPI, f. 71, op. 10, d. 407.

29. "Proshenie Vologodskomu gubernatoru o razreshenii ostat'sia na zhitel'stvo v g. Vologde po okonchanii sroka ssylki," RGASPI, f. 558, op. 1, d. 4334, l. 1; Ostrovskii, *Kto stoial za spinoi Stalina*, p. 344.

30. Kun, *Stalin: An Unknown Portrait*, p. 113; RGASPI, f. 558, op. 4, d. 647; Edelman, *Stalin: Biografiia v dokumentakh*, pp. 750–751; "Iz vospominanii S. P. Kriukovoi, RGASPI, f. 558, op. 4, d. 647, ll. 41–43.

31. "Delo departamenta politsii deloproizvodstvo ob Iosife Vissarionoviche Dzhugashvili, klichka 'Koba', August 17, 1911," RGASPI, f. 558, op. 1, d. 5377, ll. 1–44.

32. RGASPI, f. 558, op. 1, d. 5377, ll. 5–8.

33. Kun, *Stalin: An Unknown Portrait*, p. 113; RGASPI, f. 558, op. 4, d. 647.

34. Edelman, *Stalin: Biografiia v dokumentakh*, pp. 758–759; "Iz zapisi besedy s. P. G. Onufrievoi (Fominoi)," July 7, 1944, RGASPI, f. 558, op. 4, d. 647, l. 78; Kun, *Stalin: An Unknown Portrait*, pp. 115–116; RGASPI, f. 558, op. 4, d. 647.

35. Kun, *Stalin: An Unknown Portrait*, p. 117; RGASPI, f. 558, op. 4, d. 547.

36. Kun, *Stalin: An Unknown Portrait*, p. 117; RGASPI, f. 558, op. 4, d. 547.

37. Kun, *Stalin: An Unknown Portrait*, p. 117; RGASPI, f. 558, op. 4, d. 547; Edelman, *Stalin: Biografiia v dokumentakh*, p. 759.

38. Ostrovskii, *Kto stoial za spinoi Stalina*, p. 349; Memoirs of P. G. Fomina-Onufrieva, RGASPI, f. 558, op. 1, d. 647, ll. 70–81.

39. Kun, *Stalin: An Unknown Portrait*, p. 118; RGASPI, f. 558, op. 4, d. 547.

40. *Rabochaia gazeta*, no. 1, October 30 (November 12), 1910; V. I. Lenin, "Uroki revoliutsii," *PSS*, XIX, pp. 416–424.

41. Ostrovskii, *Kto stoial za spinoi Stalina*, p. 345; RGASPI, f. 558, op. 1, d. 30, l. 1.

42. "K istorii prazhskoi konferentsii," *Krasnyi arkhiv*, no. 6 (97), pp. 98–99.

43. "Svodka agenturnykh svedenii po Baku (gorodu) po partii Sotsial-Demokratov za aprel' mesiats 1911 goda, August 1911," GARF, f. 102, op. 1911, d. 5, ch. 6lBII, ll. 36–410b; *Rabochaia gazeta*, no. 7, December 22, 1911 (January 4, 1912); Arutiunov, *Rabochee dvizhenie v Zakavkaz'e v period novogo revoliutsionnogo pod"ema*, p. 134; G. A. Arutiunov, "Uchastie zakavkazskikh bol'shevistskikh organizatsii v podgotovke VI (Prazhskoi) Vserossiiskoi konferentsii RSDRP," *Teghekagir* ("Newsletter of the Armenian SSR Academy of Sciences"), no. 11 (1957), p. 92.

44. *Rabochaia gazeta*, no. 7, December 22, 1911 (January 4, 1912).

45. B. I. Nikolaevskii, *Materialy. Vokrug prazhskoi konferentsii*, HIA, B. I. Nicolaevsky Collection, p. 124; *Rabochaia gazeta*, no. 4–5, April 15 (28), 1911; GARF, f. 102, op. 1911, d. 5, ch. 6, ll. 10b–10v.

46. Shahumian's letter to Krupskaia, September 1911 [Shaumian, *Pis'ma*, p. 164.].

47. Arutiunov, "Uchastie bolshevistskikh organizatizatii . . . ," pp. 91–100; Shahumian's article, signed "K," in *Rabochaia gazeta*, no. 7, December 22 (January 4), 1911.

48. B. I. Nikolaevskii, *Materialy. Vokrug prazhskoi konferentsii*, HIA, B. I. Nicolaevsky Collection, pp. 128–130.

49. Arutiunov, *Rabochee dvizhenie v Zakavkaz'e v period novogo revoliutsionnogo pod"ema*, p. 138.

50. GARF, f. 102, op. 1911, d. 5, ch. 6, ll. 12–16; Boris Nikolaevskii, who had come to Baku in September 1911, took over the center of the underground Social Democratic organization. [B. I. Nikolaevskii, *Materialy. Vokrug prazhskoi konferentsii*, HIA, B. I. Nicolaevsky Collection, pp. 129–132.]

51. "Delo departamenta politsii deloproizvodstvo ob Iosife Vissarionoviche Dzhugashvili, klichka 'Koba', August 17, 1911," RGASPI, f. 558, op. 1, d. 5377, ll. 3–4.

52. A. S. Allilueva, *Vospominaniia*, pp. 109–110.

53. Memoirs of V. L. Shveitser [written for the fiftieth birthday of Stalin], "Nelegal'no v Moskve" and "Nelegal'no v Pitere," *Komsomolskaia Pravda*, December 21, 1929; RGASPI, f. 161, op. 1, d. 9, ll. 1–6.

54. A. S. Allilueva, *Vospominaniia*, pp. 107–108.

55. RGASPI, f. 71, op. 10, d. 407.

56. RGASPI, f. 71, op. 10, d. 407.

57. Stalin was never formally expelled from the Baku Bolshevik group. Uratadze may be referring to the judgment of the Zhordania-Danishevskii commission critical of Stalin's role in the splitting of the Baku organization.

58. Uratadze, *Vospominaniia gruzinskogo sotsial-demokrata*, pp. 234–235.

59. V. L. Shveitser memoirs, *Krasnyi arkhiv*, no. 2 (105) (1941), p. 17; Ostrovskii, *Kto stoial za spinoi Stalina*, p. 354.

60. Ostrovskii, *Kto stoial za spinoi Stalina*, p. 355.

61. Ibid., p. 357; RGASPI, f. 558, op. 2, d. 75, l. 2; d. 7, l. 1.

62. See Michael Melancon, *The Lena Goldfields Massacre and the Crisis of the Late Tsarist State* (College Station: Texas A&M Press, 2006).

63. Victoria E. Bonnell, *Roots of Rebellion: Workers' Politics and Organizations in St. Petersburg and Moscow, 1900–1914* (Berkeley and Los Angeles: University of California Press, 1983), pp. 434–438, 450.

64. On the labor movement in Russia during the years just before World War I, see Leopold H. Haimson, *Russia's Revolutionary Experience, 1905–1917: Two Essays* (New York: Columbia University Press, 2005), pp. 117–229; Bonnell, *Roots of Rebellion*; Heather Hogan, *Forging Revolution: Metalworkers, Managers, and the State in St. Petersburg, 1890–1914* (Bloomington: Indiana University Press, 1993); Leopold Haimson and Charles Tilly (eds.), *Strikes, War, and Revolutions in an International Perspective: Strike Waves in the Late Nineteenth and Early Twentieth Centuries* (Cambridge: Cambridge University Press, 1989).

65. "Census society" refers to those who possessed the *tsenz*, the wealth and property qualifcation that gave voters the right to a full vote to the duma.

66. Haimson, *Russia's Revolutionary Experience, 1905–1917*, p. 207.

67. Haimson, who in his early and very influential work had concurred with the Menshevik analysis, revised his view after decades of quantitative research on the composition of the working class. See his "'The Problem of Political and Social Stability Urban Russia on the Eve of the War' Revisited," *Slavic Review*, LIX, 4 (Winter 2000), pp. 848–875.

68. The subsequent fate of the delegates to the Prague Conference is indicative of the turbulence and violence of Soviet history. Spandarian died in a tsarist exile in 1916. Iakov ("Pavl") Zevin, a Menshevik-partyite, became a Bolshevik, was commissar of labor in Shahumian's government known as the Baku Commune in 1918, and was executed by anti-Bolsheviks as one of the famous Twenty-Six Baku Commissars. The other Menshevik-partyite, David Shvartzman ("Viktor"), died in 1949. Roman Malinovskii was executed by the Soviets as a police spy when he returned to Russia in 1918. The other police agent, A. S. Romanov, left Russia, his fate unknown. Orjonikidze committed suicide after a quarrel with Stalin in 1937. Grigorii Zinoviev, Petr Zalutskii, Leonid Serebriakov, A. I. Dogadov, F. I. Goloshchekin, and Aleksandr Voronskii were all victims of Stalin's Great Purges of the 1930s. Lenin died after a series of strokes in 1924.

69. "Protokoly VI (Prazhskoi) Vserossiiskoi konferentsii RSDRP," *Kommunist*, no. 8 (May 1988), p. 63; G. E. Zinov'ev, "Vospominaniia: Praga (18–30 ianvaria 1912g.)," *Izvestiia TsK KPSS*, no. 5 (292) (May 1989), pp. 187–202. These memoirs were written by Zinoviev during his exile in Kustanai in 1933.

70. "Protokoly VI (Prazhskoi) Vserossiiskoi konferentsii RSDRP," p. 61.

71. Ibid., p. 61.

72. "Protokoly VI (Prazhskoi) Vserossiiskoi konferentsii RSDRP," *Kommunist*, no. 9 (June 1988), p. 72.

73. V. I. Lenin, "Organ liberal'noi rabochei politiki," *Zvezda*, no. 11 (347), Febuary 19, 1912; *PSS*, XXI, pp. 157–160.

74. "Protokoly VI (Prazhskoi) Vserossiiskoi konferentsii RSDRP," *Kommunist*, no. 9 (June 1988), p. 78.

75. Ralph Carter Elwood, *Roman Malinovsky: A Life Without a Cause* (Newtonville, MA: Oriental Research Partners, 1977), pp. 15–18.

76. V. I. Lenin, *PSS*, XLVIII, p. 140.

77. Elwood, *Roman Malinovsky*, pp. 26–27.

78. Ibid., p. 32.

79. Letter from A. Chkhenkeli in Franzensbad to S. Semkovskii, July 3, 1914 [HIA, B. I. Nikolaevsky Collection, box 186, folder 3]. Chkhenkeli (1874–1969) was born into a noble family and was a major Georgian Menshevik leader, elected as a deputy to the Fourth State Duma. He served as foreign minister in the independent Georgian Republic and went into exile in France after the Soviet invastion of Georgia in February 1921.

80. See the resolution passed by the conference of Bolshevik groups abroad, held in Paris, December 27–30, 1911: "Our duty is to support the unity between Bolsheviks and Mensheviks being established in Russian practice, examples of which are the organizations in Baku, Kiev, Ekaterinoslav, etc." [Cited in Arutiunov, *Rabochee dvizhenie v Zakavkaz'e v period novogo revoliutsionnogo pod"ema*, p. 107.]

CHAPTER 22. THE MAN OF STEEL

1. S. T. Beliakova and A. M. Volodarskaia, "Iz perepiski TsK RSDRP s mestnymi bol'shevistskimi organizatsiiami, 1911–1912 gg.," *Voprosy istorii KPSS*, no. 10 (October 1964), p. 78; L. A. Slepov and S. A. Andronov, "Prazhskaia konferentsiia RSDRP i bor'ba bol'shevikov za edinstvo partii," *Voprosy istorii KPSS*, no. 2 (February 1965), p. 39; GARF, f. 102, OO. 1910, d. 5, pr. 2, l. 190.

2. Carter Elwood, *The Non-Geometric Lenin: Essays on the Development of the Bolshevik Party, 1910–1914* (London and New York: Anthem Press, 2011), p. xiii.

3. Ostrovskii, *Kto stoial za spinoi Stalina*, p. 357; *Krasnyi arkhiv*, no. 6 (97) (1939), pp. 55–56.

4. Sergei Ivanovich Kavtaradze, "Vospominaniia," SShSSA, f. 8, op. 2, ch. 1, d. 19, ll. 43–45; Kavtaradze, "Iz vospominanii o tovarishche Staline," *Pravda*, no. 38 (6644), February 8, 1936, pp. 2–3; Ostrovskii, *Kto stoial za spinoi Stalina*, pp. 358–359; S. I. Kavtaradze, *Iz vospominanii o tovarishche Staline* (Voroshilovgrad, 1936), pp. 3–4.

5. Resolution published in *Rabochaia gazeta*, no. 8, March 17, 1912.

6. Edelman, *Stalin: Biografiia v dokumentakh*, p. 807; "Perliustrirovannoe pis'mo Stalina N. K. Krupskoi," March 7, 1912, published in *Iz epokhi "Zvezdy" i "Pravdy,"* 3 vols. (Moscow, 1921–1924), III, pp. 234–235.

7. Edelman, *Stalin: Biografiia v dokumentakh*, pp. 807–808; "Iz vospominanii T. Sukhovoi," RGASPI, f. 558, op 4, d. 647, l. 274.

8. B. I. Nikolaevskii, *Materialy. Vokrug prazhskoi konferentsii*, HIA, B. I. Nikolaevsky Collection, p. 149.

9. Ibid., pp. 144–145; Police report from Baku, April 4, 1912, GARF, f. 102, op. 1912, d. 5, ch. 6, ll. 21–22.

10. Shveitser, "Nelegal'no v Moskve (Iz vospominanii)," RGASPI, f. 161, op. 1, d. 9, ll. 4–6; [B. I. Nikolaevskii, *Materialy. Vokrug prazhskoi konferentsii*, HIA, B. I. Nikolaevsky Collection, pp. 144–145, 149; I. V. Stalin, *Sochineniia*, II, pp. 162, 213–218, 219–224.

11. "Svodka agenturnykh svedenii po Baku gubernii (gorodu) po partii Sotsial-Demokratov za aprel mesiats 1912," GARF, f. 102, d. 5, ch. 6b, ll. 38–43; B. I. Nikolaevskii, *Materialy. Vokrug prazhskoi konferentsii*, HIA, B. I. Nikolaevsky Collection, pp. 132–136.

12. *Sotsial-Demokrat*, no. 26, April 25 (May 8), 1912. This article, written by Koba, is not included in his *Sochineniia*, but it was later published in Guliev and Strigunov, *Rabochee dvizhenie v Azerbaidzhane v godakh novogo revoliutsionnogo pod"ema*, pp. 201–202. Arutiunov argues that Stalin's actions at this conference prove that at this time he was a "conciliationist" willing to merge the Bolshevik organization with the Menshevik organization then led by *likvidatory*. [*Rabochee dvizhenie v Zakavkaz'e v period novogo revoliutsionnogo pod"ema*, p. 201.] But, in fact, the Baku Mensheviks were led by those moderates who were willing to cooperate with *likvidatory* while continuing to work within the underground party organization.

13. B. I. Nikolaevskii, *Materialy. Vokrug prazhskoi konferentsii*, HIA, B. I. Nicolaevsky Collection, pp. 136–138.

14. Lev Sosnovskii (1886–1937) worked as a journalist and was in Soviet times the editor of *Bednota* (Poverty), a paper directed to peasant readers. He joined the Left Opposition in the 1920s, was expelled from the Communist Party in 1927, and was executed in the Stalin purges.

15. B. I. Nikolaevskii, *Materialy. Vokrug prazhskoi konferentsii*, HIA, B. I. Nicolaevsky Collection, pp. 150–151.

16. Ibid., pp. 145–146.

17. Ibid., pp. 153–154.

18. Ibid., p. 155.

19. Ibid., pp. 155–159.

20. Ibid., pp. 159, 160.

21. Letter (intercepted by the police) from "Zel'ma" in Tiflis, April 5, 1912, to Kiev, Mikhailovskaia, 14, Mr. N. T. Omel'ianenko, for Petr, GARF, f. 102, op. 1912, d. 5, ch. 6, ll. 28–29; the handwritten originals of the letter, and the letter from Stalin, from Baku (March 30) are in RGASPI, f. 558, op. 1, d. 5085, ll. 1–4; an unsigned article, "Baku (konets Marta)," reproduces most of the letter in *Sotsial-Demokrat*, no. 26, May 8 (April 25), 1912, p. 9.

22. In general the Baku Bolsheviks at this time were conciliatory toward the Mensheviks. See the letter from Baku, to A. in Saint Petersburg, for the editorial board of the newspaper *Zhivoe delo*, GARF, f. 102, op. 1911, d. 5, ch. 6, ll. 30–300b; see also Edelman, *Stalin: Biografiia v dokumentakh*, pp. 811–812; "Pis'mo E. D. Stasovoi chlenam Russkogo Biuro TsK," April 5, 1912, which included a letter from I. Jughashvili, March 30, RGASPI, f. 558, op. 1, d. 5085, ll. 1–2; GARF, f. 102, DO. 1912, d. 5, ch. 6, ll. 28–29.

23. GARF, f. 102, OPO. 1912, d. 5–7-V, l. 290b; Ostrovskii, *Kto stoial za spinoi Stalina*, p. 359.

24. M. Liadov, *Iz zhizni partii nakanune i v gody pervoi revoliutsii* (Moscow: Izdatel'stvo kommunisticheskogo universiteta imeni Ia. M. Sverdlova, 1926), p. 3.

25. Kun, *Stalin: An Unknown Biography*, p. 132; RGASPI, f. 17, op. 4, d. 647.

26. RGASPI, f. 85, op. 3, d. 3, ll. 45–46.

27. For an excellent discussion of the relations of *Pravda* with the émigré leadership, see Ralph Carter Elwood, "Lenin and *Pravda*, 1912–1914," *Slavic Review*, XXXI, 2 (June 1972), pp. 355–380.

28. *Sto sorok besed s Molotovym*, pp. 241–242.

29. Edelman, *Stalin: Biografiia v dokumentakh*, pp. 814–815; "Chernovik pis'ma, napisannogo I. Dzhugashvili ot imenii TsK RSDRP k Klare Tsetkin, nachalo aprelia 1912," RGASPI, f. 558, op. 1, d. 35, ll. 1–2.

30. Kun, *Stalin: An Unknown Biography*, p. 133; RGASPI, f. 71, op. 10, d. 407.

31. Elwood, "Lenin and *Pravda*," p. 363.

32. I. V. Stalin, *Sochineniia*, II, pp. 219–224.

33. K. S., "Novaia polosa," *Zvezda*, no. 30 (66), April 15 (28), 1912; I. V. Stalin, *Sochineniia*, II, pp. 225–226.

34. K. S., "Tronulas'! . . . ," *Zvezda*, no. 32, April 19 (May 2), 1912; I. V. Stalin, *Sochineniia*, II, p. 238.

35. K. Salin, "Zhizn' pobezhdaet," *Zvezda*, no. 30 (66), April 15 (28), 1912; I. V. Stalin, *Sochineniia*, II, pp. 232–233.

36. "Nashi tseli," *Pravda*, no. 1, April 22, 1912; I. V. Stalin, *Sochineniia*, II, pp. 248–249.

37. *Pis'ma Aksel'roda i Martova*, p. 231.

38. Ibid., p. 235.

39. V. I. Lenin, *PSS*, XLVIII, p. 95.

40. Ibid., pp. 70–71.

41. Letter to Orjonikidze, Spandarian, and Stasova, March 28, 1912, V. I. Lenin, *PSS*, XLVIII, p. 53.

42. Kun, *Stalin: An Unknown Portrait*, p. 158; RGASPI, f. 17, op. 4, d. 647. Kun is mistaken when he claims that Stalin took the name, which comes from the Russian *stal'* [steel], because *juga* in Georgian means steel.

43. Edelman, *Stalin: Biografiia v dokumentakh*, p. 816; "Pis'mo Stalina [agentu TsK RSDRP v Parizhe]," April 18, 1912, GARF, f. 102, DO. 1912, d. 5, ch. 57, L.B.L. 103.

44. Filipp Goloshchekin (1876–1941) [Isai Isaakovich Goloshchekin] was a Bolshevik, later notorious as an organizer of the execution of the Romanov family in 1918 and as the head of the Communist Party of Kazakhstan during the famine of the early 1930s. He was executed in 1941.

45. Kun, *Stalin: An Unknown Biography*, p. 136; RGASPI, f. 558, op. 4, d. 647.

46. RGASPI, f. 558, op. 1, d. 4354, l. 1.

47. Kun, *Stalin: An Unknown Biography*, p. 136; RGASPI, f. 558, op. 4, d. 647.

48. Ibid.

49. Ibid.

50. Konstantin Chernenko (ed.), *I. V. Stalin v sibirskoi ssylke* (Krasnoiarsk: Kraevoe izdatel'stvo, 1942), p. 79.

51. S. I. Kavtaradze, "Iz vospominanii," *Oktiabr*; no. 11 (1942), p. 100; Edelman, *Stalin: Biografiia v dokumentakh*, pp. 892–893; S. Kavtaradze, *Iz vospominanii o tovarishche Staline* (Voroshilovgrad, 1936), pp. 3–13. Anna Allilueva claims that Koba escaped from Narym with Iakov Sverdlov, but this was an erroneous impression on her part. [A. S. Allilueva, *Vospominaniia*, p. 113.]

52. Police report from Baku, April 6, 1912. [GARF, f. 102, op. 1912, d. 5, ch. 6, ll. 23–230b.]

53. A. S. Allilueva, *Vospominaniia*, pp. 113–114.

54. Nikolai Krestinskii (1883–1938) was a Bolshevik from the time of the initial party schism. He was briefly people's commissar of finance in 1918. In the 1920s he was a supporter of Trotsky, a member of the Left Opposition until 1928. He served as a Soviet diplomat until his arrest in 1937. Tried in the last Great Purge trial along with Bukharin, Rykov, and Genrikh Iagoda, he was executed in 1938.

55. N. Krestinskii, "Starye pravdisty," *Iz epokhi "Zvezdy" i "Pravdy,"* I, p. 18.

56. G. Safarov, "Nasha piterskaia organizatsiia pered vyborami v IV Dumu," *Iz epokhi "Zvezdy" I "Pravdy,"* II, p. 126. Inessa Armand (1874–1920) was a French-born Bolshevik, who

worked closely with Lenin and Krupskaia from 1908 until her death. She was active in the women's organization Zhenotdel' in the early Soviet period. Deeply loved by Lenin, it is likely that they were lovers at some point, and he grieved deeply when she died. [Elwood, *The Non-Geometric Lenin*, pp. 111–124.]

Georgii Safarov (1891–1942) was born of a Polish mother and Armenian father and was a Bolshevik from 1908. In 1917 he traveled with Lenin on the famous "sealed train" from Switzerland back to Russia. In the early Soviet period he was a member of the Workers' Opposition and worked in the Urals and Central Asia. He joined Trotsky in the opposition and was expelled from the Communist Party in 1927. He was executed in 1942.

57. Elwood, *The Non-Geometric Lenin*, pp. 126–127.

58. Haimson and Tilly (eds.), *Strikes, War, and Revolutions*, p. 508.

59. This is the thesis, widely held by scholars, of the "dual polarization"—the distancing of most of society from the state along with the widening gap between the upper classes [the *verkhi*] and the lower classes [the *nizy*]—that Leopold H. Haimson argues characterized both 1914 and the revolutionary year 1917. [Haimson, "The Problem of Social Stability in Urban Russia, 1905–1917," Part I, *Slavic Review*, XXIII, 4 (December 1964), pp. 619–642; and Part II, ibid., XXIV, 1 (March 1965), pp. 1–22.]

60. K. Stalin, "Vybory v Peterburge (Pis'mo iz S.-P.B.)," *Sotsial-Demokrat*, no. 30, January 12 (25), 1913, pp. 3–5; I. V. Stalin, *Sochineniia*, II, pp. 271–284.

61. V. I. Lenin, *PSS*, XLVIII, p. 113.

62. *Sotsial-Demokrat*, nos. 28–29, November 5 (18), 1912, pp. 9–10; I. V. Stalin, *Sochineniia*, II, pp. 250–252.

63. V. I. Lenin, *PSS*, XLVIII, pp. 102, 124.

64. Badaev (1883–1951), who was later honored by the victorious Soviets by having a beer factory named in his honor, wrote a widely read memoir in which he praised Stalin as behind both *Pravda* and the victories in the 1912 elections. [A. Badaev, *Bol'sheviki v gosudarstvennoi dume. Vospominaniia* (Leningrad: Priboi, 1930).]

65. Konrad Zelinski, "Impact of the Elections to the Russian State Duma in 1912 on the Polish-Jewish Relations in the Kingdom of Poland," *Annales Universitatis Mariae Curie-Skłodowska*, XX, 1 (2013), p. 179. In the elections to the duma the Warsaw Polish curiae had to choose between the rabidly anti-Semitic Roman Dmowski, who had been elected to the Third Duma, or Jan Kucharzewski. Jewish electors voted for Jagiełło. Though Zelinski claims that the Bolsheviks opposed Jagiełło because of his support by the Jewish bourgeoisie, the texts of the Bolshevik opposition to seating him did not reflect the ethnoreligious aspect of his election.

66. Article by Stalin, "Iagello, kak nepolnopravnyi chlen s.-d. fraktsii," *Pravda*, no. 182, December 1, 1912; this article was not included in I. V. Stalin, *Sochineniia*.

67. Nikolai Shegov (1882–1918), for example, was born a peasant, became a worker and a Bolshevik. He became ill in Turukhansk exile and died in June 1918.

68. *Molotov Remembers*, p. 102.

69. Badaev, *Bol'sheviki v gosudarstvennoi dume*, pp. 35–36.

70. Edelman, *Stalin: Biografiia v dokumentakh*, p. 902; "Zapis' besedy S. Pozner s S. Todriia," July 1948, RGASPI, f. 558, op. 4, d. 647, ll. 342–343.

71. V. I. Lenin, *PSS*, XXII, p. 207.

72. Ibid., XLVIII, pp. 117–118, 123–124.

73. I. V. Stalin, *Sochineniia*, pp. 266–270.

74. A. S. Allilueva, *Vospominaniia*, p. 115.

75. Stanislaw Kot, *Conversations with the Kremlin and Dispatches from Russia*, trans. and arranged by H. C. Stevens (London: Oxford University Press, 1963), pp. xxiii–xiv.

76. Ibid., pp. 115–116.

77. Kot, *Conversations with the Kremlin*, pp. xxiii–xxiv.

78. Matvei Muranov (1873–1959) was a metal worker and Social Democrat when he was eleced to the Fourth State Duma. In Soviet times he was a member of the Central Control Commission (1922–1934) and later worked in the judicial system.

79. See Lenin's letters to Stalin, V. I. Lenin, *PSS*, XLVIII, pp. 117–118, 122–125, 126–127, 127–129; and Stalin's letters: "Pis'mo v Peterburg v izdatel'stvo 'Prosveshchenie,'" RGASPI, f. 558, op. 1, d. 41, ll. 1–2; "Iz perpiski TsK RSDRP (1912–1914 gg.)," *Istoricheskii Arkhiv*, no. 2, 1960, p. 20.

80. Elwood, "Lenin and *Pravda*," p. 369; Letter from Krupskaia to Stalin, December 10, 1912, *Iz epokhi "Zvezdy" i "Pravdy,"* III, p. 203.

81. Elwood, "Lenin and *Pravda*," p. 369; V. I. Lenin, *PSS*, XLVIII, p. 127.

82. Elwood, "Lenin and *Pravda*," pp. 369–370.

83. V. I. Lenin, *PSS*, XXII, p. 126.

84. Ostrovskii, *Kto stoial za spinoi Stalina*, p. 378; GARF, f. 102, op. 102, d. 532, ll. 101–1010b.

85. Ostrovskii, *Kto stoial za spinoi Stalina*, p. 378; GARF, f. 102, op. 102, d. 532, ll. 134–1350b.

86. Ostrovskii, *Kto stoial za spinoi Stalina*, p. 379; GARF, f. 102, OO. 1912, d. 5–58-B, ll. 630b, 64–65.

87. Ostrovskii, *Kto stoial za spinoi Stalina*, p. 380.

88. RGASPI, f. 558, op. 1, d. 4899, l. 1.

89. Ostrovskii, *Kto stoial za spinoi Stalina*, p. 381; RGASPI, f. 4, op. 3, d. 42, ll. 15–150b. Badaev does not include Stalin at this conference. [*Bol'sheviki v gosudarstvennoi dume*, p. 89.]

90. Olga Veiland memoirs, RGASPI, f. 558, op. 4, d. 647; Kun, *Stalin: An Unknown Portrait*, p. 150; Edelman, *Stalin: Biografiia v dokumentakh*, pp. 910–911; RGASPI, f. 558, op. 4, d. 647, ll. 433–434.

91. V. I. Lenin, *PSS*, XXII, p. 269. The conference lasted from December 29, 1912, to January 1, 1913 (January 10–14, 1913).

92. V. I. Lenin, *PSS*, XLVIII, p. 156.

93. Shaumian, *Pis'ma*, pp. 29–30; Kh. A. Barsegian, *Stepan Shaumian: Dokumental'naia letopis' zhizni i deiatel'nosti* (Erevan: Aiastan, 1973), pp. 147–148; *Iz epokhi "Zvezdy" i "Pravdy,"* III, pp. 145–147; Elwood, "Lenin and *Pravda*," p. 372.

94. Letter from Stalin in Kraków, to Saint Petersburg, Aleksandr Efimovich Aksel'rod, January 12, 1913, RGASPI, f. 558, op. 1, d. 46, l. 1.

95. Il'ya Muromets is a legendary Russian knight (*bogatyr'*) from the Russian epic tales (*byliny*), who gained his strength late in life. Fighting the infidel Tatars, he seized a Tatar by the heels and began to beat the Tatars with a Tatar.

96. RGASPI, f. 558, op. 1, d. 5391, l. 3; *Bol'shevistskoe rukovodstvo. Perepiska, 1912–1927* (Moscow: Rosspen, 1996), p. 16. The correspondence between Bolshevik leaders 1912–1927 is available online: https://leninism.su/revolution-and-civil-war/4197-bolshevistskoe-rukovodstvo -perepiska-19121927.html.

CHAPTER 23. THE EXPERT

1. Jones, *Socialism in Georgian Colors*, p. 196; "tsinat da akhla, *dasatsqisi*, March 21, 1908, p. 4.

2. See, for example, the collection of speeches in *Kavkazskii zapros v Gosudarstvennoi Dume: Polnyia rechi vsekh oratorov po ofitsial'nym stenogrammam* (Tiflis: Kh. G. Khachaturov, 1909).

3. Michel Löwy, "Marxists and the National Question," *New Left Review*, no. 96 (March–April 1976), p. 81.

4. Erik van Ree, *The Political Thought of Joseph Stalin: A Study in Twentieth-Century Revolutionary Patriotism* (London: Routledge, 2002), pp. 49–50.

5. Karl Marx and Friedrich Engels, *The Communist Manifesto*, with an introduction by Gareth Stedman Jones (London: Penguin Books, 1967), p. 223.

6. In an excellent review of Marx and Engels's view on the nation, Erik van Ree shows how "Marx more or less defined nations as states, or as societies capable of state formation." ["Nationalist Elements in the Work of Marx and Engels: A Critical Survey," *MEGA-Studien* (2000/2001), no. 8, pp. 25–49; quotation on p. 31.]

7. V. I. Lenin, *PSS*, XXIV, pp. 386–388.

8. I. V. Stalin, *Sochineniia*, I, pp. 6–7.

9. *Chetvertyi (Ob"edinitel'ny) s"ezd RSDRP*, pp. 454–455.

10. V. I. Lenin, *PSS*, XXII, pp. 267–269.

11. Ibid., XLVIII, pp. 147–148.

12. Shaumian, *Izbrannye proizvedeniia*, I, p. 135.

13. Ibid., p. 136. His Soviet editors, decades after his death, would chide him for his "inaccurate and unclear" discussion of the nation that veered away from the historical and social toward the natural.

14. Ibid., p. 421.

15. Ibid., pp. 153–154.

16. Ibid., p. 154.

17. Letter from Lenin to Shahumian, July 6, 1913, in V. I. Lenin, *PSS*, XLVIII, pp. 233–234. For a discussion of the Lenin-Shahumian relationship, and on Shahumian's prerevolutionary career, see Ronald Grigor Suny, "Stepan Shaumian and the Bolshevik Movement in Transcaucasia," master's thesis, Columbia University, May 1965.

18. V. I. Lenin, *PSS*, XLVIII, pp. 234–235.

19. Ibid.

20. Elie Kedourie, *Nationalism* (London: Hutchinson, 1960); Ernest Gellner, *Nations and Nationalism* (Oxford: Blackwells, 1983); Benedict Anderson, *Imagined Communities: Reflections on the Origin and Spread of Nationalism* (London: Verso, 1983); and Eric J. Hobsbawm, *Nations and Nationalism since 1780* (Cambridge: Cambridge University Press, 1990), pp. 3–37.

21. For a review of developments in theories of nations and nationalism, see Ronald Grigor Suny, "History," in Alexander J. Motyl (ed.), *Encyclopedia of Nationalism, vol. I, Fundamental Themes* (San Diego: Academic Press, 2001), pp. 335–358; and Geoff Eley and Ronald Grigor Suny, "Introduction: From the Moment of Social History to the Work of Cultural Representation," in Eley and Suny (eds.), *Becoming National: A Reader* (New York: Oxford University Press, 1996), pp. 3–37.

22. Miroslav Hroch, *Social Preconditions of National Revival in Europe: A Comparative Analysis of the Composition of Patriotic Groups among the Smaller European Nations* (New York: Columbia University Press, 2000).

23. Erik van Ree argues that Stalin was inspired by Pannekoek's pamphlet, which Lenin admired but which Stalin could not read. Stalin like Pannekoek considered the nation to be a cultural community, as did Otto Bauer, whom Stalin would criticize. [*The Political Thought of Joseph Stalin*, p. 67.]

24. Otto Bauer, *The Question of Nationalities and Social Democracy*, trans. Joseph O'Donnell (Minneapolis: University of Minnesota Press, 2000).

25. Ibid., p. 107.

26. Ibid., p. 99.

27. Ibid. p. 19.

28. Ibid., p. 110.

29. Jones, *Socialism in Georgian Colors*, p. 231; "erovnuli kitkhva," *khomli* (Constellation), July 30, 1908.

30. Jones, *Socialism in Georgian Colors*, pp. 232–234.

31. K. St., "Na puti k natsionalizmu (Pis'mo s Kavkaza), *Sotsial-Demokrat*, no. 30, January 12 (25), 1913; I. V. Stalin, *Sochineniia*, pp, 285–289.

32. GARF, f. 102, op. 265, d. 532, l. 96.

33. V. I. Lenin, *PSS*, XLVIII, p. 131.

34. Ibid., p. 134.

35. V. I. Lenin, *PSS*, XLVIII, p. 143.

36. Aleksandr Troianovskii (1882–1955) was close to Lenin before World War I but joined the Mensheviks and defended Russia's participation in the war. He later served as the first Soviet ambassador to the United States (1933–1938).

37. Oleg Aleksandrovich Troianovskii, *Cherez gody i rastoianiia: Istoriia odnoi sem'i* (Moscow: Tsentropoligraf, 2017), p. 25.

38. Veiland memoirs, RGASPI, f. 558, op. 4, d. 647, ll. 427–428; Bruno Frei, "Stalin v Vene," ibid., l. 419.

39. Kun, *Stalin: An Unknown Portrait*, p. 156; Veiland memoirs, RGASPI, f. 558, op. 4, d. 647.

40. Kun, *Stalin: An Unknown Portrait*, p. 150; RGASPI, f. 558, op. 4, d. 647. Nikolai Bukharin (1888–1938) became a leading Bolshevik during and after World War I, a member of the Left Communists in the early Soviet years, and a close ally and friend of Stalin's in the 1920s until their break over economic policies in 1927–1929. Bukharin supported peasant self-development and a slower pace of industrialization. Stalin defeated Bukharin and his allies and toyed with him until his arrest in 1937 and his trial and execution in 1938.

41. Trotsky, *Stalin*, p. 244.

42. Leon Trotsky, *Portraits, Political & Personal* (New York: Pathfinder Press, 1977), p. 208; L. D. Trotskii, *Portrety revoliutsionnerov* (Moscow: Moskovskii rabochii, 1991), p. 47. Kun suspects that this meeting of Stalin and Trotsky in Skobelev's apartment never took place but was pieced together from fragmentary memories by Trotsky. [*Stalin: An Unknown Portrait*, p. 156.]

43. RGASPI, f. 558, op. 1, d. 47, l. 1; Edelman, *Stalin: Biografiia v dokumentakh*, p. 916.

44. Much of the discussion here is indebted to Erik van Ree, "Stalin and the National Question," *Revolutionary Russia*, VII, 2 (December 1994), pp. 214–228; Troianovskii's letter, RGASPI, f. 30, op. 1, d. 4.

45. RGASPI, f. 71, op. 10, d. 266, l. 251.

46. V. I. Lenin, *PSS*, XLVIII, p. 162.

47. Ibid., p. 169.

48. Ibid., p.173.

49. K. Stalin, "Natsional'nyi vopros i Sotsial-Demokratia," *Prosveshchenie*, nos. 3–5, March–May 1913; I. V. Stalin, "Marksizm i natsional'nyi vopros," *Sochineniia*, II, pp. 290–367.

50. I. V. Stalin, "Marksizm i natsional'nyi vopros," *Sochineniia*, II, p. 296.

51. Ibid., p. 303.

52. Ibid., p. 301.

53. Ibid., p. 328.

54. Ibid.

55. Ibid., p. 312.

56. Ibid., p. 329. For the argument that the Soviets "made nations," particularly in the 1920s and 1930s, see Suny, *The Revenge of the Past* (1993); Yuri Slezkine, "The USSR as a Communal Apartment, or How a Socialist State Promoted Ethnic Particularism," *Slavic Review*, LIII, 2 (Summer 1994), pp. 414–452; Terry Martin, *The Affirmative Action Empire: Nations and Nationalism in the Soviet Union, 1923–1939* (Ithaca, NY: Cornell University Press, 2001); and Francine Hirsch, *Empire of Nations: Ethnographic Knowledge and the Making of the Soviet Union* (Ithaca, NY: Cornell University Press, 2005).

57. I. V. Stalin, *Sochineniia*, II, p. 329.

58. Ibid., p. 340.

59. Ibid., pp. 361–362.

60. Ibid., pp. 349–350.

61. Ibid., p. 351.

62. In a highly suggestive article Alfred J. Rieber argues that Stalin's Georgian origins and upbringing on the edge of the Russian Empire shaped his identity, and as he moved from Caucasia to Russia he adopted a "hegemonic Russian" identity. ["Stalin, Man of the Borderlands," pp. 1651–1691.] While Stalin certainly identified with Russia in the large sense of country and state, my own argument here, indebted to discussions with Alexander Semyonov and only in nuance differing from Rieber's, is that Stalin's identification was more imperial than national, recognizing the persistence of diversity even as he valued the superior and cohesive qualities of Russian culture and language in building a strong state.

63. I. V. Stalin, *Sochineniia*, II, p. 333.

64. Ibid., p. 342. On the Bund and Zionism, see Zvi Gitelman (ed.), *The Emergence of Modern Jewish Politics: Bundism and Zionism in Eastern Europe* (Pittsburgh: University of Pittsburgh Press, 2003).

65. I. V. Stalin, *Sochineniia*, II, p. 295.

66. Leon Trotsky, *Stalin: An Appraisal of the Man and His Influence*, trans. and ed. Alan Woods (London: Wellread Books, 2016), p. 200. This edition of Trotsky's biography of Stalin

differs in some ways from the early edition by Charles Malamuth and was approved by the estate of Leon Trotsky. References are to the earlier edition unless otherwise noted.

67. K. St., "K natsional'nomu voprosu: Evreiskaia burzhuznaia i bundovskaia kul'turno-natsional'naia avtonomiia," *Prosveshechenie*, no. 6 (June 1913), pp. 69–76.

68. Letter from Stalin in Kostino to Malinovskii, November 1913, RGASPI, f. 558, op. 11, d. 1288, ll. 13–130b.

69. Zinoviev to Troianovskii, March 12 (25), 1914, Ostrovskii, *Kto stoial za spinoi Stalina*, p. 400; RGASPI, f. 30, op. 1, d. 20, l. 1.

70. Kun, *Stalin: An Unknown Portrait*, p. 170; RGASPI, f. 30, op. 1, d. 8.

71. Letter from Stalin to Lev Borisovich Rosenfel'd [Kamenev], February 5, 1916, RGASPI, f. 558, op. 11, d. 1288, ll. 33–35.

72. Ibid.

73. Ibid.

74. Ibid.

75. Ibid. Historian Erik van Ree argues that "In his final letter of 1916, [Stalin] was actually closer to Luxemburg's position than to Lenin's. It foreshadowed the debate between Lenin and Stalin on the union of Soviet republics in 1922." [Van Ree, "Stalin and the National Question," pp. 225–226.] Van Ree also suggests that Stalin's "organicism in thinking about the nation—as an organism with its own psycho-cultural unity—was influenced in part by his reading of the Austro-Marxists and even more by the concept of "organic wholeness" found in Russian thinkers like the Slavophile Aleksei Khomiakov (1804–1860), the Orthodox philosopher Konstantin Leont'ev (1831–1891), and the Panslavist Nikolai Danilevskii (1822–1885). [Ibid., pp. 226–229.]

76. RGASPI, f. 558, op. 1, d. 56, ll. 1–3. Sections of this letter, taken from the Enisei Provincial Gendarme Archive, are reproduced in *I. V. Stalin v sibirskoi ssylke* (Krasnoiarsk: Kraevoe izdatel'stvo, 1942), pp. 178–181.

77. V. I. Lenin, "Sotsialisticheskaia revoliutsiia i pravo natsii na samoopredelenie (tezisy)," *PSS*, XXVII, p. 256.

78. The United States of Europe was a popular idea among left and liberal thinkers in the years before World War I, among them Giuseppe Mazzini, Victor Hugo, Mikhail Bakunin, and Giuseppe Garibaldi. Favored by Karl Kautsky, it was criticized as utopian by Rosa Luxemburg. Soon after the outbreak of the war, Lenin proposed, "The formation of a republican United States of Europe should be the immediate political slogan of Europe's Social Democrats. In contrast with the bourgeoisie, which is ready to 'promise' anything in order to draw the proletariat into the mainstream of chauvinism, the Social-Democrats will explain that this slogan is absolutely false and meaningless without the revolutionary overthrow of the German, the Austrian and the Russian monarchies." ["Voina i Rossiiskaia sotsial-demokratiia," *Sotsial-Demokrat*, no. 33, November 1, 1914: V. I. Lenin, *PSS*, XXVI, p. 21.] He rejected the slogan a few years later.

79. RGASPI, f. 558, op. 1, d. 57, l. 1.

80. Lenin, "O natsional'noi programme R.S.-D.R.P.," *Sotsial'demokrat*, no. 32, December 15 (28), 1913.

81. V. I. Lenin, *PSS*, XXV, p. 316.

82. Ibid., p. 319.

CHAPTER 24. THE EXILE

1. Ostrovskii, *Kto stoial za spinoi Stalina*, p. 385; Edelman, *Stalin: Biografiia v dokumentakh*, p. 919; GARF, f. 102, op. 265, d. 882, l. 251; OO. 1913, d. 5–57-B, l. 21.

2. *Pravda*, no. 47, February 26, 1913; A. E. Badaev, *Bol'sheviki v gosudarstvennoi dume. Bol'shevistskaia fraktsiia IV Gosudarstvennoi Dumy i revoliutsionnoe dvizhenie v Peterburge. Vospominaniia* (Leningrad: Priboi, 1929), p. 164.

3. HIA, Okhrana Files, Index no. XVIIc, folder 2. When this letter was discovered in the police archives in 1921, the head of the party archive, Mikhail Olminskii, asked Trotsky whether it should be published. Trotsky was opposed since it revived old controversies. [Isaac Deutscher, *The Prophet Armed. Trotsky: 1879–1921* (Oxford: Oxford University Press, 1954), p. 233.]

4. *Iz arkhiva L. O. Dan*, pp. 101, 104.

5. Ostrovskii, *Kto stoial za spinoi Stalina*, pp. 386–388; Edelman, *Stalin: Biografiia v dokumentakh*, pp. 919–920; GARF, f. 102, OO. 1913, d. 5–57-B, l. 36.

6. RGASPI, f. 71, op. 10, d. 407; Ostrovskii, *Kto stoial za spinoi Stalina*, p. 388.

7. I. S. Rozental', *Provakator Roman Malinowski: Sud'ba i vremia* (Moscow: Rosspen, 1996), p. 107.

8. Letter of N. K. Kupskaia in Kraków to N. I. Podvoiskii in Saint Petersburg, March 10, 1913, GARF, DP., 1913, d. 639, l. 363.

9. Letter of N. K. Kupskaia in Kraków to N. I. Podvoiskii in Saint Petersburg, March 14, 1913, GARF, OO., d. 5, 1913, pr. 3, l. 201.

10. Arutiunov, *Rabochee dvizhenie v Zakavkaz'e v period novogo revoliutsionnogo pod"ema*, p. 208.

11. From an account of essentially the same journey, made later by Fedor Samoilov, "Bol'shevistakaia fraktsiia IV gosudarstvennoi dumy v eniseiskoi ssylke pered fevral'skoi revoliutsiei," *Proletaraksaia revoliutsiia*, nos. 2–3 (61–62) (February–March 1927), pp. 209–239.

12. The Sami people, also known as Lapps, were related to various peoples in the Russian north and Siberia. In Finnish *tunturi* refers to a large hill in the north. [My thanks to Hanna Smith for this clarification.]

13. K. T. Sverdlova, *Iakov Mikhailovich Sverdlov* (Moscow: Molodaia gvardiia, 1985), p. 172.

14. Ostrovskii, *Kto stoial za spinoi Stalina*, p. 393.

15. Ibid., p. 394.

16. Edelman, *Stalin: Biografiia v dokumentakh*, p. 959; "Vospominaniia T. M. Shadrinoi," written in March 1942, RGASPI, f. 558, op 4, d. 667, ll. 50–52.

17. RGASPI, f. 558, op. 1, d. 48, l. 1; GARF, f. 102, OO. 1913, d. 5, ch. 69, l. B, l. 103.

18. RGASPI, f. 558, op. 11, d. 1288, ll. 13–130b; Ostrovskii, *Kto stoial za spinoi Stalina*, pp. 397–398.

19. Letter from Ia. M. Sverdlov to Malinowski, September 27, 1913, Ia. M. Sverdlov, *Izbrannye proizvedeniia*, 3 vols. (Moscow, 1957), I, pp. 231–232; RGASPI, f. 558, op. 4, d. 220, l. 1.

20. Stalin is referring to the pamphlet by Noe Zhordania, *natsionaluri kitkhva chvenshi* (The National Question in Our Country) (Kutaisi: i. kiladzis stamba, 1913).

21. Stalin's postcard to Zinoviev, December 7, 1913, Ostrovskii, *Kto stoial za spinoi Stalina*, p. 399; RGASPI, f. 558, op. 1, d. 49, ll. 1–2.

22. November 20, 1913, RGASPI, f. 558, op. 1, d. 4313, ll. 1–2.

23. Stalin's letter to G. Belinskii, February 27, 1914, RGASPI, f. 588, op. 1, d. 51, ll. 1–2; Ostrovskii, *Kto stoial za spinoi Stalina*, p. 399.

24. Tatiana Slovatinskaia (1879–1956) is identified by Kun as "his sweetheart at the time." Slovatinskaia was the grandmother of Iurii Trifonov, author of *Dom na naberezhnoi* [*The House on the Embankment*]. Slovatinskaia lived in the famous House, where top party officials resided, worked in a secret department of the Central Committee, was a member of the Central Control Committee, and worked for a time for Lazar Kaganovich, but in 1937 her daughter was imprisoned, her son-in-law executed, and she and two of her grandchildren were forced to leave the House. Yuri Slezkine identifies her as an "orthodox Bolshevik sectarian." Stalin inscribed his gift copy of *Lenin and Leninism* to her, "To Dear Comrade Slovatsinkaya, in memory of joint work underground, from the author." [Kun, *Stalin: An Unknown Portrait*, p. 46; Slezkine, *The House of Government*, pp. 167, 239–240, 829, 933, 971.]

25. Kun, *Stalin: An Unknown Portrait*, p. 41; RGASPI, f. 558, op. 4, d. 5392.

26. Ostrovskii, *Kto stoial za spinoi Stalina*, p. 396.

27. Kun, *Stalin: An Unknown Portrait*, p. 41; RGASPI, f. 558, op. 4, d. 5392.

28. Kun, *Stalin: An Unknown Portrait*, p. 41; RGASPI, f. 558, op. 4, d. 5392.

29. Stalin's postcard to Zinoviev, December 9, 1913, Ostrovskii, *Kto stoial za spinoi Stalina*, p. 399; RGASPI, f. 588, op. 2, d. 89, l. 1.

30. Stalin's letter to Zinoviev, January 11, 1914, RGASPI, f. 588, op. 1, d. 5168, l. 1; Ostrovskii, *Kto stoial za spinoi Stalina*, p. 399.

31. Ostrovskii, *Kto stoial za spinoi Stalina*, p. 398.

32. RGASPI, f. 558, op. 11, d. 1228, l. 37; Ostrovskii, *Kto stoial za spinoi Stalina*, p. 400; RGASPI, f. 588, op.1, d. 4235, ll. 1–2.

33. Ostrovskii, *Kto stoial za spinoi Stalina*, p. 401.

34. Ibid., p. 401; GARF, f. 102, OO. d. 5–25-B, l. 27.

35. V. Shveitser, *Stalin v turukhanskoi ssylke. Vospominaniia podpol'shchika*, 2nd edition (Moscow: Molodaia gvardiia, 1943), p. 10.

36. Ia. Shumiatskii, *Turukhanka: Iz zhizni ssyl'nykh turukhanskogo kraia 1908–1916* (Moscow: Moskovskii rabochii, 1925), pp. 87–89.

37. Chernenko (ed.), *I. V. Stalin v sibirskoi ssylke*, p. 141; Edelman, *Stalin: Biografiia v dokumentakh*, pp. 968–969, 976; "Iz rasskazov A. S. Taraseevoi," recorded in 1940–1941, RGASPI, f. 558, op. 4, d. 581, l. 8; "Vospominaniia M. A. Taraseeva," written in May 1940, RGASPI, f. 558, op. 4, d. 667, ll. 530b.–54.

38. "Rasskazy krest'ian s. Kureika o tovarishche Staline," *Pravda*, December 18, 1939, p. 4.

39. RGASPI, f. 558, op. 1, d. 52, ll. 1–2; Ostrovskii, *Kto stoial za spinoi Stalina*, pp. 402–403.

40. Stalin's letter to Petrovskii, March 20, 1914, GARF, f. 102, OO. 1914, d. 307, ch. 1, l. 244; RGASPI, f. 558, op. 1, d. 52, ll. 1–2; Ostrovskii, *Kto stoial za spinoi Stalina*, pp. 402–403.

41. Edelman, *Stalin: Biografiia v dokumentakh*, pp. 972–974; RGASPI, f. 558, op. 1, d. 5394, ll. 6–8.

42. Letter from N. I. Bukharin to V. I. Lenin, December 13, 1913, *Izvestiia TsK KPSS*, no. 4 (291) (April 1989), pp. 206–207; RGASPI, f. 2, op. 5, d. 810.

43. Troianovskii, *Cherez gody i rasstoianiia*, pp. 25–29.

44. From Lenin's "Deposition in the case of R. V. Malinovsky, 26 May 1917," in Pipes, *The Unknown Lenin*, pp. 36–37.

45. Elwood argues that Dzhunkovskii wanted to weaken the Bolsheviks by removing their most effective orator and to discredit the faction that was gaining worker support. [*Roman Malinovsky*, pp. 43–44.]

46. Lenin's Letter to Inessa Armand, May 25, 1914, V. I. Lenin, *PSS*, XLVIII, p. 293. The last lines are in English in the original.

47. Pipes, *The Unknown Lenin*, p. 31.

48. Elwood, *Roman Malinovsky*, p. 63.

49. Sverdlov, *Izbrannye proizvedeniia*, I, pp. 268–269.

50. A. S. Allilueva, *Vospominaniia*, p. 115.

51. Edelman, *Stalin: Biografiia v dokumentakh*, p. 975; N. S. Khrushchev, *Vremia, liudi, vlast': Vospominaniia*, 4 vols. (Moscow: Moskovskie novosti, 1999), II, pp. 118–119.

52. Sverdlov, *Izbrannye proizvedeniia*, I, pp. 276–277, 280.

53. Ibid., pp. 278–279, 298.

54. Ibid., p. 298.

55. Ibid., pp. 248, 288.

56. RGASPI, f. 558, op. 1, d. 5169, l. 1; Ostrovskii, *Kto stoial za spinoi Stalina*, p.409.

57. Postcard from Stalin to Zinoviev, May 20, 1914, RGASPI, f. 558, op. 1, d. 5169, ll. 1–1 ob.

58. Maiia Aleksandrovna Ulanovskii, *Istoriia odnoi sem'i* (Saint Petersburg: Inapress, 2003), p. 12.

59. "Iz proshlago Stalina," *Vozrozhdenie* (Paris), no. 1321, January 13, 1929, p. 3. This article reports the memories of the Socialist Revolutionary G. I. Karganov, who claimed to have known Stalin in exile, first meeting him in 1911 and seeing him again in Turukhansk.

60. Chernenko (ed.), *I. V. Stalin v sibirskoi ssylke*, p. 148.

61. Ibid., pp. 142–144. For a vivid account of the Stalin's clashes with his guard, see Montefiore, *Young Stalin*, pp. 244–245.

62. "Rasskazy krest'ian s. Kureika."

63. Chernenko (ed.), *I. V. Stalin v sibirskoi ssylke*, p. 144.

64. Edelman, *Stalin: Biografiia v dokumentakh*, pp. 976–980; "Vospominaniia byvshego strazhknika Merzliakova Mikhaila Aleksandrovicha," recorded in March 1941, RGASPI, f. 558, op. 4, d. 667, ll. 35–40.

65. Chernenko (ed.), *I. V. Stalin v sibirskoi ssylke*, pp. 143–144.

66. Ostrovskii, *Kto stoial za spinoi Stalina*, p. 410.

67. Boris Shumiatskii (1886–1938) was a long-time party activist, worked in Siberia, and later became the chairman of the Soviet committee on cinematography. He was arrested in 1937 and executed in 1938.

68. Shumiatskii, *Turukhanka*, pp. 95–96.

69. Ostrovskii, *Kto stoial za spinoi Stalina*, p. 410.

70. Ibid., p. 417; RGASPI, f. 558, op. 4, d. 662, ll. 112–118.

71. The letter, written on February 27, 1930, is reproduced in V. Sveitser, *Stalin v turukhanskoi ssylke: Vospominaniia starogo podpol'shchika* (Moscow: Molodaia gvardiia, 1943), pp. 33–34; Kun, *Stalin: An Unknown Portrait*, p. 169; RGASPI, f. 558, op. 4, d. 662.

72. A. S. Allilueva, *Vospominaniia*, p. 117.

73. RGASPI, f. 558, op. 1, d. 55, l. 1–3; f. 558, op. 11, d. 1288, l. 28; A. S. Allilueva, *Vospominaniia*, pp. 117–118.

74. A. S. Allilueva, *Vospominaniia*, pp. 144–145.

75. *Iz arkhiva L. O. Dan,* pp. 101, 104–105.

76. Ostrovskii, *Kto stoial za spinoi Stalina,* pp. 412–413; RGASPI, f. 558, op. 1, d. 54, ll. 1–3. *Natsional'nye problemy* was issued in memory of Fedor Korsh (1843–1915), a prominent philologist who defended the rights of Ukraianians, and featured the work of liberals.

77. Kun, *Stalin: An Unknown Portrait,* p. 168; Montefiore, *Young Stalin,* p. 244; RGASPI, f. 558, op. 4, d. 662.

78. "Rasskazy krest'ian s. Kureika."

79. Ostrovskii claims Peregrygina was between thirteen and sixteen [ibid., p. 408]; Montefiore uses thirteen for her age [*Young Stalin,* p. 244]; Kun says she was fourteen [*Stalin: An Unknown Portrait,* p. 168].

80. Edelman, *Stalin: Biografiia v dokumentakh,* pp. 942–943; Montefiore, *Young Stalin,* pp. 244–247.

81. Edelman, *Stalin: Biografiia v dokumentakh,* p. 943; "Memo from General I. Serov, to Nikita Khrushchev," June 4, 1956, RGASPI, f. 558, op. 11, d. 1288, ll. 14–16.

82. Ostrovskii, *Kto stoial za spinoi Stalina,* p. 412; B. Ivanov, "Vospominaniia," GARF, f. 5449, op. 1, d. 75, l. 28.

83. V. Sveitser, *Stalin v turukhanskoi ssylke,* p. 25.

84. Shumiatskii, *Turukhanka,* pp. 95–96.

85. V. Sveitser, *Stalin v turukhanskoi ssylke,* p. 26.

86. Ibid., pp. 26–27. This appears to be a classic fish story, more likely than not a semifictional exaggeration.

87. V. Sveitser, "Velikii Stalin v Turukhanske," RGASPI, f. 161, op. 1, d. 10, [ll. 1–125], l. 4. The archival version of this memoir differs considerably from the published book editions of 1940 and 1943, which were effectively Stalinized and are not reliable on political matters. For example, Shveitser quotes Stalin condemning Kamenev and saying, "One should not trust this person. Kamenev is capable of betraying the revolution." This supposedly occurred at a time when Stalin trusted and relied on Kamenev. For a discussion of Sveitser's memoirs, see Edel'man, *Stalin, Koba i Soso,* pp. 102–105.

88. Svetlana Allilueva, *Dvadtsat' pisem,* p. 114.

89. V. Sveitser, *Stalin v turukhanskoi ssylke,* p. 36.

90. A. S. Allilueva, *Vospominaniia,* p. 167.

91. Shumiatskii, *Turukhanka,* pp. 102–103.

92. "Iz proshlago Stalina," *Vozrozhdenie* (Paris), no. 1321, January 13, 1929, p. 3."

93. Shumiatskii, *Turukhanka,* pp. 104–106.

94. Ibid., pp. 109–111.

95. B. Ivanov, *Vospominaniia,* GARF, f. 5449, op. 1, d. 75, ll. 92, 96, 107–108; Sverdlov, *Izbrannye proizvedeniia,* p. 325; Sverdlova, *Iakov Mikhailovich Sverdlov,* p. 196; Slezkine, *The House of Government,* pp. 48–54.

96. S. S. Spandarian, *Stat'i, pis'ma, dokumenty* (Moscow: Izdpolit, 1982), p. 284.

97. Ibid., p. 285.

98. V. I. Lenin, *PSS,* XLIX, p. 101.

99. Ibid., p. 131.

100. Ibid., p. 161.

CHAPTER 25. FAR FROM THE FRONT

1. Jules Humbert-Droz, *L'origine d'Internationale communiste: Du Zimmerwald à Moscou* (Neuchâtel: Edition de la Baconnière, 1968), p. 52; R. Craig Nation, *War on War: Lenin, The Zimmerwald Left, and the Origins of Communist Internationalism* (Durham, NC: Duke University Press, 1989), pp. 24–25.

2. For excellent discussions of the socialist opposition to war before 1914, see George Haupt, *Socialism and the Great War: The Collapse of the Second International* (Oxford: Oxford University Press, 1972); and Wolfe, *Three Who Made a Revolution*, pp. 594–637.

3. V. I. Lenin, *PSS*, XLVIII, p. 155.

4. V. I. Lenin, *PSS*, XLIX, p. 13.

5. V. I. Lenin, *PSS*, XXV, p. 450.

6. V. I. Lenin, "Zadachi revoliutsionnoi sotsial-demokratii v evropeiskoi voine," *PSS*, XXVI, pp. 1–7.

7. Stephen F. Cohen, *Bukharin and the Bolshevik Revolution: A Political Biography, 1888–1938* (Oxford and New York: Oxford University Press, 1971), p. 23.

8. Michael Melancon, *The Socialist Revolutionaries and the Russian Anti-War Movement, 1914–1917* (Columbus: Ohio State University Press, 1990), p. 175.

9. Ascher, *Pavel Axelrod*, pp. 304–319.

10. Michael Eugene Shaw, "The Nashe-Slovo Group and Russian Social Democracy during World War I: The Search for Unity," PhD dissertation, Indiana University, 1975.

11. Zhordania, *Moia zhizn*, pp. 64–66.

12. Eradze interviews, XI, continuation, p. 6. Stephen Jones, in a note to me, suspects that this was wishful thinking on Eradze's part. In his research he found no evidence of Zhordania advocating independence. But both Zhordania in his memoirs and the Georgian nationalist Revaz Gabashvili in his remember that nationalists Giorgi Machabeli and Mikhako Tsereteli met with Zhordania and Gegechkori in Kutaisi in 1914 and discussed the overture of the nationalists in favor of independence under German auspices. Zhordania, who was committed to working through reform of Russia, told Gabashvili that they each should pursue their own path. [Zhordania, *chemi tsaruli* (My Past) (Tbilisi, 1990), pp. 71–72; Revaz Gabashvili, *rats makhsovs* (Whatever I Remember) (Tbilisi, 1992), pp. 149–150.]

13. Melancon, *Socialist Revolutionaries and the Russian Anti-War Movement*, pp. 22–27.

14. V. I. Lenin, *PSS*, XLIX, pp. 13–14.

15. V. I. Lenin, *PSS*, XLIX, p. 27.

16. G. L. Shklovskii, "Nakanune konferentsii," *Proletarskaia revoliutsiia*, no. 5 (1925), p. 137; Alfred Erich Senn, *The Russian Revolution in Switzerland, 1914–1917* (Madison: University of Wisconsin Press, 1971), p. 33.

17. Trotsky, *My Life*, pp. 233–234.

18. Shumiatskii, *Turukhanka*, p. 116.

19. Ibid., p. 119.

20. Ibid., pp. 119–120.

21. V. Sveitser, "Velikii Stalin v Turukhanke," RGASPI, f. 161, op. 1, d. 10, l. 4; V. Sveitser, "Tovarishch Stalin v turukhanskoi ssylke," *Proletarskaia revoliutsiia*, no. 8 (1937), p. 162. Edelman

considers much of Sveitser's many memoirs to be untrustworthy, and reading through them I concluded that only specific plausible or corroborated parts should be considered reliable.

22. RGASPI, f. 558, op. 1, d. 53, ll. 1–3; V. Sveitser, "V turukhanskoi ssylke," RGASPI, f. 161, op. 1, d. 10, ll. 17–39 [memoirs written in December 17, 1939]. The articles referred to are: Petr Kropotkin, "Pis'ma o sovremennykh sobytiiakh," *Russkie vedomosti*, no. 206, September 7 (20), 1914; no. 229, October 5 (18), 1914; and Georgii Plekhanov, "Otkrytoe pis'mo v redaktsiiu gazety *"Rechi,"* *Rech'*, no. 265, October 2 (15), 1914. Marcel Sembat (1862–1922) was a French socialist, who joined the government of national unity in 1914.

23. V. I. Lenin, *PSS*, XXVI, p. 168.

24. Nikolai Shagov (1882–1918), born a peasant, became a worker and a Bolshevik. He fell ill in Turukhansk exile and died in June 1918.

25. F. Samoilov, "Bol'shevistskaia fraktsiia IV Gosudarstvennoi dumy v eniseiskoi ssylke pered fevral'skoi revoliutsiei," *Proletarskaia revoliutsiia*, nos. 2–3 (61–62) (1927), pp. 221–222; Shumiatskii, *Turukhanka*, p. 123; Sverdlova, *Iakov Mikhailovich Sverdlov*, pp. 199–200.

26. Stalin's Baku associate, Shahumian, took a defeatist position on the war. [A. Gukasian, "Suren Shaumian 'O Stepane Shaumiane' (Zametki dlia biografa)," *Bakinskii rabochii*, September 20, 1928 [found in Haiastani Azgayin Arkhiv (Armenian National Archive), f. 1937, op. 1, d. 289, ll. 1–4.]

27. Trotsky, *Stalin*, p. 178.

28. Trotsky claims that Stalin was opposed to the war but did not accept Lenin's defeatist position or the idea of turning the imperialist war into a civil war. [Ibid., pp. 174–178.] My research indicates that he was correct in this assessment.

29. Ostrovskii, *Kto stoial za spinoi Stalina*, pp. 413–414; RGASPI, f. 5449, op. 1, d. 75, ll. 77–89.

30. "Iz proshlago Stalina," *Vozrozhdenie* (Paris), no. 1321, January 13, 1929, p. 3."

31. I. V. Stalin, "Rech' v kremlevskom dvortse na vypuske akademikov krasnoi armii," May 4, 1935, *Sochineniia*, XIV, p. 76.

32. Letter, March 12, 1916, RGASPI, f. 558, op. 1, d. 58, l. 1.

33. RGASPI, f. 558, op. 1, d. 56, ll. 1–3. For a discussion of this letter, see chapter 23 in this volume.

34. A. S. Allilueva, *Vospominaniia*, p. 118.

35. RGASPI, f. 17, d. 1676, l. l; f. 71, op. 10, d. 407; f. 17, d. 1866, l. 1.

36. See Erik van Ree, "Lenin's Conception of Socialism in One Country: 1915–17," *Revolutionary Russia*, XXIII, 2 (December 2010), pp. 159–181.

37. Van Ree sees such tendencies in the work of Bukharin, Trotskii, Akselrod, and Martov, among others. [Ibid.]

38. V. I. Lenin, "Referat na temu 'Proletariat i voina,'" *Golos*, nos. 37, 38, October 25, 27, 1914; *PSS*, XXVI, p. 35.

39. V. I. Lenin, "O lozunge soedinennykh shatov Evropy," *Sotsial-Demokrat*, no. 44, August 23, 1915; *PSS*, XXVI, pp. 351–355.

40. Van Ree argues that Lenin's defense of "socialism in one country" included the possibility of such an outcome for developed capitalist states and made it worthwhile for backward, agrarian Russia at least to initiate the first steps toward socialism even if it could not complete it on its own given the overwhelming presence of the peasantry. Stalin, van Ree, claims, was

closer to Lenin's formulation than was Trotsky in the debates in the 1920s. ["Lenin's Concept of Socialism in One Country," p. 173.]

41. Trotsky, *My Life*, p. 249.

42. V. I. Lenin, *PSS*, LXIX, pp. 80–82.

43. Besides Lenin and Zinoviev representing the Bolsheviks, the Russian delegation included Martov and Akselrod from the Mensheviks; Chernov and Natanson from the SRs; Trotsky; a Bundist observer, Leibmann Hersh (Lemanskii); a Latvian Social Democrat, Jan Berzin; and representing the various Polish socialist parties, Karl Radek, Pavel Lewinson, and Adolf Warski.

44. Nation, *War on War*. Much of my discussion of the socialist anti-war movement during World War I is indebted to this excellent account.

Karl Radek (Karol Sobelsohn) (1885–1939) was born in Lemberg (Lviv) and worked in the German, Polish, and Russian Social Democratic movements. He returned to Russia with Lenin on the sealed train, was active in the Comintern, and joined the Left Opposition. He was expelled from the Communist Party in 1927, but after capitulating to Stalin he was readmitted to the party. He was tried in the last major show trial in 1938 and executed in 1939.

45. Ibid., p. 101.

46. Lewis H. Siegelbaum, *The Politics of War Mobilization in Russia, 1915–1917: A Study of the War-Industries Committees* (Basingstoke: Palgrave Macmillan, 1984).

47. Rex A. Wade, "Irakli Tsereteli and Siberian Zimmerwaldism," *Journal of Modern History*, XXXIX, 4 (December 1967), pp. 425–431; Ziva Galili y Garcia, "The Origins of Revolutionary Defensism: I. G. Tsereteli and the 'Siberian Zimmerwaldists,'" *Slavic Review*, XLI, 3 (Autumn 1982), pp. 454–476.

48. Eric Lohr, Vera Tolz, Alexander Semonov, and Mark von Hagen (eds.), *The Empire and Nationalism at War* (in the series Russia's Great War and Revolution, vol. 2) (Bloomington, IN: Slavica, 2014).

49. Georgii Piatakov (1890–1937) joined the Bolsheviks in 1912 and was often on the left wing of the party. A critic of Lenin's views of nationality, he joined the Trotskyist opposition in the 1920s, was expelled from the party, but later renounced Trotsky and was reinstated. He was close to Orjonikidze and worked with him on the industrialization of the USSR in the 1930s. He was tried in one of the major show trials and executed in 1937. Evgeniia Bosh (1879–1925) worked primarily in Ukraine and was Soviet Ukraine's first interior minister. She later joined the Left Opposition in the 1920s, but sick and depressed she committed suicide in 1925.

50. Nation, *War on War*, p. 108.

51. V. I. Lenin, *PSS*, XLIX, p. 312.

52. Nation, *War on War*, p. 141.

53. Stepan Shahumian, "Mer Suren," *Paikar*, no. 38, September 18, 1916 [S. G. Shahumian, *Erkeri liakatar zhoghovatsu*, 2 vols. (Erevan, 1975–1976), II, pp. 386–387; Shaumian, *Izbrannye proizvedeniia*, I, pp. 507–508].

54. Edelman, *Stalin: Biografiia v dokumentakh*, p. 994; RGASPI, f. 558, op. 4, d. 218, l. 22.

55. Sverdlov and Goloshchekin continued to be close friends and worked together after the Bolshevik seizure of power in October 1917. In July 1918, when Sverdlov was the key organizer of the Bolshevik party network and official head of the Soviet state, he and Goloshchekin organized the execution of the tsar, Nicholas II, his family and servants in Ekaterinburg, a city that

would carry Sverdlov's name until the fall of the USSR. For an account of their relationship and activities, see Slezkine, *The House of Government*, pp. 49, 147, 155.

56. Cited in Kun, *Stalin: An Unknown Portrait*, p. 173. Ivanov's memoirs are also in RGASPI, f. 554, op. 4, d. 662.

57. V. Sveitser, *Stalin v turukhanskoi ssylke*, pp. 54–56.

58. V. Sveitser, "Tovarishch Stalin v tsarskoi ssylke v Krasnoiarskom krae (Iz vospominanii o bor'be bol'shevikov v period imperialisticheskoi voiny 1914–1917g.)," RGASPI, f. 161, op. 1, d. 10, ll. 85–100.

59. RGASPI, f. 558, op. 1, d. 4357, l. 1.

60. Anatole V. Baikaloff, *I Knew Stalin* (London: Burns Oates, 1940), p. 27.

61. Edelman, *Stalin: Biografiia v dokumentakh*, p. 1006; "Iz stenogrammy besedy so starymi bol'shevikami v Muzee Lenina," April 10, 1950, RGASPI, f. 558, op. 4, d. 582, ll. 22–23.

62. Ibid., pp. 28–29.

63. Edelman, *Stalin: Biografiia v dokumentakh*, pp. 1005–1006; A. Baikalov, "Moi vstrechi s Osipom Dzhugashvili," *Vozrozhdenie* (Paris), 1950, no. 8, pp. 117–118.

64. Nikolaevskii, *Tainye stranitsy istorii*, pp. 159–160.

65. Cited in Kun, *Stalin: An Unknown Portrait*, p. 174; RGASPI, f. 554, op. 4, d. 662.

66. Edelman, *Stalin: Biografiia v dokumentakh*, pp, 1006–1007; RGASPI, f. 558, op. 4, d. 582, ll. 6–8.

CHAPTER 26. THE REVOLUTIONARY

1. V. I. Lenin, *PSS*, XLIX, p. 428.

2. Robert M. Slusser, *Stalin in October: The Man Who Missed the Revolution* (Baltimore and London: Johns Hopkins University Press, 1987), p. 3.

3. Petr Zalutskii (1887–1937) was from a peasant family, joined the Bolsheviks in 1911, and worked in the Red Army and the party until he was expelled for oppositional activities in 1927. Restored to membership in 1928, he was arrested in 1934 and executed in 1937.

Aleksandr Shliapnikov (1885–1937) was a Bolshevik from 1903 and served as people's commissar of labor in Lenin's government. A leader of the Workers' Opposition along with Aleksandra Kollontai, Shliapnikov was the author of an important memoir of the 1917 revolution. Expelled from the Communist Party in 1933, he was tried and shot in 1937.

4. Note that the word *demokratiia* in Russian has both a political and a sociological meaning. It may refer to what we understand by the English word "democracy," a form of representative government, or to a social group, the lower classes (in Russia, the workers, soldiers, poorer urban dwellers, and peasants). For the Bolsheviks a "democratic dictatorship" was a government of the lower classes, whereas a "bourgeois democracy" as in the United States would be a "dictatorship of the bourgeoisie." For a discussion of the prevalence of the word "democracy" in 1917 Russia, see Boris Ivanovich Kolonitskii, "'Democracy' in the Political Consciousness of the February Revolution," *Slavic Review*, LVII, 1 (Spring 1998), pp. 95–106.

5. Letter from Aleksandr Guchkov to General Alekseev, March 1917, cited in Joel Carmichael, *A Short History of the Russian Revolution* (New York: Basic Books, 1964), p. 69.

6. Ziva Galili, *The Menshevik Leaders in the Russian Revolution: Social Realities and Political Strategies* (Princeton, NJ: Princeton University Press, 1989), p. 66. In his *History of the Russian*

Revolution, Trotsky argues that workers were prepared to take power in February 1917 but were betrayed by moderate leaders who surrendered power to the bourgeoisie. Galili has shown that the dual power arrangement was not a betrayal but a realistic position given workers' attitudes and strength at that time (pp. 45–68).

7. For a detailed and compelling study of the conflicts among the Bolsheviks, see E. N. Burdzhalov, *Russia's Second Revolution: The February 1917 Uprising in Petrograd,* trans. and ed. Donald J. Raleigh (Bloomington: Indiana University Press, 1967).

8. A. S. Allilueva, *Vospominaniia,* pp. 164–168.

9. Ibid., pp. 168–170, 172–173.

10. "Protokoly i rezoliutsii Biuro TsK RSDRP (b) (Mart 1917 g.)," *Voprosy istorii KPSS,* no. 3 (1962), p. 146.

11. Service, *Stalin: A Biography,* p. 119; "Protokoly i rezoliutsii Biuro," p. 143.

12. "Protokoly i rezoliutsii Biuro," p. 146.

13. *Molotov Remembers,* pp. 91–92.

14. "Protokoly i rezoliutsii Biuro," pp. 136–137. There was agreement between the Russian Bureau and the Vyborg District Committee on the kind of government preferred, but they differed slightly on the means to achieve a revolutionary provisional government. The Russian Bureau sought to form it through negotiations with the leaders of the Soviet, which soon proved to be a nonstarter, while the Vyborgtsi wanted it to emerge from the election of the soviets. On the intricacies of Bolshevik tactics and strategy at this moment, see D. A. Longley, "The Divisions in the Bolshevik Party in March 1917," *Soviet Studies,* XXIV, 1 (July 1972), pp. 61–76; and Erik van Ree, "Stalin's Bolshevism: The Year of the Revolution," *Revolutionary Russia,* XIII, 1 (June 2000), pp. 29–54.

15. "Protokoly i rezoliutsii Biuro," p. 140.

16. V. N. Zalezhskii, "Pervyi legal'nyi Pe-Ka," *Proletarskaia revoliutsiia,"* 1923, no. 1 (13), pp. 145–146.

17. V. I. Lenin, *PSS,* XXXI, p. 7.

18. "Protokoly i rezoliutsii Biuro," p. 145.

19. Ibid., p. 150.

20. *Pravda,* no. 8, March 14, 1917.

21. K. Stalin, "O sovetakh rabochikh i soldatskikh deputatov," *Pravda,* no. 8, March 14 (27), 1917; I. V. Stalin, *Sochineniia,* III, pp. 1–3.

22. Nikolai Sukhanov, *Zapiski o revoliutsii* (Berlin-Petrograd-Moscow: Z. I. Grzhebin, 1922), II, pp. 265–266; N. N. Sukhanov, *The Russian Revolution 1917: Eyewitness Account,* ed., abridged, and trans. Joel Carmichael (Oxford: Oxford University Press, 1955), pp. 229–230. My translation is an edited version of Carmichael's, based on the original Russian text.

23. Robert Paul Browder and Alexander F. Kerensky (eds.), *The Russian Provisional Government 1917: Documents,* 3 vols. (Stanford, CA: Stanford University Press, 1961), II, pp. 1077–1078.

24. Longley, "The Divisions in the Bolshevik Party," p. 72; A. G. Shliapnikov, "Fevral'skie dni v Peterburge," *Proletarskaia revoliutsiia,* no. 1 (13) (1923), pp. 181–182, n. 61.

25. L. Kamenev, "Bez tainoi diplomatii," *Pravda,* no. 9, March 15, 1917.

26. "Protokoly i rezoliutsii Biuro," pp. 148–149; Longley, "The Divisions in the Bolshevik Party," p. 73. Stalin would serve temporarily until long-time party journalist Konstantin Eremeev

returned. Since Stalin and Olminskii had been unable to write up a platform for the bureau as they had promised, that task was turned over to Kamenev and a secretary of the bureau. Stalin was elected to the presidium of the bureau along with Petrov, Muranov, Belenin, and Stasova.

27. P. F. Kudelli (ed.), *Pervyi legal'nyi Peterburgskii komitet bol'shevikov v 1917 g. Sbornik materialov i protokolov zasedanii Peterburgskogo komiteta RSDRP (b) i ego ispolnitel'noi komissii za 1917 g.* (Moscow-Leningrad, 1927), pp. 49–52; Longley, "The Divisions in the Bolshevik Party," pp. 65–66, 73.

28. K. Stalin, "Ob usloviiakh pobedy russkoi revoliutsii," *Pravda*, no. 12, March 18 (31), 1917; I. V. Stalin, *Sochineniia*, III, pp. 11–15.

29. "Protokoly i rezoliutsii Biuro," pp. 153–154.

30. "Protokoly i rezoliutsii Biuro," pp. 152–153; Longley, "The Divisions in the Bolshevik Party," pp. 68–69; van Ree, "Stalin's Bolshevism," pp. 38–39.

31. K. Stalin, "O voine," *Pravda*, no. 10, March 16 (29), 1917; I. V. Stalin, *Sochineniia*, III, pp. 4–8.

32. *Molotov Remembers*, p. 92.

33. Isidore Ramishvili, *mogonebebi*, p. 525.

34. Trotsky, *My Life*, p. 289. Tsereteli is spelled Tzereteli in the English translation of Trotsky.

35. Kolonitskii, "'Democracy in the Political Consciousness of the February Revolution," pp. 99–100, 103.

36. Ibid., p. 106.

37. For developments among soldiers and officers, see the excellent account by Allan K. Wildman, *The End of the Russian Imperial Army: The Old Army and the Soldiers' Revolt (March–April 1917)* (Princeton, NJ: Princeton University Press, 1980).

38. Browder and Kerensky, *The Russian Provisional Government*, II, pp. 1083–1084.

39. V. I. Lenin, *PSS*, XXXI, pp. 11–22; *Pravda*, nos. 14 and 15, March 21 and 22, 1917. Some historians claim that because Lenin's views were so radical, the letters were cut, but Lars Lih argues that the editors actually were not censoring Lenin but making his position clearer.

40. Sukhanov, *The Russian Revolution*, p. 304.

41. "Protokoly Vserossiiskogo (martovskogo) soveshchaniia partiinykh rabotnikov, 27 marta–2 aprelia 1917 goda," *Voprosy istorii KPSS*, no. 5 (1962), p. 112; Leon Trotsky, *The Stalin School of Falsification*, trans. John G. Wright (1937; New York: Pathfinder Press, 1971), p. 239.

42. Ibid.

43. Ibid.

44. "Protokoly Vserossiiskogo (martovskogo) soveshchaniia," pp. 112–114; Trotsky, *The Stalin School of Falsification*, pp. 240–242. In Russian the word "control" [*kontrol'*] in this context is close to the English word "supervision" and referred to a degree of regulation, monitoring, and oversight. State control would be contrasted with workers' control, but the latter did not necessarily mean the full ownership and running of factories by workers but rather their playing a supervisory role over the owners and managers. In time, however, supervision could easily gravitate into full control in the English sense.

45. Wladimir Woytinsky (1885–1960) was an important editor and economist. He was close to Tsereteli and fled to Georgia after the Bolshevik takeover in Petrograd. He edited the Menshevik newspaper, *Bor'ba* (Struggle), before immigrating first to Germany and then to the United States.

46. "Protokoly Vserossiiskogo (martovskogo) soveshchaniia," p. 120; Trotsky, *The Stalin School of Falsification*, p. 255.

47. "Protokoly Vserossiiskogo (martovskogo) soveshchaniia," *Voprosy istorii KPSS*, no. 6 (1962), p. 141; Trotsky, *The Stalin School of Falsification*, pp. 300–301.

48. "Protokoly Vserossiiskogo (martovskogo) soveshchaniia," *Voprosy istorii KPSS*, no. 6, p. 134; Trotsky, *The Stalin School of Falsification*, p. 267.

49. "Protokoly Vserossiiskogo (martovskogo) soveshchaniia," *Voprosy istorii KPSS*, no. 6, pp. 139–140; Trotsky, *The Stalin School of Falsification*, pp. 274–275.

50. "Protokoly Vserossiiskogo (martovskogo) soveshchaniia," *Voprosy istorii KPSS*, no. 6, p. 140.

51. Ibid.; Trotsky, *The Stalin School of Falsification*, p. 276. Ivan Teodorovich [Iwan Teodorowych] (1875–1937) was a Bolshevik of Polish origin, who was appointed people's commissar of agriculture in Lenin's first Soviet government. He opposed the forced requisitioning of grain during the Civil War. Close to the economist Nikolai Kondrat'ev (1892–1938), he was condemned along with him and executed in 1937.

52. "Protokoly Vserossiiskogo (martovskogo) soveshchaniia," *Voprosy istorii KPSS*, no. 6, p. 147; Trotsky, *The Stalin School of Falsification*, p. 287.

53. Sukhanov, *Zapiski*, III, pp. 7–37; *The Russian Revolution*, pp. 269–285.

54. F. F. Raskol'nikov, *Kronshtadt i Piter v 1917 godu* (Moscow and Leningrad: Gosizdat, 1925), p. 54; Alexander Rabinowitch, *Prelude to Revolution: The Petrograd Bolsheviks and the July 1917 Uprising* (Bloomington: Indiana University Press, 1968), p. 37.

55. Trotsky, *Stalin*, p. 195. Trotsky was one of the key authors to write about the radical approach of Lenin that shocked the Petrograd Bolsheviks. Lars Lih "considers Trotsky (in his work *Uroki Oktiabria* [Lessons of October], 1924) to be one of the originators, along with Sukhanov, of the myth that Lenin's "April Theses" was a break with prewar Bolshevism and a radical turn toward a socialist revolution. [Lars Lih, "Bringing Bolshevism Back into the Bolshevik Revolution: The Myth of the April Theses," unpublished paper.] For the controversy over Trotsky's reading of 1917, see Frederick C. Corney (trans., annotated, and intro.), *Trotsky's Challenge: The "Literary Discussion" of 1924 and the Fight for the Bolshevik Revolution* (The Hague: Brill, 2016).

56. Slusser, *Stalin in October*, p. 52.

57. Sukhanov, *Zapiski*, pp. 37–42; *The Russian Revolution*, pp. 285–287.

58. Zalezhskii, "Pervyi legal'nyi Pe-Ka," p. 156.

59. Sukhanov, *Zapiski*, p. 40; *The Russian Revolution*, p. 287; Zalezhskii, "Pervyi legal'nyi Pe-Ka," p. 156. Mikhail Bakunin (1814–1876) was a leading Russian anarchist, an opponent of Marx, and an influential political thinker. His daring escape from Siberian exile after suffering for years in Russian prisons and his rivalry with Marx in the First International made him an international celebrity.

60. Zalezhskii, "Pervyi legal'nyi Pe-Ka," p. 156.

61. *Molotov Remembers*, p. 94.

62. Trotsky, *The Stalin School of Falsification*, p. 291.

63. V. I. Lenin, *PSS*, XXXI, pp. 103–112; Trotsky, *The Stalin School of Falsification*, pp. 289–299.

64. Trotsky, *The Stalin School of Falsification*, p. 296.

65. Ibid., pp. 291, 293.

66. *Tretii s"ezd RSDRP, Protokoly*, p. 208.

67. *Molotov Remembers*, p. 122.

68. Iu. Kamenev, "Nashi raznoglasii," *Pravda*, no. 27, April 8, 1917.

69. Iu. Kamenev, "O tezisakh Lenina," *Pravda*, no. 30, April 12, 1917.

70. "Protokol zasedaniia Tsental'nogo Komiteta RSDRP (b), 6 aprelia 1917 g.," *Revoliutsionnoe dvizhenie v Rossii v aprele 1917 g.: Aprel'skii krizis* (Moscow: Izdatel'stvo AN SSSR, 1958), p. 15.

71. "Petrogradskaia obschegorodskaia konferentsiia RSDRP (Bol'shevikov), 14–22 aprelia (27 aprelia–5 maia) 1917 g., Protokoly," *Sedmaia (aprel'skaia Vserossiiskaia konferentsiia RSDRP (Bol'shevikov), Protokoly)* (Moscow: Gosizpolit, 1958), p. 10.

72. Ibid., pp. 34–37.

73. For a clearer statement of Lenin's position, see his polemic against Plekhanov: V. I. Lenin, "Odin iz korennykh voprosov (Kak rassuzhdaiut sotsialisty pereshedshie na storonu burzhuazii)," *PSS*, XXXI, pp. 300–303; *Pravda*, no. 37, April 21, 1917.

74. I. V. Stalin, "Trotskizm ili Leninizm?" I. V. Stalin, *Sochineniia*, pp. 333–334; *Pravda*, no. 269, November 26, 1924. Stalin's defense of Zinoviev is not to be found in the version published in *Sochineniia*.

75. Ibid., p. 334; the entire speech in its censored form can be found in I. V. Stalin, *Sochineniia*, pp. 324–357;

76. Speech on April 18 (May 1), 1917, I. V. Stalin, *Sochineniia*, III, pp. 39–42.

77. K. Stalin, "O soveshchanii v Mariinskom dvortse," *Pravda*, no. 40, April 25 (May 8), 1917; I. V. Stalin, *Sochineniia*, III, pp. 43–47.

78. K. Stalin, "Zemliu—krest'ianam," *Pravda*, no. 32, April 14, 1917; I. V. Stalin, *Sochineniia*, III, p. 36.

79. K. Stalin, "Otstavshie ot revoliutsii," *Pravda*, no. 48, May 4, 1917; I. V. Stalin, *Sochineniia*, III, p. 63.

80. Browder and Kerensky, *The Russian Provisional Government*, II, p. 1098.

81. Rabinowitch, *Prelude to Revolution*, pp. 43–45.

82. Rabinowitch, *Prelude to Revolution*, p. 50; *Vtoraia i tret'ia Petrogradskie obshchegorodskie konferentsii bol'shevikov v iiule i oktiabre 1917 goda: Protokoly* (Moscow-Leningrad: Gosizdat, 1927), p. 15. In his fundamental trilogy on the revolution in Petrograd in 1917–1918, Rabinowitch emphasizes the centrality of winning over and maintaining support of the military for victory.

Vladimir Nevskii (Fiodosii Krivobokov) (1876–1937) was a long-time Bolshevik, worked in military affairs, and was people's commissar of communications in the first Soviet government. He was the founding rector of Sverdlov Communist University and was executed after a trial in 1937.

83. Browder and Kerensky, *The Russian Provisional Government*, III, p. 1267; I. G. Tsereteli, *Vospominaniia o fevral'skoi revoliutsii*, 2 vols. (Paris and The Hague: Mouton & Co., 1963), I, p. 132.

84. Tsereteli, *Vospominaniia o fevral'skoi revoliutsii*, I, pp. 141–142.

85. William G. Rosenberg, *Liberals in the Russian Revolution: The Constitutional Democratic Party, 1917–1921* (Princeton, NJ: Princeton University Press, 1974), pp. 119, 125.

CHAPTER 27. REAPING THE WHIRLWIND

1. *Sedmaia (aprel'skaia) Vserossiiskaia konferentsiia RSDRP*, p. 63.

2. Ibid., p. 69.

3. Ibid., pp. 72–73.

4. Ibid., pp. 101, 104, 106.

5. Ibid., p. 112.

6. He had recently reintroduced the subject in two articles in *Pravda*: K. Stalin, "Ob otmene natsional'nykh ogranichenii," *Pravda*, no. 17, March 25, 1917; "Protiv federalizma," ibid., no. 19; March 28, 1917; I. V. Stalin, *Sochineniia*, III, pp. 16–19, 23–28.

7. *Sedmaia (aprel'skaia) Vserossiiskaia konferentsiia RSDRP*, p. 209.

8. Ibid., p. 210.

9. Ibid., pp. 211–212.

10. Ibid., pp. 281–282.

11. Ibid., pp. 214–215.

12. Ibid., pp. 217, 219.

13. Ibid., p. 219.

14. Feliks Dzierżyński (1877–1926) was active in both the Polish and the Russian socialist movements. Known as "Iron Felix," he joined the Bolsheviks in 1917 and was appointed the head of the secret political police, the Cheka, a position he held from 1917 until his death in 1926.

15. *Sedmaia (aprel'skaia) Vserossiiskaia konferentsiia RSDRP*, pp. 224–226.

16. Ibid., p. 227.

17. Ibid.

18. Ibid., p. 228.

19. *Molotov Remembers: Inside Kremlin Politics. Conversations with Felix Chuev*, ed. and intro. Albert Resis (Chicago: Ivan R. Dee, 1993), p. 137. Service mentions that Lenin supported Stalin for election: "We've known com[rade] Koba for very many years. We used to see him in Kraków where we had our Bureau. His activity in the Caucasus was important. He's a good official in all sorts of responsible work." [Service, *Stalin: A Biography*, p. 131.] I have been unable to find the source for this quotation in the text of the Seventh Conference, but Molotov gives a similar account.

20. *Sedmaia (aprel'skaia) Vserossiiskaia konferentsiia RSDRP*, p. 115.

21. Ibid., p. 121. Mikhail Tomskii (1880–1936) was a Bolshevik closely associated with the Soviet trade unions. A member of the Central Committee and Politburo, he was close to Bukharin, allied with Stalin in the 1920s against the Left Opposition, but was portrayed as part of the Rightist deviation in the late 1920s to early 1930s. As persecutions of former "deviationists" intensified, Tomskii committed suicide.

22. Ibid., p. 120.

23. The myth that the Bolshevik Party in 1917 was monolithic, centralized, and under the dominance of Lenin has long been discounted, particularly in the close analyses of the party in the revolutionary year by Alexander Rabinowitch.

24. A few weeks earlier (May 10) Stalin, who by this time stood somewhere near the center of the Bolshevik Party and was respected enough to convince others to go along with his views,

met with the Petersburg Committee as it set up its organizational structure and advised them not to divide the committee into groups separating economic from political work "because it is impossible to separate economics from politics." The committee voted in favor of Stalin's proposal. [*Pervyi legal'nyi Peterburgskii komitet*, p. 99.]

25. Galili, *The Menshevik Leaders in the Russian Revolution*, pp. 248–249.

26. Ibid., p. 151.

27. Ibid., p. 299; on printers, see Diane P. Koenker, *Republic of Labor: Russian Printers and Soviet Socialism, 1918–1930* (Ithaca, NY: Cornell University Press, 2005), pp. 1–44.

28. Galili, *The Menshevik Leaders in the Russian Revolution*, pp. 301–302.

29. K. Stalin, "Munitsipal'naia kompaniia," *Pravda*, nos. 63, 64, 66, May 21, 24, 26, 1917; I. V. Stalin, *Sochineniia*, III, pp. 67–79.

30. K. Stalin, "K itogam munitsipal'nykh vyborov v Petrograde," *Biulletini Biuro pechati pri TsK RSDRP*, no. 1, June 15, 1917; I. V. Stalin, *Sochineniia*, III, pp. 91–95.

31. K. Stalin, "Vchera i segodnia (Krizis revoliutsii)," *Soldatskaia pravda*, no. 43, June 13, 1917; I. V. Stalin, *Sochineniia*, III, pp. 80–87.

32. Ibid., p. 86.

33. Ibid., p. 87.

34. Sukhanov, *The Russian Revolution*, II, pp. 378–379.

35. V. I. Lenin, *PSS*, XXXII, pp. 266–267.

36. Ibid., p. 267.

37. G. I. Fedorov (1891–1936) was a Bolshevik party official, active in the civil war as chair of the Nizhnii Novgorod soviet. He joined the Trotskyist opposition in the 1920s, was expelled and then reinstated in the party before being tried and executed in 1936.

38. Rabinowitch, *Prelude to Revolution*, p. 60; *Pervyi legal'nyi Peterburgskii komitet bol'shevikov v 1917 g.*, pp. 136–145.

39. The same proclamation, with some changes, was later used for the June 18 demonstration. That version was published in *Pravda*, no. 84, June 17, 1917; I. V. Stalin, *Sochineniia*, III, pp. 96–99.

40. An excellent account of the "June Crisis" is given in Rabinowitch, *Prelude to Revolution*, pp. 54–96.

41. Leon Trotsky, *The History of the Russian Revolution*, trans. Max Eastman (Ann Arbor: University of Michigan Press, 1957), pp. 447–448.

42. Sukhanov, *The Russian Revolution*, pp. 396–401.

43. Rabinowitch, *Prelude to Revolution*, pp. 85–86. Ivar Smilga (1892–1938) was active in the revolutionary movement in the Baltic region. A member of the Central Committee in 1917, he joined the Left Opposition in the 1920s, was arrested in 1935, and was tried and executed in 1938.

44. Ibid., pp. 84–94; *Pervyi legal'nyi Peterburgskii komitet bol'shevikov v 1917 g.*, pp. 153–168.

45. While some historians are convinced that Lenin was aiming to make a bid for power in June 1917, others, like Rabinowitch, have shown more convincingly that the Bolsheviks were pushed into action by their most radical followers, that they estimated that they did not have enough popular support to seize or hold power, and that they pragmatically, wisely backed down when the planned demonstration appeared headed for a bloody denouement. [Rabinowitch, *Prelude to Revolution*.]

46. K. Stalin, "Protiv razroznennykh demonstratsii," *Pravda*, no. 81, June 14, 1917; I. V. Stalin, *Sochineniia*, III, pp. 88–90.

47. Sukhanov, *The Russian Revolution 1917*, II, p. 414.

48. Ibid., II, pp. 416–417.

49. K. St., "Na demonstratsii," *Pravda*, no. 86, June 20, 1917; I. V. Stalin, *Sochineniia*, III, pp. 100–103.

50. Allan K. Wildman, *The End of the Russian Imperial Army, Vol. II: The Road to Soviet Power and Peace* (Princeton, NJ: Princeton University Press, 1987), pp. 29–30.

51. Wildman, *The End of the Russian Imperial Army: The Old Army and the Soldiers' Revolt*, p. 372.

52. Rabinowitch, *Prelude to Revolution*, pp. 114–115; N. I. Podvoiskii, "Voennaia organizatsiia TsK RSDRP(b) i voenno-revoliutsionnyi komitet 1917 g.," *Krasnaia letopis'*, no. 6 (1923), p. 76.

53. Rabinowitch, *Prelude to Revolution*, pp. 121–122.

54. Much of what follows in the narrative about the "July Days" is deeply indebted to the careful reconstruction and analysis of the events in Rabinowitch, *Prelude to Revolution*.

55. *Shestoi s"ezd RSDRP (Bol'shevikov). Avgust 1917 goda: Protokoly* (Moscow: Gosizpolit, 1958), p. 17; Rabinowitch, *Prelude to Revolution*, p. 157.

56. Rabinowitch, *Prelude to Revolution*, p. 158; *Vtoraia i tret'ia Petrogradskie obshchegorodskie konferentsii bol'shevikov*, p. 50.

57. Demian Bednyi, "Strikhi," in *Stalin: Sbornik statei k piatidesiatiletiiu so dnia rozhdeniia* (Moscow and Leningrad: Gosizdat, 1930); Slusser, *Stalin in October*, p. 155. Slusser provides a long, thorough analysis of the so-called pencil story, pp. 155–162.

58. Rabinowitch, *Prelude to Revolution*, p. 188.

59. Semion Lyandres, *The Bolsheviks' "German Gold" Revisited: An Inquiry into the 1917 Accusations* (The Carl Beck Papers in Russian and East European Studies, 1995).

60. Ibid., p. 194; *Izvestiia*, July 6, 1917, p. 3.

61. *Shestoi s"ezd RSDRP*, p. 20.

62. I. V. Stalin, *Sochineniia*, III, pp. 111–112.

63. N. B. Bogdanova, *Moi Otets—Men'shevik* (Saint Petersburg: NITs "Memorial," 1994), p. 58.

64. Rabinowitch, *Prelude to Revolution*, p. 215; A. F. Ilin-Zhenevskii, *Ot fevralia k zakhvatu vlasti: Vospominaniia o 1917 g.* (Leningrad: Priboi, 1927), p. 82. Aleksandr Ilin-Zhenevskii (1894–1941) later became one of the founders of the Soviet chess movement and perished in the Leningrad Blockade.

65. Bogdanova, *Moi otets—Men'shevik*, p. 58.

66. Sukhanov, *The Russian Revolution 1917*, II, p. 455.

67. Rabinowitch, *Prelude to Revolution*, p. 184; M. I. Kalinin, "Vladimir Il'ich v dvizhenii," *Krasnaia gazeta*, July 16, 1920, p. 3.

68. A. S. Allilueva, *Vospominaniia*, pp. 175–179.

69. Ibid., p. 181.

70. Ibid., pp. 183–184.

71. *Molotov. Poluderzhavnyi vlastelin*, ed. F. Chuev (Moscow, 1999), pp. 216–217, 297; *Molotov Remembers*, p. 164.

72. A. S. Allilueva, *Vospominaniia*, p. 184.

73. Ibid., p. 185.

74. Ibid., p. 186.

75. Ibid.

CHAPTER 28. THE DARK BEFORE

1. This phrase comes from his notes written around this time. [V. I. Lenin, "Politicheskoe polozhenie (Chetyre tezisa)," *PSS*, XXXIV, pp. 1–5.] This piece was first published in *Proletarskoe delo*, no. 6, August 2 (July 23), 1917, signed "W." Slusser has a detailed discussion of its publishing history [*Stalin in October*, pp. 165–166.]

2. V. I. Lenin, "Politicheskoe polozhenie (chetyre tezisa)," July 10 (23), 1917, *PSS*, XXXIV, p. 5.

3. V. I. Lenin, "K lozungam," written in mid-July 1917, *PSS*, XXXIV, p. 16.

4. Rabinowitch, *Prelude to Revolution*, pp. 216–217; Podvoiskii, "Voennaia organizatsiia TsK RSDRP (b)," pp. 84. See also, Lenin, "K lozungam," pp. 10–17.

5. Pictured in Alexander Rabinowitch, *The Bolsheviks Come to Power: The Revolution of 1917 in Petrograd* (New York: W. W. Norton, 1976), p. 18.

6. Ibid., p. 19; *Edinstvo*, July 9, 1917, p. 1.

7. Rabinowitch, *The Bolsheviks Come to Power*, p. 41.

8. Ibid., p. 45.

9. V. Volodarskii (Moisei Goldstein) (1891–1918) was a Bundist, a Menshevik, and a *Mezhraionets* (member of the Interdistrict Group) before joining the Bolsheviks. He was a gifted orator and editor of *Krasnaia gazeta* (Red Newspaper). He was assassinated by a Socialist Revolutionary in 1918.

10. *Rabochii i soldat*, no. 1, July 23, 1917; Robert H. McNeal (ed.), *Resolutions and Decisions of the Communist Party of the Soviet Union, Vol. I, The Russian Social Democratic Labour Party, 1898–October 1917*, ed. Robert Carter Elwood (Toronto: University of Toronto Press, 1974), pp. 247–249.

11. Rabinowitch, *The Bolsheviks Come to Power*, p. 61; A. M. Sovokin, "Rasshirennoe soveshchanie TsK RSDRP(b), 13–14 iiulia 1917g.," *Voprosy istorii KPSS*, no. 4 (1959), pp. 125–138.

12. V. I. Lenin, *PSS*, XXXIV, pp. 10–12.

13. *Molotov Remembers*, p. 165.

14. I. V. Stalin, *Sochineniia*, III, p. 109. The speech can be found in *Vtoraia i tret'ia petrogradskie obshchegorodskie konferentsii bol'shevikov* (Moscow-Leningrad: Gosudarstvennoe izdatel'stvo, 1927), pp. 53–55. Specific quotations are from Stalin's collected works.

15. I. V. Stalin, *Sochineniia*, III, pp. 110, 112–113.

16. *Vtoraia i tret'ia petrogradskie obshchegorodskie konferentsii bol'shevikov*, pp. 64–68.

17. I. V. Stalin, *Sochineniia*, III, p. 118.

18. Ibid., p. 122.

19. Ibid., p. 123.

20. Ibid., p. 125. Moisei Kharitonov faulted Stalin for not mentioning the international situation. "We say everywhere that if there is no revolution in the West, our cause will be lost." The deeper the crisis develops, he said, the clearer it is how stable the bourgeoisie is. "The forces of

the imperialists of all countries can bring about an imperialist peace, and only then will the hands of the world revolution be untied." [*Vtoraia i tret'ia petrogradskie obshchegorodskie konferentsii bol'shevikov*, pp. 70–71.]

21. The "July Theses" have never been found, though Soviet historians reliably reported that they were basically reflected in Lenin's articles of the time: "Tri krizisa," V. I. Lenin, *PSS*, XXXII, pp. 428–432, and "K lozungam," ibid., XXXIV, pp. 10–17. [*Vtoraia i tret'ia petrogradskie obshchegorodskie konferentsii bol'shevikov*, p. 145, n. 69a.]

22. *Vtoraia i tret'ia petrogradskie obshchegorodskie konferentsii bol'shevikov*, p. 71.

23. Ibid., p. 72.

24. Ibid., pp. 73–75.

25. Ibid., pp. 77, 144–145.

26. Volodarskii as the representative of the special conference defended the resolution presented by Stalin. A radical amendment from Molotov stating that the soviets and the Provisional Government supported the counterrevolution won out over the more moderate version of the Central Committee resolution. But when Molotov proposed condemning the "petty bourgeois Soviet majority" for not resisting counterrevolution, he was defeated. The delegates unenthusiastically backed the cobbled-together resolution. Almost half the delegates abstained (28-3-28), some upset that Lenin's theses had not been revealed, others annoyed that the reporter, Stalin, had not been there to defend the resolution. Molotov abstained because the resolution was too vague for such an important time. [Ibid., p. 79.]

27. Ibid., pp. 101–105.

28. "Chto sluchilos," *Rabochii i soldat*, no. 1, July 23, 1917; I. V. Stalin, *Sochineniia*, III, pp. 127–129.

29. "Pobeda kontrevoliutsii," *Rabochii i soldat*, no. 1, July 23, 1917; I. V. Stalin, *Sochineniia*, III, pp. 130–133; "Pobeda kadetov," *Rabochii i soldat*, no. 2, July 24, 1917; I. V. Stalin, *Sochineniia*, III, pp. 134–136; "Novoe pravitel'stvo," *Rabochii i soldat*, no. 3, July 26, 1917; I. V. Stalin, *Sochineniia*, III, pp. 146–148.

30. Rabinowitch, *Prelude to Revolution*, p. 226; V. I. Nevskii, "V oktiabre: Beglye zametki pamiati," *Katorga i ssylka*, no. 11–12 (96–97) (1932), pp. 28–30.

31. *Protokoly tsentral'nogo komiteta RSDRP(b), Avgust 1917–Fevral' 1918* (Moscow: Gosizpolit, 1958), pp. 4, 247, n. 6, 7.

Grigorii Sokolnikov (Girsh, Brilliant) (1888–1939), a Bolshevik from 1905, returned to Russia with Lenin on the sealed train. He served as people's commissar of finance and as Soviet ambassador to the United Kingdom. Tried in one of Stalin's show trials, he was murdered in prison in 1939.

Vladimir Miliutin (1884–1937) was a Bolshevik from 1910, who served as people's commissar of agriculture in the first Soviet government. He wanted a coalition of socialist parties to form the government after the October Revolution. He was executed in 1937.

32. Ibid., pp. 24–25.

33. Ibid., pp. 23–25, 27; Rabinowitch, *The Bolsheviks Come to Power*, pp. 74–75; Slusser, *Stalin in October*, pp. 214–215.

34. *Shestoi s"ezd RSDRP*, p. 20.

35. Ibid., pp. 27, 36, 71, 100.

36. Ibid., pp. 111, 113.

37. Ibid., p. 111.

38. Rabinowitch, *The Bolsheviks Come to Power*, pp. 85–86. Stalin's resolution, probably first drafted by Lenin, can be found in *Golos sotsial-demokrata* (Kiev), August 13, 1917; and in A. M. Sovokin, *V preddverii oktiabria* (Moscow: Mysl', 1973), pp. 336–341.

39. *Shestoi s"ezd RSDRP*, pp. 114–115, 118. Nikolai Klestov ("Angarskii") (1873–1941) was a middle-rank party member who adhered to the Bolsheviks after February 1917. Although criticized by Stalin in the year of revolution, he survived through the years of the Great Terror as a foreign trade representative and publisher of foreign books permitted by the Soviet censorship.

40. Ibid., pp. 118–119.

41. Ibid., pp. 119–120.

42. Ibid., pp. 121–122.

43. Ibid., pp. 124.

44. Ibid., pp. 124–125. On the revolution in Baku, see Suny, *The Baku Commune, 1917–1918*.

45. Andrei Bubnov (1883–1938) was a Bolshevik activist and a member of the Central Committee and Politburo, but later joined several oppositions in the early 1920s. He served as people's commissar of enlightenment (1929–1937) before being tried and executed.

46. Ibid., pp. 241–251.

47. *Shestoi s"ezd RSDRP*, p. 250; I. V. Stalin, *Sochineniia*, III, pp. 186–187. Robert C. Tucker sees this spontaneous statement as revealing "Stalin's underlying Russocentrism." [Tucker, *Stalin as Revolutionary*, pp. 174–175.]

48. For a full discussion of Marxist views on the question of "socialism in one country," see Erik van Ree, "Socialism in One Country: A Reassessment," *Studies in East European Thought*, L, 2 (June 1998), pp. 77–117.

49. *Shestoi s"ezd RSDRP*, p. 251.

50. Ibid., pp. 144–145; Rabinowitch, *The Bolsheviks Come to Power*, pp. 88–89.

51. Ibid., p. 285. The full final version of the resolution can be found in ibid., pp. 381–385.

52. Ibid., p. 252. The number of votes received by others was not recorded.

53. *Protokoly tsentral'nogo komiteta RSDRP(b)*, p. 4.

54. Ibid., pp. 6, 13, 16, 20, 22.

55. Ibid., pp. 28–29.

56. "K vyboram k uchreditel'noe sobranie," *Rabochii i soldat*, no. 4, July 27, 1917; I. V. Stalin, *Sochineniia*, III, pp. 149–155.

57. I. V. Stalin, *Sochineniia*, III, p. 152.

CHAPTER 29. ON THE EVE

1. Sukhanov, *The Russian Revolution*, II, p. 529.

2. "Dve konferentsii," *Rabochii i soldat*, July 24, 1917; I. V. Stalin, *Sochineniia*, III, pp. 144–145.

3. Rabinowitch, *The Bolsheviks Come to Power*, p. 90.

4. William G. Rosenberg, "The Russian Municipal Duma Elections of 1917: A Preliminary Computation of Results," *Soviet Studies*, XXI, 2 (October 1969), pp. 131–163; Rosenberg, *Liberals in the Russian Revolution*, pp. 220–221.

5. Rosenberg, *Liberals in the Russian Revolution*, pp. 200–205.

6. Ibid., p. 209; *Russkie vedomosti*, August 4, 1917.

7. Rosenberg, *Liberals in the Russian Revolution*, p. 210.

8. *Poslednie novosti*, no. 5668, September 30, 1936.

9. "Chego khotiat kapitalisty?" *Rabochii i soldat*, no. 13, August 6, 1917; I. V. Stalin, *Sochineniia*, III, pp. 188–192.

10. Rosenberg, *Liberals in the Russian Revolution*, p. 215; *Gosudarstvennoe soveshchanie* (Moscow, 1930), p. 78.

11. Rosenberg, *Liberals in the Russian Revolution*, p. 218.

12. "Kuda vedet moskovskoe soveshchanie?" *Proletarii*, no. 1, August 13, 1917; I. V. Stalin, *Sochineniia*, III, pp. 200–205; "Itogi moskovskogo soveshchaniia," *Proletarii*, no. 4, August 17, 1917; I. V. Stalin, *Sochineniia*, III, pp. 214–217.

13. David Mandel, *The Petrograd Workers and the Soviet Seizure of Power* (London: Macmillan, 1984), p. 229.

14. V. I. Lenin, "Zagranichnomu biuro tsentral'nogo komiteta," August 17 (30), 1917, *PSS*, XLIX, p. 447.

15. V. I. Lenin, "O vystuplenii Kameneva v TsIK po povodu stokgol'mskoi konferentsii," *PSS*, XXXV, p. 71.

16. "Eshche o Stokgol'me," *Rabochii i Soldat*, no. 15, August 8, 1917; I. V. Stalin, *Sochineniia*, III, pp. 196–199.

17. "Pravda o nashem porazhenii na fronte," *Proletarii*, no. 5, August 18, 1917; I. V. Stalin, *Sochineniia*, III, pp. 217–220.

18. "Kto zhe vinovat v porazhenii na fronte?" published as a brochure in Petrograd, 1917; I. V. Stalin, *Sochineniia*, III, pp. 227–231.

19. "Polosa provokatsii," *Proletarii*, no. 8, August 22, 1917; I. V. Stalin, *Sochineniia*, III, pp. 241–243.

20. "Soiuz zheltykh," *Rabochii*, no. 1, August 25, 1917; I. V. Stalin, *Sochineniia*, III, pp. 248–250.

21. "Ili-ili," *Rabochii*, no. 1, August 25, 1917; I. V. Stalin, *Sochineniia*, III, pp. 251–255. Riabushinskii made his remark on August 3, 1917, at the Second All-Russian Commercial and Industrial Congress in Moscow. For a discussion of the "bony hand" remark, see Lars T. Lih, *Bread and Authority in Russia, 1914–1921* (Berkeley: University of California Press, 1990), pp. 99–102.

22. Rabinowitch, *The Bolsheviks Come to Power*, p. 109; A. S. Lukomskii, *Vospominaniia*, 2 vols. (Berlin: Otto Kirchner, 1922), I, p. 227.

23. Rabinowitch, *The Bolsheviks Come to Power*, pp. 126, 129.

24. Ibid., p. 131.

25. Sukhanov, *The Russian Revolution*, II, p. 505.

26. "My trebuem," *Rabochii*, no. 4, August 28, 1917; I. V. Stalin, *Sochineniia*, III, pp. 256–260; "Zagovor prodolzhaetsia," *Rabochii*, no. 5, 2nd extra edition, August 25, 1917; I. V. Stalin, *Sochineniia*, III, pp. 261–265.

27. K. Stalin, "Zagovor protiv revoliutsii," *Rabochii put'*, nos. 27, 28, 30, September 29, 30; October 4, 5, 7, 1917; I. V. Stalin, *Sochineniia*, III, pp. 337–357.

28. I. V. Stalin, *Sochineniia*, III, p. 343.

29. *Protokoly tsentral'nogo komiteta RSDRP(b)*, pp. 37–38; Rabinowitch, *The Bolsheviks Come to Power*, pp. 159–162.

30. "V tsentral'nyi komitet RSDRP," August 30, 1917, V. I. Lenin, *PSS*, XXXIV, pp. 119–121; *Protokoly tsentral'nogo komiteta RSDRP(b)*, pp. 43–45.

31. "Krizis i direktoriia," *Rabochii put'*, no. 1, September 3, 1917; I. V. Stalin, *Sochineniia*, III, pp. 268–271.

32. K. St., "O razryve s Kadetami," *Rabochii put'*, no. 3, September 6, 1917; I. V. Stalin, *Sochineniia*, III, pp. 275–278.

33. V. I. Lenin, "O kompromissakh," *PSS*, XXXIV, pp. 133–139.

34. Ibid., p. 134.

35. Ibid., p. 135.

36. Ibid., pp. 138–139.

37. "Russkaia revoliutsiia i grazhdanskaia voina," ibid., pp. 214–228.

38. K. Stalin, "Vtoraia volna," *Rabochii put'*, no. 6, September 9, 1917; I. V. Stalin, *Sochineniia*, III, pp. 279–285.

39. "K demokraticheskomu soveshchaniiu," *Rabochii put'*, no. 10, September 14, 1917; I. V. Stalin, *Sochineniia*, III, pp. 289–293.

40. *Protokoly tsentral'nogo komiteta RSDRP(b)*, pp. 49–54.

41. Rabinowitch, *The Bolsheviks Come to Power*, p. 178.

42. Rosenberg, *Liberals in the Russian Revolution*, p. 245.

43. *Protokoly tsentral'nogo komiteta RSDRP(b)*, p. 67.

44. "Dve linii," *Rabochii put'*, no. 12, September 16, 1917; I. V. Stalin, *Sochineniia*, III, pp. 294–296.

45. "Vsia vlast' sovetam!" *Rabochii put'*, no. 13, September 17, 1917; I. V. Stalin, *Sochineniia*, III, pp. 297–299.

46. "Zhdat' vam—ne dozhdat'sia," *Rabochii put'*, no. 23, September 29, 1917; I. V. Stalin, *Sochineniia*, III, pp. 320–323; "Vysekli sebia," *Rabochii put'*, no. 27, October 4, 1917; I. V. Stalin, *Sochineniia*, III, pp. 335–336.

47. "Otkliki," *Rabochii put'*, no. 23, September 29, 1917; I. V. Stalin, *Sochineniia*, III, pp. 324–327.

48. V. I. Lenin, "Bol'sheviki dolzhny vziat' vlast'," *PSS*, XXXIV, pp. 239–241.

49. "Marksizm i vosstanie," ibid., pp. 242–247.

50. *Protokoly tsentral'nogo komiteta RSDRP(b)*, p. 55.

51. V. I. Lenin, *PSS*, XXXIV, pp. 248–256, 264–268; Rabinowitch, *The Bolsheviks Come to Power*, p. 192.

52. V. I. Lenin, *PSS*, XXXIV, pp. 340–341.

53. Their declaration can be found in *Protokoly tsentral'nogo komiteta RSDRP(b)*, pp. 77–79.

54. "Komu nuzhen Predparlament?" *Rabochii put'*, no. 32, October 10, 1917; I. V. Stalin, *Sochineniia*, III, pp. 364–366.

55. "Vlast' sovetov," *Rabochii put'*, no. 35, October 13, 1917; I. V. Stalin, *Sochineniia*, III, pp. 367–370.

56. Present were: Lenin, Trotsky, Zinoviev, Kamenev, Stalin, Dzierżyński, Sverdlov, Uritskii, Aleksandra Kollontai, Bubnov, Sokolnikov, and Georgii Lomov (Oppokov).

57. *Protokoly tsentral'nogo komiteta RSDRP(b)*, p. 85.

58. Ibid., pp. 86–92.

59. Ibid., p. 86.

60. *Protokoly tsentral'nogo komiteta RSDRP(b)*, p. 94.

61. Mandel, *The Petrograd Workers and the Soviet Seizure of Power*, pp. 287–309.

62. *Protokoly tsentral'nogo komiteta RSDRP(b)*, p. 100.

63. Ibid., p. 103.

64. Ibid., p. 109.

65. Ibid., p. 113.

66. Ibid., p. 107.

67. Ibid., p. 268, n. 141.

68. Ibid., pp. 114–115.

69. Ibid., pp. 107–108.

70. Sukhanov, *The Russian Revolution*, II, p. 578.

71. Rabinowitch, *The Bolsheviks Come to Power*, p. 232.

72. Ibid., p. 234.

73. Ibid., p. 236.

74. "Shtreikbrekhery revoliutsii," *Rabochii put'*, no. 37, October 15, 1917; I. V. Stalin, *Sochineniia*, III, pp. 375–380.

75. *Protokoly tsentral'nogo komiteta RSDRP(b)*, p. 118.

76. Sukhanov, *The Russian Revolution*, II, p. 586.

77. Rabinowitch, *The Bolsheviks Come to Power*, p. 252.

78. Ibid., p. 253.

79. "Chto nam nuzhno," *Rabochii put'*, no. 44, October 24, 1917; I. V. Stalin, *Sochineniia*, III, pp. 387–390.

80. "Pis'mo chlenam TsK," October 24, 1917; V. I. Lenin, *PSS*, XXXIV, pp. 435–436.

81. Rabinowitch, *The Bolsheviks Come to Power*, p. 266.

82. Ibid., pp. 272, 279.

83. Ibid., p. 291.

84. Ibid., p. 294.

85. Ibid., p. 295.

86. Sukhanov, *The Russian Revolution*, II, p. 639.

87. Ibid., p. 646.

CONCLUSION: THE ROAD TRAVELED

1. "Empathy is our ability to identify what someone else is thinking and feeling and to respond to their thoughts and feelings with an appropriate emotion." [Simon Baron-Cohen, *The Science of Evil: On Empathy and the Origins of Cruelty* (New York: Basic Books, 2011), p. 16.]

2. Van Ree, *The Political Thought of Joseph Stalin*, p. 107.

3. In 1865 in answer to a questionnaire Karl Marx wrote that his motto was Descartes's *De omnibus dubitandum (Doubt everything)*. [Karl Marx's "Confession," April 1, 1865, Zalt-Bommel, The Netherlands; https://www.marxists.org/archive/marx/works/1865/04/01.htm.]

4. Adopting a term coined by Robert Tucker, Erik van Ree believes that "Stalin was indeed a Russian red patriot, if this term refers to his insistence on Russian leadership as the most advanced nation of the multinational state. He used a purely Marxist argument, proceeding from the progressive socio-economic and state development of Russia compared with the border lands, which at the same time harmonised perfectly with the traditional centralism of the Russian state." [*The Political Thought of Joseph Stalin*, p. 82.]

5. "Der Besitz der Gewalt das Frie Urteil der Vernunft unvermeidlich verdibt." [Immanuel Kant, *Zum ewigen Freiden: Ein Philosphischer Entwurf* (On Eternal Peace) (1795).]

6. Van Ree, *The Political Thought of Joseph Stalin*, pp. 1–17.

HISTORIANS LOOK AT STALIN: A HISTORIOGRAPHICAL DISCUSSION

1. Parts of this essay appeared in longer versions as "Making Sense of Stalin: Some Recent and Not-So-Recent Biographies," *Russian History*, XVI, 2–4 (1989), pp. 435–448; and "Making Sense of Stalin: His Biographers," in Ronald Grigor Suny, *Red Flag Wounded: Stalinism and the Fate of the Soviet Experiment* (London and New York: Verso, 2020).

2. Roy A. Medvedev, *Let History Judge: The Origins and Consequences of Stalinism* (New York: Alfred A. Knopf, 1972; revised edition: New York: Columbia University Press, 1989); Robert C. Tucker, *Stalin as Revolutionary, 1879–1929: A Study in History and Personality* (New York: W. W. Norton, 1973); Adam B. Ulam, *Stalin: The Man and His Era* (New York: Viking, 1973; 1989); Ronald Hingley, *Joseph Stalin: Man and Legend* (New York: McGraw-Hill, 1974); Robert M. Slusser, *Stalin in October: The Man Who Missed the Revolution* (Baltimore: Johns Hopkins University Press, 1987); Robert H. McNeal, *Stalin: Man and Ruler* (New York: New York University Press, 1988).

3. Robert Payne, *The Rise and Fall of Stalin* (London, 1966); Edward Ellis Smith, *The Young Stalin: The Early Years of an Elusive Revolutionary* (New York: Farrar, Straus, and Giroux, 1967); H. Montgomery Hyde, *Stalin: The History of a Dictator* (New York: Farrar, Straus, and Giroux, 1971); Alex de Jonge, *Stalin and the Shaping of the Soviet Union* (New York: William Morrow, 1986).

4. From Trotsky, *Moia zhizn'*, II, pp. 213–214, quoted in Dmitri Volgogonov, *Stalin: Triumph and Tragedy*, translated by Harold Shukman (New York: Grove Weidenfeld, 1991), p. 57.

5. Peter Beilharz, "Trotsky as Historian," *History Workshop Journal*, XX, 1 (October 1985), pp. 46–47.

6. Deutscher, *Stalin: A Political Biography* (Vintage paperback edition: New York, 1960; second edition: Oxford-New York, 1966), p. xv. [Page references to Deutscher are from the second edition.] The phrase "unrepentant Marxist" is that of one of Deutscher's most severe critics, Leopold Labedz. See his two-part article, "Deutscher as Historian and Prophet," *Survey*, no. 41 (April 1962), pp. 120–144; "Deutscher as Historian and Prophet, II," ibid. (Summer 1977–1978), pp. 146–164; as well as "Stalin and History: Perspectives in Retrospect," ibid., XXIII, 3 (104) (Summer 1977–1978), pp. 134–146; and Isaac Deutscher's "Stalin: An Unpublished Critique," *Encounter* (January 1979), pp. 65–81.

7. Bychowski, "Joseph V. Stalin," pp. 123–125, 139.

8. Tucker, *Stalin as Revolutionary*, pp. 119, 120, 134–135, 137, 140, 142.

9. Thomas A. Kohut, "Psychohistory as History," *American Historical Review*, XCI, 2 (April 1986), p. 338.

10. Ulam, *Stalin*, p. 33.

11. Ibid., pp. 12, 9.

12. Ibid., p. 13.

13. Montefiore, *Young Stalin*, p. 15.

14. Ibid., p. 16.

15. Ibid., p. 11.

16. Stephen Kotkin, *Stalin: Paradoxes of Power, 1878–1928* (New York: Penguin Books, 2014), p. 394.

17. Ibid., p. 400.

INDEX

A NOTE ON THE TYPE

This book has been composed in Arno, an Old-style serif typeface in the classic Venetian tradition, designed by Robert Slimbach at Adobe.

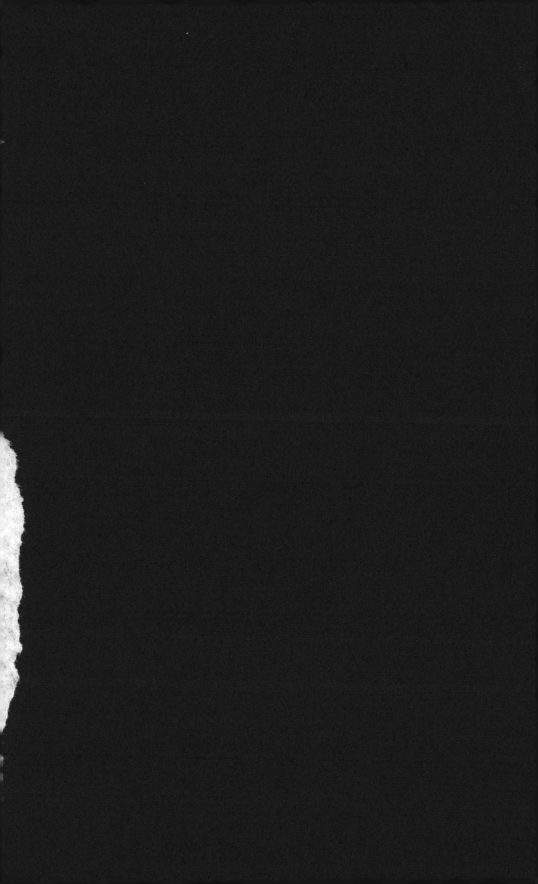